THE ENCYCLOPEDIA OF
BRITISH BIRDS

This is a Parragon Book
This edition published in 2001

Parragon
Queen Street House
4 Queen Street
Bath BA1 1HE

ISBN 0 75256-564-8

Produced for Parragon Books by
Foundry Design & Production, a part of
The Foundry Creative Media Company Ltd,
Crabtree Hall, Crabtree Lane,
Fulham, London SW6 6TY

Special thanks to Polly Willis and Dave Jones

A copy of the CIP data for this book is available in the British Library.

Printed and bound in Spain

THE ENCYCLOPEDIA OF
BRITISH BIRDS

DONALD CAMPBELL

CONTRIBUTING EDITOR
MARTIN WALTERS

p

Contents

How to use this book

This book contains a number of important features:

- **An introductory section** 'The World of Birds' containing detailed information on all aspects of birds and ornithology. Photographs, illustrations, informative captions and 'bird fact' boxes provide extra detail on every page.
- **Descriptions of over 300 bird species** organised by habitat within one of seven groups, such as Town and Garden or Mountain and Moorland.
- **'Species Information' boxes** cover scientific names for species, details of related species, behaviour, bird calls and habitats.
- **Icons provide additional information** about size, identification marks and population.
- **The reference section** comprises a reading list, useful contacts, a glossary of vital terms and an extensive index.

KEY TO SYMBOLS

SIZE

SMALL   MEDIUM   MEDIUM-LARGE   LARGE   VERY LARGE

IDENTIFICATION

Arrows point to distinctive features of the outlined bird

HABITAT

Six main headings of habitat have been identified that relate to the sections within the book. Within these there are, therefore, further categories:

BUILDINGS   CLIFFS   CONIFEROUS   DECIDUOUS   ESTUARY   FIELDS   GARDENS

GRASSLAND   HEDGES   ISLANDS   LAKES   MARSHES   MOORLAND WTH MOUNTAINS   MOUNTAINS

OPEN WATER   REEDS AND EMERGENT VEGETATION   RIVERS   SAND   SCRUB   SHINGLE   HEATH

POPULATION

ABUNDANT 50,000 PAIRS OR A MILLION IN WINTER

LARGE 50,000 OR 100,000 IN WINTER

MEDIUM 5,000 OR 1,000 IN WINTER

SMALL 500 OR 1,000 IN WINTER

PRESENT BUT A SMALL POPULATION

DISTRIBUTION

A green outline map of Britain and Ireland using the following colours:
   red to show the species is present in summer – breeding
   blue to show the species is present in winter
   pink to show the species visits during spring or autumn migration but
     will not spring or overwinter in Britain and Ireland
   orange to show the species will visit but only in very small numbers

Introduction

THIS ENCYCLOPEDIA PRESENTS a concise introduction to British birds, and is aimed primarily at the amateur or general reader with an interest in birds and natural history. In part it is intended to help with the identification of birds in the field, and therefore to act as a companion to the many excellent detailed field guides which are now available. It also explains something of the biology of birds, with accounts of their anatomy, ecology and behaviour, and thus presents birds as active, living animals, rather than simply as species to be ticked off a list and named.

At the heart of the encyclopedia is a conservation thread, reflecting our awareness of the vulnerability of so many of our bird species to changes in the landscape, be these agricultural, industrial, or perhaps climatic. The work of various organisations – notably the British Trust for Ornithology (BTO) and the Royal Society for the Protection of Birds (RSPB) – constantly helps to support birds and their habitats and monitor the changes (often quite subtle) in their populations, some of these findings are reflected in the book.

One of the unusual features of the book is that the identification section is divided up by habitat. Thus, those species most likely to be seen in woodland are grouped together, whilst those more typical of the coast will be found in a different section. This gives the reader a valuable insight into which species to expect to see in a given habitat. Of course, birds are mobile (often highly so) and will cross over between these somewhat artificial compartments, but this habitat approach helps to accentuate an ecological view of wild birds, so vital for successful conservation.

Naturally, many species would qualify, perhaps equally, for inclusion in more than one habitat – thus great spotted woodpecker is increasingly a bird of gardens as well as woodland, and other birds, such as wren and chaffinch, are at home in a wide range of habitats. However, the choice in the main is of those species most typical of each habitat.

The first part of the book covers the biology of birds – topics such as how birds evolved, their anatomy, reproduction, flight, migration, and songs. It then goes on to look at their ecology, with information about changes in bird populations, before discussing techniques of birdwatching and identification, and ending with a short section about the main groups (orders) of birds and their classification.

The main part of the encyclopedia contains the bird descriptions and illustrations, grouped by main habitat. Each section opens with an introduction to that habitat and its associated birdlife. Then, within each habitat, the species are presented roughly in conventional 'systematic' sequence, with, as far as possible, related species put close together, for ease of comparison.

Each species is described concisely, with information about size, related species, calls, main habitat, and status. Occasionally, a literary reference relating to the species in question is also included here. The species descriptions are enhanced by colour photographs, clear diagrams indicating size and habitat, and by distribution maps showing the main geographical range of each bird within the British Isles.

The final two sections in the main part cover rare or local birds, those which are only likely to be seen under exceptional circumstances, or where one knows exactly where or when to search for them. The first of these looks at those species which breed in Britain or Ireland, but only in small numbers. Some of these are at the edge of their range, and in many cases the numbers breeding here fluctuate from year to year. The other main category of rare species are those birds seen mainly as occasional migrants or as vagrants blown off course by adverse weather.

Evolutionary Background

THE EARTH IS about 4.5 billion years old. The oldest sedimentary rocks, originally laid down in layers, as sediments accumulated on the bottom of the seas, are 3.75 billion years old and contain some of the first signs of life. Fossils of bacteria and blue-green algae appeared in these rocks 3.5 billion years ago. Then, for over 2 billion years, little appears to have happened in terms of evolving life, but in rocks 1.4 billion years old the first true cells appear.

APPEARANCE OF ANIMALS

MOST OF THE cells found in rocks of this age, and for the next 0.8 billion or 800 million years, are fossils found in the last 40 years. Until then it was thought that the life of the Cambrian period, which included most of the present day animal phyla, or major groups of related animals, appeared as if from nowhere. The Cambrian, began some 570 million years ago.

The animals did appear suddenly in geological terms, and so did a whole host of soft-bodied groups that didn't survive. These are the extraordinary animals of the Burgess shales in British Columbia, and in *Wonderful Life* (1989) Stephen Jay Gould reappraises the importance of this incredible array, and makes an unfamiliar model of the way living things have evolved and died out. He goes on to write 'The maximum range of anatomical possibilities arises with the rush of diversification. Later history is

Top
Many animals, like this fossil trilobite, lived over 500 million years ago.

Bottom
Tyrannosaurus is probably the most famous of the dinosaurs. Birds evolved from a kind of early reptile stock.

a tale of restriction as most of these early experiments succumb and life settles down to generate endless variants upon a few surviving models'. We will meet a similar situation with the evolution of birds.

FOSSILISED RECORDS

GOULD'S MODELS ARE evolutionary trees. There is nothing new about that, for Darwin had just such a tree in *The Origin of Species*. We need to be able to find out about the organisms that go to make up these trees, and the dates at which they were alive. Fossils are certainly the surest way to tell us about the past, but there are plenty of other clues to be picked up from the comparative anatomy of different animals, from their geographical distribution and from a growing armoury of biochemical methods, often involving neucleic acids.

We have seen that the Cambrian period, which was also the start of the Palaeozoic era, began with an apparent evolutionary explosion. The Palaeozoic ended 345 million years later in disaster, as the fossil record indicated that 96 per cent of marine species became extinct at a time of great earth movements and mountain-building. The survivors had the opportunity for rapid evolution in the absence of competition, and reptiles flourished and diversified during the Mesozoic era. At the end of that time disaster struck again and the dinosaurs were gone, but by then there were feathered animals to carry on the dinosaur line. It is still often easier to say that an event happened during the Jurassic period than that it happened 160

GEOLOGICAL TIME SCALE IN RELATION TO THE EVOLUTION OF BIRDS

ERA	PERIOD	EPOCH	MILLIONS OF YEARS BEFORE PRESENT	BIRD EVENTS
Cainozoic	Quaternary	Recent		Ice age influences migration patterns
		Pleistocene	2	
	Tertiary	Pliocene	6	
		Miocene	22	Much bird diversification
		Oligocene	36	Origin of song birds
		Eocene	45	
		Palaeocene	65	Origin of modern birds
Mesozoic	Cretaceous		135	Extinct toothed sea birds
	Jurassic		200	*Archaeopteryx* and
	Triassic		225	*Protoarchaeopteryx*
Palaeozoic	Cambrian (earliest)		570	
Proterozoic	Precambrian			

million years ago, for, despite modern techniques, dating can be controversial. One method, carbon dating, involves the fact that radioactive carbon decays at a steady rate. However, virtually all the carbon has gone after 50,000 years so this technique can only be used to date geologically recent fossils, like those of Neanderthal man. For older fossils, the decay of potassium and the changing magnetic field in associated rocks can be used, but rare fossils, like those of birds, will often be assigned to a geological epoch by their association with animals that have left a clearer record, as they change gradually through the different geological strata or layers of rock.

THE ORIGINS OF BIRD SPECIES

THINKING ABOUT ANIMAL evolution must be linked to an awareness of geological change. The world is far from stable, the Himalayas and the Andes are of recent origin and continents are still on the move. The Himalayas and the world's great oceans are now effective barriers to the movement of most animals, including birds, and therefore the different regions evolve their different faunas.

The Atlantic did not exist until the continental land masses of North America and Eurasia separated. At that stage, Antarctica was warm, and linked Australia and Africa. Australia has been on its own for a relatively long time and has had time to evolve its very special fauna. New Zealand's two islands have completely different origins. North America and Europe still share far more bird groups than north or south America because of their shared past geological history.

Top left
The Himalayas form an effective barrier to bird movement.

Top right
The isolation of New Zealand has resulted in the evolution of many strange birds, such as this brown kiwi.

Bottom right
Another formidable barrier to birds is provided by the high Andes of South America.

9

ARCHEOPTERYX

FINDING OUT ABOUT the origins of birds presents some of the same difficulties as discovering the details of human origins. Fossils are not common, the interpretation of fossil evidence is open to different opinions, and periodically new evidence is found to throw everything into confusion. I will mention doubts about the exact position of *Archeopteryx* in the story of bird evolution, but a fossil makes a good starting point.

This bird, of magpie size, was an anomaly, for its skeleton was that of a reptile, with reptilian jaws and teeth, a reptilian tail with 20 vertebrae and solid bones, without the air spaces characteristic of birds. We therefore look to reptiles for the origins of birds and, for reasons of comparable skull structure, look to the ancestors of pterodactyls, crocodiles and dinosaurs. Birds and reptiles also share nucleated red blood corpuscles and their eggs develop in a similar way.

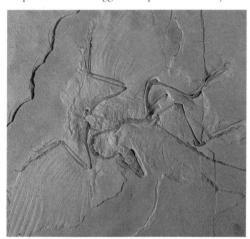

Competition is a driving force for evolutionary change and a long held-theory believed it may have forced some of these ancestral reptiles into the trees, where insects would form a likely diet. The demands of life in the trees, in pursuit of insects, could have led to a reduction of teeth and jaw muscles, and to an association between limbs and eyes to judge distance, which could have led in turn to an increase in the visual areas of the brain. This life-style could also have led to feathers, for tree-jumping would be more effective for any reptile which had slightly larger scales along the hind edge of the forearm. Alternatively, feathers arose initially for protection, and later for insulation, as suggested by Gill (1995).

FORMATION OF FEATHERS

REPTILES SCALES GIVE protection, and Gill's hypothetical steps in their evolution towards feathers starts with the elongation of scales to promote colour reflection. Splits in the elongated scales could provide flexibility and allow greater size. If the long flexible scales became frayed and pigmented they could have dual use for insulation and display. Elongation of the feathered forelimbs and tail could then allow balance and flight and later, secondary splitting, together with the appearance of hooklets, leads to the modern feather with its varied functions.

Archaeopteryx certainly had feathers very similar to those of modern birds, and had the same arrangement of primary feathers on the hand and secondaries on the equivalent of the forearm. Other features of its skeleton that were bird-like included a big toe of the sort that could grasp or perch, and clavicles which were fused to form a wishbone. By contrast, we have seen that it had reptilian teeth and tail, reptilian joints between the bones of its back, and claws on its fingers.

FOSSILISED FEATHERS

INSTEAD OF AN origin in the trees, Futuyma (1988) maintains that a sure requisite for flight is the ability to generate lift by moving the forearms down and forward. *Coelurosaur* dinosaurs had long

Top
Fossil Archeopteryx, with the feathers clearly visible.

Bottom right
Although the specialised grass snake looks far from bird-like, birds and reptiles are closely related.

Bottom left
This reconstruction shows how Archeopteryx may have looked in life.

BIRD FACT:
Birds almost certainly evolved from a group of medium-sized and small dinosaurs, called coelurosaurs, some of which were rather chicken-like. Their arms were small and not used for locomotion.

forelimbs capable of just these movements for, equipped with claws, the forelimbs of these bipedal, running carnivores were used to grasp prey. Incidentally, there were plenty of *coelurosaurs* in the book and film, *Jurassic Park*. Into these muddied and hypothetical waters comes a new fossil. Two specimens from China are of short-armed dinosaurs, which had feathers. The arms were too short for flight, so the feathers seem even more likely to have evolved for insulation purposes, with flight coming later. One of the fossils, called *Protoarcheopteryx*, is actually more recent than *Archaeopteryx*, so we are still far from a totally clear picture.

Another early bird from China, found in 1987, is *Sinornis santensis*, toothed and sparrow-sized and sharing many features with theropod dinosaurs and with *Archaeopteryx*. It was more advanced, in having stronger 'hands', forearms and pectoral girdle and in having a larger pygostyle for the support of the tail fan.

PERCHING BIRDS EVOLVE

BY 6.5 MILLION years ago there had been a great radiation of bird species, producing most of the major groups or orders of birds that we have today. The Miocene, some 20 million years ago, was the time of another phase of diversification in which the passerines, or perching birds, mainly adapted for life in dry environments, probably evolved.

A more recent diversification, which demonstrates this principle of adaptive radiation is shown by the honey-creepers on Hawaii. They apparently evolved from a flock of small finches from Asia or North America millions of years ago. Having landed on one island they did well and spread through the archipelago. Small changes in bill shape and size led to a proliferation of bill types and related feeding behaviours. Some had heavy bills for cracking large legume seeds, in total contrast to the long sickle-like bills of others. These are for sipping nectar from flowers or probing bark crevices for insects. On the island at that time there were all sorts of opportunities available and the honey-creepers were able to make use of these in the absence of competition.

Top
Winged and swimming reptiles – a scene from the Cretaceous period.

Bottom
Hawaiian honey-creepers, showing variation in bill shape.

11

Evolution by Region

> *'Almost all aspects of life are engineered at the molecular level, and without understanding molecules we can only have a very sketchy understanding of life itself.'*
> Francis Crick WHAT MAD PURSUIT (1988)

IT IS CONVENIENT, if simplistic, to think of evolution as taking place in six major faunal regions, each, to a degree, with its own characteristic birds.

The Nearctic (essentially North America) and the Palearctic (including Britain and extending to Japan) form the Holarctic, with endemic orders like divers and auks. European 'warblers' are different from American 'warblers' or wood warblers. The latter are usually small, brightly coloured insectivores which rarely warble, and which have a different number of primary wing feathers. The Palearctic ends to the south with the Sahara desert, not the Mediterranean, and this desert is the northern boundary of the Ethiopian region, with its unique ostriches and secretary birds – 95 per cent of Madagascar's birds come from here, but five per cent have Indian origins, coming from the Oriental region of tropical Asia. Australasia has cockatoos and kiwis, and the Neotropical region of Central and South America has toucans and rheas.

SOME DIFFICULTIES WITH CLASSIFICATION

AS LONG AS YOU watch birds in Europe it is relatively easy to assign any bird to its family: 'That is a crow, that is one of the finches and that is a wagtail'. As you do this you are classifying, dividing birds into sub-groups on the evidence of their appearance and behaviour. Wagtails have long claws and tail, are insectivorous, have relatively simple songs and wag their tails.

If you travel to Guyana you could find long-toed, short-billed black and white birds which run and wag their tails. These are not wagtails, but have come to look like them because of convergent evolution. Birds may look alike not because they share an ancestor, but because they play the same sort of role in nature.

Above
Icterine warbler –
a typical European
species.

Right
The huge ostrich is at
home in the dry
grasslands of Africa.

with dull green backs and yellow bellies, but vary in size, depth of colour and bill size. Further afield, in the Eastern Palearctic, in Japan and Manchuria, the birds are green-backed and white-bellied, while, over the Himalayas, in the Oriental region they are grey- backed and white-bellied.

There are also areas of hybridisation between the races, and areas of overlap where the races do not interbreed and therefore appear like separate species. Where this type of variation exists in a more or less continuous way, say with birds getting larger further north, we talk of a cline, but where the populations are more definitely separated, as on islands, we are more likely to refer to races or subspecies. Both forms of variation remind us that species are not fixed entities, nor would we expect them to be so if we think in evolutionary terms.

With some 10,000 species, however defined, there must be some way of dividing them into smaller groups, either for convenience, or because we want to work out their present relationship and past history. The basis of modern bird classification dates from 1892 and the work of Gadow who made an assessment of 40 anatomical characteristics using 'conservative' ones which he believed did not change easily in the course of ecological adaptation. T. H.

VARIETIES OF THE SAME SPECIES

CONVERGENCE IS ONLY one difficulty in classification. Many species have very extensive ranges but are not, as individuals, very mobile. These species may show great variation throughout their range. The familiar great tit breeds in most of the Western Palearctic with enough variation for ten races to have been described. These are all recognisable as great tits,

Huxley had pioneered this approach with a study of bones of the palate, the partition between the nasal cavities and the mouth. Other 'conservative' features may appear equally trivial, like the structure of the leg muscles, the tendons of the feet, the number of scales on the tarsus or the presence or absence of a fifth secondary feather on the wings.

Above left
The red-bellied toucan is a fruit-eating forest bird from Brazil.

Left
Grey wagtail, showing the characteristic long tail of members of this family.

13

Using Science to Classify Birds

THE NEW systematics, or approaches to classification, used in the 1940s and 1950s, accepted all the difficulties associated with geographical variation and replaced the species defined by anatomical features, by the species defined by its ability to interbreed and produce fertile offspring.

DNA IS USED

THE BIOCHEMICAL APPROACH, which started in the 1950s, gave no perfect answers, It involved the analyses blood group genes, egg white proteins and, later, enzymes, gave no perfect answers. Later DNA became the most useful classification tool, and Sibley and Ahlquist, who compared the DNA of 1,700 species, made only minor changes to the relationships suggested previously. Molecular biology is a more precise tool than comparative anatomy, and it did show that many Australian birds, not surprisingly, share an ancestor, just as marsupial mammals do. Australian nuthatches, warblers, flycatchers and wrens are not closely related to their European look-alikes. More surprisingly the technique of DNA-DNA hybridisation suggested that all crows originated from an Australian song bird that colonised Asia 35 million years ago. The two workers hoped to measure the true 'genetic distance' between species and thence to draw an evolutionary tree showing when they diverged from common ancestors.

Top right
Young great tit – a common European songbird.

Top left
Red-breasted flycatcher at its nest. This species is a rare vagrant to Britain.

Bottom
The hooded crow replaces the all-black carrion crow in the north and west, but they sometimes interbreed where they meet.

GROUPING BIRDS

IN THE PAST there have certainly been difficulties in making evolutionary trees which also try to show which birds are 'primitive' and which 'advanced'. Part of the trouble stems from the fact that mosaic evolution occurs, with one part evolving rapidly (like beaks or feet) while other parts are conservative. These can include plumage, and the sort of anatomical features mentioned earlier.

To make these trees, by whatever method, any group of similar birds, believed to be related, are put in the same taxon. This may be a large group, like an order, or a small one like a genus, which provides the first word of each name in the Linnean binomial nomenclature. Related taxa form a lineage, and there are 29 major lineages or orders, as described later. With a poor fossil record it is difficult to do more than theorise about the relationships of the orders or the times at which they separated, but the hope of the molecular biologists was that they would solve this.

The double-stranded DNA, extracted from birds' red blood cells, can be separated by heat before the resulting single strands from different species are combined to give a double

hybrid strand. This is not as firmly held together as the original, and therefore separates at a lower temperature than pure DNA from either species. This temperature difference can, hopefully, be translated into the date when the two species diverged from a common ancestor

THE WAY NEW SPECIES EVOLVE

THE ESSENTIAL IDEA when explaining the way new species evolve is that populations need to be separated from each other and to remain isolated. Among flowering plants this can happen rapidly when, as sometimes occurs, the chromosome number changes, perhaps doubling, making the new plant separate from its parents, and others of their species, because it cannot cross-pollinate with them. If it can itself reproduce asexually, without pollination, it can perpetuate its new gene combination in isolation.

Among animals, the isolation depends on some physical barrier between the populations. The sea is the most obvious barrier, hence the number of species that have evolved on remote islands and even more on archipelagos. Mountain ranges and deserts, and even relatively dry areas separating forests, and therefore forest species, are other types of barrier. Once separated, the birds will live in slightly different habitats subject to slightly different climates, predation levels and food supplies and will therefore change gradually as different gene combinations are favoured by natural selection. The ability of this natural selection to bring about rapid change is discussed later in relation to recent work on the beaks of ground finches in the Galapagos.

When the two populations are sufficiently different and unable to interbreed they are regarded as new species. It may be that the original barrier still remains, so that there is no way that the possibility of their interbreeding can be tested, but it may be that the ice melts or the desert

retreats and the reproductive isolation of the birds can be proved. Reproductive termination means that birds cannot interbreed for a variety of reasons. Courtship behaviour may have changed in terms of display, plumage or voice, so that members of one species will not be able to attract a mate from the other. If breeding times have altered or preferred breeding habitat changed the species may still not meet, despite an overlapping breeding area, and no interbreeding can occur.

It is as well to remember that in the last million years the ice has advanced and retreated ten times. Ice barriers at times of cold and higher sea-levels during warmer periods have separated populations in our latitudes. These have evolved along their own lines, as with certain closely related sibling species. The movements of ice will also have had momentous effects on bird movements as behaviour evolves as well as structure. Arctic waders have migration patterns that developed as the ice retreated. If global warming continues, a species like the knot will face all sorts of new challenges.

SOME POSSIBLE ORIGIN DATES USING DNA

60 million years ago: Divers, petrels, herons, gannets
40 million years ago: Gamebirds, waterfowl, woodpeckers
25 million years ago: Songbirds
20 million years ago: Swifts, pigeons, rails

> **BIRD FACT:**
> When birds sleep they often open their eyes at regular intervals, to check out their environment for danger. It has been claimed that some birds, such as swifts, which spend much of their time on the wing, actually sleep while flying – but this is difficult to prove.

Top left
The medium ground finch of the Galapagos has quite a heavy bill.

Top right
Green woodpeckers often visit sandy lawns to search for ants.

Bottom
The sharp claws of the swift enable it to cling to cliffs and buildings with ease.

Anatomy of the Bird

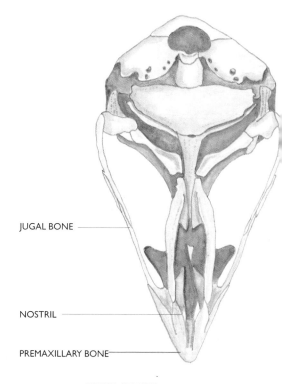

JUGAL BONE

NOSTRIL

PREMAXILLARY BONE

SKULL OF BIRD

M Y FEELING ON first looking at a feather under the microscope was much the same as when I first saw blood corpuscles moving along living capillaries; a feeling of total wonder that is not provided by most routine microscope work. Perhaps a head louse, climbing along a hair, or the massed ranks of ciliates and rotifers in stagnant water aroused something of the same feeling about the dynamic nature of life.

SKELETON

Top left
This pigeon skeleton shows clearly the structure of a typical bird's wing.

Top right
Bird skull – note the spaces for the large eyes, and the nasal cavity.

Bottom
Part of a bird's skeleton (goose), showing the rib region and the wing bones.

ALTHOUGH FEATHERS PROVIDE the essence of birds and are the single feature that separates them from all other living things, birds would not be able to show their versatility but for the skeleton that moves and supports them.

Bird bones are hollow and often fused together, gaining their strength from their shape rather than their weight. The skull bones are indivisibly united in the adult, forming a structure with large eye sockets and a large nostril. This leads into a nasal cavity, with projecting cartilage all covered in moist membranes, housed inside the bones of the bill. Five bones are joined to form the lower mandible and these are covered with a hardened, cornified 'skin' to give that typical, but not unique, feature, a beak.

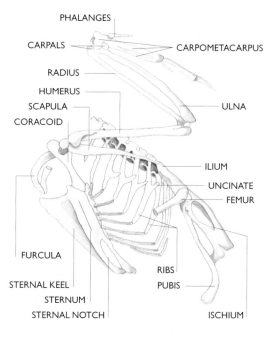

PHALANGES

CARPALS

CARPOMETACARPUS

RADIUS

HUMERUS

SCAPULA

CORACOID

ULNA

ILIUM

UNCINATE

FEMUR

FURCULA

STERNAL KEEL

RIBS

PUBIS

STERNUM

STERNAL NOTCH

ISCHIUM

SKELETON OF BIRD

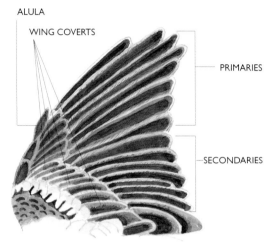

ALULA

WING COVERTS

PRIMARIES

SECONDARIES

THE WING

THE BONES OF the wing are identifiable as being the same as those of a land mammal. There is a short humerus, two longer parallel bones, the radius and ulna, two carpal or wrist bones existing free, with the others fused to form a carpometacarpus. Indications of three fingers remain.

These bones, as the foundation of the wing, are obviously vital for flight, but other skeletal features, and muscles, are also needed. The ribs have large processes for the attachment of muscles, but the more powerful ones for flight are attached, in a very clever way, with appropriate tendon pulley systems when needed, to the sternum or breast bone. To keep this part of the body firm, the vertebrae of the thorax and sacrum, at the base of the back, are nearly all joined together, but the neck, with a variable number of bones, 23 in the mute swan, is very flexible.

REMARKABLE STRUCTURE

THE WINGS ARE supported by a tripod forming the pectoral girdle: the bones involved are the scapula, coracoid and clavicle. The long scapula, our shoulder-blade, is attached to the ribs by ligaments, and the heavy coracoid, in front of the scapula, joins the sternum. Where the scapula and coracoid join, a shallow cavity fits the head of the humerus bone, allowing free wing movement. You will know the two clavicles as the wishbone which you pull apart to get your wish. Strong fliers have their clavicles spread wide to form a strut to keep the wings apart.

Just as the pectoral girdle must be strong to support the bird in flight, so the pelvic girdle is rigidly attached to the backbone to support the walking or hopping bird. Of the three bones that make up the vertebrate pelvis, the pubis is most unusual for it lies parallel to the ischium, as in some dinosaurs, and the two pubic bones do not unite in the front to form a protected pelvic outlet: perhaps because of the size of eggs.

Our foot has a series of small bones, the tarsals, between the ankle joint and what might be called the true bones of the foot, the metatarsals. In birds, some of the tarsals appear to have fused with the tibia, while others have joined the already fused and lengthened metatarsals to provide, in effect, an extra joint in the bird's leg. The fused nature of this tarsometatarsus can be seen at its lower end where there are three individual processes joining with the second, third and fourth toes. The first toe or hallux, corresponding with our big toe, has only two bones and tends to be reduced in birds that do not use it for perching. Some of the many variations in the arrangement of toes will be mentioned in the section on the orders of birds. Most birds have lost their fifth toe.

Altogether the skeleton has evolved a remarkable series of features that adapt the vast majority of bird species for flight, most for effective movement on land and many for swimming. The main features are essentially conservative, not changing much with time, so that bird skeletons are comparatively uniform, except that natural selection acts quickly and effectively on beaks, wings and legs, enabling different species to colonise a wide variety of habitats and to adapt to changing conditions.

Top right
Great skua, with wings spread in flight.

Top left
Sparrow's wing, showing the main groups of flight feathers.

Legs and Feet

LEGS AND FEET are usually covered by scales and these are moulted in much the same way as feathers. The claws, vital for gripping, digging, fighting and scratching are, like scales, made of the protein keratin.

NECESSARY MODIFICATIONS

WE TALK OF perching birds, the Passerine order, which perch by virtue of their toes and associated muscles and tendons. The term 'opposable', as with our thumb which can meet our other fingers to grip, is used for their first toe.

Some of the most obvious modifications are for swimming, where three toes are often linked by a web which can displace water backwards. This feature has evolved several times and does not indicate a relationship between ducks, gulls and auks, any more than the lobed toes of moorhens, grebes and phalaropes indicates that they are related. The position of the legs and feet is also important, and in grebes and divers they are so placed, well to the rear, that swimming and diving is perfected at the expense of walking. High degrees of specialisation of this type have their evolutionary dangers, and there are plenty of advantages in being generalists like the gulls which can fly, walk and swim with no extreme adaptations.

SPECIALISED FEET

PREDATORS ARE ANOTHER group to show specialised feet and the osprey provides a classic example. It has a reversible outer toe and large spicules on its soles to grip slippery fish prey. The sparrowhawk has wide spreading toes, harriers long legs, golden eagles really heavy, sharp claws, while the peregrine's leg is short, presumably because of the risk of damage as it strikes large birds to kill in flight.

Woodpeckers have two toes facing forwards and two back, which helps them climb, while ptarmigan, often walking on soft snow, need a good spread of broad toes helped by their feathering.

BIRD FACT:

It is now known that many birds (perhaps all) can detect and 'read' the Earth's magnetic field, which helps them find their way, even in the dark, and on cloudy days.

FIBULA

TIBIA

BONES OF THE LEG

TARSOMETER TARSUS

DIGITS

Top left
Right leg of hen, showing the main bone structure.

Top right
Black-headed gull — note the webbed feet.

Bottom
Song thrush with berries. Its feet have sharp claws for grasping firmly onto branches.

TENDONS AND JOINTS

TENDONS ARE THE strong bands of protein, largely collagen, that link muscles to bones, and in birds, with the muscles of necessity concentrated in the upper leg, the tendons are long. In an isolated foot their upper end can be pulled to make the toes close around some object.

What a leg and its toes can do will also depend on the nature of the joints, be they simple hinges or allowing the greater range of movement needed for preening. Although a bird's legs may seen rather thin and fragile, they need to absorb the shock of landing, and in swimming species the legs are equipped with strong muscles. The rather short legs of most hawks, eagles and other birds of prey end in sturdy talons.

> 'The strangest thing about the Coot
> Must surely be its funny foot.
> Can there be anyone who knows
> Why it has long, lobate toes?
> Presumably, the Coot has found
> They help him over soggy ground,
> While, as he swims, being quite long legged,
> They're much more useful than if webbed.'
> Robert S. Morrison WORDS ON BIRDS

Legs vary just as much, with birds that wade, whatever their origin, having long legs. The avocet combines long legs with webbed feet, while divers add to their adaptations by having their lower leg, the tarsus, compressed from side to side for minimum resistance when the swimming foot is brought forward. Swifts have four toes which all point forward to help them grip on vertical surfaces.

REDUCING HEAT LOSS

ANOTHER FEATURE, NOT anatomical but physiological, is characteristic of birds' legs. As most of the leg and foot is usually unfeathered, it is going, under many conditions, to lose heat. To reduce heat loss, arteries can be deeper, but in a narrow leg that still leaves them exposed to cold. If, however, they are surrounded by, and intertwine with, the veins which are returning blood from the feet, the heat from the arteries can be transferred to the cooler blood returning in the veins, rather than being lost to the surroundings.

Top left
Female lesser-spotted woodpecker at nest-hole. Woodpeckers use their claws and stiff tails to help them cling to tree trunks.

Bottom left
Mallard drake – a typical duck, with well webbed feet.

Bottom right
The long legs of the black-winged stilt allow it to wade easily in mud and shallow water.

Beaks

IT WAS THE beaks of the ground finches in the Galapagos Islands that started Darwin along the path to his theory of natural selection. It is the beaks of certain ground finches on Daphne Major that have given Peter and Rosemary Grant, and their team, as good an insight as anyone into the power of natural selection, and its ability to bring about evolutionary change. They have studied the birds for 20 generations.

Almost every finch was ringed and had had its tarsus, wing and beak length measured as well as the depth of the bill. Later every bird would be individually known. Looking at the beak data after the drought, the Grants found that the average medium ground finch beak had been 10.68 mm long and 9.42 mm deep before the drought while survivors averaged 11.07 mm by 9.96 mm. Of the 600 males, which are about 5 per cent larger with correspondingly larger beaks, more than a quarter were still alive, but of the 600 females, with smaller beaks, fewer than 30 survived.

A CASE HISTORY

IN THE FIFTH year of their study, in 1977, a drought began to develop, the crops of the young cactus finches were empty, the leaves shrivelled and there were few flies and moths. In June 1976 there had been ten grams of seeds per square metre of volcanic lava but by December 1977 there were only three grams; the seeds that were present needed working for.

In the open the temperature was 50°C (122°F) and finches could not forage between eleven o'clock and three because of the heat. All the cactus finch fledglings died before they were three months old, not a single medium ground finch laid an egg or built a nest. Just as seed numbers fell and their hardness increased so the finch populations declined. From 1,500 in March 1976 to 1,300 in January 1977 and down to 300 in December.

SURPRISING RESULTS

THE NEXT SURPRISE was that young, big, deep-beaked birds had been dying during the drought. If a beak was 9.45 mm at 8 weeks that would be its adult size. It was found that if the average at 8 weeks was 9.45 mm, a bit later it was 8.73 mm not by shrinkage but by the death of big-billed birds. A big beak in a young bird is useless for cracking big seeds because its skull is not strong enough. Big birds need more food but are not very good at getting it; that was one of the reasons why young birds had been dying even if big-billed.

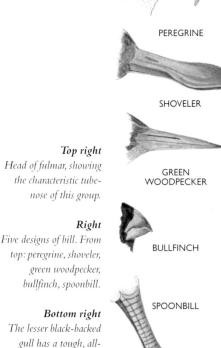

BEAKS

PEREGRINE

SHOVELER

GREEN WOODPECKER

BULLFINCH

SPOONBILL

Top right
Head of fulmar, showing the characteristic tube-nose of this group.

Right
Five designs of bill. From top: peregrine, shoveler, green woodpecker, bullfinch, spoonbill.

Bottom right
The lesser black-backed gull has a tough, all-purpose bill, enabling it to eat a variety of foods.

With few finches left, the males had to compete even more fiercely for mates. Some succeeded, while others failed. It turned out that the males that were most successful were the larger individuals, with the biggest bills, and these birds were winning the most mates. It was now time for the bills to get larger once more. In December 1982, more rain came than at any time since 1960, with stupendous thunderstorms as El Niño brought in warm water. Instead of dry lava everything grew to record size but it was too wet for cactus. By June, after a breeding frenzy, there were 2,000 finches on Daphne Major and young birds were breeding earlier than ever before.

NATURAL SELECTION

BECAUSE OF THE cactus failure most of the seeds were small but they were everywhere, even when another drought started. Natural selection began to operate strongly again as the huge finch population looked for food. Later analysis of results from that time showed that now the big finches were dying, and the big males were dying most. With less cactus the cactus finches, too, were low in numbers.

All this, and much more, demonstrates beautifully how natural selection operates, with tiny differences of fractions of a millimetre making the difference between life and death, and how its effects can oscillate so that there is, here, no overall trend. The plant life on the island and the seed supply also changed. A complicating factor was that hybridisation between species also occurred. Before El Niño, hybrids did not survive, but a cross later between a small finch, or a cactus finch, with *G. fortis*, does the genes of *G. fortis* a favour. In an oscillating environment, hybridisation and new gene combinations can flourish for a while, but when stability returns, the sharing of genes will slow again. Briefly, the second of Gould's evolutionary trees, the standard model, or the tree of survivors in the first, stops being a tree and becomes a tangled, interweaving creeper.

BEAKS OF BRITISH BIRDS

BRITISH FINCHES CONCENTRATE on whatever size of seed they can de with most effectively. Thus a hawfinch, with massive conical beak, can split exceptionally hard fruits. Linnets and greenfinches, both with short, broad beaks, pick seeds from the ground or off plant stems, while the goldfinch and siskin avoid competition by having different bill lengths, although both have long, narrow ones. The goldfinch with its longer beak can probe more deeply into thistle or teazel.

Later in this book the distinctive beaks of birds like shoveler, razorbill, spoonbill and waders, which avoid direct competition by having bills that can probe to different depths and select different food items, will be used to help identification. More subtle differences, like those of different divers or grebes, are vital to help identification of different species in winter. No doubt the variations in colour found in geese, ducks and gulls have their own significance, perhaps helping intraspecific recognition; they certainly help us with recognition.

> **BIRD FACT:**
> Wilson's petrel is probably the world's most numerous seabird, with an estimated global population of a staggering 50 million pairs.

Above left
The tough bill of the greylag goose is used for grubbing and grazing.

Above right
The greenfinch has a typical seed-eater's bill – a bit like a pair of pliers.

Left
The smaller siskin has a more delicate bill, often used for extracting seeds from cones.

Breeding patterns

AMONG ANIMALS THERE is a variety of mating systems and which one is favoured by a particular bird species will depend on factors like the resources available, the level of predation, whether female breeding behaviour is synchronised, and how well the young are able to look after themselves.

MONOGAMOUS PAIRS

MOST BIRDS are monogamous, with both parents working together to raise their young. About 10 per cent are polygamous, which means they have more than one mate. When a male mates with more than one female, this is termed polygyny (as in some harriers); when a female mates with more than one male it is termed polyandry; when more than one male mates with more than one female it is termed polygynandry (as in the dunnock). A final category, promiscuous, is the term used for a free arrangement with no fixed pair-bonds (as in some hummingbirds).

Monogamy tends to evolve where the male's help is needed for successful chick-rearing. He might need to protect the nest, or to help gather sufficient food. In colonial gulls, for example, one parent needs to be constantly at the nest to protect the eggs or chicks, while the other gathers food.

BIRD FACT:
Numbers of many birds of prey – notably peregrine and sparrowhawk – declined sharply in the 1950s and 1960s due to poisoning by organochlorine insecticides. Happily, numbers have recovered following a ban on these chemicals.

REARING THE CHICKS

IF RESOURCES ARE abundant however, a single parent is able to raise a family alone, and the other parent, usually the male, can obtain further matings (polygyny). If the young are able to look after themselves quickly, then polygamy may again be favoured, but on the whole birds are monogamous, perhaps because both eggs and chicks need heavy parental involvement. Even so, DNA analysis of, for instance, dunnocks and reed buntings, often shows that offspring do not share genes with their supposed fathers. Where predation is a major risk as it often is females may come into breeding condition together, as they do in colonial birds. An advantage of this is shown in colonial nesting kittiwakes, where a stable pair-bond is maintained for years, and reproductive success increases with age.

Herring gulls, sharing incubation, defence and food collection, have fairly equal roles, whereas male mallards and pheasants are not the most attentive of mates. In fact mallards are monogamous, perhaps because the males have to defend their mates from other males.

In most birds of prey the female is larger, sometimes, as in sparrowhawks and goshawks, markedly so.

Top right
Many marsh harriers are polygamous, with one male mating with two or more females.

Right
Arctic terns are fiercely defensive at their nest-sites.

The female initiates most territorial and courtship behaviour but, perhaps unexpectedly, she is also the main incubator and protector of her young brood.

DIFFERENT BREEDING STRATEGIES

AMONG HARRIERS, POLYGYNY is common, with a male defending a large territory, and attracting more than one female to nest within the defended area. Another form of polygyny is the lek system, seen in birds as varied as black grouse and ruff. In this system, the males gather to display in small territories, and the females visit these leks to select a mate and then bring up the young on their own. This has tended to evolve in species in which the young are born well formed and almost independent (i.e. easy to rear), as in grouse and some waders.

The fact that within a single order, the waders, there are a number of breeding strategies, shows the difficulties of generalising. Although woodcocks maintain their pair-bond for a time, the males may successively mate with four females, polygyny again, but there is no plumage difference. In the dotterel, females are brighter plumaged than males, initiate the courtship and leave the males to incubate, before mating with another male (polyandry). Similarly, in phalaropes the female is brighter and more clearly patterned, and will often leave the male to incubate after a period of pair-bonding and lay a repeat clutch with another male. Lapwings and curlews are essentially monogamous, but the ruff is decidedly polygynous, with certain dominant males having far more matings than the less successful and less distinctively ruffed males; this has led to a growing differentiation between the sexes, with male plumage and behaviour becoming progressively more exotic.

There are always advantages and disadvantages in different patterns of reproductive behaviour, but whatever tends to leave most parental genes in future generations will be favoured. In red-legged partridges, as with other ground-nesters vulnerable to predators, both sexes may mate with more than one partner during one breeding season. Each sex incubates eggs in separate 'scrapes' and if rearing the nidifugous young is successful, the pair are soon ready to mate again with the original or a different partner. If one nest fails, the incubator goes on the search for a new mate.

Some birds, like the well-studied dunnock, may show a range of different mating strategies, from monogamy, to polygyny and polyandry, and this may depend on many factors, including the nature of the habitat.

Top left
Like most species, adult reed warblers work hard to satisfy their hungry offspring.

Top right
Young coot are vulnerable and stick close to their parents.

Bottom left
Snow buntings often nest amongst boulders on high mountain plateaux.

Bottom right
Newly-hatched gulls, like this herring gull chick, have soft, downy plumage.

23

The Breeding Process

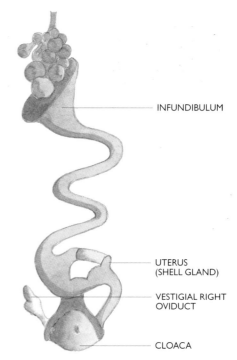

INFUNDIBULUM

UTERUS
(SHELL GLAND)

VESTIGIAL RIGHT
OVIDUCT

CLOACA

FEMALE REPRODUCTIVE SYSTEM

MUCH IS KNOWN about the factors that initiate seasonal behavioural changes in birds, and these are mainly linked with growth and recession of the reproductive organs.

FACTORS AFFECTING BREEDING

ALTHOUGH SECONDARY FACTORS, like sudden cold or warm spells which may slow down or speed up, the rate of gonadal development, there is no experimental evidence that these factors can initiate gonad growth in the absence of appropriate light regimes. The ratio of hours of daylight to darkness is the main cue which changes as spring develops. Most birds have both breeding and migrating behaviour suppressed in the absence of appropriate light stimulation.

Research workers have been helped by a behavioural peculiarity of caged migrant birds, which develop a marked nocturnal restlessness as they came into the migratory state. This provides a measurable quantity, the amount of hopping, to test experimentally the effectiveness of environmental and physiological factors in releasing the urge to migrate; this, of course, is a preliminary to breeding behaviour. Activity patterns are generally recorded by means of a spring perch attached to a micro-switch incorporated into an electrical circuit.

Gonads do not only produce eggs and sperm, but also sex hormones, and it is the level of these that determine territorial and courtship behaviour. There is an interplay of factors for final ovarian development. Egg laying may not occur unless there are other appropriate stimuli, such as the appearance of a breeding mate, or of fellow colonial nesters, or of courtship itself. As usual, there are species differences, with some birds being ready to have two breeding seasons in a year, following appropriate light stimuli, but others retaining an autonomous rhythm of gonad size according to the season, even if kept in complete darkness.

PHYSIOLOGY OF REPRODUCTION

UNDER THE RIGHT conditions, ovaries and testes can increase in weight by up to five hundred times. Except in ducks and the ostrich, which have a penis, sperm released from the testes are moved to a cloaca which, following courtship, can be brought close to the female cloaca. Fertilisation of the egg takes place in the females in the infundibulum (see diagram). As the fertilised egg travels down the oviduct, it gains food from the uterus or shell gland, and the egg, now surrounded by membranes, gains water and salts before being covered by a shell.

Top right
The reproductive system of a female bird, showing the developing eggs at the opening to the infundibulum.

Bottom left
Cross-section of egg with developing embryo.

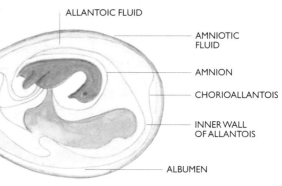

ALLANTOIC FLUID

AMNIOTIC
FLUID

AMNION

CHORIOALLANTOIS

INNER WALL
OF ALLANTOIS

ALBUMEN

FERTILISED EGG WITH EMBRYO

The large enclosed eggs of birds and reptiles are devices to allow the processes of feeding, respiration and excretion to continue as development proceeds from single cell to complex chick. Initially the actual living matter is only a thousandth of the mass of the egg, with the rest being devoted to protection and storage.

FORMATION OF THE EGG

CELL DIVISION STARTS before the egg is laid, and the growing cluster of cells moves to the tip of the egg where it will be nearest to the warmth of the brooding mother. By the tenth day, in the hen, embryonic membranes, delicate sheets of tissue, extend from the blastoderm, which can now be called the embryo. The yolk and albumen, the egg white, act as food supplies, in the form of fat and protein, and water which is steadily lost through the porous shell.

MATING

MATING CAN APPEAR very haphazard in birds, but certain behavioural techniques help to make it more efficient than it looks. One explanation, even if a rather special one, is provided by work on dunnocks. Females have a precopulatory display, involving crouching, ruffling body feathers, shivering the wings, and raising the tail to expose the cloaca for up to two minutes. Copulation is extraordinarily brief, with the male appearing to jump over the female as cloacal contact lasts only a fraction of a second.

Stuart Smith (1950) describes an 'invitation' display by the female yellow wagtail when she is ready for mating: 'The cock bird may be pirouetting around the hen ... when she suddenly crouches on the ground, puffs out her feathers, half opens and depresses her wings and elevates her tail until it is vertical. When in this position, she begins to twirl round and round on the ground ... After gyrating thus for several complete turns she stops, and the cock, if he is ready, will mount the hen and copulate.'

Above
A cock linnet displays his breeding plumage.

Bottom left
Mallard's nest with eggs and newly-hatched ducklings.

Bottom right
Mating, as in this pair of shags, is a brief and seemingly haphazard affair.

Feathers

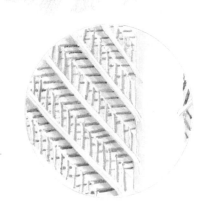

THERE ARE SEVERAL generations of feathers, from the fluffy, simple, heat-retaining feathers of the very young, through various juvenile types, to those of the adult.

CONTOUR FEATHERS, including the primaries and secondaries of the wing, the tail feathers and those that cover the ears, form the visible cover. Down feathers, hidden below, have vital insulation functions, while others are specialised, such as the rictal bristles around the beak of a nightjar that help it to catch the moths of the late evening as it flies.

In his book *Life on Earth* (1979) David Attenborough gives a clear and straightforward description of feathers: 'The feather is an extraordinary device. Few substances can equal it as an insulator, and none, weight for weight, whether man-made or animal-grown, can excel it as an aerofoil. Its substance is keratin. The same horny material forms a reptile's scales and our own nails, but the exceptional qualities of a feather come from its intricate construction. A central shaft carries on either side a hundred or so filaments; each filament is similarly fringed with about a hundred smaller filaments or barbules. Flight feathers have an additional feature. Their barbules overlap those of neighbouring filaments and hook them on to one another so that they are united into a continuous vane. There are several hundred such hooks on a single barbule, a million or so in a single feather.'

Top right
Feathers are very light, but their surfaces are kept rigid by an intricate system of interlocking barbules, as shown in the close-up.

Middle left
This young redshank is covered in soft down feathers.

Bottom right
Replacement of feathers during the moult may change the plumage from winter (behind) to summer (foreground), as in this dunlin.

OBSERVING FEATHERS

AMONG THOSE WHO observe feathers most closely are artists. Charles Tunnicliffe drew a lot of dead birds, measured to exact life size, and depicted in a variety of media to achieve an accurate impression of feather texture. His *Sketches of Bird Life* (1981) include a series of nightjar paintings of this type, but when drawing and painting from life, artists still observe in a way that most of us do not. I love watching a redshank pair but I do not notice the 'very marked difference of size and plumage in these two birds. Female larger and with neck and breast much more striped than male. Her scapulars much more patterned. Male breast had a ground colour almost vinous. The female lacked this colour on upper front of breast.'

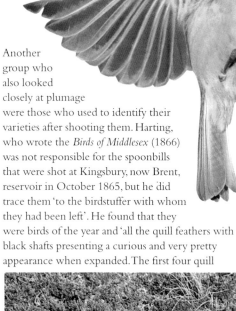

FEATHER COLOUR

THE COLOUR OF THE feathers can be vital, sometimes obviously so, but at other times in ways that are yet to be explained. Because birds live in a largely visual world, we can understand their behaviour more easily than we can the behaviour of the scent-dominated and often nocturnal mammals. Much courtship is visual, with the movements evolving to show off bright colours, like those forming the speculum on the wings of ducks. The elaborate movements of male black grouse and ruffs at their leks are further examples. Movements linked with coloured feathers serve as signals which may warn off a rival male, attract a mate or maintain a pair bond. Moorhens for instance show quite complex behaviour, but the flicking of their tails, to show the white feathers beneath, seems an obvious enough cue for the young birds to follow.

By contrast, cryptic coloration, most common among female ground-nesters like the ducks and game birds, conceals the birds. Good examples are nightjar and woodcock, which rest and incubate among the bracken fronds and dead leaves on the ground during the day, before feeding at dusk.

The way that the colour is produced is either through pigmentation or through the structure of the feather. The commonest pigment is melanin, which appears either black or brown. Carotenoid pigments show red or orange, and porphyrins and other pigments lead to some of the other colours. Feather structure can cause scattering of light waves to give iridescent colours like those of magpies and starlings. The intensity of a flamingo's pink feathers depends on the shrimps they have eaten.

Another group who also looked closely at plumage were those who used to identify their varieties after shooting them. Harting, who wrote the *Birds of Middlesex* (1866) was not responsible for the spoonbills that were shot at Kingsbury, now Brent, reservoir in October 1865, but he did trace them 'to the birdstuffer with whom they had been left'. He found that they were birds of the year and 'all the quill feathers with black shafts presenting a curious and very pretty appearance when expanded. The first four quill

feathers white with dark brown tips as follows — first with dark brown stripe on outer web; second first half of outer web brown then white; third and fourth outer webs nearly all white. The first quill shortest; the second largest in the wing.' Museum workers and some ringers will observe feathers with the same precision, but most of us operate more on impression, except in special circumstances. However there is much beauty to be seen in little details.

Top left
This blue tit clearly shows the outspread flight feathers.

Middle left
The brown plumage of a female eider helps conceal it during incubation.

Bottom right
Moorhens flash their white under-tail feathers as they display to each other.

Preening

When not a strain is heard through all the woods
I've seen the shilfa Chaffinch light from off his perch
And hop into a shallow of the stream
Then, half afraid, flit to shore, then in
Again alight and dip his rosy breast,
And fluttering wings, while dew like globules coursed
The plumage of his brown empurpled back.
William Graham (1918–86)

FEATHERS NEED regular maintenance, hence much elaborate preening to remove dirt, parasites and old preen oil and to zip the feather barbules back into place, thereby repairing the vane. Bathing is usually the first stage in feather maintenance, and most will have watched the whole-hearted activities of robins and blackbirds in bird-baths. The object would seem to be to wet as much of the body as possible without wetting it so much that damage results.

BIRD FACT:
Research has shown that male sedge warblers with the most elaborate songs are more successful in attracting a mate than those with simpler songs. This has led to the evolution of a long and varied song in this species.

BATHING

WATERBIRDS ALSO NEED to bathe, but they must also dry afterwards, and have their wing flapping movements to help them. Cormorants, as is well known, follow this up by holding their wings out for a period after bathing. But cormorants get wetter than most birds, for by driving the air from between their feathers when they dive, they can swim deeper and faster in pursuit of food. They also lack the oil which keeps most bird feathers from getting really wet — another adaptation to diving. Having dried, it is finally time for an application of oil from the preen gland at the base of the tail. Most species stimulate preen oil with their beaks, twisting their heads round to meet their twisting tails; it helps to have a long neck. A dust bath or a dose of formic acid from ants, placed strategically under the wing, or wherever, can also help parasite control.

Top
This blackbird has fluffed out its feathers during a preening session.

Bottom
Even the sleek kingfisher may look a little scruffy during the moult.

PARASITES

FEATHER LICE ARE the only parasites that feed primarily on the keratin of feathers. They are flattened from above downwards, so they can run fast enough to escape some preening; if they settle on the head or neck they can avoid the beak. Rothschild and Clay in their delightful book on an undelightful subject (1952) mention that lice have been taken from chicken dust-baths, so dust bathing does seem to help with parasite control. The fact that birds tend to be more heavily infested if they are sick also suggests that their bathing, oiling and preening activity does keep the lice in check.

A robin with most of the upper mandible missing was infected with 127 lice, but numbers rarely exceed 15 in normal robins.

Feather lice usually feed on the downy parts of larger feathers, using their legs to direct feather barbules towards their mandibles. Once the ancestors of lice had moved onto birds, or moved from scaly reptiles onto the evolving birds, their evolutionary potential was considerable. Not surprisingly, blood from any site may be part of the diet, but more exciting moves took them inside the throat-pouches of cormorants for blood and, for

part of the life cycle of one species, into the inside of the shaft of the flight feathers of curlew, to feed on dried feather cores.

Mites can also damage the plumage, while plenty of fleas will move between the feathers, if only to get to a new blood source. Luckily for birds, however, fleas have never done so well on them, as they have on mammals.

MOULT

DESPITE ALL THE dusting, bathing and preening, feathers are subject to wear. Sometimes a degree of wear can bring a bird to its conspicuous best, as when the pale edges of feathers wear off as a linnet develops its red breast before breeding.

Eventually though, replacement is needed, making for a period of difficulty, when birds may even become flightless if all flight feathers are lost at once, as happens to ducks entering eclipse plumage. More often, moulting begins with the primaries of the wing, followed by the secondaries and tail feathers, with symmetrical loss on the two sides of the body, thus reducing, but not eliminating flight. The coot is another species which becomes flightless during the moult, and on the Ukrainian coast of the Black Sea for example, the August moulting flocks may extend for several kilometres.

Moult occurs when the new feather follicle is stimulated to grow. As the new feather begins to form, the old one is pushed out. Being an actively growing structure, the new one needs blood, but this is withdrawn as the feather matures and hardens. The stimulus for follicle growth in temperate regions seems to be changes in day length, with the thyroid gland also involved, but as there is a variety of moult patterns and as the stimulus in the tropics must be different, with little variation in day length, the regulating factors may well vary.

Garden birds become much less obvious at the time of their moult, as is suggested by many of the observation frequency curves in the *Garden Bird Watch Handbook*. Some seabirds disappear out to sea, away from their main predators, where they can swim in relative safety. Many northern waders moult in two phases; if there is not time to complete a moult as the short arctic summer draws to an end, the moult is completed after the migratory flight when hopefully there is plenty of food for the energy-demanding process.

Top left
Many birds, such as this house sparrow, take regular dust baths, probably to discourage parasites.

Middle left
Water birds, such as this Canada goose, need to preen regularly to keep their feathers in good condition.

Middle right
Kingfisher preening its wing feathers.

Bottom
Some water birds, like this shag, need to spread their wings out to dry between bouts of diving.

Flight

WHETHER WATCHING FULMARS around the cliffs of Hebridean Mingulay, whooper swans leaving Irish Tory Island for Iceland, or a spotted flycatcher over the village pond in Combpyne, Devon, bird flight can always amaze. The fulmar glides apparently effortlessly and it is gliding flight that is easier to explain.

MECHANICS AND WING STRUCTURE

IN CROSS-SECTION, the part of the wing nearest the body is shaped so that air movement leads to a build up of pressure below and reduced pressure above. The resulting force is lift, and it is this which enables a bird to stay in the air. To get more lift, in a model, one can increase its surface area, or its speed relative to the air. Alternatively, the angle of attack or the camber of the wing section can be changed. Eventually, increasing the angle of attack leads to stalling, but in birds the wing slots of the bastard wing and the emarginated primaries act as effective antistalling devices. On the cliffs where fulmars

breed, the air rises as sea winds reach the cliff face, while at sea level the air is in constant motion above the waves: in either case the long-winged fulmar needs only a minimum of flapping. Around the cliff it often uses a foot to help it to steer.

Having a long, narrow wing, the fulmar's aspect ratio is high. Another important ratio gives the wing loading, the bird's weight divided by the wing area. A heavy bird with a relatively small wing area will have to do a lot of rapid flapping. With their great weight, swans will always have to flap.

Top right
Fulmar riding on an updraft of air from a cliff. Note the foot spread out as a rudder.

Bottom right
Vertical sea-cliffs such as these are ideal habitats for fulmars and gulls.

PHOTOGRAPHING FLIGHT

AT THE TIME when Gray gave the Royal Institution Christmas Lectures in 1959 the technology of photography was already able to allow the wing movements of pigeons to be followed, as they flew towards a camera or past it, along a corridor. More recent photographs give an even more remarkable image of the movements of birds' wings. They are constantly altering, due both to the suppleness of the feathers and to the birds own internal muscular movements. The main muscles are the breast or pectoral ones, attached to the sternum. The *pectoralis major*, which pulls the wing down, is a large muscle, but those that move the wrist and raise the wing are smaller.

Perhaps the peak of flying is the ability to hover in still air. A kestrel, searching for voles, will sometimes have an almost vertical body, so that wings go backwards and forwards rather than up and down. The powering of the back-stroke demands a great deal of the smaller pectoral muscle. Although most auks, like puffins, can fly fast and direct, it is the use of their wings in swimming that is their speciality.

ADAPTING FOR FLIGHT

WHATEVER THE METHOD of flight, the lightness of the bones and other adaptations of the skeleton and feathers are vital, but so are the physiological

features. A large heart is important for long flights, and a bird's high temperature (40°C/104°F) links with their high metabolic rate and this, in turn, is linked with the respiratory system. Although the lungs are small, the air sacs connected to them may form 15–20 per cent of the body volume. The air sacs are not directly involved in gas exchange, but act as bellows for the lungs which operate, not on an in and out system, but with a through flow of air. Schmidt-Nielsen (1988) points out that the finest branches of the bronchi do not end in sacs like the mammalian alveoli, but are open at both ends and gas exchange takes place in air capillaries which surround these bronchi.

Water levels need to be regulated. As birds excrete uric acid as a paste, rather than urea dissolved to form liquid urine, they do not lose so much water. If, however, they spend time at sea, as many do, they need to drink sea water but do not have kidneys efficient enough to get rid of salt. As Schmidt-Nielsen says: 'all marine birds – gulls, albatrosses, penguins and so on – have a gland in the head that can excrete a highly concentrated solution of sodium chloride. This gland, which has a structure entirely different from the kidney, can excrete a salt solution up to twice the concentration of sea water. When the birds ingest food with a high salt content or drink sea water, the gland secretes the excess salt; the secretion flows through the salt gland ducts into the nasal cavity and drips off from the tip of the beak.'

Without these physiological adaptations, life at sea or birds' extensive migratory flights would simply not be possible.

Top right
The barn owl uses its soft, broad wings in silent, hovering flight.

Top left
The streamlined wing of a duck – in this case a smew.

Middle
The long, broad wing of an eagle.

Bottom left
Pheasants are reluctant fliers, usually coming down to land again after a short distance.

Migration

AMONG ALL THE aspects of bird life, their ability to orientate themselves accurately, to fly huge distances without stopping and to return to their identical nest site has perhaps aroused the most wonder. The fact that many of the best places to study migration and see migrants are spectacular in their own right, makes migration study even more obviously exciting, while for some, the unexpected appearance of rare migrants is the very essence of birdwatching.

PATTERNS OF BIRD MOVEMENT

A CLOSE WATCH in your own garden or familiar patch of woodland, heath or estuary will reveal the ever-changing pattern of bird movement. Pied wagtails that nested on the front of the house may

soon be down on the marshes, and many woods which have song thrushes in summer, lose them to coastal areas in the winter. Almost all birds move, but it is the

spectacular long-distance flights that excite the imagination, and the two way movement, there and back, that is true migration.

REASONS FOR MIGRATION

DESPITE THE HAZARDS of these long flights, the bird population concerned must survive better by moving than by staying put, or such behaviour would not have evolved. When conditions get hard, with shorter days in which to search for more elusive food, there are two options for any bird that is going to stay for the winter.

The first option is to specialise, as the treecreeper does, with its long fine beak for reaching invertebrates dormant in crevices in the bark. The second is to change diet, as for example the change in

the digestive system of the bearded tit as it switches from summer invertebrates to winter reed seeds. From late September, the gizzard grows more muscular so that seeds can be crushed.

Alternatively, a species can migrate, as the whinchat does, unlike the closely-related stonechat that makes only local movements. Analysis of the BTO nest record cards shows that the stonechat has time for three broods, rather than the whinchat's two, and that twice as many stonechat nests produce young, giving stonechats a three to one advantage in productivity. Despite this, and the whinchat's extensive migration across the Sahara, whinchat populations are not subject to the violent fluctuations that cold weather can produce in stonechats. Avoiding food shortage can be more successful than facing the risks that cold weather brings.

BIRD FACT:
Although birds suffer many pressures, including hunting, pollution and poisoning, loss of habitat is the biggest threat to bird diversity.

Top right
Male bearded tit, feeding on a reed head, its main source of food during the winter.

Middle left
Most stonechats (female shown here) move only short distances during the winter, rather than migrating.

Bottom right
The migratory urges of the starling have been closely studied.

FINDING THEIR WAY

PRESUMABLY MIGRATION STARTED as small-scale movements, perhaps as the last ice age lifted, though no doubt there had been different patterns earlier. As the ice retreated, a bird moving further north to breed would have longer days and less competition for food. As the distances grew greater, knowledge of a familiar area, and known visual cues, would no longer be adequate for orientation. Movement in relation to the sun, particularly perhaps at dawn and dusk, and the stars, would become more important. Experiments confirm this type of orientation and link it to a bird's time clock. There is also evidence that birds can obtain directional information from the earth's magnetic field. Salmon certainly use the smell of their home river as a navigational guide, and birds, particularly hole-nesting petrels, may well use this sense in the final stages for finding their own burrows.

Smell would not however be sufficient for a breeding Welsh shearwater to find its way home from long distance. G. V. T. Matthews showed the powers of these migrants by releasing them far from home and timing their return. From relatively featureless landscapes the birds circled and set off in the right direction. Some birds were able to return at rates of 402 km (250 miles) a day, coming back to their own burrow.

In the case of shearwaters, individual birds could be traced, but another approach was to trap, ring and re-locate large numbers of a common bird whose normal migratory movements were known.

A. C. Perdeck trapped 11,000 starlings in Holland, transported them to Switzerland, and released separate flocks of adults and young. The young continued on a course parallel to their original line of migration and ended up in the South of France and in Spain. Those ringed adults which were later re-trapped had re-orientated, and were found in their normal wintering areas of northern France and Britain. There must be an inherited tendency to orientate in a given direction, but experience can modify this instinct so that they can find a particular area.

Another approach, having accepted the fact of orientation, is to experiment with birds under controlled conditions. Again using starlings, Kramer had observed that captive birds were more restless at migration times, and that this restlessness was not random. This led him to design special cages in which he could alter the sun's position, as seen by the birds, with mirrors. The restless starlings maintained the same angle to the sun's rays whether receiving them directly or reflected by the mirrors. Obscuring the sun, whether naturally by cloud or artificially, led to the birds being disorientated, just as migrants get lost when cloud or mist suddenly descends.

Top
Even in winter the treecreeper can still winkle out dormant insects from crevices in the bark.

Bottom
Some birds, like this Manx shearwater, may use smell to help them find their own burrow in the dark.

Migration Heights and Speed

MIGRATION IS DETERMINED by internal rhythmicity linked with light, and by an internal physiological clock. We have seen too that migrants in captivity show restlessness and there is a clear positive correlation between the distance of migratory flight and the degree of restlessness. Longer migratory journeys involve longer-lasting restlessness, and the migrant halts when the restlessness fades out.

> **BIRD FACT:**
> The grey heron has one of the slowest wingbeats of any bird – just 2 beats per second.

Top
The lesser whitethroat is an unobtrusive summer visitor to our woods and hedgerows.

Middle
Every few years large numbers of waxwings invade from Scandinavia.

Bottom
The house martin migrates mainly to tropical Africa.

OBSERVING MIGRATING BIRDS

IT IS THE SPEED of the bird relative to the air that determines its energy costs, but the speed and direction of the wind determine the absolute speed of the bird, and therefore the distance that it can fly. Radar observations have contributed to our understanding of these speeds, with warblers flying at 30–40 km/h (20–30 mph), larger songbirds 50 km/h (30 mph) and waders and ducks at 60–80 km/h (40–50 mph). The height of flying birds can be linked to wind speeds, and again radar has helped to find this out. Birds often start at 1,000–2,000 m (3,280–6,561 ft) over land, but move up to 6,000 m (19,658 ft) on long flights over water. Apart from there being different wind patterns at different altitudes, high flight is also useful in that heat is dissipated at height

without any loss of water; if cooling involved any water loss there could be dangerous dehydration.

Another way of looking at speed is to plot the rate at which a wave of migrants crosses a land mass. Conder (1954) illustrates the progress of two waves of wheatears in relation to British and Irish Observatories in 1952. The first wave reached Lundy and Dungeness on 3 April, Bardsey and Cley on the 4 April and Monk's House (Northumberland) on the 5 April. By 7 April they were past the Isle of May in the Firth of Forth. The second wave were seen at Saltee (Wexford) and Skokholm on the 9 April, Monk's House on the 10 April, and were clear of the Scottish mainland by 11 April.

MIGRATION PATTERNS

MIGRATION TAKES MANY forms. Long distance migration to Africa or Asia, or rather lesser distances within the northern hemisphere, special seabird movements for those which are mobile whenever they are not at their breeding sites, partial migrants when some move and others do not, altitudinal migrants and irruptive species which only move distances when food shortages force them on. If these do not move back it is not a true migration.

DIFFERENT DESTINATIONS

THE HOUSE MARTIN goes to Africa, the lesser whitethroat stays in the northern hemisphere and the arctic tern is always quoted as one of the longest bird migrants. Redwings are typical winter visitors to this country, and although a ten-year-old chaffinch may be ringed within 180 m (600 ft) of its birthplace, others move into the country from Scandinavia. The stonechat and song thrush have been mentioned as moving locally, whereas waxwing and common crossbill may irrupt over large distances. The movements of some of these selected species are illustrated.

The migration of the lesser whitethroat involve weight changes during their complex movements. Birds leave their overwintering areas and pass through Ethiopia as early as January, but only put on substantial weight in preparation for their move to Asia at the end of February. There they put on weight again before moving on, but lose it all as they fly across Europe, before flying into the south of England in mid to late April.

Their summer is busy and short with two broods characterised by weight fluctuations and a moult to be fitted into some 15 weeks. Then they start their return migration, with associated weight loss, to Italy before moving on to Egypt, where more feeding provides the energy for a final flight into winter quarters elsewhere in the warmth of the north and east of Africa.

UNEXPECTED ARRIVALS

HOWEVER EFFICIENT MIGRANTS may be at reaching their destinations, they often turn up unexpectedly elsewhere. Post breeding dispersal of young birds may mean they move in a direction away from their winter quarters. Reverse migration, for whatever reason, sends migrants off at 180∞ to their normal course, while overshooting, particularly in spring and sometimes with a following wind, can bring a bird, on the right bearing, to a land fall far beyond its breeding range, as when Iberian migrants reach Devon or Cornwall.

'Migration study, complex though it is, still depends – and always will depend – on the observatory and field man, the island lover, the cape haunter, the bunk sleeper and the sandwich eater.'
James Fisher SEA BIRDS

Top
Arctic terns are famed for one of the longest migration routes of all birds – from northern Europe and the Arctic right down to the Southern Ocean.

Bottom
Redwings are regular winter visitors from northern Europe.

Bird Observatories and Migration

THE BIRD OBSERVATORY in Britain stems from R. M. Lockley who, in the 1930s, combined farming with birdwatching on the small Welsh island of Skokholm, where he built traps for catching and ringing birds. Then in the late 1940s a surge of interest was shown, and a chain of observatories developed, providing what Williamson (1965) considered one of Britain's major contributions to ornithology.

FAIR ISLE

DR WILLIAM EAGLE CLARKE, in the early 1900s, visited Fair Isle, The Flannans and St Kilda, and his thinking about bird movements led to his *Studies in Bird Migration*, a standard work for many years. He believed that migrants followed great 'trunk routes' along prominent geographical features such as escarpments, river valleys and the coast. The east coast of England could have been one of these routes. Later came the contrasting idea that the birds set out on a broad front, in a preferred direction towards their goal, but they might be diverted by mountains or the sea and so be concentrated along leading lines.

After Eagle Clarke, others kept a watch on Fair Isle, which is 40 km (25 miles) from both Orkney and Shetland. When Kenneth Williamson arrived as the first warden in 1948, its position on migration routes had already allowed it to gain ten new species for Britain. There was no addition to these until 1953 when Williamson 'thought the world had gone mad' when, opening a bag in which a trapped bird had been kept, he saw 'a dwarf thrush no bigger than a skylark with a uniformly brown back and tail and heavily spotted whitish underparts'. It proved to be a

North American species, found once before in Europe, a young grey-cheeked thrush. That autumn also brought Siberian newcomers, citrine wagtails and a Baikal teal, at a time when other rare eastern birds turned up at Fair Isle.

Much has changed at observatories over the years, but perhaps nothing indicates change so much as the fact that Williamson shot his first rarity, to prove identification. Identification skills developed quickly, and have continued to do so, as is indicated by a letter from R. F. Ruttledge to Williamson after they, and others, had identified a Pallas's warbler. 'Perhaps the thing that struck me most of all, was the wonderful opportunity one gets to practice making field identifications and the chance of making rapid notes of essential characters.' That Pallas's warbler avoided not only the fate of being shot, but also that of being trapped, for it was far from any of Fair Isle's permanent traps, and mist-nets had not been developed.

Top

The tiny Pallas' warbler is a rare, though regular, visitor to our shores from Siberia, usually in late autumn.

Bottom

Birds, like this song thrush, are weighed as well as being ringed at observatories.

RINGING BIRDS

TRAPPING, TO ALLOW ringing and laboratory studies, is a major activity at observatories. Heligoland traps, first used on the North Sea island of that name, are large, permanent wire-netting cages, usually set among shrubby cover. They have a

wide, 20 m (65 ft), opening between wings, and the wire narrows to a covered funnel, perhaps 4 m (13 ft) high. The birds are then driven through a swing-door to an ever-narrowing lock up and, finally, to a windowed catching box.

In the mid 1950s, trapping birds for ringing was revolutionised by the introduction of mist-nets from Japan, where peasant farmers had used them for catching birds for eating. These nets, stretched upright between supporting poles, are so fine as to be almost invisible. Birds flying into them pocket themselves over taut nylon strands threaded through the loose panels of the net. Given appropriate dexterity the birds can be extracted unharmed, and the great advantage of these mist-nets is their lightness and therefore mobility.

Williamson mentions that the justification for trapping birds is to learn more about them. One way is by attaching a numbered metal ring to the bird's leg before freeing it, and hoping that someone else will find it later, perhaps brought in by the cat, trapped for eating or recovered by another ringer. From such recoveries, details of life expectancy, migration routes, and cause of death, can be accumulated. Captured birds are also measured and weighed and variations, state of moult and external parasites are examined.

IMPORTANCE OF OBSERVATORIES

IT BECAME CLEAR to Williamson that knowledge of weather and the movements of air masses was central to migrants, as adverse winds was what brought migrants to Fair Isle and other observatories. Impressive 'falls' of migrants, both in spring and autumn, took place when the wind was easterly. All the observatory observations supported the importance of wind, and this was particularly so for isolated Fair Isle. Bird movement there is accidental, due either to lateral deflection from the migrant's true heading, or to a down wind displacement in mist, when orientation is not possible, and in fine weather when birds are dispersing at random from their breeding haunts. These wind orientated dispersal movements are sometimes phenomenal.

Williamson left Fair Isle in 1957 to become Migration Research Officer for the BTO, and by the time he wrote Fair Isle and its Birds there were 26 observatories on islands and peninsulas around Britain and Ireland.

Top left
A heligoland trap on Lundy Island.

Bottom left
Ring on leg of house martin

Bottom right
Mist nets are efficient devices for catching birds – like this blue tit.

> *Bird ringing in Britain and Ireland is co-ordinated by the British Trust for Ornithology (BTO). It takes two years for volunteers to train to ring on their own and interested parties should write directly to the BTO for information.*

A TRIP TO CAPE CLEAR

IN THE SPRING of 1959 I was asked to join Garth Pettitt who wanted to explore the possibilities of Tory Island off the Donegal coast as an observatory. It was there that I had my only experience of mist-netting and my only chance to climb around a lighthouse at night, catching birds attracted to the beams.

IRISH RARITIES

IN THE AUTUMN of that year J. T. R. Sharrock and four others turned up at Cape Clear at another corner of Ireland. Sharrock (1973) describes how in 11 weeks the five of them found 17 species regarded as major rarities in Ireland, sea passage on an unsuspected scale and massive diurnal migration. If Fair Isle was associated with rare birds and the concept of drift, Cape Clear came to be associated with seabird movements. These were very poorly understood, and the only real gain in knowledge from early observatory work was the demonstration that the Balearic race of the Manx shearwater made a remarkable migration up the west coast of Europe to moult in late summer.

The Cape Clear observations began systematically in 1959, and by the time that Bourne (in Sharrock 1973) wrote *Cape Clear and Sea Bird Studies* he could base his analysis on 11 years and 2,952 hours of sea watching. This systematic work, together with the frequent recording of supposedly rarer species, stimulated interest in other sites, and co-operative observations along the length of the west coast of Europe were organised by Garth Pettitt, when the seabird group was formed in 1965.

BIRDS SEEN FROM CAPE CLEAR

AFTER FOUR YEARS it was possible to set Cape Clear in a wider context. Because they fly low, seabirds are particularly likely to be diverted by any barrier and to be concentrated along 'guiding lines', but much of the time, away from breeding areas and in good weather, they stay out at sea, which is a very uniform and featureless habitat. At the Cape, with onshore

winds and poor visibility, birds approach the shore. Passage is much more marked in a westerly direction, with the Blananarra headland concentrating the birds.

Easterly movement, except for Manx shearwaters and auks on feeding flights from Kerry colonies, is less frequent, as birds moving south along the west coast of Ireland can be seen from Erris or Brandon heads but then stay out at sea. Gannets, kittiwakes and fulmars tend to occur with onshore winds and poor visibility, local Manx shearwaters move east in the morning and west in the afternoon when they return to Kerry, and rarer shearwaters move into the area when shoaling fish reach their peak in late summer.

Skuas are only seen moving west, as are storm petrels. There may be up to 1,000 of these in an hour when there are south-westerlies with rain in late summer. Arctic and American breeders, including Sabine's gull, phalaropes, Leach's petrel and most skuas, migrate in the central Atlantic and normally have little trouble avoiding lee shores.

Rarer shearwaters, sometimes in large numbers and occasionally feeding, mainly occur between August and October. More than 1,000 great shearwaters may move west during a long seawatch, and sooty, little and Cory's shearwaters also occur, with the last species being seen earlier than the others, often in June.

Top
Great skuas may often be seen on passage during a seawatch from a vantage point.

Bottom
Redstarts breed in western woods, but often turn up in coastal scrub on migration.

VARIETY OF SPECIES

EARLY APRIL IS an exciting time on the island, with summer migrants and weather to show that spring has really arrived. It needs only the lightest of easterly or south-easterly winds to bring a rush of migrants to the island. Such movements bring the largest

numbers of sand martins hawking over the bogs, ring ouzels and wheatears, together with the first whimbrels, arctic terns and grasshopper warblers. This is the most likely time to see peregrines, jack snipe and hoopoes. Rarities have included little crake and white-throated sparrow, and choughs are very obvious, indulging in their delightful communal acrobatics.

Later in the year, no time can compare with early October, when some of the largest movements occur, and wind direction becomes everyone's obsessional interest. After evening log-writing someone is bound to look outside the Observatory and on his return a chorus of voices chants 'Where's the wind?'

A touch of easterly wind, or a calm day following a blustery day may be enough. Each clump of bushes in turn is surrounded by ornithologists twitching with excitement. Redstarts, lesser whitethroats, yellow-browed warblers, goldcrests, firecrests and red-breasted flycatchers are all in their highest numbers in October. It is almost impossible to stay on the island at the time and not see one rarity such as a spotted crake, bluethroat, Blythe's reed warbler, greenish warbler or a rare pipit. If the wind is in the west there should be few complaints, as American birds can appear, and Sharrock listed dowitcher, white-rumped sandpiper, yellow-billed cuckoo, olive-backed thrush, red-eyed vireo, American redstart and rose-breasted grosbeak.

Middle left
Whimbrels are regular on migration, especially in early spring.

Top right
Leach's petrel nests in Shetland and St Kilda, but spends most of its time out in the open Atlantic.

Bottom
The dainty yellow-browed warbler is a regular autumn visitor to Cape Clear.

BARDSLEY

SOME OF THE BIRDS flying west past Cape Clear could well have passed Bardsey, Ynys Enlli, on their way. It is a smaller island, under 200 ha (494 acres) compared with Cape Clear's 630ha (1,556 acres), but the stone walls, salt-sprayed cliffs and small fields are similar.

VARIETY OF BIRDS RECORDED

I FIRST VISITED Bardsey in 1947, and remember the puffins flying to and from Ynys Gwylan. Since 1954 there has been regular recording of all migrant and breeding birds within the main observatory season of March to November. When Peter Roberts wrote Birds of Bardsey (1985), 276 species had been recorded and over 100,000 birds ringed, and these totals are now more than 300 and over 200,000. It is interesting to compare the occurrence of some passerine migrants on Cape Clear and Bardsey.

Modern organisations are fond of quoting their aims and objectives, and the monitoring objectives of Bardsey were described in the 1996 observatory report (Adroddioid Gwylfa Ynys Enlli). Peter Hope-Jones, for long associated with the island, asks 'what precisely is the objective behind the observatory's collection of data?'

LOOKING AT BIRD MIGRATION

TO SAY 'the study of bird migration' is, he thinks, too unfocussed. Monitoring has sometimes been viewed like ringing as a 'good thing to do', but without clarifying reasons for doing it. He suggests that a major reason is that 'habitat managers, landowners, biologists and politicians can have quantified data on which to base further action.' Another outline of his objectives, accepted by the Observatory Council at its meeting in November 1996, indicates a little more of the scientific running of a modern observatory.

The aim is to carry out monitoring studies on the breeding and migrant birds at Bardsey.

Objective 1: To record numbers and biology of breeding species
Regular census of breeding birds
Productivity of breeding birds
Habitat usage by breeding landbirds
Regular habitat monitoring
Ringing as a support tool

Objective 2 : To record numbers and phenology of migrant species
Regular census of migrant birds
Standard sample – ringing of migrants
Stopover ecology of migrant land birds
Lighthouse attractions

Objective 3 : To ensure the competent documentation and storage of records
Collection of records
Collation of records
Production of Annual Report
Storage

VALUABLE REPORTS

THIS MAY SEEM a bit arid, but it is good to know what one is trying to do. Looking at a single report, no 39 for 1995, there are special reports on aspects of the ecology of choughs, herring gulls and Manx shearwaters, as well as detailed notes on landbird nesting habitats and the breeding birds of Welsh islands. Every year there is a ringing report, an account of birds at Bardsey lighthouse, and decisions from the Rarity Committee. The breadth of interest of visitors is indicated by further accounts of non-avian animals, butterflies and moths, the vegetation of two grazing areas and a botanical survey of ploughed fields to see whether arable

Bottom
The puffin is one of our most attractive seabirds. It nests mainly on offshore islands.

weeds would appear in fields which had not been ploughed for several decades. Archeological studies and a brief account of one of my favourites, an

enormously under-recorded woodlouse, *Platyarthrus hoffmannseggi*, complete the diverse diet, except of the systematic bird list and warden's report.

The warden, Andrew Silcocks, reported exciting changes, including the relaxation of grazing on the heathland which was showing wonderful regeneration, and a return to mixed farming with some arable fields to enhance plants and wildlife. He reports a heartening increase in landbirds, with three pairs of stonechats having good breeding success, and choughs fledging 18 chicks from five nests.

ARRAY OF SPECIES

CONCENTRATING ON ONE month, September, he reports reasonable sea watching, with Sabine's gull, a spate of Mediterranean gulls and two Leach's petrels, these at the lighthouse, as well as three Risso's dolphins passing close. Raptors included excellent views of an osprey and a red kite

which was watched for several hours. Dotterel and Lapland bunting, short-eared owl and little stint indicate the variety, and although there was no heavy passerine migration, there was a day of 15 redstarts, 100 goldcrests, 18 pied and 20 spotted flycatchers. Multiply that by eight, for the observatory is not usually manned in winter, and you have plenty of birds.

Observatories on islands are not only about science, or even only about birds, for their magic is linked with the sea, an ancient way of life and shared experience. Sitting among the sea pinks and vernal squills at the south end of Bardsey, admiring the evening sun on the Rhinog mountains behind Harlech, is as valued a memory as the tumultuous seas, generosity of islanders and views towards Muckish and Errigal from Tory Island.

Top left
The ringing cries of herring gulls punctuate any visit to the British coast.

Top right
Sabine's gull is a beautiful, if rare visitor – though not often seen, as here, in breeding plumage.

Middle left
Lapland buntings may be spotted on passage at sites such as Bardsey.

Bottom
Spotted flycatchers are regular migrants, in spring and autumn.

Songs and Calls

BIRDS LIVE IN a highly visual world, but however much colour, shape and visual signals matter, there is also vital communication by songs and calls. Krebs (1976) attempts to answer the question why some songs are so complex, describing some of his experiments with great tits.

SONG BIRDS

TRUE SONG IS restricted to the perching birds, about half of the world's species. In Britain, these are particularly well represented in gardens, woods and farms. In contrast to more simple calls, song is largely produced by males. Song is seasonal, and the great tits' 'teacher, teacher, teacher' song can be heard from January to May. Because of time correlations, most people associate song with claiming territory or attracting a mate, but there is little direct evidence for the attraction claim.

If woodland territory-holders are removed, new arrivals appear within hours from less desirable territories or from non territory-holders who are probably younger birds. This speedy appearance suggests they had been monitoring the woodland, listening for empty spaces. To test this, Krebs trapped and removed eight pairs from a six ha (14.8 acre) copse in Wytham Wood, Oxford. He had previously plotted the territories, well established by February. Loudspeakers playing great tit song for eight minutes per hour all day were placed in three territories, tin-whistle song substituted in two territories, while three were left silent. After eight hours of daylight, the areas without loudspeakers had been occupied by four newcomers, but it was 20 daylight hours before the loudspeaker areas were colonised. If song carries the simple 'keep out' message why is it so complex?

RANGE OF SONGS

EACH GREAT TIT or chaffinch has a small repertoire of songs, while a song thrush has a complex range. Perhaps by singing a repertoire of songs, the territory-holder causes the potential new arrivals to overestimate the density of singing males, or perhaps a big repertoire does not only mean there is a great tit here, but also that there is a dominant great tit here.

Whatever the exact function, each bird will have its own time for singing. In the dawn chorus of early summer, different species start at different times, and as Simms (1978) illustrates, each species will sing at its appropriate time of year. The early singing mistle thrush, as is well known, will sing almost regardless of weather, but territory-holders are usually most vocal on calm, bright days. There is often another burst of song as dusk approaches, with robins and thrushes being particularly active. It is not only nightingales that sing at night, sedge warblers often do so, and, where there are street-lights, robins and blackbirds may sing at any time.

Middle left
The chaffinch is one of our commonest birds; its song is a pretty sequence of descending notes, ending in a flourish.

Top right
The silvery song of the willow warbler can be heard in many of our woods and heaths in the summer.

Bottom
The song thrush has a loud, bold song, with short, repeated phrases.

CALLING

CALL NOTES, BY contrast with song, are produced by almost all birds, and are significantly simpler, although sometimes, as with the curlew, complex enough to be hard to distinguish from song. The complex versions, and some non-vocal sounds like 'drumming' of woodpeckers using their beaks, or of snipe letting air whistle through their tail feathers as they descend, serve the same function as song. Curlews, like many birds of open spaces, will advertise their territory by making themselves conspicuous in the air, as do larks and pipits, while woodland birds are more likely to rely on song alone.

ALARM CALLS

RETURNING TO THE simple calls: they are usually intraspecific signals, but sometimes involve other species as well. The alarm notes of many woodland birds – warblers, redstart, chaffinch and tits – can be very similar, with any bird that spots danger signalling to a wide range of species. This interpretation can be challenged as being too altruistic: genes are selfish. Perhaps the calls have come to resemble each other since all have evolved to be clearly audible, but difficult for a predator to locate. Similarly, wandering tit flocks, so common in autumn and winter, communicate about food supplies as no doubt do many of the waders, so busily calling as they move about the estuary at different stages of the tidal cycle.

DESCRIBING BIRD SONG

TRADITIONALLY, SONGS HAVE been described in prose. Thus Peterson, Mountfort and Hollom (1954) describe the blackcap's as a 'remarkably rich warbling more varied but less sustained than the garden warbler's, often louder at the end'. Writers attempt to describe calls so that the same book calls the voice of the green sandpiper a ringing 'tluitt, weet wet' and the greenshank's a ringing 'tew-tew-tew'.

Varied attempts to get over the lack of precision in such descriptions have been made. Harting (1866) writes how 'wherever it has been practicable I have reduced the notes to a key by means of a small whistle. The musical expression thus obtained I have introduced into the text, but the reader must not attempt to interpret these notes by the piano; for by this means he will not obtain the faintest notion of the sounds which they are intended to convey. A flute or flageolet will give a proper sound, but the most perfect expression will be obtained with a small whistle, two and a half inches long and having three perforations, similar to the whistle used by the Sardinian Picco who performed so wonderfully in London some years since.'

THE SONOGRAM

MORE MODERN AND more precise is the sonogram, by analysis of which direct comparisons can be made between the songs of subspecies, the alarm calls of birds which sound similar, the local dialects of chaffinches, or different versions in the repertoire of song thrushes. For those who want to listen and learn about songs, a large range of tapes and CDs is now, of course, available. Although some like to listen to them purely for pleasure, the real pleasure is to have birds in their natural surroundings and to try to become familiar with as many as possible. I have heard it said that a great tit has 92 separate vocalisations, and no doubt each of them has a clear meaning to other great tits.

BIRD FACT:
The bones which make up the skeleton of a bird are rigid, but they are also very light. They achieve this by having cavities inside them which are filled with air.

Top
The rock pipit's song resembles that of meadow pipit, but with a stronger trill at the end.

Middle left
The mistle thrush starts singing early in the year, usually from high up in a tree.

Bottom
The great tit is another early songster – often starting as soon as the days begin to lengthen.

Display

IN MEMORIES (1970), Julian Huxley mentions that 'scientific bird watching' was of much greater importance to his career than 'stupidly wading through Butschli's enormous German work on Protozoa'.

REDSHANKS

HE WAS STUDYING redshanks, and the male's remarkable display 'in which the wings were opened to show the white undersides and the head

advanced slowly towards the female, his conspicuous red legs repeatedly raised, while he emitted a continuous rattling note. Finally he vibrated his wings even more rapidly, until he raised himself into the air, settled on her back and, still fluttering, succeeded in copulation. I also repeatedly saw the conspicuous display flight, warning rival males off the chosen nesting area, in which the male indulges in a series of switch backs, giving vent meanwhile to a loud and melodious song.'

That was in 1910 when he published his first paper on bird courtship in relation to Darwin's theory of sexual selection. He was proud of himself for using the word 'formalised' for some of the male's actions, for we now know that much courtship behaviour is indeed stereotyped. He was much prouder of having made field natural history scientifically respectable.

GREAT CRESTED GREBES

HE PUBLISHED HIS paper on great crested grebe courtship in 1914, and was the first to apply the term 'ritualisation' to their formalised ceremonies, and to record what is now called a 'displacement activity'. Towards the end of a long spell of head-shaking the birds would make as if to free their wings, not actually preening, but just raising the tip of the wing with their beaks. This meaningless activity was also ritualised when the urges to continue displaying or to break away were in conflict.

Top
Great crested grebes have an elaborate head-shaking display in the breeding season.

Middle
A pair of gannets greet each other with ritualised gestures.

Bottom
Black-headed gulls signal to each other using a variety of different postures.

GULL BEHAVIOUR

NIKO TINBERGEN UNDERTOOK pioneering work on gull behaviour and published *The Study of Instinct* (1951), the manuscript for which had been completed in 1948. Bryan Nelson, whose gannet studies are quoted later, suggests that one reason Niko Tinbergen is held in such high esteem among ethologists, students of behaviour, and ornithologists in general is that he really let us see how birds behave, and made convincing sense of what caused the behaviour and what it meant. Tinbergen's implicit dictum that natural selection is all pervasive is in contrast with an earlier gannet-watcher who wrote 'the gannet may work off surplus energy in harmless posturing'. Gannets behave in particular ways, at particular times, because a complex set of internal and external events make them do so. It would be wrong, says Nelson, to conclude that gannets know what they are doing.

Tinbergen's films of gull behaviour, black and white and rather jerky in the style of the time, showed how the 'ritualised' and 'formalised' movements Huxley had described in courtship behaviour permeated all sorts of activities, and were evident whenever there were interactions between individuals. With black-headed gulls, the various postures act as symbols, each conveying a message of some kind to fellow black-headed gulls.

DEFENDING ITS TERRITORY

A BLACKBIRD WILL defend territory by stretching its neck up, fluffing out its feathers, except those of the head which are smoothed, and raising the beak above the horizontal. Blackbirds are one of the few species which will actually fight regularly, but it seems to me they do it more at the meeting points of densely-packed garden territories than they do in woods. Because song is such an important aspect of territorial advertising, song-posts, be they television aerials, lamp-posts or rooftops are another focal point for blackbirds, and for young ones, may be more important for a time than a nest site.

For a blackbird, song and aggressive gestures are part of territorial behaviour, and time and again a characteristic movement is linked with a characteristic sound. This is so when lapwings tumble and call, when peregrines dive and shriek, or when a moorhen makes 'crake' calls with vertical neck. Any call, or display, or combination, must give an increased chance of gene survival, even when it appears to make a bird more vulnerable. Some therefore have argued that an alarm call given in a flock of unrelated individuals may manipulate these into a position of danger when the caller itself has made its getaway.

BIRD FACT:
The beaks of birds tell us a lot about their favourite food. The range of beak shape is huge – from the sharp, hooked bill of birds of prey, to thin, narrow bill of many waders.

Top left
Blackbirds are highly territorial and often squabble over a patch of garden.

Top right
Chaffinch showing an aggressive posture at a territorial boundry. This is linked with side to side movements.

Bottom
The spring displays of lapwings are a delight, involving tumbling flights and cat-like mewing calls.

Nests

O NCE THE HOURS of daylight increase, and the anterior pituitary gland sends the appropriate stimulating hormones to the sex glands, all sorts of bird behaviour starts to change. Eventually after migration, territorial defence and courtship, comes nest-building and egg-laying, and in many ways a species' success will depend on the outcome of the events that are now set in train. How many eggs will be laid, will the nest be destroyed, and if it survives how many young will survive to fledging and become independent individuals ready for their own reproduction next year or in future years?

TYPES OF NEST

SOME BIRDS MAKE no real nest, while others make nests that are large or complex or beautifully constructed. It is usually the passerines which make the most elaborate ones based on a basic cup shape. With the long-tailed tit this is elaborated to form an enclosed dome, and the different behaviour patterns that are necessary to build so complex a structure have been analysed. This building is summarised by Perrins (1979): 'After the birds have chosen a site for their nest, they start to put pieces of moss there; although much of this may fall off, they continue until some pieces stay. When sufficient moss has adhered to the site, the birds switch to collecting spiders' webs which they pass back and forth across the moss until it sticks, when they bind it to the branch.'

Once a platform has been built they sit in the middle of it and tuck new moss around

Bottom left
Cross-section of woodpecker's nest, showing cavity inside.

Top right
The nest of the reed warbler is carefully woven around the surrounding stems.

Bottom left
Though quite small, the reed warbler's nest has quite a deep cup.

themselves, weaving moss and web into the sides of the nest, turning as they weave so as to produce a circular nest. This is only the start, for another seven or eight different movements and the incorporation of lichens and feathers are still needed.

CHAFFINCH'S NEST

THE CHAFFINCH MAKES a compact and neat nest, with a deep cup. It is so well made that it is pliable, so well lichened that it is almost invisible, and so well sited that it is firmly held in the fork of a tree or bush. All sorts of things are brought together to achieve this, a mix of bark and fibre, spiders' webs and hair, rootlets and grass.

Another cup, with the added creativity of being woven round the supporting stalks, is produced by reed

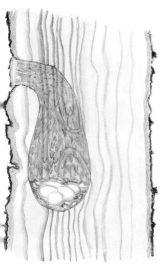

warblers and, in one form or another by other passerine reed dwellers. The non-passerines may get nearer the water, with grebes having accumulations of vegetation floating on the water, water rails adapting their cup of plant stems according to rising water levels, and bitterns adding reeds to their platform nest as the young grow.

WOODPECKER'S NEST

IN CONTRAST TO the soft and wet, could be the hard, dry heavily-worked woodpecker nests made in firm trees, or those of tits, crested and willow for instance, in softer rotten tree stumps. Even harder, but not necessarily dry, are those of guillemots which lay on bare rocks, or perhaps a bit of loose gravel, on a ledge of a vertical cliff. Most of the other cliff-breeders do make some attempt at a nest, with kittiwakes, for instance, using mud, grass and seaweed to make an elaborate cup. The steepness of the cliffs on which these birds are found gives good protection, except against skuas, but holes can be even better, and many other seabirds, Manx shearwaters and puffins for example, use rabbit-holes, and storm petrels may do the same, or use natural crevices or those in dry-stone buildings.

> 'Birds I beheld building nests in the bushes
> Which no man had the wit even to begin to work
> I wondered where and from whom the pie could have learned
> To put together the sticks in which she lays and broods,
> For there is no craftsman, I know, who could construct her nest'
> William Longland PIERS THE PLOWMAN

Top left
Woodpecker's nest from the side, showing how the entrance hole connects with the nest cavity.

Top right
The chaffinch builds a neat, soft nest, often sited close to the trunk of a tree.

Bottom
Puffins usually nest in abandoned rabbit burrows.

Eggs

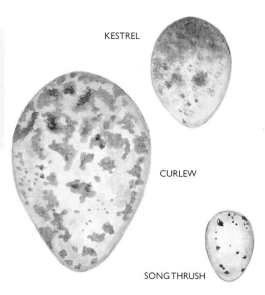

KESTREL

CURLEW

SONG THRUSH

EGGS, OF COURSE, vary in size, shape and colour. Bigger birds not surprisingly lay bigger eggs, particularly if the young are nidifugous and have to be active as soon as they hatch. A cuckoo, which is considerably larger than any of its hosts, lays relatively small eggs, and a bird that lays lots of eggs, like a partridge, also cannot produce very large ones.

VARIETY OF SHAPES

WITHIN ANY TAXONOMIC group, the shape of eggs will be basically similar, so that gulls and waders produce eggs which narrow abruptly towards the smaller end, while grebe eggs are pointed and similar at both ends. Where four eggs are laid, the narrow ends converge towards the clutch centre to form a compact group for brooding.

Top left

Mallard's nest with clutch of six eggs.

Top right

Eggs of (from left to right) curlew, kestrel and song thrush.

Bottom

Skylark's nest with clutch of four eggs.

COLOURS OF EGGS

TWO MAIN PIGMENTS are responsible for the range of egg colour: blue-greens, perhaps derived from bile pigments, and red-browns from haemoglobin of the blood. Apart from background colour, often white in hole-nesting birds, there are bands, mottlings and scribblings due to varying pressure in the oviduct. The white of woodpecker eggs is enhanced by their gloss, and the surface texture of other eggs can have as wide a range as paints – matt, vinyl silk or gloss.

NEST RECORD SCHEME

IN A BOOK CELEBRATING 50 years of the BTO, P. G. Davis in Hickling (1983) describes this scheme, the brainchild of Julian Huxley and James Fisher, which started slowly but became so successful that it has been the basis of many studies of breeding biology. As early as 1943, working on single-species studies of the robin and the wren, David Lack and E. A. Armstrong were using the material available. It was also one of many areas where computer analysis has made information much more easy to extract; as 40,000 cards were completed in 1997 alone, the accumulated number since 1939 can be appreciated.

By 1970, enough cards had been completed to achieve much of the original objective 'the collection of information on the dates of the various stages, and on incubation and fledging periods', and it was time for Henry Mayer-Gross to produce a guide to the Nest Record Scheme, which explained the instructions and requirements which appear on the cards. The guide included charts to show the length

RESULTS OF THE RECORDS

AS A FINAL EXAMPLE, the hot weather throughout much of August coupled with damp soils, high water tables and good sources of aerial insect and soil invertebrate food supplies, triggered off late nesting attempts. Great crested grebe, stone curlew, nightjar, dunnock, wren, woodlark, house martin, linnet, yellowhammer and corn bunting often raised twin sets of young.

The vital thing is that these reports are not based on anecdotal reports from a couple of sites, but from standardised observations of many nests throughout the breeding season. After analysis, the government's Joint Nature Conservation Committee can be alerted to worrying declines in breeding

of the breeding season from the first egg date to the last record of a young bird still in the nest. From those facts we see that two single-brooded species, the marsh warbler and nightingale, have the shortest breeding seasons, of nine and 11 weeks respectively. By contrast, whitethroats, also migrants, have a breeding season spread over 16 weeks, sometimes giving time for two broods, while stonechats, back on their breeding grounds by late February, may have time for three broods, spread over 21 weeks.

When Davis wrote, the emphasis was changing, as computing came in, and he hoped the nest record scheme would take on the role of a barometer in measuring the success or failure of each season, and would help to explain some of the reasons for the fluctuations that the Common Birds Census was demonstrating.

That this had been achieved can be seen by a look for example at *Nest Record News* (April 1998). A few examples show the sort of detail involved. April 'spanned a remarkably mild and dry spell in most districts with temperatures reaching 24/25°C. At first, fair conditions helped many birds, notably sawbills, mallard, moorhen, stonechat, siskin, pied and grey wagtails, to raise early large broods.' Later persistent downpours, in June, saturated the downy bodies of young waterbirds, leading to local heavy losses through hypothermia and drowning. Similarly, these torrential downpours, together with deliberate human interference, accounted for losses among the exciting raptor trio, merlin, hobby and goshawk.

> *'A hen's egg is, quite simply, a work of art, a masterpiece of design and construction with, it has to be said, brilliant packaging.'*
> Delia Smith 1998

performance. The hen harrier decline is mentioned and explained elsewhere, but reed bunting nest survival has fallen by 33 per cent in the last 25 years. Sadly, there have also been significantly increased losses in lapwing nest contents, moorhen brood size has declined by nearly one nestling, and such different birds as red-throated diver and greenfinch continue to have increasing nest failure rates.

Top
The eggs of the dunnock are a clear blue.

Middle
The tapered egg of the guillemot makes it less likely to roll off the cliff.

Bottom
Nest of common gull with clutch of two eggs.

A Bird's Year

THERE ARE MANY books about single species, and the number of individual studies of mammals and birds has grown steadily since the early New Naturalist monographs on the badger by Ernest Neal in 1948, and on the yellow wagtail by Stuart Smith in 1950.

LIFE OF BIRDS

HERE, THREE BIRDS and their activities throughout the year will be looked at, in more detail than the very brief outline sometimes provided in the species sections. The lesser whitethroat is a long-distance migrant whose weight changes in relation to migratory movements were summarised earlier. By contrast the chaffinch is an example of a familiar resident which rarely moves far from its birthplace. More detail of the chaffinch can be found in Ian Newton's *Finches* (1972), and Eric Simms in *British Warblers* (1985)

gives more detail of the lesser whitethroat's life and breeding activities. Colonial nesters provide another contrast, and the huge gannet, in its vast nesting masses, has a completely different set of behaviour patterns.

Top
Lesser whitethroat on bare branch.

Bottom
More typically, lesser whitethroats skulk about in the bushes.

month of arrival, by early June, the young will be able to flutter from the nest. If danger threatens, the female will often try to distract a potential predator with an injury-feigning display. At this time, the repeated 'tac-tac' call is often heard. By the middle of July, some birds may begin to moult. Some first-year birds seem to wait until they are wintering in Africa to change their tail feathers, but wings are moulted before migration, which peaks at the end of August.

PATTERNS OF POPULATIONS

DUNGENESS HAS FAR more birds passing through in the autumn than in spring, and there are other indications that departure is from the south-east on the first stage of movement, via Switzerland and Israel, to areas east of the Nile, which it reaches in mid-October. Eastern European populations end up in India, Sri Lanka and Iran; both populations move south-east. As early as late January some will have begun to return.

Judging by the pattern of singing in the thick bramble and blackthorn of my garden, and surrounding hedges, some of the birds in east Devon, on the fringes of the bird's range, are unsuccessful in finding mates. Having failed in one place, they move on after a few days, to sing somewhere else, leading to possible over-recording of singing males. However, being inconspicuous and often poorly known, there are also plenty of reasons for under-recording.

LESSER WHITETHROAT

EVIDENCE FROM OBSERVATORIES show that lesser whitethroats arrive in the south and south-east during a ten-day peak after 26 April, when Dungeness and Portland notice a good passage. Fair Isle's much later birds are overshooting their target areas in Germany, Denmark and Scandinavia.

Within 12 days of arrival, eggs may be laid, so that the establishment of territories, the necessary courtship, and the building of the nest are rapid events. The male's rattling song, from tall hedgerows, often with ash trees, is often our only indication of his presence, but Simms has observed courtship, when the male 'swells out his breast and the feathers thereon, raises the feathers on his crown, and fans and beats his wings, lowering the bill at the same time. There is an even greater state of ecstasy in which he tumbles and falls about, often with a leaf or grass stem in his bill.'

THE NEST

THE MALE USUALLY starts the nest, which is completed by the female. It is frequently in bramble, built from dry grasses, stalks and roots, and lined with finer roots, horsehair and catkins, and is often decorated with spiders' cocoons. Once the eggs are laid, the male helps with incubation and later helps with feeding the young, on small insects. Within a

Top
Lesser whitethroat with hungry brood.

Bottom
A female lesser whitethroat brings food to her nestlings.

Chaffinch

A N OLD COCK chaffinch will return to its territory in mid-February, advertising his arrival with his 'chink' call and by song. The same territory may well be occupied for several years, with little change in its boundaries if neighbours also survive.

THE SONG OF THE CHAFFINCH

A YOUNG BIRD will have a different approach, moving in quietly and using his subsong, which will only develop into the typical adult song with its three parts when the bird is ten months old. Male aggression is shown by flight towards any definite intruder, exposing the white wing-patches. Recognisable postures and vigorous display are shown at territorial boundaries. If a male is joined by a female, she gives a 'tupe' call. With body sleeked and horizontal he tilts it and raises the wing nearest to her to expose his red flank. If, after his 'moth flight', which involves rapid beats of small amplitude, she wanders away, he then resumes singing. If she remains, they indulge in sexual chases and ground feeding.

ESTABLISHING TERRITORY

THROUGHOUT MARCH, WITH territory and mate established, activity, involving feeding and preening, is all confined to the territory. Courtship intensifies and the hen becomes dominant, with priority at any food.

Mild weather in April leads to a frenzy of sexual chases, and the female starts to build the nest, which has four concentric layers. The outer shell is of lichen and spider silk, ideal for concealment, and the next two layers are of moss and grass, and of grass alone. The lining is made up of thin roots and feathers. Nest building takes about seven days, with up to 1,300 visits. The male follows her very persistently, even if she attacks him near the nest tree. He also attempts to mate, but is unsuccessful until she adopts the crouching, soliciting position.

Top
The hen chaffinch is duller than the male, but still shows the white wing-bar.

Bottom right
Juvenile chaffinch

Bottom left
Female chaffinch, showing almost sparrow-like plumage.

When the young do start to feed themselves they have little success, and when they attempt song it is a rambling subsong. They will hear adults and experiments suggest that this is part of the learning that will eventually lead them to a full adult repertoire when they are ten months old. By 50 days they are independent, collect into groups, and begin to moult.

RANGE OF THE CHAFFINCH

YOUNG BRITISH CHAFFINCHES rarely stray more than 5 km (3 miles) from the nest site, but a few first-year birds may wander up to 50 km (30 miles). The adults, free of young in late June or July, stop any reproductive behaviour but they may, briefly, attack other adults in their territory. When the moult begins, even this stops, and they skulk inconspicuously.

From a taxonomic point of view it is interesting that the chaffinch and its relative the brambling (both fringilline finches) have a very different pattern of territorial behaviour from the cardueline finches, like the goldfinch and linnet.

Fringillines have large territories, spreading themselves evenly over suitable habitat, while the carduelines nest in loose colonies, within which each pair defends a small territory. Compared with chaffinches, spread through the ash woods, it is very hard to count linnet territories among the shrubby blackthorn for example.

LAYING EGGS

IN LATE APRIL or May she starts laying at daily intervals, and begins regular incubation when the penultimate egg is laid. The nidicolous young are born blind, helpless and naked, but can just raise their heads. They are soon arranged with hind ends out and heads inwards, always ready to make begging calls. Eighty five per cent of feeding is done by the hen, with six to nine feeds of insects per hour; faeces are removed after each visit.

In mid to late May, the young leave the nest and continue to be fed in scattered positions.

Top
Male chaffinch in full breeding plumage, visiting a pool.

Bottom
A female chaffinch brings food to her young.

Gannet

ONE CANNOT SAY that gannets are either poorly known or inconspicuous, but most people have only seen them at sea and not at their spectacular breeding colonies. Bryan Nelson, introducing the gannet, describes the stuff of a gannet's life as 'rock, wind, waves, seaweed, guano and fish together with constant interaction with its fellows'.

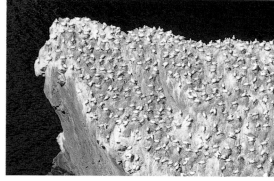

RETURNING HOME

YOUNG GANNETS, coming up to their second birthday, return to home waters but are unlikely to find space to settle on the island cliffs where they were born. At first they sail around in the busy air traffic, learning about cliff winds and fishing grounds. They may join a club of non adults, using a ledge near the breeding birds and interacting with other club members, with low-intensity territorial and sexual behaviour.

Years later, perhaps in his fourth, fifth or sixth year, a male begins to look seriously for a breeding site. After many flights over the potential plot he will settle uncertainly, often well within pecking distance of other birds, but the real challenge for the site will come from the air, particularly if the site was only vacant because the owner was away fishing. If our male survives without challenge for two or three days, the site becomes his and the confidence with which he flies in with loud calls, or performs an aggressive display on landing, increases. If there is still no serious challenge, he may spend three quarters of the daylight hours guarding and displaying, with much 'jabbing' by means of vigorous forward lunges at neighbours, and 'menacing' with exaggerated forward thrusts with an open beak.

A gannet 'bows' thousands of times a year, and each performance uses energy. The fact that evolution has produced such a complex and polished display also indicates that it is an important signal, but why does the gannet do it? It does not appear aggressive, but the author can assert, with a high degree of certainty, that 'bowing' is an aggressively motivated display, signalling ownership of the site.

ATTRACTING A MATE

RELATED TO THE bow, but with aggressive components greatly suppressed, is 'sexual advertising' for our bird has not got a mate yet. A female approaching will initially trigger the response for any gannet approaching, but once seen as a female the bow is changed to an inconspicuous 'headshake and reach' of the greatest importance. Although a variety of responses may follow, the female will often respond by approaching, followed by mutual bill-touching

Top
Aerial view of a gannetry in the Shetlands – note even spacing of birds.

Bottom
A gannet calls from its nest.

and by her 'facing away' – an appeasement gesture to reduce the risk of wasteful fighting. There are so many display signals in a complex gannetry that we will assume further pair-bonding with 'meeting ceremonies', 'sky pointing' and 'mutual fencing' leads onto copulation, which is closely linked with nest building. This is an important activity, adding flotsam and weed to a pre-existing 'drum' raised above the muddy mire of the colony.

LAYING EGGS

WHEN THE EGG is laid it is, extraordinarily, incubated beneath the webs of the feet which overlap above the egg. Both parents share incubation, with average stints of over 30 hours, which shorten as hatching approaches. As the embryo grows and the chick gets nearer to hatching, the parents' behaviour changes towards shorter incubating stints, and therefore shorter feeding trips, which is adaptive, in that when the chick does hatch it will not have to wait long for food. It is vital that the egg is transferred onto the tops of the webs at the right time before hatching, but some young breeders may not have developed the appropriate neural mechanisms for this innate action and so crush the hatching chick.

CARE OF THE YOUNG BIRD

THE ADULTS BROOD, preen and feed the young bird. Initially, as with our previous species, the newly-hatched gannet is too weak and wobbly to influence the parents, but soon the intensity of its begging manipulates the parents to produce the required amount of food. To get its regurgitated, semi-digested food, the chick gropes in the trough of the parent's lower mandible. Brooding becomes impossible after three weeks of growth and therefore in bad weather three to six week old chicks are at risk of chilling.

The parents maintain their care for 13 weeks and it is no lack of care on their part that ends this phase of life. After days of wing-flapping and looking out to sea, the chick makes the decision and reaches the traumatic moment when it rushes headlong to the cliff-edge and jumps, topples or is pushed over, and despite no practice is usually quickly airborne. For some the cliff-edge is far away, and these birds will be attacked by adults on their way to the edge and may well crash among other nesting birds, to be attacked again, but once in the air the young gannet flaps and wobbles and soars and may even fly as far as 3 km (1.8 miles) at its first attempt.

Landing on the sea is rarely a success, and if the landing is among adults it may be attacked again. Because it is so fat and the wings are not yet fully developed, it cannot fly up from the water but must swim away from the colony for two weeks, plunge-diving inefficiently for food. Once weight is lost, flight is again possible and in two weeks the young birds may have reached Morocco.

BIRD FACT:
The Arctic tern makes one of the longest regular journeys of any bird, migrating from its breeding grounds around the Arctic to the Southern Ocean and back, a round trip of up to 36,000 km.

Top left
Gannets are majestic in soaring flight as they scan the sea for shoals of fish.

Top right
This close-up shows the dagger-like bill.

Middle left
Adult gannet with down-covered young.

Bottom
Young gannets gradually lose their down and take on a grey plumage.

55

Ecology of Habitats

ECOLOGY IS THE study of populations, communities and ecosystems. Eco-systems include not only the living components of a habitat, but also the non-living ones like climate and soil and, nowadays, the endless combinations of chemicals we add to the environment.

ECOLOGICAL NICHES

WITHIN AN ECOSYSTEM each bird has its own niche, which is what it does, rather than where it is; its place in the natural grand scheme of things. If one thinks of a dunnock's niche, it is everything included within the job of 'dunnocking'. A garden or woodland or hedge is needed for a modern, British dunnock, and the right climate, roughly like that in which ancestral dunnocks grew up. It will need enough small insects and seeds on the ground to feed on, and not too many enemies.

They need to be good at 'dunnocking' to survive, and the fact that wrens are also good at 'wrenning' does not matter, because they have a different, if fairly similar, niche.

Within one habitat, niches will be limited, so the number of birds in that habitat will be limited, but habitats are often isolated from each other by distance, mountain ranges or the sea. Some birds can overcome these barriers, but many small ones, or weak fliers like rails, are limited to a special niche in an isolated habitat somewhere in the world, so there are lots of different rails. Where there are lots of niches, for instance in woodlands or coral reefs, there are lots of animal species, but in the arctic tundra or in a paved city, species are less numerous.

ROLE OF NATURAL SELECTION

EACH SPECIES HAS its niche fixed by natural selection, and, once fixed, its numbers are also relatively fixed. Surprising though it may seem, the way an animal breeds has very little to do with how many of it there are. If circumstances change, or gene frequency changes within a population, then the size of that population may change, but the reproductive effort makes no difference to the size of the eventual population. Slowly reproducing fulmars, laying one egg a year, with the first when they are six to 12, have been able to increase their British population, from the original stronghold of St Kilda, by 12 times in the last 50 years, and this after an earlier period of prolonged increase. The fulmar's niche has changed, with more food being available. Calculations suggest the availability of an extra 200,000 tonnes of offal and whitefish remains every year from the fishing industry, but it may also be that fulmar genes have changed, with immigration into Britain from Icelandic populations, rather than from St Kilda.

Top left
Fulmar's egg on its rocky sea-cliff habitat.

Top right
Introduced Canada geese have adapted to a wide range of wetlands and parks.

Bottom
Juvenile dunnock.

Birds have evolved what some ecologists call the 'large young gambit' as opposed to the 'small egg gambit' favoured for example by flies, mosquitoes and salmon. So dunnocks lay their eggs and try to raise their young until they are big and strong, but however efficient the parents are, there is a limit to the dunnock population because there are limits set by the opportunities within the dunnock niche. Every parent must still make every effort to ensure its genes are represented in the next generation.

FOOD CHAINS AND WEBS

BECAUSE A BIRD spends much of its life feeding, a niche can often be defined in terms of what a bird eats and how it sets about getting its food. Food and who eats what is at the centre of a study of ecosystems. Some birds are plant-eaters, with seeds as a favourite food because of their high energy content. These birds and the grazing ducks, geese and swans, are herbivores, like those you may feed with peanuts and sunflower seeds.

Having fed their favourites, many people resent the sparrowhawk which also occasionally visits the bird table, but carnivores, flesh-eaters, are just animals that feed differently, and are higher up the food chain. In the breeding season your bird table tits will become carnivores, synchronising their breeding with the emergence of woodland caterpillars. A song thrush eating snails is just as much a carnivore as a sparrowhawk. Sparrowhawks eat lots of different birds, and blue tits, even in the best supplied garden, do not live on peanuts alone, so a food web, showing feeding alternatives, is a better way of representing who eats what.

BIRD FACT:
Many migrating birds travel at altitudes of 2000m or more, probably because they find higher following winds at this height. If they encounter strong headwinds or bad weather systems they may fly at a very low level. The bar-headed goose has been spotted at 9000m when flying over the Himalaya Mountains.

Top left
A female sparrowhawk keeps a wary watch in the woods.

Top right
Great tits are regular visitors to bird tables.

Bottom
The oystercatcher is most at home along rocky shores.

DIFFERENT PREY FOR DIFFERENT BIRDS

DIFFERENT WADING BIRDS feed on different prey, with a few extremely numerous invertebrates being important food for many estuary birds, but most prey items being selected by only a few birds. A short-billed dunlin cannot catch a lugworm unless it is on the surface, but a curlew can reach it in its deep burrow. A stout-billed bird like a turnstone can turn over stones to find crabs, while a bird with a sensitive bill-tip, like a curlew, can rely on probing for its prey, but an oystercatcher, hammering on cockles, would do any sensitive nerve endings no good and feeds in a very different manner.

IMPORTANCE OF THE FOOD WEB

FOOD WEBS ALSO show the flow of energy through the ecosystem; a flow because there must always be new energy inputs from the sun to keep the system going. These inputs may however come rather indirectly, or in a delayed manner. The great tits and chaffinches in a winter beech wood are using last summer's energy when they pick up beech nuts, while a blackbird, scattering the beech leaves, may be

using energy from the summer before that as it searches for invertebrates feeding in the decomposing litter. On a river bed, particularly in an estuary, sediments, inorganic and organic, will be deposited from elsewhere. The organic sediments supporting the ragworms and lugworms are not obviously sun-related but they can be traced back in time and place to earlier solar inputs, somewhere upstream. Often what goes on underground, in the so-called decomposer food chain, involves a greater flow of energy than in the green world above.

NUTRIENT CYCLES

IN CONTRAST TO the flow of energy is the cycling of elements like carbon and nitrogen. The carbon dioxide of the air, through photosynthesis, becomes the carbohydrate, sugar or starch of a plant, which, when eaten, becomes the fat or glycogen reserve of a bird.

The leaves and roots of the plant, like the bird, will eventually die and decompose. This decay depends on scavenging animals and decomposer fungi and bacteria. As they and other organisms respire, the carbon dioxide is released back into the air. We fear now about an excess of carbon dioxide in the air, and the probability of global warming, but we also fear the results of other cycles which no longer 'balance' so that surplus nitrogen and phosphate appear, for instance, in aquatic ecosystems.

NUTRIENTS AND THE NORFOLK BROADS

THE EFFECT OF a surplus of these nutrients is demonstrated by a consideration of the Norfolk Broads. When E. A. Ellis wrote *The Broads* in 1965, he

started a chapter on flowering plants by saying: 'One does not have to be a botanist to enjoy the peculiar beauty and diversity of plant life throughout this wilderness of swamps and waterways ...Thus the blue waters of Hickling, bounded by the great belts of reed

reveal in their depths a fantastic water garden of crisp leaved stoneworts ....' Elsewhere he wrote frequently of the Broads 'which abound in submerged water weeds', and of herds of wild swans. He was a most unfortunate author, for much of his book was out of date in less than ten years, as pollution changed the Broads.

Before the 1970s, there were relatively low inputs of nutrients, with more nitrate than phosphate. This kept fertility low, which in turn meant that plant plankton, drifting algae in the water, was not dense, nor did it form a cover over the leaves of the large plants below the water. With a low algal density, there were few toxic ones of the type that can kill fish. Fish could therefore thrive, and so could the great crested grebes that feed off them. The large plants provided safe fish spawning sites and cover for large numbers of large invertebrates such as nymphs and beetles.

Young fish particularly favoured the opossum shrimp *(Neomysis)* in their diet, and by keeping its population down allowed its chief food source, water fleas *(Daphnia)*, to remain common and to graze effectively on the algae that were there. When winter came there was plenty of underwater plant material for the coots and pochards and swans to eat. However much they ate, enough remained next spring to act as an 'inoculum' to set off next spring's growth. Overall there was clear water, and an abundance of attractive water plants – water milfoil, bladderwort and yellow waterlilie – these provided cover for fish, and food for birds so the whole healthy ecosystem was in balance.

> **BIRD FACT:**
> Most songbirds reach a speed of about 35 k/h (20 mph) when migrating, but waders and ducks fly faster, reaching a maximum of 80 km/h (50 mph). They often fly non-stop for several days and nights, losing weight as they go.

Above left
Pochard (this is a male) are an important part of the ecosystem at sites such as the Norfolk Broads.

Above right
Winter floods at Slimbridge – ideal for wildfowl such as Bewick's and whooper swans.

Bottom
Coot's nest in a reedy lake.

Suddenly everything changed when the nutrient levels went up and the phosphate to nutrient ratio reached a critical point. Algae flourished, and included some toxic ones which periodically killed fish. The algae covered the water plants so that their photosynthetic rates fell, and there was less plant cover in which the remaining fish could spawn and the invertebrates feed and shelter. With fewer fish, *Neomysis* populations rose and ate more water fleas, which grazed less effectively on the rising levels of algae. These made the water a 'scummy' green, reducing light to the underwater plants still further. When the birds returned there was less food, and they left too little to get the spring growth effectively under way. Within a year a broad like Hickling had become visually less attractive, had lost many of its characteristic flowering plants and stoneworts, and was able to support fewer fish and birds. The

changing nutrient levels due to sewage from boats, agricultural run-off and droppings from the increasing numbers of roosting gulls had set the Broads on a sudden downward spiral.

SUCCESSION AND ZONATION

TWO OTHER ECOLOGICAL concepts are those of succession and zonation. Both could be illustrated by the Broads, but anyone with a garden is familiar enough with succession. Bare ground, carefully dug over for your flowering plants or vegetables is soon colonised by weeds, and in a year some of the short-lived annual ones will be replaced by deep-rooted docks and thistles. This is primary succession, the colonisation of bare ground, but your lawn fares little better. Unmown, it soon changes, not only because the grass is longer, but because plants that would not survive being cut are now able to thrive, and first one sort then another will colonise; a succession of different plant communities with

each species competing for its own niche in the new conditions. In time your neglected lawn, or the lawn of the unsold house next door, becomes scrub, and scrub develops by steps towards woodland, which in most of Britain would be the climax vegetation.

In nature, bare land, ready for primary succession, is unusual, and most of our abundant weeds were themselves presumably rarer, surviving for example on shingle-beds exposed by a river flood or on recently wind-blown sand. In nature too, unless there are herds of large grazing animals, grasslands are rare, but on farms, in gardens and on nature reserves we often attempt to stop the successional processes for our own purposes. In the conservation context we often want to do this to establish a particular ecosystem, by coppicing hazel, removing bramble or brush-cutting rank vegetation which we hope will create the habitats and diversity that we want.

CREATING DIVERSITY

ZONES ALSO INCREASE diversity, with different plants flourishing at different heights up a mountain for example, or different distances into a sand-dune system or at different levels below the high-tide

Top
Redshank preening on rocky shore.

Middle
Oystercatcher in flight, making alarm calls.

Bottom
Woodpigeons are common birds of open country, and are increasingly found in parks and gardens.

Top
Heathland is a threatened habitat which provides a home for many interesting birds.

Bottom left
Hundreds of thousands of knots visit Britain in the winter, returning to the high Arctic to breed.

Bottom right
Brent geese like to feed in flocks, particularly on saltmarshes and adjacent mudflats

mark. If mussels can only exist low on the beach they are not available to many birds, except at certain stages of the tide. A wading bird that fancies mussels may feed a bit in a higher zone, waiting its time for the mussel meal, while a worm-eater may have its priority zone higher up the shore.

Redshank and knot have been shown to favour the upper and middle shores, but when only the upper shore is available, curlew and oystercatchers 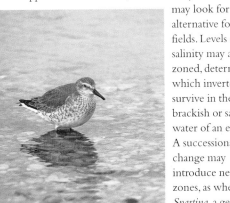 may look for alternative food in fields. Levels of salinity may also be zoned, determining which invertebrates survive in the fresh, brackish or salt water of an estuary. A successional change may introduce new zones, as when *Spartina*, a genus of cord-grass spreads, or is introduced, onto estuarine mud at a certain tidal level. In Strangford Lough, the 12,000 light-bellied brent geese from the Canadian arctic, which refuel there every autumn before dispersing across Ireland, may be in danger as their main food, the eel-grass, is being replaced by *Spartina*.

Birds at the top of food webs will tend to be rarer because energy is lost at each stage up the web as animals burn up fuel to do the work of living. Birds higher up food webs will tend also to be larger because, in general, animals need to be larger than the things they eat, particularly if they eat other animals. There is not as much energy available for as many peregrine falcons as pigeons, or for as many redshanks as marine worms. As to why they do such peculiar things, anything that help them to feed helps the individual to survive, and anything that helps them to mate helps the species to survive. Courtship behaviour is usually the most peculiar.

> **BIRD FACT:**
> Migration takes up huge amounts of energy. For this reason birds feed voraciously before setting off and build up large reserves of fat. A small songbird may weigh twice as much as normal just before migration.

Bird Habitats

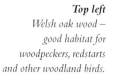

A HABITAT IS THE place where an organism lives. A cowpat can be a dung beetle's habitat, while a broad swathe of Arctic tundra is the breeding habitat of many northern waders. Within any habitat there will be a community of living things made up of flowering plants and invertebrates as well as the populations of birds with which we are concerned.

DIVISION OF HABITATS

A HABITAT, IN the broad sense of a heath or wood, will vary according to where it is, but the woodland habitat varies more than the heathland, for woods, dominated by different tree species, can grow on almost any soil and to considerable altitude. A heath, by contrast, as defined by Webb (1986) is 'an area of ericaceous dwarf shrubs growing at lower altitudes, below 250 m, in acidic nutrient-poor, mineral soils'.

Most habitats can be subdivided: apart from different types of woods, there are different layers in any wood, with different bird communities in the canopy and in the shrub layer. Similarly, with lakes, unproductive, oligotrophic lakes are very different from productive, eutrophic lakes.

DIFFERENCES IN HABITATS

AQUATIC HABITATS ARE clearly different from terrestrial ones. Among the latter, the woodlands are the most complex, with their structure separating them from more open habitats. Urban areas can be highly structured, with high-rise buildings and wooded parks, but their artificiality separates them from all others. The simpler open areas can be divided into the more natural uplands, moors and heaths, and the agricultural land which has been modified to greater or lesser extent by farming and other human activities. There are, of course, plenty of overlaps, with lakes and reservoirs in towns, sheep on the moors and open areas in the middle of a wood.

ADAPTING TO HABITATS

SOME OF THE adaptations of birds to their habitats are obvious: the webbed feet of ducks, the long legs of wading birds and the powerful beaks of woodpeckers. It is not so obvious that woodland birds tend to have short wings, that each seed-eater will have a slightly different bill, or that a number of our species have adapted to local conditions that are different from those they meet in the rest of their range. The merlin on a world scale is a bird of open forest, forest edge and low-shrub tundra, but has adapted to our heather moors derived from the forest (Ratcliffe 1990).

The classic book on plant ecology, A G Tansley's *The British Isles and their Vegetation* was written in 1939, but not until Fuller (1982) were the habitats of birds the subject of a book. This was based on information gathered during the BTO's project The Register of Ornithological Sites. Because the aim of the project was to provide conservation bodies with

Top left
Welsh oak wood – good habitat for woodpeckers, redstarts and other woodland birds.

Bottom left
Grazed, wooded landscape – ideal for rooks and buzzards.

Bottom right
Young great spotted woodpecker.

particularly in the breeding season, may in itself make a site valuable. Rarity can be judged objectively, perhaps being defined by there being fewer than 1,000 pairs in Britain, but there are also points of subjective interest. Would one prefer a few curlew, dunlin and snipe in the bogs with merlin and grouse in the heather, or sitka spruce with lots of coal tits and goldcrests and, perhaps, some siskins and crossbills? It cannot be denied that afforestation has sometimes brought more birds to the hills.

A few ecosystems are so localised that it is reasonable to mention them separately from the major habitats described later. Machair, the Gaelic word for the grassland ecosystem that has developed on wind-blown sand, typically in the Hebrides, is one such, and limestone pavement, found mainly in the north of England and the west of Ireland, another. The limestone of the Burren of County Clare and the Aran Isles of Galway Bay form a very special ecosystem. Shingle beaches, often extending into banks like Chesil Beach and Orford Ness, reach their extreme, perhaps, at Dungeness, the largest expanse of shingle in Britain. While machair and limestone are famous for their beauty and their flowers, Dungeness has long been known for its birds.

information about sites, there was a bias towards 'good' ones, and a concentration on natural and semi-natural habitats.

GOOD OR BAD SITE?

A 'GOOD' SITE can gain its status in several ways. The sheer number of birds may make a site have conservation value, whether the birds are breeding reed warblers, chattering in the *Phragmites*, or wintering knot on an estuary. The species richness of the habitat, indicated by the now much used word biodiversity, is also a valuable guide to habitat quality. Examples are given in the sections on woodland and upland habitats. The presence of rare birds,

Top left
Heron patiently stalking fish.

Top right
Female merlin amongst upland heather.

Bottom
Coastal shingle – the nesting habitat of little tern and ringed plover.

DUNGENESS AND SHINGLE

BETWEEN WINCHELSEA AND Hythe the shingle forms a great triangular projection into the English Channel. It is made up of a complex of ridges where shingle has piled up at different times. It seems that all the stones have arrived from the west, but whatever its origins Dungeness has always been a convenient arrival point for migrants and is now a surprisingly wet place.

Despite a nuclear power station and a long history of gravel digging, it is man's activities that have increased the biodiversity here, not just of birds, and the gravel-pit restoration, both of old, steep-sided pits and the more rewarding shallow-sided ones, that have brought in the water birds. David Tomlinson (1988) writes about the chance of seeing all five species of grebe, of groups of wintering smew and of up to 500 shoveler. Recent winters have brought penduline tits, while breeding birds include Mediterranean gull, garganey and that gravel favourite, little ringed plover. David also maintains that 'familiarity soon starts to engender an affection for its unusual landscape for there is nothing else remotely like it in Europe. There is genuine beauty in its bleakness. If you don't believe me go and see for yourself. You are unlikely to be disappointed.'

MACHAIR AND SAND

WHILE DUNGENESS RESULTS from moving gravel, machair develops from moving sand; white shell-sand, blowing over coastal peat, has influenced land-use and culture on many Scottish islands. Tiree has a third of its land surface covered with sand dunes or machair, sometimes tilled and sometimes not, partly dry and partly wet, and ranging from the alkaline influence of the sand to the acidity of the peat. The western coasts of South Uist, Barra, Oronsay and Coll among others demonstrate the ecological principle of

zonation to perfection and, like other ecosystems, the interplay of human and other influences on the plants and animals.

Boyd and Boyd (1990) describe the Monach Isles in summer as a 'blaze of flowers; daisies, bird's foot trefoil, white clover, buttercups, eyebright, sea pansies and many others', and as being 'alive with birds; gulls, terns, shelducks, eiders, red-breasted mergansers, oystercatchers, ringed plovers, rock pipits, pied wagtails and starlings'. The typical machair zones start with sand dunes before, on the landward side, the 'plain' at the start of true machair.

As with other grasslands, the right grazing regime is vital, for few plants flower or seed when pressures are high, but too much neglect soon leads to the suppression of the attractive flowers by more aggressive grasses. Lapwing, oystercatcher and ringed plover are the breeding waders of the 'plain' and are

replaced by dunlin, snipe and redshank, nesting on grassy tussocks, when wetter grasslands appear further from the sea. In the lochs, little grebes, ducks and the rarer red-necked phalaropes, with common terns on islands, provide a different bird community. Inland again, where the buildings of the crofts are found, starlings and sparrows and wall-nesting twite occur.

Top
Little ringed plover may be seen breeding on sandy river banks and at gravel pits.

Middle
Redshank at its nest in a damp meadow.

Bottom
The red-necked phalarope is a rare breeding bird, mainly in N and NW Scotland.

more birds, with the lake system along the east being good for winter wildfowl, having almost 5,000 wigeon and plenty of teal, and with whooper and Bewick's swans outnumbering the mutes. At the north west extremity of the Burren is Black Head, where seabirds come in close during periods of westerly winds. Some are local birds, but there are shearwaters from the Mediterranean and South Atlantic, phalaropes from the Arctic, storm petrels and skuas.

In winter it is a fine place for great northern and other divers. Like much of Ireland's west coast this, like the cliffs of Moher, further south, is also chough country. These cliffs are of shales and flagstones, and therefore not truly Burren, but their precipitous ledges are full of guillemots and kittiwakes, and the lower levels have their shags, puffins and black guillemots. The Burren and surrounding area is not full of rare birds, but its landscape is unique, and to see the abundance of mountain avens and spring gentians, mocking the efforts of most rock gardeners, makes one hate even more the destruction of much of England's limestone so that rock gardens can be built.

Apart from corncrakes, who arrive to shelter among the iris and breed among the crops that are not mown until late July, the waders are the conservation speciality of the machair, with 25 per cent of Britain's dunlin. The RSPB report that these ground-nesting birds are now at risk from what many would think an unlikely source – introduced hedgehogs. By 1995, dunlin, snipe, redshank and ringed plover had declined by 50 per cent since the 1970s through egg predation by hedgehogs .

THE BURREN AND LIMESTONE

IF THE CRAVEN district of West Yorkshire is the botanist's best limestone in northern England, then the Burren in County Clare and the Aran Isles in Galway Bay offer the finest limestone of Ireland. Perhaps the most impressive feature is the vast extent of exposed limestone rock, on which there appears to be very little vegetation. In deep frost-free crevices, sheltered from the winds, there is however a fascinatingly diverse flora.

Gordon D'Arcy (1992) admits that the open limestone has few birds; plenty of wheatears and stonechats, and a scattering of whinchats. The edges of the area provide

Top
Hedgehogs are unlikely predators of birds' eggs in some areas.

Middle
Cliffs of Moher, Co. Clare, Ireland. Ideal breeding cliffs for a multitude of seabirds.

Bottom
Limestone formation in the Burren, Co. Clare, Ireland.

Bird Populations

D ARWIN STRESSES THAT populations are capable of rapid increase and makes calculations, based on simple assumptions, as figures for animal population changes were not available to him. He also pointed out that the fulmar, that only lays one egg, was perhaps the commonest bird in the world, illustrating the fact that even slow breeders would be very abundant if there were not checks to their natural rate of increase.

COUNTING BIRDS

POPULATION FIGURES are frequently quoted, and we need to know how the figures are arrived at and still want to know what are the factors that affect populations. We may read that a species has decreased by 68 per cent in the last 25 years, or that another species is extending its range. It is relatively easy to see how the evidence for the second statement is gathered, but much less easy to see how a precise statement like the first one can be justified. Similarly, we often hear from one person that there are more swallows around this year, while another laments that she never sees any swallows these days.

Impressions about populations, like memories of the weather, are notoriously unreliable, and there are those who might maintain that figures about populations, quoted as facts, are equally uncertain. This is often so if figures for the absolute numbers of a species are quoted, but more often we need to know the relationship numbers — is a species commoner or rarer than it was, and by how much? Several methods of monitoring population levels have stood the test of time, and frequently the results of different methods can be compared, to produce an 'integrated population index'.

Top
Densely packed gannets at a colony in the Shetlands.

Bottom
Assessing populations of some inconspicuous species, like reed warbler, may be best done through ringing schemes.

> *'Although some species may be now increasing, more or less rapidly, in numbers, all cannot do so for the world would not hold them.'*
> Darwin ORIGIN OF SPECIES

COUNTING LARGER BIRDS

EVEN LARGE, CONSPICUOUS birds like grebes and herons, with restricted habitat, are not as easy to count as you might expect. To be certain how many heron nests are occupied in a small local heronry, set in two rather leafless trees, is virtually impossible. Other large birds can present different difficulties, with many raptors occurring at very low densities and in remote areas. At their nesting colonies, gannets are so mobile, so densely packed and in such large numbers, that estimates without photographic support can be very misleading. For each bird, one can refer to a counting unit, and for fulmar pairs a breeding site is 'an apparently occupied nest-site, defined as an individual sitting tightly on a reasonably horizontal area large enough to hold an egg'.

Woodcock are fairly large, but sit very tight. Those out on a pheasant shoot will see, and perhaps shoot, even more, and their shooting bags may indicate that woodcock populations are much higher than birdwatchers would believe. The increase in numbers of woodcock shot through the 1970s and 1980s may however be misleading, and due to an increase in pheasant shooting rather than a genuine increase in woodcock winter populations.

COUNTING METHODS

IN THEIR BOOK *Bird Census Techniques* (1992) Bibby, Burgess and Hill summarise these various counting techniques, and the assumptions and possible inaccuracies inherent in them all, and stress that some sort of sampling is always needed. Sometimes the sample may originally have had a different objective, as when ringing totals are used to reflect changing population levels. The ringing was done to find out about migration patterns, moult and longevity, but if twice as many mistle thrushes, allowing for changing numbers of birds caught, were ringed in one decade compared with another, it suggests twice as large a population.

Some inconspicuous birds may be best estimated by the constant effort scheme, which involves catching and ringing birds, using the same type and size of net at the same site, on a year-by-year basis. This not only monitors a population level, the number of adults trapped, but breeding success, the ratio of juveniles to adults in late season, and survival, birds re-trapped in subsequent years. As always, standardisation is vital, and other aspects of this are that no other netting is carried out within 400 m (1,312 ft), no baits are used to attract birds and 12 ringing visits are carried out between May and August. On this scheme, reed warbler populations stayed steady throughout the 1980s, while chiffchaffs started and finished high, but had a decline in between.

SAMPLING AN AREA

A VERY SIMPLE sampling method involves standing at one place and counting all birds seen or heard. If point counts like this are repeated, the birds of an area can be sampled. The limitations of the method are obvious, as soon as one tries it in the garden, with wrens singing loudly and often, being far more noticeable than the secretive bullfinches. Even with the bullfinches there would be difficulties in comparing their populations at different times of year, because of moult, tree leaves and frequency of calling for instance, but it could be perfectly adequate for comparing populations from one year to the next.

In woodland, of course, the need to be able to recognise every call and song variation, is important. Point counts might be thought to be more accurate in open country, where birds are more visible, but they are not all equally visible. On grassland in northern England, noisy and conspicuous golden plover can be located up to 500 m (1,640 ft) away. They react to the observer and may flee quietly and unnoticed from close to a transect line, but dunlin sit tight and are not detected more than 100 m (330 ft) from the transect.

> **BIRD FACT:**
> Many of the bird monitoring schemes are organised by the British Trust for Ornithology (BTO). Over the years its members and other volunteers who take part in its bird surveys have contributed significantly to the conservation of Britain and its birds.

Top
Chiffchaffs are usually first located by their song.

Middle
Bullfinches, despite the bright plumage of the male, can be hard to locate.

Bottom
Golden plover are noisy and easily spotted on their breeding grounds.

Population Change

UNTIL THE LAST 30 years, population changes could only be indicated by range changes, and these, particularly in Ireland and the remoter parts of Scotland, were often little known. In areas with larger populations, and more birdwatchers, local or county bird reports would have records of interesting birds.

ACCURACY OF REPORTS

JUST AS THE CBC index could be misleading about meadow pipits, as most of these breed in areas with few census plots, so county bird reports could be misleading because few people bothered to submit records about meadow pipits. *The London Bird Report* for 1950 has no mention of them, but has a page on the 17 breeding pairs of woodlarks, and almost a page giving all records of stonechats. By 1996, with increasing attention to common birds, the *Devon Report* has records of meadow pipits from 122 locations, a large increase over 1995. This increase probably means nothing at all, although the breeding records given, and the size of flocks reported, might be used to compare with something written in 1950.

Top

The meadow pipit is a common species, especially on heath and moorland.

Bottom

Grasshopper warbler – one of several species whose range has contracted in recent years.

IMPORTANT PUBLICATIONS

FOLLOWING PILOT STUDIES like the *Atlas of Breeding of Breeding Birds of the West Midlands* (1970, the *Atlas of Breeding Birds in Britain and Ireland* (1976),) 'represented a giant step forward in our knowledge of the distribution of British and Irish birds' and was 'by far the biggest co-operative effort ever undertaken by field ornithologists in these islands, indeed, probably, anywhere in the world'. It was followed by a *Winter Atlas*, which was ambitious enough to attempt to bring numbers into the mapping work, and the *New Atlas* (1993), took this a step further, using 'innovative colour cartography techniques' with the colour representing regional variation in relative abundance.

Although only 20 years after the original atlas, it also revealed the speed with which distributions can change, emphasising, as Humphrey Sitters said in the preface, that 'bird distribution patterns are dynamic, changing more rapidly than was previously thought'. Among other changes he mentions are the spread of the hobby, the goosander's extension into Wales and the south west, and the worrying contractions of black grouse, nightingale, grasshopper warbler and corn bunting.

FACTORS INFLUENCING POPULATION LEVELS

WITH ALL THE changes, in both range and abundance, it is even more vital to understand the factors that control bird populations. A possible starting point, highlighted by the *Winter Atlas's* attempts to estimate numbers, is that a breeding population of 50 pairs could lead to an autumn population of 300.

Early in Ian Newton's *Population Limitation in Birds* (1998) he quotes some old great tit figures to illustrate population levels at different times of the year over a five year period. Sometimes the adult population was only a quarter of the total adults plus fledged young. Taking these sorts of thing into account A. G. Gosler writes in the *Winter Atlas* 'The *Breeding Atlas* estimated the British and Irish population at something over 3,000,000 pairs, since then the population has risen about 11 per cent, based on CBC counts. Assuming that five chicks fledge per pair, some 15,000,000 first year birds might be included in the winter population.' After a couple of other assumptions and calculations he comes to a mean winter population of about 10,000,000 birds.

After mentioning Lack's earlier books, Newton describes his work as another attempt at a synthesis, incorporating the vast recent literature on bird populations and some new ideas. A number of the figures he quotes will appear under the species headings, but some are needed here to give a better idea of why numbers vary and what limits population growth. He lists the limiting factors as resources, interspecific competition, predators, parasites and the interactions between these factors, as when a bird weakened by food shortage dies of disease.

In addition, the weather impacts, and human influence might be thought to affect the whole population rather than being selective.

RESOURCES INCLUDING FOOD

ONE INDICATION OF the effect of food, the most obvious resource, is the variation in breeding success in rodent-eating raptors; another is the sudden catastrophic collapse in seabird breeding success, linked with a collapse in fish stocks. Because of the shortage of corpses, finding out about the cause of death of adult birds is not easy, but if autopsy reveals low weight, absence of body fat and emaciated muscle, starvation can be accepted. Kestrels and barn owls often seem to die of starvation, with 35 per cent and 40 per cent of birds analysed having died in that way.

Starvation linked with cold weather is familiar, and is marked by population declines of small insectivorous birds, including wrens, long-tailed tits, stonechats and Dartford warblers. Aquatic birds also suffer losses. When corpses, often of the larger birds, can be analysed, deaths are often found not to be random. An oystercatcher study in the Netherlands showed that 61 per cent of those that died in cold weather were handicapped by anatomical abnormalities, particularly of the mandible. Some of the others that died were still in moult two months later than usual.

Top
Barn owls often die of starvation in cold weather.

Middle
Long-tailed tits and wrens may also suffer losses in hard winters, when their insect food becomes hard to find.

Bottom
The great tit is one of our commoner breeding birds.

Predation

PREDATION WOULD appear an obvious limiting factor, but it is not always that simple. Predation in autumn could lead to a smaller winter population which survived better on a fixed and limited food supply.

BIRD FACT:
The marsh warbler incorporates phrases from the songs of up to 100 other species in its repertoire, even some it hears only when on migration in other countries.

EFFECTS OF PREDATORS

THOSE WHO DISLIKE sparrowhawks for 'killing all the little birds' are reluctant to accept evidence that sparrowhawks actually have little effect on the populations of their prey. Long-term population monitoring can become of value in unexpected ways. In one study, where blue and great tits have been counted each year for 50 years, their numbers were known before the sudden sparrowhawk decrease of the 1960s, known during the period of sparrowhawk absence and known for the 20 years since sparrowhawks have reappeared. Even if the peak great tit population was in a year of sparrowhawk absence, neither tit did significantly better in the absence of the hawks.

A fascinating insight into the effect of predators also involves sparrowhawks and great tits. It might be thought that a great tit at the top of the pecking order would gain most weight, to give it the best chance of surviving the winter. This was so when sparrowhawks were absent, but on their return, dominant tits, averaged over the years, were lighter and therefore more mobile and better able to escape. Being dominant they had more chance of gaining food whenever they needed it, but subordinate birds had to stock up when it was easy to get, gained weight and became at risk from predation.

Magpies are even less popular than sparrowhawks, and as versatile food gatherers they eat all sorts of young birds and eggs. Studies indicate that they actually have little influence on bird populations. However, an obsession with neat gardens can make hedge-nesting birds vulnerable to excess predation of their eggs and young.

Top
The numbers of garden and woodland birds, like this blue tit, have been little affected by increases in the sparrowhawk population.

Bottom
Female sparrowhawk with its woodpigeon prey.

RELATIONSHIPS BETWEEN PREDATORS

A CONTROVERSIAL AREA involving predators is the relationship between red grouse and raptors such as hen harriers and peregrines. The *Joint Raptor Report* (1998), a five year study in Scotland, had been widely quoted as saying that high predator levels reduce grouse populations. On one moor, predator levels went up when no illegal killing was carried out, and the autumn grouse 'bag' went down, so much that driven grouse shooting was no longer viable. There is no doubt that predators eat grouse and grouse chicks, but the breeding grouse population did not actually fall during the study period. In effect, the predators had eaten the birds that would have been shot.

There are also other factors operating; predators eat plenty of other things, and grouse depend very much on heather. For years, the grouse 'bags' have been going down, and the heather cover has decreased, as sheep grazing has favoured grass at heather's expense. This in turn encourages pipits and voles, good predator food, so their population can increase, in the absence of illegal killing and nest destruction. What is needed is better management of moorland, so that heather, grouse and predators can flourish together, perhaps with the economic benefits that shooting can bring.

Grouse are highly territorial, and if population levels are higher than the heather can support, the dominant birds gain all the territories. This in turn means that subordinate birds are forced out, and if there is not suitable heather habitat available they will die by being shot, by being predated or through eventual starvation.

EFFECTS OF A PARASITE

ANOTHER INFLUENCE on grouse numbers is a parasite. A virus transmitted by ticks, which also need sheep, causes louping ill, which can kill adult grouse but has more effect on the chicks. Chick survival in northern England was about half as high in areas with ticks and louping ill. Red grouse also suffer from nematode worms, and these may cause massive periodic reductions in populations, just as avian cholera can with waterfowl. Exceptionally, parasites can cause local extinctions, but more often they have little effect on populations, or at most reduce breeding success.

Top
Weighing a goldcrest after ringing on Lundy Island.

Bottom left
Magpies take a range of prey, including eggs and nestlings.

Bottom right
Young tawny owl.

Birdwatching

BIRDWATCHING IS NOT a new hobby. Over the last 70 years, it has gone from strength to stregth, gaining in popularity. Now, with better identification guides, easier travel, and the marvellous images of television, birdwatching has become popular enough to help support a series of industries.

Birds, the RSPB magazine, looking only at half-page and full-page advertisements, found the equivalent of 27 full-pages promoting binoculars, telescopes and cameras, 14 pages of bird-related supplies, and 12 pages of wildlife-related holidays. There were six pages on clothes and boots, and six more on what might loosely be called nature art. Five pages featured videos and CD-Roms, while a fascinating half-page invited you to 'Get Bittern' at the Lea Valley Bittern Watchpoint, where 4–7 bitterns, from a maximum, national winter population of 100, could be seen. This short list indicates the diversity of the wants of birdwatchers. Each type of birdwatcher, the home enthusiast, the habitat explorer, the 'twitcher' with immense identification skills, or the counter, who likes to contribute to research, will get their own satisfaction from birds.

Despite the comments about industries and money, birdwatching can be as cheap as you want it, and you can do it almost anywhere. Without

REQUIREMENTS OF THE BIRDWATCHER

Middle
Pied flycatcher at nestbox; Wales.

Bottom
A robin nesting in old piping might be found in your own garden – an ideal place to start birdwatching.

THOSE WHO FEED birds can spend large sums attracting them to their gardens, and many spend more by providing nest-boxes. Most birdwatchers will have binoculars, and many will have telescopes and cameras. A quick look at advertisements will tell of the amount of clothing they may claim to need, to keep them warm, and the boots to keep their feet dry.

The 'twitcher' may be ready to travel anywhere, at a moment's notice, when he hears that a new 'tick' is to be had, and helps the travel industry on the way. A superficial search through three recent issues of

binoculars you can identify birds that come to feed, and also enjoy their songs and calls. On holidays you meet new and unfamiliar species; then you will need the help that binoculars bring. I remember the excitement of my first sea and mountain birds, my early longing for rarities, and my compulsion to make lists. Many enthusiasts remain collectors; of birds seen, of photographs, of places visited or of numbers counted. Others develop special interests in behaviour or conservation, in ringing, or the study of a single bird or a bird group like owls. The choices are endless, but at some stage you will need to decide where you are going to watch your birds.

WHERE AND WHEN TO WATCH

THE SIMPLE ANSWER is at anytime and anywhere. I have seen curlew and common tern over Lords cricket ground, plotted the movements of gulls as I walked into lectures, and had redwing pointed out to me in a maths lesson, and hawfinch during biology. Another simple answer is near your home, satisfied, at least initially, with getting to know the local birds.

Many people will use birds as an opportunity to visit new places. The north Norfolk coast is a magnet at any time of year, but particularly during migration, while mountains and islands have a different lure. A week on Bardsey or Cape Clear, Fair Isle or the Scillies is unique, not only for any birds you may see, but for exposure to a special way of life.

The series of *Where to Watch Birds* books provides another set of answers. For any particular area there may be a brief habitat description, a sample of the main species to be seen at different times of year, a section on timing your watching, and details of access. In the Devon and Cornwall book (Norman and Tucker 1997) for example, the timing section directs you to dawn or dusk for migrating passerines at Prawle Point and tells you that overcast days with cool easterlies can produce rarer species in late autumn.

Above
Some birdwatchers get a thrill from spotting rarities, like this white stork.

Below
Birdwatchers at a seabird colony at the Cliffs of Moher, Ireland.

Top

Hides are excellent for birdwatching and photography.

Bottom

A well-stocked table brings the birds in to your garden where you can watch them up close.

HIDES AND THE RSPB

GUIDE BOOKS TELL YOU where to find birds but the RSPB can make it easier still. Hides, and a dedicated and skilful management, guarantee that you can see birds well. At the RSPB reserve of Leighton Moss in Lancashire, four out of seven hides are accessible by wheelchair, and the reserve centre has a tea room, shop and live video link – 1618 ha (4,000 acres) with bitterns and marsh harriers, bearded tits and a pair of Mediterranean gulls attract 80,000 visitors a year. A carpeted hide with soft seats is only a hundred metres from the car park.

Coastal National Nature Reserves looked after by English Nature include the Farne Islands and Lindisfarne in Northumberland, the Ribble marshes in Lancashire and east coast reserves further south on the Colne estuary and at Scolt Head. Separate national agencies manage scenically dramatic National Nature Reserves in Snowdonia, the Cairngorms and around Beinn Eighe in Ross and Cromarty.

A new and growing set of ventures aim to see more seabirds; the RSPB had trips this year from Torquay out into Lyme Bay. Steve Dudley in the Birdwatcher's Year Book (Ed Pemberton 1998) writes of how sea-birding can be a supplement to the sea-watch. His description of this in the past is evocative for 'to see shearwaters, skuas and petrels you glued your eyes to your telescope and your backside to some godforsaken, windswept, sea-sprayed headland. After hours of misery you might be lucky enough to see an "auk sp" shooting past.' Some of the best sea-birding he mentions

seems equally unattractive, as we will see in the seabirds section, but comfortable trips, although at sea one can never tell, take 300 birders from the Scillies to see ten or more seabird species that would never be more than distant images from land. Other trips take watchers from Bempton to see a seabird colony from the sea.

FINDING SUITABLE SUBJECTS TO WATCH

PERSONALLY I LIKE to find my own birds and, usually, to find them near home. Many lovely but mainly smaller reserves are managed by the County Wildlife Trusts which do such vital work for conservation, but you do not need to rely on the reserves when there are town parks, reservoirs, gravel pits, woods and estuaries. Watchable birds are everywhere, but do remember that you will not see many at all, if you do not watch when the sun is in the right place.

BIRDWATCHING FOR ALL

THE FACT THAT you can watch birds anywhere is exemplified by a note from David Glue in a recent *BTO News*. He has been a wheelchair-bound since 1971, but has seen 321 species in Britain since his accident. He offers a number of tips to those who cannot get

about much, including the elderly and housebound. His first two suggestions might seem obvious, but by adding well-placed nest-boxes to the bird table by the window, the range of activities to be watched is increased. He then advocates the use of pishing and squeaking techniques to draw secretive species like goldcrests, warblers and flycatchers into the open. Before leaving home, if you can, study maps closely to

find the best spots from where you can gain easy access to lakes or estuaries, and when there make full use of the car as a mobile hide, improved by using telescope accessories and other devices to clamp optics firmly to the car window. The essence of his message is be bold, take the risk of a seabird trip, make a personal approach to landowners and consult RADAR (Royal Association for Disability and Rehabilitation). He also has a message for me; overactive able-bodied watchers often miss much, and for all of us – 'use birds to help keep your mind and body active and provide enjoyment while contributing to science in a useful way.'

*Sanderlings are pretty birds, quite small
and very neat,
They move about incessantly on little
clockwork feet.
They run before advancing waves then back
when they recede,
And there they find the tiny things on which
they like to feed.
They never get their feet wet, their
movements are so fast.
You stand and watch to see if they will get
them wet at last.
They never do. And then with one accord
they take to flight,
They fly a hundred yards or so and then
they all alight
And start to feed again before a different
set of waves.
It's fascinating watching how this little
bird behaves.'*

R. S. Morrison WORDS ON BIRDS

Top right
*Herring gulls will
sometimes take food from
passengers on a ship.*

Middle left
*Seabird colony with
guillemots; Farne Islands.*

Bottom
*The small, active
sanderling is a common
shorebird.*

Birdwatching Equipment

> 'Binoculars are the instruments that define birding – like the functional equivalent of the first baseman's glove, the musician's instrument, the plough in the hands of the frontier farmer.'
> Peter Dunne OPTICS FOR BIRDING

BINOCULARS REALLY ARE needed. The fact that two of the pairs I use have been in action for 50 years is a reminder that once you have them they can last a long time, but in those years lenses and design have completely changed. Many people think that magnification is the important thing, but light-gathering and weight can matter just as much.

TYPE OF BINOCULAR

POOR LIGHT IS hardly rare in Britain, while heavy binoculars can be tiring and hard to keep still. Another problem is that high magnification can make for difficulties with close viewing. I tend to use heavier 10 x 50 binoculars on an estuary, and 8 x 30s in woodland. The first figure gives the magnification, and the second the objective lens diameter in mm. This, usually a complex of lenses, is at the opposite end from the eye-piece. If you divide the objective lens diameter by the magnification you get an indication of light-gathering power, with a higher figure making for greater usefulness in poor light.

Having said that, the modern multicoated lenses and phase coated roof prisms, both expensive, have changed the old perspectives. If you pay the price you will get the superior brightness. Before coating, 5 per cent of light striking polished glass was reflected away. With 10–16 glass surfaces inside the binocular, the net result was dark images. Coating reduces the 5 per cent to 1 per cent, and multiple coating, in thin layers,

further reduces light reflection to a fraction of 1 per cent. 'Fully coated' or 'multicoated' means all surfaces, lenses and prisms, inside and out, are coated.

FEATURES TO LOOK FOR

TRADITIONALLY WIDE-BODIED parroprism binoculars, the prisms turning inverted images the right way up again and giving the glasses their 'kink', have fewer internal surfaces and therefore transmit more light, but newer roof-prism binoculars are very tough. Their objective and ocular lenses are in line, making for a streamlined shape which some find easier to hold. Comfortable holding is important, but fast and easy focusing is vital, and central focusing with a well-positioned wheel that can move you from close to distant quickly and easily, is invaluable.

If you have limited arm strength or finger movement investigate these new lightweight binoculars, as David Glue suggests, and if you select a pair with great depth of field you will not have to alter the focus so often. Glasses wearers have different problems, but with high 'eye

Top
A telescope is essential for successful identification of seabirds and waders.

Bottom
Binoculars and telescope – the best of both worlds.

As with binoculars, the higher the magnification the narrower the field of view, and with greater weight a support system needs to be very rigid. In most cases, unless used from a car, the telescope and tripod will need to be carried so weight is significant. Always try and test out a 'scope' before buying it. Special optical field days, advertised in birdwatching magazines, give you a good opportunity to check for possible good and bad points.

CHECK LIST FOR TELESCOPES

Image brightness: dependent on lens size and coating quality, where coating is a covering of the lens by non-reflecting material
Colour coats: yellow, green or blue
Chromatic aberration: giving coloured fringes to your bird
Image sharpness: which may easily be judged by trying to read a distant poster
Field of view: a wide-angled eye-piece may make it easier to find your bird.

relief', the distance between ocular lens and eye, they can keep their glasses on. Rubber cups or 'twist in' eye cups may help.

Apart from quoted figures like magnification and objective lens diameter, there are a range of features which are often not quoted, but which determine the quality of a pair of binoculars and therefore the quality of the image you will see. You need to use the binoculars under trial conditions to test their resolving power, alignment and transmission and the absence of colour fringes and distortions. In addition you may want to pay for protection features that may make your purchase dust-, water- or fog-proof.

BENEFITS OF A TELESCOPE

UNTIL VERY RECENTLY I have not owned a telescope – not very convenient or useful in Welsh mountains or woodlands. Furthermore I had memories of the difficulties using the old tubular ones, propped on the railings of the causeway at Staines Reservoir or on an unsteady shoulder peering out to sea and hoping for skuas or shearwaters at Blakeney. While binoculars have improved, telescopes are unrecognisably better and easier to use, and even on a small estuary I am already gaining the benefit of extra detail to sort out identification and give extra pleasure with even the commonest waders.

OTHER EQUIPMENT REQUIRED

YOU WILL ALSO need to have a field notebook as well as a larger one in which you keep your permanent records. In the field I like little waterproof ones in which you really can write in pencil, even when it is wet. Avoid the more brightly coloured of modern waterproofs, and make sure your feet stay dry in the wet places that birds love. In all aspects of your birding equipment you will need to resist at least some of the heavy advertising aimed at you.

Top
Good bird artists work from detailed field notes and sketches.

Bottom
A birdwatcher's field notebook.

Whether this advertising is on behalf of the birds or their watchers it becomes more colourful, imaginative and persistent year by year. Seed storage feeders, squirrel-proof feeders, stainless-steel feeders, those that take 3.5 kilos of sunflower seeds or even one ready to take 6.4 kilos and feed 16 birds at a time! Many of these are in polycarbonate tubes which are tough, see-through and provide feeding points with perches.

New foods like sunflower hearts, foods for swans and ducks developed with help from the Wildfowl and Wetlands Trust with minerals, trace elements and vitamins, together with mealworms and earthworms full of good protein. With the emphasis now on summer feeding as well, your budget can be well stretched, but the resulting pleasure is enormous and the value to the birds incalculable. If you try to estimate, making your own assumptions, how may weed and cereal seeds used to be left in a 2-ha (five-acre) arable field, or how many berries might be available along half a mile of hedge that was not cut back so often, you will see that the way you manage your garden can have as much influence on food supplies as a number of new feeders. They are wonderful but only part of the story of bird survival.

reducing condensation and humidity: tits certainly love the ones I use but I am still waiting for a nuthatch to move in. Do not forget that you can make your own boxes, that pallets can often be found for free, while cheap offcuts of wood may also be available. Some details of nest-boxes will appear later, mainly in the town and garden section.

Booklets on bird guides are equally rich in choice and special offers – the latest, most exciting CD-Roms, videos and books, David Attenborough's marvellous *Life of Birds* on video, CD-Roms allowing you to compare plumage and calls, and with video-clips and freeze frames. Birdwatchers have never had so much on offer, but do remember that you do not need it all, or even any of it, to enjoy your birds, and that a pocket identification guide that can go everywhere with you may cost relatively little to purchase.

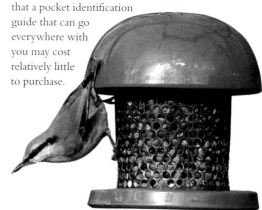

NEST BOXES

NEST-BOXES ARE a great addition to garden or woodland, but try to develop natural sites and cover as well. There is no doubt the expensive 'woodcrete' boxes do last well and are alleged to 'breathe',

RECORDING

ONCE YOU START identifying the more unusual birds or monitoring numbers of common ones on your patch, you will need to share your records by

Top
Blue tits are usually amongst the first to appear at the feeder.

Middle
A more unusual sight – a nuthatch attracted by peanuts.

Bottom
Redwings often come into gardens to feed on holly berries, especially in cold winter weather.

passing them on to someone who holds a file of local or county records. County recorders have never had an easy time. There would be a great deal of work even if every record was genuine, and every birder punctilious in the presentation and punctuality of their submissions, but Bowey and Smith (1998) write of new difficulties. They wonder how a system can be devised in which all watchers submit records which can be used nationally in the interests of conservation. They mention 'black sheep' who may be competent rarity-seekers but who never pass on their records except by hearsay, and local societies who are too insular and only think about their local area with no regard to the national scene. They also mention visitors to reserves who assume that a warden or ranger will see everything and report everything and that, therefore, their observations are not needed.

As county recorders, they see their job getting more difficult in that, 'with the advent of commercialisation, through colourful, professionally designed magazines, telephone bird lines and pagers, there has been a drift away from the local bird club, as old and new birdwatchers have realised they have up-to-date information from other sources'. The clubs need to 'think about demographic trends and gender imbalance in their membership and about youth policies, in particular working with the RSPB's YOC and Phoenix groups. These, after all, are the birders of tomorrow.'

The authors would like to see the profile of county recorders raised, and an organisation to take overall responsibility for bird recording in the country as well as a total refusal to accept hearsay records. Many, like me, are against the growing standardisation of many aspects of life but, if recording is to be effective, some sort of standard approach will have to be adopted. There are many like me who have accumulated personal knowledge of an area but have submitted few records. In my case, years of counts at different times of the year in conifer plantations and oak woods in Wales, together with estimates of grassland breeding populations at different altitudes have been lost, and only the results of BTO surveys submitted. This sort of approach does not help the conservation cause, however much pleasure it may bring. All information about nationally important sites, widespread but threatened habitats, and your local patch, need to be shared if the hard facts that influence decision makers are to be available.

Bowey and Smith hope that computerisation of county databases, hopefully to become universal if the National Biodiversity Network takes off, will create a powerful tool for conservation.

Top
A bird-friendly garden, with varied shrubs, lawn and a pond.

Middle
Birdwatcher consulting his field guide.

Bottom
Nestboxes can help boost the bird numbers in your garden.

Bird Identification

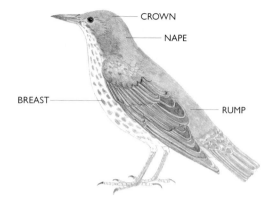

CROWN

NAPE

BREAST

RUMP

WHEN PEOPLE DESCRIBE to me a bird they have seen I often have to tell them, somewhat unhelpfully, that it must be new to science as their description fits no bird I know. When a more experienced watcher describes a bird, there is more chance of helping, for they include the details that are needed for identification.

CORRECT IDENTIFICATION

THE USE OF THE correct terms for the parts of the body, the observational ability to notice inconspicuous features, an awareness of comparable species and their size and some method of recalling sounds, all help in making a good description. There is great merit in this methodical approach, but how do you actually recognise your friends? Do you know all the details of their nose profile and ear lobes? I doubt it. You spot something distinctive about the way they move or they have some special feature and you know it is them even if they are a long way off. It is the same with birds, and when we refer to their JIZZ we mean distinctive shape and movement. 'Little brown jobs' can always cause difficulties, but even with tree, rock and meadow pipits their gestures, calls and habitat tell you which is which although they look so similar.

QUICK IDENTIFICATION

RECENTLY, IN SOME flooded fields I had an immediate 'feel' that three small waders by a muddy pool were little ringed plovers. I had not seen the species for years, but something about their jizz alerted me. Confirmation was needed and it would have been easy to make a proper field sketch, including details of plumage, leg and bill colour and features of the eye. Idly I only jotted brief notes about pale legs and back, bobbing action, the horribly vague 'ring extending downwards' and the not at all helpful 'black through eye'. Luckily the birds flew, had no wing bar and gave their distinctive call, so my 'feel' had been right.

LEARNING FROM EXPERIENCE

WATCHING WITH SOMEONE who knows more than you is the best way to learn. You may have a friend to teach you or you may decide to join a local group who watch the likely localities. If it is easier to learn the appearance of birds with help, it is even more useful to have someone to teach you the calls and songs, but ultimately you will have to develop the confidence to make your own decisions.

Top
This standard bird (thrush) shows some of the features to watch out for when identifying a bird.

Bottom
A trio of winter-plumage grebes – red-necked, black-necked and Slavonian (left to right).

Some of the sounds are clearly distinctive, but many, alarm-calls for instance, are very similar, and among flocks of waders it is hard to tell which calls are associated with which birds. To many people, one warbler singing in the brambles is much like another. Finding the garden warbler that is lurking there and seeing it well enough to identify it may require great patience. Whatever the difficulties, sounds are vital for identification and surveys. Once the leaf cover has developed on the ash trees of the Lyme Regis Undercliff, where I do a Common Bird Census, I rarely see a bird, never use binoculars, but record some 150 individuals in a three-hour count.

Knowing what species are likely to be around can also be a great help. A booklet on the local area, particularly when you go somewhere new, can indicate likely birds, and more or less rule out others. Last year in Menorca a little guide by Hearl (1996) told me about good sites and Balearic specialities. Nearer home Stan Davies (1987) has provided a useful guide to the Exe.

WHAT TO LOOK FOR

KNOWING WHAT TO look for can have a different meaning. The classic *Handbook of British Birds* was, and is, valued for many things, but the field character section was the most notable feature for most bird watchers. Later Peterson introduced the judicious use of arrows in highlighting fieldmarks in his American guides, and contributed the same with his illustrations for the *Field Guide to the Birds of Britain and Europe* (1954). An arrow to the black axillaries, arm-pits, of the winter grey plover, to the long bill of a spotted

redshank or to the light edge of a willow tit's wing ensure you know what to look for.

Some field marks are more reliable for identification than others, there are three categories of field mark. There is the diagnostic feature that is absolute, like those highlighted by Peterson and in many guides since. Peterson might also use an arrow to indicate that species A has longer wings or a darker back than species B, but there is another sort of field mark where we get into greater difficulties. There are percentage differences, where A usually has a dark iris (but not always) while B usually does not, but sometimes does. This is the sort of area where the gull experts are happy mentioning that herring gulls sometimes have yellow legs or this, that or the other wing feather.

Top
Spotted redshank –
note the rather long,
narrow bill compared
with common redshank.

Bottom
Herring gull overhead –
note the black wing tips,
with white flecks, and
the heavy bill.

Identifying Rare Birds

THE FACT REMAINS that identification experts, describing rare birds which they cannot identify by jizz, need to observe and record with precision if their records are to be accepted by the Rarities Committee of British Birds.

DIFFICULTY OF CORRECT IDENTIFICATION

REPORTING ON RARE birds in Great Britain in 1996, M.J. Rogers and members of the Rarities Committee say how 'it grieves us to receive a report of a really "good bird" that is clearly unacceptable on the skimpy details provided, or to hear of something rare and special that never sees the light of day of a submitted report'. Commenting later on the photographs that are now so often taken to support rare bird identification he continues 'some twitching episodes resemble a car boot sale and many observers can buy a photograph of a particular rarity on their way to see it: little wonder, perhaps, that field notes and drawings seem to some people to be superfluous.' However, they indicate the level of accurate observation needed by the good field worker who is really interested in identification.

PERSONAL OBSERVATIONS

BECAUSE OF THE sort of birdwatcher I am I have hardly added to the repertoire of two hundred or so birds I can identify easily for 40 years. A trip to Kenya gave me a mass of new birds, but they did not help my identification skills in Britain, and while a series of holidays, not primarily birdwatching, to southern Europe and its islands have given me chances to see hoopoes and woodchat shrikes, bee-eaters and black-winged stilts, rock thrushes and vultures, assorted eagles and wheatears, most of these are easy birds or are not likely to turn up here. I have had to try to get to grips with the skulking *Sylvia* warblers, of which there are so many, but have not grappled with most of the volumes of song that come from reedbeds, or with the larks that are often everywhere. If I really did want to improve my identification, then travel and hard work would be the way to do it, and many of our best birdwatchers, writers, recorders and members of Rarities Committee have continually extended the range of birds with which they are familiar in the field.

> 'Look at them turkeys in the water' said Olive
> 'Those aren't turkeys,' said her father. 'They're ducks. You can tell by the bill. India-runner ducks, that's what they are.'
> They weren't. They were Canada geese.
> Oh, Lord! I do hope I don't seem unkind. We all make such fat headed mistakes that we can all afford to smile at others.
>
> Robert Gibbings
> SWEET THAMES RUN SOFTLY

Top
Black-winged stilt – showing its remarkably long legs in flight.

Bottom
Canada goose – escaped or feral birds sometimes confuse the unwary.

DEVOTED TO RARE BIRDS

THEY WOULD ALSO be regular readers of *British Birds*, a monthly magazine devoted, among other things, to the identification and recording of rare birds. This publication is being revamped, with more colour and new design, for the bird magazine world is highly competitive and all have good coverage of rarities. I have a photocopy of a couple of pages from

BB, as it is always known, for February 1996, with an article about the identification of little and Baillon's crakes by three authors (Christie, Shirihae and Harris) who have gathered material over many years observations of hundreds of individuals of both species, as well as extensive examination of skins.

With that sort of background it is possible to be a real expert. After dealing with habitat, general features and structural differences, including a detailed look at wing structure, they move on to separate adult males, with details of how to distinguish little crake from Baillon's for example. But despite all the sophistication of the modern birdwatcher, identification remains an art as well as a science and it is still possible for different interpretations of the same bird to take years to resolve.

Above left
This is the fleeting glimpse a lucky birdwatcher might have of the rare hoopoe.

Above right
It is worth checking out wheatears during migration – this is the standard model!

Below
The tiny Baillon's crake is a rare and secretive bird – seldom seen, let alone photographed.

Bird Classification and Names

NAMES, AS CAIN (1954) says, are arbitrary, and there tend to be a great many of them. Peter Conder's book on the wheatear (1989) lists almost a hundred local names, many in the chacker, chicker, chatchock line, because of the wheatear's call, but including coney sucker, underground jobler and whitestart.

MOST OF THESE seem perfectly applicable, in one way or another, and perhaps more reasonable than wheatear. But 'wheatear' itself can be analysed, and Conder tells us that 'wheat' is a corruption of the Anglo Saxon 'hwit' meaning white, and 'ears' is a corruption, or Bowdlerisation, of 'aers', meaning rump – hence an old English name of 'white arse'.

VARIETY OF NAMES

BRYAN NELSON (1978) writes of the range of gannet names, stressing that the gannet is essentially a Scottish bird and that 'Solan goose' was for a long time the proper name. Variants of solem, solen, solan, soland, solent and sollem existed, and all may derive from the Gaelic 'suil' or eye, linked with the gannet's keen sight. A vernacular Welsh name was Gwydd Lygadlon (clear-eyed goose), and a lovely Gaelic name 'Ian ban an Sgadon' (the white bird of the herring). Gannet, with its obvious links to gander, is a modification of the ancient British 'gan' or 'gans', corresponding with modern German 'Gans', Latin 'anser' and Sanskrit 'hansa'. Many birds have

fascinating local or regional names, some quite different from the modern English name, and this provides a rich field for research. The most productive sources for the such names are Greenoak (1997), Boyd (1951) for Cheshire names, Berry and Johnston (1980) for Shetland, Kearton (1908), and the poems of John Clare (1793–1864) for traditional Northamptonshire names.

SCIENTIFIC NAMES

THE ARBITRARY AND often local nature of bird names has caused difficulties for those attempting classification and, while Latin was the language of the educated, attempts were made to produce brief, accepted, Latinised descriptions as names. No coherent system emerged until Linnaeus, and our accepted animal nomenclature stems from the date of the publication of the tenth edition of his *Systema Naturae*, effectively the first of January 1758. Previous names, even involving two words like his, had no standing. The 'Law of Priority' states that the correct name for any form is that which conforms to the binomial systerm and is the first validly published in, or since, *Systema Naturae*. In the binomial system, the generic name is written first, using an initial capital, thus *Morus* for a gannet, and the specific or trivial name follows without an initial capital, in this case *bassanus*, to complete the gannet's species name or binomial.

Top left
Common gull – something of a misnomer, as this species is usually less common than black-headed and herring gull.

Top right
The wheatear takes its English name from its white rump, not its ear.

Bottom
The name 'dunnock' has widely ousted the somewhat misleading name 'hedge sparrow'.

AMERICAN NAMES

THIS BRINGS US to another problem for birds found on both sides of the Atlantic are often given different names. In America 'divers' are 'loons', their sparrowhawk is a falcon, and a sand martin is a bank swallow. Another common situation is that the American name has an added adjective, to separate different species found there, where we only have a single one. Many Australasian birds have been given English names, even when the birds concerned are not related to any in Europe.

We have only one wren, but *Peterson's Field Guide to Western Birds* illustrates nine species. Our wren, *Troglodytes troglodytes*, is known there as the winter wren, while others in the same genus are the house wren and brown-throated wren. Marsh wrens, rock wrens and short-billed marsh wrens are in a different genus, but still within the wren family. The American dipper is a different species from ours, but is sometimes referred to simply as 'dipper'. A classic cause of confusion is the American robin, which is actually a species of thrush.

Although most modern bird guides agree on the English names, there are still some variations, and in an attempt to deal with these difficulties, the Records Committee of the British Ornithologists' Union has drawn up a list of new English names to meet the need for international acceptance. Some changes are minor, thus the wheatear becomes the northern wheatear, but others are greater and likely to meet more popular resistance – winter wren, black-billed magpie and willow ptarmigan may be among these.

CHANGING ENGLISH NAMES

MOST OF US do not use either local names or binomials, but call birds by their English names, which we see as part of the language. As such they change with time under the influence of both books and people. E.M. Nicholson in *Birds and Men* (1951) was keen to change several of the names that had been used in the *Handbook of British Birds*. He preferred dunnock to hedge sparrow, throstle to song thrush and pied and barred woodpecker as names for our two spotted woodpeckers. The preference for dunnock seems to have been widespread, partly because it was certainly never a sparrow. Interestingly, in the light of recent events, Nicholson wanted to replace common gull, which is certainly rarely common, with mew gull which is the accepted American name.

Top
The gannet's name involves a complex history. It is sometimes known as 'Solan goose'.

Bottom
Our wren is called the winter wren in North America.

The Orders of British Birds

THIS SECTION SUMMARISES the main orders of birds found on the British list. It also includes a short summary of the features of the different orders, and includes a few examples.

GAVIIFORMES

Red- and black-throated Diver, Great Northern Diver

SPEAR-SHAPED BILLS, stocky necks, streamlined bodies and can dive down to 75 m (250 ft), staying under water for a possible eight minutes. The male and female are similar, the young have a second coat of down, before developing their adult feathers. The loud calls of these long-lived birds are often regarded as evil omens in northern cultures.

Top

Red-throated diver in winter – note upturned bill-tip.

Bottom

Fulmar – note the tube-shaped nostrils on top of the bill.

PODICIPEDIFORMES

Dabchick, Great Crested Grebe, Red-necked Grebe, Black-necked Grebe, Slavonian Grebe

SMALL TO MEDIUM-LARGE swimming and diving birds. They have a short tail tuft, flattened tarsi, and three of the toes are broadly lobed. Many have display markings on the head. An unusual behaviour feature is that the young are initially carried by the parents and have downy plumage, usually with stripes.

PROCELLARIIFORMES

Fulmar, Manx Shearwater, Storm Petrel

PELAGIC SEA BIRDS with long, narrow wings, fly more than they swim and are very vulnerable on land. Sometimes known as 'tubenoses', referring to the nostrils being in dorsal tubes in the hooked beak.

They are colonial breeders, making a minimal nest and laying white eggs. Petrels are much smaller, with short, rounded wings and black plumage; they are long-distance migrants.

PELECANIFORMES

Gannet, Cormorant, Shag

FISH- AND SQUID-EATING aquatic birds which are usually colonial nesters. The toes are unique in that all four are joined by webs. The group have a more or less distensible pouch of bare skin between the branches of the lower mandible. Cormorants and gannets have closed external nostrils and breathe through their mouths. The members of the group have diverse feeding methods.

CICONIIFORMES

Grey Heron, Bittern, Little Egret
LONG-LEGGED, long-necked wading birds like
herons, bitterns, egrets and spoonbills which are often
colonial nesters. Different families are often separated
by their bill structure. Herons have modifications to
the bones of the neck, allowing a spearing mechanism
and letting it fold into an S-shaped curve.

ANSERIFORMES

Mallard, Mute Swan, Greylag Goose
WEB-FOOTED, LONG-NECKED swimming birds. The
feet are webbed in a different way from the previous
order, with the fourth, hind, toe being somewhat
elevated and not, therefore involved in the web. The
flattened, blunt-tipped bill has fine lamellae along the
margins of the maxilla and mandible. The feathers are
in distinct tracts, with down underneath.

FALCONIFORMES

*Sparrowhawk, Buzzard, Golden Eagle,
Kestrel, Peregrine, Merlin*
BIRDS OF PREY, with sharp,
curved talons and hooked
beaks and highly adapted
sight and flight. They have
unfeathered skin, the cere, at
the base of the bill. They often
soar in flight.

GALLIFORMES

Red Grouse, Grey Partridge, Pheasant
GAMEBIRDS, WITH SHORT, rounded
wings, a well developed keel and
sturdy legs with four toes. In pheasants the
hind toe is not in contact with the ground.
The tip of the upper mandible overlaps the
lower mandible. Two other characteristics,
not unique, are a large muscular
gizzard and the laying of
large clutches.

Top left
Cormorant in
typical silhouette.

Top right
The pure white little egret
is typically heron-shaped.
Note the yellow feet.

Bottom
This buzzard shows
the classic bird of prey
features of hooked bill
and heavy talons.

GRUIFORMES

Water Rail, Coot, Moorhen, Crane

THIS IS AN OLD, widely dispersed order, with few unifying characters. Most of our members, the crakes and rails, have slightly webbed toes and tend to be highly secretive; something that can hardly be said of the large bustards and cranes which also belong here.

CHARADRIIFORMES

Curlew, Black-headed Gull, Guillemot

THE WADERS, GULLS and auks are clearly waterbirds or, if not, like the lapwing, derived from water birds. They are united by characteristics of skull, vertebral column and syrinx. Of the three sub-orders, the waders rarely have webbed toes but usually have a good hind toe, the gulls either lack a hind toe or have a small one, are web-footed and have a salt-gland above the eye. Auks are stocky marine birds with webbed feet and no hind toe, and a distinctive upright stance.

COLUMBIFORMES

Woodpigeon, Stock Dove, Collared Dove

DOVES AND PIGEONS have small heads, short legs with small scales and a fleshly cere at the base of the bill. They have a muscular gizzard and large crop, the lining of which secretes a unique 'milk' to feed the young. The two eggs hatch into nearly naked young. As pigeons can drink by sucking, they do not have to tilt the head back to swallow.

PSITTACIFORMES

Ring-necked Parakeet

AN ORDER WITH a single large family, the parrots, mainly confined to the tropics, except for some introductions. Mainly vegetable feeders with a stout, strongly hooked bill with a woodpecker-like arrangement of their toes, they are good climbers and despite a large range in size are an extremely uniform group. Gregarious, noisy and intelligent.

Top
Water rail in typical habitat.

Bottom
Auks, such as these guillemots, are rather penguin-like in shape – but they can fly.

CUCULIFORMES
Cuckoo
USUALLY LONG-TAILED and long-billed. Many, including the European species, are brood-parasites. Cuckoos have a slightly decurved bill and are insectivorous, favouring hairy caterpillars. This order also contains the peculiar hoatzin of South America, whose young have two functional claws on their wings to help clamber in the trees, and the turacos of tropical Africa.

STRIGIFORMES
Barn Owl, Tawny Owl, Little Owl
MAINLY NOCTURNAL, with large, rounded heads and big eyes. Most can turn their heads to look sideways or over their shoulder. The eye is strengthened and lengthened by a cylinder of bony plates that help provide telescopic vision. The large facial disc of feathers concentrates sound. Owls have hooked bills, with the base covered in bristles.

CAPRIMULGIFORMES
Nightjar
NOCTURNAL, FAVOURING DUSK and dawn. Small weak feet, a short bill but with a large gape, surrounded by long bristles. Eggs are laid on bare ground. The highly specialised oilbird of South America also belongs here, as do the frogmouths, owlet-nightjars and potoos.

APODIFORMES
Swift
THE RELATIONSHIP BETWEEN swifts and the mainly tropical hummingbirds (also classified in this order) is uncertain, but they share a specialised wing structure and a unique egg-white protein. They have tiny feet, short humerus bones, but long bones in the outer portion of the wing. The crop is lacking in swifts.

CORACIIFORMES
Kingfisher, Bee-eater, Hoopoe
ALTHOUGH THIS APPARENTLY diverse group, which includes rollers, kingfishers and hoopoes, share peculiarities of the palate and leg muscles and have their front toes fused at the base, they may not be monophyletic, that is they may stem from more than one ancestral form.

PICIFORMES
Green Woodpecker, Great Spotted Woodpecker, Wryneck
WE HAVE NO honeyguides or toucans (also included in this order), but woodpeckers also have unique feet, with two toes pointing forwards and two back. True

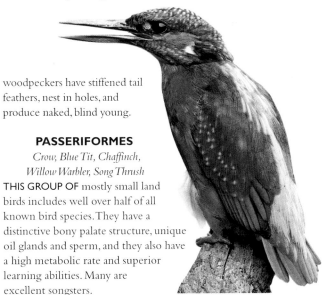

woodpeckers have stiffened tail feathers, nest in holes, and produce naked, blind young.

PASSERIFORMES
Crow, Blue Tit, Chaffinch, Willow Warbler, Song Thrush
THIS GROUP OF mostly small land birds includes well over half of all known bird species. They have a distinctive bony palate structure, unique oil glands and sperm, and they also have a high metabolic rate and superior learning abilities. Many are excellent songsters.

Top
Pigeons and doves are all very similar in general shape. The collared dove is common in towns and farmland.

Bottom left
Tawny owls are more often heard than seen. Owls have a rounded head and large eyes.

Bottom right
Many a birder's favourite, the kingfisher redefines the term brilliant.

Town and Garden Birds

NINE OUT OF TEN people in Britain live in towns. The idea of the concrete jungle is however something of a myth, and in most towns and cities private gardens and parks provide large areas of green space. In the Black Country of the West Midlands, for example, woodland doubled between 1977 and 1989 as neglected 'derelict' land was colonised. Such 'brownfield' sites are under heavy threat from further housing, but for all of us, wherever we live, it is important that the urban majority have greenery, and birds, within reach. In many newly planned urban areas, wildlife corridors provide relatively unbroken green links between the countryside and the centre of the city.

BIRDS FOUND IN CITIES

SUBURBAN NORTH LONDON has changed somewhat since Harting was able to write of 'whinchats in every grassfield; willow wrens and whitethroats in the green lanes; and the handsome Butcher-bird in the tall tangled hedges'. Nevertheless the variety of urban habitats still yields enough birds to interest most birdwatchers today.

The *Birds of the London Area* (1957) includes 245 species seen within 32 km (20 miles) of St Paul's Cathedral. Fitter dealt with a smaller, almost wholly built-up area, the administrative county of London, but still listed 45 residents, 13 summer visitors and 34 regular winter visitors and passage migrants. Red-backed shrikes sadly are now gone, grey partridge and hawfinch are rarer, and not everyone would see the gain of magpies and collared doves as fair exchange. The opportunist magpie is ready to 'tidy up' dog litter, clear roads of the victims of cars, and take away food leftovers and the contents of fragile plastic bags. The collared dove, another versatile feeder, is now one of the top ten garden birds; it had only reached the southern Balkans at the turn of the century, and it was only in 1952 that it reached Britain.

A quick look at some regional Bird Reports shows that London is not alone. Greater Manchester, stretching from Wigan to Oldham and Rochdale to Trafford, reported its usual clutch of rare birds in 1996.

Working through the year these included Iceland gull, red-necked grebe, bittern, Mediterranean gull, osprey, garganey, firecrest, dotterel, Savi's warbler, marsh harrier, bee-eater, Arctic skua, purple sandpiper, blue-winged teal, hoopoe, hen harrier, snow bunting and twite. On the other side of the Pennines the 1993/1994 report of the Barnsley and District Bird Study Group had records of great northern diver, bittern, eider, crane, pomarine skua, long-tailed skua and yellow-browed warbler in one year, and purple heron, great white egret, honey buzzard and Temminck's Stint in the next.

Top
The smart black-and-white plumage of the magpie is seen increasingly in both towns and gardens.

Middle
The blackbird is now one of the most common garden birds in Britain.

Bottom
The number of collared doves has increased rapidly over the last 30 years.

GARDEN INHABITANTS

BUT FOR MOST of those who love birds it is the ones found in town gardens that are most important.

Recent BTO research reports that the blackbird tops the list of visitors to gardens large and small, with 96.4 per cent of gardens being visited. The other most commonly seen birds are blue tit, robin, great tit, chaffinch, house sparrow (decreasing), collared dove, dunnock, starling and greenfinch. The *Bird Table*, newsletter of the Garden Bird Watch scheme, reports seasonal fluctuations among birds which would have been thought rare in gardens until a few years ago. Goldfinches come in twice as much in late spring, a time of seed shortage, blackcaps turn up in winter in up to 40 per cent of town gardens, and the appearance of wandering winter siskins, redwings and bramblings depends on such remote events as the scarcity of food in Scandinavia. These facts, together with a host of others from the first three years of the scheme are brought together by Andrew Cannon in the *Garden Bird Watch Handbook* (1998). This book, based on weekly observations by over 10,000 garden birdwatchers will be much quoted in the species section.

TOWN BIRDS

TITS AND ROBINS are probably the garden favourites. With four million pairs in Britain and Ireland, for a time they replaced the blackbird as the top garden bird. blackbirds' panic alarm calls at breeding times are a headache for anyone worried about the survival of young birds, but their beautiful song produces no such headache, unless it is too early in the morning and too loud, when densely-packed suburban blackbirds defend their territories in the dawn chorus.

House sparrows used to be thought of as the typical urban bird, and at times the noisy flocks of roosting starlings have taken over city centres, as well as the chimney pots of suburbia. Perhaps feral pigeons are now the true urban birds. These are descended from the rock doves of wild coastal cliffs, and they are well able to use the year-round food supply of towns to help prolong their extensive breeding season. They may have five broods a year, and attempts to reduce numbers and the damage caused to buildings have met with little success.

The black redstart is also urban. This rather secretive and local species chooses derelict industrial sites, gas works, power stations and other places with little normal appeal to birdwatchers. Equally unexpected, until recently, would have been the noisy screeching of a gorgeously coloured parrot, but ring-necked parakeets have settled well, notably in south-east London, and the 1997 *Surbiton Bird Report* has the extraordinary record of 1,507 Parakeets roosting at Esher Rugby Club.

Top
Robins are very adaptable and will happily nest in an abandoned pot or kettle.

Middle
The once ubiquitous house sparrow has suffered a steep decline in numbers over recent years.

Bottom
The distinctive plumage of the great tit makes the species easily recognisable among garden birds.

THE GARDEN VISITOR

APART FROM FEEDING birds, many people put up nest-boxes and it is not difficult to make your own. Humble garden nest-boxes are important, as gardens now cover more land area than nature reserves. There are various reference books, including, *Nest boxes*, that contain practical details about construction, siting, maintenance and protection against predators.

Gardeners can also help by not being too tidy; by leaving some shrubs to grow, by leaving dead flower-heads to provide seeds, saving piles of wood for invertebrate food and sheltering wrens, and cutting down on or abandoning pesticide use. If

gardeners can help, so too can councils, who can save money by not mowing all their parks, and by some healthy neglect of odd corners, providing shelter and food sources. Do not leave it to others, if you are an urban enthusiast you will want to work, preferably as part of a group, to protect valued oases so that birds can continue to adapt to town and city life.

Top
Most garden birds enjoy the provision of clean water for bathing in as well as drinking.

Middle
Blue tits will look in garden beds and on lawns for caterpillars with which to feed their hungry brood.

Bottom
All birds enjoy the provision of nuts and other scraps in the garden, especially in winter.

GARDEN BIRD WATCH 'TOP TEN TIPS'

1. Only put out as food that will be consumed in a day or two. Never allow food to accumulate; reduce it at quiet times.

2. Keep feeders reasonably clean and move them around the garden periodically, to avoid infectious droppings building up.

3. In the nesting season avoid presenting whole peanuts. Chop them, or use a mesh feeder from which adult birds can only take small fragments.

4. Try to have reasonably clean water available at all times for bathing as well as drinking – never add salt or any chemicals in winter.

5. Do not put out salted snacks, highly-flavoured foods, uncooked rice, whole bacon rinds or unsoaked, desiccated coconut which can be fatal to birds.

6. Keep food away from any cover where cats might lurk and consider electronic scarers, which need relocating weekly for best results.

7. If sparrowhawks are present, place feeders next to shrubs to allow birds to escape. Clip the shrubs back so cats cannot hide.

8. Provide a variety of foods in different positions and types of feeder. Offer unmixed foods in different positions and types of feeder. Offer unmixed foods separately rather than mixtures.

9. Cereal grain attracts pigeons. Use better quality, pure foods – black sunflower seeds or peanuts – if pigeons are a problem.

10. Stick to natural foods, rather than chemically altered or processed foods like margarine.

like protein-rich caterpillars, is available for the young. Coal tits occur in over 50 per cent of gardens in the survey at peak times, usually just before New Year; the period of highest attendance, depending on weather conditions in January and February. Our long-tailed tits, which do breed in the garden, start visiting the sunflower seeds, and any available fat, in November.

With an equally small body, wrens are also extremely vulnerable to the weather. A low level seems to occur at the time of moult, when birds are very wary and hard to see, but this is much more evident in the song thrush population.

THE GARDEN BIRD WATCH SCHEME

THIS GARDEN BIRD recording project, running all year round, aims to record changes that may occur among the birds visiting our gardens. Each observer fills in two lists weekly. For ten very common species there are four levels of abundance, and each week one of these levels is marked. The second list, of less frequent visitors, includes 31 species. Clear patterns have emerged after only three years of the scheme but good numbers of participants in any project make for meaningful results.

Some surprising patterns have emerged. The great spotted woodpecker, which might be expected to turn up most in winter, actually occurs most often in early June. Then the base rate of 20 per cent of gardens increases slightly, as young woodpeckers, as part of their apprenticeship, are shown how to peck at peanuts; another good reason to keep feeding through the summer, for they are spectacular birds to see at close quarters.

Tits are in almost every garden, with blue tits the most abundant. If adult birds have a good supply of food made available, from artificial sources, any natural food,

With the threats hanging over song thrush populations it will be interesting to see how the recording frequency, at present peaking at nearly 60 per cent of gardens, changes in the future.

Two final birds, which would not have been expected in gardens 30 years ago, are the magpie and the collared dove. The very consistent levels of both suggest how suitable the garden environment is for them. If 50 per cent of gardens have magpies then 50 per cent do not, and, in those gardens, it cannot be the magpies that are damaging eggs and young!

The whole of this scheme is organised by the BTO – more participants are always welcome, and interested parties should write directly to the the BTO address in the Further Information section.

Top
Long-tailed tits are seen mostly in gardens during the autumn and winter months.

Middle
Wrens will search out dense vegetation in which to hide their nests, which are built mainly of moss.

Bottom
Great spotted woodpeckers can often be seen in gardens, especially when there is woodland nearby.

Feral Pigeon

33 cm (13 in)

○ ○

SPECIES INFORMATION

SCIENTIFIC NAME	Columba livia
RELATED SPECIES	Rock Dove (the wild ancestor), Stock Dove
CALL	Cooing courtship call 'doo-roo-dooo'
HABITAT	Found in towns and cities; originally rocky sites and sea-cliffs (rock dove)
STATUS	Resident, some wild colonies on cliffs of north-west England

SIZE

IDENTIFICATION

HABITAT

POPULATION

MAP

A VERY FAMILIAR BIRD of towns and cities, with very variable plumage, from blue-grey to rusty-brown, or even very dark, or pure white; double black wing-bar. The wild rock dove always has white patch on rump.

FERAL PIGEONS HAVE come to substitute city ledges and shop-fronts for their ancestral cliffs. Accumulated droppings at nesting sites or roosts can cause serious economic problems as they have a corrosive action on stonework, particularly limestone. Pavements and ledges fouled by droppings are slippery and dangerous to pedestrians and workmen, and feathers and nest material may block gutters and drains.

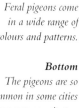

Top left and right
Feral pigeons come in a wide range of colours and patterns.

Bottom
The pigeons are so common in some cities that they may constitute a health hazard.

Collared Dove

32 cm (12.5 in)

SPECIES INFORMATION	
SCIENTIFIC NAME	Streptopelia decaocto
RELATED SPECIES	Turtle Dove
CALL	Flight-call a nasal 'shvair-shvair'. Courtship song a monotonous tri-syllabic 'coo-cooo, coo', accented on the second syllable (sometimes causes confusion with cuckoo, if third syllable omitted)
HABITAT	Towns and villages, especially where there is an abundance of food, as in parks, zoos, grain stores, farmyards. Often visits bird tables
STATUS	Most of Europe, except far north-east (rather patchy in south-west Europe). In BI about 230,000 pairs

SOME PEOPLE MISTAKE the persistent trisyllabic calls of collared doves for the previous species, but many more try to turn them into cuckoos. These elegant, long-tailed doves with black half collars in contrast to their pale greyish buff, pale pink and subtle blue grey are now familiar in gardens.

SIZE

IDENTIFICATION

HABITAT

POPULATION

MAP

THE COLLARED DOVE'S colonisation of Britain, such a success since 1952, may have been helped by the chicken runs and feeding on house balconies, which were too close to human activities for woodpigeons to use. The collared dove now seems very much a bird of the bird table and less a bird of the farmyard.

In its Indian heartland it favours open, dry, cultivated country, even semi-desert, so it has adapted well to new habitats. In his note Goodwin mentioned changes in colonial roosting in response to sparrowhawk predation, so the bird seems adaptable in every way.

As well as adaptability, a long breeding season helps it to flourish, with eggs being laid from March to October. Courtship involves a steep upward flight, followed by slow descent, accompanied by the nasal flight-call. The nest is a flimsy platform, usually in a tree, but sometimes on a building, and once the young have fledged they soon seem to be on their way so that a new brood can be produced.

Top left and right
Collared doves are commonly seen in gardens and public parks.

Bottom
The preening bird spreads its tail into a fan shape and shows the white tips to the tail feathers.

Swift

16–17 cm (6.5 in)

SPECIES INFORMATION

SCIENTIFIC NAME	Apus apus
RELATED SPECIES	Alpine Swift
CALL	High-pitched shrill squeals; very vocal in breeding season
HABITAT	Originally a cliff-nester, but now breeds mainly in buildings such as church towers, chimneys and tower blocks; also under the eaves of houses. Common, especially in towns, but declining
STATUS	Summer visitor; most of Europe. In BI about 100,000 pairs

SIZE

IDENTIFICATION

HABITAT

POPULATION

MAP

BLACKISH PLUMAGE WITH pale chin and neck, and long, sickle-shaped wings. Juveniles have pale brow and paler markings on head. Swifts spends most of their lives in the air, often for weeks at a time outside breeding season. They are also very sociable, often flying fast in tightly knit flocks. In summer they may circle to a great height in the evening, even apparently sleeping on the wing.

THE FIRST BIRD BOOK in the main New Naturalist series was *Birds and Men* (1951) by E. M. Nicholson. In his preface he said that he 'tried in each case to bring out the different character and way of life of each species'.

'No other British bird is so aerial as the swift, a species which not many people can claim ever to have seen at rest. Except at the nest the swift's life is spent flying in a layer of air which stretches from just above the ground to fully 1,000 ft above it. This layer is rather deeper than a swallow's but is more briefly tenanted because to support the type of insect life on which the swift depends it must not normally drop to a temperature below a critical level.'

I changed my views on a swift's life when I found a grounded swift in the Close in Salisbury. It did not take much to make a diagnosis for darting among its feathers were louse flies. Closer examination found 12 of these 6 mm (0.25 in) blood-sucking parasites. Rothschild and Clay (1952) compare two of these insects creeping about the feathers 'to a man with a couple of large shore crabs scuttling about in his underclothes'.

I have never fancied being a swift quite so much since, but still admire and love them screaming around a church or large Victorian house. When the sun is out the dark birds cover a wide area on swept back wings, but when it is damp and cold they may find it hard to feed their young which become almost torpid as they reduce their metabolic needs to survive.

Top
Swifts are often found nesting under the roofs and eaves of buildings.

Bottom
Because of their agility, swifts find it easy to cling to the side of vertical buildings.

House Martin

12.5 cm (5 in)

SPECIES INFORMATION	
SCIENTIFIC NAME	*Delichon urbica*
RELATED SPECIES	Swallow, Sand Martin
CALL	Flight-call 'prrt, trr-trr'. Song a simple twitter
HABITAT	Towns and villages. Also in quarries and in mountains to 2,000 m (6,500 ft). Builds mud nest with entrance hole
STATUS	Summer visitor, wintering in tropical Africa. Throughout Europe. In BI about 400,000 pairs

METALLIC BLUE-BLACK above, with white rump and pure white underside. Smaller and more compact than swallow, with short, only weakly forked tail, and flight is more fluttering; often glides. Usually feeds at a higher level than swallow.

GILBERT WHITE WROTE of house martins, 'House martins are distinguished from their congeners by having their legs covered with soft downy feathers down to their toes. They are no songsters; but twitter in a pretty soft manner in their nests. During the time of breeding they are often greatly molested with fleas.'

House martins have moved nearer city centres since the Clean Air Acts encouraged the return of aerial insects. Their white rumps are the clearest features to distinguish them from other insectivores who spend time in flight, but the blue back and slightly forked tail are also characteristic.

House martins are summer visitors to most of Europe, and across central and northern Asia to southern China. The European birds are almost totally linked with man's buildings and with the need for mud. Martin lovers may make muddy pools or brew up their own mud mixes and leave them on an appropriate flat roof, but do beware of cats if you do this to encourage martins.

Mud, building sites and insects can all be limiting factors, and in cold, wet summers the last broods may still be in the nest in September. When insects are around the house martins will search at higher altitudes than the swallow, but below the swift, picking off flies and aphids which are often drawn up high. Our birds arrive in mid April and the male selects the nest site and starts to build. There is no doubt that the birds produce plenty of mess from the nest, and that many nests are destroyed because of this, but as far as I am concerned the martins deserve every bit of help as they share their lives with us.

SIZE

IDENTIFICATION

HABITAT

POPULATION

MAP

Top right
House martins have a distinctive white chest and are plumper than swifts.

Top left and bottom
House martins gather damp mud with which to make their adhesive nests.

Wren

9–10 cm (3.75 in)

SPECIES INFORMATION	
SCIENTIFIC NAME	Troglodytes troglodytes
RELATED SPECIES	Only European member of family
CALL	Alarm call a loud 'teck-teck-teck' or 'tserrr'. Song a loud, clear warble, with trills
HABITAT	Woods, hedgerows and scrub; also in parks and gardens
STATUS	Resident. Summer visitor in north and east of range. Throughout Europe. In BI nearly 10,000,000 pairs

SIZE

IDENTIFICATION

HABITAT

POPULATION

MAP

ONE OF OUR commonest (and smallest) species. Tiny, with short tail (often cocked). Creeps mouse-like close to the ground or in vegetation or among tree roots. Flight is direct, with rapid wing-beats.

ITS TINY SIZE and cocked tail are unmistakable, despite the fact that its colour could make it one of 'the little brown jobs'. In fact the rufous brown and fine barring are attractive when seen at close quarters. Wrens often search among dense cover for insects and spiders. The long thin bill enables it to probe in crevices in bark, rocks and walls and only in hard weather, when much heat is lost from its tiny body, does the death rate rise. One of their strategies for coping with winter cold is for lots of them to pack into a confined space, often nowadays a bird box, and share the generated heat.

Despite the small wings and their normally short, low flights wrens can move extensively away from winter cold, with Swedish birds moving up to 2,500 km (1,550 miles). It is not so surprising then that it has become a good

coloniser of islands, but presumably this colonisation is not that frequent as a complex of island races has evolved. Fair Isle, St Kilda and Shetland birds form a cline, with wing, tail, bill, tarsus and foot found to be longer as one moves north.

Apart from the vehement rattling territorial song, wrens have a softer courtship song and a series of loud 'ticks' and 'churrs', for almost any situation, but particularly threat from predators.

It seems that wherever one goes there are wrens; on plenty of my woodland surveys among conifers or in all sorts of deciduous woodland they are among the commonest, often the commonest, birds. High in the mountains, as long as there is cover, from boulders or heather, or on precipitous Hebridean cliffs there are wrens. They rattle away in the garden, love heathery heaths and do as well as any bird in farmland hedges.

Edward Armstrong, who wrote both about wrens and folklore, described annual wren hunts, often to coincide with twelfth night and the tradition of Lord of Misrule when all the usual order of things was set topsy-turvy. Armstrong reckoned there was a cult of the wren from pagan times and its ritual slaughter was a sign of the death of the old year and ensured the fertility of the new.

In most circumstances however it has been seen as bad to harm a wren; it was the Druidic bird of augury, and in Cornwall they say 'hunt a robin or a wren, never prosper man or boy'.

Top right
The wren often nests on heathland but is just as happy in a hedgerow.

Top left and bottom
The dainty, rather mouse-like wren gathers spiders' webs to incorporate in its nest; it also includes spiders in its diet.

Dunnock
14 cm (5.5 in)

SPECIES INFORMATION	
SCIENTIFIC NAME	Prunella modularis
	Alternative Names: Hedge Sparrow, Hedge Accentor
RELATED SPECIES	Alpine accentor
CALL	Alarm-call is a thin 'tseek'. Song a pleasant
	warble, gently rising and falling
HABITAT	Woodland, parks and gardens
STATUS	Resident. Most of Europe, except the far south.
	In B about 2,800,000 pairs

UNOBTRUSIVE, rather nondescript, with sparrow-like plumage but robin-like shape. Head and breast are slate grey, the flanks with darker streaks. Bill thinner than house sparrow's.

DUNNOCKS MAY BE unobtrusive birds, but they have real character as they peck for almost invisible food items under the bird table or half hidden in garden shrubbery. The slim bill shows that it is no sparrow, and the uniform pale blue–grey face and underparts contrast with delicate streaks elsewhere.

After all the extraordinary colours and peculiar antics filmed with such breathtaking patience and skill by David

Attenborough's photographic team for the 'World of Birds', it was good to see the Dunnock. It may have taken almost equal patience to record their peculiar breeding behaviour, for it is only in recent years that it has been recorded, despite the Dunnock's readiness to show itself, at times, in almost every garden.

As Andrew Cannon reports in the *Garden Birdwatch Handbook*, 'Many dunnocks are polyandrous, which means the females lay eggs fertilised by more than one male. Professor Nick Davies of Cambridge University showed that even more complex "mating systems" are quite common, in fact, only about a third of female dunnocks are monogamous. This partly depends on how cold the winter has been. More females die in cold winters as males tend to monopolise the available food, so there are often extra males in the spring population. It was generally thought that male birds set up territories and females chose between them, but studying dunnocks revealed that in this species the females compete amongst themselves for territory without reference to the males, which then have to compete with each other to "move in" A dominant (alpha) and subordinate (beta) male whose territories overlap the larger territory of a female, often both join forces with her and cease to compete, defending the single territory as a trio.'

 SIZE

 IDENTIFICATION

 HABITAT

 POPULATION

 MAP

Top left and right
Dunnocks are familiar birds in parks and gardens, especially those with plenty of cover.

Bottom
The Dunnock has a pale blue-grey face and a slim bill, which distinguish it from the house sparrow.

Robin

14 cm (5.5 in)

○ ○

SPECIES INFORMATION

SCIENTIFIC NAME	Erithacus rubecula
RELATED SPECIES	No close relatives in BI
CALL	Sharp 'tick', often rapidly repeated; also a high-pitched 'tsee'. Tuneful song, heard from autumn, is a clear descending series of rippling notes
HABITAT	Woodland, especially broadleaved woods with rich undergrowth. Also in parks and gardens
STATUS	Resident and partial migrant. Throughout Europe. In BI about 6,000,000 pairs

SIZE

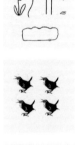

IDENTIFICATION

HABITAT

POPULATION

MAP

THIS FAMILIAR GARDEN bird has a rather rounded shape, relatively long legs, and obvious red breast (sexes similar). The juvenile lacks the red, and is mainly mottled brown.

BECAUSE THEY SING so close to us as we dig or tidy up the garden most people know the song, with its melodic warble. Fewer people spot the sharp 'tick' or high-pitched 'tsee' which indicates territorial defence or alarm.

We are lucky that we can see our individuals at close quarters, but most continental birds are noticeably less tame and inclined to skulk. As well as this difference in behaviour, other races are usually paler, have different intensities of rufous on the upper

Robins traditionally covered the dead with leaves, linking up with the legends of the babes in the wood. The first postmen who wore red waistcoats, were called robins, and so we get robins on Christmas cards, often with letters in their beak.

'In the first mild day of March:
Each minute sweeter than before,
The red-breast sings from the tall larch
That stands beside my door.'
William Wordsworth

tail coverts, and vary in size. Further afield there are populations in Tunisia, the Urals and the Caucasus, as well as a more isolated one in the Canaries which is more distinctly different. Wherever they are they like a good deal of cover, some patches of open ground, and a song post or two.

Because we have a mild, oceanic climate, many of us are surprised by the amount of movement of northern and eastern populations, but some of our robins move as far as Iberia. When all goes well, a high-flying, nocturnal migrant gives little away.

Top and middle
Perhaps our best-loved and most famous garden bird, the robin is fiercely territorial and may be quite violent against its own kind.

Bottom
The male robin does not gain its famous red breast until it reaches maturity.

Starling

21 cm (8.25 in)

```
○○○○○○○○○○○○○○○○○○○○○○○○○○
        SPECIES INFORMATION
SCIENTIFIC NAME   Sturnus vulgaris
RELATED SPECIES   Spotless Starling replaces Starling (both present in
                  winter) in Spain, Portugal, Corsica, Sardinia and
                  Sicily. It lacks spots in breeding plumage
CALL              Shrill 'rairr' or 'shrii'; alarm-call 'vett-vett'. Song
                  is very varied, with whistles, interspersed with
                  crackling, snapping and rattling calls, and many
                  imitations of other birds and sounds
HABITAT           Broadleaved and mixed woodland, cultivated areas,
                  urban areas, parks and gardens
STATUS            Resident and partial migrant. Most of Europe,
                  except extreme south and south-west. In BI about
                  3,000,000 pairs
```

FAMILIAR DUMPY GARDEN bird with rather long, pointed yellow bill. In winter heavily spotted with white and with dark bill. Breeding plumage has glossy green-violet sheen. Juvenile grey-brown. Flight direct, showing pointed, triangular wings. Roosts in large flocks, in trees or reedbeds. Often visits bird tables.

STARLINGS APPEAR BLACKISH whether searching grassland for leather-jackets or flying to roost. In flight the pointed wings and short tail make for a triangular silhouette. When well seen all sorts of spots and shiny speckles and reflections appear, and even if you did not like them before you briefly have to admit to admiration.

Starlings have done very well by taking advantage of human settlements and they have been spreading in the north of their range for more than 100 years. The possible peak winter British population was in 1967, with some 37 million birds. The significant decrease since could be because of the reduction in permanent pasture. The starling is one of the birds that has been successfully introduced elsewhere, so that it is now familiar in America, Southern Africa, Australia and New Zealand, as well as natural homes east of the Urals, and from Iran to Pakistan. With this extensive range, variation is not surprising, with differences in gloss, juvenile plumage, foot and bill structure, and size.

The nest can be bulky if in a big cavity, and is situated as far as possible from the cavity opening. Almost anything can go to make up the lining if it is not too coarse but the base contains tougher grasses and twigs.

Although they are hole nesters they do not like low, dense vegetation except for where they roost in reedbeds. Seasonality of habitat has already been suggested and the same applies to diet, with animal food dominating in the spring and being fed to nestlings when the adults yellow bills may have legs of insects and spiders sticking out in all directions. They also take a lot of plant foods, including soft fruits and seeds.

Why people do not like starlings is not clear. Some call them reptilian, and some blame their apparent greed and bossiness at the bird table. Others may find that their noisy nesting not far from a bedroom window makes for little summer sleep, while the mess their roosts can cause in cities or in country copses make further causes for unpopularity.

Nicholson in his *Birds and Men* emphasised not only their sociability with their own kind but their readiness to mix with other species. He reckoned that the closest attachment is to lapwings, whether in the fields or less convincingly in the air where the different styles of flight cause comic awkwardness. Starlings are happy with rooks and jackdaws and redwings in fields, and with oystercatchers and turnstones foraging on the sea shore, and they do not limit themselves to birds, for a quick parasite grazing on a sheep's back is always in order.

SIZE

IDENTIFICATION

HABITAT

POPULATION

MAP

Top left and right
Starlings are seldom far away from house or garden. They sometimes gather at large communal roosts in the winter.

Bottom
Starlings have a bright yellow bill and, in the winter months, a distinctive spotted chest.

Blackbird

25 cm (10 in)

SIZE

IDENTIFICATION

HABITAT

POPULATION

MAP

VERY COMMON GARDEN bird, with all black (male) or all brown (female) plumage. Bill and eye-ring of male orange-yellow. Female has weakly speckled breast. Juveniles reddish-brown and strongly speckled beneath.

THE RICH BLACKBIRD song, and equally rich orange bill, setting off the glossy plumage of the male are well known but the brown female may be less so. The alarm note when a cat or other predator is around, and the mess they make as they search for food make blackbirds among the most noticeable of birds.

As usual Nicholson has apposite comments based on his own observations. 'The alarm of the blackbird is much more than a note, having the length and pattern of a song, but not the function or the music. Beginning with two or three throaty chuckling protests, it suddenly rises in pitch and accelerates into a shrill excited chatter, to which as an anti-climax two or three more chuckles are often added. The chuckle is also used by itself as a note of caution, and the familiar "mik-mik-mik" expresses suspicion and emotional tension on such occasions as going to roost in winter or mobbing an owl or cat.'

Blackbirds are very suburban birds, and Garden BirdWatch reports a comparison with blackbirds in more natural woodland habitat. 'Woodland nests suffered a high predation rate of around 80 per cent with corvids (magpies, jays etc) mainly responsible, but wild mammals such as weasels also very active. In gardens, the rate of predation was much lower, at around 50 per cent, which might be expected, as there are generally fewer wild predators in inhabited areas, cats and magpies being the chief culprits.'

'Sing a song of blackbirds,
Who will not let me keep
Orange peel or tea bags
On my compost heap.
When the heap is opened,
Upon the worms they sup.
I wouldn't mind the mess they make
If they would clear things up.'
Robert S Morrison WORDS ON BIRDS

Top and bottom left
Blackbirds enjoy gardens with lawns, as they spend quite a lot of time searching for earthworms.

Bottom right
The male blackbird, with its yellow beak, has become a familiar sight in suburban areas.

Song Thrush

23 cm (9 in)

SMALL THRUSH WITH brown upperparts and large, dark eyes. Underside covered with small dark spots. Often feeds on fields close to woodland. Also eats snails, sometimes using a stone as an 'anvil' to break the shell.

A VERY POPULAR species. A vote in 1997 made the song of this thrush the favourite one in Britain. Snow (1998) describes it as 'a loud, clear, vigorous succession of simple but mainly musical phrases distinguished by their repetitive character, great variety and clear enunciation; more penetrating and less rich than Blackbird, lacking wild skirling quality of Mistle Thrush. Unmusical, harsh, or chattering sounds regularly intermixed with pure notes, also mimicry of other species.'

'With shorter bill and slighter build than the blackbirds', Cannon writes in the *Garden BirdWatch Handbook*, 'Song thrushes take a more limited range of prey than their bigger relative, extracting smaller worms from lawns and generally only from January to June, whereas stronger blackbirds can manage to pull them out of even quite dry summer grass.' The one resource which song thrushes do have available that blackbirds do not is snails, and many will have heard the cracking shell with relish as another garden pest is destroyed. How many who hate the snails and slugs have used pellets which are not safe for other wildlife, and have therefore contributed to the song thrush decline?

Many people remember song thrushes as being more common than blackbirds. Part of the change has been an increase in blackbirds, but since the mid 1970s the song thrush has suffered more than a 50 per cent decline, so that the BTO and RSPB have it among those birds on the red list of conservation importance. Even in woodlands, numbers are down by 45 per cent.

The song thrush has a special place in history for 'On the tenth day of April, eighteen hundred and ninety two' wrote Richard Kearton in 1908, 'my brother photographed the nest and eggs of a song thrush in the neighbourhood of London, and the result appeared to me to be so full of promise that I at once determined to write a book on British birds' nests and get him to illustrate it from beginning to end by photographs taken in situ.' He was writing then in a new and revised edition of *British Birds Nests*, the first book of its kind to be illustrated throughout by means of photographs taken direct from nature and showing things 'as they are and not as they are supposed to be'. A letter about 'this truly sporting method of studying Nature' emphasises one result. 'I consider that the birds ought to be extremely grateful to you for inventing bird photography. I never knew anything that has done so much for their protection during the nesting season as your example. I myself have for several years given up egg collecting entirely, and know many others who have done the same.'

SIZE

IDENTIFICATION

HABITAT

POPULATION

MAP

One of our finest songbirds, the song thrush has suffered a puzzling decline in recent years.

Blue Tit

12 cm (4.75 in)

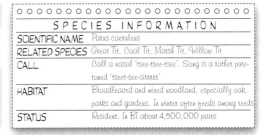

<table>
</table>

SPECIES INFORMATION	
SCIENTIFIC NAME	Parus caeruleus
RELATED SPECIES	Great Tit, Coal Tit, Marsh Tit, Willow Tit
CALL	Call a nasal 'tsee-tsee-tsee'. Song is a rather pure-toned 'tseet-see-sirrrrr'
HABITAT	Broadleaved and mixed woodland, especially oak, parks and gardens. In winter often feeds among reeds
STATUS	Resident. In BI about 4,500,000 pairs

SIZE

IDENTIFICATION

HABITAT

POPULATION

MAP

SMALL, COMPACT TIT with blue and yellow plumage. Female slightly less colourful than male. Juvenile much paler, with greenish-brown upperparts and yellow cheeks. Blue tits have blue crown, wings and tails and yellow underparts. The bill is short, the wings round and short, and the tail short, so not surprisingly it is a small bird which is vulnerable to cold weather. Its song is not as loud or distinctive as the 'teacher, teacher, teacher' of the great tit, and its wide range of calls is not quite so extensive. Scolding or churring alarm calls followed by a 'tsee', a high-pitched contact call, and a special alarm call for flying predators are among these.

'NATURE IS CRUEL – but not so cruel as the Book of Genesis' wrote Robert Gibbings (1940) thinking about the great flood. 'What harm had a wren or a blue tit ever done that they should be destroyed. I mentioned this once to a man who engaged me in religious conversation. His reply was that probably God was human like the rest of us, and that after all it was the first world He had ever made, and that it was only natural that there should have been a few mistakes.'

Whatever one's views on that, there is no doubt that we make plenty of mistakes and that we have only one world to damage. The decrease of so many species, the destruction of so many habitats, and the belief that nature is to be conquered, all tell us that we, and our government and the leaders of the world have got to learn and to change.

Luckily, despite all, 'the bluecap' still 'tootles in its glee' (John Clare) and a garden reporting rate of nearly 100 per cent, in winter, of this abundant and still increasing species, is an encouraging sign. We are learning too. Chris Perrins has studied tits in nest-boxes for many years and discovered a great deal about the biology of these common birds. Each tit species illustrates basic ecological principles mentioned earlier – each has its own ecological niche. The average size of insect and the height at which tits feed differ, with blue tits foraging in winter among twigs, but great tits often feeding on the ground.

Top
Blue tits are frequently the first to appear at the bird table, and often scare off larger birds.

Bottom left and right
The blue tit is a small compact bird with a colourful plumage.

SPECIES INFORMATION	
SCIENTIFIC NAME	Parus major
RELATED SPECIES	Blue Tit, Coal Tit, Marsh Tit, Willow Tit
CALL	Wide repertoire. Chaffinch-like 'pink' or 'tsi-pink', alarm-call 'tsher-r-r-r'. Song (variable) is a loud simple phrase such as 'tee-cher, tee-cher'. Starts singing as early as January
HABITAT	Woodland, parks and gardens
STATUS	Resident. In BI about 2,000,000 pairs

Great Tit

14 cm (5.5 in)

THE LARGEST EUROPEAN tit, with black and white head, yellow underparts, and a broad (male) or narrow (female) black stripe down centre of belly. Juvenile paler, with yellowish cheeks.

examples of birds from all round the world, were about great tits in Oxford's Wytham Woods, and Newton's recent *Population Limitation in Birds* has 67 page references to great tits.

All this erudition is fascinating, but has little to do with most people's appreciation of the bird. The yellow underparts with black central stripe, wider in males, is as familiar as the white cheeked black head and essentially green back. Variation in the black breast stripe one of the features which other great tits use to assess the dominance of competitors.

Birds maintain a dominance hierarchy in which those at the top of the 'pecking order' have preferential access to food. The hierarchy is continuously being challenged, especially in winter when the flocks of great tits that form in the autumn often aggregate together at food resources such as beech mast or in gardens with feeding stations.

LIKE BLUE TITS, great tits like nest-boxes as long as the opening is of adequate size. Whether nesting there, in a natural tree hole, or in a man-made drainpipe or crevice, great tits make a mossy nest thickly lined with hair, wool and feathers. This is much the same as the blue tit's in structure and contains a similarly large number of eggs, usually in the 6–11 range.

The great tit has given rise to a voluminous literature, much of it based on British nesting birds, many of them living near Oxford. Three of the 15 chapters in Lack's *Population Studies of Birds* which used

SIZE

IDENTIFICATION

HABITAT

POPULATION

MAP

Top
Great tits will often happily use nesting boxes in which to rear their broods.

Bottom left and right
The handsome great tit, with its striking colouring, is the largest of the European tit family.

House Sparrow

14.5 cm (5.75 in)

SPECIES INFORMATION	
SCIENTIFIC NAME	Passer domesticus
RELATED SPECIES	Tree Sparrow, Spanish Sparrow (parts of Spain, S. Italy, Greece and Turkey)
CALL	Chirps – repeated as song
HABITAT	Houses, villages, towns and farmyards
STATUS	Resident. In BI about 6,000,000 pairs

SIZE

IDENTIFICATION

HABITAT

POPULATION

MAP

A VERY FAMILIAR SMALL bird of towns. The male has grey cap and black bib; the female and juvenile are a drab grey-brown. House Sparrows, as seed eaters, have heavy bills, and they are tubby birds with broad wings and square-ended tails. On close inspection, the male is boldly patterned, with a grey crown and black eye-stripe and bib, dull white cheeks, dark streaks on the back, grey rump and greyish underparts. Females are, admittedly a little featureless and in Spain are hard to tell from Spanish sparrows.

IT IS ALWAYS THOUGHT that sparrows were everywhere, whether in London gardens and streets or in farm stackyards. The stackyards are mainly gone, and whereas 1950 counts, in Bloomsbury and Lambeth, gave densities of 4.3 and 4.0 birds per acre,

Formerly, this species was so common that it was widely regarded as a pest. In one Suffolk village 2,587 dozen sparrows earned a reward of 2d per dozen over 15 years, and in the 1860s the Sussex Express reported 'The thirteenth anniversary of the Sparrow Club, Rudgwick, was celebrated with a dinner at the Cricketers' Inn, on Tuesday last. On reference to the books it was ascertained that 5,321 birds' heads had been sent in by members during the year, 1,363 being contributed by Mr W. Wooberry, to whom was awarded the first prize.'

Turning from Man and Birds to *Birds and Men*, Nicholson as usual has a sparrow's eye view of sparrows. 'Free of the drains on time and energy represented by territory holding, competitive song and migration, and being intelligent enough to live where living is easy, the sparrow has a different daily timetable from almost any other small bird. His great outlet is social activity of many kinds. Nesting, roosting, feeding, bathing, dusting, quarrelling and even pairing are, for the sparrow, naturally social occasions; wanting to be alone, or to be out of the gang, are foreign to sparrow temperament.'

Top

The male sparrow is a boldly patterned, tubby little bird with a square tail.

Middle and bottom

House sparrows are still common in many towns and on farmland, but they have declined markedly in recent years.

there were signs that London populations were already on the way down. House sparrow populations have not been effectively monitored by woodland or farmland common bird census work but the New Atlas showed a retraction in range in Scotland, Ireland and North Wales. Although still a numerous bird, the once ubiquitous house sparrow is now a bird of high conservation concern.

Chaffinch

15 cm (6 in)

```
 o o o o o o o o o o o o o o o o o o o o o o o o o
         S P E C I E S   I N F O R M A T I O N
```

SCIENTIFIC NAME	*Fringilla coelebs*
RELATED SPECIES	*Brambling*
CALL	*Call a loud, short 'pink'. Song is a pleasant, descending phrase, accelerating towards the end*
HABITAT	*Woodland, gardens, parks and scrub; in winter flocks to farmland*
STATUS	*Resident and winter visitor. In BI about 7,000,000 pairs*

OUR COMMONEST finch. Breeding male has blue-grey crown, brown back and pinkish breast. Female is olive-brown above and grey-brown below. In flight shows white wing-patch and wing-bar, and white outer tail feathers (rump not white).

DOMINANT FEATURES OF chaffinch appearance, demonstrated in the section on a bird's year, are the white panels on the wing coverts and other bars on the secondaries and primaries. While outer tail feathers are also conspicuous. There is plenty of additional colour in males with blue-grey crown, pale red to pink face and underparts and dark back-ground to the white wing and tail marks.

Chaffinches are primarily woodland birds, but they are found in a wide range of habitats and have adapted well to farm hedges, orchards, parks and gardens.

Although widespread through Europe and the East into Russia, the chaffinch is replaced by the brambling to the north. In winter flocks the two are often together, feeding off seeds on the ground in woods or open fields and flying up with a flurry of white wing bars (chaffinch) and white rumps (bramblings).

'While the chaffinch sings on the orchard bough
In England - now!'
Robert Browning
HOME THOUGHTS
FROM ABROAD

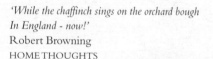

SIZE

IDENTIFICATION

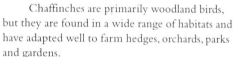
HABITAT

POPULATION

MAP

Top left and right
Chaffinches are one of our most cosmopolitan species – at home in most habitats, including parks, gardens, orchards and woodland.

Bottom
The striking little male birds have a pinkish breast and brown back with black and white striping on the wing.

107

Greenfinch

15 cm (6 in)

○○○○○○○○○○○○○○○○○○○○○○○○○○○○○

SPECIES INFORMATION

SCIENTIFIC NAME	Carduelis chloris
RELATED SPECIES	Goldfinch, Linnet, Twite, Redpoll, Siskin
CALL	Include 'chup-chup-chup', and a nasal 'dzweee'. Song consists of canary-like trills, with whistles and wheezing notes, often in slow song-flight
HABITAT	Mixed woodland, farmland, hedges, parks, orchards and gardens. Common at bird tables in winter
STATUS	Resident (and winter visitor). In BI about 700,000 pairs

SIZE

IDENTIFICATION

HABITAT

POPULATION

MAP

A LARGE, YELLOW-GREEN or brownish finch. Shows yellow wing patches, especially in flight. Female mainly grey-green with less yellow on wings and tail. Juvenile heavily streaked. The plump shape and cleft tail with yellow patches are always distinctive in flight.

IN SPRING, GREENFINCHES indulge in the so-called 'bat flight' with deep, slow wing beats. The body rolls from side to side and the bird weaves around the breeding area singing and calling. Hollom, wisely, avoids any attempt at description of the song saying just it is based mainly on calls, but *Birds of the Western Palearctic* (BWP) is braver: 'Song consists of groups of rolling tremolos ... punctuated by more slowly delivered repetition of tonal and more noisy units also by single longer and rather nasal "chew lee" and the familiar nasal or buzzing wheeze.'

In winter, hungry flocks move into gardens to feed on peanuts or sunflower seeds.

Hedge flailing does not leave many tough seeds on wild shrubs in later winter, so garden feeding then can lure them to breed if you have a stout hedge, creeper or dense conifer available. The nest, like the bird, is robust, made with grass, moss and lichen, with a lining of hair, feathers and fine grasses.

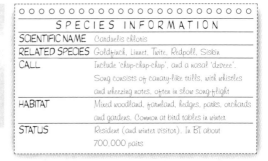

*'Thou linnet! In thy green array
Presiding Spirit here to-day
Dost lead the revels of the May
And this is thy dominion'*
William Wordsworth THE LINNET

Bottom left
Greenfinches are a greeny brown in colour and the males have yellow patches on their wings.

Top right and bottom right
Greenfinches often make their presence known by their nasal, wheezing calls.

Bullfinch

15 cm (5.75 in)

SPECIES INFORMATION	
SCIENTIFIC NAME	Pyrrhula pyrrhula
RELATED SPECIES	No close relatives in BI
CALL	A quiet, rather plaintive 'dyuk'. Song is a soft, whistling twitter
HABITAT	Forest, scrub, plantations, mixed woodland, parks, gardens and orchards
STATUS	Resident and winter visitor. In BI about 200,000 pairs

MALE UNMISTAKABLE, WITH bright, salmon-pink underparts, blue-grey back, black head and white rump. The female is brown-grey; the juvenile brownish, without black cap. Often looks plump, especially in cold weather. White rump prominent in flight.

THE BULLFINCH IS THE only finch of economic importance in Britain and Newton wonders why it has never become a major pest. It takes a greater proportion and variety of buds and for a longer period than any European bird and it does so with a beak, feeding technique and digestive system that have evolved for the job. A single Bullfinch can remove the buds of fruit trees at a rate of 30 per minute, and it can be remarkably systematic in the way that it does it. Bullfinches enter orchards from nearby woods and hedgerows, attack the nearest trees first and penetrate by stages into the orchard, stripping every tree in turn.

In the late 1950s Newton started a six-year study of bullfinch biology near Oxford. He found that six plants formed the basis of bullfinch winter diet – dock, nettle and bramble were consistent seed producers in late summer, whereas privet, birch and ash varied their production. This was particularly so for ash. Inevitably, seed supplies dwindled during the winter, and buds became increasingly important, with a preference for hawthorn.

During short days the birds could not eat enough buds to maintain their weight so some seeds were essential and it was necessary, both for Newton and for bullfinches, to know how many there were. He therefore measured the decline in seed stocks during a winter when the ash crop was good. By the end of the winter, 99 per cent of ash remained, together with some bramble and dock, but the next winter the ash crop was poor and few seeds, except 7 per cent of the bramble, remained at the end of that winter. In the first year no buds of native trees were eaten before March, and damage to fruit farms was negligible, but in the second winter tree buds were stripped from mid-December and fruit farm damage was severe. Ash tends to fruit in alternate years, and national enquiries about fruit damage indicated alternate year problems.

SIZE

IDENTIFICATION

HABITAT

POPULATION

MAP

Bottom right
The male bullfinch is a very attractive bird with a salmon-pink under-carriage and contrasting dark blue back.

Top and bottom left
Bullfinches adapt well to a variety of environments but are known to be voracious eaters.

109

Pied Wagtail

18 cm (7 in)

○○○○○○○○○○○○○○○○○○○○○○○○○○○○○

SPECIES INFORMATION

SCIENTIFIC NAME	*Motacilla alba*
RELATED SPECIES	*Yellow Wagtail, Grey Wagtail*
CALL	*'Tsick', 'tsilipp', often repeated. Song is a rapid twitter*
HABITAT	*Open country, especially near water. Towns and villages, farms and gravel pits. Also seen on lakes, rivers, meadows, fields and wet areas*
STATUS	*Resident and partial migrant. In BI about 430,000 pairs*

SIZE

IDENTIFICATION

HABITAT

POPULATION

MAP

LONG, BLACK TAIL with white outer feathers, and long black legs. The continental race, sometimes known as white wagtail (*M. alba alba*), has light grey back and rump. The British race (*M. alba yarrellii*), has a black back. Female less contrasty, and with less black on head. In winter has white chin and dark breast-band. Juveniles brown-grey above, without black. Overhead their call is as distinctive as their looping flight – a few flaps followed by a descending glide.

PIED WAGTAILS really live up to their name, with black upper parts, throat and breast and white forehead, face and chest. The long tail is in constant motion. The female has a slate grey back which is not as pale as the back of the white wagtail, the European subspecies counterpart of our bird.

These fine birds often visit gardens, especially to pick flies and other insects from lawns, or to take scraps fallen from the bird table. In the winter, they often gather at communal roosts, which may number many hundreds of birds. These may be in a reedbed, copse, or even in built-up areas. Pied wagtails make local movements, often dispersing after breeding, to wet meadows or riverside marshes. With so much food there, they can indulge in aerial flycatching, quick darts after insects, often among the legs of the cattle or in searches among the vegetation in shallow pools.

Top right and left
Pied wagtails are often found near water, but they also like to feed on garden lawns.

Bottom
Pied wagtails are opportunist, feeding their young with a combination of insects and scraps from gardens.

Magpie
46 cm (18 in)

```
○○○○○○○○○○○○○○○○○○○○○○○○○○
        SPECIES INFORMATION
SCIENTIFIC NAME   Pica pica
RELATED SPECIES   Carrion Crow, Jay, Rook
CALL              A chattering 'shak-shak-shak'. Song is a low,
                  babbling chatter, with rattling calls and whistles
HABITAT           Open country with hedges and fields, villages, parks
                  and gardens with trees, even in urban areas; avoids
                  dense woodland
STATUS            Resident. In BI about 800,000 pairs
```

A LARGE, RATHER SHOWY bird with shiny black and white plumage and a long, graduated tail. Rather sociable and often seen in small groups. The adult is a handsome bird indeed, with its very long green and bronze purple tail and black and white wings and body. In flight there is an almost African impressiveness about the outline, the spectacular silhouette and the noisy chattering. Young birds have shorter tails and duller black plumage with little gloss. The most frequently used adjectives applied to magpies: aggressive, noisy, intelligent and adaptable could be used about many of the crow family, but the long tail is less typical. It has to be said that many would use less restrained adjectives about them and, while many garden birds are almost universally loved, magpies are widely disliked.

MAGPIES PREFER OPEN woodland or scrub and their complex domed nests can easily be seen in winter when not hidden by leaves. Mud, twigs, roots, hair, feathers and leaves may all be part of the core of the nest, while sticks, often thorny, protrude in a bulky mass around the underlying bowl. There are often two entrances.

Magpies are very successful birds, and this is in part due to their opportunistic feeding, taking a range of prey, from worms and insects, to nestlings, eggs and scraps. They are now enjoying the extension of free-range pig farming.

Magpies have been blamed by many for the widespread decreases in farmland birds, but this is not supported by the latest evidence. Does their opportunism bring about the decline of smaller species? Tree sparrows are declining fast, on red-alert, but nesting in holes their eggs and nestlings are usually safe from magpies so magpies are probably not to blame. Bird prey for magpies is mainly at the egg and nestling stage and the nest record cards, completed by BTO volunteers, provide a great deal of data on the success rates of nesting songbirds over a long period of time. This information is vital if we are to understand the cause of change in bird populations. For a number of declining songbirds, including the song thrush, nest records show us that breeding success has not really changed, so other factors, not nest predation, must have caused the declines.

SIZE

IDENTIFICATION

HABITAT

POPULATION

MAP

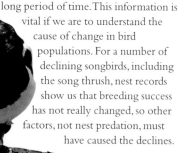

Bottom
Magpies are noisy, conspicuous birds; they are also rather clever, like other members of the crow family.

Top
Magpies are showy birds with a smart black and white plumage.

Jackdaw

33 cm 13 (in)

SPECIES INFORMATION

SCIENTIFIC NAME	*Corvus monedula*
RELATED SPECIES	Carrion Crow, Rook, Raven
CALL	Very vocal. Short, loud 'kya' or 'kyak', often repeated. Song (seldom heard) is a quiet warble with crackling and miaowing calls
HABITAT	Old, broadleaved woodland, cliffs, quarries, isolated trees in fields, parks with old trees, churches, castles and ruined buildings. Also breeds on houses, especially in chimneys
STATUS	Resident and partial migrant. In BI about 600,000 pairs

SMALL AND CROW-LIKE, with mainly black plumage, grey nape and back of head, and pale eye. Its small size, pale eyes, ash grey nape and distinctive call at once distinguish the jackdaw from other crows. In winter they often form mixed flocks on fields with rooks.

SIZE

IDENTIFICATION

HABITAT

POPULATION

MAP

THE JACKDAW IS a familiar species of towns, especially those with plenty of old buildings, such as a ruined castle or old church. Half the feeding time is on grassland, where invertebrates are an important part of the diet, with seeds also significant. When feeding their young they may move to trees in search of defoliating caterpillars and, later, for pupae. If adequate food is in short supply at that time nest sites are also often limiting and competition leads to typical noisy, jackdaw squabbling.

These sites are nearly always holes, but these may be in buildings or trees, nest boxes, or even rabbit burrows. The *Garden Bird Watch Handbook* reports research which shows how hard it is for a pair of jackdaws to find enough food to raise all their brood. Urban jackdaws are fairly frequent visitors to bird tables or to gardens where scraps are available. They also scavenge readily at rubbish dumps.

Top left and right
Birds of town and country, jackdaws are particularly fond of chimneys, church towers and similar sites, as well as cliffs and quarries.

Bottom
Jackdaws have a distinctive grey hood over the nape of their necks.

'There is a bird who,
by his coat
And by the hoarseness of his note,
Might be supposed a crow,
A great frequenter of the church,
Where, bishop like,
he finds a perch
And dormitory too'
William Couper THE JACKDAW

SPECIES INFORMATION	
SCIENTIFIC NAME	Corvus corone corone
RELATED SPECIES	Hooded Crow, Rook, Jackdaw, Raven
CALL	Hoarse monotonous cawing, often repeated three times, sometimes more
HABITAT	Open country
STATUS	Resident. In B about 800,000 pairs (absent from most of Ireland)

Carrion Crow

47 cm (18.5 in)

CARRION CROWS LIVE up to their name by including some carrion in their diet, helping for example to clear the corpses of birds or mammals killed on the roads. But they will eat almost anything, from seeds and fruit to insects and worms.

Although the hooded crow is a race of this species, it is included in the uplands section, despite its occurrence at all altitudes in Ireland.

In England people say of the magpie 'one for sorrow, two for joy', in Wales the same is said of the crow. There is also a Saxon tradition that deemed seeing a crow on your left was a portent of disaster:

ALL BLACK, WITH rather powerful bill. Lacks 'trousers' of rook. Not colonial, and less sociable than rook. Some say a crow-bar is so called because of the power of a Crow's bill, which is not quite up to a raven's. This bill, coupled with the all black plumage and harsh call, is usually sufficient to identify a crow. In flight the wing fingers are less spread than those of a rook, and the tail much squarer than a raven's. The flight silhouette shows a distinct bulge to the rear edge of the wing.

'The carrion crow, that loathsome beast,
Which cries against the rain,
Both for her hue and for the rest
The Devil resembleth plain'
George Gascoigne 1573

SIZE

IDENTIFICATION

HABITAT

POPULATION

MAP

Top and bottom right
The carrion crow is all black, with a harsh call and a square tail.

Bottom left
The rather featureless carrion crow is an opportunist feeder, taking a wide range of food, including small dead animals.

Woodland Birds

WHEN BRITAIN SEPARATED from the main continent, much of it was covered with deciduous forest, although pine was probably common in Scotland. Four thousand years later Neolithic man had opened up large areas on Breckland and on the chalk, and by Domesday the country was only sparsely wooded. Today woodland is even more patchy, following further deforestation for industrial charcoal and for building. Such woodland as has been replanted, particularly since 1920, has been largely coniferous.

MORE RECENTLY, AMBITIOUS plans for replanting with native trees have been drawn up, adding a welcome diversity to the newer forests. Many woodland birds also visit gardens, and there is much

DIVERSITY OF WOODLAND BIRDS

IN ANY ONE 'plot' in Chaddesley Woods NNR in Worcestershire I never met more than 30 species during a year of sampling by transect. To the 30 found along woodland edge adjacent to an old meadow, different species could be added from a plot of denser oak, others from a damp plot with alders, and more from spruce and pine. The diversity was greatest along the woodland edge, and least in the conifers. Different types of wood have their own distinctive bird communities. This is illustrated in the following table compiled by Simms shows the relative abundance, expressed as the number of contacts with a species per 100 birds seen, for different woodlands.

RELATIVE ABUNDANCE OF BIRDS IN DIFFERENT WOODLANDS

PEDUNCULATE OAK (ENGLAND)	SESSILE OAK (ENGLAND AND WALES)	SPRUCE (SCOTLAND)	BEECH (IRELAND)
Chaffinch 13	Chaffinch 17	Woodpigeon 38	Chaffinch 16
Robin 11	Pied flycatcher 7	Goldcrest 15	Blackbird 11
Wren 10	Willow warbler 7	Chaffinch 8	Woodpigeon 11
Blackbird 8	Wood warbler 6	Wren 6	Robin 8
Willow warbler 7	Wren 6	Crow 5	Song thrush 7
Woodpigeon 6	Robin 5	Coal tit 4	Starling 7

Top
The willow warbler is a common summer visitor to broadleaved and mixed woodland.

Bottom left
Woods with plenty of old timber are attractive to great spotted woodpeckers.

Bottom right
Oakwoods such as this support healthy populations of woodland birds.

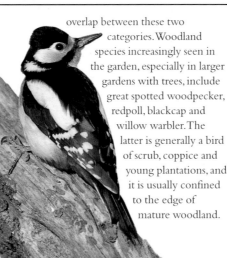

overlap between these two categories. Woodland species increasingly seen in the garden, especially in larger gardens with trees, include great spotted woodpecker, redpoll, blackcap and willow warbler. The latter is generally a bird of scrub, coppice and young plantations, and it is usually confined to the edge of mature woodland.

SUPPORTING A RANGE OF SPECIES

REGARDLESS OF GEOGRAPHY and tree type, woods also differ in size, altitude and structure. The amount of undergrowth, the nature of the field layer (such as bluebells or mosses) and the density of the canopy, are all aspects of the structure. Management can affect some of these variables, and the ideal is to maintain wildlife-rich open spaces, in effect to increase the edge effect, and to keep a full range of age-classes of trees within a wood.

In some of Snowdonia's sessile oak woods, which are full of pied flycatchers and redstarts in summer, there are no young trees because of grazing by sheep. Such woods cannot survive in the long term unless regeneration occurs. Many woods have a very different problem: there is not enough dead wood to provide a habitat for the beetle larvae which are food for woodpeckers and other birds, and not enough holes for the very many species which could nest in them.

CONIFER PLANTATIONS

CONIFER PLANTATIONS HAVE aroused strong feelings over the years, partly because of the earlier tradition of planting in straight rows, regardless of contour and landscape, and of clear-felling when the trees were needed, leaving almost a battlefield scene of desolation. Plantations do however demonstrate beautifully the ecological principle of succession, whereby as one aspect of an ecosystem changes with time, it causes other associated changes.

A recently established plantation, with sheep excluded, develops thick ground vegetation regardless of the young trees. Here insects flourish, small mammals can thrive along with birds such as meadow pipits. The mammals may in turn encourage predators like short-eared owls and hen harriers. After ten years or so the trees are pushing through the vegetation and will soon begin to suppress it, by claiming most of the light. Until they do, there are still plenty of invertebrates associated with the ground vegetation and others linked with the growing trees, so insectivorous birds can flourish. Whinchats and the rare woodlark may do well at this stage, using the young conifers as perches and song posts, but they in turn will be replaced by willow warblers, chaffinches and eventually, after 30 years or so, by coal tits and goldcrests. Many moan that nothing except coal tits and goldcrests are there but, in Wales, siskins and crossbills have moved in. Bird diversity in winter is actually comparable with the oakwoods, and in cleared areas grasshopper warblers and black grouse provide a contrasting pair of species.

A high proportion of British woodlarks and nightjars are now found in young plantations. For the woodlarks this is mainly an East Anglian phenomenon, with Breckland larks having abandoned their normal heathland habitat. Both species like some bare ground – woodlarks for feeding as they walk, and nightjars for nesting.

Left
The beautiful redstart is a relatively rare speciality bird, found mainly in oak woods.

Top right
Dead or decaying trees provide huge numbers of insects and other invertebrates, in turn supporting bird populations.

Bottom
Crossbills are mainly associated with pinewoods. They sometimes come down to drink at woodland pools.

Woodland Management

ENGLISH NATURE WOULD like to see at least 5,000 ha (12,355 acres) of ancient woodland restored over the next 10–20 years, and members of the Woodland Trust believe that conservation of ancient woodland is a top priority. Ancient woodland is land that has been continuously wooded since 1600, but it may well have been replanted, even with conifers.

which allows flowering plants to flourish to the benefit of woodland butterflies and other wildlife.

The most likely sequence of bird communities that will form the succession following coppicing will be as follows. Initially, as regrowth starts, and before ground vegetation thickens, conditions favour whitethroat and tree pipit, dunnock and yellowhammer. As the canopy of shrubs begins to close, after some three to seven years, optimum conditions for a host of migrants develop. Nightingale, garden warbler, blackcap and willow warbler all thrive, but if the coppice is left to mature, conditions change again, becoming more suitable for tits and robins. The age and density of standard trees also influence the bird life – old trees have more holes, and dense trees cast more shade. A possible ideal would have old, sparse standards, set among coppice shrubs which are cut back every seven to ten years, and with different areas of the wood being cut in different years, so that a mosaic of habitats is maintained.

RENEWING WOODLAND

WHILE SOME WOODS, and dependent organisations such as fungi, mosses and leaf-litter spiders can thrive on minimum interference, most woodland needs active management. Coppicing is one management technique, historically widely used, which, while not ideal for wildlife in all circumstances, can maintain a high density of trees and shrubs, a spectacular array of spring flowers and a succession of conditions suitable for breeding birds. Large single-trunked trees, standards, are left to mature, with a probable eventual use as timber, while the woodland shrubs, such as hazel and sweet chestnut are cut to near ground level, every few years, to produce wood for burning, hurdles or fences. These coppiced shrubs regenerate with multiple stems, but, before they do, light has been let in,

Top

The pied flycatcher is one of the prettiest woodland birds native to Britain.

Middle

The male blackcap lives up to its name, whereas the female's cap is brown.

Bottom

Green woodpeckers have started to increase in numbers since woodland conservation began.

A WOODLAND NATIONAL NATURE RESERVE

WOODLAND NEAR TO towns has many attractions, one of which is its ability to 'lose' people. There may be lots of people there, but they are much less visible

than on the beach or in open parkland. Wyre Forest, close to the towns of the Black Country and only 32 km (20 miles) from the centre of Birmingham, has 25,000 visitors a year, but little damage is caused by disturbance or trampling. It is hard to say what we mean by 'natural'. For centuries the oaks of Wyre Forest were coppiced to produce charcoal for iron smelting, which meant that few of those standing today grew directly from acorns, but have sprouted from the stumps of felled trees. The use of scrubby oak for charcoal had its compensations for wildlife, as open clearings and broad rides, together with sheltered pastures and hayfields to supply fodder for horses, created a fine mosaic of habitats.

Wyre Forest has the added benefit of the Dowles Brook, whose valley divides the forest, and which is home to dipper, grey wagtail and kingfisher, while the steep slopes and acidic soil make conditions ideal for sessile oak woodland, with redstarts and pied flycatchers. Since the mid 1960s, pied flycatchers have increasingly made use of nest-boxes here. Also found here are nightjars, woodcock, long-eared owls, woodpeckers and warblers.

SESSILE OAKWOODS

WELSH SESSILE OAK woods have a special attraction, with their interestingly shaped trees, carpets of moss and abundance of lichens. Those in the Vale of Ffestiniog for example have a long-standing reputation. One of these, Coed-y-Maentwrog, was declared a National Nature Reserve in 1966, and is one of a series of oak woodland reserves designated by the then Nature Conservancy Council to represent the range of woodland types that occur in the variety of conditions to be found in North Wales.

Transects of this reserve to find about the age structure of the oaks showed that most were well over 100 years old, reflecting past management practices and the all-pervasive effects of grazing. Boulders and tree roots beneath the canopy are well covered with woodland mosses. The numerous crevices and knot holes in the mature trees provide an abundance of nest sites for tits, nuthatches, great spotted woodpeckers, redstarts and pied flycatchers. Wood warblers and tree pipits are other summer visitors, while goldeneye and pochard visit Llyn Mair in winter. Early studies showed that a good acorn crop, perhaps every four years, could give 40 acorns per square metre, often distributed and buried by jays. As in many woods, effective fencing and the destruction of alien rhododendrons have been vital management priorities.

Top
Damp woods may develop a rich ground flora, rich in mosses.

Middle
The spreading branches of an oak tree provide a multitude of cracks and crevices.

Bottom
Nuthatches are unusual in being able to clamber down tree trunks as well as upwards.

Red Kite

60–70 cm (24–28 in)

○○○○○○○○○○○○○○○○○○○○○○○○○○○○

SPECIES INFORMATION

SCIENTIFIC NAME	*Milvus milvus*
RELATED SPECIES	Black Kite (not I)
CALL	Whistling cries, often heard in spring; also single 'deeair' or 'yeee' calls
HABITAT	Hilly, wooded landscape, with open areas such as small wetlands and clearings
STATUS	Resident in Wales, where there are some 80 pairs. Currently being re-introduced to Scotland and England

SIZE

IDENTIFICATION

HABITAT

POPULATION

MAP

LONG WINGS AND long, deeply forked tail. Light grey head, pale patches towards ends of wings, and red-brown body. Soars with slightly raised wings; sometimes hovers with deep, relatively slow wingbeats; often twists tail in flight

WHILE BREEDING DIVERS and Slavonian grebes are Scottish specialities, the kite has for long been associated with Wales, although in earlier days it was abundant everywhere. Recent re-introductions, in Scotland and England, are making the bird more familiar once more.

In 1970, Colonel H. Marrey Salmon reviewed the story of the kite's preservation in Wales. First he described why, within half a century after 1800, a widespread and relatively common bird had ceased to exist throughout almost the whole of Britain. 'Those who brought this about were the game preserving landowners and their indiscriminate and destructive agents, the gamekeepers, who pursued their calling with a callous indifference for anything but game, and an appalling amount of cruelty exercised with the connivance and, in some cases, the active participation of their masters.

By the middle of the second half of the nineteenth century the last remaining kites were confined to central Wales, which was wild, mountainous and rugged, remote and sparsely populated: here the steep-sided valleys of the main and tributary rivers were still well wooded, chiefly with mature, if scrubby, oaks.'

By 1889, kites were increasing around Brecon but then Scottish gamekeepers were brought into local estates and nine or ten kites were killed in the spring of that year. Some landowners were horrified for they had been trying to protect the birds. Around that time J. H. Salter, Professor of Botany at Aberystwyth took steps to bring into being an organisation for the protection of Welsh kites which has continued in one form or another up to the present.

In the 1976 *Atlas* there were only 26 pairs and some young seemed to emigrate to the south-east. By the 1993 *Atlas* figures of 77 proven pairs in 1991 could be quoted, but birds were still being killed by illegal poisons spread for crows and foxes.

These Welsh haunts are essentially upland, but kites could well flourish, as they used to, elsewhere and the Welsh birds hunt over low intensity farmland, rough grassland and heath. Red kites fly magnificently, with buoyant wing action, soaring gracefully with their long, broad wings and deeply forked tails. It is a wonderful thought that all the dedicated work of kite enthusiasts is making this one of the pleasures of British birding.

Top left and right
The red kite is an elegant bird, with agile flight, aided by its long, deeply forked tail.

Bottom
Red Kites have recently been reintroduced into England and Scotland from Wales.

SPECIES INFORMATION

SCIENTIFIC NAME	Buteo buteo
RELATED SPECIES	Rough-legged Buzzard
CALL	Almost cat-like mewing, especially in spring
HABITAT	Wooded regions with fields, marshes and hedges. Hunts over open country, nesting mostly at woodland edges
STATUS	Resident and partial migrant. Absent from most of Ireland (except north), and much of south and east England (but gradually spreading eastwards)

Buzzard

43–55 cm (17–22 in)

MEDIUM-SIZED BIRD of prey with short neck and large, rounded head. Wings are broad, and the tail is rounded when spread. Very variable in plumage, from almost white to uniform dark brown, but usually brownish, with paler breast-band. Eye dark brown to yellow. Rather compact in flight with wings held somewhat stiffly, and wingtips noticeably upturned when soaring. Occasionally hovers.

BUZZARDS WILL TAKE a wide variety of prey. In many parts of the British Isles rabbits and other smaller mammals form the major part of their diet but birds are also taken, especially newly fledged young in the summer. Their diet also includes worms, larvae and beetles. Buzzards often grub about in fields in wet or misty weather but one thinks of them soaring, with the 'fingers' of their broad wings extended. Those who live in Devon often think that they are 'home' when they start seeing plenty of buzzards but visitors to the south-west are now more frequently saying 'we see buzzards too', whether they live in Basingstoke or Midhurst, Worcester or Shrewsbury. The *New Atlas*

shows gains as well in Scotland, and a good foothold has been established in Ireland. Despite their varied plumage buzzards are easy to identify as medium-sized soaring raptors with broad wings, short head and relatively short tail. When perched the tail only protrudes slightly beyond the wing tips. The yellow base to beak and yellow feet may show as it sits, paying little attention to cars, on a roadside telegraph pole. When soaring, the dark border to the two-toned underwing is clear, however dark or light the plumage, and the dark almost terminal tail-band is another feature.

Buzzards are territorial when breeding, often displaying in interlocking spirals, but group soaring of nearby territory holders also occurs in spring and if all birds are making their far reaching 'meow' calls the sky can seem to be full of buzzards. When the young are calling later in the year a valley may again seem buzzard-saturated, but the birds may be harder to find at that time.

Nest are bulky affairs, usually in trees, and made of tree or heather twigs in which a shallow cup is lined with green foliage.

From September to February Dartmoor buzzards hunt mainly from perches. Later they hover more than they perch, except when visibility is poor, but in the New Forest they seldom do. These sort of details, painstakingly gleaned by ardent buzzard watchers show the difficulties of totally valid generalisations, but a buzzard soaring is unlikely to be hunting. Even if a buzzard can see a rabbit from a mile away it is not conspicuously successful and has to spend a lot of time hunting to get sufficient food.

SIZE

IDENTIFICATION

HABITAT

POPULATION

MAP

Top and middle

Buzzards often hunt by soaring, but may also be seen watching the ground from a low perch, or even grubbing for worms.

Bottom

The tail of a buzzard is only just visible beyond the wing tips when the bird is perching.

Sparrowhawk

30–40 cm (12–16 in)

SIZE

IDENTIFICATION

HABITAT

POPULATION

MAP

MALE SMALLER THAN female. Wings rounded, tail long, narrow and square-ended. Underparts narrowly banded, rust-brown in male. Female brownish-grey above, male blue-grey. Juveniles dark brown above, barred below.

THERE ARE MIXED views about sparrowhawks but I love their sudden appearance and silent flight. When overhead their barred underparts are clear and the short blunt wings most unlike a kestrel's; they are seen at their best when they soar as they often do. The sexes differ markedly in size, with the grey-brown backed female larger than the male with his bluish back. After severe decreases when organochlorine pesticides were passed along the food chain, sparrowhawks are now very successful.

Leslie Brown (1978) quotes figures which indicate the amount of food a sparrowhawk pair and their brood need during the year. To achieve the 30 kg (66 lb) of food killed per adult per year and the 20 kg (44 lb) eaten, getting on for 800 average sized or 1,600 small birds need to be killed each year. For the three months that a brood of two is fed another 400 small birds are needed. It might well be thought that the 3,600 birds taken would make serious inroads into local populations, but the evidence quoted in the population section indicates that great and blue tits are no less common when sparrowhawks are about than when they are absent. Many of the birds fed to the young are young themselves, and tits have large broods, and many of those caught at any time will be older, less fit or less well fed than those they miss.

Top

A female sparrowhawk crouches over her prey – a male chaffinch. Female sparrowhawks are capable of catching prey up to the size of a pigeon.

Bottom

A woodland ride in the New Forest, which is classic sparrowhawk habitat.

Housemartins and long-tailed tits most often warn of sparrowhawks, but the house martins fly too well and the long-tailed tits stay too close to cover for either to be major prey items.

Sparrowhawks often pass within a couple of feet of my head, which brings them very close to bird rich cover. A local watcher here saw one kill a bird as large and apparently well protected as a kestrel, but only a large female would have any chance of this. In one study Newton found that 85 per cent by weight of prey items was made up of finches, thrushes, starlings and pigeons but more tits (10 per cent of diet by number) than pigeons (6 per cent by number) would be caught.

Top
A juvenile sparrowhawk perches on a tree branch in woodland.

Bottom
The adult male sparrowhawk is much smaller than the female and feeds on smaller prey, such as tits and finches.

121

Tawny Owl

38 cm (15 in)

SPECIES INFORMATION

SCIENTIFIC NAME	*Strix aluco*
RELATED SPECIES	Long-eared Owl, Short-eared Owl
CALL	Territorial song of male, a shuddering, tremulous 'hoo (pause) huuu-hu-hukuhuh', heard mainly in early spring. Female (and sometimes male) has loud 'ke-wick'
HABITAT	Deciduous and mixed woodland. Also in parks, cemeteries and gardens with old trees
STATUS	Resident. In B about 20,000 pairs. Absent from Ireland, and also from Isle of Man and Isle of Wight

SIZE

IDENTIFICATION

HABITAT

POPULATION

MAP

TAWNY OWLS ARE dark eyed, medium-sized, relatively broad-winged owls with rather uniform mottled brown plumage. There are two colour forms: a bark-coloured grey form and a red-brown form (the latter commoner in BI). More often heard than seen. Our commonest woodland owl. In many views the shape is critical, and the large, rounded head, compact body and long flat glides on broad wings are identifying features. They like plenty of lookout posts for hunting, and favour woodland with clearings, hedges and mature trees.

WELL KNOWN IN children's stories and familiar for its hooting in gardens and parks, it is the most spectacular bird that will actually nest in a suburban garden. Woodland owls take mainly small mammals, but in parks and gardens they will catch small birds as they roost and will even forage on the lawn at night looking for earthworms. They listen alertly, then hop forward like a gigantic but not very skilful blackbird, breaking most of the worms pulled from the ground. In damp weather half the owls' pellets may be brown, fibrous worm remains rather then the normal grey fur and bones.

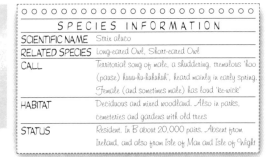

'Sweet Suffolk owl, so trimly dight
With feathers like a lady bright.
Thou singest alone sitting by night
Te whit, te whoo, te wit, te wit.
The note, that forth so freely rolls
With shrill command the mouse controls
A sings a song for dying souls.'
Thomas Vanter (1616)

Top and bottom right
Tawny owls are more often seen than heard, preferring to stay under cover until dark.

Bottom left
These owls have large, rounded heads and are either bark-grey or reddy-brown in colour.

Long-eared Owl

36 cm (14 in)

SPECIES INFORMATION

SCIENTIFIC NAME	*Asio otus*
RELATED SPECIES	Short-eared Owl, Tawny Owl
CALL	Male has low 'huh', heard as early as February. Alarm call a barking 'wick', repeated. Contact call of young birds is a high-pitched 'tsee'
HABITAT	Breeds in coniferous forests and plantations, also in light woodland. In winter often in communal roosts of over 20 birds
STATUS	Resident. In BI about 5,000 pairs

SLIM, MEDIUM-SIZED long-winged owl with orange eyes and long 'ear' tufts. Plumage with tree-bark pattern. Nocturnal and rarely seen. In flight, the wings are longer and the head narrower than the tawny while, when perched, its shape alters markedly with posture. It is long and slender when alarmed but fluffed out when relaxed. The long ears, buff facial disc and white divide between orange eyes are fine if seen well but the ear tufts may be invisible. The song has been described as similar to the sound made by blowing across the top of an empty bottle, but for much of the year the birds are silent.

LONG-EARED OWLS, particularly favouring conifer plantations, are one of the least familiar woodland birds, and the scattered distribution shown in the Atlases might reflect under-recording for they sit very still by day, often close to a tree trunk with which their cryptic plumage merges, and they favour dense conifer woodland. How many of us go searching for owls in plantations soon after the New Year when they start to call?

They have two alternative habitats: shelterbelts and small mature woodlands in northern Britain, and broad-leaved fen woodland, including sallow and thorn scrub in the south. In Scotland they favour deep heather in open hilly sites and they are obviously versatile in choice of habitat. In Ireland, Ruttledge (1966) found long-eared owls breeding in every county, being thinly distributed where suitable woodlands exist. More recently it seems to have thinned out in the west.

In most ways their biology is similar to the tawny owl with competition over food and nest sites likely. Voles are important but birds and shrews are also taken. Both owls often use old magpie nests but tawny owls favour holes in trees and long-eared will nest on the ground, so the two can, and do, co-exist.

SIZE

IDENTIFICATION

HABITAT

POPULATION

MAP

Bottom
Few birdwatchers have had a good view of a long-eared owl – this species is even more elusive than the tawny owl. Dense conifer woodland is one preferred habitat.

Woodcock

34 cm (13 in)

○○○○○○○○○○○○○○○○○○○○○○○○○○○○○
SPECIES INFORMATION

SCIENTIFIC NAME	Scolopax rusticola
RELATED SPECIES	Snipe
CALL	Occasional high-pitched 'tsveet' when disturbed. Roding male alternates deep 'kvorr-kvorr-kvorr' with very high-pitched sharp 'pitsick'
HABITAT	Mixed woodland with clearings, rich herb- and shrub-layer, and damp areas
STATUS	Resident and winter migrant. Estimates of BI population around 25,000 pairs

SIZE

IDENTIFICATION

HABITAT

POPULATION

MAP

S HORT-LEGGED, LARGE-HEADED wader with long, straight bill and highly camouflaged plumage. Flight soft and usually silent, almost owl-like. In display flight ('roding') male describes low circuits in weak zig-zag curves, grunting and clicking as he flies. Wings broad and rounded, bill held angled towards ground. Crepuscular and nocturnal.

THE RUFOUS, MARBLED plumage cannot really be appreciated at distance, but the dumpy shape and bat-like evening flight are so distinctive that description is superfluous. A snipe like 'schaap' is characteristic of night-time disturbance, but the roding 'song' of two to five growling sounds, followed by a sneeze is more exciting but again not easily described.

'Despite the brilliance of its plumage a woodcock is wonderfully difficult to see on the nest. The markings so brilliant when seen at close quarters form one of the very best examples of camouflage in the world of nature, and a sitting woodcock is to all intents and purposes invisible at a distance of only a few feet. She knows it, too,' writes Brian Vesey Fitzgerald (1946) 'and generally sits so close that you can pass her day after day and be unaware of her presence.' Like many of those interested in country sports (he was editor of the Field) Vesey Fitzgerald was obviously a very good and persistent observer and knew his game. 'It is very unusual to see a woodcock feeding in the daytime, but I have watched them feeding at midday in very frosty weather.

Top
Woodcock favour woodland with clearings as their natural habitat, especially if there are damp areas under the trees.

Bottom
The woodcock has remarkable camouflaged plumage which makes it hard to spot against the woodland floor.

Woodcock walk like snipe with the neck drawn in and the bill inclined downwards, but the walk is not nearly so easy and they seldom walk very far. When flushed from cover during the day they rise with a great swish of wings, but generally they do no more than dodge through the trees to come down again at a safe distance.'

Woodcock like moist woods, with oak, birch, larch and spruce, and woods with open glades and rides, a good cover of bracken and bramble and evergreen bushes. The abundance map in the *Breeding Atlas* shows a very scattered distribution of breeding birds but the *Winter Atlas* shows a wider distribution as birds from Scandinavia move in. At that time extensive conifer plantations can suit woodcock and they will also turn up on bracken and heather covered hillsides, parks and large gardens.

Green Woodpecker

32 cm (12 in)

SPECIES INFORMATION

SCIENTIFIC NAME	Picus viridis
RELATED SPECIES	Great Spotted / Lesser Spotted Woodpecker
CALL	Flight-call (and near nest) a hard 'kjek' or 'kjook'. Laughing territorial song, 'klee-klee-klee-klee-klee', carrying over long distance. Drums only very rarely, and then weakly
HABITAT	Broadleaved and mixed woodland, in copses in fields, orchards, parks and gardens with old trees. Fondness for ant-rich pasture. Sometimes visits garden lawns
STATUS	Resident. In B about 15,000 pairs (absent from Ireland)

A LARGE WOODPECKER with green and yellow plumage and a bright red crown. Male has red moustache with black edging, black in female. Juveniles are heavily barred below, with less intense red on head. Shows conspicuous yellow rump in flight. The crimson crown and black face are as striking as the green back and yellow rump. The male had red below the black eye patch, but the female lacks this.

WOODPECKERS ARE HIGHLY specialised for life in the trees and for extracting insects from crevices with their long tongues with barbed tips. The arrangement of toes, with two pointing up and two pointing down, when climbing, is another adaptation, as is the structure, and pattern of moult, of the tail feathers; these help to stabilise upward movement.

The green woodpecker can stretch its tongue out 10 cm (4 in) beyond the tip of its beak. Using its tongue, it can probe deep into the galleries of an ants nest. Ants adhere to the sticky saliva which coats the tongue as it wriggles, worm-like into the underground chambers. The most mobile part of the tongue is the extreme tip which has developed into a wide, flat sort of lip, and which can be moved about independently of the rest. The spoon-like lip feels the location of the ant pupae and then scoops the prey up.

In a garden with ants and ant-hills, or in old grassland, green woodpeckers find rich pickings, often making a blackbird seem a tidy gardener. But its beauty compensates for any damage caused.

On tree trunks it will spiral upwards with jerky hops, pausing to chip at the bark or peep over its shoulder.

'But most the hewel's wonders are,
Who here has the Holt – festers
(Forester's) care,
He walks still upright from the root.
Meas'ting the timber with his foot;
And all the way, to keep it clean
Doth from the bark of wood moths glean
He with his beak; examines well
Which fit to stand and which to fell.'

Andrew Marvel (1621–78)

SIZE

IDENTIFICATION

HABITAT

POPULATION

MAP

Top
Green woodpeckers excavate their nest holes in old and rotting timber, and rear their brood in the holes.

Bottom
Like all woodpeckers, they use their stiff tails as balance to help prop themselves upright when climbing.

Great Spotted Woodpecker

22 cm (9 in)

SPECIES INFORMATION	
SCIENTIFIC NAME	Dendrocopus major
RELATED SPECIES	Lesser Spotted Woodpecker, Green Woodpecker
CALL	Metallic 'kick', repeated as alarm-call. Most rapid drumming of all our woodpeckers. Drums on hollow trees, dry branches, posts
HABITAT	Woodland, copses, parks and gardens
STATUS	Resident. In B about 28,000 pairs (absent from Ireland)

OUR COMMONEST woodpecker. Black and white plumage, with white shoulder patches; lower tail coverts bright red, flanks unstreaked. Male has red patch at back of head; juveniles have red crown. Flight undulating.

IN FLIGHT, FIVE or six flapping wingbeats alternate with closure of the wings to give the typically undulating performance, which demonstrates well the pied pattern of the wings. It has the typically broad wings of a woodland bird. On a tree trunk it is less chequered but equally black and white, with black crown and upper parts and bold white ovals on the scapulars. The black bar from bill to nape distinguishes it from other pied European woodpeckers. The female lacks the male's small red nape patch. Both have a bright red patch under the tail, while young birds have more red on the head.

Great spotted woodpeckers drum much more than green woodpeckers in advertising territory, usually from mid-January through to the end of June.

The great spotted woodpecker's tongue has its own adaptations for spearing insect larvae and pupae

inside their chambers. The end of the tongue is like a hardened stiletto with a great number of small barbs at its horny tip. This species uses its beak more than the last, hacking and pecking at bark and wood, knocking off loose material in the search for insects. In winter, conifer seeds become an alternative diet, as do nuts and other foods supplied in gardens.

Apart from their drumming, these are noisy woodpeckers which often utter their sharp alarm or flight call. Harsh chattering court-ship chases are much more noisy, but the young in the nest make most noise of all.

Top and bottom right
The thrush-sized great spotted woodpecker can often be seen in British woods and, increasingly, in parks and gardens as well.

Bottom right
The male of the species has a red patch at the back of its neck.

Lesser Spotted Woodpecker

15 cm (6 in)

SMALLEST EUROPEAN woodpecker, sparrow-sized. Back is black, with horizontal white bands; no red on underside. Male has red cap with black margin, female has no red colour at all.

THIS SPECIES IS much more retiring than great spotted, but again its call is often the first sign of its presence. Having heard the high-pitched call, it is worth searching small branches for a woodpecker-shape with barred back and, depending on gender, a crimson or a pale crown. There is no red on the underparts. This is as much a bird of parkland, old hedgerow trees and riverside alders as of true woods. When near these habitats in the spring listen for its drumming which is a much less aggressive sound than that of its larger relative.

Lesser spotted woodpeckers are essentially birds of England and Wales, with a markedly south-eastern preference. There are far fewer in the Midlands or Devon than around London, and there is a marked decrease in a band from the Wash to Lands End which might correlate with the death of hedgerow elms. When elms were first diseased, the abundance of beetles and beetle larvae helped raise the BTO's Common Bird's Census index, but once substantial elm felling had taken place the woodpecker lost not only food but also a favourite nesting tree.

Just as these little birds often feed in the smaller branches, very largely on insects, their holes are often not in the trunk but in a rotten side branch. This emphasises again the need to leave some rotten wood in situ in any woodland management plan. As with so many other hole nesters, the eggs, usually four to six, are white, and the chicks hatch in a nest some 15 cm (6 in) below the nest hole.

Both the spotted woodpeckers are associated with rain, and for some reason legends abound about woodpeckers disobeying God or Gods.

> 'Zeus won't in a hurry restore to the woodpecker tapping the oak, In times prehistoric 'tis easily proved, by evidence weighty and ample
> That birds and not Gods were the rulers of men
> And the lords of the world.'
> Aristophanes THE BIRDS

SIZE

IDENTIFICATION

HABITAT

POPULATION

MAP

Top
Lesser spotted woodpeckers are surprisingly small, being only sparrow-sized. They drum quietly in the spring.

Bottom
Since the advent of Dutch elm disease, the lesser spotted woodpecker has fallen in number.

Nuthatch

14 cm (5.5 in)

SPECIES INFORMATION	
SCIENTIFIC NAME	Sitta europaea
RELATED SPECIES	No close relatives in British Isles
CALL	Call a liquid 'twit-twit-twit'. Song a whistling 'vivivivivi...' or 'peeu-peeu-peeu'
HABITAT	Broadleaved and mixed woodland, parks and gardens. Shows fondness for old oaks
STATUS	Resident. In B about 50,000 pairs (absent from Ireland)

SIZE

IDENTIFICATION

HABITAT

POPULATION

MAP

D UMPY, WOODPECKER-LIKE with short tail and powerful bill. Blue-grey above, creamy yellow or rusty below. Scandinavian race has white breast and belly. Climbs well, up, across and down trees.

WITH ITS POWERFUL bill, short tail, long claws and sturdy legs, the Nuthatch is well adapted for climbing up and down large trees. The blue-grey upperparts and salmon pink underparts are very smart, but often no colour is to be seen, only a distinctive silhouette, going about its business, usually noisily, searching the branches or flying from tree to tree in parkland. In flight the round wings, sharply pointed head and the short square tail aid identification.

Top

Nuthatches apply mud around the edges of natural holes to make the entrance to the nest just the right size.

Bottom

The agile, beautifully balanced nuthatch can climb along, up or even down branches with equal ease.

Nuthatches are among the most exciting garden visitors, but are equally welcome calling all year round as they maintain their territory in lowland woods or parks with well grown or mature trees; if there is a bit of decay then so much the better. Oak tends to be favoured but they are happy with ash. The territorial trilling 'song', and a series of whistles intergrade with each other, but the excitement call is clearly separate as is a tit-like contact call which is very clear and loud.

The nesting hole is often that used before by a woodpecker, but may be natural or even a nest-box, the hole often plastered with mud to narrow it to the required specifications, and the nest itself is largely loose flakes of bark, preferably from Scots pine. A happy nuthatch will therefore need an old deciduous tree, a barky pine and a supply of mud within its territory.

Treecreeper

12.5 cm (5 in)

SPECIES INFORMATION	
SCIENTIFIC NAME	Certhia familiaris
RELATED SPECIES	Short-toed Treecreeper (central and southern Europe)
CALL	High-pitched 'srii'. Song is rather scratchy, ending in a trill
HABITAT	Broadleaved woodland, mixed woodland, also coniferous woods (especially in south), parks and gardens
STATUS	Resident. In BI about 245,000 pairs

SIZE · IDENTIFICATION · HABITAT · POPULATION · MAP

HEARING A HIGH pitched call was enough to make me glance up and see a treecreeper moving to the base of another tree as dusk fell one chilly December evening. By the time I got home I had made a few calculations, based on assumptions that I fear are pure guesswork, to concentrate my mind on the difficulties for small insect eaters facing a winter night. Such a small bird probably needs to eat thousands of tiny insects and spiders each day.

Whatever the realities, the treecreeper, like the coal tit and every other small bird is hard pressed in winter. Commenting on BTO Common Bird Census trends, Marchant points out that treecreepers suffer particularly when freezing rain or persistent freezing fog leads to pronged ice coating of tree trunks. These conditions caused a major decline for example in the winter of 1978–79.

WOODPECKER-LIKE BIRD with long, distinctively decurved bill. Plumage brown above and white below, with rust-brown rump. Creeps in spirals up tree trunks. Treecreepers use their lengthy stiff graduated tail as a support. Mouse-like in appearance and movement they need vertical trunks, preferably with loose bark as, like a mouse, they can use the smallest crevice beneath for nesting. Assorted debris in a crevice or behind bark forms the nest into which the bird fits tightly. The song is reminiscent of the goldcrest, but louder.

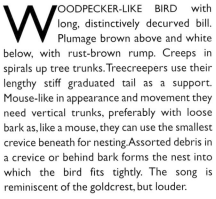

Top
The treecreeper climbs in a steady spiral up a tree trunk, flits down to the base of an adjacent tree and starts again.

Bottom
The treecreeper has a curved bill and white and brown plumage.

Jay
34 cm (13 in)

SPECIES INFORMATION	
SCIENTIFIC NAME	Garrulus glandarius
RELATED SPECIES	Magpie and other members of crow family
CALL	Loud, raw screaming calls. Song a varied, low chatter
HABITAT	Mixed woodland, wooded parks and gardens
STATUS	Resident. In BI about 170,000 pairs

SIZE

IDENTIFICATION

HABITAT

POPULATION

MAP

LARGE COLOURFUL crow-relative. Very conspicuous in flight, with black tail, white rump, and white and blue wing-patches. Body buff, with black moustache.

DESPITE THEIR COLOURFUL plumage, jays behave in such a way that they can often be missed, being heard more than seen during the breeding season. The most typical sound is the harsh screeching call, but jays make a range of other mewings and clickings, sometimes augmented by mimicry.

It is a southern bird, in as much as it is mainly English and Welsh; it is expanding its range in the Great Glen but declining in Ireland, despite a build up in county Kerry. Although never abundant, in Fuller's analysis of woodland birds it occurs in over 80 per cent of the woodland sites investigated.

Jays also now use parks and gardens, perhaps most frequently in autumn when, particularly in irruption years they can be seen overhead with undulating flight and broad wings. Jays everywhere arouse contrasting feelings, with some disliking their predatory cunning and nest-robbing, while others admire the pinkish plumage and intense blue patch on the wing. For recognition the white rump is crucial for they are shy birds often seen flying away.

An important interaction with human activities is the jay as oak planter. When acorns are freely available the birds spend much time hoarding them and carry up to six at a time with one in the bill and the remainder in the oesophagus, to hiding places in the forest floor. Many of these are later recovered, but many are not and germinate instead. By April or May only a few buried acorns can be found, and the proportion of these in the birds' diet falls from more than three quarters in January to less than a fifth.

At first, adults feed their young on larvae, but as jays breed later than many woodland birds the next lot of acorns will be on their way before the young jays are grown. Jays also act as a dispersal agent for beech, and so have a major impact on the regeneration of natural European forests.

> 'From bush to bush slow sweeps the screaming jay
> With one harsh note of pleasure all the day.'
> John Clare SELECTED POEMS

Top right and left
For such a large, brightly-coloured bird, the jay is surprisingly hard to spot; it can occasionally be seen burying acorns in a lawn.

Bottom
Jays come in for some adverse criticism for their nest-robbing ways, but others admire their showy looks.

Nightingale
16.5 cm (6.5 in)

SPECIES INFORMATION

SCIENTIFIC NAME	*Luscinia megarhynchos*
RELATED SPECIES	Bluethroat (same genus) and other members of thrush family
CALL	'Huit'; alarm-call a grating 'karrr'. Song loud and very varied, with warbling and clear fluting phrases, interspersed with deep 'tjook-tjook-tjook', and chirps. Also long crescendo sections, such as 'hiu-hiu-hiu'
HABITAT	Broadleaved or mixed woodland with thick undergrowth, river-valley woodland and fen
STATUS	Summer visitor, wintering in tropical Africa. In B about 5,500 pairs (absent from Ireland)

INCONSPICUOUS PLUMAGE and retiring habits make it hard to spot. Uniform brown above, except for red-brown tail. Underside slightly paler. Juveniles resemble young robins, but are larger and have russet tail. The nightingale is famed for its wonderful song.

THE BTO HAVE had a good initial response to their Nightingale Appeal, which is aimed not only towards nightingale research and conservation, but to all woodland birds in decline, such as spotted flycatcher, dunnock, bullfinch and marsh tit. More management guidelines are needed for enhancing the quality of scrub and woodland habitat.

Fuller looks at some of the peculiarities of nightingale requirements. 'Its occurrence in coppiced woods is extremely patchy even where underwood of a suitable age is available. Not only does the bird eschew chestnut but it is absent from a high proportion of woods with apparently suitable mixed coppice. It is a mystery why particular sites with high density are so favoured. It is possible that the reasons lie not so much with current habitat quality but with the behaviour of the birds themselves.' His hypothesis is that individual birds may show strong fidelity to particular sites or be attracted to sites already holding birds and therefore the species is slow to recolonise even when the habitat is right.

Despite the owl's words in the poem below, nightingales are not without beauty once you can see them. The rounded, rusty tail is rich and when seen in full song, for they sing by day as well as by night, the white throat vibrates as if with enthusiasm. Their wintering grounds in the African tropics are not well known, but spring movement along the north African coast and on Mediterranean islands is on a broad front.

'... besides you're filthy, dark and small
Like a sort of sooty ball
You have no loveliness or strength
And lack harmonious breadth and length,
Beauty somehow passed you by
Your virtue, too, is in short supply.'

John of Guildford
THE OWL AND THE NIGHTINGALE (1225)

 SIZE
 IDENTIFICATION
 HABITAT
 POPULATION
 MAP

Top left and right
Nightingales prefer woodland with a rich undergrowth, and are only found in the south and east of Britain.

Bottom
The nightingale is probably our most famous songbird, and is more often heard than seen.

Redstart

14 cm (5.5 in)

<table>
<tr><td colspan="2" align="center">S P E C I E S   I N F O R M A T I O N</td></tr>
<tr><td>SCIENTIFIC NAME</td><td>Phoenicurus phoenicurus</td></tr>
<tr><td>RELATED SPECIES</td><td>Black Redstart</td></tr>
<tr><td>CALL</td><td>'Hooit' or 'hooit-teck-teck'. Song is short, pleasant and robin-like, usually beginning with 'hooit-tuee-tuee'</td></tr>
<tr><td>HABITAT</td><td>Broadleaved, coniferous and mixed woodland, heathland, parks, large gardens and orchards with old trees</td></tr>
<tr><td>STATUS</td><td>Summer visitor. In B about 150,000 pairs (virtually absent from Ireland)</td></tr>
</table>

SIZE

IDENTIFICATION

HABITAT

POPULATION

MAP

B REEDING MALE HAS blue-grey crown and back, black face and throat, and orange-chestnut breast, flanks, tail and rump. Female has paler underside and is grey-brown above. Juveniles strongly mottled below.

OUR BIRDS WINTER in tropical Africa north of the equator, and another race, with variable white areas on the wings, winters to the east, in Sudan and Ethiopia and moves up to breed around the Black and Caspian Seas.

On passage, the warbler-like 'hweet' call is less likely to give it away than its tail and on arrival in breeding woods, parkland or among the drystone walls of the Pennines, the distinctive but

undistinguished song marks out the breeding territories. Redstarts often sing from perches, some favoured throughout the breeding season, but later there is a quicker song as part of a nest-showing display involving both his ends, the white forehead as he looks out and the red tail as he looks in.

A feeding bird likes some bare areas among the trees, flitting down to pick up small beetles and spiders and returning with its prey to the branch it came from. At other times birds will make aerial sallies or search the trunks or leaves for invertebrates.

Since my first searches for one in Richmond Park, through landfalls of drifted migrants on the Norfolk coast, to years of summer companionship in the sessile oaks of Eryri's valleys I have loved redstarts. A pair even nested in a hole in our kitchen wall one year. Few commentators from the past, mythologists or poets, seem to have celebrated the ever-quivering red tail, the black face set off by a white forehead and orange underparts. Even the grey back, which sounds dull, has a perfect texture to contrast with the darker wings. Females have the same pert and lively posture and like the mottled young have the diagnostic red tail.

Bottom
The male redstart has a characteristic, ever-quivering red tail and a black face.

Middle and Top
Redstarts thrive in woodland, heathland and increasingly in parks and gardens.

Mistle Thrush

27 cm (10.5 in)

LARGEST EUROPEAN THRUSH, greyer than song thrush and with longer wings and tail. Grey-brown above with large spots below; outer tail feathers tipped white. Juveniles spotted above with pale markings and whitish neck.

THE WILD CHALLENGING song is its most spectacular feature, but when looked at closely the combination of confident posture, large clear breast spots, grey back and, in flight, white underwing make it an attractive bird. Even though the nest is large, with sticks, mud and fine grasses, it is easily missed high in a tree fork.

Mistle thrushes have large territories in open woodland. They are very conspicuous in the breeding season, singing loudly from visible positions and making endless noisy complaints about magpies and other potential dangers. A little later they often seem to disappear, but in some areas, where bilberries grow among the heather, late summer is when they appear.

Mistle thrushes have gradually spread, becoming more tolerant of people, and also more suburban, being found in towns as well as plantations.

All sorts of people have said all sorts of things about mistle thrushes. In the fourth century Aristotle was already writing about its fondness for mistletoe, and there is an old belief that mistle thrushes could speak seven languages. In the west country local names often associate it with holly, and the berries on our tree are certainly often defended in winter. Holen is the Old English for holly and holm thrush, holm cock or holm screech were local Devonshire names.

> 'In early March, before the lark
> Dare start, beside the huge oak tree
> Close fixed agen the powdered bark,
> The mains' nest I often see;
> And mark, as wont, the bits of wool
> Hang round about its early bed;
> She lays six eggs in colours dull,
> Blotched thick with spots of burning red'

John Clare SELECTED POEMS

SIZE

IDENTIFICATION

HABITAT

POPULATION

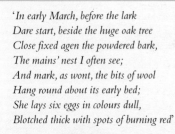

MAP

Larger and more wary than the songthrush, the mistle thrush is less often seen in gardens. In winter, they are partial to ripe berries, such as crabapples.

Spotted Flycatcher

14 cm (5.5 in)

	SPECIES INFORMATION
SCIENTIFIC NAME	Muscicapa striata
RELATED SPECIES	Pied Flycatcher
CALL	Call a sharp 'pst' or 'tseck', or longer 'tees-tuck-tuck'. Song is an unremarkable series of squeaky notes
HABITAT	Light, broadleaved and mixed woodland, wooded pasture, parks, and larger gardens
STATUS	Summer visitor, wintering to tropical Africa. In BI about 150,000 pairs

SIZE

IDENTIFICATION

HABITAT

POPULATION

MAP

SLIM AND INCONSPICUOUS, with large, dark eyes and streaked crown. Grey-brown above, whitish and streaked below. Juveniles spotted above. Makes repeated agile forays from perch to catch insects in the air.

SPOTTED FLYCATCHERS ARE perhaps more typical of large gardens than of woodlands (or at least more often seen there) but, if there are good gaps among the trees, if it is a warm day and if you listen as well as look, you may easily find them. On colder days, rather than making their typical aerial flights, they have to make do with smaller insects or spiders in the trees. Perhaps it is a shortage of larger insects that has caused their population to fall to a quarter of its former level.

When Nicholson wrote in 1951 they were far more common, and he contrasted their style with that of other birds that lived off aerial insects. 'Instead of cruising about to seek the flies, midges, gnats, butterflies, moths or other insects on which it preys, the flycatcher picks some commanding perch and waits for its food to come along. Its design for living is only less economical than the spiders; its plumage, its posture, its haunts and its migrations are all determined by that design.'

The nest is a loosely built cup of twigs, rootlets, lichens, hair and feathers, sometimes in creepers or on top of a flat branch and sometimes in an open-fronted nest-box. As Nicholson points out, they are exceptional among strongly territorial birds in not having developed a territorial song, but they do spend a lot of time patrolling in their food search and can therefore chase off any intruders. They do have a contact alarm call but unless you know it well, it can seem much like a myriad of other bird sounds; if you do know it you will see many more spotted flycatchers.

Spotted flycatchers are long-distance migrants, wintering south of the equator and being one of the last of our summer migrants to arrive back in Britain. Their breeding area spreads over much of Europe, with the usual passerine gap in Iceland, and well into Asia. There seems to be a migratory divide, with birds from western Europe moving south-west towards Iberia, while Central European birds have a more easterly route through Italy and the Aegean.

Possibly habitat degradation or more plausibly a widespread use of insecticides have had their impacts on decreasing flycatcher populations. They also have to cross the Sahara twice a year. Anything that could stem the decline of this much-loved visitor would be welcome, and we can hope that the Nightingale Appeal helps us to find out more.

Spotted flycatchers were once much commoner, and have certainly declined in recent years – possibly due to problems encountered in their winter quarters.

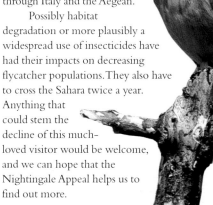

Pied Flycatcher

13 cm (5 in)

SPECIES INFORMATION

SCIENTIFIC NAME	Ficedula hypoleuca
RELATED SPECIES	Spotted Flycatcher, Collared Flycatcher and Red-breasted Flycatcher (both rare vagrants)
CALL	Alarm-call a sharp 'bit'. Song is an ascending and descending 'voo-ti-voo-ti-voo-ti', rather reminiscent of the Redstart's
HABITAT	Broadleaved, coniferous and mixed woodlands, parks and gardens (uses nest boxes in woodland)
STATUS	Summer visitor, wintering to West Africa. In B about 40,000 pairs, locally in north and west (virtually absent from Ireland)

MALE BLACK OR grey-brown above, white below, with clear white wing-patch and white spot on forehead. Female grey-brown above, wing-patch and underside dirty white. Winter male like female but with white forehead.

IN FOREST REFRESHED Norman Hickin writes how Professor Steele Elliot persuaded the pied flycatcher to nest in Wyre Forest by providing suitable but artificial nesting sites. 'In 1963, two pairs nested in an old overgrown orchard, their nearest neighbours being in the Forest of Dean. As we stood immobile against an old damson tree in the hedge, a cock, in his black and white, delighted us by fluttering down from a moss-covered crabapple and, hovering like a humming bird, picked a fly from a buttercup and then returned to his perch. The beauty of this little action was most exhilarating and I find myself recalling it to mind and reliving the breathless thirty seconds.'

Soon after Hickin's book, David Lack devoted a chapter of his *Population Studies of Birds* to the breeding of the pied flycatcher, and the main study area was the Forest of Dean from which Hickin's Wyre Forest birds had come.

Because of the ease with which nesting-boxes can be examined, the pied flycatcher was one of the earliest subjects of population studies in birds, and Lack points to two advantages over the great tit. It can freely be caught at the nest without deserting, and the black and white cock is readily distinguished from the much browner hen.

In summer, the pied flycatcher feeds on both caterpillars and adult insects. It can catch the adults in the air at times, but more often hunts for caterpillars in the foliage or drops on insects on the ground from a perch above. In the Forest of Dean, caterpillars formed about half the diet of one nest studied. Despite their liking for caterpillars, they usually breed two or three weeks after the great tits, thus missing the best caterpillar time. Yarner Wood, in Devon, is another good site for this species.

Despite scattered areas of breeding in France and Spain, where it prefers damp, hilly areas with sessile oak, they are essentially northern birds, and outside the Palearctic extend to Siberia. As long-distance migrants, wintering in West Africa, they have a major fattening area in Iberia so that initial migration direction is often south-west before turning south.

SIZE

IDENTIFICATION

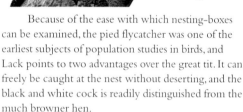

HABITAT

POPULATION

MAP

Pied flycatchers are birds of the western oakwoods. Their populations have been boosted locally by the use of nest boxes.

Garden Warbler

14 cm (5.5 in)

SPECIES INFORMATION	
SCIENTIFIC NAME	*Sylvia borin*
RELATED SPECIES	Blackcap, Whitethroat, Lesser Whitethroat, Dartford Warbler
CALL	'Vet-vet-vet' or 'tsharr'. Song is soft and musical, with blackbird-like phrases
HABITAT	Tall scrub, damp thickets, bushy woodland margins, woods and parks with rich undergrowth, large gardens
STATUS	Summer visitor. In BI about 200,000 pairs (about 200 in Ireland)

SIZE

IDENTIFICATION

HABITAT

POPULATION

MAP

PLUMP AND RATHER drab, with no obvious markings. Head rounded, bill relatively short. Grey-brown above, somewhat paler below, with the hint of an eye-stripe, and pale eye-ring. The garden warbler really has very little distinctive about it and as it skulks more it is vital to get familiar with the song.

THE DURATION OF the garden warbler's babble (perhaps an unkind word, but brook babbles are lovely) is much more prolonged but the song is softer, and lacking the rich variation of the blackcap's.

When counting birds in Chaddesley Woods in Worcestershire there were quite as many garden warblers as blackcaps, but in north Wales and in my Devon CBC plot blackcaps were, and are, much more common. They are both sylvia warblers with songs that are easy to muddle after a winter without them. *Sylvia* warblers are very much a feature of Mediterranean scrub, where they make up a much higher proportion of the bird community than they do in temperate scrub. In the south of France they can be the commonest birds in scrub of 1–6 m (3.2–19.7 ft) tall. The species concerned are dartford, sardinian and subalpine warblers and they, together with nightingales, can reach very high densities. Most Mediterranean *sylvia* warblers are resident, but of ours, the garden warbler and the two whitethroats are trans-Saharan migrants, the blackcap is a medium-distance migrant, and only the dartford warbler is resident.

Left
The garden warbler is one of our most featureless birds, but it has a very pleasant song, rather like a muted blackbird.

Right
Garden warblers like damp woodland with rich undergrowth.

Blackcap

14 cm (5.5 in)

```
○ ○ ○ ○ ○ ○ ○ ○ ○ ○ ○ ○ ○ ○ ○ ○ ○ ○ ○ ○ ○ ○
    S P E C I E S   I N F O R M A T I O N
```

SCIENTIFIC NAME	Sylvia atricapilla
RELATED SPECIES	Garden Warbler, Whitethroat, Lesser Whitethroat, Dartford Warbler
CALL	Alarm-call a hard 'tack'. Song is very pretty, starting with a soft twitter, and developing into a loud, clear fluting phrase (higher-pitched towards the end)
HABITAT	Open broadleaved and coniferous woodland, river-valley woodland, plantations, parks and gardens
STATUS	Summer visitor (some overwinter). In BI about 800,000 pairs

SIZE

IDENTIFICATION

HABITAT

POPULATION

MAP

GREY-BROWN, with cap black (male), or red-brown (female and juvenile). The blackcap's song period, as opposed to the length of the individual song, is longer than the garden warbler's, extending into July, but its loud wheatear-like 'tack' is to be heard for even longer as it searches among the blackberries in September.

BLACKCAPS TEND TO establish their territories before the arrival of garden warblers and they also choose slightly different sites. Garden warblers are more numerous in downland scrub and six- or seven-year old coppice scrub, while the blackcap is found in taller, older scrub and is more frequent in true woodland; garden warblers are often confined to

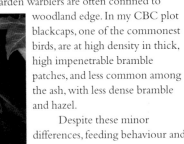

woodland edge. In my CBC plot blackcaps, one of the commonest birds, are at high density in thick, high impenetrable bramble patches, and less common among the ash, with less dense bramble and hazel.

Despite these minor differences, feeding behaviour and food itself seems much the same, with insects, in the breeding season, found mainly in the shrub layer, and fruit at other times. Blackcaps are quite happy to include berries, apples and even peanuts in their winter diet. Garden warbler nests tend to be a bit lower, in bramble or nettle, than blackcap's which may be in shrubs or a low branches.

Both male and female blackcaps have good diagnostic visual features and are quite happy to show them at times. Paler below than above, the cap is the distinctive feature, reaching down to the eye; in the female it is a rich russet.

Blackcaps turn up in gardens in winter much more than they used to. A German team, using lightweight coloured rings that could easily be spotted at bird feeders, found that many of their ringed birds ended up here and it turns out our small wintering population is completely different from the summering one.

Cannon, in the *Garden Bird Watch Handbook*, writes that 'Experiments show that migration direction in Blackcaps is genetically controlled and inherited, hence subject to natural selection. West European blackcaps migrate south-west and eastern birds south-east but in central Europe there is a small intermediate population which migrates north-west and so tended not to survive. However in the last forty years wintering conditions in Britain and Ireland seem to have improved, possibly helped by garden feeding, so instead of all these blackcaps dying, more and more of our wintering birds are surviving to breed the next spring and pass this unorthodox migration to their offspring.' This then is an opportunity to witness evolution in action.

Only the male blackcap has the black cap – that of the young birds and adult female is chestnut brown.

Wood Warbler

12.5 cm (5 in)

SPECIES INFORMATION	
SCIENTIFIC NAME	*Phylloscopus sibilatrix*
RELATED SPECIES	Willow Warbler, Chiffchaff
CALL	Alarm-call a soft 'diuh' or 'vit-vit-vit'. Song a descending trill, beginning 'sip-sip-sip-sipsirr...', often including melancholy whistling 'diuh-diuh-diuh-diuh'
HABITAT	Tall, open deciduous or mixed woodland (especially upland oak and beech)
STATUS	Summer visitor, wintering in Africa. In BI about 17,000 pairs, mainly in the west (the small Irish population of around 30 pairs is increasing)

SIZE

IDENTIFICATION

HABITAT

POPULATION

MAP

SOMEWHAT LARGER THAN willow warbler and chiffchaff, and with longer wings. Greenish upperparts contrast with yellow neck and breast, and with white belly. Yellow stripe over eye. The legs are yellowish. Lives mainly amongst the crowns of tall trees.

WOOD WARBLERS HAVE two somewhat different songs. The most common is the trill song, one of the joys of western oak woods, which is a delicate series of similar 'sip' or 'tip' units fusing into a shorter, faster shivering trill. The piping song, a slowing series of many piping 'few' notes descending in pitch is less frequent. Although western, it rarely reaches Ireland. Wood warblers have a special song flight around conspicuous branches within its territory. The bird starts to sing as it flies with shallow wing beats, keeps singing until it lands and finishes with a trill.

The wood warbler distribution coincides largely with upland oakwoods, usually with little ground cover, although beech stands are also favoured in some parts.

If *Sylvia* warblers present their difficulties, then *Phylloscopus* or leaf warblers can be a greater challenge. Our three have fairly distinct habitat preferences, but there are several more species between the British Isles and the Bering Straits, and another 15 in the mountain forests of the Himalayas and Burma.

These include a number of vagrants which sometimes reach us, notably the Arctic, greenish and yellow-browed warblers, which are pushing into Europe from Asia. Pallas's and Radde's warblers can turn up from Siberia, although Radde's extends to lake Baikal and Korea. Another vagrant, Bonelli's warbler, is from southern Europe.

W. H. Hudson describes the song of the wood warbler as 'long and passionate ... the woodland sound that is like no other'.

Top left and right
Wood warblers spend much of their time in the treetops, where their silvery song often betrays their presence.

Bottom right
Tall beechwoods are the favoured habitat in some areas.

Goldcrest

9 cm (3.5 in)

SPECIES INFORMATION	
SCIENTIFIC NAME	Regulus regulus
RELATED SPECIES	Firecrest
CALL	High-pitched 'sree-sree-sree-sree'. Song is short, very high-pitched, with a clear, somewhat deeper, end section: 'sesim-sesim-sesim-sesim-seritete'
HABITAT	Mainly coniferous forest or groups of conifers in mixed woodland, parks and gardens
STATUS	Resident and partial migrant. In BI about 860,000 pairs

TINY AND DUMPY – with firecrest, Europe's smallest bird. Olive-green above, with double white black-edged wing-bar. Head rather large, bill small and thin. Male has bright yellow crown, edged orange-red; female has light yellow crown. No stripe through or above eye. Juvenile lacks head markings.

IT IS PERHAPS odd, looking at the histograms in the Birds of Bardsey to see a clear spring peak, averaging 10–15 goldcrests a day, and an autumn one showing at least 20, from September through October. A small west coast island and yet the tiny goldcrests are moving through, sometimes in their hundreds. Most of our birds do not migrate, but an extra million goldcrests arrive in Britain in the autumn, at east coast observatories in far higher numbers than at Bardsey.

As the smallest bird in Europe, with a correspondingly high surface area to volume ratio, it loses heat very fast, and is extremely vulnerable to cold winters. Looking at BTO Common Bird Census indices the resulting fluctuations are clear, with a

huge fall in 1986 so that, on farmland, the index fell to around 20, a tenth of what it had been 12 years before, and a fifth of the previous year. Farmland being a secondary habitat, its fluctuations are greater than in woodland. The effects of cold weather vary considerably according to its duration and geographical pattern. Marchant *et al.* say of the goldcrest: 'Cold periods interrupted by brief thaws are less likely to prove damaging than those of continuous freeze, and temperatures probably matter less than snow and ice conditions. Also important is whether or not an ice-coating or hoarfrost persists on trees.' After its population decimation in the 1916–17 winter T. A. Coward wrote that the goldcrest 'could have little more than an obituary notice'.

The woods it prefers are coniferous, with optimum conditions in spruce, silver fir and pine, and goldcrests make good use of the many coniferous plantations around the country.

Goldcrests often visit gardens, but not bird tables, and you have a better chance of seeing them well there than in conifer plantations. Unless the bird is below you, the yellow-orange crown can be less clear than the dark eye, set in a pale face and two white wing bars. The olive back and buff below could well suggest a tiny warbler, but its acrobatic behaviour, in its constant search for minute insects and spiders, is really more tit-like.

SIZE

IDENTIFICATION

HABITAT

POPULATION

MAP

Top
Although goldcrests are quite tame, these tiny birds are hard to see as they flit about amongst the foliage of conifers.

Bottom
Only rarely do they come down to feed on the ground, or to drink or bathe at a puddle.

Willow Warbler

11 cm (4.25 in)

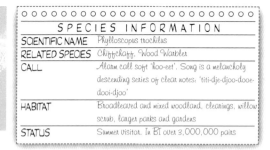

SPECIES INFORMATION	
SCIENTIFIC NAME	Phylloscopus trochilus
RELATED SPECIES	Chiffchaff, Wood Warbler
CALL	Alarm call soft 'hoo-eet'. Song is a melancholy descending series of clear notes: 'titi-dje-djoo-dooe-dooi-djoo'
HABITAT	Broadleaved and mixed woodland, clearings, willow scrub, larger parks and gardens
STATUS	Summer visitor. In BI over 3,000,000 pairs

SLIM AND DELICATE warbler; best separated from almost identical chiffchaff by its very distinct and pretty song. Somewhat yellower than chiffchaff, with clearer stripe over eye, and a less obvious eye-ring. Legs normally (but not always) light brown. Juvenile uniform yellowish below. The bill has a pinkish lower mandible and dark upper mandible. Our most numerous summer visitor.

WILLOW WARBLERS HAVE bright greenish-olive upperparts, yellow-white underparts and yellow-brown legs. Unless seen at close quarters, they are impossible to separate from chiffchaffs, except by song, and neither species is easy to observe as they flit quickly from leaf to leaf searching for insects and spiders.

Willow warblers are very adaptable, being found in heathy woodland, fen carr, and even large gardens with scattered trees. They can be very common in young conifer plantations, love birch woods and also thrive in a variety of scrub. They normally arrive in early April, leaving in late September. Most overwinter in tropical Africa, south of the Sahara.

T. A. Coward, on the willow warbler: 'a tender, delicious warbler with a dying fall – it mounts up round and full, then down the scale and expires upon the air in a gentle murmur.'

Chiffchaff

11 cm (4.25 in)

SPECIES INFORMATION	
SCIENTIFIC NAME	Phylloscopus collybita
RELATED SPECIES	Willow Warbler, Wood Warbler
CALL	Alarm-call 'hweet'. Song is a monotonous and somewhat irregular repetition of two notes 'chiff-chaff-chiff-chiff-chaff...'
HABITAT	Broadleaved and mixed woodland, with plenty of undergrowth, river-valley woodland, tall scrub, parks and gardens
STATUS	Summer visitor. In BI over 900,000 pairs

VERY LIKE WILLOW warbler, but looks less slim, with shorter wings, and more rounded head. Legs usually dark. Olive-brown above; underside whitish. The bill is dark, with a paler base and the eye has a thin white ring around it (compare willow warbler).

THE CHIFFCHAFF IS more of a true woodland bird, liking tall deciduous trees. Occasionally seen (or heard) in larger gardens. Chiffchaffs arrive early and this is often the first visitor to be heard, as early as

March. Some birds overwinter, but most migrate to the Mediterranean or Africa.

John Fowles wrote of 'newly arrived chiffchaffs and willow warblers singing in every bush and tree' in the *French Lieutenant's Woman*, but only the chiffchaff stays in any numbers in the Lyme Regis Undercliff where the book was set.

> '*The uncrested wren, called in this place chif-chaf is very loud …. It does only two piercing notes.*'
> Gilbert White

SPECIES INFORMATION	
SCIENTIFIC NAME	Parus palustris
RELATED SPECIES	Blue Tit, Great Tit, Coal Tit, Willow Tit, Crested Tit
CALL	'Pitchew' or 'psiche-che-che-che...' Song made up of rattling phrases such as 'tji-tji-tji-tji...' or 'tsivit-tsivit-tsivit...'
HABITAT	Broadleaved and mixed woodland, copses, parks and gardens
STATUS	Resident. In B about 140,000 pairs (absent from Ireland, and most of Scotland)

Marsh Tit

11.5 cm (4.5 in)

MARSH TITS ARE small and rather chunky, mainly a dull grey-brown, except for the extensive shiny black cap and white cheeks, and small black bib. They are best distinguished from the often similar-looking willow tit by their calls.

IN THE GARDEN Bird Watch Scheme marsh and willow tits are counted together because of their similarity but they do have rather different habitat preferences. Marsh tits tend to occur in open woodland, especially damp woods, copses, and in parks and gardens. The name marsh tit is not really suitable, for there is no need for dampness as long as it has open woodland with a rich understorey.

Marsh tits are great storers of food. They often cache seeds for a short time, generally a day or less, rather than storing them away for the winter. Their reason for hiding them thus may be to keep them from dominant great tits. Seeds are hidden among grass, moss or leaves. Marsh tits certainly take a lot of black sunflower seeds from bird tables, and are seen with them up to 200 m (656 ft) from the feeding station.

SPECIES INFORMATION	
SCIENTIFIC NAME	Parus montanus
RELATED SPECIES	Marsh Tit, Blue Tit, Great Tit, Coal Tit, Crested Tit
CALL	Characteristic nasal, buzzing 'chay-chay-chay'.
HABITAT	Damp woodland, especially alder and birch scrub, such as fen carr. Usually in wetter sites than marsh tit.
STATUS	Resident. In B about 60,000 pairs (absent from Ireland, and most of Scotland)

Willow Tit

11.5 cm 4.5 (in)

VERY SIMILAR TO marsh tit, but has a duller black cap, a larger black bib, and a pale wing panel. Often has a large-headed, or bullnecked appearance.

WILLOW TITS PREFER rather damp, scrubby areas of elder, alder and birch, with plenty of dead stumps. These are short-lived trees that rot rapidly, and therefore are good for nest excavation. Both marsh and willow tits nest in holes, but willow tits usually excavate their own, in rotten wood. In the nest there is less moss than is usual among tits and a lot of wood chippings may be used.

Long-tailed Tit

14 cm (5.5 in)

SPECIES INFORMATION	
SCIENTIFIC NAME	*Aegithalos caudatus*
RELATED SPECIES	No close relative in the region; bearded tit has similar shape
CALL	Flocks keep up contact calls: 'tserr, si-si-si'. Song is a thin trill
HABITAT	Woodland with rich undergrowth, often near water, parks and gardens
STATUS	Resident. In BI about 250,000 pairs

SIZE

IDENTIFICATION

HABITAT

POPULATION

MAP

VERY SMALL, BUT has long, graduated tail, making up more than half of total length. Broad, blackish stripe over eye (but note that the race found in north-east Europe has a pure white head). Juvenile has dark cheeks.

IF THEY COME, as they increasingly do, to food at a bird table, you can see, apart from a mass of tails, that they are not just black and white but have a rosy pink tinge to shoulders, flanks and belly. When they move they communicate with excited contact calls.

Chris Perrins (1979) examined studies of the preferred feeding areas for British tits. The long-tailed tit is usually found among the thinner twigs of the trees, pecking in and around the buds. It practically never comes down to the ground in its search for food. In Marley Wood, the year begins with most birds in oak and ash, but whereas oak remains popular (over 30 per cent of feeding birds) ash drops out of favour, spindle berries become important, and both birch and hawthorn have 10–5 per cent of feeding birds. Dependence on oak drops in April when the twigs and branches of ash, and maple hold food for more than 20 per cent of birds. By June, a wide range of trees are searched, with sycamore contributing the aphids which so often cluster on their leaves. In July and August birch is favourite, with hazel, maple and elder attracting over 10 per cent of feeding birds. In autumn, hawthorn is important. The value of a range of trees and shrubs to provide a selection of invertebrate foods at all times is evident. Long-tailed tits also eat a few seeds, the flesh of fruits, and sap exuded from broken branches of birch and maple.

Long-tailed tits are most familiar as extended family parties wandering through winter woods like so many flying teaspoons with their extraordinary tails as handles. If not flying teaspoons then perhaps 'bumbarrels'.

The long-tailed tit is an active, lively bird. They build delicate, oval nests, woven from mosses, lichens and spiders' webs.

'*And coy bumbarrels twenty in a drove*
Flit down the hedgrows in the frozen plain
And hang on little twigs and start again.'
John Clare EMMON SAILS HEATH IN WINTER

Coal Tit

11.5 cm (4.5 in)

SPECIES INFORMATION	
SCIENTIFIC NAME	Parus ater
RELATED SPECIES	Blue Tit, Great Tit, Marsh Tit, Willow Tit, Crested Tit
CALL	Contact-call is a high-pitched, thin 'see' or 'tsee-tsee-tsee'. Song is of repeated phrases such as 'tsevi-tsevi-tsevi' or 'sitiu-sitiu-sitiu'
HABITAT	Coniferous and mixed woods and in parks and gardens with conifers. Also found in broadleaved woods outside breeding season
STATUS	Resident. In BI about 900,000 pairs

SMALLEST EUROPEAN TIT, with a relatively large head, white cheeks and large white patch on the back of its neck. Grey above and buff below. Juveniles have yellowish undersides and cheeks. The coal tit's song is sprightly, repetitive and piping, and the alarm and contact calls are essentially based on units of the song.

SIZE

IDENTIFICATION

HABITAT

POPULATION

MAP

provided a chapter in Lack. In *Coal Tits in Breckland*, breeding success appeared to have little influence on the subsequent breeding population. After breeding, the population fell by about a half each autumn as tits dispersed to other habitats even if, at that time, there was still plenty of food in the conifers.

In a nine hour day an individual may search more than a thousand trees, taking ten food items from each, at a rate of one every 2.5 seconds.

COAL TITS ARE familiar visitors to many bird tables, identified by the white patch on the nape, contrasting with the black crown. The double white wing bars are often not noticed, and the overall impression, especially in flight, is of a dull grey-brown. Although associated with conifers, they turn up anywhere, advertising themselves with noisy calls. The very narrow bill is adept at searching for insects between conifer needles, and the ability to search for food under branches is useful when twigs are frozen.

Most early work on tits and the factors regulating their numbers was done on breeding populations, so a year-round study of coal tits

One of the best fieldmarks of the tiny coal tit is the white stripe along the back of its head.

143

Siskin

14 cm (4.75 in)

SPECIES INFORMATION	
SCIENTIFIC NAME	Carduelis spinus
RELATED SPECIES	Redpoll, Linnet, Goldfinch, Greenfinch
CALL	Melancholy 'tseelu'. Song a hurried twitter, with 'tooli' calls, and often ending in a sustained note
HABITAT	Spruce forests and mixed woods, especially in the mountains up to the tree-line and conifer plantations. In winter often feeds in birch and alder trees, and also visits bird tables (likes peanuts)
STATUS	Resident and partial migrant. In BI about 360,000 pairs

VERY SMALL, GREENISH-yellow finch, with dark wings and a yellow wing bar. Male has black crown and small black chin patch. Female is grey-green, more heavily streaked and without black on the head. Juvenile is browner above and even more heavily streaked.

A FEW DECADES ago siskins were not often seen outside their scattered breeding sites in upland coniferous woods (mainly in Scotland), but they have

increased markedly in recent years, and have now spread to many mature plantations. There have been major expansions in Wales, southern Scotland and in and around the New Forest, and increases also in Ireland and in the Breckland of East Anglia.

Another major change is that they have become garden birds, frequently coming to feed, even during the summer if the garden is near conifers, especially on peanuts. Surprisingly, they can even 'see off' greenfinches at the bird table. When feeding you may

notice their sharp beaks, very different from the greenfinch as it is adapted for feeding in conifers, extracting tiny food items from tight spaces.

Siskins are very attractive birds at close quarters, with their intricate pattern of black and yellow on the wings and tail. The male has black crown and bib, streaked green upperparts and broad yellow wing bars. The female has no cap or bib but is more streaked and has a pale lemon chest. There are even more spots and streaks on young birds. Siskins are also attractively acrobatic as they feed at the tops of birches or alders. The song is thin and high, but has a peculiar yodelling quality with a characteristic 'dluee' note and often a strange wheezing note at the ends of phrases.

> '*They fed wholly on the alder and looked beautiful, hanging like little parrots, picking at the drooping seeds of that tree.*'
> J. Thompson
> NATURAL HISTORY OF IRELAND

Siskins are often attracted to peanuts, especially in cold winter weather. They are aggressive birds, and will often keep away larger species from the bird table.

Redpoll
13 cm (5 in)

```
○ ○ ○ ○ ○ ○ ○ ○ ○ ○ ○ ○ ○ ○ ○ ○ ○ ○ ○ ○ ○ ○ ○
```
SPECIES INFORMATION
SCIENTIFIC NAME	*Carduelis flammea*
RELATED SPECIES	*Siskin, Linnet, Goldfinch, Greenfinch*
CALL	*Flight-call is a rapid, buzzing 'dshe-dshe-dshe'. Alarm-call a nasal, drawn out 'vaiid'. Song is a twitter mixed with buzzing notes and musical whistles*
HABITAT	*Moorland and heath, especially with birch, alder and willow scrub, and lowland coniferous plantations. Also northern and mountain birch and coniferous woodland. Increasingly in gardens*
STATUS	*Resident and partial migrant. In BI about 230,000 pairs.*

A VERY SMALL finch with grey-brown, streaked plumage, red forehead and black chin. Breeding male also has pink on breast. Juvenile lacks red.

REDPOLLS ARE STREAKY little brown finches with yellow bills and deeply notched tails. Breeding males have plenty of pink on breast and rump, while the female has a brownish rump and virtually no pink except for the forecrown. At times the pale wing bars become conspicuous, but very often colour is less important in identification than bouncy flight of busy feeding parties noisily calling as they move among birches or riverside alders.

further explanation. There was certainly a time when redpolls seemed everywhere if you knew their flight call, that used to fill the birchwoods or young forestry plantations.

For students of variation or collectors of records of rare subspecies, redpolls are ideal, and some of the races have even gained long-standing English names. Our race, found in Europe and Southern Sweden and Norway, is the lesser redpoll, which is smaller than a Linnet, whereas the mealy redpoll from further north is linnet-sized. The Greenland race is larger still. The Arctic redpoll, or Hornemann's redpoll, is regarded as a separate species.

Redpolls feed on seeds whose supply varies, and the birds generally concentrate wherever their food is plentiful at the time. Thus their numbers in particular localities fluctuate from year to year, partly in response to changes in local seed crops.

In recent years, redpoll levels have risen roughly four-fold from the mid 1960s through the 1970s, but after 1980 a downward trend began, and by 1990 levels were back to those of the late 1960s. The rises coincide with the age of many conifer plantations but the falls, which have continued, need

SIZE

IDENTIFICATION

HABITAT

POPULATION

MAP

Redpolls are lively little finches, often seen in gardens as well as in woodland and heathland.

Common Crossbill

16.5 cm (6.5 in)

SPECIES INFORMATION	
SCIENTIFIC NAME	Loxia curvirostra
RELATED SPECIES	Scottish Crossbill, Parrot Crossbill
CALL	'Gip-gip-gip', also a soft 'tjook'. Song is rather like that of Greenfinch, with repeated phrases and twitters
HABITAT	Coniferous woodland, especially spruce forests or plantations
STATUS	Resident. Occasionally shows population irruptions, after which may range widely. In BI population at least 1,000 pairs (variable)

SIZE

IDENTIFICATION

HABITAT

POPULATION

MAP

DUMPY AND RATHER large-headed finch, with short, forked tail, and crossed mandibles. Adult male is brick-red; female olive-green with yellow rump. Juvenile heavily streaked.

CROSSBILLS SHOW ONE of the most marked sexual dimorphisms, the adult male being rusty red and the female greenish-yellow. Both sexes are chunky, with a blunt-looking head and short forked tail so outline is very characteristic as they pass with bounding finch flight. A good look at a male will show a red bird with a brighter red rump, whereas the female is greener above and yellowish below, with a clear greenish-

The rare Scottish crossbill of the native pine forest is our only endemic bird. Another relative, the slightly larger parrot crossbill has a heavier and deeper bill. It is an occasional visitor to Britain, and has bred.

yellow rump. Young birds are coarsely streaked above and below, without the colour of either bird. All of them have the distinctive crossed mandibles, with which they deftly extract the seeds from cones – mainly spruce in the case of the common crossbill.

At the time of the last *Atlas* there was breeding evidence of crossbills in 462 squares in Britain and Ireland, they were present in another 457 squares. There are large numbers in Scotland included plenty outside the range of the Scottish crossbill. Common crossbills also have concentrations in the developing forests of Wales, in Breckland and in the New Forest and Kielder Forest. In Ireland, common crossbills are beginning to colonise the conifer plantations.

The crossed mandibles of the crossbill enable it to probe between the scales of pine cones and extract the edible seeds.

SPECIES INFORMATION	
SCIENTIFIC NAME	Coccothraustes coccothraustes
RELATED SPECIES	Other finches
CALL	Sharp 'tsik'. Song (rarely heard) is a jerky, tinkling mixture of call-like notes
HABITAT	Broadleaved and mixed woodland, parks and gardens with tall deciduous trees
STATUS	Resident and partial migrant. In B about 4,000 pairs, mainly in SE (absent from Ireland)

Hawfinch

18 cm (7 in)

LARGE, HEAVY-BODIED finch with large head and very large bill. Female has slightly duller plumage. Juvenile brownish-yellow. Looks thick-set in flight, and shows pale areas on wings, and white tip to tail. Rather shy.

HAWFINCHES SEEM TO have decreased but it is not an easy bird to census, or even to see, and once again the calls, explosive tickings, must be known. The massive head and bill, bull-neck and short tail combine to give the birds a stocky, top heavy appearance. The general coloration appears orange-brown with mainly blackish wings and large white shoulder patches. In the male the head is chestnut, the nape pale grey and the back a rich brown, while the underparts are pinkish-brown shading to white beneath the tail.

The flight feathers are iridescent and close observation, in the hand, shows the four inner-

primaries to be notched and curled at the ends. Like many special features, in this case shown by no other finch, these are used in courtship.

The internal structure of the hawfinch's beak is one of the secrets of its capacity to deal with hard objects. There are ridges on the palate, and behind them a pair of knobs which overlie a similar pair in the lower jaw. Large seeds are held between these four knobs and the strain of cracking the seeds is shared by the muscles on both sides. The four knobs are horny and do not develop immediately as young birds are fed on insects and softer seeds.

SIZE

IDENTIFICATION

HABITAT

POPULATION

MAP

This largest of our finches has a truly massive bill, strong enough to crack open even cherry stones. Hawfinches are shy birds and are seldom spotted.

Farmland, Downland and Heathland Birds

FARMING SYSTEMS HAVE produced some of our most distinctive habitats: lowland heaths, chalk downs and upland moors have all been produced by grazing. The moors will be considered with the rest of the uplands, but downs and heaths fit in best here. On the whole, farmland means fields and their associated hedges or walls, and the farm buildings and copses which are part of the agricultural scene.

FIELDS HAVE ALWAYS been liable to change, in size and shape and in arable to pasture ratio. Modern agriculture started in earnest in the eighteenth century, with population doubling and a move to the towns creating the first need for commercial agriculture.

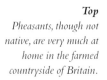

Top
Pheasants, though not native, are very much at home in the farmed countryside of Britain.

Bottom left
Sparrowhawks were very badly hit by the use of toxic pesticides applied to crops.

Bottom right
The sterile landscape of herbicide-treated fields.

EFFECTS OF MODERN FARMING

CHANGES IN FARMING practice have had dramatic effects on the birdlife of farmland, notable effects being the loss of permanent pasture in many regions, stubble burning and ploughing, which reduces seed and insect levels, and the disappearance of corn ricks and chaff heaps, reducing food for finches in particular. The use of chemical pesticides has also taken its toll of wildlife.

From a wildlife point of view, the declines of grain-eating birds, stock doves, pheasants and partridges, following the treatment of cereal seed with organochlorine insecticides, aimed at pests such as wireworms and wheat bulbfly, initiated public concern. Soon predators such as sparrowhawks, badgers and foxes, died, and evidence from autopsies and laboratory feeding experiments showed that dieldrin, taken by the grain-eating birds and small mammals, was being passed through the food-web with lethal effects. Population declines of peregrines, sparrowhawks and kestrels were observed.

POPULATION DECREASES

MOST FARMLAND BIRDS have decreased in the last 30 years. The birds have less food because of herbicide use which is effectively cumulative, depleting the seed bank in the soil. Seeds on the surface of newly ploughed land, as on vegetable patches, used to

Hedges are of great importance for the birds of farmland, as they provide shelter, food and nesting sites for many species, and are home to insects and plant life. Old hedges, with their variety of trees and shrubs, are of particular value, though any hedge is better than none at all.

Some 289,674 km (180,000 miles) of hedges have been removed since 1940, and although 450,604 km (280,000 miles) remain, hedgerows continue to be lost at a rate of 3,218 km (2,000 miles) a year. Just as bad is the quality of many that remain, leggy, over-cut or neglected, which has contributed to significant declines of not only many farmland birds, but also plants and butterflies.

number thousands per square metre, but have now almost disappeared in cereal growing regions. The best documented example of population effects through reduction of food supply concerns the grey partridge. Field trials with reduced herbicide use have led to increased weed and insect populations, better chick survival and greater partridge densities. Once again it can be demonstrated that it is possible to reverse population trends, but much depends on economics as well as effective research.

Species of open country, such as the skylark, have suffered particularly through changing land use. Thus, since 1970, the UK population of skylarks has declined by some 68 per cent. They are not alone, for 10 species monitored by the Common Bird Census decreased by more than half in the 25 years up to 1994, and were danger-listed by the conservation organisations in their leaflet *Birds of Conservation Concern* (1996). Tree sparrow, partridge, cornbunting, linnet, song thrush and lapwing populations have all halved in that time.

DOWNLAND AND HEATH

DOWNLAND AND HEATH are also, in the main, the creation of man; of his work long ago when chalk was the easiest land for Neolithic man to clear, and where his burial barrows and hill forts remind us of his activities. Heathland was also created by clearance, but because of its acid soil produces very different plants. It also often shows signs of stone-age man. Neither of these habitats suffered from hedgerow removal nor from the direct results of insecticides, but they have suffered other pressures, with ploughing and house building being the most widespread. Even so, our remaining fragments of these two vulnerable habitats are the most extensive in Europe, and a valuable heritage.

Top
Skylark numbers have dropped alarmingly with recent changes in land use.

Middle
A healthier landscape, with grazed fields and well-maintained hedges.

Bottom
Lapwing numbers have halved in the last 25 years.

PRESERVATION OF DOWNLANDS

SHEEP USED TO maintain much of the chalk of southern England as well-grazed grassland and extensive flower meadows. The shepherd's life involved bringing the sheep back to the farm at night, where their droppings would fertilise the fields by the house. By day, watched by the shepherd, they could drift across the extensive grasslands.

Because remaining chalk grassland is mainly on steep slopes, we tend to forget that the downs used to reach extensively across the lowlands, as they still do for example on Salisbury Plain. Army activities here

land encircled by Neolithic hill forts has often been ploughed, and on this flinty land nothing would grow without the heavy use of fertilisers. Some of downland turf, full of orchids and vetches, yellow-wort and rock-rose, may survive on the round, raised, rim of the fort, along with some butterflies, but in limited areas like this, isolation from other suitable habitat may lead to their extinction.

The magnificent great bustard (now sadly extinct in Britain) once roamed on Salisbury Plain, and that classic downland bird, the stone curlew, has sometimes seemed to be going that way too. It was

Top

Chalk downland provides excellent habitat for a range of birds, including skylark and kestrel. Sadly, much has now been ploughed and planted with crops, as in the foreground.

have saved the Plain from the plough and from fertilisation, just as they have on Lulworth ranges in Dorset. Similarly, Porton Down, with its restricted access, has preserved some of the best downland in Europe for flowering plants and butterflies. In most other areas, except for a few nature reserves, downland is fragmented and limited to steep slopes which the plough cannot reach. Even the enclosed

never great birding country, too dry and too uniform, but lapwings, larks and wheatears loved it. Among the shrubs which would always have been invading, corn buntings would rattle and linnets dance. Martin Down near Salisbury, Wiltshire, is still excellent for nightingales, and one can still see the occasional wintering hen harrier or short-eared owl on the Berkshire Downs.

Bottom left

Skylark at its nest hidden amongst ground vegetation.

Bottom right

The cock linnet is a handsome bird when seen at close quarters.

been in the past: 'Heathland was much more prominent in Anglo Saxon England than it is today. There are 14 places called Flatfield, Heathfield or Hadfield (field being Old English field, an open space), at least 15 called Hadley or Headley (heath-clearing), and others called Hatton (heath town). More than 100 place names allude to broom (Brampton, Bramley, Bromley) and 26 to gorse (or furze or whin). These show that

Top

Lowland heath, with clumps of heather in the foreground. Another semi-natural habitat which has sadly reduced in extent over recent decades.

DAMAGE TO HEATHLAND

THE PLOUGH HAS damaged much heathland, particularly in war at a time of food shortage, but more recently it has been seen as land for forestry or for housing – too unproductive for the farmer but still in demand. The loss of much of the Dorset heathland, largely due to the expansion of Bournemouth, has been frequently described, but now, at last, there are moves to conserve much existing heath and to restore, usually from forestry, past heathland.

Neolithic man probably started the process of heathland creation, and there must have been factors acting against trees if heath was to remain open. Human factors, fire and grazing, seem most likely, or perhaps the absence of trees led to still further deterioration and acidification of the soils.

In the nineteenth century, when transport improved, it became possible to obtain fuel, timber, animal feed and fertilisers from elsewhere, and the use of the heaths began to decline. Since then heathlands have been neglected, scrub and bracken have invaded and the vegetation composition has changed.

BIRDS OF THE HEATHLAND

IN WINTER, DEPENDING on the heath, one might find wrens, meadow pipits, stonechats and Dartford warblers and an occasional predator, while summer could be more productive with linnets and willow warblers and perhaps tree pipits, nightjars and hobbys, with a chance of woodlarks.

Oliver Rackham (1944) concludes how much more widespread heathland must have

heathland occurred all over Anglo Saxon England and lowland Scotland.' No doubt these heaths would have had their populations of black grouse and red-backed Shrikes.

Although heathlands are not as important for birds as they are, for instance, for reptiles and for invertebrates like silver-studded blue butterflies, dragonflies, and species of grasshopper, their birdlife does have plenty of interest, and heathland has enormous amenity value as well. Management is therefore often vital to reduce bracken, with rotational burning on large sites to maintain heather plots of different ages. Hardy native ponies and certain rare sheep breeds may also be good for long term grazing regime.

Middle

The resident Dartford warbler is virtually restricted to mature lowland heath in Britain, where it is at the northern limit of its range.

Bottom

Stonechats are typical birds of scrub and heathy habitats.

151

Kestrel

28–32 cm (11–13 in)

SPECIES INFORMATION	
SCIENTIFIC NAME	*Falco tinnunculus*
RELATED SPECIES	Merlin, Hobby, Peregrine
CALL	High-pitched rapid 'kikikiki'
HABITAT	Open countryside, breeding in trees in fields and at woodland edges. Also in rocky country, and in villages and cities
STATUS	Resident. In BI about 60,000 pairs

SIZE

IDENTIFICATION

HABITAT

POPULATION

MAP

COMMONEST SMALL BIRD of prey, often seen by main roads; hovers frequently. Small falcon with long tail, long, pointed wings and brown upperparts. Male has weakly speckled red-brown back, grey head, and grey tail with broad terminal band. Female uniformly red-brown, with barred upperparts.

THE STREAKED UNDERPARTS and a black band near the tip of the tail are visible when overhead, while the pointed wings help to distinguish it from sparrowhawk. The facial pattern is not striking, but a dark 'moustache' below the eye shows on all birds.

Kestrels are highly adaptable and are, perhaps, most familiar hovering over motorway verges where vole populations are high. As small mammals are widespread so are kestrels, hunting over waste ground and farmland, where they breed in old trees or outbuildings.

It is amazing to think of the levels of persecution that kestrels used to suffer in the game preserving era. Despite this, with good-sized broods and breeding in their first year they always kept their numbers up, except for a dip, in southern and eastern England, in the pesticide era of 1960–63. As they have always been ready to use railway sidings and industrial wasteland there were always safe populations even in the most intensively farmed parts of England.

Its range is widespread, including much of Asia and sub-Saharan Africa, with a large part of the northern and eastern populations moving to, for instance, Angola, Zambia and Malawi in the winter. There are areas it avoids, dense forests, precipitous mountains and treeless wetlands, but if there are small mammals that can be seen from the air kestrels are likely to be there. Attenborough (1998) reports on how some species of bird can see over a wider colour spectrum than we can and of how it is useful to a kestrel to be able to detect ultra-violet light. Voles mark their tracks through the grass with squirts of urine, which reflect ultra-violet light. This in turn, is detectable by a hunting kestrel.

Kestrels can be quite noisy, particularly when the young are exercising their wings and there is a possibility of nest disturbance.

> '... by the Two Brewers pub I watched them – flickering arrowheads – quartering their territory on chestnut-red, slender wings and hovering at bus roof height.'
> Kenneth Allsop SUNDAY TIMES MAGAZINE

Bottom left

This kestrel shows the long tail and pointed wings so typical of falcons.

Bottom right

By hovering into an updraft or headwind, the kestrel can keep its head perfectly still as it searches the ground below for signs of small mammals such as voles.

Hobby

28–35 cm (11–14 in)

SPECIES INFORMATION

SCIENTIFIC NAME	*Falco subbuteo*
RELATED SPECIES	Kestrel, peregrine, merlin
CALL	'Kew-kew-kew' and 'ki-ki-ki-ki'
HABITAT	Wooded country with heathland, damp meadows and lakes or gravel pits. Breeds in light woodland, at forest edges and in lone trees in fields
STATUS	Summer visitor. In BI mainly in S and E England, where increased in recent years (from about 60 pairs in 1950s to over 1,000 pairs in the 1990s)

FLIGHT OUTLINE LIKE a large swift. Kestrel-sized, but with shorter tail and long, sickle-shaped wings. Upperparts blue-grey, head with conspicuous moustache. Leg feathers and under tail coverts rusty-red.

HOBBIES TOO CAN be highly vocal when greeting during courtship or warning young. The piercing call is difficult to describe.

The hobby has specialised requirements, and is a bird of heaths and farmland with scattered pine and preferably a good population of dragonflies. If more poets knew about them there would be writings on the flight of these experts who can even catch swifts and swallows after pursuit on swept-back wings; these manoeuvres can even make it look like a swift. With this diet and the odd bat and any bird rash enough to have an aerial song flight, it is not surprisingly a summer visitor, returning late to northern Europe from southern Africa. A lot of farmland breeding hobbies are probably overlooked, and populations may be higher than we think.

Hobbies are elegant and long-winged, with heavily streaked underparts, rufous under the tail and upper legs and with head markings that recall peregrine.

SIZE

IDENTIFICATION

HABITAT

POPULATION

MAP

It has a fast and regular wing action when hunting birds, but will almost close the wings as it stoops. When hunting insects the flight pattern is different, slower and with flatter wing-beats, occasionally almost stalling to catch its prey. When perched, it has an upright posture and the wing tips reach the end of the short tail.

The hobby is slimmer and more delicately built than the kestrel. It can catch dragonflies and other airborne insects in its nimble talons.

Grey Partridge

30 cm (12 in)

SIZE

IDENTIFICATION

HABITAT

POPULATION

MAP

SPECIES INFORMATION

SCIENTIFIC NAME	Perdix perdix
RELATED SPECIES	Red-legged Partridge, Pheasant, Grouse
CALL	Alarm call a loud 'kerriptiptip'. Territorial males make a hoarse, repeated 'girreck', mainly in morning and evening
HABITAT	Lowland cultivated country, with agricultural fields, pasture, hedges and overgrown field margins, also heaths
STATUS	Resident. In Britain rather rare in extreme west. Rare in Ireland. Declining due to more intensive cultivation and decrease in food and cover

SMALL AND DUMPY, with short tail. Rusty-brown stripes on flank, and dark, horseshoe-shaped patch on breast. Flight rapid. Glides with wings bowed.

GREY PARTRIDGES ARE dumpy runners and fast, noisy fliers. The vermiculated brown and grey plumage of the body contrasts with the orange head and grey neck. Males, and some females, show a dark lower breast. The absence of flank bars separate both from red-legged partridges, and in flight the grey partridge is paler on the back and wings.

Richard Jefferies writing in 1879 when partridges were abundant, adds partridges 'to the number of those birds whose call is more or less apparently ventriloquial; for when they are assembling in the evening at their roosting place their calls in the stubble often sound some way to the right or left of the real position of the bird, which presently appears emerging from the turnips ten or fifteen yards further up than was judged by the ear.' This call is a repeated metallic 'girreck' used as self advertisement or threat, with other calls to summon a mate, gather the chicks or when suspicious.

Grey partridges are widespread but declining in Europe and into central Asia; their natural distribution pattern is often confused by sporting introductions. Apart from the cover that it needs, some bare dusty ground, which can be ploughed land, is enjoyed. For most of the year the food is plant material, green leaves, cereals and clover and grain and weed seeds, particularly bistorts if available.

Top left

A partridge stretches upwards to deliver its hoarse territorial call.

Bottom

Partridges are rather shy birds which skulk close to the ground for long periods, flying reluctantly.

Nests are on the ground, often in hedge bottoms and are shallow depressions lined with grass and leaves. The clutch size is large, sometimes more then 24.

As long ago as 1951 Nicholson was able to say that partridges were 'like many other birds, increasingly troubled by the inconsiderate tendencies of farmers to mess about with their farms in spring and early summer, when complete quiet is desirable, and to seek to tidy up and bring into cultivation all sorts of rough fringes and waste patches which their forefathers were content to leave untouched from generation to generation.'

He describes the partridge as being 'the most content of all our birds to stay on the earth, and moreover to stay on that part of the earth where they first saw the light. Strong on the wing though they are, they rarely seem to fly farther than across a few fields or higher than they must to clear some ground obstacle.'

Grey Partridges were at one time so common that, had it not declined, it would now be the tenth most common species in Britain and Ireland.

Extensive research has shown that chick survival rates can be increased by the use of unsprayed 'conservation headlands' or by the traditional system of undersowing cereals with a ley pasture. This system is of great benefit to sawflies, a favourite chick food.

Red-legged Partridge

33 cm 13 (in)

SPECIES INFORMATION	
SCIENTIFIC NAME	*Alectoris rufa*
RELATED SPECIES	Grey Partridge, Pheasants, Grouse
CALL	'Chuk-chuk-ar', also a grating 'shreck-shreck'
HABITAT	Prefers dry, stoney fields, sandy heaths, also chalk downland
STATUS	Resident. Introduced to Britain where commonest in south and east

ROUNDED SHAPE, BARRED flanks and distinctive white, black-bordered face mask. Flies low, with wings bowed.

THE INTRODUCED RED-LEGGED partridge, which in 1950 was outnumbered by grey-partridge by twenty to one, is now the commoner species. The first recorded introduction here was in 1673, and a successful colonisation from Sussex started in 1790. It can cope with dry mountain foothills, marginal cultivation and all kinds of arable land.

Its distinctive barred flanks, red legs and bill and rufous chest separate it from the grey partridge. It likes the drier south-east, and fields of sugar-beet, but is adaptable over its range.

The *Concise BWP* describes aspects of its behaviour as 'territorialism announced by a "steam engine call" delivered in upright posture with swollen throat. In aggressive self assertive displays, given by male to opponent or mate and by female to male or female intruders, birds stands sideways on, with head held high, drawn back, and inclined away from object of display, white bib and black borders erected and twisted towards it.' The steam engine or advertising call of the male is described as 'go chak-chak-chak go chak-go chak chak' and a rally call as a harsh, grating 'go chok-chok-chokorrr'.

 SIZE

 IDENTIFICATION

 HABITAT

 POPULATION

 MAP

The handsome red-legged partridge is sometimes known as the French partridge as it was introduced to Britain from the continent.

Pheasant

55–85 cm (22–33 in)

SPECIES INFORMATION	
SCIENTIFIC NAME	Phasianus colchicus
RELATED SPECIES	Golden Pheasant, Lady Amherst's Pheasant; Partridges, Grouse
CALL	Male has explosive 'gergock', often followed by wing flapping
HABITAT	Cultivated areas, edges of light woodland, reedy areas and fen carr
STATUS	Resident. Introduced to Europe, mainly for 'sport'

SIZE

IDENTIFICATION

HABITAT

POPULATION

MAP

MALE HAS STRIKING, bronze plumage, red face wattle, shiny green neck (sometimes with white ring) and a very long, pointed tail. Female is yellow-brown with dark speckles, and somewhat shorter tail.

It can run extremely fast, and when running carries its tail a little above the horizontal: the faster the run the more vertical the position of the tail. The flight is strong, direct and fast – but in my experience nothing like as fast as that of blackcock.'

' Feasants were brought into Europe from about the Caspian Sea. There are no feasants in Spaine, nor do I heare of any in Italy.'
John Aubrey
NATURAL HISTORY OF WILTSHIRE

EVERYONE RECOGNISES THE pheasant, a bird of arable land and woodland edge, whose numbers are maintained at a high level by breeding and release for shooting interests. Its explosive flight when disturbed, the male's green head and, usually, white neck ring, and the cryptically coloured female with shorter tail, are all well known.

Vesey Fitzgerald (1946) describes 'its normal gait as a walk, not unlike that of the domestic fowl only more stately, and it flies only on extreme provocation, much preferring to crouch in cover.

It is hard to believe that pheasants were introduced, since they are now so much a part of the country scene. Most populations are still fed food supplements to keep them going, and they are vulnerable to hard weather.

Lapwing

30 cm (12 in)

SPECIES INFORMATION	
SCIENTIFIC NAME	*Vanellus vanellus*
RELATED SPECIES	Golden Plover, Grey Plover
CALL	Whiny, hoarse 'peewee' or 'kee-vit'; wings make humming noises in courtship flight
HABITAT	Damp meadows, bogs, coastal pasture, wet heath, fields and farmland
STATUS	Resident and partial migrant in BI. Commonest breeding wader in BI, about 250,000 pairs

BLACK AND WHITE plumage, with long, curved crest on head. Female has shorter crest and paler chin. Outside breeding season upperside paler and crest shorter. Tumbling courtship flight in spring. Forms large flocks in the autumn and winter (sometimes with black-headed gulls and golden plovers).

THE LAPWING IS indeed a handsome bird, whether as a black and white aerial acrobat or as a crested wader. The green and iridescent upper parts, black throat and breast-band, long crest and cinnamon under tail coverts make it a very special bird. Because of their diet of ground-living invertebrates they were much loved by farmers, who often marked the position of their nests so that they could avoid them.

Over the period of 1962 to 1982 there was a steady decline in lapwing numbers in areas of England and Wales dominated by cereals. Lapwings prefer nesting on spring-tilled land but like to be able to move their chicks to grassland for feeding; old style mixed farming thus suiting them well. As lapwings protect their eggs by aggressive defence of their nest site a need to see approaching predators is critical, which may be one reason they prefer relatively bare to well vegetated areas. With the switch from spring-sown cereals, crops are taller at breeding time and breeding densities and clutch size are both lower. Autumn sowing brings changes, with

many tractor visits using tram-lining techniques to spread autumn herbicides, early nitrogen dressings and foliar fungicides.

Adults disperse from many breeding areas as early as late May or June, moving west long before the juveniles who move west or south-west on a broad front from September to November. Many coastal areas therefore get their highest populations in early winter before colder weather has driven birds west to Ireland or south to Iberia or north Africa.

'Upon approaching the old bird flies up, circles round, and comes so near as almost to be within reach, whistling 'pee-wit, pee-wit' over your head. He seems to tumble in the air as if wounded and scarcely able to fly; and those who are not aware of his intention may be tempted to pursue, thinking to catch him. But so soon as you are leaving the nest behind he mounts higher, and wheels off to a distant corner of the field uttering an ironical 'peewit' as he goes.

Then you have a good opportunity of observing the peculiar motion of their wings, which seem to strike simply downwards and not also backwards, as with other birds; it is a quick jerking movement, the wing giving the impression of pausing the tenth of a second at the finish of the strike before it is lifted again. If you pass on a short distance and make no effort to find the nest, they recover confidence and descend. When the peewit alights he runs along a few yards rapidly, as if carried by the impetus. He is a handsome bird, with a well marked crest.' Jeffries (1879)

SIZE

IDENTIFICATION

HABITAT

POPULATION

MAP

Top
When seen at close range the lapwing is a striking bird, with its unusual upturned crest.

Middle
Lapwings have broad wing-tips and a characteristic floppy flight.

Bottom
For its nest it makes just a simple scrape on the ground.

157

Woodpigeon

41 cm (16 in)

SPECIES INFORMATION	
SCIENTIFIC NAME	Columba palumbus
RELATED SPECIES	Stock Dove, Rock Dove and Feral Pigeon
CALL	Owl-like 'goo-goo-gu-gootoo'. Also loud wing-clapping when flushed, and in courtship flight
HABITAT	Woods, meadows and fields (often in trees at field margins). Increasingly in urban parks
STATUS	Resident. In BI about 3,520,000 pairs

SIZE

IDENTIFICATION

HABITAT

POPULATION

MAP

LARGE PIGEON WITH white patches on wings and neck, visible in flight. Longer-tailed than the rock dove or feral pigeon. Often form large flocks on fields outside breeding season.

ALTHOUGH WOODPIGEONS WERE originally woodland birds, they have adapted well to changes brought about by agriculture. Pigeons and doves can feed on a wholly vegetarian diet, even when they have young, for they can secrete protein-rich 'pigeon's milk' from their crops.

The major arable farming areas of Britain used to have extensive cereal stubbles which could be searched as a prelude to the winter cereal sowings. It is interesting that earlier attempts to limit Woodpigeon numbers failed, because autumn shooting, by reducing numbers, made relatively more food available for the survivors. Shortage of food between January and March is the limiting factor on population growth. Woodpigeons may be no more popular with gardeners than with farmers, being very destructive of cabbages and some other vegetables.

Woodpigeons flock to farmland and fields, but are equally at home in woodland and, increasingly, in parks and larger gardens.

Unlike other pigeons and doves they will take green leaves, even when there is a good supply of alternative foods, like seeds or acorns.

While many country folk may not like woodpigeons, many town-dwellers love them for their size, gently contrasting colours and character. In open space the flight is fast and direct and the white wing-patches show clearly. On the ground, the white neck-patches and pink chests make them attractive at close quarters.

Woodpigeons build bulky nests, usually in large trees, but in other respects they have now become birds of farmland as much as woods, with a more recent move to towns. It is interesting that urban birds, perhaps because of increased light and warmth, but also because of a ready supply of food at a time of shortage in the country, may breed somewhat earlier than rural birds.

Most people know, and many love, the assorted 'coos'. Some of these are associated with the impressive territory-holding display flight when, after a clatter of wings as the bird rises steeply, it glides down gently with tail spread.

> '*Coo – coo – coo*
> *It's as much as a pigeon can do,*
> *to bring up two;*
> *but the little wren can maintain ten*
> *and keep them all like gentlemen.'*
> TRADITIONAL

SIZE

IDENTIFICATION

HABITAT

POPULATION

MAP

SPECIES INFORMATION

SCIENTIFIC NAME	Columba oenas
RELATED SPECIES	Rock Dove, Feral Pigeon and Woodpigeon
CALL	Alarm call a short 'kru'. Song (heard as early as March) is a quiet, rapidly repeated 'gooo-roo, gooo-roo, gooo-roo'
HABITAT	Deciduous and mixed woodland and parks with old standard trees. Also in trees at field margins and orchards. Nests in holes in trees and needs open country nearby for feeding. Outside breeding season often flocks to fields
STATUS	Resident. In BI about 270,000 pairs

Stock Dove

33 cm (13 in)

RESEMBLES GREY FERAL pigeon, but somewhat slimmer and with grey rump, and thin black wing bars (often not prominent). In flight, distinguished from the larger woodpigeon by narrower wings with black margins and tips, and lack of white wing-patches. Flight straight and rapid.

Though stock doves rarely feed in trees, holes in trees are a favourite nest site, along with buildings and cliffs, and the occasional rabbit burrow.

When organochlorine seed dressings came in, stock dove numbers fell steeply because of their preference for newly-sown grain. The worst-hit habitats and regions were largely abandoned at the time. Conditions are still not ideal, with the loss of breeding sites in elm trees after elm disease, with fewer autumn stubbles, fewer weed seeds and the introduction of tram-lining techniques which make for a more even density of cereal crops and therefore fewer bare areas.

The stock dove had a period of range expansion in Europe in the nineteenth century when agricultural practices suited it. It did not breed in Ireland until 1877. They have an extensive range outside the Palearctic to include Siberia, central Asia and Iran, and not surprisingly many of those birds are migrants.

'They rose up in a twinkling cloud
And wheeled about and bowed,
To settle on the trees
Perching like small clay images.
Then with a noise of sudden rain
They clattered off again.'
Andrew Young THE STOCKDOVES

THESE BLUE-GREY doves easily escape notice and it is a negative feature, the absence of white on the wings, which is most distinctive. The small wing bars, grey rump and green sheen on the neck are positive things to look for. Some feral pigeons, always highly variable, can cause problems, but the pale-centred, dark-rimmed wings and grey (not white) rump are distinctive.

They are often gregarious, even in the breeding season, with flocks gathering on thinly vegetated patches in cereal fields where, if they had their way, there would be plenty of weed seeds, particularly bistorts. Recently, set-a-side has provided more habitat suitable for winter flocks.

Stubble-field with a line of trees nearby — ideal stock dove habitat.

Turtle Dove

26 cm (10 in)

SPECIES INFORMATION	
SCIENTIFIC NAME	Streptopelia turtur
RELATED SPECIES	Collared Dove
CALL	Song a soft, purring 'turrr-turrr'; alarm call a short 'ru'
HABITAT	Breeds in wooded country, orchards, and sometimes in well wooded parks and gardens. Prefers warm, dry lowland sites
STATUS	Summer visitor and passage migrant. Winters in Africa, south of Sahara. In BI about 75,000 pairs. Recent decline, perhaps due to droughts in winter quarters. Very common in Spain (about 1,000,000 pairs)

SIZE

IDENTIFICATION

HABITAT

POPULATION

MAP

OUR SMALLEST DOVE, with rather delicate build. Plumage rusty-brown, speckled wings and black and white markings at side of neck. Juveniles browner and lacking neck marking. Tail shows black feathers and white margin when spread. Flight rapid with slight rocking motion.

TURTLE DOVES ARE elegant birds, with long, rounded tails with white rim and dark patterned backs. There is a black and white neck patch, orange eye and grey cap. In flight, rapid and agile as befits a long-distance migrant, the blue-grey mid-wing panel and similar coloured rump are distinctive. The very clearly different tail rim, separating it from doves, is particularly well exposed on take-off or landing.

The turtle dove's contented 'purring' is heard so much less in the land now, and the rapid decrease has put the bird on the red list of birds of conservation concern because of a decrease of more than 50 per cent in the last 25 years. Decreases are also reported in Portugal, Belgium, Netherlands, Germany and Greece.

Apart from the shortage of weed seeds on a modern clean farm, turtle doves have long been shot, like many another migrant, on their way to Britain, and they have not always been safe when they reach here. Harting (1866) writes of them 'as timid and hard to approach but by sending some one round to the other side of the field to drive them you may obtain a good shot as they pass over your head. They are very fair eating.

> 'For lo, the winter is past, the flowers appear on the earth; the time of the singing of birds is come, and the voice of the turtle is heard in our land'
>
> THE SONG OF SOLOMON

The turtle dove is one of our prettiest summer visitors. Its song has a soft, purring quality — once learned, never forgotten.

SPECIES INFORMATION

SCIENTIFIC NAME	Cuculus canorus
RELATED SPECIES	Great Spotted Cuckoo (Spain)
CALL	Familiar 'cuck-oo' call is the territorial song of the male, normally heard from the end of April through July. Female has a loud, bubbling trill
HABITAT	Found from high mountains right down to coastal dunes, fenland and reedbeds. Prefers varied landscape with plenty of cover
STATUS	Summer visitor. Winters in tropical Africa. In BI about 30,000 pairs

Cuckoo

33 cm (13 in)

SLIM, WITH LONG wings and tail. In flight, cuckoos have kestrel-like shape, but markings more like sparrowhawk. Normally grey, but sometimes red-brown. Brood-parasite of smaller birds (commonly meadow pipit, reed warbler or dunnock).

CUCKOOS ARE MOST often seen flying quite fast and low over scrub or reedbed, when the long tail and long, narrow, pointed wings are distinctive. They fly with low wing-beats, interspersed with glides, spending as little time as possible in the open, and regaining cover as quickly as possible.

Cuckoos are found quite commonly throughout most of Britain and Ireland (and Europe, except for Iceland), but they are rare in Orkney and Shetland. Their range is determined mainly by the distribution of the host species which they parasitise, but also by the availability of their favourite food – hairy caterpillars, a food that most birds will not eat. The fat fox moth caterpillars on bilberry and heather are common most years on moorland, but are rejected by most birds except cuckoos. The last 20

years have seen a decline in numbers, especially in Ireland and in north-west Britain, perhaps reflecting a decline in meadow pipit numbers.

When on the look-out for a suitable host, the female cuckoo uses a tree or other convenient tall perch as a spying post. She is a patient and careful observer of her host's behaviour, especially during the breeding season, and may spend hours watching and waiting for the right moment. Once a nest has been located, she moves in quickly and stealthily to deposit a single egg into the nest, while the host bird is still in the process of completing her own clutch, but before incubation has started. A cuckoo can lay her egg in just a few seconds and be away again before the host has even detected her presence.

If a host does see a cuckoo at or near its nest, it will attack it and try to drive the cookoo away, and will also then be more likely to desert the clutch. It therefore pays the cuckoo to lay its egg very rapidly in the host's nest.

The adults begin to leave in mid-July, at a time when their young are still being cared for by their foster-parents. The young birds make their first migration a little later, in August or September, never having seen their own parents. The precise wintering grounds are not known, but most birds probably cross the Mediterranean Sea and the Sahara desert, to spend the winter months in equatorial Africa, where there are abundant supplies of insect food.

Although the biggest group of brood parasites are the cuckoos, with 47 parasitic species, about 80 species of bird (including some widow-birds and Cowbirds) depend on other species to rear their young. Worldwide there are 127 species of cuckoo, so about a third of all cuckoo species are in fact parasitic.

SIZE

IDENTIFICATION

HABITAT

POPULATION

MAP

Top and bottom right
With its sleek body, barred plumage and pointed wings, the cuckoo has a hawk- or falcon-like appearance. It is a threat to small birds, but only as a brood parasite.

Bottom left
A tree pipit feeds a cuckoo chick; the latter will soon be bigger than its exhausted foster parent!

Barn Owl

35 cm (14 in)

SPECIES INFORMATION	
SCIENTIFIC NAME	*Tyto alba*
RELATED SPECIES	No close relative in region
CALL	Very vocal at breeding site. Snarling and screeching sounds, such as 'khreehreehreeh'. Chicks make snoring noises
HABITAT	Mainly in open, cultivated areas; breeds in hollow trees or church towers, barns and derelict buildings
STATUS	Resident. In BI about 5,000 pairs (declining)

SIZE

IDENTIFICATION

HABITAT

POPULATION

MAP

MEDIUM-SIZED OWL with long legs, black eyes and no ear-tufts. Conspicuous pale, heart-shaped facial disc. In flight shows long, slim wings and very pale underparts. Usually seen when hunting over fields or ditches at dawn or dusk.

WITH FEWER BARNS to nest in and mercury from fungicides having possible toxic effects, barn owls are a species in decline. There were perhaps 12,000 pairs in an RSPB survey in 1930, but now there are only around 5,000.

Many are seen as 'white owls' in car lights, but there is plenty of buff in the plumage too. They are less frequently noisy than tawny owls but make eerie screeching calls. Being dependent on small mammals, numbers fluctuate. By dissecting owl pellets for bones (not an unpleasant activity) much can be learned about the relative population densities of shrews, voles and mice around their habitat. I have only found occasional rat or bird, usually sparrow, bones in the pellets. The Barn Owl and Hawk and Owl Trusts works hard in support of the species, providing nest-boxes and information, and encouraging land owners to leave enough grassland suitable for the small mammals that they need.

Barn owls are among the most widely distributed birds in the world, even reaching Madagascar, South America and Australia. These birds have been considered in the section on farmland and open habitats section but these open habitats can be of almost any type as long as there are rodents and not too much snow.

Top right
Barn owl in classic location. These owls can seem almost ghost-like when suddenly spotted in the night.

Bottom left and right
The facial disc of the owl's face helps it to detect even the faintest of rustles as it flies in search of prey.

SPECIES INFORMATION

SCIENTIFIC NAME	*Athene noctua*
RELATED SPECIES	*No close relative in region*
CALL	*Alarm call a loud 'kiu'. Male's territorial song is a drawn out, nasal 'guhg'*
HABITAT	*Open country with trees, copses or hedgerows. Meadows and pasture with pollarded willows, orchards and the edges of small, open woods*
STATUS	*Resident. Absent from Ireland and north-west Britain. In B about 10,000 pairs*

Little Owl
22 cm (9 in)

SMALL, SHORT-TAILED owl with smooth crown and large yellow eyes. Flight is undulating, rather like woodpecker. Often active by day it can be seen sitting on fence posts or telegraph poles.

SIZE

IDENTIFICATION

HABITAT

POPULATION

MAP

WHILE BARN OWLS are very good for whooping cough when made into a broth (Yorkshire) and their eggs, hard-boiled, charred and powdered do wonders for eyesight, salted little owl is very good for gout! Furthermore eating little owls will cure drunkenness, alcoholism, madness and epilepsy. Most of these gems of information came from Greenoak (1997), but a marvellous 'factoid' is reported by Robert Gibblings who had found the beetle ridden corpse of a mole. 'No doubt' he wrote 'the little owl who owned the larder was watching us, but we failed to see him. As is well known, the owls pounce on the moles when they are working near the surface, but instead of eating the body they leave it near their lair and feed on the beetles which congregate about the corpse.' Considering that little owls were only introduced in Yorkshire, from Italy, in 1842, it is surprising that they had built up such reputations in the fields of gout and drunkenness before

slightly more rational times emerged. Further introductions took place in Bedfordshire, Northamptonshire and elsewhere and by 1900 they were breeding regularly in the wild.

Little owls were greatly disliked by gamekeepers, although they pose little threat to gamebirds, feeding as they do mainly on insects, voles and mice. Nicholson (1951) reports: 'little owls are on the whole noisy birds, both by day and by night, calling to each other with a variety of notes which have little of the mysterious and unworldly quality of many owl voices'. In flight, they show 'a series of strong strokes alternating with long pauses producing a conspicuously up and down motion. When alarmed they bob comically up and down. They sit very upright.'

These birds of hedges, copse and orchards are plump, flat-headed and white eye-browed, with a plumage of two tints – a dark chocolate brown background with buffish white spots, bars and mottlings.

Top right
Little owls eat a lot of insects. This one has caught a yellow-underwing moth.

Top left and bottom
They often sit bolt upright on a post or tree stump, and are frequently active by day.

Nightjar

28 cm (11 in)

SPECIES INFORMATION	
SCIENTIFIC NAME	Caprimulgus europaeus
RELATED SPECIES	Red-necked Nightjar (Spain and north Africa)
CALL	Flight-call a liquid 'kuik', or when disturbed a raw 'vack'. Male's song is a continuous two-toned purring – 'errr...orrrr-errr', mainly heard in the evening
HABITAT	Heathland and light pinewoods on sandy soil. Also in thick forest with clearings or felled areas, and in dunes
STATUS	Summer visitor. Winters in tropical Africa. In B about 3,000 pairs (fewer than 30 in Ireland)

SIZE

IDENTIFICATION

HABITAT

POPULATION

MAP

SLIM, LONG-WINGED and long-tailed nocturnal bird, with flat head and large, dark eyes. Plumage highly camouflaged, with bark-like pattern. Small bill opens wide to reveal large gape, surrounded by bristles. Male has white spots on wing tips and tail. Rather cuckoo-like in flight.

A BIRD OF the summer night is the nightjar which, when well seen, shows its very small bill, white spots near the wing tips and on the outer tail feathers. Often, at dusk, it is just a silhouette or, more often, an evocative 'churr' in early succession woodland. It needs bare ground for its nest site and, perhaps because its exact needs are known, management is helping a recent increase after a long period of very little success.

Fuller, writing of the importance of young plantations for nightjars, says that they occupy a wider range of plantation ages than woodlarks, which are flourishing in plantations in Breckland. Nightjars will use restocks throughout the establishment and pre-felling stages. The highest densities are in three- to five-year-old pine, but they will use considerably older growth. In Thetford Forest and elsewhere, densities remain fairly high until at least ten years, with birds continuing to use some stands for up to 15 years. Being an aerial feeder, the nightjar is not as critically dependant on the vegetation structure for feeding as is the woodlark. Nonetheless it does need bare ground or sparse vegetation for nesting.

A bird that sounds and looks as strange as a nightjar has not surprisingly gained many names and been written about in many contexts. The Yorkshire name, gabble ratchet, or the Norfolk, scissors grinder, are typical, but why is it a corpse bird? It seems there was a belief in Nidderdale that the souls of unbaptised children went into nightjars.

> '*To hear the fern owl's cry, that whews aloft*
> *In circling whirls … she wakes her jarring noise*
> *To the unheeding waste.*'
> John Clare SELECTED POEMS

Centre
The nightjar's plumage is so cryptically patterned that the bird seems to blend into its background when sitting on the ground.

Below
The nightjar has a very wide gape, allowing it to scoop up flying insects such as moths.

Woodlark

15 cm (6 in)

SMALLER AND SHORTER-TAILED than the skylark. Has pale eye-stripes, meeting at nape, and black and white markings at the bend of wing. Crest rather small and rounded, often inconspicuous. Often nests near tree pipit.

THE JIZZ OF a woodlark may give it away when feeding with skylarks on winter seeds. Something about the fine bill, the short tail and the broad, rounded wings may say 'woodlark' even if their features are not analysed. Analyses might add the long white eye-stripe and black and white marks on the wrist or carpal feathers. The cheeks are rufous, and the streaky upper breast is clearly separated from white below. The wrist pattern is also clear in flight, while wing shape, hesitant flight and white end to short tail are distinctive. In song-flight it does not rise as high as does the skylark, but circles widely before spiralling in descent, or sings from a perch. Song-flight is often started from a tree-top.

Being confined to milder latitudes, woodlarks only reach the southern part of Scandinavia and there has been range retraction there as in Britain. Northern and eastern populations, like our Breckland ones, are migratory, moving into the breeding range of the southern and western populations. This migration is very inconspicuous with no large flocks.

While the French call the woodlark alouette lulu, the Germans call it Heidelerche, heath lark, and some of its strongholds here are certainly on heathland. The 1997 woodlark survey, showing a great upsurge in population, had 46 per cent of larks in heathland, 40 per cent in forestry plantation, a perverse Devon population on low intensity farmland, and a 'new' habitat where woodlarks bred on bare ground around old mine workings. When times were bad, heath fires helped the Surrey/Hampshire population in the 1970s by providing bare ground, while the felling of Breckland conifers did the same, so the British populations rose to 400 pairs in 1981. Severe weather reduced this and a woodlark survey in 1986 found only 241 territories.

In 1997 the New Forest population, although increased to 183, was smaller than the Suffolk Breckland (457), the Suffolk coastal sandlings (245) and Norfolk (245). Woodlark populations have always fluctuated and I remember a lovely surge in breeding birds in the London area in the 1940s. There having been none in the area in 1940, they were up to 45 pairs in 1950, including a pair quite close to a main road on Putney Heath which is only about 10 km (6 miles) from St Paul's Cathedral.

If the occasional sight of a hoopoe is one reward for a southerly visit, then hearing the song of the woodlark is surely another. While the song is as always impossible to describe, Kightly *et al* (1998) attempts this: 'song outstanding for its clarity and sweetness, comprises short fluty phrases; dilee – dilee – , lu – lu – lu; may last several minutes but sound seems to come and go'. The 'lu lu lu' part is adapted by the French who call the bird lulu.

SIZE

IDENTIFICATION

HABITAT

POPULATION

MAP

The woodlark is a much daintier bird than the skylark, and is associated with lowland heath and forestry clearings.

Skylark

16 cm (6.5 in)

○○○○○○○○○○○○○○○○○○○○○○○○○○○○
SPECIES INFORMATION
SCIENTIFIC NAME	*Alauda arvensis*
RELATED SPECIES	Woodlark
CALL	Flight-call a pleasant 'chee' or 'cheeoo'. Song, usually delivered in vertical song-flight, is a long-lasting, almost continuous mixture of trills and whistles
HABITAT	Open country, especially agricultural fields and pasture, meadows and downland
STATUS	Resident and partial migrant. In BI about 2,500,000 pairs

SIZE

IDENTIFICATION

HABITAT

POPULATION

MAP

COMMON LARGE LARK of open country, with camouflaged plumage and small crest. Trailing edges of wings and outer tail feathers white.

THE SONG AND SONG-FLIGHT of the lark seem to tempt the poets to verse more even than the song of the nightingale, but the skylark got an equally abundant press from those who have revelled in trapping and eating them.

The decline of he skylark, highlighted by surveys by BTO volunteers, has been the stimulus for

much research into the birds of farmland, especially by the BTO and RSPB. Using Common Birds Census data it was evident that declines in coastal and upland habitats had not been as great as on farmland. The timing of the farmland decline coincided with agricultural intensification, with big changes in winter feeding opportunities. A set-aside survey showed plenty of larks there, as well as on stubble and saltmarsh, but in winter–wheat the numbers of larks decreased as winter went on. The Breeding Bird Survey is beginning to produce vital habitat data for skylarks, with more larks where farms are more diverse. Recently surveys have shown worrying declines in upland areas too, and the reasons for this are still far from clear.

Nicholson (1957) writes that 'skylarks, when they are not on the wing, like to have their feet firmly on the ground, and are remarkable among passerine birds in not only refusing to perch on trees

Bottom right
Skylark atop a post. Note the obvious crest.

Top left
A skylark returns to its nest which is hidden amongst the long grass.

but in usually keeping a good distance away from them.' He goes on to mention the great flocking and migratory movements of larks. 'Their flight on such journeys is dogged but purposeful, with spasms of wing flapping interrupted by longish rests. When flying about the fields the action is quite different from either the song flight or the migratory flight and the broad triangular sail shaped wings are fluttered as if their power were an embarrassment in the short, slow, deliberate flights which often seem to serve for patrolling and looking round.'

On migration flights and in the fields they produce a constant 'chirrup' call. Their movements do not take them that far, for few winter far south of the Mediterranean, while many make no more than local movements.

'We have great plenty of larkes and very good ones especially in those parts adjoining to Coteswold. They take them by alluring them with a dareing glass which is whirled about in a sun shining day, and the larkes are pleased at it, ass at a sheepe's eye, and at that time the net is drawn over them' writes Aubrey in 1847 in the Natural History of Wiltshire. Greenoak (1998) mentions that the song 'Allouette, gentille allouette' goes into great details about plucking the birds and the saying 'the land where larks fall ready rosted' would be equivalent of land flowing in milk and honey.

'And still the singing skylark soared
And silent sank and soared to sing.'
Christina Rosetti SKYLARK

SPECIES INFORMATION

SCIENTIFIC NAME	*Anthus trivialis*
RELATED SPECIES	Meadow Pipit, Rock Pipit
CALL	When flushed 'psee' or 'tsitt', often repeated. Song louder and more musical than meadow pipit's, with long canary-like phrases. Usually sings in parachuting display-flight from and returning to a perch in a tree
HABITAT	Heath with scattered trees and bushes. Also margins of broadleaved and coniferous forest, and in clearings
STATUS	Summer visitor. In B about 120,000 pairs (virtually absent from Ireland)

Tree Pipit
15 cm (6 in)

SLIM, WITH YELLOWISH breast and neck, streaked heavily with dark brown. Legs reddish. Slightly larger and paler than Meadow Pipit.

TREE PIPITS LIKE trees rather than woods, but woodland fringes and young forestry plantations are as acceptable as scattered birches and pines on heathland. In two of the places I have known Tree pipits best, an English railway embankment and an open field in north Wales, they have used telegraph wires as the base from which to launch themselves into their song flight which, though beautiful and distinctive, is impossible to describe. Kightley *et al* (1998) attempts it with 'cheery song is much stronger than meadow's; opens like a chaffinch and concludes with terminal flourish: seeurr – seeurr – seeurr – seeurr'.

Tree pipits have large territories, 1.5 ha (3.7 acres) in one study, within which the nest, a cup of dry grass stems, is made either on the ground or in low cover.

Tree pipits breed up to the Arctic fringes and south until conditions became too dry. It is a summer visitor to Europe, wintering in Africa, west as far south as the equatorial rain forest and in the east as far south as Natal.

> '*Its a pity pipits have*
> *No diagnostic features*
> *Specifically they are the least*
> *Distinctive of God's creatures.*'
> BULLETIN OF THE BRITISH MUSEUM

 SIZE

 IDENTIFICATION

 HABITAT

 POPULATION

 MAP

Top
The tree pipit is slim and graceful, with paler plumage than the meadow pipit, and a much more tuneful song.

Bottom
A tree pipit brings home a juicy grub for its brood.

Swallow

18 cm (7 in)

SPECIES INFORMATION

SCIENTIFIC NAME	*Hirundo rustica*
RELATED SPECIES	House Martin, Sand Martin
CALL	Flight-call 'vid-vid' or 'tsi-dit', often repeated. Song is a pleasant twittering and warbling
HABITAT	Open countryside, villages and farms. May flock in wetlands on migration
STATUS	Summer visitor, wintering in Africa. In BI about 800,000 pairs

SIZE

IDENTIFICATION

HABITAT

POPULATION

MAP

SLIM AND ELEGANT, with long tail streamers. Metallic blue above, with red-brown chin and forehead. Juveniles less brightly coloured and with shorter tail streamers. Flight rapid, and rather more direct than the house martin's and often feeds at low level. Its nest is a mud half-cup.

SWALLOWS ARE MANY people's idea of the country bird and the essence of summer. Where there is warmth, insects and somewhere to nest swallows are to be found, showing their long wings and forked tails in flight. Perched on telephone wires the chestnut-red throat and forehead, dark chest-band and pinkish belly are clear.

Swallows are extensive migrants, even if a few winter in southern Spain. Ronald Hickling (1983) says how the swallow has always been an especial favourite of ringers. Its nests in farm buildings are easy to discover and are readily accessible; large numbers of nestlings can thus be ringed with little effort. In addition, the mist-net has enabled many swallows to be ringed at their autumn roosts, when for brief periods enormous numbers gather nightly in reedbeds. By the end of 1980 over three quarters of a million had been ringed. The recovery rate of birds from their winter quarters

in southern Africa has also been gratifyingly high. Few recoveries can have caused such excitement as the first swallow found in South Africa. It was caught in a farmhouse at Utrecht, Natal, on 27 December 1911, 18 months after being ringed as a nesting adult. Autumn recoveries of British ringed swallows have ranged from western France, eastern Spain, the Straits of Gibraltar and in Nigeria, en route to South Africa.

Swallows begin their return flight in February, and by mid-April they will be back taking their flying prey after aerial pursuit in characteristic swoops and sweeps. Just as welcome will be their chattering warble of a song and 'witt witt' call in flight. By the end of April they will be laying in their cupped mud pellet and feather nests set on a beam or window ledge and as they brake, by spreading their tail, on approach to the nest they show the white spots on the tail. Usually there will be a second brood with the young birds recognisable by their shorter tail streamers, patchy breast-band and altogether duller plumage.

Top right
Swallows build a cup nest of mud and feathers, usually inside a barn or similar outbuilding.

Bottom
A young swallow begs for food on a twig.

> 'Sister, my sister, O fleet, sweet swallow
> Thy way is long to the sun and the south.'
> Swinburne ITYLUS

Yellow Wagtail

17 cm (6.5 in)

SIZE

IDENTIFICATION

HABITAT

POPULATION

MAP

SPECIES INFORMATION

SCIENTIFIC NAME	Motacilla flava
RELATED SPECIES	Pied Wagtail, Grey Wagtail
CALL	Flight-call a sharp 'pseep'. Song of short chirping elements
HABITAT	Boggy ground, marshes, heathland, damp meadows and pasture
STATUS	Summer visitor. In B about 50,000 pairs (virtually absent from Ireland, and much of Scotland). Somewhat smaller and shorter-tailed than pied wagtail

THE YELLOW WAGTAIL (1950) was the first of the *New Naturalist* monographs on birds and arose from a seven-year study of 'this attractive species, so lovely to look upon, and so full of a dainty and buoyant airiness of stance and flight' along a strip of so called green belt, the vegetable plots of the market garden country flanking the Mersey south of Manchester.

'THE COCK YELLOW wagtail is an extremely handsome bird, and when it first arrives in the spring is a joy to see. It has a bright yellow head, with crown and ear coverts more or less greenish, through there are wide variations in the plumage of the head ....There is an eye stripe which is yellow, while the chin and throat are a bright yellow which extends down and under the belly. Certain cocks however, especially those which have not completed the spring moult, may appear so poorly coloured as to resemble hens.'

This species shows some of the most marked and complex colour variations among a European species. Such variation involves the use of subspecific or trinomial names because male birds from the different areas are distinctive. Some might argue that

they should therefore be different species, but there are zones of hybridisation and therefore it is best to consider the Yellow Wagtail a polytypic species. Yellow Wagtail (*M. flava flavissima*), the British race, has yellow-green upperparts and yellow stripe above eye. Blue-headed wagtail (*M. flava flava*), the central European race, has slate-grey head and white stripe above eye; female somewhat duller with somewhat brownish head. The blue-headed occurs in a band

through temperate Europe, the grey-headed (*M. f. thunbergi*) is found to the north, and the black-headed (*M. f. feldegg*) to the south-east.

For a summer visitor with such an extensive northern range there are different winter quarters, but our birds head for African tropics and, like moving skylarks or tree pipits, can often be heard overhead as they tend to move by day, making a drawn out 'tsweep' which many find difficult to distinguish from the call of pied or grey wagtails.

All wagtails are insectivorous, and yellow wagtails collect their insect food from the ground when walking (often among cattle) or by more rapid pursuit, or by short flycatching flights. Although half yellow wagtail nests are by water, where insect food is often abundant, I have known Midland populations on sandy fields growing sugar-beet.

The reliance of yellow wagtails on insect food has made then vulnerable to the instensification of British farming, especially the improvement and reduction of pasture.

Top left
The Somerset Levels – these wet meadows are good habitat for yellow wagtails.

Top right and bottom
The yellow wagtail is pure yellow underneath, greenish grey above.

Fieldfare

26 cm (10 in)

○ ○

SPECIES INFORMATION

SCIENTIFIC NAME	Turdus pilaris
RELATED SPECIES	Redwing, Blackbird, Song Thrush, Mistle Thrush
CALL	Flight-call a loud, raw chatter: 'shack-shack-shack'. Song fairly quiet warbling and twittering, often given in flight
HABITAT	Mountain forests, tundra also and tall trees in parks. In winter flocks to open fields, farmland and occasionally gardens
STATUS	Winter visitor (some breed). In B about 20 pairs, mainly in the north (absent from Ireland)

SIZE

IDENTIFICATION

HABITAT

POPULATION

MAP

CHESTNUT BACK AND wings, grey head and rump and black tail. In flight shows contrast between black tail, light grey rump and white lower wing coverts.

FIELDFARES HAVE GREY heads and rumps and dark tails. The typical thrush speckling is darker on the upper breast. Being large and bold and constantly noisy with their 'chack chack chacking' they are part of many winter county walks. The flight can be described as 'noticeably loose and leisurely with bursts of wing beats alternating with brief glides on extended wings'.

Their Anglo Saxon name 'Felde Fare' makes them travellers over fields, and pasture and open fields are certainly their favourite winter feeding grounds.

By contrast with the noisy colonies of the northern birch and pine forests

Fieldfares are partial to apples, and they sometimes come into gardens to feed during frosty weather. Redwings take a range of berries in the winter; a flock can strip a holly tree in just a few days.

David Snow in the *New Atlas* writes that 'isolated breeding pairs, as all those recorded so far in Britain have been, are much less easy to find. The song a feeble

warble interrupted by wheezes and chuckles, is of little help for it is not persistent or audible from afar. Also, in late spring, pairs tend to wander, presumably in search of a suitable nesting area.' He suggests that the breeding population over the years of the Atlas might be 25 pairs, scattered widely.

In winter there might be a million birds here, but where they will be depends on the stage of winter and the weather, with a tendency for these highly mobile and nomadic birds to move further south later and in cold weather. Ringing recoveries in Italy and Spain, of birds ringed here, show possible alternative destinations. No doubt such large numbers of a large bird make great inroads into food supplies, and it is tragic that so many hedges are flailed so frequently so that no berries have a chance to appear or to survive. As ground feeders for much of the time, however, they seek out a wide range of invertebrates, turning over small stones in their search.

Redwing

21 cm (8.5 in)

```
○○○○○○○○○○○○○○○○○○○○○○○○○○
       SPECIES  INFORMATION
SCIENTIFIC NAME  Turdus iliacus
RELATED SPECIES  Fieldfare, Blackbird, Song Thrush, Mistle Thrush
CALL             Distinctive 'tsweep' flight-call, audible during
                 autumn migration at night. Alarm call 'rrt'. Song is a
                 rapid, melancholy, descending series of notes,
                 followed by a short twitter
HABITAT          Light birch and coniferous forest in the north, up to
                 the edge of tundra. In winter flocks to fields and
                 open woods, and parks and gardens
STATUS           Winter visitor (some breed). In BI about 50 pairs
                 (mainly in Scotland)
```

SIZE

IDENTIFICATION

HABITAT

POPULATION

MAP

SLIGHTLY SMALLER AND darker than Song Thrush, and with whitish stripe over eye, red-brown flanks, and streaked, not spotted breast. In flight shows the red-brown under wing coverts.

THE REDWING'S VERSION of thrush plumage involves parallel rows of dark streaks on the breast. Its underwing is red in flight and this colour shows as rusty flanks as the bird devours holly berries or is tempted into gardens by fallen apples. Given the opportunity redwings are also great worm eaters. Their high pitched call as they migrate overhead at night is frequent in October but also around the hedges and fields throughout the winter, and particularly when they plunge suddenly into roosting quarters.

The winter range of redwings is from only just outside the western Palearctic to the east of the Black Sea so birds from eastern Siberian have long, 6,500 km (4,000 miles), south-westerly flights but European birds have relatively short movements. As with fieldfare ringing returns show little fidelity to one wintering area, with British-ringed birds appearing in subsequent winters in Italy and Greece.

Whereas singing fieldfares are inconspicuous, the song of the redwing is rather more distinctive and penetrating. It consists of a series of four to seven, but most commonly five, descending, fluted notes of such tone and volume as to be clearly audible at a considerable distance.

The first British nest record is from Sutherland in 1925. There were breeding records in only 17 of the next 41 years, but with 20 pairs in Wester Ross in 1968 a firm foothold was established. Fluctuations followed, with many nesting in remote parts.

You will be able to sight redwings on clear October nights and hear them call as they migrate south.

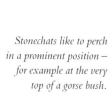

Stonechat

12.5 cm (5 in)

SPECIES INFORMATION	
SCIENTIFIC NAME	*Saxicola torquata*
RELATED SPECIES	Whinchat
CALL	Scratchy 'trat'. Song is a short, hurried phrase with coarse, rattling and whistled notes, sometimes in short, dancing song-flight
HABITAT	Open, stoney country; heaths, especially those with gorse or broom; raised bogs and pasture; to 1,400 m (4,593 ft) in mountains
STATUS	Resident and partial migrant. In BI about 20,000 pairs

MALE IS DARK above, with black throat, white half-collar and orange belly. Female and juvenile paler, but still with dark head and ruddy colour below. Often sits at top of bush. Flight low and jerky.

THE WHITE WING-flash and the constant twitching of wings and tail are very distinctive. Females, and males in winter until they have worn away the brownish new feather tips, are duller, with the female's head grey-brown rather then black. Young stonechats are robin-like with a hint of rufous, and pale flecks on the back. The call, aptly and frequently likened to two stones being struck together, greets your approach, as birds move from perch to perch on rapidly whirring broad wings.

The stonechat has a markedly western and coastal distribution reflecting areas with the mildest winters and least habitat change, but even parts which rarely expect freezing conditions can suffer. The stonechat population of Cape Clear in County Cork was between 50 and 150 pairs in 1961, but was down to three pairs in 1963 after two really cold winters. Fortunately stonechats are resilient, and there were 33 pairs by 1967. By the time of the *New Atlas* the breeding range had retracted enormously, with many losses in Ireland, the south-west and southern and eastern

Scotland, which were attributed to habitat loss, disturbance on the marginal, gorse-clad land beloved of stonechats and the growing maturity of many forestry plantations, colonised when the plantations were young.

On breeding territories, where gorse and bare patches are often favoured, males make distinctive song-flights, with brief hovers, involving a dunnock-like variable rattle. The nest is sited near to the ground in thick vegetation and is a loose cup of grass and leaves. Fledging success is often remarkably high, up to 80 per cent, and with two broods and a clutch size of four to six, stonechat populations can increase rapidly. Gorse-covered cliffs on the Lleyn Peninsula of north Wales can seem delightfully alive with young stonechats.

Stonechats like to perch in a prominent position – for example at the very top of a gorse bush.

Whinchat

12.5 cm (5 in)

```
○ ○ ○ ○ ○ ○ ○ ○ ○ ○ ○ ○ ○ ○ ○ ○ ○ ○ ○ ○ ○ ○ ○ ○ ○
```

SPECIES INFORMATION

SCIENTIFIC NAME	Saxicola rubetra
RELATED SPECIES	Stonechat
CALL	Hard, very short 'tek-tek' or 'tsek-tsek'. Song is a mixture of short, hurried phrases made up of scratchy, warbling and fluting notes; includes mimicry
HABITAT	Open bushy meadows and wasteland. Often near wet habitats, but also on dry heath
STATUS	Summer visitor. In BI about 20,000 pairs

SQUAT AND SHORT-TAILED. Male has white stripe above eye, paler in female. Male dark above, with orangey breast.

WHINCHAT MALES WITH their streaked brown upperparts, reddish underparts and dark face are attractive. The white eye-stripe and white sides at the base of the tail are more useful in identification as they are shared by female and young. The upright posture, short tail and sharp call are typical of chats, as is its pleasant warble. Breeding whinchats perch and dart, often among bracken, in open country, while on passage they may turn up in cereal fields and coastal marshes.

Whinchats are slimmer than stonechats, with whom they often share coastal and upland habitats, and females of the two could be mistaken, but the stonechat is darker and the whinchat has the eye-stripe. Young birds, too, are paler than stonechats. The diet of the two species, mainly invertebrates, is much the same.

Unlike stonechats, whinchats are long-distance migrants, moving from a wide area of northern and central Europe to winter in Africa, with many birds crossing the Sahara to Senegal, Nigeria and Uganda.

 SIZE

 IDENTIFICATION

 HABITAT

 POPULATION

 MAP

Top
The whinchat enjoys a diet of insects and their larvae, together with spiders and worms.

Bottom
The bold eyestripe helps to distinguish the whinchat from the rather similar stonechat.

173

Whitethroat

14 cm (5.5 in)

○○○○○○○○○○○○○○○○○○○○○○○○○○
SPECIES INFORMATION

SCIENTIFIC NAME	Sylvia communis
RELATED SPECIES	Lesser Whitethroat, Dartford Warbler, Blackcap, Garden Warbler
CALL	Alarm-call 'voit-voit-vit-vit', also repeated 'tsheck'. Song is a rather rushed warble, from bush or in short song-flight
HABITAT	Scrub, hedgerows, embankments, woodland edges
STATUS	Summer visitor. In BI about 780,000 pairs

SIZE

IDENTIFICATION

HABITAT

POPULATION

MAP

Lively warbler with white throat, grey head and back and chestnut wings. Relatively long tail with white outer feathers. Narrow white eye-ring. Female drabber, with brownish head.

WHITETHROATS ARE CLASSIC hedge and scrub birds. Their jerky display flight and urgent chatter can also be found in early successional stages of woodland. The male's rich rusty back and ashy head contrast with the white throat; the female is browner. The longer tail, more slender build and white outer tail feathers, which are common to both sexes, distinguish the autumn male, the females and the young from the garden warbler. During the summer the male whitethroat has a delicate pink suffusion overlaying his buffish breast and flanks, but a few females may display some pink as well. The bill is brownish-grey and the feet and legs a paler brown.

Whitethoat populations are strongly influenced by conditions in their African wintering grounds – the Sahel region to the south of the Sahara Desert. Numbers fell markedly in 1969, and have fluctuated since, but at a lower general level.

As extensive migrants, 'falls' are a feature at many bird observatories and much pioneering work on navigation was carried out on this and other *Sylvia* warblers, showing that nocturnal migrants depend partly on the stars, and establishing the concept of a 'star compass'.

> '*And after April, when May follows*
> *And the whitethroat builds, and all the*
> *swallow …*'
> Robert Browning
> HOME THOUGHTS FROM ABROAD

Top
This whitethroat, perched in the open, clearly displays its pure white throat.

Bottom
A whitethroat pours out its chattering song, throat distended.

SPECIES INFORMATION	
SCIENTIFIC NAME	Sylvia curruca
RELATED SPECIES	Whitethroat, Dartford Warbler, Blackcap, Garden Warbler
CALL	'Tjeck' and, when alarmed, an irregularly repeated 'tack'. Song is in two parts: a quiet, hurried warble, followed by a loud rattle all on one note. From a distance, only the second section is audible
HABITAT	Scrub, hedgerows and bushes and hedges in larger gardens
STATUS	Summer visitor. In B about 80,000 pairs (virtually absent from Ireland)

Lesser Whitethroat

13.5 cm (5 in)

SLIGHTLY SMALLER THAN whitethroat, and without chestnut on wings. Has indistinct mask-like dark cheeks, contrasting with white chin, and a relatively short tail.

LESSER WHITETHROATS ARE greyer with dark cheeks and no rusty wings. They are noticeably smaller and more compact than whitethroats and the sexes are similar, with shorter white-edged tails. Their 'tuks' and 'churrs' among a variety of scolding calls are not that different from whitethroat but their rattling song, somewhat like an unfinished yellowhammer's, is their best identification feature. Once known you will find lesser whitethroats more common than you perhaps thought.

Their habitat is overgrown railway embankments, hedgerows and scrub; they may also be found in such places as disused mineral workings, and even derelict industrial sites.

Naturally occurring examples of this habitat are largely confined to chalk grassland scrub. They like taller and more scrubby hedges than whitethroats, and can be found occasionally in hedges in larger gardens and parks.

'A rare, and I think a new little bird, frequents my garden. This bird much resembles the whitethroat but has a more white silvery breast and belly; is restless and active, like the willow wrens and hops from bough to bough examining every part for food.'
Gilbert White
NATURAL HISTORY OF SELBORNE

SIZE

IDENTIFICATION

HABITAT

POPULATION

MAP

Top right and left
Lesser whitethroats tend to be more secretive than whitethroats, and they often stay hidden in the foliage.

Bottom
Habitats such as this old hedge are favoured by lesser whitethroats.

Dartford Warbler

13 cm (5 in)

SPECIES INFORMATION	
SCIENTIFIC NAME	Sylvia undata
RELATED SPECIES	Whitethroat, Lesser Whitethroat, Blackcap, Garden Warbler
CALL	Call 'tchairr'. Song is a short, scratchy warble, from bush-top or flight
HABITAT	Heath and scrub, especially with gorse
STATUS	Resident. In B about 900 pairs in southern England (absent from Ireland)

SIZE

IDENTIFICATION

S MALL, LIVELY WARBLER, with dark plumage. Slate-blue above and brown-maroon below. Tail is long and often held cocked; wings are rather short. Red eye-ring.

FEMALES ARE PALER above and less chestnut, more buff, below. Its short scratching warble and drawn out alarm calls can often be heard when the elusive bird cannot be seen; it may even be down on the ground looking for invertebrate prey. The nest, a compact cup, will also be in deep cover and made up of grass, leaves and stems, and often some heather.

HABITAT

The Dartford warbler is the classic bird of southern heathland, and is therefore included here, even though it is rather rare. Such mature heath habitat is in short supply, with constant pressure to burn off this element of the vegetation at a greater rate than it is replaced. Uncontrolled burning kills individual animals, or flushes them from refuges, after which they can be picked off by predators (notably kestrels and buzzards). Grazing widely checks gorse regeneration, and trampling by livestock also damages mature heath.

POPULATION

Although Cetti's and a growing number of blackcaps and chiffchaffs overwinter in Britain, Dartford warblers have, historically, been the only warbler to remain in Britain throughout the winter.

MAP

Their food is mainly beetles, spiders, lepidopterous larvae and bugs, with nestlings fed on large spiders and caterpillars mainly caught among gorse.

Whereas Dartford warblers breed in areas with July temperatures up to 30°C (86°F) and above, they barely survive if January temperatures fall below an average of 4°C (39°F). They are therefore limited to the maritime areas of France, as well as being on the extreme of their range in Britain.

W. H. Hudson, writing early in the century, describes the Dartford warbler: 'To some who have glanced at a little dusty, out of shape mummy of a bird, labelled "Dartford warbler", in a museum, or private collection, or under a glass shade, it may seem that I speak too warmly of the pleasure which the sight of the small furze lover can give us. He is of the type of the whitethroat, but idealised; ....A sprite-like bird in his slender exquisite shape and his beautiful fits of excitement, fantastic in his motions as he flits and flies from spray to spray, now hovering motionless in the air like the wooing goldcrest, anon dropping on a perch, to sit jerking his long tail, his crest raised, his throat swollen, chiding when he sings and singing when he chides, like a refined and lesser sedge warbler in a frenzy, his slate black and chestnut plumage showing rich and dark against the pure and luminous yellow of the massed furze blossoms. It is a sight of fairy-like bird life and of flower which cannot soon be forgotten.'

Top
Dartford warbler
in typical pose atop
a gorse bush.

Bottom
Shades of maroon and
blue-grey characterise the
male Dartford warbler in
breeding plumage. Also
prominent is the bright
red eye-ring.

Grasshopper Warbler

13 cm (5 in)

SPECIES INFORMATION	
SCIENTIFIC NAME	Locustella naevia
RELATED SPECIES	Savi's Warbler
CALL	Alarm call 'tschek-tschek'. Song is an even, almost mechanical reeling often continuing for minutes, by day and at night
HABITAT	Thick scrub in marshy areas, damp meadows with tall grass, swampy and river-valley woodland. Also on heathland and in dry woodland clearings
STATUS	Summer visitor. In BI about 16,000 pairs (rather local)

SMALL, OLIVE-BROWN, streaked above, and with narrow, rounded tail. Underside pale, weakly striped, frequently identified by its song.

MORE OFTEN HEARD than seen, grasshopper warblers tend to skulk in thick undergrowth, except when singing, when they usually perch on the very top of a bush or thicket. Even then they can be difficult to pick out as their song is difficult to

pinpoint. The ventriloquist's effect is increased as the singing bird moves its head from side to side. This serves to broadcast its territorial song and to make it less easy for a predator to locate.

Rook

45 cm (18 in)

SPECIES INFORMATION	
SCIENTIFIC NAME	Corvus frugilegus
RELATED SPECIES	Carrion Crow, Hooded Crow, Jackdaw, Raven.
CALL	Range of cawing calls – 'krah' or 'korr' – much more varied than Carrion Crow's
HABITAT	Open country and farmland, edges of broadleaved and coniferous woodland, parks and urban areas with tall trees
STATUS	Resident. In BI about 1,375,000 pairs

BLACK, WITH PALE bill and bare grey bill-base, and steep, angled forehead. Belly and thigh feathers tend to be loose, giving trousered effect. Nests colonially and often flocks.

NOWADAYS ROOKS ARE most familiar to many as scavengers along motorway verges and roadsides. They will take a wide range of food, like most members of the crow family, and they often feed in open fields.

Back in 1866 Harting wrote that 'we should not be too hasty in condemning them ... for during the year they destroy innumerable quantities of slugs, snails, worms, beetles and grubs. And when we reflect

upon the ravages committed by a single species, the wire-worm, which is greedily devoured by rooks, we can hardly fail to arrive at the conclusion that the amount of evil committed on the one hand is counterbalanced by the good rendered on the other.'

Rooks are real specialists at extracting invertebrates from below the soil surface, digging with

the bill and probing deep in the ground. Their noisy rookeries have always fascinated the country observer.

Tree Sparrow

14 cm (5.5 in)

SIZE

IDENTIFICATION

HABITAT

POPULATION

MAP

SPECIES INFORMATION	
SCIENTIFIC NAME	Passer montanus
RELATED SPECIES	House Sparrow
CALL	Flight-call a hard 'tek-tek-tek'. Song similar to house sparrow's, but shorter
HABITAT	Less dependent on houses and people than house sparrow. Breeds in open country with hedges, copses and orchards, in parks and at edges of towns and villages
STATUS	Resident. In BI about 285,000 pairs

SOMEWHAT SMALLER and slimmer than House Sparrow, and with brighter plumage. Chestnut crown and nape, black spot on white cheek, and small black chin spot. Juvenile has grey-brown head and dark grey chin.

THE BROWN CROWN and black cheek spot of the tree sparrow separate it from its commoner relative, and its sharp flight note is often the first indication that it is around. Many of us have treated it like the stock dove as a bird 'that is around somewhere' in the farming landscape and, but for routine monitoring of its numbers by the band of farmland Common Birds Census workers, we might not have realised that the population has actually fallen by a staggering 89 per cent in the last 25 years.

Old orchards, willows, hedgerow trees with holes, quarries and outbuildings all provide possible nest sites. Elm disease and the subsequent death and felling of the trees may have reduced the numbers of breeding holes, but reduced food supply seems to be the main cause of their decline.

The key features of the tree sparrow are the chestnut brown crown and the black spot on a white cheek.

They mainly feed on the ground, favouring seeds of small weeds At all times feeding tends to be in groups. Colonial nesting groups may disappear suddenly for no apparent reason. Out of the breeding season, tree sparrows mix with other finches and are highly mobile in their search for suitable food. Perhaps it is this mobility, following a build-up of continental populations, that occasionally boosts our numbers.

Brambling

15 cm (6 in)

SPECIES INFORMATION	
SCIENTIFIC NAME	*Fringilla montifringilla*
RELATED SPECIES	*Chaffinch*
CALL	A rather wheezy 'eeekp'. Song is a soft combination of greenfinch-like calls and rattling sounds
HABITAT	Breeds in northern birch woods and coniferous forests. In winter often in large flocks to fields and under beech trees
STATUS	Irregular winter visitor. In BI a handful of pairs breed, usually in Scotland (absent from Ireland)

BREEDING MALE HAS black back, head and bill, with orange breast and shoulders. In winter male loses most of black. Female has grey cheeks, black streaks on crown and brown back. Shows white rump in flight and has less obvious wing bar than chaffinch.

THE BRAMBLING IS one of the most migratory of finches, and over much of Europe is entirely a winter visitor. In a mixed flock it can be distinguished from the chaffinch by its white rump, darker patterned head, tortoiseshell shoulders and scaly black back as well as by distinctive wheezing call notes. The females are paler, with buff grey heads, and young birds are paler still. Tail is shorter and more forked than chaffinch's.

In the birch woods of northern Europe, the brambling is usually the commonest bird after the willow warbler. It is strongly territorial, but where chaffinch and brambling overlap there is not interspecific territorial aggression. Under ideal conditions bramblings may breed at densities of 50 per square kilometre. Breeding densities fluctuate, as do in turn the winter populations in Britain. If the bramblings have bred well, feeding their young on insects, and then the tree crops fail there are enormous irruptions, as opposed to the regular brambling migrations.

Wintering bramblings feed very largely on beech-mast. This is only used by chaffinches if they chance upon it, but bramblings roam in search of it. The brambling here is more of a specialist, for it can open the nuts more easily with a bill that is one tenth deeper and has sharper edges than the chaffinch's.

Bramblings have established a tenuous foothold in Britain, with ten or so proven records of breeding in Scotland, and a scattering of singing males have been heard down the east of the country.

SIZE

IDENTIFICATION

HABITAT

POPULATION

MAP

A beechwood in winter – typical brambling country, if the beechmast crop has been good.

179

Goldfinch

12 cm (4.75 in)

SPECIES INFORMATION	
SCIENTIFIC NAME	*Carduelis carduelis*
RELATED SPECIES	Linnet, Greenfinch, Siskin, Twite, Redpoll
CALL	High-pitched 'deed-lit'. Song is a high-pitched rapid twitter
HABITAT	Parks, orchards, hedgerows, gardens and cultivated fields. Often feeds on thistles
STATUS	Resident. In BI about 300,000 pairs

SIZE

IDENTIFICATION

HABITAT

POPULATION

MAP

COLOURFUL, SMALL FINCH with black and yellow wings and red face. Juveniles lack head colours, but do have the characteristic yellow wing bars.

THE GOLD OF the name shows on birds of all ages, with the shining panel along the centre of the black wing, but the head pattern is, perhaps, even more striking with near vertical bands of red, white and black. The back and tail have three bands too; brown back, whitish rump and black tail with white spots. Young birds have plain faces and lack the white tips to the tertials and primaries that feature on the adults. The pointed bill enables the bird to feed off its favourite seeds, such as those of thistles and teasel.

Nicholson writes:'They further recommend themselves by their fondness for feeding on the seeds of the thistle, groundsel, knapweed and other plants objectionable to both the farmer and the gardener.' It is interesting to see how he saw the future of farming:- 'Greater use of science, improved equipment and education and

The goldfinch must be one of our prettiest birds, but they seldom keep still long enough for one to appreciate their plumage.

higher prices make for more intensive farming and may be expected to involve more wholesale eradication of weeds and the diminution of waste patches, banks and even hedges on many farms. The ploughing and reseeding of grassland aims at results which will leave little food for birds such as goldfinches.'

In fact goldfinches have not done badly, perhaps because of their flexibility. As an alternative to weed seeds they join siskins and redpolls among the birch and alder seeds and recently they have become more ready to use garden feeders in time of need. In addition if conditions become difficult, particularly in response to cold, a large part of the population may move south-west.

Many European devotional paintings include goldfinches, which are apparently a symbol of fertility and healing powers.

'Who can stay indoors when the goldfinches are busy among the bloom on the apple trees? A flood of sunshine falling through a roof of rosy pink and delicate white blossom overhead; underneath, grass deeply green with the vigour of spring, dotted with yellow buttercups and strewn with bloom shaken by the wind from the trees. Listen how happy the goldfinches are in the orchard. Summer after summer they build in the same trees, bushy – headed codlings; generation and generation has been born there and gone forth to enjoy in turn the pleasures of the field.'

Linnet

14 cm (5.5 in)

```
○ ○ ○ ○ ○ ○ ○ ○ ○ ○ ○ ○ ○ ○ ○ ○ ○ ○ ○ ○ ○ ○ ○ ○ ○ ○
  S P E C I E S   I N F O R M A T I O N
```

SCIENTIFIC NAME	Carduelis cannabina
RELATED SPECIES	Goldfinch, Greenfinch, Siskin, Twite, Redpoll
CALL	Flight-call rather bouncy 'ge-ge-geg'. Song is rather pretty, beginning with a series of calls, and developing into rapid trills and fluting
HABITAT	Open, cultivated country, hedgerow, heathland, parks and gardens
STATUS	Resident. In BI about 650,000 pairs

MAINLY BROWN, ACTIVE finch. Breeding male has red forehead and breast; duller in winter with no red on head. Female lacks red, is streaked and dark brown above. Juvenile more heavily streaked. Often forms flocks in open country outside breeding season.

IT IS EASY TO take linnets for granted and they are often overlooked, perhaps because they are nearly always on the move. Seen close, they are attractive, especially a male in full breeding plumage.

Although linnets are found over most of lowland Britain, but more scattered in Ireland, the abundance map in the *New Atlas* shows a marked coastal bias, particularly along the east.

'Over the years' as Newton (1998) reports 'herbicide use has enormously reduced the populations of various farmland weeds, on which many seed-eating birds depend and once common arable weeds have now become rare in lowland

Britain. Each application of herbicide depletes the soil's seed bank with seeds turned to the surface being killed before producing seeds. Linnets thrive on fat-hen, persicaria and chickweed which could at one time be counted in thousands per square metre on newly turned farmland soil whereas now, after years of herbicide use, they have almost disappeared from the soil of cereal growing regions.'

SIZE

IDENTIFICATION

HABITAT

POPULATION

MAP

Top left
Cock linnet in full breeding plumage.

Top right
Gorse scrub and woodland edge in Dorset — excellent habitat for linnets.

Bottom
Feeding a nest of young linnets.

181

Yellowhammer

16 cm (6.5 in)

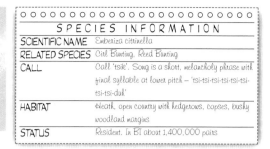

○ ○

SPECIES INFORMATION

SCIENTIFIC NAME	Emberiza citrinella
RELATED SPECIES	Cirl Bunting, Reed Bunting
CALL	Call 'tsik'. Song is a short, melancholy phrase with final syllable at lower pitch – 'tsi-tsi-tsi-tsi-tsi-tsi-tsi-tsi-duh'
HABITAT	Heath, open country with hedgerows, copses, bushy woodland margins
STATUS	Resident. In BI about 1,400,000 pairs

SIZE

IDENTIFICATION

HABITAT

POPULATION

MAP

SLIM, YELLOW-HEADED bunting with long tail and cinnamon-brown rump. Female and juvenile less yellow, with dark streaks on head and throat. White outer tail feathers obvious in flight.

THE BRIGHT YELLOW head of the breeding male is what people think of in the plumage of yellowhammers, but the chestnut rump and long,

white-edged tail are equally distinctive. Females and non breeding males are duller but yellow on head and streaky belly can usually identify, although some first winter females are rather nondescript.

In Gaelic, the yellowhammer is the yellow broom bird and the association between yellowhammers and gorse or broom is close, even if the development of farming with tall hedges and scruffy patches of scrub helped it to spread originally. Now its world is changing again and like the linnet it no longer has the food supply it used to have.

Nicholson (1951) writes that 'those who go about with their eyes open find themselves constantly crossing invisible lines on one side of which there are plenty of yellowhammers and on the other few or none. These lines are less distinct than those bounding the tribes of corn buntings, for the cock yellowhammer, although conspicuous in plumage, is less dominating in voice and in choice of singing posts, and is moreover sufficiently widespread and common to be easily taken for granted unless the observer takes the trouble to notice where yellowhammers are not as well as where they are.'

Top and bottom right
The cock yellowhammer has a russet rump and a bright yellow head.

Bottom left
The female, here at its nest, is much less brightly coloured.

He then gives same examples of these 'invisible lines' and is once again ahead of his time in stressing the value of negative records, and in setting up a problem for investigation. As we get to know more of the ecology of individual species we are more able to explain declines and to help to bring about recoveries.

Everyone knows the common rendering of the yellowhammer's song: 'a little bit of bread and no cheese', but in Scotland this is said to be rendered as 'may the devil take you'.

Apart from the song, the common contact call, given in flight or perched, is particularly useful to us when birds feed in mixed winter flocks.

Most populations are partial migrants, with part of the north of its range being vacated and wintering birds moving to northern Spain, Italy and Greece. British birds though are largely sedentary, few moving more than 5 km (3 miles). The few ringing recoveries indicate passage of a few Scandinavian birds along the east coast in spring and autumn.

> '*In early spring when winds blow chilly cold*
> *The yellow hammer trailing grass will come*
> *To fix a place and choose an early home*
> *With yellow breast and head of solid gold.*'
> John Clare SELECTED POEMS

Corn Bunting

18 cm (7 in)

LARGE BUNTING WITH lark-like plumage. Cream coloured below, with brown streaks on throat and flanks; no white in tail (compare larks). Is often seen sitting on telephone wires.

Food is taken on the ground, with seeds, mainly cereals, featuring importantly, together with invertebrates. Because of the importance of cereals, the range has retracted not only in Britain but in many parts of Europe.

In winter there are local movements, and information about the whereabouts of food supplies may be shared among birds at winter roosts in gorse, scrub or reedbeds. On a wider scale, the central European birds are most migratory, heading south or east, while other populations show a westerly tendency.

THE SONG OF THE corn bunting is a great deal more conspicuous than its rather drab plumage. This is usually likened to the rattling of a bunch of keys. It also has distinctive 'quit - it – it' flight-call, and a harsh 'chip' as contact call.

The corn bunting in a bulky bird, which often sits in a conspicuous position, on a wire or bush-top. It has a fluttering flight, and sometimes dangles its legs.

Although mainly associated with agriculture, any open country with song posts can be corn bunting country. As the nest is usually on the ground, little cover is needed, although protection in rank vegetation is helpful.

SIZE

IDENTIFICATION

HABITAT

POPULATION

MAP

Corn buntings, once ubiquitous in farmland, have decreased in recent years following changes in agriculture and in particular the decrease in barley growing.

Mountain and Moorland Birds

LOOKING TOWARDS THE Cuillins of Skye or across many a Scottish loch, the highlands and islands seem to extend for ever. Many of the islands have their hills, and even those that do not retain their upland character with moorland often reaching to sea level. In fact, hills cover a third of all Britain, while Ireland is ringed by uplands.

BIRDS OF THE REGION

MOUNTAIN BIRDS MAY be few, but they can be exciting. The calls of red-throated divers along coast evoke the lonely hills and the jingling of Snow buntings hints at the hardness of life among the summits. One of the finest of all mountain bird sounds is the whistling song of the dotterel, a wader of the high mountain summits of Scotland.

The birds at the top of the mountain and moorland food chains are the birds of prey, such as kestrel, merlin, golden eagle, buzzard and hen harrier, and the raven which is a general scavenger.

THE UPLANDS ARE made up of a variety of habitats, with zones at different altitudes, each with its characteristic birds. Species, as well as individuals, are few, even in summer, for under the dual influence of poor soil and harsh climate food is short. When winter comes, wheatears and ring ouzels will have migrated, and the meadow pipits moved down from the hills, making these habitats seem even more deserted.

If Scotland, with its remains of post ice-age arctic tundra, has most of the gems, from ptarmigan to rare breeding waders, Wales has its choughs and kites, the pennines have golden plover and twite, and the most southerly dunlin in the world still breed on Dartmoor.

Top left
Meadow pipits are common birds of mountain and moorland .

Top right
Merlins like to nest in deep heather – but you would be lucky indeed to spot one.

Bottom right
Golden plover is another species which breeds on high moorland – mainly in Scotland and the northern Pennines.

Two northern areas need special mention for their climatic peculiarities lead to bird habitats of the utmost importance. The blanket bogs and wet heaths of Shetland and the 'flow country' of Sutherland and Caithness hold a significant percentage of a number of British birds.

Shetland lies in the track of depressions that sweep westwards across the North Atlantic and is in the same latitude as southern Greenland. Not surprisingly, northern birds are the speciality here, with 95 per cent of Britain's breeding whimbrels, 70 per cent of great skuas and 60 per cent of arctic skuas. Including the coastal areas as well as the moorland, Shetland also holds a significant percentage of eiders, ringed plovers, oystercatchers and dunlins. Where the drainage is better and ling gives way to bell heather, crowberry, bilberry and cranberry, the golden plover breeds, with 5-10 per cent of the British population.

The Flow Country, where the undulating moorlands of east Sutherland gradually descend into Caithness, includes, to the west, higher peaks and ranges projecting from the peat. As on Shetland, moor and water are inseparable. The importance of this country as our nearest equivalent to the wet tundras of the Low Arctic is seen by their recognition as of 'outstanding universal value' on the UK's new tentative list of world heritage sites for submission to UNESCO.

Detailed study of the area only began in 1979, when the then Nature Conservancy Council launched a breeding bird survey of this difficult terrain. Ten species of wader were widespread, but breeding wood sandpipers, red-necked phalaropes, Temminck's stints and ruffs have also been found. Native greylag geese, red- and black-throated divers, common scoters and Arctic skua are important, with the black-throats making up some 20 per cent and the common scoter 40 per cent of the British breeding populations.

CWM IDWAL

This reserve, the first National Nature Reserve in Wales, is one of the most easily accessible mountain areas in Britain, and has some of the most exciting arctic alpine plants south of Scotland.

As soon as one starts along the path into the Cwm from April on, wheatears will 'chack' and show their white rumps. Quite soon, if one is lucky, the ringing song of ring ouzels will carry from the lower crags, and grey wagtails will flit after flies along the stream. From the rocky slopes of Tryfan or the crags of the Glyders, ravens or peregrines glide across the cwm, while in winter the occasional whooper swan or goldeneye will turn up on Llyn Idwal. A small island gives some indication of what the vegetation might be like with fewer sheep.

Apart from meadow pipits, there are birdless times as one climbs towards the botanist's mecca, Twll Du, black chasm or the Devils Kitchen. Emerging onto wet grassland above the Kitchen and turning towards the summit of Y Garn, outside the reserve, skylarks sing. In late summer choughs come to feed in the short grass, searching for insects particularly where grass meets stone and the crevices can be explored with their long, curved bills. In winter, when snow covers the slopes, snow buntings may feed on seeds on isolated rush heads jutting through.

Top
Whimbrel breed in the north of Scotland, mainly Shetland, where they are increasing.

Bottom
Red-throated divers like to nest close to small lakes.

Unless there is a great reduction in the emission of greenhouse gases, global warming is likely to be with us for some time, and although its consequences for birds can be debated, our mountain birds will probably not benefit. In Scandinavia the tree-line is already rising, and if we had a 300 m (984 ft) shift in altitude of the upland zones and a longer growing season even the Scottish mountains could well lose their mossy *Racomitrium* heath, their solifluction terraces and their snow-beds.

Des Thompson, Principal Advisor on the Uplands in Scottish National Heritage sees three likely consequences: the numbers and breeding distribution of upland species will change, upland birds will breed earlier and patterns of migration and overwintering behaviour will also be influenced.

Ravens are already breeding earlier and, as greenshank breeding is linked with soil temperature, they will probably follow suit. The upward movement of grasses will change grazing practices with consequences for dotterel, while snow bunting and the occasionally breeding purple sandpiper might be

lost. Although oystercatcher, hen harrier, lapwing and twite may benefit, the spread of arable at lower levels and of scrub at higher levels, will need imaginative conservation measures. If the threat to the uplands in the 1980s was afforestation and in the 1990s agricultural change and overgrazing, it is now climate change that could lead to a different Cairngorm bird community by 2050.

Middle left
The raven, largest of our crows, favours remote, rocky uplands.

Middle right
Moorland – typical golden plover country.

Bottom
Greenshank, here seen on migration, nest in parts of north-west Scotland.

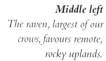

THE HIGHLANDS

IN THE *Highlands and Islands* Fraser Darling describes the delights of the arctic-alpine grassland for the human observer. 'The high grasslands on a summer day have an idyllic quality. They are remote and quiet. They are green and kind to the eye. They are easy to the feet. The very pebbles among which the flowers grow have a sparkle and show of colour. To climb on one of these alps of grass and descend again in a few hours is not enough.'

He goes on to say, 'Take a little tent and remain in the quietness for one night at least. It is a magnificent experience to rise in the morning in such a place and feel fresh, knowing that your enjoyment of the peat-free plateaux is not to be spoiled by a gruelling climb and the necessity of going down the same day. The only sounds breaking the silence, if you can get the best of the early July weather, will be the grackle of the ptarmigan, the flute-like pipe of the ring ouzel, perhaps the plaint of a golden plover or a dotterel and the bark of the golden eagle. These are good sounds, and do not

disturb what is for the moment a place of peace. See how the deer, now bright-red-coated, lie at ease in the alpine grassland. Listen, if you have stalked near enough, to the sweet talkings of the calves who are like happy children. Here is new herbage over which no other muzzles have grazed: the very soil has been washed by fifty inches of rain since the deer were here before, in November.'

THREATS TO THE ENVIRONMENT

EVEN THOUGH MANY mountain and moorland sites are rather remote, nevertheless the threats to them are real enough. Forestry schemes have reduced the wildlife value of parts of Flow Country for example, perhaps the nearest to a unique British habitat, leading to reductions in breeding waders. Access to the summit plateaux of the Cairngorms grows ever easier, while leisure activities everywhere, together with intensive grazing, acidification of rivers, drainage and fertilisation of marginal land, have all had their effects.

The Pennine moors now lack many of the plants that normally make up the upland community, partly as a result of decades of acid rain, and the destruction of the soil through erosion. But the news is not all bad, and many mountain birds are beginning to show increases as awareness grows of the value of these marvellous upland habitats.

Top left
Golden plover – camouflaged amidst the lichens and mosses of high moorland.

Top right
Upland farmland is good curlew habitat.

Bottom
Curlews use their long bills to probe in the ground for worms and grubs.

Red-throated Diver

50–65 cm (21–26 in)

SIZE

IDENTIFICATION

HABITAT

POPULATION

MAP

SPECIES INFORMATION	
SCIENTIFIC NAME	Gavia stellata
RELATED SPECIES	Black-throated Diver, Great Northern Diver
CALL	Wailing on breeding grounds, occasional ringing 'ah-oo-ah' in winter and goose-like flight call. Long like cooing of collared dove, but harsher and louder
HABITAT	Small lakes in moorland and tundra, coastal in winter
STATUS	Breeds in North Britain. Winters mostly on North Sea and Baltic coasts; rare but regular on inland lakes, reservoirs and larger rivers

SOMEWHAT SMALLER THAN black-throated diver, with slimmer head, neck and bill (latter slightly upturned). Head normally tilted upwards. In breeding plumage with red-brown patch on neck, looking black from a distance. In winter very like black-throated, but back lighter. Less distinct border between dark and pale colours on the head and neck.

FOR MOST OF US, divers only occur as winter excitements around the coast, and seeing the red-throat of the one and the black of the other of our breeding divers is just a hope of pleasure to come. The red-throated diver is a bird that likes small lochs for breeding and needs to fly, often far, to collect food, whereas the black-throated, with its distinctive blacks and whites and neck streaks, prefers bigger expanses of water and therefore does not need to fly so much.

The red-throated diver only has a red throat in breeding plumage. In winter a distinctive feature is the up-turned bill-tip.

Both have similar calls, but description can do no justice to the sounds which epitomise the wild, open northern spaces. These sounds are mainly responsible for the place divers play in folklore, but not for their Shetland name of rainbird or, for red-throated diver, learga-chaol, the slender raingoose.

It is at sea that most of us will see divers, and on cold winter days with chilly fingers on the binoculars, with birds half hidden behind waves and never as close as you would like them, you need to know what to look out for.

Divers, grebes and cormorants have features in common. Cormorants swim low in water with bill pointed slightly upward, grebes of comparable size hold their thin necks quite erect and ride higher in the water, while the thicker-necked divers are longer-bodied and larger-billed. Those of red-throated divers appear uptilted because of an angled lower mandible, while black-throats are straight-billed.

There should be no such difficulty in summer, as the red-throated, appropriately, has a wine red patch on its neck and uniform grey brown upperparts, whereas the upper parts of the black throated are chequered black and white. Black and white also feature on the side of the neck bordering the black throat. At all times the bill of the black-throated is heavier and the forehead higher. In flight in winter they are hard to tell apart, but the red-throated diver has a thinner neck and pale face. In flight the black-throated has slower wing beats. Both birds are largely silent in winter.

Black-throated Diver

58–73 cm (23–31 in)

SPECIES INFORMATION

SCIENTIFIC NAME	*Gavia arctica*
RELATED SPECIES	Red-throated Diver, Great Northern Diver
CALL	Seldom heard in winter. Long drawn-out wail, also miaowing call when disturbed. Croaking call: long, pulsed and hoarse, like raven. Wailing call: three brief notes given in territorial encounters. Long call: resembles low-pitched whistle composed of two notes with marked pitch increase in longer second note
HABITAT	Large lakes in summer. In winter usually on coastal seas
STATUS	Breeds mainly in north-west Scotland. Winters on North Sea and Baltic, more rarely on large inland lakes

DUCK-LIKE, WITH rather snake-like head. Bill held straight, head upright. In breeding plumage has grey head, black throat and striped neck. Back with striking black and white markings. In winter uniform dark above, pale underneath, with clear border on head and neck; bill black; juveniles in winter rather paler.

BLACK-THROATED DIVERS choose to breed on larger lochs which, although often nutrient deficient, have enough small trout, and a range of invertebrates such as crustaceans, molluscs and insect larvae, to feed adults and young. In the past, the link between black-throated divers and trout led to direct persecution, but now disturbance is more of a problem with birdwatchers being quite as disturbing as fishermen.

The main breeding area of both divers is Scandinavia, as well as northern Russia and across northern Asia. In winter they spread out around coasts as far south as France, Italy and the Black Sea.

SIZE

IDENTIFICATION

HABITAT

POPULATION

MAP

The usual view of a black-throated diver is a distant bird in winter, at sea or on a reservoir.

Golden Eagle

75–89 cm (30–35 in)

○ ○

SPECIES INFORMATION

SCIENTIFIC NAME	*Aquila chrysaetos*
RELATED SPECIES	White-tailed eagle
CALL	Occasional yelps, but rarely heard
HABITAT	Mainly restricted to remote mountain areas
STATUS	Mainly resident. Young birds may wander. Mainly Scotland but occasionally breeds in Lake District. British population about 450 pairs

SIZE

IDENTIFICATION

HABITAT

POPULATION

MAP

LARGE, DARK, AND powerful, with heavy bill and strong talons. Crown and neck golden brown, wings long and relatively narrow. Tail rather long and broad. Juveniles dark with large white patches on wings; tail white with broad black tip.

GOLDEN EAGLES OUGHT to be easy to identify, but many a buzzard has been turned into an eagle when watchers in remote hills were over hopeful. With the return of white-tailed eagles there is another possible source of error, but the squarish tail of the golden sets it apart from the white-tailed, which has a wedge-shaped tail with a dark end. Apart from size, golden eagles have relatively larger heads than buzzards, and young birds have a helpful white wing patch and rounded tails.

Adult birds are uniform dark brown but with some golden on the crown and hind neck. It soars with its wings raised slightly on either side of the body, the wings narrow at their base and the body is noticeably darker than the flight feathers. Leslie Brown suggests that an average home-range might be of the order of 5000 ha. Another point he makes is that no one can give a good account of how a golden eagle spends its day, or the proportion of time spent

hunting, for one sees an eagle about once a day, and if lucky for one minute, when on the hill.

The Scottish birds form about per cent of the European population, which is widely spread but scattered, with Spain and Norway each having more than per cent. Although aerial displays are less developed than in some other eagles, this is a fine bird with a history of devoted supporters.

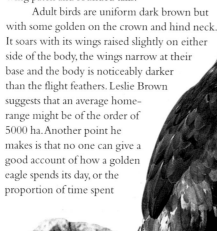

The golden eagle, our largest bird of prey, is truly magnificent, with a huge wingspan and massive hooked bill.

> '*The clinching, inter locking claw,*
> *a living fierce gyrating wheel,*
> *Four beating wings, two beaks,*
> *a swirling mass tight grappling,*
> *In tumbling turning, clustering loops,*
> *straight downward falling.*'
> Walt Whitman THE DALLIANCE OF EAGLES

Peregrine Falcon

39–50 cm (15–20 in)

SIZE

IDENTIFICATION

HABITAT

POPULATION

MAP

SPECIES INFORMATION	
SCIENTIFIC NAME	*Falco peregrinus*
RELATED SPECIES	Kestrel, Hobby, Merlin
CALL	'Kek-kek-kek' at or near nest-site
HABITAT	Hilly and mountainous areas, and at coast. Needs steep rocks or cliffs for nest-site. Estuaries and other wetlands in winter
STATUS	Resident. In BI about 1500 pairs, mainly in north and west

CROW-SIZED, POWERFUL falcon. Pointed, broad-based wings; short, tapering tail. Broad, dark moustache. Underparts pale, with dark barring. Juveniles dark brown above, yellow-brown beneath, with heavy dark streaks. Normal flight relatively slow, with powerful, shallow wingstrokes, and periods of gliding.

APART FROM SPEED and power, the dark head and relatively short tail are characteristic, and at close quarters the head can be seen to be almost completely dark except for white on the neck up to the bill, with another white extension of the pale chest towards the rear side of the head. Between these two white areas, a distinctive curved V of black covers the side of the neck. Adults are slate-coloured above and barred below, while young birds are dark brown above with small, but noticeable, pale tip to their tails.

The peregrine is a large falcon exuding strength, and the success of its population recovery brings pleasure to all except the most ardent pigeon fancier. The problems with persistent organochlorine insecticides were outlined in the introduction to farmland birds, and peregrines were among those most affected, as the long-lived residues moved up the food chain to end in the top predator. A decline began around 1956, when southern populations had almost recovered from egg destruction and shooting, resulting from its liking for homing pigeons during the war. By 1962 it was down to 68 pairs, and was extinct over much of its former range. Now, apart form returning to many traditional and new cliff haunts, it is even using buildings such as cathedrals, churches and office blocks, as breeding sites.

Whether chasing, soaring or just flying by, peregrines are spectacular, but when they indulge in high circling or flight-play together, or when the male displays in undulating flight or with downward plunges, it is appreciated by almost everybody. The noise it makes can make it more impressive. These calls, mainly near the eyrie, are essentially a harsh chattering, repeated rapidly, and carrying far, so that the bird itself can be hard to find against a background of mountain crags. It is on record that some eyries occupied in medieval times were still being used in 1939.

As indicated by references to pigeon fanciers and homing pigeons, peregrines feed largely on birds largely taken on the wing and often over the sea. Most frequently they are caught from above, with a rapid stoop, but pigeons often need hectic pursuit, during which they too may show acrobatic ability. Breeding auks may be the target at some breeding sites but, over winter estuaries, waders and ducks are important prey and the appearance of a peregrine can cause estuarine chaos.

Peregrines have made a steady recovery from the earlier effects of pesticides and persecution. They have even started to nest in some of our cities.

Merlin

25–30 cm (10–12 in)

○ ○

SPECIES INFORMATION

SCIENTIFIC NAME	*Falco columbarius*
RELATED SPECIES	Kestrel, Peregrine, Hobby
CALL	Very rapid 'kikiki', usually near nest
HABITAT	Upland birch woodland, heather moors, and dunes. In winter often at coast or washland
STATUS	Resident. Wanders in winter. In BI recent decline to about 600 pairs

SIZE

IDENTIFICATION

HABITAT

POPULATION

MAP

SMALLEST OF OUR falcons, with low, rapid flight. Male is grey above; rusty yellow underneath with long dark streaks. Female has larger streaks below, and is dark brown above, with a barred tail. Juveniles very like female.

BY CONTRAST WITH the heavy power of eagles, we have the dashing forays of merlins in pursuit of moorland birds. Merlin prey is usually caught after a short distance by surprise attack, but sometimes they may be chased to exhaustion.

Ratcliffe mentions two great difficulties with merlins. The first is the complex interplay of facts, afforestation, organochlorines, mercury, and unknowns, involved in trying to explain the decline in merlin numbers and range, and the second is the difficulty in finding out what their numbers actually are.

A pair may apparently be interested in one part of a moor and then move elsewhere, while sitting birds may sit so tight that they will not move even with a hopeful observer hand clapping or shouting from 25 m; the off-duty bird may also leave the nesting area for hours. Why do merlin much prefer heather moor to grassmoor, when meadow pipit populations are much the same in both? The answer may be that merlins like tall heather for nesting sites, but old crow nests in bushes will do on grassmoor.

Merlins are dark, uniform-looking falcons with apparently long tails. If seen well the male has dark slate-blue back and pale streaked pinkish underparts, while the larger female has a distinct head pattern with contrasting dark and white. In flight both sexes have dark but barred underwings and pointed wing tips, but the tail of the male ends in a single subterminal bar whereas those of females and immatures are strongly barred. A typical falcon alarm call near the nest and other calls are used in courtship.

The merlin has a markedly northerly distribution, with Scandinavia and Iceland its European stronghold, so not surprisingly many birds migrate. Even among our western populations most leave the summer's heather for the coast; this is not so true of Ireland.

Top left
The sharp-eyed merlin catches mainly small birds such as meadow pipits.

Top right
A brood of merlin chicks, still covered in soft down.

Bottom
Open moorland is favoured by merlins, with tall scrub and heather for nesting.

Hen Harrier

43–50 cm (17–20 in)

SPECIES INFORMATION

SCIENTIFIC NAME	Circus cyaneus
RELATED SPECIES	Marsh Harrier, Montagu's Harrier
CALL	Male has a high-pitched 'piuu piuu' in courtship flight; female a hoarse 'pik-e'. Alarm call 'chek-ek-ek-ek'
HABITAT	Open landscapes – heather moor, dunes, marshes and damp meadows; also in young plantations. In winter regular in open marshland and wet heath
STATUS	Resident and partial migrant. In BI mainly in N and W about 800 pairs. Ranges south in winter

SLIM AND LIGHT in flight. Male has ash-grey plumage, with contrasting black-tipped wings and white rump. Female is dark brown above, pale yellow-brown beneath, with striped wings and tail, and clear white rump. Flight buoyant and gliding.

THERE ARE BOTH Welsh and Scottish hen harriers, a good Irish population and some in northern England, on heather moor and young forestry. All harriers fly low on long wings and the female of this species, larger than the male, is not easily distinguished from the more delicate (and rarer) Montagu's, but she does have a broader white rump. The male has 'clean' grey back and upper wings with black tips. His combination of black on all primaries, decidedly broader wings with dark trailing edge below should distinguish him from male Montagu's harrier.

Like the red kite, hen harriers suffered much in the interests of game preservation, and by the turn of the century had a few refuges on Scottish islands and Irish uplands. As a rarity it suffered at the hands of egg collectors, but the Second World War reduced the gamekeepers, and increased young forestry plantations, to such an extent that in 20 years the hen harrier had again become a widespread breeder in the uplands of Britain and Ireland. Since then a decline has set in, certainly driven by illegal persecution, for it is the most hated of raptors for those with interests in grouse populations. In fact, meadow pipits and small mammals form a high percentage of its prey in upland areas.

One unusual feature is the relatively high level of polygamy, with some males pairing with more than one female.

From their summer breeding haunts hen harriers spread more widely to coasts and lowland downs and heaths, avoiding trees (except for roosting) because of their hunting method of low-level flight. Similarly, forestry plantations are used only for breeding and not for hunting. There are often small winter roosts, collecting birds from a wide feeding area. These roosts, often in reedbeds, are on the ground or on platforms of vegetation.

In parts of its range there are more extensive movements, and in France, it is sometimes known as St Martin's bird as it passes through on or around St Martin's Day, 11 November.

 SIZE

 IDENTIFICATION

 HABITAT

 POPULATION

 MAP

Top
Downland sometimes attracts visiting hen harriers during the winter.

Bottom
Hen harriers are very buoyant in flight as they quarter the moorland for small mammals and birds.

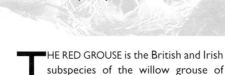

Red Grouse

38 cm (15 in)

SPECIES INFORMATION	
SCIENTIFIC NAME	Lagopus lagopus
RELATED SPECIES	Ptarmigan, Black Grouse and Capercaillie
CALL	'Go-back, go-back, go-back'
HABITAT	Upland heather-moor and bog
STATUS	Resident. In BI commonest in northern England and Scotland, about 250,000 pairs

SIZE

IDENTIFICATION

HABITAT

POPULATION

MAP

THE RED GROUSE is the British and Irish subspecies of the willow grouse of Scandinavia and North Asia. Both sexes are reddish-brown, with black barring. Flies strongly and glides on drooping wings.

BRITISH RED GROUSE were thought to be an endemic species, but are now considered as an isolated race of the willow grouse which is found all round the arctic. Because of shooting interests grouse are among the most studied of birds, and their fluctuating populations have been well documented. It would seem that numbers are influenced by a complex of factors with the activities of predators, gamekeepers and parasites interacting with territorial behaviour of the birds and the quality of the heather. Red grouse are dependant on heather at all times, and their explosive flight and noisy 'go back, go back' calls are quite enough to identify them when disturbed.

MacGillivray in his *History of British Birds* (1837-52) wrote that 'the Celts, naturally imagining the moorcock to speak Gaelic signify it (the call) as 'co co co co mo chlaidh, mo chlaidh' i.e. who, who who goes there, my sword, my sword.'

Some of the highest densities are found in north Yorkshire, but elsewhere in England there are areas where too many grazing sheep have converted grouse moor to grassland. This has also happened in Wales and the Scottish borders, and in all these places

heather has also been lost to afforestation. The greatest range retraction had been in Ireland. Paradoxically perhaps, high densities of red grouse are very dependant on shooting and the associated management of the heather.

When looking for grouse it may be only a head that is visible above the heather, when the bright red wattle in spring may be conspicuous, but the white woolly feet are less likely to be seen. Females lack the wattle and are paler and browner but most frequently grouse are only seen as they 'explode' with a clatter of wings and noisy calls, showing a characteristic profile from behind with dumpy body and wings forming a shallow inverted U during the gliding phases of their flight.

Red grouse are at home on upland heather moor. Their call is a highly characteristic 'go-back, go-back'.

Ptarmigan

36cm (14 in)

```
○○○○○○○○○○○○○○○○○○○○○○○○○○○
        S P E C I E S   I N F O R M A T I O N
SCIENTIFIC NAME   Lagopus mutus
RELATED SPECIES   Red Grouse, Black Grouse and Capercaillie
CALL              Characteristic grating call of male 'arrr-arr-krrr-ak-
                  ak-ak'
HABITAT           Above tree-line in rocky sites. At lower levels in
                  winter
STATUS            Resident. Scottish highlands about 15,000 birds
```

SLIGHTLY SMALLER THAN red grouse. Wings are white at all seasons. Breeding male marbled dark brown-grey on upperside and breast, otherwise white, with small red comb. Female yellow-brown, with darker crescent-shaped markings. In winter pure white, except for jet black tail, male with black stripe through eye.

VERY SUITABLY THIS peculiar name is derived from the Gaelic name 'tarmachan'. Going back somewhat further, some 10,000 years, we come to the ending of the ice-age, at which stage British ptarmigan became separated from other populations. Like many of the arctic-alpine plants, which have become isolated as relicts near the summits of the hills, the ptarmigan is a true survivor. Despite this period of isolation, Scottish birds are much like their relatives in the Alps, Pyrenees, Iceland and Scandinavia.

One might expect this bird of the high tops to be plumper and larger than the red grouse, so that it could conserve heat better, but in fact it is smaller and slimmer, with narrower wings and a more slender bill. In summer the males can look like stones. The wings and underbody are white, and in winter the whole body becomes white, except for the black tail which is hidden until the bird flies. The male has a red comb over the eye; more prominent in spring. The female, when not white, has more obvious

dark barring than the male and a yellow rather than grey back. The calls of the two birds have a different pitch, the female's higher; both involve peculiar cyclic clicks and creaks.

Ratcliffe describes how the ptarmigan has a claim to being the hardiest bird on earth. 'It endures the appalling severity of winter throughout the high Arctic region, with mean January temperatures down as low as -40° C. Even in these inhospitable wastes the ptarmigan appears to move little in seeking to escape the terrible cold, but burrows into the snow for shelter and access to its buried food supply. Scottish haunts must be mild by comparison, for at 1,200 m, mean January temperature is only -5° C, even though the extreme windiness of the highland climate can give additional adversity in winter.'

In much of its Arctic habitat, where food webs are simplified, the ptarmigan faces further danger as the chief food of the gyr falcon which has few alternative food items in winter and even in summer targets the ptarmigan as its favourite single item of prey.

Ptarmigan populations have suffered from the rising density of sheep, whose grazing converts dwarf shrub heath to grassland. Ptarmigan need the dwarf shrubs as providers of shoots, buds, berries, twigs and seeds, and indiscriminate burning does not help their cause either. Another problem is that easier human access makes for more litter of one sort or another, which encourages crows, which then eat ptarmigan eggs. Nevertheless, this tame attractive grouse can be one of the commonest bird of the tops where it occurs.

SIZE

IDENTIFICATION

HABITAT

POPULATION

MAP

Top and bottom left
In winter the ptarmigan change to an almost pure white, blending in with the snow and ice.

Middle right
In summer, the belly and wings remain white, but the upper parts are grey-brown.

Black Grouse

40–55 cm 16–22 (in)

SPECIES INFORMATION	
SCIENTIFIC NAME	Lyrurus Tetrao
RELATED SPECIES	Capercaillie, Red Grouse, Ptarmigan
CALL	Male song at display ground (lek) is a bubbling coo, interspersed with hissing or sneezing
HABITAT	Heather moor and bog, open wooded areas and dwarf shrub heath near tree-line
STATUS	Resident. In Britain about 10,000 breeding females (in steady decline) absent from Ireland

MALE HAS SHINY blue-black plumage and lyre-shaped tail feathers, fluffed out during courtship to reveal white under tail coverts. Female is smaller, with camouflaged grey-brown plumage. Bill slightly hooked. Flight involves rapid wingbeats, interspersed with periods of gliding. Often perches in trees.

THE VERY SPECIAL tail may not be conspicuous, but the white shoulder patches of the male are. The black body is glossed with blue. Almost as distinctive as plumage, behaviour and the dove-like bubbling is the flight which may be high, gliding on stretched wings or, as with other woodland grouse, involve rapid wing-beats as the short-winged bird rises among trees. Females in flight have a whiter underwing than red grouse, a notched tail and often a whitish bar on the upperwing. On the ground her larger size and longer tail distinguish the so called 'grey hen' from a female red grouse.

The black grouse is one of our finest birds, and also sadly now rather rare. The males pirouette and spread their feathers in an elaborate lekking display.

Black grouse country has tall heather or young conifers to nest and hide in, together with patches of forest edge and rushy meadows that have not been improved for sheep grazing. These grouse like an abundance of shoots, buds and leaves, especially of heather and bilberry to keep the adults well fed. The young chicks need spiders and beetles and moth caterpillars and sawfly larvae; these are found among bog myrtle and the rushes and grasses of wet places.

In upland areas where rough grazing, moorland edge and heather have disappeared under conifers, and where fields have been 'improved', with the heather, boggy hollows and rushy fields enclosed by wire fences, black grouse have problems. They have little to eat, and few places to hide or nest. Other species such as lapwings, curlews, redshanks and snipe face similar difficulties.

Black grouse are famous for their leks in which the male birds gather to court the females. The leks are usually found in an open area of bog, marsh or forest glade; the males have their own territory within this open area, with low status young birds visiting as intruders. Those with central territories gain the majority of matings; they are usually the older birds. In display the males fan their tails wide: the white under tail converts form a circle as seen from behind. All this is accompanied by a cacophony of 'rookooing' song which carries for up to 3 km (1.8 miles) but is extremely hard to locate. There is also much rushing to and fro within the territory, and fighting at the boundary, which seems to attract the females. They have been at the periphery of the lek, perhaps in nearby trees, watching the males and sometimes preening. Successful matings also attract more females, so one success is likely to precede another.

SPECIES INFORMATION

SCIENTIFIC NAME	Pluvialis apricaria
RELATED SPECIES	Grey Plover
CALL	Soft 'dui'. Alarm call a sharp 'tlie', also a plaintive, musical 'tlooi-fee'. Song consists of high, trilling whistles
HABITAT	Breeds on moorland. Moves to open fields, meadows, pasture and estuaries in winter, often in large flocks
STATUS	Resident and partial migrant. Numbers swelled by migrants from further north in winter. In BI mainly breeds in Scotland and north Pennines. British population about 23,000 pairs. Ireland about 400 pairs

Golden Plover

27 cm (11 in)

I N BREEDING PLUMAGE speckled gold above, jet black neck and belly with white curving dividing line from face to tail. Amount of black on underside is variable and sometimes lacking completely. In winter plumage much duller, without black. Winter flocks on fields can look very thrush-like, both in coloration and behaviour.

As their habitat suggests, they are northern birds with large populations in Iceland, Scandinavia and Russia. All their populations are migratory, mainly moving to western maritime regions as far south as North Africa.

'A golden plover's golden music calls
Across the moor. A heady fragrance spills
From freshly opened peat, then silence falls.'
R. S. Morrison WORDS ON BIRDS

BREEDING GOLDEN PLOVER really are golden, when seen well, but the dusky face and black belly are more noticeable from a distance, when the back looks brown rather than golden. A description of non-breeding birds would make them seem rather drab, but the upright posture, fast, jerking running and plaintive call always help with identification. In winter, large flocks gather, often with lapwings, on stubble fields, floodlands, extensive grazed grass and aerodromes. Frost prevents them getting to the earthworms which are their staple diet, although other invertebrates and even berries and seeds may be eaten.

SIZE

IDENTIFICATION

HABITAT

POPULATION

MAP

Bottom right
The golden plover in full breeding plumage is golden-yellow above and jet black beneath.

Top right
A flock of golden plover in winter.

197

Curlew

50–60 cm (20–24 in)

○ ○

SPECIES INFORMATION

SCIENTIFIC NAME	Numenius arquata
RELATED SPECIES	Whimbrel
CALL	Flight-call a fluting 'tlooi'. Spring song consists of loud fluting calls accelerating into a trill, given by male during rising and falling song-flight
HABITAT	Open bogs and upland moors, overgrown lake margins and damp meadows. Also breeds on damp hay meadows and wet meadows. Mudflats and estuaries outside breeding season
STATUS	Resident in BI about 50,000 pairs. Winters to coast, when numbers swelled by migrants from further north

SIZE

IDENTIFICATION

HABITAT

POPULATION

MAP

LARGE WADER, WITH long, decurved bill. Speckled brown plumage, with white rump and lower back. Legs long and strong. Flight strong and gull-like, often in lines or formation.

CURLEWS ARE EUROPE'S largest waders, and with their size and bills they need little more description. The intricate markings at close range disappear into a general grey-brown when seen from a distance, as the long-legged wader wanders at the edge of the tide. In flight, which is slightly gull-like, the white rump and lower back is conspicuous.

Spring in the Welsh uplands, or winter by a west country estuary and the curlew calls. It may be its bubbling, rippling call or the rich whistling 'corlee corlee corlee' that enlivens the winter day, but better still is the 'song' delivered in undulating display flight with long downcurved beak open to deliver accelerating whistles which turn to bubbling.

A comparison of breeding densities on improved and unimproved hill grasslands in the north Pennines showed that snipe virtually disappeared after drainage, fertilising and, sometimes ploughing and re-seeding. Curlew showed an 82per cent reduction, redshank 81 per cent and lapwing 74 per cent. On the unimproved grassland, with plenty of rush clumps, densities of waders of up to 140 pairs per square kilometre could be found, so the scale of the losses was considerable. Curlews like damp soil so that they can insert their bills into soil or mud to extract invertebrates.

In the last century, curlews spread north in Europe, but more recently there have been declines. They are only scattered in France and Denmark, but become more widespread in Scandinavia and Russia, and other populations extend across Siberia and into north Central Asia. Many of them are migrants, with western birds wintering on European and African coasts. Ireland has a good population wintering inland, but British wintering birds are mainly coastal, with populations of international importance in Morcambe Bay, where there may be 14,000 in March, the Wash and in the estuaries of the Solway, Severn and Dee.

E. A. Armstrong, in his *Birds of the Grey Wind* recalls the birds of Ulster: 'When scattered skeins of curlew passed over in the night their mournful calls chilled and yet thrilled me. They were the very spirit of loveliness wandering homeless through the empty spaces and trackless ways. In later years when I discovered that the Gael consider the curlew to be one of the ominous, dreaded Seven Whistlers and call him by names which signify, Wail of Sorrow, Wail of Warning, Death Cry and Wailing Music I understood and was glad; for I then realised that the wild beautiful sadness which I heard throbbing in the curlew's cry was not born of mere childish apprehension but an intuition shared by a people highly sensitive to mystical images…But if the curlew's is a lonely call, it is the Spirit of the Wild in music, as full of changeful meaning as the voice of the wind, as mysterious and fascinating as the song of the sea.'

The curlew is usually heard before it is spotted, but when seen, the long, decurved bill is distinctive.

SPECIES INFORMATION

SCIENTIFIC NAME	*Numenius phaeopus*
RELATED SPECIES	Curlew
CALL	Flight call a stammering trilled 'pu-hu-hu-hu'. Song rather like curlew's, but trill section harsher
HABITAT	Breeds on moorland and wet heath in coniferous forest zone and tundra. Migrates to coasts, mainly mudflats, but also to rocky coasts
STATUS	Breeds in north of Scotland, about 465 pairs, increasing. Coastal on migration

Whimbrel

40–46 cm (16–18 in)

LIKE A SMALLER version of curlew, with somewhat shorter, less smoothly curved bill. Upperparts more contrastingly patterned; head with two broad, dark brown stripes. Faster wingbeats than curlew.

THE PLUMAGE IS very curlew-like, but darker, and the crown, if seen closely, has a pale central stripe, and the face a noticeable eye-stripe. Unlike the curlew, whimbrels rarely probe deeply, taking insects from the upper layers of soil, and worms from the mudflats.

Most frequently one hears the tittering call of seven notes, and looks up to see a small party of curlew-like birds with faster wing-beats than their larger relatives. You may notice the darker back or dark barring on the underwing, and sometimes the party will stay to give pleasure for a few days. Spring passage is mainly from mid April to May, and in autumn the birds are moving through from July, with a peak in August. Very few stay here as the main wintering area is south of Sahara.

SIZE

IDENTIFICATION

HABITAT

POPULATION

MAP

Breeding whimbrel extend up to the arctic, often far inland. Britain is at the extreme south of their breeding range, with Shetland the stronghold, where some 500 pairs breed among short heather or blanket bog. Elsewhere they are rare, with just a handful on Orkney and scattered in north Scotland and the Western Isles. Whimbrel often breed in loose groups, and make shallow nests lined with fragments of vegetation.

Like a small version of a curlew, the whimbrel's trilling flight-call often gives it away.

Greenshank

30 cm (12 in)

○ ○

SPECIES INFORMATION

SCIENTIFIC NAME	Tringa nebularia
RELATED SPECIES	Redshank, Spotted Redshank, Green Sandpiper, Wood Sandpiper
CALL	Flight-call a fluting 'tew-tew-tew'. On breeding ground a harder 'kji-kji-kji'. Song a fluting 'klivi-klivi-klivi', often in flight over territory
HABITAT	Breeds on open moorland or on heath with bushes or isolated trees close to water. Outside breeding season mainly coastal, in small groups or individually
STATUS	North-west Scotland about 1500 pairs. Migrates to coasts in autumn and winter

SIZE

IDENTIFICATION

HABITAT

POPULATION

MAP

LARGE, RATHER PALE grey wader with long, slightly upturned bill and long, greenish legs. Outside breeding season (and juveniles) paler and greyer above, white beneath. In flight the legs extend well beyond the tail.

GREENSHANK OFTEN LOOK very pale, and the legs usually do look green. Like many waders, there is nothing remarkable about the plumage, but there is an attractive mix of grey brown and black on the back and wings, a streaked breast turning to spots and then to pure white underparts.

The long, slightly upturned bill, used for feeding in the shallows, is very distinctive. A wide range of food is taken, including small fish, shrimps, shore crabs and worms. Greenshanks often feed by sweeping the bill from side to side, with the tip just in contact with the surface and opening and closing gently. On its breeding grounds it takes mainly insects and other small invertebrates.

Ratcliffe describes the contributions made by the Nethersole Thompson family to understanding the breeding biology of what he calls 'the most special bird of the deer forests'. 'Greenshanks' writes Ratcliffe 'mostly return to their Scottish breeding haunts

An elegant wader, the greenshank has quite a long, very slightly upturned bill.

during early April and for two to three weeks afterwards are conspicuous and vocal in pairs as they court and stake out territories. It is then that the male gives his thrilling song dance in undulating flight high over his chosen area, advertising his possession to all his neighbours. This is a water's edge feeder, probing and picking for the wide range of invertebrates along the margins of lochs, lochans, bog pools and rivers or on the seashore.

By early May, greenshanks are to be found nesting singly. They rise to the intruder with an alarmed 'tew-tew-tew' and rapidly distance themselves before pitching to resume their quiet search for food. The absent mate is sitting on eggs in some secret place on the moor: it may be near or far but there is not the least clue to suggest where.'

Greenshank country is the high rainfall areas of western Scotland – notably Sutherland, West Caithness, Wester Ross, west Inverness and the Western Isles, dominated by pools and blanket bogs.

Among the haunts loved by Nethersole Thompson and greenshank are places where 'great cliffs and precipices, grim, moist, black and forbidding, soar above a wilderness of scree and rock table overlooking the scars, pocks, furrows and craters of a bog, in which the roots of an ancient forest project like the snouts of primeval monsters snuffing in ebony, porridge like scum'.

Short-Eared Owl

38 cm (15 in)

SPECIES INFORMATION

SCIENTIFIC NAME	Asio flammeus
RELATED SPECIES	Long-eared Owl
CALL	Territorial males have soft 'doo-doo-doo-doo' in spring, female replies with 'tjair-op'. Alarm call at nest is a barking 'kwe'
HABITAT	Open country with low vegetation. Moorland, heath, overgrown lake margins, damp meadows and reedbeds
STATUS	Resident and partial migrant. In BI about 2,000 pairs (almost absent as breeding bird in Ireland)

MEDIUM-SIZED, LONG-WINGED owl, often active by day. Has short 'ear' tufts, often invisible. Plumage light brownish-grey. Eyes yellow and surrounded by broad black circles. In flight appears pale and narrow-winged. Wing tips dark; often glides with wings held in V shape; tail wedge-shaped.

SHORT-EARED OWLS breed on heather moors, coastal marshes and young plantations where new growth gives cover to small mammals. When voles do not occur, as in Ireland, there are few owls. In winter these long-winged diurnal hunters can turn up on downland, heath or coastal dune, and when they settle, the boldly streaked underparts and yellow eye may be seen.

Wintering birds are highly nomadic, and half of the ringing recoveries mentioned in the *Winter Atlas* were more than a hundred kilometres from where they were ringed. These wanderers will take what food they can, but small mammals dominate, although some birds also feature.

If food supplies of small rodents are steady, owls will be consistent in their breeding but where voles come and go, as they often do among young forestry plantations, the owls do likewise. Their real favourite is heather. Here short eared owls can be conspicuous whether sitting on a roadside post, beating about slowly over the ground in search of prey, or showing their aerial antics in courtship and territorial display.

The short ears of the name are usually invisible, but the face, buff white with black patches is striking enough in its own right. Striking also is the advertising call of the male, a hollow 'doo doo doo', likened to the distant puffing of a steam engine, frequently repeated. A barking call, hoarse and hissing, is used in a variety of contexts.

The Scandinavian countries have good populations, up to 10,000 pairs in Norway and Finland, while the extensive Arctic tundra of Russia has many more. The range extends across Northern Asia and North America, and it is one of few Palearctic birds that breeds in South America.

SIZE

IDENTIFICATION

HABITAT

POPULATION

MAP

Top left and right
Despite its name, the short tufts (which are not ears) of the short-eared owl are usually invisible.

Bottom
They sometimes turn up on downland in the winter.

Ring Ouzel

24 cm (9.5 in)

SPECIES INFORMATION

SCIENTIFIC NAME	*Turdus torquatus*
RELATED SPECIES	Blackbird, Song Thrush, Mistle Thrush, Redwing, Fieldfare
CALL	Alarm call 'tok-tok-tok'; flight-call 'tsreet'. Song consists of short, repeated rather rough-toned fluting phrases
HABITAT	Hills, moorland and mountains. On migration also in lowland and coastal pasture
STATUS	Summer visitor. In BI about 10,000 pairs (only about 200 in Ireland)

SIZE

IDENTIFICATION

HABITAT

POPULATION

MAP

SIMILAR IN SIZE and shape to blackbird, but with white breastband (male), slightly longer wings and tail and 'scaly' underside, particularly in winter. Female has fainter breastband and browner plumage. Juveniles are speckled brown below and on throat.

EVERYONE WHO LOVES the hills and knows something of their birds loves the ring ouzel. One reason, as Ratcliffe describes, is that it 'shares with the wheatear the claim of being the earliest of our upland summer migrants to arrive, usually towards the end of March. From this time onwards, dawn chorus in the mountains often begins with the clear triple note of a cock ring ouzel carrying far across the hill.

While evidently preferring heathery hills, ring ouzels are typical birds of the sheep walks, especially where there is much

The scaly plumage and white throat crescent distinguish this upland species from the blackbird.

rocky ground. Nesting habitat varies widely, but one of the most favoured is the steep, rocky bank of a secluded little stream, preferably grown with long overhanging heather or other rank vegetation ... The nests are beautifully made and durable structures of tough hill grasses such as *nardus*, and will last for several years in sheltered sites.' These secluded little streams are often free of sheep, and the mountain plants, roseroot and mountain sorrel, globeflower and starry saxifrage survive to add to the ambience of the ring ouzel's haunt.

Ring ouzels really are blackbird-like, although the scaly plumage has not the gloss of its lowland relative. The males white bib is 'cleaner' than the female's and she is not as dark. Both have pale yellow bills. Autumn migrants, which may turn up where there are good berry supplies, have almost lost their crescent bibs, but the silvery wings, due to pale fringes on the wing coverts, help identification. Ring ouzels turn up regularly in early spring along the coasts, especially on grazed pasture. Our birds may only move as far as Southern Spain, but some may go on to winter in the Atlas mountains.

SPECIES INFORMATION

SCIENTIFIC NAME	*Oenanthe oenanthe*
RELATED SPECIES	*No close relatives in British Isles*
CALL	*Alarm-call 'chak'. Song, not often heard, is a short, rapid, warbling phrase made up of hard notes and soft whistles*
HABITAT	*Open stoney or rocky country, pasture, moorland and heath*
STATUS	*Summer visitor. In BI about 70,000 pairs*

Northern Wheatear

15 cm (6 in)

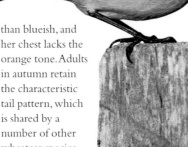

RATHER ACTIVE, STURDY bird with striking white rump and tail markings, long, black legs and upright posture. Male has grey back, black cheeks and wings, and white stripe above eye. Female and autumn male brownish, without contrasting head markings. Juveniles finely speckled.

SIZE

IDENTIFICATION

HABITAT

POPULATION

MAP

WHEATEARS ARE BIRDS of rocky grassland, particularly if there are loose boulders or screes. Hiding among these screes, or showing themselves on close-cropped turf the striking males, a pattern of pale orange, grey-blue and black, with striking whiteness on rump and sides of tail, are good company. Where the male's wings are black, the female's are browner, her back is brownish grey rather than blueish, and her chest lacks the orange tone. Adults in autumn retain the characteristic tail pattern, which is shared by a number of other wheatear species, but the birds are essentially buff, with the vaguest trace of the breeding male's pattern of black face and white eye-stripe.

Frank Fraser Darling (1940) describing bird life in the *Summer Isles* wrote about wheatears: 'It would be impossible to pass through the springtime country of sea pinks, where heaps of lichened stones add their saffron and green to the brilliance of the whole, without seeing wheatears. They are brilliant also, and no bird more graceful. Would that their voice equalled their plumage.'

Peter Conder (1989) explains that 'one of the actions which has prime significance in a wide range of displays is the exposure of the rump by fanning the tail out sideways and drooping the wings a fraction.' On all occasions of excitement the tail is fanned and the rump exposed. He also mentions bobbing at the approach of any intruder, including rabbits and sheep, when the 'tuc tuc' call is usually given.

'The wheatears come in early spring
And sit on tufts of higher ground
Bobbing smartly as they sing
Synchronously with the sound'
Robert S. Morrison WORDS ON BIRDS

The usual sight of a wheatear is of a lively bird flitting close to the ground or landing on a pile of rocks. Watch for the tell-tail white rump.

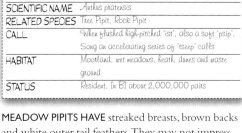

Meadow Pipit

14.5 cm (5.5 in)

 SIZE

IDENTIFICATION

HABITAT

POPULATION

MAP

SPECIES INFORMATION	
SCIENTIFIC NAME	Anthus pratensis
RELATED SPECIES	Tree Pipit, Rock Pipit
CALL	When flushed high-pitched 'ist', also a soft 'psip'. Song an accelerating series of 'tseep' calls
HABITAT	Moorland, wet meadows, heath, dunes and waste ground
STATUS	Resident. In BI about 2,000,000 pairs

SMALL, RATHER FEATURELESS common bird of open country. From similar tree pipit mainly by voice and habitat. Breast has less yellow, and is more delicately streaked. Flight rather undulating.

MEADOW PIPITS HAVE streaked breasts, brown backs and white outer tail feathers. They may not impress one, but their friendly presence, 'tseep' call and tinkling song as they glide down to grassy slopes is part of the hill scene in summer. On many walks in the mountains they are just about the only bird to be seen. In autumn many leave for Iberia, while others winter in loose flocks in lowland fields or by the sea.

Irish legend has it that if a meadow pipit host climbs into a cuckoo's mouth, which it often appears to be trying to, the end of the world will come.

Meadow pipits are common on upland pasture and moorland.

Twite

14 cm (5.5 in)

○ ○

SPECIES INFORMATION

SCIENTIFIC NAME	Carduelis flavirostris
RELATED SPECIES	Linnet, Siskin, Redpoll, Goldfinch, Greenfinch
CALL	Call is a nasal 'chweet'. Song is a rattling twitter, slightly slower than Linnet's
HABITAT	Breeds on rocky coasts, in mountains and moorland. In winter on coastal meadows, saltmarsh and stubblefields; rarer inland
STATUS	Resident and partial migrant. Winters mainly on north and east coasts. In BI about 68,500 pairs

VERY SIMILAR TO female Linnet, but browner, and with less white on wings and tail; has yellow-brown, not pale chin. Male has pinkish rump.

AT A DISTANCE, twites and linnets are very similar, but the male twite's pink rump, more distinct wing bars and honey buff face, together with longer tail are good field characters.

A gathering of twites on telephone wires in north Skye is my only lasting memory of these inconspicuous finches that are as much birds of coastal rough pastures as of mountains,

heather and bracken offer the birds safe and concealed nesting places. Throughout the breeding season they travel to and from agricultural pastures where they feed on weed seeds.

particularly in winter. The 'chweet' call may separate them from linnets but they have the same bouncy flight and twitters. Always as inconspicuous as female or juvenile linnets, their yellow winter beaks and honey-coloured throats may set them apart. Twites are in long term decline in Ireland and, like other finches, suffer as so much agriculture, even in the hills, becomes cleaner.

The main breeding areas are on the Scottish coasts and highlands, and the Pennines. Those breeding on the English moors move to the coast for the winter, whereas the Scottish birds tend to be sedentary. On their return, the S. Pennine flocks rely heavily on patches of burnt purple moor grass where they exploit its fallen seeds, before dispersing to heather-dominated parts of the moors. Here the

SIZE

IDENTIFICATION

HABITAT

POPULATION

MAP

The linnet-like twite is a rather unobtrusive moorland bird, sometimes seen in winter on saltmarshes.

Raven

65 cm (25 in)

SPECIES INFORMATION	
SCIENTIFIC NAME	Corvus corax
RELATED SPECIES	Rook, Carrion Crow, Hooded Crow, Jackdaw
CALL	Call a deep, hollow 'grok', or 'krrooap'
HABITAT	Mainly mountains and other rocky sites
STATUS	Resident. In BI about 10,500 pairs

SIZE

IDENTIFICATION

HABITAT

POPULATION

MAP

LARGEST BLACK CROW, with very deep call and wedge-shaped tail. Very powerful black bill.

WHEN, IN THE 1930s, only one pair of ravens bred in Dorset, Llwelyn Powys, quoted by Hawkins (1991), described how, 'Their dark shadows cross and recross the sloping shoulders of the downs, but they are always flying alone, the male and the female, with solitary, mutual love. In February, when they prepare for the first clutch of eggs, they are self sufficient, and in mid winter, when they come in Swyre Head after a morning's scavenging on the Chesil Beach, it is the same. What a massive self absorption is suggested by the croak of a raven: no wonder to primitive minds this harsh utterance seemed to conceal hidden meanings, dark occult messages, decrees of a dolorous fate.'

Aloof though the ravens are, there is one bird that breaks in upon their proud isolation. For some obscure reason the heavy, dark flight of these giants of the air is exasperating to peregrine falcons. A peregrine falcon will pester a raven in its flight for several miles together, soaring high up above it and then with a deadly swoop darting downwards. I have seen them knock feathers out of the ravens body, but never do serious harm and it is astonishing how the great bird knows when to turn upon its back in mid air at the very instant when in its downward rush the peregrine is ready to strike.

There are certainly plenty of raven stories and superstitions. To the old St Kildans it meant battles, mayhem and death in a big way, and wayward children in Yorkshire are still told 'the black raven' will get them. In Denmark, ravens contain the unbaptised dead, and in Languedoc it is wicked priests. There was the hoarse raven in *Macbeth* and a swarthy one in the *Anglo Saxon Chronicle of 938.*

John Fowles maintains in *The Nature of Nature* that 'if I see or hear ravens something in me always rises with and to them'. They are good, if often distant company on even the worst day in the mountains. Obviously large crows, their guttural call, wedge-shaped tail and acrobatic flight distinguish them.

Top left and right
Large size and very heavy bill typify the jet-black raven.

Bottom
In flight, the wedge-shaped tail is a good field character.

'The boding raven on her cottage sat,
And with hoarse croakings warned us of our fate'
John Gay THE DIRGE

SPECIES INFORMATION	
SCIENTIFIC NAME	Corvus corone cornix
RELATED SPECIES	Carrion Crow, Rook, Raven, Jackdaw
CALL	Hoarse cawing call, often repeated three times
HABITAT	Open country
STATUS	Resident and partial migrant. Replaces carrion crow in north, east and south-east Europe, and in north-west Scotland and Ireland. In BI about 450,000 pairs

Hooded Crow

47cm (19 in)

AN IMPRESSIVE BIRD to spot out of context, for example flying over Bardsey, or at a refuse dump in north London or, where there are no carrion crows, rampaging among the seaweed on an Irish beach.

BELONGS TO THE same species as carrion crow, but clearly different in plumage, with grey back and underbody. They are sufficiently alike in physiology and behaviour to be able to interbreed along a line across Britain, northern Europe and the Mediterranean. Although the hybrid zone moves, it is surprising that it does not widen. In Britain most hybrids are found in central Scotland, the north-east tip of mainland Scotland, and in the Isle of Man.

Pure hooded crows live mainly in Ireland, the Isle of Man and western and northern Scotland.

SIZE

IDENTIFICATION

HABITAT

POPULATION

MAP

Hooded crows, like ravens, often nest in rocky sites.

Freshwater amd Marsh Birds

THE RIVER I have known best is the Lledr, a tributary of the Conwy in north Wales. It collects first from wet deserted grassland in the hinterland between the Crimean Pass and Moel Siabod, cascades through a deserted village at the point the railway disappears into a tunnel in the hillside and flows peacefully through the farmland of, so-called, Roman Bridge.

AFTER ANOTHER CHANGE, a surrounding of sessile oaks, it is joined by two tributaries, both now thickly planted around with conifers. Just below Dolwyddelan is a meandering stretch, where for several years I carried out a Waterways Bird Survey, and then torrential falls below Pont-y-Pant bridge.

It is a typical young upland river, with shingle banks and rapids, but 'my' stretch was not typical for the gradient is slight, allowing marshy areas and emergent riverside vegetation. The resident moorhens and a pair of reed buntings must have been the only ones for miles around, as was the occasional sedge warbler. By contrast, the dippers, grey wagtails and common sandpipers were typical of rivers in the hills. As dippers declined, perhaps because of increasing acidity, goosanders appeared, to produce another welcome touch of impressive colour.

THE RIVER THAMES

THE THAMES IS very different, an old lowland river with a tendency to accumulate mud. It has a long history of pollution, and not only in the very lowest reaches. In 1940 Robert Gibbins mentions a walk along Strand-on-the-Green 'The houses are charming, but the river is filthy. Talk about the sacred Ganges. It is nothing to the Thames at Chiswick. And there were children bathing, swimming in water the colour of beer, with a sediment on its surface thick enough to be the beginning of a new continent.'

Twenty years on the accumulated mud was black, smelly and oxygen-deficient outside the Houses of Parliament, and so was the water. The lower river was an avian void except for gulls.

Top
The grey wagtail is almost always associated with water, usually flowing water at weirs, or along a stream.

Bottom left
Bewick's swans are regular winter visitors to open water, such as at Slimbridge or the Ouse Washes.

Bottom right
The smart dipper lives up to its name by ducking underwater and feeding along the river bed.

THE CLEAN-UP OPERATION

THE START OF the cleaning-up operation was described in the *London Bird Report* of 1972. In the late 1950s, the Port of London Authority and the Greater London Council had started an anti-

pollution programme involving the closing down of small overloaded sewage works and establishing regulations that made sure that polluted wastes should be channelled through new plants.

By 1963, dissolved oxygen was present throughout the year, although locally in very small quantities, and the foul smells, often due to hydrogen sulphide, were decreasing. It was still dirty enough for tubifex worms, who thrive on organic waste, so there was plenty of food for ducks. Peak counts over the five years from 1968, along what had been a birdless stretch of river, were 1,490 mallard, 1,500 teal, 200 wigeon, 388 pintail, 800 tufted duck, 4,000 pochard and 3,000 shelduck. In the 1960s, some 2,500 dunlin

took to roosting on new dredging beds and soon birds actually started feeding; 7,000 dunlin, 800 redshank and 100 ruff by 1972–73.

The creation of this prime new bird habitat in what seemed a hopeless situation gave hope for other polluted waters, but it involved plenty of scientific research, a vast input of money and the drive of the Chairman of the Port of London Authority.

Paradoxically, when waters get cleaner bird populations may fall. There was a time when 20,000 scaup thrived on distillery discharges in the Firth of Forth, but they are gone and tubifex worms, often used as indicators of pollution, are often a duck's best food in the Mersey. London, perhaps because the evil-smelling water passed the terrace of the House of Commons, had shown what could be done, and other rivers have followed the Thames to a far healthier state.

Top
Wigeon sometimes gather in enormous flocks at suitable feeding sites.

Middle
A female tufted duck. This species feeds mainly by diving below the surface.

Bottom
Shy and unobtrusive, the teal (female shown) is our smallest duck.

Cotswold Water Park

ANOTHER WAY THAT man can create good wildlife habitat is as a product for his search for minerals. In this section Jim Harris, Head Ranger at The Cotswold Water Park describes this situation.

OLD GRAVEL PITS

THE COTSWOLD WATER PARK is an unusual and unique place formed as a result of man's activity. Gravel quarrying, which started in the early 1900s and peaked in the 1970s, has created what is now a fascinating area of lakes and wetlands. There are now well over 100 lakes within an area of approximately 100,000 ha (25,000 acres) on the boder of Wiltshire and Gloucestershire border which includes over 1,000 ha (2,500 acres) of open water. The gravel deposits were laid down in the Jurassic era (some

Top
Tufted ducks are common at the Cotswold Water Park.

Middle
Coots build their nests close to the water, using reeds and other vegetation.

Bottom
This coot is accompanied by a young bird.

165 million years ago) by glacial meltwaters in what now forms the Upper Thames Valley. The quarrying has created the largest area of man-made lakes in Britain, about half as large again as the Norfolk Broads. Every year over two million tonnes of gravel are excavated, opening up approximately 55 ha of new ground which will later flood and form new lakes, hence the area will continue to grow for many years. The deposits and therefore the resulting lakes are not particularly deep, being between two and seven metres, provide an ideal habitat for a wide variety of wildlife.

Not only wildlife benefits from all this open water, humans flock to the area, as it is a mecca for watersports enthusiasts, naturalists and families visiting the Country Park. Watersport clubs and facilities: jet ski-ing, sailing and angling use some 40 per cent of the lakes. This causes fewer problems to wildlife than might be expected as much of the disturbance happens after the breeding season and before the winter, when there is a huge influx of over-wintering wildfowl. However there is a policy for zoning the different recreational activities to keep those ones which cause most disturbance away from the best lakes for wildlife. English Nature has drawn up conservation guidelines for 64 lakes including nine which have Site of Special Scientific Interest (SSSI) designation. These SSSIs are an unusual feature of the area as they are 'Marl Forming' lakes. Normally only found in upland limestone areas, they deposit

calcium carbonate out of the water which accumulates on the lake bed resulting in an unusual flora including often rare species such as stoneworts. These provide a very important food source for over-wintering diving ducks.

BIRDWATCHING IN THE AREA

Birdwatchers find it daunting to know where to start, but it is worthwhile persevering, especially from late autumn, when large flocks of wildfowl can be seen through to when the spring migrants arrive to breed. However all year round there can be surprises – squacco heron, red-footed falcon and white-winged black tern to name a few. In summer a huge variety of insects, especially dragonflies and damselflies, can be seen. These attract birds such as hobbies and sand martins which nest in the quarry faces. The bird life becomes very tolerant of the large quarrying

machinery and often the bare quarry floors can be worth scanning carefully to spot waders such as a visiting Temminck's stint or perhaps a nesting little ringed plover. This should only be done from the safety of the extensive rights-of way-network. In the lake margins you may be lucky enough to spot a real rarity, a little egret or even an overwintering bittern.

In autumn hundreds of golden plover arrive to feed on the surrounding farmland and then, as winter starts to bite, flights of wigeon can be heard whistling as they fly in at dusk. This is the start of the winter

build-up. The Water Park is nationally important (having over one per cent of the total GB population) for six species: gadwall, pochard, tufted duck, great crested grebe, shoveler and coot. There are many other ducks that you are likely to see, such as goosander, smew, goldeneye and the unusual red-crested pochard, which has its UK stronghold in the Water Park.

There is a Ranger Service that operates from Keynes Country Park, which covers the whole of the Cotswold Water Park. A wide variety of conservation work is done to improve habitats, often with help from volunteers, including woodland management, lake management and general landscape improvements, such as hedgelaying. One particularly large scheme, started in 1997, is attracting a lot of interest; the creation of the largest inland reedbed in southern England – some 10 ha (24 acres) of reed on 17 ha (42 acres) of land that has been quarried and partially infilled. The hope is that the bitterns that overwinter at present will no longer need to leave the area to breed, and the otters that have been sighted occasionally will become resident. A Biodiversity Action Plan has been devised with various target species and habitats.

Top
Great crested grebe. The beautiful head feathers are spread out during spring displays.

Middle
Goldeneye is a pretty winter visitor to the coast and some inland lakes.

Bottom
Pond with a good range of aquatic habitats.

211

Ponds, Fens and Marshes

APART FROM RIVERS and gravel pits, the range of freshwater habitats is extensive, with vast man-made reservoirs and extensive natural lakes ranging in size from Lough Neagh in Northern Ireland to the smallest mountain lochan, and from the wet vegetation, nutrient-rich meres to the clear, almost plant-free, nutrient-poor lakes in the north and west.

Top right
Chesil Bank and the Fleet, Dorset. This coastal lagoon attracts large numbers of wildfowl.

Middle
A farm pond – a typical moorhen habitat.

Bottom
Redshank are still common marshland birds, although their numbers have declined in many areas.

PONDS

THERE ARE THE numerous ponds which people have made for a variety of reasons; these are constantly filling naturally, being used as dumps, or cleared in the interest of tidiness or agricultural convenience. Their reduction has not had the same effect on birdlife as the draining of extensive marshes and fens: moorhens may suffer, but not as much as newts and frogs.

THE FENS

OLIVER RACKHAM (1994) DESCRIBES three great phases to draining the Fens through which the Great Ouse flows. The Romans, he explains, had the most elaborate fen engineering technology that Europe has experienced and they created the Car Dyke, the biggest artificial watercourse the Fens have ever seen, a channel that ran for 145 km (90 miles) between Lincoln and Cambridge. When they left, their drainage system largely lapsed.

Viking place names show their involvement in the next long phase, with Anglo-Saxons and then Normans helping to make the Fens the most prosperous part of rural England by the fourteenth century. The Normans created a 96 km (60 mile) earthwork that stood for 500 years and protected more than a million acres of land.

The third drainage phase is well known, with the creation of the Old and New Bedford rivers in 1637 and 1651, not for immediate local benefit, but in the hopes of good profits, through improved grassland and arable land.

Other wet areas, such as the Somerset Levels or Romney Marsh, have similar long histories of use and periods of lapsed management. Most of the great river estuaries were not embanked so they too were wet in a way we find hard to grasp. Lagoons are formed where a river is deflected by beach material like the Fleet behind Chesil Beach in Dorset or

Slapton Lea in Devon. Flashes are shallow ponds produced by subsidence when disused mines collapse or, as in Cheshire, when rock salt is pumped out, while the Norfolk Broads were holes left by a large industry of peat digging. The population density of Norfolk and Suffolk in the eleventh century was high and they had little wood, hence the use of vast amounts of peat for fuel. They could only dig because sea levels were lower then. Peat can accumulate on slopes, retaining water and forming blanket-bogs, while if it accumulates on level ground, raised bog, a great dome of sphagnum moss, results as it did over much of Ireland before peat-fired powerstations and bog reclamation began.

BIRDLIFE

WHAT BIRDS MIGHT have been in these wet habitats as human life ebbed and flowed and prosperity came and went? Fitter (1945) gives an interesting list of birds consumed in the household of a Tudor nobleman in 1512. They included 'crannys (cranes), redeshankes, fesauntes, sholards (spoonbills), knottes, bustards, great byrdes, hearonsewys (herons), bytters (bitterns), reys (reeves), kyrlewes, wegions, dottrells, ternes and smale byrds' all of which, except the bustards for which they might have had to go to the wild heaths of Hounslow, would have been obtainable in the marshes flanking the Thames.

Three hundred years on Fitter mentions G. Graves who recorded all three harriers from the south London marshes. The hen harrier was no uncommon sight skimming over fields by the Kent Road. The bearded tit seems to have been a common bird from Oxford to the Thames estuary, and the spotted crake was said to occur in great abundance. The large number of black terns that used to nest on the Norfolk Broads are another indication of the birdlife the old wetlands supported.

RECREATION OF OLD WETLANDS

ONE OF THE most encouraging things is how the recreation of old wetlands can so rapidly bring birds

back. In the winter of 1997–98, the RSPB had almost 50,000 waterfowl of 22 species at their West Sedgemoor Reserve on the Somerset Levels, including 10,000 teal and 20,000 lapwings, while more than 5,000 waterfowl, mainly teal and wigeon, were attracted to newly-created lagoons at Pulborough Brooks in West Sussex. It is the speed with which birds colonise that is so impressive. At Holkham, Norfolk, the co-operation between English Nature, the Earl of Leicester, Lord Coke, and the tenants of the estate, has transformed a large, relatively dull area into one of high value to wildlife as Marren (1994) describes: 'There have been immediate and in some cases dramatic increases in visiting and nesting birds, including exciting ones like marsh harrier and avocet. In 1993 the nesting density of redshanks, at around 15 pairs to the square kilometre was as high as anywhere in Britain... The greater depth of water in the dykes has benefited birds like little grebe and coot. The biggest increases have been achieved by geese and wigeon.'

Many of these successful reserves are where sea and land meet, so it will be fascinating to see how the RSPB develop their reserve in the heart of England at Otmoor, and it will be interesting, too, to see how climate change influences that vital zone at the edge of the sea.

Top

The male bearded tit is a beautiful, almost exotic-looking bird. Bearded tits are reedbed specialists.

Middle

Little grebes love weedy lakes, and are adept at diving for their food.

Bottom

An adult coot leads its newly-fledged young out onto the open water.

Lough Neagh

MANY NATURAL LAKES are rich in bird life, and the largest of them all has plenty. It is years since I have been to Lough Neagh, but it is ancestral country and E. A. Armstrong, writing in 1940, uses an approach that takes history, a long history of folklore and fairy, as part of his way of looking at birds.

'IF YOU VISIT Lough Neagh expecting to see scenery like that of the English Lakes or Scottish Lochs disappointment awaits you. No craggy headlands jut forth into it, no lofty mountains mirror their high tips in its waters.

In days to come when planes and speedboats have turned Lough Neagh into a Bedlam and nobody hearkens to the wind nor heeds the fairies songs, what I have written may seem foolishness. But I testify of what I have seen and felt; and still those who care for simple things and quiet places may prove my testimony is true.'

VARIETIES OF BIRDLIFE

AFTER A NIGHT by the Loughside 'a redshank, passing hurriedly with a gleam of silver, whistles "Look out!" I do look out from my blankets and behold a pair of wagtails tripping over the stones with frequent eager leaps into the air after some luckless insect. Where there are wagtails there is peace. With noisy pinions a pair of red-breasted mergansers fly quacking along the treetops fringing the lough "QUORK, QUORK, QUORK, quork, quork." The receding calls remind me absurdly of the coughing diminuendo of a

locomotive pulling out of a station. From the heronry in the wood behind comes an uproar like the quarrelling of the damned, it is only mother disgorging her morning's catch to the youngsters!

As I swim out into the Lough there is discomfiture amongst the birds. "Kittie Needie" cries a sandpiper, the daintiest of water sprites, fleeing low with attendant reflection in the limpid lake. Moorhens sneak away with huge strides through the alders, coots call off their ginger-headed young,

crested grebes, scandalised, crane their necks and dive, a distracted shoveler quacks in agitation to her brood by the waterside amongst the yellow flags.

Top
A stately heron strides through the shallows in search of fish or frogs.

Middle
Common sandpipers can often be spotted along the banks of lakes or reservoirs.

Bottom
Radipole Lake, near Weymouth, Dorset is an RSPB reserve, excellent for wildfowl, and also passage birds during the migration.

THE DUCK POPULATION

IN MAY AND JUNE ducks are busy with domestic affairs. The shoveler is much more plentiful than formerly. On the reedy islands the tufted duck's nest is

fairly common – yet half a century ago it was unknown in Ireland as a breeding bird. The pintail has been reported from several counties; happily this bird of refined colouring and elegant figure has been found nesting on Lough Neagh. "There seems to be a kind of natural modesty in it which you do not find in other ducks," said Audubon. May it thrive and multiply.'

Now that the Government accept the diversity of birds as an indicator of the quality of life let us press for wetter wetlands and help the Environment Agency to make river quality and associated marshland a top priority.

TRANSFORMATION OF WETLANDS

SIXTY YEARS AFTER Armstrong's writing we know so much more, but in Britain and Ireland as a whole the ordinary countryside, the ordinary rivers, the margins of the ordinary lakes grow more boring, more uniform, more sterile; we must make more of the ordinary places more like the best.

> 'What would the world be, once bereft
> Of wet and of wildness? Let them be left
> O let them be left, wildness and wet;
> Long live the weeds and the wilderness yet.'
> Gerard Manley Hopkins INVERSNAID

Top
The male shoveler is a very smart bird – note the large, spoon-shaped bill.

Middle
Female pintail – note the marbled plumage.

Bottom
Water meadows such as this provide nesting sites for birds such as redshank, snipe and yellow wagtail.

Great Crested Grebe

50 cm (19 in)

SPECIES INFORMATION	
SCIENTIFIC NAME	Podiceps cristatus
RELATED SPECIES	Red-necked Grebe, Black-necked Grebe, Slavonian Grebe, Little Grebe
CALL	Raw 'gruck-gruck', hoarse 'rah-rah', mostly in spring
HABITAT	Large lakes with reedy margins, sometimes on small lakes or reservoirs
STATUS	Mainly central, southern and eastern England. Absent from much of Scotland. In Ireland mainly in the north and central areas. In winter often in flocks on large lakes, rivers and coastal seas. In BI about 12,000 birds

SIZE

IDENTIFICATION

HABITAT

POPULATION

MAP

OUR LARGEST GREBE. Striking head and neck feathers form a ruff in breeding season. In winter has dark cap, white cheeks and front of neck and a clear white stripe above eye. Juveniles have striped head and neck. Swims deep in water.

GREAT CRESTED GREBES were among the first birds to have their populations monitored by a national survey as reported in *British Birds* (1932). At that time the grebes were increasing due to the digging of gravel pits and the end of persecution for their feathers.

'Grebe furs', particularly the breast feathers, had been a fashion item supplied from the continent for many years before, and in the middle of the nineteenth century it was realised that to some extent the market could be supplied from home.

From 1870, the year of the first bird protection Act, several measures were introduced in rapid succession:-

    1870 'Act for the preservation of sea birds'
    1873 'Act for the protection of certain inland birds during the breeding season'
    1877 'Act for the preservation of wildfowl'
    1880 'Wild Birds Protection Act'

THE 1880 ACT created the first reasonable length of 'close season', from March to July, and grebes began to increase. The value of grebe 'furs' also went up, and the fashion for them did not end until 1907 or 1908.

Great crested grebes have another role in ornithological history because of Julian Huxley's pioneering work on behaviour and courtship, during

which their black crests and chestnut and black tippets come into their own. The mutual head-shaking display is the commonest, but the weed ceremony – when their long pink bills gather weed, to present to each other they rise out of the water is just as impressive. At this time grebes are unmistakable, but in winter they lose their ornaments, become decidedly pale and could be mistaken for red-necked grebes but for their much whiter faces and necks and pink bills. In flight the great crested has a longer neck and larger white wing-patches.

Today great crested grebes are spread over much of lowland Britain with an increasing Irish population. In England almost 50 per cent nest on gravel pits while more natural sites, with peripheral emergent vegetation, are favoured in Scotland. The nest is a bulky mass of aquatic vegetation with spare material available for covering the eggs. Despite a repertoire of guttural clucks and growls it is not so vocal as many grebes. It is mainly a fish eater.

Populations are found in a broad swathe across the Palearctic as far as China and it also breeds in Australasia and parts of Africa. In much of its British range it is migratory with many moving to the coast. Large numbers remain at extensive inland waters like Rutland Water, Chew Valley Lake and Queen Mary Reservoir, while Lough Neagh and Belfast Lough have outstanding populations of more than 1,000.

Top
Great crested grebes perform delightful courtship dances, involving head shaking.

Bottom
Seen up close, this species is very attractive with its head plumes.

Little Grebe

25 cm (10 in)

SPECIES INFORMATION

SCIENTIFIC NAME	Tachybaptus ruficollis
RELATED SPECIES	Great Crested Grebe, Red-necked Grebe, Black-necked Grebe, Slavonian Grebe
CALL	Long, vibrating trill, mainly in spring; also a high-pitched 'bi-ib'
HABITAT	Well-vegetated ponds and small lakes, slow rivers
STATUS	In winter often in small flocks on rivers, lakes and ponds. In BI about 15,000 pairs

OUR SMALLEST GREBE, dumpy and short-necked. In breeding plumage has chestnut brown head and sides of neck, and an obvious bright spot at base of bill. In winter uniform grey-brown, somewhat lighter on flanks.

DESPITE THE WHINNYING call, the little grebe (or Dabchick) can be elusive in the breeding season appearing with young on small lakes where you have no previous suspicion of their presence. The little grebe seems just about tail-less, and hardly any neck either so that its name is very apt. They are smart birds in breeding plumage, with a yellow spot on the bill and chestnut neck, but less distinctive in winter when essentially a dull brown.

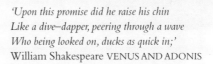

Little grebes like shallow-water breeding lakes, and can tolerate far smaller bodies of water than other grebes, as long as there is plenty of emergent vegetation and sufficient clear water surface to allow them to swim and dive.

When above the water it swims buoyantly with feathers often fluffed up to give a plump appearance. When it dives there is a distinct splash and when it flies, which it seems quite ready to do on a winter estuary, it goes low on rapid wing-beats. The fact that it appears on unlikely waters suggests more mobility than expected.

BWP describes its voice on its breeding grounds as 'wild sounding, shrill, rippling peal of notes like high pitched whinny of horse, with certain quality of laughter'. Perhaps its highly vocal summer is linked with strongly territorial nature. Little grebes are fond of molluscs and of any of all normal submerged, floating and aerial inhabitants of nutrient-rich lakes – insect larvae and crustaceans, amphibian larvae, whirligig beetles and adult flying insects snatched as the grebe swims rapidly to and fro.

> 'Upon this promise did he raise his chin
> Like a dive–dapper, peering through a wave
> Who being looked on, ducks as quick in;'
> William Shakespeare VENUS AND ADONIS
>
> 'Now up, now down again that hard it is to prove
> Whether underwater most it liveth or above'
> Michael Drayton POLY-OLBION

SIZE

IDENTIFICATION

HABITAT

POPULATION

MAP

Top and middle
Little grebe's nest, safely surrounded by water.

Bottom
A young little grebe seeking food from its parent.

Grey Heron

92 cm (36 in)

○ ○

SPECIES INFORMATION

SCIENTIFIC NAME	*Ardea cinerea*
RELATED SPECIES	Bittern, Little Egret
CALL	Flight call a raw, hollow croak
HABITAT	Breeds in colonies in tall trees, occasionally in reedbeds. Feeds in shallow water of ponds, rivers, lakes, saltmarshes, estuaries and rocky coasts. Also hunts frogs and small rodents in damp fields
STATUS	Mainly resident, but migrates in cold winter areas. About 1,500 pairs in BI. High mortality in hard winters

SIZE

IDENTIFICATION

HABITAT

POPULATION

MAP

COMMONEST AND LARGEST heron. Long neck and legs; long, pointed, yellowish bill. Plumage mainly grey; black stripe above eye, continued as two long drooping feathers. Young birds lack eye-stripe and plume feathers. Flies slowly, with heavy wing-beats and S-shaped neck, legs outstretched behind.

THE IMPRESSION CREATED by a solitary heron rising from a remoter pool is very different from that given by a group resting on the Thames foreshore, but the long legs, neck and bill and grey plumage are the same. As a large, gregarious tree-nester, with possible influence on fish populations, census work started even earlier than for great crested grebes, in 1928. Dips in population since then have often indicated cold winters.

As counting began along the Thames it seems appropriate to quote from Robert Gibbings (1940). 'Watching the second bird I soon saw the cause of the trouble, for across the bird's beak was a large fish. The broad wings beat the air, the long legs of the bird trailed in the rushes, but the weight in its beak prevented it from raising its head. What misgivings there must have been in the poor creature's mind as it tried to rise, and what disappointment when it was compelled to drop its burden! In the momentary glance I had of the fish as it fell, I estimated it to be about two pounds in weight, but pink, trout or chub I failed to mark it.'

After early returns to breeding sites, the males issue far-carrying advertising call, perched conspicuously with head raised. Away from the heronry the harsh 'frarnk' call is common.

Top and middle
Typical views of herons standing or wading in shallow water

Bottom
In flight herons are heavy and ponderous, with slow wingbeats.

> 'The old heron from the lonely lake
> Starts slow and flaps his melancholy wings.'
> John Clare SELECTED POEMS

SPECIES INFORMATION

SCIENTIFIC NAME	Botaurus stellaris
RELATED SPECIES	Grey Heron, Little Egret
CALL	Foghorn-like booming during breeding season. Flight call a raw croak
HABITAT	Breeds in large reedbeds near lakes, marshes and bogs
STATUS	Mainly resident. Rare and decreasing over most of range. British population now down to about 15 pairs, mainly in Norfolk and Suffolk

Bittern
76 cm (30 in)

A SQUAT, BROWN HERON, with relatively short neck. Plumage reed-coloured, legs and toes green (camouflage). Flight owl-like, with head stretched out in short flight, tucked in for longer flight. Clambers slowly among reeds. Stands motionless with head erect when disturbed, often for long periods.

THE BITTERN POPULATION is dangerously low with possible causes including pesticides, neglect of traditionally managed reedbeds, increased leisure boating and a decrease in the reedbeds themselves. It is included here as, even though rare, it is a keystone wetland species.

The booming call carries an extraordinary distance, but it is hard to find the caller. Bitterns may show themselves in open water in winter or be seen flying over the reeds when feeding young. Their ability to regurgitate frogs and fish of a size appropriate to their different-sized young is a special one, as is their ability to 'freeze' so that their mottled golden plumage merges with the reeds.

Because of their significance to birds, the proper management of reedbeds is important, particularly as fewer are now cut to produce a crop of thatching reed. Reedbeds, dominated by the common reed *Phragmites australis*, can be tidal or freshwater; neglected freshwater ones tend to dry out as dead vegetation builds up. The control of water level, by sluices and ditches, makes management possible for the reedbed must not dry out in summer. A regime that lowers the water level below the soil in autumn can allow cutting and prevent the build up of litter. Open water areas may add to habitat diversity, bitterns can feed in water up to 20 cm (8 in) deep and bearded tits flourish in beds of over 20 ha (49 acres); all these factors need consideration.

While traditional management for thatching might involve annual or biennial cutting, management for birds involves longer rotations, leaving plenty of cover, for species such as marsh harriers. As with grasslands, all cut material needs to be removed, but burning adds unwanted nutrients and piling around the fringes is labour intensive. The latter option may however create nesting sites for wildfowl as well as a habitat for beetles and hibernating grass snakes.

The varied diet of the bittern includes fish, amphibians, worms, leeches and molluscs as well as birds, lizards and crustaceans, but in winter sufficient food may be hard to find, and in most years reports of emaciated bitterns occur, often in unlikely places. In cold winters more continental birds arrive in Britain, and if there was enough suitable habitat perhaps more of them would stay. Foreign ringed birds tend to have come from north-west Europe where the Netherlands and Germany have good populations.

SIZE

IDENTIFICATION

HABITAT

POPULATION

MAP

Bitterns are very secretive, skulking amongst the reeds, where their camouflaged plumage makes them hard to spot.

Mute Swan

150 cm (60 in)

SPECIES INFORMATION	
SCIENTIFIC NAME	Cygnus olor
RELATED SPECIES	Whooper Swan, Bewick's Swan
CALL	Fairly silent, occasional hissing in defence. Wing noise in flight
HABITAT	Mainly freshwater. Lakes, gravel pits and ponds, even in urban areas. In winter often in large numbers on lakes. Breeds in lakes with rich vegetation and reedy banks; also banks of slow rivers and near the coast. Makes large nest of old reeds and other plant material. Semi-domesticated in many areas
STATUS	Partial migrant. In BI about 40,000 birds

SIZE

IDENTIFICATION

HABITAT

POPULATION

MAP

LARGEST AND HEAVIEST waterbird. Pure white plumage, bill reddish with black base; obvious knob on bill, more developed in male, especially in spring. Juveniles grey-brown; bill grey, without knob. Swims with neck held in S-shaped curve. Flies with powerful wing-beats, with neck stretched out. Wings make distinct swishing sound.

SWANS ARE IMMEDIATELY recognisable, and the vast majority are of this species. The orange-red bill with its black knob, larger on the male when breeding starts, is diagnostic, as are the arched wings of aggression of swimming males and their graceful curved necks. Young birds, in their first year, also have a black base to their bill but grey-brown plumage. As the name implies, this species is normally silent but makes a distinctive throb, peculiar to the mute swan, with its wings as it flies and it hisses readily to protect nest or young.

In western Europe many swans are semi-tame, and very used to human activities, so that in parks they will readily take food, and on urban rivers, not only the Thames, they have built up large populations. On the Severn, and elsewhere, a rapid decline was linked to the ingestion of lead weights used by fishermen, but publicity about the deaths changed fishing practice. There are still problems with nylon fishing line.

The largest breeding colony, over 600 years old, at Abbotsbury in Dorset, is a popular tourist attraction. The brochure indicates the level of their wildness, encouraging visitors to help feed them at 12 and 4 pm daily, and visitors find the major attraction between mid-May and the end of June when over a hundred nests with six eggs each produce young.

Mute swans tend to like gentle waters, but whether these are river, gravel-pit, natural wetland or

Top
Mute swans are often seen sailing slowly along a river or lake.

Bottom
Mute swans traditionally congregate in large numbers at Abbotsbury, Dorset.

urban lake, does not seem to matter. There needs to be a supply of vegetation, of rushes and reeds, to create the large mounded nest which can be more than 2 m (6.5 ft) in diameter and which, as well as vegetation, has a lining of down.

Although not migratory in western Europe, there are local movements, Northern European birds are much more mobile, with movements from Scandinavia and northern Germany down to warmer wintering quarters, where water plants are not iced over. Much grazing, however, is at the water's edge, and on land, and some of the food is animal, including frogs, snails and worms.

Thames swans have been protected, at least since the time of Edward III in 1387, but even so, during that reign, swans were available in London markets at ten times the price of a goose. Swan upping, when young birds are caught and have their beaks marked, must have been very active in Elizabethan times for there were 900 recognised swan marks. A surviving aspect of this is any pub called the

'*Generally speaking, I do not like swans. I think they are self opinionated and the flattery of human beings. Whenever they go they are pampered or treated with respect and indulgence. They have been glorified in the mythology of many countries.... But whatever may be said for or against the birds, there is no doubt that a swan on her nest has a truly regal appearance; and in the spring there are plenty of them to be seen on the islands in the Thames. There they sit, under canopies of budding willows, proud as queens upon their thrones, while their ever vigilant consorts sail majestically up and down the stream.*'
Robert Gibbings SWEET THAMES RUN SOFTLY

'Swan with Two Necks' which is a corruption of 'Swan with two nicks', for the Vintners Company marked their birds with two nicks on the bill. Royalty have always been associated with swans, and in the time of Henry VII one could be imprisoned for a year and a day, as well as being fined, for stealing a swan's egg, but attempts to restrict the ownership of the swans seem to have failed, and swan stealing was rife. Since the end of the eighteenth century only the Crown and the Dyers and Vintners Companies have exercised their swan rights.

Introduced birds have made this already widely distributed swan even more widespread and with its capacity to live with man, but less happily with his dogs, this, our heaviest resident bird, must be our most conspicuous.

Top
A mute swan's nest is often a huge mound of vegetation, usually close to the river bank or lake side.

Middle
One of the heaviest of all flying birds, a mute swan needs a long run for successful take off.

Bottom
Mute swan courtship is a romantic sight.

221

Whooper Swan

150 cm (60 in)

SIZE

IDENTIFICATION

HABITAT

POPULATION

MAP

AS LARGE AS MUTE swan but slimmer. Bill has yellow wedge-shaped patch and lacks knob at base. Neck held straight. Juveniles greyer than young mute, bill flesh-coloured with darker tip. Flocks often fly in formation.

SPECIES INFORMATION	
SCIENTIFIC NAME	Cygnus cygnus
RELATED SPECIES	Mute Swan, Bewick's Swan
CALL	Calls frequently. Swimming flocks have goose-like nasal calls, loud trumpeting calls before and during migration
HABITAT	Breeds in bogs and around tundra lakes. Winters to washland and wet marshes
STATUS	Regular winter visitor in large flocks to North Sea and Baltic coasts, as well as to lakes and flooded rivers. Large numbers visit Ireland and Britain (mainly from Iceland). A handful breed each year in BI (about 5 pairs)

THESE MOST ELEGANT swans like shallow water and extensive grass and in favoured areas occur in large flocks. Our birds come from the western part of their tundra breeding range while Eastern birds move to Japan and China. Our whooper swans breed mainly in Iceland. Both whooper and Bewick's swans have yellow and black beaks with the Bewick's having more black than yellow, and the whooper the reverse.

Whooper swans gain their name from the bugle-like trumpetings, produced through a particularly long trachea, which are highly characteristic of flocks on the move or on the water.

A few whoopers stay in Britain for the summer and breeding has been recorded, as it has in Donegal.

The whooper swan has a large triangular patch of bright yellow on its bill.

○○○○○○○○○○○○○○○○○○○○○○○○○
SPECIES INFORMATION
SCIENTIFIC NAME — *Cygnus columbianus*
RELATED SPECIES — *Whooper Swan, Mute Swan*
CALL — *Family groups make yodelling calls*
HABITAT — *Washland and flooded meadows*
STATUS — *Winter visitor*

Bewick's Swan

125 cm (48 in)

BEWICK'S SWAN IS smaller than whooper, and has a variable yellow/orange bill patch. Regular winter visitor to north-west Europe from Siberian breeding grounds.

THE EXACT PATTERN on each individual Bewick's swan's beak is different, and students of Slimbridge birds, which have come to winter in the luxury of that Severnside reserve, having learned and named the individuals, can identify them on migration, on their distinct breeding grounds or on their annual return to Gloucestershire. Over a third of these Slimbridge birds carry some level of lead shot despite extensive protection.

Apart from bill colour and size, Bewick's are shorter-necked and shorter-bodied than other swans, and their bills are smaller than those of whoopers. The different bill size does not seem to reflect much difference in diet for both are largely vegetarians with leaves, shoots, roots and the like gathered by upending or grazing on land. Despite this their winter habitat seems very different,

although they overlap in protected areas like the Ouse Washes. Whoopers are far more northerly, happy with impoverished upland lakes of no great size and ready to graze on estuary eel-grass as well as agricultural land.

The Bewick's distribution is patchy, with very few in Scotland, but in Ireland there are plenty of whoopers.

Britain and Ireland are internationally important for both birds with eight English sites for Bewick's and 12 British and Irish sites for whoopers having more than one per cent of the international population. In 1995–96 there were almost 5,000 Bewick's on the Ouse Washes and almost 2,000 on the Nene Washes, while Lough Neagh and the Ouse Washes each had over 1,000 whooper swans.

'Here in my vaster pools, as white as snow or milk
In water black as Styx, swims the wild swan, the ilke
Of Hollanders so termed, no niggard of his breath
(As poets says of swans who only sing in death);
But, as other birds, is heard his tunes to roat
Which like a trumpet comes, from his long
arched throat.'
Michael Drayton

Top
The patch on Bewick's swan's bill is variable in shape, but is normally smaller than whooper's; it is also more orange-yellow.

Bottom left
Wintering pairs are often accompanied by their offspring.

223

Canada Goose

100 cm (40 in)

SIZE

IDENTIFICATION

HABITAT

POPULATION

MAP

○○○○○○○○○○○○○○○○○○○○○○○○○○○○○

SPECIES INFORMATION

SCIENTIFIC NAME	Branta canadensis
RELATED SPECIES	Brent Goose
CALL	Flight-call a nasal trumpeting, accented on the second syllable
HABITAT	Reservoirs, lakes, fishponds and ornamental lakes in parks. Introduced from North America; original habitat is marshy lakes and river banks, right up into tundra region
STATUS	Resident and partial migrant. About 60,000 pairs in Britain; about 700 in Ireland, where very local

VERY LARGE GOOSE (though the species is variable, with some small races) with long, black neck. Head black and white, tail, bill and feet black. Flocks often fly in V-formation.

THE LARGE CANADA goose has become familiar over most of England, and increasingly in southern Scotland, Ireland and lowland Wales. It has a dark head and white face patch, white belly and grey-brown body, and a dark tail. Canada geese are commonly found grazing in town or country. The winter flocks are highly mobile, making noisy honking calls as they fly.

This species was introduced into England in the seventeenth century and a glance at a selection of books will indicate its increase and change to a wider range of breeding sites. *Witherby's Handbook* (1939) says 'breeding local and to a great extent artificial'. Hollom (1952) in the *Popular Handbook* said much the same: 'widespread but local, breeding chiefly on private lakes'. The West Midlands has been a centre of increase, and the *Atlas of Breeding Birds in the West Midlands* says how flocks of 40 were noteworthy in 1950, whereas by 1970 flocks of 400 were to be found on some occasions. The first *Breeding Atlas* (1976) reported that 'following transportation by man there was a more marked tendency to breed on reservoirs with natural margins, flooded gravel pits, rural meres and town lakes', and by the *New Atlas* (1993) it had a catholic taste in breeding sites and was widespread in all English counties.

Although our introduced birds are mobile, they are not migratory except for moult migrations which have recently developed, with Yorkshire birds moving to Inverness. In North America there are northern moult migrations and extensive autumn movements to the south, with birds reaching Mexico. American birds cause taxonomic disagreements, with some authorities claiming four different species, and others claiming a varied range of subspecies. British birds are mainly of the subspecies *B. canadensis canadensis* but some seem too large for that. A white neck collar distinguishes some of these subspecies.

Canada geese breed close to water; very close if there are no islands on which to build their nests of a pile of vegetation, which may be on a raft of twigs or branches.

Top left
The white patch on the black neck is characteristic of the Canada goose.

Top right
Canada geese are fond of grazing.

Bottom
Pair with their brood of goslings.

Mallard

58 cm (23 in)

SPECIES INFORMATION	
SCIENTIFIC NAME	Anas platyrhynchos
RELATED SPECIES	Gadwall, Pintail, Shoveler, Wigeon, Teal, Garganey
CALL	Displaying males have a quiet 'yeeb' and a thin, high-pitched whistle. Females the well-known quack, 'waak-wak-wak-wak-wak'
HABITAT	Still or slow-flowing water. Common as feral bird in parks
STATUS	Resident and partial migrant. In BI around 125,000 pairs

BEST KNOWN DUCK, the world's commonest, and ancestor of most domestic duck breeds. Breeding male has shiny green head with yellow bill, reddish-brown breast and curly black central tail feathers. Female brown and speckled.

THE MALLARD IS common on a wide variety of water, in town and country. The green head and white collar of the male is most familiar, as are the browns and buffs of the speckled females. Both have the violet speculum on the wing, while the purplish breast of the male is also distinctive. Males and females in eclipse are similar to other surface-feeding ducks so examine the beaks closely; the fine bill of the gadwall has orange patches pintail have a blue-grey bill, and wigeon much shorter ones. Mallards have longer bills than these, with the male's essentially yellow and the female's more orange.

Being highly adaptable, but liking shallow water, mallard can be found in town parks where artificially supplied food is welcome, or on small and even remote lochs, as long as there is vegetation. Some of this is used in nest building, as is down, but once again the bird is adaptable with some nesting in trees, some among ground vegetation and some under the shelter of logs or boulders. The downy young make spectacular descents from tree nests and often have to make substantial journeys to water; hence the newspaper's favourite pictures of policemen helping the birds across the road.

A very successful species across Europe and beyond it has also done well after being introduced in the southern hemisphere. As many breed in arctic tundra there are extensive winter movements. Those moving to Britain are more ready to use brackish and estuarine habitats in winter than for breeding. Here, and on island waters, there may be extensive flocking with much upending, surface dabbling and terrestrial grazing for plants which make up much of the food.

There is much variation through interbreeding with domestic ducks, and in some parks, or even small estuaries where feeding takes place, the range in size and colour is extensive, with few typical wild birds to be found. Whether wild or not, male sexual behaviour can be aggressive which could be the basis for the mallard having become a symbol of male promiscuity and fertility in the thirteenth century. Pope Gregory IX preached a crusade against a devil-worshipping cult whose symbol was a drake.

SIZE

IDENTIFICATION

HABITAT

POPULATION

MAP

Like many ducks, male and female mallard have markedly different plumage.

Wigeon

46 cm (18 in)

SPECIES INFORMATION	
SCIENTIFIC NAME	*Anas penelope*
RELATED SPECIES	Mallard, Gadwall, Pintail, Shoveler, Teal, Garganey
CALL	Highly distinctive whistling 'whee-oo', with accent on first syllable (male). Rattling 'rarr' (female)
HABITAT	Lakes, muddy shores and estuaries
STATUS	Breeds on lakes, bogs and river deltas in northern Europe. In BI, about 450 pairs, mainly in the north. Regular winter visitor to North Sea and other coasts

SIZE

IDENTIFICATION

HABITAT

POPULATION

MAP

MEDIUM-SIZED DUCK with tucked-in head, high forehead and short bill. Breeding male has chestnut head with golden crown stripe; female similar to mallard female, but slimmer, with rusty-brown plumage and more pointed tail. In flight note the long wings and white belly, also large white wing-patches of male. Often forms large flocks in winter. Wigeon are vegetarian, grazing on land, or taking food from at or near the water surface.

WHETHER ONE HEARS them by a large reservoir, moving around on the edge of floodwater or on the mud of an estuary as the tide retreats, the whistling of wigeon is one of the great sounds of winter. They first arrive on our local estuary, visible from the road, in September, unimpressive in their eclipse plumage and unimpressive in numbers, but later there may be a couple of hundred and from the car, in the morning when the light is right, you can see the detail on the males. They now have yellow forecrowns on their chestnut heads.

The body is gently patterned grey, the silhouette distinctive, the chest pink and the rear end a contrast of black and white. As they dabble at the water's edge they whistle contentedly, paying no attention to the traffic and the female is seen to be just as distinctively shaped with her small bill, pointed

Above right
A large group of wigeon take to the air. The drake has a highly distinctive whistling flight-call.

Centre and bottom right
The drake wigeon is one of our prettiest waterfowl.

Bottom left
Grazing wigeon. At distance, the pure white at the base of the tail stands out clearly.

tail and high forehead. When the tide, or a passing dog, makes them fly, her white belly is characteristic. Both sexes have pointed wings and the white forewings of the males can still be seen as they gently descend some way off in the saltmarsh.

These birds will have come from Scandinavia, Finland, or Russia to winter on the Axe where, if we are lucky, we have 200 birds. More than 300,000 have made the journey to Britain. Estuaries, river valleys and areas of low-lying marsh will have more than 2,000, while the Ribble will sometimes have 100,000 feeding on eel-grass, sometimes called wigeon-grass, or grazing on grassland.

Of all the wintering wigeon, only some 300 pairs may be British breeding birds, mainly of Scottish origin. They breed scattered about upland bogs and lakes, in the Flow Country or on Loch Leven, with a few in northern England. Courtship is rather different from most dabbling ducks with hostility between courting males. The dominant males displays yellow crown in forehead-turning display. A tussock or a bit of shelter from scrub is needed to shelter the nest, a depression of grasses lined with down.

SPECIES INFORMATION

SCIENTIFIC NAME	*Anas strepera*
RELATED SPECIES	Mallard, Wigeon, Pintail, Shoveler, Teal, Garganey
CALL	Male has nasal 'arp' call and whistle; female a mallard-like quack 'kaak kaak kak kak kak', in diminuendo
HABITAT	Breeds on freshwater lakes with rich vegetation and on slow rivers. Winters to estuaries and other wetlands
STATUS	Resident and partial migrant. Winter numbers swelled by migrants from further north. Patchy distribution over much of Europe, except the north. About 800 pairs in BI, mainly in south-east

Gadwall

48–54 cm (19–21 in)

SIZE

IDENTIFICATION

HABITAT

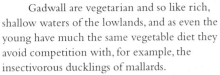

POPULATION

MAP

MALLARD-LIKE BUT slightly smaller and slimmer, with steeper forehead. Male relatively drab, with obvious black 'stern'. In flight both sexes show white belly and white speculum. Female has yellow-orange edges to bill.

THE DABBLING DUCKS have much in common so details of size and bill colour will be considered together. Male gadwall usually appear grey-brown with black back ends, and can easily be missed among duck as the white wing-patch is often obscure. In flight this becomes the identification feature while in good light the grey-brown, as Tunnicliffe mentions, becomes a complex of fine lines.

Gadwall are vegetarian and so like rich, shallow waters of the lowlands, and as even the young have much the same vegetable diet they avoid competition with, for example, the insectivorous ducklings of mallards.

The male Gadwall's most striking feature is its jet black stern.

227

Teal

34–38 cm (13–15 in)

SPECIES INFORMATION	
SCIENTIFIC NAME	*Anas crecca*
RELATED SPECIES	Mallard, Wigeon, Pintail, Shoveler, Garganey, Gadwall
CALL	Melodious 'krick', often in flight (male). Female has a higher-pitched quack
HABITAT	Breeds on lakes with thick bank vegetation
STATUS	Widespread in N and E Europe, rarer further south. About 3,000 pairs in BI. Northern breeders move south for winter. Commoner outside breeding season, especially on flooded meadows and marshland

SIZE

IDENTIFICATION

HABITAT

POPULATION

MAP

OUR SMALLEST DUCK, with rapid, wader-like flight. Breeding male has chestnut and green head, and yellow triangle (bordered black) at side of tail. Female has yellow-brown spots and dark grey bill. Both sexes show white wing bar and green speculum in flight.

TEAL ARE THE smallest of the dabbling ducks. The male looks grey, with a brown head and buff black end. The green mark through the eye is often obscure but the white stripe along the scapulars is seen whether swimming, walking or flying past in a compact flock. The female, as with most ducks, is mottled brown with her green and black speculum and wing bars her most distinctive features. The very clear 'krit krit' call in flight is as good a winter sound as the wigeon's whistle and the two are often found together.

Any area of winter flooding may be the place for teal, and even smaller rivers get a few visitors. This implies a mobile population, moving according to weather and food supplies, and ringing recoveries confirm this. Hard weather movements to Ireland are characteristic. On their wanderings, seeds will be important, whether those of estuarine plants or farm weeds, but insects and molluscs, some flooded out of the soil, form a quarter of the diet.

Although they are wanderers, there are significant aggregations in suitable fresh water or estuarine conditions. While Mersey populations have fallen, the 1995–96 population on the Somerset Levels, where attempts are being made to keep water levels higher, rose to a peak of 24,000. Average populations on the Mersey, Ribble and Dee are also of international importance, while Lough Neagh and Strangford Lough have important populations in Northern Ireland. The breeding distribution is thinly scattered, concentrated on upland areas, where it is undisturbed, close to small moorland pools and bogs.

As already implied, most populations are migratory with northern populations moving south-west to winter to Britain and the Netherlands. The American subspecies, the green-winged teal, is an extensive migrant, moving as far south as the West Indies and Central America and sometimes appearing over here, as a vagrant. Adult males are recognisable by the absence of the white horizontal stripe on scapulars and the presence of a white crescent at the sides of the breast.

Top and middle
The drake teal has bright, pretty plumage.

Bottom
Teal in typical pose, resting close to the water.

Garganey

37–40 cm (14.5–15.75 in)

SPECIES INFORMATION	
SCIENTIFIC NAME	*Anas querquedula*
RELATED SPECIES	Teal, Mallard, Wigeon, Pintail, Shoveler, Gadwall
CALL	Breeding male has dry 'klerreb'; female a high-pitched, nasal quack
HABITAT	Breeds on shallow water or marsh with rich vegetation. Outside breeding season on lakes, flooded meadows and marshes
STATUS	Summer visitor to much of Europe (but absent from most of north-west and south Europe). Winters in Africa. In BI rare breeding bird, about 50 pairs

SLIGHTLY LARGER YET slimmer than teal. Breeding male has broad white eye-stripe reaching to back of head. Female like teal but with rather striped face pattern. Male in eclipse like female, but with blue-grey front of wing. Flight not as rapid as teal.

BWP SAYS THE garganey voice 'is characterised by the peculiar call of the male who lacks pure whistles in his repertoire and whose main utterance is a unique mechanical sounding rattle recalling the crackling noise of breaking ice'.

The drake garganey is a very beautiful bird, mainly mottled brown, with fine crescent markings on the breast, and a broad white band from the eye to the nape of the neck. The breast is brown, and sharply divided from the grey flanks and white underparts. The scapulars are blue-grey, black and white. The speculum is a bright metallic green, bordered with white in front and behind. On the wing the pale bluish-grey forewing is often conspicuous.

Garganey are unique among the *Anas* ducks in being wholly migratory, wintering in sub-Saharan Africa, even as far south as the Transvaal. In Britain it is on the edge of its range, and the small numbers fluctuate. Breeding is in sheltered, shallow waters with plenty of floating and emergent vegetation. The main movement to these breeding areas is in March and April, with eggs laid in late April.

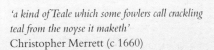

'a kind of Teale which some fowlers call crackling teal from the noyse it maketh'
Christopher Merrett (c 1660)

SIZE

IDENTIFICATION

HABITAT

POPULATION

MAP

Male garganey, showing the prominent white eyestripe – its most obvious feature.

Pintail

55–65 cm (22–25.5 in)

○○○○○○○○○○○○○○○○○○○○○○○○○○○○○○

SPECIES INFORMATION	
SCIENTIFIC NAME	Anas acuta
RELATED SPECIES	Mallard, Wigeon, Shoveler, Gadwall, Teal, Garganey
CALL	Breeding call of male a low whistle; female a grating quack
HABITAT	Breeds mainly on shallow lakes in northern coniferous forest or tundra. Outside breeding season mainly on the coast, or flooded washland
STATUS	Summer visitor to breeding grounds. Winter visitor further south (mainly coastal areas). Rare breeder in BI, about 50 pairs

SLIMMER THAN MALLARD. Male has chestnut head, grey body and long, pointed tail feathers. Female similar to mallard, but has more pointed tail and smaller, grey bill. Eclipse male very similar to female, but darker above. In flight (which is rapid) note long, pointed wings, slim body, long neck and white-edged speculum.

TUNNICLIFFE'S ANGLESEY PAINTINGS emphasise the black rear end of pintail males. They also have an elaborate vermiculated pattern on the back and flanks, which both appear grey at long range,

contrasting with dark head and clear white band down the side of the neck. When displaying, the drakes exhibit this striking nape and neck pattern, as a reminder that most or all the colours of birds have their appropriate significance. Slimbridge is a marvellous place to watch such elaborate duck displays, which focus on the brightly coloured parts

being exhibited by ritualised movements. The male pintail's tail is long and pointed but the female's is also pointed enough to help identification.

Although a few pintail do breed in Britain, they are essentially northern ducks ranging into tundra with a preference for moderately productive shallow pools and floods. Perhaps the often temporary nature of these explain why this mobile bird often nests as outlier populations well beyond its normal range. Pintail nest on the ground, usually but not always close to the water, lining a grassy nest with down.

The winter populations here are about half of the north-west European population, with Strangford Lough in Northern Ireland and Dublin Bay in the Republic holding significant numbers, but nothing like the 15 internationally important sites in England and Wales. The largest average populations recently have been 6,500 on the Dee and 3,300 on the Ribble. Pintail populations in the north-west emphasise the importance of that part of the Lancashire coast for estuarine birds.

Top and middle
The drake pintail has a very richly-textured breeding plumage, and the long, pointed tail which gives the species its name.

Bottom
In flight the long tail is very obvious.

Shoveler

47–53 cm (18.5–21 in)

<table>
<tr><td colspan="2" align="center">○○○○○○○○○○○○○○○○○○○○○○○○○○○○
SPECIES INFORMATION</td></tr>
<tr><td>SCIENTIFIC NAME</td><td>Anas clypeata</td></tr>
<tr><td>RELATED SPECIES</td><td>Mallard, Wigeon, Pintail, Gadwall, Teal, Garganey</td></tr>
<tr><td>CALL</td><td>Usually rather silent. Male has a deep 'tuk-tuk'; female a two-syllable quack</td></tr>
<tr><td>HABITAT</td><td>Breeds on shallow lakes bordered by rushes, sedges or reeds, and in marshy areas with open water. Outside breeding season also at coast</td></tr>
<tr><td>STATUS</td><td>Resident and partial migrant. Winter numbers swelled by migrants from further north. Scattered, mainly N and E Europe. In BI about 1,500 pairs</td></tr>
</table>

SQUATTER THAN MALLARD, with more pointed wings and long, broad bill. Male has dark head, white breast and chestnut belly and flanks. Female rather like mallard, but has pale blue forewing.

THE MALE HAS very distinctive plumage, but even the drab female can be identified with ease from the broad, flattened bill.

COMPARISON OF BILLS OF SEVERAL SPECIES

SPECIES	SIZE OF BILL	DESCRIPTION OF BEAK
Gadwall	50 mm (2 in)	Orange at sides (female)
Teal	36 mm (1.4 in)	Dark grey
Garganey	38 mm (1.5 in)	Grey; pale spot near base (female)
Pintail	56 mm (2.2 in)	Slim, grey
Shoveler	51 mm (2 in)	Broad, flattened
Mallard	58 mm (2.3 in)	Black and orange patches (female) Yellowish (male)
Wigeon	48 mm (1.9 in)	Small: grey-blue with dark tip

Male Shovelers, apart from their top heavy look, have green heads and a most distinguished contrast of chestnut flanks with white in front and behind and dark back. The blue forewing and green speculum are more visible in flight when wings appear small and pointed.

The bill can be used on the surface as a filter, being swept from side to catch crustaceans and other drifting invertebrates. The shoveler's filters are made up of intermeshing hair-like structures associated with both jaws, while the large bill allows much water to be sucked in.

Their breeding populations are scattered, being dependent on just the right sort of shallow water close to rough pasture or marshland. It is more territorial and less impressive in display than other ducks.

The main Palearctic populations are to the east, and it is some of these birds that make up our winter populations. These are nearly all freshwater, and there can be 500 or more on the Ouse Washes, at Abberton Reservoir, Rutland Water, Loch Leven or the Somerset Levels.

SIZE

IDENTIFICATION

HABITAT

POPULATION

MAP

Top right
A pair of shovelers living up to their name.

Bottom
Apart from the bill-shape, drake and duck look rather different.

Pochard

46 cm (18 in)

SIZE

IDENTIFICATION

HABITAT

POPULATION

POPULATION

MAP

PLUMP, COMPACT DUCK with domed head and steep forehead. Male has contrasting silver-grey back and flanks, black chest and tail, and chestnut-brown head. Female brown, with blackish bill and pale eye-ring.

MALE POCHARD, with brown head, black breast and patterned grey back and sides are handsome ducks. Females are rather nondescript brown, like many another duck, but the amount of grey among the brown, and the grey-banded bill make her recognisable. Like females, males have pale blue-banded bill and dark legs. They are fairly unusual among ducks in that there is no wing bar in flight, which is fast, with rapid beats of the broad wings.

The genus *Aythya* and relatives are medium-sized, diving ducks usually found on fresh water. Heads are distinctly large and bodies short; two features which are very clear when pochard and tufted duck flocks swim peacefully with beaks hidden as they doze on park lake, gravel pit or reservoir. As expert divers they have large toes and the legs are widely separated and set far back on the body, so are much more reluctant to move on land than mallards.

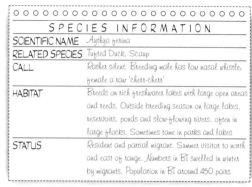

If sufficient food is offered, as it often is in town parks, they will move out near the water.

Although an expert diver, mainly to collect plant material, it is also a dabbler and upender, and its mixed feeding methods may have led to the name, with the old French 'pocher' meaning to poke about. The name pochard was not used until 1544.

Pochards breed in a broad band across Europe, avoiding the tundra and liking extensive shallow water as befits their feeding methods. They normally breed in thick vegetation, making a shallow nest of leaves and reed stems with the usual duck addition of down. In Britain there are only some 400 pairs, with a markedly eastern bias, but in winter a major arrival of migrants is heralded by the males, who arrive a fortnight before females in early autumn. Perhaps because of this, males and females often overwinter separately.

Top
Grey, black at both ends, and a rich chestnut head – defines the drake pochard.

Bottom left
Pochard in flight.

Bottom Right
Duck pochard has drabber plumage.

Tufted Duck

44 cm (17 in)

SPECIES INFORMATION

SCIENTIFIC NAME	Aythya fuligula
RELATED SPECIES	Pochard, Scaup
CALL	Breeding male has guttural 'gee-gee-gee'; female a grating 'kreck-kreck'.
HABITAT	Lakes and reservoirs
STATUS	Resident and partial migrant. Numbers in BI swelled in winter by migrants. Relatively common breeding bird, occasionally in urban areas too. In BI population stands at about 10,000 pairs

SMALL, COMPACT DIVING duck. In flight shows white wing bar. Male black with white flanks, and long plume on back of head (which has purple sheen). Female dark brown, with head plume very short or absent, and sometimes with white spot at base of bill. Often forms large winter flocks. Not so quiet as pochard, the male whistles during the breeding season when females also call softly.

TUFTED DUCK MUST be among the most popular of park birds; plenty of character, distinctive plumage and a spectacular dive help to make them attractive. The tuft is clear in breeding males but is little more than a bump on the back of the head of the female. The clear black and white pattern and black back of the male are unmistakable, but the dark brown female could be confused with similar, but white-faced, scaup or even a young male pochard, but it also has a paler face. The conspicuous yellow eye adds to their attraction, and the broad white wing bar in flight is very noticeable.

By becoming tolerant of humans, and ready to adapt diet to their offerings, the tufted duck has added park lakes to the other habitats, reservoirs, gravel pits, natural lakes and lowland lochs where it can be seen in winter. The number at Lough Neagh is of international importance, and with over 25,000 there early in the year it is almost as big a gathering as the pochards that feed there in November. Other large counts, with over 2,000 in 1995–96, were at Loch Leven and Rutland Water in early autumn.

Tufted ducks dive deeper than pochard and eat more animal food, some being sieved from bottom mud and some, like molluscs, being picked off underwater vegetation.

Although they need open water for feeding, without too much marginal encroachment, a degree of cover is needed for nesting to keep predation levels within bounds. Grassy tussocks close to water are favoured, but on islands, the ideal breeding site, they may make their nest of rushes and down further from the water. They will sometimes nest in the open among gulls and terns which give more protection to nests. After breeding, flocking starts early, with males collecting first after the break-up of the pair bond.

SIZE

IDENTIFICATION

HABITAT

POPULATION

MAP

Top right
Tufted ducks show a prominent white wing-bar in flight.

Bottom
The delicate crest trailing down the back of its head gives the tufted duck its name.

233

Marsh Harrier

48–56 cm (19–22 in)

○ ○

SPECIES INFORMATION

SCIENTIFIC NAME	*Circus aeruginosus*
RELATED SPECIES	Hen Harrier, Montagu's Harrier
CALL	Male has squawking 'quiaair', alarm-call a snarling 'kike-kike-kike'
HABITAT	Marshes and lakes with extensive reedbeds. Hunts over reeds, water meadows, fields and open country
STATUS	Resident. In BI, mainly in south and east about 100 pairs

SIZE

IDENTIFICATION

HABITAT

POPULATION

MAP

BUZZARD-SIZED, BUT slimmer and narrower-winged and with longer tail. Male has pale grey tail and upper wings, contrasting with otherwise dark plumage and black wing tips. Female dark, with cream coloured head and shoulders. Flight slow, interspersed with buoyant gliding, wings held in a V-shape.

MARSH HARRIERS SHARE their reedbed habitat with the even rarer bittern, and both nest mainly in protected and managed reserves. The population is now recovering from a disastrous low, probably due to pesticides in the food chain.

They fly over the reeds with characteristic harrier glides, long tails and distinctive V silhouette of the wings. The male has grey patches on the wings and tail, and the larger female has a pale crown and throat. With one male often partnering more than one female we can talk of nests rather than pairs. In fact, some 15 per cent of males are polygamous and this may help explain the increase in recent years.

Brown (1976) describes their spectacular display: 'From this height they tumble earthwards in spectacular dives, during which they twist violently from side to side, or spin through 360°. The erratic movements display the contrasting grey and brown of their wings to advantage and the whole process is not only visible but the rushing sound made is audible for some distance. At the completion of the dive the male mounts again steeply, to repeat the

Top left
A female marsh harrier looks out over the reedbeds from a vantage point nearby.

Top right
Typical harrier outline – very buoyant in flight, with a fairly long tail.

Bottom
Female marsh harrier – note the long, yellow legs.

performance, sometimes after further acrobatics which may include looping the loop at the top of the swift steep upward swoop.'

He also describes the food pass, which is characteristic of all harriers: 'The male arriving with food calls the female off the nest with a characteristic mewing whistle. The female may answer with a higher pitched whistle. She rises from her perch, or from the nest and flies to meet the male. He often drops the food, which the female flying below him then

catches with a dextrous twist in mid air. Sometimes however, she flies up to him, turns over, and receives the prey by a foot to foot pass, a spectacularly agile and beautifully timed movement.'

In reedbeds the food passed may be a rodent, particularly voles, a bird or perhaps an amphibian. These are caught in low flight which is checked before descent with long legs extended. In arable fields, small birds, including young game birds, and rabbits are favoured.

SPECIES INFORMATION

SCIENTIFIC NAME	Pandion haliaetus
RELATED SPECIES	No close relatives
CALL	Whistling calls, usually heard near nest
HABITAT	Lakes, slow-flowing rivers and coasts. Regular at lakes, reservoirs and rivers on migration
STATUS	Summer visitor. Stable but small population in Scotland (about 80 pairs)

Osprey

55–69 cm (22–27 in)

VERY PALE BENEATH in flight, with long, narrow, angled wings. Dark brown above, mostly white underneath, with brown breast-band. Hovers and plunges to catch fish in talons. Dives almost vertically with wings half closed, often submerging for a short time.

OSPREYS HAVE RECEIVED much protection, particularly when they first returned to Scotland to breed, mostly in the form of direct protection of the nest site rather than of their habitat. This spectacular 'fish hawk' nests mainly in pines and, as it fishes, its white head, kinked wings and black wrist-patch make it easy to identify. More birds now appear at coastal and inland waters on migration.

In 1954, ospreys returned to build a nest near Loch Garten in Speyside and as Brown describes it: 'despite one failure through the maniac efforts of an egg collector which might have halted the entire process of re-establishment, the pair persisted, produced young in 1957, and the site is occupied to this day, observed day and night, and by many thousands of people annually. Never can any individual pair of birds anywhere in the world have given so much pleasure to so many people and never can any pair of birds done more for the cause of bird conservation.' By the early 1990s there were over 70 pairs.

Brown also describes its fishing habits: 'On sighting a fish it checks briefly in flight, sometimes hovers for a moment or two, then plunges nearly vertically towards the prey. It appears to dive head first ... but actually, at the last moment, the feet are thrown forward in front of the head and the osprey crashes feet first.' Short thick tarsi, spicules on the toes, long curved talons and a large cere which can close over the nostrils help this specialist fish eater.

Ospreys are very widely distributed over the northern hemisphere and also breed in Australia. Apart from some Mediterranean birds, those breeding in Europe are migrants, wintering along African river systems south of the Sahara. Migrant birds often delay at a suitable lake or estuary on the way, which is when most are seen.

> 'I will provide thee of a princely osprey,
> That, as he flieth over fish in pools
> The fish shall turn their glistening bellies up'
> George Peele THE BATTLE OF ALCAZOR

SIZE

IDENTIFICATION

HABITAT

POPULATION

MAP

Top
In flight, the osprey has rather angled wings.

Middle
In some areas osprey numbers have been boosted by the provision of platforms.

Bottom
Osprey bringing a fish back to the nest.

235

Moorhen

33 cm (13 in)

○○○○○○○○○○○○○○○○○○○○○○○○○○

SPECIES INFORMATION

SCIENTIFIC NAME	*Gallinula chloropus*
RELATED SPECIES	Coot, Water Rail
CALL	Alarm call a guttural 'krrrk', or penetrating 'kirreck'
HABITAT	Still and slow-flowing water, ditches and small, overgrown ponds. Also common on streams and in ponds in urban parks and gardens. Feeds mainly on land
STATUS	Resident. In BI common except in north-west Scotland, about 315,000 pairs

SIZE

IDENTIFICATION

HABITAT

POPULATION

MAP

S MALLER AND SLIMMER than Coot, with red, yellow-tipped bill and red frontal shield. Legs and toes long and green. White under tail coverts displayed as tail bobbed. Juveniles grey-brown with pale chin. Trails legs in flight. Nods head while swimming and walking, and repeatedly bobs tail.

IN TOWN PARKS moorhens are easy to spot with their flicking tails, red shield above the beak and white stripes below the wing. On land, collecting any additional food offered, their long flattened toes and smart green legs are easy to see, as they are if the birds are moving over water lilies or other surface vegetation. In reedy rivers they are often much more elusive, showing white under tail coverts as they head for cover.

Along the Lledr, in North Wales, it was surprisingly difficult to map their territories because of their elusive, sheltering behaviour, but on a winter evening they were often easy to count as they gathered to roost at the top of riverside willows. A breeding pair on the pond opposite our house in Devon was even more arboreal and

had their first nesting attempt about 9 m (30 ft) up an ash, concealed in ivy. They appeared most incongruous walking along the branches with long twigs for nesting material. This attempt was abandoned and later two broods were reared in more conventional sites. As so often happens with moorhens, the members of the first brood were most attentive helpers in the rearing of the second, but the apparently harmonious family life ended, with many chases over several days and a lot of noise, when the parents drove off the first lot of young birds.

British birds do not usually move far, whereas those from the north and east of the range, which extends across most of Europe south of 60∞, move extensively; a Scandinavian bird could reach north Africa or even south of the Sahara.

Moorhens are not demanding about breeding conditions, and are therefore widespread wherever water has sufficient emergent vegetation and is rich enough to provide adequate food. They therefore avoid upland areas and acid lakes.

The main features of the moorhen are the bright red bill and the white patches under the tail.

'Planing up shaving of silver spray
A moorhen darted out
From the bank there about,
And through the stream shine ripped his way.'
Thomas Hardy

Coot

38 cm (15 in)

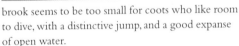

SPECIES INFORMATION

SCIENTIFIC NAME	*Fulica atra*
RELATED SPECIES	Moorhen, Water Rail
CALL	Male an unmusical 'tsk', and a sound rather like a cork popping. Female has a loud, barking 'kurff'. Alarm call a sharp 'psi'
HABITAT	Lakes, reservoirs, ponds, and slow-flowing rivers with well-developed fringing vegetation. Also on gravel pits and on lakes in urban parks
STATUS	Resident and partial migrant. In BI common except in NW Scotland, about 55,000 pairs

BLACK, RATHER DUMPY waterbird with grey-green legs and white frontal shield above white bill. Toes lobed at edges. Dives for submerged food. Often gather in large flocks in winter.

COOTS ARE LESS LIKELY to be celebrated in verse as they are noisy, quarrelsome birds with some insulting names. Michael Drayton in the sixteenth century wrote of the 'brain-bald coot' as well as casting aspersions on their sexual proclivities. Tennyson's brook came 'from haunt of coot and hern' but unless there were some lakes at the headwater it sounds an unlikely habitat. Perhaps there was an oxbow, but a

brook seems to be too small for coots who like room to dive, with a distinctive jump, and a good expanse of open water.

Coots are larger and dumpier than moorhens, with all-black plumage, contrasting with their white bill and frontal shield. Juveniles can be very pale and are always less black, while the downy young, like moorhens, have distinctively coloured heads.

Arrivals of birds from northern Europe lead to some huge winter flocks. At the start of the breeding season there is much squabbling. The conspicuous shield is advertised when an aggressive bird lowers its head and raises neck and back feathers; if this is not sufficient and an intruder does not withdraw, actual foot-to-foot and beak-to-beak combat, with much splashing, follows.

SIZE

IDENTIFICATION

HABITAT

POPULATION

MAP

Top left and right
The coot is sooty black, with a white bill and frontal shield.

Bottom
In winter, coot often congregate in large numbers at lakes and reservoirs.

237

SIZE

IDENTIFICATION

HABITAT

POPULATION

MAP

Water Rail

25 cm (10 in)

SPECIES INFORMATION

SCIENTIFIC NAME	Rallus aquaticus
RELATED SPECIES	Moorhen, Coot, Corncrake
CALL	Like squealing pigs – 'kriek kruuie kruuie'; in spring a sharp 'zik-zik-zik' call, often ending with an extended, throaty 'tjuier'
HABITAT	Thick reed and sedge beds, especially at river or lake margins. Sometimes along ditches
STATUS	Resident. In BI commonest in Ireland and in parts of E Anglia. Total BI population probably around 3,000 pairs

SLIM MARSH BIRD with long, slightly decurved red bill and black and white striped flanks. Upperparts brown with black markings; face, neck and breast slate grey; under tail coverts white. Juveniles pale brown below, with delicate stripes on neck and breast, and less stripy flanks. Secretive and difficult to observe.

WATER RAILS ARE noisy but elusive and live in well vegetated swamps. May be spotted for example as it searches the edge of a reedbed in shallow water, when the long red bill and impressively barred flanks, coupled with an actively jerking tail make it an attractive bird. When flushed it flutters off with trailing legs. When heard it is usually the grunts, groans and screams that are described, but the repeated 'pik pik' call is just as good an indication of a rail in the reeds. These noises are most frequently made at dawn or dusk. If one wants to see the bird in detail than a hide among the reeds can provide the answer.

Water rails, whose lateral compression allows them to stalk through reedbeds, have a very varied diet, including a wide range of wetland invertebrates, ranging in size from insects and their larvae to shrimps and molluscs, as well as vertebrates such as frogs and newts, and some vegetable matter.

Water rail are secretive, but sometimes come into the open, especially in the evening.

Common Snipe
26 cm (10 in)

MEDIUM-SIZED WADER with very long bill and camouflaged plumage. Back brown, with black and yellow markings. Dark stripes on cap. When flushed, tends to fly up suddenly, then pitch sideways, calling.

SNIPE ARE USUALLY hard to see on the ground, but the long straight beak and patterned upperparts are their most striking features when they are seen, often staying very still, beside a shallow pool. More often they are put up from a bog, calling as they zig-zag

away. With all snipe, on the ground or in the air, the long straight bills are the most noticeable features, but when well seen on the ground the cryptic patterning of browns, blacks and whites is marvellous.

Today breeding snipe look to be fairly widespread if one thinks in terms of 10 km (6 mile) squares, as in the *Atlas*, but even on that scale much of the west country, a swathe from there up to the Midlands, and many areas in the south-east are entirely without breeding snipe.

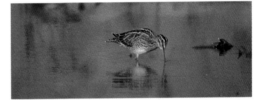

Jack Snipe
19 cm (7.5 in)

IT IS HARD to get a good view of jack snipe on the ground. They are usually seen when flushed from cover, when they make a brief low flight, showing a dark, wedge-shaped tail, and shorter bill.

SMALLER THAN THE SNIPE and much more secretive only taking flight at the very last minute. It has a slower, less zig-zagging flight than snipe and often flies back over the head of any intruder or diving in to cover. Despite apparently extraordinary noises it makes when breeding, any jack snipe here are likely to be quiet giving only a faint snipe like call. The head and back pattern show more clearly than on the snipe paticularly on a flying bird.

Common Redshank

26 cm (10 in)

SIZE

IDENTIFICATION

BRIGHT RED LEGS, white rump and broad white trailing edge to wings (prominent in flight). In breeding plumage upperparts brownish, with darker speckles; at other times paler grey-brown above, and less speckled. Juveniles lack the red base to bill, have yellower legs, and are more reddish-brown above.

WADERS OF the genus *Tringa* are noisy, but some are heard more widely than others. Although breeding redshank in wet grassland are decreasing inland, their alarm calls there, or in winter estuaries, are a feature of the habitat, and their flight 'song' of sweet yodelling notes, often given in aerial display, seems joyous.

HABITAT

'A cry half of challenge, half lament, the very spirit of the estuary, of a life that chances and changes with wind and tide … No one who has ever heard the redshank cry in the wind over the saltings will ever after think of those waste spaces of water and ooze and sunlight without that haunting voice … and the lovely curves of that swift and slanting flight.'
Eric Parker ENGLISH WILDLIFE

POPULATION

MAP

SPECIES INFORMATION	
SCIENTIFIC NAME	Tringa totanus
RELATED SPECIES	Greenshank, Spotted Redshank, Green Sandpiper, Wood Sandpiper
CALL	Loud, fluting 'tleu-hu' or 'tleu-hu-hu' flight-call is one of the most characteristic sounds of wetlands and coasts. Alarm call 'tjuk-tjuk-tjuk'. Song a yodelling 'tooli tooli tooli', often given in flight
HABITAT	Breeds in open marshes, mires and saltmarsh with short vegetation, especially near coasts. Outside breeding season on low-lying coasts, often in flocks on mudflats, or smaller groups in wet sites inland. Feeds mainly in shallow, muddy water
STATUS	Resident and partial migrant. Numbers in BI swelled in autumn and winter by migrants. About 35,000 pairs in BI. Declining over most of range

Bottom right
Redshank at its nest in marshland.

Top
The redshank takes its name from its long, red legs.

Bottom left
Redshank feeding in shallow water.

Little Ringed Plover

15 cm (6 in)

SMALL ROTUND WADER with black and white face pattern (breeding season), muddy yellow legs and yellow eye-ring. Smaller than ringed plover and lacking white wing bar.

LITTLE RINGED PLOVER and ringed plover are rather similar, and if you do not know them well or have not seen them for some time, they can be confused.

POINTS OF COMPARISON BETWEEN THE ADULT RINGED AND LITTLE RINGED PLOVERS

FEATURE	LITTLE RINGED PLOVER	RINGED PLOVER
Body	Slim	More robust
Eye-ring	Bright yellow	Faint orange
Legs	Pale flesh colour	Orange
Chest-band	Varied, but often narrow in centre	Wide
Head pattern	White border behind black crown	White eyebrow
Bill	Black	Orange at base

The crucial differences are that the little ringed plover has no wing bar in flight and 'pee-u' call rather than 'too-eep'. Young birds are brown where adults are black and have a uniform brown cap.

Here is a bird that has made great use of man-made habitats including gravel pits and reservoirs in their early days as they fill. The bird did not breed in Britain until 1938 but is now widespread, with recent colonisation of Wales along river shingle.

A similar picture emerges in Europe, with its versatility allowing it to spread in many countries, but with the largest populations in the north and east. To all these areas it is a summer visitor, mainly wintering in north Africa. Birds return to Britain in early April, display with territorial song-flight and lay from April onwards on bare ground.

SIZE

IDENTIFICATION

HABITAT

POPULATION

MAP

Top
Little ringed plover – note the prominent eye-ring.

Bottom left
Pair of little ringed plover at their nest in shingle.

Bottom right
The female settles down on her eggs.

Black-tailed Godwit

38–44 cm (15–17 in)

○○○○○○○○○○○○○○○○○○○○○○○○○○○○○

SPECIES INFORMATION

SCIENTIFIC NAME	Limosa limosa
RELATED SPECIES	Bar-tailed Godwit
CALL	Flight call 'eeka-reeka-reeka'. Song, in flight, a repeated 'reeveeyoo-reeveeyoo'
HABITAT	Breeds mainly in water meadows. In winter on estuaries, marshes and also on inland shallow water
STATUS	Summer visitor and migrant. Winters mainly around coasts. Breeds in Iceland, Netherlands, N Germany, southern Baltic, and scattered elsewhere. About 50 pairs breed in Britain, and a handful in Ireland

SIZE

IDENTIFICATION

HABITAT

POPULATION

MAP

LARGE, LONG-LEGGED, long-billed wader. Adult in breeding plumage has rust-brown neck and breast. In winter both sexes are a uniform grey. In flight shows white wing bar and white base to black tail. Legs longer than those of bar-tailed godwit, and bill longer and straighter.

AFTER MORE THAN a hundred years' absence black-tailed godwits nested sporadically in the 1930s when numbers were increasing in the Netherlands. They have nested on the Ouse Washes since 1952, with a peak of 64 pairs, from which birds may have spread to the Nene Washes, where the RSPB can maintain appropriate water levels for breeding waders. When water levels are right on the Somerset Levels black-tailed godwits occasionally nest there, as they do in Kent and Shetland.

'At the Ouse Washes, godwits begin returning to their breeding grounds in March, and the first nests are usually in the first two weeks of April. When breeding, they are loosely colonial (4–5 pairs per 100 ha) and such groups provide effective communal defence of eggs and young against crows, kestrels and other predators. Godwits nest in damp, tussocky pastures which have been grazed fairly heavily by cattle the previous summer.'

They feed mainly on earthworms, which they find by probing. Sites with a fairly high water table and

The black-tailed godwit is a majestic wader, with its long legs, long bill and russet summer plumage.

soft, peaty soils facilitate this method of feeding. They also take aquatic insects in shallow pools and ditches.

These large, graceful waders are very distinctive when flying, with their bold white wing bar, large white area of rump and tail-base and black terminal tail-band that gives them their name.

Black-tailed godwits are more commonly seen on our estuaries in the winter, when birds from western Europe are replaced by birds of the Icelandic race, the latter with shorter bills. British estuaries are vital feeding grounds for these birds. Prime sites include the Stour estuary in Essex, the Dee, Swale (Kent) and Poole Harbour.

Ruff

26–32 cm (10–12.5 in) (male)
20–25 cm (8–9 in) (female)

SPECIES INFORMATION

SCIENTIFIC NAME	*Philomachus pugnax*
RELATED SPECIES	No close relatives
CALL	Usually silent. A low 'wek' flight-call
HABITAT	Breeds on open bogs, damp meadows and on wet heaths; favours damp meadows with ditches and ponds, especially near to coast.
STATUS	Summer visitor to north of range. Mainly NE Europe (Finland holds about 50,000 pairs). Also Norway, Sweden, Denmark, N Germany and Holland. Rare breeder in Britain (about 5 females each year)

SIZE

IDENTIFICATION

HABITAT

POPULATION

MAP

BREEDING MALE HAS remarkable ruff of feathers around neck, and head tufts, for lek displays. This varies in colour and pattern between individuals. Front of face with naked skin. Female and non-breeding male plumage dingy grey. Head small, and neck rather long. In flight shows narrow wing bar and white base to outer tail feathers.

MALES ARE LARGER than females and, in the breeding season they develop elaborate plumage, with a ruff of puffed out neck feathers. Different individuals have a different pattern of coloration – some being red, while others are white, black, mottled or barred.

The flamboyant males strut about, showing off their multicoloured ruffs and elaborate ear-tufts. Different coloured birds have different roles in the lek, with white-ruffed ones being 'satellites' who do not defend territories and serve mainly to attract females to the site. 'Independent' males, usually dark-coloured, may either be 'residents' who defend territories, or 'marginals' who do not. To complicate matters further, the satellite males are allowed on the residences, while the marginals are not. All this means, that a few males are responsible for all the matings, often with several females in a few minutes, and that the males play no part whatever in any subsequent incubation or chick rearing. It might be thought that the whole scheme would be an evolutionary disaster and that, following a different line of thought, genes for white ruffs would die out. Satellites however are quite good at sneaking in to mate, without any display.

In Britain, ruffs are most often seen on their wintering grounds – muddy lakes, rivers and ponds, or at the coast. Features to watch for are the longish neck, medium-short bill, scaly back plumage, and, in flight, the white sides to the base of the tail.

Ruffs as breeding birds were once much commoner. An eighteenth-century Lincolnshire fowler netted 72 ruffs in a single morning, and 40–50 dozen between April and Michaelmas. These, when fattened, would sell for two shillings, or two shillings and six pence as table birds. No doubt this was one reason for their decline, but land drainage was probably more important, as this species likes hummocky marshes with shallow water for feeding, drier zones for displaying, and some cover for nest building. Another factor is that Britain is on the extreme western edge of the ruff's range, and any contractions of that range would mean a loss to us.

Top and bottom
Ruff are relatively short-billed, with characteristically scaly plumage on the back.

Middle
In spring, male ruffs show a wide variety of plumages – this one has developed pure white feathering.

Common Sandpiper

20 cm (8 in)

○○○○○○○○○○○○○○○○○○○○○○○○○○○
SPECIES INFORMATION

SCIENTIFIC NAME	Actitis hypoleucos
RELATED SPECIES	Green Sandpiper, Wood sandpiper
CALL	Shrill 'hee-dee-dee' when flushed. Song, given mostly in flight, 'heedee-titti-veedee-titi-veedee', often at night as well
HABITAT	Clear rivers, streams, lakes and on rocky islands with relatively sparse vegetation. Also on rocky shores with loose tree stands. Outside breeding season on gravelly or stoney ponds, lakes and rivers, and at sewage farms and estuaries
STATUS	Summer visitor and passage migrant. Scattered throughout most of Europe, becoming commoner towards N and NE (common in Finland and Scandinavia). In BI about 18,000 pairs

SIZE

IDENTIFICATION

HABITAT

POPULATION

MAP

A SMALL, SHORT-LEGGED wader with rather short, straight bill and dark rump. White wing bar is clearly visible in flight. Often bobs tail. Flies low over water with whirring wing-beats, interspersed with gliding on down-curved wings.

COMMON SANDPIPERS ARE white below, with the white looping up between brown wing and chest. There is a hint of an eye-stripe.

If redshank are the spirit of the lowland wetlands and estuaries, then common sandpipers fill a similar role by upland lakes and rivers.

Breeding sandpipers, with their excited calls and low flight on stiff wings, are welcome indeed when they return in April. Their presence, bobbing

The common sandpiper tolerates an extremely wide climate range. Its range, always favouring the same fairly fast headwaters, extends across Asia to Japan. These eastern birds move into Australia, while European birds usually winter in the far south in Africa.

up and down on shingle banks, is very noticeable throughout the summer. On their return south they turn up wherever there is water, the concrete edge of a reservoir or the muddy margins of a lowland river, still repeating their triple call and bobbing up and down.

Along upland rivers, the amount of gravel exposed may vary rapidly after rain, and excited parents sometimes have to take their young into grassy cover after floods. The chicks are cryptically patterned, and difficult to spot amongst the stony banks, where food, in the form of beetles and fly larvae, can be found.

This rather short-legged wader typically sits, bobbing, close to the water's edge.

Green Sandpiper

23 cm (9 in)

MEDIUM-SIZED WADER with dark upperparts and white base of tail. Tail white, with 3 or 4 brownish bars. Juveniles have yellowish spots above. Shy, often sitting tight until flushed.

GREEN SANDPIPERS ARE largely passage migrants moving between their breeding areas in Norway (15,000 pairs), Sweden (30,000) and Finland (60,000) and wintering areas around the Mediterranean and into Africa. The huge Russian population moves to Turkey and Iran and on into China and the Philippines. Most migrants turn up around freshwater sites, which may be extensive wetlands, a steep-sided ditch or a river's edge: they can surprise you anywhere.

Surprise it can be for they rise steeply and noisily, calling 'klueet' or an extended 'tluit-tit-tit'. Apart from the white tail, rump and belly, the bird often appears almost black, flies fast and erratically before plunging back, snipe-like, to some hidden watery spot. The green of the name is never very evident, for the back, even of well-observed birds, is never more than an optimistic green-brown, peppered with small white dots. The neck and breast is streaked, with a clear boundary between breast and white belly.

Watercress beds or sewage farms are popular winter haunts and, as with passage birds, it is usually a singleton or couple who remain faithful to a chosen site for many weeks. The winter sites are likely to be southerly, whether in Ireland or in Britain, and may be abandoned if cold weather makes it difficult to get at the aquatic invertebrates and occasional small fish that make up the diet.

Green sandpipers' breeding habitat also requires freshwater, but often in very small amounts, with muddy margins and the presence of bogs and stands of alder, birch or pine. These trees are vital for nesting; some other bird's nest, or a squirrel's drey is often used.

SIZE

IDENTIFICATION

HABITAT

POPULATION

MAP

At a distance the green sandpiper can look very dark above, contrasting with its pure white plumage below.

245

Kingfisher

17 cm (6.5 in)

SPECIES INFORMATION	
SCIENTIFIC NAME	*Alcedo atthis*
RELATED SPECIES	*No close relatives in region*
CALL	*Flight-call a high-pitched 'tiekt', or 'tii-tee', often repeated*
HABITAT	*Clear streams, lakes and rivers with steep banks in the vicinity (for nest tunnel). Outside breeding season on rivers, lakes, ponds, and also at the coast in hard weather*
STATUS	*Resident and partial migrant in west and central Europe. Summer visitor in north-east of range (avoids hard winters). Most of Europe, except far north. In BI about 6,000 pairs*

SIZE

IDENTIFICATION

HABITAT

POPULATION

MAP

BRIGHT BLUE ABOVE, with rapid flight, low and straight over the water. Easily overlooked when sitting quietly on a branch, and most often seen in flight.

APART FROM THE azure back, large bill and distinctive shape, the orange underparts and complex head pattern of blue, orange and white contribute to the appearance of a unique bird. Often, however, particularly on a misty winter's day it is the shrill call, frequently repeated, that makes you look up to see the bird disappearing down some estuarine creek. At that time of year more birds are down by the coast, but in summer, a fish supply, sandy bank and fishing post or branch are the requirements. The eggs, laid in the tunnel in the sandy bank, are usually round and, like many well hidden ones, are white and smooth.

Richard Jefferies (1879) has plenty to say about Kingfishers: 'Though these brilliant coloured birds may often be seen skimming across the surface of the mere, they seem to obtain more food from the brooks and ponds than from the broader expanse of water above. In the brooks they find overhanging branches upon which to perch and watch for their prey and without which they can do nothing.

His azure back and wings and ruddy breast are not equalled in beauty of colour by any bird native to this country. The long pointed beak looks half as long as the whole bird: his shape is somewhat wedge like, enlarging gradually from the point of the beak backwards.'

In Athens, when dried and hung up, kingfishers would ward off Zeus's lightening, they could calm storms, particularly during the halcyon days, the seven days they brood the eggs.

People in the Loire area knew that when hung up their beaks would turn to whichever way the wind blew. I like particularly the advice of Giraldus Cambrensis in 1186, 'these little birds ... if they are put among clothes and other articles ... preserve them from the moth and give them a pleasant odour'. I wonder how many of our present day activities will be seen as equally ridiculous.

Hopefully not the activities of the Environment Agency who, in our Local Biodiversity Action Plan needed to encourage and maintain the steep sandy banks favoured by kingfishers and sand martins for breeding. A 'well canalised', 'well disciplined' river would not create such things as it would not be allowed to erode and behave as rivers should. The Agency also works hard to keep rivers well-oxygenated, to prevent or clean up toxic spills and overflow from silage clamps. They are also much concerned with preventing fish-spawning gravels from being covered with sediment. In all these ways they help kingfishers, for without fish the fish-eating birds would starve.

Many eastern kingfishers, where population densities tend always to be lower, are migrants to the south-west. Not surprisingly if it is cold and the water icebound, kingfishers suffer and our relatively mild oceanic climate helps to make the British and Irish populations of great importance.

Top left
A kingfisher holds a fish lengthways in its bill, after a successful dive.

Top right
Watching the water below for suitable prey.

Bottom
When seen from behind, the shiny back contrasts with the somewhat darker wings.

Sand Martin

12 cm (4.75 in)

SPECIES INFORMATION	
SCIENTIFIC NAME	Riparia riparia
RELATED SPECIES	House Martin, Swallow
CALL	Very vocal. Scratchy 'tshrr' and repeated 'brr-brr-brr'. Song is a series of soft twitters
HABITAT	Sandy banks and quarries, usually close to water. Sometimes flocks gather in large numbers at reedbeds in late summer
STATUS	Summer visitor, wintering in tropical Africa. Throughout Europe, but distribution rather patchy. In BI about 200,000 pairs

SMALLEST EUROPEAN MARTIN. Tail is only weakly forked. Brown above and white below, with brown breast-band.

THEY ARE ONE OF the first of our summer visitors to arrive back, and seeing a brown martin with distinct chest-band over river or lake at the end of March is a hopeful sign of more spring arrivals soon. Colonies can be large, and are constantly alive with their twittering calls. Loss of habitat, and drought in the African Sahel where many of the birds winter, have combined to reduce numbers periodically. Notable crash years were 1968–69 and 1983–84.

A small nest area is defended, but essentially breeding birds are as gregarious as those on migration. Being early breeders, with eggs laid by the end of April, there is usually time for two broods. Sand martins dig out their tunnels in vertical sand or gravel banks, and a single colony may consist of hundreds or exceptionally thousands of pairs. In many urban areas, where rivers have been canalised and drains are needed to control water movements, artificial sites such as these drainpipes are sometimes used. Nests in Salisbury of this type usually seemed to be successful.

Sand martins rarely fly high, and although particularly associated with water are quite prepared to catch their insect prey wherever it is abundant.

'… the desolate face
Of rude waste landscapes far away from men
where frequent quarries give thee dwelling place
With strangest taste and labour undeterred
Drilling small holes along the quarries side'
John Clare SELECTED POEMS

SIZE

IDENTIFICATION

HABITAT

POPULATION

MAP

Sand martin nesting burrows in the sandy bank of a gravel workings.

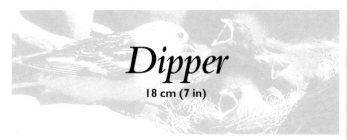

Dipper

18 cm (7 in)

○○○○○○○○○○○○○○○○○○○○○○○○○

SPECIES INFORMATION

SCIENTIFIC NAME	*Cinclus cinclus*
RELATED SPECIES	*None in region*
CALL	*Flight-call 'zit'. Song a series of quiet whistles, trills and twitters*
HABITAT	*Fast-flowing, clear streams and rivers. In winter also seen at slower rivers and lakes*
STATUS	*Resident and partial migrant. Scattered throughout Europe in suitable habitat. In BI about 20,000 pairs*

SIZE

IDENTIFICATION

HABITAT

POPULATION

MAP

DUMPY, LIKE A large wren in shape. Short tail and powerful legs and feet. Black and brown, with large white bib. Juveniles slatey-grey above with dirty white breast and chin. Often sits on stone in the water, bobbing. Flight is rapid, direct and low.

ON SOME WELSH streams I have found dippers with grey wagtails, but on others, where extensive forestry around the headwaters had led to acidification, the fall in invertebrates led to a consequent fall in the dipper population. Newton (1998) quoted studies from Wales and Scotland that showed that territories were longer and densities therefore lower, where the water was acid. This was in turn associated with decreases in suitable food items, such as mayfly nymphs and caddisfly larvae. Luckily, a recent survey in the Axe and its tributaries showed neutral water and plenty of invertebrates, but such dippers as there are prefer the shallower tributaries.

The territorial behaviour and unreadiness to move onto a neighbour's territory make dippers easy to map, and they are often easy to see if you stop, look and listen for instance on an old stone bridge. From there you may hear, as well as the murmur of the stream, the dipper's gentle babbling or its 'zit' call when disturbed from a mid-stream boulder. If you see one before disturbance, its bobbing action is as characteristic as its large wren-like shape, bright white chest, bordered below by chestnut, and the blackish back. It is the back, and whirring wings, that are most evident as it flies low to a new boulder or shingle bank.

In Ireland and western Scotland dippers have less chestnut below, and are darker above, while the Scandinavian bird that Linnaeus named has no chestnut at all. Four other races with a degree of overlap and variation are described within its European distribution, which appears scattered because of its preference for rapid flowing hill streams.

Dippers are very early breeders with laying eggs from the end of February, in a domed nest of moss and grass stems, often concealed behind a waterfall frequently on a ledge overhanging the water.

Turner in 1544, as many others since, called it a water ouzel, and the more appropriate dipper name did not appear until *Tunstall's Ornithologica Britannica* in 1777.

Top right
Dippers usually nest close to a river, such as underneath a waterfall or bridge.

Top and bottom left
The dipper is a rotund bird, with grey-brown plumage and obvious white bib.

> '*Peradventure he may have the good fortune to see the common dipper walking, literally walking, at the bottom of the water in pursuit of its prey ... precisely as if upon dry land.*'
> George Pulman BOOK OF THE AXE (1875)

Grey Wagtail

40 cm (16 in)

SPECIES INFORMATION

SCIENTIFIC NAME	Motacilla cinerea
RELATED SPECIES	Yellow Wagtail, Pied wagtail
CALL	Sharp 'tseet-tseet'. Song is made up of high-pitched twittering phrases
HABITAT	Breeds along fast-flowing streams, shallow rivers, at reservoirs and gravel pits. Outside breeding season also on lakes and ponds
STATUS	Resident and partial migrant. Most of Europe, except for north and east. Absent from most of Scandinavia. In BI about 56,000 pairs

YELLOW BENEATH, LIKE yellow wagtail, but has much longer tail, a grey back and dark wings. Male has black chin; in winter male, female and juveniles the chin is white. The bright yellow of the chest turns to even brighter yellow on the vent, and the smart grey head contrasts with white moustache and eye-stripe and black bib, which the female lacks.

THE GREY OF the name is wholly appropriate in winter when only rump and under-tail coverts are yellow. At that time grey wagtails are quite ready to move into towns where they may appear unexpectedly, especially where there is water.

In summer they often feed along rivers, but tend to breed up tiny tributaries, among rocks, by a bridge, or in a drystone wall. The song, an excited elaboration of its basic call is often delivered in flight, and may turn into a peaceful trill as the bird descends.

Away from the uplands, weirs and sluices can provide the breeding holes and cascading water that it likes and, using these, it has been spreading east in the lowlands.

Unlike dippers, they do not seem to suffer from acidification of watercourses, probably because they take a wide range of prey, including many of non-aquatic origin.

SIZE

IDENTIFICATION

HABITAT

POPULATION

MAP

Top right
A grey wagtail brings back a beakful of insects to its nest.

Top left
The grey-blue back contrasts with the bright yellow underside.

Bottom
This bird has caught a damselfly.

249

Goosander

58–66 cm (23–26 in)

S P E C I E S I N F O R M A T I O N	
SCIENTIFIC NAME	Mergus merganser
RELATED SPECIES	Red-breasted Merganser, Smew
CALL	Normally silent. Breeding male has various high-pitched calls, and breeding female a harsh 'skrrark'
HABITAT	Breeds on fish-rich lakes and rivers in forested areas, right up into the tundra. In winter on large lakes and rivers, and at coast
STATUS	Resident and partial migrant. In Britain about 2,500 pairs, mostly in Wales, N England, the border country and scattered in Scotland

SIZE

IDENTIFICATION

HABITAT

POPULATION

MAP

LARGEST EUROPEAN SAWBILL, with long, hook-tipped red bill. Male mostly white, with salmon pink flush underneath, greenish-black head and black back. Female mainly grey, with brown head and upper neck and white chin and neck.

THERE ARE FEW better colours than the pale pink underparts of male goosander. The combination of green head, long red bill and contrasting black back and white, merging with pink underparts are not always so clear, for it often seem a black and white bird. Females are rather merganser-like, but are more thick-set and have clearer demarcation to their white chin and a similarly clear separation between brown of head and blue-grey body.

It is not always popular with fishermen for the diet is almost entirely of fish. Photographs of goosanders fishing underwater show them as streamlined, with head and neck held out straight in front, strong-footed and versatile in the use of the saw-edged bill. When a fish is caught across the middle it needs realignment before swallowing.

Its distribution in winter is mainly on freshwater, spreading into southern England. As the evidence suggests that breeding birds do not spread far from their origins, the southern birds may be migrants from Scandinavia and Germany. The highest numbers are at Scottish sites, with several gatherings of 150 or more.

This large, fish-eating duck, has a long bill equipped with sharp saw-like projections. The male is handsome indeed, with black, grey and pinkish-white, and a dark green head. The female is duller, with a brown head.

Smew

40 cm (16 in)

SPECIES INFORMATION	
SCIENTIFIC NAME	Mergus albellus
RELATED SPECIES	Red-breasted Merganser, Goosander
CALL	Fairly silent. Male has rasping 'kairrr' as alarm call, or in courtship. Female a quacking 'gagaga'
HABITAT	Breeds on woodland edges and at lakes. Coastal in winter. Also at inland lakes and reservoirs
STATUS	Summer visitor in breeding range – northern and eastern Scandinavia. Winters south to coasts of North Sea, Baltic and Channel

SMALLEST OF THE sawbill ducks. Steep forehead and relatively short bill. Male pure white, with black lines on body, black eye-patch and back. Female grey, with red-brown cap, and white cheeks. Eclipse male like female, but with larger amounts of white on wings. Immature male has brownish-white wing patches. Sometimes seen with goldeneye in winter. Dives frequently, and flies fast.

THE DRAKE SMEW is truly impressive, with dazzling white plumage. In flight, both sexes show clear flickering white wing-patches. First winter males and females are 'red heads' and can be mistaken for grebes or goldeneye, as they are mainly grey, but the white on front of neck and side of face should identify them.

On their breeding grounds, smew, like goldeneye, like well-grown trees with holes but their southern limit is further north. Like goldeneye, also, they are divers with a winter fish diet appropriate to a 'sawbill'.

SIZE

IDENTIFICATION

HABITAT

POPULATION

MAP

Top right
Female smew has a dark head, with bright white cheek.

Top left
Male smew has beautiful snow-white plumage.

Bottom
A flock of smew at sea. From a distance, the drakes look as pale as seagulls.

Red-breasted Merganser

52–58 cm (20–23 in)

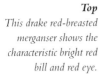

SPECIES INFORMATION

SCIENTIFIC NAME	Mergus serrator
RELATED SPECIES	Goosander, Smew
CALL	Normally silent. Breeding male has nasal 'qui-qui-air'. Female a grating 'aark-aark-aark'
HABITAT	Breeds on clear lakes and rivers of northern Europe, and on shallow sandy or stoney coasts. Outside breeding season mainly at coasts
STATUS	Resident and partial migrant in Britain, summer visitor to breeding areas in northern Europe. Winters south to most coasts. Mainly in north and west Scotland, north-west England and Wales, and west Ireland. Total British and Irish population about 3,000 pairs.

SLIGHTLY SMALLER THAN goosander, with similar long, narrow bill. Both sexes have ragged double crest. Female has indistinct boundary between head and neck colouration.

MALE MERGANSERS HAVE contrasting black and white and grey bodies with green heads, a fine double crest, and an impressive red bill. The red breast is much the colour of the female's ginger head. She can be told from a goosander by slighter frame, crest and absence of white chin.

E. A. Armstrong thinks that mergansers have never received the appreciation they deserve. 'Thousands of poets, artists and writers have lavished praise on the kingfisher, yet hardly a voice has been raised in honour of the merganser. The very name is clumsy, ugly and repellent.'

Some of the peculiar behaviour which delights him is described: 'As the birds career back and forth they constantly open wide their slender, serrated, red bills. They bob quickly and then shoot up head and neck into the air, gaping widely. It looks almost as if the birds were having spasms or retching uncontrollably towards the heavens. The females, too, will occasionally stretch up their necks with a quick pump handle motion. Grace and pride of beauty are set aside and the agitated birds jerk and belch with what seems to the spectator painful vigour and intensity. "A mad world my masters", one might be inclined to say on first seeing this ludicrous pantomime amidst the still beauty of the Irish springtide.'

Top
This drake red-breasted merganser shows the characteristic bright red bill and red eye.

Bottom
The white double wing patch is clearly visible on this female merganser.

Sedge Warbler

13 cm (5 in)

SPECIES INFORMATION	
SCIENTIFIC NAME	*Acrocephalus schoenobaenus*
RELATED SPECIES	Reed Warbler, Marsh Warbler
CALL	Alarm-call a hard 'tseck' or rattling 'karrr'. Song is lively and scratchy, quite varied, usually beginning with a short 'trr' and with long trills.
HABITAT	Reedbeds, marshy scrub, carr, banks and ditches
STATUS	Summer visitor. In BI about 360,000 pairs

SMALL BROWNISH WARBLER with clear white stripe over eye and dark crown. Streaked above, with unmarked rump.

THE MOST WIDESPREAD and numerous of the *Acrocephalus* warblers, whose cheerful chattering song livens up many a walk in marshy and reedy habitats. Sedge warblers also nest in scrub and bramble thickets, but usually require damp or swampy ground nearby.

Found over most of Britain and Ireland, but absent from upland country. The main strongholds are in south-east England, and the east coast of Britain generally, lowland Scotland and central Ireland.

SIZE

IDENTIFICATION

HABITAT

POPULATION

MAP

Sedge warblers nest hidden amongst damp scrub.

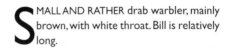

Reed Warbler

13 cm (5 in)

SPECIES INFORMATION	
SCIENTIFIC NAME	Acrocephalus scirpaceus
RELATED SPECIES	Sedge Warbler, Marsh Warbler
CALL	Alarm call hard 'kra' or 'vet'. Song similar to sedge warbler's but quieter, less penetrating, more continuous and faster
HABITAT	Mainly reedbeds, but also damp scrub
STATUS	Summer visitor. In BI about 60,000 pairs (fewer than 50 in Ireland and few in Scotland)

SMALL AND RATHER drab warbler, mainly brown, with white throat. Bill is relatively long.

THE REAL REEDBED specialist is the reed warbler, whose large foot-span helps it grip as it sidles among the reed stems. The nest is slung between adjacent reeds, or built in nearby scrub. Oddly, reed warbler's nests away from the reedbeds are often more successful, perhaps because fewer are parasitised by cuckoos. Grasses and reed leaves are wound around vertical stems to produce a deep cup, often lined with dead reed heads.

Reed warblers are found mainly in the south and east of Britain, especially in East Anglia, but are gradually expanding in range towards the north and west.

The song is easy to confuse with that of the sedge warbler but it is less grating, and full of repeated phrases. Reed warblers, like the very similar but rarer marsh warbler, often mimic other birds. They also have a longer song period, probably because many start to sing again when they breed for a second time.

Reed Bunting

15.5 cm (6 in)

SPECIES INFORMATION	
SCIENTIFIC NAME	Emberiza schoeniclus
RELATED SPECIES	Yellowhammer, Cirl Bunting.
CALL	Call is 'tsieh'. Song is a short phrase 'tsip-tsip-tete-tsink-tet'
HABITAT	Lake and river margins with reed and sedge beds, and damp willow scrub
STATUS	Resident. In BI about 350,000 pairs

BREEDING MALE HAS black head, chin and throat, white collar and white moustache. In winter head and neck are mottled brown. Female and juvenile have streaky brown plumage with black and white moustache.

BOTH SEXES ARE rather sparrow-like, but the male's bold head markings stand out, with the white moustache accentuating the black. The rest of the bird is unremarkable, but the white-edged tail, with a clear fork, often helps to pick out birds in mixed winter flocks. Females have a distinctive face pattern with pale eye-stripe and a pale patch where the male has his moustache.

At a time of population growth in the 1960s, when many farms were losing damp areas of marginal land, reed buntings adapted to far drier breeding conditions, moving into young forestry plantations, farmland and even scrub on dry chalkland, beginning to overlap with the yellowhammer's niche. They avoid really wet reedbeds as they nest on the ground.

SPECIES INFORMATION

SCIENTIFIC NAME	*Panurus biarmicus*
RELATED SPECIES	*No close relatives*
CALL	*Flight-call is a very distinctive nasal 'ting', often repeated. Song is short and squeaky*
HABITAT	*Extensive reedbeds*
STATUS	*Resident. In B about 400 pairs (virtually absent from Ireland)*

Bearded Tit

16.5 cm (6.5 in)

L ONG, CINNAMON TAIL. Male mainly cinnamon-brown with grey head and broad black moustache, yellow bill and eyes. Female less colourful and without moustache. Juvenile similar to female, but with dark back and sides of tail.

BEARDED TITS OR reedlings are very strongly associated with reedbeds, and their 'pinging' call and flight, like little arrows with their long tails, can create excitement when they turn up unexpectedly, and consistent pleasure when in familiar situations.

Males have lavender-grey heads with a black moustachial stripe and yellow bill. The body is mainly tawny-brown. The female is duller and lacks the male's head pattern. In the reeds they move jerkily or descend to feed among the detritus below. They suffer

severely in cold, snowy winters, and only a few pairs were left in Suffolk after the 1946–47 winter, but good recruitment from Dutch polder reedbeds helped recovery, despite further setbacks with east coast floods in 1963.

As with other reedbed species, population estimates are difficult, but when numbers do build up, autumn movements may help to colonise new sites. A new design of 'reedling box' might also encourage higher breeding densities.

The main sites for this species are Humberside, which has the largest colony, and the coastal reedbeds of Norfolk, Suffolk, Kent and Essex.

Bearded tits are mainly insectivorous, gathering midges from wetter areas, or moth larvae and pupae from reed stems and litter. Their nests are built near the ground, in drier areas where sedge or fallen reed stems provide cover, and their long breeding season enables them to rear a large number of young, if the conditions are good.

SIZE

IDENTIFICATION

HABITAT

POPULATION

MAP

Bearded tits perch on reed stems and feed from their seedheads.

255

Coastal Birds

AN ESTUARY AT the mouth of a river may sometimes appear desolate and lacking in life, but beneath the extensive tidal mud are usually a mass of worms, molluscs and crustaceans – there may be as many as 25,000 tiny *Hydrobia* snails per square metre. The larger lugworm may, despite much smaller numbers, provide an equal mass of food. The importance of wetlands such as estuaries is indicated by the 1.5 million waders which were counted in January 1996.

location of the birds. They are often tiny dots in a vast expanse of sea and, except in bad weather, are seldom visible to the naked eye.'

A NEW RESERVE

A 1998 ACTION UPDATE from the RSPB told of their excitement about one of their newest reserves. Belfast Lough is an oasis for wildlife in the middle of an industrialised harbour. It is also within easy reach of more than half a million people.

The mudflats and lagoons of this Northern Ireland site are surrounded by docks, development and

ESTUARY SITES OF INTERNATIONAL IMPORTANCE FOR WINTERING WADERS

SPECIES	SITES	MAIN SITE	AVERAGE MAXIMUM	MONTH
Redshank	24	Dee	7,000	Dec
Bar-tailed Godwit	18	Ribble	17,000	Feb
Knot	18	Wash	170,000	Nov
Dunlin	14	Morecambe Bay	53,000	Mar
Grey plover	14	Wash	10,000	Mar
Black-tailed Godwit	12	Stour	2,200	Jan

SEA-WATCHING

J.T.R.SHARROCK (1972) describes how sea-watching is an art: 'Put an ornithologist, even a real expert, on a cliff, point out a sooty shearwater half a mile away and watch him fail to see it. A Manx shearwater is only slightly larger than a cuckoo. Yet identification at a range of three miles is simple. The major problem encountered by the beginner however is the initial

wasteland, but the potential of the area for birds is enormous. A feature on the Lough in the Wetland Bird Survey report for 1995–96 also mentions problems of refuse disposal, pollution and general disturbance.

The feature reported that the Lough was of international importance for redshank and turnstone – 2,000 redshank were counted at low tide with the main concentration, at more than 15 birds per hectare, close to the city itself. Oystercatchers were more on

Top
The oystercatcher is ever-present at most estuaries and coastal sites.

Bottom left
An estuary at low tide. An excellent habitat for many birds, including waders and shelduck.

Bottom right
Drake goldeneye. This attractive duck often visits estuaries in winter.

the east shore but the 5,600 counted were well spread and represented a population in Ireland second only to those in Dundalk Bay in the Republic. Nationally important numbers of lapwing were near the Belfast Harbour Pools where there were also plenty of dunlin, enough again to be of national importance. Populations of both godwits, curlew, ringed plover and knot were also of national importance.

E.A. Armstrong (1945), growing up there, found the Lough of great interest and could remember the din of the shipyards, a diffused clamour carried for miles on warm summer morning breezes. He was taken on board the Titanic. It was a memorable experience to peep over the embankment as the sun was sinking below the purple Antrim hills. 'There not far from land, swim the silent swan flotillas, a vast, scattered fleet. The wine red dimples of the lazy wavelets form a perfect foil for the snowy birds as they placidly float or dip their necks to feed ... Beyond, appearing only as dark lines on the rippled sea lie squadrons of ducks – wigeon, mallard, scaup, goldeneye and scoter. A belated heron flaps away into the glowing sky leaving loneliness in his wake. There is hardly a sound: only the lapping of the water on the rocks and the occasional whistle of a redshank or curlew.'

Of the ducks he mentions, scaup and mallard are present today in numbers of national importance, as are shelduck, eider and red-breasted merganser. Belfast Lough is one of the most important sites for great crested grebes in the British Isles, and low-tide counts found 1,112 in February 1996. It also found 169 scaup, 481 eiders, 20 long-tailed duck, 260 goldeneye and 173 red-breasted merganser.

CLIFF BIRDS AND THEIR FOOD

ONLY THE NUMBER of birds and the coastal situation link the estuaries with the steep cliffs and rocky islets that are home to large segments of the world's storm petrels, gannets, razorbills and Manx shearwaters. Britain and Ireland form one of the outstanding seabird stations in the North Atlantic, and to experience the birds on an exposed Hebridean island or the corner of western Ireland is unforgettable.

Nesting cliffs need to be associated with rich feeding grounds. When important food sources

decline, as Shetland sand-eels did in the late 1980s, birds suffer and few kittiwake or Arctic tern young were reared in those years. Whether the sand-eel fisheries, now closed, were responsible is uncertain.

Sand-eels are food to Arctic tern, shag, puffin and kittiwake, but also to the dwindling stocks of cod, haddock and whiting. There are commercial fisheries for these on the East Coast. Other groups of organisms liking sand-eels are minke whales, harbour porpoises, dolphins, sea trout and salmon.

The sand-eel fishing had been uncontrolled, but following pressure from RSPB and other pressure groups it was set at one million tonnes in 1998. Efforts are being made to control the sand-eel fishery so that sufficient food remains to support our internationally important seabird colonies. It would indeed be excellent if another marine food web could return to something nearer a proper balance between the interests of man and wildlife.

Top left

Shelduck liven up many an estuary, especially on the North Sea coast.

Top right

A gannet colony at Hermaness, Shetland.

Bottom

The strange beak of the puffin is actually perfectly adapted for catching and carrying small fish and sand-eels.

BIRDS OF THE HEBRIDES

THE HEBRIDES SUPPORT a million pairs of breeding seabirds, while one Hebridean island, Islay, can feed up to 90 per cent of the barnacle geese from east Greenland and 50 per cent of the white-fronted geese from the west of that massive land mass.

The petrels that breed in the Hebrides are pelagic for most of the year, the auks, apart from the black guillemot, are offshore species, but the gulls, with the exception of the kittiwake, are essentially coastal. All find the Hebrides among the best of breeding areas, and the large numbers make up 50 per cent of the seabirds of Britain and Ireland. Even so, of all the possible sites, few are used, for food is the limiting factor. At the southern end of the Outer Hebrides, where inshore water from the sea of the Hebrides or the Minch, meets oceanic water, south-west of Barra Head there is a rich food supply. Here the vertical cliffs of Mingulay and Bernsey have getting on for 10,000 kitttiwakes, 10,000 razorbills and 15,000 guillemots.

By contrast with Mingulay, the Shiants, in the Minch and Treshnish Isles, off Mull, have cliff terraces with plenty of talus, loose material that has fallen from the cliffs above, providing ideal conditions for crevice-lovers like puffins, shearwaters and storm petrels. The Treshnish Isles, with 14 species of seabird challenge the 15 of St Kilda, which has most of the annets, 50,000; most of the fulmars, 65,000; storm petrels, 10,000; and thousands of the virtually uncountable Leach's petrels. Rum, with its extraordinary mountain Manx shearwaters, challenges St Kilda for shearwater numbers.

When these birds have returned to sea, almost 30,000 barnacle geese arrive in November to fill the fertile fields of Islay, just 20 km (12 miles) wide. Numbers are reduced when some disperse to Ireland and to Scottish coasts, but most remain, with the RSPB farm at Gruinart as their centre. They feed on improved pasture. Grazing is restricted elsewhere so numbers build up again and birds gain weight before their return migration in April. These numbers, concentrated on improved pasture, caused resentment among farmers who shot some birds themselves and let some shooting rights to others until, in the mid 1980s, Sites of Special Scientific Interest were established, with compensation paid to farmers whose land was in these protected areas.

When Irish populations of wintering white-fronted geese suffered from drainage, disturbance and shooting, the population of these geese increased in Scotland with Islay holding 5,000, or 50 per cent of British birds. They feed and roost at different sites from the garnacle geese, and in the late 1980s were threatened when their peat roosting grounds were wanted by Islay's distinguished whisky distillers and moorlands were wanted by forestry interests. After national debate and much strong feeling, legal and political pressures eventually favoured the geese.

Top
Barnacle geese are regular winter visitors, mainly to Scotland and Ireland.

Bottom
Kittiwakes roosting on a rocky headland.

CLIMATE CHANGE

'SOFT' COASTS; ESTUARIES, saltmarshes, sand dunes and anywhere a sea defence wall is needed are highly vulnerable to the consequences of global warming. With a rise in sea level, together with more storms and increased wave height, 100 ha (250 acres) of saltmarsh are already being lost each year and the

be coastal squeeze' as the sea rises, with a narrower belt of sand or shingle on which terns or ringed plover can breed.

English Nature firmly believes that these coastal habitats need to be allowed to move. If vital habitats are lost, and many are protected as Special Areas of Conservation under the Habitats Directive, they must be recreated. Much of the coastline between the Humber and Poole Harbour is subject to various degrees of flooding, with over 3,000 ha (7,400 acres) of wet grassland, 500 ha (1,200 acres) of saline lagoons, 200 ha (500 acres) of reedbed and over 100 ha (250 acres) of shingle and sand-dune likely to go. Those involved with shoreline management planning and the recreation of habitats are going to be kept busy.

maintenance of many sea walls, make no economic sense. The Essex coast is at present the most vulnerable, and managed retreat or realignment means a new sea-wall further back and flooding of grazing marshes and other land behind the old wall. The nature of what is lost will have different consequences for birds, for grazing marshes can be an important feeding ground, and reedbeds, quite likely to be lost, are a most valued habitat for bitterns, bearded tits and marsh harriers among others. Sea level rise can also threaten sand dune systems, saline lagoons and shingle – all vital habitats. There will also be gains, for after the flooding new intertidal mudflats, suitable for waders, will soon develop, while plants are quick to colonise, creating new saltmarsh. It the old sea wall were to be maintained there would

> '*There heard I naught but seething sea,*
> *Ice cold waves, awhile a song of swan.*
> *There came to charm me gannets' pother*
> *And whimbrels' trills for the laughter of men,*
> *Kittiwake singing instead of mead.*
> *Storms there the stacks thrashed, there answered*
> *them the tern*
> *With icy feathers, full oft the erne wailed round*
> *Spray feathered …'*
> Anon 'THE SEAFARER' (c 680 AD)
>
> *Translated by James Fisher – this may refer to the Bass Rock in the Firth of Forth*

Top
Low tide on an estuary, which is good habitat for brent geese and many other species.

Middle
Seabirds have to contend with fierce seas along the Dorset coast.

Bottom
Ringed plover eggs are very difficult to spot amongst the shingle.

Manx Shearwater

34 cm (14 in)

SIZE

IDENTIFICATION

HABITAT

POPULATION

MAP

```
○○○○○○○○○○○○○○○○○○○○○○○○○
        SPECIES  INFORMATION
SCIENTIFIC NAME   Puffinus puffinus
RELATED SPECIES   Sooty Shearwater, Great Shearwater
CALL              Weird screaming and wailing at breeding colonies
HABITAT           Oceanic, except when breeding. Feeds in flocks
                  offshore
STATUS            Coasts and islands of Iceland, western BI, France
                  and Mediterranean. Ranges widely over open sea
                  outside breeding season. In BI about 300,000
                  pairs breed
```

BLACK AND WHITE seabird with long, narrow, stiffly held wings. Glides low over the waves; wing-beats shallow, rapid and intermittent.

MANX SHEARWATERS ARE nocturnal island visitors making a selection of weird gruff sound effects suitable for a horror film. On Bardsey Island the birds nest where the soil is deep enough for a burrow, and also along low-lying field boundary walls; 'rafts' of thousands of birds build up at sea in summer evenings. Away from their breeding haunts the long-winged tilting flight, using every movement of the wind, reveals at one moment, the black back and at another the white underparts. All shearwaters share this distinctive flight, but separation into species often requires great skill.

The largest colonies are on Rum in Scotland, Skomer and Skokholm in Wales and the islands off the coast of Kerry in Ireland. The British and Irish sites account for over 90 per cent of the world total.

Apart from Manx shearwaters, British waters are visited by a number of other shearwater species. Cory's is sometimes described, being rather featureless, as the garden warbler of the oceans.

Top

Manx shearwaters come ashore to breed.

Bottom

A sandy slope showing Manx shearwater nesting burrows.

CORY'S
45 CM (17.7 IN)

Heavy appearance with grey hood, brown back; white below. Scattered breeding around the Mediterranean

GREAT
43–51 CM (17–20 IN)

Dark brown-grey above with white collar; white below, with some dark markings. Breeds in south Atlantic

SOOTY
40–51 CM (15.7–20 IN)

Almost uniform dark plumage; pale panel below (mostly dark). Breeds in southern hemisphere

YELKOUAN
36 CM (14 IN)

Duller than Manx shearwater, with little contrast Breeds on Mediterranean islands

LITTLE
25–30 CM (9.8–11.8 IN)

Compact shearwater black above, with white face; white below. Nearest breeding sites Canaries, Madeira and Azores

One way to see these birds is described by Steve Dudley in the *Bird Watcher's Year Book* 1998: 'You need to find a boat, with a skipper who knows where fishing boats are operating. If fish are gutted on board or if you have an evil mixture of fish scraps and offal to throw overboard, gulls, and then petrels and shearwaters, are attracted to the commotion and by the smell, picked up miles away with their specially evolved "tube noses". Within minutes your very own group of feeding seabirds is trailing your boat, with views more akin to watching blue tits in the garden.'

SPECIES INFORMATION

SCIENTIFIC NAME	Hydrobates pelagicus
RELATED SPECIES	Leach's Petrel
CALL	Strange purring and squeaking at breeding colonies
HABITAT	Open sea, except when breeding at offshore islands
STATUS	Coasts and islands of Iceland, western BI, France and Mediterranean. In BI from Shetland through the west of Ireland, south to Scilly. Outside breeding season ranges widely over open sea. In BI probably about 160,000 pairs

Storm Petrel
15 cm (6 in)

VERY SMALL, DARK seabird with obvious white rump. Flight fluttery, dipping to surface sometimes with legs dangling. Pale wing bar, most obvious on underside.

THE SMALL PETRELS are virtually impossible to locate at their breeding grounds on remote boulder-covered islands, where they are active at night. Even on well-watched Bardsey the best evidence of breeding is a pathetic predated corpse. The storm petrel has a distinct white rump and a square-ended tail. May sometimes be seen on sea-watches from a prominent headland or from a boat. When flying in storms, petrels appear to pat the water with alternate feet as if walking on the water. The name 'petrel' comes from St Peter, who also allegedly walked on the water.

 SIZE

 IDENTIFICATION

 HABITAT

 POPULATION

 MAP

SPECIES INFORMATION

SCIENTIFIC NAME	Oceanodroma leucorhoa
RELATED SPECIES	Storm Petrel
CALL	Purring song, interrupted by sharp whistles; cackling
HABITAT	Open sea, except when breeding at offshore islands
STATUS	Much more local than storm petrel, with main colonies in Shetland, Foula, Flannan Islands and St Kilda. In BI population around 50,000 pairs (may be more – difficult to census)

Leach's Petrel
20 cm (8 in)

LARGER AND PALER than the storm petrel and with more pointed wings and less obvious white rump (V-shaped patch), and forked tail (may look ragged).

USUALLY SEEN AFTER storms on the western coasts of the British Isles, particularly on the islands of the west coast of Scotland between April and November. Leach's petrel spends much of its time out on the open sea but comes in to breed and nest on the cliffs and rockfaces along the coastline. A characteristic of the Leach's petrel is its bounding flight in relatively short bursts; it is also given to changing speed and direction. The Leach's is silent at sea but is given to making high-pitched churrs when in colonies.

 SIZE

 IDENTIFICATION

 HABITAT

 POPULATION

 MAP

Cormorant

90 cm (35 in)

MAINLY BLACK WATERBIRD with white chin and cheeks, and long hooked bill. White patch on thigh in breeding season. Juveniles brownish, with whitish underside. Swims low in water, like divers. Often perches with wings spread out.

SPECIES INFORMATION	
SCIENTIFIC NAME	Phalacrocorax carbo
RELATED SPECIES	Shag
CALL	Raw, grating, gurgling and crowing, usually only heard on breeding ground
HABITAT	Breeds in colonies on rocky coasts, also inland, usually on islands in large lakes, often in tall trees. Regular on larger lakes in winter, and in shallow coastal waters
STATUS	Resident and partial migrant. In BI about 12,000 pairs

CORMORANTS AND SHAGS are similar in many ways but avoid competition, with the smaller shag taking more free-swimming fish off rocky coasts, and the cormorant taking flat fish and shrimps in estuaries and 'soft' coasts. Perhaps there is less cormorant food there, for they are certainly gaining ground inland much to the chagrin of many fishermen. The white throat and, when breeding, white thigh patches of the cormorant, and the crest and green sheen of shags, when seen well, are clear distinctions. Young birds are harder to separate, but cormorants have more white. Both birds swim low in the water, and fly strongly with neck extended, but the shag avoids overland routes and stays close to the water.

Shag

70 cm (28 in)

SPECIES INFORMATION	
SCIENTIFIC NAME	Phalacrocorax aristotelis
RELATED SPECIES	Cormorant
CALL	Grunts and hisses at breeding site
HABITAT	Strictly coastal. Rocky coasts and cliff-bases
STATUS	Mainly resident, sometimes seen inland in winter. In BI more northern and western than cormorant; about 48,000 pairs

SMALLER THAN CORMORANT. Black plumage with a greenish tinge; upturned crest in breeding season. Breeds in colonies on rocky coasts. Less widespread than cormorant, but breeds in larger colonies. THIS BIRD IS normally found on the open sea rather than sheltered water or estuaries; its nests on rocky shorelines but is seen inland after storms and galeas along the coast. It may disperse along the coast in winter.

Gannet

92 cm (36 in)

SPECIES INFORMATION

SCIENTIFIC NAME	Morus bassanus
RELATED SPECIES	None in this region (Boobies of the tropics)
CALL	Barking and growling at breeding site
HABITAT	Open sea. Breeds in often huge colonies on inaccessible rocky islands
STATUS	North-west Europe. BI population about 187,000 pairs. Ranges widely outside breeding season, south to the west of the Mediterranean Sea

LARGE, GRACEFUL BLACK and white (adult) seabird, with pointed head and tail and long, rather narrow, black-tipped wings. Juveniles brown, gradually turning whiter over five years. Glides and soars, occasionally plunge-diving for fish.

GANNETS, WHICH REALLY are visible when sea-watching, are among our most spectacular birds with their size, distinctive shape and pattern, and magnificent diving making them unique.

The shape, with pointed tail, beak and wings is common to all gannets, but the pattern of black wing tips, contrasting with white plumage is for adults only, and takes up to five years to achieve. Before that the young will show various degrees of speckling and whiteness.

Our few large colonies are home to 70 per cent of the world's gannets, with half of the whole population in just five sites – St Kilda, Bass Rock, and Ailsa Craig in Scotland, Grassholm in Wales, and Little Skerrig in Ireland.

A fascinating feature of gannet breeding behaviour is that the egg is incubated below the webs of its feet. Nelson describes how 'the webs are placed in overlapping fashion over the egg ... They are adjusted by rocking movements, whilst the bird is slightly lifted, after which it settles back into the cup.'

SIZE

IDENTIFICATION

HABITAT

POPULATION

MAP

Top
Gannet colony on the Bass Rock, Firth of Forth, Scotland.

Bottom right and left
Adult gannet and the downy young.

Fulmar

45 cm (18 in)

SPECIES INFORMATION

SCIENTIFIC NAME	*Fulmarus glacialis*
RELATED SPECIES	*No close relatives in area*
CALL	*Rasping calls and also a softer flight call*
HABITAT	*Breeds in colonies on cliffs, rocky coasts and islands. Outside breeding season often at sea far from coasts*
STATUS	*Around coasts of northern Europe, Iceland and Norway, BI and south in to northern France. Seen mainly in Atlantic Ocean and North Sea; occasionally in Baltic. Population in BI about 575,000 pairs*

GULL-LIKE, BUT stockier, with thicker head and neck. Bill short and broad. Glides on stiffly held wings with occasional wing-beats.

FULMARS, WITH THEIR white heads and grey backs look a little like herring gulls on their breeding ledges, but the 'tube nose' bill and the straightness of the wings in flight make identification easy. Except for a time at the end of the year when they are at sea their distinctive flight, with flaps and long glides, can now be seen around most cliffs, for in just over a hundred years they have spread right round our coasts, from their St Kilda stronghold. Fulmars return from the ocean as early as the turn of the year.

> 'Our most elegant companions were the fulmars, the premier acrobats of the waters, who glided in endless loops and circles around us for hour after hour riding close to the waves on stiff wings, their fat fluffy bodies like huge moths.'
>
> Tim Severin THE BRENDAN VOYAGE

SIZE

IDENTIFICATION

HABITAT

POPULATION

MAP

Top left
A fulmar glides in the wind on its stiff, narrow wings.

Top right
The tube-like nostrils are clearly visible on the beak of this bird.

Bottom
A fulmar pair going through the elaborate courting ritual.

Brent Goose

59 cm (23 in)

SPECIES INFORMATION	
SCIENTIFIC NAME	Branta bernicla
RELATED SPECIES	Barnacle Goose, Canada Goose
CALL	Deep nasal 'rott-rott-rott' or guttural 'rronk' when disturbed. Flight-call a short, hard 'ack', mixed with quieter, higher-pitched calls
HABITAT	Winters on mudflats and coastal fields
STATUS	Autumn and winter visitor to coasts of north-west Europe. Breeds in colonies near lakes in coastal arctic tundra

SMALL, DARK, RATHER duck-like goose with black bill and legs. White 'stern' contrasts with the rest of plumage.

TWO RACES VISIT Europe, a dark-bellied and a (rarer) pale-bellied form. Irish birds, and those in north east England are mainly of the pale-bellied race, while those visiting southern England and continental Europe are mostly dark-bellied. Usually forms large, loose flocks. Flight rapid. The dark-bellied form breeds in W Siberia, while the pale-bellied breeds in E Greenland and Svalbard (Spitzbergen).

The naturalist Armstrong describes the brent geese of Strangford Lough in Ireland:

'They come up in the mornings to feed if the mud banks are uncovered. What a sight it is as they advance! – flying in wide spreading arcs or chevrons, skein after skein, coming into view as long lines of tiny specks high above the water and swerving grandly as they come down to the slob land. As the smaller gaggles draw near, their resonant travel talk is heard, a virile "onk, onk, onk, orrck", but when the large flocks are resting on the water this busy chatter reaches the fascinated listener as a hoarse continuous clamour, rising and falling like the tumult from a vast encampment.'

SIZE

IDENTIFICATION

HABITAT

POPULATION

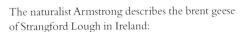

MAP

Top
Brent geese are rather restless and move about the estuary in small flocks.

Middle
At distance, brent geese appear very dark, with a white stern.

Bottom
Brent geese spend much time grazing in small flocks on saltmarsh and coastal grassland.

Barnacle Goose

64 cm (25 ins)

○ ○

SPECIES INFORMATION

SCIENTIFIC NAME	*Branta leucopsis*
RELATED SPECIES	Brent Goose, Canada Goose
CALL	Flight-call a soft, puppy-like, yapping
HABITAT	Winters on saltmarshes, mudflats and coastal pasture.
STATUS	Regular winter visitor to Scotland, Ireland, and south-east North Sea. Breeds in far north, on cliffs above river valleys or fjords

SIZE

IDENTIFICATION

HABITAT

POPULATION

MAP

MEDIUM-SIZED GOOSE with small, black bill. From a distance looks black above, white below. The white face contrasts with the black neck. First year juveniles have a grey-white face and dark brown neck. Flocks of barnacle geese are usually unstructured in flight.

THIS SPECIES BREEDS mainly in East Greenland, Svalbard and Novaya Zemlya. Svalbard birds winter to Solway Firth, while those from Greenland migrate to West Scotland and Ireland.

Top
Barnacle geese are rather short-necked, with a large white patch on the face.

Bottom
A flock of barnacle geese grazing on coastal grassland, Islay, Scotland.

SPECIES INFORMATION

SCIENTIFIC NAME	Anser anser
RELATED SPECIES	Pink-footed Goose, Bean Goose, White-fronted Goose, Lesser White-fronted Goose
CALL	Rather vocal, a nasal 'ga-ga-ga', 'angangang', or similar
HABITAT	Breeds on large inland lakes with thick fringing vegetation such as reeds, rushes or swampy thickets, or in bogs. Winter habitat coastal marshes and fields
STATUS	Resident and partial migrant. Iceland, Scandinavia, and patchily from Britain to E and SE Europe. In BI total population about 22,000 pairs, a large proportion (especially in the south) not of truly wild origin. Also resident as feral park bird, often with Canada Geese

Greylag Goose
75–90 cm (30–35 in)

SIZE

IDENTIFICATION

HABITAT

POPULATION

MAP

LARGEST OF THE grey geese, and the ancestor of the familiar farmyard goose. Bill orange-yellow (western race) or flesh-coloured (eastern race), with intermediates; feet flesh-pink, grey in juveniles. In flight shows clear silver-grey leading edge to the broad wings.

SOME POPULATIONS ARE feral and semi-tame. However, those that fly into Scotland from Iceland or breed in the Outer Hebrides are truly wild. Graze on pasture or feed on estuaries and saltmarshes.

> 'And let us not forget
> The hopping gander
> Who gave a few quills to Bishop Morgan
> Giving the haven of its wings to the Welsh
>   language.'
>
> Gwilym R. Jones PSALM TO THE CREATURES

Top
The greylag is a large bird with a powerful bill.

Middle
A flock of greylag feeding on coastal meadow.

Bottom
In flight, the greylag goose appears heavy-headed.

White-fronted Goose

65–6cm (25.5–30 in)

SIZE

IDENTIFICATION

HABITAT

POPULATION

MAP

SMALL GOOSE, WITH black horizontal barring on belly. Forehead white. Bill long and pink in Russian race; orange-yellow in Greenland race. Juveniles lack black belly markings and white patch, and bill has darker tip.

THE WHITE-FRONTED GOOSE is a medium-sized goose with sharp, angular wings and a square head. Juvenile birds do not have any white on their faces. The goose has a shrill, cackle-like call and is mainly a winter visitor to the grasslands of the British Isles, spending the summer months in arctic tundra. The nest is a shallow scrape on the ground, lined with vegetation and down from the female bird. Numbers have risen dramatically since the establishing of hunting restrictions in Europe.

SPECIES INFORMATION	
SCIENTIFIC NAME	Anser albifrons
RELATED SPECIES	Greylag Goose, Pink-footed Goose, Bean Goose, Lesser White-fronted Goose
CALL	High-pitched rapid 'kwi-kwi-kwi', or 'keowlyow'
HABITAT	Feed on coastal meadows and saltmarshes by day, spending the night on the water
STATUS	Winter visitor in flocks to British Isles – notably Ireland, W Scotland (Greenland race). Also North Sea and channel coasts of England, France, Holland and Germany (mainly Russian race). Breeds in tundra of northern Russia and Greenland

Bean Goose

66–88cm (26–35 in)

SIZE

IDENTIFICATION

HABITAT

POPULATION

MAP

THE BEAN GOOSE is much rarer than pink-footed. It is also larger, and has an orange bill and feet. The wings are browner, and uniformly dark.

THERE ARE TWO populations of bean goose in Britain; one in the Norfolk Broads and one in central Scotland. The total British wintering population in less than one thousand birds. The call of this bird is louder than that of the greylag but quieter than the other geese, and it has a distinctive deep call. The nest consists of a shallow scrape on the ground which is lined with moss.

The goose is less laboured in flight than the greylag, and although slightly shy as a species, will feed among other types of goose.

SPECIES INFORMATION	
SCIENTIFIC NAME	Anser fabalis
RELATED SPECIES	Greylag Goose, Pink-footed Goose, White-fronted Goose, Lesser White-fronted Goose
CALL	Nasal cackle: 'kayakak'
HABITAT	Breeds in wooded tundra. Winters to coastal pastures and marshland
STATUS	Breeds in NE Scandinavia. Winters around coasts of Europe. In BI mainly SW Scotland (Solway) and E Anglia (but numbers small)

SPECIES INFORMATION

SCIENTIFIC NAME	*Anser brachyrhynchus*
RELATED SPECIES	Greylag Goose, Bean Goose, White-fronted Goose, Lesser White-fronted Goose
CALL	Very vocal. Musical calls include 'unk-unk' and a higher-pitched 'wink-wink-wink'
HABITAT	Breeds on rocky sites and tundra. Winters to pasture, stubble-fields and saltmarsh
STATUS	Breeds in Greenland, Iceland and Svalbard. Winters in large flocks to traditional sites in N Britain, notably Scotland, Lancashire and Norfolk

Pink-footed Goose

60–75 cm (24–30 in)

A RATHER SMALL, compact grey goose, showing pale leading edge to wing in flight (like greylag). Head is dark, and white upper tail shows clearly in flight. Legs pink; bill small and pink, dark at base.

IN 1939 PETER SCOTT wrote and broadcast about a pink-foot he called Annabel who had arrived one September at his lighthouse haven on the Wash.

'Greenland, Spitzbergen, and Iceland, the breeding grounds of all the pink-feet in the world, are dangerous places for a single goose. There are arctic foxes, and falcons, and men for all of whom a goose is just a very good meal. As October began I became apprehensive. There were also the dangers of the early autumn to be overcome, when the geese are stubbling in Scotland, and later in Yorkshire; a hundred possible fates might have overtaken Annabel. But none of them had, and, at noon on October 9th, I heard her shout high up in a dappled autumn sky. She was a tiny speck when I first saw her, almost straight above me, and with bowed wings she hurtled downwards. I called to her and she walked straight up to me. There she stood, a plump little round person, with her queer angular forehead, her unusually pink bill pattern and the few white feathers at its base.'

Fifteen years later Peter Scott was in Iceland to find out more of the breeding secrets of the pink-footed goose and to ring them during their flightless moult. Their breeding grounds in Spitzbergen had been found in 1855, in Greenland in 1891 and in Iceland in 1929 but the known sites could not account for the wintering numbers. Furthermore, the Severn Wildlife Trust had developed a technique of catching geese under rocket nets and in October 1950, 634 had been ringed in Scotland and perhaps a new Icelandic site would have some of these birds.

Eventually the expedition ringed and tagged 1,151 geese, estimated the population at 5,500 adults and 7,500 goslings, a major contribution to knowledge of pink-footed geese and their populations.

In 1950–51 there was a total of 30,000, including Greenland birds; by the 1990s there were over 200,000 in Britain and Iceland, an increase attributed to more favourable conditions in Britain in winter, where farming changes have led to an increased food supply, especially in east Scotland.

Their winter distribution correlates closely with areas of lowland farmland, where barley stubble, potato fields, winter-sown cereals and pasture provide them with their winter food. The low-lying farmland around the Wash was attracting flocks of 50,000 , to feed mainly on harvested sugar beet fields.

The contrast between the dark neck and pale chest can be seen again in flight, when the dark underwing, grey forewing, shape and sound all help identification. The roosting sites used to be on the sandbanks and mudflats of estuaries but are now often on freshwater lochs and reservoirs. In the morning they will fly up to 20 km (12 miles) to find suitable feeding grounds.

SIZE

IDENTIFICATION

HABITAT

POPULATION

MAP

Top
A flock of pink-footed geese is a wonderful sight, accompanied by their musical calls.

Bottom
Pink-footed geese are regular winter visitors to several sites in Britain and Ireland.

269

Shelduck

61 cm (24 in)

○○○○○○○○○○○○○○○○○○○○○○○○○○○○○

SPECIES INFORMATION

SCIENTIFIC NAME	Tadorna tadorna
RELATED SPECIES	Ruddy Shelduck
CALL	Piping 'tyutyutyutyu', and a trill (male). Female calls much deeper 'ga-ga-ga-ga' or 'ark'
HABITAT	Muddy and sandy coasts, and coastal lakes. Nests in holes and rabbit burrows
STATUS	Resident and partial migrant. Coasts of NW Europe, and patchily in Mediterranean. Common breeding bird of North Sea and Baltic. About 12,000 pairs in BI

SIZE

IDENTIFICATION

HABITAT

POPULATION

MAP

A LARGE, GOOSE-SIZED bird, looking black and white in the distance. Note the broad chestnut band around the body at chest region. Male has a knob at base of bill. Juveniles mostly grey-brown above, whitish below, with light grey bill and feet. Goose-like in flight, with relatively slow wing-beats, in lines or wedge formation.

SHELDUCK ARE EASY to identify, with both sexes having a dark green head and red bill above contrasting black, white and chestnut body. Young birds and adults in eclipse can cause identification difficulties however.

Tunnicliffe wondered where the Anglesey shelduck went from September to January, a time when many of them move to the Wadden Sea, where most of Europe's shelduck moult. Others go to Bridgwater Bay, but the succession of shelduck movements is very complex.

Shelduck need good feeding habitat for their mollusc and crustacean food, and also access to sand-dunes, for nesting. The nest burrows may be some way from water, so the ducklings may need to walk some distance. Once there, a number of young birds may form a crèche, with one or two parents who appear to have very large families.

Top left and right
The drake shelduck has an obvious knob at the base of its bill and distinct stripey patterning.

Bottom
In flight, the striking black and white pattern is very clear.

Eider
50–71cm (20–28 in)

SPECIES INFORMATION

SCIENTIFIC NAME	Somateria mollissima
RELATED SPECIES	King Eider
CALL	Breeding male has a crooning 'ohuuo' or 'hu-huo'. Female a raw 'korr'
HABITAT	Breeds on coasts and nearby islands; outside breeding season in shallow bays and estuaries
STATUS	Summer visitor in breeding range. Winters mainly to adjacent coastal waters, south to English Channel. Coasts of Iceland, Scandinavia, northern BI about 32,000 pairs

LARGE SEA-DUCK, heavier than mallard, but more compact and shorter-necked. Breeding male mainly black and white. First-year males dark with partially white feathers, giving 'dappled' pattern. Female brownish, with darker stripes. Very sociable; often flying low over the water in long, straggling flocks.

THE EIDER HAS a peculiar head shape and the male has a black, white and lime-green head that distinguishes them from other ducks. They are highly social birds, spending all their time on sea water, and can often be seen around shorelines and on islands, chattering away between themselves. Take-off is laboured and their flight is relatively slow.

 SIZE
 IDENTIFICATION
 HABITAT
 POPULATION
 MAP

SPECIES INFORMATION

SCIENTIFIC NAME	Melanitta nigra
RELATED SPECIES	Velvet Scoter, Surf Scoter
CALL	Male has short fluting 'pyer' courtship call; female 'how-how-how' or 'knarr'
HABITAT	Breeds on lakes, mostly in tundra zone. Outside breeding season mainly at sea, often far from coast
STATUS	Summer visitor in breeding range. Winters to Atlantic and North Sea coasts, south to Gibraltar. Breeds in Iceland and Scandinavia; also a rare breeder in Scotland and Ireland (about 150 pairs)

Common Scoter
46–50cm (18–20 in)

SQUAT, SHORT-NECKED sea-duck. Male is uniform black; bill black, with orange-yellow spot at base. Female dark brown with pale head and sides of neck. Flight rapid, in irregular strings.

COMMON SCOTERS AND the somewhat rarer velvet scoter are both strongly marine in winter when they will be seen as distant little blobs on a grey sea. Common scoter males are all black except for a yellow patch on the bill, but velvet scoters have a white wing-patch visible when they flap on the water. A few common scoter nest by limestone lakes in western Ireland and in the Flow Country of Scotland. Velvet scoters may join flocks of common scoters at sea in the winter.

 SIZE
 IDENTIFICATION
 HABITAT

Scaup

48 cm (19 in)

SPECIES INFORMATION	
SCIENTIFIC NAME	Aythya marila
RELATED SPECIES	Tufted Duck, Pochard
CALL	Display call of male is a whistling 'pe-a-oo'. Female 'arr...arr'
HABITAT	Breeds on lakes in Scandinavia and Iceland. Winters to shallow seas and sheltered bays
STATUS	Regular winter visitor. A handful of pairs breed most years (mainly in Scotland)

SIZE

IDENTIFICATION

HABITAT

POPULATION

MAP

S CAUP ARE ONE of the few ducks where females are easy to recognise, in this case by the white band around the base of her bill. The male, with dark head and breast and lighter body, can be confused with tufted or pochard, but black head and shoulder, pale grey back and white flanks should be sufficient for identification if well seen. In flight the wing pattern of white bars is similar to tufted.

'*There is not a Shetland ornithologist who would not throw away his binoculars to confirm the calloo as a breeding bird*'

J. L. Johnston

NATURAL HISTORY OF SHETLAND

('calloo' is a local name for scaup)

Scaup may be confused with tufted ducks, but the grey back is distinctive.

Goldeneye

45 cm (18 in)

SIZE
IDENTIFICATION
HABITAT
POPULATION
MAP

<table>
<tr><td colspan="2">○○○○○○○○○○○○○○○○○○○○○○○○</td></tr>
<tr><td colspan="2">SPECIES INFORMATION</td></tr>
<tr><td>SCIENTIFIC NAME</td><td>Bucephala clangula</td></tr>
<tr><td>RELATED SPECIES</td><td>Barrow's Goldeneye (Iceland and N America)</td></tr>
<tr><td>CALL</td><td>Male has nasal quacking call. Female a grating 'berr-berr-berr'</td></tr>
<tr><td>HABITAT</td><td>Breeds near lakes and fast-flowing rivers in the coniferous forest zone. Outside breeding season mainly coastal; also on lakes, reservoirs and larger rivers, especially at the coast</td></tr>
<tr><td>STATUS</td><td>Mainly winter visitor to BI (around 15,000 birds). Breeds mainly in Scandinavia and NE Europe. In BI increasing: about 100 pairs, mainly in Scotland</td></tr>
</table>

VERY COMPACT DUCK with large, domed head and yellow eye. Male black and white, with oval white patch between eye (yellow) and bill, and glossy green head. Female mainly grey, with brown head and yellow-tipped bill. Juvenile male similar to female, but with darker head, hint of white head-patch and uniformly black bill. Flight level, with rapid wing-beats.

THESE DUMPY DUCKS with their distinctive head shape have been increasing as breeders since nest-boxes have been provided to make up for a shortage of tree holes.

The idea of ducks in nest-boxes is peculiar to most of us, and the idea of boxes with porches and ladders that much more so, but Scandinavian boxes are of that type. Le Feu writing in the BTO's *Nest Box Guide*, 1993 describes the need for rough wood inside for the ducklings to get a firm hold, and a dark interior, and asks you not to worry about height as the ducklings can descend from great heights quite safely.

Goldeneye need molluscs, crustaceans and insect larvae, but they also like grain discharged from breweries and seed processing plants in Scotland, where sewer outlets are a favourite winter feeding place. At that time of year plenty do feed at sea, but they are also widespread inland, with a huge aggregation of up to or above 10,000 at Lough Neagh.

> '*Or sadly listen to the tuneless cry*
> *Of fishing gull or clanging golden eye.*'
> George Crabbe (1754–1832) PETER GRIMES

The drake goldeneye is one of our most attractive ducks, with its shiny green head, bright yellow eye and white face patch.

Long-tailed Duck

40–55cm (16–22 in)

SPECIES INFORMATION

SCIENTIFIC NAME	Clangula hyemalis
RELATED SPECIES	No close relative
CALL	Vocal. Male has melodious goose-like call, audible from a distance. Females 'ark-ark-ark'
HABITAT	Breeds on small lakes and slow rivers in Scandinavian tundra, and at coast. In winter usually well out to sea
STATUS	Common winter visitor to southern North Sea, Baltic and coasts around northern BI. Breeds in Iceland, Scandinavia and east Baltic

SIZE

IDENTIFICATION

HABITAT

POPULATION

MAP

AN ELEGANT, SHORT-BILLED sea-duck with striking brown and white plumage. Plumage variable through season, but male nearly always has long tail streamers. In winter plumage mainly white, with brown patch on head, dark brown breast and wings. Breeding plumage male has brown upper parts and white area around eye. Females have mottled brown back and, most noticeable, a dark patch on the upper neck.

DRIFT NETS OF microfilament nylon are estimated to kill more than a million seabirds a year. Among British species some 10–20 per cent of long-tailed duck, velvet scoter and eider were killed in the southern Baltic between 1986 and 1990.

In winter, the drake long-tailed duck has very elaborate plumage. In summer, it is much darker on the head and back.

Avocet
42–46cm (16.5–18 in)

ELEGANT BLACK AND white wader with long, upturned bill and bluish legs. Juveniles have brownish cap and back markings. Legs extend well beyond tail in flight.

THE RETURN OF the avocet is for many people a symbol of the RSPB and of the growing interest in birds and conservation since the Second World War. It is as white and black as the oystercatcher, but totally different in every move and gesture. The liquid call is melodious.

They have favourite winter estuaries in the west, but Suffolk, Norfolk and the Thames are equally important. In winter, there is an average of 700 on the Alde complex, and nearly 400 on the Exe and in Poole Harbour.

Avocets breed near or in shallow water, and one of the main roles of the RSPB is in maintaining water levels to provide optimum conditions for breeding and feeding. The splendid bill is used to catch invertebrates by sideways sweeps, with the curved part, slightly open, passing through mud or water.

They are highly social birds with impressive displays as males circle females, getting closer and closer. This is followed by a lot of dipping and shaking of the bill in water. There are also complex distraction displays.

Avocets are normally found in shallow saline pools, muddy deltas and the like. There is a wide distribution outside Europe to Iran, Pakistan and Africa. Although the British wintering population is increasing, it is only about 6 per cent of the European birds.

 SIZE

 IDENTIFICATION

 HABITAT

 POPULATION

 MAP

Top
The avocet, symbol of the RSPB, is quite unmistakable, with its unusual upturned bill.

Bottom
An avocet taking a bath.

Bar-tailed Godwit

33–42 cm (13–16.5 in)

SPECIES INFORMATION	
SCIENTIFIC NAME	Limosa lapponica
RELATED SPECIES	Black-tailed Godwit
CALL	Flight call 'kirrik-kirrik'. Small flocks often silent
HABITAT	Breeds on damp tundra and mires at edge of conifer limit. On migration mainly on coastal mudflats
STATUS	Summer visitor to breeding grounds, the far north of Scandinavia and Russia. Winter visitor and passage migrant to coasts of western Europe. About 80,000 birds visit BI each winter (the main wintering area, along with the Netherlands coast)

MEDIUM-SIZED WADER with rather long legs and long, very slightly upturned bill. Female has longer bill than male. Breeding male mainly rust-red, speckled brown and black on the back; female and winter male buff coloured. In flight legs extend slightly beyond tail. No wing bar. Tail with narrow bars.

BAR-TAILED GODWITS are one of those birds that turn up on those often beautiful but relatively bird-free sweeps of sand like those on the Northumberland coast, or along Cardigan Bay. Unlike the sanderling, which also occurs there, godwits really prefer a good muddy estuary, although they leave it to roost, sometimes some way off, on the safest sand-bar available. Not only will they fly to roost, but they are mobile in response to food supplies. Some 18 British estuaries hold more than 1,000 birds, with the Ribble averaging 17,000.

Not as tall as their black-tailed relatives, these godwits are still taller than most of the waders they spend their time with. The typical winter wader plumage of streaked breast, brown upperparts, eye-stripe and pale belly is not distinctive against the mud, but when it flies, the long upturned beak, white rump and beautifully barred tail is easily recognised. The long bill, of course, is vital when probing, often in fairly deep water, for molluscs, crustaceans and annelid worms.

Breeding birds are much more spectacular, with much of the male's plumage over head, breast and belly being richly rufous. They have elaborate ceremonial display flights and a range of confusing calls. These can be seen and heard in Norway, Finland and Russia, and across Siberia into Alaska.

Top
A bar-tailed godwit in rarely-seen russet breeding plumage.

Middle
Here the bird is in the common winter plumage.

Bottom
Flock wading in an estuary.

SPECIES INFORMATION

SCIENTIFIC NAME	Pluvialis squatarola
RELATED SPECIES	Golden Plover
CALL	Flight call 'tlee-u-ee'
HABITAT	Breeds in arctic lichen tundra. In winter mainly on mudflats or sandy shores
STATUS	Regular migrant and winter visitor to most coasts. Breeds in high arctic of north Russia

Grey Plover
30 cm 12 (in)

SIZE

IDENTIFICATION

HABITAT

POPULATION

MAP

SLIGHTLY LARGER THAN golden plover, and with heavier bill. Greyer than golden plover in winter plumage. Breeding plumage (rarely seen) richly contrasting black, white and grey. Always has black axillaries ('armpits') and white rump. Often solitary.

GREY PLOVER NUMBERS peak in different months at different sites: as early as November on the Norfolk marshes, and as late as March on the Wash or in Chichester Harbour. In the 1995–96 winter it was present in internationally important numbers at 14 sites, at which at least one per cent of the international population wintered.

Large muddy estuaries are its favoured habitat, and there its short, stout bill separates it from most of its fellow waders. In winter, the plumage is pretty uniform grey, without the black chest and back 'spangling' of summer, but the black axillaries as it flies prevent confusion with the golden plover. The white rump of the young, which are more like golden plover because of their patterned backs, should also help to prevent confusion.

Top left and right
Grey plovers look timid and have rather a meek expression.

Bottom
A flock of four grey plover feed alongside a dunlin.

Knot

25 cm (10 in)

○○○○○○○○○○○○○○○○○○○○○○○○○○
SPECIES INFORMATION

SCIENTIFIC NAME	*Calidris canutus*
RELATED SPECIES	Dunlin, Sanderling, Curlew Sandpiper, Purple Sandpiper, Stints
CALL	Rather muted 'wutt-wutt'
HABITAT	Mainly sandy and muddy shores (winter)
STATUS	Winter visitor, mainly to NW European coasts. Mainly BI, Netherlands and France. About 90 per cent of European wintering birds (about 300,000) in Britain (notably in the Wash). Breeds in the high Arctic of Greenland and Canada

SIZE

IDENTIFICATION

HABITAT

POPULATION

MAP

MEDIUM-SIZED RATHER stocky, short-legged wader with short, straight bill. In breeding plumage rust-brown, with speckled upperparts. In winter pale grey upperparts, pale below. Wings rather long and narrow. In flight shows narrow white bars, and grey rump. Gathers in large, dense flocks, which in flight can seem almost cloud-like.

RESEARCH HAS SHOWN how knots, and no doubt other waders too, can detect crustaceans and molluscs under wet mud. When it pushes its bill into wet mud it creates a pressure wave in the water between the particles. This wave is reflected back and detected by cells in the horny layer at the end of the beak. Any objects larger than a grain of sand show up like aircraft on a radar screen.

The genus to which the Knot belongs, *Calidris*, is made up of small, short-billed Arctic breeders. They are extensive migrants, and while some winter here, others only occur on passage. All comparisons below are with dunlin.

KNOT
25 CM (10 IN)
Appearance: Stocky. Rusty underparts when breeding; short straight bill; pale grey rump; inconspicuous white wing bar in flight
Habitat: Feeds in masses on estuaries
Winter and passage

The knot is a medium-sized wading bird with few distinguishing features.

SANDERLING
20 CM (8 IN)
Appearance: Pale with black shoulder-patch; short straight heavier bill; very conspicuous broad white wing bar across dark wing
Habitat: Runs fast on sandy shores
Winter and passage

CURLEW SANDPIPER
22 CM (8.5 IN)
Appearance: Taller, scaly back, eye-stripe; larger, decurved bill; clear white rump and wing bar
Habitat: Often wades. Muddy shores and estuaries
Passage

LITTLE STINT
13 CM (5 IN)
Appearance: V on marked upperparts; tiny straight bill; grey outer tail feathers and narrower wing bar
Habitat: Often wades. Muddy shores and estuaries
Passage

PURPLE SANDPIPER
21 CM (8.25 IN)
Appearance: Dark, slatey and compact with yellow legs; yellow base to bill; Darker in flight
Winter

SPECIES INFORMATION

SPECIES INFORMATION	
SCIENTIFIC NAME	Calidris alpina
RELATED SPECIES	Knot, Sanderling, Curlew Sandpiper, Purple Sandpiper, Stints
CALL	Flight-call a nasal 'krree'. The song, in flight, is a purring trill
HABITAT	Breeds in tundra, marshes and bogs, coastal grassland, and upland moors. Gathers in flocks (sometimes large) on mudflats outside breeding season
STATUS	Resident in south of range; summer visitor further north. Winters around coasts of Europe. BI have the highest winter populations in Europe (about 750,000 birds). Breeds in N and W Europe, north into Arctic, and south to BI. Main numbers in Iceland and N Russia. In BI (about 9,000 pairs) mainly in Scotland and Pennines

Dunlin

18 cm (7 in)

COMMONEST WADER IN northern Europe. Bill relatively long and slightly downcurved at tip. In breeding plumage belly is black. In winter grey-brown, without black belly patch. Juveniles brown above, with pale feather edges. Forms large flocks; flies in tight formation.

MOST PEOPLE WITH an interest in birds know the often abundant, but not very distinctive, dunlin and its tight flocks which so impress as they manoeuvre over winter estuaries. Many fewer know them on the wet grouse-moors and well developed blanket-bog of their breeding grounds.

Ratcliffe describes their return in spring: 'Pairs or threes or fours will suddenly appear weaving their way at high speed through peat haggs with a thin, sizzling call. Alternatively flashing pale underparts and darker back as they zig-zag close to the ground, they are gone again...The nest will later be in a tussock, usually quite well hidden, and the neatest little cup, lined with cotton-grass leaves and containing four eggs.'

Adult dunlins in breeding plumage are smart little waders with quite a long, slightly decurved bill, streaked chestnut upperparts and a black belly. The first returning migrants, reaching estuaries in July, may still have this black belly, but when it is lost winter birds merge well with murky mud. The shrill flight call is a feature of autumn and winter estuaries.

Most winter on the coast, but passage birds will turn up at many inland waters, and sewage farms. At that time many moulting birds congregate in the Wash. The abundance of the bird, and the importance of British estuaries to it, is indicated by the facts that 14,000 or more are needed at one site to make the site of international merit, and that we have 14 sites of that importance. In 1995–96, the leading ones were Morecambe Bay (53,000 March), Mersey (44,000 Feb), Severn (41,000 Jan), Ribble (40,000 Jan) and Wash (36,000 Nov), while in Ireland the peak count of 5,316 was at Strangford Lough in February.

SIZE

IDENTIFICATION

HABITAT

POPULATION

MAP

Top
A flock of dunlin in flight; the black bellies are very apparent.

Bottom right and left
The dunlin's bill is very slightly decurved.

Purple Sandpiper

21 cm (8.25 in)

SPECIES INFORMATION	
SCIENTIFIC NAME	Calidris maritima
RELATED SPECIES	Dunlin, Knot, Curlew Sandpiper, Knot, Stints
CALL	Usually silent in winter. Flight-call 'veet' or 'vitveet'. Song fluting, from ground or in whirring song-flight
HABITAT	Breeds on bare, stoney plateaux, usually far from coast. Outside breeding season in small flocks on stoney and rocky coasts and jetties, often in surf zone
STATUS	Resident and partial migrant. Locally regular in autumn and winter at rocky coasts of north-west Europe, including BI. Breeds mainly in Iceland and Scandinavia. Very rare breeder in Scotland (two-three pairs)

SIZE

IDENTIFICATION

HABITAT

POPULATION

MAP

S MALL DARK, DUMPY wader with highly camouflaged plumage. Larger and shorter-legged than dunlin, with rather plump, rounded breast. Bill about as long as head, dark, with yellow base and slightly decurved. Legs grey-green.

IN BREEDING PLUMAGE back is blackish, flecked with rusty-brown and pale markings. In winter mainly dark brownish-grey with a pale belly, and pale orange legs. Dark in flight, with narrow white wing bar, black centre to rump, edged white. Relatively tame.

Fraser Darling gained constant pleasure from their tameness. 'The winter habitat is the barnacled rocks washed by the waves of every tide and there, apparently indifferent to the weather, the little bird quickly follows the receding wave, gathering small life unseen by us. And then a short fly back again as the new wave breaks on the rocks once more. How the ceaseless rhythm of the sea must have become part of the purple sandpiper, for in winter she is concerned wholly with the turbulent, changing strip of the intertidal zone.'

The purple sandpiper has dusky grey plumage and frequents rocky shores in winter.

Ringed Plover
18–20 cm (7–8 in)

SMALL WADER WITH sandy-brown upperparts, black and white face pattern and orange-yellow legs. In flight shows clear white wing bar. Bill orange, tipped with black. Outside breeding plumage bill is black with orange mark at base. Juveniles resemble winter adults, but upperside feathers look scaly. Runs rapidly over sand, often stopping abruptly.

RINGED PLOVER ARE one of the few waders to be found on shingle beaches, but they also like sand. Disturbance is therefore a major problem, and breeding numbers have fallen on well-trodden beaches. As some compensation, the species has colonised some inland gravel pits and river shingles.

Males have a lovely 'song' and display flight, but you are most likely to hear liquid flight-call as it flits from one of the sandier parts of a winter estuary. Apart from the black ring across the white chest, which can immediately disappear when birds are among shingle, it has orange legs and bill and a brown back. The points separating it from the little ringed plover are listed in the freshwater section.

SIZE

IDENTIFICATION

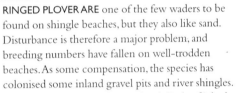
HABITAT

POPULATION

MAP

Top
Stony ground near the coast is the preferred nesting habitat of ringed plover.

Middle
A ringed plover at its nest on the stoney beach at Dungeness.

Bottom
Close-up showing the bird's head patterning.

Spotted Redshank

30 cm (12 in)

SOMEWHAT LARGER THAN redshank, and with a longer bill and legs. In breeding plumage (rarely seen) mainly blackish, with fine white spots on back (hence the name); legs dark red. At other times resembles redshank, but paler, and with black and white streaks from beak to eye. Lacks wing bar, but shows white in rump and back.

SPOTTED REDSHANK ARE among the pleasant, and very vocal, surprises when passage movements are on, and a few linger in the winter rather than heading on for Africa. Like other waders they often feed on rich tidal mudflats along the coastal wetlands.

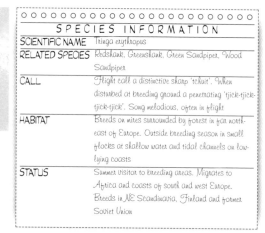

SPECIES INFORMATION	
SCIENTIFIC NAME	Tringa erythropus
RELATED SPECIES	Redshank, Greenshank, Green Sandpiper, Wood Sandpiper
CALL	Flight call a distinctive sharp 'tchuit'. When disturbed at breeding ground a penetrating 'tjick-tjick-tjick-tjick'. Song melodious, often in flight
HABITAT	Breeds on mires surrounded by forest in far north-east of Europe. Outside breeding season in small flocks at shallow water and tidal channels on low-lying coasts
STATUS	Summer visitor to breeding areas. Migrates to Africa and coasts of south and west Europe. Breeds in NE Scandinavia, Finland and former Soviet Union

Wood Sandpiper

20 cm (8 in)

MEDIUM-SIZED WADER, resembling green sandpiper, but more delicate and with slightly longer legs (visible beyond tail in flight).

SPECIES INFORMATION	
SCIENTIFIC NAME	Tringa glareola
RELATED SPECIES	Redshank, Spotted Redshank, Greenshank, Green Sandpiper
CALL	Flight call 'jiff-jiff-jiff'. Song incorporates 'tleea-tleea-tleea', delivered in high song-flight over territory
HABITAT	Breeds near water on mires with individual trees, in swampy woodland and in the tundra. On migration in small flocks on open mud, flooded meadows; often at coast
STATUS	Summer visitor to breeding grounds. Migrates to Africa and south Europe in autumn. In BI small numbers visit regularly as passage migrants (mainly autumn). Breeds mainly in north-east Europe (notably Finland and Sweden). Also a very rare breeder in Scotland (about six pairs)

ALSO HAS PALER, more heavily spotted plumage, and paler head and neck. Heavily spotted with white above, less clearly marked in winter. Juveniles with regular yellowish markings on back. Otherwise distinguished from green sandpiper by pale underwing and less contrasting upperparts. May nest in an old nest in a tree, but usually on the ground.

Oystercatcher

43 cm (17 in)

S P E C I E S   I N F O R M A T I O N

SCIENTIFIC NAME	Haematopus ostralegus
RELATED SPECIES	No close relatives in region
CALL	Very loud 'kileep', often repeated. On breeding grounds an insistant, piping trill
HABITAT	Breeds on sandy and shingle beaches, and also in some areas at inland lakes and rivers. Outside breeding season often in large flocks on mudflats, and coastal fields
STATUS	Summer visitor to north of range, resident in south. Migrant to coasts of W and S Europe. Breeds mainly around coasts of N Europe. In BI about 50,000 pairs (increasing)

other countries, is thought to be genetic, and involves earlier breeding to coincide with a time of good food supplies.

LARGE BLACK AND white wader with long, red, slightly flattened bill, and red legs. Juveniles have pale throat markings and a dark tip to bill. In flight shows broad white wing bar and white rump.

NOISY OYSTERCATCHERS, with their black and white plumage and startling orange bills enliven many a rocky coast and estuary, but are also spreading as breeding birds inland, along northern rivers. This change, which has its parallels in

SIZE

IDENTIFICATION

HABITAT

POPULATION

MAP

Sanderling

20 cm (8 in)

S P E C I E S   I N F O R M A T I O N

SCIENTIFIC NAME	Calidris alba
RELATED SPECIES	Dunlin, Knot, Curlew Sandpiper, Purple Sandpiper, stints
CALL	Short 'plitt', often repeated in flight
HABITAT	Breeds on bare lichen tundra. Outside breeding season at coast, mostly on sandy shores
STATUS	In BI common passage migrant and winter visitor. Breeds in high Arctic

SMALL WADER (roughly dunlin-sized), with straight, black bill and black legs. In breeding plumage, back, neck and upper breast rust-red with darker spots; white below.

VERY PALE IN winter plumage, with dark shoulder-patch. In flight silver-grey, with bold white wing bar. Often runs rapidly in and out of waves at the edge of the surf, and tends to stay close to the edge of the sea. The sanderling often nests in small hollows on the ground.

SIZE

IDENTIFICATION

HABITAT

POPULATION

MAP

Arctic Skua

41–45 cm (17 in)

SPECIES INFORMATION	
SCIENTIFIC NAME	Stercorarius parasiticus
RELATED SPECIES	Long-tailed Skua, Pomarine Skua, Great Skua
CALL	Gull-like 'ee-air', often repeated
HABITAT	Breeds in open tundra and moorland with low vegetation, usually at the coast, or on grassy islands, and in some regions inland on boggy moorland, heath and in the tundra. Outside breeding season at sea
STATUS	Passage migrant, wintering in Atlantic. Regular off coasts of BI, mainly in autumn and spring. Breeds in Northern Europe and Arctic, south to Scandinavian coasts and N Britain (latter about 3,500 pairs)

SIZE

IDENTIFICATION

HABITAT

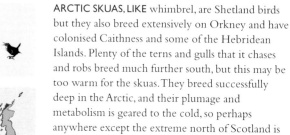

POPULATION

MAP

COMMONEST EUROPEAN SKUA. Two colour phases occur, with intermediates. Light phase (commoner in north) has whitish underside and dark neck band (sometimes missing). Dark phase (mainly in south) is uniformly dusky brown. Two pointed central tail feathers extend beyond tip of tail. Juvenile has shorter central tail feathers.

ARCTIC SKUAS, LIKE whimbrel, are Shetland birds but they also breed extensively on Orkney and have colonised Caithness and some of the Hebridean Islands. Plenty of the terns and gulls that it chases and robs breed much further south, but this may be too warm for the skuas. They breed successfully deep in the Arctic, and their plumage and metabolism is geared to the cold, so perhaps anywhere except the extreme north of Scotland is too warm for them.

Another peculiarity is that they exist in two forms, or phases. They are all dark sea birds with white wing flashes, like several other skuas, and most, 70 per cent or more, of the southern birds are dark phase individuals, which may be wholly dark below. Light phase individuals are pale below. Both phases are falcon-like in flight, well able to pursue terns and

kittiwakes with agile twists and turns. Their chases often cause the victim to regurgitate its food, which the skua then consumes.

The ratio of light to dark phase birds increases as one moves north, with those in Greenland and Svalbard being virtually all pale. In 1977 Berry put forward an explanation based on a study of the Fair Isle birds. Dark male birds are less aggressive in relation to females, who initiate mating behaviour, and therefore dark males breed earlier as it takes less time before the male accepts the female.

When they first mate, those that pair with dark birds lay eggs some 11 days earlier. On the other hand, pale birds have an advantage over dark ones because they start to breed at a younger age and have a higher chance of surviving to breed, but their breeding season will be later. In the north, a late breeding season coincides with the peak population of lemmings and voles, while in the south early breeding helps the birds to time their breeding season to coincide with that of the gulls and terns.

Whether this version is true or not, most of us who see Arctic skuas see them on passage – for example harrying terns on the north Norfolk coast at Blakeney Point.

> ' … a pair of skuas arrived and this time there was no contest. The two terns fled for their lives, jinking and turning at wave crest level as the powerful skuas struck at them.'
> Tim Severin THE BRENDAN VOYAGE

Arctic skuas come in different colour phases: dark (below, left), pale (below, right) and intermediate (above).

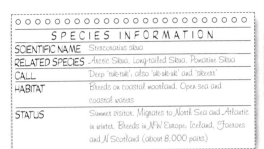

SPECIES INFORMATION	
SCIENTIFIC NAME	Stercorarius skua
RELATED SPECIES	Arctic Skua, Long-tailed Skua, Pomarine Skua
CALL	Deep 'tuk-tuk'; also 'uk-uk-uk' and 'skeeer'
HABITAT	Breeds on coastal moorland. Open sea and coastal waters
STATUS	Summer visitor. Migrates to North Sea and Atlantic in winter. Breeds in NW Europe: Iceland, Faeroes and N Scotland (about 8,000 pairs)

Great Skua

58 cm (23 in)

SIZE

IDENTIFICATION

HABITAT

POPULATION

MAP

L ARGEST AND BULKIEST of the skuas, with short tail. Looks rather like juvenile herring gull, but wings more rounded. Wings show flashes of white at base of primaries. Chases other seabirds for food, and also eats fish, birds and eggs. Very aggressive at breeding grounds (will attack people).

GREAT SKUAS ARE BIRD pirates, chasing gulls, gannets, terns and auks to a point when the hapless victim disgorges the contents of its crop, upon which the skua swiftly swoops. They are also predators of other seabirds, killing adults and pillaging eggs and nestlings.

The great skua (or bonxie) can kill a bird as large as a gannet, and is the boldest of birds in defending its own nest site against an intruder – sheep and sheep-dogs can be harried and cowed by the diving bonxies and chased from the nesting area. Nearby, there are usually pools at which the bonxies bathe, preen and stand with raised wings, cackling. They rise to meet the intruder and then suddenly swoop in attack, sometimes striking the head with their feet before climbing away with a guttural 'tuk-tuk-tuk'. Though the birds are unlikely to cause serious injury to a person, they can draw blood and the onslaught takes nerve to resist, usually resulting in a hasty, head-down retreat.

Apart from its aggression, great skuas are remarkable for their distribution. In the western palearctic, populations are dotted around mainly remote islands, avoiding summer ice. In winter, birds may move at least as far as Brazil and the Gulf of Guinea.

Great skuas, as well as being pirates, predators and great travellers, are sturdy, brown, agile gull-like birds that look very dark in the distance, as when sea-watching, but with the darkness contrasting with white wing-flashes, both above and on the underwing. Outside the breeding season they are usually quiet.

Top left and below
The great skua is quite a bulky bird, with uniform brown plumage.

Top right
In comparison, the juvenile bird shows a rather streaky plumage.

285

Common Tern

34 cm (13 in)

○○○○○○○○○○○○○○○○○○○○○○○○○○○○○

SPECIES INFORMATION

SCIENTIFIC NAME	Sterna hirundo
RELATED SPECIES	Arctic Tern, Sandwich Tern, Roseate Tern, Little Tern
CALL	Very vocal. Flight-call a short, repeated 'kick'. Alarm call 'kee-yah'
HABITAT	Breeds in colonies on sandy coasts, in dunes, and on islands. Also inland on gravel banks of undisturbed rivers, lakes and ponds
STATUS	Summer visitor and passage migrant. Scattered throughout, most numerous in north and east. In BI about 16,000 pairs

SIZE

IDENTIFICATION

HABITAT

POPULATION

MAP

COMMONEST EUROPEAN TERN. Very slim and elegant. Bill bright red, with black tip. Tail streamers do not extend beyond wing-tips when sitting. Winter adults and juveniles have dark bill and whitish forehead. In flight the dark outer primaries contrast with paler inner primaries.

TERNS RESEMBLE GULLS in their mainly white plumage, but are more graceful in flight, have pale grey backs and black crowns in the summer, when they breed on sand, shingle or low islands. This makes them very vulnerable to summer storms and to predators like foxes, rats and kestrels. Humans can disturb the birds too, sometimes causing them to abandon a site. Being long-lived, however, one successful breeding season can compensate for a series of bad ones.

Scolt Head Island in Norfolk is a typical tern nesting site. This is a natural ridge of sand and shingle about 6 km (4 miles) long, and separated from the mainland by a kilometre of intertidal mud and saltmarsh. As an uninhabited island which is also a National Nature Reserve it is ideal for nesting terns, and with protection the island became one of the largest tern colonies in western Europe, with several thousand pairs of sandwich, little and common terns in a good year. Since 1985 however, foxes have been crossing to the island at night and at low-tide, and an endless battle has gone on between the reserve manager and the foxes. All sorts of means, including electric fences, snares, cage-traps and a range of other inventive ideas have had to be employed to try to cope with this threat.

Top
The common tern's bright red bill has a black tip.

Middle
A pair of common terns copulating during the mating season.

Bottom
The common tern is extremely graceful in flight.

Arctic Tern

34 cm (13 in)

```
○ ○ ○ ○ ○ ○ ○ ○ ○ ○ ○ ○ ○ ○ ○ ○ ○ ○ ○ ○ ○ ○
        S P E C I E S   I N F O R M A T I O N
```

SCIENTIFIC NAME	*Sterna paradisaea*
RELATED SPECIES	Common Tern, Roseate Tern, Sandwich Tern, Little Tern
CALL	Not quite as harsh as common tern, and usually shorter and higher-pitched 'kree-errr'; also a soft 'gik'
HABITAT	Breeds entirely on coast, usually with other terns, in large colonies on sand and shingle banks
STATUS	Summer visitor. Famous for its long migration route – wintering around Antarctic pack-ice. Breeds mainly around Arctic region, south through Iceland to Scandinavia, BI and south North Sea. In BI about 46,500 pairs

SIZE

IDENTIFICATION

HABITAT

POPULATION

MAP

VERY SIMILAR TO common tern, and often hard to distinguish in the field. Uniformly red bill, shorter legs, and greyer underside. Tail streamers are longer, extending beyond wing-tips when sitting. In flight shows translucent primaries.

COMMON AND ARCTIC terns are often recorded in county bird reports as 'comic' terns because they are so hard to distinguish. Both are smaller, lighter birds than the sandwich, have red beaks and legs and forked tails. At close quarters in summer the arctic can be seen to have a uniformly red bill, while the common has a black tip to the bill, and, if seen perched, the short legs of the arctic are clear, if you are already familiar with the longer ones of the common. Arctic terns also have longer tail streamers, the length of which can be judged in relation to the wings when birds are perched: tail beyond wing-tip in arctic, but not in common. With their calls, too, familiarity with both species is the surest guide, but there is much to be said for enjoying the birds and not worrying about which is which.

Top right
*Arctic tern's
nest in Shetland.*

Top left and below
*Arctic terns have a red
bill, greyish underparts
and long tail streamers.*

Sandwich Tern

40 cm (16 in)

SIZE

IDENTIFICATION

HABITAT

POPULATION

MAP

RELATIVELY LARGE TERN, with long, black, yellow-tipped bill and shaggy crest on back of head. In winter has white forehead. Slim and narrow-winged in flight, with deep wing strokes.

THESE ARE THE largest British terns, less buoyant in flight than the others, and with relatively long, narrow wings. At its breeding sites the elongated feathers at the back of the crown may be seen, but most often birds will be seen flying out at sea and periodically diving for food. The black crown gains a white forehead after the breeding season; the beak remains black with a yellow tip. The noisy, rather creaking, calls have the second syllable higher pitched than the first, in contrast to common and arctic terns.

John Latham (General Synopsis of birds 1781–1790) said the sandwich tern was so called because some boys in that town told him about the birds.

Top
This is the largest of our local terns and has a white forehead in winter.

Bottom
A crowded breeding colony of sandwich terns.

Little Tern

23 cm (9 in)

SMALLEST OF OUR TERNS, with white forehead even in breeding plumage, and yellow bill with black tip. Crown whitish in winter, grading into black of back of head. Juveniles have brownish crown and upperparts, with dark wavy markings. Wingbeats much quicker than those of other terns. Hovers frequently, often just before diving.

ALTHOUGH ALL TERN calls have plenty of similarities, the quick 'kirri-kirri, kirri-kirri' of this species on its breeding grounds is easier to distinguish than many. Little terns are often seen fishing, with characteristic hovering before diving. Little tern nests are extremely vulnerable, as they are placed so close to the high tide mark, and the terns also choose the same sorts of beaches that holiday-makers like: disturbance is therefore a major problem. In some places breeding sites are fenced off during the summer to reduce human (and canine) disturbance.

SIZE

IDENTIFICATION

HABITAT

POPULATION

MAP

Top
Little Terns flying and wading in shallow water.

Middle
A juvenile little tern.

Bottom
Our smallest tern, the little tern has a white forehead, even in summer, and a yellow bill.

Turnstone

22 cm (9 in)

○ ○

SPECIES INFORMATION

SCIENTIFIC NAME	Arenaria interpres
RELATED SPECIES	No close relatives in region
CALL	Flight call a rapid 'triititi' or 'tuk-a-tuk'. Song a nasal 'tivi-tivi-tititi', from song-post or in flight
HABITAT	Breeds on rocky coasts, islands, and in moss and lichen tundra of northern Europe and Arctic Canada. Winters on stoney or pebbly coasts.
STATUS	Summer visitor to breeding grounds. Winters mainly to coasts of North Sea and Atlantic. Breeds on coasts of Scandinavia and N Baltic

SIZE

IDENTIFICATION

HABITAT

POPULATION

MAP

SHORT-LEGGED AND dumpy wader. Breeding plumage is a very colourful chequered pattern. In winter duller brownish-black, with pale feather edges. In flight shows broad white wing bar and white tail with black band near tip.

Top left

A turnstone nest situated in the open tundra.

Top right

A turnstone at its nest in chequered summer plumage.

Bottom

The turnstone uses its strong bill to probe beneath stones and pebbles.

TURNSTONES ARE BIRDS of rock and seaweed. In spring, as they head for their northern breeding lands, they show a splendid contrast of black and white patterned head, black breast-band and chestnut back. They are more often seen in winter plumage, still with black breast-band, a suggestion of the summer face markings, but now with browny-black back. The orange legs provide the colour.

Turnstones are rather tame, but when they eventually move they fly off with a twittering call, and usually settle quickly, having shown their bold, pied flight pattern.

Armstrong describes the turnstone which frequent Strangford Lough all winter: 'They butt and bore into the wrack, using head and bill like a ram or ploughshare. Running briskly hither and thither the plump little birds poke under stones and generally behave as if they thoroughly understand the business of finding and devouring small marine organisms.'

Black-headed Gull

36 cm (14 in)

SPECIES INFORMATION	
SCIENTIFIC NAME	*Larus ridibundus*
RELATED SPECIES	Common Gull, Mediterranean Gull, Little Gull; other *Larus* gulls
CALL	Very vocal 'kvairr' or 'kverarr'; also 'ke-ke-ke' and high-pitched 'piee'
HABITAT	Breeds in colonies (often large) at reedy lakes, and on small islands and coastal marshes. Very common at coast and on inland waters (and fields) during the winter, also in built-up areas
STATUS	Summer visitor to north-east of range; resident and winter visitor further south. Breeds throughout Europe, especially in north and east. In BI about 200,000 pairs

COMMONEST OF THE smaller gulls, and the commonest gull inland. Chocolate brown face-mask (not extending down back of neck), with crescent-shaped white mark around eye. Wing-tips black, bill and legs dark red. In winter has white head with dark ear-patch. Juveniles speckled brown above, with dark trailing edge to wings and dark tip to tail. In flight the narrow, pointed wings show a highly characteristic white leading edge.

NOTHING IS MORE recognisable than a gull, but the identification of individual species often causes problems. Even the attractive, common and widespread black-headed gull can create difficulties, as it has no dark head for much of the year, and, despite its name, never has a black head. Black-headed gulls are frequent visitors to park ponds, urban rivers, reservoirs, and rubbish tips, and will even take food in gardens. The *Garden Bird Watch Handbook* shows that ten to fifteen per cent of gardens have black-headed gulls early in the year.

The patterns of the wings of gulls in flight is crucial to their identification. Black-headed gulls are buoyant fliers, with pointed wings, which have a white leading edge when seen from above or below. There is a dark trailing edge to the upper wing and a generally dusky under wing. Young birds are very pale brown and white with dull orange legs and bill and they retain their mottled backs and distinctive tail-band into their first winter.

Breeding, which is always near shallow fresh water, occurs in a band across European middle latitudes.

Breeding behaviour is complex and much studied, with the head posture playing a crucial role. The nest around which all the display takes place is usually on the ground – a shallow scrape lined with vegetation. Where it is really wet, a mound may be built up.

Most of Europe's birds are migratory, avoiding the eastern continental climate and Scandinavian winters by moving as far south as the Persian gulf and the West African coast. Many also winter in inshore tidal waters around the North Sea, Baltic and Mediterranean.

Part of the success of the bird stems from the variety of its feeding methods, and of its food. All gulls, to varying degrees, share this versatility. They walk, as when following the plough, searching for worms, or investigating rubbish tips, fly with agility as when circling for flying ants in up-currents, for crusts thrown from London Bridge or for tideline detritus, or swim to feed at or just below the water surface.

SIZE

IDENTIFICATION

HABITAT

POPULATION

MAP

Top
The chocolate-brown head of this gull appears black from a distance.

Bottom left
A black-headed gull proudly incubates its clutch of eggs.

Bottom right
When in winter plumage, only tiny smudges of dark remain on the head.

Herring Gull

60 cm (24 in)

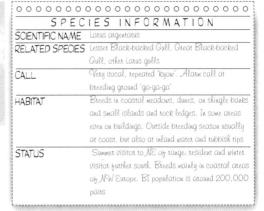

SPECIES INFORMATION	
SCIENTIFIC NAME	Larus argentatus
RELATED SPECIES	Lesser Black-backed Gull, Great Black-backed Gull, other Larus gulls
CALL	Very vocal, repeated 'kyow'. Alarm call at breeding ground 'ga-ga-ga'
HABITAT	Breeds in coastal meadows, dunes, on shingle banks and small islands and rock ledges. In some areas even on buildings. Outside breeding season usually at coast, but also at inland water and rubbish tips
STATUS	Summer visitor to NE of range; resident and winter visitor further south. Breeds mainly in coastal areas of NW Europe. BI population is around 200,000 pairs

COMMONEST LARGE GULL. White, with pale grey back and wings, and black wing-tips. Bill powerful, yellow, with red spot; eyes yellow; feet flesh pink. In winter, head has brownish streaks. Juveniles speckled brown, with black terminal tail-band, gradually attaining full adult plumage in the fourth year.

SIZE

IDENTIFICATION

HABITAT

POPULATION

MAP

BOTH THE HERRING gull and the closely related lesser black-backed gull have begun to become more and more urban. Indeed, in some cities, such as Bristol, their populations have risen to the level at which they have become a bit of a problem. Herring gulls tend to remain fairly local, whereas lesser black-backed gulls wander further, more randomly and rather more inland.

Herring gulls, like many other gulls, have developed a great liking for refuse tips, sewage outlets and fish-quays; in fact for anywhere which provides rich pickings.

Top left
This young herring gull still shows signs of brown in its plumage.

Top right
A herring gull soaring overhead.

Bottom
A herring gull at its nest on a cliff-face in Wales.

Lesser Black-backed Gull

52–62 cm (20–24 in)

SPECIES INFORMATION	
SCIENTIFIC NAME	Larus fuscus
RELATED SPECIES	Herring Gull, Great Black-backed Gull; other Larus gulls
CALL	Similar to Herring Gulls, but slightly deeper in pitch
HABITAT	Breeds on low-lying coasts and islands, usually with higher vegetation than Herring Gull; also on inland moors and bogs. Outside breeding season mainly at coasts, but regular at inland lakes as well. Hunts over open sea; occasionally visits rubbish tips
STATUS	Summer visitor, migrant and winter visitor from further north. Similar to herring gull, but breeds further N (to Arctic) and further south (to coasts of Spain and Portugal). BI population is around 90,000 pairs

British lesser black-backs have lighter slate-grey backs than Scandinavian ones, so their wing-tips, which are black, provide a contrast. Apart from the back, the yellow legs in summer contrast with the pink of herring gulls and of the much larger great black-back. The legs in winter are a rather indeterminate grey. Young birds retain the mottled plumage typical of young gulls for a couple of years, but are always distinctly dark.

SIZE AND SHAPE of herring gull, but with dark slate-grey back, and proportionately slightly longer wings. Legs yellow. In winter has streaky head and yellowish-pink legs. Juveniles difficult to separate from young herring gulls, but tend to be darker. Shade of colour on back and wings deepens from grey in south of range to black in Baltic area.

LESSER BLACK-BACKED GULLS used to be summer visitors to well vegetated cliffs and islands, but now some 80,000 winter on arable land, refuse tips and estuaries. The taxonomy of lesser black-back and herring gulls presents a complex picture on a world scale, with all sorts of grading of different coloured backs and legs, producing intermediate forms. Although this species can interbreed with the herring gull, it normally behaves as a good species, with differences in habitat, behaviour, leg, beak and back colour.

SIZE

IDENTIFICATION

HABITAT

POPULATION

MAP

Top
In comparison with the great black-backed gull, the back of this species is somewhat paler than the jet-black wingtips.

Bottom
Lesser black-backed gull in full cry, with slate-grey back and yellow legs.

Great Black-backed Gull

68–78 cm (27–31 in)

SPECIES INFORMATION

SCIENTIFIC NAME	Larus marinus
RELATED SPECIES	Lesser Black-backed Gull, Herring Gull and other Larus gulls
CALL	A chuckling 'krau-krau-krau', deeper and slower than Herring Gull; also 'owk'
HABITAT	Breeds on rocky and stoney coasts, particularly on small rocky islands. Outside breeding season at coasts, often at rubbish tips
STATUS	Summer visitor to north-east of range; resident and winter visitor further S. Breeds in Iceland, Scandinavia, Finland, south to BI and north-west France. BI population about 23,000 pairs

O UR LARGEST GULL, with back and wings black. Wings broader than those of lesser black-backed. Head large, bill deep, legs flesh-coloured. Juvenile similar to young herring gull, but larger, and head usually paler. Flight slow, with regular wing-beats and long periods of gliding.

THE VERY MUCH larger great black-back is more strictly maritime, has a genuine black back and can be beastly to almost anything that moves. Conservationists regret the killing that goes on at seabird breeding stations by this rather aggressive predator. Solitary nesters seem to be more bird directed in their food preference than colonial nesters. In fact great black-backs take a huge range of food, from live birds and small mammals to carrion, fish, eggs and worms. Along with crows and other gulls, they play an important role in cleaning up the bodies of sea animals from our beaches.

> 'It prefers a flesh diet, either recent or ancient, a dead rat, dog or whale is alike acceptable to the corpse eater.'
> T.A. Coward

SIZE

IDENTIFICATION

HABITAT

POPULATION

MAP

Bottom left
A nest of great black-backed gulls on a rocky headland.

Top and bottom right
This powerful predator of the seaside has a back which is as dark as the wingtips, and flesh-coloured feet.

SPECIES INFORMATION

SCIENTIFIC NAME	Larus canus
RELATED SPECIES	Black-headed Gull, Herring Gull, other Larus gulls
CALL	Higher and more penetrating than herring gull. Flight-call nasal 'kyow-kyow', alarm call 'gleeu-gleeu'
HABITAT	Chiefly breeds near coast, in colonies in coastal meadows, bog and heath with low vegetation. Mainly coastal outside breeding season, but also on inland waters
STATUS	Summer visitor to NE of range; resident and winter visitor further S. Breeds mainly in N and NE Europe. Common in Scandinavia, and around Baltic Sea. Occasional breeder inland in central Europe. In BI mainly in N and W; about 70,000 pairs

Common Gull

40–43 cm (16–17 in)

LIKE A SMALL herring gull, but lacks red spot on bill. Rounded white head, relatively narrow yellow bill and dark eyes, giving rather a meek expression. Feet greenish-yellow. In winter head speckled brownish. Juvenile brownish above, with dark bill. In flight shows black wing-tips with white spots, and white trailing edge to wing. Back and wings of adult slightly darker grey than herring gull.

ALTHOUGH PLENTY OF herring, black-backed and black-headed gulls follow the plough, the common gull is the one most closely linked with farms, and earthworms, in the winter. It is fairly common at that time, but the name refers more to the absence of distinguishing features than any abundance anywhere or anytime.

The *Winter Atlas* shows a wide distribution in Britain, away from the mountains, but most Irish birds are around the coasts. J. D. R. Vernon, writing in the *Atlas* describes a 'preference for feeding at well grazed grassland, particularly on well-drained limestone soils, and often above 100 m in altitude. The short kept turf on airfields and playing fields is also exploited.' After heavy rain, flooded lowlands are visited for worms, often with black-headed gulls. Most of the wintering birds come from Scandinavia, Denmark and Germany.

The *Breeding Atlas* shows a very different picture. Most Irish populations are towards the north, and the main British concentration is in Scotland. Amazingly, 50 per cent of this population is in two colonies, on low heather-covered hills.

The common gull is usually identified on features of legs and bill, but those interested in gulls often rely more on features of wing and tail patterns. The small bill, like the legs, is yellow or greenish, while the wings, narrower than those of herring gull, have bold white wing mirrors on the outer primaries. Young gulls are always more difficult, but size, smaller bill, whiter underparts, white rump and contrasting black tail-band should distinguish from herring gull.

The common gull's diet is largely invertebrates, taken from land and water, fish, and eggs. The call is described as more 'mewing' than the herring gull's.

SIZE

IDENTIFICATION

HABITAT

POPULATION

MAP

Top
A common gull at its nest guarding its eggs.

Bottom left
The common gull is a daintier version of a herring gull with a lesser bill and green legs.

Bottom right
This common gull has made its nest among the wooden slats of a pier.

Kittiwake

38–40 cm (15–16 in)

○○○○○○○○○○○○○○○○○○○○○○○○○○○○○
SPECIES INFORMATION

SCIENTIFIC NAME	*Rissa tridactyla*
RELATED SPECIES	*No close relative in region*
CALL	*Flight-call a raw 'ke-ke-ke'. At breeding site a loud, repeated 'kiti-wa-ak'*
HABITAT	*Breeds in colonies on steep cliffs (sometimes on buildings). Otherwise a bird of the open sea*
STATUS	*Summer visitor to breeding areas. Winters in North Sea and Atlantic. Scattered around coasts of N and W Europe. In BI breeds on all coasts, except much of S and E (total about 545,000 pairs)*

SIZE

IDENTIFICATION

HABITAT

POPULATION

MAP

GRACEFUL, MEDIUM-SIZED gull. Resembles common gull, but wings ('dipped in ink') lack white patches at tips. Legs black, bill yellow. Juveniles have dark zig-zag pattern on upper wings (see juvenile little gull), and black band across nape.

KITTIWAKES HAVE NO white tips to their primaries in flight, while black bands along the front of the wing and a dark patch behind the neck characterise young birds. Adults at the nest site might be mistaken for common gulls but for the site itself, their black legs, yellow bill and darker back. Non-breeding adults, like young birds, have a black 'splodge' behind the eye.

They are unusual among gulls in that they have adapted to life on vertical cliffs, while most gulls nest more or less on the level. The nest needs depth, and a firm base so parents trample mud to make the foundation. Unlike other gull chicks, kittiwake chicks remain fairly immobile – this keeps them safe on their precipitous nest site. Young kittiwakes also face the cliff wall. As they are always on the nest, there is no special parental food call and the parent recognises the nest not the young birds. This cliff-nesting which also calls for anatomical adaptations like strong claws and foot muscles, is an anti-predator device but some skuas have perfected the art of catching kittiwakes from the ledges. Kittiwakes get their name from the call, which can dominate the vicinity of their breeding cliffs.

Top

The kittiwake, arguably our prettiest gull, has a greenish-yellow bill and black legs.

Bottom

A pair of kittiwakes at their nesting site.

ADULT GULLS IN WINTER

BLACK-HEADED
Head: Dark mark behind eye; pale red bill
Back: Pale grey
Wings: White flash along front
Legs: Pale red

COMMON
Head: Streaked; grey–green bill
Back: Dark grey
Wings: Large white mirrors
Legs: Grey green

KITTIWAKE
Head: Spot behind eye; yellow bill
Back: Dark grey
Wings: White below with pure black tips
Legs: Short, black

LITTLE
Head: Dark eye patch; slight black bill
Back: Pale
Wings: Rounded, dark below
Legs: Reddish

MEDITERRANEAN
Head: Dusky side of face; strong red bill
Back: Very pale
Wings: Wholly white
Legs: reddish

GREAT BLACK-BACKED

Head: White; yellow, red-spotted bill
Back: Dark black
Wings: Very black
Legs: Pink

LESSER BLACK-BACKED BACK

Head: Some streaking; yellow, red-spotted bill
Back: Grey-black (but depends on race)
Legs: Yellow
Wings: Grey-black

HERRING

Head: White or streaked; yellow, red-spotted bill
Back: Grey
Wings: White mirrors to black tips
Legs: Pink

ICELAND

Head: Dirty streaking; yellow; red spot
Back: Very pale grey
Wings Pale: White-tipped
Legs: Pink

GLAUCOUS

Head: Dirty streaking; yellow, red-spotted bill
Back: Very pale grey
Wings: Pale, white-tipped
Legs: Pink

NB Iceland gull is size of herring gull; glaucous gull is size of great black-backed gull.

Top
A kittiwake soaring overhead, showing the 'dipped in ink' pure black wingtips.

Middle
Kittiwakes nest on precarious cliff faces; there is a dark neck band on the young bird.

Bottom left
At favoured breeding cliffs kittiwakes seem to occupy every ledge.

Bottom right
With dusty grey plumage and their yellow bills, these gulls are attractive.

Guillemot

40 cm (16 in)

SPECIES INFORMATION	
SCIENTIFIC NAME	Uria aalge
RELATED SPECIES	Razorbill, Puffin, Black Guillemot
CALL	Grating 'aaarrr', 'varr' at nesting site
HABITAT	Breeds in dense colonies on narrow ledges and small ridges on rocky sea-cliffs. Outside breeding season at sea
STATUS	Breeds on coasts of north and west Europe. Leaves breeding grounds in August to return in January. In BI over 1,200,000 birds

SIZE

IDENTIFICATION

HABITAT

POPULATION

MAP

BLACK AND WHITE seabird with narrow, pointed bill. Sits upright, penguin-style. Often has white eye-ring and narrow stripe behind eye (bridled form). In winter, cheeks, chin and neck white, and has a dark line behind eye.

THEY ARE HIGHLY specialised and distinctive swimmers and divers who spend most of their time at sea. The guillemot is most easily told from the razorbill by its slender bill and its rather paler grey-black upperparts.

Guillemots are specialist fish-feeders and they nest close to seas rich in fish, which they bring in one at a time to their young. The largest colonies are in Scotland, where many have more than 10,000 birds each. On the east coast, the most southerly colony is at Flamborough Head, and there are no colonies between there and the Isle of Wight.

Top left
Guillemots standing, penguin-like, on a rock in the Shetland Isles.

Top right
A guillemot colony in the Farne Islands.

Bottom
The guillemot's streamlined body helps it swim and dive with ease.

'*The guillemot and other auks all nest on rocky ledges.*
Their eggs are conical to stop them rolling off the edges,
They sit in groups in coats of black like elders at a wake
But differ from the elders in the kind of noise they make'
Robert S. Morrison WORDS ON BIRDS

SPECIES INFORMATION	
SCIENTIFIC NAME	Alca torda
RELATED SPECIES	Guillemot, Puffin, Black Guillemot
CALL	Grating calls such as 'arrr' and 'orrr'
HABITAT	Breeds in small groups on steep cliffs, often with guillemots
STATUS	Breeds at coasts of NW Europe. Leaves breeding grounds in July, to return in February or March. In BI about 182,000 birds

Razorbill

38 cm (15 in)

SIZE

IDENTIFICATION

HABITAT

POPULATION

MAP

SIMILAR TO GUILLEMOT but has larger head, shorter neck and heavier bill. Juveniles with smaller, uniformly black bill; easily confused with juvenile guillemots, but bill shorter and less pointed.

RAZORBILLS ARE BLACK on the back with white underparts and an odd bill, as its name implies. The bill is laterally compressed, looks a bit formidable, and is crossed by a white line; another white line runs towards the eye. Separating the two in winter is harder, but the guillemot is more pointed in front, the beak, and the razorbill at the rear, its tail. Flight appears fast, is usually low, and the wings are also used under water in pursuit of fish and crustaceans.

Top
Although they have narrow wings, razorbills and guillemots can fly quite well.

Middle
The razorbill has a thicker neck and wider bill than the guillemot.

Bottom
A group of razorbills perched on a seaside rock.

299

Puffin

28 cm (11 in)

SPECIES INFORMATION	
SCIENTIFIC NAME	*Fratercula arctica*
RELATED SPECIES	Guillemot, Razorbill, Black Guillemot
CALL	Long growling at nest
HABITAT	Nests in colonies in rabbit burrows (or digs its own) on grassy islands or cliffs
STATUS	Summer visitor to breeding sites. Winters at sea (Atlantic, North Sea and west Mediterranean). Breeds at coasts of north and north-west Europe. In BI about 940,000 birds

CLOWN-LIKE FACE, and unusual heavy, colourful bill. Dumpy, black and white seabird with bright red legs and feet. In winter, bill becomes smaller and darker. Flight straight, with rapid wing-beats.

THE PUFFIN IS the only one of our auks that does anything about preparing a home. It digs effectively, using its bill as a pickaxe, and its webbed feet as shovels to fling earth, or even soft sandstone, backwards. Having made the hole, or enlarged a rabbit burrow, it will take feathers, grass or seaweed into the burrow but may just as easily drop them at the entrance.

Everyone has seen pictures, tea towels or cards of puffins, with their remarkable triangular, brightly-coloured bills, but few are able to see these sociable birds at their breeding colonies. One of the pair spends much of the day in the isolation of the burrow, but when the egg is abandoned, for an hour or two on a summer evening, the pairs parade together, showing their bright orange legs among the orange lichens, or flap down to join rafts of birds on the sea below.

With their unusual bills, puffins are able to carry several small fish, such as sprats, at a time back to their young.

Top left and right
The puffin's bill is designed to catch and carry several sand-eels at once.

Bottom
Puffins at their burrows in the colony on the Shetland Islands.

Black Guillemot

30 cm (12 in)

SPECIES INFORMATION	
SCIENTIFIC NAME	Cepphus grylle
RELATED SPECIES	Guillemot, Razorbill, Puffin
CALL	High-pitched whistle, 'ssiii' or 'piiiih', also repeated 'sist-sist'
HABITAT	Breeds in small colonies among rocks at the base of steep cliffs, on the lower slopes of bird cliffs and on small, rocky islands. Outside breeding season mostly in shallow coastal waters
STATUS	Resident or partial migrant. Coasts of N Europe. In BI about 40,000 birds

SMALL SEABIRD WITH black plumage and white wing-patches; feet bright red. In winter, white beneath, grey above, with pale feather edging. In flight the white wing-patches are conspicuous.

BLACK GUILLEMOTS SEEM to love their rocks and seaweed, and display beautifully early in the morning, near little islands in the north west. Their bright red feet, white wing-patch, slender bill and black summer plumage make them as distinctive as the almost pure white non-breeding adults, with dappled black and white backs in winter. Not surprisingly the white wing-patch is at all times a feature, but white underwings add to the bird's pied contrast when it flies or flaps in the water.

The main concentrations of black guillemots are in Shetland and Orkney, and along the western seaboard of Scotland.

In a chapter called the 'Playboys of the Western World' E.A. Armstrong describes the black guillemot: 'He is a quaint, jolly little fellow. The more you know him the queerer and the more likeable you find him to be. You appreciate him, indeed, because of his odd ways....If the black guillemot has his little whimsies and foibles it is only to say he is a real personality.'

> '*There is no more charming bird on Clerach than the black guillemot or tystie. The little bird is classed as an auk, but it is the least representative of the family in type. It is gregarious on the sea, or at least given to making up playful parties, but it nests in private, deep in some cranny and not necessarily directly above the sea.*'
> Fraser Darling

The black guillemot stands out clearly in summer plumage with its contrasting black and white colouring and the vivid red of the legs.

Chough

40 cm (16 in)

S P E C I E S I N F O R M A T I O N	
SCIENTIFIC NAME	Pyrrhocorax pyrrhocorax
RELATED SPECIES	No close relatives in region (Alpine Chough in mountains of S Europe)
CALL	Jackdaw-like calls
HABITAT	Rocky sites in mountains; also on rocky coasts in west Europe
STATUS	Resident. Range includes S Europe, particularly Spain, Greece and Turkey; also Sardinia and Sicily and north-west France. In BI about 1,100 pairs, mainly in Ireland

GLOSSY, BLUE-BLACK plumage, with long, curved red bill and red legs. Acrobatic in flight, showing deeply fingered wings and square tail.

*'How fearful
And dizzy 'tis, to cast one's eyes so low!
The crows and choughs that wing the midway air
Show scarce so gross as beetles: half way down
Hangs one that gathers samphire, dreadful trade..!'*

KING LEAR William Shakespeare

THE RED, CURVED bill and red legs make the chough instantly recognisable, but its call can be confused with a jackdaw's. In no sense is it a water bird, but over most of its British range it is closely associated with the sea, and there are few nest sites on mainland Britain, except in west Wales. RSPB research has shown a clear link between the length of grass sward and chough populations on Ramsey Island and Islay. On Bardsey chough populations have recently fallen, in line with a decline in rabbits, while a previous increase was linked to the introduction of a more intense grazing regime.

As well as low intensity agriculture, with short grass rich in beetles, choughs need caves, quarries or derelict buildings in which to nest. Welsh, Scottish and Irish islands can produce this combination, and Islay, the Isle of Man and Ireland hold the majority of birds. Choughs are obvious 'corvids' and fine fliers, deftly using air currents up sea-cliffs and soaring, with well spread primary feathers.

I had always been led to believe, whether in English lessons or by birdwatchers who knew, that those caught were jackdaws, and that Shakespeare was wrong. However, there is a reference in *A History of Kent* (Dunkins, 1857): 'before the war of extermination was ruthlessly waged against the chough or red legged crow or Cornish chough – this bird was very plentiful among the Dover cliffs.'

The chough is a rather unusual member of the crow family, with its narrow, curved, bright-red bill. This rare bird is restricted to coastal sites in the extreme west of Britain and Ireland.

Rock Pipit
16 cm (6.5 in)

SPECIES INFORMATION

SCIENTIFIC NAME	Anthus petrosus
RELATED SPECIES	Meadow Pipit, Tree Pipit
CALL	Call 'weest'. Song given in flapping song-flight resembles that of meadow pipit, but with stronger trill at the end
HABITAT	Stoney and rocky shorelines
STATUS	Resident and partial migrant. Winters regularly around North Sea and Baltic. Breeds at coasts of north and west Europe. In BI about 45,000 pairs

LARGE AND DARK, with long bill and dark legs. Outer tail feathers are grey.

ROCK PIPITS ARE easy to miss, with their inconspicuous greys, olives and buffs blending with the seaweed as they search for food, among the boulders. Habitat alone is a good indicator when you do see them, but when joined by meadow pipits the more streaked back of the latter should be clear. The rock pipit has grey, not white, outer tail feathers and a call that is distinctive once you know it.

Rock pipits are very strongly linked to rocky shores and nest in rather inaccessible sites, on cliffs and among boulders. Their food includes a large proportion of marine animals, such as sandhoppers, small worms and marine molluscs.

'A sudden flip of olive green wings as we pass some stone or bunch of heather, and there for the trouble of kneeling and delicately parting the herbage with our hands we see a perfect, round nest of smoothed fibres and four mottled eggs. Happy and welcome little pipit! In our island winters you have become tame and graced our doorstep and only we can tell how grateful we are, for the island dweller in windswept places can have no fun from watching tits and robins and exciting newcomers at a bird table in the garden.'

Fraser Darling

 SIZE
 IDENTIFICATION
 HABITAT
 POPULATION
 MAP

The rock pipit lives up to its name – making its nest in rocky sites along the coast. It is larger and darker than its close relative, the meadow pipit.

Rare or Local Breeding Birds

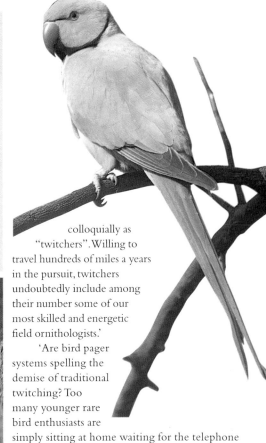

IN HIS INTRODUCTION to *Rare Birds in Britain and Ireland*, Sharrock maintains that: 'Most birdwatchers are fascinated by rarities. To some the occasional rarity is an unexpected but welcome excitement in the course of a normal year's birding, but to others the finding of rare birds becomes the *raison d'être* of their hobby.'

colloquially as "twitchers". Willing to travel hundreds of miles a years in the pursuit, twitchers undoubtedly include among their number some of our most skilled and energetic field ornithologists.'

'Are bird pager systems spelling the demise of traditional twitching? Too many younger rare bird enthusiasts are simply sitting at home waiting for the telephone to ring.'

ONCE KNOWN AS tally-hunters, tick-hunters or tickers, these rarity-seekers are now known

RARITIES AND VAGRANTS

IN 1974, SHARROCK had written a book on scarce migrants, defined as those which occur annually or nearly so, in numbers ranging from a handful to a hundred or more. Two spectacular and one rather dull bird started this survey, with the striking hoopoe and equally striking but more elusive golden oriole being linked with the tawny pipit which, as he said, is distinctive as pipits go. Altogether he analysed some 7,000 records of 25 species, together with a collective look at the records of American waders and landbirds that appeared in Britain and Ireland. For most of us these are rare birds, but they do occur regularly, and many twitchers will have seen them.

Sometimes rarities and vagrants are just described and listed, but Cottridge and Vinicombe have attempted to make sense of the

Top
The exotic ring-necked parakeet is now firmly established, notably in the southern suburbs of London.

Bottom
The ortolan bunting breeds over much of mainland Europe, but is only a rare vagrant to Britain.

competition following population falls of trans-Saharan migrants. They also ask the very pertinent question: 'If 615 yellow-browed warblers are recorded in Britain and Ireland in one autumn how many actually reach western Europe? As an extension of that, how many more left their breeding grounds heading in the wrong direction, and why? Similarly, if 25 red-eyed vireos from America reach this side of the Atlantic, how many set out?'

VAGRANTS FROM EUROPE

THEY THEN CONSIDERED short-range vagrancy from Europe, citing pre-migratory dispersal as a cause of autumn records of woodchat shrike, ortolan bunting and melodious warbler and, while not liking drift as a universal answer to the arrival of vagrants, used it to explain the spring arrival of bluethroats and icterine warblers. Some 15,000 redstarts, 8,000 wheatears, 4,000 pied flycatchers, 40 wrynecks, together with great reed warbler, icterine warbler, barred warbler, tawny pipit and ortolan bunting, were drifted onto a 3 km (1.8 mile) stretch of Suffolk coastline at Walberswick on 3 September 1965, so how many other vagrants could arrive?

Without adverse winds, birds can still make errors of judgement, with hoopoes not having to overshoot far to arrive from France, and bee-eaters, woodchat shrikes and southern herons sometimes arriving in the west country, having overshot from Iberia.

Bottom
The golden pheasant is a gaudy bird which breeds in small numbers at a few sites.

movements of vagrant birds. The increased records of Cetti's warbler as it spreads from the south, were a prelude to its colonisation, so will great white egrets and black kites be future colonists? They list ten eastern migrants that are occurring more frequently, and these may include species which will breed regularly in Britain in the future: citrine wagtail, thrush nightingale, river warbler, paddy-field warbler, Blythe's reed warbler, greenish warbler, penduline tit, rosefinch, and rustic and little buntings.

Perhaps their spread is linked with climate change, or perhaps, the authors suggest, with reduced

EFFECTS OF THE CLIMATE ON RARE BIRDS

CLIMATIC CHANGE WILL influence patterns of vagrancy, and perhaps has already done so through changes in wind patterns. It is possible that the surge in American landbirds recorded between 1950 and 1970 was not due to increased observers but to changes in the Atlantic weather systems.

Increased wind speeds at the spring and autumn equinoxes could affect spring over-shooting and autumn vagrancy from the east. It is also evident that some winter visitors like pink-footed geese, Greenland white-fronts, barnacle geese and Bewick's swan may winter nearer their breeding sites if conditions change.

LOCATION OF SCARCE SPECIES

SHARROCK PRODUCED A SERIES of maps showing where the scarce species turned up. Autumn icterine warbler, autumn greenish warbler and autumn pectoral sandpiper had a high incidence in Ireland, while spring icterine warbler, ortolan bunting and bluethroat were particularly Scottish. In autumn, barred, arctic and yellow-browed warblers and scarlet rosefinch were also more frequent in Scotland. Red-breasted flycatchers occurred on the east coast, hoopoes on the south coast, and autumn Richard's' pipits had two favourite areas, in Scotland and the south-west.

Bluethroat and red-breasted flycatcher are among the commonest and most attractive of the

AMERICAN VISITORS

RARE AMERICAN MIGRANTS are perhaps of particular interest because of the distance flown and the possibility of the birds having had assisted passages. Of the waders, most have been making landfalls in Ireland and south-west England. Tacumshin Lake, a brackish lagoon on the Wexford coast, has recorded almost all these American waders, with frequent buff-breasted sandpipers, and periodic lesser yellowlegs. American landbird records are concentrated on Scilly, Lundy, Skokholm, Bardsey and Cape Clear, in the first three weeks of October. There is good evidence that the majority of these, other than the seed-eating 'sparrows' and buntings, reach Britain and Ireland naturally.

Whether from the Atlantic or from the north, weather or food shortage can bring invasions, as with the 1995 irruption of arctic redpolls which led to 236 records, or the 315 nutcrackers in 1968.

Top

The little egret is a rare but increasingly regular visitor, now breeding in small numbers.

Middle

Little egrets are easily identified, even at some distance.

Bottom

Another rare breeding bird, the goshawk has taken advantage of coniferous plantations.

scarce migrants, with common rosefinch, barred and icterine warbler, wryneck and red-backed shrike also frequent. Both of these last two were still breeding in Britain when the original *Breeding Atlas* was produced, having been much more widespread before. Now, instead of breeding on south-eastern heaths, red-backed shrikes turn up in Shetland and Orkney, mainly in spring, while wrynecks, which have bred in every English and Welsh county, tend to appear on south and east coasts around September.

A long list of genuinely rare birds, in more or less increasing order of rarity might read: red-footed falcon, white-rumped sandpiper, subalpine warbler, alpine swift, night heron, rose-coloured starling and American wigeon. These are birds from a good spread of taxonomic groups, adapted to a range of habitats: will any of them come to stay?

Many species are seen only rarely, either because they breed here only in very small numbers, or because they appear infrequently on migration, or as rare vagrants. This section is divided into two parts – the first deals with rare breeders, and the second with rare birds which are mainly seen on migration or when blown off course by unusual weather systems.

Top far left and bottom
The snow bunting breeds in small numbers in the Scottish highlands, but winter flocks may be seen at the coasts further south.

Top right
The drake wood duck is a handsome bird. This species was introduced from North America, and now breeds wild in a few places.

Slavonian Grebe

35 cm (14 in)

SPECIES INFORMATION	
SCIENTIFIC NAME	Podiceps auritus
RELATED SPECIES	Black-necked Grebe, Red-necked Grebe, Great Crested Grebe
CALL	Trills and squeals on breeding ground (recalls water rail)
HABITAT	Breeds on shallow lakes
STATUS	Regular but rare winter visitor to BI, mainly to coasts and estuaries. Northern Europe (Iceland, Norway, Sweden, Finland); small population in Scotland (about 75 pairs)

SIZE

IDENTIFICATION

HABITAT

POPULATION

MAP

SMALL, SLIMMER AND somewhat longer-necked than little grebe. In summer it has black head, with golden 'horns', neck and rusty red underparts. In winter, grey with white neck and lower face, and black cap.

SLAVONIAN GREBES ARE as vulnerable to disturbance as the divers, and, as rare, beautiful birds, it can often be the birdwatchers who do the disturbing. As the *New Atlas* points out, there are hides on RSPB reserves where the birds can be safely watched without causing difficulties. From the hide you might see the chestnut red breast, neck and flanks, but most eye-catching is the contrast between the dark cheeks and golden crest tufts. Overall, this is a small, dumpy, rather stubby-billed grebe, with trilling calls and elaborate display. If you were lucky you could watch these and see the stripy-headed, downy young. Unfortunately, breeding success is not high, partly because of disturbance, but also due to predation and changing water levels which can flood or leave nests stranded.

Slavonian grebes are far less distinctive in their winter plumage, and, as they may then occur with other similar grebes, identification features which differentiate them are summarised within the coastal birds section. Arthropods form a significant part of their diet when breeding, but fish are important at all times of year. When birds breed on more productive lakes they may reach breeding condition earlier, allowing the possibility of second broods. As a northern bird, breeding is determined by the period when lakes are frost-free, so second broods further north are rare. The nest is typical of grebes in being a heap of water weed and, in Scotland, is usually situated among sedges in a shallow bog.

In Western Europe, Finland has the highest population, but its extensive range in Russia, across Siberia, makes for many more birds. From their northern breeding quarters they move to mainly coastal wintering areas, with a few on the Atlantic coast south of Brittany, but other populations in the Adriatic and northern Black Sea. They usually stay within sheltered coastal waters, and in Britain few of these would have more than ten birds. However, internationally important sites in the Moray Firth and Forth estuary peak at more than 50, while Lough Foyle is an important site in Northern Ireland.

Top
The Slavonian grebe in winter plumage, as it normally appears outside the breeding season.

Bottom left and right
In breeding plumage it is very striking, with a golden tufted crest from its eye to the back of its head.

SPECIES INFORMATION

SCIENTIFIC NAME	Podiceps nigricollis
RELATED SPECIES	Slavonian Grebe, Red-necked Grebe, Great Crested Grebe
CALL	Squeaky whistles
HABITAT	Shallow lakes with vegetation and little open water
STATUS	In BI breeds locally, in small numbers (about 30 pairs)

Black-necked Grebe

30 cm (12 in)

SLIGHTLY SMALLER THAN Slavonian, with upturned bill. In winter, neck and face are dusky grey. In summer, mainly black, with rusty flanks, and golden fan of feathers behind eyes. Look for the steep forehead, smudgy markings, and upturned bill. The red eye is sometimes visible. Summer birds look very different, with a genuine black neck and a less impressive spray of golden plumes than the Slavonian grebe.

SIZE

IDENTIFICATION

HABITAT

POPULATION

MAP

BLACK-NECKED GREBES are mainly passage migrants, but south-coast wintering, in a few sheltered waters, is regular, with Langstone Harbour and Studland Bay, for example, having good numbers. Also seen at reservoirs, such as Staines.

Like the little grebe, it is elusive even when present, and breeding haunts seem to change: a large Irish colony did not re-establish elsewhere after drainage, new birds have appeared in the English Midlands, and even in Scotland it is rarely certain where it will breed.

Disturbance and pike have been blamed for breeding failure, and drainage and natural succession for a moving population. It breeds in a wide swathe across Russia, and has some huge colonies in N America. In winter many birds move south to western coasts or the Mediterranean; with larger numbers further east.

The black-necked grebe has less yellow on its head than the Slavonian. The bill is slimmer and slightly upturned at the tip, and the forehead steeper.

Little Egret

48–53 cm (19–21 in)

SPECIES INFORMATION

SCIENTIFIC NAME	*Egretta garzetta*
RELATED SPECIES	Other herons and egrets
CALL	Raucous gurgling and snoring noises at nest
HABITAT	Breeds in colonies in large wetlands with bushes and trees
STATUS	Increasingly common visitor. A few now breed in BI

SIZE

IDENTIFICATION

HABITAT

POPULATION

MAP

WHITE WITH BLACK bill, black legs and yellow feet. Long plumes on head and shoulders in breeding season, raised during displays. In flight has relatively rapid wing-beat, and rounded wings. Yellow feet most visible in flight. Sometimes runs rapidly in shallow water, stabbing to left and right for small fish, frogs and aquatic insects.

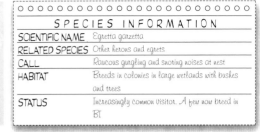

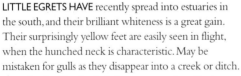

LITTLE EGRETS HAVE recently spread into estuaries in the south, and their brilliant whiteness is a great gain. Their surprisingly yellow feet are easily seen in flight, when the hunched neck is characteristic. May be mistaken for gulls as they disappear into a creek or ditch.

In the *Handbook*, little egrets are described as very rare vagrants, and when Sharrock described scarce birds in 1974 there had only been 12 records. They first bred in Dorset in 1996 and in Ireland in 1997. Twelve young were raised on Brownsea Island in 1997, and what 60 years before had been a vagrant was established as a breeding bird. In 1998 it bred in Somerset and Devon.

The little egret is a typical heron, but stands out well in its pure white plumage. The legs are dark, but the feet a bright yellow, though sometimes obscured by mud.

SPECIES INFORMATION

SCIENTIFIC NAME	*Alopochen aegyptiacus*
RELATED SPECIES	*No close relative*
CALL	*Deep 'kek-kek'*
HABITAT	*Freshwater marshes*
STATUS	*Introduced in East Anglia. Breeds in the wild, mainly in Norfolk and Suffolk – about 750 birds*

Egyptian Goose

68 cm (27 in)

PINKISH-BROWN BIRD with large, dark eye patches and huge white wing-flashes. The population is very much based in East Anglia, but it has bred at scattered English sites elsewhere, and on Anglesey. They need a gravel pit or similar refuge, short grass for the goslings, and a hole or old nest of buzzard or crow in which to breed.

SIZE

IDENTIFICATION

HABITAT

POPULATION

MAP

The large, dark eye patches and brown breast markings clearly distinguish the Egyptian goose.

311

Mandarin Duck

45 cm (18 in)

SPECIES INFORMATION	
SCIENTIFIC NAME	Aix galericulata
RELATED SPECIES	Wood Duck
CALL	High-pitched, coot-like 'tweek'
HABITAT	Wooded freshwater sites, such as ponds and rivers
STATUS	Has steadily increased. Now probably 4,000 birds in Britain

SIZE

IDENTIFICATION

HABITAT

POPULATION

MAP

MALE MANDARINS LOOK exotic, with their orange-yellow necks and wing sails, maroon breast with white stripes behind, multicoloured crown and red bill. By duck standards the female is also distinctive. Grey-brown above, distinct white spots below, and a white spectacle and eye-stripe.

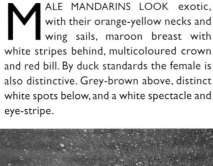

Originally from Japan, China and Eastern Russia, the British feral population stems from birds that were released in various home counties in the 1920s and 1930s. By 1971 they were admitted to the British and Irish official list, and by the time of the first *Atlas* they were breeding, or suspected of breeding, far from their original centre. The Isle of Wight, Cheshire and Norfolk had birds, but these had not spread from the Surrey source, but from other wildfowl collections. The mandarin's stronghold is in Berkshire, Surrey and Buckinghamshire.

ONLY THE WOOD duck is similar. Being small and compact, mandarins rise easily from land or water, fly with agility and perch readily. The spectacular sails are, of course, linked with breeding behaviour, and they and the crest are raised on many social occasions.

It is many years since I saw the only 'wild' mandarin ducks I have met, by Virginia Water in Surrey. This, and the neighbouring Windsor Great Park, has their preferred habitat, with old deciduous trees with holes, together with a mix of ponds and streams. As well as nesting holes, the trees produce the acorns, nuts and mast which are winter food for a species which lives very differently from any of our native ducks. Living among trees they need high manoeuvrability, which is partly provided by their relatively long tails.

Top
The duck mandarin has much more sombre plumage than her mate.

Middle and bottom
Almost cartoon-like in its elaborate breeding plumage, the drake mandarin is a splendid sight.

SPECIES INFORMATION

SCIENTIFIC NAME	Aix sponsa
RELATED SPECIES	Mandarin
CALL	Female has squealing flight-call
HABITAT	Water with trees nearby
STATUS	Introduced, and breeding wild, mainly in SE England, but in much smaller numbers than Mandarin

Wood Duck
45 cm (18 in)

WOOD DUCK MALES have extraordinarily marked green heads, clear white throats, richer red, wine-coloured breasts, and dark patches under the tail. The female has some green on the crown, a broader but shorter spectacle and a white line around the base of the bill.

ALTHOUGH VERY SIMILAR to the mandarin in being a woodland, perching duck, the wood duck stems from America and has not been nearly as successful as the mandarin. A peculiar aspect of the relationship between the two, whose English ranges concentrate on Berkshire and Surrey, is that mandarins sometimes dump their eggs in wood duck clutches and leave the parent wood ducks with extra ducklings. The wood duck is not included on the British and Irish list, as most records are explicable in terms of movements of birds from free-flying collections, with breeding only occurring close to 'home'.

SIZE

IDENTIFICATION

HABITAT

POPULATION

MAP

Top
The female wood duck lacks the white spots along the flanks of the similar female mandarin.

Ruddy Duck

40 cm (16 in)

SPECIES INFORMATION	
SCIENTIFIC NAME	Oxyura jamaicensis
RELATED SPECIES	White-headed Duck (mainly south Spain)
CALL	Male makes low chuckling.
HABITAT	Reservoirs, lakes
STATUS	Introduced from North America. Probably at least 600 pairs, mainly in West Midlands

SIZE

IDENTIFICATION

HABITAT

POPULATION

MAP

THE RUDDY DUCK has been in the news recently. From its very successful expansion in Britain, it has now spread to the continent, including Spain, putting the scarce, closely-related native white-headed duck at risk through competition and hybridisation. Control measures are being introduced in Britain in 1999.

THE OUTLINE OF the ruddy duck is highly distinctive, with its partly cocked tail used in display and broad, concave bill. Males have a chestnut body, and clear white cheeks, surrounded by black head and neck. Female is duller than the male with patterned face.

Top
The drake ruddy duck, showing its blue bill and obvious white lower face.

Middle
The short, stiff tail is so characteristic of this species.

Bottom
The female ruddy duck exercises its wraps.

Red-crested Pochard

55 cm (22 in)

SPECIES INFORMATION	
SCIENTIFIC NAME	Netta rufina
RELATED SPECIES	Pochard.
CALL	Breeding male has loud 'bait' or slow, nasal 'geng'; female a harsh 'kurr'
HABITAT	Breeds at reedy lakes, mainly in drier regions
STATUS	Summer visitor, but resident south Spain and south France. Breeds in only a few places in Europe, mainly in southern Spain and Camargue (France), but also in Netherlands, Denmark, and south Central Europe (Lake Constance and southern Bavaria). Sometimes escapes from collections.

L ARGE, THICK-HEADED diving duck, sitting rather high in the water. Breeding male has chestnut head (crown paler) and bright red bill. Female is uniform grey-brown with pale grey cheeks, (see also female common scoter).

THE HEADQUARTERS FOR this duck seems to be the Cotswold Water Park, and birds now breed in small numbers elsewhere in Britain. The females resemble common scoter. There is also a free-flying population in St James' Park, London.

The main world population is in Central Asia, west to the Caspian and Black Seas.

SIZE

IDENTIFICATION

HABITAT

POPULATION

MAP

Top
The female, though less colourful, is also distinctive, with pale cheeks and brown top to the head.

Bottom
The drake red-crested pochard has a prominent orange crown of erectile feathers.

315

White-tailed Eagle
80–95 cm (31–37 in)

SPECIES INFORMATION

SCIENTIFIC NAME	Haliaeetus albicilla
RELATED SPECIES	Golden Eagle
CALL	Very vocal, with a loud raucous 'kyowkyowkyow', especially near nest
HABITAT	Rocky coasts. Also near large forested lakes and rivers, even a few kilometres from water
STATUS	Resident and partial migrant. Regular on certain large lakes (e.g. in foothills of the Alps) outside breeding season. Norway, northern Germany and Poland. Re-introduction in west of Scotland is slowly proving a success, with about a dozen pairs now breeding

SIZE

IDENTIFICATION

HABITAT

POPULATION

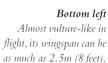

MAP

HUGE, WITH VERY broad, parallel-sided wings, head well extended, tail short and wedge-shaped. Powerful yellow bill and short white tail. Juveniles (up to 4 years) dark, even on head, tail and bill.

THE WING SHAPE of the white-tailed eagle, sea eagle or erne, is very different from the golden eagle, being broad, rectangular and deeply fingered. The bill is huge, the tail short, wedge-shaped and white in adult. Young birds are darker, with dark tails.

A reintroduction project started in 1975 and, for 11 years, eight-week old birds from Norway were taken to Rum for rearing and release. This involved fine levels of co-operation between many organisations, including the Royal Air Force who brought the young birds over. The species prospers in the Bodo district of Norway and taking birds from eyries with two eaglets, poses no threat to the Norwegian population.

The eagles needed to survive for five or six years to breed. By the early 1980s there were attempts, and in 1985 the first Scottish-bred sea eagle for 75 years flew in the Hebrides. There is now a young population there – in 1995 there were nine clutches and seven young, and in 1998, 15 clutches, with 13 chicks being fledged by 9 pairs.

'He clasps the crag with crooked hands;
Close to the sun in lonely lands.
Ring'd with azure world he stands
The wrinkled sea beneath him crawls:
He watches from his mountain wall,
And like a thunderbolt he falls'
Alfred Lord Tennyson THE EAGLE

Top and bottom right
The white-tailed eagle is a very powerful bird which feeds mainly on fish and carrion.

Bottom left
Almost vulture-like in flight, its wingspan can be as much as 2.5m (8 feet).

SPECIES INFORMATION

SCIENTIFIC NAME	*Pernis apivorus*
RELATED SPECIES	
CALL	On breeding ground a high-pitched, melodious 'kee-er'
	Mixed woodland with clearings, pasture and fields.
HABITAT	Usually nests at woodland edge, hunting in open areas
STATUS	Summer visitor. Most of Europe, except far north
	and west. Rare bird (at edge of range) in Britain
	(about 20 pairs)

Honey Buzzard

55 cm (21 in)

SIZE

IDENTIFICATION

HABITAT

POPULATION

MAP

BUZZARD-SIZED, BUT slimmer and longer-winged and with longer tail. Plumage variable – upperside usually dark brown, underside pale, almost white, or uniform brown. Head grey, eye yellow. In flight shows outstretched head, relatively narrow wings and long, narrow tail with one or two clear dark bands and black tip.

FOREST DESTRUCTION OCCURRED early in Britain and Ireland, and there is a long history of disturbance through hunting interests, and the demands for timber and more agricultural land. Honey buzzards may have been among the birds of prey to suffer from change and disturbance but they are on the fringes of their range here so climate too is important.

Fuller quotes its preference for forests larger than 250 ha (620 acres), for mixed forests in the Netherlands, although often nesting in fir or spruce, and a general preference for broadleaved woodland.

The scattered population of British summer visitors is spread over the south and east of England, with none in Ireland. It is unique in its diet, with its summer dependence on larvae and adults of bees and wasps; the larvae are crucial to the survival of the young.

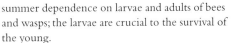

In flight, the honey buzzard shows its long, banded tail, splendid patterned wing span and rather narrow, almost pigeon-like head.

317

Goshawk

48–60 cm (19–24 in)

○ ○

SPECIES INFORMATION

SCIENTIFIC NAME	*Accipiter gentilis*
RELATED SPECIES	Sparrowhawk
CALL	In breeding season 'gik-gik-gik', buzzard-like 'kiair', accented on the first syllable
HABITAT	Wooded country, particularly coniferous forest
STATUS	Resident. Widespread (but secretive) in most of Europe. In Britain rare (about 200 pairs)

SIZE

IDENTIFICATION

HABITAT

POPULATION

MAP

LARGE SIZE (Especially the female which is buzzard-sized); long tail and relatively short and rounded wings. Male smaller and lighter than female. Upperparts of male grey-brown to slate-grey, female brown. Underside pale, with horizontal speckles, in juveniles yellowish, with dark brown spots. Look out for marked S-curve on trailing edge of wing, due to bulging secondaries, and remember that a male goshawk may be smaller than a female sparrowhawk.

GOSHAWKS ARE LARGER than sparrowhawks, and have more patterned faces and slate coloured backs. The rounder tail and longer wings, help separation from our other *Accipter*. Goshawks are on the increase, particularly in conifer woodland, but its exact status is difficult to verify because of its secrecy and doubts about the true status of some birds, which have escaped from hawking stock. It is unlikely that there are many more than 200 pairs, compared with over 40,000 pairs of sparrowhawks.

Sometimes British pairs breed as close together as 1.5 km (0.9 miles), so there is a potential for a very large population. It would be good to see more of these fine birds displaying over their nesting territories.

Top right and left
The goshawk is a powerful woodland predator, whose favourite prey is woodpigeon.

Bottom
A large eye and heavy bill are vital for an efficient bird-hunter.

Montagu's Harrier

43–47 cm (17–18 in)

SPECIES INFORMATION

SCIENTIFIC NAME	Circus pygargus
RELATED SPECIES	Hen Harrier, Marsh Harrier
CALL	Shrill 'kek-kek-kek'
HABITAT	Breeds in low vegetation near water, but also in damp heath, especially on fens, and increasingly in open fields. Hunts mainly over wetlands with low cover, and in cultivated fields
STATUS	Summer visitor. Much of central and southern Europe. Rare breeder in BI (about ten pairs)

SIZE
IDENTIFICATION
HABITAT
POPULATION
MAP

VERY SLIM AND GRACEFUL in flight (recalls seagull, or even tern). Male similar to hen harrier, but with narrower wings and longer tail, black band on wings, and brown stripes on belly. Female almost identical to female hen harrier, but wings narrower and white rump less marked. Juveniles like female, but with red-brown undersides.

ITS BEAUTY, AS with all harriers, is partly in its movement, on narrow, pointed wings. Kearton referred to it as the ash-coloured harrier, with the implication of a touch of dirty mottle to the male's grey upperparts. The dark wing-tips are shared with the hen harrier, but a black bar across the upperwing is diagnostic. The rump varies from pale grey to whitish. There are also black bars on the underwing, and brown streaks on the underside and underwing. Females can be distinguished from female hen harriers by their smaller size, narrower wings and narrower white rump; again there is a black bar on the wings, but as they are darker it is not so evident.

Montagu's harriers are summer visitors to Europe, wintering in sub-Saharan Africa, while an Indian wintering population summers well to the east. It is essentially a lowland species which will breed in dry as well as wet fields, including farmland, heaths, moors and peat bogs. Crops, given appropriate protection, provide the undisturbed taller cover it needs for breeding but when hunting it prefers lower vegetation.

Brown describes their hunting method: 'They fly low and slowly over the ground gliding against the wind if they can, but flying slowly and gliding if there is no wind, repeatedly checking in flight, hovering briefly above suspected prey, and dropping into the grass to catch it if it is finally located, or passing on if it is not.' He reckons that a day's winter hunting could involve 150 km (93 miles) of flying; certainly enough to take it a long way from its roost. Their manoeuvrability allows them to catch small birds, but voles and young rabbits are also important.

In an area of Dorset arable farmland, little groups of bird watchers can often be seen in summer in a lay-by on the main road. Although there is a magnificent National Nature Reserve nearby, that is not where the harriers breed. With co-operation between local farmers and RSPB this area of farmland has been one of the few strongholds for British Montagu's harriers in recent years. Rather than leaving uncut crops around the nest which might show where it was, the young are transferred to a box when harvesting, and this is tolerated by both parents and young. They are then returned to the nest after harvest.

Formerly associated with heath and wet fenland, Montagu's harriers now nest mainly amongst crops, ideally with rough ground nearby for hunting. They are still very rare in Britain however.

Capercaillie

82–90 cm (32–35 in) male
58–64 cm (23–25 in) female

SPECIES INFORMATION

SCIENTIFIC NAME	Tetrao urogallus
RELATED SPECIES	Black Grouse
CALL	Courting male has strange explosive, grinding and gurgling calls
HABITAT	Coniferous and mixed forests, with small clearings.
STATUS	Resident. Scandinavia, Scotland (about 1,500 birds), central and south-east Europe. Declined due to destruction of natural Scots pine forests, and through disturbance.

SIZE

IDENTIFICATION

HABITAT

POPULATION

MAP

LARGEST GROUSE. MALE is turkey-sized, black, with long spreadable tail. Female smaller, with orange-brown breast-band and rusty-red, black-banded tail. Take-off noisy, flight rapid with powerful wing-beats and long glides.

GIRALDUS CALLED THEM 'peacocks of the woods' and described them as 'abundant', but few of us get a chance to see the huge capercaillie in the mature pine forests of Scotland. Not only is it very big but its tail and wings are broad and the beak heavy. The male is dark with rich brown back and wings, velvet green shield on chest and white patches on the shoulder and on the flanks. The much smaller female could be confused with black grouse but is twice the weight and is paler. In flight, initial crashing among the branches gives way to agile but powerful flight between trees or away across a valley.

The song of the male is more complex than that of the black grouse. A tapping phase precedes a drum-roll of shortened clicks, often followed by a cork popping note. The end of the song is a rapid rhythmic gurgling or strangled squealing. The male also has a belch call, while females 'bray' at display area and 'cackle' when watching or anticipating display.

The capercaillie, except in its youth, is almost entirely vegetarian. From October until April it feeds on the buds and shoots of conifers, but during the summer months its diet is extensive and includes flowers, leaves, shoots of bracken, seed pods and berries.

Recent years have seen a marked contraction in range and numbers. The *New Atlas* suggests a reduction in blueberries, wetter June weather, more foxes and crows, collisions with deer fences, overshooting and habitat change as possible causes, pointing out also that over much of its wide range it is decreasing, as mature Scots pine and oak forests are felled.

Capercaillie males provide a wonderful spectacle in the mating season. Recent years have seen a decline in their numbers.

SPECIES INFORMATION

SCIENTIFIC NAME	Chrysolophus pictus
RELATED SPECIES	Lady Amherst's Pheasant
CALL	Noisy 'kercheck'
HABITAT	Young coniferous woodland
STATUS	Native of China. Introduced and now established, mainly in Breckland, South Downs, Anglesey and Galloway. About 1,500 birds

Golden Pheasant

60–115 cm (23–45 in), of which tail 30–75 cm

GOLDEN PHEASANTS RUN rather than fly and, being rather secretive birds, are hard to spot, despite their bright plumage. In February the males form small flocks on suitable territories and display to each other to claim ownership. By March these territories are established and the males dispersed throughout the suitable habitat, calling at dawn and dusk.

SIZE
IDENTIFICATION
HABITAT
POPULATION
MAP

SPECIES INFORMATION

SCIENTIFIC NAME	Chrysolophus amherstiae
RELATED SPECIES	Golden Pheasant
CALL	Similar to Golden Pheasant
HABITAT	Young conifer plantations and rhododendron scrub
STATUS	Native of China. Introduced and now established, mainly near Woburn Abbey. About 200 birds

Lady Amherst's Pheasant

60–120 cm (23–47 in), of which tail 30–95 cm

LADY AMHERST'S PHEASANT is another Chinese bird and is arguably even more beautiful than the golden. It has an even longer, highly barred tail, scale-like pied feathers on neck, and a red and yellow rump (male).

SIZE
IDENTIFICATION
HABITAT
POPULATION
MAP

Quail

18 cm (7 in)

SPECIES INFORMATION	
SCIENTIFIC NAME	Coturnix coturnix
RELATED SPECIES	Partridges and pheasants
CALL	Male territorial call is a repeated 'wick-wick-ic' (accented on first syllable), heard by day or night
HABITAT	Mixed fields with rough margins, hedges. Breeds in winter wheat, clover and lucerne crops, and in hay-meadows
STATUS	Summer visitor. Resident in Mediterranean. Mainly south and central Europe, north to BI. Widespread in lowlands, but generally decreasing. Normally rather rare in BI (about 300 pairs), but population fluctuates

SMALLEST EUROPEAN MEMBER of the partridge family. Dumpy, almost tail-less, with camouflaged plumage. Male has black markings on head and chin; female has heavily speckled chest. Secretive and more often heard than seen.

QUAILS ARE LONG-distance migrants, and their wings, relatively longer than those of gamebird relatives indicate this fact. They are, in effect, miniature partridges, and are easily confused, should you see them, with young partridges. More often the distinctive call is the only indication of their presence.

The 1988-91 *Atlas* included a 'quail year' in 1989, when instead of a few birds calling in Dorset and Wiltshire there was evidence of breeding in 233 10-km (6-mile) squares, and quail were present in another 571 squares. Male quail arrive first, set up territory, often among winter wheat, and call distinctively, with a sound that is often represented as 'wet-my-lips'.

SIZE

IDENTIFICATION

HABITAT

POPULATION

MAP

Top
Arable landscape is the preferred habitat of quail, but they are almost impossible to spot.

Bottom left and right
The tiny quail likes to skulk close to the ground, under cover and seldom flies, except on migration.

Corncrake

26 cm (11 in)

```
○○○○○○○○○○○○○○○○○○○○○○○○
      S P E C I E S   I N F O R M A T I O N
SCIENTIFIC NAME   Crex crex
RELATED SPECIES   Other crakes, Water Rail
CALL              Male has rasping 'rerrp-rerrp', often continuing for
                  hours, by night as well as in the daytime
HABITAT           Damp grassland, traditionally-cropped hay
                  meadows; also in crops such as cereals, lucerne and
                  clover
STATUS            Summer visitor. Mainly C and E Europe. In BI
                  highly endangered and declining (about 450 pairs);
                  mainly in Ireland and Hebrides. Populations in
                  decline following habitat destruction, and
                  mechanised hay-gathering
```

SLIM, LONG-LEGGED. Upperparts light grey-brown, with dark brown streaks on back. Flight ungainly and fluttering with trailing legs and showing chestnut wings. Rarely seen, as usually remains hidden in vegetation.

RICHARD JEFFERIES writing in 1879 told how 'the grass in the meadow or home field as it begins to grow tall is soon visited by the corncrakes, who take up their residence there. In this district they generally arrive about the time when it has grown sufficiently high and thick to hide their motions. This desire for concealment is apparently more marked in them than in any other bird; yet they utter their loud call of "crake, crake, crake!" not unlike the turning of a wooden rattle, continuously.'

It is not hiding now that makes corncrakes hard to see, for it is almost gone from Ireland, and only the activities of the RSPB and crofters allow it to maintain a precarious hold in Hebridean machair.

> '*In the valley a corncrake calls*
> *Monotonously*
> *With a plaintive unalterable voice, that deadens*
> *My confident activity.*'
> D. H. Lawrence
> END OF ANOTHER HOME HOLIDAY

SIZE

IDENTIFICATION

HABITAT

POPULATION

MAP

The persistent, rasping song of the corncrake has almost disappeared from our countryside now that this fascinating bird has become such a rarity.

Spotted Crake

23 cm (9 in)

SPECIES INFORMATION	
SCIENTIFIC NAME	Porzana porzana
RELATED SPECIES	Other crakes, Water Rail
CALL	Male's spring song is characteristic – a short, repeated, 'huitt', like a whiplash, usually at dusk and at night. Other sounds include 'keck' or growling 'brurr'
HABITAT	Fenland, edges of rivers and lakes, particularly where reeds give way to sedges; also in wet meadows and ditch margins
STATUS	Resident in south of range, summer visitor further north (including BI). Most of Europe, except far north and south. Rare and decreasing, absent over large areas. In BI a rare breeder (about 20 pairs)

SIZE

IDENTIFICATION

HABITAT

POPULATION

MAP

SMALL MARSH BIRD, scarcely as big as blackbird, with dark, speckled plumage. Flanks barred white; undertail coverts yellowish. Bill much shorter than water rail's. Juveniles have whiter chin and paler undersides. Very rarely seen; lives in thick vegetation.

> 'Impossible little brutes to see'
> John Buxton about the Norfolk Broads (1950)

IF THE BIRD IS seen, running away perhaps, the undertail coverts will not be as white as those of water rail, and the white freckles over the body plumage might be seen. With a better view, short yellowish bill with orange patch at base and yellow legs are very different.

Spotted crakes are summer visitors and probably were common when Britain and Ireland were wetter. By the time of the *New Atlas* there was breeding evidence from 11 squares, mainly in Cambridgeshire and eastern Scotland, and in 1989 there had been 21 singing males at ten sites.

Modern technology has come into crake-watching, and among the incredible crake numbers on the Ouse and Nene Washes in 1998, 15 were heard on one night, and two were caught and radio-tagged so that their use of the habitat could be investigated. They were followed for six weeks.

Spotted crakes rarely show themselves in the open, preferring to stay hidden in swamp vegetation. They dip around the river banks and are rarely seen.

SIZE
IDENTIFICATION
HABITAT
POPULATION
MAP

SPECIES INFORMATION

SCIENTIFIC NAME	Burhinus oedicnemus
RELATED SPECIES	None in region
CALL	Curlew-like, fluting 'keerlee'; often as duet at dusk; flight-call 'gigigigigi'
HABITAT	Dry, open heathy areas with sparse plant cover and sandy or stony soil and low vegetation. Sometimes on arable fields. Occasional at coast during migration
STATUS	Resident in south Mediterranean, summer visitor elsewhere. Patchy distribution in west, central and south Europe (mainly Spain, Portugal and France). Absent from north Europe (including Ireland). Rare breeder in Britain (about 150 pairs).

Stone Curlew

43 cm (17 in)

LARGE WADER WITH short bill, large yellow eyes and long, relatively thick, yellow legs. In flight shows double white wing bars and black and white primaries.

its eggs are well camouflaged. Another factor may be the tendency for free-draining soils to warm up early in the spring, and hence to have enhanced availability of the invertebrates upon which stone curlews feed. Many of the remaining patches of open ground with sparse vegetation only survive because of the activities of the military on Salisbury Plain and Breckland.

THEY ARE LARGE-HEADED, long-tailed, thick-kneed birds with a striking wing pattern. In flight the black flight feathers contrast with the white patches on the primaries. Lovely though they are to see, their magic stems from the wailing calls which are striking by day, but positively haunting as dusk falls and the birds call in chorus.

More often heard than seen; secretive in behaviour and highly camouflaged in plumage. As T. A. Coward wrote in 1950, they are hard to see as 'from egg onward the life of the stone curlew is spent in hiding itself from view'.

There are two main population centres – the Breckland of Suffolk and Norfolk, and an area centred on Salisbury Plain. Stone curlew like free-draining, sandy soils with a high proportion of chalk rubble or flints, giving a background upon which the bird and

> '*He begins with the witching hour when the sun is down but the light not yet quite gone, the hour when the older shrubs and juniper bushes seem to take on uncanny shapes of things that do not appear in the hard light of day. Then from one side of the valley the quiet cour-lee steals forth, to be taken up afar by another bird out upon its evening business.*'
>
> G. K. Yeates
> BIRD HAUNTS IN SOUTHERN ENGLAND

Top
The stone curlew at its nest in completely open country.

Middle
Although it often squats down low, the stone curlew has quite long legs.

Bottom
Stone curlew spend much of their time sitting very still, relying on camouflage for protection.

Dotterel

21 cm (8.5 in)

SIZE

IDENTIFICATION

HABITAT

POPULATION

MAP

SPECIES INFORMATION	
SCIENTIFIC NAME	Charadrius morinellus
RELATED SPECIES	Ringed Plover, Little Ringed Plover, Kentish Plover
CALL	Flight-call 'kirr' or 'plitt'. Song a repeated 'pit-pit-pit', in display flight
HABITAT	Breeds on open tundra or mountain tops. Outside breeding season seen in small groups on dry, rocky areas, short pasture and on river banks
STATUS	Summer visitor. Regularly seen on passage at traditional sites. Breeds in northern Scandinavia, northern Britain (mainly Scottish Highlands). Also in a few places in the Alps, Apennines, and, more recently, on the Netherlands coast. British population about 900 pairs

PROMINENT WHITE STRIPE above eye, meeting behind head to form V-shape. Female slightly larger and more colourful than male. Black belly in breeding plumage. In winter much paler with yellow-grey upperparts, white belly and less clear breast band and eye-stripe. Dumpy and short-tailed in flight, with no wing bar. Often very approachable.

THE FEMALE IS the more highly coloured and larger of the pair, and she takes the initiative in the establishment of territory. White face and eye-stripe, dark cap, pinkish-grey chest with narrow black and white bands above makes for a mosaic of colour that is hard to describe. The yellow legs, white eye-stripes and chest band are present in all plumages, but non-breeding birds are far from conspicuous when they turn up on grassy hills, poor agricultural land or coastal heaths. These migrant birds winter in the Middle East and North Africa.

Brewer's Dictionary of Phrase and Fable tells us that a dotterel is a doting old fool, an old man easily cajoled, and this plover is so called as it is easily approached. Despite this tameness, dotterel are not easy to count, partly, as Ratcliffe says, because their nesting habitat includes some of the bleakest terrain in our country – the windswept summit plateaux or broad ridges and upper spurs of the higher hills. Here the ground cover is sparse, with moss carpets, lichen heaths or open stony fell-fields. Sometimes the males, which do the incubating, sit tight until almost trodden upon. Knowledge of past population levels are sketchy and contradictory, but it seems now that almost 1,000 pairs may breed in Scotland. A further complication is that some birds attempt to breed in Norway and Scotland in the same year.

Right
Young dotterel can be hard to spot in rocky terrain.

Left
In all plumages, the broad white eyestripe is a tell-tale feature.

Red-necked Phalarope

18 cm (7 in)

SMALL, DELICATE WADER with fine, needle-like bill. Female has showy breeding plumage, with white chin and bright rust-brown band at sides of neck and breast. Male less colourful. Winter plumage is grey with dark on top of head and dark patch through eye. In flight shows prominent white wing bar. Often swims when feeding, turning abruptly on its own axis to stir up food items from sediment.

 SIZE

 IDENTIFICATION

 HABITAT

 POPULATION

 MAP

Top
With phalaropes, it is the male which sits on the eggs and cares for the young.

Middle
Phalaropes swim and dabble in shallow pools.

Bottom
The female has the brightest colours in the breeding season.

327

Roseate Tern

36 cm (14 in)

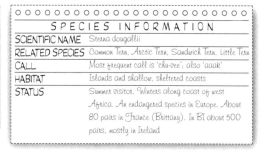

SPECIES INFORMATION	
SCIENTIFIC NAME	Sterna dougallii
RELATED SPECIES	Common Tern, Arctic Tern, Sandwich Tern, Little Tern
CALL	Most frequent call is 'chu-vee'; also 'aaak'
HABITAT	Islands and shallow, sheltered coasts
STATUS	Summer visitor. Winters along coast of west Africa. An endangered species in Europe. About 80 pairs in France (Brittany). In BI about 500 pairs, mostly in Ireland

SIZE

IDENTIFICATION

HABITAT

POPULATION

MAP

DIFFICULT TO DISTINGUISH from common and arctic terns, but paler grey above, and with faint rose tinge to belly in breeding season. Tail streamers extend well beyond wing-tips when sitting, like arctic, but legs are longer. Bill mainly black, and usually only red towards base.

However, it is rarely as rosy as some illustrations make out, and the amount of red on the mainly black bill varies: all red is lost after breeding. The call is said to be distinctive, but the impression of greater whiteness and the very long streamers are probably the best field characters.

The roseate differs from the similar common and Arctic terns in having a mainly black bill, and longer tail streamers.

Black Tern

23 cm (9 in)

SMALL TERN, WITH very dark breeding plumage; head and upperparts grey-black, wings light grey, above and below. With its forked tail, looks rather like a large, dark swallow. In winter white below, with dark on top of head. Juveniles similar, but darker above, and with dark mark on body near base of wing. Hovers and skims water, taking prey from surface.

WHEN THE EAST ANGLIAN fens were more extensive, black terns bred in good numbers. They are, therefore, one of our lost breeding birds, except for an occasional success in sites such as the Ouse Washes.

Black terns are one of the marsh terns, liking fresh or brackish waters with plenty of vegetation and insects and perhaps amphibian and fish food. Most of the birds we see are on migration, with more in autumn, when they are certainly not black.

Spring passage birds are black, or rather dark grey, with whitish underwing coverts, and a rather square tail. Small and slim, they dip down to the surface of the water of lakes, reservoirs or estuaries to pick up insects or crustaceans. At any other time look for the long, slim bill, blackish shoulder smudge and grey rump and tail. Black terns may also be seen during seawatches as they head for coastal areas in tropical west Africa.

White-winged black tern, *Chlidonias leucopterus*, is similar, but with more contrast in plumage, a whiter rump (also a white leading edge to wing), and black underwing coverts. Rare vagrant to BI (mainly May–September) from breeding grounds North of the Black Sea.

SIZE

IDENTIFICATION

HABITAT

POPULATION

MAP

Top
The white-winged black tern breeds in eastern Europe and is a rare vagrant to Britain.

Middle and bottom
Black terns are dainty birds with a hovering flight pattern.

Ring-necked Parakeet

40 cm (16 in)

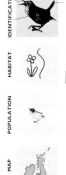

UNMISTAKABLE, WITH GREEN plumage and long tail. Flies fast and straight, usually singly or in small groups.

FIRST RECORDED IN 1969, it has spread and increased steadily. Although not featured in detail in the original *Atlas of Breeding Birds*, it had a page to itself by the time of the *Winter Atlas*. The populations are mainly in suburban areas, indicating its dependence on man for survival in this northern environment. It seems to manage well, even in hard winter weather.

It nests in holes, and therefore might compete with owls, jackdaws and woodpeckers, but there is no evidence that they are harming the prospects of any of these birds.

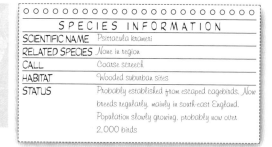

SPECIES INFORMATION	
SCIENTIFIC NAME	Psittacula krameri
RELATED SPECIES	None in region
CALL	Coarse screech
HABITAT	Wooded suburban sites
STATUS	Probably established from escaped cagebirds. Now breeds regularly, mainly in south-east England. Population slowly growing, probably now over 2,000 birds

Snowy Owl

55–65 cm (22–26 in)

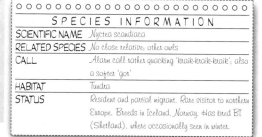

VERY LARGE AND white (male) or white with black flecks (female). Flies powerfully on rather pointed wings.

There is always the chance that this magnificent predator will breed again in northern Scotland, but at present it is only a rare visitor.

SPECIES INFORMATION	
SCIENTIFIC NAME	Nyctea scandiaca
RELATED SPECIES	No close relative; other owls
CALL	Alarm call rather quacking 'kraik-kraik-kraik'; also a softer 'gor'
HABITAT	Tundra
STATUS	Resident and partial migrant. Rare visitor to northern Europe. Breeds in Iceland, Norway. Has bred BI (Shetland), where occasionally seen in winter.

SPECIES INFORMATION

SCIENTIFIC NAME	*Phoenicurus ochruros*
RELATED SPECIES	Redstart
CALL	Alarm call 'hit-tek-tek'. Song is a short, rapid phrase, starting with 'jizz-ti-ti-ti-ti', and ending with a scratchy sound, a bit like sliding gravel
HABITAT	On buildings in towns, villages and even in the centres of cities. Original habitat is mountain rocks and scree to over 3,000 m (10,000 ft) – now mainly in south of range
STATUS	Resident in south and west of range; summer visitor to north and east. Breeds in most of Europe, except for the far north and east. In BI about 100 pairs, mainly in the south (absent from Ireland)

Black Redstart

14.5 cm (5.5 in)

MALE HAS DARK, sooty plumage with a pale wing-patch, and red rump and tail. Females are dusky grey-brown rather than dusky black, as are immatures, who also lack the white wing-panel of males.

OVER MUCH OF its range it favours cliffs and boulder-strewn terrain, but the presence of many potential nesting sites in walls and roofs of buildings has also led to a close association with people. Building sites often have weedy and bare areas as well as song-posts to recommend them.

Black redstarts attracted attention when they moved into London bombsites in the late 1940s, but their colonisation of Britain as breeding birds had started earlier. Taking examples from *Birds of the London Area* some salient stages in the London story appear. The book claims 'London is the metropolis not only of man but of the black redstart in the British Isles. The story begins with three pairs taking up their abode within the Palace of Engineering in (1926) the year after the end of the Wembley Exhibition, and nesting on breeze-slab ledges about 18 feet from the ground every year... until 1941. In 1940 came the first breeding record for inner London, when a pair brought off two broods within the precincts of Westminster Abbey, and at least five other cocks were reported to be holding territories.'

The hoped for take-off in numbers, which might have led to colonisation of towns and villages as on the continent, has not occurred, but three pairs have recently (January 1998) turned up to interfere with work on the Millennium Dome.

David Glue, in his introduction to the species in the 1993 *Atlas* writes: 'The flash of bright orange-chestnut quivering tail announces the welcome spring arrival of a full-plumage male black redstart to brighten a scattering of built up environments. Others betray their presence through a scolding "tucc tucc" alarm call, still more by the short warbling song with characteristic metallic terminal flourish.'

Whereas breeding areas tend to be in the east of England, it often winters in the south-west, where it is closely associated with the sea. Cliffs have their own microclimate, as do city centres, and for a bird at the edge of its range this extra warmth may be important.

SIZE

IDENTIFICATION

HABITAT

POPULATION

MAP

Top
Black redstart are often now found in a typically urban setting.

Bottom
Sea-cliffs provide another suitable habitat for this species in some areas along the coast.

Cetti's Warbler

14 cm (5.5 in)

SPECIES INFORMATION

SCIENTIFIC NAME	Cettia cetti
RELATED SPECIES	No close relative
CALL	A very distinctive, rather explosive, loud and abrupt 'chut-chut-chutti-chutti-chutti', usually delivered from dense cover
HABITAT	Damp, overgrown habitats such as fen carr, swamps and ditches
STATUS	Resident. Breeds mainly in south and south-west Europe. Rare breeder in Britain, Netherlands, Belgium, and Switzerland. In B about 450 pairs, in south England and Wales. Absent from Ireland

CHESTNUT AND GREY warbler, with rather rounded tail. More often heard than seen. The male is some 30 per cent heavier than the female, and another strange feature is that the eggs are bright red. The rounded tail and dark chestnut upper parts can help separation from other reedbed warblers.

VERY DIFFICULT TO see among the reeds, and other dense vegetation. This interesting species has colonised the south of England and Wales, since the early 1970s, and now breeds locally in suitable sites. Suffers badly in hard winters, like Dartford warbler, which is another rare resident warbler at the edge of its range.

Savi's Warbler

14 cm (5.5 in)

SPECIES INFORMATION

SCIENTIFIC NAME	Locustella luscinioides
RELATED SPECIES	Grasshopper Warbler, River Warbler (rare vagrant)
CALL	Alarm call a short 'tsik'. Song reeling: shorter, faster and deeper than grasshopper warbler's, often beginning with accelerating ticking notes: 'tik-tik-tik-tik...'
HABITAT	Mainly reedbeds. Sometimes in rushes, and at overgrown lake margins
STATUS	Summer visitor. Mainly central, south and east Europe (notably Hungary and Romania). In Britain about 15 pairs, mainly in the south-east (absent from Ireland)

TAIL BROAD, ROUNDED and graduated. Plumage is unstreaked, rather like nightingale (but without chestnut on tail), or a dark reed warbler; inconspicuous stripe over eye.

THIS REEDBED BIRD, sounding rather more insect-like than the grasshopper warbler, disappeared from England for almost a hundred years, but finally returned in 1954. It broadly resembles the reed warbler but is in fact related to the grasshopper warbler.

The closely related river warbler, *Locustella fluviatilis* is a rare vagrant. It breeds in East Europe (mainly Poland and Hungary), West to Germany. Unstreaked above, but with spotted or streaked breast.

SPECIES INFORMATION

SCIENTIFIC NAME	Acrocephalus palustris
RELATED SPECIES	Reed Warbler, Sedge Warbler, Aquatic Warbler
CALL	Alarm-call 'tschak'. Song is loud, pleasant and very varied, mixed with squeaking and rattling notes: an unstructured medley, famously incorporating much mimicry. Often sings at night
HABITAT	Lush scrub near water, in tall-herb communities and nettle-beds
STATUS	Summer visitor. Mainly C and NE Europe. In B only about 12 pairs (but varies from year to year). Absent from Ireland

Marsh Warbler
13 cm (5 in)

 SIZE

 IDENTIFICATION

 HABITAT

 POPULATION

MAP

VERY LIKE REED warbler, except for song. More olive-brown above and not quite so flat-headed.

MARSH WARBLERS ARE said to mimic 70 different species, from summer and winter haunts, in half an hour's singing. In addition, they blend these into their song, which is of striking beauty and vivacity.

Marsh warblers like sites with dense vegetation – such as nettles, meadow-sweet, umbellifers and willow-herbs. Plenty of such habitat is available, and the rarity of this species is something of a mystery. The main areas for breeding marsh warblers are now the Severn and Avon valleys in Worcestershire, and, more recently, Kent.

SPECIES INFORMATION

SCIENTIFIC NAME	Loxia scotica
RELATED SPECIES	Common Crossbill, Parrot Crossbill
CALL	Flight-call 'chip-chip-chip'
HABITAT	Scottish pine woods
STATUS	Resident. About 1,500 birds

Scottish Crossbill
17.5 cm (7 in)

 SIZE

 IDENTIFICATION

 HABITAT

 POPULATION

 MAP

THE SCOTTISH CROSSBILL is very similar to the common crossbill, but is slightly larger, and it has a somewhat heavier bill. It breeds only in the ancient Scots pine woods of the highlands of Scotland. It is Britain's only endemic species.

THE PARROT CROSSBILL, *Loxia pytyopsittacus*, is slightly larger, at 18 cm (7 in), with an even heavier bill. It breeds in north-east Europe, but has bred in East Anglia. It feeds mainly on pine seeds and, like a parrot, breaks a cone with its beak, then holds it with one leg to empty the contents.

Firecrest

9 cm (3.5 in)

○ ○

SPECIES INFORMATION

SCIENTIFIC NAME	Regulus ignicapillus
RELATED SPECIES	Goldcrest
CALL	Very high-pitched, sharp 'see-seesee'. Song is a high-pitched crescendo of rather similar notes: 'see-see-see-see-See-See-Sirrr'
HABITAT	Breeds in coniferous forest, but also found in parks, gardens and scrub
STATUS	Resident and partial migrant. Summer visitor in north of range. Mainly central and southern Europe. In BI a varying population of about 50 pairs, mainly in south and east (absent from Scotland and Ireland)

SIZE

IDENTIFICATION

HABITAT

POPULATION

MAP

SAME SIZE AND shape as goldcrest, but has black stripe through the eye and white stripe over the eye. Male has orange-red crown, female yellow. Juvenile lacks head markings, but has dark eye-stripe.

IN MOST RESPECTS firecrests are much like goldcrests, but a good view shows their beauty, with brighter plumage, striped head with white eye-stripe, and bronze shoulder patch. They are less committed to conifers than goldcrests, but some of the recently colonised British sites are in spruce, while others are in oak, beech and holly. To spot breeding birds the persistent, high-pitched song needs to be recognised.

Between the two *Breeding Atlases*, the firecrest had made large gains, with breeding records into Wales and as far as the Mersey, but the concentrations were in seven main areas: the New Forest, south-east Kent and the Suffolk coast. These birds would seem to be summer visitors wintering in the western Mediterranean.

The *Winter Atlas* shows a very different pattern, with a majority along the south coast and in the west country. Writing there, Marchant, who is obviously a firecrest enthusiast, says the places to look are in sheltered scrub or woodland edge near the coast. Many such sites hold small parties.

Top and bottom right
Firecrests are difficult to pick out as they flit amongst the branches, often in the company of goldcrests or tits in autumn or winter.

Bottom left
Look for the obvious eyestripe, which is characteristic.

SPECIES INFORMATION	
SCIENTIFIC NAME	Parus cristatus
RELATED SPECIES	Blue Tit, Great Tit, Coal Tit, Marsh Tit, Willow Tit
CALL	Alarm call 'tzee-tzee-gurrr-r'. Song is similar to call, at alternating pitches
HABITAT	Pine, spruce or fir forests. In Britain, restricted to native Scots pine forests of the Scottish highlands and mature pine plantations of the Moray coast
STATUS	Resident. Breeds throughout Europe, except far N. and much of SE. In BI about 900 pairs (Scotland only)

Crested Tit

11.5 cm (4.5 in)

SIZE

IDENTIFICATION

HABITAT

POPULATION

MAP

BROWN ABOVE, whitish below, with cream coloured flanks, and black and white speckled crest. Juveniles have shorter crests.

THE BACKWARD POINTING crest is unique among our small passerines, giving it a distinctive silhouette. The crest is black and white, the patterned head with black 'C' on the ear coverts is also black and white, and the rest brown and white or brown and buff. It often draws attention to itself with its trilling, rolling call, which acts as a contact and alarm call.

Although widespread in Europe, in Spanish cork oak, Pyrenean beech, or other mixed southern woods, it prefers pine forest in Scotland. There it does also breed in pine plantations, but as a highly sedentary species any spread is slow, and the extensive mature and native pine along Deeside in Aberdeen has not been colonised. Martin Cook in the *New Atlas* asks, were they never there, is there some subtle ecological factor missing, or is it just the difficulty of dispersion across difficult ground?

The ecological conditions that do favour crested tits are extensive needle canopy, sufficient light to support ground cover or heather, and dead stumps for the excavation of nest holes. As with other tits, different times of year demand different feeding strategies, including the storage of seeds from pine cones, secreted under lichens on the branches.

Top right
Crested tits dig their nest holes in dead tree stumps.

Top left and bottom
This species is well named, as it has a prominent crest at all times of the year.

Golden Oriole

24 cm (9.5 in)

○ ○

SPECIES INFORMATION

SCIENTIFIC NAME	*Oriolus oriolus*
RELATED SPECIES	*None in region*
CALL	*Call harsh 'kraa', or cat-like mewing. Song is a clear, plaintive, fluting whistle: 'peeloo-peeleoo'*
HABITAT	*Deciduous woods, parks, plantations (often poplar)*
STATUS	*Summer visitor. Throughout Europe except far N and NW. In B about 40 pairs, mainly in SE England (absent from Ireland).*

SIZE

IDENTIFICATION

HABITAT

POPULATION

MAP

BEAUTIFUL, WITH (MALE) bright yellow body and mainly black wings and tail. Female is green and yellow. Flight undulating (female can be confused with green woodpecker in flight).

FOR A LARGE, brightly-coloured bird, the golden oriole is notoriously hard to see. As the *New Atlas* says: 'in spite of the male's bright yellow and black plumage, the golden oriole is a bird more often heard than seen, even where it is known to have a nest. When eventually seen it is arguably one of the most spectacular of British breeding passerines. The female is a much duller green and black and is far more difficult to see against a leafy background. The cat like contact squawk or alarm call is the best indication that a bird is present.'

Golden orioles reach Britain mostly during early May, arriving all along the coasts from Cornwall to Suffolk, and then filter northwards to varying degrees. Many of these will be non-breeding first-year males.

The RSPB and the Golden Oriole Group monitor population levels in their stronghold of the East Anglian fens, and at the time of the *New Atlas* were hoping to promote the planting of new poplar cultivars, suitable both for commercial use and for golden orioles. In 1990 there were ten confirmed and 32 possible breeding pairs, but only 7–11 young were reared in 1995 because of bad weather.

A candidate for being one of our most beautiful birds, the male golden oriole looks quite stunning, and also has an attractive fluting call.

SPECIES INFORMATION

SCIENTIFIC NAME	Serinus serinus
RELATED SPECIES	None in immediate region; Citril Finch, Canary
CALL	Flight-call high-pitched trilling 'tiu-ri-lillit'. Song is a high-pitched, rapid, jingling twitter
HABITAT	Parks, gardens, orchards and vineyards
STATUS	Resident in southern Europe; summer visitor further north. Breed in central and southern Europe; absent from most of north and north-west Europe. In BI about five pairs (south and south-east England)

Serin

11 cm (4.25 in)

SIZE

IDENTIFICATION

HABITAT

POPULATION

MAP

THE SMALLEST EUROPEAN finch, with a very short bill, yellow head and breast (male), and streaked flanks. Female more grey-green. Shows yellow rump in flight.

THIS BOUNCY CHARACTER is everywhere on the continent, with its wheezy jingle-jangle song and erratic display flight making it a most conspicuous bird.

Since its range has now extended to northern France and southern Scandinavia, for a long time people have been predicting its arrival in Britain as a regular breeding bird, but it seems stubbornly unable to make the necessary leap across the channel.

The first *Breeding Atlas* (1976) had a map to show it spread across Europe from a Spanish and Italian base in 1800, until it had reached north and east to France, except Brittany, and southern Scandinavia by 1970. There had been some 185 occurrences in Britain by 1974, including two confirmed breeding reports. The *Winter Atlas* only had records from four 10-km(6-mile) squares, and the 1993 *Breeding Atlas* mentioned breeding pairs in Devon in the early 1980s, and the successful colonisation of Jersey.

The serin is rather like a tiny canary. Its hurried, jingling song is a characteristic sound further south in Europe, though rarely heard in the British Isles.

Snow Bunting

17 cm (6.5 in)

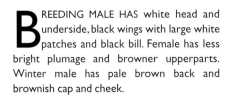

○○○○○○○○○○○○○○○○○○○○○○○○○○
SPECIES INFORMATION

SCIENTIFIC NAME	Plectrophenax nivalis
RELATED SPECIES	No close relative: other buntings
CALL	Flight-call a trilling 'tirr'. Song simple and tinkling
HABITAT	High mountains and tundra. Regular on north European coasts in winter, on open areas with low vegetation
STATUS	Resident in Iceland and Scotland. Elsewhere mainly summer visitor, wintering to shores of north and north-west Europe, and further inland in eastern Europe. In BI about 80 pairs (Scotland only)

SIZE

IDENTIFICATION

HABITAT

POPULATION

MAP

BREEDING MALE HAS white head and underside, black wings with large white patches and black bill. Female has less bright plumage and browner upperparts. Winter male has pale brown back and brownish cap and cheek.

THE MALE IS predominately white, strikingly pied on back and wings. The female is also white below, but has grey head and dark streaked back. More of us will see them not in the mountains in summer but perhaps on winter hilltops, or more likely on east coast saltmarshes or shores. On the ground they may not appear as bright as in summer, but as soon as a party takes wing; flickering and drifting, the white tail and wing markings inevitably remind the observer of a blizzard of snowflakes. When settled, they run fast and use their orange beaks to collect seeds, and when they fly again the musical rippled twitter is as attractive as the flying bird.

Derek Ratcliffe writes: 'last of the high mountain breeders in Britain, but by far the rarest and most elusive. This is a true Arctic species, with a virtually continuous circumpolar distribution'. Those breeding in Iceland, Scotland and southern Scandinavia, are more or less sedentary in winter, when the coastal migrants probably consist mainly of birds from northern Europe and perhaps Greenland.

Their summer haunts in the Highlands are the upper slopes with boulders and rocky outcrops, where snow patches linger in sheltered spots until late in summer, or may even last the whole year through. The nest sites are deep inside crannies among the rocks.

Nethersole Thompson found that male snow buntings, which go through the motions of territorial behaviour, are concerned more with seeking and holding a mate than with defence of an area. In the Cairngorms it is usual for there to be surplus, unpaired cock buntings, which continue to sing and display, often ranging over large areas, while paired birds have eggs or young.

Top
A female snow bunting approaches its nest amongst the rocks.

Middle
Snow buntings can sometimes be seen along the sea shore in winter.

Bottom
Female snow bunting feeding her young in a nest in a craggy rockface.

SPECIES INFORMATION	
SCIENTIFIC NAME	Emberiza cirlus
RELATED SPECIES	Yellowhammer, Reed Bunting
CALL	Call a high-pitched 'tsiih'. Rattling song, somewhat reminiscent of lesser whitethroat's, but higher-pitched and more ringing, often all on one note
HABITAT	Open, bushy country with isolated trees; vineyards, avenues of trees, gardens
STATUS	Resident. Mainly S and SW Europe. In B about 300 pairs in SW England, and a few in Cornwall and Jersey (absent from Ireland)

Cirl Bunting

16 cm (6.5 in)

MALE YELLOW BELOW, with greenish breast-band and yellow and black markings on head and neck. Female much drabber, rather like female yellowhammer, but with less yellow and with greybrown (not chestnut) rump.

MALES START SINGING their rapid rattling song reminiscent of the lesser whitethroat in mid-March. They become more conspicuous, often perching openly but, even then, only a head may protrude from the tip of a tree. At other times, cirl buntings are often secretive in tree cover but will feed in the open for winter seeds.

'A map of the Roman Empire would give a tolerable idea of the distribution of the cirl bunting', wrote Nicholson. 'It is a bird of the Mediterranean but spreads some way across Asia Minor, up the Danube valley and through the mildest parts of western Europe. Like the Roman colonists it conveys an impression of tolerating best the most benign and genial spots in this dank northern island, in which it reaches both the most northerly and most westerly points of its breeding range.' He finds it difficult to define their exacting tastes. 'Their choice seems to fall not on a particular type of country but on the kind of spot to which a discriminating man might wish to retire after spending a good deal of his life in some much warmer climate than ours.'

A bit earlier than that the *Handbook* had given a map of cirl bunting distribution, with the bird widely distributed in north Wales, the Malvern–Cheltenham area, and from Cornwall to Kent, with an extension northwards into the Chilterns. Earlier in the century it had extended to Yorkshire and Cumberland. Now this attractive species is restricted to an area centred on south Devon, and it is counted amongst one of our rarest breeding birds.

The RSPB Cirl Bunting Project provides advice to land managers on beneficial management, and grants available, through site visits, demonstration sites and publications. The project officer draws up management plans and helps with grant applications that will benefit cirl buntings and other farmland wildlife. Of particular importance has been the MAFF Countryside Stewardship Scheme, which gives payment for provision of stubbles, vitally important for birds during the winter months. Cirl buntings seem to require weed-rich stubble fields in the winter months, a habitat which has declined considerably.

Top and bottom right
Black chin and dark eyestripe distinguish the male cirl bunting, but it is hard to spot in among the branches.

Bottom left
South-facing farmland in the south west of England provides some suitable sites for this rare breeding bird.

Great Northern Diver

69–91 cm (27–36 in)

SPECIES INFORMATION	
SCIENTIFIC NAME	*Gavia immer*
RELATED SPECIES	Red-throated Diver, Black-throated Diver
CALL	Silent; in flight a barking 'kwuk'
HABITAT	Rivers and large freshwater lakes
STATUS	Winter visitor to coastal waters, may remain for summer months and has bred, but rarely, in Scotland

SIZE

IDENTIFICATION

HABITAT

POPULATION

MAP

L ARGER, AND WITH heavier bill than red- and black-throated. Seen mainly in winter on coasts of north-western Europe. Usually seen at sea where they look really bulky, with heavy heads and powerful bills, and in winter with a dark crown and white throat. A comparison with other divers may be helpful.

THE GREAT NORTHERN DIVER has a steep forehead, with a dark collar that is almost complete. The back is slate-grey and covered with large spots. Preferred habitat is large lakes in remote areas during the summer months and they are often seen off sea coasts in the summer. The **black-throated diver** shows a clear contrast between white front and dark back of the neck. The **red-throated diver** has a whiter neck and face, and an upturned bill.

SPECIES INFORMATION

SCIENTIFIC NAME	Podiceps grisegena
RELATED SPECIES	Great Crested, Slavonian and Black-necked Grebes
CALL	A loud, whinnying display call; sharp alarm call 'eck-eck-eck'. Usually silent in winter
HABITAT	Breeds on reedy, shallower lakes. In winter on lakes and coastal sea, occasionally on rivers
STATUS	Breeds mainly eastern Europe, to Denmark and north Germany

Red-necked Grebe

46 cm (18 in)

MORE COMPACT THAN great crested grebe, with shorter, thicker neck. In breeding plumage has rusty-red neck, white cheeks and throat and a black bill, yellow towards base. In winter plumage very like great crested, but with greyer neck and lacking the white stripe over the eye.

THE GREAT CRESTED GREBE is pale of plumage, with a long white neck. The flanks are pale brown and the back is dark grey. They are found in shallow waters such as large lakes with plants emerging from them, normally at low levels. Their courtship is intricate; they make extravagant use of their head plumes. The red-necked grebe has a yellow bill, with a medium-length neck, and is only slightly smaller than great crested. The **Slavonian grebe** is black and white, with a flat forehead. It is of medium size, between little grebe and great crested. The **black-necked grebe** is fairly uniform in colour, with a steep forehead, and is slightly longer than the little grebe.

SIZE

IDENTIFICATION

HABITAT

POPULATION

MAP

The red-necked grebe winters in the British Isles sometimes, but still not in large numbers. It does not have the crest of the crested grebe.

341

Purple Heron

75–85 cm (30–33 in)

SPECIES INFORMATION

SCIENTIFIC NAME	Ardea purpurea
RELATED SPECIES	Grey Heron.
CALL	Flight-call rather higher pitched than Grey Heron's
HABITAT	Extensive reedbeds; marshy areas with thick scrub
STATUS	Summer visitor. Breeds mainly in southern Europe, but north to Holland. Rare, but regular, visitor, mainly to SE England

SIZE

IDENTIFICATION

HABITAT

POPULATION

MAP

SLIMMER AND LONGER-NECKED than grey heron; plumage very dark, especially in flight. Often holds neck in snake-like curve (neck looks angular in flight). Juveniles paler, lacking black head and neck markings; easily confused with grey heron from a distance.

Night Heron

58–65 cm (23–26 in)

SPECIES INFORMATION

SCIENTIFIC NAME	Nycticorax nycticorax
RELATED SPECIES	Other herons
CALL	
HABITAT	Reedbeds, marshes
STATUS	Rare in northern and central Europe, with a few small colonies in Holland and southern Germany; somewhat commoner in Hungary and Czechoslovakia. Vagrant to Britain

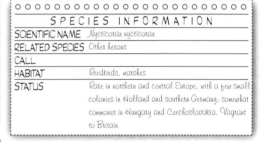

SMALLISH HERON, GREY and black (juvenile brown).

AS ITS NAME suggests, the night heron spends its days hidden in cover and is nocturnal. Although it can be seen feeding during the day the bird leaves its roost a dusk, setting out to hunt for food and thus avoids competition with diurnal heron species.

The night heron's bill is very thick, wide and rather short, this relates directly to its feeding habits as its varied diet includes not only fish, frogs and insects but even the chicks of marsh birds. The adult is balck on crown and back, wings are dove-grey and underparts white with yellowish legs and large reddish eyes. A vagrant from southern Europe.

SPECIES INFORMATION

SCIENTIFIC NAME	Ixobrychus minutus
RELATED SPECIES	Other herons
CALL	Flight-call a short, raw croak. Male also has low, repeated bark in breeding season
HABITAT	Thick reedbeds on lakes, damp, riverside willow scrub, marshes and flood-plain woods
STATUS	Summer visitor. Breeds in central and southern Europe. Local, and mostly commoner in the east of range. Vagrant to Britain (mainly in spring)

Little Bittern
33–38 cm (13–15 in)

EUROPE'S SMALLEST HERON. Male has dark cap and upperparts. Female less contrasting, streaked on neck, breast and flanks. Pale wings obvious in flight, especially in male. Flies low over reeds with rapid wing-beats, quickly diving down into fresh cover. Found in marshes, little bitterns climb up reed streams rather than walk along the floor of the reedbed. They migrate to Africa and spend the winter south of the Sahara and in Britain only odd birds turn up during migration

SPECIES INFORMATION

SCIENTIFIC NAME	Platalea leucorodia
RELATED SPECIES	None in region
CALL	Nasal grunts and wailing sounds at nest
HABITAT	Marshy areas, with reedbeds and shallow water
STATUS	Summer visitor (resident Spain). Often at coasts outside breeding season. Rare breeding bird in Holland, Austria, Hungary and Greece. Also SW Spain. Rare but regular visitor to Britain

Spoonbill
78–85 cm (31–33 in)

LONG SPOON-SHAPED bill with yellow tip. White plumage, with yellow-ochre chin. In breeding season has crest behind head and yellowish breast-band. Juveniles lack crest, yellow chin spot and breast-band, and wings have dark tips. In flight, head and neck outstretched; neck sagging slightly. Stands in water and sieves small animals by swishing bill from side to side. Flocks often fly in long lines or in V-formation.

White Stork

95–105 cm (37–41 in)

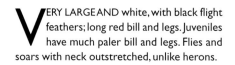

○○○○○○○○○○○○○○○○○○○○○○○○○○○

S P E C I E S   I N F O R M A T I O N

SCIENTIFIC NAME	Ciconia ciconia
RELATED SPECIES	Black Stork (even rarer visitor).
CALL	Noisy bill clapping during breeding displays. Occasional hissing.
HABITAT	Damp meadows and fields in open lowland.
STATUS	Summer visitor. Resident in S Spain and Portugal. Breeds mainly in NE Central Europe, and in SW Spain and Portugal.

VERY LARGE AND white, with black flight feathers; long red bill and legs. Juveniles have much paler bill and legs. Flies and soars with neck outstretched, unlike herons.

THE WHITE STORK breeds mainly on buildings and chimneys, often on a wheel provided specially for the birds. Sometimes nests in trees in river-valley woodland.

In western Europe has been decreasing markedly for decades, mainly because of habitat destruction, collisions with power lines and shooting in winter quarters. Occasional in Britain, and is found mainly April to August.

Crane

106–118 cm (42–46 in)

○○○○○○○○○○○○○○○○○○○○○○○○○○

S P E C I E S   I N F O R M A T I O N

SCIENTIFIC NAME	Grus grus
RELATED SPECIES	None in area
CALL	Loud bellowing or trumpeting call 'krooi-kruh', often in early morning.
HABITAT	Extensive wetlands, marshy lake margins, swampy woodland, bogs and isolated forest lakes. On migration also found in cultivated areas, or roosting on shallow water
STATUS	Summer visitor. Mainly in Scandinavia, N Germany, Poland and Baltic States. Irregular breeder in Britain (1–2 pairs)

TALL, ELEGANT, AND long-legged with long bill (but relatively shorter than heron or egret). Mainly grey, with black and white on head and neck. In flight neck is extended and legs trail well beyond tail. Migrating flocks often fly in wedge formation.

THROUGHOUT THE YEAR, especially during spring, close to their breeding grounds they perform a distinctive mating ritual in which they leap up with raised wings, their tail plumes fluffed and erect and trumpet loudly.

They breed in open bogs on marshland, where they also take insects and other animal food.

Lesser White-fronted Goose

53–66 cm (21–26 in)

SPECIES INFORMATION

SCIENTIFIC NAME	Anser erythropus
RELATED SPECIES	White-fronted Goose; other Anser geese
CALL	Higher-pitched than White-fronted Goose
HABITAT	Breeds in the tundra. In BI winters to estuaries and flooded fields
STATUS	Breeds in Siberia and far N of Scandinavia. Rare, yet regular, winter visitor to BI. Normally winters in Balkans

HAS A LARGER WHITE shield than its larger and much commoner relative. Smaller and shorter-necked, with rounder head and shorter bill. The white patch extends above eye, which has a characteristic yellow ring. Flight very agile. Numbers of these have risen dramatically in areas where hunting restrictions have been imposed, usch as in the Netherlands, Flanders and parts of Germany and the numbers wintering in Britain have remained stable.

RED-BREASTED GOOSE

Breeds in Siberian tundra; winters on estuaries and flooded fields, mainly around black sea. Very rare visitor to Britain, usually with barnacle geese. Small, mainly black and white, but with red breast and cheek-patch.

SNOW GOOSE

Very rare visitor from North America, but most are probably birds escaped from collections.

SIZE

IDENTIFICATION

HABITAT

POPULATION

MAP

These three species may be seen, though rarely, usually as single birds turning up in mixed flocks with other commoner geese.

Ring-necked Duck

37–46 cm (15–18 in)

SPECIES INFORMATION

SCIENTIFIC NAME	*Aythya collaris*
RELATED SPECIES	Pochard, Tufted Duck, Scaup, Ferruginous duck
CALL	Wheezy whistle (male), growl (female)
HABITAT	Freshwater; estuaries
STATUS	Rare but regular visitor

SIZE

IDENTIFICATION

HABITAT

POPULATION

MAP

THE MALE IS BLACK with pale grey flank, outlined in white and extending up the neck. Takes its name from the dark neck-band (not obvious in the field). Female like female pochard, but has white eye-ring and black tip to bill. Both sexes have more peaked crown, and show pale trailing edge to wing in flight. Behaviour is much like pochard.

VAGRANT FROM North America, with a social disposition; often found consorting with other diving ducks. The species has been spreading throughout the USA and eastern Canada, which may help to explain, together with the growing expertise of birders, the increasing number of records.

Ferruginous Duck

38-42cm (15-17in)

SPECIES INFORMATION

SCIENTIFIC NAME	*Aythya nyroca*
RELATED SPECIES	Pochard, Tufted Duck, Scaup, Ring-necked Duck
CALL	'Err-err-err' (female); 'chuck-chuck' (male)
HABITAT	Shallow lowland lakes
STATUS	Rare winter visitor, mainly to south-east England

SIZE

IDENTIFICATION

HABITAT

POPULATION

MAP

THIS SMALL RELATIVE of our other diving ducks has very dark plumage with a chestnut tinge, contrasting with a pure white or pale undertail. The male also has a white iris. In flight it shows a white patch on the belly and a broad, white wing-bar. Note also the rather long bill and sloping forehead. It breeds mainly on ponds and lakes in eastern and central Europe.

SPECIES INFORMATION

SCIENTIFIC NAME	Melanitta fusca
RELATED SPECIES	Common Scoter, Surf Scoter
CALL	In breeding season female has a nasal 'braa-braa'; male a piping 'kyu'
HABITAT	Breeds at lakes in mountains, especially in northern coniferous forest and tundra zones; coastal waters outside breeding season
STATUS	Breeds in Scandinavia and around Baltic Sea. Summer visitor in breeding range. Mainly to North Sea and Baltic coasts as passage bird and winter visitor. Rarer than common scoter

Velvet Scoter

53–58 cm (21–23 in)

LARGER THAN COMMON SCOTER, and has white wing-patches (may be hidden when swimming). Male black, with white patch below eye. Female dark brown with pale patches at side of head (sometimes absent). Sometimes accompanies the common scoter or eider in winter flocks and in flight are immediately identifiable by the white speculum. In marine areas, their food consists of molluscs, but in freshwater they eat insects.

SPECIES INFORMATION

SCIENTIFIC NAME	Melanitta perspicillata
RELATED SPECIES	Common Scoter, Velvet Scoter
CALL	
HABITAT	Open sea
STATUS	Rare, but regular, vagrant from North America

Surf Scoter

45–56 cm (18–22 in)

THIS SEA DUCK is about the same size as the common scoter, and smaller than the velvet scoter. In flight, the wings are dark, with no pale area or wing-bar. Male has heavy, orange and white bill with a black patch at the side, and a white patch on the back of its neck. Female is more like common scoter, but has heavier bill and more angular head. It is most often seen off the north coast of Britain, mainly between September and April.

Rough-legged Buzzard

53–63 cm (21–25 in)

SIZE

IDENTIFICATION

HABITAT

POPULATION

MAP

SPECIES INFORMATION	
SCIENTIFIC NAME	Buteo lagopus
RELATED SPECIES	Common Buzzard
CALL	Cat-like mewing. Usually silent in winter
HABITAT	Mountains and tundra of northern Europe, mostly above or beyond tree-line. Numbers increase after rodent population explosions. In winter found mainly on moorland and heaths
STATUS	Breeds mainly in Scandinavia and Finland. In some winters it migrates south in large numbers, especially to eastern Europe, but also (in small numbers) to east coast of BI

TAIL WHITE, WITH wide dark band at tip; hovers much more frequently than buzzard. Plumage variable, but usually has pale head, and more contrast than buzzard. Legs feathered to toes. Wings and tail relatively long, belly black, contrasting with pale undersides of the wings.

MOST BIRDS THAT reach Britain in an ordinary winter remain close to the east coast, in East Anglia or Kent. The rough legs and feathered tarsi, are not easy to spot, but the pale tail with broad terminal band, the very dark upperparts, and the dark belly patch are good field marks.

Rodent cycles have their influence on breeding success. A good spring lemming or vole population can lead to large clutches and, if the rodents continue to breed through the summer, the large clutches become successful broods. After years like that, more rough-legged buzzards are likely to reach Britain, but the main movement is south to south-east, taking birds to the Black Sea and Caucasus.

One of the best rough-legged buzzard winters was 1966–67 when there were 67 records. It seems that these were due more to a crash in vole numbers than to an unusually high rough-legged buzzard population. Even better was 1974, when the wintering population may have been 100 birds, and more were seen in passage in October.

East Anglian coastal heathland is a favoured haunt of wintering rough-legged buzzards. They pause and hover as they search the ground below for rodents.

SPECIES INFORMATION

SCIENTIFIC NAME	*Falco vespertinus*
RELATED SPECIES	Kestrel, Hobby, Peregrine, Merlin, Gyr Falcon
CALL	Usually silent
HABITAT	Heaths and wetlands
STATUS	Rare, but regular, visitor to Britain, mainly in May–June

Red-footed Falcon
21–31 cm (8–12 in)

LIKE A SMALL, dainty kestrel. Female rusty orange beneath, grey with dark barring above. Adult male all grey. Adults have bright red feet. Often found perching on wires and posts.

A HANDFUL OF THESE elegant falcons reach Britain almost every year and causing a stir amongst keen birdwatchers. Agile in flight and reminiscent of the hobby, but also hovering frequently in the manner of a kestrel, they catch insects either in flight or on the ground. The female and male look very different, the former is almost all dove-grey, but with red under tail coverts, while the latter is grey above, with rufous crown and underparts. The falcon is the same size as the hobby but has a blunter profile.

SPECIES INFORMATION

SCIENTIFIC NAME	*Falco rusticolus*
RELATED SPECIES	Peregrine, Kestrel, Hobby, Merlin, Red-footed Falcon
CALL	Coarse 'kerreh-kerreh-kerreh'
HABITAT	Breeds in tundra (Iceland and Scandinavia). Rare visitor to BI, mainly in winter, when seen most often at coast
STATUS	Vagrant to BI

Gyr Falcon
55–60 cm (22–24 in)

LARGEST EUROPEAN FALCON, the size of a goshawk. Wings are broader at the base than peregrine's, and wing-beats slower. Plumage mainly grey, pale grey or even white (mainly Greenland birds).

SIMILAR IN FLIGHT to peregrine, but heavier and with slower, more deliberate wingbeats. There is much variation in plumage, with the pure white form found mainly in Siberia and Greenland, a light grey form in Iceland and a darker grey type in northern Scandinavia. Although it is a rare winter or spring visitor, each year will usually bring a couple of exciting sightings of the magnificent Gyr falcon in the British Isles.

349

Curlew Sandpiper

18–23 cm

○ ○

SPECIES INFORMATION

SCIENTIFIC NAME	*Calidris ferruginea*
RELATED SPECIES	Dunlin, stints, Purple Sandpiper, Pectoral Sandpiper
CALL	Flight-call a trilling 'krillee', softer and less nasal than dunlin's
HABITAT	Breeds in arctic coastal tundra. On migration, mostly on mudflats, more rarely on inland muddy sites and salt lakes
STATUS	Regular passage migrant in small numbers on coasts, especially North Sea. Larger flocks in eastern Mediterranean. Breeds in High Arctic of east Asia

SIZE

IDENTIFICATION

HABITAT

POPULATION

MAP

DUNLIN-SIZED, BUT less dumpy, with longer legs and neck. Bill also longer and more decurved. Breeding plumage brick-red (like knot). In winter plumage it resembles Dunlin, but has paler belly. In flight shows white wing bar and white rump.

CURLEW SANDPIPERS BREED in the far north of Asia – in the Siberian Arctic. In Britain they turn up regularly on passage to their wintering grounds in Africa, in spring or, more commonly, in autumn. They tend to be single birds, and are often seen in mixed flocks, especially with dunlin. Easily confused with dunlin, especially since some dunlins have longer, more curved bills than others. Look also for the longer neck of the curlew sandpiper, and the more obvious eye-stripe. Unmistakable in spring or summer plumage, with brick-red plumage on neck and belly.

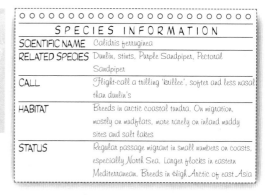

Curlew sandpipers are closely related to dunlins and look very similar; however, they are slightly larger in size.

SPECIES INFORMATION	
SCIENTIFIC NAME	Calidris melanotus
RELATED SPECIES	Knot, Dunlin, Sanderling, stints, Purple Sandpiper, Curlew Sandpiper
CALL	'Chrook'
HABITAT	Breeds in N American and E Siberian tundra. Visits muddy and grassy shores
STATUS	N American species, but the most frequently seen American wader in Europe – mainly July–October

Pectoral Sandpiper

19–23 cm (7.5–9 in)

LARGER THAN DUNLIN, with a stance that often resembles a ruff. It has rich black and brown upper parts with pale stripes down the back. The pectoral band, with upper breast distinctly streaked, makes a sharp contrast with the white lower breast.

OFTEN TURNS UP in Ireland, at sites such as Akeragh Lough in County Kerry. However, as a quarter of records for pectoral sandpiper are from the east coast, some birds could be of Siberian rather than American origin. The legs are of a distinctive greenish colour. In small numbers, this sandpiper has become a regular transatlantic migrant, especially in the autumn months.

SPECIES INFORMATION	
SCIENTIFIC NAME	Charadrius alexandrinus
RELATED SPECIES	Ringed Plover, Little Ringed Plover
CALL	Alarm call 'brrr brrr'; flight-call 'pit'. Song a trill, often in flight.
HABITAT	Most coastal of plovers, usually seen near to tidal zone on sandy coasts. Also on lagoons and saltpans
STATUS	Resident and partial migrant. Breeds in Spain, Portugal, France, and scattered around Mediterranean, Atlantic and (more rarely) southern North Sea. Also breeds inland in Hungary and E Austria, and further east around Black Sea. Rare visitor to BI on migration (mainly April–May or August–October)

Kentish Plover

16 cm (6 in)

LONGER-LEGGED THAN other ringed plovers, and with less black on face. Breeding male has chestnut on head. Bill and feet are dark, and neck band is incomplete. Female and winter male has paler plumage. In flight shows white wing bar.

OTHER FIELDMARKS USEFUL for distinguishing Kentish plover from ringed or little ringed plover are the sightly longer, narrower bill, the broad, rather flat-crowned head and the long, black or dark grey legs. In flight, look for the obvious white wing-bar and white sides to the tail. The plover's nest is a minimal scrape which has almost no lining, and both sexes help to incubate the eggs (normally two or three) for the 24 days that they take to hatch.

Grey Phalarope

SPECIES INFORMATION	
SCIENTIFIC NAME	Phalaropus fulicarius
RELATED SPECIES	Red-necked phalarope
CALL	
HABITAT	Breeds in high-arctic, south to Iceland. Winters to sea, mainly off west Africa
STATUS	Very rare coastal visitor to BI, mainly September–November; sometimes driven inland by storms

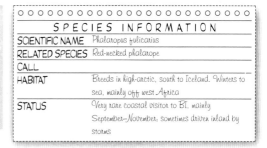

USUALLY SEEN SWIMMING like a miniature gull the grey phalarope is larger than the red-necked, and with thicker bill, often yellow at the base and pale greyish or black legs. Paler grey in winter than red-necked; bright brick-red summer plumage rarely seen in this country.

Little Stint

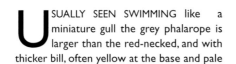

13 cm (5 in)

SPECIES INFORMATION	
SCIENTIFIC NAME	Calidris minuta
RELATED SPECIES	Temminck's Stint, Knot, Dunlin, Sanderling, Purple Sandpiper, Curlew Sandpiper
CALL	Quiet vibrating 'tirr-tirr-tirrit' when flushed. Flight-call 'bit'. Song a soft, tinkling trill, in flight
HABITAT	Breeds in damp tundra. On migration mainly at coast (especially muddy estuaries) in small or mixed flocks
STATUS	Breeds on tundra of high Arctic. Summer visitor to breeding grounds. Migrates to Africa and S European coasts in autumn. In BI small numbers (mostly juveniles) visit regularly as passage migrants (mainly autumn)

TINY WADER WITH short, black bill and black legs. In breeding plumage has reddish-brown upperparts with black and brown spots on the back; white below. V-shaped cream marking on upper back (very clear in juveniles). Dark streak along centre of crown. In winter, grey above, with greyish tinge to sides of breast.

SCIENTIFIC NAME	Calidris temminckii
RELATED SPECIES	Knot, Dunlin, Sanderling, stints, Purple Sandpiper, Curlew Sandpiper
CALL	Flight-call 'tirr'. Tittering song-flight
HABITAT	Breeds on rivers and lake margins in willow and birch zones of northern Europe. On migration on banks of inland pools and lakes, as well as at coasts. Breeds in high Arctic and Scandinavian mountains. Very rare breeder in Scotland (about four pairs).
STATUS	Summer visitor to breeding grounds. Migrates to S and SE European coasts in autumn. In BI rarer than little stint

Temminck's Stint
13 cm (5 in)

SIMILAR TO LITTLE stint, but slightly more elongated and shorter-legged. Legs paler, plumage greyer above. At the southern edge of its range in Scotland, where there is a tiny population, but plenty of suitable habitat. The Scandinavian population stands at over 100,000 birds, but few visit these shores.

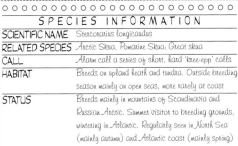

 SIZE
 IDENTIFICATION
 HABITAT
 POPULATION
 MAP

SCIENTIFIC NAME	Stercorarius longicaudus
RELATED SPECIES	Arctic Skua, Pomarine Skua, Great skua
CALL	Alarm call a series of short, hard 'kree-epp' calls
HABITAT	Breeds on upland heath and tundra. Outside breeding season mainly on open seas, more rarely at coast
STATUS	Breeds mainly in mountains of Scandinavia and Russian Arctic. Summer visitor to breeding grounds, wintering in Atlantic. Regularly seen in North Sea (mainly autumn) and Atlantic coast (mainly spring)

Long-tailed Skua
35–58 cm (14–23 in) includes tail 12–20 cm (5–8 in)

MORE DELICATE THAN other skuas, with narrower wings. Very elegant in flight. Has sharply defined dark cap, with a white neck and upper breast. Tail streamers are longer than those of arctic skua. Juvenile has shorter central tail feathers.

THE LONG-TAILED skua is one of several Arctic and northern species whose populations fluctuate with the abundance of their prey – in this case mostly small rodents, especially lemmings. Records of passage birds in Britain increase following good breeding seasons.

 SIZE
 IDENTIFICATION
 HABITAT
 POPULATION
 MAP

Pomarine Skua

65–78 cm (25.5–31 in) includes tail 8 cm (3 in)

SPECIES INFORMATION	
SCIENTIFIC NAME	*Stercorarius pomarinus*
RELATED SPECIES	Arctic Skua, Long-tailed Skua, Great Skua
CALL	'Gek-gek', or 'yee-ee'
HABITAT	Breeds on tundra. Winters mainly at sea (Atlantic)
STATUS	Breeds in arctic Russia. Summer visitor to breeding grounds. On passage off coasts, mainly in late autumn and late spring

LARGER AND HEAVIER than Arctic skua, with broader wings and heavier bill. Central tail feathers twisted into a blob. Pale phase and (rarer) dark phase occur. In juvenile the central tail feathers hardly visible (tail looks rounded).

Mediterranean Gull

38 cm (15 in)

SPECIES INFORMATION	
SCIENTIFIC NAME	*Larus melanocephalus*
RELATED SPECIES	Black-headed Gull, other *Larus* gulls
CALL	Mostly silent outside breeding season. 'Eu-err' – more nasal, and shriller than black-headed gull
HABITAT	Nests in colonies at lagoons and lakes
STATUS	Scattered from S Baltic, through C Europe, to N Mediterranean. Rare breeder in England, with about 12 pairs, mainly in SE. Summer visitor to breeding grounds. Winters around Mediterranean, north to Channel.

SIMILAR TO BLACK-HEADED gull, but has paler and broader wings. In the summer the head is a true black (black more extensive than black-headed's brown); face has dark mask in winter.

THE MEDITERRANEAN GULL can easily be hidden in a huge breeding colony of black-headed gulls in summer or in winter. Either way, identification presents a challenge to the gull enthusiast.

Little Gull

26 cm (10 in)

SPECIES INFORMATION

SCIENTIFIC NAME	Larus minutus
RELATED SPECIES	Black-headed gull, other Larus gulls
CALL	Soft 'kik-ki-ki' or tern-like 'kyek'
HABITAT	Breeds on shallow lakes with rich vegetation, often with black-headed gulls. Outside breeding season at sea and regularly on large inland lakes
STATUS	Mainly NE Europe, east of Baltic Sea. A few pairs in the Netherlands and north Germany. Mainly summer visitor to breeding areas (resident towards south). Winters around coasts. In BI regular on passage (has bred)

O**UR SMALLEST GULL** is rather tern-like in flight. In breeding plumage resembles black-headed gull, but cap is black, and extends further down neck. The little gull also lacks white near eye, and has rounded wing-tips, without black tips. In flight, shows slate-black beneath wings, and white trailing edge to wings. Juveniles have dark, zig-zag pattern on upper wings (compare juvenile kittiwake), and dusky cap.

OUT OF THE breeding season, for instance when storm-driven winter birds are forced inshore, adult and young have a dark cap and ear-patch. Little gulls are buoyant fliers, and show their dark underwings and plain white wing-tips as they dip for food at the water surface.

SIZE

IDENTIFICATION

HABITAT

POPULATION

MAP

Top and Middle
The juvenile little gull has a dark cap and a broad, black neck-band.

Below
The little gull in its winter plumage, with a dusky cap, dark ear-spot and general tern-like appearance.

Glaucous Gull

62–72 cm (24–28 in)

SPECIES INFORMATION	
SCIENTIFIC NAME	Larus hyperboreus
RELATED SPECIES	Iceland Gull, other Larus gulls
CALL	Similar call to herring
HABITAT	Breeds in high arctic – e.g. Greenland, Iceland, Svalbard
STATUS	Rare but regular visitor – mainly in winter

Glaucous gulls and Iceland gulls both have uniquely white wings, even at the tips. Immature birds have pale brown plumage, and in wintering adults there is a degree of brown streaking on the head. Immature birds mainly show a pink bill with a dark tip. Glaucous is slightly larger than herring gull, and the wings are relatively broader than Iceland's. Most glaucous gulls are ponderous, pot bellied birds although small birds may be seen. A winter visitor occurring in numbers around Shetland.

Iceland Gull

52–63 cm (20–25 in)

SPECIES INFORMATION	
SCIENTIFIC NAME	Larus glaucoides
RELATED SPECIES	Glaucous gull, other Larus gulls.
CALL	Similar call to herring
HABITAT	Breeds in high arctic – mainly Greenland.
STATUS	Rare but regular visitor – mainly in winter, mostly to NW of BI.

Rather smaller than herring gull, with a slightly shorter, less heavy bill. Note that the wing tips are pure white. When resting, the long wings extend well beyond the tip of its tail. Immature birds are mottled brownish, but always have pale primaries. Iceland gulls prefer to stay over or close to the sea.

Wryneck
17 cm (7in)

STRANGE-LOOKING WOODPECKER relative with nightjar-like, bark-coloured plumage and short bill. Could be mistaken for barred warbler, or possibly immature red-backed shrike.

THE WRYNECK AVOIDS dense woodland and feeds mainly on the ground. It is an uncommon but regular passage migrant to the British Isles.

The complex patterning of its plummage is unique. Its undulating flight is woodpecker-like and it nests in tree holes feeding on insects licked up with its long tongue. A sky-pointing display is used in courtship or when threatened.

Lapland Bunting
16 cm (6 in)

THE BREEDING MALE is streaked above, with black head and face and chestnut nape. In winter similar to reed bunting, but has chestnut patch on wing, framed by two white wing bars with a yellowish.

THE LAPLAND BUNTING has bred in Scotland. Regular winter visitor, mainly along the east coast of England.

Hoopoe

26–28 cm (10.5 in)

SPECIES INFORMATION	
SCIENTIFIC NAME	Upupa epops
RELATED SPECIES	No close relatives
CALL	Raw, scratching territorial call. Song is a soft, but far-carrying 'poo-poo-poo'
HABITAT	Warm, dry, open country, especially cultivated areas, such as vineyards, light woodland, parks, orchards and pasture. Nests in holes in old trees, or in crevices in rocks and walls
STATUS	Breeds across much of continental Europe, north to Channel and Baltic. Rare but regular spring visitor to Britain (has bred)

SIZE

IDENTIFICATION

HABITAT

POPULATION

MAP

THIS BIRD IS unmistakable. Often seen in flight, when seems floppy, almost like a huge butterfly, showing contrasting black and white barred wings and tail. Can be hard to spot on the ground. It has a fan-like erectile crest with a long, curved bill.

ONE OF THE JOYS of a continental holiday is to see and hear Hoopoes. The first sign is often the 'hoop-hoop-hoop' call, that excites with the prospect of a flying bird, boldly pied, and cinnamon-coloured, or of a bird feeding on the ground, using its long decurved bill and fanning its extraordinary crest. On Bardsey the rare possibility of a spring bird flying past the observatory and down the lane can clear the breakfast table, and a stray bird in a southern village soon gets known.

Although resident in southern Spain and North Africa, hoopoes are migratory over most of their range, and birds reaching Britain in the spring have probably overshot from France where it breeds in most areas.

Most European birds winter in sub-Saharan Africa.

Where it has declined, intensification of agriculture is probably responsible, for the larger insects and their protein-rich larvae and pupae are much scarcer in this insecticide age. Perhaps cool, wet summers have not helped, for it is decidedly a bird of warm, dry country, although it breeds successfully in a wide range of habitats.

Hoopoes have bred in Britain, for example four pairs in 1977, and nests are usually in a tree-hole. Territory is advertised with a 'pooping' display, involving calls and head movements from some conspicuous position.

Top right and left
The hoopoe cannot be mistaken for any other bird. The long crest is usually held furled, but is sometimes fanned forward.

Bottom
This lovely bird has begun to breed in the British Isles again and numbers may perhaps increase in the future.

Waxwing

18 cm (7 in)

SPECIES INFORMATION	
SCIENTIFIC NAME	Bombycilla garrulus
RELATED SPECIES	None in region
CALL	Flight-call a buzzing 'sree'. Song a mixture of humming and chattering calls
HABITAT	Breeds in open spruce or birch woods with rich undergrowth. May occur almost anywhere in winter
STATUS	Breeds mainly in NE Scandinavia and Russia. Summer visitor to breeding grounds. In autumn and winter, mainly to Scandinavia and E Europe. Further S and W (as far as Britain) in small numbers; in some years in much larger numbers, during 'irruptions'

LOOKS BROWN FROM afar, but colourful when close. Starling-like in build and in flight, when white edges to primaries and the trilling calls, as a flock leaves its feeding place, help to distinguish them. The waxwing has sleek, pinky-brown plumage and crest of the same colour, black throat and black mask from bill and over the eye, and two bright yellow patches under the tail. The wings have bright red spots, like sealing wax, on the tips of the secondaries. Female has smaller red wing markings.

OCCASIONALLY, MANY WAXWINGS visit, as in 1996, when it was estimated that more than 10,000 birds arrived in Britain. Most records are from the east coast. In waxwing years, the birds can be easy to spot as they are tame and tend to congregate at berry-rich shrubs, often in parks and gardens.

SIZE

IDENTIFICATION

HABITAT

POPULATION

MAP

Top and bottom right
Suburban gardens with plenty of berry-bearing trees and shrubs are the places to watch for waxwings, which invade Britain from time to time in large numbers during the autumn and winter.

Bottom left
Waxwings have a distinctive pinky-brown crest with a black mask on the face.

359

Icterine Warbler

13 cm (5 in)

○ ○

SPECIES INFORMATION

SCIENTIFIC NAME	Hippolais icterina
RELATED SPECIES	Melodious Warbler
CALL	Call is a musical 'deederoid' or 'taytaydwee'. Song very varied, with musical whistling calls and much mimicry
HABITAT	Broadleaved and mixed woodland, river-valley woods, parks with undergrowth, copses and gardens
STATUS	Breeds mainly in C, N and E Europe, where summer visitor. Scarce migrant to BI

SIZE

IDENTIFICATION

HABITAT

POPULATION

MAP

THIS BIRD IS a little larger than wood warbler, its plumage mainly yellowish; and its posture reed warbler-like. It has a long orange bill with a pale patch on its wings

COULD WELL GO unnoticed unless trapped, or unless you hear the beautiful song – unlikely as most turn up in autumn.

Difficult to identify unless you are familiar with migrant birds, the icterine warbler is a rare visitor that turns up occasionally, mainly at coastal sites in autumn.

MELODIOUS WARBLER

Slightly shorter-tailed than icterine, and with shorter wings, lacking pale patch (13 cm (5 in). Only reliably distinguished from icterine in the field by song, a prolonged babbling warble although some individuals include mimicry

AQUATIC WARBLER

This rare visitor from central Europe is occasionally seen, mainly when caught at observatories. At 13 cm (5 in) tall, it resembles a sedge warbler, but is slightly yellower, with a darker crown with a central yellow stripe. Likes bushy country - olive groves, gardens, plantations and is often found in willows near water. Replaces icterine in S and W Europe. Summer visitor. Scare migrant to BI.

BARRED WARBLER

Large warbler, 15.5 cm (6 in), with powerful bill, double white wing bar and white tip to tail. Eye is yellow in adult. Female less barred beneath. Juvenile has dusky white underside, with indistinct barring, and dark eye. Young autumn birds are big, as warblers go, and have a heavy bill, but their sandy-grey plumage is not very distinctive. Breeds mainly in C, E and SE Europe, west to S Scandinavia and Germany. Summer visitor, wintering in E Africa. Scarce migrant to BI (mainly E coast, in autumn).

ARCTIC WARBLER AND GREENISH WARBLER

These two belong to an intriguing group, as several members of the genus *Phylloscopus* are so similar that identification sets a challenge. Greenish warblers, 11

cm (4.3 in), are the same size as chiffchaffs and willow warblers, with Arctic warblers slightly larger, 12 cm (4.75 in). The two species are greenish-brown above, whiter below than the common species, and with more prominent stripe over the eye, and small whitish wing bars. Arctic warbler has straw-coloured legs, while those of greenish are dusky.

Top right, middle right and bottom
Arctic and greenish warblers are two species from north-east Europe, both rare autumn vagrants to Britain. They are very similar, and migrants are only reliably identified in the hand.

Bluethroat

14 cm (5.5 in)

SIZE

IDENTIFICATION

HABITAT

POPULATION

MAP

SIMILAR TO THE robin in shape and size, but with slightly longer legs. The base of its tail is rust-red with a pale stripe above the eye.

THE CENTRAL EUROPEAN race (*L. svecica cyanecula*) has a white spot on the blue throat, while the northern European race (*L. svecica svecica*) has a red spot. Female and winter male have white throat. Juveniles are similar to young robins, but with a red base to the tail. It is an extremely shy bird that likes to keep to the cover of its low vegetation habitat.

SPECIES INFORMATION

SCIENTIFIC NAME	*Luscinia svecica*
RELATED SPECIES	Nightingale, Thrush Nightingale
CALL	Alarm-call a hard 'tack'. Song is made up of pure, sharp calls, together with imitations of other species, and often with an accelerating series of bell-like notes at the start
HABITAT	Breeds in birch or willow thickets, often by water. In lowlands often near swampy lakes and ditches
STATUS	Breeds mainly in N and E Europe, but scattered S to C Europe, W France, and N Spain. Summer visitor. In BI scarce passage migrant

Red-Breasted Flycatcher

11.5 cm (4.5 in)

SIZE

IDENTIFICATION

HABITAT

POPULATION

MAP

SMALLEST OF THE European flycatchers, it is grey-brown above, creamy white below, with pale eye-ring and white at base of outer tail feathers.

ADULT MALE RED-BREASTED flycatcher has an orange-red throat bib with a greyish head. Female and first year male lack red bib.

SPECIES INFORMATION

SCIENTIFIC NAME	*Ficedula parva*
RELATED SPECIES	Pied Flycatcher, Collared Flycatcher
CALL	Alarm call 'dootii', and wren-like 'tsrrr'. Song is a descending, whistling phrase, a little like Willow Warbler's towards the end
HABITAT	Breeds in tall deciduous or mixed woodland. Also in parks in some areas
STATUS	Mainly C and E Europe, W to Germany. Summer visitor to breeding range. Scarce migrant to Britain (mainly E coast in autumn)

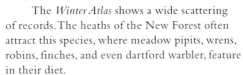

Great Grey Shrike
24 cm (9.5 in)

SPECIES INFORMATION

SCIENTIFIC NAME	Lanius excubitor
RELATED SPECIES	Red-backed Shrike, Woodchat Shrike
CALL	Sharp 'vaird' or 'shrrie' in two or three syllables. Sometimes a magpie-like chatter. Song consists of short metallic or vibrating phrases, and continuous warbling
HABITAT	Breeds on moorland and heath; also in hedgerows and orchards
STATUS	Breeds from N and NE Europe, through C Europe to SW Europe. Absent from NW, S and SE Europe. Resident; summer visitor to NE of range. In winter ranges over most of Europe, to suitable sites

LARGER THAN RED-BACKED shrike, with relatively short wings, and a long, somewhat graduated tail. Looks black and white from distance. Juvenile is rather duller, and darker below. Often sits on a high look-out perch. Flight slow and undulating; often hovers. Sometimes wedges food in tree branch, or impales it on thorns or barbed wire.

LIKE STONECHATS, great grey shrikes perch openly on heathland vegetation, but there the likeness ends. They are spectacular birds, particularly as they can appear suddenly, on a bleak winter's day, in a habitat where there appears to be little birdlife. As, particularly later in the winter, much of their diet is small birds, this means that a large hunting territory with appropriate hunting posts, is needed. On arrival in one of these territories, often heathland, there may still be insect life available, but as winter draws in, small mammals may be an alternative. As they too become less active and less visible, and as some birds weaken on a thinning diet, smaller birds may then become the chosen food.

The *Winter Atlas* shows a wide scattering of records. The heaths of the New Forest often attract this species, where meadow pipits, wrens, robins, finches, and even dartford warbler, feature in their diet.

The large insects which make up much of the summer diet are declining over most of Europe, with the intensification of agriculture and use of pesticides. Where these and small reptiles and mammals are available, they are caught following a wait and watch strategy from a good vantage point. After swooping flight and vertical pounce the shrike may eat the prey immediately or impale it for future use. Most British birds have Scandinavian origins, but the population centre is in the vast subarctic ranges of Russia which might hold a million pairs.

 SIZE

 IDENTIFICATION

 HABITAT

 POPULATION

 MAP

A Great grey shrike in a typical pose at the top of a bush, from which it can scan its surroundings and watch the ground below for likely prey such as large beetles.

363

Red-backed Shrike

17 cm (7 in)

THE MALE HAS bright red-brown back, grey head with thick black eye-stripe, and black tail with white outer feathers at base. The female is red-brown above, pale beneath with crescent-shaped markings. Juvenile has rather scaly markings. Impales prey on thorns (or barbed wire) when food is plentiful.

SPECIES INFORMATION	
SCIENTIFIC NAME	Lanius collurio
RELATED SPECIES	Great Grey Shrike, Woodchat Shrike
CALL	Alarm call 'dshain', 'geck' or a hard 'trrt-trrt'. Song, seldom heard, is a varied warble, with short calls, interspersed with imitations of other birds.
HABITAT	Breeds on heaths, at woodland margins with thorn bushes, and in hedgerows
STATUS	Breeds throughout Europe, except for N and W. Virtually extinct as breeding species in BI (at north-west limit of range). Summer visitor, wintering in tropical Africa. In BI regularly seen on passage in spring and autumn

Woodchat Shrike

19 cm (7.5 in)

SMALL SHRIKE WITH rust-red head and conspicuous white shoulder-patches. Blackish above, pure white below. The female is slightly paler, with browner upperparts and less clearly marked black mask. Juvenile like young red-backed, but browner above, with paler shoulder and rump.

SPECIES INFORMATION	
SCIENTIFIC NAME	Lanius senator
RELATED SPECIES	Great Grey Shrike, Red-backed Shrike
CALL	Harsh calls, such as 'kshairr'. Song varied, with trills, whistles and mimicry
HABITAT	Open country – maquis, vineyards, gardens, orchards and the like
STATUS	Breeds mainly in S Europe, but north to Poland, and S Germany. Summer visitor. Annual vagrant to BI (mainly in May)

Scarlet Rosefinch
14 cm (5.5 in)

A PRETTY FINCH. Sparrow-sized with stumpy bill. Distinctive red plumage on male, duller on female. Fairly common in Europe, rare in British Isles.

THIS BIRD HAS BEEN rapidly expanding westwards, and a pair were found with nest and eggs in the Highland Region of Scotland as recently in 1982. Singing males are becoming more common, other nests have been found on the east coast of Scotland, and it is hardly rare in the Shetland Islands in the spring months. Bright red plummage identifies adult males, but females, except for the powerful, stumpy bill, could be mistaken for the linnet as their plumage is dull. Occurs in thickets.

 SIZE
 IDENTIFICATION
 HABITAT
 POPULATION
 MAP

Shore Lark
16 cm (6 in)

SANDY GREY ABOVE, whitish below. Yellow and black head markings, less distinct in winter, especially in the female. Breeding male has small black 'horns'. Slimmer, in flight, than other larks, and with rather pointed wings.

SINCE 1970, SHORE larks have bred erratically in the central Highlands, but certainly as breeding birds they are very rare. Seen regularly in winter along the east coast, although numbers have declined in recent years, reflecting declines in Scandinavia.

 SIZE
 IDENTIFICATION
 HABITAT
 POPULATION
 MAP

Useful Adresses

The Wildfowl and Wetlands Trust,
Slimbridge, Gloucester, GL2 7BT.
Tel: 01453 890333

The Royal Society for the Protection of Birds
and **Young Ornithologists' Club** (YOC),
(junior section of RSPB),
The Lodge, Sandy, Bedfordshire, SG19 2DL.
Tel: 01767 680551

British Trust for Ornithology,
National Centre for Ornithology,
The Nunnery, Thetford,
Norfolk, IP24 2PU.
Tel: 01842 750050

Birdwatch Ireland,
8 Longford Place, Monkstown, Co Dublin.
Tel: 012 804322

The National Trust,
36 Queen Anne's Gate, London, SW1H 9AS.
Tel: 0181 315 1111

Worldwide Fund for Nature,
Panda House, Weyside Park,
Godalming, Surrey, GU7 1XR.
Tel: 01483 426444

British Trust for Conservation Volunteers (BTCV),
36 St Mary's Street, Wallingford, Oxon, OX10 0EL.
Tel: 01491 839766

Royal Society for Nature Conservation (RSNC)
and **Watch** (junior section of RSNC),
The Kiln, Waterside, Mather Road,
Newark, NG24 1WT.
Tel: 01636 677711

The Woodland Trust,
Autumn Park, Dysart Road, Grantham,
Lincolnshire, NG31 6LL.
Tel: 01476 581111

The Walter Rothschild Zoological Museum,
Department of Ornithology,
Akeman Street, Tring, Herts, HP23 6AP.
Tel: 01442 824181

Scottish Ornithologists' Club,
21 Regent Terrace, Edinburgh, EH7 5BT.
Tel: 0131 5566042

**Royal Society for the Prevention
of Cruelty to Animals** (RSPCA),
Causeway, Horsham, Surrey, RH12 1HG.
Tel: 01403 264181

Selected Bibliography

Attenborough D., *The Life of Birds,* BBC 1998

Brooke M. & Birkhead T., *Cambridge Encyclopedia of Ornithology,* CUP, 1991

Bruun B. et al., *Hamlyn Guide to the Birds of Britain and Europe, 2nd ed.,* Hamlyn, 1992

Cannon A., *Garden Bird Watch Handbook,* BTO, 1998

Cottridge D. & Vinicombe K., *Rare Birds in Britain and Ireland,* HarperCollins, 1996

Du Feu C., *Nest Boxes,* BTO, 1993

Ferns P., *Bird Life of Coasts and Estuaries,* CUP, 1992

Fuller R., *Bird Habitats in Britain,* Poyser, 1982

Fuller R., *Bird Life of Woodland and Forest,* CUP, 1995

Gibbons D. et al., *The New Atlas of Breeding Birds in Britain and Ireland,* Poyser, 1993

Golley M. et al., *The Complete Garden Bird Book,* New Holland, 1996

Greenoak F., *British Birds: Their Folklore, Names and Literature,* Helm, 1997

Hayman P. & Hume R., *The Shell Easy Bird Guide,* Macmillan, 1997

Jonsson L., *Birds of Europe with North Africa and the Middle East,* Helm, 1996

Kightley C. et al., *Pocket Guide to the Birds of Britain and NW Europe,* Pica Press, 1998

Lack P., *Atlas of Wintering Birds in Britain and Ireland,* Poyser, 1986

Marchant J. H. et al., *Population Trends in British Breeding Birds,* BTO, 1990

Mead C., *Bird Migration,* Country Life, 1983

Newton I., *Population Limitation in Birds,* Academic Press, 1998

Pemberton J.E., *Birdwatchers Yearbook, 1999.* Buckingham Press, 1998

Peterson R. et al., *Birds of Britain and Europe, 5th ed.,* HarperCollins, 1993

Rackham O., *The Illustrated History of the Countryside,* Weidenfeld and Nicholson, 1994

Ratcliffe D., *Bird Life of Mountain and Upland,* CUP, 1990

RSPB, *Birds of Conservation Importance,* 1996

Sharrock J.T. R, *The Atlas of Breeding Birds,* BTO/Irish Wildbird Conservancy, 1976

Sharrock J.T.R, *Scarce Migrant Birds in Britain and Ireland.,* Poyser 1974

Snow D. & Perrins C.M., *The Birds of the Western Palearctic., Concise Edition.,* OUP 1998

Sterry, P. et al., *AA Field Guide: Birds of Britain and Europe,* AA, 1998

Tipling, D., *Top Birding Spots in Britain and Ireland,* HarperCollins, 1996

Glossary

Archaeopteryx
The name of an early fossil bird discovered in Jurassic rocks in Bavaria. The first specimen was found in 1861, and the state of its preservation is such that the structure of its feathers is clear. Archaeopteryx lived about 150 million years ago, and shows many features linking birds with reptiles.

Adaptive Radiation
The process by which a species evolves, through the isolation of different populations, into several new species. All birds have radiated out from an ancestral form, as they gradually adapted to different environments.

Allopatric Speciation
Occurs when populations are isolated for long enough, by some form of barrier, for their genetic makeup to become sufficiently different to make interbreeding between the members of the populations impossible. The isolated populations therefore become separate species.

Anting
This involves the use of ants by birds, or of the formic acid produced by the ants, together with peculiar movements, in what is probably an attempt to control parasites.

Aspect Ratio
Aspect ratio of a bird's wings is calculated by dividing the wingspan by the average width of the wing. A long, narrow wing with high aspect ratio is good for fast gliding.

Binomial Nomenclature
Introduced by Linnaeus (1758) to help with classifying animals and plants. Each species has a binomial (double-name), made up of the genus (or generic) name, together with the species (or specific) name. Both words are in Latin form. The generic name is placed first, with an initial capital letter, and the specific name afterwards, as in *Turdus philomelus*, the song thrush. By convention, binomials are always written in italic.

British Ornithologists Union (BOU)
This organisation aims to promote ornithology within the international scientific and birdwatching communities by, among other things, meetings, conferences and the publication of the journal *Ibis*.

British Trust for Ornithology (BTO)
A research and conservation organisation in which amateur enthusiasts co-operate with professional ornithologists in national projects, to count birds and monitor populations and distribution. For more details contact BTO.

Carpometacarpus
The name given to the fused bones of the hand of a bird, which provide a firm attachment for the primary feathers of the wing.

Cere
The fleshy covering to part of the upper mandible.

Climax Vegetation
The vegetation that would result if there were no interference by man, and if succession were allowed to take its natural course. In Britain, the climax vegetation of most normal lowland sites is woodland.

Cline
Occurs when a population shows a gradation in some feature such as weight, colour or tarsus length, from one part of its range to another.

Common Birds Census
A method used for estimating bird populations in woodland and on farms. Birdwatchers visit a site regularly during the breeding season, recording every contact with a bird on a large-scale visit map.

Convergent Evolution
The evolutionary process by which unrelated birds come to look similar or to have similar attributes. One example is the hummingbirds of Central and South America and the sunbirds of Africa.

Cloaca
The shared opening for three physiological systems: digestive, excretory and reproductive.

Density Dependent Factor
This reduces survival chances in a population when that population level is high. Too big a brood could actually reduce the number fledging.

Displacement Activity
Behaviour which appears out of context, as when a gull, at the edge of its territory, does not 'know' whether to advance or retreat: it may do neither but pull up grass instead.

Eclipse Plumage
Plumage taken on for a short time following a post-breeding moult in ducks. The males assume a cryptic, female-like plumage.

Ecosystem
A habitat defined in terms of the inter-relationships of the organisms living there, and their interactions with non-living factors like climate and soil.

Emargination
Emargination of primary wing feathers leads to an asymmetrical tapering towards the tip. This can help in identification, but its significance for the bird is that air can move smoothly through the wing-tips as it flies.

Endemic
Those birds found nowhere else. Thus many birds are endemic to Madagascar, but only the Scottish crossbill to Britain.

Eutrophic
Eutrophic of a lake or river, is when it is enriched, or over-enriched, with nutrients, particularly nitrates or phosphates. Contrast oligotrophic.

Family
A unit of classification with, in theory, all members sharing a common ancestor. Thus the family Corvidae includes the genus *Corvus*, crows, but also separate genera for jay, magpie and chough. They all belong in the Order Passeriformes.

Field Characteristics
The most important diagnostic features helping with wild bird identification.

Food Web
A way of representing who eats what in nature. Plants represent the lowest level at the bottom, and carnivores make up the top level. Toxic chemicals may pass up the complex food web to end up in the largest concentrations in the top carnivores.

Intraspecific Competition
This occurs between members of the same species, and interspecific competition occurs between different species.

Garden Bird Watch Scheme
A simple but scientific project by which anyone with a garden can contribute to knowledge of the populations of common birds.

Gene Flow
The exchange of genes between members of a population. It is reduced by distance and prevented by isolation.

Imprinting
A form of behaviour by which young birds, such as ducks, follow the first moving object that they encounter.

Integrated Population Monitoring
Uses information from all BTO surveys, to give the best possible indication of the causes of population changes.

Jizz
A term given to the impression a bird makes by its behaviour: for example the way it flicks its tail, moves in the reeds, or undulates in flight.

Leks
Elaborate, ritualised displays in which males compete to attract a female. Females are a passive audience, except when one enters the lek to mate with a dominant central male.

Lift
One of two components, drag being the other, of the force that acts when a wing moves. To keep a bird in the air, the lift must equal or exceed the weight of the bird.

Metatarsals
The bones of the foot, usually with three fused together and one free. The fused trio form an ankle joint with the long bone above. There are other joints with three toes below. The fourth toe, usually the backward pointing thumb, is attached to the free metatarsal.

Monophyletic
The monophyletic group has in theory a single ancestral form. Where convergence has taken place, those with different ancestors may be classified together, for instance in a family, because they seem similar. Such a group would be polyphyletic.

Niche
The combination of conditions that allows a bird to survive and reproduce. It involves environmental conditions like climate and food and habitat resources such as nest sites.

Nidicolous
Nidicolous young are hatched naked and are dependent upon their parents for a considerable time.

Nidifugous
Nidifugous chicks are immediately active and quickly leave the nest to become independent.

Nucleic Acids
Nucleic acids such as Deoxyribonucleic Acid (DNA), famed as the double helix, carry all the genetic information that determines an organism's inherited characteristics. The more closely related birds are, the more similar their DNA, and the more genes they will share.

Photoperiodism
A response to light, particularly to an increase or decrease in day length. The eyes, brain, hypothalamus, anterior pituitary gland and sex hormones are involved in bringing about associated behaviour changes.

Pishing
The making of vague 'pshu-pshu' sounds in an attempt to lure skulking birds out into a more open position.

Polygyny
This involves a pair bond of a male bird with more than one female, while polyandry is the reverse.

Polytypic
Polytypic species occur in a variety of forms, sometimes within the same range, sometimes separated in different areas. When closely studied, most species show this type of variation.

Pygostyle
The final part of the vertebral column with caudal or tail vertebrae fused or joined together.

Race
Race or subspecies, is made up of a population which is, or has been, geographically separated from other populations and has evolved its own characteristics of plumage, migratory behaviour or, for example, wing dimensions. The populations are still capable of interbreeding.

Resolving Power
This is the degree to which the lens system, in binoculars or a telescope, can make different parts of

an object distinguishable. Magnification by itself is not enough.

Royal Society for the Protection of Birds (RSPB)

This society champions the conservation of birds and biodiversity. It has a million members, manages more than 120 reserves and produces the quarterly magazine *Birds*.

Signals

Whether visual or auditory, signals release or stimulate aspects of behaviour. The coloured gape of a young cuckoo is a signal, releasing an instinctive feeding response.

Sonograms

A way of displaying bird calls and songs graphically in such a way that they can be accurately analysed and compared. The sonogram shows the changing frequency (kHz) over a period of time, and also gives an indication of volume.

Subsong

A quiet, modified song. It is often produced in autumn, or in spring when a low, but increasing, level of sex hormones starts to induce breeding behaviour.

Succession

The sequence of vegetational changes when bare soil or rock is colonised by plants or when grazing, burning or cutting stops. In Britain and Ireland such changes would almost always end in woodland, the climax vegetation.

Syrinx

A bird's organ of voice or song. It consists of a resonating chamber and vibrating membranes.

Transect

A line along which birds, or flowers or butterflies, are counted in a standardised way.

Zonation

Occurs when conditions change along a gradient; for example as one climbs a mountain or goes down the shore at low tide.

Author's Sources and Acknowledgements

AS WILL BE EVIDENT, books resulting from BTO surveys have provided much useful information for this book, helped by another thread that has run through a lifetime of interest in natural history; the 'New Naturalist' series published by HarperCollins, which started in 1945.

Two other bird books, of very different size, have been indispensable; the *'Birds of the Western Palearctic' (Concise Edition)*, edited by David Snow and Chris Perrins, and the genuinely pocket-sized *'Guide to the Birds of Britain and North West Europe'* by Chris Kightly and Steve Madge and illustrated by Dave Nurney.

Apart from these, and a few other recent references, I have delved into the past, as that is the nature of my library, so that I hope the book takes a historical perspective of the ever-changing habitats in which birds live.

History goes back a lot further than the written word, and birds are what they are because of millions of years of evolution. The world birds live in, whether it is one particular habitat or the whole of Britain and Ireland, is equally dependent upon the past, for most of which the two islands have had nothing like their present form. Only since the geologically recent changes of sea level and the action of ice have they been approximately as they are today. The presence of sea and ice has done much to shape the movements of our birds, and these cannot be separated from the rest of the world's geography. This book attempts at times to hint at the dependence of British and Irish birds on places far away and times past.

That the book exists at all depends on many people, starting from a comment from Helena Dean, my wife during the early *Atlas* years, about my lifelong interest in birds. This comment reached Polly Willis at The Foundry, who pursued the possibility of my writing something, and who has been a great support at all times.

The following is a list of all the sources I have drawn upon during the writing of this volume.

Allen, N. and Giddens, C., 'Forty Years of Exmoor's Wildlife', *Exmoor Review*, Vol. 40, Exmoor Society, 1999

Armstrong, E.A., *Birds of the Grey Wind*, OUP, 1940

Attenborough, D., *The Life of Birds*, BBC, 1998

Aubrey, John, *Natural History of Wiltshire*, David and Charles, 1969

Bains, C., 'Urban Areas', *Managing Habitats for Conservation*, Sutherland, W.J. and Hill, D.A. (Editors), Cambridge

Baker, R. (Editor), *The Mystery of Migration*, McDonald, 1980

Berry, R.J., *Inheritance and Natural History*, Collins, 1977

Berry, R.J. and Johnston, J.L., *The Natural History of Shetland*, Collins, 1980

Bibby, C., Burgess, N. and Hill, D., *Bird Census Techniques*, Academic Press/Collins, 1992

BOU, *The British List*, based on checklist of birds of Britain and Ireland, 1998 6th edition

Boyd, A.W., *A Country Parish*, Collins, 1951

Boyd, J.M. and Boyd L.I., *The Hebrides*, Collins, 1990

Brooke, Rupert, *Poetical Works*, Faber

Brooks, D. and Birkhead, T., *Cambridge Encyclopedia of Ornithology*, CUP, 1991

Brown, L., *Birds of Prey*, Harnlyn, 1979

Brown, L., *British Birds of Prey*, Collins, 1976

Burgess, N. et al., 'Reedbeds, Fens and Acid Bogs', *Managing Habitats for Conservation*, Sutherland, W.J., 1995

Cain, A.J., *Animal Species and their Evolution*, Hutchinson, 1954

Cain, A.J., *Nature in Wales*, National Museum of Wales, 1984, vol. 3

Campbell, P.J., *Blades of Grass*, Granary Press, 1986

Cannon, A., *Garden Bird Watch Handbook*, BTO, 1998

Chaucer, Geoffrey, *The Riverside Chaucer*, OUP, 1987

Clare, John, *Selected Poems*, Dent, 1976

Colininvause, C., *Why Big Force Animals are Rare*, Allen and Unwin, 1978

Conder, P., *The Wheatear*, Christopher Helm, 1954

Condry, W.M., *The Natural History of Wales*, Collins, 1981

Cooper, J.J. (Editor), *Brewers' Book of Myth and Legend*, Cassell, 1992

Cothridge, D. and Vinecombe, K., *Rare Birds in Britain and Ireland – a photographic record*, Collins, 1996

Cranswick, P. et al., *Wetland Bird Survey 1995-96*, BTO/WWT/RSPB/JNCC, Slimbridge, 1997

Dare, P., *A Buzzard Population*, Devon Birds, 1998

Davies, S., *The Wildlife of the Exe Estuary*,

Harbour Books, 1987

Diamond, J. , *Nature*, vol. 305, pp.17-18, 1983

Drabble, M. (Editor), *Oxford Companion to English Literature*, OUP, 1992

Du Feu, C. , *Nest Boxes*, BTO, 1993

Evans, I.H. (Editor), *Brewers' Dictionary of Phrase and Fable*, Cassell, 1987

Fisher, J. and Lockley, R. , *Sea Birds*, Collins, 1954

Fitler, R. , *London's Natural History*, Collins, 1945

Fitler, R. , *London's Birds*, Collins, 1949

Fowles, J. , *The French Lieutenant's Woman*, Jonathon Cape, 1969

Fowles, J. , *Wormholes*, Jonathon Cape, 1998

Fraser Darling, F. , *Island Years*, G. Bell and Sons, 1940

Fraser Darling, F. , *Natural History in the Highlands and Islands*, Collins, 1947

Freba, J. , *New Scientist*, 2.6.1976

Fuller, R. , *Bird Habitats in Britain*, Poyser, 1982

Fuller, R. , *Bird Life of Woodland and Forest*, Cambridge, 1995

Futuyama, D. , *Evolutionary Biology*, Sinaner Associated Ltd. , 1986 2nd Edition

Garner, M. , 'Identification of Yellow Legged Gulls', *British Birds*, vol. 90 Nos. 1 and 2, 1997

Gerald of Wales, *The Journey through Wales, The Description of Wales*, Penguin, 1978

Gibbings, R. , *Sweet Thames Run Softly*, Dent, 1940

Gibbons, D. et al. , *The New Atlas of Breeding Birds in Britain and Ireland 1988-1991*, Peyser, 1993

Glaves, D. (Editor), *Devon Bird Report*, 1996, 1998

Glegg, W. , *A History of the Birds of Middlesex*, Witherby, 1935

Gray J. , *How Animals Move*, Penguin, 1959

Greenoak F. , British Birds, *Their Folklore, Names and Literature*, A and C Black, 1979

Hale, W.G. , *Waders*, Collins, 1980

Harding, D.J.L. (Editor), *Britian since Silent Spring*, Institute of Biology, 1988

Hardy, Thomas, *New Wessex Selection of Poems*, Macmillan, 1978

Hardy, Thomas, *The Return of the Native*, Penguin, 1967

Harrison, T. and Hollom, P. , *The Great Crested Grebe Enquiry 1931*, Witherby, 1932

Harting, *Birds of Middlesex*, 1866

Hawkins, D. , *Hardy's Wessex*, Macmillan, 1983

Hayward, J. (Editor), *The Penguin Book of English Verse*, Penguin, 1983

Hearl, G. , *Bird Watching Guide to Menorca, Ibiza and Formentera*, Arlequin, 1996

Hickin, N.E. , *The Natural History of an English Forest*, Huychinson, 1971

Hickling, R. (Editor), *Enjoying Ornithology*, Poyser, 1983

Hollom, *Popular Handbook of British Birds*, Witherby, 1952

Hutchinson, C. , *Birds of Ireland*, Poyser, 1989

Huxley, J. , *Memories*, Penguin, 1972

Jeffries, R. , *Wildlife a Southern County*, Moonraker Press, 1978

Jones, G. (Editor), *The Oxford Book of Welsh Verse in English*, OUP, 1977

Jones, Hope and Bardsey, P. , *Observatory Report*, No. 40, 1996

Kaufman, K. , *Advanced Birding*, Boston, 1990

Kearton, R. and Kearton, C. , *British Birds Nests*, Cassell, 1908

Kennedy, P.G. , Ruttledge, R.F. and Scroope C.F. , *Birds of Ireland*, Oliver and Boyd, 1953

Kind, A.S. and McLelland J. , *Form and Function in Birds*, Academic Press, 1979

Kightly, C. et al. , *Pocket Guide to the Birds of Britain and Northern Europe*, Pica, 1998

Lacey, W.S. , *Welsh Wildlife in Trust*, North Wales Naturalist's Trust, 1970

Lack, D. , *The Natural Regulation of Animal Numbers*, OUP, 1954

Lack, P. , *Atlas of Wintering Birds in Britain and Ireland*, Poyser, 1986

Landsborough, Thomson A. (Editor), *New Dictionary of Birds*, Nelson, 1964

Leake, J. , *The Sunday Times*, July 10 1998

Lee, Laurie, *My Many Coated Man*, Andre Deutsch, 1955

Lee, Laurie, *The Sun My Monument*, Chatto and Windus, 1969

Le Feu, *Nest Boxes*, BTU, 1993

Lightowlers, P. , *New Scientist*, 5.5.1988

Lofts, B. , *Animal Photoperiodism*, Arnold

London Natural History Society, *The Birds of the London Area since 1900*,

Collins, 1957

Marchant, J.H. , Hudson, R. , Carter S. and Whittington P. , *Population Trends in British Breeding Birds*, BTO, 1990

Marren, P. , *England's National Nature Reserves*, Poyser, 1994

Mead, C. , 'Bird Migration', *Country Life*, 1983

Mitchell, F. , 'Shell Guide to Reading the Irish Landscape', *Country House*, 1986

Morrison, R.S. , *Words on Birds*

Mosley, J. and Hillier, C. , *Images of the Downs*, Macmillan, 1983

Moss, C. , 'Climate Change', *British Birds*, vol. 91 No. 8, 1998

Muldoon, P. (Editor), *Faber Book of Beasts*, Faber, 1997

NFU Countryside, *Conservation Frustrations*, NFU, 1996

Nelson, B. , *The Gannet*, Poyser, 1978

Nethersole-Thompson, *The Greenshank*, Collins, 1951

Newton, I. , *Finches*, Collins, 1972

Newton, I. , *Population Limitation in Birds*, Academic Press, 1998

Nicholson, E. M. , *Birds and Men*, Collins, 1951

Norman, D. and Tucker ,V. , *Where to Watch Birds in Devon and Cornwall*, Helm, 1997

Nuttall, N. , 'Ban on Eel Fishing', *The Times*, 30.9.1998

O'Conner, R. and Shrubb, M. , *Farming and Birds*, Cambridge, 1986

Oglivic, M. , 'Rare Breeding Species 1995', *British Birds* vol. 91 No. 8, 1998

O'Sullivan, M. , *Twenty Years A' Growing*, Chatto and Windus, 1933

Parker, M. , *Avian Physiology*, Zoological Society of London, 1975

Pemberton, J.E. , *Birdwatchers Yearbook 1999*, Buckingham Press, 1998

Perrins, C. , *British Tits*, Collins, 1979

Peterson, R. et al. , *A Field Guide to the Birds of Britain and Europe*, Collins, 1954

Potter, S. and Sargent, L. , *Pedigree; Words from Nature*, Collins, 1951

Prater, A. J. , *Birds of Estuaries Enquiry*, BTO/RSPB/WT

Pultman, G. , *The Book of the Axe*, Longman, 1875

Rachan, O. , *The Illustrated History of the Countryside*, Weidenfeld and Nicholson, 1994

Ratcliffe, D. , *Bird Life of Mountain and Upland*, Cambridge, 1990

Ravenscroft, N.O.M., 'The Status and Habit of the Nightjar', *Bird Study*, vol. 36, 1989

Ricks, C. (Editor), *The New Oxford Book of Victorian Verse*, OUP, 1987

Rigg, D. (Editor), *So To The Land*, Headline, 1994

Roberts, M. (Editor), *The Faber Book of Modern Verse*, Faber, 1965

Roberts, P., *Birds of Bardsey Bird and Field Observatory*, 1985

Rogers, M., Rarieties Committee, *Report on Rare birds in Great Britain in 1996*, British Birds vol. 90 No. 10, 1997

RSPB, *Birds of Conservation Importance*, 1996

RSPB, *Birds Magazine*, 1998

Ruttledge, R.F., *Ireland's Birds*, Witherby, 1966

Salim, A., *The Book of Indian Birds*, Bombay Natural History Society, 1964

Schmidt and Neilson, K., *How Animals Work*, Cambridge, 1988

Scott, P. and Fisher, J., *A Thousand Geese*, Collins, 1953

Scott, P., *Wild Chorus Country Life*, 1939

Severin, T., *The Brendan Voyage*, Abacus, 1978

Sharrock, J.T.R., *The Atlas of Breeding Birds*, BTO/Irish Wildbird Conservance, 1976

Sharrock, J.T.R., *Rare Birds in Britain and Ireland*, 1976

Sharrock, J.T.R., *The Natural History of Cape Clear Island*, Poysner, 1973

Sharrock, J.T.R., *Scarce Migrant Birds of Britain and Ireland*, Poysner, 1974

Shrubb, M., 'Birds and Farming Today', *Bird Study*, vol. 17, BTO, 1970

Simms, E., *British Thrushes*, Collins, 1978

Simms, E., *British Warblers*, Collins, 1985

Simms, E., *Woodland Birds*, Collins, 1971

Smith, M., 'Squawk on the Wildside', *The Independent*, 28.11.1998

Smith, S., *The Yellow Wagtail*, Collins, 1950

Snow, D. and Perrins, C.M., *The Birds of the Western Palearic*, 1998 Concise Edition OUP

Spearman, D., *The Animal Anthology*, John Baker, 1978

Sutherland, W. and Hill, D., *Managing Habitats for Conservation*, CUP, 1995

Tinbergen, N., 'Behaviour, Systematics and Natural Selection', *Ibis*, vol. 101 Nos. 3-4, BOU, 1959

Tinbergen, N., *Curious Naturalists*, Penguin, 1974

Tinbergen, N., *Herring Gulls World*, Collins, 1978

Tubbs, C., *The New Forest*, Collins, 1986

Tunnicliffe, C., *Shorelands Winter Diary*, Robinson, 1992

Vaux, C., *Why Big Fierce Animals are Rare*, Allen and Unwin, 1978

Vosey-Fitzgerald, B., *British Game*, Collins, 1946

Vickery, J., Chamberlain, D. and Henderson, I., 'Farming and Birds', *BTO News*, vol. 216/217, 1998

Wardle Fowler, W., *Kingham Old and New; Studies in a Rural Parish*, Blackwell, 1913

Webb, N., *Heathlands*, Collins, 1986

Weiner, J., *The Beak of the Finch*, Cape, 1994

Wildland News, Nos. 43-44, Scottish Wildlife Group, 1998

Williams, I., 'Boosting Black Grouse', *RSPB Birds*, Winter, 1998

Williams, M. (Editor), *The Way to Lords*, Willow Books, 1983

Williamson, K., *Fair Isle and Its Birds*, Oliver and Boyd, 1965

Witherly, H.F. et al., *The Handbook of British Birds*, Witherly, 1941

Wordsworth, William, *Selected Poetry*, Penguin, 1992

Weiner, J., *The Beak of the Finch*, Cape, 1994

Wildland News, Nos. 43-45, Scottish Wildland Group, 1998

Wyatt, J., *Bird Watching*, July 1997

THE BOOK ITSELF would have taken a very different form but for the suggestions of Polly, the editor at The Foundry, which led Nicky, my present wife, into research on the non-ornithological aspects of wildlife; verse, folklore and the amazing world of bird names. Francesca Greenoak's book on *'Folklore, Names and Literature'* has been a rich source, and John Clare must have written more bird verse than anyone.

Nicky was also deeply involved in later stages, as deadlines approached, and she became tied to proof-reading, printer and computer. Her daughter Sarah was at the control of the computing world, converting my appalling scribble and constant changes of mind into a legible and coherent form.

The enormous contributions of Colin Varndell and Val Baker, from across the county border in Dorset, are enormously appreciated.

Finally many thanks to my father, my birdwatching companion for more than twenty five years until his eyes began to fail and he returned to plants. To have been able to show him four arctic-alpine species that were new to him, high in Cwm Idwal, was a special treat as he moved into his eighties. My brother Christopher abandoned birding after leaving our sandwiches on the train but was my companion in watching sport and drinking beer.

Nicky and I now run a bed and breakfast business in Devon which we advertise as 'friendly and different'; the aim of this book is to be the same.

NOTES ON THE EDITOR

MARTIN WALTERS is a keen ornithologist and naturalist, with a special interest in ecology and conservation. After studying zoology at Oxford, he has since worked mainly in biological publishing. He has travelled extensively and watched birds in many different regions, both in Europe and further afield. Martin has written and edited several books on birds, wildlife and natural history.

Picture Credits

Illustrations by Valerie Baker: 16 (tr), 14 (br), 17 (tl), 18 (l), 20 (l), 24 (t,b), 26 (tr,l,br), 31 (tl,mr), 45 (tr), 46 (bl,tr), 47 (tl,tr), 48 (tr) 80 (t,b), and **General Illustrations** by Jennifer Kenna and Helen Courtney.

Ardea London Ltd: 10 (t,bl), 11 (t,br), 12 (b), 13 (t), 14 (tr,br), 15 (l,br), 16 (l), 21 (tr), 36 (b), 37 (bl), 39 (tr), 41 (tr), 51 (b), 60 (b), 62 (tl), 64 (t,m,b), 70 (b), 73 (a), 74 (t), 76 (b), 77 (t,b), 79 (m), 115 (b), 146 (t,m,b), 155 (t,b), 161 (t,br), 172 (t,b), 174 (t,b), 175 (tl,b), 176 (t,b), 177 (b), 178 (b), 179 (tl,tr,b), 180 (t,b), 181 (tl,tr), 190 (b), 239 (b), 307 (tr), 313 (t,bl,br), 321 (tl,tr,bl,br), 324 (tl,tr,b), 332 (b), 333 (bl,br), 336 (bl), 344 (tl,tr,b), 345 (tr), 346 (bl,br), 347 (bl,br), 349 (t,b), 354 (tl,tr), 361 (tr,mr), 365 (t), 368 (b), 381 (t),

A-Z Wildlife Library: 17 (r), 20 (br), 23 (tl,tr,bl), 25 (l), 27 (ml), 29 (b), 33 (b), 34 (b), 38 (b), 40 (b), 43 (b), 44 (b), 46 (br), 47 (b), 48 (tl,b), 49 (t,m,b), 54 (t), 55 (tr,ml,b), 56 (tl,tr), 59 (b), 62 (br), 63 (tr), 64 (m,b), 66 (t), 67 (bl,br), 68 (t), 69 (t,mr,b), 72 (b), 84 (tl), 85 (t,b), 86 (r), 87 (tl), 96 (b), 97 (tl), 98 (tl), 99 (tr), 100 (m,b), 102 (t), 104 (br), 105 (bl), 107 (tl), 109 (br), 112 (tr,b), 114 (t), 115 (tl), 132 (t,b), 140 (t), 149 (t), 150 (bl), 157 (b), 161 (bl), 162 (br), 164 (c), 166 (tl), 167 (t,b), 171 (b), 181 (b), 182 (bl), 183 (r), 184 (tl), 188 (tl,tr,b), 190 (t), 184 (tr,br,bl), 185 (t,b), 192 (rl,tr), 197 (m,br), 204 (tl), 207 (l,r), 210 (m), 211 (t,m), 216 (b), 217 (t,m), 220 (t), 221 (t), 222 (t,b), 223 (t,bl,br), 224 (t,bl), 237 (b), 240 (br), 242 (t;.tr), 246 (tl), 251 (b), 253 (tl,tr,b), 254 (t), 256 (t), 257 (tr,b), 315 (t), 327 (t,m,b), 330 (bl,br), 333 (t), 335 (tr), 338 (t,m,b), 345 (tl), 353 (tl,b), 357 (bl), 373 (t), 379 (b),

Foundry Arts: 195 (mr),

Natural Image: 37 (tl,br), 50 (t), 51 (t), 53 (t,b), 71 (t), 72 (m), 73 (b), 74 (b), 75 (tr,ml), 76 (t), 78 (t,b), 79 (b), 96 (t), 97 (tr,b), 108 (tr), 110 (tr,b), 147 (t), 164 (b), 180 (m), 337 (t,bl,br), 346 (t), 365 (b), 382 (b),

RSPB: 118 (tl,tr,b), 124 (b), 131 (tr,b), 145 (t,m,b), 147 (b), 154 (tl,b), 159 (m), 160 (t,b), 165 (l,r), 169 (tr,b), 173 (t,b), 178 (tl,tr), 193 (m,b), 194 (t,b), 195 (tl,bl), 196 (t,m,b), 201 (tl,tr), 202 (t,b), 205 (t,m,b), 219 (b), 308 (t,l,r), 309 (tl,tr,b), 311 (t,b), 316 (t,bl,br), 317 (t,b), 318 (tl,tr), 319 (t,m,b), 320 (b), 322 (bl,br), 323 (t,m,b), 325 (t,m,b), 326 (br), 328 (tl,tr,b), 329 (t,m,b), 332 (t), 335 (tr,b), 336 (t,br), 339 (t,br), 340 (t,b), 341 (b), 343 (t), 348 (b), 354 (bl,br), 355 (t,m), 364 (bl,br), 366 (b), 370 (b), 378 (b),

Colin Varndell: 10 (br), 13 (b), 14 (l), 15 (tr), 18 (tr,br), 19 (tl,bl), 20 (tr), 21 (tl,br), 22 (b), 23 (br), 25 (t,br), 27 (tl,br), 28 (t,b), 29 (tl,ml,mr), 30 (tr,br), 31 (tr,bl), 32 (tr,ml,br), 33 (t), 34 (m), 35 (t,b), 39 (tl,ml), 41 (tl,b), 42 (ml,tr,b), 43 (t,ml), 44 (t,m), 45 (tl,b), 52 (t,bl,br), 54 (b), 55 (tl), 56 (b), 57 (tl,tr,b), 58 (tl,bl,br), 59 (al,ar), 60 (t,m), 61 (t), 62 (bl), 63 (tl,b), 64 (t), 66 (b), 67 (t), 69 (ml), 70 (t), 71 (m,b), 78 (m,b), 79 (t), 81 (b), 82 (b), 84 (b), 87 (b), 88 (b), 89 (t,bl,br), 94 (tl,tr,b), 95 (tl,tr,b), 98 (tr,b), 99 (tl,b), 100 (t), 101 (tl,tr,b), 102 (bl,br), 103 (t,b), 104 (t,bl), 105 (t,br), 106 (t,m,b), 107 (tr,b), 108 (bl,br), 109 (t,br), 110 (tl), 111 (b,t), 112 (tl), 113 (t,br,bl), 114 (bl,br), 115 (tr), 116 (t,m,b), 117 (t,m,b), 119 (t,m,b), 120 (t,b), 121 (t,b), 122 (t,bl,br), 123 (b), 124 (t), 125 (t,b), 126 (t,bl,br), 127 (t,b), 128 (t,b), 129 (t,br,bl), 130 (tr,tl,b), 131 (tl), 133 (t,m,b), 134 (t), 134 (bl), 134 (br), 135 (tl), 135 (tr), 135 (b), 136 (r), 137 (t), 137 (bl), 137 (br), 138 (br), 139 (t), 139 (b), 140 (b), 141 (t), 142 (tl), 142 (tr), 142 (b), 143 (tl), 143 (tr), 143 (b), 144 (t), 144 (bl), 144 (br), 148 (t), 148 (bl), 148 (br), 149 (m), 149 (b), 150 (t), 150 (br), 151 (t), 151 (m), 151 (b), 152 (bl), 152 (br), 153 (l), 153 (r), 155 (m), 156 (tl), 156 (tr), 156 (b), 157 (t), 156 (m), 158 (t,m), 158 (b), 159 (b), 162 (tr,bl), 163 (tr,tl,b), 166 (br), 168 (tl,tr,b), 169 (tl), 170 (tl,tr,b), 171 (tl,tr), 182 (t,br), 183 (l), 186 (ml,mr,b), 187 (tr,b), 191 (t,m,b), 184 (rl), 192 (b), 193 (t), 197 (tr), 198 (t,b), 199 (b), 201 (b), 203 (tl,b), 204 (b;.br), 206 (tl,tr,b), 208 (t,bl,br), 209 (t,m,b), 210 (t,b), 211 (b), 212 (t,b), 213 (t,m,b), 214 (t,m,b), 215 (t,m,b), 216 (t), 217 (b), 218 (tl,tr,bl,br), 220 (b), 221 (m,b), 224 (br), 225 (t,b), 226 (ar,cl,cr,b), 227 (t,b), 228 (t,m,b), 230 (t,m,b), 231 (tr,bl,br), 232 (tl,tr,bl,br), 233 (tr,b), 236 (t,m,b), 237 (t,m,b), 239 (t), 240 (tr,br), 241 (t,br,bl), 243 (t,m,b), 244 (t,m,b), 246 (tr,b), 247 (b), 248 (tr,tl,b), 249 (tr,tl,b), 250 (tl,tr,b), 251 (m), 252 (t,b), 254 (b), 255 (l,r), 256 (bl), 257 (tr), 310 (tr,l), 312 (t,m,b), 318 (b), 322 (t), 326 (r), 331 (l,r), 339 (bl), 345 (b), 347 (t), 351 (t), 352 (b), 353 (tr), 357 (t), 359 (t.bl.br), 306 (m,b), 307 (b), 367 (b), 369 (t), 371 (r), 372 (b), 380 (b),

Colin Varndell/Martin Cade: 234 (tr),

Colin Varndell/Peter Coe: 12 (t), 19 (br), 22 (t), 34 (t), 38 (t), 41 (ml), 50 (b), 61 (br,bl), 68 (b), 72 (b), 75 (b), 81 (t), 82 (t), 83 (al,ar), 84 (tr), 86 (l), 87 (tr), 88 (t), 132 (m), 136 (l), 138 (tl,tr), 141 (b), 175 (tr), 177 (tl,tr), 186 (b), 189 (t,b), 199 (ml,mr), 200 (t,b), 203 (tr), 229 (t,b), 234 (tl,b), 235 (t,mb), 238 (b), 242 (t), 245 (b), 251 (t), 256 (br), 306 (t), 307 (tl), 310 (br), 314 (t,m,b), 315 (m,b), 330 (tl,tr), 334 (t,bl,br), 342 (tl,tr,b), 343 (b), 350 (t,b), 351 (b), 352 (t), 355 (b), 356 (t,bl,br), 357 (br), 358 (tl,tr,b), 360b) 361 (tl), 362 (t,bl,br), 363 (b), 364 (tl,tr), 383 (t), 384 (b).

Colin Varndell/Peter Leigh: 36 (t), 39 (b), 83 (b), 361 (ml),

Windrush Photos: 361 (br).

Every effort has been made to contact the copyright holders and we apologise in advance for any ommissions. We will be pleased to insert appropriate acknowledgements in subsequent editions of this publication.

Index

INDEX

Contents

Wales

Scotland

[Title page image: Greg Martin]

About the Author

With five highly acclaimed surf travel titles under her belt, Demi Taylor is one of Britain's most authoritative voices on surf travel and a regular contributor to national magazines and newspapers. The idea for *Adventure Britain* crystalized on a back to basics surf trip powered by public transport and pedals, camping out and foraging for the fruits of the land, a journey based on the philosophy of enjoying the natural environment without leaving a lasting impression on it. The book draws on her experiences climbing, mountain biking, canoeing, hiking, surfing and foraging in the great outdoors, linking up with like-minded individuals and organizations. She has co-authored Footprint's *Surfing Britain & Ireland* and *Surfing Europe* and lives in Cornwall overlooking the sea. halfnelson.co.uk.

Acknowledgements

I'd like to say thank you to all those who contributed their time, thoughts, knowledge, wisdom, support, words and images to the project. I'd especially like to thank my co-author of *Surfing Britain* Chris Nelson, wordsmiths and deadline chargers Clare Howdle and Hayley Spurway, Darren Saxton of Mountain Aspirations, Andrew Bateman of Mountain Innovations, Swim Trek's Brad Andersen, SAS campaign's Director Andy Cummins, Ruth Somerville of the Ramblers, photographers extraordinaire Wig Worland and Seb Rogers. I'd also like to thank climber Alex Palmer, Mal Dickson of Southwest Adventures, Marcus Harrison of the Wild Food School, Roger Knight at the Bike Barn, Nick Webb, Adrian Boots at Walk the Mendips, Eric Wallis MBE of the SWCPA, Layla Ashworth and Robyn Davies at the National Trust, Kerenza Townsend of the DNPA, Waterbourne's Drew Pilley, Matthew Wheadon of Cornish Rock Tors, the Extreme Academy's Carl Coombes, Sarah Cullen at Nuts4Climbing, Laura Preece at the BHF, Hannah Curzon at the YHA, Robin Renwick, Mrs Tee, Chris Bull at HIKS, climber Claudia Sarner, Polly Robinson of Wild Food Safari, Caroline Holmes of the Great Swim, Ollie Jay at Active4seasons, Nick and Jill at More than Mountains, Adam at Joint Adventures, Paul Tatersall of Go Further Scotland, Mike Pescod of Abacus Mountaineering, Mike Gale at G2 Outdoor, Polly McClure and Tim Willis of Wilderness Scotland, Kirstin Reeve of Nae Limits, Bill Strachan of Scotch on the Rocks, Synergy's Mark Davies, Keith Gault of Hillways, Glenmore Lodge's Scott Webster, Call of the Wild's Dave Thomas, Charli Holder and Alice Middleton at TYF, John Harold at Moelyci, Andrew Lamb of Wales Outdoors, Claire Carlile at Preseli Venture, Mark Hanford of Snowdonia Adventures, Sylvia Fitzpatrick of the Rock Climbing Company and the brilliant Dave Cheetham at Plas y Brenin for their invaluable input, insight and guidance. Special thanks as always to Mum, The Big Dog and Claire King.

Huge appreciation goes to the whole Footprint crew who epitomize the real spirit of adventure travel: they've been robbed in Costa Rica, crashed motorbikes in Nam, caught Dengue Fever in Venezuela and been shot in a hold up in Mexico – all in the name of research. Special thanks to the dream team: Al Murphy, Angus Dawson, Dav Rungasamy, Pat Dawson and Rob Lunn.

Contributors

Additional editorial and research by Chris Nelson, Clare Howdle and Hayley Spurway.

Photographic contributions by Wig Worland, Seb Rogers, Greg Martin, Alex Messenger, Andy Ward, John Sparshatt, Alex Williams, Andy McAndlish, Russ Shea, Jordan Weeks, Layla Astley Ashworth, Bike Barn, Nick Webb, Geoff Tydeman, Ben Rowe, Tim Nunn, Dartmoor National Park, The Gill, Estpix, Gary Knights, Mike Baldwin, Elizabeth Tom, Bedruthan Steps Hotel, Belle Tents, Fat Hen, The Landmark Trust, Roger Powley, Chris Bull, BHF, Annie Mitchel, Kim Gilmour, John Cullen, Dncan Kendall, Stef Kerswell, Les Andrean, Sarah Cullen, Nuts4Climbing, Joss Bay Surf School, Stuart Evans, Hidden Spring, The Duke of Cambridge, Beech Hill, The Real Eating Company, Neil Dotti, The Canoe Hire Company, Simon Pattison, Andrew Dunwood, Swim Trek, Wild Food Safari, Dale Reynolds, Mark Dann, Great Swim, Dave Tyrell, Darren Saxton, Susie Norris, Neil Mansfield, Paul Reynolds, Adam McCluskey, Stu Norton, Natural England, Ollie Jay, C2C Surf School, Tony Marsh, Nae Limits, Glenmore Lodge, Paul Tomkins VS/Mountain Innovations, Synergy, Scotch on the Rocks, Tim Willis, Wilderness Scotland, Keith Gault, James Laver, Andy Law, Go Further Scotland, Howard Walker, Pete Roberts, MacNeill and D Taylor.

Our island is an alluring array of tarn-decked peaks and depressions. It is riven with rivers and interlaced by a spider's web of trails and paths exploring hidden wooded pockets and connecting vast, open tracts where village inns are reassuring beacons of hope and refreshment. The coastline is a confusion of hard jagged edges, soft sands, sheer cliffs, and shapely dunes. Vast public, sandy bays neighbour private coves whose secrets are only revealed to those willing to wait for an ebbing tide.

Standing on top of the grassy hill, boots caked in mud, a granite tor rises in the foreground with a climber pushing for the summit. Scanning 360 degrees, eyes log miles and miles of singletrack potential roller-coastering across the moorland, occasional mountain bikers speed-blurring down bone-shaking descents. The hike in skirted wooded valleys, the air heavy with the scent of wild garlic, kayakers edging into fast-flowing rivers that snake away into the distance to create cool pockets and plunge pools for swimmers. Beyond, the rivers empty into the sea where there are cliffs to be scaled, winds to be harnessed and waves to be ridden with each new swell. For us adventurists, when we look at Britain we see summits, valleys, rivers, coastline and a landscape of endless possibilities – a natural outdoor playground waiting to be explored. Whether we're surfers bored in a flat spell, MTBers looking for water not mud, hikers wanting to scale new heights and climb, or just want to maximise our time outside, this is our domain.

The ethos involves reconnecting with the landscape, translating the terrain and seeing the endless opportunities for fun laid bare. It's about getting out there and experiencing Britain's natural heritage without leaving a lasting impression on it, treading lightly where possible. It's about common sense: respecting access issues or climbing restrictions, not disturbing wildlife or trampling the flora, foraging for just what is needed as opposed to picking branches clean, sticking to trails or giving them a wide berth when local guidelines advise and being aware of erosion and the impact increased footfall can have on an area. It's also about taking care of rubbish and leaving an area in a better state than when found, even if that means taking just one piece of litter from the beach after a morning of kiteboarding or picking up a thoughtlessly

Alex Messenger

Wig Worland

Wilderness Scotland

Wild swimming

Wild swimming is about finding a natural body of water where you can enjoy either a dip or a nice swim and feel yourself go as you relax, fully absorbed in the moment and the environment.

Essential kit The swim cap. In the UK especially where the water can be sometimes a little chilly it is important to always go into the water with a nice bright/thick swim cap. This not only alerts other people that a swimmer is in the water but will help keep your body warm because most of your body heat is lost through your head.

Preparation It is as much physical as mental. You can be a great swimmer or a recreational paddler but should have previously swum the distance you would like to swim on an outdoor expedition at least 3 times beforehand to ensure you are able to comfortably cope with the distance. If you are underprepared you will feel tired and not enjoy the all-round experience. Going into the unknown can be frightening; know your boundaries and take it slowly to ensure you are always moving forward and take the positives out of each new adventure.

Planning Choose a swim that interests you, ensure you are allowed to swim in this area and that the water is clean. Arrange a friend to swim with watch you; never swim alone. Assess the area: are there any hazards or boat traffic. Have the correct equipment for the type of swim: wetsuit, sunblock, swim cap, hot drinks at the end, boat support, blankets, first aid. Always prepare for the worst. Enjoy yourself and always swim within yourself.

Technique Start your stroke near the surface of the water in front of you and make sure you finish with a full stroke exiting the water past your hips. This will ensure you are getting everything out of your stroke each time.

Advice Have a goal whether it be to work on your breathing during your training session or having one special swim a year that gives you something to train for. Your swims will have a purpose and you will feel that every swim you do gets you closer to your goal, whether it be a dip in cold water or a 2-mile ocean swim.

Brad Andersen, SwimTrek, swimtrek.com, T01273-73971.

SwimTrek

discarded drinks can after topping out on a clifftop climb. We are essentially the keepers of our own natural world. There are also of course the implications of the impact that the environment can have on us – negatives as well as positives. As a result it's important to go armed with all the facts necessary for enjoying the landscape and be mindful of potential risks that you can avoid without affecting your enjoyment. Dress appropriately for conditions which could quickly alter, when walking and climbing bear in mind ticks and the risk of Lyme disease, check weather and sea conditions and assess for danger areas such as sewage outflows, groynes or rip currents before jumping in, be mindful of the quality of inland waters from blue green algae in lakes to the risk of Weil's disease in more urban locations. Know your limits in terms of when to push them and when to be guided by them.

These adventures are about people power not petrol power and considering the impact of where, when and how you undertake them. And while the thrills aim to be guilt free they certainly aren't light on excitement or adrenaline. The CRoW Act of 2000 has improved and clarified our access to areas of open land as well as improving nature conservation and wildlife protection, (see the Ramblers on page 8 for more details). However, our rights to access

and navigate the waterways of England and Wales are much more limited (see riversaccess.org for full details). Accompanied by a trusty OS map, walking is our greatest tool, allowing us to explore those hidden realms that lie off-road and it can be as easy or as challenging as you want it to be. Walking is about the journey not just getting from A to B, it can often reveal other unexpected delights along the way. A walk may lead you to a crag just begging to be climbed, it could take you to a surf break away from the tarmaced paths and the masses, it may reveal a tarn or a river where a quick dip can be snatched or take you along a trail to later explore on two wheels.

It's about considering how you embark upon your big escape into the great outdoors and the way you choose to travel; taking the start of your adventure as the moment you close your door behind you. For example, taking the sleeper train to Inverness as opposed to hopping on a cheap flight is going to have more impact on you, allowing you to absorb the terrain through which you're passing, and make less impact on the environment. But there are of course times when going public just won't get you where you need to be. Look at car pooling – you can share the cost and share the ride as well as the stoke of the adventure. The aim in putting this book together has been to give you the best alternatives for reaching your destination – listing the nearest or most convenient train station, highlighting local transport links or even providing the number of a bio-fuel cab company.

It's about thinking about how and where you stay. There are accommodation awards such as the Green Tourism Business Scheme which recognises those who are attempting to operate their businesses in a sustainable way. This means those who support the local economy and local suppliers, enhance the natural environment and are actively engaged in limiting their impact through energy efficiency, water and waste management. The David Bellamy Conservation Awards recognise those campsites and parks that are actively working to protect and enhance Britain's environment through the creation of wildlife meadows and woodlands as well as employing sustainable practices in terms or water and energy. And while we've included accommodation recommendations that have received these accolades, these aren't

Alex Messenger

Climbing

Climbing is ascending a piece of rock. You could be sport climbing, 'trad' adventure climbing or bouldering. You could be on a relatively small boulder, a roadside single-pitch crag, an isolated mountain or an exposed sea cliff. It is not just about taking risks, finding adventure, being in the outdoors, overcoming a challenge or having fun. It is all these things and more.

Essential kit Well fitted climbing shoes that are appropriate to the style and level of climbing that you undertake are essential. For example, beginners would need a 'broad-lasted' shoe that won't squash up the toe — comfort over performance. It's no use having the latest most technical pair of shoes if they are so uncomfortable that the pain stops you enjoying your climbing. Also a helmet — but don't forget to use it whilst you're climbing to help keep you safe!

Preparation Being strong doesn't mean you will always climb well. A high overall level of aerobic fitness will be of great help along with having achievable goals to aim for, such as a particular route you aspire to climb so that any training is focused and worthwhile. In terms of mental preparation, overcome the fear of falling whilst lead climbing so you know that if you were to fall, the protection that you've placed is going to work.

Planning Consult the relevant guidebook for the crag, this will contain access information and any restrictions such as those imposed by the landowner or for environmental reasons for nesting birds etc. Think about what protection is necessary to take with you on the climb. There's no need taking a set of massive 'cams' to weigh you down if the route follows a finger width crack all the way. Before you set off up your route, break it down into smaller sections and try to visualize where you could place some protection, where you could get a rest, what type of move you should do at a particular point.

Technique Think about your balance when climbing. Understanding where your centre of gravity is in relation to your hand and most importantly your footholds will help to increase the efficiency and effectiveness of your movement.

Advice Climb the style of routes that you struggle on and often shy away from. For example, if your climbing standard on 'slabby' routes is letting you down, then go and force yourself to climb 'slabby' type routes. Face your challenges head-on and it will improve your overall performance.

Darren Saxon, Mountain Aspirations, T01302-888842, mountainaspirations.co.uk.

The Art of Rambling
Ruth Somerville, The Ramblers

Nothing beats the sheer freedom of setting out armed with just a pair of boots, a cagoul(!) and a map, in one of the world's most walk-friendly countries. One crucial piece of advice, however, is never overreach yourself; it's better to underestimate your abilities and have energy left at the end of a walk, than overestimate them and end up in trouble. Just because it's in the UK, doesn't mean it's not dangerous. If in doubt, join a walking group. They might be able to teach you how to map read too…

There are many, many reasons why it is green to walk; on bank holidays for example, the average reveller will travel around 304 miles, releasing around 85 kg of CO_2 emissions into the atmosphere. A walking holiday, however, reached by train or even on foot, will cost the environment nothing and save you an average 5½ hours on a jam-packed road. In everyday life too you can make a huge amount of difference by walking; a quarter of all car journeys are under two miles – imagine how much greener and safer the country would be if these journeys were taken on foot. At base, however, is a logical but crucial point; walking fosters a love of the environment, and people who love their environment are more likely to protect, maintain and fight for it.

Walking has negligible negative environmental impacts, especially when the will is there. The Ramblers encourages two types of behaviour: to walk local and/or use public transport and to follow the countryside code. In popular places (such as Hadrian's Wall) we suggest you follow local advice, and follow the local code of practice.

Access: England and Wales Around 1.4 million ha of land in England and Wales are designated as access land, where the public has a right to walk under the Countryside and Rights of Way Act 2000. The exact areas of land covered are shown on official maps prepared by the Countryside Agency and the Countryside Council for Wales. Access land may be signed on the ground with the access symbol.

The rights apply to specific areas of land classed as mountain (over 1968 ft), moor, heath, down and registered common land (areas of land which were historically used communally by local residents). In addition landowners are now able voluntarily to dedicate other categories of land for public access.

Landowners can restrict or prevent access for up to 28 days a year without special permission, and can apply for additional restrictions for purposes such as land management, conservation and fire prevention. These closures apply only to the wider right of access. For example where land closed under the 28-day rule is crossed by a footpath that is a public right of way, you still have a right to use the footpath.

You might also see a sign indicating the end of wider access. This should only be used where the boundary between access land and non-access land is unclear. It applies only to wider access, not for example to rights of way that continue beyond the sign.

Access: Scotland Traditionally in Scotland people have roamed free for years, but it was not laid down in law and there were disputes. Scotland does have rights of way (routes used by the public for 20 years, which link two public places) but there is no official map of public paths.

The access ethos was enshrined in law via the Land Reform (Scotland) Act 2003, in February 2005. This establishes a statutory right of responsible access to almost all land and water, so long as you behave responsibly. Ramblers Association Scotland was instrumental in getting this passed. The only access-free areas are 'domains', which is land set out as private, such as gardens. Scotland doesn't have a comprehensive, statutory path network and it's this sweeping freedom which, ironically, causes the problems and disputes

The Ramblers make walking available to everyone through improving places for walking and encouraging people to walk – we are Britain's walking charity. As a member, your £29.50 per year will buy: a choice of 28,000 walks around the country; a network of 20s and 30s groups to join, subscriptions to award-winning *Walk* magazine and discounts at many outdoor stores. Possibly most importantly, your money will support our vital and unique work, quite simply ensuring that there is a rights-of-way network for people to go walking on. The Ramblers, T020-7339 8500, ramblers.org.uk. Find us on Facebook and Twitter.

The Countryside Code: respect, protect, enjoy

❶ Be safe, plan ahead and follow any signs
❷ Leave gates and property as you find them
❸ Protect plants and animals and take your litter home.
❹ Keep dogs under close control.
❺ Consider other people.
For further details see naturalengland.org.uk.

the only bastions of green holidays or the only ways to limit the size of your footprint. We've also included sites which allow you to camp simply and off-grid meaning you impact less on and connect more with your local environment. We've included many good B&Bs that support regional producers, featuring local, seasonal goodies at the breakfast table which not only limits food miles but gives you a real taste of the region of you're in. Sometimes, it's just about staying as locally as possible, limiting your daily miles, and embracing the food and produce that's there on your doorstep.

Through our enjoyment of our natural heritage, we are more inclined to want to protect, conserve and enhance it – it is after all our playground, our own backyard. There are also numerous groups and charities who work hard behind the scenes, lobbying on our behalf for access to landscapes and waterways as well as improvements and enhancements to our environment. These bodies are worth supporting wherever and whenever possible – find the group that is most relevant to you and get involved, they need your support.

This is a growing movement. There are now more of us than ever getting out into the great outdoors, seeking the mental and physical

challenges and escapes that our countryside and coastline affords. And it's not just there for the people who live close by. Whether you live in central London, Leeds or Edinburgh, the outdoors is closer than you think; after all no British city is more than two hours from the coastline and the green countryside is often just a short hop away. There are even hidden oases within urban confines if you know where to look. Ultimately, it's about getting out there, getting active and enjoying your environment. It's about being an outsider.

G2Outdoor

Hill walking

Hill walking. It's the term we use in Britain for hiking up the hills and mountains and it's fantastic! It's the physical challenge, the stunning views, a sense of freedom and adventure, an opportunity for solitude and a chance to experience wilderness and nature.

Essential kit Walking boots aside, it's hard to single out one piece of kit. The conditions can be very changeable (4 seasons in one day) so you need to be prepared to cover a good number of eventualities: waterproof jacket and trousers, warm hat and gloves, map and compass (and know how to use them), food and drink, warm fleece, sun block, etc.

Preparation Endurance and stamina is what you need rather than a high level of aerobic fitness. The best training is walking itself so it's a case of building up the difficulty of the walk over time. Activities like cycling and running are also good.

Planning Start with a good topographic map of the area and a guidebook can also be a great help. There's lots to consider but the 2 most important are the available time or daylight and

what the mountain weather is likely to be. Both the Met Office and MWIS provide bespoke mountain forecasts. A proper plan provides you with an opportunity to consider and plan for any likely difficulties en route as well as letting other people know where you're going.

Technique It's vitally important you pace yourself. In the mountains a fit hill walker wouldn't expect to go any faster than 3 mph on the flat. An average would be closer to 2½ mph with extra time for stops and breaks. If you're ascending you need to add on an additional 5-10 mins per 300 ft. If you plan to walk over the mountains tops I would aim to do no more than 7-10 miles in a day to start off. Walk at a pace that allows you to hold a conversation. If you can't you're probably going too fast

Advice Our mountains may not be very high on a global scale but don't underestimate them. They can provide plenty of difficulties for the ill prepared.

Andrew Bateman, Mountain Innovations, T01497-831331, scotmountain.co.uk.

Surfing

Surfing is a lifestyle that draws you in. Handle with care, it's addictive. Britain is a great place to be a surfer – no city is more than 2 hrs from the nearest stretch of an 11,075-mile coastline and there's a whole infrastructure designed to help get you in the water.

Essential kit A good wetsuit is an essential – and recent developments in neoprene technology mean they are warmer and more flexible than ever. The key is to get one that's a good fit; too big and the water will flood in, too tight and you'll not be able to move properly, the neoprene will stretch too much and not keep you as warm. Look at what the local surfers are wearing, they usually gravitate to the brand and type of suit that works well for their region.

Preparation Surfing engages a whole range of muscles that you never normally work. Take the fittest person you know, put them on a surf board for the first time and they will be exhausted before they know it. The best training for surfing is more surfing. Get in the water whenever you can, even when the surf's pretty crappy; that way you'll improve your paddle fitness and your stamina, which will pay dividends when the surf gets good.

Planning On the surface surfing seems pretty green: no noisy engines, just you and a wave. But unless you cycle to the beach and ride a wooden Mal in your boardies, we do have a guilty secret – wetsuits, boards and our transport are all based on oil derivatives, which means while we may be eco minded, our eco credentials are pretty poor. We can try and minimize our carbon footprint in a number of ways. Fewer long-haul flights, more local surf trips. Car pooling saves on petrol and parking costs, but is also better for the environment. Learn how to read a weather chart, it can help you score when the swell prediction sites get it wrong, and save you a journey when it's going to be flat or howling onshore. Watch out for new wetsuits and board technologies that are trying to pioneer more environmentally friendly materials – support them if you can.

Technique One of the most underestimated yet difficult skills to perfect is the duck dive. Work on your technique, get some advice and watch how good surfers do it. Nail it and you'll be able to pass beneath waves while paddling out as opposed to getting worked by each breaking wave, helping you spend more time out back and less time in the white water.

Advice Get a good board that suits where you surf and the actual level you're at (be honest with your shaper). That's the most important thing. Then, if you're determined to progress, watch good surfers and analyze where they place their feet and how they use their bodies when taking off, generating speed down the line and turning. Then get a (patient) friend to video your technique and compare your stance and style. It'll be immediately obvious what you're doing wrong.

Chris Nelson, author of the surfer's ultimate travel guides
Surfing Britain and Ireland and *Surfing Europe.*

Surfers against Sewage
Andy Cummins, SAS Campaigns Director

Surfers Against Sewage (SAS) has come a very long way since its launch in 1990. In the process, it has achieved huge successes for the UK's water quality, acting as a pivotal player in the fight to ensure the country's waves, oceans and beaches are protected from environmental abuse. Now approaching its 20th anniversary, and still commanding the biggest membership base of any European green boardriders' pressure group, SAS remains the most important organization protecting the interests of surfers, wave riders and recreational water users in the UK.

With the world's ocean environment under increasing pressure, and emerging threats to our coastline from climate change and other industrial practices, SAS's remit today reaches further and wider than ever, addressing critical issues from marine litter to climate change. Along with the growing number of new threats, some of the great campaign successes of the 1990s could go into reverse without SAS's ongoing vigilance and experience to take on government and industry at the highest level. And this includes the threat of returning sewage and reversal of sewage treatment levels.

SAS campaigns originated and remain based in the direct experiences surfers and many other recreational water users have whilst enjoying the seas around the UK. We are all lucky to have caught the bug for a sport that takes us into the heart of the natural world and that taps into the pulses of green energy that criss-cross our seas. As such, we all get first-hand experience of the damage that is inflicted on the coastal and oceanic environment. This is perhaps why SAS's grassroots action is so popular and attracts support from far and wide. On a very basic level, we've all seen litter on the beach and perhaps even had our board smudged with a stain of crude oil occasionally. This first-hand experience impassions us and motivates us to take direct action. It heightens our senses about what should be done, which abusers need to be hunted down and, increasingly, the part we all play in protecting the stuff we love: oceans, waves, beaches, dunes – the natural world that surrounds us when we surf.

You could be forgiven for thinking SAS just tackled sewage issues and represented only surfers. Our name today is almost a misnomer but its heritage is strong, and helps us open doors to the media and decision makers and instils fear in those who abuse the UK's coastal heritage. A name change might help better describe what's in the tin but could never replace the 20 years of campaigning and recognition that has been so hard fought and won. So SAS it is and will remain, just don't let it mislead you.

SAS campaigns help protect the UK's oceans, waves, beaches and coastlines for everyone to enjoy as safely as possible. Whether you're a family visiting the beach for a week every summer, a surfer in the water year round, a kayaker or undertaking any other sport or pastime that brings you into contact with the UK's coastline or sea, you'll already have benefited from SAS tireless campaigning.

SAS is also playing an important part in encouraging the 'surf industry' to improve its own environmental record. We are, of course, well aware of the paradox of surfing and the environment – it's a sport with the natural world at its heart but heavily reliant on the petrochemical industry: the travel, boards, wetsuits, wax and all the associated paraphernalia, all of which directly and indirectly have an impact on the environments we cherish. But companies are changing, making steps forward, some tentatively, some in leaps and bounds, and this should be recognised and encouraged. Surfers should do their part and take these green options where possible to help accelerate their transition to the mainstream markets.

Whether SAS is taking on industry, lobbying Parliament, applying pressure to local governments or making sure the renewable electricity industry is considering surfing communities when developing its new offshore installations, one thing can be sure – SAS is fighting the corner for surfers, recreational water users and the environment, basing its arguments on scientific fact and proposing the positive, achievable, sustainable solutions to deliver protection for our beloved waves, oceans, beaches and coastlines.

SAS, campaigning for clean, safe recreational waters for EVERYONE. Get involved: sas.org.uk.

Slowcoast
Nick Hand

Summer 2009, I cycled 4600 miles clockwise around the British coastline, starting at my home in Bristol on 21st June and finishing on 3rd October. On the way I met, photographed and interviewed potters, basket makers, film stars, musicians, other cyclists, tea tasters, artists, fishermen and sculptors.

I can't think of a better way of finding out about Britain. Journeys are about discovery, finding out about ourselves mostly, but also learning new stuff everywhere you look. There is no doubt that you miss so much flying along roads in a car. On a bike you can stop pretty much anywhere, you drift through landscapes and miss very little.

Hemingway, as he would, puts it very nicely:

'It is by riding a bicycle that you learn the contours of a country best, since you have to sweat up the hills and coast down them. Thus you remember them as they actually are, while in a motor car only a high hill impresses you, and you have no such accurate remembrance of country you have driven through as you gain by riding a bicycle.'

When I started out I had planned to do about 50 miles a day. I liked the roundness of the figures 100 days, 50 miles a day. But as it happens it was a good kind of target. It is achievable by the average leisure cyclist (which is how I would describe myself), and in the summer months of long days, you can take your time, stop at any little café that takes your fancy and still achieve your 50 miles.

The hills are interesting. Even with a fully laden bike (one that is pretty difficult to lift at all), you can get up the steepest of hills. Sometimes I would stop four or five times on a big hill, but got there eventually. And with that heavy bike you can celebrate by bombing down the other side. I got to quite enjoy the hills and kind of missed them in the flatlands of Norfolk and Suffolk. Though as any end to ender (Land's End to John O'Groats) will tell you that Devon and Cornwall offer some big old climbs and lots of them.

Since I finished the ride, there is a question that people have asked regularly: 'what's the best place that you have visited?'

I would say that our coastline is beautiful and amazing and it's hard to pick a single place. What is easy for me, though, is a favourite time of day. There is an hour or so in the evening that is magical. The time before sunset, when things calm down and the wind drops. The skies are amazing and often the low sun will pick out and light a single building on the horizon or throw huge shadows across the fields.

It's a great time to ride: on Anglesey you are alone on the ancient hills, in Cumbria the hedgerows come alive with birds, the west coast of Scotland has vast dramatic sunsets, and in Norfolk and Suffolk the huge skies light the rich farmlands.

I loved riding around the islands, they have their own character and are beautiful places. So Anglesey, Arran, Mull, the Orkneys and the Isle of Wight all come to mind. I also loved the ferry experiences, always good fun and generally very cheap for a bloke and a bike.

If you are thinking of a long bike journey. Here is a list of 10 things to consider.

❶ You need to decide whether to go solo or with mates. On your own you can go at your own pace, stop where you like, and you'll meet more folks. With friends you'll have company, share some costs, and some luggage (tent, etc).

❷ Pack and then pack again. Take out absolutely anything you don't really need. You can always add to what you have. You don't need too many clothes, but what you do take should be good (Merino base layers are a good tip).

❸ You eat a lot when you are on a bike all day. You will need to eat three good meals a day, just to maintain weight. I picked up a porridge habit.

❹ Where you get one hill, you get lots. You will get fitter and stronger on a long trip. You need to stretch and look after your back well. Hours on a bike mean you need to look after yourself. Changing riding positions is a good idea. I found spinning classes useful before the ride.

❺ Our country is beautiful. Stop lots, take lots of photos. You can stop pretty much anywhere on a bike, so make the most of it.

❻ Camping is better than B&Bs (unless you need to charge batteries). Your sleeping bag and tent is your home. It's cheaper and again it's worth spending money on a good sleeping bag and mat.

❼ You can get a good cake anywhere in Britain. Explore the cafés of Britain, we must be the best cake makers in the world. You just don't know what you are missing passing a café. My tip here is explore as many as possible. And my absolute favourite? C-side in Bexhill-on-Sea.

❽ Going slow is better than going fast. If your bike is heavy, you are not going to break any records. Enjoy travelling slowly (though make the most of going down hills).

❾ I had a bike made for me in Bristol. It fits me like a glove. I guess I was lucky because I could afford it. But even so, if you are sitting on it for up to 10 hours a day. Make sure it's well built, has good tyres, look after the chain, and most of all make sure it's comfortable to ride.

❿ There are golf courses everywhere – why? It's a mystery.

For details of Nick's trip, see slowcoast.co.uk.

∧ Scory, Scotland.
❯ Camping up.

❯ Nick, St Mawes ferry .

All images: Nick Hand

Greg Martin

< Classic Cornwall.

Southwest England

The southwest has long been celebrated as a surf destination but this region is no one-trick pony. With a little forethought and a bag tucked into your wetsuit key pocket, an afternoon of waveriding can quickly translate into some shoreline foraging, swimming out to mussel-crowned rocks where the juicest of bivalves reside – provided of course that there is a 'R' in the month. A walk along the South West Coast Path can yield sea cliffs whose pink and golden crystalized surfaces appear to glint and crackle in the morning sun as if in memory of their fiery origins, enticing climbers to scale their heights and coasteerers to leap from the safety of their ledges into the cool Atlantic beneath. Inland, the limestone ridge of the Mendips Hills is a natural pull to cavers and climbers drawn by the gorge – while the undulating terrain is also woven with exciting singletrack potential where technical climbs are matched by bone-shaking descents. But deep in the heart of Devon, the granite plateau of Dartmoor deserves its elevated position: far from the fast flowing sections that delight the kayakers you slip into the cool waters. Mesmerized by the sunlight dancing on the surface of the hidden pool you are free to contemplate whether to climb the nearby lofty tor or hit the MTB trail before setting up your wild camp for the night.

∨ Somerset Sessions.

Environment

The southwest is an exciting mix of terrain. What it lacks in mountain ranges and high peaks it makes up for in epic granite tors rising from moorland plateaux, limestone gorges cut by fast flowing rivers and high sea cliffs washed by the restless Atlantic. Pockets of woodland protected by the Forestry Commission, from Haldon Forest to Hundred Acre Wood, have experienced regeneration where mountain bikers have been allowed to develop and build their own trails. It is home to some of the country's best loved surfing real estate – the quality beaches, points and reefs off Exmoor and North Devon, the classic beach breaks of Cornwall that spawned the UK's burgeoning surf industry back in the 60s as well as Dorset's reefs hidden behind the firing lines. Crossing rivers and flooded estuaries, passing through deeply wooded vales and climbing steep, singletrack summits, the 630-mile South West Coast Path threads its way along shoreline sewing these wide open beaches and intimate coves together. Leading away from the coast, the chalk downlands of the Purbeck Hills and Wiltshire's ancient Salisbury Plain give way to the 100-mile limestone ridge of the Cotswolds with views across the River Severn. The region is home to a high concentration of AONB's as well as national parkland, national forests, Braunton Burrows Reserve UNESCO biosphere and UNESCO Natural World Heritage Site, the Jurassic Coast.

For the shoreline forager or ocean-going adventurer, it is worth remembering that the semidiurnal tides that occur twice daily are large so bays revealed at low tide may quickly get cut off or even swallowed up as the tide pushes back in. Check local press for tides plus: bbc.co.uk/weather/coast/tides/southwest.shtml.

Coastal erosion is a threat, not least to sections of the South West Coast Path. This natural occurrence is only exacerbated by global warming and the rising sea levels, flooding and increase in storms it brings. Other high-risk areas highlighted by the Environment Agency include Porlock in West Somerset, Dawlish and Slapton Sands in South Devon as well as Dorset's landslip-shaped Jurassic Coast.

Climate

The southwest peninsula is directly influenced by the Atlantic, benefiting from the warming effects of the North Atlantic Drift (the Gulf Stream that brings with it the warm waters from the equatorial region). As a result, coastal regions enjoy an early spring, temperate summers and mild winters where snow and heavy frosts are rare.

As demonstrated by the sculpted trees the predominant wind direction is southwesterly and this moisture-laden air also contributes to making the southwest warmer but often wetter and windier than much of the UK. While Cornwall endures the full force, Dorset is less affected by the Atlantic storms, resulting in higher temperatures, drier conditions and more sunshine than its cousins to the west. Winter and Spring see low pressure systems track off the Atlantic across the UK bringing with them unsettled, damp and blustery weather to the region, sea temperatures fall to around 9°C making 5/4 mm wetsuits, boots, gloves and hoods essential for those braving the water. Air temperatures fall a few degrees further, although wind chill can make it feel considerably colder. In summer, the southwest can benefit from the blocking Azores high which can see temperatures soar; however the Atlantic helps temper this with seasonal averages of 17°C. The sea warms to around 15°C so 3/2 mm wetsuits can be broken out and streams and rivers begin to lose their frigid edge. Autumn however is often a golden time: early in the season, the sea will be at its warmest with groomed ground swells beginning to march in from the lows tracking to the north, winds are often light with occasional fronts moving through and air temperatures can remain high well into October – perfect conditions for everyone from climbers to surfers.

Resources

itsadventuresouthwest.co.uk South West Tourism site with suggestions on further adventures in the region.

feelgood.visitsouthwest.co.uk South West Tourism guide to enjoying an environmentally-friendly visit to the region.

cstn.org.uk COAST Cornwall Sustainable Tourism Project.

dartmoor-npa.gov.uk Dartmoor National Park Authority with up-to-date information on everything from wild camping and bike routes to planning your visit.

activeexmoor.com Comprehensive site detailing active adventures on Exmoor.

activemendipvenues.co.uk Individuals, businesses and organizations supporting and offering sustainable activities in the wild beauty of the Mendip Hills.

southwestcoastpath.com Official site for the SWCP offering information and advice on everything from short walks to long trips.

forestry.gov.uk Forestry Commission site with details on dedicated walks and MTB trails.

sas.org.uk Surfers Against Sewage, environmental campaigners for clean safe seas and recreational waters.

Surfing Sennen

Provider DIY	
Skill level Novice-advanced	
Time frame Dawn till dusk	
Equipment Surfboard, wetsuit	
Exertion level ●●●●○	

The black tarmac of Cove Hill urges a pause as it drops over the edge into the steep descent towards the ocean, just as time stands still for the briefest of seconds as a roller coaster stalls, before plunging into that first heart-stopping dive. From here, the large horseshoe of Sennen Cove is revealed in all its beauty. To call it a cove is probably underselling it somewhat, for it's a bay, and a glorious one at that. Grass-swathed cliffs angle down to the large expanse of white sand, groomed by an azure Atlantic that, on a clear, sunny morning will do a startling impression of Caribbean waters. To the south, the village huddles, sheltered behind the headland, the roundhouse and harbour wall distract but not

for long. To the north the beach is backed by a ramp of green and brown hues. Black dots bobbing in the line up signify it's time to drop into the car park and climb into your wetsuit.

Sennen has always drawn surfers, from the embryonic days of British waveriding, when swimming caps and short wooden belly boards were essential equipment. Visiting lifeguards first trimmed along these crystal faces in the early 1960s followed by a hardy band of locals and visiting patrons of Skewjack Surf Village in the mid 70s. Today Sennen is the hub of a burgeoning surf scene around the southwestern tip of Cornwall. The beachfront car park at the bottom of the hill is alive year round, whenever the surf pumps.

Sitting on the toe of Britain, jutting out into the Atlantic just north of Land's End, this stretch of beach is probably England's best swell catcher – which means if there isn't a wave here, there probably isn't one anywhere in the southwest.

> Sam Bleakley enjoying the crystaline delights of Sennen.

⌄ Penwith pleasures.

Greg Martin

Alex Williams

Small to medium swells from the southwest through to the northwest can make for excellent conditions, especially when combined with east winds that will blow offshore. Sennen delivers waves through the tidal range, though they may get a bit fat on a full tide. Walking north from the car park, a number of peaks should be apparent. During the high summer season the waves tend to be smaller, more crowded but the lifeguard presence should reassure those who fall into the beginner to improver category. (If you are unsure of conditions, it's always worth having a chat with one of the RNLI beach lifeguards – most of whom are surfers). On special days there might even be a cruise through by one of the local basking shark community. These huge specimens may resemble their film star cousins, but they are in fact harmless and toothless – feeding on plankton.

For those more confident in the line-up, the autumn season can see classic surf, when this beach break throws up reeling, hollow lefts and rights. The middle of the bay and towards the north is always worth checking, and the car park provides a good vantage point. To the very north, the beach at Gwynver is revealed as the tide drops away. It can pick up more swell than Sennen and the punchy waves here are best left to the experienced waverider. The long walk to this end tends to put some of the crowds off. It is also true of the drive down to this western-most extremity of Kernow. The throng crowds of Newquay are a world away, and while popular, there is plenty of space to enjoy sitting on your board, floating in the crystal blue waters, admiring the rugged Cornish coastline from this unique perspective and waiting for your next wave.

Practicalities

Sennen is a small seafront village just a mile north of Land's End, complete with fishing harbour and RNLI lifeboat station. There are a few amenities here including a pub, fish and chipper, café and restaurant plus surf shop and large beachfront car park. The market town of Penzance, 10 miles east along the A30, is the area's main commercial hub.

Transport   Penzance train station is 10 miles away. An intermittent bus service runs to Sennen Cove (about 40 mins), firstgroup.com.

Sleeping   **££-£** **Whitesands Lodge**, T01736-871776, on the A30 and less than a mile from Sennen Cove, is a friendly and popular spot with an on-site café and full range of accommodation options from budget dorms to doubles and full B&B. Camping also available. For a premium experience with a conscience **£££** **Global Boarders**, T01736-711404, based in Penzance, offers the full high-end package including transfers from the station and to the beach for lessons, equipment, tuition from beginners through advanced at a number of beaches including Sennen, plus a range of beautifully placed 4- or 5-star B&B options. Champions of sustainable tourism, they are carbon neutral and hold the silver award for green tourism. Long weekends from £385.

Eating & drinking   **The Old Success** is a St Austell Brewery pub serving local ales. **The Beach Restaurant** on the seafront serves beautiful views with a mixture of simple, tasty staples and daily specials which take advantage of Cornish reared meats and locally caught fish. Facing west, **The Beach** is a special spot to enjoy a post-surf sundowner.

Resources   **Chapel Idne Surf Shop**, T01736-871192, chapelidne.com, in the car park, is well stocked with a full range of surf hardware and accessories. They also offer a demo centre where you can test-drive a Surftech surfboard before buying it. Check the site for the Sennen web cam. For surf lessons **Smart Surf**, T01736-871817, smartsurf.co.uk, is an excellent family run school with BSA approved instructors – both male and female – who have competed in surfing at national level. They also offer wetsuit and soft board hire – ideal for beginners from ½ day up to a week.

Also try   The **South West Coast Path** and granite cliffs of Penwith make for wonderful walking. Land's End is a mile south of Sennen. The views along this wild stretch of water governed by Longships lighthouse are spectacular, however the 'attraction' at Land's End may be an amusement too far. A 4-mile walk north will bring you through quiet valleys to the wild and windswept Cape Cornwall – once thought to be the most westerly point in England.

> **Lowdown**

⊕ **Prices**
Free (or from £10/half day board and wetsuit hire).

⊗ **Season**
Year round.

⊕ **Don't miss**
A walk along the coast to Gwynver.

⊗ **Avoid**
The right turn into the car park at the bottom of the hill is pretty sharp – don't over shoot it.

Surfing Godrevy

Provider	DIY
Skill level	Novice-advanced
Time frame	Dawn till dusk
Equipment	Surfboard, wetsuit
Exertion level	●●●●●

The National Trust car park attendants at Godrevy are a patient lot. They're used to cars rolling to a stop at their kiosk, winding down the window and asking, "Can we just check the surf first." The wide expanse of St Ives Bay isn't visible until you crest the dunes on the wooden boardwalks, so it often pays not to pay until you've seen the pay-off. To be honest though, you can usually gauge how good it's going to be just by looking at the furrows of cars and vans, or the dripping wetsuits and towels hanging from fences. Still, it's always satisfying to see for yourself.

Godrevy nestles at the northern head of one long, continuous stretch of sand that reaches four miles south to the rivermouth at Hayle, giving plenty of room to spread out. Godrevy Lighthouse stands as a solitary sentry out front while to the southwest, on the far edge of this L-shaped bay, the town of St Ives reclines around its bustling harbour.

∨ Jayce Robinson, bluebird days at Godrevy.

Jordan Weeks

A ridge of dunes and crumbling cliffs fringe the land between, looking out over one of Cornwall's best surfing locations. At low tide the sand appears endless and occasional kite buggies will race along its open canvas. The section of beach at Godrevy tends to hoover up the most swell so is first port of call on smaller days when longboards and fish are popular weapons of choice. On bigger days however, the waves and paddle out can be challenging. Add to this the rips formed by the Red River and it's probably best for those who are less confident to head south where wave size will gradually decrease.

Optimum conditions for Godrevy would see a southwesterly, westerly or northwesterly swell running in the two to four feet range, with offshore winds blowing out of the southeast or east. A high and dropping tide will reduce the size, but a low tide on the push will see the wave size increase. Looking south to where the cliffs begin, Gwithian is usually where the swell size begins to diminish, especially south of Ceres Rock. There is a large car park outside the Sunset Surf Shop, and on solid swells this will quickly become a bustling hive of surf checks and board waxing. From here there's an unimpaired view south towards the river with three miles of peaks to choose from. A slightly bigger swell is needed for this stretch to work, but outside the summer season that isn't uncommon. Head south along the cliff top walk and access points will lead down onto the sands. As with Godrevy, this stretch also has a summer RNLI Beach Lifeguard service.

A once underrated stretch of sand, Godrevy and Gwithian have become popular spots with both local and visiting surfers as they offer easy access, plenty of parking and good cafés to grab a cup of something warm post surf. You won't find the perfect barrels of Supertubes in Portugal or the endless reeling lefts of Mundaka, but you'll certainly enjoy fun waves and a line-up where the vibe is mellow and most will be happy to strike up a conversation. If you're lucky, a pod of bottle nosed dolphins may cruise through and put on a show of real waveriding prowess.

Practicalities

The pretty village of Gwithian is small with few amenities other than a pub – which helps to keep the scene at the beach relaxed. Along the 3 miles of beach there are also several good cafés plus a surf shop and beach bar which answer most calls of nature. If you need to feel the buzz of a town with galleries, bars and shops, arty, café-cultured St Ives at the southwest edge of the bay is just 9 miles from Gwithian.

Transport Hayle train station is 3 miles away. The 515 bus operates a limited service from Hayle to Gwithian, westerngreyhound.com.

Sleeping A short walk from the beach and the heart of the village, **££ Gwithian Holiday Suites**, T01736-755493, gwithianholidays.com, are modern, self-catering flats sleeping up to 5 with board store and wetsuit drying facilities. For campers, **Gwithian Farm**, T01736-753127, opposite the local pub, is a relaxed, simple site a 15-min walk to the beach, open Apr-Sep. In nearby St Ives, **£££ Primrose Valley Hotel**, T01736-794939, holds a gold award for green tourism. This former Edwardian seaside villa, thoughtfully converted into a sleek retreat, locally sources the best produce for their fantastic breakfasts and supports the MCS plus Cornwall Wildlife Trust. B&B from £125.

Eating & drinking The cool, popular **Godrevy Café**, National Trust car park delivers views across the bay from the upper deck – ideal for tucking into home-made cake or some seriously good home cooking. **Sunset Surf**, Gwithian Towans, has a great little beach café – good cakes and hot chocolate. **Red River Inn**, Gwithian, is the local pub which also serves up decent grub utilising seasonal local produce where possible.

Resources Sunset Surf Shop, T01736-752575, sunsetsurfshop.co.uk, in Gwithian Towans is well stocked with hardware. They also offer board and wetsuit hire ½ day to 24 hrs and have a licensed café next door. Check the site for the Gwithian web cam. **Gwithian Academy of Surfing** (T01736-755493, surfacademy.co.uk), is a Level 4 surf school run by former competitive surfer Tyson Greenaway, open Apr-Sep.

Also try For an unrivalled birds eye view of St Ives Bay, book in for a paragliding or hang gliding session with Graham Phipps of **Cloud 9**, flycloud.co.uk, BHPA registered Phippsy has more than 25 years experience. A tandem gets you airborne with an instructor – the flight lasting around 15 mins – while a day's taster session gives a great overall feel of the sport finishing up with a flight.

> Lowdown

◉ Prices
Free (or from £10/half day board and wetsuit hire).

◉ Season
Year round.

◉ Don't miss
At low tide follow the coast path round from the car park at Godrevy Head to Mutton Cove to see the seal colony from the cliff top.

◉ Avoid
Surfing here after heavy rains.

Kayaking Helford Passage

Provider	Waterborne
Skill level	Novice-intermediate
Time frame	½ day to 4 hrs approx
Equipment	All equipment provided including wetsuits, kayaks and buoyancy aids. Bring a bottle of water (plus your own wetsuit and boots if you have them)
Exertion level	●●○○○

The gentle fingers of early morning mist curling around the river seem to have been art directed into place to emphasise the peaceful beauty of the little village. Gweek Quay and Boatyard is quiet and still except or a small group of wetsuited people huddled round a raft of brightly coloured kayaks and paddles scattered across the slipway. From this dry land launching site, Waterbourne founder Drew Pilley gives an induction to kayaking and a safety briefing. "In the unlikely event that you do capsize, stay calm, bang the bottom of the kayak three times and push yourself out," he says, demonstrating how easy it is to release the neoprene spray skirt and, with your hands on the deck, to straighten your legs and slide out of the cockpit.

The Helford River is a fabulously beautiful and magical waterway of hidden coves and creeks. A vast stretch of ancient woodland runs along the

> Nearing Helford, the riverbank becomes peppered with houses and moored boats.

˅ Going with the flow on the idyllic Helford River.

Layla Astley

Practicalities

On the upper reaches of the Helford River, tiny, pretty Gweek, with its quay boatyard, is a one-pub village while the nearby town of Helston has all the usual amenities including banks.

Transport For Gweek, the nearest train stations are Truro and Redruth. From Redruth firstgroup.com run a service to Helston with a connection on to Gweek.

Sleeping **Trelowarren**, Mawgan, TR12 6AF, T01326-221224, is a demonstration of how holiday cottages should be: set on 1000-acre estate of woodlands and gardens leading to the river, cottages have been built using timber frames, local sustainable materials and abandoned buildings restored to high environmental standards that don't skimp on comfort, class or design. Biomass technology heats the estate while water comes from their own borehole and is aerated to minimize waste. Around 20 cottages completed sleep 4-10 from £450-2000+ per week. The stylish on-site **New Yard Restaurant**, T01326-221595, sources 90% ingredients from a 10-mile radius including game from the estate. Set lunch £16. **£££ The Hen House**, Manaccan, Helston, TR12 6EW, T01326-280236, holds a gold award for green tourism and is in a peaceful, private spot, Tai-chi and reflexology available. **Gear Farm Campsite**, St Martins, Helston, TR12 6DE, T01326-221364. Based on an organic farm (also the home of Spiezia Organics) the 1½ acre site overlooks the Helford with trails leading to the river. Open year round with organic food shop on site.

Eating & drinking **The Gweek Inn**, Gweek serves well-priced pub grub with a good selection of real ales. **The Green House**, in nearby St Keverne, T01326-280800, serves up rustic modern cooking using seasonal organic and local produce including locally caught fish. Wed-Sat evenings until 2100. Sunday roasts 1200-1400. **Kota** in Porthleven, T01326-562407, is also a special spot giving local produce an Asian twist – lunch is the more affordable option here.

Resources Waterbourne may be a small family-run business but the quayside shop is well stocked with wetsuits, quality kayaking hardwear and beach wear. If you're making a special visit to the shop T07773-322273 to ensure they will be open.

Also try For an alternative experience, Drew also offers coastal kayaking trips and his base in Mounts Bay means there are a wealth of launch sites along the coast. A half-day trip from Praa Sands to Porthleven takes in an exploration of the fantastic caves at Rinsey and the Trewarvas Copper mines while full day trips launching from Penzance and taking in St Michael's Mount are also available.

northern banks, the gnarled, stunted sessile oaks rising from just above the water line. An occasional snort of heavy breathing accompanied by the feeling of being watched usually signals that the log floating on the surface nearby is actually a seal newly released from the national sanctuary at Gweek. An hour into the journey, Drew encourages the expedition to 'raft up' in the middle of the empty river and take stock of the environment. Launching on an outgoing tide means that you can take advantage of the natural flow and momentum of the river as it carries the raft of kayaks gently downstream, and an early morning launch means very few people are up and out, adding to the tranquillity of the situation. Closing your eyes for a few moments in the safety of the situation gives you the space to really switch off and tune in to your natural surroundings, noticing the calls of the birds that occupy the air space, branches and river bank for the first time. Breaking away, the trip continues downstream, passing the grassy, wood backed Tremayne Quay, built for a planned visit Queen Victoria didn't actually make in the 1840s and which today makes an ideal spot for a picnic. As the waterway winds closer to Helford, the river becomes busier with the occasional passing gig, the crew rowing in unison, while idyllic country homes and the houses of the rich and famous begin to dot the riverbank. On the northern bank the Ferry Boat Inn backing the strip of sand at Helford Passage is a tempting sight, while having passed Frenchman's Creek, The Shipwright's Arms beacons from the other shore. Where to go first? Difficult decisions still have to be made, even in the most beautiful locations.

> Lowdown

❶ Directory
Waterborne, Breageside Quay, Mount Pleasant Road, Porthleven, TR13 9JS, T07773-322273, kayakingcornwall.co.uk.

❸ Prices
£45 for ½ day.

❸ Season
Year round.

❸ Don't miss
The Lizard Peninsula is a beautiful spot to explore – head out on the SW Coast Path to discover idyllic coves.

❸ Avoid Gweek is home to a National Seal Sanctuary so try to avoid careering into anything resembling a large floating log, chances are it is a seal newly released into the wild.

Mountain biking Mineral Tramways Coast to Coast Trail

Provider DIY	
Skill level All	
Time frame 3-4 hrs	
Equipment Mountain bike, helmet, map, snacks, water, a map and a repair kit/spare tube	
Exertion level ●●●○○	

Looking at Portreath it's hard to believe it was once the heart of a trade route with trams and a steady stream of cargo ships feeding what some called 'the richest square mile to be found anywhere on the Earth'. On a hot summer's day the seafront may still bustle with parking cars, however trades now revolve around ice creams and multi-coloured windbreaks, while only

shimmering rock pools are mined by small hands hunting for treasures. The village has undergone a creeping re-model: during the seventies new houses sprouted by the harbour, a peppering of bungalows have filled the sides of the valley and blinking amusements compete with the rolling Atlantic for the attention of visitors.

But not all the remnants of the region's golden age have been lost. This historic harbour was once linked to the prosperous mines inland by an arterial tramway that carried out metals to be shipped to Swansea for smelting and brought in Welsh coal, mining supplies and timber. The tram road opened

∨ Coast to coast.

in 1812 and, with carts drawn by horses, they ran to the main copper-producing region around Gwennap and other mines around Redruth. The area was also serviced by a railway that opened in 1825 and connected the mines with the harbour at Devoran. Although the routes ceased operating in the early 1920s, the disued tramway has recently seen a renaissance. The path infrastructure now forms a cycle way called the Cornish Coast to Coast Trail, linking the tramway from Portreath with the former railway that runs down to Devoran.

Leaving the north coast behind you'll pass the Portreath Arms and a granite marker that signals the start of the trail. The route then heads inland avoiding the busy coast road and past the village of Bridge, until the trail eventually crosses the Portreath to Porthtowan road. Soon you'll be at the Bike Barn, which offers refreshments and technical assistance. From here head east towards the Embankment, built around 1810 to cross the valley, and then on past the appropriately named Wheal Plenty and Trevennen's East Shaft. Next up is Wheal Rose where the track passes behind the Rodda's Creamery, home of Cornwall's famous clotted cream, before crossing the A30 at Scorrier and passing under the railway bridge by the Crossroads Hotel. Take care traversing the junction by the Fox and Hounds – this is a fast and busy road – then follow the route marker back onto the trail and into the Poldice Valley. Now the cycle way takes in some bleakly eye-catching scenery. From woods, to tumbledown arsenic works, to mine shafts, chimneys and viaducts, this route traces a line through the region's industrial past. The tombstone like remnants of Brunel's Carnon Valley viaduct stand next to its modern counterpart, signalling that the village of Devoran draws near, with it's calm waters and waiting Inn.

The route is flat, with the opportunity to insert some more demanding loops, so really is suitable for riders of all abilities. Although quieter during the week, it pays to be aware that the trail is also popular with walkers and horse riders. This 11 mile ride through the 'Copper Kingdom' offers an up-close personal view of the uniquely hard worked Cornish landscape, just try not to work your elbow too hard at the Inn at Devoran because it's an 11-mile cycle back again!

Practicalities

Portreath is a classic seaside village with local pubs and village store. The nearby village of Porthtowan is a real draw for surfers.

Transport For Portreath the nearest mainline railway station is Redruth. First Group firstgroup.com operate an hourly bus service on to Portreath. Bikes are not permitted but it's only a 4½ mile cycle along the B3300 from Redruth Station to Portreath.

Sleeping £ **Elm Farm**, small holding near Portreath, T01209-891498, cornwallcycletrails.com, offers excellent value B&B accommodation with locally sourced breakfast including eggs from their chickens. Camping available on their Camping and Caravan Club certified site. Part of the Bike Barn, their farm shop also sells cream teas, local beers and ciders to be enjoyed in the beer garden plus other essentials. £££ **Rose Hill Lodges**, T01209-891920, at nearby Porthtowan sports the gold award for green tourism and offers ch-eco, grass-roofed, solar-panelled, wooden lodges sleeping 4-6. The individual hot tubs aren't exactly eco but do soothe away aches and pains. A week self-catering for 4 from £450-1500.

Eating & drinking The **Old Quay Inn**, Devoran overlooks the creek and is a welcome sight at the end of your ride with good local ales and home-cooked food that champions Cornish suppliers. Open Apr-Oct all day and lunchtime and dinner only out of season. In Portreath, **Gwel an Mor** luxury lodges, Tregea Hill ,T01209-84354, also have a terrace bar and restaurant with, as their name suggests in Cornish, views of the sea. They serve up light lunches and more substantial dinners focusing on utilising local suppliers. Ride on to the nearby village of Porthtowan to enjoy the beach side **Blue Bar**, an ideal spot to watch the sun sink beneath the horizon while you sink a beer or two. Regular live music and good food seals the deal and with a gold green tourism award, you can feel good about being here too.

Resources The **Bike Barn**, Elm Farm, Cambrose, TR16 5UF, T01209-891498, cornwallcycletrails.com, excellent bike shop with work shop and bike hire (from £12) that sits conveniently on the trail not far from Portreath. SMBLA qualified, they also offer skills training for beginners through advanced. B&B and camping also (see above). Further south **Bike Chain Bissoe Bike Hire**, TR4 8QZ, T01872-870341, also on the C2C trail nr Bissoe with a café.

Also try There's a walking trail that heads along the cliff-lined coast from Portreath to Porthtowan and on to St Agnes. You can stop at the National Trust café at Chapel Porth for some lunch and continue on past the engine houses at Wheal Coates and around the headland to Trevaunance Cove. A great way to spend the day.

Bike Barn

∧ The trail is popular with cyclists, walkers and riders.

❯ Lowdown

❸ Prices
Free/from £12 MTB hire.

❸ Season
Year round.

❸ Don't miss
If you're desperate for dirt tracks with ramps, dirt jumps and slope style head to The Track near Portreath, TR16 4HW, T01209-211073, bike hire and instruction also available.

❸ Avoid Riding on the fragile landscape off the track.

Swimming Porthtowan

Provider	DIY
Skill level	Novice-advanced
Time frame	3-4 hrs depending on the tides
Equipment	Towel, bathers/wetsuit (depending on season/hardiness)
Exertion level	●●○○○

Porthtowan is not a quaint Cornish village, it is practical and evolving, with two distinct faces and two distinct personalities. It has been industrious and the old mine workings topping the surrounding cliffs and the shafts that riddle the rock faces attest to that fact. With its cool Atlantic waters and golden sands protected by a gently sloping valley carpeted in grasses, thrift and picnic blankets it has also been a place of holidays, kicking back and taking five. While the cliffs on the southwest side are shaded by afternoon shadows, the northeast basks in the warm glow of the setting sun. When the tide is in, Porthtowan is a small, dune-backed bay with a pebbled high tide line. As the receding waters draw back, its potential is revealed: more than 1½ miles of beach stretches out in a series of scallop-edged, cliff-backed coves, mussels clinging to their extremities, linking the village with neighbouring Chapel Porth. At the foot of the cliffs a newly replenished salt-water swimming pool has been left behind.

The sea pools dotted around Britain's coastline come in all shapes and sizes: from naturally formed to enhanced or engineered, from small plunge pits to generous bathing pools where generations have learnt to swim. There are those that take centre stage and draw a well-seen crowd and those that hide like a secret waiting to be told. All though are refilled and renewed with the ebb and flow of the tide creating a haven for a quick dip or longer swim, protected from the power of the ocean. Standing on the sand looking out to sea, the pool at Porthtowan is concealed; at beach level, only a clamber up and over the rocks on the right of the bay reveals this hidden oasis. From the cliff path above however you can enjoy an entirely different perspective, watching the rock and concrete edges emerge as the sea retires to create a pool for leisurely lengths or shrieks and screams as the waves wash over the seaward wall.

With its back protected by the copper tinged cliff walls, locals use the pool here year round whether lazily floating on their backs counting clouds in the height of the summer or earnestly taking their morning constitutional in the January chill. Some stand with their backs to the sea waiting for the next surge to crash over the wall and wash them from the safety of their perch while others jump from the rock ledges knees clasped to chests soaking those cautious paddlers on the peripheries.

If you time your swim right on a dropping tide (check the table at magicseaweed.com) you can take a post dip stroll along the beach to Chapel Porth to reward your worthy endeavours with a Hedgehog: Cornish ice cream dipped in clotted cream and rolled in roasted nuts. As the tide comes back in, you can follow the cliff top path home to Porthtowan watching as the succession of coves become cut off before disappearing underwater and if you've been really good, you may even be treated to an appearance by the dolphins or seals who cruise these waters.

⌄ The clifftop path leads down to the sea pool that provides protection for swimmers.

Demi Taylor

Practicalities

The small seaside village of Porthtowan nestles into a valley on the hard-working north Cornwall coast. The high sea cliffs on either side are topped by the shells of engine houses which watch proudly over the coast like ancient fortifications, the land in between scarred and sculpted by mine workings. With its cool beach bar, icecream parlour, local store, and takeaways, the village throngs in the summer while the powerful beach break is popular with experienced surfers.

Transport Redruth train station is 5 miles away. A limited bus service to Porthtowan is available with hopleyscoaches.com.

Sleeping £ Porthtowan Backpackers, T01209-891611, above Sick Lame and Lazy surf shop offers basic hostel accommodation with continental breakfast. **£££ Rose Hill Lodges**, T01209-891920, just opposite the Porthtowan turning sports the gold award for green tourism and offers ch-eco, grass-roofed, solar-panelled, wooden lodges sleeping 4-6. The individual hot tubs aren't exactly eco but do soothe away aches and pains. A week self-catering for 4 from £450-1500.

Eating & drinking Having been built at the perfect angle to kick back and watch the sun set over the bay, the **Blue Bar** on Porthtowan Beach is the ultimate spot to enjoy a post-dip beer. Regular live music and good food seals the deal and with a gold green tourism award, you can feel good about being here too. In the next cove north, **Chapel Porth Beach Café** is a real draw.

Resources Surf shops **Sick Lame and Lazy** and the summer opening **Tris** stock all the gear from surf hardware to beach accessories and offer wetsuit hire for the chilly.

> Lowdown

☉ Prices
Free.

☉ Season
Year round.

☉ Don't miss
A walk along the sand at low tide to Chapel Porth and a walk back along the cliff tops at high tide.

☒ Avoid
Standing on weaver fish which lurk in the shallows on the beach at low tide in the summer.

Internet Free Wi-Fi is available at the **Blue Bar**.

Also try The southwest is home to a series of salt water bathing pools from art deco lidos to natural tidal holes including:

Tunnels Beach, Ilfracombe, North Devon – a series of hand carved tunnels lead to these private beaches and Victorian tidal pool. Open Easter-Oct, nominal entrance fee (tunnelsbeaches. co.uk). Westward Ho!, North Devon – as the tide drops back, two miles of sand is revealed as well as a tidal pool with concrete edges embedded into the rocks at the southern end of the bay.

Summerleaze Beach, Bude, North Cornwall – open Easter-Sep and watched over by lifeguards, this tidal pool is so vast it almost thinks it's a lido. The sandy bottom and seaweed are a bit of a giveaway though.

Treyarnon Bay, North Cornwall – a large rock pool which can accommodate more of a dip than a swim at the base of the cliffs.

Perranporth Beach, North Cornwall – this pool lies hidden at the foot of Chapel Rock, at the southern end of a popular two-mile stretch of beach. It would seem wrong not to stop in at The Watering Hole on the beach for a quick post-plunge refresher.

Portreath Beach, North Cornwall – a small tidal pool nestles by the harbour wall for shelter while at the other end of the bay are Lady Bassetts 'baths' – a series of small pools hewn into the rocks to catch the falling tide.

Jubilee Pool, Penzance, West Cornwall – opened on The Promenade in 1935 as part of the King George V's silver jubilee celebrations this art deco, Grade II listed structure is one of the largest open air pools in the UK that is tidally filled with fresh seawater. Open Easter-Oct, entrance £3.85, jubileepool.co.uk

Priests Cove, West Cornwall – this fishing cove at Cape Cornwall is devoid of sand but still manages to be busy on a summers day thanks to the tidal pool here.

Polperro Beach, South Cornwall – at low tide, this small cove reveals the popular Chapel Pool at the base of Chapel Rock.

Tinside Lido, Plymouth, South Devon – re-opened in 2003, this is another wonderful Art Deco sea water lido – complete with central fountain – which offers views across the Plymouth Sound. Open Jun-Sep, entrance £3, plymouth.gov.uk

Shoalstone Pool, Brixham, South Devon – a lovely summer opening, life-guarded sea water pool which is completely free.

Dancing Ledge, Isle of Purbeck, Dorset – signed from the southwest coast path and a short scramble down the cliffs, the pool here was quarried from an impressive natural rock ledge which sits just above the waves at low tide.

Coasteering Lusty Glaze

Provider	The Adventure Centre
Skill level	All proficient swimmers
Time frame	Half day
Equipment	Wetsuits and safety equipment provided. Bring old trainers that you don't mind getting wet as you won't be allowed to coasteer without them (they'll also save your feet getting shredded on the rocks!)
Exertion level	●●●○○

It's a strange feeling, bobbing around like a sea otter being swept into and out of a tidal pool with the surging swell. Looking up at the cliffs from this perspective, they seem to lean forward as if trying to get a better look at this weird creature – not quite the proverbial fish out of water, but certainly one outside its natural environment. Coasteering is weird mix of magical mystery tour and theme park thrills. It's designed to get us to places we probably wouldn't normally see or experience – hidden coves, craggy rock faces, huge lagoons or exploring deep inside a cool damp cave, but then it also mixes things up by throwing in climbs, traverses and cliff jumps. Yes, sometimes floating like an otter is a most welcome break on a tour of duty.

Coasteering first evolved from a combination of cliff jumping, exploring and adventure swimming. This embryonic sport started to grow in the 90s and today its popularity has spread around the UK coastline. On the outskirts of bustling Newquay, Lusty Glaze is like an oasis; 133 steps lead down to the cliff-lined golden sands and crystal blue waters of this privately owned cove which has established itself as a leading centre to sample this sport. As well as high adrenaline moments which will see you taking a leap of faith from the comfort of a cliff, while out on the coastline there's also the chance you'll encounter seals, dolphins or even the migratory gentle giants – basking sharks.

◄ Edging out into the currents.

Nick Webb

Practicalities
Located on the edge of Newquay on the way to Watergate, Lusty Glaze Beach is open to the public 365 days of the year and is the complete package. As well as the **Adventure Centre**, showers, toilets and change facilities, there are beach-front chalets, a take away café, bar and quality restaurant.

Transport Newquay train station has direct and connecting services from across the UK. **BioTravel**, T01637-880006, biotravel.co.uk, taxi service runs on locally sourced bio diesel.

Sleeping There are plenty of cheap hostels and B&B's in Newquay especially Headland Rd near Fistral. Right on the sand at Lusty Glaze, the **Beach House** and **Beach Chalet** self-catering bungalows sleep up to 6 (no single sex groups) from £1160/week each. T01637-872444. When everyone's gone home, it's just you and your own private beach.

Eating & drinking Lusty Glaze Restaurant, T01637-879709, delivers excellent daytime beach café fare 7 days a week but turns up the gourmet dial for the evening menu available Thu-Sat using locally sourced quality produce.

Resources Newquay is overrun with surf shops of every kind. **Lusty Glaze Adventure Centre**, T01637-874620, offers surfboard and wetsuit hire.

Also try The Adventure Centre offers other on-site activities and lessons in surfing, rock climbing and kiteboarding. Guided mountain biking on exciting off road trails for all levels is offered through the excellent, environmentally minded **Mobius**, mobiusonline.co.uk, from £30 including all equipment.

> **Lowdown**

ⓘ Directory
The Adventure Centre, Lusty Glaze Beach, Lusty Glaze Road, Newquay TR7 3AE, T01637-872444, lustyglaze.co.uk.

Ⓢ Prices
£52.50 for a half day.

☀ Season
Apr-Oct.

Ⓞ Don't miss
The annual Night Surf Contest which sees Britain's best professional surfers compete in the UK's only night surf event. ukprosurf.com.

Ⓧ Avoid
Getting caught out by Newquay traffic wardens or wheel clampers! They're notorious…

Mountain biking The Camel Trail

Provider	DIY
Skill level	Beginner-Intermediate
Time frame	4 hrs plus round trip
Equipment	Mountain bike, helmet, map, snacks, water, and repair kit/spare tube
Exertion level	●●○○○

Padstow has become an epicentre, the eye of a swirling culinary cyclone. People are sucked into the town not only by the lure of its picturesque harbour and views of the lush green estuary, but also by the promise of fine fresh fish. Superchef Rick Stein's rise to fame has certainly pulled the name of this Cornish village with it, and along with the Eden Project, this seems to be a fixed point on the tourist itinerary. For those with an historical eye, a glance at the map will show why Padstow at its peak was the region's busiest harbour. As the only safe natural inlet between Bude and St Ives, it became a vital export point for local copper, tin and farm produce. A rail link followed, connecting the town with inland Wadebridge and on to Bodmin, Okehampton and London beyond. The withering of the rail network saw these branch lines close in the 60s, but the sheer beauty of the route soon led to its conversion to a trail for walkers and cyclists.

This is a route for the cruiser, not the bruiser. This gentle pedal will nurture the soul; it's a chance to blow off a few cobwebs and take in the stunning vistas of the estuary, the shrouded woodland and the views up on to Bodmin Moor. You may see the rust-crusted dredger, chugging its way through the flowing waters, keeping the channel open. Leaving the crowds of Padstow behind, the estuary is a land of herons, oystercatchers, curlews and egrets. For five miles the trails hugs the estuary as it sweeps towards Wadebridge. Cutting through are cafés, but you'll soon be back on the trail hugging the river as it winds southeast towards Bodmin. Places to look out for en route include the stone and slate cottages of Polbrock, Grogley Halt, the Camel Valley Vineyard, the Camel Trail Tea Garden and the Borough Arms pub. This stretch of the route is a leisurely and flat six miles and soon Bodmin comes into sight. Those with more time to spare can push on north to Poley's Bridge and beyond to Wenfordbridge, it's an extra seven miles but worth every pedal.

Practicalities

Pretty Padstow bustles with tourists in the summer months and has good amenities including banks, shops, pubs and cafés plus plenty of places to stay so makes a good base.

Transport   The nearest railway station is Bodmin Parkway, 3 miles from Bodmin. First Buses offer a regular service (also to Wadebridge and Bodmin, no bikes), firstgroup.com.

Sleeping   In the heart of Padstow is the gorgeous £££ Althea Library, 27 High St, Padstow PL28 8BB, T01841-532717, althealibrary.co.uk. £ The Stephen Gelly Farm, Lanivet, Bodmin PL30 5AX, T01208-831213, stephengellyfarm.co.uk, offers B&B from £20/person/night in their Victorian farmhouse. The farm has 120 acres of organic grassland and breakfast is home grown or home made. For those who want to camp, £ Cornish Yurt Holidays, Greyhayes, PL30 4LP, T01208-850670, yurtworks. co.uk, offer yurts on their organic small holding next to Bodmin Moor, just a couple of miles from the cycle route.

Eating & drinking   When in Padstow, you really do have to try something Rick Stein so head for Steins Fish and Chips, South Quay, T01841-532700, lunch 1200-1430, dinner 1700-2000. Traditional fish 'n' chips from around £6 plus a raft of fish prepared to order. In Wadebridge, Relish, Foundry Court is an excellent spot to refuel with organic brekkies and lunches.

Resources   There are two bike hire centres in the car park at the start of the trail in Padstow. Padstow Cycle Hire, South Quay, T01841-533533, padstowcyclehire.com. Trail Bike Hire, South Quay, T01841-532594, trailbikehire.co.uk. In Wadebridge there is Bridge Bike Hire, T01208-813050, bridgebikehire. co.uk, and for those starting in Bodmin try Bodmin Bikes and Cycle Hire, T01208-73192, bodminbikes.co.uk.

Also try   To cool off after your cycle, why not try coasteering on the rugged north Cornwall coastline, including climbing, swimming and cliff jumps. Contact Cornish Rock Tors, T07791-534884, cornishrocktors.com. From £30.

> **Lowdown**

⊖ Prices
Free/MTB hire from £9.

⊗ Season
Year round.

⊕ Don't miss
Fish 'n' chips at Stein's Chip Shop.

⊗ Avoid
If you are here for peace and quiet, avoid school holidays.

Stand up paddle surfing Watergate Bay

Provider	Extreme Academy
Skill level	Novice
Time frame	Half day
Equipment	Equipment and wetsuit provided but take a towel
Exertion level	●●●●○

Standing on your paddle board, the early autumn sun overhead, you study the horizon to your left, the ocean boundary is sharp against the clear, bright sky. Looking right, the bay opens out, the hotel perched on the rough, broken cliffs that rise around it and line the three miles of golden sand revealed by the low tide. You meditatively stir the waters with your paddle as silhouettes emerge from the shadows of the slipway that leads down from the car park. They are drawn to the shoreline, carrying with them an assortment of waveriding vehicles and an almost visible aura of anticipation. From this elevation you have a great perspective. Glancing left again you spot a set and that moment of inner calm is switched off by a sudden flutter of adrenaline. Turning the huge 12-ft board towards the shore

you dig in and begin to paddle, one hand on top on the T-bar grip the other half way down the carbon fibre shaft. Gathering momentum, the rush builds and the tail of the board lifts as the wave is caught. Shifting your feet into a classic surf stance you remember this time to use the paddle, guiding yourself out onto the open face. Trimming along the morning glass, feeling the energy of the ocean and the buzz of the glide you catch yourself doing inner high fives. You have just experienced the yin and yang elements of stand up paddle surfing.

Stand up paddle surfing or SUP is one of the world's fastest growing boardsports with a wide fan base. While it may not be an ancient Hawaiian art, this mid 20th-century combo of huge longboard and outrigger canoe paddle does have the kudos of having been created by the Waikiki beachboys, the original surf instructors. Standing tall and stroking out into the line up at Watergate, single blade paddle in hand, it is easy to see the appeal of this hybrid. Standing as opposed to lying prone gives

❯ Trimming along on an SUP.

Geoff Tydeman

a better vantage point for surveying the line up and spotting the sets. As surf styles altered, SUP all but died out only to be revived at the dawn of the new millennium by the world's greatest all round waterman, Laird Hamilton who brought the sport charging back into the boardriding mainstream in the huge, hollow waves of Tahiti's Teahupoo.

Just paddling out into the line up standing upright, with feet facing the nose of the board like a skier, will be an alien experience for anyone who has surfed before. "Your feet should be parallel in the centre of the board about shoulder width apart, with your back straight and knees slightly bent," explains the Extreme Academy's Sports Manager Carl Coombes. Twitch responses are tested as ankles and knees absorb the energy from the lines of water passed over, shifting weight toe to heel to maintain balance. "The trick is not to forget to use your paddle for stability as well as to generate momentum and to keep looking forward," Coombes continues. Ideal learning conditions are those one to two foot days, meaning you don't have to be an aquatic all-star to start out. It also means it's not too difficult to get out back, allowing you to trade waves with your instructor and see the right technique up close, in action.

SUPing is a two-fold experience. Because of the size of the board, the paddle element can be enjoyed on even the flattest of days, allowing you to clock up water time while everyone else is bemoaning a lack of waves. Then there's the stoke of riding waves when a swell kicks in and exploring the possibilities of what your board can do on them. "I've had endless fun riding even the smallest waves on my SUP," says 10-time British longboard champion Chris 'Guts' Griffiths and SUP convert. "And because you are constantly standing you get the most amazing view of the coastline and surrounding ocean."

With its northwesterly orientation, Watergate is open to the majority of swells that grace this stretch of coastline. Add to this the fact that there's plenty of room to spread out, and it's little wonder that this is a popular spot with surfers trying to escape the crowds of Newquay. It is also the spiritual home of British kite surfing, hosting the UK's first leg on the PKRA world kite surfing tour. "All surfcraft and watermen are welcome here," says Carl. "That's part of the magic of Watergate."

Ben Rowe

Practicalities

Watergate is like a ski resort on a beach: a cool, comfortable spot to enjoy great adventures outdoors while all your needs are catered for, whether you need a celebrity chef establishment or a low-key pub. Plus, Newquay is just down the road.

Transport Newquay train station is 3½ miles away. BioTravel, T01637-880006, biotravel.co.uk, operates a taxi service whose cabs run on locally sourced bio diesel.

Sleeping For the full 'Watergate experience' £££ **The Hotel**, T01637-860543, watergatebay.co.uk, overlooks the bay merging contemporary design and the beach lifestyle with direct access to the sands below. Twins, doubles and family B&B, some with beach balconies plus equipment lock-up, terraced bar and brasserie on-site. While they are making steps to be more environmentally conscious, the real plus is that once you've arrived it cuts the need to travel completely out of the equation. For camping try **Watergate Bay Touring Park**, T01637-860387, ½ mile from the beach, open Mar-Oct.

Eating & drinking Open till dusk, **The Beach Hut** serves up well-priced breakfasts and lunches with views that take a lot of beating. **Fifteen Cornwall**, T01637-861000, fifteencornwall. co.uk – brainchild of Jamie Oliver – is the bay's deluxe eating option. Picture windows with far-reaching Atlantic views, hip decor and the best seasonal and local produce are combined to create top-end eating experiences, all profits go to charity Cornwall Foundation of Promise.

Resources **Gone Feral**, T01637-861174, next to the Phoenix pub stocks all the surf essentials while **The Extreme Academy** on the beachfront offers equipment and wetsuit hire. **The Hotel** has free Wi-Fi access in all public areas.

Also try The Extreme Academy also offers tuition at Watergate in the following: Surfing, Waveskiing, Mountain Boarding, Traction Kiting (as a good introduction to both Kite Surfing and Kite Buggying), as well as a full on Extreme Day.

∧ Watergate Bay stretches for almost 3 miles at low tide.

> **Lowdown**

❶ **Directory**
Extreme Academy, Watergate Bay, Cornwall, TR8 4AA, T01637-860543, extremeacademy.co.uk.

❺ **Prices**
£40 half-day session.

❻ **Season**
Year round.

❼ **Don't miss**
The post-lesson hot shower at the Extreme Academy – very welcome in the winter!

❌ **Avoid** High tide – low tide sees the beach open up to the north and south giving everyone plenty of room to spread out.

Climbing Roche Rock

Provider	Cornish Rock Tors
Skill level	Novice-intermediate
Time frame	Approx 6 hrs (usually 1000-1600)
Equipment	All equipment provided including helmet and rock shoes, remember to wear comfortable clothing
Exertion level	●●●●●

At the southern end of Roche village lies a corner of rough Cornish heath land. Encircled entirely by the lush green of worked lands and playing fields, this single uncultivated parcel is instantly set apart as somewhere significant. Pushing up through the coarse, boulder-strewn carpet stands Roche Rock, an impressive granite and tourmaline outcrop which rises for some 70 ft over the surrounding countryside. Embedded into the rock and seeming to grow from it, the ominous ruins of the 15th century hermitage chapel cap the crag. These walls are the stuff of legend, both old and new. One tale links the chapel to fated lovers Tristan and Isolde, another to Cornish sinner Jan Tregeagle who, said to have made a pact with the devil, fled here in vain to try to escape the hounds of hell. More recently it has acted as a chilling backdrop in the *Omen, The Final Conflict*.

Daubs of lichen cover the surface of the hard grey granite, whose face, covered in fissures, cracks, flakes and ridges, has been worked by time to create an ideal environment for climbers. "There are a number of good lower grade climbs here as well as some more challenging routes," explains experienced climber and instructor Matthew Wheadon of Cornish Rock Tors.

After a safety briefing and explanation of the kit you will be working with, the introductory session will have you roped in and climbing before you know it. The session is broken down into a series of climbs, the first of which is attainable enough to build confidence. A goal is set, advice on which line to follow is given and with Matthew belaying from below you set off. "Climbing is an almost primordial instinct" he says, "The first climb is about

getting onto the rock, getting up there and getting a feel for it." Jamming your toes into a large crevice in one move while searching out a hand hole in the next you progress higher until you reach your objective. Tips on technique are passed on and keeping excitement levels high, the session will see you progress on to increasingly longer and more challenging climbs for your ability, pushing yourself mentally and physically, upping the risk versus reward ratio.

Having secured the rope, Matthew will abseil down the rock stopping to point out key holds or moves on the route. The climbs are done using a top rope technique, essentially the rope is anchored above you with your guide belaying or controlling the rope from below ensuring maximum safety and meaning that if and when you do slip or miss a hold, you won't fall very far. From here, when the wall simply becomes a kaleidoscope of rough crystals and you can't see your next hold, Matthew

❮ Scaling the face on a bright winters morning.

Practicalities

Cornish Rock Tors operates out of the upmarket seaside village of Polzeath, nestled in the lea of Pentire Point. Depending on conditions and individual requirements there are several climb locations available so with transport laid on, this can make a good base. There are several shops, cafés, pubs and restaurants in the village. As a popular and flexible surf spot, the beach is also a draw offering a series of lefts and rights through the tide, working best in decent west/northwest swells, off shore with east/southeast winds.

Transport   Bodmin Parkway train station is a 40-min drive from Polzeath. A bus service is available from Bodmin Parkway station to Wadebridge with a connecting service on to Polzeath with westerngreyhound.com.

Sleeping   The family run **Valley Caravan Park**, T01208-862391, valleycaravanpark.co.uk, just 2 mins from the beach is an excellent choice with good facilities, camping options plus caravans to hire. A mile from Polzeath at St Minver, **£££ Mesmear**, T01208-869731, mesmear.co.uk, provides 3 high-end self-catering options in exceedingly chic barn conversions (**The Mill** sleeping 10 comes with its own chef and house keeper, if you don't mind). **The Barn** sleeps 4 from around £1000/week. The houses are heated by a geothermal system which, they say, cuts their carbon dioxide emissions by up to 12 tonnes/year. A bore-hole provides fresh water while waste water is treated on site to water authority standards before being fed back into the streams. At Chapel Amble, 5 miles from Polzeath, **£££ David's House**, T01208-814514, davidshouse.co.uk, is an organic, chemical-free B&B.

Eating & drinking   Matthew recommends the nearby **Carruan Farm** for its excellent farm shop plus licensed restaurant serving up locally sourced, home cooked, wholesome grub from breakfasts through to afternoon tea plus supper, summer only. **St Kew Harvest Farm Shop**, St Kew Highway, Wadebridge, is another excellent farm shop selling home grown fruit and veg, Gloucestershire Old Spot pork and bacon plus local produce.

Resources   Free Wi-Fi at **Carter's Bar** on Rock Road plus access with Valley Caravan Park and Mesmear.

Also try   As well as Introductory, Intermediate and Advanced rock climbing taking you from your first tentative steps through to becoming a proficient free climber, Cornish Rock Tors also offer Coasteering and Kayaking around the rugged North Cornwall coastline.

◀ The hermitage rising almost organically from the granite tor.

coaches from below, guiding you into your next posture, encouraging you to take a leap of faith. "Don't forget to breathe as you climb," he advises. "Holding your breath really increases feelings of anxiety."

Topping out on your most extreme climb of the day, you will be filled with an almost overwhelming sense of achievement. The combination of factors that go into climbing are what make it so addictive. As well as the problem solving aspect – reading the rock and deciphering the holds – there is the sheer physicality of the climb, making your body translate the information into a series of moves. Fuelled by a healthy cocktail of fear, adrenaline and shouts of encouragement from below, you will have convinced your body and mind to pull together, to overcome waves of panic and doubt, to push yourself that little bit harder. Having focused in on the detail of the route and analysed the minutiae of every lump and crack for its usefulness you can pause at the top and take in the bigger picture, drinking in your surroundings and the feeling of triumph. Rubbing your aching forearms, and scuffed knuckles, sun on your face, the stepped landscape of the Cornish Pyramids comes into view while a ribbon of sea shimmers in the far distance.

Cornish Rock Tors was established in 2006 by friends Matthew Wheadon, a trained zoologist and Simon Carley-Smith, a trained ecologist who share a passion for climbing and outdoor activities. At the end of a session with them you will have learnt how to belay a climber, tie yourself into a rope, abseil and picked up useful tips on technique. Moreover, you will have sparked what may be a life-long affair with climbing.

› Lowdown

❶ **Directory**
Cornish Rock Tors Ltd, Surfside Café, Polzeath Beach, Polzeath, Cornwall, PL27 6TB, T07791-533569/53488, cornishrocktors.com.

❷ **Prices**
£60 introductory session, £80 intermediate (includes packed lunch).

❸ **Season**
Easter-Oct half term.

❹ **Don't miss**
Climbing the rusty ladders to explore the ruins of the chapel and take in the views.

❺ **Avoid**   Getting your climbing shoes muddy at the base of the wall.

Foraging Lostwithiel

Provider	Wild Food School
Skill level	Novice-advanced
Time frame	Approx 6 hrs (usually 1000-1600)
Equipment	Adequate footwear for rough terrain, notebook, camera
Exertion level	●○○○○

A cursory glance at Lostwithiel may render the scene a blanket of rolling green, punctuated by the grey tops of arterial routes. This south coast town lies at the head of an estuary, in a wooded valley, the surrounding countryside feeding into it with country lanes and farm tracks. On closer observation however it becomes clear that these geographical elements have combined to create not just a thing of beauty but a land of substance and sustenance – a well stocked series of wild food larders, if you know what you're looking at.

"Foraging is really about having the ability, imagination, and energy to gather your own foodstuffs from the wild," says Marcus Harrison who runs the Wild Food School. "It's no different really from going to a supermarket to pick what you want from their shelves." Only here, location, season and climate determine what's available as opposed to consumer demand and market forces.

A self-taught forager, Marcus's interest in wild foods stemmed from his experimenting with nettles more than 30 years ago. His knowledge has continued to grow with his research, following a wild food paper trail of cross-references from contemporary literature though to medieval manuscripts, all of which lead him back to his kitchen. The way in which Marcus views the countryside is different from the average Joe – while a rambler may enjoy the beauty of a hedgerow erupting with spring growth, Marcus mentally maps an area, registering current or future harvest opportunities, "In the UK alone there are over 160 edible wild plants, not counting mushrooms and fungi," he says, explaining that many of the plants we now consider to be wild or weeds were once part of our daily menu.

The Wild Food School runs a series of courses, tailor-made to the skills and needs of the group. Canoeists may want to learn how to supplement provisions with tasty riverside edibles, while some come with pure 'survival' foods in mind, , and others may simply want to learn how to bring the tastes and textures of their local surroundings into their cooking. You may find yourself foraging on the edge of a friendly farmer's field, along a hedgerow stepping in occasionally to let the odd car pass, by the banks of the River Fowey or in the surrounding woodlands. Whichever your environment, a

˅ When cooked, nettles make an excellent replacement for spinach .

Marcus Harrison's Tips for Safe Wild Plant Foraging

❶ If you cannot positively identify 100% a plant as being one of the edible species, or remember which parts are used, leave well alone.

❷ Only harvest from safe sources – study the landscape for possible sources of contamination.

❸ Wash harvested plants thoroughly before use.

❹ Avoid harvesting discoloured, diseased and dying plants. Never eat dead leaves.

❺ Test your personal tolerance to an edible wild plant before consuming in quantity.

❻ If you have a medical condition or take medication seek medical guidance before consuming wild plants.

❼ Consume edible wild plants in moderation as part of a mixed diet.

∧ Three cornered leek.

morning's harvesting will lead back to the kitchen, where Marcus can turn even the simplest staples can into exotic fare – nettles become curried nettle aloo, sorrel creates a wonderful tangy base for a crumble, while three cornered leeks excite a cream cheese spread into becoming something wonderful. From here you can see the WFS garden. To the untrained eye, this may look like a rough untended patch of scrubland but to your newly opened eyes you'll be able to see that this is a cultivated wilderness where useful 'weeds' and wild plants are encouraged to thrive while plants that trade on looks alone are out on their ear.

A day's introductory course will whet your wild food appetite and give you enough information and confidence to carefully begin to explore your wild food larders closer to home, the 'Takeaway' CD-Rom, with images of some of the species encountered on your course, acting as an excellent aide-memoire.

> Lowdown

❶ Directory
Wild Food School, Lostwithiel, wildfoodschool.com, T01208-873788.

❸ Prices
£70 starter day.

❸ Season
Year round.

❶ Don't miss
A trip to Restormel Castel with awesome views over the valley.

❸ Avoid
Eating anything until you've tested your personal tolerance.

Practicalities

Lying in a wooded valley at the head of the River Fowey the pretty former 'stannery' town of Lostwithiel was founded as an inland port by the Normans for the export of tin, at a time when the river ran deep. Today canoes and kayaks make up the main shipping this far up into the tidal reaches of the estuary and with its mix of medieval bridges and churches, antique shops, restaurants and pubs plus amenities such as banking and shops it makes a great base. It's also around 7 miles from the gardens and biomes of the Eden Project, edenproject.com.

Transport Lostwithiel train station is on the main Plymouth to Penzance line.

Sleeping Set in 2 acres in the heart of the village ££ Benthams, T01208-872472, unfussy with free Wi-Fi and excellent breakfasts. At Lanivet, the organic, working £ Stephen Gelly Farm, T01208-831213, stephengellyfarm. co.uk, is run by the Collinge family who also offer year round farmhouse B&B. Breakfast is mostly home grown and includes milk, butter and yoghurt from the house cow, honey from Susan's bees, plus jams, juice and stewed fruits from the fruit trees. In summer a yurt is available as is camping. The farm shop sells their produce. Three minutes down the road, the family run Eden Valley Holiday Park, T01208-872277, powderhamcastletouristpark.co.uk, in Lanlivery is a quiet, low-key site complete with stream and generous pitches. No bar/shop/restaurant on site leaving you to practice foraging skills!

Eating & drinking There are several good pubs here including the Globe Inn, North Street specializing in home-cooked fare using locally sourced fish, meat, game and produce and the St Austell Brewery Kings Arms. B&B at both.

Resources Excellent, downloadable free WFS foraging guides available at wildfoodschool.co.uk, including urban, riverside and Cornwall.

Internet Free Wi-Fi available in public areas of Lostwithiel Hotel, Golf & Country Club, Lower Polscoe.

Also try Encounter Cornwall, T01208-871066, encountercornwall.co.uk, run a series of activities including canoe and kayaking trips for all abilities along Fowey's beautiful river valley departing from Lostwithiel's medieval bridge. Alternatively they can organize a cycling trip to the Eden Project, including bike hire, route maps and drop off if required, taking in the Clay Trails before enjoying a £3 discount at the project for arriving in an environmentally friendly way.

Walking Bodmin

Provider	DIY
Skill level	All
Time frame	2 hrs
Equipment	OS Map, walking books, provisions
Exertion level	●●○○○

Bodmin Moor is all smoke and mirrors. Despite the idea of a wilderness expanse and the feelings of remoteness it generates, Bodmin Moor covers an area of just 10 sq miles and is cornered by four bustling towns. While bisected by Cornwall's main artery, it is often simply passed by; hypnotized drivers with tunnel vision barely register the blurred moorland mass as they are lured on by the region's more obvious attractions. To understand the secrets of the moor, study it not from behind glass but from on high and you'll see that the smoke is just a fast descending fog and the mirrors are the waterways reflecting the sky.

For a great perspective head to the high moors and the twin peaks Rough Tor (pronounced 'Rowter') and Brown Willy. From the A39 take the sign for Tregoodwell for good parking and easy access. There is a clear path across the grassy moorland leading to the ridge from which the granite-capped Rough Tor and its smaller sister summits, Little Rough Tor and Showery Tor, rise. The base is littered with the defined remains of ancient settlements while the lush green slope is strewn with absent-mindedly discarded granite lumps. The summit is a carefully crafted proposition. Here nature has created neat granite stacks before precision smoothing and sculpting each layer to create often logic-defying formations that wouldn't seem out of place in a Japanese contemplation garden. Search out a 'logan rock', apply gentle pressure and contemplate. Across the valley and the De Lank River is Brown Willy, Bodmin's highest point at 1375 ft and your next destination. Follow the permissive path to its zenith (the land is privately owned and farmed) and drink in the views. But this is just one perspective, one walk. There are plenty more secrets to be revealed on Bodmin as well as paths to follow.

Practicalities

On the western edge of the Moor, the pretty village of Blisland centres around a village green. Four towns corner the Moor — Bodmin, Camelford, Launceston and Liskeard so if you're looking for more bustle, banks and shops it's in easy reach.

Transport The nearest mainline station is Bodmin Parkway — just under 9 miles from Blisland but buses on Bodmin Moor are few and far between.

Sleeping ££ **Little Keasts Farmhouse**, Draynes nr St Neot T01579-320645, littlekeasts.co.uk, offers B&B on their small-holding. Breakfast includes their own sausages, bacon and eggs plus home-made breads and preserves. For camping, the 200 acre organic **South Penquite Farm**, T01208-850491, is a natural, relaxed site working with the environment including solar heated rainwater showers. Open May-Oct, yurts plus VW campervan hire available.

Eating & drinking The **Blisland Inn** is all about real ales, basic grub also available. For local produce and supplies, head to **Taste of the West Country Farm Shop**, St Cleer, nr Liskeard.

Resources OS Explorer Map 109 shows the full potential of the Moor at a scale of 1:25 000.

Also try Kayaking on nearby Siblyback Lake with the **Watersports Centre**, T01579-346522, swlakestrust.org.uk. Camping on water's edge Apr-Oct.

∨∧ The carefully crafted summit of Rough Tor.

Surfing Bude

Provider	DIY
Skill level	Novice-advanced
Time frame	Dawn till dusk
Equipment	Surfboard, wetsuit
Exertion level	●●●●●

Bude is ice creams, deck chairs and a summer jazz festival. It's home to an impressive tidal sea pool and stacked tiers of sun terracing, it boasts a sea lock allowing visiting boats to tie up opposite the row of white B&Bs. The River Neet, around which the town was built, arcs lazily towards the seafront while two beaches provide open access to the Atlantic. Spines of rock frame these golden arches of sand, worn fingers pointing out to sea. And for the surfer, back turned on the hustle and bustle of the popular beach and pretty town, this is where the focus is, the ocean: here the Atlantic conspires with the local geography to provide both the sandbanks and the swell to break over them.

Bude is a draw for local and visiting surfers, and the summer crowds are a testament to this. RNLI Beach Lifeguards and ample parking help draw those keen to learn or improve, while bigger swells show why some of Cornwall's top surfers choose to call this place home.

The walk down to the water at low tide can be a long one at Summerleaze, especially if the surf is taunting you from afar. The quality left that breaks at low needs a bigger swell to kick in, however a number of peaks can crop up along the beach as it extends north, past rock outcrops, towards the open sand of Crooklets. Here a right towards the northern edge and a left near its southern fringe are ample reward for the walk, but beware of rocks as the tide pushes into the bay. The bays are also cut off from each other at high tide. At low tide you can walk two miles north along the beach to the National Trust owned, cliff backed Sandymouth – a good place to escape the crowds. All work best in small to medium NW to SW swells and are off shore in easterly winds. The mile long bay south at Widemouth is another popular option best in NW to W swells with E and SE winds.

Demi Taylor

∧ Josh Crook,
sundown sessions.

Practicalities

Cornwall's northernmost town, Bude was built around a 19th century canal and golden sands. This pretty spot has been a popular seaside resort since Regency times. Although large with all the usual facilities including banks and shops, it's also a relaxed spot and with a number of good surf shops and schools, the town is well used to catering to surfers.

Transport Exeter St David's is the closest train station at 43 miles away. The First North Devon X9 bus service on to Bude takes 1¾ hrs, firstgroup.com.

Sleeping £££ **Bangors Organic** in Poundstock, T01288-361297, bangorsorganic.co.uk, is a special place. Five miles south of Bude it offers grown-up, Soil Association certified organic B&B set in a 5 acre organic holding providing produce for its home cooked breakfasts and licensed restaurant. £££-££ **Atlantic House Hotel**, overlooks Summerleaze beach, T01228-352451, atlantichousehotel.com, with bike storage, drying room and a silver award from green tourism. Many of the campsites here are very family orientated with lots of activities and facilities, one of the more simple, relaxed sites is **Willow Valley** in Bush, T01288-353104, 2 miles south of Bude, open Mar-Oct.

Eating & drinking **Life's A Beach** bar and bistro perches on cliffs overlooking Summerleaze making it a great spot for a sun-downer, evening meals focus on utilising the best locally sourced produce. The slick, **Elements Surf Hotel**, T01288-352386, overlooks Widemouth Bay and incorporates local reared meats, produce and locally caught fish into its bistro-style menu.

Resources There are several good surf shops here on Belle Vue Rd including **Zuma Jays**, zumajay.co.uk, T01288-354956, who also offer equipment hire – check the site for a surf forecast. Former National Champion Mike Raven runs the level 4 **Raven Surf School**, T01288-353693, ravensurf.co.uk, tutoring beginners through to experts.

Also try The canal system of Bude is a good spot to get to grips with paddling and kayaking basics before trying sea or surf kayaking. **Shoreline Activities**, T01288-354039, shorelineactivities. co.uk, run kayaking, sea and surf kayaking courses all year from £27. If you're lucky you may get a lesson with partner and former world surf kayaking champion Simon Hammond.

> **Lowdown**

⊙ **Prices**
Free (or from £10/half day board and wetsuit hire).

⊙ **Season**
Year round.

⊙ **Don't miss**
A dip in the tidal sea pool.

⊙ **Avoid**
Aug during the Jazz festival as accommodation gets booked up.

Climbing Dewerstone

Provider	Southwest Adventures
Skill level	Novice-experienced
Time frame	Full day
Equipment	All necessary equipment provided such as helmet and rock shoes, remember to wear comfortable clothing
Exertion level	●●●●●

With its great, grey tors rising like monuments in wild, open expanses and hard granite faces emerging from deep within dark, wooded creases, Dartmoor is home to some serious climbing real estate. While the climbing here is uniformly granite, the moods and personalities it caters to are wonderfully varied, providing stages for those looking to perform public climbs in exposed locales and for those seeking refuge, the opportunity to enjoy more secluded ascents.

On the southwestern extremities of the national park and 10 miles from busy the port and bustling city of Plymouth, Dewerstone Rocks seem like the perfect balancing act. "Dewerstone is a real surprise tucked away in a wooded valley just north of Plymouth," explains instructor Mal Dickson of Southwest Adventures.

Although hardly an unknown entity – there are in excess of 100 routes of varying difficulty charted across their surface, the idyllic setting and route in makes them feel like a carefully preserved secret. Shaugh Bridge is the access point as well as the meeting place of the rivers Meavy and Plym. The wooden footbridge leading from the car park gives way to a rough, steep track heading up through the wild woods, with the River Plym babbling on its journey well below. Having persevered and followed the right path, you

❯ The Dewerstone's Raven Buttress.

Mark Glaisler

Mark Glaister

◄ Tackling The Dewerstones Climbers Club Direct route.

are rewarded with a view through the trees of this impressive crag which rises for over 150 ft.

Although the Main Face is popular, the outcrop is comprised of a number of equally appealing, quality slabs and buttresses including Pinnacle Buttress which has some beautiful multi-pitch climbs as well as a death-defying leap back on to the main crag for the seriously insane and experienced. The area also offers some decent opportunities for bouldering meaning that provided people can be flexible, fair and patient, there is plenty of rock to go around.

"I love climbing here," says Mal who has been a climber for more than 20 years. "It escapes much of the wind and rain that you can experience on the top of the moor so I work here throughout the year. The River Plym flows past the base of the main cliffs and when you are on the top of the crags you can see Plymouth Sound in the distance. You are also climbing in a beautiful wooded valley on fast drying solid granite with a lot of routes that are suitable for beginners."

And after a hard day's climb in the mid-summer sunshine, it's only a short walk downhill to take a quick dip in the reviving waters of Dartmoor.

> **Lowdown**

ℹ **Directory**
Southwest Adventures, Devon, T01398-331921 M07870-451827, southwest adventures.co.uk.

💲 **Prices**
£120 covers 2 people for a day of climbing multi-pitch routes.

☀ **Season**
Year round (weather permitting).

◎ **Don't miss**
A post climb plunge in the Plym.

✖ **Avoid**
Walking off the path – due to popularity some areas are suffering from erosion which the landowning National Trust are trying to curb.

Practicalities

One of the real joys of Dartmoor National Park is that considerate wild camping is permitted on much of the common land, which accounts for roughly a third of the park's 368 sq miles — pack a tent and a spirit of adventure and anything is possible. See dartmoor-npa.gov.uk for information. Part of Dartmoor is used by the military for training (the rounds they fire on the ranges are live); check details regarding access at dartmoor-ranges.co.uk. For a more conventional stay, there are a number of villages that act as good bases such as Horrabridge to the west and Ivybridge to the south. Ivybridge is also the starting point for the 102-mile Two Moors Way walk which runs through Dartmoor and Exmoor before finishing at Lynmouth, twomoorsway.org.uk for more info.

Transport The mainline Plymouth train station is around 10 miles from Shaugh Bridge and a regular bus service is available with plymouthcitybus.co.uk. For buses to Horrabridge see firstgroup.co.uk. Ivybridge has its own train station.

Sleeping Wild camping on open land for a night or two is allowed on Dartmoor provided the camping code is followed. See dartmoor-npa.gov.uk/vi-wildcamping.htm for details. There are also a number of sites including **Dartmoor Country Holidays** in nearby Horrabridge, T01822-852651, open to campers and tourers Mar-Nov. Lodges sleeping 4 also available from £185/week. **£££ Overcombe House**, Horrabridge, T01822-853501, backs onto Roborough Down and has the gold award for green tourism for their commitment to local, homemade and fairtrade food. Mar-Nov the lovely **££ Hillhead Farm B&B**, in Ugborough, Ivybridge, offers proper farmhouse B&B with a silver green tourism award. Caravan Club site also — NB showers 20p.

Eating & drinking The **Ship Inn**, Ugborough uses local produce to create decent pub grub. Near Horrabridge, the market town of Tavistock is home to a number of cafés including the veggie **Robertson's Organic Café and Pizzeria** on Pepper Street and **Food Dreckley** based in the Cattle Market who serve up excellent brekkies and lunches Tue-Sat.

Also try The **National Nature Reserve of Wistman's Wood** nestles near the heart of the national park. This copse of stunted oaks looks like a scene created by Tolkien: moss covers the boulder-strewn valley floor and gnarled tree trunks in great folds while lichen hangs beard-like from the branches. This dynamic eco-system is protected so visitors are asked to enjoy it from the edges. A 3-mile walk from Two Bridges takes you along the valley of the West Dart to the woods and back again.

Surfing Saunton, Croyde & Putsborough

Provider	DIY
Skill level	Novice-advanced
Time frame	Dawn till dusk
Equipment	Surfboard, wetsuit
Exertion level	●●●●●

Saunton

Mention Saunton Sands to any longboarder and it won't be the three miles of long flat sands that spring to mind. Nor will it be the beach's muso credentials: they won't have a 'Momentary Lapse of Reason' and break out a stash of metal beds in an attempt recreate Pink Floyd's album cover or break into Robbie William's 'Angels' and imagine themselves swirling on this open beach. Well they might, but if they do, run… run as fast as you can. To anyone who delights in the art of the glide, it is the waters breaking off Saunton Sands they will picture, for these are a true longboard heaven.

< Golden sands of Saunton.

The tidal range is great and the beach flat; it's these elements that conspire to produce waves that, although less powerful than those of neighbouring breaks, cannot be beaten for length of ride. Don't expect gaping barrels or speeding walls, the waves here are long and mellow, perfect for finding your feet, mastering the cross step, drop knee turns or practising noseriding. Between the sets there is the backdrop of Braunton Burrows to drink in, a UNESCO Biosphere Reserve and one of Britain largest dune systems. The waters closest to the point are always the busiest, but with so much room to spread out, it's not difficult to find a quiet peak. Swells from the west in the two to three foot range mean plenty of waves and not too punishing a paddle out. If it's much bigger the lack of any real channels can make it a draining experience. The open exposed nature of the beach means that wind is also crucial. Light easterly offshores will help groom the waves into clean, feathering peelers. Be warned, if blustery, a momentary lapse may find your board being blown down the beach in a Robbie Williams style spiral with you in hot pursuit.

Croyde

Low Tide Croyde – it's a mantra repeated in hushed tones by both hardcore locals and visiting surfers from across the country. It's what the best surfers flock here for, what they dream of as the autumn swells kick in and the offshore winds fan the line-up. This chocolate-box village would always have enjoyed a popular following even if the art of waveriding had never been invented, but since this beach happens to be one of Britain's best surf spots, the streets and pubs now see numbers swell year round. And low tide is when the waves are at their heaviest and most hollow – it's the time that draws the most committed to do battle. Not all emerge from the line-up unscathed. In a macking swell, when waves way over head high are drawing water off the shallow sandbanks, and producing pitching, hollow barrels, broken boards are not uncommon. This is a place to come when you are ready for the fight. Off shore in easterly winds, the beach turns

Practicalities

Croyde, with its thatched roofs and narrow streets, has that chocolate-box appeal. It is also Devon's own 'surf city' with a large population of local surfers who generally rip. Nearby, the market town of Braunton has excellent amenities including banks.

Transport Barnstaple is the closest train station – 8 miles from Saunton. Stagecoach Devon 308 regular bus service runs from Braunton to Saunton and on to Croyde, stagecoachbus.com.

Sleeping There is plenty of B&B accommodation here. The 400 year old thatched **£££-££ Vale Cottage**, T01271-890804, valecottagecroyde.co.uk, is chocolate-box but not twee with comfortable doubles plus twin surf annex with board store and drying facilities. Breakfasts use locally sourced produce where possible. The organic, family run **Little Comfort Farm**, T01228-352451, littlecomfortfarm.co.uk, West Down, Braunton, holds the gold award from green tourism for their converted cottages sleeping 2-12. Home reared and home-made produce and meals available from the farmhouse. From £350/week for 4. There is plenty of camping – although it's not a particularly cheap option. One of the simpler sites is the friendly **Lobb Fields** nr Saunton, T01271-812090, open Mar-Oct, on-site surf hire. In Croyde, **Bay View Farm**, T01271-809501, has good access to the beach plus statics to hire – families only.

Eating & drinking **The Thatch** is the focus for Croyde – it's always busy in the summer so be prepared to wait for that pint. **The Corner Bistro**, on the Square, Braunton, combines quality local and free-range produce with good simple cooking to create excellent breakfasts, lunch and dinners. Closed Mon.

Resources There are several surf shops in Croyde including **Little Pink Shop** and **Redwood Surf Shop** with hardware and surf hire. In Braunton, **Loose-Fit**, Exeter Rd, loose-fit.co.uk, pride themselves on their ethical, environmental approach to hardware and lifestyle products. Unsurprisingly there are plenty of surf schools, the well-established 4-star **Surf Southwest**, surfsouthwest.com, have Croyde's top surfers as instructors and aim to minimize their environmental impact. Wi-Fi available at the posh **Saunton Sands Hotel**.

Also try South of the River Taw, the excellent **EBO Fremington**, fremingtonadventure.com, T0800-781 6861, run a number of activities designed to get the most out of the coastline including climbing the popular sandstone crag at Baggy Point and coasteering.

on in northwest to westerly swells and is capped by a reef at either end – Baggy Point to the north and Downend Point to the south. Like the beach they are busy when they're on and best left to experienced waveriders.

^ Peel tucking into a Woolacombe wonder wall.

Putsborough

On the northern edge of Baggy Point, accessed via winding country lanes, is Putsborough Sand, a beach break living in its neighbour's shadow. Although this stretch of sand may be second choice, it doesn't mean it's second rate. The banks here are often overlooked, which is a treat for those willing to forego the lure of the big name for a potentially more satisfying surf. The waves here tend to be smaller than those to the south, but the headland also offers some protection from southerly winds that can blow out other spots. The waters of Morte Bay offer plenty of space to spread out, all the way to Woolacombe, and great rides can be snagged all the way through the tidal range. Only on the biggest days, when Croyde is maxed out, will the crowds descend here and the banks hustle with urgency and static. However, when the swell drops, the lure of Croyde will work its magic again, leaving Putsborough to the lovers of the glide. Putsborough work best in medium northwesterly to westerly swells, off shore in easterly winds. The daily parking charge is around £6 so it's worth packing a picnic and staying until you are truly surfed out.

> Lowdown

⊙ Prices
Free (or from £25/day board and wetsuit hire).

⊙ Season
Year round.

⊙ Don't miss
Exploring Braunton Burrows – one of the UK's largest dune systems.

⊗ Avoid
Surfing anything other than a longboard, mini-mal or fish at Saunton; surfing at Croyde if you're anything less than proficient.

Swimming Dartmoor

Provider	DIY
Skill level	Novice-advanced
Time frame	All day
Equipment	Towel, bathers (depending on season/hardiness wetsuit)
Exertion level	●●○○○

Covering 368 sq miles, Dartmoor National Park is the southwest's largest area of open countryside. Made up of a mosaic of farmland, pony-grazed open moorland, deep valleys shaded by dense forest canopies, undulating hills, ancient woodlands harbouring rare lichens and mosses, peat bogs ready to snare the unsuspecting and vast granite surfaces rising to magnificent tors, it is also one of the wildest. And it is this unique geography rising to a plateau above the surrounding countryside that also means that Dartmoor gets more than its fair share of rainfall and has an almost perpetual air of dampness to it, be it via downpours, mist, fog or just the saturated peaty land that retains pockets of water like a sponge. But this is no bad thing, with 8 reservoirs and countless streams and rivers radiating from its heart, it has made the area one of the southwest's most important sources of water – but not just for domestic consumption. The wild salmon and trout transform it into a natural larder, while industries from tin to gin have benefited from its purity and flow but for those water babies who are wild at heart the fast flowing streams, cascades and meandering rivers also make for an excellent playground.

The Dart, which gives the area its name, begins life as two separate tributaries, East and West Dart, which rise without too much fanfare on the high moors before converging at Dartmeet. From here it twists and turns as one through shaded valleys, lush in spring with the sights and smells of bluebells and wild garlic, before flowing on to Dartmouth and releasing into the sea. It rises and falls quickly according to rainfall but along its length are plenty of opportunities for a carefully considered splash or a serious swim with calm pools and gentle pockets found alongside wilder sections. To Holne Bridge, the river has been pretty much left to run its own course while to the south there are a series of weirs.

❮ Stroking out into a cool pool on the River Dart.

Dam building

Building a dam on a fast flowing river or a gentle stream can cause irreparable damage.

1. Erosion is caused by the stones being removed from the riverbank.
2. Silt builds up behind the dam resulting in a loss of fish spawning grounds.
3. Fish get trapped in the pools and become easy targets for predators.
4. Returning salmon and sea trout cannot get back to their spawning grounds.
5. Damming rivers is illegal.
6. The Environment Agency cleared away over 60 dams last year.

Parking at Newbridge, to the west of Ashburton gives easy access to several wonderful swimming holes some of which are conveniently nestled alongside clearings on which to peg yourself out and recharge your batteries post swim. A short walk down stream sees you emerging from the trees onto Deeper Marsh or Spitchwick Common, which has long been a popular spot for picnicking and plunging. Here the generous grassy clearing gives way to a rocky bank groomed by cool, clean, peat-stained waters and, with mellow pools for the uninitiated and deeper recesses for the committed, it can quickly become busy on a warm summer's day. Walking up-stream from Newbridge can yield quieter returns: a hidden island complete with sandy beach lies in wait around a river bend, under a wooded canopy while deep, damp, shady pools whose hard grey edges have been softened by green blankets of moss and algae such as Sharrah or Mel Pool call to the adventurous from further upstream. (For these pools also park at Venford Reservoir for quicker access.)

In the southwest corner of Dartmoor, the exposed Plym, which lends its name to Plymouth, Plymstock and Plymouth Gin, and winds its way past the impressive Dewerstone, also affords some excellent opportunities for taking the plunge in fresh, peaty waters. On the edge of the national park Cadover Bridge near Shaugh Prior has a good car park making it an excellent starting point from which to explore the pools of the area – take a stroll, take your time and take your pick.

The Loop which runs between Newbridge and Holne Bridge and encircles Holne Woods is popular with intermediate canoeists and kayakers.

> Lowdown

● Prices
Free.

● Season
Year round.

● Don't miss
A post swim bask in the sunshine at Deep Marsh to warm the soul.

● Avoid
Disturbing the spawning salmon around Dartmeet or being caught out by rapidly rising water levels and fast flowing rivers following rainfall high on the moors.

∧ Leap of faith at Spitchwick Common.

∧ The river banks are strewn with bluebells.

Practicalities

Dartmoor covers 368 sq miles and is managed by the Dartmoor National Park Authority, dartmoor-npa.gov.uk. Just over a third of this is common land meaning, thanks to the Dartmoor Commons Act 1985, that considerate wild camping by those following the backpacking code is permitted on much of it. For for those looking for a more substantial place to lay their hat, the ancient stannery town of Ashburton, is an ideal base for exploring the Dart.

Transport Newton Abbot and Totnes train stations are both about 7 miles from Ashburton. Stagecoach offers service to the town from either station, stagecoachbus.com.

Sleeping For those wanting to connect with the environment, wild camping on open land for a night or two is allowed on Dartmoor provided "you don't pitch your tent on farmland, on moorland enclosed by walls, within 100 yards of a road, on flood plains or on archaeological sites", explains the Dartmoor National Park Authority. Part of Dartmoor is used by the military for training (the rounds they fire are live) so it's essential to check their site carefully for details on where you can and can't free camp: dartmoor-npa.gov.uk/vi-wildcamping.htm. There are a number of local sites from the basic but wonderful **Beara Farm**, T01364-642234, on the river's edge in nearby Buckfastleigh, to **River Dart Adventures**, T01364-652511, riverdart.co.uk, combining camping and caravanning with an adventure playground on the river which flows through the grounds and also powers their hydro turbine, producing a great deal of their electricity. There are a number of hostels including the **£ Bellever YHA**, T0845-3719622, open all year, offering home cooked foods using local ingredients, plus the self-styled eco-hostel, **£ Sparrowhawk**, Moretonhampstead, T01647-440318, with dorms, doubles and solar powered showers. **££ Cuddyford B&B**, T01364-653325, Broadpark, Ashburton is a simple, family run vegetarian B&B – home-made bread and apple juice plus honey from their hives are a highlight.

Eating & drinking If you're not cooking up a storm on your camping stove then head to the fantastic **Field Kitchen**, Buckfastleigh, T01803-762074. You are driven by tractor to the barn (restaurant) to enjoy organic produce, dug from the farm's ground that day and turned into 2 set courses of something special! Feb-Dec, weekends lunch £16, dinner £20.

Also try Oct-Mar if heavy rainfall has caused the Dart to flow too fast for swimming, try whitewater rafting with **CRS Adventure**, Ashburton, crsadventures.co.uk, T01364-653444. Half day from £35/person, minimum 4.

Mountain biking Dartmoor

Provider	DIY
Skill level	All
Time frame	2 hrs +
Equipment	Mountain bike, helmet, map, snacks, water, a map and a repair kit/spare tube. Conditions on Dartmoor change quickly so carry foul weather gear
Exertion level	●●●○○

On a sunny day the vast open landscape of Dartmoor can appear to challenge the notion that civilization ever made it out of the Iron Age and into a modern era. A rest stop here may consist of a lichen-covered wall in a shady, wooded valley, a small granite bridge that neatly steps over a babbling brook, or a sun-warmed summit slab that offers far-reaching sea views south over the distant Plymouth Sound. Criss-crossed with sound trails, a day's riding on Dartmoor can deliver breathtaking terrain, epic vistas, challenging climbs, hell-for-leather descents or relaxing touring.

Princetown is excellent for a MTB-based trip with access to the region's most enticing landscapes. The 368 sq miles of Dartmoor are a mosaic of private, public, military, farm and common lands, but the right to roam allows access to the majority of it. For bikes, there are rideable trails, tracks, roads, abandoned rail lines and pathways – check the Dartmoor Off-Road Cycling Map for details.

From Princetown, there's a circular trail of around 12½ miles, excellent for all levels. Leaving the campsite, the outward stretch climbs south out of the village bearing in the direction of Burrator Reservoir. The track then heads through the heart of Dartmoor. Continuing across the moor, the twin peaks of Sharpitor and Leathertor are companions before the track drops towards Burrator Reservoir. The woodland trail loops around towards Yellow Mead Down, the village of Sheepstor and round past the Sheepstor peak. The home stretch runs up through the bleak Eylesbarrow Tin Mine and north via South Hessary Tor. Dartmoor is an open and exposed expanse – don't underestimate it.

Wig Worland

> ∧ Threading through the granite strewn landscape.

Practicalities

Transport Plymouth station is 15 miles from Princetown. You can bike or bus via Yelverton, firstgroup.com (no bikes).

Sleeping £ Fox Tor Café, Two Bridges Road, PL20 6QS, T01822-890238. Basic bunkhouse with beds for £10; bring your own bedding. Drying room, plus bike storage. **£ Bellever YHA**, T0845-3719622, in nearby Postbridge has a discount for those arriving by bike, bus or on foot. **££ The Oratory B&B**, Tavistock Rd, Princetown run by outdoors enthusiasts. For camping try the **Plume of Feathers Inn**, The Square, T01822-890240. NB Avoid the bunkrooms.

Eating & drinking The **Prince of Wales** is popular and offers food and good beer. **The Dartmoor Inn**, Merrivale, has a great atmosphere and serves food. The **Old Police Station Café** serves traditional food through the day.

Resources **Devon Cycle Hire**, Sourton Down near Okehampton, T01837-861141, devoncyclehire.co.uk. Guided rides for all levels, MTB hire (can deliver). Easter-Sep but out of season hire can be arranged in advance.

Also try The less demanding 11-mile Granite Trail runs along the northwestern edge of Dartmoor between Okehampton and Lydford. Free route map available: devon.gov.uk/cycling.

> **Lowdown**

> **⊖ Prices**
> Free or from £15/day MTB hire.

> **⊙ Season**
> Spring to autumn.

> **⊕ Don't miss**
> A post-ride dip in the nearby river.

> **⊗ Avoid**
> To prevent damage and erosion to this ecologically sensitive land, it's not permitted to range over open moorland unless you are following one of the linear routes.

Climbing Southwest: best of the rest

Provider	Various
Skill level	Novice-advanced
Time frame	1½ hrs to 2 days
Equipment	See details
Exertion level	●●●●●

The geology, geography and climate of the southwest have conspired to create a wealth of natural architectural delights with which to tempt even the most reluctant climber. From pink granite sea cliffs warmed by Cornwall's autumn sun to the cool, grey tors of Dartmoor and the angled limestone of the Avon or Cheddar Gorges there is something for everyone.

Avon Gorge & Cheddar Gorge

While Isambard Kingdom Brunel's Clifton Suspension Bridge linking Bristol and North Somerset is iconic, it is the gorge which it spans that attracts the climber. More than a mile long, the Avon Gorge, skirted by the busy A4 road, cuts through a ridge of limestone along the River Avon to create some exciting climb locations with a number of good routes at lower grades on more angled rock and a wonderfully bizarre mix of city and nature. "The Avon Gorge is THE big city place to climb," enthuses instructor **Barry Donavan**. "Go climbing and drink a perfect mojito in a cocktail bar on the same day. The climbing is like ballroom dancing except it's a bad idea to put a foot wrong!" A day climbing with Avon based Barry costs £130 for two people with all equipment supplied. T07876-565159, bjdclimbing@hotmail.com. 2008 saw Bristol crowned as the UK's most sustainable city, it has also become Britain's first cycle city with new cycle ways and 24 hour bike hire planned. See hourbike.com for details on bike hire from Parkway station. To the south is Somerset's impressive **Cheddar Gorge**. Gaining household fame for Chris Bonnington's mid-sixties televized ascent, this vast limestone gorge deep in the Mendip Hills is home to some breathtaking climbs. With the cathedral-like Cheddar Caves, it is also a popular visitor spot and with sections of the road running directly beneath some of the buttresses, there are several climbing

restrictions in place including restrictions on commercial climbing with paid instructors, making this a spot for the experienced. See the BMC Regional Access Database for details. **Rock Sport Adventures**, cheddarcaves.co.uk, run 1½-hour taster climbs and abseiling for £17.

Baggy Point, Croyde, Devon

On the northern edge of the popular Croyde Bay, Baggy Point, edged by the South West Coast Path, is more than just a wind break for the beachgoer. Washed by the Atlantic, the south facing, lichen daubed sandstone slabs are home to some

ⵗ Good instruction is essential for making your first steps on a rock face or improving your technique.

Demi Taylor

Dartmoor National Park Authority

excellent sea cliff climbing with something for most levels, provided you time it right with the tides (from mid tide, most routes are accessible). From March-July, the cliffs are also home to nesting birds when a ban is in place – see the BMC access database for full details thebmc.co.uk. Park at the National Trust car park. Those with some experience can arrange sea cliff climbing with **Mal Dickson**, southwestadventures.co.uk, £120 for up to two people (includes equipment for a day's climb). **Baggy Lodge** on the Baggy Point coast path, T01271-890078, baggys.co.uk, offers B&B and surf lodge accommodation from £20.

Bosigran, Penwith, Cornwall

On the edge of a turquoise sea, on the toe of Cornwall, between the magical sounding villages of Zennor and Morvah rises an exquisite granite wall. Its wonderful cracked face, mottled with rich bands of colour from stark white to ochre and dark brown interspersed with occasional bands of grass and heather is home to some excellent single and multi-pitch routes. "Bosigran offers the middle grade climber a wealth of multi-pitch routes on great rock and in a perfect situation," explains instructor Mal Dickson. "A real sun trap, the cliff offers climbing over the sea but without the tidal dangers." It's little

wonder that it can get busy during the summer and bank holidays. Access from nearby NT car park. Those with some experience can arrange sea cliff climbing with **Mal Dickson**, southwestadventures.co.uk, £120 for up to two people (including equipment for a day's climb). **Old Chapel Backpackers**, Zennor, T01736-798307, is a handy spot with beds from £15. In the nearby village of St Just, **Kelynack Holidays**, T01736-787633. offers camping, bunkhouse plus B&B with breakfasts featuring local produce accommodation March-October.

Chair Ladder, Penwith, Cornwall

The journey to Porthgwarra winds down ever decreasing country lanes and muddied tracks before reaching the tiny, sheltered cove around which a handful of cottages and a little café cluster. The Atlantic pounds the base of this tidal crag whose golden granite face is so riddled with useful, solid cracks and fissures it looks as though it is a series of giant rock cubes stacked one on top of the other. "Chair Ladder offers climbs up to 220 ft long on perfect granite," says climber Mal. "But be careful with tides and freak waves as the base of the cliff can only be accessed at low tide. This is not somewhere for the beginner." Nearby Sennen Cove poses other wonderful sea cliff alternatives. "There are shorter climbs up to 90 ft long at Sennen Cove on single pitch routes only a five-minute walk from the white sand and surf of the beach," Mal advises. "Many of these are in the VD – E1 category." Stay at the nearby **Old Chapel Backpackers**, Zennor, T01736-798307, with beds from £15.

Haytor (also Hay Tor) and Low Man, Dartmoor, Devon

These twin peaks emerge from green baize muddled with smaller lumps of rock to dominate the surrounding east Dartmoor skyline, calling visitors to its brain-like mass of crack riddled grey granite. With excellent access and nearby parking, this is a very public, very popular spot attracting walkers and sightseers as well as plenty of climbers in peak summer. "Hay Tor has a handful of single pitch routes that are ideal for the novice with flakes and cracks but they all have their difficult moves and do not give in easily," explains Mal Dickson of the rock's appeal. "At first sight Low Man appears to be the smaller relation but on NW side, a large 150 ft wall with some classic climbs can be found. These routes are multi-pitch and require some experience before you attempt them." Contact Mal for a day's climbing (see page opposite). Responsible wild camping is permitted on some of Dartmoor's common land, dartmoor-npa.gov.uk/vi-wildcamping.htm for details.

Chudleigh Rock, Devon

Nestling in a sheltered valley just east of Dartmoor and within easy reach of Exeter, Chudleigh is home to some high quality limestone with some fine climbs across the grades from moderate to extreme. "This is an inspiring spot which makes you feel as though you are standing next to giants," says experienced climber Alex Palmer and UKC crag moderator who began his climbing career here. "You can see what you'll be climbing tomorrow while standing next to the wall you're going to climb that day." This is a popular spot for good reason: the South Face is a real sun trap so on a bright, clear January day you can easily believe it's the middle of summer and as you climb out of the trees and look out over the canopy the feeling is epic. The popularity of the area means that the limestone has become polished but increased difficulty is a small price to pay – just watch out for the bees nesting in the wall and you'll be fine. Book a two-day beginners/improvers course with **Ben Bradford** from £110, T07709-432014, ben-bradford.co.uk. The North Face of Chudleigh is owned and run by **The Rock Centre**, rockcentre.co.uk, who have developed their 10 acre grounds into a climbing facility with everything from an indoor wall to bolted sports climbs; they also offer instruction. They offer on-site parking (please sign guest book) and lovely low-key camping from £1.50 a night as well as tipis for hire.

> The impressive, brain-like Haytor rising from Dartmoor.

Demi Taylor

Canoeing Wimbleball Lake, Exmoor

Provider	DIY
Skill level	Beginner-intermediate
Time frame	4 hrs
Equipment	Sun block. Canoe and safety equipment at hire centre
Exertion level	●●○○○

Wimbleball Lake on Exmoor may be one of the region's most popular sailing and kayaking locations, but here on the southern arm there's not a soul in sight as I paddle through the lush canopy of reflected oak and beech towards the point where the Haddeo brings life to this majestic lake. Wimbleball from the air is a slightly misshapen capital E, but from the water it offers over 7 miles of ever-changing shoreline to follow. It's fringed by green open fields, ancient sessile oak woodlands, sleepy lagoons where birdwatchers wait with binoculars at the ready and anglers creep sweeping the surface for tell tale signs of the one that got away.

From the jetty at the Watersports Centre it's plain paddling south but rounding the headland you'll find the reason for this body of water's existence in this high valley, the 161-ft high dam completed in 1979 which holds back 21,000 megalitres of water. At the northern end of the lake lies Bessom Bridge and next to it a causeway leading to a popular bird hide. Wimbleball is quite a large body of water and as such can get choppy on a windy day. The waters here can be alive with all kinds of human- and wind-powered craft – if you want to experience peace and quiet then weekdays outside the summer are the times to come. But even on the busiest of days, it's great to be out on the water. The Angling and Watersports Centre offers craft to hire, from Canadian canoes and kayaks to double kayaks. If you've never tried canoeing or kayaking before, they have qualified instructors on hand to offer lessons and encouragement. And after some liquid refreshment of the visual kind, it's just a short walk to the tea room for some cake and the sort of liquid refreshment you CAN drink.

Practicalities

Near Dulverton, Wimbleball Lake sits high on Exmoor and offers an excellent day out with walking, sailing, fishing and bird watching opportunities year round. Wimbleball is part of the South West Lakes Trust Charity swlakestrust.org.uk, created to encourage, promote and enhance sustainable recreation, access, nature conservation and education on and around over 50 inland waters in the Southwest. Parking £2/day.

Transport The local railway station is Tiverton Parkway, with direct services to mainline hubs such as Plymouth, Bristol Temple Meads or Birmingham. From here there's a bus to Tiverton bus station and a connection on to Dulverton, however buses don't run out to the lake.

Sleeping £ Wimbleball Lake Camping, TA22 9NW, T01398-371257, has 30 pitches overlooking the lake, some with electric hook-up. From £6 pp/night. Open Mar-Oct. ££-£ Harton Farm, Oakford, EX16 9HH, T01398-351209, hartonfarm.co.uk, is a working livestock farm with quiet farmhouse B&B and a gold award for green tourism. Evening meals available featuring home-grown vegetables, home-reared meats and traditional home cooking.

Eating & drinking There is a café on site at Wimbleball, but for something a bit special, **Woods Bar and restaurant**, Bank Square, Dulverton, with its open fire and local produce is a great spot to sink a local ale, glass of wine or enjoy some hearty fare.

Resources Canoe hire: **Angling and Watersports Centre**, Wimbleball Lake, nr Dulverton, TA22 9NW, T01398-371460, swlakestrust.org.uk (plus kayak hire available by the hour plus half and full day rates). Taster courses as well as one to one tuition is also available.

Also try The dramatic Valley of the Rocks near Lynton is home to some good climbing for all levels. For novices, **The Mill Adventure Centre**, Hacche Mill, South Molton, T01769-579600, offers a good introduction to climbing here (as well as courses for more experienced climbers). On-site they have a café plus the well-stocked **Rock and Rapid** climbing store T01769-572020, as well as an excellent indoor climbing wall. Accommodation also available from £15 pp.

> **Lowdown**

◷ **Prices**
Canadian canoe £40 half day, £60 full day.

☀ **Season**
All year.

✪ **Don't miss**
The 9-mile walk around the lake is beautiful.

✖ **Avoid**
This body of water can get pretty choppy so check to avoid launching in the wrong conditions for your ability.

Walking Cotswolds

Provider	DIY
Skill level	Novice-experienced
Time frame	2 hrs to 5 days
Equipment	OS Map, walking books, provisions
Exertion level	●●●○○

∧ Belas Knap.
< Autumnal moods, Leckhampton.

Huge skies watch over the gently rolling hills and river valleys. Surrounded by open pasture, patches of woodland and manicured village greens, pretty clusters of honey-hued thatched cottages with welcoming village pubs and wealthy market towns signal their location with church spires reaching skyward. Yes, the views across this 790-sq mile Area of Outstanding Natural Beauty are quintessentially English and classically Cotswold. The southern and eastern-most reaches of the limestone hills gently undulate to their conclusion while the north and west are marked by the arresting feature of the escarpment or the Edge – an uplifting of limestone that has shifted and tilted dramatically to expose its broken edge.

At just over 100 miles, the Cotswold Way stretches south from the market town of Chipping Campden to Bath. Following the impressive ridge, the trail affords vistas across the River Severn towards the Brecon Beacons. Skirting pastureland parcelled into fields with local dry stone walling, descending into bluebell-carpeted valleys and beech woodlands, the trail undulates past striking features from ancient burial barrows and iron age forts to Leckhampton Hill's lore-etched limestone pinnacle, the Devil's Chimney. Heading north to south, the trail starts with a series of longer climbs, taking in the 1040 ft Cleve Hill – the highest point in the Cotswolds before being replaced by a number of gentler hills. Despite the distance, this is a gentle introduction to hill walking, and the full distance can easily be covered in around 6-7 days. A baggage transfer company can shuttle non-essentials to your next resting stop. There are also excellent short walks in the Cotswolds that make the most of the views, terrain and local pubs.

Practicalities

The trail runs between Bath and Chipping Campden with plenty of B&B and camping opportunities along the way. It can be walked in either direction, some preferring the walk south to north keeping the sun on their backs.

Transport   Bath Spa is the city's mainline station. Moreton-in-Marsh is 5 miles from Chipping Campden with an onward bus service with **Johnsons Coach & Bus.**

Sleeping   There are plenty of places to stop off along the way nationaltrail.co.uk/Cotswold is a good starting place. As a first/last night stopover, the **£££-£ White Hart Inn**, Winchcombe T01242-602359, wineandsausage.co.uk, takes some beating with rooms from £40 to en suites from £75, plus there is a well-priced restaurant below. For camping, try **Hayles Fruit Farm** T01242-602123, year round with excellent farm shop (includes Hayles Cider) and tea room.

Resources   The Cotswold Way National Trail has its own dedicated website: nationaltrail.co.uk/Cotswold and guide companion. Local company **Cotswolds Walks** (cotswoldwalks. com, T01242-518888) organizes walking breaks from self-guided to luxury tours. **Sherpa Van**, T0871-520 0124, sherpavan. com, offers a baggage transfer from £7 per bag per day, Apr-Oct.

Also try   For a walking break with a twist check out **The Three Ways Hotel Pudding Club**, Mickleton, Chipping Campden, GL55 6SB, T01386-438429, puddingclub.com. They run all-inclusive weekend walking breaks to coincide with their Pudding Club nights — an evening meal where a parade of 7 great British puddings follows an 11-mile guided walk on the Saturday with a shorter 8-mile walk on the Sun.

> **Lowdown**

⊙ **Prices**
Free.

⊙ **Season**
Year round (weather permitting).

⊙ **Don't miss**
The area is riddled with almost 100 limestone chambered tombs including the Neolithic Belas Knap Longbarrow of 3800 BC near Charlton Abbots.

⊗ **Avoid**
While the Cotswolds is generally about gently rolling hills – don't get caught out by the odd steep climb!

Mountain biking Quantocks & Exmoor

Provider	DIY
Skill level	All
Time frame	3-4 hrs
Equipment	Mountain bike, helmet, map, snacks, water, a map and a repair kit/spare tube
Exertion level	●●●○○

Resting on handlebars and sipping water high on the Quantocks, you realize just what makes this area so special – after all it was the first region to be awarded the status of Area of Outstanding Natural Beauty in England back in 1956. The compact nature of the area belies the huge amount of terrain on offer to riders of all abilities. Though the Quantocks measure a mere twelve miles by four, there are combes and hidden snaking tracks that can take years of exploring to discover. Wide, open heathland tops the high spine before disappearing into a series of shady, broadleaf woodlands where sessile oaks and beech shroud the deep cut valleys and lead out on to the open farmland and small villages that nestle in the lee of these undulating hills. This is an area of not only outstanding beauty, but outstanding terrain and riding potential.

The views on a clear day are legendary, across the Bristol Channel into Wales and over to Exmoor, and the high track offers access into a network of paths and trails that criss-cross the area offering everything from leisurely touring and gentle climbs following well-defined routes to intense, condensed riding of testing ascents and downhill blasts negotiating tree roots, boulders and streams that are technical enough to test the best. John Charlesworth of Mountain Bike Crazy has been riding these tracks for many years and offers guided days out. "Very few mountain bike venues have such a diversity of tracks in such a compact area, offering exciting riding to all levels of rider. Steep technical downhill's, singletrack routes that seem to go on forever and wide open trails, whatever your riding preference, you'll find it on the Quantock Hills and never have far to the next thrill. There is so much riding here you will never tire of it."

> Tim Flooks, Quantocks down time.

< Birds eye view on a prime strip of Quantocks trail.

Seb Rogers

There are plenty of starting and stopping off points, but the village of Holford, just off the A39 is easy to access and well placed to unlock the potential of Hodders Combe and Holford Combe valleys to the southwest. A good route for an afternoon's riding takes you out through Holford Combe along a wooded track that climbs to about a thousand feet, then takes in a 360 degree loop past an ancient fort site, before striking out along Robin Uprights Hill onto the spine track. Once up high you can follow this route as it arcs round to the northwest for about three miles, before looping back round to the head of Hodders Combe. This is a challenging descent through trees, with technical sections peppered with roots and boulders, which then fords the stream and leads out to a leisurely drop to the village. A route like this will run between ten and twelve miles, but can be extended or shortened.

To the west of the Quantocks the expanse of the Exmoor National Park spreads out over 267 sq miles across the northern borders of Somerset and Devon. The terrain here may seem similar at first sight but this is a real change of scene: Exmoor is more of a high plateau and lacks the high number of combes with which the Quantocks are riven. And while the riding is varied and exciting, it is more spread out. "Exmoor offers miles of country tracks that are ideal for a family day out, or a day building up your cross country endurance," explains John Charlesworth. " On the whole Exmoor is more of a sedate ride, the fast downhill sections are placed farther apart than on the Quantocks, but they are there for the riding none the less." From a bone shaking blast through the Brendon Hills, a relaxing cycle through the Vale of Porlock or a day out on the heights of Exmoor, the National Park offers myriad paths and routes.

Dunster is one popular starting point and there are tracks that climb up around Croydon Hill and on into the Brendon Hills. Passing to the south of Luxborough, it's then possible to head northwest towards Luccombe and sweep round to the southeast back to Dunster. A route like this will take in climbs over a thousand feet and extend over twenty plus miles, but the terrain will include some challenging climbs and swift descents, and roam through woodland, fields and along country lanes. A good OS map will show just how much potential there is here to enjoy. Go, explore.

∧ Descending toward the dramatic Exmoor coastline.

> Lowdown

⊖ Prices
Free or from £14/day MTB hire.

⊗ Season
All year.

◐ Don't miss
The Exmoor Explorer Mountain Bike Marathon takes place on 1st Sun in Aug. Long distance reliability trail across Exmoor – suitable for all levels, exmoorexplorer.com.

⊗ Avoid
The riding around the Quantocks is pretty demanding to both your body and bike – avoid cycling without a decent repair kit.

Practicalities

The Quantocks are compact with a number of good bases depending on your needs: north of the hills, Bridgwater is a classic market town with full amenities while the Quantocks proper is home to a collection of smaller villages. Exmoor meets the sea at the coastal town of Minehead, the starting point for the Southwest Coast Path and a good base. Take a walk out on to the parade for pubs, cafés and restaurants.

Transport   For the Quantocks, Bridgwater is a good access point with train connections via Taunton, Bristol or Weston-super-Mare. For Exmoor, Taunton is 23 miles from Minehead by bus, firstgroup.com. NB no bikes permitted.

Sleeping   Quantocks: ££-£ Huntstile Organic Farm, Goathurst, nr Bridgwater TA5 2DQ, T01278-662358/07725-278280, huntstileorganicfarm.co.uk. Huntstile is a farm with lake and woodlands with B&B, self-catering and camping. ££-£ Parsonage Farm, Over Stowey, TA5 1HA, T01278-733237, parsonfarm.co.uk, is a B&B with discount for visitors who arrive by bike, public transport or on foot. Exmoor: ££ Hindon Organic Farm, nr Selworthy, Minehead, TA24 8SH, T01643-705244, hindonfarm.co.uk, offers B&B as well as self-catering accommodation. Evening meals and organic produce. £ YHA Exford nr Minehead, TA24 7PU, T0845-3719634, dorms, a double plus camping with on-site restaurant. Camping Westermill Farm Campsite, Exford, TA24 7NJ, T01643-831238, westermill.com, is riverside with a shop selling local produce.

Eating & drinking   In the Quantocks for something special try Clavelshay Barn, North Petherton, T01278-662629. This restaurant specializes in seasonal, locally sourced ingredients. The Smugglers Inn, Blue Anchor, nr Minehead TA24 6JS, T01984-640385, also uses locally sourced quality produce.

Resources   Mountain Bike Crazy, T07974-933140, mountainbikecrazy.com, ABCC MTB coach John Charlesworth offers guided tours of Quantocks and Exmoor plus courses to hone MTB skills from £79/5 hr session. Pompy's Cycles, Minehead, Exmoor, TA24 5BJ, T01643-704077, MTB hire from £14/day plus guided rides from £60 (not Sun). JustRide Exmoor, Lynmouth, EX35 6EP, T01598-752529, bike hire from £15, delivery also available, hire including GPS units with pre-loaded routes £30. Guided rides from £30/person. Well stocked shop, refreshments plus Wi-Fi access.

Also try   The Exmoor Cycle Route 60 mile circular. Starting at Minehead heading west gives you a chance to warm up on the flat before the route rollercoasters taking in 3 substantial "King of the Mountains" challenges; activeexmoor.com for route map.

Mountain biking The Mendip Hills

Provider	DIY
Skill level	Novice-experienced
Time frame	Full day
Equipment	Mountain bike, helmet, map, snacks, water, a map and a repair kit/spare tube
Exertion level	●●●●●

The significant AONB takes the focus of the Mendips – an area of almost 125 sq mile stretching from the Bristol Channel eastward to Wells. The area is rich with architectural and archaeological wonders from Neolithic monuments and bronze age barrows to roman hill forts and WW2 bunkers. However, it is the natural architecture of the land that is perhaps more impressive to the mountain biker. The limestone range which rises to a central undulating plateau is riven with gorges and caves, deep valleys and combes to deliver a variety of terrains in a small area, from dense forest to open grassland and trails, from country roads and bridleways to singletrack for all levels. "The Mendips are a hidden gem containing some of the best singletrack in the southwest topped off with incredible views over the Bristol Channel to south Wales," enthuses leading photographer and hills local Seb Rogers. "But it's an area best avoided after prolonged periods of rain, since the trails tend to get boggy very quickly."

In contrast to the main plateau the highest point rises from steep slopes to the moorland summit of 1065 ft at Black Down, the spot at Beacon Batch marked by an OS trig point. This area is home to some of the best Mendip riding where steep, fast singletrack descents are matched by tough climbs. As this is an ecologically sensitive area, stick to the trails. mendiphillsaonb.org.uk have produced some circular trail maps, which don't skimp on thrills: the Black Down bike card and Mendip Fat Tyre Trails. For experienced riders, the 12 mile Black Down circular kicks off from Charterhouse (parking but be aware there have been a number of break-ins) and takes in a combination of challenging trails through Black Down and Rowberrow forest.

Way Warcing

< Tall trees and singletrack descents.

Practicalities
Cheddar has shops, banks, pubs and accommodation.

Transport Bristol has 2 main train stations Temple Meads and Parkway, 20 miles from Cheddar. Weston-super-Mare station is just over 12 miles away. Bus services with firstgroup.com. NB Bikes not permitted on the bus.

Sleeping **Cheddar Camp**, Shipham, BS25 1RW, T01934-743166, basic, pitches £5, no showers. **Broadway House Lodge**, Cheddar BS27 3DB, T01934-742610, statics, pitches plus BMX track and skate park, Mar-Nov. **££ Ashcroft House B&B**, Blagdon, T01822-853501, cottagebandb.co.uk. Relaxed cottage. Bike storage, guided walks (see Forage Mendips, page 60).

Eating & drinking **Bank House Café**, Axbridge Main Square, T01934-733004, for lunches and dinners. **The Plume of Feathers**, Rickford nr Blagdon, for quality pub fare Fri-Sat. On the trails, **The Swan Inn**, Rowberrow (handy car park to set off from) serves local ales plus standard pub grub.

Resources mendiphillsaonb.org.uk for route maps (used with OS Explorer Maps 153 and 141). **Bike the Mendips**, T01761-463356, bikethemendips.co.uk, guided rides from £25. Skills session, followed by challenging trail. **Cheddar Cycle Store**, T01934-741300, cheddarcyclestore.co.uk, bike hire £12/day near Strawberry Line national cycle route sustrans.org.uk.

Also try The 50-mile Mendip Way links Weston-super-Mare and Frome. With views across the Somerset levels, the walk combines climbs before dropping down to the Cheddar Gorge, Wells and wooded valleys near Frome.

> **Lowdown**

⊙ Prices
Free or from £12/day MTB hire.

⊗ Season
Year round (weather permitting).

⊕ Don't miss
If you love a challenge and a good cause check out the 24-hr endurance ride: clic24.org.uk.

⊗ Avoid
This is not somewhere to attempt in the wet.

Kite surfing Weymouth

Provider	Paraacdemy Extreme Sports Centre
Skill level	Beginner/intermediate
Time frame	3 days
Equipment	Towel, swimming trunks/one piece and sun block; everything else is provided
Exertion level	●●●●●

Pulling into the car park there's a tell tale scattering of boxy VW vans, always a good sign that you're in the right place. This dusty patch looks out over the harbour, its back to the wind-whipped sea surging up the steep angled pebbles that form Chesil beach shoreline. Ahead is a perfect maritime enclosure nearly two and a half miles long and two miles wide, big enough to stretch your seafaring wings, but not so big you can disappear into shipping lanes or wash up on some foreign beach. Kite surfing developed as an offshoot of windsurfing and kite buggying. It's come a long way in the last decade, from its origins in southwest France, to its growth in the balmy waters off Maui. This is now officially an Olympic venue so Portland Harbour seems as natural a place as any to 'sheet in'.

Weymouth has become something of a Mecca for kite surfing – the waters off Weymouth Bay offer great freestyle, hangtime and waveriding opportunities from October-March, while the harbour at Portland sees those looking for some freestyle fun or straight-line speed launching year round. For first timers, British Kite Surfing Association schools offer courses designed to help you pick up the basics and get out there. These usually run over a three day period with the first day mastering the theory behind kite surfing and handling a kite on land, day two getting in the water for some kite dragging and then on day three putting all you've learnt together whilst strapped in on a board.

"The great thing about Portland Harbour is that it's a large area of enclosed shallow water," says Spencer Whyte of Paracademy Extreme Sports Centre. "It's not choppy and you don't have to

deal with a shore dump, which means it's good for beginners. It's also very consistent here – last season was great, we only had to cancel four lessons in the whole year." Spencer thinks that most people will get the basics after a three-day course, especially those who have previous experience of a boardsport. You'll certainly have fun trying. The key to getting started in kite surfing is getting good tuition – it should get you up and riding and will help you avoid any kitemares.

Practicalities

The former navy town of Weymouth is a vibrant, buzzy seaside resort. To the south the huge limestone mass of Portland sticks into the sea joined to the mainland by the improbable-looking 18-mile stretch of pebbles that is Chesil Beach.

Transport   The local mainline railway station is Weymouth.

Sleeping   ££ **Sundial Cottage**, Gorwell Farm, Abbotsbury, DT3 4JX, T01305-871401, gorwellfarm.co.uk, is a great spot for those looking for a quiet self-catering option. With the bronze award for green tourism and nestled in its own wooded valley, it sleeps five and is just a couple of miles from Chesil Beach. For those who want to camp, **£ East Fleet Farm**, Chickerell, Weymouth DT3 4DW, T01305-785768, eastfleet.co.uk, has a David Bellamy gold award and is at the heart of a 300-acre organic dairy farm overlooking Chesil Beach and Fleet Lagoon. There is also a fully licensed bar with local ales and bar menu featuring organic beef.

Eating & drinking   The **Blue Fish Café**, 17a Chiswell, Portland, Weymouth DT5 1AN, T01305-822991, offers excellent locally sourced food.

Resources   **Paracademy Extreme Sports Centre** sells hard-wear and beach wear, has a café plus showers, toilets and lockers for students.

Also try   Portland is all about sport climbing (relying on permanent anchors such as bolts fixed to the rock for protection) so is a great place to be introduced to this style of climbing. Introduction with **Dorset Climbing Activities**, dorsetclimbingactivities.co.uk, from £175. Trad climbing also available.

> Lowdown

❶ **Directory**
Paracademy Extreme Sports Centre, Weymouth, DT5 1AL, T01305-824797, paracademyextreme. co.uk. The large centre is on the south side of Portland harbour.

❸ **Prices**
3-day course from £250.

❂ **Season**
Mar-Nov.

❂ **Don't miss**
Check out Pulpit Rock on the southern tip of Portland.

❌ **Avoid**
This isn't a sport to DIY, get some good instruction under your belt.

Walking Salisbury Plain

Provider	DIY
Skill level	All
Time frame	3 days
Equipment	Walking boots
Exertion level	●●○○○

The countryside is awash with colour as a sea of wild flowers and tall, bleached grasses ripple in the summer breeze. The vast, open stretch of Salisbury Plain is home to one of Europe's largest expanses of uncultivated, unfarmed chalk downland. The unimproved grassland, punctuated with small hilltop woodlands, is a refuge for rarities from marsh fritillary butterflies to purple milk-vetch and an important site for birds. The perimeters of this plain have also acted to protect and preserve some 2000 ancient monuments – burial mounds to Romano-British settlements – that may otherwise have fallen prey to the ravages of modernisation: intensive farming and road building. It is odd to think then that this protective cotton wool barrier and natural countryside has been created as a happy by-product of war games played out on a grand scale. Salisbury Plain Army Training Estate covers just over 38,000 hectares and while some of the land has been let to farmers, access is severely restricted to the majority for good reason. The army has utilized the area since the 1890s to test devices and train troops and the resulting lethal cocktail of live firing range and unexploded hidden shells has rendered vast tracts of land off limits and somewhat bizarrely unspoiled.

The 30-mile Imber Range Perimeter Path delivers the ultimate war and peace experience. Circling the western half of the impressive Salisbury Plain, it reconciles up-close wildlife visual feasts with panoramic vistas across the Wiltshire and Somerset countryside while skirting the MoD's off-limits Imber Live Firing Range. It is little wonder then that the way-marked trail of tracks, paths and sections of road is mainly well defined. Westbury enjoys decent transport links making it a good starting

point from which to tackle the path, but it isn't the train station or the bus connections that seals its appeal as a gateway to the plain. It is the sight of the magnificent Westbury White Horse which signals that this is the start of something special. Cut into the escarpment, originally revealing the white chalk beneath, this is one of Wiltshire's oldest and best-known white horses. Above, Bratton Camp Iron Age Hill Fort protectively stands guard over the grand equine etching while hang gliders circle in the thermals like the hen harriers who come here to hunt. The trail continues onwards taking in the villages of Heytesbury, Chitterne, Tilshead and Gore Cross, affording far reaching views across the plain and surrounding countryside.

Practicalities

The trail can be walked in 2-3 days. Westbury is a good jumping off point with long-term parking in town and bus connections. Handy overnights include Heytesbury and Tilshead.

Transport   Westbury train station.

Sleeping   In Heytesbury there are a couple of inns on the high street plus, **££ The Resting Post B&B**, with pretty rooms. For good year round camping near Tilshead try **Stonehenge Touring Park**, Orcheston, SP3 4SH, T01980-626304.

Eating & drinking   Heytesbury: **The Angel**, T01985-840330, is known for its steaks from the local Pensworth Farm – steak burger from £10. The River Wyley runs along the bottom of the **Red Lion** beer garden, food also, T01985-840315.

Resources   OS Explorer Map 130 and 143 at scale 1:2,000.

Also try   Head west to the Frome valley, home to the **Farleigh and District swimming club** – the county's only river swimming club. With a lovely deep water pool above the weir, it has been going strong for more than 75 years and today boasts some 2000 members. Camp at the idyllic **Stowford Manor Farm** just upstream, from Easter-Oct. Wingfield, Trowbridge, Wiltshire, BA14 9LH, T01225-752253, stowfordmanorfarm. co.uk. B&B also available (££), T01225-781318.

Demi Taylor

∧ Poppies – just one of the many wild flowers that paint Salisbury Plain in a riot of colours.

> **Lowdown**

θ **Prices**
Free.

⊙ **Season**
Year round but for recorded info on access and live firing, T01980-674763.

⊙ **Don't miss**
Westbury White Horse.

⊗ **Avoid**
Sections of the perimeter path follow the edge of the Imber Firing Range Danger Area where there is strictly no access for good reason (live fire, buried, unexploded munitions) be careful not to stray off the path.

Foraging Mendips

Provider	Walk the Mendips
Skill level	All
Time frame	6 hrs
Equipment	Decent footwear, outdoor clothing, packed lunch
Exertion level	●●○○○

"There are only a few really wild places left in the southwest and the Mendips figure in there," says landscape ecologist and wild food expert Adrian Boots. "It has a lot in common with a wide range of areas in Britain but in a short distance you encounter heathland, woodland, grasslands, meadow, hedgerows, limestone habitats, rocky outcrops making it a constant fascination. The landscape alters with the seasons and you never know exactly what you're going to find so there's a real joy of discovery."

Adrian trains bushcraft instructors and, having grown up in the New Forest, spending happy days blackberrying and apple picking as a lad, it is clear that he is a natural in this environment. It's easy to warm to him as he shares his knowledge and enthuses about the wide-ranging wild food larder on his doorstep. "As well as hawthorn and elder, we have bilberries here, wiry little plants with thick waxy leaves, which are like blueberries and stain your mouth black. They're pretty special." He's also passionate about fungi, "St George's mushrooms are one of the first edible mushrooms of the year, and usually appear around 23 April – St George's Day, hence the name. You first notice them as fairy rings or dark circles in an unploughed meadow then, as you approach, you see their oatmeal coloured caps, which smell quite mealy as well."

> Landscape ecologist and wild food expert, Adrian Boots.

∨ Jelly Ears are often found lurking on the useful elder.

> **Lowdown**

❶ **Directory**
Walk The Mendips,
Ashcroft House,
Ellick Rd, Blagdon,
Bristol, BS40 7TU,
T 01761-463356,
walkthemendips.com.

❷ **Prices**
£50 day's Wild Food
Foray & Camp Cook Up.

❸ **Season**
Spring-Autumn is best
but Winter also.

❹ **Don't miss**
A trip to Burrington
Combe to see the
awesome Rock of Ages.

❺ **Avoid**
The emphasis is on
careful and thorough
identification. Never
eat something unless
you are confident
about its identification.

< Cooking up a storm after a morning's forage.

The forage covers only about five miles but it's easy to lose track of time and distance as Adrian gets you thinking about the landscape – the history of the land and how our ancestors ate, while talking passionately and knowledgeably about the different species encountered in this altering terrain. "I think it's important to have a sense of place and connection with the history of our land. I worry that we've lost that connection as we've become more urban and insular. We don't have such an intimate knowledge of the land. "

The day is based on a code of ethics, picking only common and dominant species, including plenty of nettles, dandelions and handfuls of sorrel however Adrian is quick to point out the rarer plants and discuss their qualities and usages. After the foray, wood is collected while Adrian sets up a tarp canopy between the trees providing shade from the sun's rays and a feeling of camaraderie for those who gather beneath it and get down to the business of making fire. Wild foods are combined with ingredients that Adrian has brought along to create a wonderful stew, or other feast, which may taste all the better for the connection you now have to the land you have just walked, foraged and understand a little better.

Practicalities

Home to the Big Green Gathering – a festival celebrating music, culture and all things green, the Mendips is a pretty eco-minded region. On the northern edge of this AONB, the village of Blagdon is home to Yeo Valley Organic yogurts and the brown trout-stocked Blagdon lake while nearby Cheddar has a little more hustle and bustle.

Transport Bristol has 2 main train stations – Temple Meads and Parkway. **Eurotaxis** bus 672 or 674, T0871-2503333, to Blagdon follows the scenic route and takes just over an hour – the walk up the hill to the B&B is pretty steep but a lift up the hill can sometimes be negotiated.

Sleeping Adrian and his partner Renee run the lovely, eco-minded **££ Ashcroft House B&B**, T01822-853501, cottagebandb.co.uk. This pretty Victorian cottage set in an acre of gardens and paddock offers fantastic views and a relaxed stay with Wi-Fi and continental style B&B using mainly local and organic produce. Recommended. For **Camping Broadway House Lodge**, Cheddar, BS27 3DB, T01934-742610, has the Bronze award for green tourism, open Mar-Nov.

Eating & drinking If you're not full of forage, **The Plume of Feathers**, Rickford near Blagdon, works with local suppliers and produce where possible to create quality pub fare plus home cooked pizzas Fri and Sat.

Also try Adrian is also a keen MTBer and with lead instructor Dave Parke, runs **Bike the Mendips** offering guided rides for all levels from £25/person. Following a skills session you'll be taken on a trail that matches your experience to challenge, thrill and entertain.

▼ Mustard garlic is great in salads.

Surfing Bournemouth

Provider	DIY
Skill level	Novice-advanced
Time frame	Dawn till dusk
Equipment	Surfboard, wetsuit
Exertion level	●●●●●

Bournemouth doesn't seem like a promising place to go searching out adventure or thrills. Looking out over the seafront of this Victorian resort, resplendent in autumnal sunshine, it may be hard to believe that this stretch of sea front, popular with retirees actually sits at the cutting edge of surfing. The sandy beach, dissected at intervals by the intervention of groynes, may not seem an ideal spot to launch into the white water and paddle out for a few enjoyable waves, but as with so much in surfing, it's all about what's going on below the surface.

The twin piers of Bournemouth and Boscombe have always attracted surfers. The supports plunged into the seabed help to sculpt sand bars and when a westerly swell rolls down the Channel, these sudden shallow banks will cause waves to peak and break. The waves can be short but fun and proved so popular that they drew surfers from across the south of the country to the resort. It wasn't long before the council started to see the financial repercussion of this influx. Sandbanks are by nature, shifty things and surfers can often be

∨ Board walk.

Greg Martin

◄ Small but perfectly formed at Bournemouth Pier.

thwarted by the lack of good sandbars to produce waves. But what if there were a world-class reef off the Bournemouth coast, something that would produce epic waves whenever the Channel came alive? This was a question put to Bournemouth Council. So in 2008 they embarked on an ambitious project to produce the northern hemisphere's first artificial reef. Huge computer designed, sand filled sausages have been laid down in layers taking up an area roughly the size of a football pitch just over 655 ft from the shore at Boscombe. Spinning Atlantic depressions, which can often be thousands of miles away, generate corduroy lines of swell, which roll into the bay. When each pulse nears the reef, the sudden change in depth cause waves to pitch and break. The design of the ocean bottom produces waves that break to the right and left, ideal for intermediate and advanced surfers, but the size of the waves all depends on the size of the swell. "Surfing first hit our beaches in the 1960s," says Paul Clarke from the Bournemouth Surfing Centre. "Today Bournemouth has the third largest population of surfers in the country. For the 10,000 locals and a catchment that includes London, the reef promises to be a huge attraction, the nearest thing to an Atlantic roller this side of Cornwall." The aim is also to have beginner friendly waves nearer the shore so that surfers of all abilities can find waves to suit their ambitions. The scheme has seen the Boscombe seafront redeveloped with cool cafés and apartments as well as achingly hip sea front Surf Pods in which you can chill between surfs. As well as balconies with reef views, these Wayne Hemmingway designed beach huts have small kitchens so if (and when) the weather takes a turn for the worse, you can sit back, watch the action from the comfort of your pod and enjoy a nice, warm brew. Grandma would approve.

> **Lowdown**

💲 **Prices**
Free (or from £10/half day board and wetsuit hire).

☀ **Season**
Year round.

◉ **Don't miss**
Packing your beach cruiser bike or longboard skateboard – the promenade is a lovely place to cruise in the sunshine.

✖ **Avoid**
The groynes!

Practicalities

Sheltered between Swanage and the Isle of Wight, Bournemouth's golden beaches were traditionally a pull for those drawing their pensions. Just 2 hrs from London and with a strong student culture, this seaside resort is changing its image. Not least in Boscombe, where £10.3 mn has been invested into the reef scheme to lure the savvy surfer, including redevelopment of the seafront with cafés, and Wayne Hemmingway-designed surf pods (beach huts).

Transport Bournemouth Boro has 2 handy train stations – Bournemouth is only a couple of miles west of the reef development while Pokesdown is just over 1 mile to the east – easy walking.

Sleeping £££ **Urban Beach Hotel**, Argyll Rd, Boscombe, T01202-301509, urbanbeachhotel.co.uk, small, laid-back boutique hotel, just back from the beach – minimizing transport issues. Room size varies but the luxury of the styling doesn't. Room includes an excellent locally sourced breakfast. Free Wi-Fi plus board storage. Also on site – popular bar and bistro (worth considering this when making your room choice if you want an early night). £££-££ **Beach Lodge**, Grand Ave, Southbourne, T01202-23296, Edwardian guest house 20-min walk east of the reef and just back from the sea front with board and wettie storage. They support a local organic farm meaning you can tuck into your breakfast with a clear(ish) conscience! Camping here isn't great and involves a drive to the breaks. **Grove Farm Meadow**, Stour Way, Christchurch, T01202-483597, is the best bet Mar-Oct. No tents.

Eating & drinking The **Urban Beach Bistro** uses fresh, seasonal produce from local suppliers – from New Forest beef to local crayfish tails – to create good simple food. Mains cost around £10.

Resources **Sorted Surf Shop**, Sea Rd, Boscombe Pier, T01202-399099, sortedsurfshop.co.uk, is well stocked with hardware and essentials as well as offering equipment hire and lessons. **Bournemouth Surfing Centre**, Bellevue Rd, Southbourne, T01202-433544, also has a good range of boards and wetties. Check both sites for local area webcams.

Also try The World Heritage Jurassic Coast lies west of Bournemouth and is a visual and geological delight. If the waves aren't pumping, take a sea kayaking trip along this stretch of coastline for a great perspective of the incredible rock formations such as the arch of Durdle Door and the fossil forest at Lulworth Cove. Book a trip with **Jurassic Kayak Tours**, T01305-835301, from £45, launching from Lulworth Cove.

Surfing Southwest: best of the rest

Provider	DIY – see details
Skill level	All breaks beginner-advanced
Time frame	Dawn till dusk
Equipment	Surfboard, wetsuit
Exertion level	●●●●●

The southwest, with its surf history, warm days, consistent swell and miles of golden sands carved into coves or left as generous swathes, is a natural lure for waveriders. RNLI lifeguards operate at the these beaches in peak season unless otherwise stated. For more information on the beaches the RNLI patrol check rnli.org.uk

Woolacombe, Devon

In the lee of Morte Point these mellow, golden sands stretch out to join up with Putsborough three miles to the south. With peaks along its length there's plenty of room to spread out making it an ideal spot for beginners and improvers. It works in all W through SW swells, offshore in E winds. Plenty of beach parking plus shower and toilets. There are a number of surf shops in the relaxed resort town including **Hunter Surf**, at The Red Barn, Barton Rd, T01271-871061 – equipment hire from £15/½ day. Lessons with Nick Thorn's BSA surf school, nickthorn.com, from £30, T01271-871337. **The Boardwalk** on the Esplanade, open March to November uses locally sourced meats and fish to good effect.

Polzeath, Cornwall

This flexible bay protected from light northwesterly winds by Pentire Point is a very popular spot with surfers and holiday makers. The beach break works through the tides with a decent right breaking by the point at the northern end. Works best in medium W to NW swells, off shore in E to SE winds. Surf shops, schools and hire at the beach entrance including **Ann's Cottage**, annscottagesurf. co.uk (web cam). **Surf's Up Surf School**, T01208-862003, surfsupsurfschool.com, run excellent courses for beginners through to advanced, coaching from £25.

Watergate, Cornwall

At low tide Watergate opens out to the north and south creating a vast stretch of cliff backed golden sands and an inviting proposition for escaping the crowds that converge on the beaches of Newquay proper. The middle of the bay is always popular but a walk in either direction will usually yield a quieter peak. Works best in small to medium NW to SW swells, off shore in E to SE winds. A ski resort at the beach, Watergate has several quality bars, restaurants, cafés, surf shops, hire and lessons readily available. Learn with the **Extreme Academy**, T01637-860543, extremeacademy.co.uk, from £30, equipment hire also available.

Fistral, Cornwall

The heart of Newquay's surf scene, the summer-thronging Fistral is watched over by the **National Surfing Centre** housing cafés, surf shops, the BSA headquarters and surf school and perhaps more importantly, warm showers! The beach break plays host to an annual leg of the surfing world tour and can produce high quality hollow barrels or speeding walls in the right swell. Works best in NW to SW swells, off shore in E to SE winds while

∨ Grab a lesson.

Learn to surf

South Fistral offers some shelter in SW winds. Learn with the official BSA surf school, T01637-850737, nationalsurfingcentre.com, from £30. Hit the chilled **Windswept Café** overlooking South Fistral for lovely home-made, locally sourced fare. They have free Wi-Fi and will look after your keys for £1 deposit, which they'll take off a post-surf takeaway coffee. Not a bad bunch really!

Perranporth, Cornwall

This huge expanse of westerly facing beach break stretches north from Droskyn Head to Penhale Corner, is offshore in E winds, picks up pretty much any westerly swell going and is generally less competitive than others nearby. It works through the tides and can produce anything from mellow peelers to hollow barrels depending on the banks and swell size, although over 4 ft it can become pretty rippy making the paddle out a bit of a mission. The holiday town has a number of surf shops offering surf hire on the high street including **Piran Surf** and **Bathsheba**. Learn with perranporthsurfschool.com, T01872-571259, from £25. For locally sourced produce, head to **Seiners** bar/restaurant at the southern end of the beach.

Porthmeor, Cornwall

Nestled in the heart of the picturesque town of St Ives, and watched over by the curving white façade of the Tate Gallery, this sheltered, north facing bay is the place to head for when the bigger swells kick in, or when the southwesterly winds turn the beaches to the north into an onshore mass of white water. The sandbanks here can produce some great lefts, rights and peaks – especially when the surf is in the two to four foot range. You can learn with the nearby **Gwithian Academy of Surfing**, T01736-755493, surfacademy.co.uk, April-September. To rest and refuel, head to the tiny **Blas Burger Works** in The Warren for Cornish free range beef, chicken

^ Paying homage during the summer solstice.

and veggies converted into beautiful burgers. The packaging is recycled and the furniture reclaimed – fabulous fast food with a conscience.

Praa Sands, Cornwall

Backed by sand dunes, this popular south coast spot is a mainstay of Cornish winter surfing. When big swells pound the north coast and northerly winds kick in, Praa will be offshore, producing powerful, often barrelling waves that will draw crowds. It works through the tides but the shore break can become heavy at high. **Stone's Reef** surf shop on the beach, T01736-762991, offers equipment hire while the Sand Bar overlooking the beach does a good line in hot chocolate and Sunday afternoon acoustic sessions. NB Watch the traffic wardens at the main car park, they sure can be efficient!

Whitsand Bay, Cornwall

Backed by gently sloping cliffs carpeted in a heathland baize, the four miles of sand on offer here are an excellent ending to Cornwall. They also ensure that when the region's surfers converge on this popular beach break in decent W to SW swells, there are plenty of peaks to go round. Best from low on the push and off shore in NE winds there is parking off the coast road – just follow signs to Freathy. Be aware that the area around Tregantle is regulated by the MOD which has a firing range here. Stop by the **Purely Cornish Farm Shop** at St Martins in nearby Looe to stock up on local goodies for a beach picnic.

Bantham, Devon

South Devon's most consistent spot, this beach break is home to excellent banks which can produce heavenly, long, reeling rides in big SW to W swells. Watched over by the art deco Burgh Island Hotel, it is especially popular with longboarders and is one of the region's best-known spots. Watch for rips near the river. Inland is **Tri-Ocean Surf Shop**, South Hams Business Park, Churchstow, T01548-854676, with a good range of hardware plus board hire. Learn with **Discovery Surf School** from £35 who also run lessons at nearby Whitsand Bay, T07813-639622. Eat at the **Venus Café** at Bigbury beach. They hold a gold award for green tourism and serve excellent, locally sourced (plus organic, free range, fairtrade where possible) breakfasts and simple lunches at good prices.

◄ Micah Lester tucking into a slice of north Cornwall perfection.

Mountain biking Forest of Dean

Provider	DIY
Skill level	Novice-experienced
Time frame	2-3 hrs
Equipment	Mountain bike, helmet, snacks, water, a map and a repair kit/spare tube
Exertion level	●●●●●

The Forest of Dean, some 27,000 acres of woodlands and ancient forest stretches between the snaking River Severn and the Wye Valley creating a wooded border between England and Wales. This rich and varied treasure chest, which has acted as a hunting ground for nobility, has been mined for the coal and iron that lies beneath it and is now home to a wealth of mountain biking possibility.

For experienced riders, the Forest of Dean Cycling Association trail is a three-mile loop designed, built and maintained by the association in partnership with the Forestry Commission. What this CTC red graded trail lacks in length, it makes up for in variety and quality with challenging singletrack mixing up switchback climbs, decent drops and hairpin bends. There are more trails in the offing as well as some freeride features and excellent downhill tracks to be discovered meaning that with a bit of exploring and some creative thinking there are plenty of challenges to be unearthed. For something more leisurely, the circular 11-mile Family Cycle Trail is a picturesque route that gently winds its way along specially laid singletrack, following the former Severn and Wye Valley Railway line passing former railway stations and remnants of former coal mines. The route takes around two to three hours and is suitable for all levels.

Whether you're looking for an afternoon's scenic pedal through bluebell valleys or an intense session with plenty of challenges the forest delivers and the Cannop Valley Cycle Centre near Coleford is an ideal jumping off point. The two trails are well marked from here plus there is all day parking for £3, bike hire as well as a café for after your work is done.

< Mud tracks and forest trails.

Practicalities

The pretty market town of Coleford makes an excellent base.

Transport Gloucester is the nearest mainline train station, 19 miles away. Stagecoach bus to Coleford (no bikes). Lydney train station also — just 7 miles ride to Coleford.

Sleeping There are plenty of campsites including the **Forest Holidays Bracelands Caravan and Camping Site**, Christchurch, Coleford GL16 7NN, T01594-837258, meadow and surrounded by trees, open Mar-Sep. The **Cherry Orchard Farm Campsite**, Newland, Coleford, GL16 8NP, T01594-832212, is a lot cheaper, open year round. **£ Fountain Inn and Lodge**, Parkend, GL15 4JD, T01594-562189, in the Cannop Valley Nature Reserve offers dorm accommodation sleeping 2-12 from £11, own bedding required/bed kits available to hire. Next door to pub, B&B also available.

Eating & drinking Ostrich Inn, Newland, Coleford — pub serving huge portions and real ales; bar meals £6-10, restaurant mains around £15. On the trails there is a café at the **Cannop Cycle Centre and Beechenhurst Lodge** at Broadwell.

Resources Trail maps available from Pedalabikeaway plus Forest of Dean offices. OS Leisure Map 14 also has the Cycle trail marked. **Pedalabikeaway**, Cannop Cycle Centre, T01594-860065, offers bike hire by hour/day. Easy, moderate and difficult guided rides available from 10-mile stoned tracks to 20-mile singletrack with steep climbs and descents.

Also try Go Ape is a high-wire forest adventure at Mallards Pike Lake — a tree-top obstacle course of bridges, ladders, walkways and zip lines. Usually 2-3 hrs, £25, open Mar-Nov, T0845-643 9215, goape.co.uk.

> Lowdown

❸ Prices
Free or from £15/day MTB hire.

☀ Season
Year round (weather permitting).

➕ Don't miss
Peregrine falcons nest nearby and can often be spotted hunting overhead from Apr-Aug.

✖ Avoid
The FODCA is not much fun after there has been heavy rain.

Mountain biking Southwest: best of the rest

Provider	(see details)
Skill level	Beginner-advanced
Time frame	From 2 hrs +
Equipment	Bike, helmet, map, repair kit, inner tube, snacks, water
Exertion level	●●●●●

Isle of Purbeck, Dorset

Purbeck isn't exactly an island but you can still access it via a ferry that shuttles back and forth on chains between Sandbanks and Shell Bay in Studland. The small range of hills here provide stunning views over the countryside and Jurassic coastline and make for a day's fun riding with not too many challenges, mixing country lanes, forest tracks and decent grassy down hills with sections of the Priest's Way and Purbeck Way. There are plenty of tea shops and pubs to revive the weary including the excellent **Square + Compass** at Worth Matravers – definitely worth a detour. Bike

hire at **Cycle Experience**, Wareham Station, T01929-660440, purbeckcyclehire.co.uk, for £15.50/day including helmet, map, tool kit and spares. Delivery can be arranged plus pre-arranged collection from Norden Park & Ride.

Haldon Forest Park, Devon

Follow the A38 south from Exeter and you will hit Haldon Forest Park that, thanks to the work of the Forestry Commission and Haldon Freeride, is now home to some excellent 'red' and 'black' rated XC trails that will test the best plus a challenging freeride area that really is for experienced riders only. For intermediates and beginners, mellower family cycle trails and adventure trails have been created. This excellent trail centre has been designed and built with the local environment in mind and relies on volunteers to maintain the area: T01392-834251 to get involved. Trails are sometimes closed for essential repairs check forestry.gov.uk/

❮ Cara Coolbaugh and Cass Gilbert, Leigh Woods, Bristol.

Seb Rogers

❮ Mud, sweat and gears –
the poetry of a day well spent.

❮ This limestone range
translate into technical climbs
and long sweeping descents.

haldonforestpark or haldonfreeride.org before
heading over. Parking £1.50/day. Bike hire at **Forest
Cycle Hire**, The Hub, near the Ranger's Office,
T01392-833768.

Cotswolds, Gloucestershire
This area of outstanding natural beauty is a 50-mile
stretch of rolling limestone hills matched by pretty
wooded valleys. At 1072 ft and with views over
the River Severn, Cleve Hill north of Cheltenham is
the highest point in the Cotswolds and home to
the steepest riding while on the south side of the
city, Leckhampton Hill is a veritable playground
with swooping singletrack, technical climbs and
steep downhill track. Further south still, Birdlip
and Cranham Woods are excellent jumping off
points from which to explore the potential of
the area with plenty of wooded singletrack, fun
descents and good climbs. For a decent two-hour
blast, from Birdlip head out towards Popes Wood
which is flatter but more technical than nearby
Leckhampton Hill, continue to the upland area
Painswick Beacon, with views to the Malvern Hills
before heading back. Nearby Winchcombe is the
staging post for "The Hell of the North Cotswolds"

spring reliability trial which covers 30-60 miles; honc.org.uk for details. MTB store: **Leisure Lakes**, Town Centre, Cheltenham, leisurelakesbikes.com.

Salisbury Plain, Wiltshire

Famous for Stonehenge and extensive army training, the 300-sq-mile chalk plateau of Salisbury Plain is also home to some exposed tracks and decent downland riding. Much of the riding is on broad fire track however, steep technical descents can be found between Westbury White Horse and West Lavington. **Skyline Adventures** offer

❯ Chalk highs on Dorset's Jurassic Coast.

guided rides on Salisbury Plain with MIAS Level 4 Instructor/Guide Neil Haskinsskylineadventures. co.uk. If you want to practice your XC skills, then head to Chippenham. The working **Naish Hill Farm** at Spirthill has diversified to create some decent mountain trails of 2½ and four miles. The trails are varied with a good mix of terrain including woodland and arable land for intermediate riders as well as those just starting out. Sections of singletrack with raised tree roots, bridges and jumps. Day pass £3, spirthilltrail.uk.com.

Ashton Court, Bristol

The Forest of Avon's seven-mile Timberland Trail circles Ashton Court Estate and the nearby 50 Acre Wood. The yellow trail is ideal for getting to grips with riding on rough terrain, while the pink trail in 50 Acre Wood links up with it and includes more challenging singletrack and features such as berms, jumps and drop-offs. The trails are best avoided in wet weather. Nearby Leigh Woods has some tight singletrack and challenging cross country loops. See forestofavon.org.uk for more details and Timberland Trail route map.

Puddletown, Dorset

Puddletown Woods is an example of the good that can happen when local riders work with the Forestry Commission to create well thought out trails. Just three miles from Dorchester, aside from forest road bridleways the woods are home to huge areas of natural singletrack plus well-maintained downhill and cross country trails. And because the Forestry Commission maintains the land through felling, the trails area is a constantly shifting and altering playground. ridepuddletown.co.uk. Bike Hire at **Cycloan**, London Road, Dorchester, from £12.50/day, cycloan.co.uk. They also offer guided rides and suggest mellower routes from Dorchester. (Dorchester can also be a starting point to explore the Isle of Purbeck).

Walking The South West Coast Path

Provider	DIY
Skill level	Novice-advanced
Time frame	From a few hours to 8 weeks
Equipment	Boots, OS map, SWCP Association Guide
Exertion level	●●●●○

Demi Taylor

Some scour the trail unknowingly, backs to the wind and eyes to the horizon, pondering over the potential of a hidden cove or a long forgotten reef awakened by a new swell. On warm, still, autumn mornings those equipped with rope and karabiners hardly notice the reassuring path underfoot as they draw along it, mesmerized by the glinting granite sea cliff ahead. Others combing its edges for seasonal delights focus in on the minutiae of the forage barely acknowledging the trail they have strayed from as they delight in the year's first blackberries. Yet this unassuming track is literally the crowning glory of the southwest. Running from Minehead on the edge of Exmoor National Park the South West Coast Path winds its way around 630 miles of twisting, turning coastline before reaching its conclusion at the shores of Poole harbour in Dorset. You don't have to pass through the national parkland or one of the officially recognized AONB's, through which more than half of the trail runs, or find yourself on a piece of Heritage Coast, accounting for 56% of the trail, or explore the stretch traversing England's first natural World Heritage site to appreciate that this is the gateway to an outstandingly beautiful landscape.

Until the 1850s coastguards patrolled the footpath, scanning for smugglers for whom the southwest peninsula was so notorious. "It was the essence of their job that the coastguards had literally to be able to see into every cove and inlet on the coast," explains Hon Secretary of the South West Coast Path Association (SWCPA), Eric Wallis MBE. "This meant that their path had to hug the cliff top, so providing the splendidly scenic coastal views we get today." Signalled by an Acorn waymark, Britain's

∧ The path hugs the coastline and in spring is edged with wild flowers.

longest National Trail must surely also be one of its most diverse and spectacular. In the space of a day you can cross moorlands or high plateaux incised by steep coastal valleys and dotted with dramatic mine workings, bypassing vast sandy beaches and pebble ridges before exploring an intimate cove released from the reaches of the Atlantic for a few short hours. There are rugged cliff tops to climb and drowned estuaries to cross – some by ferry some carefully by foot. The path weaves around busy harbours and though pretty, bustling villages which can quickly be forgotten along wild, remote stretches, where only the cry of gulls punctuate the silence. The path has evolved and continues to do so, bending to accommodate not only a landscape shaped by erosion, landslips and shifting boundaries but the personalities that seek it out.

There are sections for casual strollers, weekend walkers or serious journeymen, ones that will delight Jurassic Coast fossil hunters and those who want to explore Axmouth's undercliff. Between Polzeath and Porthcothan, North Cornwall is considered to be one of the easiest sections of the path to tackle and a good starting point for those with less experience. Just to the north the 15-mile section between Hartland Quay in south Devon and Bude has been graded 'severe' and deemed by the SWCPA, 'probably the most difficult section of the whole Coast Path'. Crossing ten river valleys and the Devon/Cornwall border is not without its rewards – this section also takes in the dramatic waterfall at Speke's Mill Mouth.

From the tiny cove at Porthgwarra in Cornwall's West Penwith a beautiful, moderate three-mile circular follows the granite coastline east to Porthcurno and the Minack Theatre cut into the golden cliffs here. In late spring the cliff top walk which delivers stunning vistas along the coast is scented with wild garlic and punctuated with bluebells and dusky pink clumps of thrift. It winds past St Levan with its holy well and Porth Chapel beach, which hides away in plain view down a short scramble path. Circling back to Porthgwarra, for a snack it is worth following the path westward out to Gwennap Head. Basking sharks are often spotted in the turquoise waters along this stretch while the moaning of the Runnelstone Buoy provides a wistful commentary.

In east Devon the undercliffs are an experience. The seven-mile moderate walk between Seaton

∧ An evening's meander along the SWCP.

> Golden grasses mingle with heather, violets and the gently coconut-fragranced gorse on the coastal heathland.

and Lyme Regis though delivers what estate agents would term 'sea glimpses'. After crossing the River Axe, the path descends into the uneven terrain of the undercliffs, an area of often humid, dense, tangled, woodland created through landslips and which is now a National Nature Reserve. The region is also noted for its geology and fossils. Unsurprisingly, due to the slippery nature of the clay spoil which is responsible for causing the slides, it's best tackled in dry weather. This is also not a section you can cut out on so once you've committed you have to push through to the end which can take anywhere between 2 and 4 hours. This coastal path offers diversity, hemming the four counties it runs through, completing them and is definitely a trail to be savoured.

> **Lowdown**

$ **Prices**
Free .

☀ **Season**
Year round.

○ **Don't miss**
Catch the wild flowers in spring, the open cafés in summer, the migrating birds in autumn, and, as the vegetation dies back, the archaeological features in winter.

⊗ **Avoid**
Be realistic about how much you can walk in a day and consider the weight of any equipment you carry.

Practicalities

The South West Coast Path is 630 miles long and runs between Minehead in Somerset and Poole in Dorset. The path has a mixture of terrain from easy plateaux to steep valley ascents for more strenuous walking and can be broken into sections for casual strolls, day walks, weekends or long-distance challenges. The entire trail can be walked in around 8 weeks.

Transport   For the trail start at Minehead, Taunton is the nearest main line station 23 miles away with a regular bus service, firstgroup.com.

Sleeping   Plenty of accommodation along the length of the path. If you have booked ahead but are unable to reach your evening's accommodation make sure you call to explain to avoid the coastguards being sent on a mission to 'save' you! The South West Coast Path Association Guide is invaluable for trip planning with contacts for B&Bs, hostels and campsites, indicating those which offer kit transfer and pick-ups.

Eating & drinking   There are a plenty of pubs and cafés along the path, but cafés in more remote locations are likely to be seasonal and may be closed in the quieter winter months.

Supported walking   With the silver award for green tourism, the excellent **Encounter Cornwall**, T01208-871066, encountercornwall.com, design well thought out tailor made itineraries for self guided and supported walking trips along the Cornish section of the path from 2 to 14 days, including baggage transfer and accommodation (CoAST affiliated where available).

Resources   For route information: southwestcoastpath.com is a dedicated resource for the long distance trail with route suggestions plus news on temporary route changes. With around 4000 members, the South West Coast Path Association swcp.org.uk, is a charity that works on behalf of walkers and users of the path to preserve and protect it including lobbying bodies to ensure that the path is well maintained and seeking realignments of the path to the coast. The site is an excellent resource detailing news about route closures, ferry crossings and army ranges as well as suggested itineraries. Membership of £11 supports the association's work and includes their annual guide (usual price £8.50) detailing all the essentials from descriptive route information to accommodation.

Also try   The path weaves its way past some of Britain's premier surfing destinations many of which carry full surf hire – from beginner's foamies to performance sticks. Check out the surfing pages for more information and inspiration about spots to check.

Best of the rest Southwest: activities

Kite surfing, Cornwall	
Provider	Mobius
Skill level	Novice-experienced
Time frame	2 hrs +
Equipment	Equipment provided
Exertion level	●●●●●

Unlike surfing, kite surfing requires a steady cross or onshore wind, and with beaches facing north, south, east and west, when the wind blows, Cornwall can offer up countless kite surfing possibilities. Making the most of their location and approved by the BKSA, **Mobius** run lessons across a number of beaches including Perranporth, Hayle, Marazion, Pentewan and St Mary's on the Isles of Scilly, guided by wind direction. With a broad spectrum of qualified and skilled instructors, they offer everything from a 2-hour taster session for novices which will take you through the basics of kite surfing and equipment, three day BKSA courses designed to get you up and riding, through to progression sessions which will see you learn new tricks or take your kiting to the next level. Mobius work hard to ensure that their business is as environmental as possible, they ask students to donate £1 to SAS, offset their carbon emissions through Carbon Care and hold the silver award for Green Tourism. Intro session from £65. mobiusonline.co.uk. Excellent guided MTB tours for all levels also available.

Walking, Devon	
Provider	DIY
Skill level	All
Time frame	1 day
Equipment	Boots
Exertion level	●●●○○

Twelve miles off Hartland Point, just two hours by boat from north Devon, Lundy is England's only statutory marine nature reserve and home to one of the southern England's largest sea bird colonies – gulls, guillemots, puffins. Basking sharks cruise by and a colony of grey seals have taken up residence.

^ A sea shore forage with Fat Hen.

Owned by the National Trust, and managed by the Landmark Trust this granite outcrop is only three miles long and half a mile wide with dramatic cliffs rising up to 400 ft. Lundy's own ship MS Oldenburg sails from Bideford and Ilfracombe. Day Returns: £32.50 or longer stays £56, T01271-863636. Camping as well as B&B accommodation available. The island warden offers free walks and talks year round – donations to the Lundy Fund are always gratefully received. Lundy Shore Office, T01271-863636.

Blokarting, Cornwall	
Provider	Cornwall Blokart Centre
Skill level	Novice-experienced
Time frame	2 hrs
Equipment	Provided
Exertion level	●●●○○

Reaching speeds of up to 60 mph as you zoom along just inches above the ground in a light, wind-powered blokart is utterly exhilarating. A steering arm controls direction while the sheet rope, attached to the sail, controls your speed, making the experience somewhat like sailing on land. Book in for a two-hour session at **The Cornwall Blokart Centre**, based at Perranporth Airfield (and away from walkers, dogs and tides) to learn the finer points of controlling the lightweight, triple-wheeled sharkfin-sailed kart. Enthusiastic instructor Kevin Myers is a UK blokart heavy weight who has competed internationally and even blokarted across the Mongolian desert! Two-hour session for 2-4 people, £55 per person, T07971-856468.

Letterboxing, Devon	
Provider	DIY
Skill level	All
Time frame	2 hrs +
Equipment	Walking boots
Exertion level	●●○○○

A combination of hiking, orienteering and treasure hunting, letterboxing has been taking place on Dartmoor for more than 150 years. In the 1850s guide James Perrott placed a bottle in a cairn at Cranmere Pool and encouraged hikers that made the walk to the site to leave a calling card as a record of their achievement. Later, a tin box containing a visitor's book replaced the bottle and

⌃ Wild food forager extraordinaire, Caroline Davey.

today thousands of 'letterboxes' have been hidden across Dartmoor. Clues to their locations are spread by word of mouth and through an informal group known as the Letterbox 100 Club which publishes a catalogue of letterboxes twice a year, coinciding with a 'meet'. For info see: letterboxingondartmoor.co.uk. Guidelines have been set up to avoid damage to the moor; for information see: dartmoor-npa.gov.uk/index/visiting/vi-enjoyingdartmoor/vi-letterboxing.htm.

Foraging, Cornwall	
Provider	Fat Hen
Skill level	Novice-experienced
Time frame	3 hrs-weekend
Equipment	Decent footwear
Exertion level	●○○○○

On the edge of Cornwall, surrounded by seashore, woodlands, hedgerows and ancient bridleways professional ecologist and wild food forager Caroline Davey reconnects people to their landscape and their food. From her **Fat Hen HQ** she runs short Taster Walks from £10 for novices lasting 3-4 hours as well as Wild Food Taster days running from 10-4 for £40 – a morning's foraging in West Penwith followed by a communal 'cook up' of the wild produce in the kitchen at Fat Hen's beautifully converted granite barn HQ. But for those who want to immerse themselves in a foraging and feasting nirvana, book in for a Gourmet Wild Food Weekend. Run over two days you enjoy three foraging excursions, exploring different environments followed by three gastronomic meals prepared by the chefs Matt and Claire who also demonstrate traditional and contemporary cooking techniques. Saturday night's feast in the Goat Barn, by fire and candlelight, includes live folk music, hedgerow cocktails and almost certainly a pinch of magic. **Fat Hen**, Gwenmenhir, Boscawen-noon Farm, St. Buryan, Penzance, TR19 6EH, T01736-810156, fathen.org.

⌄ A birds eye view of Lundy Island.

The Landmark Trust

Troytown Farm, Isles of Scilly
St Agnes, Isles of Scilly, TR22 OPL, T01720-422360.

Just yards from the water's edge on the western shore of the tiny island of St Agnes, this campsite location takes some beating. Just getting here feels like an adventure – a ferry crossing followed by a catamaran, followed by a 20-minute hike while your bags take a ride on the tractor. It's an exposed spot, but that's the point so come prepared or come prepared to spend some quality time in the island's Turk's Head pub. Farm shop sells goodies including milk, ice cream and veggies.

Bell Tents Camping, Cornwall
Owls Gate, Davidstow, Camelford, Cornwall, PL32 9XY, T01840-261556, belletentscamping.co.uk.

You may feel as if you've run away to the most fabulous, yet civilized circus: three private encampments of candy-striped tents nestled on this small site on the edge of Bodmin Moor. The camps, comprising a kitchen tent and two bedroom tents sleeping up to six (in real beds) are ready erected and designed for comfort with rugs, carpets and solar lighting. The bar/social tent comes complete with woodburner, campfire and table football. Camps from £510 week May-September.

Miss Peapod's Kitchen Café, Cornwall
Jubilee Wharf, Commercial Road, Penryn, Falmouth, T01326-374424, misspeapod.co.uk.

Jubilee Wharf champions sustainability meaning that this cool café has been built using pioneering techniques of eco-development including wind turbines, solar panels and super insulation. The furniture, china, even the floor (formerly a night club's) are recycled. Produce is sourced with a priority to organic, Fairtrade, sustainable and local ingredients creating meals from tofu burritos to organic steaks £5-10, plus delicious home-made cakes. Check site for details of live music and events on selected evenings.

Bedruthan Steps Hotel & Spa, Cornwall
Mawgan Porth, TR8 4BU, T01637-860555, bedruthan.com.

Set on the cliff tops with views towards the setting sun and across the golden sands of Mawgan Porth below, the four-star, family friendly hotel is in an enviable position. Their long-term commitment to sustainability has seen them rightly rewarded with a gold award for green tourism but that certainly doesn't mean that they have skimped on comfort and style. Rooms as well as villas and apartments are available and all have access to the outdoor (solar panel) heated pool.

Blas Burger Works, Cornwall
The Warren, St Ives, TR26 2EA, blasburgerworks.co.uk.

Blas might be small, but it's a beautiful vision of how burgers should be created: using local, free-range beef and fresh, seasonal produce to make something sustainable and delicious for under a tenner that is eaten on furniture made from reclaimed timber or sustainable sources. Wash it down with a local cider or beer. Free range chicken and veggie burgers also available.

Plan-it Earth, Cornwall
Chynea, Sancreed, Penzance, TR20 8QS, T01725-810660, plan-itearth.org.uk.

This smallholding and orchard in an idyllic location near Mounts Bay, Penzance is home to two yurts sleeping two adults (plus children) The yurts include beds, rugs and woodburners. The toilet is composting and the shower wood burning. Open May-September with discounts for those arriving by public transport from £265/week.

Rezare Farmhouse, Cornwall
Rezare, Launceston, PL15 9NX, T01579-371214, rezarefarmhouse.co.uk.

This is a wonderful spot from which to explore the Tamar valley. With a silver award for Green Tourism,

∧ One of the wonderful Belle Tents encampments.

∧ The Bedruthan Steps Hotel reflected in its solar-heated pool.

∧ Cornish Tipi.

this welcoming farmhouse B&B has lovely touches like home-made quilts thrown over comfortable beds and evening meals on offer utilising only local ingredients and produce – down to the beer, cider and wine! They can suggest some lovely circular cycle trails from the B&B which go via the odd pub or two…

Cornish Tipi Holidays, Cornwall
Tregeare, Pendogget, St Kew, Cornwall, PL30 3LW, T01208-880781, cornishtipiholidays.co.uk.

Combining a beautiful location with old-fashioned camping and a very modern desire to be more environmentally friendly, this is a very special place. Between Bodmin and the coast, 17 tipis are dotted around the wooded valley. The lake in the centre is great for a dip, fishing or canoeing. The site is family focussed. Tipis sleep 2-10 and come with a camping stove and cool box. Apr-Oct from £475 a week for two. Short breaks also available.

∧ The lake at Cornish Tipis will lend itself just as well to an evening's swim as a morning's row.

The Lookout Café, Dorset
Durlston, Swanage, T01929-426473.

Sourcing most of its ingredients locally and set in the country park on Durlston Head with views across the water, this tea room serves up café classics from jacket spuds and pasties to daily specials. The rolls and cakes are baked locally, the eggs are free range, the cheese and meats come from local suppliers but the views are out of this world.

Hive Beach Café, Dorset
Burton Bradstock, near Bridport, Dorset, T01308-897070, hivebeachcafe.co.uk.

Set on the edge of the beach on the Jurassic Coast, this spot is definitely in the running for the ultimate seaside café. While not cheap, the food is simple and sophisticated utilising the best local ingredients whether they are serving up a breakfast bap or hand dived Lulworth scallops. Fish is bought from a family-run fishmonger in Bridport, with the emphasis on sustainability. For something delicious and affordable, take your seafood soup and local bread (£5.65) down on to the beach (most dishes are available as takeaways), or have a scoop or two of Lovingtons local ice-cream.

Yarde Orchard Café and Bunkhouse, Devon
East Yarde, Petersmarland, Torrington, EX38 8QA, T01805-624007, yarde-orchard.co.uk.

At the highest point on the Tarka Trail, this is the perfect place to stop for a home-made pie and a pint. Open weekends (weather permitting) and through the week July-August, the little café seats about 20 and focuses on local and seasonal produce. The timber bunkhouse (£12/night dorm, £40 family room) minimizes its impact on the environment with solar water heating, wood fuel stove, rainwater harvesting, a waste water system using composting and reedbed purification as well as super-efficient insulation.

Wheatland Farm, Devon
Winkleigh, EX19 8DJ, T01837-83499, wheatlandfarm.co.uk.

On the edge of North Devon's UNESCO biosphere these Scandinavian lodges are set in a nature lover's paradise – this farm is run for wildlife, one third is an SSI. They hold a gold award for Green Tourism, have bikes to borrow if you want to explore, or can organize bike hire if you want to go off road, they'll happily collect from the nearby Eggesford Station. Just up the road, **Fiona's Farm Fayre**, T01837-83382, is a local farm shop selling organic produce and nearby are some good pubs specializing in local produce and local real ales.

Fernhill Farm, North Somerset
Cheddar Road, Compton Martin, BS40 6LD, T07903-584695/07712-616797, fernhill-farm.co.uk.

Set in the heart of the Mendips, this working farm operates with the environment at its forefront. Local craftsmen renovated the 18th century stone barns using materials sourced on site to create a beautifully designed, eco-friendly, camping barn that can sleep (in beds) groups of up to 32. The open-plan barn, divided into areas that are just as good for barn dances as they are for bunking down, is kept warm using their efficient wood burner while wool from their sheep acts as insulation. Beds are made from the farm's wood, and they operate a water-catchment policy recycling rainwater for their grey water supply while reed beds clean up the waste water. This is a cool comfortable space where you can appreciate your natural environment.

Southeast England

Seb Rogers

❮ Pausing for thought as early evening washes over the Downs.

This may not be a region that immediately leaps to the forefront of one's mind as being a playground for those who want to get outside and experience active adventures. Dominated by the sprawling conurbations of the capital and the surrounding metropolis, it can sometimes feel a long way from tree-lined tracks, winding trails and testing pitches, but salvation can be closer than you think. Even within the confines of the city and its suburbs lie some excellent opportunities for swimming, climbing, canoeing, mountain biking and walking. Heading away from the capital, one can soon be out in the rolling hills or resting by lapping shores. The lush green canopies and wide open valleys of the New Forest, South Downs and Surrey Hills are havens for walkers, foragers and mountain bikers while water lovers make a bee-line for White Isle where surfing, kayaking, kite surfing and SUPing are thriving. Brighton has become a bustling hub for waveriders who hit the water with enthusiasm with each new swell. There are tranquil pools swimming with opportunity all across the southeast, resting in wooded glens or cascading through narrow valleys while southern sandstone crags offer lofty challenges for climbers. On the very southern fringe of the southeast sits the Seven Sisters, spectacular landmarks turning their vast chalky faces against the Channel. The walk along one of the country's most iconic landscapes lasts long in the memory and must rank as a must on anyone's to-do list.

❯ South coast swell lines.

Environment

The geology of the southeast is predominantly sedimentary in nature and sculpted from the remains of the Wealden Dome, a weathered uplift that has created ridges that run through the region. From Kent to Sussex there are ridges of chalk, calcareous green sandstone, red sandstone and finally the chalk of the South Downs. The countryside across this corner of England is a rich and diverse blanket, sculpted by nature and shaped by the hand of agriculture. The New Forest is a quilted patchwork of broadleaf woodland, heath and pasture. Rare species are found within each setting, from the smooth snakes and sand lizards that bask within the heather to the soaring red kite and skulking polecat. Ponies and cattle graze the common land while regimented legions of conifers corralled by the Forestry Commission make up tall plantations. Telegraph Hill, at 550 ft is the tallest summit and much of the area, over 220 sq miles falls within under the control of the National Park. Chalk downlands dominate the South Downs, with an open landscape of rolling green carpet complemented by glens of shady woodland. By 2011 this will all be brought together as the country's newest national park within a 628 sq mile border. These rolling ridges tempt those who travel by two wheels or two feet, or even search for a quiet pool to shake off the warm day in cool waters. Close to the bustling city the Surrey Hills are a mountain biker's haven blending broadleaf woodland with wildflower freckled grasslands. Leith Hill towers 965 ft, offering grand views and the promise of a good cup of tea at the top. Beneath the towering chalk faces of the Seven Sisters sits the English Channel, one of the world's busiest waterways, but one also rich with marine life, from whales and dolphins, through to seals and basking sharks. With such busy sea lanes, pollution is an issue here, as is bathing water quality. Check out the Marine Conservation Society's Good Beach Guide for up-to-date advice: goodbeachguide.co.uk

Climate

The southeast is England's warmest region, helped by the proximity of the continental landmass. Counties like Kent are famed as the basket of England, due to the fertile soils and their traditional abundance of orchards and hops. Summertime temperatures within the Thames Valley see average maximums between 21 and 22°C whereas the south coast, although sunnier, only muster 17 to 20°C. The mass of London's urban sprawl has a distinct effect on localized weather patterns by creating a microclimate around the city. This is most obvious in winter when Central London sees an average minimum of between 3 and 5°C where as the nearby suburbs of Surrey have an average minimum of only 1.5°C.

There are also wide ranging regional variations in precipitation patterns. The area around the South Downs sees an average annual rainfall of between 950 and 1250 mm while between 450 and 650 mm falls on the capital.

During the winter easterlies blowing off the continent can send temperatures plummeting in the southeast, and although snow is traditionally quite rare in this area, prolonged easterlies or northerlies can see a widespread winter blanket of the white stuff, as in the winters of 2009 and 2010.

For those who brave the waters of The Channel, winter is a time for brave constitutions. Sea temperatures can drop to around 6°C making 5/4 mm wetsuits, boots, gloves and hoods a recommended safeguard for surfers and kite surfers. The shallow waters here and the cooling effect of the North Sea means that even in the summer the water may only climb to around 12°C so a 4/3 mm is advisable. Weather patterns during the warmer months mean the chance of scoring some swell is very small, anywhere but the west coast of the Isle of Wight.

Foraging New Forest

Provider	Mrs Tee's Wild Mushrooms
Skill level	All levels
Time frame	A full day
Equipment	All foraging equipment provided. Remember to wear sturdy shoes
Exertion level	●○○○○

Crunching through golden leaves and trailing fingers over rough, lichen-laden bark, bright afternoon sunlight pours through the trees as the group steadily makes its way forward. Each armed with a small basket their eyes are open wide, scouring the forest for the treasures they learnt about this morning, before striking out into the ancient woodlands. A rustle in the distance stops them in their tracks, silently whipping out their cameras to capture the wild deer as it trots across their path. Moments later the group leader, slightly ahead of the rest, waves everyone over to see what she has found. A blanket of creamy coloured mushrooms spreads across the ground, thousands of them clustered together on the forest floor. With smiles on their faces, the group bends down and starts to pick.

The New Forest is renowned for its wild mushrooms. Around 2700 species of fungi nestle in the warm, damp pockets of the national park, which stretches 94,000 acres across Hampshire. Originally established as a royal hunting ground by William the Conqueror in the 11th century, today it's hunting of a different nature that draws people amongst the trees. Foraging for flavoursome mushrooms is a great way to see the forest close up but deciphering the dangerous from the delicious is difficult so it's essential you take someone with expert knowledge with you.

Enter Mrs Bridgette Tee, the New Forest's resident wild mushroom expert who has been foraging the woodland for fungi for over 35 years. She is the only licence holder entitled to pick and sell the many diverse wild mushrooms that grow in the New Forest and supplies restaurants across the UK. However, it's not only professional chefs

that can make the most of Mrs Tee's knowledge – she also runs wild mushroom seminars so that individuals can learn about foraging before heading into the forest with her to have a go themselves.

"Every day in the New Forest is different and you never know what you are going to find," explains Mrs Tee about what makes foraging so special. "The weather, the season and even the smallest deviations in the route you take can affect what you come away with – foraging is the tale of the unexpected which makes it hugely rewarding."

The day-long seminars start with a lecture about identification, seasonality and the preparation of both wild and cultivated mushrooms followed by a delicious home-cooked lunch where guests can sample some of Mrs Tee's gathered mushrooms and enjoy listening to her many anecdotes about famous chefs and celebrities that she has taken foraging. It's also a great opportunity to quiz Mrs Tee personally before pulling on the wellies and heading out for an afternoon's guided excursion into the forest, to put all your new found knowledge to the test. Using her expert

⌄ The New Forest has always been a place where hunters have gathered. Around 2700 species of fungi nestle in warm, damp pockets of the forest and in order to decipher the dangerous from the delicious, it's essential to take some expert knowledge with you.

Jane Jones

understanding of the Forest, Mrs Tee will take the group to the best spot for that day's conditions and advise on what's safe and what's not, how to tell the difference and when a mushroom is ripe for picking.

"Some days we'll only find a few mushrooms and other days there are thousands to be picked," she continues, "that's the nature of it, but whatever happens you are sure to see the beautiful nature of the New Forest close up. Because we are a small group going off the beaten track we regularly see owls, deer and other wildlife – it's all part of the foraging experience."

Whether it's a handful or a hundred, at the end of the day whatever you pick you can take away with you to cook up and enjoy at home, along with the knowledge you need to head out into the countryside near you and see what you can find.

< The alluring gills of New Forest mycelium.

Jane Jones

Practicalities

Lymington is a pretty Georgian market town on the coast of the Solent and the southern edge of the New Forest. With two large marinas, the town gets a lot of sailing visitors year round as well as tourists looking to explore the ancient woodland of the forest itself. With a busy high street crammed with independent shops, major retailers and designer boutiques along with plenty of pubs and accommodation, it's a good place from which to start your foraging adventure.

Transport Lymington train station is 2 miles away from Gorsemeadow, Mrs Tee's base.

Sleeping Stay with Mrs Tee herself at the pretty **££ Gorse Meadow Guest House**, T01590-673354. The rooms are large with beautiful views across the Hampshire countryside and you can sample more of Mrs Tee's mushrooms at dinner and breakfast. With its roaring log fire, elegant yet comfortable furnishings and scattered antiques and curiosities, **££ Passford House Hotel**, T01590-682398, on the outskirts of Lymington has an elegant yet homely feel. The hotel offers spacious, comfortable rooms, extensive gardens to enjoy, and a range of evening dining options as well as a fresh, locally sourced breakfast. A privately owned boutique hotel in the centre of Lymington, **££ Stanwell House**, T01590-677123, is contemporary and stylish, with modern decor. The rooms are a good size and equipped with all mod cons, with bottles of locally sourced mineral water for every guest an extra

special touch. The hotel has a vodka martini bar, offers champagne afternoon teas and is home to a well respected seafood restaurant so it is easy to indulge yourself during your stay. **Camping** Why not get back to nature and try out a Mongolian yurt at **£ Hurst View**, T01590-671648, a quiet, family owned campsite on the edge of the New Forest. Each yurt sleeps 4 people comfortably and comes complete with large wood burning stoves for cooking and added warmth.

Eating & drinking Lanes of Lymington, T01590-627777, in a former church and school offers a tucked away, intimate dining experience in central Lymington. Serving a range of fresh fish and seafood as well as other dishes, Lanes' alcoves, nooks and balconies make it ideal for romantic, affordable dining. Just like the hotel, **Stanwells**, T01590-677123, is stylish and slick, serving the best fresh seafood in town. Renowned for its mind blowing breakfasts, at the **Vanilla Pod Café**, T01590-673828, you can get everything from blueberry pancakes and home baked muffins to croquet monsieur, almond torte and Belgian waffles. All using the finest locally sourced ingredients, where possible. Also serves light lunches and dinner.

Also try Enjoy the forest on horseback and get a different perspective. Whether you are a beginner or a seasoned rider, Burley Villa stables, 10 mins drive from Lymington, burleyvilla.co.uk, offers lessons, hacks and full on treks throughout the national park.

> Lowdown

🛈 Directory
Mrs Tee's Wild Mushrooms, Gorsemeadow, Sway Road, Lymington, Hampshire, SO41 8LR, T0208-133 1622, wildmushrooms.co.uk.

🕑 Prices
£120/person.

🕑 Season
May-Dec.

⊙ Don't miss
The chance to pick Mrs Tee's brains personally, over lunch.

⊗ Avoid
Picking alone, you need an expert to help you decipher edible from poisonous.

Mountain biking South Downs Way

Provider DIY	
Skill level 2	
Time frame 2-3 days	
Equipment MTB, helmet, padded shorts, water bottle	
Exertion level ●●●●○	

Blue butterflies flutter over the rolling chalky downs, the patchwork of arable fields, beech woods and grazing land stretching to the horizon where a line of turquoise blue promises a distant downhill run to the seafront at Eastbourne. The picturesque redbrick villages which peppered the Meon Valley seem like a lifetime away, separated from the open downland by steep wooded scarp slopes and challenging climbs.

The South Downs Way, which runs for 100 miles from Winchester to Eastbourne has long been popular with walkers, cyclists and horseriders. The trail itself is a great introduction to mountain biking and follows the old droveways used in medieval times along the chalk escarpments and ridgeways of the Downs, though some parts of the landscape date back even further, to the Ice Age when glaciers carved out deep valleys from hill to sea. Ninety per cent off road with undulating grasslands, wooded bridleways and smooth open stretches, to complete the South Downs Way by mountain bike usually takes around three days (although some have conquered the trail in just a single day). The landscape and abundance of wildlife ensures the route will keep your interest while the 9843 ft of ascent, that your legs will know about by the end, means it is a serious challenge.

First capital of England, Winchester, where the trail begins, is steeped in history. Dating back to the

∨ Over rolling hils...

∧ … and through golden pastures, the south Downs Way urges you on.

reign of King Alfred the Great the city retains many of its ancient buildings and monuments, all worth a look before pedalling off into the countryside. From Winchester the route heads east through the Meon Valley and towards Petersfield. Two Bronze and Iron Age farm sites overlook the route and a short detour away, the Iron Age fort on Winchester Hill is well worth a look. Further historic intrigue awaits on the stretch from Queen Elizabeth Country Park to Upwaltham, where mounds and ditches pepper the trail before it weaves into the dense plantation woodland around Heyshott Down, where glimpses of the Isle of Wight and the English channel can be caught through the trees.

Onwards through the deep dry valleys and steep slopes of Upwaltham to Upper Beeding, the trail passes through cornfields and grassland where two 19th-century windmills can be seen. The final stretch of the route progresses over the arduous Ditchling Beacon before turning south and dropping down into the Ouse Valley stretching towards the Seven Sisters country park and then on to Eastbourne seafront.

The length and undeveloped nature of the South Downs Way means you can ride all day without passing anyone, even though the trail is popular at all times of the year. This enhances the sense of getting away from it all, with some sections of the route feeling remote, exposed to the elements and without a building for miles. But because most people take the self-guided approach to the South Downs Way there are plenty of signposts and information boards along the way to help you keep track of where you are.

After arriving weary-legged but bubbling with pride on completion of the trail, the seafront at Eastbourne beckons, the perfect place to stretch out your calves and relax with a paper full of fish and chips and some well deserved pats on the back. However, if self appreciation isn't enough for you, the National Trail website has a downloadable certificate that you can print off and put up on your wall, to show off the mammoth two-wheeled feat you have achieved.

Seb Rogers

Practicalities

At the trail head, heritage city Winchester is just an hour southwest of London with winding streets, old buildings, and plenty of amenities set in pretty Hampshire countryside. At the far end of the South Downs Way, Eastbourne is a large seaside resort near Beachy Head, with the usual tourist facilities.

Transport Winchester train station is served by Southwest Trains, Eastbourne is served by Southern Trains, southernrailway.com.

Sleeping In Winchester, **££ 58 Hyde Street B&B**, is clean, friendly and within easy walk — or cycle — of the train station. **££ The Dell**, T01962-714710, is a pretty 15th-century renovated building 10 mins from Winchester town centre and on the edge of the South Downs. Decorated to a high standard and with Wi-Fi throughout, the bed and breakfast is comfortable, stylish and welcoming. **£ Wetherdown Hostel**, East Meon T01730-823549, sustainability-centre.org, is a green award-winning sustainability centre with amazing views over the South Downs offering simple, clean rooms as well as camping pitches, tipi or yurt hire in their peaceful field. The building itself is converted navy accommodation with many environmental features including a bio-mass boiler, triple glazing and wool fleece insulation. There's a help yourself breakfast each morning and for £4.50 they'll even prepare you a packed lunch. Camping also. Reward yourself in Eastbourne at the **£££ Guesthouse East**, T01323-722774, theguesthouseeastbourne.co.uk. The listed Regency villa delivers modern suites with luxurious bedrooms, spacious bathrooms

and kitchens. Self-catering or B&B, they are cycle friendly, green aware and within a stone's throw of the seafront.

Eating & drinking The **Black Rat**, T01962-844465, Winchester combines modern British cuisine with seasonal, locally sourced produce. **The Chesil Rectory**, T01962-851555, in Winchester's oldest building, a unique historic Grade II listed building delivering plenty of character. It's relaxed and informal serving honest, robust, British classics. En route, the friendly, popular **Plough Inn**, serves fresh, seasonal Italian food.

Resources nationaltrail.co.uk/southdowns for route information. There are plenty of bicycle hire shops on the South Downs Way to choose from if you don't have your own, including **M's Cycle Hire**, m-cyclehire.co.uk, who will deliver the bike to your hotel and pick it up from a different location. Baggage transport also.

Also try If you don't feel quite ready to tackle the three days of lung-bursting ascents and giddy descents of the South Downs Way, try finding your feet at The Queen Elizabeth Country Park. Just off the A3, Hampshire's largest country park is home to two short but decent way marked mountain bike trails of around 3½ miles each. The 'purple' novice loop sticks mainly to forest tracks and with little in the way of climbing is a good gentle introduction. For more experienced riders, the challenging singletrack of the 'orange' trail tackles some technical rooty sections, looping and climbing through the stunning woodland.

> **Lowdown**

Prices
Free.

Season
Year round.

Don't miss
The poppy fields which line the route across the South Downs, worth a photograph.

Avoid
Coming up quietly on horseriders. Give a friendly shout to let them know you're there so they don't get spooked.

Walking The Arun Valley

Provider	DIY
Skill level	All levels
Time frame	1 hr to 8 days
Equipment	Good walking boots
Exertion level	●●●○○

The river wraps and turns, meandering its steady way south, drawn to the sea. The uplands wear their summer coat of sun-withered browns and lush greens laced with wildflower. Clumps of oak form shady glens while villages queue in an ordered row along the river's course, sandstone towers, white Tudor frontage and red tiles glinting in the afternoon light. Laughter rises from the beer garden as sunbrollies are angled to offer slowly shifting shade. Dreamy afternoons strolling by the riverbank, thoughts caught by skimming kingfishers, there are few better paths to follow, than those that weave through the Arun Valley.

The River Arun, the 'flowing one', winds through the chalk heartlands of West Sussex, before reaching the Channel at Littlehampton. Along its way there are footpaths and trails waiting to be explored, from the lush green spring dawn, through to winters frosty evening light. There are myriad of opportunities, such as the stretch running from Amberley over Westbury and Bignor Hills to Cocking, a 12 mile trail delivering riverside walks through lush flood plain, hill top views, hedgerows alive with chattering wrens, woodland pathways that run below high canopy and wide open pasture where skylarks sing their presence to challengers. Finally one can sit and bathe tired feet in the cool stream in the shade of Cocking Church.

For most, a 12 to 15 mile trail is a reasonable day's walk. There are many other options for those with less time to spare, including a hike up Bury Hill from the George and Dragon in Houghton, delivering far reaching views across the Downs, followed by rewarding refreshment below. Arundel itself is there to explore, this picturesque market town home of an impressive Norman citadel that rose in 1067. The streets bustle in the summer, but a quick glance at the map reveals an impressive selection of routes out into the green. The only dilemma, which one today.

Practicalities

Shared by walkers, cyclists and horse riders, The South Downs trail crosses the Arun Valley but continues either side to a total of 99 miles. There are towns and villages to explore in the valley and while they can get busy during summer weekends, are great spring and autumn escapes.

Transport Amberley is well served by a train station. For Cocking, buses run to nearby Chichester station.

Sleeping South of Amberley on the banks of the Arun lies the converted 17th-century **££ The Thatched Barn**, Wepham, West Sussex, BN18 9RA, T01903-885404, thehatchedbarnwepham.co.uk, with magnificent views across the Arun Valley towards Arundel Castle. To the east of Cocking on the river is **££ The Old Railway Station**, Petworth, GU28 0JF, T01798-342346, old-station.co.uk, a gloriously quirky converted station complete with 3 restored Pullman carriages resplendent in period decor. It's like travelling without moving. Camping Just south of Bignor, National Trust **Gumber Bothy Camping Barn**, BN18 0RN, is simple with good facilities including kitchen and good hot showers. Camping also. Mar-Oct.

Eating & drinking The Black Horse Inn, Byworth, T01798-342424, is an untouched 16th-century hostelry with a large fireplace and huge beams. The restaurant serves fresh local produce updated seasonally – from fresh soups to substantial burgers and more exotic fare at good prices. Wide selection of real ales – a destination pub. Four miles south of Cocking in nearby East Dean, **The Star and Garter**, PO18 0JG, T01243-811318, is a restored 18th-century freehouse with a reputation for fresh quality local fish and seafood, including Selsey Crab – main from around £12 plus lighter lunchtime bites. Good ales.

Resources See nationaltrail.co.uk/southdowns and southdownsway.co.uk for trail information.

Also try The Monarchs Way, a route of over six hundred miles that is said to follow the route taken by King Charles II after his defeat in the battle of Worcester. The trail passes through Arundel, where it crosses the river, before continuing on to Shoreham-by-Sea.

> **Lowdown**

🕑 **Prices**
Free.

☀ **Season**
Year round.

✪ **Don't miss**
The Romans – the Stane Sreet road linking Chichester to London as well as Roman remains at Bignor.

✖ **Avoid**
If you are going peak season it's best to book accommodation beforehand.

Surfing Isle of Wight

Provider	DIY
Skill level	All
Time frame	As long as you like
Equipment	Surfboard, wetsuit
Exertion level	●●●●●

From the cliff top, the golden arc of Compton Bay sweeps into the distance, met by green trimmed cliffs and sun-flecked sea. In the water, a smattering of black shapes can be picked out against the backdrop of chalky white rocks, waiting patiently for the next set to hit. Lines roll into the bay as one by one the shapes shift, and paddling to gain momentum, they absorb the pulse of energy, slipping and dancing their way across the face of the wave before paddling back out, their laughter and chat drifting high on the evening air.

Never as crowded as Devon or Cornwall but with more than 60 miles of coastline and a surprising consistency – given its English Channel location – the Isle of Wight has been something of a UK surf secret for years. With many mainland surfers put off by the effort of a ferry crossing, the island has seen its surf tourism kept to a happy minimum and managed to retain a friendly, laid back atmosphere reminiscent of the Southwest in the 60s and 70s. But in true 'island style', this rock delivers probably the best and most consistent breaks to those seeking out surf in these narrow waters. Sticking out into the channel the southern side of the Isle of Wight picks up any swell that's heading past while the convenient 'V' bottomed coastline provides welcome shelter and an offshore alternative in those pesky prevailing southwesterly winds.

∨ Compton: Down the line.

Roger Powley

< Freshwater: Dusk washes the sky above the classic point break.

With beach breaks, reef and point breaks to choose from there are waves to be had whatever your ability level. Quieter and less touristy than the eastern side, West Wight has the pick of the island's best surfing and a short trip along the coastline when a southwesterly swell rolls in should yield positive results. Best in medium sized swells and off shore in northerly winds, Compton Bay works through the tide, producing everything from playful knee-ticklers perfect for beginners to powerful head high peaks and is possibly the most consistent spot on the island. Because it can work even in a small swell it is popular year round and irresistible on an August day when the sun's out, the water's warm and the summer glass starts drifting in. But with three main set ups – from mellow A-frame reef to punchy beach break , there should be room for manoeuvre.

Next to Compton, Freshwater Bay is one of the best-known breaks on the island with a right-hand point on the western fringe of the bay capable of producing quality, walling right-handers when the swell wraps in. As the tide pushes in, the backwash from the cliffs can affect the waves so it's best caught around low when it can deliver long, quality rides.

Further south and one to leave to the experienced, Chilton Reef is worth watching when a powerful southwesterly swell heads in; a heavy reef with hollow lefts and rights, it allows the local talent to show off what they do best.

Not so much on the southeast coast where seaside resorts Ventnor and Shanklin offer shelter should a storm hit but don't do much in the way of waves otherwise. On the most southerly point of the island and between east and west, Niton's right hand point delivers in clean southwesterly groundswells, but this is one to watch for rips.

> Lowdown

 Prices
Free or from £35 for a 90-min surf lesson.

 Season
Best swell season is autumn/winter.

 Don't miss
Sunset in West Wight, illuminating the white chalk cliffs. A spectacular sight best viewed from the water.

 Avoid
High summer in Shanklin and Ventnor. Little chance of waves and maximum chance of holidaymakers.

Practicalities

Covering an area of 23 by 13 miles, the Isle of Wight is best known for its prestigious yachting event, Cowes Week when the little rock heaves. B&B's are dotted along the coast path and in the villages nearby. Freshwater town, about 10 mins inland, is the main shopping centre for West Wight with shops, pubs and places to stay plus easy links to the island's other major towns like Yarmouth and Cowes.

Transport The nearest ferry port to Freshwater is at Yarmouth, where Wightlink Ferries, wightlink.co.uk, dock from Lymington on the UK mainland. The crossing takes 30 mins. Lymington has a train station served by a branchline from Brockenhurst. Ferries to the Isle of Wight docking at Fishbourne and Ryde are also available.

Sleeping ££ **Seven B&B**, T01983-740296, in the pretty village of Brighstone, just moments away from Freshwater Bay and Compton is 7 miles from both Freshwater and Yarmouth, hence the name. **£ Totland Bay YHA**, Hurst Hill, PO39 0HD, T0845-371 9348, is a couple of miles from Freshwater with bike hire and drying room. **Three Sea Breeze Cottages**, T01983-740993, near Brightstone has stunning sea views. 250 yards from the coast path and beach it's well kitted out and the owners even offer a ferry pick up and drop off service. **Camping** Holding a David Bellamy Gold Award for Conservation, **Grange Farm Campsite**, PO30 4DA, T01983-740296, perched on the cliffs at Brighstone Bay a few miles from Compton is one of the few non-commercialized campsites on the island.

Eating & drinking To sample the Isle of Wight's cream teas, head to **Warren Farm**, T01983-753200, where they are made on site. Lunches and snacks also available. **High Down Inn**, T01983-752450, is well known for its seafood. Daily specials available. For something more unusual, try **The Garlic Farm**, T01983-865378, over on the east coast. One of the UK's premier growers of garlic, the farm has recently opened an on-site café.

Resources **Offshore Sports**, Shanklin, T01983-866269, and **X-Isle Sports**, Bembridge T01983-761678, xisle.co.uk, both carry a limited range of hardware and accessories. For lessons contact BSA qualified surf coach and native Wighter Chris Mannion who operates a mobile surf school, **iSurf**, T07968-609169, iowsurf.com, taking you to the best waves for your ability according to conditions. **Wight Water Adventures**, T01983-866269, wightwaters.com, also offer lessons.

Mountain biking New Forest

Provider	DIY
Skill level	All levels
Time Frame	From a couple of hours
Equipment	Bikes, helmets and route maps can be hired. Waterproofs, drinks and snacks are a good idea
Exertion level	●●●○○

New Forest purifying mud mask.

Mountain biking in a flat region might seem at odds with the essence of the sport, but the New Forest offers a diverse spectrum of biking opportunities. Long winding tracks meander across miles of open countryside offering mellow days out, but for those who prefer to get into the muddy thick of it there are the woodland tracks with sharp berms and sculpted challenges to test even the strongest nerve. The New Forest, England's newest and smallest national park roams over some 220 sq miles of woodland, heathland and pasture, a countryside moulded by the ancient pastoral system allowing free roaming cattle and ponies to graze here. Local 'commoners' livestock helps maintain the grassland, bogs and wooded pasture that is the hallmark of this region, an area that is quickly becoming known as one of the UK's cycling hotspots.

A network of trails are now actively promoted signposted and well maintained making this ideal territory for the MTB novice . There are many to choose from including Land of the Rising Sun, a fifteen mile route that follows part of the disused railway from Brockenhurst, before looping back around via the poetic sounding villages of Tiptoe and Sway. The Bolderwood Double is an off road ride starting from Boldwerwood car park, one of the highest points in the New Forest and following a loop that links to Burley. This run can be tailored to a short five mile ride or enjoyed as a longer thirteen mile circuit. For the more adventurous there is the Watchmoor Wood Bike Park in Verwood Wood near Poole. This area offers a track with an impressive number of lines that weave through an assortment of banks, berms, jumps with wooden tabletops and boardwalks.

> **Lowdown**

$ Prices
Free/adult MTB hire from £15.50/day.

⊘ Season
All year.

✪ Don't miss
The wildlife along the way including the infamous ponies.

⊗ Avoid
Don't stray off track and into the forest on bikes as they are trying to maintain the fragile ecosystem.

Practicalities

The village of Brokenhurst is an ideal base with pubs, restaurants and places to stay from sublime spas to a clutch of homely B&B's.

Transport Brockenhurst is the most convenient station for those looking for bike hire.

Sleeping Green Tourism Gold Award Holder, £££-££ **Cottage Lodge** in Brockenhurst, has a lovely old school feel in that it doesn't shy away from chintz. They serve a New Forest breakfast using locally sourced quality produce. If you're looking for a special break where relaxation is as important as blasting around trails, £££ **Careys Manor Hotel and Senspa**, SO42 7RH, T01590-625201, careysmanor.com, is the ultimate. The rooms are luxurious, the food locally sourced and the spa experience, including the hydrotherapy pool to ease your aching limbs, heavenly. It's not cheap but ease you conscience with the fact they have the Gold Award for Green Tourism. Cycle breaks from £85/person. Keep an eye out for offers. **Camping** Forest Holidays have 8 cracking sites across the forest one of which is the large, simple and sublime **Hollands Wood** site, Lyndhurst Rd, Brockenhurst, SO42 7QH, T01590-622967, also a David Bellamy Conservation Gold Award winner. Mar-Sep.

Eating & drinking Foresters Arms, Brockenhurst is a popular pit stop for a reviving beverage or twol. Out on the trails **The Turfcutters Arms**, Boldre, Hants, SO42 7WL, T01590-612331, with roaring fires is a welcome sight on a winter ride. The inn serves decent pub fare plus seasonal game dishes. The on-site barn has been renovated to house three comfortable apartments sleeping 2 or 3 with kitchenettes available on a B&B basis.

Resources Country Lanes, The Railway Station, Brockenhurst, SO42 7TW, T01590-622627, countrylanes.co.uk, offer bike hire as well route maps and guided rides. **Cyclexperience**, Brookley Road, Brockenhurst, T01590-623407, newforestcyclehire.co.uk, also offer bike hire and great route advice.

Also try There are miles and miles of forest to explore, head out on foot to discover secret patches of moorland and ancient woodland. Head south from Brockenhurst station towards Lymington river, crossing it by Roydon Manor before circling back towards the station passing the edge of Hatchet Moor and crossing the river again.

Paragliding Isle of Wight

Provider	High Adventure
Skill level	All levels
Time frame	2 days on the introductory course
Equipment	All paragliding and safety equipment provided
Exertion level	●●○○○

Pulling up to the gentle slope of one of the Isle of Wight's many paragliding sites it's clear conditions must be good. Shadows dance over the car bonnet as hundreds of feet above, canopies soar on the air currents rising up from the land. With its variety of terrain, mild climate and regular summer sea breezes, the Isle of Wight is known as a great spot for paragliding, with a concentration of quality flying sites on the southwestern shore. The island's rolling hills, towering cliffs and long sandy beaches make for perfect takeoff and touchdown sites, while the panoramic vistas of chalk white cliffs blurring into an azure haze see novice and experienced pilots return year on year.

Staring up at the curving wings as they dart across the sky, it's easy to feel like the skills required for paragliding sit far out of reach, however, under the watchful eye of an experienced instructor, you could be soaring high before you know it.

Phil, the chief flying instructor at High Adventure, has been taking students sky high for years, offering everything from one off tandem flights to full blown qualifications. However if it's a quick route into solo flying you are after, High Adventure's two-day introductory paragliding course is the one to go for.

From basic equipment handling through some short ground-skimming sessions to radio instruction-led flights, High Adventure's instructors help you pick up the skills, theory and knowledge required to finish the course high in the air on your first solo flight. And, if your fledgling flight sparks off an airborne addiction, the introductory course can be converted into a week's training to gain your student, then club pilot, qualification, a chance to deepen your knowledge and earn a licence which will enable you to continue flying and feed you habit when you return home.

<High lines over the white isle.

Roger Powley

Practicalities

Historic Yarmouth, with an active community all year round, makes an ideal base.

Transport Wightlink Ferries from Lymington dock in Yarmouth, wightlink.co.uk.

Sleeping The 18th-century **££ Rockstone Cottage**, T01983-753723, provides quality accommodation in Freshwater, close to Yarmouth. With locally sourced breakfasts and pretty Colwell Bay at the end of the road, it's a good bet for a comfortable stay. **£££ The George**, T01983-760331, in Yarmouth itself is a 17th-century farmhouse. The hotel has an outdoor deck overlooking Yarmouth pier and a brasserie which uses local organic produce. **Camping** Compton Farm Camping, T01983-740215, is next door to High Adventure's main training site and practically on top of Compton Bay. In a sheltered valley, the small, site is part of a working farm.

Eating & drinking Salty's Harbourside Restaurant, Yarmouth, T0871-963 3079, serves freshly caught fish as well as crab and lobster from the family fishing boat. Alternatively the **Bugle Inn**, T01983-760272, another 17th-century building serves real ales and good food made with fresh island produce.

Resources For flight information see flywight.com.

Also try On the south coast of the island, **Butterfly Paragliding**, Chale, T01983-731611, paraglide.uk.com, holds an annual Solstice Cup — an event for novice paraglider pilots where skills are tested followed by a party. Accommodation with organic brekkies available year round: camping from £5, camping and breakfast £12/person B&B from £25/person.

> Lowdown

ⓘ Directory
High Adventure, Chilton green Cottage, Hoxall Lane, Brighstone, Isle of Wight, PO30 4DT, T01983-741484/07796-231316, high-adventure.uk.com.

ⓢ Prices
£185 for a 2-day introductory solo flying course.

Season
Mar-Dec.

Don't miss
The view over The Needles from Compton Whites flying site.

Avoid
Some of the sites here are sensitive with flying restrictions at some sites during nesting season. See flywight.co.uk for details

Kite surfing Hayling Island

Provider	Hayling Island Kitesurf School
Skill level	All levels
Time Frame	1-2 days introductory course
Equipment	All kite surfing and safety equipment provided. Remember to bring a warm dry change of clothes
Exertion level	●●●●○

Standing on the seafront staring at the white caps as the frantic flap of billowing material fills the air, it's clear to see why Hayling Island is popular with wind sport enthusiasts. It's approaching mid tide and the West Winner sandbank is just visible, stretching out for a mile into the Solent and providing shallow, sheltered conditions ideal for learning how to kitesurf.

On the beach, huge inflated sails, narrow boards and hefty harnesses lie dormant as their owners take a breather, readying themselves for an afternoon skitting across the waves. Among them a cluster of beginners eager to feel the whip of water against their skin get to grips with their equipment, while top UK kitesurfer Chris Bull looks on and advises.

Kite surfing has taken off in the last decade, with British Kite surfing Association schools springing up countrywide, but for Chris, there's nowhere better than Hayling Island when it comes to learning the ropes. "We almost always have good conditions here," he explains, "at West Beach the water is knee deep for about half a mile out to sea and our wind statistics are consistently high. And we can make the most of the winds whatever the direction – a luxury you don't get on the mainland."

Chris set up HI Kitesurf School in Hayling in 1999, and for the last ten years he has helped novices learn what they need to know to become safe, competent kite surfers. This starts with a one day kiteboarding session that familiarizes students with the fundamentals, followed by a two-day kite surfing course building on that knowledge, giving students the chance to take to the water.

From here it's just a case of taking what you've learned and getting out there. You'll be sheeting in with the best of them before you know it.

> Ankle deep and learning the ropes. "Always check the forecast, work out when conditions are best and safe. Always double check your equipment prior to launch and never go out alone." Sound advice that Chris and his instructors drum into those keen to master kite surfing.

> **Lowdown**

> ℹ **Directory**
> Hayling Island Kitesurf School, 222 The Seafront, Hayling Island, PO11 0AU, T023-9242 2570, hikitesurfschool.co.uk.

> 💲 **Prices**
> From £100/person for the 1-day introductory course.

> ☀ **Season**
> Mar-Dec.

> ✓ **Don't miss**
> Warming up with a hot chocolate at the Inn on the Beach after a session.

> ✗ **Avoid**
> Peak travel times in the summer. The road to Hayling Island is easily jammed.

Chris Bull

Practicalities

Thanks to its shallow waters and breezy coastline, Hayling Island is popular with wind sport enthusiasts. At just 4 miles long and 4 miles wide, it's a small island, although still large enough for a decent spread of pubs, restaurants, shops, facilities and accommodation. Most of this is concentrated around South Hayling, which stretches back from the seafront.

Transport Havant is the nearest train station with regular bus links to Hayling: havant-travel.info

Sleeping ££ Cocklewarren Cottage Hotel, T02392-464961, is a small, stylish hotel right on the seafront and within a stone's throw of a couple of great pubs. Owner Kate cooks up a well-celebrated, locally sourced full English. The converted 18th-century farmhouse of £££ Newtown House Hotel, T02392-466131, is away from the hustle and bustle of the seafront. Their Garden Room restaurant serves fresh local food.
Camping Try small, inland campsite £ Fleet Farm, PO11 0QE, T02392-463684. Surrounded by oaks and with a tidal creek where small boats and windsurfers can be launched.

Eating & drinking For pub lunches, snacks and dinners teamed with views across West Beach, try the Inn on the Beach, T023-9246 0043. Marina Jaks, T02390-469459, is popular with locals and visitors for its modern British cuisine and seafood dishes

Resources Ocean Addiction, Seafront, oceanaddiction.co.uk, for kite surfing hardware and accessories.

Also try There are plenty of good walks. Take the Hayling Billy trail which starts at the former railway station in West Town and passes Langstone Harbour and the island's oyster beds en route, or head inland to discover the many lanes that connect the north and south of the island.

Kayaking Isle of Wight

Provider	Isle of Wight Sea Kayaking
Skill level	All levels
Time frame	2 hr sessions to 4 day excursions
Equipment	All sea kayaking and safety equipment provided. Remember to bring a warm dry change of clothes
Exertion level	●●●●○

Paddles rhythmically plunge in and out and droplets of water splash upwards as a small group of brightly coloured kayaks meander through the shallow waters of the creek. Clinging to the river bank, the party moves swiftly forward, basking in the dappled sunlight and savouring their surroundings before paddling out towards open sea. Strikingly different from the huge tidal races and rough conditions more commonly associated with the sport, when it comes to sea kayaking in the Isle of Wight, no two trips are the same.

The white island has an incredible range of different coastal areas to explore, and a reputation as a top sea kayaking location as a result. From sheltered bays and creeks of scientific interest, to towering cliffs, fast paced surf beaches and tumultuous seas, there are conditions to suit every taste and ability level

"Because of the variety the Isle of Wight offers we can kayak in all weather, all year round," explains Owen Burson, experienced kayaker and founder of Isle of Wight Sea Kayaking. "It means you have a real choice, whether you are looking to learn in a sheltered spot or want to tackle something more challenging, like an excursion across the Solent."

Of course the classic trip for those who have put in a bit of water time is to go out to the Needles. Lying off the westernmost tip of the island, this distinctive row of chalk stacks, eroded by time into sharp edged pinnacles, reach out into the sea like a semaphore code warning of the dangers that lie in these waters. Stroking out through rough waters to these towering monuments to wrecked ships and lost souls is certainly enough to get the heart racing. And if this has whetted your appetite, there's always the island to circumnavigate – the three day camping and kayaking expedition can involve up to eight hours

of paddling a day, so be sure you can sustain that level of output to go the distance. Closely linked to the island's Canoe Club, Isle of Wight Sea Kayaking also offers courses delivering good solid grounding; half day entry level sessions using sit-on-top kayaks are ideal for those who want to learn the basics and gain confidence while half day sea kayak expeditions are aimed at those who have some paddle experience but are yet to sample saline pleasures.

Practicalities

Freshwater is a busy town with great facilities and home to a beautiful sandy beach flanked by the towering white sea cliffs which this stretch of the coast is famous for.

Transport A mile north, the nearest ferry port is Yarmouth, with Wightlink Ferries docking from Lymington. Lymington train station is served by a branchline from Brockenhurst.

Sleeping The **£££ Sentry Mead**, T01983-753212, is a classic country house hotel. Traditional decor and comfortable rooms. There are plenty of B&Bs including the good value **££ Buttercup B&B**, Camp Rd, T01983-752772, with 3-course breakfast to rave about. **£ Totland Bay YHA**, Hurst Hill, T0845-371 9384, is in a quiet residential area but is close to the Needles and provides a good base. **Camping** Winner of the David Bellamy Gold Award for conservation **Heathfield Camping**, T01983-407822, spreads across 9 acres of unspoilt countryside.

Eating & drinking King's Manor Farm Café, T01983-756050, just outside Freshwater serves up its very own Aberdeen Angus Beef gourmet burgers as well as other snacks and light meals made from ingredients grown on the farm. **The Fat Cat on the Bay Restaurant**, T01983-758500, part of the Sandpiper Hotel, serves homecooked Aga-baked food using local ingredients.

Resources Southeast England Sea Kyakers is an online space for sea kayakers to network, share stories, organize excursions and upload images, sesk.co.uk.

Also try Jumping over rock archways, swimming through wave filled gaps, climbing up cliffs and ducking down into underwater caves. Isle of Wight Sea Kayaking also run day-long coasteering excursions from their base in Freshwater Bay; a great way to see another side of the island.

Roger Powley

∧ The iconic Needles.

> Lowdown

❶ Directory
Isle of Wight Sea Kayaking, The Sandpipers, Freshwater Bay, Isle of Wight, PO40 9QX, T01983-752043, iow-seakayaking.co.uk.

❷ Prices
£70 for an introductory course to £250 for a 4-day circumnavigation.

❸ Season
Year round.

❹ Don't miss
Paddling around the stacks and in and out of the caves around Freshwater Bay.

❺ Avoid
Heading out without a plan. Weather is fickle and conditions can change; it's best to be prepared.

Mountain biking Surrey Hills

Provider	Surrey Hills All Terrain MTB Tours
Skill level	All
Time Frame	4 hrs
Equipment	Mountain bike, helmet, map, snacks, water and a repair kit/spare tube
Exertion level	●●●●○

The tight trail weaves between needle straight trunks, speeding faster as the drop accelerates away across the descent. Orange brown blurs of withered bracken are peripheral markers, the surreal green of rhododendrons lean close, but the myriad of trees hem in the narrow track as it suddenly throws a contrary change of direction through a tightly angled berm. Weathered roots, jumps, drops and an acceleration into the new end section brings the climax of the trail and waiting friends into focus. Here in the Surrey Hills, a region rich in rolling chalk downs and sandstone hills with flower-scattered grasslands and ancient woodlands, the winding descents of Hurtwood are hard to beat. Perhaps Barry does Know Best.

As one of Britain's first Areas of Outstanding Natural Beauty, the Surrey Hills truly is a green and pleasant land. This is an area of hills that climb up to 984 ft, criss-crossed by trails and tracks, woodland warrens of runs with names like Abba Zabba, Blind Terror and Barry Knows Best. As with surf breaks and climbing routes, the naming of a trail makes it easier to identify its position, discuss the intricacies of how difficult it is and the route it follows. Some, like Yoghurt Pots/the Rollercoaster are so good they have been named twice. Most of the major trails are easy to find, but for those new to the sport, would like to try a guided tour, or feel they would like to develop their off-road skills with the help of a qualified instructor, companies like Surrey Hills All Terrain Mountain Bike Tours can help.

> The North Downs.
> A warm glow tackling Tilford: one of the Surrey Hills Classics.

Wig Worland

Practicalities

Yet this area of outstanding natural beauty set around the triangle of Leith Hill, Holmbury Hill and Pitch Hill is a mountainbiker's dream. Large areas of land fall under the control of the National Trust, Forestry Commission and local estates such as Hurtwood, Shere Manor and Wotton Estate. There are a number of good bases from towns such as Guildford and Dorking as well as the little villages scattered in between.

Transport Gomshall is the closest station for the guided rides, which can be tailored to leave from here. Other nearby stations include Dorking 6 miles to the north and Holmwood, 4 miles east of Leith Hill.

Sleeping In a prime location between Guildford and Dorking, in the village of Shere £££ **The Rookery Nook**, GU5 9HG, T01483-209399, is in the heart of the hills. The breakfast uses local goodies where possible. Secure bike store also. The starting point for one of the rides £ **Holmbury St Mary YHA**, RH5 6NW, T0845-3719323, is a handy base with a bike store. Camping available.

Eating & drinking Leith Hill Tower is the highest point in South East England, but it serves up tea, cake and sandwiches on weekends. Peaslake Village Stores deli/tea shop is a bit of a weekend Mecca for mountain bikers. There are many MTB friendly pubs in the area including the Stephen Langton, Friday Street, Abinger Common, in a valley a few miles from Dorking. The menu features home-made soups as well as more substantial fare. Other good spots include **The Plough**, Coldharbour, nr Dorking, T01306-711793 home to the Leith Hill Brewery and close to the hills, serving up their own real ales as well as gourmet grub.

Resources Nirvana Cycles, The Green, Guildford Rd, Westcott, Surrey, RH4 3NH, T01306-740300, nirvanacycles.com, is well stocked and carries a full range of hire bikes from £25/day as well as trail maps on sale for those wanting to explore the Surrey Hills area alone. To link up with the local crew that ride here, check out: mtbsurreyhills.com. In Dorking **Head for the Hills**, West St, T01306-885007, is also well stocked and offers bike hire.

Also try There are plenty of opportunities for those looking to explore the area. The Redlands Trails crew are usually out clearing, building and improving trails, redlandstrails. wordpress.com. Leith Hill is home to a number of classic trails – pore over OS Explorer 145 and 146 for inspiration while at Coldharbour, the steep woodlands provide plenty of single and doubletrack to enjoy. Then of course there are sections of the North Downs Way that are ripe for exploration.

Their guides offer everything from open group rides, to MTB skills training catered to experienced levels. Level 1 covers fundamentals, core skills and helps build confidence, level 2 develops the skills needed for riding singletrack, level 3 helps master rhythm and flow, an understanding of energy management while level 4 is aimed to take riding to another level on steeper terrain and bigger obstacles. Surrey Hills All Terrain MTB also offer Skill Development Weekends that run from Friday evening through to Sunday. For those who are yet to take the plunge and buy an off-road bike, they can be hired and instructors will happily pass on advice for your future purchase. Much of the riding here takes place in the private oasis of Hurtwood, a mountainbike Mecca and woodland retreat that belies the fact it rests on the fringe of bustling London. So if you have a spare weekend, maybe make time for a trip down the Widowmaker, Deliverance or Cliff Richard – so called because Richard found it, and it's a cliff.

∧ Home Counties comforts Part 1: autumn leaves crunch beneath fat tyres.

∧ Home Counties comforts Part 2: This is snacking Surrey style.

> Lowdown

ⓘ Directory
Surrey Hills All Terrain MTB Tours, T07976-353963, mountain-bike-guiding.co.uk.

Ⓢ Prices
£55 for a 4-hr lesson.

Ⓢ Season
Year round.

Ⓞ Don't miss
A cup of tea at the Tower.

Ⓧ Avoid
The Hurtwood Control Trust manages the 3000 acres of land in the heart of the hills, maintaining a large network of trails. They have recently decided to disallow the building of new unsanctioned trails – they've closed 2 and put them out of use. Don't waste your efforts here, they're not wanted!

Swimming Frensham Ponds

Provider	DIY
Skill level	Novice-advanced
Time frame	2 hrs +
Equipment	Swimsuit, towel
Exertion level	●●○○○

On first thoughts, Surrey with its tidy edges governed by the strict timetable of commuters rushing to catch the 0753 to Waterloo may not seem like a natural escape. But to see the county that borders Greater London as a mere facilitating cog in the wheel that powers the capital is to miss the point. The real Surrey, although under threat of erosion, is green belt, not commuter belt, with 37,564 hectares of land under a leafy canopy. The Surrey Hills Area of Outstanding Natural Beauty stretches east to west through the heartland as if to hold back the encroaching city, bolstering support from the chalk slopes of the North Downs.

On the western fringes of this AONB lies Frensham Common, some 900 acres of heathland, woodland and pond. This natural conservation area and SSSI is a draw for twitchers who come to spy green woodpeckers, reed warblers, nightjars and woodlarks. Those with a keen eye may spot a sand lizard, grass snake or blue butterfly. But in the warmth of long, lingering summer days, the shores of the watering hole are home to an entirely different species, the brightly coloured major and minor pond plungers whose tell-tale squeals of horror and delight can be heard on the approach from the Bacon Lane car park. Formerly a 13th Century fish farm, the large, man-made Frensham Great Pond regularly finds itself transformed into a modern day beach scene complete with buckets and spades, soggy towels and families who have pitched up for the day. And why not, the cool, calm waters that lap against the gently sloping shoreline are backed by a sandy bay – perfect for a spot of sun bathing or sand castle construction. The waters are shared with anglers and sailing boats so two swimming zones have been designated going out to about 4½ ft in depth. Lying back post dip to examine the clouds slowly scudding by may strike you as wonderfully at odds with the 0753 to Waterloo, and it is.

Practicalities

The pretty market town of Farnham is well served by amenities if not overrun with good pit stops.

Transport From Farnham train station, 19 Stagecoach links to Frensham, stagecoachbus.com.

Sleeping Less than 2 miles from the pond, **Mellow Farm**, Dockenfield, Farnham, GU10 4HH, T01428-717815, is as it sounds, a simple campsite in the heart of a working farm. Basic facilities (portaloos) but fires are allowed – bags of wood £5. On the banks of the River Wey with a little 'beach' making access easy for those looking to indulge in an early morning dip. ££ **The Old Post House**, Priory Ln, Frensham, GU10 3DW, T01252-794466, is very villagey and rather quaint. The National Trust rents out the idyllic **Frensham Common Cottage**, T0844-800 2070 whose large garden backs on to the common, sleeping 5 from £463/week.

Eating & drinking The Holly Bush, Frensham and the **Blue Bell**, Dockenfield both serve up real ale and your regular pub grub. **The Barn**, Old Kiln Courtyard, Farnham is a music venue and members only arts club by night. During the day they serve up tasty organic and fair trade fare to nourish body and soul from home-made soups to pitta parcels. Head south towards Grayshott to **Applegarth** farmshop and café, GU26 6JL – serving up seasonal and organic goodies fresh from their fields as light lunches and afternoon teas.

Also try Stretch your legs along the North Downs Way the 153 mile National Trail linking Farnham, Surrey with the far reaches of Kent including Canterbury and Dover. It weaves its way along the highest line of the downs to take in the picture perfect and quintessentially English countryside of Surrey and Kent, matching rolling hills and areas of outstanding natural beauty with ridiculously pretty villages where it would be terribly bad manners not to pause for afternoon tea or stop for a ploughman's and a swift half. If you don't have time to stay the distance – around 12 days – there are a number of excellent shorter walks such as exploring the woodland around White Down in the Surrey Hills. nationaltrail.co.uk.

> **Lowdown**

ⓘ Directory
Bacon Lane, Churt, Surrey.

⊗ Prices
Free/parking from £2.50.

⊘ Season
Year round.

⊕ Don't miss
A walk around the nearby Frensham Little Pond, a sanctuary for waterfowl and wildlife. Setting out from Great Pond you'll pass through woodland dominated by alder as well as areas of birch and Scots pine.

⊗ Avoid
Tested by the EA, the bathing waters are usually good. However, do not swim here after heavy rains as water quality can be questionable at best. Blooms of blue-green algae can build up in the summer which makes for a hazardous swimming environment so heed the warnings.

Cycling London to Brighton

Provider	DIY
Skill level	All
Time frame	All day
Equipment	Bicycle, helmet, water bottle
Exertion level	● ● ● ● ●

After 53 miles of winding country lanes, a glut of open roads flanked by poppies and steep climbs, Brighton's seafront flashes into view. The welcome rush of air as the bicycle picks up pace on its five mile descent into the town kindles a genuine sense of achievement; setting a contrast to the gradual, gear-grinding grunt of the Ditchling Beacon just moments before.

The London to Brighton cycle route has been made popular by the British Heart Foundation, which organizes a massive sponsored cycle from the country's capital to the seaside resort every June. Tens of thousands take part each year, making their way from Clapham Common in London across the North and South Downs towards Brighton promenade some 56 miles away. The annual ride has raised £40 million since its inception in 1980, and has inspired many cyclists to tackle the route on their own. Avoiding the A23 and sticking to back roads is accepted as the way to do it, because although the A23 is flatter, the lanes that weave between London and Brighton are far more picturesque and offer more opportunities to stop and catch your breath.

For those who prefer the organized approach, London based Redspokes run regular day trips to Brighton. Differing from the BHF ride, but just as pretty, Redspokes' route sets out from Coulsdon South train station before heading on quiet roads through Surrey and Sussex towards the Ditchling Beacon and down into Brighton itself. Lunch, maps, a guide and a bike mechanic are all provided plus it's a chance to meet fellow riders.

However you decide to do it, leaving the heaving metropolis behind and spending a day cycling through the countryside feels mighty good, as does the well earned ice cream and seaside paddle at the other end.

∧ In the UK around 2.6 million people are living with coronary heart disease. In 2009, the Ride raised just over £3.9 million for the British Heart Foundation. Wigs not compulsory.

> **Lowdown**

❸ Prices
Free or £20 if completed with Red Spokes, redspokes.co.uk.

❹ Season
Year round.

❺ Don't miss
The poppy fields which line the route across the South Downs; worth a photograph..

❻ Avoid
A sore bottom. Wear padded shorts to steer clear of saddle sore.

Practicalities

Weaving along the country lanes from London, this ride ends up in the seaside resort of Brighton – an eclectic mix of contemporary style, chintz and underground culture. There's a wide range of tourist facilities, pubs, bars, restaurants and accommodation to choose from, as well as a long promenade and shingle beaches.

Transport Southern Trains serves Brighton station to London Victoria, bicycles accommodated free of charge outside peak times, southernrailway.com.

Sleeping The award-winning **££ Brighton House**, T01273-323282, in the heart of Brighton has clean comfortable hotels and an impressive environmental policy. From low energy bulbs in all rooms to using eco electricity suppliers, religious recycling to making compost from kitchen waste, they've thought of everything. Breakfast is organic, locally sourced, with vegetarian options available. **££ Paskins Townhouse**, T01273-601203, is a gold award winning green hotel which gives 10% room discounts to members of the Vegetarian, Vegan Society and Amnesty International. Rooms are comfortable and modern. Organic, locally sourced breakfasts. **Camping** Idyllic **Blackberry Wood**, Streat, BN6 8RS, T01273-890035, at the foot of the South Downs is a small friendly campsite where campfires are actively encouraged.

Eating & drinking The **Real Eating Company Restaurant**, Western Rd, Hove, T01273-212444, focuses on British classics with a seasonal, modern slant, using the best local producers, seeking out quality handmade specialities. Or try their café, Ship St, Brighton for a light bite or a smoothie. **The Gingerman**, Norfolk Sq, T01273-326688, is a small and modern restaurant which creates full-flavoured food made from the freshest, highest quality, seasonal produce – 2 course lunch from £15.

Resources Register at: bhf.org.uk. See freewebs.com/cycleroutes for useful route info.

Also try Rolling down a hill, head over heels in a big inflatable ball! The longest orbing site in the country is just outside Brighton, where you can aquaslide or free-orb down 1½ miles of hillside building up to speeds of 30 mph, orb360.co.uk.

Outdoors London

A diverse, sprawling metropolis, London isn't the first place you would think of as an outdoor adventure playground, space is at a premium and open spaces are a seemingly limited resource. But look a little deeper, with a fresh perspective and no end of delights can be found; there are patches of green lighting up the urban landscape, places where shoes can be kicked off during snatched lunch breaks and grass can be felt underfoot. Alexandra Park in the north of the capital comes complete with nearby weekend farmers' market whose tasty morsels temporarily whisk the shopper off to greener and more pleasant lands, while to the south the green dream of Clapham Common throngs in early summer evenings with picnickers, skaters and gig goers reconnecting

with the outdoors. Indeed many of the open parks, canals, river banks and lakes spread across the capital boast some sort of activity and for those looking for a social escape there are clubs, associations and centres tucked away.

Open Air Swimming, Hampstead Heath	
Provider DIY	
Skill level All	
Time frame Dawn til dusk (or until you turn into a prune)	
Equipment Swimsuit, towel	
Exertion level ●●○○○	

Stepping out of the tube and onto the streets of North London, the baking summer sun beats down and the air refuses to move, the dense reality of

‹ Photographer Annie Mitchell has documented a group of women who quietly swim the outdoor pools of Hampstead Heath every day of the year. The result is a captivating collection of images and stories. anniemitchell.co.uk.

Annie Mitchell

city living weighing it down. Striding up Parliament Hill a welcome breeze picks up and anticipation begins to mount as the slope's brow gets closer and shrill laughter of those indulging in a spot of city swimming filters through the trees.

For those in need of a natural plunge, glide or splash, Hampstead Heath Ponds are a real hidden treasure; a series of three wooded ponds that have been tempting city dwellers into their waters for over 150 years. Made popular in the 1930s and still a big hit today, the ponds are segregated into male, female and mixed, each one veiled from public view by sweeping willows and lush undergrowth. In a secluded spot, Highgate Men's Pond has springboards for diving and a separate fenced in area which is a naturists' (not to be confused with naturalists') delight. Outside the fencing, swimsuits are required. The Kenwood Ladies' Pond is the highest up the hill and surrounded by sprawling foliage. Being nearest to the natural springs at Kenwood it has the clearest, cleanest water and is popular with swimming clubs who use the pool year round. The mixed pond pulls the crowds on a hot summer's day, with everyone free to enjoy the water whenever they want. The open fields of the heath mixed with the elevated views out across London make this a pretty special spot. Tufnell Park and Belsize Park are the nearest tube stations – around a 20 minute walk. Open year round dawn-dusk, T0207-485 4491.

If outdoor swimming grabs your imagination, you are not alone. There are a number of places you can indulge your pleasures across the city. The **Serpentine Lake Swimming Club** meets regularly to take a dip in the waters of Hyde Park – the club has its own changing facilities and swims all year round, whatever the weather, serpentineswimmingclub. com. There is also a wide range of lidos dotted across the city from **Parliament Lido**, Hampstead Heath's unheated 60 m by 28 m pool for serious swimmers, **Brockwell's Art Deco lido**, in the southeast and **Tooting Bec**'s brightly coloured **lido** in the southwest, to **London Fields** Olympic-sized open air pool near Dalston. Lido entry varies from around £2-4.50.

◄ Canoeing by Camden.

Bouldering, Shoreditch	
Provider	DIY
Skill level	All
Time frame	As long as you like
Equipment	Bring climbing equipment, appropriate footwear.
Exertion level	●●●○○

Installed in 2008 as part of the regeneration of Shoreditch, two huge rock sculptures jut out proudly from the flat grassland of Shoreditch Park and Mabley Green. But these are no ordinary works of art. Weighing somewhere in the region of 100 tonnes and standing almost 12 ft high, each chunk of granite is part of an ambitious public realm sculpture project by artist John Frankland. These rocks are just made for bouldering with just enough scars, holes and holds for climbers to get excited over but they are no tease; an experienced climber himself, the artist's concept focused around people physically engaging and interacting with the boulders. And in fact, since they were unveiled in 2008, the ground beneath has rarely been free from crash pads, with able bodies tackling problems across rockface. All in the name of art, of course.

This is no organized space; there is no regular club held here – it is much more a case of just rocking up and having a go. If you're interested in learning more about bouldering before tackling it you can join a climbing club to learn the ropes. There are a number of clubs in the area, each with indoor walls, active members and regular trips to sites like the Shoreditch Boulders on offer. Afterwards, reward yourself with lunch on the pavement at nearby vegetarian Italian deli Saponara, Prebend Street.

Canoeing, Regent's Canal	
Provider	Regent's Canoe Club
Skill level	All
Time frame	As taster evening from 1830
Equipment	Canoe equipment provided on taster days, bring a change of clothing, a towel and trainers to paddle in
Exertion level	●●○○○

The tucked-away waters of the Regent's Canal which wind their way around the city centre are one of London's best kept secrets. Nine miles of water stretching from the aptly named Little Venice near Paddington to Limehouse in the docklands, linked together in a network of well-used waterways, tunnels and city basins. From the water, peering in through the gateways of the properties in Little Venice as you paddle by is a real case of seeing how the other half lives. And sure, while there are river cruises and boat trips that tour the waterways, the best way to experience the canal is by canoe. If you do manage to capsize your craft, try not to swallow too much of the river water. It might look alright, but there are definitely some nasties in it.

The active, friendly Regent's Canoe Club meets twice weekly in Islington, taking to the water every Thursday evening at the City Road Basin. Sharing facilities with the Islington Boat Club, the Canoe Club has no formal coaching at its weekly get-togethers, but there's always a club member on hand to show you around and assist you in getting on the water if you are keen. Once a month there's an open evening for non-members to experience what the club is all about, before deciding whether to become a member. If you choose to join, all sorts of courses are available, from an introduction to white water courses where you can get used to your craft in the calm waters of the river basin, to full-on excursions further afield in search of adventure. **Regent's Canoe Club**, Graham St, N1 8JX, regentscanoeclub.co.uk. Angel is the closest tube, around a 10-minute walk. Membership from £120/year, entitles you to paddle the river, hire equipment and join club trips.

Walking, Primrose Hill	
Provider	DIY
Skill level	None
Time frame	As long as you like
Equipment	A sturdy pair of shoes.
Exertion level	●○○○○

Whether it's strolling the back streets of the city centre, yomping through parkland or meandering along the riverbank, London is packed with interesting city walks to while away an hour or two. Even for Londoners born and bred, there's a lot to be got out of slowing down and taking the time to explore behind the shop fronts and pavements that get the majority of the urban perambulars' attention.

A particularly good central walk takes in Primrose Hill. Starting out at Chalk Farm the best route leads down Regent's Park Road through upmarket neighbourhoods lined with cafés and delicatessens, deviating briefly down Fitzroy Road to number 23 where WB Yeats lived, before ascending Primrose Hill. Don't miss the view from the top to Battersea Power Station and beyond. With every footstep the bustle of London falls away, spilling out in the near distance to be gawped at from the summit, where a handy information plaque points out the sights. The remnants of over-ambitious kite flying mishaps can be seen flapping in the trees, bright coloured tails and wings constantly added to as the wind has its mischievous way. From here the descent leads through the wealthy streets of Queen's Grove before hitting Abbey Road and a chance to read the heavily graffitied walls of the famous studio before the obligatory walk across the most famous zebra crossing in the world. For other ideas, see walklondon.org.uk

∨ Wandering up the Primrose Hill.

Kim Gilmour

∨ The Green credentials of Acorn House on display.

Duncan Kendall

Duncan Kendall

Practicalities

As an urban centre the range of accommodation, restaurants and facilities is vast so it's easy to find somewhere that suits your tastes and budget.

Transport Getting around London in an eco-friendly manner is relatively simple as the public transport links are so good. If you are staying for a while, it's worth investing in an Oyster Card which gives you freedom of the London underground system, the bus network and much of the overground train network, across zones 1-6, much cheaper than buying individual day tickets, tfl.gov.uk/oyster.

Sleeping £££ **Base2Stay**, Kensington, T0207-244 2255, base2stay.com, combines the design sensibility of a boutique hotel with the ease of a self service apartment within an ethical framework. The townhouse and mews have been converted into 67 different guest rooms, some interconnecting, all with en suite bathroom, kitchen units and free Wi-Fi. There is a 24-hr reception and daily maid service. With the Gold Award for Green Tourism and a member of Hospitable Climates, a government initiative to reduce carbon emissions in the hospitality industry, Base2Stay ensures their air conditioning and heating don't circulate unnecessarily, its lighting is all low energy and its cleaning materials are all ecologically sound. £££ **The Zetter**, St John's Square, Clerkenwell, EC1M 5RJ, T0207-324 4444, in is an award-winning eco hotel near the Shoreditch bouldering sites. A converted Victorian warehouse the cool 58 bedroom luxury hotel has paid attention to detail, with natural pigment painted walls, duck-down duvets and even wool-knit covered hot water bottles but at a starting price of £180 a night, you'd expect them to. Most rooms are double glazed and compact, while on the top level studio rooms with floor-to-ceiling windows and wooden decking have great views across London. Sustainable and recycled materials were used in the renovation of the building, while the air conditioning uses water pumped from the hotel's own bore hole, which also flushes toilets. £££ **KWest Hotel**, T0870-0274343 in Shepherd's Bush is a chic, urban hotel popular with the media and music set, with BBC TV centre and Endemol studios just minutes up the road. In fact the KWest used to be BBC premises until it was transformed into a slickly designed 222 bedroom hotel with a subtle but ever present green conscience. The hotel has five ground source boiler pumps that draw heat from the earth, and has reduced its hot water temperature by 2 degrees to save energy. A third of all water used in washing and rinsing is recycled as is all paper and all the hotel's lights are low energy. At the other end of the scale, £ **Earls Court Hostel**, T0845-371 9114, is a clean, basic and friendly hostel with growing green credentials. Part of the £1.7 million modernization of the building, a new energy efficient boiler and pipes have been installed as well as low energy bulbs throughout. Out in the garden a compost recycling system in planned along with rainwater collection and a new organic vegetable plot. The hostel sleeps 186 in 2, 3, 4, 6 and 10-bedded dorms and all shared accommodation is in single sex dormitories.

Eating & drinking London is literally awash with organic pubs, cafés, restaurants and eateries. A city-wide chain of 9 restaurants, **Leon**, leonrestaurants.co.uk, aims to bring full flavoured, ethically sourced food to the mass market, with quick, tasty and delicious meals served in stylish surroundings. They've gained recognition from the RSPCA for their responsible sourcing, have a slant on seasonal produce and a team committed to recycling and composting their packaging, something which is soon to be rolled out to all their stores. Fresh and Wild, part of the Whole Foods Market have organic supermarket-cum-deli-cum-cafés across London. Their fresh seasonal produce and ethically sourced treats could see your wallet emptied all too easily, while their deliciously tempting deli counter and smoothie bar are ideal for a fast refuel or for gathering together some organic fodder for some al fresco dining. Alternatively if you fancy a quality sitdown meal which leaves your conscience gleaming, try the **Waterhouse** restaurant, T0207-003 0123. Based in east London and run by the award-winning charitable regeneration organization The Shoreditch Trust, this restaurant not only serves up delicious, ethical fare, it is also a social enterprise reinvesting in the community and delivering for planet, people and profit. On top of all that, they also produce their own bottled water on site, using a premium Greencare filtering system. **Acorn House Restaurant**, Swinton St, WC1X 9NT, T0207-812 1842, another social enterprise created and run by the Shoreditch Trust, the restaurant aims to be environmentally conscious and sustainable in every aspect of their business whether buying local, seasonal, organic produce from independent suppliers, buying sustainable fish and seafood, using bio-diesel transport in London, limiting water and energy use and waste or recycling up to 80% of their waste. But it's not just a 'worthy' cause, the quality, modern, exciting food they produce backs up their endeavours. Mains around £10. **Mildred's**, Lexington St, serves fantastic vegetarian fare from wholesome, tasty curries to cleansing yet filling salads in relaxed, unpretentious surroundings. They showcase is perhaps the huge veggie burger of the day with fat chips for less than £8. The make an effort to use organic ingredients sourced from small independents. Definitely one to hunt out.

Also try If swimming, bouldering, canoeing or walking don't take your fancy – why not try taking to two wheels. London's parks are perfect for cycling, with long flat pathways, winding past lakes, along rivers, through woodland and across open grass. There's also an endless network of cycle paths which runs across the capital. Check out lcc.org.uk for more details.

Surfing Brighton

Provider	DIY
Skill level	Novice-advanced
Time frame	All day
Equipment	Surfboard, wetsuit.
Exertion level	●●●●●

The sky glows crimson through the clouds as the sun drops down below the horizon, the seafront sucking every last drop of colour out of the day. Stretching out to sea, the glimmering lights of Brighton pier illuminate the water below, where waist high glass rolls in set after set. The sea bobs with people eager to lap up every last moment of a rare surf day in the seaside resort. One after the next, long, cruisy lefts peel off the pier, their smooth surfaces and foaming lips causing those in the water to salivate as they wait their turn to take off, nip into trim and glide down the line. Hands up high, the more nimble footed in the line-up dance their way up and down their logs, smiles broad on their faces until they can no longer see their feet and dusk demands that it's time to paddle the short distance into the shore.

Surfing in Brighton can be a somewhat tricky affair. Abundant patience is needed to wait out flat day after flat day until the faintest trickle of hope pulses in on a southwesterly swell. And whatever it brings, if there's a wave the water goes wild; crammed full of people eager to catch their share of 2 ft onshore mush. The good days do happen though and when they do there are a number of different spots along the coastline that can work. The Wedge, sheltered from westerly winds, breaks off the large stone breakwater and is popular with bodyboarders, while The Piers can produce a build up of sand around the pilings providing rolling rights and lefts – rich pickings for longboarders. Further to the west The Marina is considered the area's best break, producing short, powerful rights and lefts when a channel storm pushes through.

"We can get some great waves down here when it's on," explains Stu Brass, Brighton surfer and owner of Soulsports.co.uk, "but to get these waves you'll have to be dedicated to checking the surf reports and flexible enough to actually surf it. I'm always astounded by the number of people that manage to bunk off for a quick surf in the middle of the day…it goes to show the force is strong in Brighton." The number of people paddling out when the surf hits can mean fierce competition. "The anticipation is huge. You can get up to 50 people in the water, even if it's just a one foot wave dribbling through," Stu continues, "localism does strike now and again but so long as you respect each other's waves you'll find there's no trouble."

However there's more to stay on the watch for aside from the odd hint of localism. "Brighton has 80 Olympic swimming pools-worth of raw sewage dumped into the sea daily which obviously has a negative impact on the environment," says Andy Cummins, from Surfers Against Sewage. "There's also the run-off from the land after heavy rains, look out for CSOs and rivers as sources of harmful bacteria and viruses."

∨ Cutting back in Brighton.

But, it's not all bad. Despite the water being the colour of chocolate milkshake, the beaches are relatively clean on a day to day basis – a number of the beaches have a achieved a basic pass from the Marine Conservation Society in their Good Beach Guide. And while the waves may not be world class, the surf scene is vibrant and the high level of stoke running on a daily basis is truly infectious. Emerging from a one foot day amped and excited you'll know that some of that local enthusiasm has rubbed off and perhaps encouraged you, subconsciously, to re-examine just what surfing is all about.

Stef Kerswell/photoslags

◄ Summer's annual Paddle Round the Pier.

Practicalities

A cool blend of urban and surf culture and just 1½ hrs from London, Brighton is burgeoning as a surf destination. When it's on, the locals are out in force and there is plenty of fun to be had. There is an ever-growing number of surf shops and shapers as well as surf friendly cafés and diners. Of course, Brighton has plenty of places to stay along with all sorts of pubs, bars, clubs and facilities to keep you happy when it's flat.

Transport Brighton's train station is served by Southern Trains with regular services to London Victoria. Surfboards are welcome on board outside of peak times, southernrailway.com. Brighton can also be reached by coach from most major UK cities, nationalexpress.com.

Sleeping For budget surf friendly accommodation try £ **The Grapevine**, T01273-777717, with 2 locations seafront and north it has clean shared, and private, rooms and is seconds away from the water. NB can be popular with stags. Quirky, kooky £££ **Paskins Townhouse**, Charlotte St, T01273-601203, has the gold award for Green Tourism. The brekkies are local, organic, freerange and served in their art deco breakfast room. If self-catering suits you better, try **Brighton Holiday Homes**, brightonholidayhomes.co.uk, which has a range of different apartments, cottages and chalets on its books for you to choose from. They vary from compact seafront one bedroom's with all the basics to 3 bedroom cottages in the Lanes, boasting stylish interiors, open fireplaces and cute courtyards. **Camping** 20 mins away from Brighton seafront, **Blacklands Farm Campsite**,Henfield, BN5 9AT, T01273-493528, is a quiet meadow backed by tall trees and a carp lake. A family-run farm it's basic but comfortable with views out over rural Sussex. Year round. **Sheepcote Valley Caravan Site**, BN2 5TS, T0127-626546, is within walking distance of Brighton marina and because of this a little pricier, open year round.

Eating & drinking **Bill's Produce Store**, The Depot, North Rd, T01273-692894, is an outstanding organic produce shop-cum-café where you can stock up on fruit, vegetables and herbs before sitting down to a well priced home-made, organic lunch or a wholesome brekkie washed down with a freshly whizzed smoothie. Ooh, did I mention the brownies? **Woodies Longboard Diner**, Kingsway, Hove, T01273-430300, (by Ocean Sports), is a 1950s inspired theme diner where you can get a stack of pancakes or a generous burger and fries to sate your post surf hunger. **The Real Eating Company** which is all about quality local, free range and fair trade produce as well as top notch home cooking has a cracking restaurant in Hove, Western Rd, T01273-221444 – breakfasts, lunch and dinner – from an affordable soup of the day to a £16 Sussex rump steak. Café in Brighton, Ship St simple sarnies and yummy cakes.

Resources For south coast surf reports check out sharkbait. co.uk. If you're looking to make a purchase, head to **Ocean Sports Boardriders**, Kingsway, Hove, boardriders.co.uk, or **Filf**, West St in nearby Rottingdean, T01273-307465, filf.co.uk, both with a good range of hardware and experience. For lessons, **Pure Spirit Surf School**, T01273-605384, purespiritsurfschool.com, is run by 2 times English Masters Champion Cliff Cox. Private one on one coaching or lessons, including equipment, from £55.

Also try Brighton is home to the annual Paddle Round the Pier beach festival, which takes place in Jul and sees all manner of people launching into the water on all types of craft from surfboards to inflatables in order to raise money for organizations including RNLI and Surfaid International. See paddleroundthepier.com for more information.

> Lowdown

⊖ **Prices**
Free or £15 with Pure Spirit Surf School.

⊘ **Season**
All year round, although swells are far more likely in autumn and winter.

⊕ **Don't miss**
The chance to see yourself surfing, check out photoslags.co.uk to see if your efforts have been caught on camera.

⊗ **Avoid**
Unless you are an experienced surfer, avoid the marina.

Mountain biking Southeast: best of the rest

Provider	(see details)
Skill level	Beginner-advanced
Time frame	From 2 hrs +
Equipment	Bike, helmet, map, repair kit, inner tube, snacks, water
Exertion level	●●●●●

Epping Forest

Offering salvation to the capital's MTB community, Epping Forest delivers around 6000 acres of off-road riding, right on the edge of the sprawling city. While the forest doesn't deliver much in the way of long climbs and intense descents, the 12 miles stretch of undulating terrain draped in a grassland carpet and ancient woodland canopies of oak and beech provides plenty of opportunity to lose yourself. A network of bridleways running through the forest make for easy riding while there is plenty of singletrack and the odd short, sharp climb for the adventurous to seek out. The Central Line of the London Underground system passes the forest with Woodford and Buckhurst Hill being the most convenient stations. Bikes are only permitted on over ground sections of track meaning only from Stratford heading eastwards. At High Beech, there's a tea hut which also sells forest maps and the Royal Oak Pub for refuelling post ride. **Heales Cycles**, Hale End Road, E4 9PT, T0208-527 1592, is well stocked with hardware and accessories and organizes a weekly ride in the forest every Sunday, 0900.

Aston Hill Bike Park

In the Chiltern Hills, this area of Outstanding Natural Beauty is also home to an area of outstanding MTB park potential. Taking over the steep slopes of some prime Forestry Commission woodland just outside Wendover, the park features five graded down hill tracks all of which include some quality, steep and challenging sections, four cross track as well as a stunning six mile cross country loop

> A bit of south coast down time.
< Jenny Copnall, Chilterns.

which combines swooping, undulating singletrack descents and a switch-back climb. **Aston Hill Bike Park**, HP22 5NQ, T0844-736 8451, rideastonhill.co.uk. For those living nearby, annual adult membership costs £68 and includes full access to the park, CTC membership and third party insurance. Alternatively pay to play on a day to day basis, £6 in advance or £7 on the door. **Mountain Mania**, Tring, HP23 4BX, T01442-822458, is the nearest MTB shop. They are well stocked and offer service and repairs. For skills courses contact **Firecrest**, T07711-638195.

Isle of Wight
Shaded woodland valleys and gentle cycle ways isn't all the Isle of Wight has to offer, the chalk downland throws up plenty of long challenging ascents matched by equally fast descents to make this an interesting and well-rounded MTB destination. If you're after a decent bit of singletrack head to Brighstone Forest, alternatively the island is riddled with well marked, quality bridleways and cycle ways to follow that thread their way across the landscape and circumnavigate the coastline. Ride coast to coast between Yarmouth and Freshwater Bay following sections of the old railway line before

heading over the Downs from where you can take in the sights of the island or try the Tennyson Trail with incredible views out across the channel. Rent MTB from **Wight Cycle Hire**, T01983-761800 – prices start at £8/half day or £60/week.

Bedgebury Forest, Kent
Over nine miles of singletrack featuring switchbacks and berms, a freeride area, dirt jumps and north shore are some of the delights created to tempt the MTB fraternity to this 2000-acre Forestry Commission woodland in deepest, darkest Kent. If you're after something a little less challenging there's always the 5½ miles family cycle trail. The facilities are also quality. **Quench**, T01580-879694, are well stocked and provide repairs and servicing as well as bike hire, and if the going has been tough on you and your bike you can hose off post ride in the on-site showers before grabbing a quick cuppa. Locals may want to join the Bedgebury Forest Cycle Club who get involved in trail building and influence the development of the MTB facilities here. As well as meeting for night rides and a bit of a social, benefits include discounts at Quench, annual parking pass and free showers. boarsonbikes.co.uk

◄ The Ridgeway passes through the Chilterns.

Wig Worland

Walking The Seven Sisters

Provider	DIY
Skill level	All
Time frame	4 hrs
Equipment	Walking boots
Exertion level	●●○○○

In the valley summer sits heavy in the air, not a breeze to disturb the humming throng, busy about their morning round, perfunctorily ticking off their daily roster of blooms. The wild flowers growing through the fields of long grass are greeted with equal enthusiasm as the tidy tangle of sweet peas marshalled on neat trellises and the heavy cascades of rambling roses that have been coerced by green fingers into arches. Nearby, the contents of the Tiger Inn spill on to the green where satisfied walkers who have conquered the Seven Sisters stretch out, rewarding their efforts with a pint of Beachy Head Original or Legless Rambler.

The eight mile circular from East Dean leads you on an undulating journey across the coastal hills of the Seven Sisters. Ever since the South Downs rolled into the English Channel, time and motion has worked tirelessly to cast and reshape this stretch into an impressive wall of white cliffs. But these vast, chalk ramparts have been unable to halt the sea's energy and are steadily receding. As if enraged by its diminishing position, the coastline retaliates, claiming lives of seafarers and grounding ships that dare navigate these unrelenting waters. After climbing Went Hill there are, a little confusingly, still seven more sisters to summit but with a green carpet underfoot and an expansive blue horizon over your left shoulder, there is little to worry about – provided of course you don't stray too close to that cliff edge!

At the mouth of River Cuckmere, the path weaves inland skirting the Meanders – an ideal spot for a paddle or splash, and continues north to Exceat. Passing above the A259 the route leads through the densely wooded Friston Forest before cutting back over the road into the top of East Dean, where the promise of a Legless Rambler awaits.

❮ The Seven Sisters lit up in the glow of a day's end.

Les Andrean

Practicalities
A mile from the coast, East Dean is a little slice of heaven with a cracking village pub and a number of eateries.

Transport   Eastbourne train station is well connected. Regular onward bus to East Dean. – 712, 713.

Sleeping   In the heart of East Dean, **Beachy Head Farm**, T01323-423878, has 3 self-catering cottages, beautifully converted from 18th-century farm buildings. Sleeping 4-6 they have the gold award for Green Tourism and come with thoughtful welcome packs. From £360/week. **Camping**   For those wanting to pitch their tent in the peace and quiet of the Seven Sisters Country Park, The Foxhole, Exceat, Seaford, BN25 4AG, T01323-870280, is ideal if basic – there are a few loos but the shower is cold. £4.50/person, discount if arriving under own steam. Camping barn also from £6/night, booking essential. Apr-Oct.

Eating & drinking   The Tiger Inn, East Dean, BN20 0DA, T01323-423209, with thatched roof, low beams and log fires delivers a warm village pub welcome in the cold winter months. Here the ploughman's is king. Wash it down with local ale from the Beachy Head Brewery (part of the farm's diversification). Pretty B&B also available, rooms £90, T01323-423878. For a pot of tea and slice of cake, head next door to the **Hikers Rest** – they'll even do you a packed lunch for your walk. If you want to organize your own, step into the **Frith and Little Deli and Café** on the green for some of the best local and international produce. En route, tea up at the **Exceat Farmhouse** tea rooms.

Also try   The walk from Eastbourne to East Dean via the infamous Beachy Head and the Seven Sisters before cutting inland to the village – about 7 miles.

❯ Lowdown

❸ Prices
Free.

❂ Season
Year round although spring and early summer, when the white cliff edges are thrift-dappled is the showcase.

❍ Don't miss
A chocolate brownie at the Frith and Little Deli – you'll walk it off!!

❂ Avoid
If walking along the beach below the cliffs don't get cut off by the tide, check times and details locally.

Climbing Harrison's Rocks

Provider	Nuts4Climbing
Skill level	All
Time frame	From a 3-hr taster to a full 6-week course
Equipment	All climbing equipment provided
Exertion level	●●●●○

Squelching a muddy path through the fern undergrowth, warm sunlight begins to break through the birch trees as the first imposing boulder of Harrison's Rocks heaves into view. Already teaming with people, nimble bodies are making the most of the fine morning, skilfully clambering upwards as their ropes stretch high to an anchor point then fall back down. Gripped in the hands of their climbing buddy the rope remains taut, as they shout words of encouragement from the ground below.

Called 'top roping', this technique is essential at Harrison's Rocks, one of the southeast's most popular climbing sites. Formed from southern sandstone – a crumbly, fragile rock that is fighting a war of attrition – Harrison's is owned and protected by the British Mountaineering Council (BMC) which encourages and educates climbers to use the right equipment and employ the necessary techniques, like wearing the correct footwear and hanging ropes in a way so as not to see-saw through the rocks, in order to preserve the outcrop for future generations. "Correct top roping at Harrison's Rocks isn't just about preventing erosion," explains Sarah Cullen, an avid climber, who is involved in the upkeep and management of the site on behalf of the BMC, "it's also a method which means if you lose your footing you don't fall, you merely come away from the rocks – great for learning and progressing. Great lengths are taken to prevent erosion on these very soft rocks," expands Sarah who also runs Nuts4Climbing specializing in courses focused on developing the proper skills for climbing southern sandstone . "They literally are 'squashed-together-sand' with a weathered harder layer on the outside which is only a few millimetres thick."

< Sarah Cullen: "Climbing relaxes the mind in that when you are doing it, you are completely focused on what you are doing. It brings a sense of achievement and takes you to the most wonderful places that you didn't even know existed, and would never otherwise have explored."

Based in Groombridge, the majority of Sarah's courses make use of Harrison's Rocks, from the challenging overhangs to its low level boulders and caves. The three-hour taster course brings the experience and rush of climbing in a safe and relaxed environment, providing a key to climbing independently. After a safety briefing and equipment check, the course warms up with some scrambling; learning how to move on small rocks and through caves without ropes. From here the session moves on to some roped rock climbs, and having eyed up the route from below while being fixed into your safety harness you'll soon be carried away by the sensation of scaling heady heights over the tactile stone surface.

And if the taster gets you interested, Nuts4Climbing runs other courses to help you progress. One and two-day courses build on knowledge and introduce more challenging rope climbs, developing skills and rope techniques. If

> Sarah leads the way over the southern sandstone.

you want to go all the way, the full six-week course means you learn you all the skills for climbing on this terrain independently – your key to real exploration of the freedom rock climbing brings. It offers a holisitic approach, covers equipment and kit from basics like appropriate footwear to safely setting up the ropes needed for southern sandstone climbing. Environmental and preservation issues facing this type of rock are covered, which all ties back to good climbing practice.

The ledges, cracks, crags and walls of Harrison's Rocks are enough to keep you busy for a lifetime, but if, on completing the six-week course, you're bitten by the climbing bug, Sarah and her team can recommend a variety of other sites in the area and further afield for you to try out your new found techniques. "If you wanted to progress further, you would be ready to join us on weekend away trips to the Sea Cliffs of Portland Bill, or the Gritstone Edges of the Peak District." Harrison's Rocks are just the tip of your climbing adventures.

Practicalities

Groombridge is a small village between Tunbridge Wells and Crowborough just under 1 mile away from Harrison's Rocks. The village itself has a handful of shops and a number of pubs, while accommodation can be easily found in nearby Tunbridge Wells.

Transport Tunbridge Wells has a station, 3½ miles away from Groombridge. Coach services run to Tunbridge Wells from London, nationalexpress.co.uk.

Sleeping The contemporary **££ Brew House**, T01892-520587, has 10 bedrooms, individually designed with all the mod cons. Slick and stylish, it's got a cosmopolitan feel and provides free Wi-Fi for its guests. A locally sourced breakfast is served in their adjoining restaurant, **The School House**, which also offers a daily changing, seasonal dinner menu. **£ The Crown Inn**, TN3 9QH, has simple B&B in lovely beamed rooms with preferential rates for those taking one of Sarah's courses. Near the Harrison's Rocks, **£ Manor House Farm**, T01892-740279, offers camping and bed and breakfast on the farm land. The camping is basic but does the job and the bed and breakfast is comfortable with a great breakfast cooked on the farmhouse Aga using their own eggs, home-made jam and marmalade and meat from local suppliers.

Eating & drinking In Groombridge the popular **Crown Inn**, T01892-864742, serves quality home-cooked food with fresh, local fish and a daily changing specials board. The bar also has some of the area's best real ales on tap. Alternatively, in Tunbridge Wells, acclaimed restaurant **The Beacon**, T01892-524252, offers a touch of Victorian style with top end cuisine. A member of Kentish Fayre, The Beacon sources fresh local seasonal ingredients whenever possible across its set and a la carte, menus, which change daily. In the summer there are also regular hog roasts out on the veranda where you can enjoy impressive views over the Kentish countryside.

Resources The Sandstone Volunteer Group help to maintain the rocks — get involved: sandstonevolunteers.nildram.co.uk.

Also try Almost wild camping. If you fancy spending the night at Harrison's Rocks, a very basic campsite was set up years ago as a memorial to climber Julie Tullis, who died on K2 in August 1986 after reaching the summit. The campground is wardened by Chris Tullis, Julie's son, has 16 pitches and is found next to the car park. There's an honesty box for the upkeep and pitches are hidden from each other in secluded clearings among birch and fern undergrowth. There's no need to book so you can turn up, pitch and relax.

∧ Taking the next step at Harrison's Rocks.

> Lowdown

ⓘ Directory
Nuts4Climbing, Merlin's Cottage, Motts Mill, Groombridge, Tunbridge Wells, Kent, TN3 9PE, T01892-860670, rockclimbingclasses.co.uk.

ⓢ Prices
£50 for the taster session.

ⓢ Season
All year round.

ⓢ Don't miss
The chance to explore the Harrison's Rocks caves. "While climbing, hang your karabiner over the edge of the crag," reminds Sarah.

ⓧ Avoid
"We ask people not to abseil on these rocks as bouncing around on them causes holds to break off," says Sarah. "Once the outer crust of the rocks is damaged, the sand will simply wash away when it rains or with wind".

Canoeing & kayaking Medway

Provider	Kent Canoes
Skill level	All levels
Time frame	From a few hours to a full 5-day course
Equipment	All canoeing and safety equipment provided. Remember to bring a warm dry change of clothes
Exertion level	●●●○○

It's a calm day in rural Kent, and a handful of kayaks slice through the sheltered waters of the Medway, the gentle lap of river against hull the only sound as smiling faces and taut arms gradually get used to manoeuvering their craft. Two experienced canoeists paddle past, offering a taste of what's to come as they weave their way along the riverbank towards the more challenging waters downstream.

The Medway meanders through rural Kent, stretching for 70 miles across the county, with a 19 mile navigable stretch from Leigh Sluice near Tonbridge to Allington Lock near Maidstone. It has placid waters perfect for learning between Maidstone and East Farleigh in particular, while the picturesque stretches from Yalding to Tonbridge require more skill, with some pulse-racing white water and weirs to navigate.

Catering for both camps, Kent Canoes offers everything from taster sessions and BCU qualifications to open canoe guided trips and excursions further afield. The team of qualified instructors are all passionate about the sport and the area, using their knowledge and enthusiasm to get people making the most of the river.

The BCU One Star will have novices confident in the basic techniques of manoeuvring their kayak out on to flat waters in one day. Having mastered weight transference it's on to the water to get a feel for the boat's manoeuvrability, before learning the art of forward paddling.

Safety and rescue skills are a key aspect of the day – including learning how to exit a capsized boat, which should see you receive your first star.

Practicalities

The small village of Wrotham is half an hour outside London. With four pubs to revive sea legs literally yards from each other, it's a fine base.

Transport Wrotham is in the middle of the M20 and M26 and the train station there is served by Southeastern rail. Bus links between the station and village centre – a walkable mile, arriva.co.uk.

Sleeping ££The Bull Hotel, Wrotham, T01732-789800, dates back to 1385. Restored to retain original features including exposed beams, fireplaces and inglenooks. Enjoy homecooked, locally sourced full English breakfast. At nearby Sevenoaks £££ Cabbages and Kings, Church Rd, NT14 7HE, T01959-533054, is all about the extra touches – hot water bottles and wheat bags available for aching limbs and a selection of daily and seasonal specials on offer for breakfast. ££ Anchor Inn, T01622-814359, Yalding is near one of Kent Canoes common launch sites offering comfortable accommodation in a pretty thatched inn on the edge of the river. **Camping** 4 miles from Wrotham the Thriftwood Campsite, TN15 7PB, T01732-822261, is in the heart of the Kentish North Downs. Set in 20 acres of woodland with statics also available.

Eating & drinking The Bull Hotel's, T01732-789800, menu is laden with local produce from the fish straight off the boat to the meat, vegetables and selection of cheeses. There's even a local ale or two – all reasonably priced and expertly prepared. Try the bar menu if you fancy something lighter. In Sevenoaks, **The Vine**, T01732-469510, overlooks the oldest cricket ground in England and prides itself on its local supplier relationships and quality food as a result.

Resources Kent Canoes stocks a full range of equipment, and can even help source quality secondhand equipment, kentcanoes.co.uk.

Also try With medieval bridges, church spires and castles and even kingfishers to look out for, walking the Medway Valley is a great way of exploring the area on dry land. The route weaves through fields, woodland, orchards and hop gardens and there are plenty of picturesque places to stop, take a breather and even have a drink en route.

> Lowdown

ⓘ Directory
Kent Canoes,
New House Farm,
Kemsing Rd, Wrotham,
Kent TN15 7BU,
T01732-886688,
kentcanoes.co.uk,

Ⓢ Prices
From £45 per person.

Ⓢ Season
Courses run Mar-Oct.

Ⓞ Don't miss
Winter white water paddling at the sluice weir, East Peckham – if you're brave enough.

Ⓧ Avoid
Paddling below Allington on a low tide, you'll get stuck. Check with the Environment Agency for tide times.

Surfing Joss Bay

Provider	DIY
Skill level	Novice-experienced
Time frame	All day
Equipment	Surfboard, wetsuit
Exertion level	●●●●●

< A fun day at Joss Bay – the sloping geography of the sea bed can rob swells of some of their power.

The sun's early morning rays peer out from behind the cloud bank and the crisp chill of autumn hangs in the air. On the beach, dark suited figures strap on leashes and stretch, before bounding through the white water to reach the undulating calm out back. Shoulder high waves peel off the reef which juts out from the chalky white cliffs where experienced surfers line up to take off, while on the beach the first surf school of the day is shaking itself into action. A big swell is running, wrapping into Joss Bay and bringing the beach to life. The car park is full and the water is teaming with locals making the most of the mild weather and good conditions before the thickly neoprened necessity of winter kicks in.

This is a bay that sits between the traditional seaside resorts of Margate and Ramsgate, like a child squeezed between two jolly, buxom aunts on a summer's holiday. And while this region may not immediately spring to mind when thinking of potential surfing hotspots, Kent has a long history of wave sliding, with shops and chatty boardriders sharing stories and photographs of eager souls taking on the surf as far back as the 1960s. In modern times, surfing in this corner of England has boomed and Joss Bay is a key focal point.

The beach's shallow, sloping seabed makes it a good place to learn and a BSA registered school runs lessons here throughout the year. Alternatively you can hire a board and wetsuit and go it alone. However, Joss Bay isn't just for learners; when a solid easterly or northeasterly comes in the surf can really pump. For the more confident, winter can pack a punch with the beach working throughout the tide, so it's well worth checking a chart and heading down to the shoreline if you're in the area.

Practicalities
Broadstairs is a quaint little seaside resort packing everything you need, from surf shops to accommodation

Transport Broadstairs train station is well connected.

Sleeping **£££ Burrow House**, T01843-601817, offers premium boutique accommodation in a renovated Victorian townhouse. With an award for its organic, locally sourced breakfast, it's small but very well formed. To the north **£ YHA Margate**, Royal Esplanade, T0845-371 9130, is simple and affordable. In quiet Birchington village, **St Nicholas Camping**, T01843-847245, offers basic pitches in a countryside location. Farmhouse B&B also.

Eating & drinking Restaurant54, Albion St, T01843-867150, prides itself on its fresh local ingredients, inventive menu and warm friendly atmosphere. Also try **Oscar Road**, T01843-872442, a cute vintage café serving lashings of nostalgia with Fairtrade coffee, organic goods and locally sourced snacks including crab sandwiches and pints of prawns.

Resources Joss Bay Surf School, T07812-991195, jossbay. co.uk, runs surf lessons throughout the year. Run by skater and local surfer Dan Chapman, **Kent Surf School**, T07970-870098, kentsurfschool.co.uk, operates from Viking Bay, Broadstairs. Lessons £35, board and wetsuit hire also available. **Revolution Skatepark**, Oakwood Industrial Estate, T01843-866707, has a well stocked surf shop

Also try The flat 27-mile Viking Coastal Trail takes in the best of the Isle of Thanet's coastline before cutting inland to sample the countryside — ideal for a bit of casual cruising. Trail map: visitthanet.co.uk. Bike hire from **Ken's Bike Shop**, Eaton Rd, Margate, T01843-221422.

> **Lowdown**

❸ **Prices**
Free or £10/half day board and wetsuit hire.

☀ **Season**
Joss Bay works best in the autumn and winter.

◉ **Don't miss**
A stroll along the harbour pier with ice cream in hand. Seaside heaven.

✖ **Avoid**
High summer, the sea is often flat and the town is heaving and the crowds arrive.

Best of the rest Southeast: activities

SUP, Witterings	
Provider	2xs
Skill level	Novice-experienced
Time frame	2 hrs for a lesson
Equipment	All paddleboarding equipment provided.
Exertion level	●●●●●

If you've tried surfing and are looking for a new challenge, or just like the idea of mixing it up, it's worth giving paddleboarding a go. With small, gentle conditions most of the year, West and East Wittering are ideal for getting to grips with the sport. Backed by the golden sands of Bracklesham Bay and with a friendly, laidback scene there's plenty of room for everyone and, although longboards and windsurfers dominate the water, a crew of regular paddleboarders can be seen heading out here. If you want to go it alone there are a couple of places with equipment for hire, but for first-timers, lessons are definitely recommended. 2xs offer a range of SUP lessons from entry level, where you'll focus on finding your balance, mastering the paddle and taking off, and intermediate where you'll develop turning and reverse paddle skills, to advanced, where it's all about improving your take-off and bottom turn. There's also a one to one session available with video coaching, to really fine tune your technique. **2xs**, T01243-513077, 2xs. co.uk, two-hour paddleboarding lesson from £45. **£ Stubcroft Farmhouse**, T01243-671469. Camping and B&B on an environmentally-friendly sheep farm within walking distance of East Wittering. The paddock is planted with conservation trees and hedges, while the campers have use of six 'eco loos'. Arrive in an electric car, on bike, or on foot, and you'll get a 10% discount.

Canoeing, River Thames	
Provider	DIY
Skill level	All
Time frame	Whenever you like
Equipment	Canoes can be hired at numerous spots along the Thames.
Exertion level	●●●○○

Leisurely paddling along the river, idly taking in the sights and sounds with someone to share the effort and experience, Canadian or 'open top' canoeing is a popular pastime on the River Thames and there are numerous places the length of the river where you can hire a canoe for a couple of hours to give it a try. Alternatively, if you fancy something a little more in-depth, companies like Thames Canoes offer guided river trips so you can get the most out of your time on the water. With 30 years canoeing experience and ten years living on the banks of the Thames under his belt, owner Andy Jackson's knowledge and passion for both feed into every trip he runs. He explores a range of routes year round, including the rural Mapledurham to ancient Marlow Lock stretch, whose nearby corn mill is mentioned in the Domesday Book, and an urban route from Marlow to Runnymede, taking in Windsor. All the equipment is provided and as Andy knows the river so well, he always includes a pit stop at one of the excellent pubs or tearooms which the river floats past. A two-day excursion of the River Thames costs £130. **Thames Canoes**, T0162-847 8787, thamescanoes.co.uk. Alternatively, for half-day and full-day Canadian canoe hire try **Thames Canoe Hire**, T07960-973709, thamescanoehire.co.uk.

Foraging, Midhurst	
Provider	Woodcraft School
Skill level	Novice-experienced
Time frame	All day
Equipment	Provided.
Exertion level	●●○○○

With woodland, heathland and lakeside banks all in easy distance, foraging for food in West Sussex is a diverse and rewarding affair. Aside from fungi, the countryside can yield all sorts of wild food so long as you know what's edible and where it can be found. Which is where experienced bushcraftsman John Ryder and his team at Woodcraft School can help. Running classes and qualifications in bushcraft since 1997, their short courses include everything from bow making to hedgerow foraging.

Sidney Cripps

∧ Winding through Marlow.

Stuart Evans

∨ Robin Renwick climbing further north extoles the joys of southern sandstone. "The settings are always inspiring, from the cultivated park land atmosphere of Bowles to the crags at Harrisons rising out of the wooded hillside. There are literally hundreds of routes up the rocks, all of which can be safely top roped, with grades from elementary to some of the toughest around. Being the closest rock to London some of the country's top climbers can be seen working out on these rocks."

Focusing on identifying, finding and eating British countryside bounty, the one day 'Hedgerow Gourmet' course starts with a walk to find the best vittles nature has to offer, before returning to camp for a late lunch and a chance to sample what you have picked. From bark and roots, to leaves and flowers, you'll finish the day amazed at what you can eat and how good it tastes, leaving you looking at the countryside in a whole new way. **Woodcraft School**, T01730-816299, woodcraftschool.co.uk, Hedgerow Gourmet course, £75. **Camping** Nearby, **Graffham Campsite**, T01798-867476, is a thickly wooded 20-acre site which feels like wild camping with all the conveniences of a well kept campsite. Keep an eye out for badgers, rabbits, squirrels and foxes, all regularly seen scurrying past quiet pitches.

Walk the Coast, Isle of Wight	
Provider	DIY
Skill level	All
Time frame	4-6 days
Equipment	Sturdy shoes.
Exertion level	●●○○○

Walking the coastline of the Isle of Wight has a lot to offer. Stretching for 67 miles along clifftops and across downland, completing the walk takes between four and six days and covers varied terrain, although all on well maintained footpaths. Starting at the yachting resort of Cowes, the route heads anti-clockwise overlooking the Solent before weaving inland around the Newtown river estuary then on to Yarmouth. From here the trail picks up the coastline once more and heads to Brighstone, with views of The Needles, weaves through National Trust land to the Victorian promenades of Shanklin then on to the sheltered harbour of Bembridge. Next on to Ryde, before heading through woodland and along rivers to return to Cowes. En route, the Newton Creek nature reserve and Hanover Point fossil forest are two particular highlights, as is the magnificent view across Tennyson Downs. The walk can be tackled in stretches with plenty of accommodation dotted along the route. If you would prefer to have a guide to show you round the island, Step by Step Holidays offer a six-day walking break, taking care of accommodation and baggage transfers, so all you need to think about is putting one foot in front of the other. **Step by Step Holidays**, T01983-862403, step-by-step.co.uk.

∧ Walking the Coast Path by Ventnor.

Roger Powley

Climbing, Bowles Rock	
Provider	DIY, or Robin Renwick
Skill level	Novice-experienced
Time frame	½ day
Equipment	All necessary technical and safety equipment provided during lesson, remember to wear comfortable clothing.
Exertion level	●●●●○

Located on the border between Kent and Sussex, the quality, south facing Bowles Rock is popular with climbers across the country for its variety of routes. With more than 150 climbs, this stunning weather worn and element-scarred sandstone crag offers routes of up to 33 ft to suit most ability. Bowles is owned by Bowles Rock Trust and located in the grounds of their outdoor activity centre, but the rock is also open to the public for a nominal fee (around £3 with season tickets available) which goes towards the upkeep of the site. Due to the nature of the site, the use of chalk is discouraged. If you are interested in having lessons, experienced climbing instructor Robin Renwick offers private tuition at the rocks, where he covers safety and environmental awareness (the rocks are southern sandstone and very fragile so require care when climbing), as well as basic rope and climbing techniques. **Bowles Rock**, T01892-665665, bowlesrock.ac. **Robin Renwick**, T01424-434108, robinclimbs.co.uk, one-on-one half-day instruction, £50. The small, **£££-££ Yew House B&B**, Crowborough, T01892-610522, holds the gold standard green tourist award.

Swimming, Pells Pool	
Provider	Pells Pool
Skill level	All
Time frame	1200-1900
Equipment	Bathers and towel.
Exertion level	●●●○○

For a wonderful swimming experience Pells Pool, fed by a natural spring is the oldest, fresh water, outdoor pool in the country. Opened in the 1860s this 40 m by 20 m pool is a civilized affair surrounded by a tree-lined lawn and a sun terrace and set within a nature reserve by the banks of the Ouse. There's even a café on site serving fresh coffee, cakes and other home-made treats. Open May-September, 1200-1900 – now that is civilized. Adults from £3.80. Pells Pool, Brook Street, Lewes, BN27 2PW, T01273-472334.

Best of the rest Southeast: sleeping & eating

The Duke of Cambridge, London ◑
The Duke of Cambridge, St Peter's St, Islington, N1 8JT, T0207-359 3066.

The quality food cooked and created here is all about seasonal, organic produce sourced as locally as possible – no mean feat for a pub in the heart of the big smoke. Despite this, nothing arrives by air freight, in fact they manage to source 80% of their fresh ingredients from the surrounding home counties, working with small independents and farms and became the first gastropub to be certified by the Soil Association. The decor and food is rustic, British and modern with delights like rabbit, pollack and butternut squash gracing the menus – there are always two fish, two meat and two vegetarian options. Main's come in around the £13 mark meaning it isn't cheap, but while it's easy to forget, you are in London you know! They also hold an extensive organic wine list and their enthusiasm for an organic way of life is so infectious they managed to convince two local breweries to become certified so they could supply the pub with decent ales and lagers. The pub has won plenty of praise and awards for its food while the efforts of MD Geetie Singh who set up the business have been rewarded with an MBE.

Gotten Manor, Isle of Wight ◎
Gotten Manor, Gotten Lane, Isle of Wight, PO38 2HQ, gottenmanor.co.uk.

All exposed beams and lime washed walls, nestling beneath St Catherine's Down, Gotten Manor is certainly something a bit special. Well off the beaten track, this lovingly restored 14th-century manor holds the gold Green Island award thanks to the owner's ethical stance. Aside from minimizing her footprint and regulating consumption of natural resources, Caroline makes her own jams, marmalades and yoghurts which are served at breakfast and sources everything else locally and ethically. This means you can feel pretty good about yourself as you luxuriate in your roll top bath, wrap yourself in your fluffy towel, and settle in for

a weekend of country walks and romance in very fitting surroundings. Rooms from £75. Self-catering cottages are also available.

St Martin's Tearooms, Chichester ◑
St Martin's Tearooms, St Martin's St, Chichester, PO19 1NP, T01243-786715.

Calm yet eccentric – whoever thought those two words would go together? Yet, they do so splendidly at St Martin's Tearooms who specialize in creating home-made healthy wholefood bites from 100% organic produce. From freshly squeezed juices to revive, soups, vegan pasties and welsh rarebit to sustain and tasty cakes to treat, they deliver the full package. Enjoy your lunch in the old beamed medieval interior or in the pretty garden when the weather permits. Monday-Saturday 1000-1800.

Palace Farm, Kent ◎
Palace Farm, Doddington, Kent, ME9 0AU, T01795-886200, palacefarm.com.

Set on a family farm within the open fields and wooded valleys of the North Kent Downs AONB, Palace Farm delivers a quality hostel experience, while their environmental policies have also won them a Green Tourism Business Scheme gold medal. Set in converted farm buildings, the six rooms sleep between two and eight people in each dorm with access to a communal kitchen, dining room and lounge, kept toasty with a wood burner. Drying room and cycle store available for those making use of the nearby cycle routes. Beds from £18/night for adults which includes continental breakfast. Also on site is a quiet green field camping area – April-October, with an emphasis on the quiet, where pre-arranged camp fires are usually permitted. Pre-erected 'tipi' style tents also from £250/week. Bike hire is available from £5/day and maps can be borrowed.

∧ At the Duke, nothing arrives by air freight and they source 80% of their fresh ingredients from the surrounding home counties. Tascha Franklin with the fruits of the labour – strawberry and rhubarb if you were wondering.

∧ Beech Hill Coach House wrapped in a duvet of daisies.

▲ The Real Eating Company, Hove.

Roundhill Campsite, Hampshire ◉

Roundhill Campsite, Beaulieu Road, Brockenhurst, Hampshire, SO42 7QL, T0131-3146505, forestholidays.co.uk.

Follow the road into the heart of the New Forest where you'll discover a partially cleared area of heathland dotted with clumps of woodland and shrubs to create natural boundaries and haphazard hedges. The Roundhill Forestry Commission campsite is well organized with decent facilities, joyously however there are no designated pitches with edges marked out. Select a space for yourself and make camp – there are pond-side pitches for water babies and those nestled amongst the woodland for tree huggers as well as wide open expanses for those who just want to feel free. The site is huge with room for up to 500 pitches so this is no secret retreat but you can't beat the location if you want to explore the trails of the forest on foot or by bike. Remember, the New Forest ponies roam free and have been known to enter tents uninvited, on more then one occasion, to snaffle whatever edible delights they find lurking about so keep your goodies locked away… The staff can be real sticklers for rules and pre-booking in peak times is advised. Easter-September.

The Real Island Food Company, IOW ◉

T01983-731778, realislandfood.co.uk.

Delivering a clear conscience as well as your groceries, The Real Island Food allows you to buy locally and seasonally without having to spend your precious holiday time food shopping. Sourcing the best produce and working with the best suppliers

▼ Spring lambs and chicken in the valley.

on the island – from farmers, butchers, bakers, breweries, dairies and artisans – they deliver it right to your door, wherever you are on the Isle of Wight. Island Essential Welcome Pack for four costs £27.50 and includes everything you need to help you settle in from Fairtrade tea and coffee and a more-ish carrot cake to a fresh baked cob, locally made jam and Hamilton's dry cure bacon.

Beech Hill Farm, East Sussex ◉

Beech Hill Farm, Rushlake Green, TN21 9QB.

Surrounded by the ancient woodlands, deep valleys and wide, open spaces of High Weald's AONB, Beech Hill Farm is in an idyllic setting. The organically run 20-acre small holding raises rare breed sheep and their sustainable approach to their tourism off-shoot has won them a number of awards including the gold standard for Green Tourism and the SEEDA award for resource efficiency. Their 16th-century beamed coach house has been beautifully restored and the self-catering ground floor apartment sleeping is available to rent. Sleeping two, the garden room acts as a drying room and handy bike store too – the nearby Cuckoo Trail is definitely worth pushing out on two wheels to explore. From £300/week.

Hidden Spring, Sussex ◉

Hidden Spring Vineyard, Vines Cross Road, Horam, TN21 0HG, T01435-812640.

From March-October pitch up overlooking the beautiful orchards of this 23-acre working small holding, complete with an assortment of free ranging livestock from rare breed sheep to happy chickens. If all that gazing across fruity fields has whetted your appetite, fear not. Soil Association approved, they produce wine from their vines plus organic juices, cider and perry from their apple and pear varieties. The on-site shop stocks their rich bounty including honey made by the bees who live in hives in the orchard and pollinate the crops. If you'd rather take the 'camping' out of camping, opt for one of the yurts instead, with all the mod cons from a double bed to a wood burning stove (for heating and cooking!). Also available is a geodesic dome or a larger bell bent – erected on demand – which can sleep up to six. And it would seem wrong not to step into the nearby Brewers Arms for a swift pint and a locally sourced bite to eat.

Hidden Spring

< Worcestershire source.

Central England

A vast swathe bulges around the country's midriff stretching from the Welsh borders, where clans once waged bloody war, though to the coastline of East Anglia where tribes battle together to save villages from the onslaught of the ocean's violence. This belt of land has been cinched in tight by the hand of man in an attempt to redefine and recontour. Uniform ranks of cereal replace the ragged randomness of ancient woodlands whose lines in part are being refilled and replanted by green fingers; centuries have seen vast tracts of green drained and reclaimed from the grip of lakes and marsh creating rivers and waterways through which bodies and boats absentmindedly float. Maps reveal that, although cities and towns abound, there are many opportunities for getting into the wild. The Malvern Hills Area of Outstanding Natural Beauty that runs through Gloucestershire, Herefordshire and Worcestershire draws walkers and mountain bikers to its summits and slopes while the bright wings of paragliders light up the thermals above. The River Severn cuts through meandering banks and deep gorges as it winds its way towards the sea, lazy waters sliced by canoes and kayaks. Unexpected gems rest within this region like Leicestershire's hard island of rock and quarry, a playground for those with vertical ambitions. Around East Anglia's rump, where the power of the sea is demonstrated by the amount of land it claws back each year, there are some sandy havens where waveriders can glide and kitesufers find solace on windswept shallows. The motto of this area should be, expect the unexpected.

❯ Huge skies and big rides.

Environment

The Malvern Hills stand spectacular against the horizon, their green walls rising from the landscape in defiance of gravity and the forces of nature. These peaks form a line of ancient igneous and metamorphic rocks that runs north to south, less prone to forces of erosion than the land around, they stand tall against rain and wind. The highest point, Worcestershire Beacon, looms 1395 ft high. Skylarks dance here above open pasture while the eagle-eyed may spot a dormouse's retreat under lush hedgerow or a great crested newt darting through a crystal pond. The rest of the West Midlands region as a whole is dominated by sedimentary rocks such as shale, slate and sandstone with striations of limestone, while heavily quarried Lincolnshire is an island of hard, granitic rock. The landscape has a predominantly rural feel here, with the green shires of Worcestershire, Warwickshire, Staffordshire, Shropshire and Herefordshire surrounding the urban hub of Birmingham, Wolverhampton and Coventry. In the heart of the Midlands a bold environmental project is underway to transform 200 sq miles across Derbyshire, Leicestershire and Staffordshire into a new National Forest. The ambitious scheme has already seen more than seven million trees planted in an attempt to address climate change issues by sequestering carbon, conserving nature and creating new woodland habitats, producing wood to replace materials with a greater carbon footprint and ultimately regenerating the landscape.

The Eastern part of the region lies mostly on limestone, with granite outcrops such as Charnwood Forest. There are contrasts here with urban Essex and its commuter belt at odds with the wide flat plains to the north. Large areas of low lying land, such as the Fens and the Broads, were created when early peat excavations flooded to form lakes and watercourses, while other parts were drained to create pasture and arable acres. Unsurprisingly this area is of outstanding importance in terms of wildlife and home to National Nature Reserves, the RSPB Reserve as well as Special Areas of Conservation and SSSI. The marsh harrier may hover, scanning for disturbance in the grasses below, a dragonfly may skim the waters while a grass snake swims across a shady pool in search of frogs. Along the changing coastline, wetlands glimmer in afternoon sun while in front of grassy dunes legions of groynes and boulders fight in vain against current and tide, waters heavy with silt breaking on endless, open, empty beaches. Here the footprints of waders make temporary patterns before the east winds wipe clean the sands once more.

Resources

forestry.gov.uk Forestry Commission site with details on dedicated walks and MTB trails.

sas.org.uk Surfers Against Sewage, environmental campaigners for clean safe seas and recreational waters.

nationalforest.org Information on the new National Forest.

malvernhillsaonb.org.uk Information on exploring the Malvern Hills including details on the Hills Hopper bus service.

shropshirehills.info Details on visiting the Shropshire Hills including local produce and details on the Shuttle Bus service.

wyevalleyaonb.org.uk Wye Valley AONB official website.

broads-authority.gov.uk promoting sustainable tourism in the region with tide tables and details for water users.

norfolkcoastaonb.org.uk Details on sustainable exploration of the area including public transport including Coast Hopper and Norfolk Green.

visiteastofengland.com Tourist Board information with alternative suggestions for exploring the region.

Climate

The east of England is one of the driest parts of the land, so dry that parts of peaty wetland can become parched tinderboxes that risk fire during summer's peak. Precipitation levels average 100 mm for the summer and as little as 400 mm annually in some areas. Temperature ranges are fairly constant with average maximums between 19 to 20°C on the coast and 21 to 22°C inland. When the cold winters roll in mists cling to open waters and drift through hedgerows like spectres. Thermometers can hover near freezing in the central eastern region, while staying 2 or 3°C warmer near the coast. Snows can arrive where moist fronts from the southwest meet cold easterly airflows. In the West Midlands, the high grounds see the harshest weather. Areas like the Shropshire Hills have an average winter low near freezing, while below in the Severn valley and estuary the air is milder by up to 3°C. In the summer the valleys may have an average high between 21 and 22°C while on the hills it could be between 15 and 18°C.

The surf is often offshore here on the east coast, though there are days when easterly swells arrive from across the North Sea chased by a chilly tail wind. Sea temperatures are around 12°C in the summer meaning a 3/2 or 4/3 suit is the go, but winter water temperatures of 5 or 4°C makes a 5/4 mm wetsuits, boots, gloves and hoods essential for those braving the long walk down frosty beaches.

Canoeing River Wye

Provider	The Canoe Hire Company
Skill level	Novice-experienced
Time frame	½ day to 4 days
Equipment	Paddles, buoyancy aids, spray decks and dry bags are provided. Bring snacks and a change of clothing (just in case you do get wet)
Exertion level	●●●○○

Having slipped away from the historic Ross-on-Wye deep countryside flanking the river, the only sound to be heard is that of paddles breaking the surface of the murky-green water. A heron overtakes, guiding the boats downstream as it soars ahead to its next perch. On the banks a deer darts out of view into the woods.

A wide, meandering river that twists and turns through open pastures and wooded banks, the River Wye is – in the most part – a tame domain for canoeists. While the Welsh Wye is younger and more vigorous, attracting white water kayakers, by the time it crosses into England the river meanders at a steady plod, inviting even the novice paddler on a journey along a waterway lauded as one of the most stunning in the country. But it's not all slow moving this side of the border. For those that have the basics down pat or want a challenge, a bumpier ride is up for grabs on Symonds Yat rapids, where more experienced paddlers hop in to hone their freestyle manoeuvres and water skills.

There are many launching points along the banks of the Wye, but a day trip from Ross-on-Wye to Symond's Yat is a pearl of a paddle, taking in an abundance of wildlife, a smattering of historic sites and several watering holes en route. The vessel of choice on which to embark on this leisurely 12-mile voyage is an open Canadian canoe – these flat-bottomed, sturdy craft come big enough for up to a crew of four plus camping supplies, in case the mood takes you, and even the dog. Having dropped you at your starting point, the small team from The Canoe Hire Company get you kitted out and up to speed with a short talk covering river safety and etiquette

◁ Looking back across the river as it weaves away from Symonds Yat.

plus paddling techniques and useful tips before allowing you to launch off on your solo expedition. Being well genned up on the area they also crucially provide the lowdown on the best places to refuel and rest weary arms, whether you're looking for a pub stop or a private riverbank picnic. Having launched below the Riverside Inn, the waters weave away, flowing beneath bridges and past historic castles and by the time Kerne Bridge comes into sight, you'll be around a third of the way into your journey with your thoughts probably beginning to turn to food. Enter The Inn on the Wye, right on cue with beer garden and menus to tempt. Or paddle a few miles further to Lower Lydbrook mesmerized by the idyllic countryside view, and there's the option of the 18th-century Courtfield Arms, popular with the canoe crowd, or perhaps the nearby Forge Hammer Inn with a good range of real ales. Yep, you really can hop from well placed watering hole to watering hole

but remember this trip was not all about eating and drinking, honest. There was that impressive Norman fortification of Goodrich Castle you passed back by Kerne Bridge, the verdant countryside through which you passed, then there was the act of having to actually propel your canoe along the Wye. And, etched on your consciousness, maybe the best moment of all, when you craned your neck skyward beneath the staggering limestone of Yat Rock and glimpsed peregrines soaring on high.

Specialists in kayaking trips on the Wye, and operating from Hereford to Monmouth, The Canoe Hire Company will tailor a trip to individual abilities and requirements. While beginners are advised to limit themselves to just half a day paddling (more than long enough to get the arm muscles pumping), the canoes can take supplies and camping equipment to last a few days on a watery adventure.

∧ Kerne Bridge.
∨ Messing about in Canadian canoes.

Practicalities

Symonds Yat East (Gloucestershire) and West (Herefordshire) are thriving little villages bang on the River Wye and popular hubs for paddlers, walkers and fishermen. A hand-pulled rope ferry crosses the river between the two villages and there's a handful of campsites, teashops and places to stay. The ancient market town of Ross-on-Wye offers more extensive facilities.

Transport Car parking adjacent to the centre at Symonds Yat West costs £2/day. Car parking at the Ross-on-Wye car park is free. The closest train station to Symonds Yat West is at Lydney, about 10 miles from The Canoe Hire Company base.

Sleeping At Kerne Bridge (the launch point for an excellent half-day trip) the **££ Inn on the Wye**, T01600-890872, boasts views of the river and the ancient Goodrich Castle from elegant rooms that include a four-poster suite and a family apartment. On the riverbank at Ross-on-Wye **£ The Riverside Inn B&B**, T01989-564688, welcomes wet, muddy kayakers with clean, comfy rooms, overnight kayak storage, watery views and a full English cooked breakfast from the most local produce available. **£ Welsh Bicknor YHA**, Goodrich, HR9 6JJ, T0845-371 9666, is a handy spot – you pass the grounds of this Victorian riverside rectory on your float downstream. Comfortable with doubles, dorms and camping also available. **Camping** Stay under canvas at the **River Wye Camping**, HR9 6BY, T01600-890672, right by the river at Symonds Yat West – you can haul canoes out here and store them next to your tent but they can sometimes be a bit sniffy about this (they have their own canoe hire) and

amenities/toilet facilities are a bit hit and miss. **Downward Park**, HR9 6BP, T01600-890438, Easter-Sep is perhaps a better option although not bang on the river. The site is small, wooded and peaceful. Perfect.

Eating & drinking The team can organize picnics from £8/head. Don't pass up a lunch stop at **The Inn on the Wye** at Kerne Bridge, T01600-890872. A modernized country inn, it serves a good selection of real ales and locally sourced grub alongside stunning views of the river and Goodrich Castle. At **The Riverside Inn**, Ross-on-Wye, T01989-564688, tuck into Gloucester Old Spot sausages and home-made burgers washed down with local ale. En route, the **Courtfield Arms**, Lower Lydbrook, T01594-860207, is relaxed and popular serving well priced and locally sourced grub including the Hereford steak and Wye Valley Ale pie. On the banks of the river at Symonds Yat West, **Ye Olde Ferrie Inn**, T01600-890232, is a 17th-century inn with local ales on tap. Over at Symonds Yat East, **The Saracens Head** is something a bit special with ferry, waterside terraces and a modern pub/brasserie menu. The ingredients are locally sourced where possible and have been worked into light bites from lunchtime baguettes to their hearty beef and Wye Valley Ale stew. If you've had a long day you could always stay – B&B from £79/double.

Also try For those well prepped in the art of canoeing try the 4-day, 44-mile trip between the historic town of Hereford and Symonds Yat with plenty of excellent campsites and watering holes en route. Pack up your camping kit into the dry bags provided and paddle off!

> Lowdown

❶ Directory
Ross-on-Wye Canoe Hire, Symond's Yat West, Herefordshire, HR9 6BJ, T01600-890883. thecanoehire.co.uk.

❺ Prices
£30-£40/canoe/day, plus transport charges from £10/first canoe, £3 each thereafter.

❹ Season
Mar-Oct (river conditions permitting).

❶ Don't miss
The chance to spot peregrines that nest in the limestone of Yat Rock.

❽ Avoid
Paddling beyond your capabilities – if you haven't done this before, don't take on more than a half-day trip.

Walking Wye Valley

Provider	DIY
Skill level	Novice-intermediate
Time frame	12 days end to end
Equipment	Sturdy walking boots, map, food and water, waterproof, survival kit. Remember to always walk prepared
Exertion level	●●●●○

Carpeted in a deep purple, the woodland floor shifts and sways; thousands of bluebells dancing in the spring breeze. Overhead, red kites circle, while in the distance the fast flow of the river can be heard splashing over rock. Before long the densely packed broadleaved trees give way to open pastures, lush and green, stretching to the horizon where the windswept uplands await. The valley's path weaves its way into the distance, a well-worn trail traversed by walkers over the years, all eager to explore the beautiful landscape of the Welsh borders.

The Wye Valley in the English Welsh Borders is not only a Designated Area of Outstanding Natural Beauty but also historically rich. From Britain's oldest surviving stone castle in Chepstow, to the medieval longhouse in Gilfach, the valley is covered with buildings and ruins which chart Anglo-Welsh relations, or lack there of, through the centuries. It's this combination of varied landscape and fascinating history that draws walkers to the valley every year, looking to follow the river's course on the Wye Valley Walk.

Stretching for 136 miles from mountain to sea, the popular approach is to work against the flow of the river and tread north, starting in the border town of Chepstow. Heading out from the town's celebrated castle, the Wye Valley Walk weaves along narrow paths through dense woodland, its steep inclines leading to viewpoints across the valley. From here, the route takes you into the historic county town of Monmouth, before leading out into the open fields for a stretch of riverside walking.

Passing under impressive limestone cliffs and through more broadleaved woodlands, for the next 10 miles the walk clings to the banks of the Wye, before changing pace and climbing steeply over hills and valleys around Leys Hill and Howle

❮ As spring appears the woodland carpet of the Wye Valley begins its transformation.

Demi Taylor

Practicalities

The historic walled town of Chepstow, on the English-Welsh border, is commonly considered the starting point of the Wye Valley Walk. Home to the oldest surviving stone castle in Britain it's a popular destination for history fans along with outdoors enthusiasts keen to explore the beautiful scenery of the Wye Valley and Forest of Dean. The town itself has a selection of independent shops and high street retailers along with plenty of restaurants, pubs, hotels, guesthouses and tourist facilities.

Transport   Chepstow is just over the old Severn Bridge and the railway station is well served by Arriva Trains Wales.

Sleeping   ££ The Beaufort Hotel, T01291-622497, is a 16th-century coaching inn in the centre of Chepstow with bags of character. Each room is different, some sporting original low oak beams, others with more modern additions, but all clean, comfortable and well appointed. The hotel has free Wi-Fi throughout and a well-regarded restaurant where a locally sourced breakfast is served daily. Alternatively, ££ The First Hurdle, NP16 5EX, T01291-622189, is a small guesthouse in the heart of town, popular with walkers and cyclists. It offers small, comfortable rooms and has a friendly, homely atmosphere. For self-catering, try something really special at The Gatehouse, Mathern, Monmouthshire, T01291-638806. Twenty mins away from the start of the Wye Valley Walk this exclusive 1-bedroom property boasts 700 years of history, built in the time of Edward I, around 1270. The Gatehouse's spiral staircases, low oak beams, woodburning stove, gallery bedroom, deep leather sofas, thick

stone walls and ancient windows make it a quirky, romantic place to stay. There's even a tower with impressive views over the Monmouth countryside. The nearby Newhall Farm Shop brings together the best fresh, local and international produce including deli goodies, fresh baked bread and local beer and cider.

Eating & drinking   The Piercefield, St Arvans, T01291-622614, is a popular pub and restaurant in Chepstow serving top class Sunday roasts. The rest of the week its well rounded seasonal menu, drawing on local Welsh ingredients, is reasonably priced and generously portioned. Castle View Hotel, Bridge St, T01291-620349, is well known for its moules marinière as well as its locally sourced lamb dishes, while at the first stop on the River Wye Walk, Bistro Prego, Monmouth, T01600-712600, is worth a mention; a family run restaurant combining Italian cooking with locally sourced produce to create classically flavoured dishes.

Resources   For Wye Valley Walk details see wyevalleywalk.org.

Also try   If you fancy exploring the Wye Valley but don't fancy the full 136 mile stretch there are a number of circular trails that link into the Wye Valley Walk and give you a chance to take in the gorges, woodlands and riverbanks that the area is famous for. Walks along the Angiddy Valley taking in Tintern and its famous Abbey are particularly good. Look at the Monmouthshire County Council website for more details, monmouthshire.gov.uk.

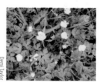

∧ A short lived river shower won't dampen the spirits, it only serves to intensify the colour palette.

Hill, eventually dropping into Ross. Again shifting from pastoral riverside to uphill scramble, the following section of the walk winds through a patchwork of farmland and orchards on to the Wye floodplain surrounding Hereford, before ambling out of the city towards Hay-on-Wye, where attentions turn briefly from walking to reading and a few hours can easily be lost browsing the town's famous bookshops.

The river gets noticeably faster after Hay, frothing its way through the fields as the walk heads into Wales. Here, it leaves the riverside, climbing higher into the Welsh uplands which give way to the exposed, rugged, final stretch of the route. Windswept and wild with mountains rising in the near distance, the landscape around Plynlimon, where the walk draws to a close, provides stark contrast to the placid lowlands over 100 miles before.

The full Wye Valley Walk takes 12 days to complete; weaving through a number of border towns and villages all well kitted out to put up exhausted walkers for the night. There are a number of baggage transfer services available for the route and plenty of maps and guidebooks, as well as regular marked signs to show you the way, if you are keen to do it off your own back. For those who prefer to be more than just pointed in the right direction, walking outfits like Contours, contours.co.uk, offer holidays which include accommodation, meals and guides, taking groups from Chepstow to Plynlimon and beyond.

Regardless of how you choose to do it – alone or guided - undertaking the Wye Valley Walk from spring through until autumn you are sure to experience the natural beauty, abundance of wildlife, tranquillity and sense of history that this rich landscape has to offer.

> **Lowdown**

⊙ Prices
Free.

⊘ Season
Year round.

⊙ Don't miss
Shouting from the ramparts of Britain's oldest surviving stone castle in Chepstow.

⊗ Avoid
Ill preparation. The weather in the Welsh borders is notably changeable, so remember your waterproofs.

Mountain biking Shropshire Hills

Provider	DIY
Skill level	All
Time frame	5 hrs
Equipment	Mountain bike, helmet, map, provisions, appropriate gear for changing weather and a repair kit/ spare tube
Exertion level	●●●●○

As the old saying goes, 'When you're tired of Shropshire, you're tired of mountain biking.' Okay, maybe that's not quite how the saying goes, but it should. While the terrain of the Marches may not be as instantly impressive as that of its Celtic cousin, the hills south of Shrewsbury deliver a wealth of riding possibilities within a tight perimeter that cater to most mountain biking persuasions.

For those in search of a classic long distance tour named after a local cad and a bounder, look no further than the Jack Mytton Way. Recently extended, to include a loop of the southern hills, the trail covers 100 miles travelling in a general east to west direction towards the Welsh Border. Depending on whether you want to include the new section, there are a number of starting points, with the traditional trail setting off from Ray's Farm by Bridgnorth. Mainly off-road, the undulating route follows rural bridleways and trails as well as some stretches on quiet country lanes. It takes in exciting features such as a decent climb up and along the impressive Wenlock Edge limestone escarpment as well as a challenging ascent of Long Mynd before descending into Clun where the May bank holiday sees the Green Man banish the Frost Queen to usher in Spring. Following Offa's Dyke, the trail concludes at Llanfair Waterdine. The route is also shared by walkers and horse riders so care needs to be taken not to startle the horses which brings us to the trail's namesake, Jack Mytton. Famous or infamous round these parts as a sportsman, a lover of the countryside and a lover of liquor, stories abound – tall or otherwise – regarding his derring-do of an equine nature – attempting to jump closed tollgates with his horse still attached to the carriage, jumping the dinner table on horseback… you get the idea.

If you're looking for a decent day's riding combining steep climbs, flat sections to draw breath, cracking views and the odd speeding descent, there are worse places to explore than Long Mynd. Owned by the National Trust, this 'long mountain' is around seven miles long and three miles wide. It is edged with steep valleys and capped by a heathland plateau which affords stunning views across Shropshire and into Wales. Setting out from Cardingmill Valley, there are a number of routes and circuits to explore following bridleways and well defined singletrack to minimize impact in the area, but make sure you don't miss Minton Batch, the highlight swooping singletrack descent.

There's also a strong downhill scene here fuelled by Dave Pearce of Pearce Cycles who has assisted

⌄ Long Mynd: steep climbs, flat sections to draw breath, cracking views and of course the odd speeding descent.

course development, runs regular track days as well as the popular annual six-part downhill series across a number of established local venues. The Forestry Commission's Hopton Wood, eight miles west of Craven Arms is one of the race venues with the testing DH tracks available to ride any time, not just on race days. Only seasoned MTBers need apply and you may want to time your visit to coincide with one of the weekends where uplift is available. If the berms, jumps and descents of this DH are too intense, the 350 hectare forest is home to 20 miles of waymarked trails to explore, covering wide open forest road as well as tighter weaving singletrack. A laminated all weather map of the trails is available from the Forestry Commission.

The Shropshire Hills are no 'one size fits all' mountain bike experience, but rather a wealth of experiences, waiting to be tailored to suit so go, explore the hills and get the measure of them.

Practicalities

There are a number of good bases from the pretty market towns of Church Stretton and Craven Arms to the smaller Clun, while nearby Ludlow is something of a foodie's delight.

Transport A series of train stations circle beneath the hills with handy stops at Hopton Heath, Craven Arms and Church Stretton.

Sleeping The 500-year-old **£££ Clun Farmhouse**, Clun, SY7 8JB, T01588-640432, has pretty beamed rooms, a welcome feel and wonderful Shropshire breakfast featuring Ludlow meats, just-laid eggs, home-made preserves and locally baked bread. **£££ Hopton House**, SY7 0QD, T01547-530885, is perfectly placed for exploring the Hopton Woods trails and pretty ideal full stop. The converted granary delivers comfortable, luxurious rooms and breakfast made with the best local ingredients. Packed lunches can be organized. **£ Clun YHA**, SY7 8NY, T0845-371 9112, is a bit of a gem. The converted mill is small and tucked away with bike store and camping on site too. Decent YHA with camping option also available at Bridges Long Mynd, Ratlinghope, SY5 0SP T01588-650656, plus small simple YHA bunkhouse at All Stretton, SY6 6JW, T01694-722593. **Camping** A number of campsites in and around Church Stretton handy for Long Mynd, the pick of the crop being the simple **Small Batch**, Little Stretton, SY6 6PW, T01694-723358, nestled at the foot of Long Mynd, open Mar-Sep.

Eating & drinking In Church Stretton, the **Acorn Wholefood Café**, Sandford Ave, T01694-722495, is a real hit serving up healthy, wholesome home-made goodies using local produce where possible (including locally picked fruit for their scrummy crumbles and jams). Open 0930-1700, not Wed. En route on Long Mynd, stop off at the lovely little 17th-century Ragleth Inn, Little Stretton, SY6 6RB for a pint and some decent home cooking whether you fancy a carb-rich jacket potato from £4 or something a little meatier say the steak and ale pie for around a tenner. On warm summer days sit out and enjoy the beer garden.

Resources For a full route description of the Jack Mytton Way search shropshire.gov.uk. OS mapping is also required. **Pearce Cycles**, Fishmore Rd, Ludlow, SY8 3DP, T01584-879288, are at the top of their game. Their well stocked shop carries bikes, hardware and accessories and as riders they offer a wealth of local knowledge. Their on-site workshop is run by a highly qualified team of mechanics offering service and repair. For hire and basics try **Terry's Cycles**, Castle Hill, All Stretton, T01694-723302, or **Onny Mountain Bike Hire**, Flowers Coffee Shop, Craven Arms, T01588-672710. With MTB bike hire from £18/day, **Wheely Wonderful Cycling**, Petchfield Farm, Elton, SY8 2HJ, T01568-770755, also offers cycling holidays where accommodation, luggage transfers (and bike hire) are all taken care of from 2-6 days.

Also try Eastridge Woods at the northern end of the Stiperstones is another Forestry Commission mountain bike trail centre which combines two short, steep DH courses as well as beginner-friendly and intermediate trails to explore.

∧ From the heather-flecked hill tops, giant vistas roll away.

> **Lowdown**

⊙ **Prices**
Free/£1 the all-weather laminated Hopton Woods maps from Forestry Commission District Office – proceeds go towards trail maintenance.

⊙ **Season**
Year round.

⊙ **Don't miss**
A pie and a pint at The Royal Oak, Cardingham.

⊗ **Avoid**
Unless you know what you're doing leave the DH to the experts. On the cross county trail, avoid spooking the horses, call out to let riders know you're coming.

Open Canoe Touring River Severn

Provider Backwaters Adventure	
Skill level Novice-intermediate	
Time frame 1 day to 1 week	
Equipment All gear including canoe, tent, sleeping bag and mat, stove and fuel, and waterproof containers are provided. Bring a change of clothing and food	
Exertion level ●●●●○	

Rising in the Cambrian Mountains the River Severn filters its way through the forests and hillsides of the Welsh landscape before joining with the River Vyrnwy to create a flood plain on the border with England. From here, it squeezes a course through the narrow sides of the Ironbridge Gorge, deepening and widening as momentum pushes it on into Worcestershire. Approaching Gloucester, the water becomes brackish and the river tidal before it releases into the Bristol Channel. Along its length the water teams with salmon and other fresh water fish while dragonflies and busy kingfishers light up the banks.

Whether you fancy spending a day lazily meandering downstream before choosing the ideal spot for a picnic, a few days splashing around on the river, or a week navigating the length of the River Severn, open canoe touring is a sublime way to experience this watery vein. Between Pool Quay and Gloucester it delivers up 130 miles of navigable potential on mostly placid waters which wind their way through unspoilt, untamed remote landscapes, devoid of hustle or bustle before twisting and turning past villages and under bridges. Rest assured, there are however a few thrills to break up all that the tranquillity; as well as weirs, there are a handful of short, faster-flowing sections as well as a Grade 3 rapid near Ironbridge to contend with.

When it comes down to a flexible, bespoke set up, Backwaters Adventure has got it nailed. Although Pool Quay is the highest point in the navigation and accessible year round to paddlers, there are a number of drop off points along the river's length from which you can set off on your voyage. The team meets you at the start point of your choice, armed

> Regular river users and behind, Worcester Cathedral.

< Autumn mist hangs heavy over the River Severn.

Neil Dorti

with your canoe plus your tent and kit packed and ready to go in water tight containers, as well as a list of recommended campsites, B&Bs and those all important riverside inns. The only decision you have to make is how much of Britain's longest river you want to tackle – what with weirs to portage, locks to negotiate and rapids to shoot, not to mention the odd pub to stop off at, around 10-15 miles a day is enough for most. When the sun goes down on the water, pitch up at a campsite, light the stove and enjoy being self-sufficient in the arms of nature, or crank up the creature comforts with a stopover at a guesthouse. Just let the crew know where you intend to finish your odyssey and when, and they'll come and collect you – leaving you free to rest your aching arms, no doubt a little damp from your adventure.

The upper reaches are narrow but rich in wildlife while a cracking five-day adventure is to take on the 75-mile stretch linking Shrewsbury and Worcester – approaching the city and seeing the impressive cathedral come into view is an awesome sight. Note: kayakers are free to navigate the river from Pool Quay to Stourport, but between Stourport and Gloucester British Waterways is the navigation authority and a licence is required.

You don't have to be a kayaking aficionado to take to the Severn, but you do need to be capable of steering your vessel around common hazards such as fallen trees. If you're unsure whether your skills are up to the job, guided tours are available, alternatively book on to a river awareness day or a skills course prior to heading off under your own steam.

A company committed to squeaky green operations, Backwaters Adventure encourages awareness of the river environment and provides clients with instruction to take measures that minimize their impact.

Practicalities

Montford Bridge, just 3 miles from Shrewsbury, has a campsite, car parking and a family pub. The medieval border town of Shrewsbury, with its historic abbey and timber-framed buildings offers a characterful place to stay with extensive facilities and plenty of accommodation from campsites to hotels.

Transport Shrewsbury train station is around 5½ miles from the launch point at Montford Bridge.

Sleeping A full list of recommended campsites and B&Bs is available from Backwaters Adventure. If you start at Montford Bridge, **£ The Old Swan Pub**, T01743-850750, has a campsite in its grounds. Just 3 miles out of Montford Bridge, **£ Hollies Farm**, T01939-261046, offers a double room in its 17th-century cottage. Breakfast here includes outdoor reared Gloucester Old Spot sausage and bacon and free-range eggs laid on site.

Eating & drinking If you launch from the highest point of the river at Pool Quay, grab a cup of tea and a slice of home-baked cake at the church tearoom, T01939-261046, before setting off (that is if you set off on a Thu, Fri or Sat when it's open). **The Old Swan Inn**, T01743-850750, at Montford Bridge serves 3 quenching cask ales alongside a daily changing menu. **The Riverside Inn**, T01952-510900, on a bend in the river 7 miles southeast of Shrewsbury, is a fine place to sample seasonal, local produce and guest beers whilst taking in the views of the River Severn.

Resources Hit the river armed with the Ordnance Survey maps covering the appropriate sections of the River Severn (Pool to Cressage – 126, Leighton to Coalport – 127, Apley Forge to Grimley – 138, Worcester to Chaceley Stock – 150, Wainlode to Severn Road Bridge – 162).

Also try If you prefer to experience the River Severn from terra firma, freewheel along the Severn Valley from Shrewsbury to Worcester on the Sustrans National Cycle Network route 45.

> Lowdown

ⓘ Directory
Backwaters Adventure Equipment Ltd, Abergavenny, T07815-542775, backwatershire.co.uk. (Note: Office address is not the location for hire. Directions of the start point will be provided on confirmation of booking).

ⓢ Prices
From £280/multi-day booking.

ⓐ Season
All year.

ⓞ Don't miss
Keep your eyes peeled and you may spot an elusive otter hiding close to the banks.

ⓧ Avoid
Make sure you check availability with campsite owners before setting off, and avoid camping anywhere other than designated sites. Be aware that the rivers rise rapidly in wet weather. Proceed cautiously where rapids and weirs are marked on the map. Beyond Stourport a fee is payable to use the river.

Walking The Shropshire Way

Provider	DIY
Skill level	Novice-experienced
Time frame	7 days to complete the full circular route
Equipment	Sturdy walking boots, map, refreshments
Exertion level	●●○○○

Golden with bracken, the undulating hills of Shropshire roll away into the distance as clouds skit across the autumn sky and a fresh wind whips through the air. The babbling rivers and sheltered, wooded valleys of the day before seem a lifetime away, distanced in the memory by the challenging climb and rewarding views of today.

Once the heart of the industrial revolution, Shropshire is now a quiet, rural county but it isn't like other walking destinations. Edging Wales, the Shropshire Hills are a product of their location, benefitting from the limelight being cast over their better known neighbours – Offa's Dyke, the impressive cross border Cambrian Mountains plus local contemporary and darling of the walking world, the Malvern Hills. As a result, Shropshire's perambulation potential is relatively untapped and yet with 2175 miles of waymarked routes in a county with striking, historic scenery that is one quarter designated an Area of Outstanding Natural Beauty, it's the perfect place for walkers looking to lose themselves in tranquil valleys and on peaceful hill tops.

There are a number of excellent day walks and circulars to explore including those that lace their way across the striking geological feature of Long Mynd – essentially a long stretch of upland plateau, riven with valleys and blanketed in moorland. Setting out from the NT-owned Carding Mill Valley, whose Pavillion tea rooms do a good line in local food, there is a decent six mile circular following the main path up the valley to the summit. The Stiperstones, steeped in legends provide a split personality of walks: setting out from The Bog, crossing familiar rolling green hills before finding yourself scrambling over the rough, glittering quartzite tors The Devil's Chair and Cranberry Rock, (which should perhaps be renamed 'bilberry rock'

due to the number of delicious blue berries that can be found littering this area in autumn)

But perhaps the county's most popular walk is the Shropshire Way, a 75-ish mile circular route which weaves through the region's hills and valleys. Broken down into seven day-long walks the route has been pulled together and developed by local walkers who have shared their knowledge, tips and favourite hikes to create an interesting and sometimes challenging path through the Shropshire countryside. The resulting Shropshire Way website is crammed with information, to download all of which should help you get the most out of the area. It's clear from the effort that has gone into the resource that local walkers are proud of their countryside and it's no wonder. From the jagged edged Stiperstones and roughly hewn tors to the bronze age cairns and Norman remains scattered across the hills, from the twin peaks of Clee Burf and Abdon Burf to the limestone escarpment and Elizabethan manor of Wenlock Edge, natural and manmade history is everywhere on the Shropshire Way, a real walk through the ages waiting to be discovered.

> **Lowdown**

⊖ **Prices**
Free.

✪ **Season**
All year round although in winter conditions can be difficult.

⊙ **Don't miss**
The chance to extend the circular route with a walk up the Long Mynd, the view over the Shropshire Hills is spectacular.

✪ **Avoid**
Leaving gates open when walking across farmland. Know the countryside code!

> From the jagged edges of the Stiperstones, Shropshire's dramatic potential is revealed.

Simon Pattison

Practicalities

Situated in the heart of the Shropshire hills, Church Stretton is a busy market town on the English/Welsh border with a good range of accommodation, restaurants, pubs and shops.

Transport   Church Stretton has a well served train station.

Sleeping   The small **££ Juniper Cottage**, SY6 6HG, T01694-723427, welcomes walkers with comfortable rooms. The stunning views of Caer Caradoc from the dining room make it a great place to enjoy the freshly laid eggs, local sausages and home-made marmalade of their tasty breakfast. **££ Victoria House**, T01694-723823, is a Victorian townhouse bed and breakfast in the centre of Church Stretton, with 6 simple but stylish bedrooms all with views over the Shropshire countryside. Free Wi-Fi throughout and breakfast is locally sourced and organic where possible; they also use only eco-friendly cleaning products. They're happy to organize a packed lunch and make suggestions on walks in the area. For self-catering near Church Stretton, **£ Willow Batch**, T01694-722358, a Swiss style chalet in the Carding Mill valley, opens straight out into 6000 acres of National Trust hill country. There's a twin and double bedroom, both with private showers, as well as a lounge, kitchen and garden complete with visiting rabbits, squirrels and badgers.
Camping   At the foot of the Long Mynd, **Small Batch Campsite**, SY6 6PW, T01694-723358, is quiet and peaceful campsite in the village of Little Stretton, surrounded by stunning landscapes. Run by the same family since '69 it's friendly and welcoming, with basic, well maintained facilities.

Eating & drinking   The Studio Restaurant, T01604-722672, in Church Stretton is an intimate neighbourhood restaurant serving modern British fare, maximizing its relationship with local suppliers to create a seasonal menu. **The Royal Oak**, Cardington, SY6 7JZ, T01694-771266, 15th-century free house is an excellent, traditional country pub with roaring fire and low beams. It celebrates local produce and is famous for its 'fidget pie,' a Shropshire speciality of gammon, apples and cider which has been handed down from landlord to landlord.

Resources   The Shropshire Way website shropshirewalking.co.uk/shropshire-way.

Also try   For those who want to enjoy touring the Shropshire landscape without the hassle of schleping your luggage between pit stops, or indeed the hassle of having to organize said pit spots, book a trip with Wheely Wonderful Cycling. The 6-day/5-night **Wild Edric Way Walking Tour** is a classic combining just the right balance of walking (49 miles in total, taking you past some decent inns to revive the weary), grand vistas (especially those afforded by Long Mynd) and cracking B&B's (such as the Green Tourism Silver rated **Old Brick Guest House** whose locally sourced breakfast will undoubtedly set you up for a day's march). £415/adult includes accommodation, luggage transfers as well as detailed route map. **Wheely Wonderful Cycling**, Petchfield Farm, Elton, Ludlow, Shropshire SY8 2HJ, T01568-770755, wheelywonderfulcycling.co.uk.

< The sun rises over Shropshire.

Mountain biking Cannock Chase

Provider	DIY
Skill level	Intermediate-advanced
Time frame	1½ hrs +
Equipment	Mountain bike, helmet plus repair kit
Exertion level	●●●●○

‹ Stile Cop rock garden.
∧ Just ask the guys who ride here, Cannock Chase is truly an Area of Outstanding Natural Beauty.

Lying north of the heaving sprawl of Birmingham, Wolverhampton and Walsall, Cannock Chase is a truly stunning Area of Outstanding Natural Beauty, a striking contrast to the urban, ordered Midlands landscape that surrounds it. Bridle paths and waymarked walking trails weave their way across Cannock Forest providing ramblers and horse riders with a respite from the city but it is the mountain bike trails carefully cut into the landscape here that offer the real thrill of the Chase.

Setting out from the Birches Valley Forest Centre, Follow the Dog is the main event – a seven mile red graded singletrack route that weaves its way through tall pines to get the pulse racing. Aimed at competent riders the trail is technical with impressive berms and fast descents as well as sections of boardwalk and a rock garden to contend with. The trails are constantly being upgraded and adapted with a new trail due to open at the time of writing – a challenging link-up with Follow the Dog creating a 13-mile epic to put riders through their paces. If you want to get involved in the regular Sunday morning trail building at Cannock Chase check out the Chase Trails site.

For less confident riders there are a couple of green graded trails that lead out from the visitor centre and offer a leisurely cycle on waymarked paths, bridleways and forest roads.

The hills here aren't huge – standing a modest 705 ft above sea level – but the effort that's been put in to the downhill trails make them well worth a visit. From Stile Cop there are a number of courses on offer ranging from intermediate to seriously insane and as the soil is well draining, there's no excuse not to ride. The advice is to walk the course before you ride it, wear proper body armour and check out racersguild.co.uk.

Practicalities

The forest is well equipped with cafés and bike hire facilities.

Transport Rugeley train station is 1½-miles east of the trails.

Sleeping ££ Haywood Park Farm, Shugborough, ST17 0XA, T01889-882736, manor house B&B with access to the trails and farmhouse breakfasts featuring home-made preserves plus local bacon and free range eggs. **Camping** Springslade Lodge, WS12 4PT, T01785-715091. A simple site within the pines of Cannock Chase giving access to the trails and possibilities further north from £10/night. Also on site the tea rooms. **Tackeroo Caravan Site**, Birches Vallery, WS15 2UQ, T01889-586593, no booking, no tents but it's on the trails and a crackingly simple site.

Eating/drinking Birches Valley Café, at the trail head, aim to keep their food miles low but their food tasty!

Resources Swinnerton Cycles Forest Centre, T01889-575170, bikechase.co.uk, good range of bikes and accessories plus demo bike hire from £30/half day. Closed Wed. **Mountain Bike Adventures**, T01889-574969, mountainbikeadventures.co.uk, run skills courses making the most of the trail, from £38/person. For information on the trail building and maintenance, see chasetrails.co.uk. To get involved in the DH scene see racersguild.co.uk.

Also try The Go Ape! tree tops trail here deliver a new perspective on familiar terrain, T0845-6439215, £30/adults.

> **Lowdown**

ⓘ Directory
Birches Valley Forest Centre, Rugeley, WS15 2UQ.

ⓢ Prices
Free/£30 demo bike hire.

ⓞ Season
Year round.

ⓞ Don't miss
A cup of Fairtrade coffee at the Birches Valley Café to revive the weary post ride.

ⓧ Avoid
The bike shop is closed on Wed so don't mistime your visit.

Climbing Leicestershire

Provider	Claudia Sarner
Skill level	Beginner-intermediate
Time frame	½ day to 1 day for beginners introduction
Equipment	Comfortable clothing and tight fitting trainers to climb in as well as drinks and snacks. All climbing and safety equipment provided
Exertion level	●●●●○

"Leicestershire is a little island of hard rock," explains Claudia Sarner, who has been coaching and guiding for the past decade. "It has pockets of beauty and somewhat ugly quarries with hidden charms." Hill Hole is one such oasis. At first sight it appears no more than a water-filled hole topped off by grassy plateaux. But there is more to this place than meets the eye. Markfieldite, a particularly hard granite used in road construction, was ripped from the ground here, but scanning rock faces it isn't long before you are mind climbing the slabs.

The quarry, once under threat to be filled, is now a nature reserve, earmarked for the National Forest scheme. It delivers climbs that aren't too imposing but offer the possibility for progression from an 36 ft to a 50 ft wall, making it a great spot for those who are keen to get to grips with climbing. For Claudia, it's important to talk to people about the location, get them thinking about their surroundings and how they can minimize their impact on their environment. After the safety briefing she sets up the route and it's onto the rocks to get your first taste. But it's not just the satisfaction of the climbing that's on offer. "I think part of the experience is being able to top out, to feel the exhilaration and experience the views that come with it, putting your surroundings into context and pushing yourself," says Claudia. While the courses are tailored to the individual, the emphasis is on laying down a foundation of basic climbing skills, getting to grips with the equipment and learning how to belay and thus rely on your climbing buddies. And when topping out, vistas are unveiled, ones that on a clear day expand from the pink, crystalline wall that has dominated your attention, opening up to wide ranging views across the Midland Plain and a new world of possibilities.

"There's the mental problem solving aspect, the natural beauty of my surroundings and there's also the enjoyment of arriving at a place through climbing that you can't otherwise reach," says Claudia on the appeal of climbing. "For me, it's all about the situation and seeing where I can get to."

Practicalities

The Hill Hole Quarry Nature Reserve is in Markfield, next to the heaving, restless M1.

Transport The nearest train station is Leicester, 9 miles east. Difficult bus connections on with Arriva Midlands.

Sleeping Just 4 miles east of Markfield, £££ Horseshoe Cottage Farm, Cropston, LE7 7HQ, T0116-2350038, delivers upmarket B&B with a conscience. The rooms are pretty, the breakfasts locally sourced, while the water is solar heated. To the west, £ National Forest YHA, Moira, Swadlincote, Derbyshire, DE12 6BD, T0845-371 9672. Newly built, the hostel has been designed with the environment in mind – water is heated by solar panels, rain water is captured for grey water use and the biofuel boiler uses sustainable locally sourced forest woodchips. It's all extremely civilized - the licensed on-site restaurant matches local ales and local produce and the en-suite rooms sleep 2-4 people.

Resources Tower Climbing Centre, Leicester, LE4 1DS, indoor wall and shop is a good way to meet local climbers and hone your skills, also check out North Leicestershire Mountain Club: northleicestermc.org. Keep an eye out for the new BMC guide to Climbing Leicestershire.

Also try Across Derbyshire, Leicestershire and Staffordshire, an exciting venture is taking root. Covering 200 sq miles, the development of National Forest has seen more than 7 million trees planted in an attempt to link the ancient forests of Needwood and Charnwood, conserve the natural environment and address the climate change issue. Get involved and plant a 2 year old sapling – oak, silver birch or ash – between Nov and Mar for £25 or grow your own tree from seed and see a great oak rise from a tiny acorns. See nationalforest.org.

> **Lowdown**

❶ **Directory**
Claudia Sarner,
Leicester,
T0116-270 1510,
claudiasarner@
hotmail.com.

❷ **Prices**
From £45.

❸ **Season**
Year round.

❹ **Don't miss**
Keep your eyes open at Hill Hole Quarry, you might just spot a native white clawed crayfish in the water filled quarry here.

❺ **Avoid**
A number of the quarries in Leicestershire have access issues make sure you have up to date information before embarking on a route.

Walking Malvern Ridge, Malvern Hills

Provider DIY	
Skill level Intermediate-experienced	
Time frame 4-5 hrs	
Equipment OS map, walking boots, waterproofs (lightweight), water, snacks and camera	
Exertion level ●●●●●	

Picture a blue-sky day walking high along English hilltops. Below, reams of rolling green countryside and seemingly endless vistas stretch into the distance and into neighbouring Wales, like excitedly unravelled bolts of fabric. Rising up in a nine-mile long ridge where Herefordshire butts up against Worcestershire, the glorious Malvern Hills are amongst the oldest rocks in Britain and recently voted home to 'The Best View in Britain'

by the Ramblers' Association, make a mighty fine place to don your boots and get walking. There are all levels of walks tracing the valleys and crests, while from the town of Great Malvern the 1394 ft Worcestershire Beacon – the highest point in the range – is accessible to those prepared for an uphill hike.

However, for the seasoned walker, the challenge that begs to be taken on is a walk along the entire Malvern Ridge from end to end. A tough 10 mile hike with 3181 ft of ascent, this classic route visits Herefordshire, Gloucestershire and Worcestershire, and every summit along this line-up of majestic hills. The list of conquests ticked off within a few hours would have any Munro-bagger gasping for

▼ Evening sky over Black Hill, Malvern.

breath – there's North Hill, Sugarloaf Hill, Summer Hill, Raggedstone Hill and Hangman's Hill to name just a few, but it's the aptly named Perseverance Hill that best sums up the mission ahead. If it all becomes too tiring once you're en route, you can choose to skirt around many of the peaks, but when good visibility is on your side the awe-inspiring views make every uphill step worth the effort.

The Malvern ridge runs from north to south making navigation a cinch, so all you have to decide is which end to start from. During the summer months many opt to take the Hills Hopper bus to the southern end and tramp back to base at Great Malvern and logistically this can be a wise decision as transport back from the more remote southern tip requires a bit of pre-planning.

Others however would rather hike against the grain enjoying the lower, more tranquil hills as a natural wind down at the end of a hard day's walking. For those canny walkers, the trail heads out from the clock tower of Great Malvern, ascending the wide track to North Hill that looms large above the town. This initial climb takes you directly, albeit quite steeply, to the highest point of Worcestershire Beacon. Head away from this reigning monarch of the Malverns and the undulating ridge beckons ahead, taking you deep into the dramatic, big-sky scenery that zigzags all the way to Herefordshire Beacon – the site of an ancient hill fort known as British Camp, and a well-visited part of the range on any weekend or bank holiday. Beyond here the route becomes less severe (and less obvious so a decent map is essential) with more woodland, gentler gradients and rocky outcrops aflame with heavy-scented gorse. If exhaustion creeps up prior to the final goalpost, there is a get-out clause where the bus stops on the A438 after Midsummer Hill. However, if your legs can take it, the exhilaration of reaching the final triangulation pillar is worth the knee-wobbling climbs up Raggedstone and Chase End Hills.

Whatever level of walk you're after you'll find it in the Malverns: be it a woodland wander in the foothills or a calf-busting climb in the peaks. Come prepared for a full-throttle dose of bracing air and landscape drama, and before setting off make sure you fill your bottles with the fresh spring waters that made this area famous.

Practicalities

Great Malvern is the closest town to the highest point of the ridge at Worcestershire Beacon with good amenities.

Transport Great Malvern train station or Malvern Link train station (the latter is marginally closer to the hills). Bus service 44B connects Worcester with the Malverns and British Camp, and a Hills Hopper bus service (244) runs throughout the Malverns (weekends and bank holidays only, between Easter and August).

Sleeping Set in 220 acres of farm land, the 600-year-old £££-££ Old Country House, Mathon, WR13 5PS, T01886-880867, provides excellent breakfasts using organic and local produce and lovely rooms with low beamed ceilings. Splash out at the 4-star £££ Treherne House & The Malvern Retreat, WR14 3QP, T01684-772445, in the heart of the Malverns. The bedrooms are pretty with double showers or roll top baths, while breakfasts involve locally produced sausages, bacon and organic eggs. B&B plus self-catering (from £375/week) at this grand, former Gentleman's Residence. **Camping** Providing you've arrived on foot, bike or horseback you are welcome at Caves Folly Eco Campsite, Colwall, WR13 6DU, T01684-540631. Pitch your tent in a quiet corner of the wildflower meadow from £6/person. Fires permitted in designated areas while on-site farm shop sells all the basics. Tent also available to hire from £30/night.

Eating & drinking For those in search of a real ale, The Nag's Head, Bank St, Great Malvern, is small if extremely obliging. Fuel up with scrumptious cakes and fresh spring water at St Ann's Well Café, T01684-560285, set in a building dating back to 1815 on the slopes of the Malvern Hills. Conveniently close to the British Camp hill fort, the Malvern Hills Hotel, T01684-540327, offers relaxed or smart dining options and serves the finest, freshest, locally sourced produce the chef can get his hands on.

Resources OS Explorer 190 or OS Landranger 150, malverntrail.co.uk. Serious fell runners looking for a challenge should check out: beaconrace.co.uk

Also try Swap your walking boots for wheels and explore the Malverns by mountain bike. Try Malvern Bike Hire (with on-site B&B, Treherne House, listed above) for bikes and local route planning, T01684-589414, malvernbikehire.co.uk. Or, if the reviving spring water has gone to your head and you're looking for more of a challenge than the ridge-to-ridge walk, sign up for the annual Worcestershire Beacon Race which sees fell runners competing over a challenging 7-mile course, beaconrace.co.uk

Swimming The Cam

Provider	DIY
Skill level	All levels
Time frame	Dawn till dusk
Equipment	Swimsuit, towel, swimming hat, goggles, wetsuits for those that feel the chill
Exertion level	●●●○○

Having revived themselves on the lawns of The Orchard, recreating quintessentially English scenes of deck chairs, picnic tables and afternoon tea taken beneath shady boughs, it is late afternoon before the crew of novice navigators begin their return journey downstream. Wooden punts, weekend canoes and university rowing teams share the waters of the River Cam which idly weaves its course northward through the meadowed landscapes of Grantchester, passing through the Backs – from Queens College to Magdalene, before pushing on through the Fens, joining the sea at the Wash. Dropping the pole to the river bed, feeding it through more practiced hands, the pilot of the flat bottomed punt slips naturally into an easy rhythm this time round. A kingfisher alights on the bank, catching the eye of those on board while swifts and swallows swoop overhead teasing the dragonflies which hover and dart for cover. Behind, the swimmer low on the water line goes unnoticed as he strokes on through the clear waters.

The clean, calm upper river between Grantchester and Newnham is an ideal stretch for those in search of a quick fresh water baptism or a more considered swim where limbs can be stretched out and the mind left to wander. The meandering, muddy, weed-lined banks here are edged with formal

< Cool pools for toe dabbles.

Practicalities

The River Cam runs through the heart of Cambridge, a thriving bustling university town. Grantchester just to the south provides a quieter respite.

Transport   Cambridge train station is well served, from here it's a short punt or walk down to the river.

Sleeping   Close to the river banks, the 17th-century **£££ Byron's Lodge**, High St, Grantchester, T01223-841003, offers great access for quiet exploration of this stretch of waterway. The rooms are pretty, as are the gardens which are open for afternoon tea. **Camping**   Just south east of Grantchester, **Cambridge Camping and Caravanning Club Site**, Great Shelford, CB2 5NB, T01223-841185, is a decent flat, open site and pretty much the closest to the city. Next to the Fens, it can get a little windy. Open Apr-Nov.

Eating & drinking   No trip is complete without a stop at **The Orchard Tea Gardens**, Grantchester, to an enjoy a well-deserved lunch time bite, like the Orchard Ploughmans or afternoon tea. The cakes are home baked and the scones heavenly. Set across a couple of acres, pull up a deck chair beneath your favourite fruit trees, close your eyes and you can imagine Rupert Brooke and his band of neo pagans running wild and free. There are a couple of decent pubs in the village, the **Green Man**, High St, which has played host to the Cambridge literati is a good choice with home-made pub fare and range of bitters. **Cotto**, East Rd, T01223-302010, in Cambridge specializes in turning local, seasonal produce into lovely Italian inspired fare from simple home-made soups to roasted racks of salt marsh lamb. The buzzy **Rainbow Café**, King Parade (opposite King College Gate), T01223-321551, serves up imaginative, quality, home cooked vegetarian fare to an appreciative and devoted crowd using locally sourced ingredients where possible. The puddings are cracking while the mains draw inspiration from across the world.

Also try   For a different, less wild approach to outdoor swimming head to the **Nantwich Outdoor Swimming Pool**, Wall lane, T01270-537255. First opened in 1934 the pool measures 30 m by 15 m, making it the largest pool in the area. It is heated to a generous 22°C and, more interestingly it is one of the only inland brine pools in the country. A natural encounter in a man made space. Open May-Sep, £3.50.

Demi Taylor

▲ Swimmers go unnoticed as they enter the realm of the neo-Pagan beneath the surface.
◄ At Newnham Riverbank Club swimsuits are a decidedly optional affair.

clipped lawns, flora-rich wild meadow perfect for impromptu picnics as well as woodlands where willows weep into the river creating private, shady pools and hidden corners to seek out. It travels through the aptly named Paradise Nature Reserve and past the steps leading to the Newnham Riverbank Club whose members enjoy the very natural delights of their locality.

The appeal of the Cam is well documented: the river was a wild playground to poet Rupert Brooke, writer Virginia Woolf and friends; it played host to Cambridge University's bathing sheds and swim club who, with diving platforms erected, regularly raced along the straighter stretches; and in more modern times, Roger Deakin's Waterlog extolled the virtues of his time spent exploring the waters here. Indeed, whether it is an idle pursuit, where a stroke here and a well-timed push there acts to aid momentum, or a rather more dynamic voyage of active engagement propelling you onwards, there are few acts more pleasurable in life than going with the flow, and few places more perfect than the upper reaches of the Cam.

> **Lowdown**

Prices
Free.

Season
Year round though it is at its best from spring to autumn.

Don't miss
A post dip afternoon tea at the Orchard to conjure up the spirit of those bygone wild swimmers.

Avoid
Byron's Pool which is now backed by a weir, not exactly idyllic.

Mountain biking Thetford Forest

Provider DIY	
Skill level Novice-experienced	
Time frame The shortest trail takes a couple of hours to complete	
Equipment Mountain bike, helmet	
Exertion level ●●●○○	

The thick dark trunks of a thousand pines tower up to the sky, filtering shards of sunshine through to the plantlife below so that heavy shadows fall across the track. Weaving through the trees the slope steepens, needles falling to the floor as a blur of bikes brush past on their painstaking ascent to the top of the incline, where pausing for breath, full of anticipation they start their speedy descent back into the depths of the forest.

In the midst of East Anglia's lowlands, the Brecks span 370 sq miles – a blend of ancient farmland, protected heathlands and new forests. In the heart, is Thetford Forest. Nineteenth century farmers unwittingly started a trend here, planting pines to protect their fragile soil from vicious winds that swept sandstorms across the plains. After WWI the Forestry Commission was formed amidst fears of timber shortages and began buying up tracts of the Brecks, planting millions of trees, developing a new forest here. And what a forest it is, covering 50,000 acres it is rich in wildlife, escapism and of course pure riding potential.

Amidst the patchwork of dense evergreens, sprawling broadleaves and open heathland are four waymarked trails, as well as plenty of 'off-piste'

❯ The Black Route provides 10 miles of technical, endurance testing singletrack.

possibilities. The Black route provides 10 miles of technical, endurance-testing singletrack matching challenging ascents with speeding descents. For less experienced riders who are still looking for some challenges, the 11-mile red routes bends its way around the trees, throwing up just enough surprises. The wide easy pathways of the Green 'High Lodge Loop' are ideal for families, while the gradients and varied surfaces of the eight mile Blue Trail, are well suited to those gaining MTB confidence – if it fails, you can always opt out with the short cut. The trails run from the High Lodge Forest Centre by the car park in the northwest of the forest, complete with bike shop and café to revive the weary.

Practicalities

While the small rural town of Brandon is closer to the High Lodge Forest Centre, the ancient market town of Thetford is the obvious place to stay if you are spending time in amongst the trees.

Transport Thetford railway station is a 5-mile ride from High Lodge Forest Centre, the gateway to the Forest trails.

Sleeping A privately owned and family run hotel in the heart of Thetford, £ **The Thomas Paine Hotel**, T01842-755631, is small and welcoming rooms. **Camping** In a secluded spot on the banks of the River Thet is the **Forest Holidays Thorpe Caravan and Camping Site**, IP24 2RX, T01842-751042. There are no shower or toilet facilities here and no set pitches, just good simple camping. East of Thetford Forest, **The Dower House Touring Park**, NR16 2SE, T01953-717314, has a David Bellamy Gold Award for conservation and offers campers spacious secluded pitches in a well-maintained park with top notch facilities including on-site pub and pool.

Eating & drinking High Lodge Forest Centre café has light snacks for post ride refuelling. In town **The Deer's Leap**, T01842-761616, delivers quality pub food at a reasonable price.

Resources Bike Art, High Lodge Centre, T01842-810090, offer bike hire from £16/day. For mapping and waymarked routes see forestry.gov.uk. **Timber** acts to improve the MTB tails and routes in the forest. Get involved at timbermtb.org.

Also try Explore Thetford forest with your feet high off the ground with **Go Ape!**, T0845-643 9215, goape.co.uk. Home to their first tree top course, it winds through the woodland canopy, 40 ft up, using ladders, walkways, bridges and zip wires. 15 Adults £30.

< Beware the Beast.

Wig Worland

< Thetford: the line weaves its way into the heart of thick, dense evergreen forest.

> **Lowdown**

❶ Directory
High Lodge Forest Centre, Thetford Forest Park, IP27 0AF.

❷ Prices
Parking from around £1.50/hr.

❸ Season
All year round although some of the tracks can get very muddy in winter.

❹ Don't miss
The steep rises and hair-raising descents of the Black Trail, not for the unfit, or fainthearted (or the under 15s for that matter!).

❺ Avoid
There is a rifle range that butts up against the red and green routes so check maps carefully before heading off-piste.

Wig Worland

Surfing East Anglia

Provider	DIY
Skill level	Novice-advanced
Time frame	Dawn till dusk
Equipment	Surfboard, wetsuit
Exertion level	●●●●○

A golden glow begins to burn, like raging fires far off over the ocean. Lines of swell emanate from far over the horizon, rolling towards the shore like ripples from some distant apocalypse. The deep red burns the peaks as they advance, rising near the shore before rising into a rainbow of spray and peeling along the waiting sandbank, a clap and rumble announcing its arrival. The summer sun rises early here, the glassy dew underfoot will be gone by the time the tide has dropped back off the sandbar. Watching figures lean against vans glistening with condensation from the cold night air. Wetsuits hang on wing mirrors, still dripping from yesterday's session. The sound of boards being waxed signals the start, awakens the sleepers. The sun has cracked the horizon now, a figure runs down the beach and launches over the approaching white water, beginning the paddle out into the vast green. The swell approaches in lined sets, rising on the peak and reeling into long walling lefts and rights. A crackle of excitement fills the air now, the paddling surfer gives scale to the scene and the rush is on for damp wetsuits and sand crusted wax. The shoreline is awake and the line-up is the destination on this most underrated coastline.

While East Anglia may not seem like the most promising surf location in the UK, it can in fact be home to some pretty good waves. The scene here dates back to the sixties and there has been a serious crew surfing here for decades. Around the breaks of Cromer and East Runton you'll find surfers in the water whenever a swell comes rolling out of the far north, or is blown in with those hard-edged easterlies. The waves at Cromer can be found near the pier, where short rights and longer lefts form throughout the tides. There are groynes here and there can be rips, so be careful in bigger swells which can pack more power than expected. Further north lies East Runton, a chalk flint reef which is home to both lefts and rights, though the lefts are generally longer. This is a break that works best from mid to three quarter tide, when waves can peel through to the sandy beach.

As a general rule of thumb, the waves in East Anglia tend to be smaller than the East coast around Scarborough, due to the shallow seafloor, which drains some of the swell's power. If Scarborough is 6 ft, East Runton will probably be about 3 ft. The water here has a greenie brown hue, although sometimes it's the colour of gravy. This isn't due to pollution, but the fine silts and sediments that are suspended within the water – evidence of a coastline in a perpetual state of flux, erosion and deposition, where the mighty sea gives with one hand and takes with the other. There are breaks to the south of Cromer but these are best left to the more advanced waveriders as rips are stronger and there are groynes in place to marshal the shoreline as well as other obstacles to overcome. The surfers here are a pretty friendly bunch, if in doubt, don't be afraid ask – striking up a conversation may reveal some hidden gems of knowledge.

⌄ Pier pressure – marshalling the banks.

< The gravy train rolls into East Anglia, the water brown with silt deposits, the swell well groomed by a distant storm.

Practicalities

The coastal town of Cromer is all about crabs and tourism. With its pretty pier, cliff top presence and faded grandeur it is a great base for exploring the area, it's also home to one of the area's premier breaks.

Transport Cromer train station is well served by connections from Norwich.

Sleeping ££ Shrublands Farm, Northrepps, NR27 0AA, T01263-579297, is 2½ miles from Cromer. A comfortable farm stay, year round B&B plus self-catering bungalow sleeping 6 and on-site camping Apr-Oct. Hearty breakfast includes their own eggs plus locally produced bacon and snorkers. On the north Coast, the environmentally conscious, Green Tourism Gold Award holding £ Deepdale Backpackers and Camping, Burnham, PE13 8DD, T01485-210256, is a popular spot delivering modern, clean, comfortable hostel accommodation Solar panels provide the under floor heating and hot water. Campsite also plus the easy camping option of tipis and very comfortable yurts, sleeping mattresses provided. **Camping** Plenty of options available including the rustic farm site Pondfarm, Sidestrand by Cromer, T01263-579326. Just off the main A140 between Norwich and Cromer, **Deer's Glade**, Hanworth, NR11 7HN, T01263-768633, deersglade.co.uk, is around 6 miles from the coast but the facilities including the Wi-Fi and showers are top notch. They have created natural wildlife havens, winning them

David Bellamy's gold conservation award. Year round. In August only Muntjac Meadow opens up to tents, with a central fire pit for chilling round. Backpackers arriving by foot/bike get a well reduced rate of £6/night (usually £13/pitch inc. car).

Eating & drinking By Deepdale, **The White Horse**, Brancaster, PE31 8BY, is something special hidden in the marshes. This chic little gastro pub has a reasonably priced bar menu offering up local, seasonal delights from mussels and crab to well-hung steak. Wash it down with one of a wide selection of cracking local ales.

Resources **Odyssey Surf Snow Style**, St Johns St, Bury St Edmunds, Suffolk, IP33 1SQ, T01284-753322, surfsnowstyle. com, is a lifestyle/cross over store but they do carry hardware including boards and accessories.

Also try Round in The Wash, get to grips with a spot of kite surfing on Hunstanton Beach. **Lost Boys**, T07897-563734, operate out of the well stocked Surface Kiteboarding shop in the Pier Amusement Centre offering beginners' lessons Mar-Oct with BKSA and IKO qualified instructors from £100/1-day course. For those who have mastered the basics but are yet to invest in some kit, they offer supervized hire from £20/hr while those looking for more advanced tuition to hone their skills can book in year round from £40/hr.

> Lowdown

⊖ Prices
Free.

⊗ Season
Year round although Autumn/winter usually most productive.

✪ Don't miss
Blakeney Point is a spectacular 3½ mile long single spit, constantly evolving and shifting with the movement of the sea. The nature reserve looked after by the National Trust is an internationally important breeding area for birds and a home to common seals.

⊗ Avoid
The rips and the huge groynes running out to sea.

Swimming Norfolk Broads

Provider Swimtrek	
Skill level Intermediate	
Time frame 2 nights, 2 days	
Equipment 2 swimsuits, goggles, suncream, towel plus sleeping bag, pillow and roll mat. Swim hat provided plus flippers as required	
Exertion level ●●●○○	

Early morning in north Norfolk; waves of heat can already be seen rising off the fields, promising warm sunshine all day long. The calm, inviting water of the River Bure flows steadily through the reeds and alongside overgrown banks, sure to offer relief from the hot summer's day come lunchtime. By the water's edge, a flotilla of swimmers are wading in, the fresh splash of legs and feet sending ripples across the surface as one by one the group plunges under and surges forward, the refreshing chill making them gasp and laugh.

One of the country's largest inland wetlands, the Norfolk Broads are a sanctuary for swimmers of wild persuasions who are eager to wash away the troubles of modern life and reconnect with the natural environment armed with little more than a smile and usually a swimsuit. The Broads were formed through the digging of peat in medieval times, later flooded by the rivers and tributaries that now make up the area's network of waterways. A wildlife haven where kingfishers, otters and butterflies are common sights, the Broads are also a popular destination for nature lovers and all manner of outdoors enthusiasts who can often be spotted keeping a low profile on the riverbanks or taking to the waterways on all manner of crafts.

"You never know what you are going to get wild swimming here," explains Simon Murie, a seasoned wild swimmer whose company SwimTrek runs swimming breaks to the Norfolk Broads. "Even in exactly the same place, your experience will be

❮ "There's a huge array of local wildlife and the landscape continually changes as you progress down the river," says Simon Murie. "You just can't get that kaleidoscope of experiences with pool swimming."

Practicalities

The holiday includes guided, swimming, breakfast, and camping. If you're looking to extend your trip, nearby Aylsham is a pretty market town with a few pubs and places to stay. Note: the food festival in Oct celebrates the region's local produce.

Transport Norwich train station is well connected to the rest of the country. Onward bus links to Goat Inn rendezvous, sanderscoaches.com. Collection from Norwich with SwimTrek around £10/person.

Sleeping Camping is included as part of the swim safari and **The Goat Inn** plays host in their well-maintained paddock over the road from the pub itself. It's basic (no showers) but comfortable and crucially close to the river. If you want to extend your stay, or up the comfort levels. **££ The Black Boys Hotel**, NR11 6EH, T01263-732122, is comfortable and spacious, while the bar and restaurant, popular with locals, were shortlisted in the Local Food Heroes awards. Recommended by Simon, the **££ Plough Inn**, Marsham, NR10 5PS, T01263-735000, is small and friendly with views over the Norfolk countryside. Breakfasts are locally sourced. Free Wi-Fi. **Bure Valley Farm Stays**, T01263-732177, has a selection of cottages sleeping 2-6 people set in an 87 acre farm. They take their environmental impact seriously employing efforts including a wind turbine to generate power and a biomass boiler to fuel the under floor heating. The cottages combine period character with modern facilities. Ecover cleaning products, fresh linen and towels are supplied as well as a freshly home-baked cake from £250/week or £80/night for 2.

Eating & drinking A hearty meal at the **The Goat Inn**, Skeyton, NR10 5DH, T01692-538600, is the first activity on the SwimTrek break, where they serve honest, traditional, homecooked food using locally sourced ingredients. The puddings are always a hit. For coffee with a conscience try the **Greenhouse** shop and café, Bethel St, Norwich, T01603-631007. Part of the environmental centre, the vegetarian café serves organic cakes, breads and soups and serves Fair-trade coffee. For something special, head a few miles north to the **Saracen's Head** in Wolterton, NR11 7LZ, T01263-768909, a wonderfully kooky mix of polka dot table cloths, country inn, roaring fires, real ales and hearty fare that celebrates all things local from crab to venison to wild mushrooms and everything in between. And if you're too full to move, the **£££ B&B** rooms are country-craft-rustic-fabulous.

Also try Explore the quiet lanes of the Broads by bike to see the wetlands from a different perspective. There are a number of places near the water where you can hire bicycles and a selection of cycle paths and bridleways to try, norfolkbroadscycling.co.uk.

∨ One of the country's largest inland wetlands, the Norfolk Broads are a sanctuary for all sorts of wildlife.

∨ Heading downstream past idle anglers.

∨ Pausing for thought.

different every time you jump in. There's a huge array of local wildlife both in and by the water's edge and the landscape continually changes as you progress down the river. What's more the water we swim in here is incredibly clear, directly filtrated by the natural reed beds and with no motor boats allowed. You just can't get that kaleidoscope of experiences with pool swimming."

With a 6 pm meet at the Goat Inn, the holiday starts with a relaxed pre-trip briefing and early evening acclimatization dip. Heading out the next morning to stroke and glide along the River Bure from Aylsham to the Burgh Mill is when the 'serious' swimming begins. Just over two miles, this stretch of the river drifts beneath old stone bridges and past sweeping trees that drape their leaves into the river to hide the river bank from view. After a wander through the idyllic countryside and lunch at a nearby pub, the afternoon sees a return to the water to swim to Oxnead Mill before returning to camp to discuss the day's experiences over, perhaps a reviving ale of two. The final day explores the channels and tributaries of the broads downstream of the Goat Inn, silently slipping past fishermen with wide-brimmed hats pulled low over their noses, lines idly dropped over the banks, waiting to snag an altogether different type of river-dweller. Hauling out by Little Hautbois for a picnic revives the weary before pushing on for the final 1¼ miles to Coltishall, remembering to pause momentarily and float between strokes in an attempt to spy kingfishers and otters, the agile and often more successful anglers, regularly seen around the waterside village.

Covering around 7½ miles of river and taking in some of the prettiest parts of the Broads, the focus is on enjoying the natural environment. But with fully qualified guides on hand to pass on coaching tips such as how to maintain a more efficient stroke, there's also the opportunity to improve your technique. "We want everyone to enjoy the holiday and come away from the experience feeling even more excited about wild swimming," Simon enthuses. "It's such a rewarding hobby we try to make sure that people leave not only enthusiastic but also better equipped to get the most out of taking a dip."

> Lowdown

❶ Directory
SwimTrek, Lansdowne Place, Brighton & Hove, BN3 1FL, T01273-739713, swimtrek.com.

❾ Prices
From £195.

◉ Season
High summer.

❂ Don't miss
Home-made banana ice cream with sticky toffee sauce from The Goat Inn the night before your first swim. Essential energy food.

✖ Avoid
Wild swimming on your own, especially if you don't know the water.

Foraging Southwold

Provider	Food Safari
Skill level	All levels
Time frame	Full day
Equipment	All foraging equipment provided. Wear sturdy shoes
Exertion level	●○○○○

Practicalities

The small waterfront village of Walberswick has good amenities including two pubs and a tea room, while fresh fish can be bought from the harbour huts. See Jacky's wild food blog: wildfoodie.com.

Transport   The nearest train stations for Walberswick are Darsham or Halesworth, onward bus service with Anglian Coaches between Halesworth and Southwold town centre angliancoaches.co.uk.

Sleeping   Recommended by Polly, **£££ The Anchor, Walberswick**, IP18 6UA, T01502-722112, where the Wild Food course meets, is a charming old inn with slate floors and low beams. Accommodation is clean and simple with 6 garden rooms and 2 smaller bedrooms in the main building. For breakfast try the smoked Lowestoft haddock with poached egg. In nearby Henham Park, an alternate foraging location, **£££ The Stables**, NR34 8AN, T07939-566714, is something a bit special – the beautiful former coach house features rooms with high vaulted ceilings and some with roll top baths. The breakfast menu is extensive, Fairtrade and locally sourced and their environmental policy is water tight. **Camping**   Just south of Walberswick, **£ Cliff House Holiday Park**, IP17 3DQ, T01728-648282, provides space for tents, caravans and tourers as well as offering self-catered accommodation in their chalets and lodges. In wooded grounds looking out over the coast they hold the David Bellamy Gold Conservation Award.

Eating & drinking   The Anchor has an extensive menu with local produce and hearty dishes as well as summer Sunday BBQ's. **The Crown Inn**, Southwold, T01502-722186, prides itself on its relationship with local farmers and fishermen, creating a fresh local, seasonal menu that changes daily.

Also try   Food Safari runs a number of courses charting the journey of Suffolk food from field to fork from butchery classes to cheese courses, foodsafari.co.uk.

< Burgeoning baskets.

< Marsh samphire: "Pinch out or snip off the tops of the plants, leaving the more fibrous stems in the ground. There's a fair chance that what you've left in the mud will continue to grow". Polly.

< Armed and dangerous.

> Keen hunters out on a mushroom safari.

Springtime in the Suffolk countryside; the mist hangs low over the land and silhouettes of wild deer can be made out in the distance. Like an efficiency of inspectors, a small group huddles close to the hedgerow, carefully assessing leaves, shoots and new growth under the watchful eye of an expert forager, choosing the best specimens to feast on later. Suffolk has long been on the foodies' map for its meat, fish and game but more recently its reputation as a prime spot for wild foods has hit the limelight. "With coast, woodland, riverbanks and open parks in close proximity there's a wealth of food to be found in the Suffolk countryside," enthuses food fanatic Polly Robinson.

Along with husband Tim, Polly runs Food Safari, offering wild food courses introducing people to the delights of foraging. Led by local connoisseur Jacky Sutton-Adam, the day starts with a three hour walk, taking in a variety of landscapes that really shows the breadth of wild food that the area has to offer. One of the region's summer treats is the salt marsh and mud flat loving marsh samphire. "It's very salty and delicious steamed or raw," says Polly. "The many unspoilt estuaries and creeks of the Suffolk coast are a great place to find it". En route, Jacky pauses to point out specific species, explaining the principles of foraging, what to look out for, what's in season and how to identify plants. Then, with eyes retuned to view the countryside as a larder, you're off and hunting, picking over the fruits of the land, before heading to The Anchor for a gastronomic wild food feast. This is where the day comes together with demonstrations of how to prepare and thoroughly enjoy the foraged bounty, with real ales and wines matched to the menu. This is also a chance to ask questions, picking up more tips on how to get the best from the countryside.

"Understanding the forager's code of practice is really important if you're going on the hunt for wild food," says Polly of a key aspect of the day. "We want people to leave the course confident in their foraging skills, learning how to identify and prepare edible wild plants." And indulging in delicious gourmet food and wine after a leisurely stroll through Suffolk's stunning countryside isn't a bad way to learn. Not bad at all.

∧ Local wild food expert Jacky Sutton-Adam picks over the days finds.

∧ Bright basket of nettle tops – ripe for wilting with some butter and devouring.

> Lowdown

ⓘ **Directory**
Food Safari, Framlingham, Suffolk, IP13 9BN, T01728-621380, foodsafari.co.uk.

💲 **Prices**
£150/person.

☀ **Season**
Spring to autumn.

⊕ **Don't miss**
The rare chance to pick wild samphire in the late spring and early summer.

⊗ **Avoid**
9 August in Walberswick – it's the British Open Crabbing Championships, a fun family event which makes the village mighty busy.

Canoeing River Waveney

Provider DIY	
Skill level Intermediate	
Time frame As long as you like	
Equipment All canoe equipment can be hired	
Exertion level ●●○○○	

The River Waveney rises west of Diss on the southern reaches of the Broads – a water lover's paradise and 117 sq miles of protected low-lying wetlands encompassing rivers, broads or shallow lakes, marshes and fens. With the Redgrave and Lopham Fen lying in its headwaters, the Waveney draws a dividing line for much of its course between Suffolk and Norfolk as it meanders eastward.

Known for its placid waters and easy navigation, canoeing the Bungay Loop section is a great way of experiencing river life. Crystal clear water and calm conditions make the stretch which runs from Earsham to Ellingham perfect for wildlife spotting with otters, swans, geese and kingfishers a common sight, alongside herons, regularly seen wading into the shallows to fish for their supper. Stable, easy to control and almost silent as they slip though the waters, Canadian canoes are the watercraft of choice for many and on a warm day in summer the river is speckled up and down with people heading out for a leisurely paddle. For the more experienced canoeist, downstream of Beccles and on to the Oulton Broad offers more adventure; subject to vigorous tidal flows through the network of the New Cut, the Yare and Breydon Water this part of the river is altogether more challenging.

However, if you're happy to leave the whitewater to the pros there are a number of places you can hire canoes along the riverbank, with Outney Meadow Camping a popular choice, thanks to its easy launch site and handy river map to help guide you round. A trip from the campsite upstream to the old railway bridge at the opposite side of the Loop takes around three hours, but with plenty of picnicking spots en route it's easy to while away a whole summer's day just mucking about on the river.

Practicalities

The market town of Bungay is ideally positioned for water activities with plenty to keep you occupied in between paddling.

Transport Beccles is the nearest station with regular buses on to Bungay.

Sleeping **££ The Castle Inn**, Bungay, T01986-892283, is a popular pub with clean and comfortable rooms. Home-cooked full English breakfast using local produce and there's always a selection of home-baked scones, cakes and sweet treats, available throughout the day. In nearby Beccles, **££ The Salmon's Leap**, T01502-476756, is an environmentally friendly bungalow with solar panels for hot water, a ground source heat pump for underfloor heating and a log burning stove for colder evenings. They grow their own salad vegetables in the summer, make their own bread, jams and preserves and use the local village butcher for the sausages and bacon in their cooked breakfasts. Rooms are well equipped and comfortable and there's ample parking. **Camping** Ideal for exploring the Bungay Loop, **£ Outney Meadow**, right on the riverbank, T01986-892338, is a quiet, well maintained campsite with good facilities.

Eating & drinking The Castle Inn has a good reputation for top notch local dishes and delicious desserts. Their evening menu changes regularly with the best of local suppliers' seasonal produce on offer. Regularly awarded Seafood Pub of the Year, **The Swann Inn**, T01502-476646, in nearby Barnby, has been praised for its use of local ingredients and imaginative menu, sourcing most of its fish from the port at Lowestoft. The fishing nets and buoys give the place a real atmosphere and the reasonable prices and decent portions make this a popular choice so booking is advisable.

Resources Canoe hire also available with **Waveney River Centre**, Burgh St Peter, T01502-677343, and **Rowancraft**, Geldeston, T01508-518208.

Also try One of the prettiest walks in the area, the south facing Bath Hills on the Bigod Way. South facing, they pick up the sunshine, which is why they made perfect vineyards in Roman times. Bigod had extensive vineyards on the land in 1240 when he built his castle in the town of Bungay. The 5 mile circular takes you into the hills delivering spectacular views.

> **Lowdown**

Prices
From £20/half day's Canadian canoe hire.

Season
Apr-Oct.

Don't miss
A trip to Bigod's Castle, ancient medieval ruins with imposing twin turrets in the centre of Bungay.

Avoid
The stretch after Beccles; best left to experienced canoeists.

Swimming The Great East Swim

Provider	Great Swim
Skill level	All levels
Time frame	From 16.25 minutes (the time of 2009 elite athlete winner) to as long as you like
Equipment	Swimsuit, towel, goggles. Wetsuits are recommended for added buoyancy and compulsory on race day if the water falls below 15°C
Exertion level	●●●●●

The shrill piercing sound of the starter horn echoes out across Alton Water and 1500 bodies rush in, keen to set a good pace for the one mile swim around the reservoir. The Great East Swim attracts swimmers of all abilities to plunge into Suffolk's largest area of inland water. Taking place every June it's hugely popular and registration fills up fast, so you need to get in early.

If you fancy a wild swim but don't like the sound of the full mile stretch, or simply aren't quick enough to register, Alton Water makes a great swim spot any time of the year. Surrounded by broadleaved woodland, wild flower meadows and reed beds, the reservoir forms a 400 acre designated Area of Outstanding Natural Beauty and plays host to thousands of wildfowl, including greater crested grebes and common terns. There are plenty of easy entry points around the water's edge with sandy beaches and grassy banks perfect for lazing on post swim. Watch out for sailboats and windsurfers though.

If flowing water is more your thing, and you're looking for an experience less 'en masse' just under an hour away, the River Waveney, a slow-moving tributary to the Norfolk Broads, is something rather sublime. Outney Common, which sits in a particularly placid loop of the river near the small village of Bungay, is particularly good for a dip, the evidence of rope swings lurking in branches are a testament to that. Its still, deep waters and picturesque river banks are great for those seeking out somewhere to enjoy a contemplative stroke and glide and, with goggles fixed tight, a duck dive cutting below the surface. If you have the stamina and enough to contemplate, swimming the full two miles around the Common offers a real sense of achievement.

∧ (Top) The one mile swim around Alton Water equates to 64 lengths of a 25 m swimming pool.
∧ Under starter's orders, and they're off.

> **Lowdown**

⊖ **Prices**
£30 registration to the Great East Swim.

⊘ **Season**
June for the Great Swim; year round river swimming, at its best from spring to autumn.

⊕ **Don't miss**
The early summertime wild flower meadows at Alton and Outney Common – quintessential English countryside.

⊗ **Avoid**
Bank holidays and half terms, both Alton and Outney Common heave with watersports enthusiasts from canoeists in the Waveney to windsurfers and sailboats on the reservoir.

Practicalities
The villages of Holbrook and Stutton are nearest to Alton Water. For Outney Common, the little market town of Bungay and nearby Beccles have a good choice of places to stay with cafés, restaurants and facilities.

Transport For Alton Water, the nearest station is Ipswich, 6 miles north. For Outney Common, the nearest station is in Beccles with regular local onward buses.

Sleeping For Alton Water, the **£ Garden Cabin**, IP9 2NH, T01473-328371, is a great summer time option. On the water's edge, it's a small but perfectly formed cabin for 2 with a basic kitchenette, bed, sofa and enclosed courtyard. Surrounded by wild flowers, it's a wildlife paradise where you can drip and dry off just yards from your front door. For Outney Common, **££ Pine Trees**, Beccles, NR34 7DQ, T01502-470796, is about as green as it gets. An energy efficient eco home built from sustainable timber, this B&B recycles its rainwater, uses solar power for its heating, has a biological sewage processor, is kept warm by environmentally friendly insulation and serves organic, locally produced or home-made breakfasts every day. Discount for those arriving under own steam or by public transport. **£ Outney Meadow**, T01986-892338, is a quiet, well maintained campsite with decent facilities, perfectly located on the riverbank meaning you can start your swim from here.

Eating & drinking Alton Water's **Café**, the Stutton carpark, serves a basic selection of snacks and light bites as well as hot and cold drinks. For Outney Common, **The Castle Inn**, T01986-892283, has a range of top notch local dishes and desserts. Their evening menu changes regularly with the best of local suppliers' seasonal produce on offer.

Resources Register for the Great East Swim at greatswim.org. For information on Alton Water, see anglianwater.co.uk.

Also try A 2-wheeled approach to Alton Water follows an 8-mile route along the edge of the reservoir, through wild flower meadows and rolling countryside. **Alton Cycle Hire**, altoncyclehire.co.uk, provides bikes and also a café for refuelling at the end of the route.

Cycling Coastal Suffolk

Provider	DIY
Skill level	All levels
Time frame	2 days
Equipment	Mountain bike, helmet, padded shorts, water bottle
Exertion level	●●●○○

Dale Reynolds

Flecked with pink and orange clouds, the sun begins to set over the heathland, turning the ground a rich purple and drawing dusk-time creatures into the air. Seagulls circle overhead as the North Sea coast stretches into the distance and winding quiet lanes dip down into Aldeburgh where the beachfront and cafés promise a welcome break from pedalling.

From the Brecks to the Sandlines, from the Broads to the estuaries, Suffolk boasts 3000 miles of waymarked paths and is a haven for outdoor enthusiasts. However, it is the Suffolk Coastal Route that draws most attention from those on two wheels, an 88-mile circular route that really shows off what the county has to offer. Relatively low lying with few challenging hills, the route's network of quiet country lanes, byways, bridleways and cycle paths weave along the coast from Felixstowe through Orford up to Dunwich, before looping inland through the market towns of Framlington and Woodbridge, then heading back to Felixstowe. Through forest and heathland, along beachfront and across rivers, cycling here is varied and interesting, with ancient landscapes and seaside heritage to admire. The county is set up for it, with cycle hire shops in almost every town and village while many of the bed and breakfasts and guesthouses are run by keen cyclists who are eager to offer top tips to help you make the most of your trip.

"The Suffolk Coastal Route is set within a designated Area of Outstanding Natural Beauty and uses mostly quiet roads and tracks," explains Nigel Brigham, Regional Director at Sustrans, "it's perfect for cycling because the estuaries which break up the coast means there's very little traffic, leaving cyclists to enjoy a relaxing, safe and peaceful ride."

It's true that the rivers which flow into the North Sea along the Suffolk coastline do require a spot of navigation, but it all adds to the character of the route, with footbridges and ferries providing regular intervals and breathing points. Between Easter and October, the Butley Ferry, south of Orford is one of the route's highlights. A rowing boat run by volunteers, it will take bicycles on board, so long as you are able to get them in to the ferry and hold them steady while you are rowed across the river. The ferry has to be booked in advance, call T01394-450374.

Cycling the whole route, with its town and village stop-offs should take the best part of two days so it's the perfect length for a weekend break. However, there are a number of spots a short distance off the main route, which might add a few extra hours but are well worth the detour. Aldeburgh, a pretty seaside resort that has inspired artists and writers for centuries, is one such rewarding sidetrack. Take the time to pick up some of the town's famous fish and chips and wander the shingled shoreline listening to the waves cracking through the pebbles.

However, detours don't just have to be about taking a load off for a few hours. If you are enjoying the Coastal Route but fancy something more challenging there are a number of off-road tracks in nearby forests which can be easily reached and provide ample opportunity for some adrenaline pumping rides. "Cycling in Suffolk is what you make it," concludes Nigel, "there are so many opportunities for different terrains, scenery and sights that no experience will be the same and whatever your preference you are sure to come away satisfied."

Practicalities

A mid-sized seaside town on the North Sea coast of Suffolk, Felixstowe sits on the River Orwell estuary and is the start of the Coastal Suffolk Route. The nearby port of Felixstowe is the largest container port in the UK which makes the town busy all year round, but in the summer it gets even busier with tourists heading in to make the most of the beach, pier and many restaurants, cafés and shops in the town centre.

Transport The town is the terminus of the main Felixstowe branchline from Ipswich, where connections can be made on to London Liverpool Street.

Sleeping Right on Felixstowe seafront, the **££ Norfolk Guest House**, T01394-2831660, is a family-owned small hotel with comfortable, affordable rooms. Free Wi-Fi for guests and a varied breakfast menu using local produce. If you take a detour into Aldeburgh, **£ Laurel House**, T01728-452775, is a quiet, small family-run guesthouse with simple, stylish rooms all with private bathrooms. Owner, Damian Risdon is a keen rider and always eager to talk route and share stories. Just inland from Dunwich, The **£££ Westleton Crown**, Westleton, IP17 3AD, T01728-648777, is very special a beautifully renovated coaching inn — all stripped wood and Farrow & Ball colours. The food here is also quality. **Camping £ High House Fruit Farm**, Woodbridge, IP12 2BL, T01394-450263, is a great little campsite in a secluded paddock on a fruit farm, surrounded by apple orchards. It's pretty basic but clean and well maintained with washbasins and toilets but no showers. However there is the added bonus of being able to pick your own fruit! Between Woodbridge and Framington, **The Orchard Campsite**, Wickham Market, IP13 0SJ, T01728-

746170, is a wonderfully kooky spot with woodland and pond sites available as well as a wooden gypsy caravan. Campfires are celebrated here.

Eating & drinking The **Alex**, T01394-282958, in Felixstowe is a friendly café-bar right on the seafront with a full menu featuring café favourites and seasonal specials — all sourced locally. Special emphasis is given to the Felixstowe catch of the day. **The Bru**, T01728-452071, in Aldeburgh, north of Felixstowe, is just a stone's throw from the beach and specializes in fish, seafood and local, seasonal dishes. Their afternoon tea is worth the detour alone. Inlands from Alderurgh, **The Crown Inn**, Snape, IP17 1SL, is a cracking 15th-century Inn well served by Adnams ale and fresh fish, meat and game. **The Station Hotel**, Framlington, is an excellent stop off serving up top notch real ale, local ciders and making the most of local produce.

Resources A map and guide book for the Suffolk Coastal Route is available from the Suffolk Council's coastal website, suffolkcoastal.gov.uk. Also check out Sustrans website for all the details you need on the Suffolk Coastal Route and to buy cycling maps and guides of the area, sustrans.org.uk

Also try If the thought of cycling 88 miles along the coast tires you out, try Rendlesham Forest for a more leisurely cycling experience. There are circular walks and trails throughout the forest and the level, even tracks mean you can just focus on admiring the scenery, forestry.gov.uk/rendlesham. Or looking out for a UFO; one was apparently seen here in 1989 and there are endless websites dedicated to it.

> Lowdown

⊖ Prices
Free, you'll need money for the ferries though.

⊘ Season
All year round, though at its best from spring to autumn.

◎ Don't miss
Picking up the Butley Ferry (book in advance) and being rowed across the river.

⊗ Avoid
The A12, it's traffic heavy and at some points it can be easy to slip on to. Make sure you plan your route carefully to stick to the more attractive country lanes.

< Through the shady Dunwich Forest, the path leads on to the Dingle Marsh nature reserve.

Dale Reynolds

Best of the rest Central: activities

Paragliding, Shropshire Hills	
Provider	Beyond Extreme
Skill level	Novice-experienced
Time frame	2 hrs
Equipment	All flight equipment provided, wear sturdy boots with good ankle support. NB. Bring a packed lunch – when the adrenaline flying round your body wears off you'll find yourself pretty peckish
Exertion level	●●●○○

Home to the Long Mynd Soaring Club, Long Mynd ridge stretches for 9½ miles providing a cracking launch site for those looking to notch up some air time in England's western fringes. Having laid out your canopy and lines, launching is a pretty straightforward affair of taking a few small steps down the hill, feeling the wind inflate the wings, the lines tension and the canopy rise overhead. Then it's just a short run and a giant leap of faith before you're, airborne, looking down on the Shropshire Hills below.

If you're not quite ready to throw yourself into the ether on a solo flight, book in for a tandem flight with Beyond Extreme. The BHPA registered school is run by Mark Dann who, with more than 20 years' flying experience, has been a member of the Great Britain Paragliding Squad so is the ideal person to give you some first-hand free flying experience. "I have worked and flown paragliders all over the world but the beauty of the Shropshire Hills always draws me back to this breathtaking place," enthuses Mark. If you want to learn the ropes, opt for a one-day taster or two-day introduction instead. After getting to grips with the equipment and learning how to assess a site and weather conditions you'll be ready to attempt your first launch – initially on reassuringly flat ground, before working up to short hops on gentle inclines and longer flights as the course progresses. And, if you've caught the bug, the time you put in now can count towards your elementary pilot's course, the first step on the way to being able to safely pilot your own flights. **Beyond Extreme**, Burway Road, Church Stretton, Shropshire, SY6 6DL, T01691-682640, beyondextreme.co.uk, tandem flight £90, two-day introduction £280. **Long Mynd Soaring**

Club, longmynd.org. **Sleeping ££ Brimford House**, Criggon, SY5 9AU, T01938-570235, delivers farmhouse B&B – breakfast featuring home-made preserves, free range eggs and sometimes even local venison sausages. Beneath regular flying sites and within stumbling distance of the pub. Camp at **Botvyle Farm**, All Stretton, SY6 7JN, T01694-722869, April-October, for views across to Long Mynd.

Horseriding, Mortimer Forest	
Provider	North Farm Riding Establishment
Skill level	Novice-experienced
Time frame	2 hrs
Equipment	All riding equipment, and horse, provided
Exertion level	●●○○○

Trotting through the broadleaves with the light dappling on to the forest floor the distinctive clip clop of horse shoes muddles with the cheerful chirp of birdsong in a melody of peace and tranquillity. Rising up in the distance, the steep slopes of the Forest's limestone ridges reach high, promising spectacular views out across Ludlow, while down below, the group treks onwards, deeper into the ancient trees to make the most of the privileged perspective that horseback allows.

The remnants of three ancient Saxon hunting forests, Mortimer Forest, as it is now known, was

▼ Paragliders above Long Mynd light up the sky.

Mark Dann

pilaged for firewood for centuries; cut down to warm the inhabitants of nearby Ludlow Castle. Now preserved and maintained by the Forestry Commission, riding through Mortimer Forest is a popular pastime; its well-kept lanes and paths make easy terrain for beginners and improvers to take to the saddle. North Farm Riding Establishment situated adjacent to the forest offers woodland horseriding all year round, with everything from fully instructed introductory classes for complete novices to solo horse hire, giving accomplished riders the freedom to explore the Forest at their own leisure.

Climbing, Grinshill, Wem	
Provider	DIY
Skill level	Intermediate-experienced
Time frame	As long as you like
Equipment	Appropriate climbing equipment for sandstone, appropriate footwear
Exertion level	●●●●○

For quality climbing and bouldering in central England, Grinshill is a good bet. Jutting out of the flat surrounds of the Shropshire Plain near the old market town of Wem, it's famous for the quality sandstone that is quarried here, an activity which has left plenty of rockfaces to scale. On top of that there are a number of natural rocky outcrops poking through the woodlands worth climbing. All under 50 ft high, southwest facing and with a range of routes and grades on offer, Grinshill is suitable for most ability levels and throws up a number of interesting bouldering problems too, although an understanding of the specific climbing techniques employed for sandstone is essential. Popular routes include Sugar Bullets and The Nebuliser which are mentioned on the UK Climbing Database (ukclimbing.com) but there is the possibility for new route development at all grades with many of the outcrops under-explored. Care needs to be taken here as there have been a few rock slides and large/organized groups are not welcome. But should you choose to climb all the way up, the views from the top are outstanding; on a clear day you can see for miles across the vale of Shrewsbury towards the Wrekin and the Black Hills. A real beauty spot, definitely worth a post climb bimble through the woodlands before heading home. See westmidlandsrock.co.uk for a more detailed overview of climbs in the area.

Sleeping In the lee of Grinshill, the traditional country pub and hotel ££ The Inn at Grinshill, T01939-220410, is a convenient, comfortable and tasty place to stay if you are planning on climbing in the area. They cook with local produce in the restaurant, serve local real ales in the Elephant and Castle bar, have spacious well-kitted out rooms and won't frown on you if you come in after a day on the outcrops covered in dirt. You can't argue with that.

Sailing, Rutland Reservoir	
Provider	Rutland Sailing School
Skill level	Novice-intermediate
Time frame	Up to 2 whole days
Equipment	All necessary sailing equipment provided. Remember to bring waterproofs and a change of clothes
Exertion level	●●○○○

Filling the air with their loud honking call, a flock of Canada geese fly overhead, their long necks undulating as their wings pad silently through the air. Near the pebbled shoreline a handful of Lasers cut and jibe across the calm water, small waves slapping hulls as they dart and turn, keen learners with their hands on the tiller, getting a feel for the wind in their sails.

Learning to sail on Rutland Water is pretty special. With a nature reserve stretching for nine miles and taking up 600 acres at the far western end of the man-made reservoir, Rutland plays home to over 20,000 waterfowl. The other 2500 acres are an open playground for sailboats, windsurfers and canoeists who can be seen almost every day making the most of the water.

Rutland Sailing School, part of the Rutland Sailing Club, offers a range of RYA courses for beginners and improvers with club facilities and top notch technical equipment to offer as well as passionate, experienced instructors eager to help you get the most out of the reservoir. From taster sessions in the newest Lasers to RYA qualifications and even personal one-on-one tuition in your own boat, there's a suite of options all of which include the provision of wetsuit, buoyancy aid and spray tops. And if you are confident in your sailing skills but don't have a boat, you can hire vessels from the Sailing Club from as little as £15. **Rutland Sailing School**, T01780-721999, rutlandsc.co.uk.

Best of the rest Central: sleeping & eating

∧ Breakfast at the mountain house wih a side order of Brecon Beacons.

Milden Hall, Suffolk
Milden, Lavenham, Sudbury, Suffolk CO10 9NY,
T01787-247235, thehall-milden.co.uk.

This is bed and breakfast and self-catering accommodation with an environmental conscience, the owner Julie Hawkins is a keen conservationist. The 16th-century farmhouse sits in acres of Suffolk countryside, surrounded by wildflower meadows and hedged farmland. The B&B side is relaxed and the rooms prettily decorated with period furnishings and stunning, far-reaching country views. Retaining original features, there are no en suites. Breakfast is served in the large sunny living room warmed in winter by a woodburner and consists of the farm's own free range eggs and home-made sausages as well as all the usual trimmings. B&B from £65/night. Alternatively large groups can hire the historic barn which sleeps up to 22 but is still comfortable, cosy, if a little kooky – what other barn do you know of that has curtained four poster beds for some of the guests?

The Warehouse Café, Birmingham
Allison St, Birmingham, B5 5TH, T0121-633 0261,
thewarehousecafe.com.

Housed in the Friends of the Earth building, you can be pretty well assured of the café's environmental credentials, but if you were in any doubt there are solar panels in the roof to provide hot water, their vegetable oil is recycled into biofuel and they use local suppliers and organic produce wherever possible as a matter of course. The food is veggie, vegan and interesting and you can either opt for a full-on sit down three-course meal for £16.95 or opt for a lighter bite like their bean burger served with a generous portion of potato wedges from £5.50. Monday-Saturday 1100-2200, Sunday 1100-1800.

The Old Hall, Norfolk
Barnsham, Beccles, Norfolk, NR3 8HB, T01502-714661,
bikeways.org.uk.

Set within a 3-acre organic small holding, the 16th-century Old Hall offers very informal, relaxed (if a little chaotic) cycle friendly B&B in the heart of the Waveney Valley. Rooms from £20/person and vegetarian evening meal can be rustled up from £7/person. Camping is again informal and basic but tranquil from £1/person with access to water and a compost toilet. Whether camping or B&B, cars are charged at £5/night to encourage guests to arrive under their own steam. The Cowshed is a great self-catering option sleeping up to eight people in two rooms, dorm style – there is however a double bed in one of the rooms. The hot water is solar heated and there a wood burner (first basket of logs free, £5 thereafter) and they can usually supply fresh baked bread as well as seasonal fruit and veggies from their organic small holding. From £100/night or £310/week. Available April-November.

Woodland Tipi and Yurts, Herefordshire
Woodlands Farm, Little Dewchurch, Herefordshire, HR2 6QD,
T01432-840488, woodlandtipis.co.uk.

Set in a wooded, car free site within the farm are three tipis and three yurts, each sleeping around 4-5 people comfortably in an assortment of raised king-sized beds as well as single foam mattresses – which can be piled up when not in use to make a rather comfortable day bed for reclining and contemplating. The tipis are heated by a central chimenea, requiring smoke flaps to be opened while the yurts are a little easier, larger and warmer as they are heated by woodburners. An outdoor fire pit and BBQ accompany each pitch and with a ready supply of firewood, it's easy to keep them burning into the starry-skied night as you gently swing in your hammock. If you'd rather cook indoors, there's also a gas stove while the kitchen area has electric ovens (for cheats) as well as fridges, kitchenware and crockery. Or try the bake house clay oven for rustling up a loaf of bread or a quick pizza! The River Wye is just over a mile away, waiting to be explored… Midweek breaks from £220, Easter-October.

Fishmore Hall, Shropshire ℹ
Fishmore Rd, Ludlow, Shropshire, SY8 3DP, T01584-875148.

The views across rolling green fields towards Clee Hill are enticing enough and when you find yourself tucking into a wonderful local market lunch created from the best local products that Shropshire can offer, you realise you've struck gold. The two-course Sunday lunch comes in at around £20 and usually features a roast rib of Herefordshire rare breed beef accompanied by a pile of seasonal goodies. If you're looking for something lighter, fresh made soups and sandwiches are also available. Then of course, there's the tea – cream tea or the whole hog afternoon tea featuring home-made scones, red berry compote, home-made biscuits, sandwiches and of course a pot of tea (£5.50 cream tea, £16.50 afternoon tea). Then perhaps supper… and if you find you've over indulged…

Well, you could always splash out and book in for a night at this little boutique hotel. Well, how else are you going to get to sample their Shropshire breakfast?

Hunter's Hall, Norfolk ◉
Swanton Morley, Dereham, Norfolk, NR20 4JU, T01362-637457.

Set on the 790 acre working Park Farm with rare breed cattle, the two acre site here is essentially just a grassy field, and that's the appeal. With a tent you can pretty much pitch up anywhere within reason, providing you leave enough space between you and the next pitch but there are also a number of electric hook-ups for vans. There's a central campfire which people tend to gravitate towards on fine summer evenings. The field next door is also a popular spot for wedding receptions so Saturday nights can sometimes be a little 'excitable'. If rustling up breakfast on the old camp stove sounds like too much effort, book in for a full-English in the B&B breakfast room on site from £7.50. And if you're after a slice of home-made cake and a cup of tea, look no further than Peggy's Pantry also in the farmhouse. Open year round.

Ty-Mynydd, Herefordshire ◉
Llanigon, Hay-on-Wye, HR3 5RJ, T01497-821593, tymynydd.co.uk.

Welsh for 'mountain house', this organic farmhouse perched on Hay Bluff, high in the Welsh Marches lives up to its moniker. Having bumped up the hillside track, the farm delivers incredible views that reach across the Wye Valley to the Black Mountains and beyond. This is a working organic farm raising pigs, Welsh mountain ewes and cows while the rooms are comfortable and really farm-house pretty. If you want a soak in the roll top bath at the end of a long day's walking, it's fresh mountain spring water that flows from the taps to ease away your aches and pains. Breakfast naturally features home baked bread plus their own organic produce where possible as well as a decent portion of views across to the Brecon Beacons reminding you that while this is only six miles from Hay-on-Wye, it's also only 10 miles from the Welsh town of Brecon. With so much walking potential, it's hard to know which way to go first! B&B from £80/night.

◅ Ty-Mynydd, Herefordshire.

◅ Ty-Mynydd interior, Herefordshire.

North England

Wig Worland

❮ Grand vistas and even grander challenges await.

The vast landscape spreads coast to coast across England's high latitudes, the fabric of the land laid down in strata. Ribbons of industrial growth; the yellow glow of night-time illuminations marking the approach of great cities while beyond lie towering peaks that pierce the thick film of vast grey sky. Knocking on Scotland's door the Lake District is the region's head boy; notching up both England's highest peak and largest lake to its name, it's potential is clear. Wrapped in a hard blanket of gritstone encrusted with climbers, walkers and mountain bikers, the Dark Peak keeps a firm grip on the region's southern reaches. Malham Cove's epic limestone face draws the walker's gaze and climber's hand while nearby the cool waters of tarns and pools call out. The peaks of Ingleborough and Pen-y-Ghent see cyclists race and ramblers push for lofty summits while the peaks close to the mouth of the mighty Tyne are devoured by wave-hungry surfers. Watched only by Northumberland's gothic castles, offshore islands lie within reach of kayakers while the Coast to Coast trail that winds and climbs through the valleys of the Lakes, the peaks of the Pennines, the heights of the Dales and the heathlands of the North Yorkshire Moors awaits the brave. Do not doubt The North as an entity for its name is writ large on the towering motorway signs that line the arterial tarmac of the M1. This is a grand region offering escape on a grand scale.

⌄ Yorkshire's very own 'Peak District'

Environment

The North is a kingdom divided. The Peaks and Pennines run like a backbone through the country, separating Yorkshire from Lancashire, Northumberland from Cumbria, local rivalries cemented by geological ascent. This strip of uplands runs from the Scottish borders down to the south of Sheffield, a lofty ridge rich in moorland, high fells and verdant valleys. Millstone grit and limestone predominate; in the Yorkshire Dales the carboniferous limestone creates a landscape of magnificent bleached pavements, deep gorges and cavernous potholes. Tracts of woodland have arisen at the hands of the Forestry Commission; Kielder Forest, at over 250 sq miles and the largest manmade forest in Europe, is an extreme example. Many have been opened up with an array of excellent mountain bike trails, centres for outdoor activities beneath lush canopies. Despite the towering cliffs that have been drawn up in an attempt to hide the golden beaches, hidden fingers of reef and classic point breaks from prying eyes, the secret is well and truly out: the northeast coast is home to some of the best surf breaks in England. What it lacks in quantity of surfable days, it makes up for in quality; swells generated by low pressures high in the North Sea find eager waveriders waiting along the shore between Saltburn and Scarborough and on the fringes of Tynemouth. Surfing after heavy rainfall should be avoided near storm drain outfalls as sewage contaminated outflow can be discharged into the sea.

Popular pathways and routes such as those that follow the 270-mile Pennine Way and tour the UNESCO World Heritage site of Hadrian's Wall suffer for their popularity and thought needs to be given regarding the impact of footfall, erosion and the timing of when journeys are undertaken.

For all that the M62 corridor bustles with urban activity, outside this ribbon there are vast areas of open space to explore. The Peak District, the Yorkshire Dales, the Lake District, the Cheviot Hills, the North Yorkshire Moors and the Pennines are just some of the upland regions that offer the chance to be lost in thought, to climb out of the norm, to escape into the great outdoors and be immersed in cool, deep waters.

In 1932 a mass trespass of Kinder Scout was staged by more than 400 ramblers pressuring for access to the then forbidden realm of Dark Peak and their right to roam over open country and common land. The impact was far reaching and has changed the way we interact with our environment. In 1951 The Peak District became Britain's first national park and in 2000 the Countryside and Right of Way act was passed.

Climate

Winters can be harsh in the north, especially on high ground where snowfall can be heavy and sudden. Climbers, walkers and mountain bikers out in the cold seasons should ensure they are properly equipped. Temperatures have been known to fall into minus double figures, especially when a bitter easterly wind blows in from Siberia. Average winter temperatures are usually in single figures on lowlands, between 7 and 8°C, but this will be nearer zero on higher ground. During the summer and autumn the days can be long and warm with temperatures soaring into the high twenties, with a summer time average around 21 or 22°C, though again, be aware that altitude will see this much lower. The western side of the Pennines receives higher precipitation due to the moist predominantly westerly winds blowing in off the Atlantic. While the cities of Liverpool and Manchester can have an annual rainfall averaging between 800 and 1250 mm per year, Leeds will receive an average less than 600 mm. The east coast also benefits from lower rainfall and with southwesterly trade winds, the surf is often offshore here. Sea temperatures are around 12°C in the summer meaning a 3/2 or 4/3 suit is the go, but winter water temperatures of 5 or 4°C makes a 5/4 mm wetsuits, boots, gloves and hoods essential for those braving the duck dives, and wind chill in the line-up can make it feel considerably colder.

Resources

forestry.gov.uk Forestry Commission site with details on dedicated walks and MTB trails

sas.org.uk Surfers Against Sewage, environmental campaigners.

nationaltrail.co.uk Useful information on planning a trip to explore Hadrian's Wall Path, the Peninne Way, Cleveland Way and Yorkshire Wolds Way national.

visitpeakdistrict.com Peak District tourist board website with details on planning a 'green' visit and outdoors adventures.

peakdistrict.gov.uk/eqm Peak District National Park Authority guide to businesses who have received their environmental quality mark.

golakes.co.uk Excellent Lake District tourism website with practical advice on visiting and suggestions on further adventures in the region.

fixthefells.co.uk Dedicated to the preservation and maintenance of the Lake District's upland footpaths.

lakedistrict.gov.uk Lake District National Park website. Check their weatherline for essential forecast information.

yorkshiredales.org.uk Yorkshire Dales National Park Authority site with information on public rights of way and exploring the park.

northyorkmoors.org.uk National Park website with useful information on visiting the area including downloadable walks.

visitnortheastengland.com Tourist board website with details of alternative walking and cycling breaks.

Climbing Peak District

Provider	Mountain Aspirations
Skill level	All levels
Time frame	1-2 days for an introductory course
Equipment	All climbing equipment provided
Exertion level	●●●○○

It's a crisp autumn day and set against the pale blue emptiness of the October sky, layers of thick dark rock fold on top of each other, crevice, over nook, over crevice. Across the crag's surface, ropes hold climbers fast as they strategically stretch and grip, edging their way up the rock face inch by inch. In the distance, yet more crags and outcrops can be seen, the dark grey of hard gritstone and the limestone valleys with their secluded glinting pale white faces stacking up high with promise of yet more routes to be discovered. This is the Peak District. This is climbing country.

Lying across Derbyshire, Staffordshire, Yorkshire and Cheshire, the Peak District, as the name would suggest, packs a seemingly inexhaustible range of challenges into a relatively small area. Squeezed between the heavy industry of Sheffield and the metropolis of Manchester the national park provides a breathing space, an escape from the grind; with well over 100,000 recorded climbs since the early pioneers first took to the crags in the 1890s, and many more attempted and unrecorded, it's popular for good reason. There are a variety of terrains with routes and problems across the grades, which means that everyone – from total beginners to experienced climbers – can find something to get excited about.

"Climbing in the Peak District very rarely fails," explains Darren Saxton, passionate climber and Peak native, "the easier grade climbs like 'Black Hawk Traverse' at Stanage Edge (grade: Difficult) or 'High Buttress Arete' at Windgather (grade: Difficult) are ideal for starting out as the crags are easily accessed, the routes maintain interest and adequate protection can be placed."

To help people get the most out of these and other climbs on the Peak and beyond, Darren runs Mountain Aspirations. "Our bespoke courses are designed to fulfil individual aspirations," explains Darren, "so that by developing confidence and building experience, combined with an understanding of the relevant techniques, climbers are equipped to head out onto the more adventurous and remote cliffs found throughout the UK."

The climbing taster is perfect for those looking to learn the ropes. The course is kept small, no more than four people at a time, and goes into plenty of detail covering essential aspects such as equipment selection, use of guidebooks and route choice as well as rope work and belaying, but most importantly getting out on the rocks and climbing. "Use your feet," coaches Darren. "Good footwork is more important than being strong." By focusing on the Peak's gritstone crags and often working on the easier routes and range of problems that Burbage and Stanage have to offer, Darren will have you

Darren Saxton

quickly going beyond the basics and beginning to develop a range of techniques from footwork to the art of 'hand-jamming' while encouraging you to be in the moment. "When starting out just enjoy being out on the rock," he says. "Don't get too caught up in trying to rush up through the grades."

With a broad knowledge of the Peak and over 18 years climbing experience under his belt, Darren has something more accomplished climbers can benefit from too. With this in mind, he also offers private guiding, ideal if there's a specific route on the Peak you want to tackle. Whether it's ticking off 'Mississippi Buttress Direct,' (grade: Very Severe 4c) an established classic which follows a steep groove and a soaring flake crack at Stanage Edge, or completing 'The Thorn' at Beeston Tor, a rite of passage for any climber operating at the Hard-Very Severe grade, Darren can help you reach your

goals, hold by hold. And if you want to experience the Peak District but don't have a route in mind, he can design a day's climbing for you, taking in a collection of the Peak's classic gritstone edges so that you come away totally satisfied.

Darren Saxton

< "The massive variety of crags and their stunning locations and just the sheer range of classic routes at all grades make the Peak a special place to climb," enthuses Darren. "The gritstone crags may be quite small, but in the words of Jim Perrin in *Hard Rock*, let them never be so short, for me there are no better climbs in the world."

Practicalities

On River Derwent, the former spa town of Matlock has been popular with climbers for over 100 years, a good base from which to explore the crags of the Peak District. Closer to the Burbage and Stanage, the village of Hathersage has a number of good sleeping options and watering holes.

Transport Matlock is just off the A6, the train here is the terminus of the Derwent Valley line. Hathersage station has decent connections from Sheffield and Manchester.

Sleeping £££-££ Ellen House B&B, Matlock, T01629-555584, combines comfortable rooms and imaginative, locally sourced breakfasts. For groups the self-catering **Top Eccles Farm Eco Barn**, Whaley Bridge, SK23 7EW, T01663-750372, is a good choice. High on the south facing slopes of Eccles Pike, the 300-year old barn sleeps 4 with a herb and vegetable garden that guests can help themselves to. Sheep's wool insulation and a wood pellet boiler keeps the place toasty on chilly nights. From £365/week. In Hathersage, there are numerous B&Bs; **£££-££ Cannon Croft**, S32 1AG, T01433-650005, is at the high end. The rooms are pretty while the breakfasts feature the best local produce and home-made preserves. **££ Hillfoot Farm**, S32 1EG, T01433-651673, also serves up locally sourced brekkies. **£ Thorpe Farm Bunkhouses**, S32 1BQ, T01433-650659, basic accommodation 1½ miles from town. Beds from £10. Camp at **North Lees**, S33 1BR, T01433-650838, in walking distance of the climbs but 2 miles from the village. The gently sloping site is simple, tranquil with a drying room available. Can get bit midgey and muddy.

Eating & drinking The family owned **Druid Inn**, Birchover, near Matlock, T01629-650302, has won a Michelin Bib Gourmand 3 years running. Eat at the bar, on the terrace or in one of the pub's 2 restaurants, all serving modern European food, using local produce sourced from within the Peak District whenever possible. It's not cheap, around £12/main, but it is a cracker. And to wash it all down try the inn's very own ale. In Hathersgage there are a number of good pubs but in terms of eating the stylish **Walnut Club**, T01433-651155, is the showcase sourcing the best local seasonal produce the Peak District has to offer and converting them into a bistro experience. Lunch is the affordable option here.

Resources Outside, Main Rd, Hathersage, T01433-651936, outside.co.uk, is well staffed and well stocked with specialist rock climbing and mountaineering equipment. On-site café. Check the site for weather report and webcam.

Also try No visit to the Peak is really complete without undertaking a pilgrimage to Kinder Scout. This steep-sided, flat-topped plateau was the site of the 1932 mass trespass that saw more than 400 ramblers stage a group walk, pressuring for access to the then forbidden realm of Dark Peak and their right to roam over open country and common land. A handful were imprisoned over scuffles with gamekeepers but the impact was far reaching – in 1951 The Peak District became Britain's first national park and in 2000 the Countryside and Right of Way act was passed. Head out from Hayfield to enjoy a challenging and dramatic 8 mile circular by passing the epic 100 ft Kinder Downfall and the beautiful gritstone outcrops. For details see nationaltrust.org.uk.

> Lowdown

ⓘ Directory
Mountain Aspirations, T01302-888842, mountain aspirations.co.uk enquiries@mountain aspirations.co.uk.

$ Prices
From £45/person for a group of 4.

☀ Season
All year.

◎ Don't miss
"A summer's evening on a gritstone crag, the sun turning everything golden and the call of curlews as you climb in near solitude," says Darren.

✖ Avoid
The aptly named 'Popular End' of Stanage Edge on a bank holiday weekend and instead go and explore the quieter parts of the crag to the left of High Neb and you'll find some hidden gems.

Rail & bike tours Yorkshire Dales

Provider	Off the Rails
Skill level	Novice-intermediate
Time frame	Around 5 hrs
Equipment	Your rail fare on the Settle to Carlisle railway, bike hire, helmet and bike lock, handlebar pannier, route map and emergency backup are included. Just bring snacks and water (or order a picnic box)
Exertion level	●●●○○

'Let the train take the strain.' Ride *up* the Yorkshire Dales onboard the Settle-Carlisle Railway (dubbed the most picturesque route to Scotland) and meet your bike, kitted out with all you need for an afternoon in the saddle, at the top. Then freewheel *down* the Dales, taking in the scenic highlights along routes that have been carefully designed to avoid all of the steepest hills. What the passionate cyclists behind Off the Rails have only gone and done is come up with the perfect solution for those of us who want to explore under peddle power but, frankly, can't muster enthusiasm for slugging up long, arduous hillsides by bike.

If you haven't been on a bike for while, these dramatic peaks might not have been the first place you thought of getting back in the saddle, but the rides set a leisurely pace on country lanes and easy terrain that welcomes even the novice cyclist. Not only is 'Rail and Bike' an easy way to see the ups and downs of the Dales, it is also surely one of the greenest tourism experiences in the area. You really can leave the car at home without missing out, each route touring past landmarks and through pretty villages where you can get a real taste of Yorkshire. To make it a real cinch you can even set off with a picnic packed into your pannier.

If 'Rail and Bike' riding sounds like your bag there are three routes to choose from: the limestone caves and waterfalls of the Three Peaks, the country lanes of Eden Valley and the ride down scenic Ribblesdale. Whichever way you go, wending along the mellow country lanes you won't be too out of breath to appreciate the awesome landscape peppered with limestone escarpments, deep valleys, jagged peaks, thundering gorges, hillside villages and market towns. But if this pleasure-ride simply doesn't sound tough enough for your taste, Off the Rails can up the ante with mountain biking trails that will really get your heart pumping.

Practicalities

A busy market town, Settle is the starting point for the Settle-Carlisle railway and the base for the Green Tourism Gold award holding 'Off the Rails'. As well as the famous Shambles, there are plenty of restaurants and places to stay.

Transport There is a mainline railway station in Settle. DaleBus network also runs throughout the Dales area, regularly servicing Settle, dalesbus.org.

Sleeping On the outskirts of Settle, £££ **The Falcon Manor Hotel**, T01729-823814, delivers the high end option of four-poster doubles and twin rooms in a former rectory. ££ **Oast Guest House**, T01729-822989, peering out to the rocky stack of Pen-Y-Ghent, this Edwardian House delivers homely B&B where you can fuel up on local produce and home-baked cakes. £ **The Hornby Laithe Bunkhouse Barn**, T01729-822240, basic accommodation in converted farm buildings within easy walking distance of Settle. There are a couple of good campsites including Knight **Stainfoth Hall Caravan and Camping Park**, BD24 0DP, T01729-822200. A few miles north at Little Stainforth it's a large relaxed spot with the added bonus of being close to the river – perfect for a post ride dip!

Eating & drinking Pre-order a picnic that packs neatly into your handlebar panniers. Options include The Yorkshire Ploughman, The Vegetarian Treat and even a (small) bottle of wine or a locally brewed ale for a special treat, T01729-824419, offtherails.org.uk. Listed in the Camra Good Beer Guide every year since 2002, **The Harts Head Inn**, T01729-822086, in Giggleswick, near Settle, serves a good selection of real ales, some of them brewed locally in Skipton. A farm, a Drovers' inn and a place frequented by Winston Churchill in its past life, the characterful **Old Hill Inn**, T01524-241256, near Ingleton (on the Three Peaks ride) serves excellent home-cooked food

Also try The Yorkshire Dales is home to some of the UK's finest limestone scenery. Explore the cave systems with Yorkshire Dales Guides, Settle, T01729-824455, yorkshiredalesguides.co.uk.

> Lowdown

❶ Directory
Off the Rails, The Cycling Centre, Settle, North Yorkshire, BD24 9RP, T01729-824419, offtherails.org.uk.

❺ Prices
From £35/half-day ride, £75/day.

❷ Season
All year.

❸ Don't miss
Visit the museum that charts the history of the Settle-Carlisle railway line – an amazing feat of construction with 72 miles of track including 17 major viaducts and 14 tunnels. .

❌ Avoid
Bringing your car. Arrive by train, explore by bike and train; a car is unnecessary on all counts.

Bouldering Almscliff

Provider	DIY
Skill level	Intermediate-advanced
Time frame	Sun up till sundown
Equipment	Bouldering mat, suitable clothing and footwear, a mate or two to 'spot' you
Exertion level	●●●●○

The sun hangs low in the sky casting deep shadows across the weatherworn surface. Clinging to the coarse rockface a climber hangs spiderlike, inching higher, overcoming the problematic holds and ridges Almscliff is famous for.

Considered by some as the purest form of climbing, bouldering involves scaling crags and cliff sections under 13 ft high, without ropes or any of the usual climbing safety equipment. Normally undertaken in groups, it requires skill, strategy and a hefty dose of courage – as well as a bouldering mat and 'spotter' should you slip.

Covered with craggy outcrops and gritstone lumps, West Yorkshire is renowned for its bouldering, with a range of sites across the Dales. Probably the most well known, Almscliff – a warty chunk of premier quality gritstone perched on a windy hillside between Leeds and Harrogate – offers steep, powerful bouldering for those keen to hone their technique. Its rough, fast drying surface is great in all conditions and it's big enough to handle all the attention it gets with climbers and boulderers taking to the crag's surfaces all year round.

If you are a novice keen to have a go, but not quite ready to take on the main sections, there are a couple of boulders either side of the entrance to popular climbing route, 'Low Man Slab' where you can develop your skills, although overall Almscliff is considered more of a place to master your craft than to learn it. Should you be just starting out, nearby Leeds Wall Climbing Club offers a Bouldering Induction where you can learn and practice with qualified instructors, gradually building the confidence to take on even the Dales' most challenging of crags.

Practicalities

Almscliff is by the small village of Huby. It is 6 miles south west of the historic spa town of Harrogate, packed with good amenities but this is not a cheap base

Transport Harrogate train station has connections to Huby every 15 mins.

Sleeping The renovated Victorian townhouse £££ **Applewood House**, HG2 9BP, T01423-544549, is pretty, homely and quiet. Free Wi-Fi and locally sourced English breakfast. **Camping** 5 miles west of Huby, **Maustin Caravan Park**, Kearby, LS22 4DA, T0113-288 6234, with the David Bellamy Gold award for conservation, is a good, if pricey choice. Statics available to rent from £455/week sleeping 4.

Eating & drinking There are plenty of places in the buzzing centre of Harrogate to eat out, from independent restaurants to High Street chains, gastropubs to cafés. **Quantro**, T01423-503034, is a modern European restaurant with a warm, lively atmosphere and a seasonal menu using locally sourced ingredients.

Resources **Yorkshire Grit**, yorkshiregrit.com, Yorkshire Gritstone Bouldering is a comprehensive guidebook to bouldering. The **Leeds Wall**, T0113-234 1554, theleedswall.co.uk.

Also try If you want to get higher in Yorkshire, Ilkley (of the famous Moor) is one of Yorkshire's great gritstone locations with technical walls, cracks and arêtes throwing up challenging lines and quality routes for the novice through to the most experienced of traditional climbers. It's northerly aspect means it is often bitterly cold and exposed to the wind, it is also fairly quick drying and the nearby Cow and Calf is there to revive. For those who are able to belay but would like to progress and learn how to set up top ropes, make anchor selections and understand the guide books The Leeds Wall run novice courses at the quarry from Jun-Oct from £55/person.

Susie Norris

> **> Lowdown**

> **⊕ Prices**
> Free.

> **⊗ Season**
> All year round on gritstone, although conditions are favourable from spring through to autumn.

> **◉ Don't miss**
> The lesser visited site of Scugdale, home to dozens of bouldering problems in a quiet, beautiful valley in east Yorkshire.

> **⊗ Avoid**
> Don't upset the locals. Don't park near the farm or block any gateways to the field instead head to the layby on road to Stainburn.

Surfing Cayton Bay

Provider	DIY
Skill level	All levels
Time frame	Sunrise to sunset
Equipment	Surfboard, 4/3 wetsuit (winter 5/3, boots gloves and hood)
Exertion level	●●●●●

The figure on the cliff raises their collars and leans into the cold winter offshore. Frost crackles underfoot, and a fine network of crystal veins seals the scattered puddles that line the track. The only noise is the periodical pulse of sound emanating from the sets unloading on the sandbar below, drifting up the steep cliff face with a salty tang that lingers on the lips. This is a place of real drama, a vista filled with the profusion of kinetic energy, the meeting of forces on a massive scale, a battle royale enclosed within the confines of a quiet horseshoe curve. The cliffs terminate dramatically at steep points, a towering bay crowned by a flat plateau of cropped grassy pasture. The northern fringe is enclosed in a shroud of green woodland, a zigzag path leading down beneath shady boughs to open sand, while the southern arc lies scoured and exposed, a sheer wall exfoliated by biting Arctic winds. Between these points a battle rages, towering walls of brown, ochre and red, the very fabric of the land under ceaseless attack, a relentless onslaught of the ocean. On the beach lies the casualties, a walkway savaged and splintered, wartime pillboxes and tank traps rolled around like giant dice, the base of the cliffs slumped forlorn, like a boxer crumpled on the ropes.

Cayton Bay is one of the finest surfing beaches on the whole of the eastern side of the UK, it faces directly into oncoming swells and the curving arc is home to a number of excellent spots. In the middle of the bay lies Bunkers, a set of sandbanks that lie

> Lowdown

🄳 **Prices**
Parking only available in pay car park £2.

🄢 **Season**
All year.

🄞 **Don't miss**
Hot showers.

🄧 **Avoid**
Thinking that surfing is limited to colder seasons.

< The consistent Bunkers, Cayton Bay.
⌄ Scarborough delights.

Greg Martin

in front of the old pillboxes. They work as the tide pushes in from mid to high tide, producing good quality rights and lefts. Winds from the southwest are offshore here and these popular waves can be crowded on a weekend. The Pumphouse is a more fickle beast, a patchy area of boulders in front of the pumping station it works best when the swell is from the southeast. The wave here is usually a left, but can be a peak depending on swell direction, it works from mid to high tide. At the northern end of the bay lies Cayton Point, a fast, hollow left that breaks over boulders in medium to big northeasterly swells. This is a powerful and heavy wave that can see grinding walls between three and ten feet. Low is too shallow, but it does work from quarter tide up to high. With dark hold downs this is definitely a wave for experienced surfers, but hook into a set wave here and it's a long, reeling pinwheel that will not disappoint.

The beach at Cayton sits just to the south of the grand Victorian resort of Scarborough. When a new swell arrives, the grassy cliff-top car park will be filled with a cosmopolitan assortment of surf mobiles, from as near as Scarborough and as far away as Manchester, Sheffield, Leeds and York. Cayton Bay Surf Shop sits by the car park entrance, and there are warm showers and changing facilities to help with those cold winter sessions. Summer swells used to be a rare beast here on the Yorkshire coastline, but changing weather patterns are bringing year round waves, and Internet forecast sites are closely monitored by the counties surfing nomads. The motto here, where the ocean battles the land, is 'be prepared'.

Practicalities

Scarborough is a popular resort town with a population of over 50,000. It has 2 large sandy beaches either side of a large headland, topped by Scarborough Castle. Cayton Bay sits just 4 miles to the south, on the fringes of the town. There is a large caravan park here and couple of shops.

Transport Cayton has, a minor train station 1 mile inland. For better connections, Scarborough station is 3½ miles north.

Sleeping The ££-£ **Waves B&B**, Esplanade, South Cliff, Scarborough, YO11 2AT, T01723-373658, scarboroughwaves. co.uk. This Victorian house sits close to the seafront on Scarborough's South Bay. They offer free parking and secure cycle store. Rooms are en suite and the focus of the menu is organic, free range and fair trade. They also offer vegetarian breakfasts as well as vegan options. The ££ **Lodge Organic B&B**, YO12 5RE, T01723-363365, lodgeorganic.com, sits on the outskirts of the town and offers a wide ranging organic breakfast with the option of an evening meal. **Camping** There are a few options close to Cayton Bay, most being full on holiday parks. In nearby Flixton, **Humble Bee Farm**, YO11 3UJ, T01723-890437, is a better alternative with a relaxed vibe, happy ducks and abundant wildlife, as well as a fire pit and an on-site shop selling local ice-cream and goodies. Wooden wigwams sleeping up to 5 also available to rent.

Eating & drinking Close to Stephen Joseph Theatre on Victoria Road sits **Nutmeg**, a friendly café that specializes in fair trade, organic and local produce for their vegetarian and vegan menu. It wouldn't be a trip to Scarborough without fish 'n' chips and the Golden Grid on the seafront in South Bay buys fresh fish directly from the market and boat skippers at the harbour.

Resources Cayton Bay Surf Shop, right on the cliffs at Cayton Bay, T01723-585585, caytonbaysurfshop.co.uk, is a well stocked shop with the added bonus of being an O'Neill wetsuit test centre so you can try before you buy. Surf hire available. Scarborough Surf School is also based here. For forecasting and webcams check out **Secret Spot Surf Shop's** website, secretspot.co.uk.

Also try If the swells are too big for Cayton, head 4 miles north to Scarborough. South Bay is a much more sheltered spot and is surfable in even the biggest swells, when it can get busy. However, there is plenty of room to spread out with peaks along the bay, the smallest towards the harbour end, the largest towards the spa.

Foraging North Yorkshire

Provider	Taste the Wild
Skill level	All
Time frame	Weekend (Fri night to Sun afternoon)
Equipment	Tuition and meals are included as well as camping (in your own tent or ready erected tipi). Wear decent footwear and bring waterproofs, plus sleeping bag, sleeping mat
Exertion level	●○○○○

Step into the magical woods of North Yorkshire and forage, prepare, cook and eat from nature's larder. Pick wild mushrooms and sweet, crisp greens, scour the foliage for berries and nuts, skin a wild rabbit, and gut and smoke fresh trout.

After a weekend with Taste the Wild you'll have learnt that you can eat a peeled thistle head and what a pig nut looks like. But this isn't a hardcore bush experience where existences hang on a knife edge, and it's not about dutifully feeding the body with survival food stuffs. This is about looking at your landscape as an extended larder, foraging for delicious seasonal edibles, creating exciting dishes which err on the side of gourmet from wild ingredients and even learning to make a tipple or two from what you find in the meadows and hedgerows. In the hands of a team who are passionate about food and the great outdoors it's about getting back to nature, nourishing the soul, exciting the palette and expanding the mind.

The courses are based between Whitby and York within 16-acres of private, peaceful woodland at the heart of which is the simple outdoor kitchen-cum dining room which the surrounding forest has helped to furnish and fuel. After a morning's foraging under the watchful eye and inspiring tutelage of Taste the Wild founder Chris Bax, it's back to the kitchen where this former professional chef shows the newly initiated how to make he most of their haul, whipping up a sumptuous feast on the open fire and clay ovens. Although roofed, the sides of he kitchen are open meaning you constantly engage with your environment, putting the food into its natural context.

What you unearth depends on the time of year, from tapping sap in spring, to making drinks and sweets from hedgerow offerings in summer to hunting for berries, fungi and nuts in autumn. Forage for a day and it will change the way you look at your environment, but to get the most out of the experience make the wild woods your home for a the weekend. As well as finding free food and learning to prepare and cook nature's ingredients, stay the night in the on-site tipi, eat around the campfire, and listen to owls hooting in the treetops.

Practicalities

Your base for the weekend is in the 16 acres of woodland owned by Chris Bax. The nearest town is Boroughbridge on the River Ure and you aren't far from the vibrant city of York or Harrogate (about 13 miles to both).

Transport The closest stations are Knaresborough and York. There is no public transport to the woods but car sharing is encouraged and in some instances pick-ups are available from Knaresborough.

Sleeping Guests undertaking weekend courses can pitch a tent or stay in communal tipis in the woods. Decked out with rugs, floor cushions and wood-burning stoves, this is camping semi-luxury style and they may be able to loan you an airbed. Alternatively **£££ Cundall Lodge**, YO61 2RN, T01423-360203, is just a couple of miles down the road. The pretty B&B is on a working family farm. Enjoy views across the Vale of York with a breakfast crammed with locally sourced produce and home-made conserves.

Eating & drinking With a chef at the helm of Taste the Wild, there's no need to head outside of the woods. However, if you want to extend your experience head to the **Crab and Lobster**, Asenby, T01845-577286, for top notch local seafood or Yorkshire venison. For something special **The Dining Room** at Boroughbridge, T01423-326426, has reaped a number of accolades including the Bib Gourmand, for its menu boasting the bold, fresh flavours of the best local produce from £28/3 courses.

Also try If it's fungi you favour opt for the one-day foraging course. Or if you want to flip fresh fish over the flames, the Coastal Foraging and Fishing course explore the shores of North Yorkshire from a base in Staithes. Harvest edible seaweed, pluck shellfish from the rocks, hunt for crabs at low tide, haul and bait lobster pots, and enjoy a spot of fishing. Coastal foraging and fishing weekend £190, 1-day foraging, £60/person.

∧ Penny Wort.

> **Lowdown**

ⓘ **Directory**
Taste the Wild, 4, Manor Court, Shaw Lane, Farnham, North Yorkshire, HG5 9JE (postal address only), T07914-290083, tastethewild.co.uk.

⑤ **Prices**
Wild Food Weekend £150/person (limited to 8/course).

◉ **Season**
Mar-Oct (winter foraging days may be available by special arrangement).

⊕ **Don't miss**
Cooking over an open fire.

⊗ **Avoid**
Eating anything from the wild without prior guidance on identification and preparation.

Mountain biking Sherwood Pines

Provider	None
Skill level	Beginner-intermediate
Time frame	2 hrs
Equipment	Mountain bike, helmet, map, snacks, water, a repair kit/spare tube, foul weather gear
Exertion level	●●●○○

Riding through the glen.

Sherwood Pines is a living resource – an active woodland. Weaving beneath the canopy there are many trails here, some have been laid down over the years by the active local mountain bike community, but recently the Forestry Commission have embarked on a project to establish a network of routes, the aim being to ultimately create a National Centre of Excellence.

They range from a green Family Cycle path, through to the blue Adventure Trail, the challenging red Kitchener's Trail and a Bike Park. The Adventure trail is a six-mile circular designed to provide a suitable challenge for those keen to experience off road riding, to push themselves and stretch their boundaries out on to unsurfaced, tough, uneven lines. The route begins by following the Family Trail, before the way-markers divert towards more demanding terrain. Expect challenging riding, but do not be put off as this is a great introduction to off-road trails. Once you've mastered this, there is always the Kitchener's red trail to test your metal. During the winter this route can get muddy and there are areas where it's a bit boggy, however the FC have an ongoing program to maintain and improve the trail. Sections are closed periodically for forestry operations and trail maintenance, but there are always old trails around to explore and a good local mountain bike scene here.

Practicalities

Sherwood Pines is the largest woodland with public access in the East Midlands, at over 3300 acres. Pay parking is available but the car park does close evenings and is then locked – check times. Visitor centre has a café, toilets plus bike shop. Just a few miles south of the park, Edwinstowe is a good village base with pubs, a bistro and shops.

Transport The nearest station is at Mansfield.

Sleeping £ **Sherwood Forest YHA**, NG21 9RN, T0845-3719139, is fairly modern and a couple of miles south of the park with small 4-bed dorms and a couple of twins. On-site restaurant plus cycle store. Nearby campsites include **Sherwood Forest Holiday Park**, NG21 9HW, T01623-823132, year round. To the south is **New Hall Farm**, Edingley, NG22 8BS, T01623-883041, open Mar-Oct, adults only. Close to the Robin Hood Way, farm produce on sale.

Eating & drinking The on-site **Sherwood Pines Café** delivers cooked breakfasts, afternoon teas and everything in between. **The Forest Lodge**, Edwinstowe, T01623-824443, does the job with bar meals and real ales – rooms also.

Resources In the park, **Sherwood Pine Cycles**, T01623-822855, sherwoodpinescycles.co.uk, is well stocked with on-site sales, servicing and repairs. Bike hire from £7/hr or £18 all day. Courses also available. For independent trail info see sherwoodpines.yolasite.com.

Also try The forest plays host to the **Go Ape!** high wire adventure park whose course weaves through the lofty trees. Steel yourself for the 460-ft zip line slide. Adults £30, T0845-6439215, goape.co.uk.

> **Lowdown**

ℹ **Directory**
Sherwood Pines Forest Park, Edwinstowe, Mansfield, NG21 9JH.

Prices
Free or from £7/hr bike hire.

Season
All year.

Don't miss
The 13-mile Kitchener double loop.

Avoid
Getting locked in the car park after it closes – check the times.

Walking Mosedale Horseshoe

Provider DIY	
Skill level Experienced	
Time frame Around 6 hrs	
Equipment Map and compass, waterproofs, food, water, a survival bag, first aid kit, hat, gloves and an extra layer of warm clothing	
Exertion level ●●●●●	

"In the combinations which they make, towering above each other, or lifting themselves in ridges like the waves of a tumultuous sea, and in the beauty and variety of their surfaces and colours, they are surpassed by none."

Few people can describe the awesome peaks of the Lake District better than Wordsworth. And standing at the mercy of these staggering hills, its little surprise that they have inspired the works of many notable writers – Beatrix Potter, Arthur Ransome and, one of the area's greatest advocates, Alfred Wainwright.

Lauded as one of the most scenic gems of Britain, the Lake District National Park boasts a mind-blowing array of walks, from easy ambles and 'miles without stiles' (ideal for buggies and wheelchairs), to technical ridge walks and rocky scrambles. There's no denying this is a popular place with the tourists, but even on the busiest Bank Holiday it's possible to find peace, quiet and a world-class view within ten minutes of parking the car. Keen walkers need see little more than a map of the topography to persuade them to head for the hills, but you don't have to be an expert hill walker or conquer the highest summits to enjoy heart-stopping panoramas, verdant slopes and gnarly crests.

Scores of visitors come here with just one mission in mind – to tick off England's highest mountain, Scafell Pike. It's a stunner all right, but pays for its beauty with the constant footfall of ramblers on its well-trodden paths. The Old Man of Coniston, Helvellyn and Skiddaw are other impressive, classic peaks to scale, but also make popular tramping ground. If you really want to experience the best

◄ Looking down over Wasdale from Red Pike, it appears as though the fells have been draped in a vast, green, velveteen blanket.

of the Lakes and get a glimpse of the landscape to yourself, veer off the beaten tracks and take on one of many lesser known, yet no less beautiful, trails, such as the Mosedale Horseshoe.

This is a corker for experienced walkers only – the beauty of it being its delivery of some of the most spectacular views without the congestion of the ambling masses. From the start point at Wasdale Head this horseshoe of towering giants prodding the clouds do indeed look out of reach to all but the hardcore walker. And in poor visibility or wet, windy weather, even the most accomplished hikers would be well advised to enjoy the peaks of Pillar, Steeple, Scoat Fell and Red Pike with a pint in hand at the Wasdale Head Inn. But on a clear day, so long as you're physically and mentally prepped for the 11½ miles, and 3000 ft of lung-busting work ahead, the ascent is surprisingly swift and quickly rewarded with an emerging panorama of staggering peaks.

Just beyond the first climb to Black Sail Pass the summit of Locking Stead offers a good viewpoint for respite. And once you've got your breath back and scaled the rest of Pillar you'll be surrounded by some of the greatest mountains of the Lake District: Scafell Pike, Scafell, Great Gable, Kirk Fell and Great End. Peer down to the valley floor and you can spot the Black Sail Hut, one of the most remote youth hostels in Britain. As you march on from here, although the exertion levels don't let up, the views still insist on blowing you away at every vantage point. It's up and down all the way to Red Pike before a welcome downhill stretch back to Dore Head, where, if exhaustion has claimed you and your knees can take it, you could cut down a steep scree slope directly back to Wasdale. But, if you can muster the energy, what's a few hundred more metres ascent to the peak of Yewbarrow for a breathtaking finish to an epic walk?

Practicalities

Aside from the awesome scenery and England's second smallest church, there's very little in the tiny village of Wasdale. But for the serious walker there's all you need – a pub, campsite, youth hostel and The Barn Door shop, which stocks all sorts of outdoorsy equipment.

Transport The nearest stations are Drigg and Ravenglass, both about 40 mins' drive from Wasdale and served by Northern Rail, northernrail.org. There is no public transport servicing Wasdale, except the **Wasdale Taxibus**, T01947-25308, that runs from nearby Gosforth.

Sleeping £ **Murt Farm** in Nether Wasdale, T01946-758198, is not only where they make the creamy Wasdale Cheese, but also home to a camping barn, which is basically a stone tent with running water, hot showers and a toilet. Open year round from £7/person. ££ **Wasdale Yurt Holidays**, Gosforth, CA20 1ER, T01946-725934, delivers a more comfortable 'camping' experience with views across the Wasdale Valley and Scafell Pike. The locally made yurt sleeps 5 in comfortable beds and is insulated with organic sheep felt lining. Breakfast provided in the house from £525/week. Regular B&B also available at their farm house from £65/double. One of the most remote youth hostels in the UK, £ **Black Sail Hut**, CA23 3AY, T0845-371 9680, is a basic shepherd's bothy at the head of Ennerdale, with good access to the Mosedale Horseshoe peaks. In terms of 'real' camping The National Trust's **Wasdale Head** site, T01946-726220, is hard to beat. Nestled beneath the mighty Scarfel mountain range and at

the head of Wastwater, it's open year round with limited hook up for campervans also and just a 20-min walk from the Wasdale Head Inn. From Mar-Oct there's also an on-site shop selling all the basics.

Eating & drinking In a world-class location surrounded by some of England's highest peaks and the deepest lake, the **Wasdale Head Inn**, T01946-726229, caters for the heartiest appetite with the likes of Herwick lamb and mutton, and will quench the thirstiest hill walkers with ales from its very own Great Gable micro-brewery. **The Screes Inn**, Nether Wasdale, T01946-726262, has a reputation for serving lashings of excellent, local food. As well as having a good selection of veggie options, the likes of Cumberland sausages and local organic lamb are just what you need after a day in the hills.

Resources **The Barn Door Shop**, Wasdale, CA20 1EX, T01946-726384, barndoorshop.co.uk, is well stocked with technical and non-technical walking and climbing gear and they also run a simple campsite opposite the inn from £2.50/night. For local infoamtion check wasdaleweb.co.uk. For seasonal walks of all levels see lakedistrict.gov.uk/walking. For guided walks try thelakedistrictwalker.co.uk.

Also try Kayaking on the deepest lake in England, Wastwater. It is an alternative way to experience the views of the country's highest peaks. For kayaks and/or tuition contact **Carolclimb Outdoor Adventures**, T01946-862342, carolclimb.co.uk.

Swimming Lakes & Tarns of the Lake District

Provider	Swimtrek
Skill level	Intermediate
Time frame	2 nights, 2 days
Equipment	2 swimsuits, goggles, sunblock, towel plus swimming wetsuit if required. Swim hat provided plus flippers as required, limited range of swimming wetsuits available
Exertion level	●●●○○

Covering some 885 sq miles of rough, rugged, fell-sculpted terrain, from the lofty heights of England's tallest peak, Scarfell Pike to the smaller but perfectly formed tors, the Lake District is the country's largest national park. The clue's in the name but it is something of an aquatic wonderland. With Grasmere at its heart the great lakes radiate from its core like the hour hand travelling round a clock face. Thirlmere at 12 o'clock; Windemere, England's largest lake takes the six o'clock prime time slot; Wastwater, the deepest of the lakes slips in before the watershed at eight while Bassenthwaite Lake, the area's one and only named lake shares its

11 o'clock billing with Derwentwater. But fluid pleasures are not only available on a grand scale. The landscape is so dappled with tarns and hidden pools that even on the dullest, dampest, day, when the boggy ground compresses underfoot like a fully loaded sponge, it is bathed in a reflected brightness. Through the drizzle and downpour its beauty can lift the spirits and convince you to head outdoors. After all, you came here to get wet. You came here to swim.

After waking up in Wordsworth's Grasmere, the remedy for the first day combines a decent dose of hiking and swimming in equal measure designed to get the blood pumping, the limbs loosened and the mind freed. Following the course of the fantastically named Sourmilk Ghyll, the trek up hill to the first swim of the weekend takes about an hour with the babbling, swirling waters encouraging you on. Cocooned by a bank of steep-sided crags, Easdale Tarn, although large, gives the impression of being an intimate, private setting;

> Gearing up and kicking back.

SwimTrek

< There's nothing like a breathtaking, eye catching, stamina testing 1½ mile swim of Grasmere to start your day.

SwimTrek

an ideal spot for making your first commune with nature. A decent kilometre swim around the tarn's perimeter slowly acclimatizes bodies to the shuddering chill of the water, reminding them of the pre-trip training and opens eyes to the beautiful natural environment. A second decent hike delivers views across Windemere before climbing to 1550 ft for the second swim of the day, the dramatic glacial corrie of Stickle Tarn which holds itself up as a mirror to Harrison Stickle rising above it. A further hike and swim is on offer to those looking to squeeze in 'just one more' before bedtime, but for the weary there is the get out clause of returning to base, if that is, they think they can stomach the, 'oh, you missed the best swim of the day,' teasing from the die-hards.

Day two is all about the swimming, the morning kicking off with a stamina testing two mile north to south swim of the 245-ft deep Grasmere, bypassing the small private island that lies in the centre of the lake. But it's not just about covering distances, it's also about taking time to pause for breath and really drink in your surrounds, allowing the stresses and strains of modern living to be washed away. "I always tell the guests that they have to stop in the middle of each Lake and enjoy the view around them," says Swim Trek's Brad Andersen. "It's a view that most visitors to the lakes never get to see – they walk around them yet never dive in which is a real shame." After a cup of something to warm the soul it's on to explore the shallow delights of the achingly pretty Rydal Water whose banks are woven with rolling meadow, shady wooded retreats and tales of a poet who used to wonder here.

Practicalities

The weekender includes guided swimming, B&B plus lunch. The trip base is the pretty village of Grasmere, once home to Wordsworth (it's a popular tourist spot and prices generally reflect this). It is however in the heart of Lake District and an excellent spot from which to explore the region.

Transport 7 miles south Windemere is the closest station with bus links on to the village.

Sleeping Included in the price of the trip is B&B at **£££ Glenthorne**, LA22 9QH, T01539-435389. Part Quaker centre, part Victorian guest house it is set within its own gardens. If you want to extend your stay, there are several good options nearby including the pricey but pretty **£££ Moss Grove Organic Hotel**, LA22 9SW, which combines beautiful rooms, organic brekkies and sustainability. There are infinite cracking campsites in the Lake District where you can really get away from it all but the closest to Grasmere are around Ambleside including **Chapel Stile**, LA22 9JZ, T01539-437150, clean, busy and spread over 3 fields. **Great Langdale NT** site, LA22 9JU, T01539-437668, open to tents and campervans year round. Although further away has to be the pick of the bunch. Yes the ground can get a little boggy after heavy rains but the valley site is in the most glorious of locations, surrounded by the Langdale Pikes to explore as well as lakes and decent pubs to dip into. For campers in need of a little more luxury there are yurts and bell tents available with solar powered lighting, wood burning stoves and more importantly for some, beds! Sleeping 6 from £385/week.

Eating & drinking The Jumble Room, Langdale Rd, Grasmere, T01539-435188, is all about ustilizing the best local and where possible organic ingredients. From local steak burgers to Fleetwood fish and chips for around a tenner or soup of the day for £5, the lunch time menu delivers hearty home-cooked fare in a brilliant county/kitsch setting while the evening menu is a little more grown up. In Great Langdale, **The Old Dungeon Ghyll**, T01539-437272, is well know and well loved by walkers who descend on the Hiker's Bar for reviving ales and tall tales.

Also try This part of the world will always be linked to master fell walker, renowned guidebook writer and philosophical muser Alfred Wainwright who created the epic 190 mile, 12 day, stunning Coast to Coast walk between St Bees, Cumbria and Robin Hood's Bay, Yorkshire. For details see: thecoasttocoastwalk.info and wainwright.org.uk. Or explore the popular Langdale Pikes and awesome Dungeon Ghyll waterfall. A decent circular sets out from the Old Dungeon Ghyll Hotel.

> **Lowdown**

ℹ **Directory**
SwimTrek, Lansdowne Place, Brighton & Hove, BN3 1FL, T01273-739713, swimtrek.com.

Prices
From £285.

Season
Jul-Sep.

Don't miss
The views over glorious Windemere from Blea Crag.

Avoid
It pays not to come underprepared – put in some time with the pre-trip raining and you'll reap the benefits.

SwimTrek

∧ Treading water.
∨ Drying off on the banks.

SwimTrek

Climbing Cumbria

Provider	More than Mountains
Skill level	Novice-experienced
Time frame	½ day to a week
Equipment	Helmets, harnesses, ropes, protection and all technical gear provided. Wear breathable, warm layers and trainers or climbing shoes, and bring waterproofs, hat, gloves, food, drink and a rucksack
Exertion level	●●●●○

Your chalky fingers clasp the rock face. Spread below is a lush valley, a patchwork of farmland peppered with boulders, babbling streams and sheep. In the distance the sea glimmers. Above towers yet more volcanic rock, clawing sky-high. You are enveloped in the pitch-perfect elements. This is rock climbing, Lake District style.

When it comes to climbing the Lake District certainly puts on a sensational performance. It was the 1886 ascent of Napes Needle in Wasdale that put the area on the map as the birthplace of climbing in Britain and today Wasdale still retains it magnetism, drawing serious climbers to classic routes etched in its majestic mountains and tumbling scree slopes. Across generations, climbers have congregated at the Wasdale Head Inn to share white-knuckle stories of rocky escapades, and the graveyard of nearby St Olaf church bears testament to a few climbers who succumbed to the perils of the sport in its early days.

While Wasdale is riddled with historic connotations and awe-inspiring climbs, perhaps a better location to kindle a passion for climbing is on the more easily accessible valley crags of Keswick. Here, around Borrowdale, climbers can notch up an impressive number of ascents on classic routes of all levels. Just footsteps from the roadside the popular Shepherds Crag boasts excellent single pitch routes basked in sunshine, while the steep, shaded walls of Goat Crag, on the western side of Borrowdale, saves its best offerings for competent crag rats looking for more difficult climbs. If you're seeking the full mountain experience, jaw-dropping views and some excellent, less populated, climbing terrain reward the longer walk into Sergeant Crag Slabs at upper Borrowdale.

< Borrowdale at dawn.

Of course if you're not a climbing aficionado it would be foolhardy to charge off into the mountains with little more than a rope and a guidebook. What you need is a climbing guide and some tuition. And whatever your ability the experts at More than Mountains, based in Keswick, are ready and waiting to take you on climbing course, or a climbing tour, on the rock of Borrowdale that they know intimately. Beginners can get a taster on a private half-day session, or secure basic skills on a one- or two-day course with a group of other aspirant climbers. While the private tuition and guiding is tailored to your time and needs – be it a day learning to lead a climb or a five-day hardcore multi-pitch rock tour – there are also a range of group courses geared towards different climbing abilities. Intermediate climbers who want to be self-sufficient in the mountain environment can learn advanced techniques on a rescue skills course led by Nick Jones, one half of the More than Mountains team and an active member of the Keswick Mountain Rescue Team.

> **Lowdown**

❶ **Directory**
More than Mountains, Keswick, CA12 4DQ, T07984-410230, morethan mountains.co.uk.

❺ **Prices**
Courses from £75/ person. Private tuition £160/day, £120/half day (the cost is split between participants. Max 6 people for single pitch climbing; max 2 people for multi-pitch climbs).

❺ **Season**
All year.

❺ **Don't miss**
Take a trip to the historic Wasdale Head Inn. It's been a local haunt of climbing pioneers over the generations and the walls are clad in sepia images.

❺ **Avoid**
Climbing in bad weather or poor visibility. Call the National Park Authority's Weatherline Service, T0870-055 0575, to check the forecast before you set out.

Practicalities

Keswick is a traditional, small market town nestled in the heart of the Lake District. Once home to no more than a cheese farm, these days it boasts a vibrant tourism scene and plenty of facilities including shops and accommodation.

Transport A number of buses service Keswick, including the LakesLink 555 and the X4 and X5 from Penrith (where the closest mainline station is located).

Sleeping Close to Keswick town centre and Derwentwater, £££ **Howe Keld B&B**, T01768-772417, is decked out in local, natural materials and has the gold award for Green Tourism. Tuck into organic, home-baked bread, free range eggs from a nearby farm, locally sourced bacon and sausages, and fairtrade coffee, and bag one of the new chalet-style rooms with solid wood floors. In a tranquil, scenic location close to the banks of Derwentwater, ££ **Cumbria House**, T01768-773171, welcomes climbers, walkers, cyclists and dogs into a homely Victorian guesthouse. Its green credentials focus not only minimizing food miles (the hearty breakfast is crammed with locally sourced ingredients) but also on 'water miles', by encouraging guests to fill up their water bottles with chilled Lakeland tap water kept in the fridge. They also offer a 5% discount for car-free arrivals. Packed lunches can be organized. **Camping** There are a number of cracking options here. Hogging a prime location overlooking Derwentwater yet just 1½ miles from town, **Castlerigg Hall Caravan and Camping Park**, CA12 4TE, T01768-774499, offers a great location to pitch your tent and watch the sun go down on a day in the hills. If you want something a little more plush, weatherproof your camping experience in a camping pod – a timber hut insulated with sheep's wool.

Eating The menu at the **Keswick Lodge**, Main St, T01768-774584, sets out to showcase the wealth of produce grown and reared in Cumbria. Take a pew by the log fire and dine on west coast salmon, fellside lamb, Cumberland sausages or local steak and Thwaites ale pie. You won't be served just any old tea and cake at **Bryson's of Keswick**, T01768-772257, a craft bakery since 1947, the treats in store here have been hand-baked according to traditional recipes. Tuck into a slice of speciality Lakeland Plum Bread with a cup of Bryson's own blend tea.

Resources A good source of information is the **FRCC** climbing guides (frcc.co.uk) with the Scafell, Wasdale, Eskdale edition and the Gable & Pillar edition covering the central massif, and the Borrowdale edition covering the area around Keswick. More information on climbing in the Lakes is available from the **British Mountaineering Council**, T0870-010 4878, thebmc.co.uk.

Also try If you're tentative about scaling awesome heights, even under expert tutelage, try scrambling. Said to be one of the purest forms of mountain adventure, this technique does away with the ropes and is all about using footholds and handholds to ascend, well, scramble up steep, rocky sections of hillsides. One step beyond hill walking yet not as far off the ground as climbing, scrambling can add an exciting edge to exploring the fells on foot. 2 day introduction to scrambling courses with More than Mountains from £170.

⌄ Eve Prickett, Shepherd's Crag, Borrowdale. "It is no coincidence that rock climbing first started in the Lake District," says More than Mountains' Jill Frankland. "With the quality of the rock and the beauty of the scenery, nothing beats it. And with 100s of easy climbs the Lake District is the perfect place for beginners to discover the joys and challenges of rock climbing."

Alex Messenger

Mountain biking Coast to Coast

Provider	None
Skill level	Intermediate-experienced
Time frame	6 days
Equipment	Mountain bike, helmet, map, snacks, water, a map, compass, first aid kit, a repair kit/spare tube, foul weather gear
Exertion level	●●●●●

The North of England is home to some of the UK's most spectacular scenery. In 1972 well known walker and writer Alfred Wainwright devised his now legendary coast to coast walk, one that climbs and descends its way over some 200 miles from the shores of the Irish Sea through three National Parks to the fringes of the North Sea in the east. Starting at the coastal village of St Bees, it winds through Cumbria, soaring high onto misty Lakeland fells, climbing through the lofty Pennine peaks, over the Yorkshire Dales windswept limestone crags, down through lush meadow and woodland pathways before climbing the Cleveland Hills and into the North Yorkshire Moors before there, in the distance, shimmering like a mirage, looms the expanse of the North Sea and the tiny village of Robin Hoods Bay. It hasn't taken mountain bikers long to realize what a challenging and rewarding route this can be.

∨ Passing though shady woodland provides some respite.

The classic Coast to Coast runs to just over 200 miles and usually takes around six days to complete, though some will naturally push it to five. There are steep climbs, rewarding descents and impressive views throughout. There are certainly sections that require a bit of hiking, but there are also super fast downhill runs to compensate. Accommodation is staggered into five or six stopovers with youth hostels and pubs well used to the late afternoon arrivals of the mud spattered and leg weary. There are companies that help facilitate accommodation and act as sherpas for your gear, but some choose to take on this challenge with a group of friends, roping in someone with a van to act as back up, leapfrogging to the next destination carrying a good supply of warm clothes and fresh supplies.

The Coast to Coast offers a unique opportunity, traversing the roof top of England from one shore to the other, through some stunning landscapes and over some demanding terrain. The rewards come not only from the endlessly changing scenery, but also from accomplishing what is a very special challenge.

< Surveying the path ahead.

Practicalities

There is no strict itinerary to follow, but the route follows right of ways, footpaths and some minor roads. The route passes through St Bees, Rosthwaite, Grasmere, Shap, Kirkby Stephen, Keld, Richmond, Ingleby Cross, Glaisdale finshes in Robin Hoods Bay.

Transport At the western end of the ride, St Bees train station is well served by the Cumbrian Coast Line (connections via Lancaster and Carlisle) except Sundays when trains terminate at Whitehaven 4 miles north.

Sleeping ££-£ **Abbey Farmhouse**, St Bees, Cumbria, CA27 0DY, T01946-823534, abbeyfarm-stbees.co.uk, is a B&B in a charming building that dates back to the 17th century. They offer a breakfast of locally sourced produce and home-made bread, an ideal way to set yourself up for the long trip ahead. At the other end of the scale, **£ Tarn Flatt Camping Barn**, Sandwith, Whitehaven, CA28 9UX, set on a working family farm has simple bunk barn accommodation from £7/person with coin operated shower and open fire for warmth. Breakfast bookable in advance. Along the route there are many **YHA hostels** such as Eskdale, Grasmere, Ambleside, Kirkby Stephen, Keld, Richmond, Osmotherly, Robin Hoods Bay (Boggle Hole). Check out yha.org.uk. At the end of the journey, camp up at the simple **Hooks House Farm**, Robin Hood's Bay, YO22 4PE,

T01947-880283. Set on a working farm there are wonderful views across the sea (blue making a change to all the green you've been seeing) and a 4 bed caravan available to rent for those who don't have their own tent.

Eating & drinking **Swell Café** in Robin Hoods Bay serves fair trade tea and coffee, as well as an assortment of light meals and sandwiches overlooking the sea. At nearly 1800 ft above sea level, Tan Hill Inn near Richmond is the highest in England and dates from the 17th century.

Resources The Coast To Coast Route Companion Pack is available and offers a choice of route variations for differing technical abilities as well as accommodation options, mbruk.co.uk.

Also try For those not ready for the serious challenge of the Coast to Coast there is the Sea to Sea cycle route. It was developed by Sustrans and opened in 1994 running from Whitehaven on the coast of Cumbria to Sunderland on the east coast. It is 147 miles long and part of the National Cycle Network that runs mostly along minor roads, disused railway tracks and cycle tracks. For more info check out c2c-guide.co.uk.

> Lowdown

🅢 Prices
Free.

🅢 Season
All year.

🅞 Don't miss
Allow time to take in some of the stunning scenery and beautiful villages along the way.

✖ Avoid
Make sure you train before hand, there are plenty of climbs and long miles.

Kayaking Coniston

Provider	Joint Adventures
Skill level	Novice-intermediate
Time frame	1-2 days
Equipment	All kayaking equipment provided. Remember to take a change of clothes
Exertion level	●●●○○

Paul Reynolds

Silently paddling away from the shore, four blue kayaks glide deep. Splashes of water catch the sun as their yellow paddles scoop in and out, thrusting them forward across the lake's calm surface. In the distance the golden brown slopes of a hundred fells rise majestically toward the sky, while closer in, thickly wooded banks and clusters of houses line the lakeside, providing shelter and intrigue wherever the kayakers decide to land.

The Lake District is made for canoeing and kayaking. With 16 lakes and countless rivers, exploring the region's famous waters under paddle power offers a unique perspective on this beautiful part of Britain. All the major lakes are kitted out for it, with Windermere, Derwentwater, Coniston, Ullswater and Bassenthwaite the most popular. As a result there are numerous places to hire canoes and kayaks dotted along the region's shorelines, as well as plenty of places to launch if you've got your own. Most are unrestricted, although on some lakes and rivers you will need a license. The waters of the many of the lakes, especially Derwentwater and Coniston, are pretty calm and require only basic handling skills to feel at ease, so hiring a canoe or kayak for a recreational half day on the water is relatively easy.

However, for the more accomplished kayaker there are some challenging spots too, particularly on the Lake District's rivers, where plentiful weirs and whitewater stretches create a kayaking adventure playground. From the grade 2 waters of River Greta with its many boulders, to the grade 3 and 4 rapids and drops of the River Sprint, it's possible to really test yourself here, especially after heavy rain.

If you fancy more than just a gentle paddle but are not quite up to tackling the fury of whitewater rapids on your own, it might be worth investing

in a kayaking course to help you step up to the next level. Joint Adventures, based on picturesque Coniston Water, offers a wide range of kayaking and canoeing courses aimed at all levels of ability, with small focused groups led by fully qualified instructors which allow students to learn at their own pace.

If you are a complete beginner, there's a one- or two-day course to get you paddling with confidence, so you'll finish happy to take on flat water by yourself. These courses cover forwards and backwards paddling techniques, steering and ruddering strokes and safe wet exits as well as looking at how to prevent a capsize. On the two-day course specifically you also learn about edging your boat and how to prepare for a kayaking journey. Both courses result in a British Canoe Union award to acknowledge your skill level. There's also an additional kayaking rolling and safety course to help you master the Eskimo roll so you feel equipped to go solo.

For the more experienced, Joint Adventure's moving water courses are structured around developing skills to handle the different grades of whitewater from 2 through to 5. On the lower level courses, there's the chance to review your flat water

∧ The cool calm, inviting waters of Coniston stretch out from the banks of the boating centre.

Practicalities

Lying to the west of Windermere, Coniston village is a pretty settlement on the banks of Coniston Water. The dramatic rising slopes of the Old Man of Coniston set against the calm waters of the lake make the village both hugely photogenic and an ideal base for walkers, climbers and watersports enthusiasts. There are plenty of places to stay in and around the village as well as a handful of shops and a range of pubs, inns and restaurants.

Transport The nearest train stations are at Windermere (13 miles) and Ulverston, with regular local buses connecting Coniston to both. Ulverston is on the Barrow-in-Furness Line and is served by First TransPennine Express, connecting with Lancaster and beyond, Windermere connects with Oxenholme, the principle Lake District station on the West Coast Main Line.

Sleeping Once home to Beatrix Potter, **£££ Yew Tree Farm**, Coniston, LA21 8DP, T01539-441433, is a superb spot delivering luxurious, 'period', farmhouse accommodation in the midst of an awe-inspiring location. There are no TVs here and quite right too but there are a couple of posters. Breakfast is as local as it comes, featuring home-made, home-reared goodies – the 660-acre farmland is well used by Jon and Caroline who naturally rear traditional breeds providing quality Herdwick Hogget, Belted Galloway Beef and porky products to the discerning, which if you stay includes you! **£££ Lakeland House**, Tilberthwaite, T01539-441303, is a contemporary, guesthouse in the heart of Coniston village. All rooms are en suite, and comfortable, with views of the village and fells. Breakfast is locally sourced and there's even an internet café on site to keep you connected. **£ Coniston Holly How**, LA21 8DD, T0845-371 9511, has simple dorm accommodation with bike store and licensed on-site café just nort of the village and

the water. For self-catering accommodation, try **Bridge Cottages**, T01539-441765, a row of interlinking historic whitewashed stone cottages that can be hired individually or as a set, sleeping anything from 2 to 18. Sympathetically restored with modern kitchens and bathrooms as well as comfortable rooms and log fires throughout, they are centrally located with extensive countryside views.

Eating & drinking The Ship Inn, T01539-441224, is a traditional country pub on the outskirts of the village, serving seasonal, local meat, fish and poultry dishes as well as a range of vegetarian meals throughout the day. The historic **Black Bull Inn**, T01539-441133, is a 16th century coaching inn with the 'toe' of Old Man Coniston protruding into the resident's lounge. The bar serves quality snacks and light meals throughout the day, with hearty, homely traditional dishes served in the restaurant in the evening. For food with a view, try **Jumping Jenny's Café**, T01539-441715, on the Brantwood Estate. Reached by steam gondola or boat across Coniston Water, the café serves wholesome freshly prepared lunches and snacks within the beautiful grounds of Brantwood House.

Resources The Lake District Authority's website is a useful resource with details about river restrictions and licenses as well as up to date weather information, lakedistrict.gov.uk.

Also try The much underexplored Cumbrian coastline is a great place to take your kayaking skills one step further and head out into the ocean. With an abundance of wildlife and coastal scenery to explore, the elemental power of nature is impossible to ignore here and, if you're a skilled kayaker, is a challenge worth rising to. There are a number of organizations that offer sea kayaking trips and courses, try westcoastseakayaking.co.uk.

> **Lowdown**

ⓘ Directory
Joint Adventures,
Coniston, Cumbria,
LA21 8EE,
T01539-441526,
jointadventures.co.uk.

₿ Prices
From £60 for a 1-day course.

☀ Season
Mar-Oct.

Ⓞ Don't miss
A summertime paddle on Coniston just before dusk. Often the water turns glassy and the reflections are awesome.

⊗ Avoid
Don't get into trouble! Some lakes and rivers are restricted and others you'll need a permit. Check the UK Rivers Guidebook for more information.

∨ Sea kayaking, Coniston Water.

skills before going into detail about how to break in and out of moving water as well as how to surf small waves and read a river. Higher level courses focus on how to stay safe in more powerful whitewater as well as how to catch eddies and improve your technique as you descend through the rapids.

Whatever your level and whatever your aspiration, kayaking in the Lake District caters for everyone – be it a gentle cruise across the glassy calm of Coniston or a breakneck thrill ride through the rushing waters of Wallow Gorge. So long as you know what you're capable of and are well prepared, you'll be duly rewarded with a chance to experience close up, the real beauty of the Lakes.

Walking Scafell, Wasdale Valley

Provider	DIY
Skill level	Intermediate-experienced
Time frame	1 day
Equipment	Sturdy walking boots, map, energy food
Exertion level	●●●●○

Clambering over the circular stack of roughly hewn stones piled one a top each other, a cluster of walkers reach the platform and their end point, breathing deeply before finally standing still, hearts pounding. The view is immense. In the distance Scotland can be seen, with the Isle of Mann also picked out in rich blue from the northwest England coast. In the foreground, the craggy, baron, beautiful slopes of the Lake District's fells rise majestically from the lush green of the valleys below, dark shadows racing across their surfaces, cast by the bright afternoon sunshine shining through a spring time's scattering of white clouds.

Rising a mighty 3200 ft above sea level, Scafell Pike is England's highest peak, delivering panoramas to take the breath away. Situated in the far west of the Lake District, Scafell Pike is just one peak rising from a spectacular range of fells, all of which are on most serious walker's to do list.

The walk starts in the remote Wasdale Valley, an area which despite Scafell Pike's popularity has managed to escape being spoiled by commercialism. Home to Wastwater, England's deepest lake from which the scree slopes of the Scafell range build, the Valley is the best place

⌄ Scafell, where towering peaks pierce the very fabric of the vast grey sky and rise into the realm of the extraordinary.

from which to start the ascent, although other, longer routes up the mountain from Eskdale, Great Langdale and Borrowdale are also possible.

From the National Trust campsite at Wasdale Head the well trodden path climbs up the valley sides with impressive views of Pikes Crag and Scafell Crag towering forebodingly ahead. The route is clear, simple, and, if you are walking in summer, very popular, so navigating your way up the mountain should be quite straightforward. If you are a moderately fit walker taking the more commonly used path northeast is the best decision, however if you are a confident walker who wants a challenge, the scree slopes of Mickledore which lie on the east path, offer a difficult and exhilarating alternative. This is terrain that should be treated with respect. Landslides that cause changes to the scree patterns are quite common and care should be taken at all times not to displace the ground. Always take what looks like the most obvious route and if you happen to kick a rock back down by accident, remember to warn fellow walkers by calling out 'Below'.

On reaching the crest of Michaeldore, England's two highest mountains, Scafell and Scafell Pike, rear up either side or you, clearly illustrating why walkers don't attempt both on one excursion. A huge slab of rock known as Broad Stand blocks the route to Scafell, impossible for walkers to traverse, but an exciting challenge for climbers and one that is regularly taken on. The path to Scafell Pike is much simpler however and, after ascending onto a plateau and weaving through the boulder-strewn landscape, you will eventually arrive at the summit. A stone circle viewing platform and an unusual stone trig point mark the top of the mountain both of which are pretty busy on clear summer days with jubilant walkers taking photographs to capture the view and document their achievement.

Snaking back down the mountain, the descent heads northwest off the summit towards Lingmell, where the amazing ravine of Piers Gill plunges deep, its huge rocky pinnacles and sheer drops like something straight from Lord of the Rings. From here a path leads west then southwest down the fell's grassy ridge with views towards the Irish Sea, before a final descent into the valley and a victory drink at the famous Wasdale Head Inn, where many a walker has propped up the bar, telling the tales of their escapades up England's highest peak.

Practicalities

Remote, wild and beautiful, Scafell is situated between 4 valleys, Wasdale, Eskdale, Borrowdale and Great Langdale. All hold small villages within them, but Wasdale Valley holds the key to the shortest summit route. Nether Wasdale and Wasdale Head, on the banks of Wastwater, have a number of places to stay as well as inns.

Transport The nearest train station is Ravenglass, 12 miles southwest of Wasdale, served by Northern Rail.

Sleeping **££ The Wasdale Inn**, T01946-726229, lies at the head of the valley and is the closest hotel to the start of the walk. With comfortable rooms, a restaurant, bar or self-catering facilities if you prefer. In Nether Wasdale the **££ Strands Hotel**, T01946-726237, is a small establishment with log fires and comfortable rooms, restaurant, bar and beer garden for those mild summer evenings. **Camping** The National Trust runs the basic but beautiful **Wasdale Camping**, T01539-463862, on the banks of Wastwater at the foot of Scafell. It's popular in the summer and is run on a first come first serve basis. They also have 'camping pods.' Built from locally sourced wood, insulated with sheep wool and double glazed to cut down on the noise of heavy rain. Don't forget your sleeping bags though as they require all the usual camping equipment minus the tent.

Eating & drinking The Strands Hotel, Nether Wasdale, T01946-726237, has a reputation for producing fine food from the best locally sourced ingredients. **The Wasdale Inn**, T01946-726229, also serves quality traditional food in hearty portions.

Resources The Barn Door Shop, Wasdale, CA20 1EX, T01946-726384, barndoorshop.co.uk, is well stocked with walking and climbing gear. They also run a simple campsite opposite the inn from £2.50/night. See lakedistrict.gov.uk for comprehensive route and weather information.

Also try If you want to enjoy the scenery of the Lake District but don't feel up to tackling England's highest mountain, a walk round Wastwater is a worthy alternative. The deepest lake in the region and surrounded by stunning fells, it's a spectacular stomp that weaves through woods and across farmland on its journey around the lake edge. And of course, it would be wrong not to stop off at an appropriately delicious spot on the banks and gently lower yourself into the lake's soft, smooth waters for a cooling dip.

> Lowdown

⊖ Prices
Free.

⊘ Season
Summer is your best chance to make it to the summit.

⊕ Don't miss
The view from the top, it really is the best in the Lakes, stretching to Scotland and the Isle of Man.

⊘ Avoid
Sending rocks flying as you scramble. If you do accidentally misplace a rock remember to shout 'Below' to warn them.

Swimming Windermere

Provider	DIY
Skill level	Novice-experienced
Time frame	As long as you like
Equipment	Swim suit, towel, goggles and hat if you want
Exertion level	●●●○○

It's dawn on the lakeside and peaceful silence hangs in the air as two lone figures drop their towels on the pebbles and wade knee deep into the mirror-like water. Disappearing briefly, they emerge metres away, their heads bobbing forward as they swim out deep, throwing ripples across the still surface behind them. The view from the water as the sun rises up over the mountains, shrouded in morning mist, seems well worth the fresh chill that took their breath away just moments before.

At 10½ miles long, one mile wide and 220 ft deep, Windermere is not only the largest body of water in the Lake District, it is also the largest natural lake in England. Due to its scale the majestic Windermere is a draw for a range of water users from canoeists and kayakers to sailors and even the odd motorboat. Speed is now curbed to 10 mph meaning that the days of world water speed records being set here are long gone and boy racers razzing around

⌄ 10½ miles long, one mile wide and 220 ft deep, Windermere is the largest body of water in the Lakes.

on jetskis chucking out exhaust fumes have been confined to the dustbin of history. It also makes for an interesting if somewhat public swim, with plenty of entry points around its course and stunning views from the water. Because of its size it's easy to find a spot for a dip and its central location makes it a good place to come back to and cool off after a day exploring the fells. However, Windermere isn't the only swimming option here. The region is packed with lakes, rivers and tarns which cater for all interests and ability levels, whether you fancy frolicking under a waterfall, taking a discreet skinny dip among the lilies, or challenging yourself with an intense six-mile open swim.

For the uninitiated, Crummock and Buttermere is a pair of small lakes perfect for those looking to begin their outdoor swimming career. With their accessible shorelines and restriction on motorboats they offer an unintimidating and relaxing swim. On top of that, the twin lakes are just a short distance away from Scale Force, the highest falls in England, where you can take a rejuvenating splash under its flow. Also good for beginners, High Dam, near the south end of Lake Windermere is a shallow tarn sheltered from the wind, so warmer than other swim spots. With rocks to jump off, hidden lily-filled bays to paddle in and a couple of nice islands to explore, it's great for either a quick dip, or a whole day lounging around.

For the more adventurous, Goat's Water – tucked between Coniston Old Man and Dow Crag – is a cold dip set 1540 ft above sea level and a 1312-ft ascent from Coniston. It takes some effort to get to, but the scenery and solitude is worth the walk. Alternatively the River Lune, near Killington, is a lively waterway flowing from north to south, cut deep through limestone. There's no beach, so you have to jump straight into the moving water from the riverside rocks, though if the water is low you can get in by the exposed boulders on the bank below the trees. Best avoided after heavy rain or when the water is running fast.

For lengthier swims its back to where we started – Lake Windermere is difficult to beat as

Great Swim Dave Tyrell

a long distance open swimming destination. The home of the Great North Swim, every year its banks see some 6000 swimmers take to the water to swim a mile and raise money for charity. The event, held in September, is hugely popular and is open to swimmers of all abilities, although you have to be comfortable and capable of going the distance. Be warned, places get booked up very early. Alternatively you can tackle the mile long swim solo, at any point in the year, or increase the distance and try swimming the full, gruelling 10½ miles – it has been done!

< Up to 6000 swimmers participate in the 1-mile Great North Swim.

Great Swim-Dave Tyrell

Practicalities

At the head of Windermere and the home of the Great North Swim, Ambleside is a good base. The lakeside town has all sorts of accommodation, a handful of restaurants, pubs and cafés and a selection of useful shops. It's pretty centrally located too so makes a good base for exploring the Lakes' other swimming holes.

Transport Ambleside can be reached from the M6 north or southbound, onto the A590 then the A591. Be wary in the summer though, the road gets packed and it might be worth seeking a different route or alternative transportation. By train, Windermere is the terminus of the Windermere branch line, connecting with Oxenholme, which is the principle Lake District station on the West Coast Main Line, served by Virgin Trains, virgintrains.com.

Sleeping Cheap and cheerful, £ **The Ambleside Youth Hostel**, T0845-371 9620, is right on the banks of Windermere and is ideal if you are looking for a clean, comfortable bed for the night. The views from the lounge and many of waterfront bedrooms are outstanding, and there are plenty of private and family rooms available as well as dorms. There is a modern café/bar on site which serves food from lunch into the late evening, using local products, and with a good selection of local ales. The hostel also has Wi-Fi. For something a little more upmarket, try £££ **The Old Vicarage**, LA22 9DH, T01539-433364, the only B&B in Ambleside with its own swimming pool, hot tub and sauna — ideal if you fancy an indoor, on top of an outdoor, dip. Its rooms are top spec, spacious and well kitted out, its breakfasts are substantial and locally sourced and best of all it's just a short walk away from Windermere pier. **Camping** Low Wray, LA22 0JA, T01539-432810, on the western shores of Windermere is a lakeside National Trust campsite. Recently gaining a Gold Award from Cumbria Business Environment Network it's green as you like, clean, friendly and well maintained.

If you don't have your own tent you can choose between staying in an eco camping pod, a tipi or a luxury Bell Tent, all quirky alternatives to hiring a room for the night. Open from Easter-Nov every year, bookings start in Jan and its worth planning well ahead to avoid disappointment. For campers, it's well worth paying the premium and camping next to the lake — there's nothing like hauling yourself out after a swim and diving straight into your tent to warm up!

Eating & drinking There are a couple of lakeside pubs to sample. **The Drunken Duck**, Barngates, Ambleside, LA22 0NG, T01539-436347, might be a bit of a trek but on arriving at this pretty spot, far from the madding crowds you'll know it's worth it. The award winning ales created by their brewery Barngates will certainly help refresh the spirits and wash down a lunchtime ploughman's or roast beef sandwich for around £6 or indeed the hand-dived scallops which feature on the quality evening menu. OK, it's not cheap but neither is the experience and if you can't face the return walk, crash over in one of the exceptionally pretty, beamed rooms from £95 including breakfast and afternoon tea — heaven.

Resources To register for the **Great North Swim** seegreatswim.org. Entry is £35 and places get booked up extremely quickly. The Lake District Authority's website is a useful resource with details about each lake as well as up to date weather information, lakedistrict.gov.uk.

Also try Getting out on the water rather than in it and give sailing a go. The Low Hotel, also the host of the Great North Swim, has a Watersports Centre, T01539-439441, elh.co.uk, with a wide range of sailing equipment. It offers short, as well as more detailed, courses to help you master Lake Windermere under sail.

> Lowdown

© Prices
Free.

© Season
Apr-Oct, or any time of year if you are hardy.

© Don't miss
A dip in Wastwater, the Lake District's deepest and most dramatic lake. Apparently it has an underwater gnome garden!

© Avoid
Skinny dipping at Seathwaite Tarn. It might look and feel remote, but it is popular with walkers and has footpaths around its edge, so best preserve your modesty and save it for somewhere else.

Surfing Saltburn-by-the-Sea

Provider	Saltburn Surf and Hire/DIY
Skill level	Beginner-advanced
Time frame	Sunrise to sunset
Equipment	Board and wetsuit provided
Exertion level	●●●●●

The seafront at Saltburn-by-the-Sea rises proud on the cliff-top, turning its face towards the wide expanse of the North Sea. This noble façade is crowned by huge terraces of fine Victorian houses, streets named after jewels feeding out onto the open cliff top promenade. Below lies the seafront, the funicular railway leading to the pier and miles of wide open beach. Saltburn is a true gem, a charming resort that has managed to maintain much of its character even as the towns to the north lost out under the spread of an industrial onslaught. The sands that once enticed the Victorians to paddle and promenade, now attract surfers from across the north of England – just as they have done since the early 1960s.

The sandbanks either side of the pier offer a great spot for beginners keen on mastering the craft of surfboard riding. Swells roll out of the far northeast, sometimes generated off in the wild cauldron of the Arctic Circle, to break on these sands through the whole tidal range, making Saltburn a flexible and fairly reliable spot for waves. Here by the renovated pier, sits one of the East Coast's most respected emporiums. In the eighties, Nick Noble and Gary Rogers started their surf shop and hire business from the back of an old Luton box van, their surf shop that they built to replace it by 1990 was one of the first on the whole East Coast. Faded images on the shop walls tell the story of the growth of the scene with enigmatic photos depicting classic days at nearby reefs. The pair have encouraged surfers for over twenty years, offering board hire and lessons to would-be grommets, backed up by advice and encouragement to help see surfers through their first winter. Today Gary focuses on shop while Nick, a BSA qualified coach offers lessons catered to groups or individuals, as well as board and wetsuit hire for those who wish to progress after they have mastered the basics. Many a surfer has now caught their first waves here at Saltburn-by-the-Sea, and with warm, modern wetsuits removing one big obstacle, there's no reason not to join them. The beach fires in all north east swells, off shore in soutwesterly winds.

Practicalities

The Victorian seaside resort of Saltburn-by-the-Sea has good transport links and all amenities such as banks, ATMs and shops.

Transport There is a train station in the centre of the town, just a short walk from the beach. There are trains approximately every 30 mins running to Middlesborough and Darlington, Monday to Saturday. The journey is just under 25 mins and connects with these mainline stations for onward journeys. Northernrail.org

Sleeping The **£ Rose Garden B&B**, 31 Leven St, Saltburn, TS12 1JY, T01287 622947, therosegarden.co.uk, is a pretty Victorian terrace just a short walk from the station and seafront. It offers 2 en suite rooms and a breakfast that is organic, fair trade and locally sourced. There isn't a lot in the way of camping, the nearest is **Serenity Camping and Caravaning Park** in Hinderwell, T01947-841122, serenitycaravaning.co.uk, and they're not partial to 'youths'.

Eating & drinking Located in Valley Gardens not far from the surf shop, **Camfields Coffee and Juice Bar** serves a selection of fresh juices, smoothies and coffee. All food served is sourced locally, organic and free range wherever possible.

Also try More advanced surfers will find Saltburn offers plenty too. Along the beach to the east of the pier Penny's Hole is a good lowtide left-hander with long walls. Saltburn Point is a classic right-hander that breaks under the headland at the eastern end of the beach. It breaks over a flat reef and involves long paddles so best left to the more experienced. Gary and Nick will happily pass on tips and advice.

Demi Taylor

∧ Looking down over Saltburn beach towards Penny's Hole reef break.

> Lowdown

ⓘ Directory
Saltburn Surf Shop, Surf Hire and Surf School, Pier Car Park, Lower Promenade, Saltburn, T01287-625321, saltburnsurf.co.uk.

$ Prices
Board, wetsuit and boots combo hire from £9/hr. Lessons from £30, all equipment included.

☀ Season
Shop and hire all year, school closed in the winter.

➕ Don't miss
Check out the funicular railway.

✕ Avoid
Surfers come a long way from towns inland. To avoid a wasted drive there's a daily surf check on T09068-545543 from 0800 (60p/min).

Mountain biking Chopwell Wood

Provider	DIY
Skill level	Intermediate-experienced
Time frame	Less than an hour for the Powerline Trail
Equipment	Mountain bike, suitable clothing, helmet
Exertion level	●●●●○

Tight fast trails twisting sharply through the dense trees; Chopwell Wood has beckoned thrill seekers to fly round its corners, splattering mud on bark and experience its punishing climbs and exhilarating downhills since 1993.

More recently Chopwell's 890 acres of mixed woodland have been recognized as a Plantation on an Ancient Woodland Site. The majority of the ancient trees were felled in the 17th- and 18th-century for boatbuilding, but some gnarled oaks held fast and since its designated status was announced, the Forestry Commission has confirmed that only native trees will be planted here from now on.

    None of this talk of ancient woodland has stopped the mountain bikers – and nor should it. The sport is welcome in Chopwell where a series of trails draw in riders of all abilities. The blue graded Outside Line trail is a pleasant route that makes its way along the woodland's paths, with waymarked signs directing you round. It's relatively easy with some impressive viewing points, although care does have to be taken as the paths are shared with other visitors including dog walkers and families.

    However, it's the red graded Powerline Trail that rightly attracts the most attention: a fast, demanding trail with flowing 'berms' (embankments), open downhill stretches and a variety of decent jumps to try out. On wet days it can get really muddy so grip is a bit of an issue and as with any wooded trail it gets a little overgrown in places but that all adds to the adventure and adrenaline rush as you bomb around. At a little over 2½ miles long, if you know your stuff you'll get around it in about 30 minutes; short but sweet – you're sure to be left hungry for more.

Andy McAndlish

< Tracing a tight line through the 890 acres of Chopwell's mixed woodland.
∨ Power Line.

Practicalities

Set right on the fringe of Gateshead, Chopwell Wood is somewhere to lose yourself and escape the city.

Transport   The nearest train station is in Blaydon, a 7-mile ride away from the wood.

Sleeping   £££ **Park Farm Hotel**, Ravensworth, T0191-4824870, 10 miles east is an 18th century farmhouse surrounded by countryside. The bedrooms are directly accessed via an outdoor courtyard. **East Byemoor Guesthouse**, Whickham, NE16 5BD, T01207-272687, is 5 miles away. Comfortable rooms with countryside views, the breakfasts are full and hearty. **Derwent Park Caravan and Camping Site**, T01207-543383, Rowlands Gill, NE39 1LG, is a clean and simple site.

Eating & drinking   Gateshead and Newcastle are packed with places to eat and drink. **Blackfriars Restaurant**, T0191-2615945 – serves a seasonal, locally sourced menu and is the oldest dining room in Britain.

Resources   There are no signs outside Chopwell Wood. See forestry.gov for directions and trail information. There are a couple of good bike shops in Gateshead including **Evans Cycles**, Metro Centre, NE11 9YS, T0191-488 3264, with a good range of hardware. Servicing available.

Also try   Explore the woodland on foot. The 890 acres of trees play home to foxes, rabbits, badgers and roe deer as well as 95 species of bird and 16 species of butterfly.

> **Lowdown**

ⓘ Directory
Chopwell Wood, near High Spen village. OS grid reference: NZ137586.

ⓢ Prices
Free.

⊙ Season
All year.

⊙ Don't miss
The open winding downhill section with decent jumps on the Powerline Trail.

⊗ Avoid
Doing the trail after heavy rain, it's too slippy and impossible to get any grip.

Surfing Tynemouth Longsands

Provider	Rise Surf School
Skill level	Beginner-intermediate
Time frame	2 hrs
Equipment	Surfboard and wetsuit provided. Bring a towel and sun block
Exertion level	●●●●●

The beach is bustling with pockets of figures, walking, running, gathered in conversation and reclined in the afternoon sun. Couples saunter down the path until there progress is slowed as they meet the soft sand underfoot. Footballs are launched into the air and a whirlwind of children chase a cricket ball towards the frothy water's edge. From the sea you gain a unique insight into the history of Tynemouth, the panorama tells a story of the ebb and flow of growth around the golden shore here at Longsands. To the south stands the stark ruins of the castle and priory, founded in the seventh century it has seen many great swells come and go in this time, waves of occupation, tides of change. The towering Victorian terraces tells of a fashion for beaches and bathing that became all the vogue at the end of the 19th century, while the red brick semi's hark back to the post war era of pastel coloured Vauxhall Victors and bronze Hillman Imps packed for a week away at the coast. The northern fringe is crowned by the towering pinnacle of St George's Church, its dark spire a monument to the grandiose aspirations of the Victorian era.

From the line-up these landmarks offer a momentary distraction when a clean swell is rolling into the bay. Generated by storms far in the Arctic north, by the time the energy arrives here it has calmed into ordered rows of clean, regimented lines, ready to break on the sandbanks that form here along the shore. Come the freedom of the weekends and surfers will be drawn here from across the north of England. The webcams and swell prediction websites studied, bands of waveriders will be in the water come first light. Dark neoprene figures sit in small groups, joined by the occasional inquisitive seal. The vibe in the line-up here is friendly, a good community spirit exists among those who brave the winter's chill and the east wind's bite for just one more wave.

Jesse Davies chose to locate his surf school here for a good reason. Yes it is his home break, but this bay has also produced some of the UK's best surfers, from Sam Lamiroy to Gabe Davies to Jesse himself, and for good reason. Tynemouth is consistent by East Coast standards and waves break all through the tidal range. The sandbanks can be excellent and are spread along the beach. This bay has also been the venue for the British Surfing Championships, an occasion that attracted a record crowd to the shoreline to watch. Rise Surf School operates from spring through to autumn and offers packages to suit all ability of surfer, from complete novice to improvers. Lessons last two hours and Jesse and his team provide everything you need including wetsuits and boards. "Rise has BSA level 1 and 2 coaches which means can coach all different levels of surfing," says Jesse. "We offer a small friendly operation in a great location." If you've never been on a board before, this is the perfect spot to try. All you need to bring is your swimsuit, a towel and a realisation that this one lesson could seriously change your life.

▼ Professor Jesse Davies, deep in thought, hard at work.

Stu Norton

Greg Martin

Practicalities

At the mouth of the Tyne, this town is a good base for exploring the delights of the area without having to venture into the city. Front St, with cafés and accommodation is the focus.

Transport   From Newcastle Central Train Station, ride the metro to Tynemouth.

Sleeping   **££ No. 61 Guesthouse**, Front St, T01912-573687, has a downstairs tea shop and walled Victorian garden serving up home-made soups and cakes plus lite bites. 'Village' rooms can be a bit noisy at weekends. In land **£££-££ Riding Farm B&B**, Kibblesworth, Gateshead, NE11 0JA, T01913-701868, delivers views towards the Angel of the North. They encourage wildlife while breakfasts feature local produce. This is not exactly camper country. For those looking to pitch a tent, **Old Hartley Caravan Club Site**, Whitley Bay, NE26 4RL, T01912-370256, is fine, sloping and overooks the sea but nothing to write home about. There are a couple of full on holiday parks nearby with statics including **Whitley Bay Holiday Park**, T0870-4429282, 2 miles north of Tynemouth, Mar-Oct.

Eating & drinking   **Crusoe's Café**, Londsands overlooking the beach is an ideal spot to grab a coffee while building up the nerve and your body temperature to head back into the North Sea. Cool, comfortable **Lui's Bistro**, Front St, serves up quality food through

out the day from the Northumberland Grill breakfast featuring local goodies, through to filling lunches and quality tapas. Put together a tasty picnic of local goodies, at the farmers market 3rd Sat of the month at the metro station.

Resources   For Longsands webcam check: tynemouth.org.uk/webcam.pl. Set up in 1995, **Tynemouth Surf Co**, Grand Parade, Tynemouth, NE30 4JH, T01912-582496, is a well stocked shop with knowledgeable staff and a great range of hardware from wetsuits to new and secondhand boards. Equipment hire also available for those looking to hone their skills.

Also try   Away from the city, the northeast is home to wide open, uncrowded spaces – where a pair of boots and a glance at an OS map can deliver an escape. To the north there are the Cheviot Hills and Northumberland National Park, to the south the North Penines AONB and England's largest waterfall, High Force. For those looking to go long haul, the 8-day Teesdale Way follows the River Tees from North Sea to its source high in the Cumbrian Fells. Covering 100 miles it weaves its way through deep wooded valleys and high across heather-dashed moorland passing villages and towns along the way where a curative ale or two and a comfortable bed for the night can easily be sought. See ramblers.org.uk for information.

Walking Hadrian's Wall

Provider	DIY
Skill level	Intermediate-advanced
Time frame	7 days
Equipment	Sturdy walking boots, map, energy food
Exertion level	●●●○○

Standing in a glass tower on the urban outskirts of Newcastle staring down at geometric patterns spread across the ground, it's hard to imagine the Roman Fort that once stood here. However, striding alongside the sturdy stone wall a few hours later, past watchtowers and milecastles, Roman Britain couldn't feel more alive.

Built between 120-128 AD to protect the northern extreme of the Roman Empire, Hadrian's Wall stretches across the country, coast to coast. Opened as a national trail in 2002, Hadrian's Wall Walk is 84 miles long and takes around seven days to complete. Starting from Segedunum Fort in Wallsend, it clings to the Tyne through the farmland of Tynedale and into Northumberland National Park. Passing the craggy rocks of the Great Whin Sill it descends into the pastures of Cumbria, coming to an end in the salt marshes of Bowness-on-Solway. There are B&Bs along the way and baggage transfer services to help make your walk more comfortable, as well as campsites and bunk barns for a more basic approach.

There are 14 major Roman sites along the wall's length, including the spectacular Vindolanda, an extensive roman settlement near Once Brewed. The wall is a valuable Roman artefact in its own right, though some areas are in far better nick than others. With this in mind, walkers are asked to help preserve it for future generations, which means no walking on it, no walking single file next to it and no walking the route in winter, when erosion is far more likely.

The sense of achievement gained from crossing England coast to coast is made even better by experiencing first hand one of the country's most important historical landmarks.

Practicalities

Hadrian's Wall stretches the breadth of the country and can be started from either end, but the popular approach is to start out in Wallsend, the busy, modern suburb of Newcastle Upon Tyne and finish in the quiet Solway estuary

Transport Newcastle is an urban hub and the main station, Newcastle Central is well served. Getting around Newcastle is easy thanks to the metro system. Wallsend is 6 stops from Newcastle Central.

Sleeping There is a wealth of accommodation in and around Wallsend, so you should have no trouble finding a place to stay. The cheap and cheerful, **£ The Albatross Backpackers**, Grainger St, NE1 5JE, T0191-233 1330, offers basic, modern dorm accommodation, ideally situated by Newcastle's Central Station and 15 mins from the start of the walk in Wallsend. Internet plus free tea, toast and coffee. Around 25 miles in, Hexham, close to the wall, has a couple of cracking places to stay including **££ Grindon Cartshed**, Haydon Bridge, NE46 6NQ, T01434-684273. With the silver award for green tourism they deliver comfortable, friendly B&B with stunning views across their 600 acre farmland plus the Northumberland National Park. They have a drying room and are well used to walkers. Packed lunches £6 also available.

Eating & drinking In the Wallsend area, the restaurant at Jesmond Dene House is worth trying if you are looking for something special — contemporary modern flavours and classic combinations using seasonal ingredients; it's a popular place with 3 AA rosettes and a number of awards to its name. **Sky Apple Café**, Heaton Rd, T0191-209 2571, is small, quirky vegetarian restaurant 5 mins away from Wallsend with a wide range of vegetarian dishes and a lively, friendly clientele. **Pizzeria Santana**, Jesmond Rd, T0191-2817849, also five minutes from Wallsend is a traditional and family run serving top notch antipasti, pizza, pasta and meat and fish dishes.

Resources See hadrians-wall.org for route information. For baggage transfer contact **Walkers Bags**, T0871-423 8803, walkersbags.co.uk.

Also try There are plenty of pools at which to enjoy an illicit dip en route.

^ Crag Lough, one of the many watering holes that line Hadrian's Wall.

> Lowdown

⊕ Prices
Free.

⊗ Season
Spring-autumn.

⊕ Don't miss
The chance to cool off enroute at one of the many watering holes. Easily visable from the walk try the large Broomlee Lough set within dramatic moorland just north of the Vercovicivm Roman Fort.

⊗ Avoid
Walking the wall in winter. It causes erosion.

Surfing Embleton Bay

Provider	DIY
Skill level	Intermediate-advanced
Time frame	Sunrise to sunset
Equipment	Surfboard, 4/3 wetsuit (winter 5/3, boots gloves and hood)
Exertion level	●●●●●

Paddling towards shore you feel the peak rising. Accelerating forward you instinctively pop to your feet, the board dropping down the face as you lean onto your toes, bringing the board round in an arching turn onto the wide green face. Ahead the wall stretches, shimmering in the light, as it sweeps towards the shore. The board rises and falls as you trim, fizzing white-water left behind. Ahead, framed perfectly by the curve of the wave and the arch of the bay towers the castle, a fractured, ragged silhouette, watching. The wave begins to speed as it reaches the inside, you aim for the lip and float over the closing section, gliding back onto the face before angling off the back of the wave and somersaulting off your board. Hair wet and a smile as wide as the bay, surfing in the ancient lands of Northumberland is something truly special.

Dunstanburgh Castle is one of English surfing's most filmic backdrops. This is a land where war was a constant, where invasion and counterinsurgency was a way of life throughout the millennia. Castles, keeps and defensive landscapes have borne attack from Roman Legions, Viking longships, Saxon armies and Celtic raiders. The bays here are well off the surfing path, a place for the soul surfer to sit in the line-up and soak in the history, feel the isolation and enjoy the waves with but a few other searchers. The sands wait for swells from the north, large arctic groundswells that bring this bay life. At all tides there will be waves and when the swell does come, this beach offers the best chance to utilize what may be a fleeting encounter. Below the headland and castle lies the Point, a boulder break that wakes with clean northerly or large southeasterly swells, producing long right-handers that may peel through to the sandy beach on good days. There are only dunes here to witness the turning of the tide, so this is a break best left to those with who have a good understanding of rips and a hunger to escape the crowds, to charge the peaks watched only by the silent battlements and to earn memories that will stay long after the ephemeral swell has passed.

Practicalities

There are a few sleeping options in Embleton village while Beadnell makes a good base from which to explore Northumberland's potential. The seaside resort of Seahouses has plenty of amenities from chippes, to shops and banks.

Transport Alnmouth, 7 miles away is the nearest station.

Sleeping 10 mins walk from the beach, **£££ Dunstanburgh Castle Hotel**, NE66 3UN, T01665-576111, is a welcoming spot that offers a 10% discount to guests arriving under their own steam or via public transport. Bike storage. Pretty self-catering cottages also available sleeping 2-4 from £250/week. The hotel supports local suppliers, serving up fresh shell fish to local meat. Mains around £10. In land near Chathill, **£ Joiners Shop Bunkhouse**, NE67 5ES, T01665-589245, is good for groups with board storage, cosy communal areas and beds from £12. **Dunstan Hill Camping and Caravan Site**, NE66 3TQ, T01665-576310, is a cracking 20-min walk though open countryside to the beach, open Apr-Oct.

Eating & drinking Just north of the bay, **The Ship Inn**, Low Newton by the Sea, T01665-576262, is something of a destination pub. The produce is local and twitchingly fresh with shellfish from the bay, meat from nearby fields and farms and ales from their own micro-brewery next door.

Resources **Ledge Surf Shop**, Seahouses, T01665-721257, sells wax, a couple of wetties and that's about it.

Also try Get your walking boots on and head inland to the wide open moorland of the beautiful Cheviot Hills. The area is riven with flowing rivers and cool mellow burns so hot bodies can find some respite. A wonderful place to explore is Linhope Spout in the Breamish Valley which cascades 60 ft into pool to calm its force.

∧ The Northumberland coastline throws up plenty of opportunities for a soul searcher's escape.

∧ Here the beaches unfurl like seemingly unending lengths of golden ribbon opening up myriad opportunities.

> **Lowdown**

⊙ Prices
Free.

⊙ Season
Year round, best Autumn-Winter.

⊙ Don't miss
Lunch at the Ship Inn.

⊗ Avoid
Watch the golf balls on the walk to the beach if you have driven down.

Mountain biking Rothbury Forests

Provider	DIY or Northumberland Bike Breaks
Skill level	Novice-experienced
Time frame	½ day to 2 days
Equipment	Bring your own kit – bike, helmet, cycling clothing, lightweight waterproof – or bike hire can be arranged
Exertion level	●●●●○

Serving up more than 10,000 hectares of forest overlooked by the majestic Cheviot Hills, it's little wonder that the oases of Rothbury forests attract mountain bikers with a sense of adventure. Simonsdale, Thrunton, Harwood, Hepburn and Wooler Common are frequented by those searching out hair-raising downhills and technical trails.

Thrunton Woods is well known for its cross-country trails zigzagging a steep escarpment with lofty views of the Cheviots. Hepburn is the home of steep sandstone crags that stare out over the countryside. Wooler Common is no longer raided by marauding Scots, as it was in the 14th and 16th centuries, but by mountain bikers who come here to race on its 4X course. The Simonside Hills, on the northernmost edge of Harwood forest, beckon bikers into wild, rugged peaks that peer out as far as the Northumbrian coastline.

While the forests serves up terrain for mountain bikers of all abilities, many of the routes aren't well marked which is ideal for looking for an expedition of exploration. However, for those looking to make the most of their time in the saddle, see the best of the scenery and eliminate the hassle of route finding, it's time to head out with a guide. Whether you're an off-road novice or a singletrack fanatic, Tim at Northumberland Bike Breaks delivers classic mountain biking adventures, give you invaluable tips on riding technique and share knowledge of the trails they know like their own back garden. You might spend a morning following a carriage road

❮ Golden challenges await those who venture north.

Wig Worland

up into the hills north of the village, or an afternoon wending south to Simonside and getting mud-spattered in the woods. If one day in the saddle just isn't enough opt for a weekend package (or stay for a week if you like) with guided rides, luxury accommodation, hearty breakfasts, packed lunches (made from tasty local produce, no less) and even a few slices of home-baked cake thrown in.

If you are intent on riding solo, armed with a decent map it only takes a couple of hours to complete an exhilarating route from Rothbury. Picture the highs and lows of a basic loop from the riverside car park, starting with a challenging grind up towards Tosson Tower, past the farm and onto the picnic area (if you're not feeling in finest fettle, cheat and drive this first bit!). As you climb on up past the mast the hard slog is rewarded by awesome views of the Cheviot Hills. Stop, look around and get a sense of your epic surrounds as well as your breath back before carrying on along gnarled track, because for the next section of downhill, you're going to want to be dialed in. Arms vibrating, acting like extra suspension, mind rushing, eventually the trail levels out, then starts to rise again. A muddy track, a technical rocky section, then a fast-flowing singletrack through the trees. This really is somewhere the up are rewarded by the downs because as you start climbing again, it's not long before you're dropping its into another classic descent. Hop over a small timber bridge, swooping out of the forest and back onto the road to the picnic area. Sweet.

Practicalities

Rothbury sits in the Coquet Valley and is a popular base for walkers and mountain bikers who flock to the Northumberland National Park. A thriving market town, it is home to a good choice of local food stores, tearooms, antique and craft shops, cafés, pubs, galleries, an arts centre and a community cinema.

Transport   Rothbury lies southwest of Alnwick, off the A697. Morpeth train station a 16-mile ride away has good bus links to the town. Other nearby train stations are Acklington (10 miles), and Alnmouth (16 miles).

Sleeping   £££ Northumberland Bike Breaks delivers comfortable, clean, luxury B&B accommodation, especially designed for mountain bikers and active outdoorsy folk. Store your bikes and equipment safely, fuel up with a breakfast of freshly made from local produce and sink into a steaming bath at the end of a day's ride. They also have a comfortable 2-bed self-catering cottage in Rothbury finished to a similarly high standard sleeping 4-6 from £225/week. **£££ Tosson Tower Farm Holidays**, NE65 7NW, T01669-620228, offers a traditional farmhouse B&B (or self-catering cottages) on a working sheep farm at the foot of the Simonside Hills. Steel away to this hamlet close to Rothbury and enjoy the views of the Cheviots over a hearty farmhouse breakfast. Self-catering **Kidlandlee**, Harbottle, Morpeth, NE65 7DA, T01669-650457. In the heart of the Cheviots the holiday cottages are off-grid getting their power from the elements and well set up for walkers and riders with drying facilities, bike stores and woodburners keeping everything toasty. Sleeping 4 from £205. **Camping**   Pitch your tent in the Northumberland National Park surrounded by the verdant scenery of upper Coquetdale, **Clennell Hall Riverside Holiday Park**, NE65 7BG, T01669-650341, is on the doorstep of trails and walks in the forests, but it is a 9-mile ride back into town for the shops and cafés. Beware the midges who come out at dusk!

Eating & drinking   Fresh fish, local lamb and own-recipe sausages are all par for the course at the **Queens Head** in Rothbury, T01669-620470. And as well as platefuls of modern pub food conjured from locally sourced ingredients you might also catch a live folk music session. Follow the old drover roads into the foothills of the Cheviots to the hamlet of Alwinton, where the rivers Alwin and Coquet meet. And here, welcoming mountain bikers and walkers off the hills, the **Rose & Thistle**, T01669-650226, serves bar meals and refreshments, and offers pub games from darts to dominoes, in a traditional country inn at the hub of the village.

Resources   The closest bike hire shops – also the best place to go for maps and trail information – are **Cyclelife** in Alnwick, cyclelife-alnwick.co.uk, and **Pedal Power** in Amble, pedal-power.co.uk. You can also get maps, guides and information from **Rothbury National Park Centre** in Church St, NE65 7UP, T01669-620887, and **Haugh Head Garage**, NE71 6QP, T01668-281316, Wooler – a petrol station cum bike sales, repair and hire shop where you can get all sorts of information about local rides. If you want to hook up with the local crew, get in touch with **Cheviot Hill Riders**, team-chr.co.uk.

Also try   If such hilly terrain isn't your bag there are more leisurely options not too far away. Head coastwards to join the Sustrans Coast and Castles route at Amble, and cruise along reasonably flat, well signposted trails, taking in the sandy beaches and North Sea scenery on your easygoing way.

> Lowdown

ⓘ Directory
Northumberland Bike Breaks, Front St, Rothbury, NE65 7UB, T01669-621167, northumberland bikebreaks.co.uk.

❸ Prices
Free or from £80/day (for 2 people riding from Rothbury) to £200 for a group (max 6, including transport to a remote start point).

❸ Season
All year.

❶ Don't miss
The remains of an Iron Age hill fort sits above Rothbury on Hepburn crag and look for rock carvings near the ancient paths and caves on Simonside peak – rumoured to be a sacred mountain.

❽ Avoid
Being caught off your guard. Rocky terrain and fast descents throw up all sorts of surprises when you're hooning along – from fallen branches to muddy bogs.

Kite surfing Northumberland

Provider	KA Kitesurfing
Skill level	Novice-experienced
Time frame	3 hrs to 3 days
Equipment	Wetsuits, kites, boards, harnesses, helmets and buoyancy aids included. Just bring swimmers, warm clothes to change into and snacks
Exertion level	●●●●○

The kite bellows, charged with the power of the wind. Hurtling over the white caps a kitesurfer heads for shore, where the silhouette of Bamburgh castle poses on the sand. A vast, un-crowded bay. An adrenaline-pumping activity. The perfect recipe for a wet, wild, beauty of an adventure.

It's little wonder that three times national sailing champ Kevin Anderson fell in love with the sport of kitesurfing: a keen windsurfer, paraglider and snowboarder, his discovery of kite surfing's thrilling combination of three of his favourite sports was somewhat of a revelation. And once he'd mastered the sport and qualified as a senior instructor, he couldn't have picked a better location than the wide, open beaches of Northumberland on which to teach. Up here there are decent locations for almost every wind direction, so KA Kitesurfing has pick of the best beaches from Budle Bay in the North, down to Bamburgh, Beadnell Bay, Druridge Bay and as far as Redcar in the south.

Whether you want a taster session to whet your kitesurfing appetite, or a comprehensive three-day course to turn you into a fully-fledged kite surfer, KA will get you up and going (safely) on the end of a kite. In three hours you can nail the basics of launching, landing, pre-flight checks and water safety. But don't expect to hop straight on a board and start skimming across the waves. First you'll learn to control the kite on land, and then take to the waves for some body dragging – a high octane, full throttle taster of the power behind a kite while your arms are mercilessly pulled from their sockets.

Three days under Anderson's tutelage and you'll be ripping on a kiteboard. And, more importantly, you'll also come away with weather and tide theory, site assessment skills and the rules of the road.

< Bamburgh Castle.

Practicalities

With sandy beaches and medieval castle, Bamburgh is a popular seaside village boasting decent (some award winning) accommodation and eateries serving good Northumbrian fare.

Transport The nearest train station is Chathill, about 5 miles away with onward bus service to Bamburgh with Arriva however there trains are few and far between. A better bet is a train to well served Berwick Upon Tweed, 20 miles north.

Sleeping In the middle of historic Bamburgh, **££ The Greenhouse**, Front St, Bamburgh, T01668-214513, delivers B&B and self-catering accommodation while trying to mimimize its impact on the environment using low energy solutions, nature toiletries and local, organic produce. **Camping** Hire a wigwam at **Waren Caravan and Camping Park**, NE70 7EE, T01668-214366, and feel good as you peak out of your sustainable wood abode to witness commanding views of the beach and the Northumbrian coastline. With electricity and insulation they are one luxury step up from tent life.

Eating & drinking An avid supporter of locally produced artisan foods, the chef at the **Mizen Head Hotel**, Lucker Rd, T01668-214254, makes the most of his location. Stargaze as you dine on the freshest produce beneath the glass roof of **Victoria Hotel's**, T01688-214431, award-winning Brasserie. **Bamburgh Castle Inn**, T01665-720283, a decent bit of pub grub.

Resources Log onto nekitesurfing.co.uk for the lowdown on all things kitesurfing in the Northeast.

Also try Spot wrecks and seals on a diving trip to the Farne Islands. **Farne Island Divers**, T01327-860895, farneislanddivers.co.uk, run dive safaris for all levels from Beadnell Bay.

> Lowdown

ℹ Directory
KA Kitesurfing, Elton, Elm Bank Road, Wylam, Northumberland, NE41 8HT, T07766-303876, kitesurfinglessons.co.uk.

⊖ Prices
£49/½-day taster, £40/hr personal coaching, to £269 for a 3-day course.

⊛ Season
All year.

⊕ Don't miss
A trip to the iconic landmark of Bamburgh Castle – once home to the kings of ancient Northumbria.

⊗ Avoid
Kite surfing outside of the water sports zone in Budle Bay – it is marked by a number of buoys. Also, take heed that Budle is closed to kitesurfers from Nov to Mar each year (as it is a nature reserve with a large migratory bird population during winter).

Sea kayaking Farne Islands

Provider	DIY
Skill level	Intermediate-experienced
Time frame	Take a whole day to enjoy it properly
Equipment	All kayaking equipment, wetsuit and money if you are planning on landing on the islands
Exertion level	●●●●○

It's 2200, mid-summer and the sun is still low on the horizon, turning the glassy water golden as it laps around the hull. The call of arctic terns, kittiwakes and guillemots can be heard from the islands, while metres away a cormorant dives deep in search of its evening meal.

Lying a few miles off the Northumberland coast, the Farne Islands are a wildlife paradise, populated with 17 species of breeding birds and both common and grey seals. Owned by the National Trust they make for a challenging but rewarding sea kayaking excursion, taking you as close to marine wildlife as you can get, above the water.

There are four suitable launch points in and around Bamburgh on the mainland, with the easiest and most consistent at Harkness Rocks, best attempted on a rising tide. To get to the Farne Islands you have to cross a tide which runs south on the flood, north on the ebb, with a two knot tidal stream in the Inner Sound increasing to four knots further out. Along with the testing landing and launching conditions and the potential for chop on the shallow water across the Sound, the Farne Islands are best left to competent kayakers seeking adventure rather than novices looking to learn.

That said, if you know how to handle a kayak at sea, the trip is well worth it. Watching a flock of puffins settle on the Inner Farnes' cliff tops as you approach is a real treat and on arrival, the tidal flows between the islands make for a paddler's playground. If you'd like to take the trip but aren't sure if your skill level is up to it, Active4Seasons run excursions where fully qualified instructors guide and support you over and back making sure you get to enjoy the unique marine environment that the islands have to offer.

Practicalities

The main launch points for the islands are scattered around Bamburgh. Seahouses, 3 miles south, has good amenities.

Transport Berwick Upon Tweed station, 20 miles north has good connections to the major cities with onward bus connection to Seahouses via Arriva.

Sleeping £££ St Cuthbert's House, T01665-720456, 1 mile south of Seahouses is a renovated former Presbyterian church, a real gem. The breakfast bacon and sausages come from the award-winning local butcher and the eggs from local farms. With a gold Green Tourism award to its name you can stay with a clean conscience. **Waren Caravan and Camping Park**, NE70 7EE, T01668-214366, also has wigwams available to rent.

Eating & drinking Blacketts Restaurant, Lucker Rd, Bamburgh, T01668-214252, seasonal, locally sourced British fare and a friendly vibe. Enjoy a real ale at **The Olde Ship Inn**, Seahouses to wash down those cracking views.

Resources For details on the Farne Islands check nationaltrust.org.uk. Run by experienced coach Ollie Jay, **Activ4seasons**, active4seasons.co.uk, offers sea kayaking courses and guided trips for those looking to explore the area.

Ollie Jay

Mountain biking Kielder Water & Forest Park

Provider	None
Skill level	Intermediate-advanced
Time frame	2 hrs +
Equipment	Mountain bike, helmet, map, snacks, water, a repair kit/spare tube, foul weather gear
Exertion level	●●●●○

This all used to be open moorland, hills purple flushed with heather, buzzards soaring on ghostlike thermals, scanning the valley below where the river danced over boulders and slowed in looping eddies. Then the hand of planners transformed the landscape. Kielder Water was created, the largest man made lake in the UK, fringed by groomed plantations thick with Sitka spruce, pine and fir. Drinking water for the northeast, hydroelectric power to light a city and timber to serve every whim. It is only fitting that within this dark canopy, this man made environment, there should be crafted a manmade playground – a network of mountain bike trails that provides some of the best riding on the land with some of the best hill top views these Isles can offer.

There are a number of trails on offer here as well as a mountain bike park and hire centre, all produced with a huge investment of time and capital. Starting out at Kielder Castle, the 12½ mile Lonesome Pine Trail is a cross country red route that heads south along the shores of the lake past Bakethin Wier before heading into the woods up the singletrack Lewisburn Valley. There is then a trail climb at Ferny Knowle and Dinmount before a descent at Capon Hassock. The route includes the North Shore trail of boardwalk, a half-mile, three foot-wide wooden track, the longest of its kind anywhere in the UK. It was constructed using five truck loads of Kielder timber. The singletrack holds various challenges such as the stages known as Stony Holes, Stairway to Heaven, Purdom Plunge and Skydive before the descent back to the castle to complete the loop.

As a red route this trail is set up for mountain bikers with good off-road riding skills. There are climbs and descents of a challenging nature with

Andy McAndlish

Andy McAndlish

some berms, large rocks, steps and drop offs but the aim of this course is to open and flowing, so there aren't too many technical features. This could be just the trail for riders making the progression onto red trails. From the Lonesome Pine section there are wide reaching views, a spectacular place to draw breath. The whole route is a one and a half hour ride, considered by some to be a hard blue but with tougher climbs.

If you've still got plenty left in the tank Kielder has more on offer. For those who can handle a serious trail, Deadwater offers a suitable challenge. There's Deadwater Fell, a nine-mile red route or Up and Over which is a 1½-mile black trail. Pop into Purple Mountain for a heads up before heading out. There is a café here as well as bike hire, advice and have a workshop for any emergency repairs that might crop up. They hold a regular night ride for those who fancy a different challenge, fuelled by some hot food and a good social gathering to boot.

∧ On the trail of the Lonesome Pine and not even a hint of the Laurel and Hardy's about it.
< Riding out of the trees through purple flushed moorland.

> **Lowdown**

ⓘ **Directory**
Kielder Castle, Kielder, Hexham, NE48 1ER.

💲 **Prices**
Free, toll road to forest though.

☀ **Season**
All year.

◎ **Don't miss**
The view from Lonesome Pine.

✖ **Avoid**
There are some steep climbs and it can be windy on the boardwalk.

Practicalities

Kielder is a large forest where planting began in the 1920's and is maintained by the Forestry Commission. There is 239 sq miles of woodland under their control. Access to the trails here is via the car park where there is also access to shops, a café and Kielder Castle, a hunting lodge built by the Earl of Northumberland in 1775.

Transport It's not easy getting to Kielder by public transport. Tue, Fri and Sat there is the 880 bus operated by Snaith's Travel from Hexham to Kielder Castle. They can carry bikes but it is advisable to book in advance, T01830-520609. Trains run via Hexham on the Tyne Valley Rail Line from Carlisle to Newcastle and Sunderland, T0845-000 0125 to book bikes on the train.

Sleeping ££ **Twenty Seven B&B**, Castle Drive, Kielder, NE48 1EQ, is the only B&B in the village, basic but is popular with walkers and the bike crowd. There is bike storage available and breakfasts are made with locally sourced produce. They can also provide evening meals and laundry washing and drying. For self-catering try **Kielder Lodges**, Kielder Water, NE48 1BT, T0870-2403549. There are a number of options available that sleep between 4 and 8, nwl.co.uk/leaplishlodges. Another option is the £ **Kielder YHA Hostel**, Butteryhaugh, Kielder, NE48 1HQ, T0870-7705898, yha.org.uk. Popular choice for groups of mountain bikers. They have a bar and offer breakfast and evening meals.

Eating & drinking On-site café serves up hearty fare and light snacks for those looking to refuel instantly post-ride.

In the southern edge of Kielder Water, **The Pheasant Inn**, Stannersburn, NE48 1DD, T01434-240382, is a cracking traditional beamed inn serving up real ales and home cooking. In the nearby village of Wark on Tyne you'll find the Green Tourism Gold Award winning **Battlesteads Inn and Restaurant**, T01434-230209, battlesteads.com. Relax by the woodburner on a leather sofa and enjoy one of the 5 cask ales or an organic soft drink. Their extensive menu features a wonderful array of seasonal, locally sourced produce. If you've over indulged and can't face the ride back they also have accommodation on offer and have secure bike storage.

Resources Purple Mountain, T01434-250532, purplemountain.co.uk, based near Kielder Castle is well stocked and offers advice, repairs, servicing and bike hire from standard hardtails from £15/3 hrs to 'posh hire' demo bikes from £35, (including helmet, repair kit and pump). Skills tuition also available. Check out the mountain biking section on the Visit Kielder website for downloadable pdf maps, visitkielder.com/site/things-to-do/mountain-biking

Also try Check out the Ospreys that are now actively breeding in Kielder Forest. These birds were hunted to extinction by 1840 but the erection of a special platform has seen nesting resume here. There are plans to set up a camera for 2010. For a more mellow ride, the 26-mile Lakeside Way circumnavigates Kielder Water on easy going trails.

Walking North: best of the rest

Provider	DIY
Skill level	Beginner-experienced (see details)
Time frame	3 hrs
Equipment	Sturdy walking boots, waterproofs, map, compass, mobile, phone, survival kit
Exertion level	●●●●●

Malham Cove and Tarn, Yorkshire Dales

Towering up to the sky the limestone cliff's sheer surface blends into the thick white clouds above; a huge curving amphitheatre of rock. On the ground, gathered walkers stare upwards in awe, the trees and bushes that surround them all dwarfed by the majesty of Malham Cove. This natural phenomenon has been a draw for walkers for hundreds of years, part of a circular route which covers some of the best limestone scenery in the country and shows off just why the Dales are such a special place. The walk, which heads out from Malham, takes in the tranquil, ethereal waterfall of Janet's Foss before striding across the bleak moorland to Gordale Scar, a gaping chasm carved out of the landscape in the ice age complete with its own waterfall pouring violently through the rock. A path leads out of the gorge towards peaceful Malham Tarn before heading on the walk's grand finale; Malham Cove itself. Taking little over three hours and with only moderate inclines to navigate, the walk is easy to complete and hugely rewarding. It also delivers the added bonus of a number of liquid delights, ideal for water babies looking for a quick reviving splash. Set in moorland, the upland lake of Malham Tarn is a decent size while relatively shallow, the average depth being around eight feet in depth, so in comparison with other tarns it is relatively mild. Below, Janet's Foss the plunge pool is cool, deep and invigorating.

Malham's popularity with walkers has seen a number of guesthouses and B&Bs spring up. The 16th-century country house, **Beck Hall**, T01729-830332, has 17 guest bedrooms, six of which are four-poster suites. The lounge has a roaring open fire while the locally sourced full English breakfasts, kippers or vegetarian fry ups are sure to set you up for a day of walking.

The Yorkshire Three Peaks, Pen-y-ghent, Whernside and Ingleborough

A demanding but rewarding walk, the Yorkshire Three Peaks is not for the faint-hearted, taking in the summits of three of Yorkshire's most imposing hills, Pen-y-ghent, Whernside and Ingleborough within a 24-mile circular route that requires 5000 ft of steep uphill climbing to complete. Over blustering uplands, boggy moorlands and limestone pavement, the walk takes in some spectacular scenery and breathtaking views.

There is no official starting place for the walk although the majority of Three Peaks challengers start in Horton in Ribbersdale, where you can clock your start time at the village café before tracking to Pen-y-ghent's steep slopes via Brackenbottom. Scaling the face of the hill to reach the trig point is tough, but not impossible, warming you up ready to tackle Whernside. Heading down from Pen-y-ghent due west the sound of gushing water may fox you until you reach the edge of Hull Pot and stare down into the deep gorge to see a waterfall plummeting onto limestone. It's an impressive sight but take care as the edge of the gorge creeps up quickly. From Hull Pot the track is less distinct but leads over to Ling Gill, a snatch of forest in a steep sided cleft, before making a course for the Ribblehead Viaduct and the long haul up Whernside. On a clear day the views are beautiful, if not daunting, clearly marking out the next challenge ahead; Ingleborough.

Walking along Whernside ridge, the Philpin Farm caravan is a welcome sight, usually wrapped in walkers clutching hot cups of tea taking a breather before tackling the final hill. After half a mile of gentle gradient, Ingleborough kicks in with a steep ascent to the top, rewarded with views across the Dales, towards the Lake District and beyond. It's then a six-mile stomp back to Horton, where you can clock back in. For most it takes an entire day but if your time sits below the two-hour threshold, you're entitled to become a member of the exclusive Yorkshire Three Peaks Club. Now there's a membership to be proud of.

> Walking on the rooftop of England.

Andy Ward

Andy Ward

∧ Cumbrian delights.

The Pendle Way, Lancashire

Gnarled and twisted, a row of leaveless trees stand defiantly vertical in the blustering wind, shadows skitting across the wild landscape as the sun's warmth teases the walkers below, trekking across limestone meadows and moor. There's no doubt about it, this Bronte Country.

A 45-mile walk circling the eponymously named Pendle Hill, The Pendle Way is steeped in history, from the notorious witch hunts of the 17th century and the founding of the Quaker movement, to Charlotte Bronte's wanderings which acted as inspiration for Jane Eyre. Weaving through huddled hamlets, across rugged moorlands and along waterways, the walk takes around four days to complete starting from and finishing at the Pendle Heritage Centre. The walk is moderately paced with the only strenuous stretch the final climb to the summit, from which impressive views over the Dales stretch into the distance.

It can easily be tackled with just a map and compass but if you'd prefer to go with a group, **Northwest Walks**, T01257-424899, offer five days holidays exploring the trail, providing B&B accommodation en route, as well as maps and guides. Packed lunches can be purchased on the day and they can sort baggage transfers too.

The Pennine Way

The word stamina could have been invented for those setting out on The Pennine Way. A colossal 270-mile long distance walk across the Southern Pennines, the Peak District and the Yorkshire Dales, finally ending up in the Scottish borders – it takes in sights of cultural and historic interest as well as beautiful landscape. The first official long distance footpath in Britain, the walk was officially recognized in 1965 after 30 years of campaigning by Tom Stephenson, secretary of The Ramblers Association.

Today, the route draws walkers from all around the world keen to take on the challenge, while the National Parks Authorities strive to maintain the footpaths and prevent damage to the surrounding environment that such constant footfall inevitably creates. Passing through some of the loneliest and loveliest high walking terrain in Britain, 'The Way' takes in high peat bog, heathlands and limestone scenery as well as deep wooded valleys, like Swaledale, ice age gorges like High Cup Nick, plunging waterfalls like Low Force and the Roman remains of Hadrian's Wall.

Most people attack the walk from south to north, in order to predominantly head with their backs to the worst of the weather, which on the highest grounds can sometimes veer into the dangerous. It's not a walk for the inexperienced as some stretches of the route are very difficult, but as one of the oldest and longest official footpaths in the country it's well worth tackling if walking is your thing. For details of the route: nationaltrail.co.uk and penninewayassociation.co.uk.

To make the walk more achievable, the **Sherpa Van Project**, T0871-520 0124, sherpavan.com, offers a door-to-door baggage moving service and can organize accommodation for you along the route.

The Cumbria Way, Ulverston to Carlisle

Devised by the Ramblers Association in the 1970s to give walkers a flavour of of Cumbria rather than just the Lake District, The Cumbria Way stretches from Ulverston in the south to Carlisle in the north. Covering 70 miles and splitting naturally into five stages each around 14 miles long, it takes in sweeping bays, rugged valleys, stunning lakes, famous fells and historic settlements offering ramblers something different each day.

Starting in the market town of Ulverston, the walk threads its way through gentle farmland and across moors before arriving on the shores of Coniston Water and the Lake District proper. From here, the famous beauty spot of Tarn Howes beckons, leading on to the Langdale Pikes, then the wild valleys of Mickleden and Langstrath, separated by one of the walks, few steep climbs over Stake Pass. A remote stretch follows, wending towards pretty Rosthwaite before entering a glorious wooded trail which emerges on the banks of Derwentwater.

From Keswick, the walk follows the flanks of Lonscale Fell before taking to the moorland around Skiddaw and on to the village of Caldbeck. The route follows River Caldew as it meanders towards the ancient border town of Carlisle and the journey's end.

Most of the walking is on established paths with only three steep ascents so it's an achievable walk for most and a good route for those who want to experience Cumbria without having to scale the region's mountains into the bargain. Passing a number of lakes, tarns and rivers, make sure you've packed your bathers or at least a towel so you can enjoy the fluid pleasures first hand and gain a different perspective on our surroundings.

If you need to rest after five days on foot, there is plenty of choice around Carlisle. **£££ Bessiestown Farm**, T01288-577219, in the Debatable Lands has self-catering cottages as well as B&B in pretty farm buildings with open fires and stunning views of the Border countryside to enjoy. The locally sourced breakfasts are highly rated.

Best of the rest North: activities

Stand up paddle boarding, Longsands

At Longsands and South Shields, Boardskillz offer an alternative to surfing – stand up paddle boarding. The SUPs are longer than regular surfboards at around 11-12 ft and can be both ridden dynamically in decent swell or taken for on a flat water cruise, exploring the coastline and mellow inland waterways. For those who are new to the sport, they offer beginners courses on the beaches from two-hour tasters from £35 to an entire weekend £110, where you can learn the basics and really begin to hone your skills. For groups looking for an approach where you can take time to appreciate your surroundings, they also run 'destination paddles' – both coastal cruises exploring Tynemouth, Beadnell Bay and beyond as well as flat water paddles exploring the Tees or Tyne. For those who have mastered the basics and want to spend time honing their skills, they have boards and paddles available to hire from £10/hour or £25/half day. **Boardskillz**, Alma Place, North Shields, NE29 0LZ, T01912-581499, boardskillz.co.uk.

Ghyll scrambling, Peak District

Some describe this as caving, without the roof on, but Ghyll Scrambling is the art of heading upstream through a gorge or ravine and taking on any obstacles that come your way. These could be waterfall climbs, rocky traverses, wading through pools or even a bit of plunging. Part of the fun is the adventure of the trek, the other part is the joy of getting wet. Here in the heart of the Peak District, Peak Pursuits offer a scramble upstream taking on several waterfalls en route to the summit of Kinder Scout. The site of the famous 1932 Mass Trespass which acted as a catalyst in the creation of England's National Parks, this upland gritstone plateau will always have a special place in the hearts and minds of walkers and all outdoors adventurists. Drink in the far reaching views across Edale and soak up the spirit of social change that took place here. The group is guided by a qualified leader and all equipment is provided. The scramble costs £44.99 per person but remember to bring a towel and change of clothing for after.

◄ 3 Peaks Cyclo Cross – stamina, endurance and the promise of a cracking cup of tea at the end.

Wig Worland

Peak Pursuits, Castle Hill, Nantwich Road, Audley, ST7 8DH, T01782-722226, peakpursuits.co.uk. Close to Kinder Scout, **Top Eccles Farm Eco Barn**, Whaley Bridge, SK23 7EW, T01663-750372, is a good base for those looking to spend a bit of time exploring the area. High on the south facing slopes of Eccles Pike, the 300-year-old barn sleeps four with a herb and vegetable garden that guests can help themselves to. Sheep's wool insulation and a wood pellet boiler keeps the place toasty and conscience clear on chilly nights. From £365/week. **£ Thorpe Farm Bunkhouses**, Hathersage, S32 1BQ, T01433-650659, basic accommodation with beds from £10.

The Three Peaks Cyclo-Cross Challenge, Yorkshire

Held in the golden days of early Autumn, this annual race combines road, trail and steep climbs in a true test of endurance, skill and stamina. The course was first completed in 1959 by a young cyclist and the seeds were planted. In 1961 the first race was held and it has since become the stuff of legend. Riders depart Helwith Bridge in an escorted start before passing through Gill Garth, leaving the road to climb the first of the peaks, Ingleborough. A fast descent follows, leading on through Cold Cotes, into Ingleton to Brunscar building up to a testing climb of Whernside, at 2414 ft this is the highest of the three peaks and the highest point in Yorkshire. The descent to Ribblehead precedes a road section to Horton for a climb of the final peak Pen-y-Ghent, before a last leg to the finish back in Helwith Bridge. The course is 38 miles long with 18 miles on road and 20 miles over unsurfaced track. Around four miles of the race are classed as 'unrideable' meaning competitors have to pick up their bikes and run with them, usually up steep climbs or descents. Past winners have completed the course, which involves 5000 ft of climbing, in under three hrs. All competitors who complete the course are awarded a certificate, with those clocking in with a sub 3½ hours time being presented with the coveted Elite Class certificate. If that has sparked your competitive spirit, check out 3peakscyclocross.org. uk for more details and if you're feeling up to the challenge, the entry forms are there to download. Entry from around £30. Limited bunkhouse accommodation available at the nearby **YSS Schoolhouse**, Helwith Bridge, BD24 0EH, informal camping also available in the finish field.

∧ It's not all uphill.

Climbing, Malham Cove/Goredale Scar, Yorkshire

The Yorkshire Dales has long been a magnet for serious climbers, dating back to the 1950's. There are two dominant rock types here, the gritstone outcrops such as those Crookrise, Rylstone and Eastby offering a range of challenges from beginners through to expert. However when most people think of climbing in the Dales, it is the limestone walls that spring to mind, intimidating cliffs like the challenges of Gordale Scar, Malham Cove and Kilnsey. These are spectacular locations, a great place to watch if you're not quite up to taking on one of the 'big three'. Malham Cove was one a huge prehistoric waterfall, but is now a huge sweeping face of vertical rock offering a range of challenges from hard sport routes through to easy trad climbs. In the winter this face catches a lot of sun, but during the summer it can really heat up. There are always routes to climb when it's raining. There are some seasonal restrictions on some of the routes due to nesting birds. Nearby Gordale Scar was created by a collapsing cave and offers some very challenging yet rewarding routes. For information on specific routes check out rockfax. com. There is camping at the entrance to Gordale Scar, one of the most spectacular sites for pitching up in the UK, **Gordale Scar House**, Malham, BD23 4DL, T01729-830333. **YHA Malham**, BD23 4DB, T0845-371 9529, is also a cracking spot, next to the Lister Arms pub well within easy reach of the tantalising limestone pavement. Cycle store, meals available.

Best of the rest North: sleeping & eating

The Eco-Lodge, Lincolnshire

The Eco-lodge, Station Rd, Old Leake, Boston, PE22 9RF, T01205- 871396.

It's a big claim to call yourself an eco lodge but this simple 2-bedroomed cottage constructed from wood grown and harvested in Lincolnshire is just that. Set in 8 acres of woodland and meadow, the lodge it is wind and solar powered while in the kitchen is a wood burning range. They also offer a 10% discount to those who arrive via train and pedal power, rewarding those who aim to minimize their carbon footprint. Be prepared, the lodge is 10 miles from Boston, the nearest train station. Sleeps 4 from £360/week, short breaks also available.

The Cross Keys, Leeds

Water Lane, T0113-2433711, the-crosskeys.com.

If you find yourself in the city at the weekend, this is a cracking spot to head for a Sunday Roast. The Sunday Feasts arrive at the table, ready to carve, just like mama used to make! There's usually the choice of an organic chicken for 4 or a whole roast leg of lamb for 6, for £105 served with all the trimmings. During the week, the quality doesn't drop and the winter lunch time menu sees comfort food like fish finger or rare breed pork sandwiches (around £6) vying for space against more substantial mains like mutton and rosemary pie or rare breed bacon chop with mash and egg (around £10). It's just the sort of grub you want to blanket yourself in during those bitterly cold winter months up north. And with a focus on quality, locally sourced and seasonal produce, it's about minimizing food miles and maximizing foody smiles. Good selection of ales from local brewery Rooster's of Knaresborough as well as hand pulled, cask conditioned porter and stout.

YHA Langdon Beck

Forest-in-Teesdale, Barnard Castle, Co. Durham, DL12 0XN, T0845-371 9027, yha.org.uk.

High in the North Pennines in an Area of Outstanding Natural Beauty, this is a hostel with impeccable green credentials. Yes it is in a windy spot, but it has certainly made the most of its position – harnessing the wind's energy through a turbine and the sun's energy through photovoltaics to power and heat the accommodation. The café is licensed serving real ales and they are committed to using fresh, seasonal produce sourced as locally as possible. They harvest rainwater while a reed bed system treats waste water. Cycle store. Beds from £13.95.

Southwaite Green, Cumbria

Lorton, CA13 0RF, T01900-821055, southwaitegreen.co.uk.

Set on the western edge of the Lakes, surrounded by fields and backed by high fells, the four converted farm cottages are in a pretty perfect location . They are close enough to Cockermouth to be convenient – a 40-min riverside walk, but secluded enough that you can detach yourself from the hustle of the outside world. The cottages sleep 4 and are squeaky green meaning you can snuggle down with a clear conscience. They are kept toasty even on the coldest days with an underfloor heating system that uses ground and air source heat pumps – so literally the environment warms the land. Water is heated by solar panels while waste water is dealt with using a reed bed system. From £430/week, short breaks also available.

Low Sizergh Barn, Kendal

Low Sizergh Farm, Sizergh, Cumbria, T015395-60426, lowsizerghbarn.co.uk.

Set in the context of an organic dairy farm, this tea room on the edge of the Lake District seems even more perfect. An ideal pick me up after a tough day in the lakes, they serve up delicious home-baked cakes and scones to be washed down with fairtrade coffee and tea specially blended to suit the local water – tea is a very serious business in this part of the world. If you need something more substantial, they also offer home-made quiches and pies as well as soups and a dish of the day, all of which have been created using meats and produce from their 250 acres of land and the farms that neighbour them. If you're after some goodies for your a picnic or packed lunch, the farm shop stocks local and home grown delights from free range eggs, meat, game and organic veggies to puddings, pies and pickles as well as an award winning range of cheeses made by small dairies and artisan producers.

The Three Fishes, Lancashire ◐
Miton Rd, Mitton, BB7 9PQ, T01254-826888, thethreefishes.com.

They're proud of who they are, where they come from and what they're part of at The Three Fishes – so much so that their menu charts 30 of the regional Lancashire 'food heroes' that supply the inn from Thwaites Brewery in Blackburn to Mrs Kirkham's Lancashire Cheese in Goosnargh and Rose County Beef in Clitheroe. The family friendly inn's main menu is on the gastro end of 'pub' serving up simple, quality, intelligent British classics, with their regularly updated 'seasonal alternatives' running alongside. Despite the quality, prices are not stupid and if you're after something lighter they also offer a menu of afternoon bites – local seafood sandwiches and hearty snacks. And don't miss the scrummy home-made ice-cream, oh, or the cask conditioned local ales and organic ciders or, for that matter, the toasty fire in the winter and the sun terrace in the summer, perfect for reviving yourself after a decent leg stretch in the Ribble Valley.

Speirs House Camping Site ◐
Cropton, Pickering, YO18 8ES, T01751-417591, forestholidays.co.uk.

Swaithes of plantation forests and native birch, ash, rowan and oak stand together in dense pockets of woodland, tight trails weaving between them. Pushing out from these shady retreats, the vast, rolling open moorland is washed in the bright purple of heather and cut by meandering, shady

becks, swollen rivers, cascades and squealingly cold plunge pools. Yes, the North York Moors, held back from the sea by the high coastal cliffs certainly deliver an exciting array of terrains in which to escape. Set within Cropton Forest on the southern edge of the moors and surrounded by a spider's web of waymarked cycling and walking trails, Speirs House Camping Site is one such great escape. To the east the spectacular glacial coombe, the Hole of Horcum is worth an explore on foot while hoping aboard a steam train on the North Yorkshire Moors Railway will give you a unique tour through the landscape. In terms of shops, pubs and restaurants, there's not much to hand, and that's the point – instead its all about 'wild' nights out. As with all Forest Holiday sites, standard pitches allocations are undefined and unregimented, meaning that within reason, you can pitch up where you like – in the trees or out in the open. If you'd rather not get that close to nature, they also have comfortable, well designed, pretty luxurious wooden cabins available to rent, kept toasty with under floor heating. From £345/week for 4, short breaks also.

La Rosa ◌
Goathland, Whitby, YO22 5AS, T01947-606981, larosa.co.uk.

Set within a 20 acre site in the North York Moors National Park, this is a wonderfully kooky camping site where the emphasis is on low-impact living – from candles and fairy lights to a composting loo – as a matter of course and reusing – breathing life into forgotten caravans, tipis and kitschy knick-knacks. The result is an effortlessly bohemian, off-grid wonderland where you can reconnect with nature. The site accommodates up to 16 people in an assortment of caravans, vans and tipis.

Wales

❮ John Cook, Llanberis Slate Quarries.

Wales is a kingdom of epic highs and deep lows, where landscapes unfurl like a giant map dominated by folds and creases. It is a place governed by epic national parks; havens, retreats, resources. Snowdonia rules the north, the huge white mass soars on a clear winters' day, a range of high potential and epic endeavour. Climbers and walkers are drawn above like moths on a moonlit night, swimmers find pools and river courses to follow on summer's days, while skiers traverse the winter's white canvas. A beacon of knowledge and inspiration Plas-y-Brenin, the National Mountain Centre, reclines by still waters in the mountain's shadow. Following the Cambrian mountain ridge south, the Brecon Beacons rise as a counterpoint and balance; lofty vistas and soaring tracts of common land with uncommon purpose. Mountain bikes descend on classic trails, cavers delve deep beneath the earth's crust while water babies bob in cool pools fed by cascades. The Pemrokeshire National Park with its sweeping bays, hidden coves, sandy havens and lofty cliffs, is the jewel of the southwest coast. It is a place where coasteering was spawned and thrives. A place where surfers tear up epic winter swells and recline, soul-arched along lazy summer lines. It is a place where climbers gaze down from their sea cliff perches and kayakers explore offshore before making landfall for the night; mussels plucked from the low water mark and just-caught mackerel crackle over a driftwood fire, while sun-freckled faces watch the last light sink into the inky depths of the Atlantic.

Managed by the Mountain Training Trust, Plas y Brenin is perfectly positioned within the breathtaking and accessible peaks of Snowdonia to offer some of the best courses in Britain for those keen to experience heady heights in the lush summer months or the crisp chill of winter.

Environment

Over 20 percent of the land in Wales falls within the boundaries of national parks. The Snowdonia National Park covers 823 sq miles and was formed in 1951. The high mountains dominate this area with the range peaking at the 3560 ft summit of Snowdon. Their complex geology mixes sedimentary, metamorphic and igneous rocks all sculpted into a series of ridges and glacial cwms. The windswept uplands predominate with moorland, grass and boulder screes, but there are also shady valleys lined with oak, ash and rowan tracing lines by tumbling rivers and streams. Snowdon is one of the country's busiest mountains and thus measures need to be taken to protect from erosion due to excessive footfall.

While south Wales has traditionally been the heart of Wales' industrial might, with some landscapes blighted by mining and other forms of manufacturing infrastructure, the Brecon Beacons are an oasis within easy reach of the main urban conurbations of Cardiff, Swansea and Newport. Wide ranging moors spread over 519 sq miles with peaks and high ridges, the largest being Pen y Fan that climbs to over 2900 ft. The Beacons rest predominantly on red sandstone but in the southern region carboniferous limestone predominates, giving rise to cave systems, cascading waterfalls and classic limestone pavements. Millstone grit makes an appearance along the southern edge to offer climbers some variation in textured slabs. Welsh mountain ponies roam wild here and the red kite is the national parks' iconic bird while rivers run with salmon.

The coastline of Pembrokeshire is rich in wildlife and wondrous landscapes. Climbers cling to sheer faces, cracked and tilted through the relentless pressure of time and geological process. Sedimentary rocks predominate though regions of igneous protrusions are present. There are wonderful folds and faults, creating intriguing and intricate cliffs and reefs. Climbing restrictions are in place to ensure nesting birds are not disturbed – see bmc.co.uk for up to date details.

In terms of water quality a number of beaches and reefs of north and southwest Wales do not benefit from full tertiary treatment of sewage and, as with beaches across Britain are further hampered by CSO's and river's carrying run off leading into them so it is best to avoid entering the sea after heavy rains. For further information see sas.org.uk.

Climate

The Welsh weather is a temperate maritime climate dominated by the moist southwesterly air flow that comes off the Atlantic. Wales has a reputation for being wet, with an increase in precipitation on higher ground. The tip of Pembrokeshire sees between 100 to 200 mm rain during the summer, where as Snowdonia and the Beacons can receive between 500 and 1000 mm rainfall. Annually these high regions may see a massive 2200 to 4700 mm of rainfall, with some kind of precipitation falling on up to two thirds of the days of the year. The flanks of Snowdon are one of the wettest places in the UK.

Seasonal temperature variations differ from summer time average highs between 19 and 22°C in the warmest lowland areas, to an average of only 10°C at higher altitudes. Winter sees high altitude averages near freezing while the coastal zones are tempered by the effect of the sea, averaging between 3 and 5°C. For those setting off for high peaks on a warm summer's day it's worth bearing in mind that summits are usually around 9°C colder than the valleys, and can be even cooler with wind chill.

For water lovers the relatively shallow waters off the Welsh coastline means sea temperatures differ greatly with season. In the summer the ocean warms quickly and delivers warmer conditions than Cornwall at 15°C, meaning a 3/2 is very comfortable and it is not unknown to see the hardy surfing in board shorts. The chill of winter sees heat energy lost so water can drop to as low as a chilly 6 or 7°C during January and February, meaning a 5/4 mm wetsuits, boots, gloves and hoods are pretty essential. Remember to pack sunscreen when out on the water, climbing or walking.

Resources

welshwildlife.org Wildlife Trust of South and West Wales.

groundworkinwales.org.uk/greendragon Website listing the criteria and businesses qualifying for the Green Dragon environmental standard award recreational waters.

Snowdonia-society.org.uk This charity works to preserve the park's landscape, scenery and wildlife.

green-snowdonia.co.uk Committed to encouraging and promoting sustainable tourism ion Snowdonia. Green Snowdonia Tourism Awards.

eyri-npa.gov.uk Excellent Snowdonia National Park website with maps and information on exploring the area.

snowdoniagreenkey.co.uk Snowdonia Sherpa Bus details.

foresty.gov.co.uk Great resource with trail guides and mapping for both MTB and walking routes.

pcnpa.org.uk Pembrokeshire National Park website.

permbokeshiregreenways.co.uk Pembrokeshire travel advice for those looking to ditch the car.

breconbeacons.org National Park website with alternative suggestions for exploring the park.

ccw.gov.uk Countryside Council for Wales with details regarding access and public rights of way.

Swimming Fairy Glen

Provider	DIY
Skill level	All
Time frame	1 hr +
Equipment	Towel, bathers (depending on season/hardiness wetsuit)
Exertion level	●●○○○

Llyn Conwy lies within a drainage basin comforted by the Migneint blanket bog that surrounds it, the moorland's sponge-like ability serving to meter water flow and continually replenish the lake's stocks. These are the upper reaches of the Afon Conwy which lends the region its name, snaking for some 27 miles through upland streams, lowland meanders and fast flowing rapids and cascades, gathering strength from joining tributaries, before discharging into Conwy Bay on the north Wales coast.

Some simply come to witness the sheer energy of the 40-ft Conwy Falls while for others it is the promise of salmon and wild brown trout that lures them to the river's banks. For a select group however it is the somewhat enchanting properties of Ffos Noddun, 'the deep ditch', that draws them to the water's edge and into the cooling currents. Fairy Glen, as it is better known, is a magical spot for a serious swim or a peaceful glide down stream – the high, steep walls of the gorge are covered in green baize while sunlight filters through the wooded banks on to the deep pool and rock perches. It is just a mile south of Betws-y-Coed and around a mile below the famous falls of the Conwy River but the sublime scenery gives it an air of seclusion.

From Betws-y-Coed head south on the A5, turning right on to the A470 for Dolgellau/Ffestiniog. Turn left for Fairy Glen parking before road crosses over the river and from here it is a 10- to 15-minute walk along the signed path.

Practicalities

With a pretty backdrop, relaxed vibe and the pick of facilities, Betws-y-Coed is an ideal base for exploring Snowdonia. This is no secret so does get extremely busy in the summer months!

Transport Betws-y-Coed train station is also an important bus interchange for the Snowdonia National Park Sherpa and Conwy Valley services.

Sleeping £££ **Bryn Bella**, bryn-bella.co.uk, T01690-710627, offers award winning, sustainable yet comfortable B&B – breakfast eggs from their rescued hens, locally sourced produce and solar heated water, balanced with Wi-Fi and drying facilities. Packed lunch available. £ **YHA Swallow Falls**, LL24 0DW, T01690-710796, west of the town is fairly average but good for groups. For camping, **Hafod Farm** north of Betws y Coed towards Llanrwst LL26 0RA, T01690-710988, is a simple site in the Conwy Valley with pitches from £6/person.

Eating & drinking The Conwy Falls Café serves up excellent home made, locally sourced grub from quality all day breakfasts and cakes to soups, flat bread wraps and pizzas. Open 0900-1600 Wed, Sun; 0900-2100 Thu-Sat (pizza evenings and BYO booze). The building was designed by Sir Clough Williams-Ellis of Portmeirion fame in the 1950's.

Also try For a bird's eye perspective of the area, get roped up and embark on a tree top tour that combines awesome views and high level obstacle negotiation with adrenaline drops through the pine canopy. Green Snowdonia Sustainable Tourism award winners **Tree Top Adventure**, operate a mile north of Betws-y-Coed, T01690-710914, ttadventure.co.uk, with courses lasting around 2 hrs. The on-site café is also a champion of local, sustainable produce (inside and out).

> **Lowdown**

> **Prices**
£1 honesty box fee towards path maintenance.

> **Season**
Year round.

> **Don't miss**
An off-season walk to the waterfalls. A mile upstream are the Conwy Falls – £1 entrance. A couple of miles east of the village along the A5, the Swallow Falls are impressive in full flood.

> **Avoid**
The wrath of the people who 'operate' the Fairy Glen – just pay your small access charge BEFORE you head down and everyone will have a nice day.

> The Fairy Glen, where dappled light dances and secret swimmers slip beneath the surface.

Mountain biking Coed Llandegla Forest

Provider DIY	
Skill level All	
Time frame 1½ hrs +	
Equipment Mountain bike, helmet plus repair kit	
Exertion level ●●●●○	

Emerging from the trees you pause for a moment, turning your head to drink in the views. Marshalled by clean, green fields, a band of open moorland fades from purple to brown as it reaches out towards the heather-clad peak in the distance. From this perspective, the hills appear to rise gently so as not to dominate the landscape yet the Clwydian chain undulates northward for around 22 miles. 'Tomorrow', you think turning your attention back to the forest trail ahead, you still have unfinished business to attend to.

Coed Llandegla forest represents more than 1600 acres of hilly woodland potential. Cut through by the Offa's Dyke Path, this privately owned Denbighshire forest has its own comprehensive, purpose-built mountain bike centre complete with well-stocked shop, a workshop to iron out any mechanical problems you may encounter, full rider facilities and even a café selling home-made goodies to help you refuel after tackling one or all of the four trails on offer here.

The green arrow waymarked family trail avoids too many hard climbs following a three-mile loop on mainly hard-packed trail – with a few muddier sections thrown in for good measure. After a gentle climb from the car park, the trail passes the reservoir delivering views over to the Clywds. Taking it up a level, the blue 7½-mile beginners trail combines gradual uphill climbs with rewarding sections of down hill. They have also thrown in a few tests, such as small humps to negotiate, in order to make the trail a more satisfying challenge for those finding their way with mountain biking and whet the appetite of those looking to up their game. While the red intermediate trail may seem to get off to a slow start, the initial climb allows the more serious mountain biker a rare chance to take in their surroundings before heading off into the forest on an 11-mile loop of decent singletrack matching tougher more technical climbs with smooth, fast descents, tricky switchbacks and short sections of northshore. Accessible from the red trail, the black run delivers four miles of good singletrack challenges – from more technical climbs to speeding downhill sections with drops for experienced riders.

Practicalities

If you want to be close to the trails, the village of Llandegla is ideal while the nearby town of Llangollen has a number of decent places to eat plus amenities.

Transport Gwersyllt, 11 miles away is the closest station for the forest while Wrexham offers easier bus links.

Sleeping ££ **Hand House**, LL13 3AW, T01978-790570, offers very 'homely' B&B with home-made cakes on arrival. Self-catering set on a working farm near the trails, Plas yn lal, LL11 3BD, T01490-450 239, yalehall.com, offers gorgeous cottage accommodation for 4 from £350-550/week. For **camping**, the family run **Llyn Rhys Farm**, LL11 3AF, T01978-790 627, is a great spot with simple pitches from £5, just 5 mins from the trails.

Eating & drinking The log cabin **Oneplanet Adventure Café** serves up excellent home-made cakes and café fare to re-fuel post ride. Open 1000-1600 Tue-Sun.

Resources **Oneplanet Adventure**, T01978-751656, oneplanetadventure.com, on-site shop stocks a good range of hardware and essentials plus bike hire from £19/half day. Repairs and servicing also available. Oneplanet also run skills sessions with CTC instructors from foundation courses to conquering jumps and drops. They've also hooked up with down hill racers The Atherton's to run special Training Days and Race Clinics. **Mountain Biking North Wales**, mbnw.co.uk.

Also try This is mountain biking country. The Clwydian Hills have been mapped out at ridetheclwyds.com. To the south Llangollen is home to some excellent waymarked trails navigating the local and neighbouring mountains including the classic 24-mile Ceiriog Trail. **Pro Adventure**, Llangollen, T01978-861912, proadventure.co.uk, run skills courses.

> **Lowdown**

ⓘ Directory
Coed Llandegla Forest, LL11 3AA, coedllandegla.com for trail map.

€ Prices
Free/£19 bike hire.

☀ Season
Year round.

❂ Don't miss
A quick trip north to the Clwydians for lung-bursting ascents and warp-speeding descents.

✖ Avoid
Parking in lay-bys just annoys local landowners and may curb further trail development so fork out the £3.50/car and use the carpark.

Mountain skills Snowdonia

Provider	National Mountain Centre, Plas y Brenin, Wales
Skill level	Novice-experienced
Time frame	2 days
Equipment	Equipment can be loaned but must be pre-booked. Appropriate warm clothing, see text for more details
Exertion level	●●●●○

The small group of figures is not immediately noticeable in the vast expanse. Shaded by the peak, they make their way slowly along the dull cold of the northeast slope, a serpentine trail stretches steadily as they advance. Above, peaks are shrouded in white, edges softened, angles erased, shorn of features and definition. Erratic clumps of boulders punch through the sterile canvas, laid bare by the wind's callous backhand swipe. Suddenly the group is on the ground, lying tight, compact. A figure in a red jacket rises first, followed by another dark silhouette. Then they are on the floor again, as if struck down by some phantom or diving to avoid detection by prying eyes. However, there are no sinister forces at work here, for this is a learning environment, a classroom, and this team from the National Mountain Centre are learning how to self arrest with an ice axe, an essential and potentially life saving skill for anyone keen to get out into the hills during the winter.

⌄ On the summit.

pyb.co.uk

Based in Snowdonia, the Plas y Brenin National Mountain Centre lies in some of the most breathtaking and accessible peaks in the UK. From its enviable position on the shores of Llynnau Mymbyr it looks out over the awesome Snowdon Horseshoe, the classic ridge walking challenge that rises over significant mountain peaks, traverses knife-edge arêtes and circles the glacial lakes of LLydaw and Glaslyn. Managed by the Mountain Training Trust – a registered charity set up by the British Mountaineering Council, the Mountain Leader Training Board and the United Kingdom Mountain Training Board – it is hardly surprising that Plas y Brenin offers some the best courses in Britain for those keen to experience the environment on high, be it during the clean, crisp winter or the lush summer months. The staff are committed and highly competent outdoor enthusiasts and amongst the most experienced instructors you could hope to be led by and it is their unique talents that make a visit to the centre so special. When temperatures plummet below zero and more than a dusting of white covers the peaks and valley floors, mountain regions like Snowdonia throw up specific challenges to the walker and the courses on offer serve to equip clients with a specific skill set including winter navigation skills, terrain and route choice, the use of an ice axe and crampons as well as winter equipment selection. The two day Winter Skills course focuses on two essentials; navigation and security on winter terrain.

Heading out on to the slopes, crunching through knee deep snow, this is a comprehensive learning experience that really gives you first-hand knowledge of the skills needed, not just for a quick

> Getting to grips with crampons and ice axe in perfect conditions.

⌄ The National Mountain Centre is perfectly positioned within some of the most breathtaking and accessible peaks in the UK.

Practicalities

Established more than 50 years ago Plas y Brenin Mountain Centre is a top class resource, in terms of the quality of instruction, the range of courses offered on site, covering mountain based activities from climbing and walking to orienteering and mountain biking as well as water based activities including canoeing, kayaking and sea kayaking and the self contained facility itself which covers all aspects of a stay from accommodation, food and a bar. The residential course is offered on a full board basis.

Transport   Llandudno Train Station is the nearest access point, and the Centre provides a pick-up service the evening before the course starts. Parking is also provided at the centre.

Sleeping   The course includes accommodation at the Main Centre, which sleeps 72 people in comfortable rooms that range from single to double and triple, most with en-suite facilities. Bedding and towels are provided.

Eating & drinking   Food is big on the agenda here. The centre serves a wide selection of home-made, locally sourced food, vegetarian options provided for every meal. The breakfasts are huge on a help-yourself basis — start with cereal and toast before pushing on through a heart fry up — well, it is going to be cold out there! Help yourself to a packed lunch and on your return tuck into home-made cake (see website for recipes). The on-site bar with awesome views of the Horseshoe lake is pretty lively and serves a good range of guest ales from local micro breweries, Wi-Fi and bar food 1200-1000 and 1900-2100 also available. Non-residential can opt for a packed lunch £5.

Also try   The centre runs two day REC Emergency courses, a practical course and qualification for those who work outdoors or for those who want to be proficient at dealing with casualty situations. A great idea for anyone spending time on the mountains. From £162/non-residential.

hike on a fine bright sunny morning when the going is good, but to be confident in poor visibility, or high winds when there's snow and ice underfoot. Having spent time on the railway sleeper mock up slope on the previous day, learning the crampon technique, building confidence and just getting used to the new feeling of crampons underfoot, you'll feel ready to begin traversing up the real slopes, crossing small rocky outcrops. This two-day course does require a degree of summer walking experience and a good core fitness level, after all, tramping through deep snow and steep terrain can be a tiring business, but the views from the top certainly make it all worthwhile, and at the end of the day the knowledge and experience gained could prove invaluable.

The kit list: ice axe & crampons (if you have already), climbing helmet (if you have already), warm outdoor wear (all times of the year), hat (all times of the year), gloves or mitts, day rucksack, rucksack liner (bin liner), small first aid kit/blister kit, water bottle, vacuum flask, head torch, compass (Silva - type 4 recommended), boots, gaiters, waterproof jacket, waterproof trousers, notebook and pens, small amount of cash, 1:25 000 OS map Snowdon + Conwy valley, snow goggles, thick walking socks.

> Lowdown

ⓘ Directory
Plas y Brenin, Wales, Capel Curig, Conwy, LL24 0ET, T01690-720214, pyb.co.uk.

Prices
£200/person.

Season
Nov to Mar.

Don't miss
Try the great climbing wall which you're free to use.

Avoid
If you need to borrow equipment don't forget to book in advance.

Swimming Snowdonia

Provider DIY	
Skill level Novice-advanced	
Time frame All day – the return walk to the summit takes approximately 6 hrs	
Equipment For swimming: towel, bathers (depending on season/hardiness wetsuit). For walking: proper walking boots, adequate protective clothing	
Exertion level ●●●○○	

Snowdonia National Park or Eryri covers 823 sq miles of northwest Wales. This vast parkland reaches between Conwy in the north and the River Dyfi in the south, its western flanks are washed by the waters of the Irish Sea while its eastern boundary disappears into the Conwy Valley. Lakes, steep river gorges, pinnacled knife-edge ridges, verdant valleys and cascading waterfalls – the complex landscape has been forged by fire and ice. Great glacial valleys have been scoured out beneath jagged peaks born of the earth's furnace. While challenging mountain ranges cover more than half of its surface it is the tallest, Yr Wyddfa, Snowdon that dominates the landscape, lends its name to the park and stands centre stage. More than 300,000 pilgrims are drawn to its summit every year, hiking, biking and racing up well worn routes; finding freedom on challenging scrambles or sitting sedately as a train carries them to the top, to an altitude of 3560 ft. Despite the steady flow of traffic, many have their eyes fixed firmly on the main prize: the zenith, leaving treasures of an altogether more aquatic nature to be passed by and overooked.

Pen y Pass is a popular starting point and during the long days of the warmer months the car park fills quickly. However those early birds who strike out for the summit via the Miners Track are rewarded with quieter walkways and plenty of opportunities for a peaceful mountainside plunge. The path up to the peak is four miles long (eight miles when factoring in the return element of the swim tour) and laced along its edge is a series of three lakes, carved into Snowdon at ever increasing elevations, meaning the greater the effort the bigger the reward. Around a mile from the start of the wide and easy path, created to service the Brittania Copper Mines in the 19th and early 20th Centuries you reach the first lake, Llyn Teryn, which serves to whet the appetite. There is something deliciously Dali-esque about the notion of swimming up the

< The breath-stopping, jaw-numbing water of Llyn Llydaw.

side of the largest mountain in Wales and England and after a refreshing dip, you will be keen to follow the pathway up the short climb to the shores of the vast Llyn Llydaw. This is a different proposition altogether and demands a pause for thought. The 'deep end' descends for 190 ft into the blue-black realm of the unknown while the frigid, breath-stopping, jaw-numbing waters of this natural swimming pool serve to remind the hardy that, while in recent years this lake has been divided by a man-made causeway, it is truly the work of ice age architects. 600 ft above, a steep section of path leads on to the final pool, Llyn Glaslyn, a deep glacial cwm of blue, blue waters bounded by crags whose sheer sides appear to have been scooped out as if by a warm spoon serving up ice-cream.

Reserve some energy post plunge for the final and most testing push to the summit.

Below, the glacial Nant Gwynant valley, watched over by Snowdon, is also home to other, more accessible watering holes. Fed by the Afon Glaslyn, the huge Llyn Gwynant is capped by a beach and campsite and is a popular spot for a summer splash by both swimmers and paddlers. One and a half miles to the southwest, connected by the river and A498, Llyn Dinas is another great spot for a glide, plunge or swim. Unlike many of is neighbours, this is a relatively shallow lake meaning that by late summer, it has lost its chill edge. There are more than 100 lakes in Snowdonia measuring more than an acre in size. Then there are the rivers, plunge pools, quarries and cwms. Snowdon is just the tip. Go. Explore.

Practicalities

Snowdon is the main draw for visitors to the Snowdonia National Park and as such there are plenty of different bases to push out from depending on which water holes draw your attention. If you want to stay in a village with good resources, accommodation options and a good vibe then Llanberis is the best bet llanberis. org for details. It also acts as a spring board for the delights of the Llyn Padarn whose twin lake Llyn Peris acts as the lower reservoir of the Dinorwig hydroelectric power station housed in 'Electric Mountain'. Lake dwellers remember your midge repellent!

Transport Porthmadog is the nearest station. From here the Snowdon Sherpa offers a bus link to destinations including Llyn Gwynant, Llanberis, Pen-y-Pass gwynedd.gov.uk for details. Bangor and Betsw-y-Coed are also handy train stations.

Sleeping Ideal for exploring lakes Gwynant and Dinas, **Llyn Gwynant Campsite**, gwynant.com, takes its name from the lakeside shores on which it resides and for water babies must surely be in the running for best site in Wales. The land was bought by national parks advocate Clough Williams-Ellis in the 30s to protect it from development along with 300 acres of mountain land which he donated to the nation. Accessed via the A498, the simple 14 acre site is on the northern shores of the elliptical lake — the site of choice being Pen Helen field bounded by lake and river. Camping from £6/person, booking for large groups only. Open Mar-Oct plus year round for large groups. Self-catering available: secluded 'Nutshell' caravan overlooks lake south of site from £175/week sleeping up to 4. Kayak and canoe hire available during peak times from £5/hr. Overlooking the southern end of the lake £ **Bryn Gwynant YHA**, LL55 4NP, T0845-371 9108, is open year round, self-catering and restaurant. For those exploring the Miners Path

lakes, £ **Pen Y Pass YHA**, LL55 4NY, T0845-371 9534, is ideal: open year round with licensed bar and on-site restaurant. Allegedly Mallory even stayed here once (before it was a YHA presumably!) At the base of the Snowdon Ranger Path and on the edge of Llyn Cwllyn £ **Snowdon Ranger YHA**, LL54 7YS, T0845-371 9695, has Wi-Fi. Open year round.

Eating & drinking From Llyn Gwynant, the nearest place for a pint is 2 miles away at **Hotel Pen y Gwryd**, T01286-870211, pyg.co.uk — somewhat of an institution for mountain explorers with plenty of climbing memorabilia and photos. Near the base of the Watkins Path **Caffi Gwynant**, Nant Gwynant is a champion of local produce and home cooking. Full Welsh breakfasts for a fiver and well priced, warming home cooked pies to tasty soups for lunch. Wed-Sun 0900-1730. In Llanberis, refuel at modern institution the legendary **Pete's Eats** on the High St with hearty, filling well priced fare. At the summit of Snowdon the new visitors centre and café **Hafod Eryri** is open in the warmer months only, offering rewards to those who have made the trek — or just jumped aboard the train from Llanberis.

Resources eryri-npa.co.uk — Snowdonia National Park website has information and maps showing the main routes to the summit of Snowdon as well as an overview of the lakes of Snowdonia — serious food for thought!

Also try If you're prepared to push out with your trusty OS map, you can find a world of wild bathing opportunities from the vast to the sublime and secluded. While the lakes are often chilly, in the height of the summer the rivers and streams that feed them can be more forgiving.

> Lowdown

⊖ Prices
Free.

⊙ Season
Late summer is the optimum time temperature-wise – plenty of sunshine and little rain is key!

⊙ Don't miss
Save some energy for the final push to the summit of Yr Wyddfa – on a clear day, the view from the top is awe inspiring.

⊗ Avoid
The deep mountain lakes can be extremely cold. Know your limits – get out before you start to give up. Avoid straying from the banks before you have acclimatized.

Fungi forage Bangor

Provider	Moelyci
Skill level	All
Time frame	2 days
Equipment	Decent footwear, outdoor clothing, packed lunch
Exertion level	●○○○○

"I think a big part of the fascination of fungi is that we know so little about them," enthuses John Harold, Conservation Officer for Moelyci, the community owned farm and environmental centre based the heartlands of north west Wales. "Their fascinating lifecycles and their importance in driving major natural processes are balanced by a powerful sense of mystery, strangeness, 'otherness'." And the people of Moelyci know all about instinctive reactions. In 2003, when this intensively grazed mountain farmland was under threat of sale to developers the community knew it had to rally round. Around 200 members from surrounding villages originally invested in the land, some 150 acres of it, forming a not-for-profit society and today there are 500 community shareholders whose conservation instincts and cash help safeguard the land. "Within a small geographical area in this corner of NW Wales we have every habitat imaginable from sand dunes to high mountain top – this means that people with an interest in natural history have an amazing richness of choice at their feet," says John. "Moelyci itself is a kind of microcosm of that diversity, with its land running from lush lowland wetlands to upland heathland on the mountain, with a range of grassland, wetland and woodland habitats all in the mix."

Accompanied by respected field mycologist Charles Aron, John leads an annual course in Edible Fungi Identification, and it is clear that this is a man who is passionate about fungi. "As someone who spends much time educating and engaging people with biodiversity, I find them an unparalleled useful resource," says John. "They are visually delightful and surprising, and prompt strong and varied instinctive reactions in people who otherwise may not have a great interest in nature". The two-day course aims to clear the mycological minefield that lies before the uninitiated. Day one is about learning the principles of fungi identification. Using samples collected beforehand, John explains about the importance of analysing the whole picture – stems, caps, gills, colours, smells and excretions, effectively learning to identify the 'tells' of the ones you can eat but more importantly, confidently recognising the poisonous ones you can't.

The second day is spent entirely in the field, foraying in the area at a site selected using the local knowledge of the course leaders. Here the emphasis is on responsible foraging, taking on board the ethics and conservation issues raised the previous day, associated with collecting fungi from the wild. It's about being mindful of the environment, leaving habitats as undisturbed as possible and not stripping an area clean. It's about employing simple techniques like using a wicker basket to hold your harvest, ensuring spores are free to scatter in the wind and find fertile new ground on which to flourish and fulfil their role in the natural process. It's about selecting your harvest carefully and identifying well. And if you are skilful in that art, the best is yet to come, cooking up some of the finds of the day on a camping stove.

> A splendid hygrocybe splendidissima.

˅ Cooking up a feast and enjoying the fruits of one's labours.

ⓘ Directory
Moelyci Farm, Lon
Felin Hen, Tregarth,
Bangor, Gwynedd,
LL57 4BB, T01248-
602793, moelyci.org.

Ⓟ Prices
£90 – strictly limited
to maximum 12
participants.

⊘ Season
Late Sep.

⊕ Don't miss
A stomp to the trig
point at the top of
the modest Moel y Ci
for wonderful views
of Snowdonia and
across the Menai Strait
and Lavan Sands to
Anglesey.

⊗ Avoid
Watch where you
put your feet when
out on a stomp – the
grasslands of north
Wales are a rich
and diverse site for
grassland fungi.

Practicalities

Just off the important A5 London to Holyhead Road, and a 5 min walk to the Moelyci Environmental Centre, the small village of Tregarth, complete with pub is in the Welsh speaking heartlands. It is the gateway to the Ogwen Valley, lying in the foothills of Snowdonia yet is just under 3 miles from the city of Bangor.

Transport Bangor station is just 3½ miles away. Two onward buses and a short walk connect you to the village arrivabus.co.uk for details. Better yet the Lon Las Ogwen cycle path, links Bangor with Tregarth and runs straight through the centre. The cycleway gently climbs taking you along a stream and through woodland before bringing you out into the open countryside

Sleeping John recommends the well priced, family run **£££-££ Pant Teg B&B**, Tregarth, LL57 4AU, T01248-602248, pantteg.co.uk, a short walk from the centre. For camping, the small, family run **Dinas Farm Site**, LL57 4NB, T01248-364227, is a good choice. Open Apr-Oct it is on the banks of the River Ogwen and just over 1 mile from the centre.

Eating & drinking The **Caban** at Brynrefail utilizes local, organic produce – including ingredients from their own kitchen garden to create simple tasty fare 0900-1600. John also recommends the **Vaynol Arms** for food at nearby Pentir, LL57 4EA. For an evening drink, pop into the local **Pant Yr Ardd** in Tregarth.

Also try The Fungi Foray. This annual event is usually held on the 1st Sun in Oct and regularly attracts over 100 people. Led by John Harold and leading North Wales naturalist and curator, Bangor University Botanic Gardens Nigel Brown, more than 150 acres of varied farmland is available to be foraged. The finds are then sorted and discussed, highlighting species of interest, be they ecologically important, scientifically interesting, edible or poisonous.

Climbing Snowdonia

Provider	Rock Climbing Company, Wales
Skill level	Novice-experienced
Time frame	Full day
Equipment	All necessary equipment provided such as helmet and rock shoes, remember to wear comfortable clothing
Exertion level	●●●●●

The rounded peak is boulder strewn, rocks fractured and tossed aside as if by some ancient prison gang on endless hard labour. The summit here is as bleak as Mars and nearly as desolate, on a clear winter's day the sun appears but seems to lack the will to impart any degree of warmth to rival the biting wind. Across the gulf of the unseen glacial valley below, the Snowdon Massif looms, all green and beige angles and points. A line of white cloud peels off the snow tipped summit of the highest point, the jagged mountain which lends its name to the region, to the National Park that spreads out around North Wales for over 827 sq miles. The 3560 ft climb to the looming cap of Snowdon is not quite the expeditionary challenge it may seem, there is even a railway to carry those not up to the brisk hike to the summit. No, for those in need of a climbing challenge look elsewhere – but not too far, for the region of Snowdonia is home to some of Britain's most challenging and most varied terrain, as well as some of its best climbers.

Whether your passion is for sports climbing or freeclimbing, or if you feel you'd like to try your hand at bouldering or sea cliffs, then look no further. "It is the huge variety of climbing in Snowdonia that makes living here so enjoyable," says Sylvia Fitzpatrick of Rock Climbing Company. Sylvia who holds the Mountain Instructor's Award has been climbing for over 22 years and her impressive CV includes several summits in Patagonia as well as some of the Alps most testing routes. "There are remote mountain crags where you can escape the heat and the crowds, roadside boulders and crags for a sociable evening's climbing with friends after work and the most amazing sea cliffs that have incredibly good weather. In addition many of these routes and crags are intertwined so deeply with the history of climbing – all of the masters have used Snowdonia as a forcing ground for cutting edge new routes – that climbing here has an extra dimension that really adds to the climbing experience."

For those who are keen to get to grips with climbing but who are yet to progress from the climbing wall out on to the rock, an experienced climbing school can really help your transition. Sylvia feels communication is the key to an enjoyable and rewarding climbing experience. "Prior to the course starting I like to be in contact with the clients in order to ensure that the course meets their requirements," she says. "Although the term 'Beginners Climbing' might seem a bit generic, people have very different needs and expectations – some want an adventurous experience for their family with the emphasis on fun and excitement, others will want to concentrate on the technical aspects of climbing so that when they finish the course they have the core skills needed to climb independently and safely." The beauty of a region

> Quarrying times.
⌄ Llanberis Pass, embedded with climbing history. "The masters have used Snowdonia as a forcing ground," says Silvia. "Climbing here has an extra dimension that really adds to the climbing experience."

Alex Messenger

like Snowdonia is the plethora of climbing areas on offer. If the weather turns, a pitch may be exposed and wet, but there are always other venues where the local microclimate can offer much more shelter. That's where local knowledge is key. "It can be blowing horribly and throwing down buckets in one valley and yet 10 miles away in another venue it can be dry and fairly still," Sylvia explains.

"The venues we favour have good access, solid rock and large safe areas at the bottom where people can gather. It is rare that we can't find somewhere dry to climb because each area has its own individual weather pattern. Clogwyn Cyrrau near Betws-y-Coed is great for beginners. It has easy access, good weather and great views but

it is also quite quiet. Tryfan Bach and Milestone Buttress in the Ogwen Valley, Holyhead Mountain on Anglesey and the Upper Tier of Tremadog are other great venues that all have different strengths," says Sylvia." Another popular venue is Lions Rock on the outskirts of Llanberis. This is a bigger crag that is great for teaching multi-pitch techniques plus it offers great views of the Llanberis lake and the Llanberis Pass between Glyderau and the Snowdon Massif. The area around here was used as the training base for the 1953 Everest Expedition that put Hillary and Tenzing on the summit. After all, if it's good enough for the first crew to successfully ascend the Himalayan peak, it'll offer challenges for even those with the most adventurous streak.

Practicalities

Snowdonia National Park consists of glacial valleys, snow scoured peaks and lush green lowland pasture. It is the venue for many adventure sports and activities. Check out Snowdonia-npa.gov.uk. The Snowdon Railway train climbs the 3560 ft to the summit of Snowdon and is open outside the winter climbing season. snowdonrailway.co.uk. The Llanberis Path is a moderate grade 6-hor walk that takes in the summit of Snowdon with excellent views on the climb across to the Llanberis Pass, the Glyderau and below to the Cwm Glas Bach. The town of Llanberis is home to a large and active climbing population. It has a good atmosphere, excellent resources, is at the head of the Llanberis Pass and is steeped in climbing history making it an ideal base for a climbing trip. See llanberis.org.

Transport Porthmadog is the nearest station. From here the Snowdon Sherpa offers a bus link to Llanberis. See gwynedd.gov.uk for details. Bangor and Betsw-y-Coed are other options with decent links.

Sleeping There are plenty of B&B's in Llanberis including the small, informal **££ Nitas B&B**, The High St, LL55 4EU, T07769-851681, surfsister.co.uk, utilising local and organic produce where possible and can organize packed lunches for £5. Half a mile from the village, opposite DMM, the small, family run **££-£ Gallt y Glyn**, LL55 4EL, T01286-870370, gallt-y-glyn.co.uk, has B&B and bunkhouse accommodation from £8. On-site bar with summertime pizza and pint nights also. Half a mile from the town **£ Llanberis YHA**, LLwyn Celyn, LL55 4SR, T0845-371 9645, is well placed while close by **Llwyn Celyn Bach**, T01286-870923, campinginllanberis.com, offers simple camping on a working farm. Three miles north, the small **££ Graianfryn Vegetarian Guest House**, LL55 3NH, T01286-871007, is comfortable while mindful

of the environment – solar panels help to heat the water. At the foot of Moel Gynghorion on a mountain sheep farm, **£ Yr Helfa Bunkhouse**, snowdonbunkhouse.co.uk, offers simple accommodation from £12/night.

Eating & drinking No self-respecting climber's visit to Llanberis is complete without a trip to **Pete's Eats** on the High St which has served up generous portions of good grub to climbers since '78. For a quick fix, the **Hot Shop** also on the High St does a cracking line in quality takeaway pizzas. Drop in for an ale or two at **The Pen-y-Gwryd Hotel**, Pen-y-Pass, Nant Gwynant, Gwynedd, LL55 4NT, T01286-870211, with history, climbing memorabilia and photos.

Resources There are 2 excellent independent climbing shops here: **Joe Brown** on the High St, T01286-870327, joe-brown.com, opened by the legendary climber in 1966 and well stocked with equipment and advice and; **V12 Outdoor**, The Old Baptist Chapel, T01286-871534 , v12outdoor.com, also has an excellent range of goods.

Also try For those looking to progress, Sylvia runs 1,2,3, and 5 day lead climbing courses based in the Snowdonia mountains, the sea cliffs at Gogarth and Holyhead Mountain on Anglesey, prices vary according to course length and student ratios. For those wanting to experience the region's classic climbs guiding is also available at a variety of levels in a range of locations from the high, sombre mountain buttresses of Clogwyn Du'r Arddu, the extensive crags in the Llanberis and Ogwen Valleys, the rain shadow crags of Tremadog, the quick drying slate in the Dinorwig quarries or the adventurous Gogarth cliffs on Anglesey.

> Lowdown

ⓘ Directory
Rock Climbing Company, Llys Gain, Crafnant Road,Trefriw, Conwy, LL27 0JZ, T01492-641430/ 0797-0016291, rockclimbing company.co.uk.

ⓢ Prices
£150 covers 1 person for a single day 1-to-1 climb outdoor course. A 2-day course for 2 is £300.

ⓢ Season
Summer.

ⓞ Don't miss
A quick dip in one of the streams of rivers to cool of post climb.

ⓧ Avoid
The midges love the warm Welsh summer days and the hills of Snowdonia – grease up with repellent.

Alex Messenger

Surfing Llyn Peninsula

Provider	DIY
Skill level	All
Time frame	Dawn till dusk
Equipment	Surfboard, wetsuit
Exertion level	●●●○○

When the topic of surfing in Wales raises its head, it is usually the Gower or Pembroke coastlines of the south that immediately spring to most people's minds. It is well known that the north is the heartlands of Welsh Nationalism and Welsh speakers, but few outside the wave riding fraternity know that it has increasingly become a surfing Mecca, drawing tribes from across the north of the country and as far afield as the northeast of England and the northwest of Scotland. Just as for centuries the Llyn Peninsula drew pilgrims from across Europe to its storm ravaged tip, eager to make the crossing to the island of Ynys Enlli, today the beaches and bays of this remote and rugged Area of Outstanding Natural Beauty have become a major draw for boardriders.

Like a giant grassy arm reaching out into the Irish sea, the long, low Llyn offers an open hand to the groundswells that roll up from the southwest. And due to its geography, you are never far from the craggy cliffs or sandy bays of the coastline. Lying near the tip, Abersoch has a real surf town feeling to it. It is a magnet for watersports enthusiasts, those lovers of wakeboarding, windsurfing and kiteboarding, playing host to the annual Wakestock – Europe's largest wakeboarding and music festival. However while the surf can be excellent, this region isn't renowned as the most consistent. Local surfers and pilgrims alike have had to master the art of swell prediction, reading the weather patterns to know just when the waves will arrive and which winds will bring those golden offshore mornings. And if the waves don't deliver, well there's always the chance to break out a kiteboard or chill on the beach with a BBQ.

Porth Neigwl or Hell's Mouth consists of a 4-mile long stretch of beach, backed by green fields and crumbling cliffs. Working in all southwest swells and off-shore in northeasterly winds, for surfers, this is the area's main draw but it also acts as an indicator as to how the other breaks will be. At high tide it is mostly pebble but from mid tide it opens into a vast expanse of sand that shifts with tide and swell to produce a variety of banks along its length. At the southern end lies the Corner, a wedgy lefthander that peels along a rocky bottom, before finishing on the sand. At the northern end sits the Reef, a good quality right that always attracts a crowd when it's working.

Moving south around the headland you will find the much smaller bay at Porth Ceriad which works in similar conditions to its neighbour. This is a popular high tide break and offers a series of peaks to choose from along the beach. One of the most popular waves is found on the eastern side of the bay.

Here swell lines can often bounce back off the cliffs and converge, jacking up to form a wedge-like left-hand barrel. Waves here are bigger and more powerful than along the rest of the beach, providing hell drops and cover-up for those more experienced surfers. The most consistent times for the Llyn Peninsula are during the autumn to spring seasons, but bear in mind that neither of these beaches is life guarded, so beginners need to take care and watch for rips.

◄ Top Welsh surfer Chris 'Guts' Griffiths fanning the flames at the southern end of Hell's Mouth.

The Gill

< Hanging five at Porth Neigwl.

Turtle

< Port Ceriad.

Practicalities

Abersoch with surf shops, bars and eateries is a natural hub and draw for visiting surfers while quieter, more secluded areas can be found towards the toe and Aberdaron.

Transport 7 miles from Abersoch, Pwllheli train station has a regular bus service on to Abersoch – the number 18 Nefyn.

Sleeping Within easy reach of Porth Neigwl, **££ Rhydolion**, LL53 7LR is just ½ mile inland T01758-712342 rhydolion. co.uk with 4 quality, self-catering cottages sleeping up to 7. Short breaks from £100 available off-season. Basic camping also available ¾ mile from the beach. **£ Tanrallt**, Llangian, LL53 7LN, T01758-713527, tanrallt.com, has comfortable bunkhouse accommodation popular with surfers from £16 inc. light breakfast. Camping for families and couples also. For camping the small, basic and lovely **Treheli Farm**, LL53 8AA, T01758-780281, overlooks Porth Neigwl, May-Sep. For a change of scene, in nearby Aberdaron, **£££-££ The Ship Hotel** is a comfortable, modernized village inn with clean, simple rooms and good bar and restaurant below.

Eating & drinking The Ship Hotel, Aberdaron serves up really decent food using local ingredients where possible. **The Sun Inn**, Llanengan, near Hell's Mouth is another great spot to grab a spot surf bite and a beer.

Resources In Abersoch, there are a number of surf shops including **West Coast Surf**, T01758-713067, westcoastsurf. co.uk, and **Lon Pen Cei** which sells a good range of hardware and offers surf hire from £10/day board and wettie. Check the site for the Hell's Mouth webcam plus surf forecast. Surf Tech demon centre **Offaxis**,T01728-454341, offaxis.co.uk, offers lessons for beginners through to advanced with BSA qualified instructors.

Also try For a different take on this AONB, organize a **coasteering** session which will see you scrambling on sea cliffs, taking leaps of faith into the Irish Sea and squeezing through rock tunnels. Who better to throw yourself off a cliff with than a former RAF man and mountaineering instructor? Chris Thorne of **Llyn Adventures**, T07751-826714, llynadventures.com, fits this bill exactly. A half-day session costs £30/person and should see you getting wet for around 2 hrs – bring a towel, some bathers and old trainers.

> **Lowdown**

☉ Prices
Free or from £10/day board and suit hire.

☉ Season
Autumn to Spring but with occasional summer swells.

☉ Don't miss
Annual Wakestock festival in Abersoch each Jul.

☒ Avoid
Beginners should avoid surfing in swells over waist high as the beaches do not have lifeguard cover.

Mountain biking Coed y Brenin

Provider	DIY
Skill level	All
Time frame	1½ to 6 hrs
Equipment	Mountain bike, helmet, snacks, water, a map and a repair kit/spare tube.
Exertion level	●●●○○

The King's Forest, Coed y Brenin lies in the southern reaches of the Snowdonia National Park. With huge Douglas firs and broad-leaf oaks, the woodland is spectacularly placed, stretching out for more than 9000 acres across the deep river valleys of the Eden, Gain, Wren and Mawddach, while bounded by dramatic peaks. The popular Cadair Idris rises to the south, Aran Fawddwy, just shy of joining the Welsh 3000's takes up the eastern flank, with the often-overlooked Rhinogs to the west. The land is striated with mined veins of gold, while the evergreen and deciduous patchwork canopy provides shelter to a king's

ransom of wildlife from fallow and roe deer on the ground and otters in the rivers to butterflies, bats and red kites circling overhead. There are also rare sightings of red squirrels and pine martens that have been known to inhabit the space in between. However it is mountain biking that has seen the Forestry Commission managed woodland regenerate – the 82 miles of cleverly devised trails have acted to pump new life and riches into the forest and seen it crowned as a Mecca for MTBers.

The first dedicated trail was opened in 1997 thanks to the pioneering efforts of Daffyd Davis who persuaded his then Forestry Enterprise bosses to allow him to build some singletrack. The overwhelming popularity of the trail saw visitor numbers explode, the original track expand, the network of trails increase to form a dedicated MTB centre and Davis awarded an MBE for his

◄ Luke Webber, draws his line though the King's Forest.

efforts. Today there are seven quality trails and counting making this a must-stop on a Welsh tour of mountain biking duty. Providing something for family fun day-ers to thrill-seeking experts, the all-weather trails are a well thought out mix of singletrack and fire roads with sections of dual track, all signed from the visitor centre and set against a backdrop of majestic pines and grand peaks.

The 7-mile family friendly Yr Afon loop follows the deep river valley, passing gold mine workings and waterfalls which feed the soul. It's easy but not effortless mixing forest road with short sections of track and pot-holed roads plus some climbs, making it a great introduction not just to MTB but to north Wales.

Stepping up a grade, there are two long red trails as well as the shorter routes Temtiwr at nearly 5½ miles and Cyflym Coch at seven miles, but with technical sections, these are not soft options. You can get round Temtiwr in under an hour – a good quick blast to get your legs warmed up while the rocky sections get the brain going – while the newer Cyflym Coch has some excellent fast descents linked by short, technical climbs. At just over 12 miles, the Tarw or 'Bull' keeps most of its 1510 ft of climbing to fire roads leaving its downhill sections as twisty, rocky, bone shaking singletrack – 'Rocky Horror Show' anyone? In contrast, the challenging MBR Trail is open and flowing with long swooping descents over decent rooty, muddy, rocky sections and passes through spectacular scenery – if you can see it through the speed blur. The infamous Pink Heifer is back and links up with the Beginning of the End descent – the most technically challenging section of this trail.

Gluttons for punishment who want to endure sustained exertion and tests of mental and physical toughness need look no further as Coed y Brenin delivers two such experts-only black runs. Llwybr Dragon's Back covers nine miles of ground, climbing 2330 ft in long, intense sections with equally challenging, heart thumping descents while the 24-mile, Beast'climbs 2559 ft – some of which is on fire road and combines a lot of the best of MBR and Dragon's Back. Those who are gluttons for cake are also well catered for here – just head for the café where you can order up your treat with a serious side order of views.

Practicalities

In the southern reaches of the Snowdonia National Park, the pretty market town of Dolgellau is a great base with supermarkets, pubs, restaurants, banks plus plenty of decent accommodation.

Transport Morfa Mawddach station on the coast is around 7½ miles from Dolgellau with a lovely, flat bike trail and footpath running along disused track following the River Mawddach.

Sleeping **££-£ Cae Gwyn Farm** and Nature Reserve, Bronaber, Gwynedd, LL41 4YE, T01766-540245/07776-019336, caegwynfarm.co.uk, 0900-1900. On the northern edge of Coed y Brenin, this 190 acre sheep farm run on organic farming principles is ideally placed for enjoying car-free adventures. With the River Eden running through it and crossed by smaller streams, it's also idyllic. Year-round accommodation for all wallets: simple camping with breathtaking views, a camping barn from £10/night to comfortable B&B. Bike wash and lock-ups, plus Wi-Fi. In nearby Dolgellau **£ Plas Isa**, T01341-421949, plasisa.co.uk, is ideal for groups with bunk rooms sleeping 4 from £60 plus one room sleeping 8 from £100. Plus lounge, pool table and bike store. Book ahead. West near Bontddu, **££ Coed Cae**, Taicynhaeaf, LL40 2TU, T01341-430628, coedcae.co.uk, is run by keen MTBers, offering sustainable B&B with a log-fuelled boiler to power the central heating and top up the solar heated water. If you're up to the challenge they'll provide you with the route card for their 31 miles Snowbikers Circuit of nearby peak Cadair Idris.

Eating & drinking The **Coed y Brenin café** serves up just the right sort of simple food you need to refuel post session. In Dolgellau, for a proper Welsh tea, head to **Aber Cottage Tea Rooms**, Smithfield Street for a slice of two of Bara Brith. For dinner **Dylanwad Da Restaurant**, T01341-422870, is pricey but the quality is excellent and features local produce. Thu-Sat.

Resources forestry.gov.uk/coed-y-breninforestpark – excellent resource including trail guide and maps. **Beics Brenin**, T01341-440728, beicsbrenin.co.uk, based at the centre offers full suspension bikes from £50/day plus entry level bikes from £25/day. Contact for opening times. **Snowbikers**, Taicynhaeaf, T01341-430628, offer guided rides from half day family circuits to XC day expeditions for experienced riders plus skills courses, weekenders and girls only sessions.

Also try Whitewater rafting on the Treweryn with the **National Whitewater Centre**, T01678-521083, ukrafting.co.uk. The 1¾ mile run is rated an exhilarating grade 3-4 (grade 1 is gentle flowing water, 6 is considered commercially un-runable). From £31. Check rafting is on before making the trek.

> Lowdown

❶ Directory
Coed Y Brenin Visitor Centre, Maesgwm, Ganllwyd, Dolgellau, LL40 2HY.

⑤ Prices
Parking £3/day. MTB hire from £25.

⊗ Season
Year round.

❶ Don't miss
The waterfalls – The family MTB trail takes in Rhaeadr Mawddach and Pistyll Cain while a circular foot trail will lead you on a 2-hr hike to the Gain waterfall.

⊗ Avoid
The Beast is over 24 miles of pure mental and physical challenge, do not take this on unless you are fit enough for this sustained level of exertion.

Kite surfing Anglesey

Provider	Turbulence Extreme Sports
Skill level	Novice to experienced
Time frame	Courses from 1-day +
Equipment	All specialist equipment supplied, but wear long sleeves and trousers to protect knees and elbows, sun cream, sunglasses and some sturdy footwear
Exertion level	●●●●○

There are few better sights than that offered along the North Wales coastline, the towering mountains a jagged backdrop, blurring in a haze of wind and spray, board skittering across the surface of the Irish Sea, the kite angling into the breeze, a sudden burst of acceleration leading into a carving turn, throwing up a rooster tail of spray. Kite surfing brings together elements of waveriding and wakeboarding into a hybrid offspring, and North Wales has established itself as something of a kite surfing Mecca for the north of the UK. This is a sport that challenges co-ordination, fitness and stamina but the pay-off is certainly worth all the effort.

There are myriad quality beaches around the Llyn Peninsula, the mythical isle of Anglesey and on to the resorts of Llandudno and Rhyl – depending on the fickle hand of tide and wind. For the novice, good advice and lessons in the basics are essential. The first skill to master is kite control, and at Turbulence Kite Academy, that's where they start, on dry land. "With starter lessons it is an ideal opportunity to understand the basics of kites and how they work," says Lukas Jones who has been involved in kiting for more than 10 years. "We'll also teach you where they develop power, how to launch and land and how to put those skills of wrapping and unwrapping lines into practice." It's only then that you'll move into the water with some intensive one-to-one training.

"As all our lessons are booked on a one-on-one or one-on-two basis for you and a partner, we also have the ability to offer coaching sessions," explains Lukas. "These sessions are again based on your level and what you want to learn."

Practicalities

On the banks of the river the walled town of Conwy, the gateway to Snowdonia, is dominated by its formidable medieval castle, renowned as one of the best in Europe.

Transport There are train stations with good links in Conwy and over the river in Llandudno Junction.

Sleeping £££ Gwynfryn B&B, 4 York Place, Conwy, LL32 8AB, T01492-576733, gwynfrynbandb.co.uk. Lovely boutique B&B in central location with broadband access. ££ Bryn B&B, Synchant Pass Road, Conwy, LL32 8NS, T01492-592449, bryn.org.uk. This excellent guesthouse sits by one of the medieval towers and offers organic locally sourced breakfasts with fresh, home-made bread. Vegetarian and coeliac options available too. Closed winter season. £ Conwy YHA, LL32 8AJ, resembles a university building but don't let this put you off. This modern hostel is just a 10-min walk to the town centre with good facilities.

Eating & drinking Conwy Bistro, not cheap but excellent locally sourced dishes. Also check out **Zanzibar Coffee Shop** on Penrhyn Road, Colwyn Bay. **The Fat Cat**, Mostyn St, Llandudno is another popular café/bar which serves up well priced grub in relaxed surroundings.

Resources The Turbulence Store, Llandudno, ukkiting. com, staffed by a knowledgeable team, carries a full range of kit from kites to boards and buggies (including second-hand equipment) as well as accessories, wetties and protection. Their site is an excellent resource with details on the best beaches to access according to wind and weather conditions.

Also try For more aquatic adventures on the northern shore, Sea Kayaking in Holyhead, seakayakinguk.com, offers guided trips that take on the tidal races of the Menai Straits and the turbulent waters at North Stack – paddler's heavens. The abundance of wildlife is perfect for anyone in search of seals, porpoises and seabirds. Rhoscolyn offers great scope for 'rock-hopping' – the opportunity to weave and paddle through small inlets and gullies while the eastern shores of Anglesey provide more sheltered paddling. For less experienced paddlers, introductory, residential weekends from £155.

> **Lowdown**

ⓘ Directory
Turbulence, 148 Conwy Road, Llandudno Junction, Conwy, North Wales, LL31 9DU, T08456-589656, ukkiting.com.

Ⓢ Prices
£40/session.

Ⓢ Season
All year.

Ⓞ Don't miss
Conwy Feast – local annual food festival in Oct. Conwyfeast.co.uk.

Ⓧ Avoid
Getting caught out by the weather, it can change quickly here.

Canoeing Llangollen

Provider	Pro Adventure
Skill level	Novice-intermediate
Time frame	2 days
Equipment	Bring warm clothing and waterproof jacket
Exertion level	●●●●○

There's something really special when the boat is trimming, gliding through the water on that sweet spot where resistance seems to disappear; the boat almost hovers, subtle oar movements seeing the nose edge to the left or right around potential hazards and glassy boils. "For comfort and efficiency move your knees towards your paddle side," advises Pro Adventure's Pete Carol. Suddenly the amount of energy input drops and everything seems to make sense, any frustration disappears and the calm surroundings seem to fade in from the background as your mind relaxes. It's a quiet moment of Zen when it all clicks.

Born in the mountains of Snowdonia, the Dee is one of Britain's best canoeing rivers and what better way to see it than by open canoe. There's something deep down inside us all that wants to give this a go, maybe it's being raised on a steady diet of westerns and Ray Mears but it has always looked like the way to get down river. And it turns out it is. "The Dee has hundreds of years of boating history from coracles to international canoeing competitions which run every winter," says Pete whose company runs a two-day course that will help those eager to get to grips with the open canoe. Day one is mastering the basics. "We start on the Llangollen Canal or a flat section of the River Dee to get turning and canoe handling skills up to speed," says Pete. "The rest of the day is spent on the river learning to work with the water, moving into and out of the current, getting across the current with a ferry glide as well as learning about river hazards." Day two is about getting down the river, running the rapids and playing with the river's waves. There are plenty of skills to master but gaining an efficient forward paddling stroke is key. "You'll be able to ferry glide, break in, break out and choose your line down the river," says Pete. "You will be able to turn the boat quickly and run grade 2 rapids in good control." Although the course is aimed at gaining useful river skills, which with four to five hours paddling a day you can't help but absorb, it's mostly just great fun. And if you avoid having to use your newly learned whitewater swimming techniques, so much the better.

Part of 1% for the Planet and holding a Level 2 Green Dragon Environmental Award, Pro Adventure live up to their mantra, 'If you're not part of the solution, you're part of the problem'.

Practicalities

The Dee Valley and Llangollen specifically is one of the UK's canoeing havens. Above town the ruin of the Castle of Dinas Bran is steeped in Arthurian legend while Llangollen Canal is part of a World Heritage Site and the river banks are an SSSI. The town has good amenities and hosts the annual musical extravaganza International Eisteddfod in July and a food festival in the autumn.

Transport   Just south of Wrexham, Ruabon train station is the nearest with a regular bus connection on to the town. Or you can arrive via narrowboat . . .

Sleeping   ££ **Dee Farm**, Rhewl, Llangollen, LL20 7YT, T01978-861598, 4 miles northwest of Llangollen, but just 1 field back from the river is this comfortable 18th-century farmhouse, set in beautiful and quiet countryside. ££ **Plas Hafod B&B**, Abbey Road, Llangollen, LL20 8SN, T01978-869225, plas-hafod.co.uk. Red brick Victorian house with a lovely tiled entrance and a warm welcome. Wi-Fi and good town access. **Riverside Mews**, T01978-861457, riversidemews.co.uk, apartments on the waterfront. **Camping Wern Isaf Farm**, LL29 8DU, T01978-860632, excellent views and laid back atmosphere on this working farm site. Field is sloped so pitch well!

Eating & drinking   Llangollen is packed with pubs and cafés, although not many on the cheaper side. Set on the rushing water of the Dee **The Corn Mill** is a renovated 18th century mill serving up very decent pub fare to be washed down by a real ale or two.

Also try   Llangollen Bike Hire, T01978-861912. Get on 2 wheels to enjoy the towpath lanes, bridleways and mountains around the town.

> Lowdown

ⓘ **Directory**
Pro Adventure, Parade Street, Llangollen, Denbighshire, LL20 8PW, T01978-861912, proadventure.co.uk.

⊘ **Prices**
£210/person. A range of overnight accommodation can be booked but is extra.

⊘ **Season**
Year round.

⊕ **Don't miss**
If you're lucky you might spot one of the local otters.

⊗ **Avoid**
Getting the right weight distribution is key to good trimming.

Mountain biking Machynlleth

Provider	DIY
Skill level	All
Time frame	2 hrs to a weekend
Equipment	Mountain bike, helmet, map, provisions and a repair kit/spare tube. Machynlleth is known for its rainfall so bring good wet weather gear
Exertion level	●●●●○

The River Dyfi rises at the foot of Aran Fawddwy and, flowing seaward towards the open sandy shores of Cardigan Bay it has carved out a natural pathway for itself. The valley that frames it is lush and green, its hills punctuated by rich pockets of forest and ancient woodland. Lying at its heart, the Centre for Alternative Technology has worked hard since its inception in the 1970s to convert its once seemingly niche ideas of sustainability into a mainstream reality of the modern day. Three miles south the town of Machynlleth has also worked with the environment, creating its own natural niche as a Mid-Wales haven for mountain bikers.

As well as excellent natural singletrack and open riding, Machynlleth and the Dyfi Forest are home to four official quality trails whose evolution came about via an organic process. A committed crew of mountain bikers worked with local businesses and the community to promote the region as a natural hub in order to raise funding to waymark three existing rotes and build a new trail. In ascending order of difficulty, Mach 1, 2 and 3 all start from the town car park, while the intermediate Cli-Machx kicks off in the nearby Dyfi Forest.

The 10 miles Mach 1 is a great introduction to the area. Looping southwest towards the village of Derwenlas this not too challenging trail skirts along the Llyfnant Valley before climbing to Bryn Coch Bach, where all three trails converge. From here it's a fast drop back into town. Next up the Mach 2, with decent fast descents combined with long, long, steep ascents – incorporating some 656 ft of climbing – caters well to the intermediate rider. For experienced mountain bikers looking for a

good three or four hour burn, Mach 3 delivers. This cross-country route covers 18½ miles of forest and moorland terrain with decent snatches of remote riding where no one can hear you scream as you take in 1640 ft of climbing which builds up to the killer descent, The Chute which is both steep and rocky. After all that, take a breather with a mellow four-mile ride along quiet country lanes to the Dyfi Forest, home of the Cli-Machx. Built by Eco Trails who specialize in sustainable MTB tracks, this 9-mile loop incorporates 5½ miles of singletrack pleasure, tight berms, flowing turns plus an excellent final descent. The forest is also the staging post for the popular Dyfi Enduro which sees 700 riders taking part in the long distance mountain bike challenge organized each year by Summit Cycles. Book in early, if you think you can stick the distance.

< Taking it to the Machx.

Jon Brooke

Jon Brooke

The testing trails of Machynlleth are a popular staging post for endurance trials.

Practicalities

The Dyfi (also Dovey) Valley played host to rock gods Led Zeppelin, allegedly spawning tracks including Bron-Y-Aur. It is also home to the switched on and somewhat bohemian market town of Machynlleth. With an active focus on sustainable tourism and sustainable living, the town has good amenities and is a hub for the environmentally minded.

Transport   Machynlleth is a mainline train station.

Sleeping   In the heart of the village, **£ Reditreks**, T01654-702184, reditreks.com, is ideal for a weekend's mountain biking with comfortable bunkhouse accommodation and beds from £15. Drying room, bike wash and lock up plus camping from £5/person. Another year round bunkhouse option is the Green Dragon awarded **£ Braich Goch Bunkhouse and Inn**, Corris, SY20 9RD, T01654-761229. Around 6 miles north of Machynlleth with beds from £16, drying room, lock up and all the usuals. Also in Corris the 2-star **£ Canolfan Youth Hostel**, SY20 9TQ, T01654-761686, corrishostel.co.uk, is environmentally minded with beds from £15. Private rooms, breakfasts and pack lunch also available. East of Machynlleth, **£ Gwalia Farm**, Cemaes, SY20 9PZ, T01650-511377, gwaliafarm.co.uk, is a tranquil spot offering homegrown brekkies and simple camping in beautiful surroundings. Also for camping, **Llwyngwern Farm**, Pantperthog, SY20 9RB, T01654-702492, next to the CAT has simple riverside pitches Apr-Oct.

Eating & drinking   There are plenty of good pubs and eateries. **The Quarry Café**, Main St, T01654-702624, an offshoot of the CAT, specializes in wholesome grub using local, seasonal and Fairtrade produce where possible. The home-made cakes are definitely worthy of sampling. **Wynnstay Arms** just along the road, T01654-702941, champions local produce to great effect from classic dishes to hand thrown pizzas.

Resources   dyfimountainbiking.org.uk is a great resource set up by some of those who campaigned to get the Mach trails waymarked and trails in the Dyfi Forest built. **The Holey Trail Bike Shop**, Maengwyn St, T 01654-700411, theholeytrail.co.uk, offers hardware, repairs plus hire. **Reditreks**, T01654-702184, reditreks.com, offer guided rides for all levels around the Dyfi Valley with half day from £20/person. The Aberystwyth based **Summit Cycles**, SY23 2JN, summitcycles.co.uk, organize the annual Dyfi Enduro – see their site for details.

Also try   If the wind is blowing, head to the beach at Aberdovey, where the River Dovey reaches the sea. **Kite surfing Wales**, T01654-791342, kitesurfwales.co.uk, offers 1-day kite-buggying sessions with IKO/BKSA instructors – a full day on the beach learning to fly traction kites and harness the wind's power to control the buggy. Kite surfing courses and taster sessions also from £25/person.

> **Lowdown**

⊖ **Prices**
Free.

⊘ **Season**
Year round.

⊕ **Don't miss**
A trip up to the Centre for Alternative Technology (with discounts for those arriving by train to the village or by foot/bike to the centre), T01654-705950, cat.org.uk.

⊗ **Avoid**
Machynlleth is well known for its rain that can fall on even the sunniest days so avoid getting caught out by the weather.

Walking The Welsh 3000's

Provider	Snowdonia Adventures, Wales
Skill level	Novice-experienced
Time frame	1 to 3 days
Equipment	If you have little experience, take the guided option. Good boots, outdoor clothing, compass, map, food and drink are essential
Exertion level	●●●●●

On a blue sky morning, only the white scars of transatlantic jets offer signs of a wider civilisation out beyond jagged peaks and rolling hills. Below, Carneddau ponies scramble down the slope with a swiftness that belies their size. These small, compact ponies live wild on the hills and mountains of Snowdonia, the last in the UK to roam truly free. The rocky summit of Tryfan awaits, just a short push now, a scramble up the left to top out by the large rocks known as Adam and Eve. From here the horizon's fringe is textured by the distant Irish coastline, the high caps of the Lake District rise to the north and the Isle of Man shimmers marooned offshore.

The Welsh 3000's is a challenge, a feat, an accomplishment: the aim being to top all the region's mountains over 3000 ft in one single journey. Luckily all the peaks are conveniently within the three mountain groups of northern Snowdonia – Carneddau, Glyderau and Snowdon. The challenge, also known as the 14 peaks, is roughly 25 miles of mountain walking and should not be underestimated – as well as gentle slopes and vast plateaus, the route takes in hard scrambles, steep ridges and of course Snowdonia's most spectacular scenery. Most choose to make the traverse following a northwards route from the tallest peak Yr Wyddfa towards Foel Fras, but there are no rules. Experienced walkers may attempt this route alone, however a guide can offer a greater insight into the landscape, and the opportunity to learn along the way. "The skills that people come away with after such a great adventure vary immensely," explains Mark Handford of Snowdonia Adventures. "It could be learning about yourself and

your limits as you push yourself up that mountain, through to having a deeper insight into mountain weather, geology, the rare plants and heathers or learning mountain skills such as map and compass navigation." Mark and his team offer a range of opportunities, with guides able to pass on local knowledge, mountain confidence and expertise. "Our guides are all qualified summer and winter Mountain Leaders," he explains. "This allows us to provide all year round mountain skills instruction and guided days for our clients in all conditions, day or night, summer and winter."

This is a rewarding challenge, but does need preparation and determination. "Those who would like to attempt the Welsh 3000's should train for endurance as the days can be long and hard depending on how many days you choose to cover the three mountain ranges," says Mark. The highly skilled and the super fit looking to take on the traverse in a single day should know that the record set by Colin Donelly stands at 4 hours 19 minutes and has remained unbroken for more than 20 years. For everyone else, a 2, 3 or even 4 day traverse is nothing to be sniffed at. "For a 2-day challenge people should have a very good level of endurance fitness, otherwise they should choose the 3-day option, which can be completed by those with a good level of fitness." The first recorded completion of the traverse of all 14 summits in a day was in 1919 by a Rucksack Club party led by Eustace Thomas. There is no right or wrong route for tackling the 14 three's, and variations and permutations are possible as long as they take in all the summits – indeed some even choose to include the new peak on the block Garnedd Uchaf. However there is a wrong way to go into the mountains. "If I was to offer just one piece of advice for people visiting the mountains it would be to learn how to read a map and use a compass," says Mark. "A high proportion of mountain rescue call outs arise from not being aware of the surroundings and getting lost in bad weather or as darkness approaches." So if you do go, be sure to go prepared and equipped – or go with a guide.

> On a knife edge on the mighty Crib Goch.

Alex Messenger

Practicalities

If traversing the peaks in a northerly fashion, Llanberis makes an ideal springboard. As well as being steeped in climbing history, the town has plenty of accommodation options as well as some excellent outdoors shops. And chances are, you'll run into someone who has already taken on the challenge and can offer a few words to the wise.

Transport Depending on your route, Porthmadog is a good station, with links to Llanberis on the Snowdon Sherpa gwynedd. gov.uk for details. Bangor and Betsw-y-Coed are other options with decent links.

Sleeping £££ Gwesty Plas Coch, High St, Llanberris, LL55 4HB. Four-star traditional B&B with 8 en suite rooms in this stone built house. Offers locally sourced organic meals as well as vegetarian and vegan options. £ YHA Pen y Pass, Nantgwynant, LL55 4NY, T0845-371 9534, right on the edge of the path is an excellent choice. Licensed bar, meals available, open year round. En route, below the Glyder mountains and on the edge of Llyn Ogwen, £ Idwal Cottage YHA, Nant Ffrancon, LL57 LZ, T0845-371 9744, also offers camping and meals. Between Tryfan and Llyn Ogwen, £ Gwern Gof Uchaf, Capel Curig, LL24 0EU, T01690-720294, offers year round camping and bunkhouse accommodation on family run hill farm. Foel Fras is fairly remote with a decent walk out. Nearest options include £ Rowen YHA,

LL32 8YW, T0845-371 9038, and, at the foot of Carneddau £ Caban Cysgu, Ffordd Gerlan, LL57 3TL, T01248-605573. Open year round.

Eating & drinking In Llanberis Pete's Eats, High St has served up generous portions of good grub to climbers since '78. At the north end of Llyn Padarn, Caban Cyf, Bryn Refail, LL55 3NR, T01286-685500, utilizes organic, fair trade and local ingredients, including produce from its own kitchen garden and bee hives to create simple, tasty, seasonal food as well as excellent full brekkies. Open 0900-1600, plus Sat evening buffet.

Resources For inspiration and information, check out welsh3000s.co.uk and 14peaks.com. They even issue a 14 peaks completion certificate. The Snowdonia Society is a charity working to preserve the national park's landscape: snowdonia-society.org.uk, membership. Ogwen Valley Mountain Rescue Organization, ogwen-rescue.org.uk. This registered charity is one of the country's busiest mountain rescue teams, on standby 24/7, 365 days a year.

Also try If you need to brush up on your navigation and map skills before pushing out on your own, Snowdonia Adventures also run a series of 1- and 2-day navigation courses for novice through to advanced as well as night navigation sessions, from £35/person.

> Lowdown

❶ Directory
Snowdonia Adventures, 4 New Street, Deiniolen, Caernarfon, Gwynedd. LL55 3LH, T01286-879044, snowdonia-adventures.co.uk.

⊘ Prices
£150/person 2-day, £185/person 3-day.

⊘ Season
May to Sep.

⊕ Don't miss
Carneddau ponies.

⊗ Avoid
Stay within your capabilities, take all the necessary equipment, some of the peaks are steep and dangerous.

Mountain biking Trans Cambrian Way

Provider	DIY
Skill level	Advanced
Time frame	3-5 days
Equipment	Maps, wet weather gear, spares and repairs, first aid kit, food, water
Exertion level	●●●●○

The great frontier earthwork of Offa's Dyke stretches north and south creating a defensive boundary and symbolic delineation between the kingdoms of Powys and Mercia, the ramparts creating the perfect platform from which to survey the land and drink in the open views of Wales. Cleaving the land once more, the Trans Cambrian Way weaves an epic trail from the English border to the Irish Sea. But this line has not been created to divide or hold back, rather it has been blazed as a pathway through the Welsh heartlands for mountain bikers seeking a real cross country experience away from the numbers.

This 100-mile modern classic runs between the stations of Knighton, whose village lies on the English/Welsh border and Dovey Junction near the coastal Machynlleth. Traversing mid Wales, it is largely off-road and pieces together moorland tracks, ridge roads, bridleways and old trails. But don't be fooled into thinking that this is going too be an easy ride. The Trans Cambrian Way was developed exclusively by mountain bikers, for mountain bikers, pioneered by an IMBA UK crew in 2005 meaning that the ride is as tough going and challenging as it is fun. Weaving west, then northward the trail navigates through the upland area of Mid Wales, rising and falling for 12,139 ft to combine the 'what goes up must come down' of steep climbs with fast, challenging descents. The Trans Cambrian negotiates the 'Welsh desert', (so called for its general remoteness and lack of population as opposed to it's rainfall, of which there is plenty) crossing remote, rolling hills, exposed and isolated moorlands as well as five major fords which can be dangerous after heavy rains, before dropping into the Dyfi Valley and reaching its

Seb Rogers

◀ On the Trans Cambrian Way, it's about a steady release of energy and holding back plenty in reserve.

conclusion. Riding away from England may mean that you don't have the wind with you but the payoff is more descents than climbs.

Although uber-fit, MTB orienteer extraordinaire and Trail Cyclists Association Chairman John Houlihan conquered the trail in a day, for mere mortals this is not recommended or indeed possible. The IMBA originally designed the trail as a three-day ride for those with reasonable fitness and good outdoor experience, taking into account essentials such as pub lunches and over night stops. Covering 31 miles and climbing 4265 ft, day one breaks at Rhayader (home of Clive Powel's Dirty Weekends). Day two is mentally and physically tougher, climbing 4921 ft and covering 43 miles before breaking at Llangurig with the final push on day three climbing 2953 ft and covering the last 34 miles. The trail can also more comfortably be covered over four or even five days so ride within your limits and if you don't want to carry all your kit, the IMBA have a list of taxi firms who offer a portage service.

▶ The trail rises and falls for 12,139 ft through the Welsh hearlands to combine the 'what goes up must come down' of steep climbs with fast, challenging descents.

Practicalities

Transport Knighton train station is actually in Shropshire. Dovey Junction is the station for the journey's end. Trains between the two require a change at Shrewsbury.

Sleeping Check out the excellent IMBA website for a comprehensive list of accommodation en route, imba.org.uk. It seems a fitting start to push out from England and cross Offa's Dyke. **££ Well House B&B**, Chapel Lawn, Bucknell, Shropshire SY7 0BW, T01547-530347, stayatchapellawn.co.uk, is around 5 miles east of the Knighton start. They happily accommodate cyclists and even offer collection from the station. The rooms are en suite, the breakfasts local and organic where possible and despite being a lovely old stone house, they try to minimize their impact on the environment using solar panels for hot water alongside other steps. Packed lunches (£5) plus evening meals also available. Around 6 miles north of Knighton, **£ YHA Clun Mill**, Clun, Shropshire, SY7 8NY, T0845-371 9112, is a recently restored mill and an excellent hostel with cycle store and café. At the finish **£ Reditreks Bunkhouse**, Maengwyn Street Machynlleth, Powys, SY20 8EB, reditreks.com, is on the doorstep of some excellent trails meaning you can spend an extra day or so burning round the Dyfi Valley.

Eating & drinking Check the IMBA site for details of cafés, pubs en route and ensure you have enough supplies with you for the day's journey. In Machynlleth there are plenty of good pubs and places to eat. Set up by the nearby Centre for Alternative Technology, cat.org.uk, the **Quarry Café**, Maengwyn St, T01654-702624, serves up well priced, wholesome, hearty food using local and Fairtrade produce Mon-Sat. Lovely cakes too.

Resources For anyone considering this trail, it is essential to check out the excellent IMBA website, imba.org.uk, for a detailed overview of the route, mapping plus comprehensive accommodation/resources list. A good bike shop near the start is **Pearce Cycles**, Ludlow, pearcecycles.co.uk, T01584-879288. Mid way, **Clive Powell's MTB's** in Rhayader, LD6 5AB, T01597 811343, clivepowell-mtb.co.uk is a well-known and trusted fixture with excellent café also. In Machynlleth stop by **The Holey Trail**, Maengwyn Street, SY20 8EB , T01654-700411, theholeytrail.co.uk.

Also try If you're not broken by the time you get to Machynlleth, there are 3 excellent cross country trails here Mach 1, 2 and 3 and a purpose-built trail, the Cli-Machx, in the Dyfi Forest north of the town. To the north, there is an excellent, trek up Cadair Idris. Following the mainly well-maintained path from the car park at Minfford, the demanding 6-mile circular takes in the dramatic views of the glacial lake Lyn Cau via Craig Cwm Amarch — a decent challenge in its own right of nearly 2625 ft — before ascending this 2930 ft peak to drink in the views (providing the clouds haven't descended!) and heading home.

> **Lowdown**

Ⓢ Prices
Free.

✖ Season
Year round – avoid after heavy rains when ford crossings can be treacherous.

✪ Don't miss
A jump in the river just south of Rhayader and down stream of the reservoirs where the Elan and Wye meet. The water can be very fresh!

✖ Avoid
Some parts of the trail are very remote; don't underestimate the supplies you'll need for a day's ride.

Swimming Abereiddy

Provider DIY	
Skill level Novice-advanced	
Time frame All day	
Equipment Towel, bathers (depending on season/hardiness wetsuit)	
Exertion level ●●○○○	

There is only so long you can stand up here, toes curled over the blackened rock, staring into the mesmerising cerulean blue depths below. There is only so long before you find yourself being pulled, by that irresistible lemming-like draw, over the edge. Only so long before you catch yourself momentarily suspended in mid flight wondering how you ended up in this position: legs clamped tight, toes pointing straight down, arms locked to your body, mouth unfortunately open wide. Only so long before you hear a strange whooping scream as the surface is punctured. Before you find yourself enveloped in a saline blanket of muffled sounds where shards of sunlight hang fractured overhead. Before, drawn to the light, you kick your way up, up, up to suck in a lung busting breath of adrenaline heavy euphoria.

To the north of St Davids Head, a long pebble ridge backs the dark, almost black sands of Abereiddy Beach. While this is a popular spot with both day tripping tourists and hard charging surfers who come to take on the reef here in big south westerly swells, for purveyors of the wild stroke and glide or indeed the rock hop and cliff jump, it is not the main draw. From the car park above the beach, follow the coastal path northward past the skeletons of stone cottages to bathers' delight, the Blue Lagoon.

Pushing off from the edge through the milky blue green tones of this drowned slate quarry you kick out into the middle of the deep waters and toward the gully that, when the tide permits, links this protected pool with the dark blue expanse of the wild open Atlantic. While the colours here merge, the conditions do not, meaning that on warm, sunshiney days the lagoon can become busy. Outside, winds whip the sea and currents run. Within, the waters

sheltered by the cliffs and abandoned workings are calm, or relatively so until another body, another lemming, finds itself pulled from the edges – ledges and platforms rising 10-40 ft from the surface of the water. The jumps can be intense, making it a popular spot with crews of coasteerers but should only be attempted when tides, conditions and confidence allow. A little bit of gleaned local knowledge goes a long way. But if the tide isn't right or perhaps you just aren't wearing the right kind of bathers, actually, then the serene waters here are an ideal spot for a serious swim or a contemplative float – just don't be alarmed if a diver pops up for air next to you!

⌄ When the tide permits the gully connects the lagoon with the open ocean, giving access to all manner of sea faring craft.

Pembrokeshire County Council

◄ Swimmer's-eye view of the cool, calm waters and the pulse-racing launch pads ahead.

Frank Whittle

Practicalities

The tiny city of St Davids with decent amenities is just 5 miles from Abereiddy but there are plenty of places to stay around this swimming hole. Around 3 miles north Porthgain has a couple of good places to eat.

Transport   Haverfordwest is the nearest train station. Onward bus connections with Richards Bros. For advice of ditching the car and getting around see pembrokeshiregreenways.co.uk

Sleeping   Half a mile from the lagoon, £££-££ **Caerhys Organic Farm**, Berea, SA62 6DX, T01348-831244, organic-farm-holidays.co.uk, offer comfortable B&B, their Welsh cooked breakfast featuring bacon and sausages from their own home bred pigs when available as well as other locally sourced produce. Cottage sleeping 6 also available. On the delicious stretch between Abereiddy and Abercastle there are plenty of excellent sites to pitch up and set up camp on. The 250 acre **Pwll Caerog Farm**, Berea, SA62 6DG, T01348-831682, celtic-camping.co.uk, is just south of Abereiddy with basic, friendly camping, fire pits and bunkhouse accommodation from £12/night, Mar-Oct. **AryMwyn**, near Trefin, SA62 5AL T01348-837892, campingwildwales.co.uk, is a basic, well priced escape with just 5 pitches. Portaloo on site, bathroom facilities in the house and campfires welcome. Wood available to buy. Amidst a conservation project, idyllic **Trellyn Woodland**

Campsite, Abercastle, SA62 5HJ, T01348-837762, trellyn.co.uk, offers camping from £170/week, 5 secluded pitches available with personal touches — picnic bench, covered outdoors area (camping and Caravanning Club members only although you can join on-site). Campfires welcomed, firewood is free. If you want to get away from it in comfort, 2 tipis from £365/week and 2 yurts from £475/week also available. Majority of water solar heated, waste-water managed by reed bed system. Strumble Shuttle coastal bus service stops off here.

Eating & drinking   If you're after fresh fish, you can't do much better than **The Shed Bar and Bistro** at Porthgain, T01348-831518. Overlooking the harbour they serve their own fish and shellfish landed daily (mains around £14/lunchtime and around £20/evenings) plus fish and chips on a Mon. **The Sloop Inn**, Abereiddy is another good choice for decent bar meals.

Also try   A walk along the Pembrokeshire Coastal path between Abereiddy and Porthgain can yield otherwise hidden coves such as the low tide treasure Traeth Llyfn. If you're after more salt water experiences, in big SW swells, Abereiddy beach is home to a testing slab that throws up wedgy, shallow left-handers, best left to experienced surfers. Mortals should head south to Whitesand Bay where the waves are a little more forgiving and boards can be hired. **Ma Simes Surf Hut**, St Davids, T01437-720433.

> **Lowdown**

Θ Prices
Free.

⊘ Season
Year round.

◐ Don't miss
Lounging on the rocks in the sunshine post swim to watch the jumpers.

⊗ Avoid
The lagoon is a lot calmer than the sea, so avoid swimming round to the beach if you are a little unsure of the conditions.

Sea Kayaking North Pembrokeshire

Provider	Preseli Venture
Skill level	Novice-experienced
Time frame	2-5 days
Equipment	All specialist equipment supplied, but bring a cozzie and some sneakers that you don't mind getting wet as well as warm clothes
Exertion level	●●●●○

On a windless, glassy, summer's afternoon, the glare from the oily sea and the rhythmic lapping sound of paddles slicing the water can have a mesmerising effect on the senses. The water is clear as glass and below seaweed dances in the deep, anchored to submerged islands of barnacle-covered rock, a verdant refuge in a furrowed acre of sand. Here in Pembrokeshire the jagged, cliff-lined coastline stretches away into the distance – a queue of grass-topped headlands, bases scattered with fractured boulders ripped from the bedrock by the Atlantic's winter fury. The coast has been sculpted and moulded into a twisting, writhing series of coves and bays, vertical inlets and huge sandy expanses, yet today these malignant forces sleep. Only the tide-shifting flecks of whitewater identify reefs lying almost totally submerged, like some predator cruising inshore. Out of the light shallows islands beckon, sea birds swoon and dive and dolphins cruise. On days like this it is hard to imagine anywhere better for enjoying an ocean adventure.

The National Park coastline of Pembrokeshire offers some of the UK's most spectacular scenery and is a perfect place to explore the coastline by kayak. "Pembrokeshire is unique in its status as Britain's only coastal National Park and as such offers a plethora of flora and fauna to be admired and viewed," enthuses Preseli Venture's Claire Carlile.

◄ Bobbing between sea stacks, catching waves through rocky channels, chilling out in idyllic sheltered coves, surfing on to secluded sandy beaches, all part of the Odyssey experience.

"It is also famous as a sea kayaking paradise, with clean Atlantic Ocean waters, the beauty and variety of the coastal scenery with fascinating features under the high sea cliffs – waterfalls, sea caves and natural rock arches. There's also the variety of fun conditions in which to play, from bobbing between sea stacks, catching waves through rocky channels, chilling out in idyllic sheltered coves, to surfing on to secluded sandy beaches. "The kayaks are a quiet and clean mode of transport meaning your chances of having a close encounter with some wild life are pretty good. The Atlantic grey seals that breed around the coast and off-shore islands are an inquisitive bunch – if you get the feeling you're being watched, chances are that fishing float you thought you saw bobbing close by comes complete with two round, wide eyes and a playful stare. "Porpoise and dolphins live in the deeper waters of Cardigan Bay," explains Claire, "while the coast is awash with sea birds: kittiwakes, razorbills, choughs, shags and cormorants, also the gannets who have their colony on Grassholm island."

For those who have a little bit of kayak experience, Preseli's five day 'Odyssey' is a special way to rediscover Pembrokeshire, offering up a fresh new perspective on a classic destination. While the emphasis of the trip is on exploration, as opposed to acquiring a pre-ordained skill set after four and a half days of coastal kayaking, you can't help but come away with a strong grasp of the basics, a good understanding of how tides and weather influence decisions made on ocean-bound voyages as well as a tip or two regarding the art of fishing for one's supper. Distances covered and itineraries are tailored to suit, depending on the group and conditions but you'll have around five hours of paddling a day sampling the delights of moving water – exploring secluded sandy bays and echoing sea caves, rock hopping or pushing the envelope in tidal rapids. While three nights are spent at the adventure lodge, the fourth under canvas at a small site brings a real expedition feeling – catching fish, cooking outdoors, and counting stars until bedtime, once the eating is over and tall tales from the day have been told that is. "Our friendly and qualified guides ensure you get the most out of this awesome opportunity to experience this National Park coastline at close hand," says Claire. All specialist sea kayak equipment is included. All you need to bring is your spirit of adventure.

∧ Strumble Lighthouse.
< Abercastle, late summer, late evening.

Practicalities

With an emphasis on sustainable adventure tourism, Preseli Venture is all about re-engaging with the natural environment. They offer the full deal from coastal tour, through to comfortable accommodation and food for the duration that is where possible locally sourced – and no, you don't get a discount for providing fish for the BBQ!

Transport Haverford west is the nearest station. Minimizing their footprint at every turn, PV encourage guests to use public transport and at certain times provide free transfers from local bus and train stations, running minibuses on locally sourced bio diesel.

Sleeping A mile from Abermawr beach, accommodation at the Eco Lodge is included in the cost of the break, otherwise shared rooms from £35 B&B or £55 full board. They hold a Level 2 Green Dragon Environmental Award. Use of a ground source heat pump to produce all the hot water in the lodge is just one of the ways they aim to reduce their impact on the environment. For the camping element bring your own tent and sleeping bag or rent a 2-man from Preseli for £10.

Eating & drinking They have a licensed pay bar on site and all food is home cooked using locally sourced ingredients where possible.

Also try If you have more limited kayak experience an 'At Sea with the Seals' weekend will help you gain confidence and develop your skills, mastering an efficient forward paddle stroke and turning your kayak while exploring the coastline from £259.

> **Lowdown**

❶ **Directory**
Preseli Venture,
Parcynole
Fach, Mathry,
Haverfordwest,
Pembrokeshire, SA62
5HN, T01348-837709,
preseliventure.co.uk.

❸ **Prices**
Sea Kayak Odyssey
£539.

❷ **Season**
May to Sep.

❍ **Don't miss**
"Enjoy the unique marine and coastal environment," says Claire Carlile. "Have fun!"

✖ **Avoid**
As the saying goes, leave only your footprints. "Be conscious of your impact as you explore along the coastline," reminds Claire.

Surfing Whitesands Bay

Provider	None
Skill level	All
Time frame	2 hrs +
Equipment	Surfboard and wetsuit
Exertion level	●●●○○

Looking down from the 600 ft summit of Carn Llidi, the curve of Whitesands Bay stretches away to the south towards the cliff-lined mass of Ramsey Island, anchored just off the coast. At the northern edge, St David's Head helps provide the perfect rugged symmetry to this sandy enclave. As the sun sinks to the west, the sky blazing red, the surfers below try to cram in one last wave before the dark descends, forcing them back to the beachfront car park and the waiting armada of vans. The sun lovers and walkers have gone now and the beach is left to the die-hards.

Whitesands Bay is one of Wales' most scenic surf locations, the kind of break that attracts a loyal crew. When charts promise easterly winds with a westerly, southwesterly or large northwesterly swell then they can be found checking the line-up from the sand dunes. The Elevator, turning over at the northern end of the beach, attracts the most faithful following, a low tide spot with drops that let you know just were the name comes from. Further down the beach a series of banks work through the tides, but will vary in quality with tide and swell direction.

For those who are keen to take to the waves for the first time there are surf schools operating from the beach and RNLI beach lifeguards patrolling during the summer months. If you're not yet fully proficient it might be best to stay within the life guarded areas and only surf during the patrolled hours. Post-surf, take a walk up on to the headland and check out the megalithic burial chambers or on a very low spring tide look out for the petrified stumps that signal the remains of an ancient submerged forest.

Practicalities

Pretty little St Davids is in fact a city — it has a cathedral you know. Home to the Really Wild Food and Countryside Festival celebrating local, wild foods and countryside craft, is in touch with its ecological side. Good amenities.

Transport   Haverford West and Fishguard train stations are around 15 miles from the city, onward bus service with **Richards Bros**, T01239-613756, richardsbros.co.uk.

Sleeping   **£** St Davids YHA, SA62 6PR, T0845-371 9141, basic but just 1 mile from the beach is an excellent option. Around the headland towards Abereiddy the family run, organic, **££ Caerhys Farm**, Berea, SA62 6DX, T01348-831244, provides comfortable farmhouse B&B and breakfasts using locally sourced and organic produce where possible. Self-catering cottage also available. There are plenty of good **camping** options from the small, (very) basic and perfectly formed farm site **Tan-y-Bryn** on the edge of Whitesands Bay, T01437-721472. **Leithyr Farm**, SA62 6PR, T01437-720245, ½ mile from the beach, has better facilities and is popular with couples and families, Easter-Oct. South of St David's, **Caerfai Farm**, SA62 6QD, T01437-720548, is 200 yards from Caerfai Bay. As well as running an organic farm and making cheeses, they offer simple but lovely camping, Whitsun-Sep. Farm shop on-site. Self-catering cottages also available.

Eating & drinking   Outside of pretty standard pub grub at **The Farmers Arms**, Goat Street, eating out in St David's here can be fairly pricey.

Resources   In St Davids, **Ma Simes Surf Hut**, High St, T01437-720433, masimes.co.uk, has a good range of hardware and offers surf hire from £20/day board and wettie from the shop and on the beach at Whitesands. Check the site for webcam and surf report. **Whitesands Surf School**, T07789-435670/01437-720433, offer beginners lessons May-Oct with BSA qualified instructors from £25.

Also try   For those proficient in sea kayaking, celebrate midsummer with a two day adventure and overnight bivvy exploring the Pembrokeshire coastline with **TYF Adventure**, tyf.com. Set out from Solva harbour and paddle to Porthlysgi Beach to set up camp. After an evening around the campfire, set off for a return adventure to Whitesands Bay. From £195.

> **Lowdown**

❸ **Prices**
Free of from £20/day board and wettie hire.

❷ **Season**
All year.

● **Don't miss**
Megalithic burial chambers and other historic remains around St David's Head and Carn Llidi.

✖ **Avoid**
Beginners should stay in lifeguarded area.

Coasteering Pembrokeshire

Provider	TYF Adventure
Skill level	All
Time frame	Half day
Equipment	Wetsuits and safety equipment provided. Bring a cozzie, towel and old trainers that you don't mind getting wet
Exertion level	●●●○○

Rock ledges, steep cliffs, abrupt drop offs, caves, waves. With a mindset like this, on an odyssey like this, these aren't obstacles to be avoided, rather they are features to seek out, to edge along, scramble up, jump off, swim in and enjoy.

"Something dark started to murmur in the caves of StNons," remembers Andy Middleton somewhat ominously. In the early eighties Andy set up a windsurfing school on the spectacular Pembrokeshire coastline which quickly blossomed into an outdoors centre – TYF – attracting surfers, climbers and kayakers to its craggy adventure-rich shores. But then when there weren't any waves, or the weather along this coastal national park just wasn't playing ball, these distinct, separate groups began to seek out an alternative and somewhat collective buzz, "something that seemed to resemble a hybrid of every adventure sport available," he says. "Coasteering. The climbers climbed, surfers swam and lemmings jumped!" This is the spiritual home of the sport, so when in Rome or St Davids for that matter…

   The courses take place at a range of breathtaking coastal locations from Abereiddy and Porthclais to St Nons – depending on conditions, which in themselves can swing from gentle rollers to rollercoaster. A Blue Line is a good introductory taster while a Green Line Coaster gets you up close and personal with insight into the flora and fauna surviving in the intertidal zone. For coasteering aficionados only, check out the White Line – a day of rough seas, powerful swells and high adrenaline or the Flat Line which is all about endurance, stamina and fitness.

   TYF is a carbon neutral company and actively encourages sustainable adventure, minimizing emissions and supports 1% For The Planet.

Practicalities

TYF supports Eco City St Davids, an organization aiming to make St Davids a carbon neutral city, eco-city.co.uk.

Transport   Haverford west and Fishguard train stations are around 15 miles from the city. For drivers, TYF encourage car sharing see switch2share.com and liftshare.org.

Sleeping   Four miles from St Davids, **£££-££ Caerhys Organic Farm**, Berea, SA62 6DX, T01348-831244, offer comfortable B&B – cooked breakfast featuring bacon and sausages from their own pigs when available plus other locally sourced produce. 10 miles from St Davids, the 5 luxury converted **Asherton Eco Barns**, Penycwm, SA62 6NH, T01348-831781, asheston.co.uk, are surrounded by rolling countryside. Sleeping 4-7, rest easy as the focus is on minimal environmental impact: wind turbine generated electricity, hot water from high speed solar panels, geo-thermal pumps provide heating, rain water is recycled and waste treated in a bio-digester. From £340/week for 4.

Eating & drinking   There are plenty of pubs and cafés here but for something a bit special **Cwtch**, High St, T01437-720491, uses the very best local produce to great effect. Mains from £15.

Also try   TYF also offers half, full day or weekend courses in surfing, sea rock climbing and sea kayaking as well as kayak trips for more experienced paddlers.

> **Lowdown**

ⓘ Directory
TYF Adventure,
1 High St, St Davids,
Pembrokeshire, SA62
6SA, T01437-721611,
tyf.com.

Ⓢ Prices
£50-60.

Ⓢ Season
Year round.

Ⓞ Don't miss
Jumping is not compulsory but is not worth missing however bad the stage fright – plunges up to 30 ft high!

Ⓧ Avoid
Don't be tempted to up the style stakes – this is not the time to break out new trainers

Walking Wales: best of the rest

Of course there is the crowning glory of Snowdon in the north. Paths and routes of varying difficulty have been etched into the wild landscape for those wishing to reach the impressive heights of her summit and drink in views, mist permitting, or if not just a mug of something warm from the glass fronted café. Comprehensive details of the paths and walks can be found at the useful: walkeryri.org.uk. To the south, trails explore the craggy peaks, rounded summits, sheltered valleys and open moorland of the Brecon Beacons, from the 101-mile Beacons Way to the comparatively modest path leading to the top of the popular Pen-y-Fan. At 2907 ft this red sandstone peak it is the highest point in south Wales. See breconbeacons.org for information. But, with its undulating terrain, Wales has plenty of opportunities for those who want to pull their socks up, put their boots on and stride out into the wild.

Pembrokeshire Coast Path

The Pembrokeshire Coast Path covers 186 miles of stunning national parkland between St Dogmaels and Amroth, skirting the shoreline, passing golden beaches, rising and falling along cliff tops. Walking north to south, feeling the sun on your face for the majority of the day seems to be the preferred route for many. Bear in mind however, these first 16 miles – taking in some 3000 ft of ascent and descent – are some of the trail's most challenging. Refreshments on this stretch are also few and far between meaning you will need to pack provisions well. For those looking for a more 'fluid' approach, the walk south to north might go against the grain but it takes in plenty of opportunities to sample it. In those first 16 miles there are still enough steep hills to challenge but there is also a pub at which to sup on a reviving ale at least every four miles or so! With the prevailing wind at your back, the distance will slip by in no time. To enjoy the walk in bite size chunks, check out the coastal bus services which run through the summer seven days a week. See pembrokeshire.gov.uk/coastbus for details.

> Chamomile lawn hidden beind the dunes of Llangennith.

Demi Taylor

Berwyn Hills

Rising up between the River Dee and Lake Vyrnwy, the heather-clad Berwyn Hills offer a decent mix of low and high level walking but are often somewhat overlooked in favour of their less lofty neighbours, the Clwydians. And herein lies their appeal – their relative isolation and of course the fact that they are home to one of the highest peaks outside the national parks. Just shy of the magic 3000 mark, Cadair Berwyn rises for 2723 ft, making it the uppermost point in the Berwyn Hills. Linked to its twin summit Moel Sych (2713 ft) by a sweeping high rocky ridgeline it more than channels the spirit of Snowdonia. There is an abundance of routes to explore here taking you through jagged hills, rolling moorland and wooded pockets. A memorable 2½ mile circular ridge walk leads from the car park and café at the magnificent, thundering 240 ft waterfall Pistyll Rhaeadr northward towards Cadair Berwyn to deliver views towards Snowdonia. Those looking for a quiet retreat can camp at the simple **Pistyll Rhaeadr** site, Llanrhaeadr ym Mochnant, SY10 0BZ, T01691-780392, pistyllrhaeadr.co.uk. Note they operate a no alcohol policy. Membership £25 plus £5.50/night.

Patrol the Anglo-Wales border

Hugging the Anglo-Welsh border, Offa's Dyke Path extends north to south from the Irish Sea to the Severn Estuary. Stretching for 177 miles between Prestatyn and Chepstow the path skirts and crosses the impressive earthwork dyke built by Offa, King of Mercia in the 8th century to draw a boundary and protect his proud nation of Celts. This National Trail, which takes most people around two weeks to complete, runs through a range of terrain that can throw up surprises and challenges to the unsuspecting. While the path crosses lowland farmland and hill pasture with a relatively flat section following the Severn and Montgomeryshire Canal between Buttington Bridge and Llanymynech, much of the area is undulating meaning plenty of switchbacks. And that's not forgetting the number of stiles this path is famous for nor that it also passes through the heart of the Black Mountains as well as the uplands of the Clwydians. Most tackle the path south to north, as designated in the majority of guidebooks. nationaltrail.co.uk for more information.

Gower Peninsula

Sticking out into the Irish Sea as though thumbing a lift, the Gower Peninsula, measuring just 16 by seven miles was designated as one of Britain's first Areas of Natural Outstanding Beauty. With vast dune backed bays, cliff lined coves, secret caves and hidden nooks marking its perimeter, it's easy to see why. Sure there are the incredible salt marshes and mudflats on its northern flank to explore as well as myriad beautiful paths to roam, moorland to meander and hills to stalk inland. However the achingly beautiful coastline is what it's all about. On the western tip of the peninsula the flagship stretch of Rhossili Bay serves up three miles of golden sands, protected in part by a high ridge of dunes which has been peppered with the long, green stalks of marram grass which bend and sway with the wind. At the southern edge of the bay, at low tide a limestone finger leads out to the Worms Head, supposedly named by the Vikings for its dragon like appearance. The jagged promontory, which is about a mile long, makes for a fantastic scramble with its flat-topped Inner Head to climb, the Devil's Bridge to cross and a low stretch leading to the Outer Head to negotiate. The causeway is only accessible for a couple of hours either side of low so check tide times before heading over. This is an important spot for nesting birds so be mindful, no access to Outer Head March-August. Follow this with a northward hike towards Hillend before cutting back on to the beach for the return leg – a great five-mile circular or, if you feel inspired, push nothward along the beach to tidal island Burry Holms. Grab a pint and a bite to eat at **The Worm's Head Hotel**, Rhosilli thewormshead.co.uk.

Black Mountains

The most easterly peaks in the Brecon Beacons National Park, the Black Mountains, despite the name, are all about rolling green hills and narrow valleys (and are not to be mistaken for the Black Mountain which also resides here). Because of this, the Black Mountains are popular with hill walkers and The Sugar Loaf (Y Fal) that dominates the skyline around Abergavenny and rises to 1962 ft is an obvious draw. The trig point on the summit deciphers beautiful views over the parkland. If you're only looking for a quick stomp of an hour or so, head out from the car park and view point south of the summit which will deliver a 3-mile round trip. Eat and drink at **The Bear**, Crickhowell, NP8 1BW, bearhotel.co.uk. The CAMRA recommended bar serves up local brews and local food to accompany – from Welsh lamb hotpot to Welsh Black Beef Steaks, perfect for re-energising after a day on the mountains. If it all gets too much, stay at The Bear, doubles from £86.

⌄ Thrift on the Pembrokeshire Coast Path.

Derri Taylor

Surfing Freshwater West

Provider	None
Skill level	All
Time frame	2 hrs +
Equipment	Surfboard and wetsuit
Exertion level	●●●●●

Every country has its surfing epicentre. In the USA it's Malibu, in England it's Fistral, and in Wales it's Freshwater West. Fresh West has a lot in common with Fistral; it's a quality beach break that works through the tides, it's consistent, and it is the regular venue for the big, national surf contests. But while its Cornish cousin practically submerges under sheer weight of numbers during the high season, and the encroaching developments edge closer and closer toward the golden sands, Fresh West spends the summer surrounded by the calm tranquillity of rolling green fields. In fact you won't even find a beachside snack shack or café providing sustenance to those visiting this sandy Welsh oasis.

This peaceful existence is thanks in part to the lords of war whose military base, lined with tanks and red-flagged warnings, takes up a vast swathe of land to the south.

Freshwater has to be the most consistent break in Wales. If there is a low pressure out there in the Atlantic, the results will be seen here in the form of some type of waves rolling ashore; if there is no surf here, it's a good bet there is no surf anywhere. The quality of the waves depends on a number of factors; offshore winds come from an easterly direction, but bigger swells tend to be too much for the banks, either closing out the bay or converting the sea into a swirling cauldron of churning water. It's at these times when the local crew go in search of one of the less exposed spots, gladly trading size for wave quality. Be aware, the beach here is also renowned for the sometimes-deadly rips and currents that can spring up. If you do get caught in a rip, don't panic but try to paddle your way out of the situation. Look at the way the current is taking

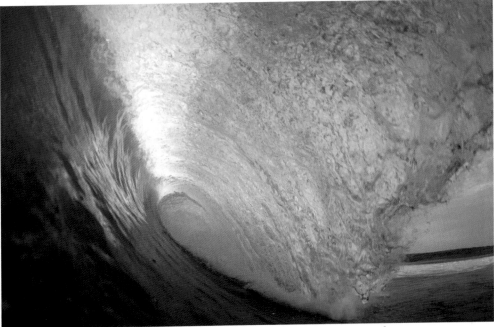

❮ Crystaline caverns and thundering barrels reward the committed at Freshwater West.

Will Bailey

∧ Back lit aerial attack .

you and instead of fighting against it, paddle across it at an angle and out of trouble. Even on calm days this is not a recommended spot for swimmers and there is no lifeguard presence on the beach.

The road angles in to run alongside this long sandy beach offering a great vantage point over the peaks to the north. On a sunny summer's day it will be lined with camper vans and cars, towels draped over bonnets and wetsuits lying on the grass. In the right conditions the wide section of reef here at the southern end can attract more experienced surfers, while further to the south stretches Frainslake Sands, often taunting with its empty peaks on a crowded day. In the past surfers would scale the fence of the military base and sneak down to the pristine haven, bringing back memories of the exploits of Mickey Dora, Phil Edwards and some of the original Malibu surfers who would break into Camp Pendleton to surf the hallowed waves at Trestles in the early 1950's. However, the increase in the popularity of the area and of surfing as a whole means that now security is tight and the risk of arrest or injury too great.

A local bus service runs out to this Pembrokeshire Coast National Park beach during the summer with a limited winter service, but for those heading out at any time it's essential to bring whatever you'll need for a day out with you. Although the occasional food van may swing by, don't count on it and there's nothing more irritating than turning up to find you've left your leash behind. There is however a toilet block in the car park, which can be a haven for those changing in the middle of a winter blizzard.

> **Lowdown**

⊙ **Prices**
Free.

⊗ **Season**
All year.

⊕ **Don't miss**
Check out the Welsh National Surf Championships held May Bank Holiday.

⊗ **Avoid**
Swimming. Quicksands are signposted on the beach.

Practicalities

The market town of Pembroke with fortified walls and a castle has amenities — banks, shops, sleeping, pubs — with good access to the surrounding breaks, making it a good base for a trip.

Transport Pembroke train station is 9 miles from the beach. The Coastal Cruiser runs year round to the beach and beyond pembrokeshire.gov.uk for details

Sleeping £££ **Penfro**, Main St, SA71 4DB, T01646-682753, penfro.co.uk, is something a bit special and is an ideal escape for couples. This grand Georgian town house is sumptuous, if a little over the top, yet comfortable, while breakfast features local produce and home-made jams. North of Freshwater West, in the little village of Angle, the pretty **Foxglove Cottage**, T01437-767930, anglecottages.co.uk, sleeps 4/5 and is a great self-catering option from £265-525/week. For **camping**, nearby **Newton Farm**, SA71 5AG ,T01646-641266, is small with basic toilet and shower facilities and is a Camping and Caravanning Club Certified Site. Another good option is east around the headland at **Trefalen Farm**, Bosherton, SA71 5DR, T01646-661643. This simple site is just above the beach at Broadhaven. B&B also available.

Eating & drinking There are a couple of decent pubs in Angle — **The Hibernia Inn** which holds a number of cask ales and the **Old Point House** overlooking the sea.

Resources Outer Reef Surf School, T01646-680070, outerreefsurfschool.com, offers lessons for beginners through to improvers and runs dedicated women's weekends. With BSA qualified instructors and a number of British and Welsh championship surfers in their ranks, they operate at a number of beaches including Fresh West and can be mobile according to conditions. Equipment hire also available from around £30/ day board and wettie with deals on longer hire. There are a couple of surf shops in Pembroke including **The Edge**, Main St, T01646-622066, edgesurf.co.uk.

Also try If there are howling on-shores at Freshwater West combined with a huge swell running, head around the coast to the sheltered Freshwater East. A huge westerly storm can turn this tranquil, easterly facing bay into an absolute keg-fest. Best around mid-tide; when big this is not a spot for the novice.

Climbing Porth Clais

Provider	TYF Adventure
Skill level	Novice-experienced
Time frame	1 day
Equipment	Ropes, helmet, harness etc provided but you'll need climbing shoes (although tight trainers are suitable for beginners' lessons), water/windproof jacket, packed lunch
Exertion level	●●●●○

The vertical slab of rock is warm to the touch, the wall's texture a roughened flatness, huge lines transform the surface into an age worn face. Like a jigsaw of interlocking blocks, the grey stone cliff is riven with angles, scars woven in simple patterns by the gigantic forces of nature and the relentless pressure of time. Reaching up and pushing off, the two huge slabs of stone tower above, a grey wall of hard sandstone to the left, red sandstone to the right. "Imagine you have a beach ball in between the rock and your chest," advises TYF instructor Charli Holder. "This gives you more spatial awareness and it also pushes your waist into the wall rather than straight down if you are hugging the wall." The lines here are easily followed but can challenge even the most experienced. Just to the west, the azure sea has mustered its fury to gouge its way into the land, opening a small tidal inlet. Hidden from view lies the tiny Porth Clais harbour, a cluster of inshore fishing boats and yachts sheltered behind its defensive wall. There are a number of climbs along this short stretch of coast, many bathed in the warmth of a southerly aspect. Their names betray the terrain, with the likes of Harbour Crack, Glaze Crack or the Cracker waiting for those with a taste for crags, as well as the crimson faces of the Red Wall and Red Adair.

Pembrokeshire is home to a diverse range of climbing experiences, from bouldering and short slabs for beginners, through to steep technical sea cliffs. Southern Pembrokeshire is renown for its vertical limestone faces, some of the most challenging in the UK. To the north, the excellent red and grey sandstone slabs and volcanic cliffs await. Many of the climbs are tidal with access via abseil, and this is true at Porth Clais. "There's the view of Skomer when you top out, the walk up the side of the harbour to get to the crag, and the contrast between the two different colour walls, " says Charli on the appeal of the location. TYF offer lessons to those with skills ranging from the novice to the more experienced, and these sea cliffs offer challenges to suit. "In a full day we teach practical skills; edging, spearing, crimping etc by bouldering and traversing," says Charli. "Then we'll do some basic routes from a top rope, moving on to harder routes, introducing gear placement and anchoring off. Port Clais is amazing for it and it is just down the road from our centre."

There are few better locations to master basic climbing skills than this ocean front terrain. A dramatic coastline that is at the very heart of the Pembrokeshire Coast National Park and the spiritual home of coasteering , it offers enough thrills and awesome views to satisfy even the hardiest outdoor adventurer.

Practicalities
The tiny, eco-minded city of St Davids has good amenities.

Transport Haverfordwest is the nearest train station. Onward bus connections with Richards Bros, richardsbros.co.uk.

Sleeping There are several good campsites nearby. South of St Davids above Porth Cla is **Harbour Porthclais Farm**, SA62 6RR, T01437-720256, a simple, quiet site with room to spread out. It is a cliff top site so fairly exposed to the elements. Deliveries twice daily from the dairy with essentials from free range eggs and milk to BBQ ready meat. Open Easter-Oct.

Eating & drinking The Italian café **The Bench Bar** serves up home-baked breads, panninis and pizzas topped with local cheeses as well as ice cream, home made using organic milk from local Caerfai Dairy. Specials include local seasonal delights from game to sea food. Internet also. The Refectory at St Davids Cathedral is a champion of local produce and home cooking, from serving up locally sourced meat for the Sunday Carvery to tasty, well priced soups, salads, sandwiches and pies.

Resources Check pcnpa.org.uk for details on climbing restrictions.

> The contrasting walls of Porth Clais appear to have been assembled by giant building blocks.

> **Lowdown**

ⓘ Directory
TYF, 1 High St, St Davids, Pembrokeshire, Wales, SA62 6SA, T01437-721611, tyf.com.

Ⓢ Prices
£100 whole day/£60 half day.

Ⓢ Season
All year.

Ⓞ Don't miss
Seals and cetaceans can sometimes be spotted cruising the coastal waters around St Davids, keep your eyes peeled, but perhaps just when you top out eh?

Ⓧ Avoid
Consider your impact on the environment. The Pembrokeshire sea cliffs are important breeding zones – do not climb routes where birds are nesting. Check for restrictions. Pembrokesire is also a bolt-free zone and no new belay stakes should be put in.

Surfing Llangennith

Provider	None
Skill level	All
Time frame	2 hrs +
Equipment	Surfboard and wetsuit
Exertion level	●●●○○

There are some surf spots in the world where their fame as a surfing destination actually outstrips the quality of the waves on offer. If the power and shape of the waiting peaks at Llangennith were matched by the degree to which its name has spread not only through the UK, but far and wide across the globe, it would be pounded by Pipeline-like lefts and Backdoor-like rights every time the swell kicked in. Along with Fistral Beach in Cornwall, this is the spot everybody knows – even people who've never even seen a surfer in their lives know that Llangennith is the place to go. Yet, the truth is, Llangennith isn't really a world class surf spot.

But don't let that put you off. The secret of just why Llangennith is a surfer's paradise lies as much in what it doesn't offer as what it does. It doesn't offer huge gaping barrels like Indo, it doesn't offer waves as long as the Superbank, and it doesn't offer a beach front urban buzz like Huntington Beach. No, the real reason Llangennith is such a great place to head for is that it offers the perfect combo of waves, sand and space. Miles of the stuff. Room to spread your surfing wings, along three miles of beach, backed by pristine sand dunes. Many of Wales's top surfers have honed their skills at Llangennith and the waves around. Former European champion Pete Jones owns PJ's in the village, and his son James can often be found setting these waters alight. There's beachfront camping meaning you can emerge bleary-eyed from the humid comfort of your tent to the sound of a new swell arriving and know that this is another great day. There's the tiny village with a great little local and a surf shop run by a legendary, sage-like surfer. What more do you need?

Alex Lewis

> ◄ Around the dragon's head lurk challenges for experienced chargers.
> ▼ Nearby Broughton Bay: have board, will travel.

Demi Taylor

The Gower stretches west from Swansea, sticking out hopefully in the ocean like a thumb hitching a ride. And when a swell rolls out of the Atlantic, the three miles of Rhossili Bay sitting on the far reaches of the peninsula act as the perfect wave catcher. Any wind out of the east will create off-shores, but the wide, open expanse also means that this exposed spot is susceptible to being blown out. The relatively large, featureless sand means that sandbank formation can be inconsistent and waves may lack the punch of other spots around but that's not really too much of a problem if you are a beginner trying to master your pop or an intermediate trying to master your first cutbacks on the open face. This consistent spot will work through all tides, but bigger swells will tend to mean the paddle out is a frustrating white water experience. Beginners should take care as Llangennith and the rest of Rhossili Bay do not have an RNLI beach lifeguard presence.

The bay is hemmed in by points at either end. At the northern edge lies Burry Holms, a lush green tidal island, connected to the shore at low tide by a causeway. At the southern fringe lies the well-known beauty spot of Worms Head, the worm in this case meaning dragon – a reference to the silhouette of the serpentine like headland. On the southern side of the Worm, Fall Bay is home to Mewslade Reef, a sucky, hollow left that's a popular spot with experienced surfers who head there at low tide and in northerly winds. Still, with three miles of golden sands at your disposal, the reef can wait until you're truly ready for it.

∧ Rhossili Bay stretching northward towards the tidal island of Burry Holms.
∨ The King's Head.

> **Lowdown**

Prices
Free or from £20 board and wettie hire.

Season
All year.

Don't miss
Check out PJ's and ask advice from former European Surfing champion Pete Jones.

Avoid
Watch out for rips and remember there are no lifeguards here.

Practicalities

Llangennith is a tiny village and not a lot is actually here, but what it does have – decent pub, good surf shop and beachfront camping – are the essentials of any good surf trip, everything else is up to you.

Transport The nearest railway station is Swansea and from here you can make the 18-mile journey by a connecting bus service via Gowerton, which takes about an hour.

Sleeping ££-£ **Western House B&B**, Llangennith, SA3 1HU, T01792-386620, westernhousebandb.co.uk. Just down the road from the King's Head, this comfortable family run B&B offers great accommodation with views across the dunes to the sea plus advice from Steve, himself a keen surfer. **£ Hardingsdown**, Lower Hardingsdown Farm, Llangennith, SA3 1HT, T01792-386222, bunkhousegower.co.uk. This renovated stone barn sits within an organic working farm and offers comfortable, self-catering bunkhouse accommodation for groups year round. Great facilities including a drying room. For camping, **Hillend Caravan and Camping Park**, Llangennith, SA3 1JD, T01792-386204, offers pitches by the dunes and a stone's throw from the beach. There's a restaurant, little shop stocking the basics and even Welsh Surfing Federation surf school here.

Eating & drinking The options are pretty limited but you haven't truly experienced the Gower until you have enjoyed a post-surf pint here at **The Kings Head**, kingsheadgower.co.uk. Sit outside on the patio, re-live the waves ridden and watch as the world goes by. Food offerings consist of traditional English, Italian or Indian options. The large **Eddy's Restaurant** at Hillend does decent cheap eats and is open seasonally.

Resources PJ's Surf Shop, Llangennith, SA3 1HU, T01792-386669, pjsurfshop.co.uk, is an institution. Open all year they offer board hire from £10 per day and wetsuit hire from £10/day. **The Welsh Surf Federation Surf School**, T01792-386426, wsfsurfschool.co.uk, is based at Llangennith and run lessons spring to autumn. A 2-hr session costs £25 with a reduced cost for further lessons.

Also try If the wind is playing havoc with the surf, it might be the perfect time to harness that frustration and try kite surfing. **Gower Kite Riders**, T01792-367453, gowerkiteriders. com, offers courses and lessons from 1-hr tasters with kite handling to 3 or 4 hrs of more intensive skills. They operate at beaches around the Gower including Llangennith.

Mountain biking Brecon Beacons

Provider DIY	
Skill level All	
Time frame 5 hrs	
Equipment Mountain bike, helmet, map, provisions, appropriate gear-changing weather and a repair kit/spare tube	
Exertion level ●●●●○	

Covering more than 500 sq miles, The Brecon Beacons National Park stretches out across southern Wales from Abergavenny in the east to Llandeilo in the west, its features carved out by glaciers long since melted. But this dull geography lesson of words and name places quickly converts into a magical, topographic, 3D playground when you realise the potential that these borders encapsulate. From the central Brecon Beacon range, Pen-y-Fan, the highest point in south Wales rises for 2907 ft. Its sandstone flanks still bear the telltale ripples from its aquatic past while its summit rewards the committed with staggering views of just what this area offers. The Black Mountains guard the park's eastern flank while to the west the great Fawr Forest gives way, somewhat confusingly, to the Black Mountain. But then in a landscape which speaks for itself, names don't count for much.

For mountain bikers looking for natural trails, open spaces and huge skies, it doesn't get much better than this. The park is home to 16 quality routes mapped out and waymarked from five main hubs with plenty of terrain to explore that will keep you smiling for at least a week without too many repeats. Brecon is the classic base with everything from a family trail through to the classic ride – The Gap. This 24-mile route circumnavigating the main Beacon ridge is rideable year round and ideal for intermediate riders looking for a challenge. Don't let the easier sections following the canal along the Taff Trail fool you. While the majority is technically straight forward, the trail crosses a very exposed and open landscape which is a test in itself. It incorporates several long ascents, climbing over 1968 ft, plus speeding down hills over terrain that quickly changes from grass, to gravel to rocks to a river valley crossing as well as the exhilarating Gap

descent which includes some tricky rock steps. The views, if you can pause for breath, are definitely worth it. The town is also the staging post for the Brecon Beast, an annual enduro event that takes on some of the toughest tracks covering around 43 or 62 miles depending on how much of a challenge you are up for. Entry costs around £25 and includes camping and other goodies with all profits going to local charities including Brecon Mountain Rescue. breconmrt.co.uk.

Sennybridge is a good hub for those finding their feet and wanting to gradually push themselves over the course of a few days while Crickhowell has two good trails – the loop serving well as a warm up before pushing out on to the Mynydd du Forest red trail. Talybont on Usk uses its position on the Taff Trail to great effect delivering quality trails for the less experienced as well as a testing red route. Talgarth, an excellent gateway to the Black Mountains, delivers a hardcore mix of trails including the only designated black route in the region which covers more than 31 miles and reaches heights of 2297 ft.

> A magical topographic three dimensional playground.

< Feeling the burn but staying focused: just one of the the testing ascents thrown up by the Beacons.

Seb Rogers

Seb Rogers

> Lowdown

Prices
£7 for the all-weather laminated maps from Brecon Beacon National Park Authority – proceeds go towards trail maintenance.

Season
All year.

Don't miss
A detour to some of the waterfalls – there is a lovely series on the Caerfanel, Blaen y Glyn on the southern edge of the trail plus some pretty falls near the trail's end on the Nant Sere at the foot of Pen-y-Fan which can provide some decent pools for a reviving plunge.

Avoid
Although technically pretty straightforward there are a number of challenges to overcome – avoid riding beyond your skill level as there are plenty of good routes in the region for all abilities.

Practicalities

There are 5 main hubs depending on the experience and the type of riding you are looking for but Brecon is a classic base with good accommodation and amenities.

Transport   Abergavenny train station (20 miles) has onward coach links with Sixty Sixty Coaches to Brecon – no bikes. May-Sep on Sunday and bank holidays a limited Bike Bus service operates with stops between Cardiff and Brecon, T01873-853254 for details.

Sleeping   ££-£ Bridge Café, Bridge St, T01874-622024, bridgecafe.co.uk, run by mountain bikers is a lovely spot with simple, comfortable rooms, bike store, a welcome feel and a great café downstairs. For groups, **£ Canal Barn Bunkhouse**, Brecon, LD3 7HH, T01874-625361, bunkhouse-brecon-beacons-wales.co.uk, has beds from £12.50/night and has been set up with MTBers and walkers in mind. For camping, **Pencelli Castle**, LD3 7LX, T01874-665451, 4 miles east of Brecon has the Gold David Bellamy Conservation Award, free Wi-Fi and is open year round except Dec. The pretty **Priory Mill Farm**, LD3 7SR, priorymillfarm.co.uk, just a 5-minute walk from town offers simple, traditional camping in a quiet, riverside site with free range eggs for sale. Showers 50p.

Eating & drinking   Mar-Oct eat at the lovely **Bridge Café** which utilizes seasonal and local ingredients to create lovely simple fare from casseroles when it's chilly to salads when it's warm and organic cakes always as well as local beers, organic wines and Brecon whisky. Or lick your plate clean in the evening at the **Castle**

Street Restaurant, T01874 624392, whether enjoying Welsh beef, locally line caught bass or some other local, seasonal delight – main around £9, pizzas £8. B&B also available.

Resources   mtbbreconbeacons.co.uk is an excellent resource with detailed route info produced by the Brecon Beacon National Park. For all-weather laminated maps of the 16 routes plus detailed information booklet splash out the £7 for the info pack – proceeds from which go towards trail maintenance, T01874-623366. **Biped Cycles**, Ship St, Brecon, T01874-622296, bipedcycles.co.uk, has a comprehensive range of mountain and touring bikes plus essentials from helmets to repair kits. They have an on-site mechanic to iron out any problems, offer Trek bike hire with delivery service for groups and do Sunday rides from the shop – call for details. Brecon based **Bikes and Hikes**, T01874-610 071, bikesandhikes. co.uk, offer bike hire – from hi-spec Gary Fishers to kids' bikes and can deliver to your accommodation with prior notice. Guided rides also available. **Brecon Mountain Biking**, T01903-743538, breconbeaconsmountainbiking.co.uk, based in Abergavenny offers guided rides for all levels from £30/person half day plus skills sessions from £50/day with SMBLA qualified guides.

Also try   If you need some help in finding your way on mountains and moorland or coping in poor visibility, book in with the experienced Kevin Walker who has been running excellent navigation courses in the Brecon Beacons for more than 30 years. One-day courses from £75, T01874-625111, mountain-activities.com.

Surfing Three Cliffs Bay

Provider	DIY
Skill level	All
Time frame	2 hrs +
Equipment	Surfboard, wetsuit
Exertion level	●●●○○

Like a golden chain lost from a giant's pocket in the lush green of the valley floor, the bronze sunlight shimmers off the meandering Pennard Pill, its waters searching for the open sandy beach and the way back home to the sea. The tumbledown ruins of Pennard Castle are dark and brooding in the evening light. Marked against the fiery sky like a slumbering dragon, looking back the eastern flank of the cliff-lined inlet wraps protectively around the left-hand side of the bay, the three rocky promontories that trail into the sea transformed into giant scales that ridge its tail. Traversing this canvas, a single track of footprints, the only clues that anyone has dared to venture into this Arthurian landscape. Making the hike out of the Three Cliffs after a day's surfing alone can feel almost more magical than the waveriding itself, for here is one of the Gower's most famous vistas, and it is yours to savour alone.

A mere twenty-minute walk can make all the difference between bustling crowds and empty peaks. Here epic scenery and sandy reaches are there for those willing to make the trek. Three Cliffs has become something of a pin-up celebrity for the tourist boards and travel feature writers, but the truth is you can still share this bay with a select few, maybe a group of passing walkers or a metronomically precise climber or two. In the water you may be dropped in on by a passing pod of dolphins, oblivious to the man made etiquette that keeps the line-up in order.

But it's worth bearing in mind that the moving tidal waters can create mid to high tide rip currents at this beach, and you will not find the watchful gaze of lifeguards here. Come on a medium sized swell with light winds out of the north, pack food and water for the day and wait for the right bank to

call. Then, with the fading light, make the trek back to the world allowing yourself one last look over your shoulder at a timeless scene that many surfers busy chasing tide and swells around the Gower's main breaks often pass without a second glance.

Practicalities

There isn't a lot here, but this is precisely why you came.

Transport Swansea Station. From Craddock St there is an onbound bus service covering the 10 miles to Penmaen with veolia-transport.co.uk.

Sleeping It's all about the camping! **Three Cliffs Bay Holiday Park**, North Hills Farm, Penmaen, SA3 2HB, T01792-371218, threecliffsbay.com, isn't how it sounds — overlooking the bay, this is simple camping geared to families and couples who want to enjoy the views. Small shop on site. Apr-Oct, busy in summer. Self-catering cottages nearby also available from £305/week for 4. **Nicolaston Farm**, Penmaen, SA3 2HL, T01792-371209, also offers camping with views across the adjoining Tor Bay plus the chance to pick your own fruit in Jun-Jul and a good on-site farm café.

Eating & drinking If you want to build up an appetite, strike out for Cefyn Bryn, the highest point on the Gower and drink in the views. Continue on to Reynoldstone and **The Arthur Hotel**, T01792-390775, where you can reward yourself with a decent local brew or two with your home cooked meal featuring seasonal, local produce. **The Gower Inn** in Parkmill is closer — about a mile away.

Resources The nearest surf shop, **Big Drop** is in Mumbles on Tivoli Walk, T01792-368861, big-drop.com, with a good range of hardware including second hand boards. Heading west into Oxwich Bay proper, which is one of the places to check for waves in west to southwest storms, **Oxwich Bay Hotel** on the seafront has a webcam, oxwichbayhotel.co.uk/webcam.htm.

Also try The angled limestone slabs of Three Cliffs are a climbers delight serving up a number of decent single pitches. Be aware that this is a tidal spot only accessible around low tide (route starts can often be a bit wet) and the sea comes in pretty quickly. Scavenger is a popular VS route.

> **Lowdown**

Prices
Free.

Season
Year round.

Don't miss
Pennard Castle, legend has it that the garrison was swamped by a sand storm generated by angry fairies.

Avoid
The rips at mid to high tide on the eastern side of the bay.

Mountain biking Afan Argoed

Provider DIY	
Skill level Intermediate-Advanced	
Time frame 1½ hrs +	
Equipment Mountain bike, helmet plus repair kit	
Exertion level ●●●○○	

The huge spinning blades of the wind farm are a welcome sight marking out Windy Point and signalling a change of pace. After 3½ miles of switch-backing, rocky, ascent, Whites Level rewards riders with almost six miles of tight singletrack that weaves in and out of forest and virtually down hill all the way home in a series of testing descents. The steep sided valley ups the stakes, delivering a real feeling of exposure. Not bad for a former south Wales coal mining area and even better when you consider that this red graded trail is just one of five testing routes waymarked around the forest.

The Afan Forest Park stretches out over 24 sq miles and shades the narrow valley in 30,000 hectares of managed woodlands. Ribbons of red and black graded singletrack and forest road spread across the park from two hubs, one of which is a dedicated MTB centre, helping to make this one of the UK's leading sites for experienced riders. From the Visitor Centre, the 10½ mile Penhydd Trail combines big climbs on forest road with flowing singletrack, and tight technical switchback to good effect. The Wall sticks pretty well to the north side of the valley along much of its 14 miles length and is all about the singletrack descents. Whites Level sets off from Glyncorrwg Mountain Bike Centre as does the epic Skyline. Climbing 6562 ft and covering 28 miles of forest road and often technical singletrack, fitness and stamina are king on this tough trail but if you do persevere, the pay-off is a roller-coastering, bone-shaking final descent. There are a couple of shortcuts but in the words of your maths teacher, the only person you'll be cheating is yourself.

Linking the two centres are the family friendly low level cycleway and the fierce, 27-mile, W2 trail.

While the cycleway bimbles along a disused train line, W2 matches 3199 ft of climbing with seriously demanding singletrack descents, combining The Wall and Whites Level to create the centre's only black route. Just make sure you don't mix the two up!

Practicalities

Everything you need is in and around the forest…

Transport Port Talbot station is around a 10½-mile ride from the park.

Sleeping For camping, Glyncorrwg Ponds, T01639-851900, has a campsite set up next to the café. Showers require a good haul of 50ps but after a hard day on the Skyline this is a small price to pay to wash away your aches and pains. The family run **££ Afan Lodge**, Afan Rd, SA13 3ES, T01639-85250, afanlodge. com, is owned by keen bikers. They have simple en-suite doubles plus self-contained units with kitchens sleeping up to 5 from £125/night. With a bar and restaurant on site that uses local produce plus bike wash and lock up and private trail access this is an idea spot. For self-catering the 1-bedroom **Bryn Bettws Log Cabins**, Gyfylchi Farm, Pontrhydyfen, SA12 9SP, T01639-642040, sleep up to 4 in single beds plus futons in the lounge. Bike lock up plus direct access to Skyline.

Eating & drinking Drop Off Café, Glyncorrwg, T01639-852005, serves nothing but home-made fare from smoothies and cakes to fresh soups and tasty pizzas and pastas to replenish energy levels. It's licensed and open till 2200 on summer weekends. Free Wi-Fi access also.

Resources At MTB centre **Skyline Cycles**, A13 3EA, T01639-850011, skylinecycles.co.uk, stocks bikes plus all the essentials. They have a professional workshop dealing with emergency repairs to servicing issues. Skyline MTB hire at the visitors centre, T01639-851100, full suspension £40/day. See mbwales.com for an overview of the centre and trails.

Also try Surfing. There are plenty of choices along this coastal stretch – Aberavon's A-frame for the experienced, the huge dune backed Margam Sands for the less so plus the popular and consistent Rest Bay. **Simon Tucker Surf Academy**, T01656-772415, surfingexperience.com for lessons.

∧ Rollercoastering singletrack challenges.

> **Lowdown**

❶ Directory
Afan Forest Park, SA13 3HG, forestry.gov.uk.

❺ Prices
Free/£40 full suspension MTB hire.

✷ Season
Year round.

❂ Don't miss
The Drop Off Café – a real social hub and welcome sight.

✖ Avoid
The midges.

Mountain biking Wales: best of the rest

Provider	DIY/see details
Skill level	Various
Time frame	2 hrs to 4 days
Equipment	Mountain bike, helmet, map, provisions, appropriate gear and a repair kit/spare tube
Exertion level	●●●●●

Llanwrtyd Wells

Mountain bike, check; lead weights, check; snorkel and mask, check, you're ready to hit that bog and start pedalling. If it sounds odd, that's because it is, but then this is Llanwrtyd Wells. Home to a series of off-the-wall events from the World MTB Bog Snorkeling Championships to the Man Versus Horse Marathon and the Real Ale Wobble (which are all exactly as they sound) this tiny town has its tongue firmly in its cheek and as such has always attracted MTBers with a real sense of fun who don't take themselves too seriously. The Red Kite Mountain Bike Bash is less odd-ball but still fun combining four days of singletrack, forest road and bridleway riding covering 15-35 miles/day with serious socializing. Check green-events.co.uk for details. It's not just about events, a decent trail network surrounds the area and the nearby Coed Trallwm Centre, LD5 4TS, coedtrallwm.co.uk, with a couple of short, waymarked XC trails makes a good springboard for exploring them. **Riverside Caravans** in nearby Llangmmarch Wells, LD4 4BY, T01591-620465, riversidecaravans.com, is a family friendly campsite with level pitches right on the banks of the Irfon open March-November.

Rhayader

Backed by the Cambrian Mountains on the banks of the River Wye, the small market town takes up its position. In the heart of Wales, its central location made Rhayader a natural stopping point for travellers from Romans to monks while today the rugged landscape and rolling hills that surround the town ensure it is a firm fixture on any mountain biking agenda. "Rhayader has some of the most spectacular

 Easy rider.

Wig Worland

and beautiful scenery in the country and makes
for really interesting riding without being scary or
dangerous," says Clive Powell, whose Dirty Weekends
delivering guided rides for all levels, are synonymous
with the region. Epic Weekends offer experienced
riders with good endurance off-road riding for up to
eight hours/day, while Standard Dirty Weekends are
catered towards mere mortals with reasonable bike
fitness. Novice Weekends still deliver real mountain
biking over exciting terrain, conquering challenging
climbs but are ideal for those with little or no off-road
experience, lapsed MTBers, or even riders looking
for a relaxed pace. "There are no man-made routes,"
enthuses Clive, "so it never gets overcrowded." Two
days from £176/person includes accommodation,
breakfast, lunch brought out by a support vehicle,
tea and cakes plus home cooked dinners by Clive's
wife Francine – a champion of local and organic
produce. T01597-811343, clivepowell-mtb.co.uk.
MTB shop and bike hire also.

Betws-y-Coed

In the heart of Snowdonia surrounded by forest,
this pretty village is the gateway to some serious
mountain biking potential – natural and man-
made. Heading north into the Gwydyr Forest Park,

the red graded 15½ miles Marin Trail combines
forest track with sections of single and double track.
Utilising tree cover, the trail matches big climbs
with decent descents. Hidden in plain view in
Gwydyr Forest to the south, Penmachno is another
quality XC loop with steady climbs and stunning
views. "The descents are incredible, rocky, fast and
scary," explained downhill world champions The
Atherton's on selecting it as one of the UK's top MTB
trails for WideWorld. **Beics Betws**, T01690-710766,
bikewales.co.uk, offer quality MTB hire for around
£25/day. Check mbwales.com for trail information
and mapping. **£££ Bryn Bella**, T01690-710627,
bryn-bella.co.uk, offers award winning, sustainable
yet comfortable B&B – breakfast eggs from their
own rescued hens, solar heated water with good
access to the Marin trail.

Brechfa

Brechfa Forest has always paid its way, turning its
hand to the needs of the day – serving as a royal
hunting ground to fuelling industrial south Wales.
Under the Forestry Commission, the woodland cut
by deep valleys still earns its keep and is home to
some excellent mountain biking – both natural
delights and man-made trails. The population is

Seb Rogers

◄ Former Welsh Champion
Rowan Sorrell, at home in
south Wales.

scattered in this corner of Carmarthenshire, the forest itself is surrounded by farmland and open grazing and there is no dedicated centre here waiting to brew you up a mug of tea. But that's part of the appeal. As are the red rated 12 miles Gorlech Trail and (Black) Raven Trail designed by MTB king and world cup winner Rowan Sorrel. And that's not forgetting the easier Green Derwen Trail which weaves through the lower woodlands from Byrgwm for 5½ miles, combining sections of singletrack with forest road as a great introduction to the area and MTB. It also links up with a loop of blue graded trail for those who want to push themselves a little more. Just outside Brechfa, the rural **££ Ty'r Cae**, SA32 7RD, T01267-202406, tyrcae.co.uk, delivers comfortable farmhouse B&B with breakfast cooked on the AGA using locally sourced produce. For groups the environmentally managed Gilfach Wen farm, T07970-629726, brechfa-bunkhouse.com, has bunkhouse-style self-catering accommodation from £15/person (midweek/late notice only) or £325/night sole use.

Snowdon

While riding up and down Snowdon on a mountain bike may have a slight novelty value, especially for any walkers who catch sight of you, this is a serious mountain – at 3560 ft it is the highest in England and Wales. As such this peak needs to be treated with respect and the implications of tackling it, in terms of weather, safety and the level of riding involved should not be taken lightly. Ascend via the Llanberis Path, which follows the Snowdon Mountain Railway to the summit, and is also used by walkers. Much of the bridleway climbing up the mountain is rough, bouldery and unsurprisingly steep. Take in the views before plotting your descent. The mountain suffers from over-popularity meaning that erosion is an issue, as such a voluntary agreement bans cycling on the mountain 1000-1700 May-September, but there are plenty of other peaks to tackle in the area. Refuel at the legendary **Pete's Eats** on the High Street, Llanberis, T01286-870 117, petes-eats.co.uk, that has been filling the weary climber up with hearty, filling well priced fare since the '70's. Self-catering and limited bunkhouse accommodation available. For a change of scene and a Mediterranean flavour (I know, but somehow it works), hit Pete's Bistro opposite.

Surfing Langland Bay

Provider	DIY
Skill level	All
Time frame	2 hrs +
Equipment	Surfboard, wetsuit
Exertion level	●●●○○

The Gower was the first part of the UK to be designated an Area of Outstanding Natural Beauty in 1956. This peninsula is one of our most picturesque and unspoilt regions, an area of green rolling hills, verdant open pasture, golden sand dunes and rocky shores, all bordered by the azure of the open ocean to the south and the Loughor estuary to the north. Crumbling bays, craggy coves and open beaches defend the southern flank from the raw power of the Atlantic's fury, linked by cliff walks that fringe the coastline, leading all the way to the open expanse of Rhossili and Llangennith.

Langland Bay, at the gateway to the Gower, has that real Victorian resort feel to it. There are the hotels and B&B's that watch out over the bay, the green and white chalets fronted by strips of manicured lawn and the ocean side promenade that has seen generations stroll hand in hand before resting, eyes drawn magnetically to the sea. The sand is wide and the bank of pebbles that delineate the high tide mark are easily negotiated. From the early part of the nineteenth century until the 1960s the Oystermouth Railway ferried weekend crowds out to Mumbles from nearby Swansea, eager to escape the city and sample the sea air, but today Langland has become known for something a lot more energetic than promenading.

Here in Langland, the surfing possibilities seem endless. This curved arch isn't just one surf break, there are a myriad of reefs, sandbanks and points all offering quality waves on their day. From Outside Point, Inside Point and Langland Shorebreak, to Langland Reef, MOTB, The Reef and Rotherslade Left. Welsh surfers are known for their hard charging in the water backed up by a wicked sense of humour – hence the fact that The Sandbar is actually a serious reef producing heavy, hollow barrels for those who have made the jacking take off while

The Reef is actually a sandbar. Medium to big westerley swells sees the bay come to life, anticipated by a committed local crew, while northerly winds create clean offshore conditions. With these breaks working on various states of tide there is usually a rideable wave to be had, if you can snag one. Yes, Langland may have a polite, Victorian feel on land, but in the water the starchiness is washed away as surfers chase down quality waves with the voracity of a 1980s city trader closing in on the deal of the century.

Practicalities

Mumbles is the largest of the Gower villages and is the general term for the Victorian resort Oystermouth. The name came about as a bastardisation of mamelles (breasts) – the term by which French sailors referred to the two offshore islands nearby.

Transport Swansea train station is around 6 miles from Langland with a connecting bus service with First Cymru from Picton Arcade.

Sleeping £££ **Langland Cove Guest House**, overlooking Langland Bay, Rotherslade Road, T01792-366003, is a pretty B&B run by legendary shaper and surf photographer The Gill and is an ideal spot for couples. For camping, heading west, Three Cliff Bay is home to the excellent **Three Cliffs Bay Caravan and Camping Park**, T01792-390777, threecliffsbay.com, overlooking the bay with its own private beach, open Apr-Oct.

Eating & drinking The **café** on Langland beach front serves up tasty bacon butties and coffees to warm the soul after a chilly winter session. There are also a number of decent spots to eat in Mumbles including **Castellamare Pizzeria**, T01792-369408, which may be a bit pricey but the views overlooking Bracelet Bay make up for that fact. Most of the pubs, including the popular **Antelope** claim a connection to Welsh poet Dylan Thomas but you can allow them some artistic licence.

Resources **Big Drop Surf Shop**, Tivloi Walk, T01792-48048, stocks all the essentials.

Also try The Gower Peninsula has excellent bridleway circuits mixing up moorland and coastal riding.

Gorge walking Brecon Beacons

Provider	Wales Outdoors Limited
Skill level	Novice-intermediate
Time frame	Usually 1000-1600
Equipment	All kit including wetsuit, buoyancy aid, helmet and boots are provided, but bring warm clothes and a packed lunch
Exertion level	●●●●○

The rushing of water echoes around the gorge, any harshness softened by leaves and a lush cushioning of moss that seems to wallpaper the surrounding vertical sides. There is a short climb above, to the left of the waterfall, rocks lubricated with algae, fingers white with pressure. Just one last push on the right leg and the rock relinquishes its vertical stance, allowing a short scramble on to a drier platform. Looking down on the gorge, branches bow a salute to the endless flow, shattered boulders lay strewn around the cascade. A swim next, then on to the leap of faith.

"The range of activities undertaken on a gorge walking day is similar to those offered on a coasteering session: scrambles, traversing, swims and jumps, the difference being that you are in a river, usually with steep cliffs on both sides, rather than in the sea," says Andrew Lamb, who has been gorge walking for 15 years and is Director of Wales Outdoors. "The first half of the day is training – moving over difficult and broken ground, traversing, rock hopping and sometimes a journey into an old silica mine." After lunch the pace picks up with a waterfall climb, swim across some pools followed by another climb. "The highlight of the day is the 20-foot jump into a cold and very deep pool," explains Andrew. "The Afon Sychryd was an old site of silica mining, which has left walls, bridges and ramparts within the river environment. There are the remains of a tram road, which runs alongside the river for all but the narrowest sections. Because of this historic use of the river we feel that this is the only choice for gorge walking in South Wales." For many the journey underground and into the mine is awe inspiring, and unlike most caving has standing room with large open spaces. But then there's the ledge-side waterfall crawl while water crashes around your ears, not forgetting that jump at the end of the session." The jump always makes most think about what they are doing there," says Andrew smiling

In 1995, Andrew Lamb opened the first mountain bike hire centre in the Brecon Beacons and his business has since grown into a multi-adventure activity centre, awarded the Level 2 Green Dragon environmental standard.

Practicalities

The Brecon Beacons National Park is an area of high peaks, making it a popular spot for climbing, walking, mountain biking and caving. The Central Massif is dominated by the mountain ridges of Pen-y-Fan — the highest mountain in southern Wales at 2,907 ft, Cribyn and Coru Du as well as the Beacon Horseshoe. On the western edge of the park Llandeilo, a small market town in the Tywi Valley makes a lovely base.

Transport   Llandeilo has its own, small train station.

Sleeping   £££ Fronlas, Thomas Street, Llandeilo, SA19 6LB, T01558-824733, fronlas.com. This boutique B&B matches chic rooms and an environmental agenda. Organic locally sourced breakfasts combine with eco-electricity and solar panels. Something very special. Self-catering **Mountain View Cottages**, Llandeilo, Carmarthenshire, SA19 7EE, T01558-685815, mountainviewcottages.co.uk, is a converted barn set on an organic farm offering stunning views and walks through a bluebell wood.

Eating & drinking   The **Brecon Beacon Mountain Centre Tea Rooms**, Libanus, LD3 8ER, is about great food created from local produce. Stock up on tea and cakes, packed lunches or a serious hearty lunch. Open 0930-1730 summer, earlier closing off in peak season. Llandeilo is flowing with pubs while just north in Llangadog, **The Red Lion** does a cracking line in ales and simple food — home cooked and locally sourced.

Resources   Breconbeacons.org.

Also try   South Wales is one of the most exciting caving areas in Britain. Head underground with **Adventure Wales**, adventurewales.com, from £35/half day.

> **Lowdown**

❶ **Directory**
Wales Outdoors Limited, Brecon Beacons, walesoutdoors.co.uk, T08454-666999.

$ **Prices**
£55/adult, £37.50/under18.

☉ **Season**
Year round.

⊕ **Don't miss**
The jump and the mine.

⊗ **Avoid**
Respect the environment around you.

Surfing Wales: best of the rest

Provider	DIY/see details
Skill level	Various
Time frame	Dawn till dusk
Equipment	Surfboard, wetsuit
Exertion level	●●●●●

There's a joke that goes around saying if Ireland wasn't in the way, Wales would be pretty good for surfing. Well Wales has a long and proud surfing tradition with some of the best beaches and surfers in the UK. Swells wrap around the southern edge of the Emerald Isle or come sweeping up from the Bay of Biscay bringing the beaches, reefs and points to life. The region is also blessed with an undulating coastline with coves and reefs facing to all four points of the compass meaning that whatever the conditions, there's always a surfable wave, somewhere, in everything from the smallest to the biggest of swells. Lifeguards operate at some of the beaches in peak season, check goodbeachguide.co.uk for a full list.

Aberystwyth

Skill level	Beginner-advanced

The waters around this Victorian resort town might not be tropical blue – more like a murky brown – but the waves can turn on the juice when a southwesterly swell rolls up the Irish Sea. Harbour Trap reef delivers hollow rights at low tide and long lefts at mid with Castle reef, opposite the Trap delivering mid-tide rights. Queens beach break is another option working on the same tides. Note it really needs to be 6 ft on the south coast to be working here. To the north, the dune-backed beach at Borth produces mellower waves and is rarely busy, making it a more beginner-friendly proposition. **Aber Adventures** run their BSA level 3 approved surf school from Borth, offering beginners lessons from £25 as well as advanced surf coaching for more experienced riders looking to hone their skills. Board and wettie hire also available from less than £10/day (T07976-061514, aberadventures. com). Stop by the lovely, organic **Treehouse** on

‹ Tucking into the Glamorgan Heritage Coast.

Baker Street, Aberystwyth for a big lunchtime bowl of home-made soup and a roll for around £4 or something more filling like a burger – veggie or freerange – for around £6.

Newgale
Skill level Beginner-advanced

Found at the northern edge of St Bride's Bay, Newgale is part of the beautiful Pembrokeshire Coast National Park so enjoys generally excellent water quality. With handy beach parking, the two miles of sands allow plenty of room to spread out and is a good spot for beginners when small. It works best in small to medium westerly swells with offshore winds from the east. For surf basics there's **Newsurf**, T01437-721398, newsurf.co.uk, who also offer lessons – check their site also for a daily surf report. If the swell is too big, try heading south to Broad Haven at the other end of the bay which can often be more sheltered.

Broadhaven South
Skill level Advanced

For those who know what they're doing and like their rides fast and their take-offs steep, BHS is the place for heart-in-your-mouth drops and short intense barrels. On the wild, beautiful south coast of Pembrokeshire, the waves bend into this small bay, and refract off the eastern side, meeting in

an intense wedge. The take-off zone is small and there is always a strong pack of competitive, local surfers, skilled in the art of hell-dropping. The bay faces southeast so needs a decent sized swell to get going. Watch out for rips and heavy close-outs. National Trust parking. For those still finding their feet or wanting to improve, book a lesson with **Outer Reef**, T01646-680070, outerreefsurfschool. com, in nearby Maiden Wells who will take you to a more friendly spot to practise your skills.

Manorbier
Skill level Beginner-advanced

The cliffs that flank the sandy bay here can offer some high tide protection on windy days where other southwesterly facing beaches can be blown out. Because of its protected aspect, swell getting into the bay is around two thirds the size of Fresh West, but that doesn't mean this spot should be underestimated. While the beach break in the middle of the bay is beginner-friendly, the high tide reef at the western edge isn't. Producing long walling righthanders that can pack a punch, the reef is a big draw card but doesn't hold a big crowd so ensure you can hold your own before trying to take it on. Park overlooking the beach or at the National Trust car park. For beginners and improvers courses, contact BSA approved **Outer Reef Surf School** (see above) who run two-hour lessons from £25 including equipment.

⌄ Sizing up the bargains at BHS.

The Gill

Crab Island
Skill level Advanced

The apex surf break in Langland Bay, this world-class righthander breaks over a rock bottom when the tide drops enough for the island to be revealed. One of the country's best waves, it will usually have a bustling line-up. Works best in a southwesterly swell from two to ten feet and a northerly wind. Expect elevator drops followed by fast walls and hollow sections for the brave. If you're not quite up to the challenge, you can always grab a coffee and watch in comfort as the gladiators do battle.

Rest Bay
Skill level Beginner-advanced

This popular beach just to the north of Porthcawl consistently produces some great peaks and is home to some excellent wave riding potential. Working best from low to three-quarter tide on the push, the beach break churns out both lefts and rights that can be surprisingly good. In the summer there are lifeguards and beginners would do best to stay in front of the car park. For those in the market for a new stick, Porthcawl is home to Freelap Custom Surfboards, crafters extraordinaire of some of Wales's finest custom boards, put out under the ODD brand, T01656-744692, oddsurfboards. com. For lessons, head to **Simon Tucker Surf Academy**, T01656-772415, run by the former British Champion. surfingexperience.com.

Llantwit Major
Skill level Intermediate-advanced

Lying on the Glamorgan Heritage Coast, this small town is home to a large, triangular boulder reef generating quality surf. As the tide shifts, a number of waves come to life. In smaller swells, at low tide the Peak will turn on, producing decent waves. Picture perfect rights peel off the edge of the reef at low to mid tide, and these can be classic on their day. From mid to high tide there can be hollow peaks on the boulders near the car park. Unsurprisingly, in a good swell, this break will be crowded with a strong local crew but for those who surf respectfully, it's always possible to snag a decent wave or two. Sign posted, the beach does have lifeguards in the summer, but water quality isn't great. **Point Break Surf, Snow and Skate** in Llantwit, T01446-794303, pointbreaksurfskateandsnow.com, stocks all the essentials.

∧ Welsh legend PJ making the most of fun waves.

Best of the rest Wales: activities

Kayaking, North Wales

Provider	DC Paddlers
Skill level	Experienced
Time frame	Up to 4 hrs
Equipment	Kayak
Exertion level	●●●●●

For the competitively minded paddler bored with 'going with the flow', the Conwy Ascent Canoe Race is for you. This annual nine-mile upstream race from Deganwy Narrows to Dolgarrog Bridge coincides with the flood tide so while yes, you still are technically going with the flow, you get to feel like a rebel as you also get to go up the river, the wrong way! The estuary setting is stunning in terms of both scenery and wildlife but the 'Le Mans' style start from the beach at Conwy Morfa should help focus your attention on the task at hand. The marathon takes place in an open water estuary and conditions can be very testing so is for experienced paddlers only – organizers recommend a Division 7 cut off. For non-competitive paddlers, there is the option of the tour event. £6 per seat plus £2.50 day ticket for non members of WCA, BCU, SCA for insurance purposes. For more information see dcpaddlers.co.uk/conwy_ascent. Stay at **Pyllau Gloewen Organic Farm's Conwy Valley Bunk Barn**, Tal-y-Bont, LL32 8YX, T01492-660504, conwyvalleybarn.com, with comfortable dorms from £15/person. Cosy cottage and private yurt in lush meadow sleeping two also available from £70/night. B&B from £45/person. Packed lunches, breakfast and BBQ also available on request.

Kite surfing, Gower

Provider	Gower Kiteriders
Skill level	Novice-experienced
Time frame	From 1 hr
Equipment	Provided
Exertion level	●●●●○

With beaches facing to all points of the compass, the Gower is an ideal kite surfing destination – the best beaches for learning or honing skills can be selected according to the conditions on the day. Gower Kite Riders operate from six main beaches, Swansea Bay, Oxwich, Horton, Llangennith, Broughton and Llanelli which, OK isn't part of the peninsula but is ideal if you're not keen on choppy conditions as very little swell can get in here. Like all the best kite surfing schools, their beginners' programme kicks off with basic powerkite flying and introduction lessons can be booked for £15/hour. "Kite surfing cannot be learnt in a single day," they advise. So for a more thorough introduction, book on to one of their Kiteboarder Programmes – a two-day course which should get you familiar with the equipment and set up, piloting kites, body dragging in the water and, more importantly up and riding on a board by its conclusion. Gower Kite Riders, T01792-367453, gowerkiteriders. com, two-day programme £180. **Hardingsdown Bunkhouse**, Llangennith, SA3 1HT, T01792-386222, rhoddssfarm.co.uk, delivers comfortable, modern bunkhouse accommodation in a former stable block on this working organic farm from £15/night. Handy drying room and lock up also.

Climbing, Dinas Rock

Provider	Call of the Wild
Skill level	Novice-experienced
Time frame	½ day plus
Equipment	All necessary technical and safety equipment provided, remember to wear comfortable clothing
Exertion level	●●●●●

"Trust your feet," says Call of the Wild's Dave Thomas. "You can stand on your legs all day. Often beginners will only commit a little weight to a foothold before deciding that it is unsafe whereas the more weight you slowly place on a foot placement the less likely it is to slip." Sound advice when you're half way up a 98 ft single pitch route. The Brecon Beacons National Park extends over more than 500 sq miles with deep ravines, wooded gorges, cave systems, rolling hills, craggy mountains and breathtaking rock faces to explore. On the southern fringe of the

∧ Wild delights of Sgwd
Gwladus

park, Dinas Rock is one such quality crag, home to, "some of the best climbing in SE Wales," enthuses Dave. "The beginners' area is ideally situated next to the car park where bouldering and bolted top roped activities take place on an east angled face but the site caters for all abilities of climber with approximately 127 rock climbs (mainly sport routes)." After a safety briefing, the beginners' course kicks off with a warm-up to get you thinking about balance and mobility as well as introducing climbing techniques at low levels before progressing on to belay techniques. By the end of a full course, students should be able to identify and utilize equipment safely, risk assess a venue and make an informed judgement on it as well as climb to a competent standard within the parameters experienced on the course. Half-day introductory courses from £45. **Clyngwyn Farm**, Pontneddfechan SA11 5US, T01639-722930, offers both simple B&B and comfortable bunkhouse accommodation with an outside BBQ pit and fire for whiling away the evening under the stars. Bunkhouse bookings for a minimum group number of four, last minute booking £17/head for smaller numbers. By Dinas Rock Car Park, Pontneddfechan Village Hall has café and toilet facilities during summer weekends, but be aware: the car park closes at 1600 daily.

Cycling, TransWales	
Provider DIY	
Skill level All	
Time frame 50 hrs +	
Equipment MTB, map, repair kit/spare tube, helmet, snacks, water	
Exertion level ●●●●●	

Lon Las Cymru National Cycle Route measures some 300 miles and runs pretty well north to south from Holyhead to Cardiff/Chepstow. Covering the length of Wales and involving around 50 hours of pedalling, this route passes through the national parks of the Brecon Beacons in the south and Snowdonia in the north, taking in the long, steady climb and descent of the impressive Nant Ffrancon Pass and following a number of former railway lines including the popular Mawddach Trail. sustrans.org.uk for details of this and other long distance cycle trails.

Swimming, Waterfall Woods	
Provider DIY	
Skill level All	
Time frame Sun up till sun down	
Equipment Towel, bathers (depending on season/ hardiness wetsuit	
Exertion level ●●●○○	

Water has sculpted the landscape of Wales, shaping its moods, its personality. Deep llyns whose glacial ancestors carved their place on the mountainscape, to the quietly babbling brooks and meandering streams that gently forge their paths on their way to becoming fast flowing, excitable forces who, under a woodland cover, have cut steep gorges deep into the rocks, rapids to race and ledges to cascade over in a thundering burst of liberated energy before plunging into a pool below. Nowhere else in Wales are these waterfalls in a greater concentration than on the southern edges of the Brecon Beacons in Coed y Rhaedr. Nowhere else in Wales is there a more exciting spot for a plunge, paddle, dive of swim where the constant rushing of moving water becomes an at times overwhelming aural sensation, adding another dimension to your experience. From the village of Pontneddfechan in the Neath Valley, a mile or so walk upstream from the Angel Pub will bring you to Scwd Gwladus, Lady Falls. The 20 ft cascade falls in a column of water from the high rock ledge into the wide, inviting pool below. Watched over by trees and cocooned by a bank of moss and ferns, it is a sight to take your breath away. The swimming here is sublime and with a little careful slipping and sliding it is even possible to walk behind the falls. NB The waterfall varies from trickle to crashing cascade. There are more falls to explore in the area including, half a mile further upstream, the seriously impressive and extremely hard to reach Scwd Einon Gam plus the smaller Horseshoe Falls on the Afon Nedd Fechan which have a dreamy pool below for plunging and swimming.

Best of the rest Wales: sleeping & eating

Foxhunter, Monmouthshire
*Nantyderry, Abergavenny, Monmouthshire, NP7 9DN,
T01873-881101, thefoxhunter.com.*

Squirreled away within a small Welsh village lies
The Foxhunter: a former station master's house
that has been transformed into a gastronomic lair
celebrating modern British cooking and all things
local, organic and seasonal. But it is also offers the
full deal: foraging, eating and sleeping rolled into
one special package. The two self-catering cottages
from £145/night are close by, the fridges are stocked
with breakfast goodies and, if you'd prefer a cosy
night in, some of the restaurant dishes are available
on a takeaway basis. Explore the woodlands with
a professional guide searching out berries, herbs,
leaves, mushrooms – depending on the season –
before heading to the restaurant to enjoy the fruits
of your labour from £130/two people, £40 each for
subsequent people. Alternatively opt for someone
else to do the hard work and simply sample a set
menu of locally foraged goodies at this modern
gastro pub from £30/person.

Gwern Gof Isaf Farm, Snowdonia
*Capel Curig, Betws-y-Coed, Snowdonia, LL24 0EU,
T01690-720276, gwerngofisaf.co.uk.*

Lodged in the peaks of the Snowdonia National
Park between between Capel Curig and LLyn
Ogwen lies this traditional 750 acre National Trust
hill farm and family run campsite. Close to the
base of the impressive Tryfan which rises for more
than 3000 ft, it has long been a draw for walkers
and climbers keen to challenge themselves, in fact
Sir John Hurt used this base as a proving ground
in preparation for leading the 1953 ascent of
Everest. As well as a camping for tents, campervans
and caravans they also offer simple bunkhouse
accommodation in converted farm buildings
sleeping six and 16 – own sleeping bags and
cooking tools are essential. Open year round, this is
a jaw droppingly dramatic location in which to lay
your head after a days adventure.

Knowles Farm B&B, Pembrokeshire
*Lawrenny, Kilgetty, Pembrokeshire, SA68 0PX,
T01834-891221, lawrenny.org.uk.*

Set on a working organic dairy farm, this bed and
breakfast basks in the sunshine for most of the day
and is a simple pleasure. It rests above the Cleddau
Estuary which affords the opportunity for a splash
or a swim as it which winds its way towards Milford
Haven. If you ask nicely, camping is also available
as are organic evening meals operating on a BYO
booze policy.

Felin Fach Griffin, Powys
*Felin Fach, Brecon, Powys, LD3 0UB, T01874-620111,
eatdrinksleep.ltd.*

Working with seasonal and locally sourced produce
including ingredients from their organic kitchen
garden, chef Ricardo, a supporter of the slow food
movement creates fabulous fare. For the more
affordable option at this Welsh country inn, enjoy
a two-course set lunch from £15.90 or push the
boat out with the a la carte where wild venison and
line caught sea bass grace the menu. Stop by for a
drink, a bite to eat, and, if it all gets too much, stay
for the night.

⌄ Farm stores.

Graig Wen, Snowdonia ⊜
Arthog, Dolgellau, LL39 1BQ, T 01341-250482, graigwen.co.uk.

Overlooking the Mawddach Estuary and with views to Snowdon, Graig Wen was awarded the most sustainable campsite by Green Snowdonia in 2009. In the height of the summer, tents can be pitched in the hidden glades of the lower fields while the small touring site is open right through the chilly winter months. For those looking to travel light, the ready erected Bell Tent, sleeping up to four, is a little haven and if you want to ditch the car, Sarah and John will happily collect from the local train station. From March-October yurts with wood burning stoves and creature comforts bridge the gap between indoors and outdoors. And if the 'wild' gets too much, you can always elect to stay in their stylish, relaxed B&B whose breakfasts are from 100% locally sourced produce.

The Yurt Farm, Ceredigion ⊜
Crynfryn, Penuwch, Tregaron, SY25 6RE, T 01974-821594, theyurtfarm.co.uk.

Escape to Laurie and Thea's 150 acre organic farm whose careful trails lead you through wildflower meadows, lofty woodlands and along streams. The farm is home to Hereford cattle, Cheviot sheep and rare breed pigs not to mention the chickens or the four acres given over to the art of veggie growing, the results of which are available in their farm shop. The farm and yurts have been engineered to have minimum impact on the environment – the locally made yurts are hidden in a secluded corner between crab apple trees and blackcurrant bushes, and the furniture in them is made from farm timber. The wooden 'social cabin' houses solar heated showers while the toilets are composting with a reed bed drainage system. The two yurts sleep 4-6 and 6-8 and are available April-October from £55/night, including a basket of farm produce on arrival. Organic duvets and pillows cost a further £10/person. They will happily collect anyone arriving by bus or train from Aberystwyth, Aberaeron, Lampter or Tregaron.

Fforest Camps, Cardigan ⊜
Teifi, SA43 3AA, T 01239-623633, coldatnight.co.uk.

On their 200 acre forest farm next to the Teifi Marshes Nature Reserve, this is place to sleep under canvas, enjoy the simple pleasures in life and connect with the natural environment without having to deal with any of the inconveniences that nature and the environment can throw up – like mud, or trying to pitch your tent in a force 8 gale in the rain. So it's a little like cheating, but just because it's easy doesn't mean it isn't good. They have three types of 'tents', the geodisic dome being the real highlight as it comes complete with arm chair, wood burner, double bed…heaven. All come ready erected on timber decks with undisturbed countryside views (read privacy) and have separate, covered camp kitchens. Then of course there's the 'crogloft', simple, stylish accommodation sleeping four in a converted farm building. If cooking seems likes chore, fear not the Fforest Lodge in the centre serves up brekkie every day using locally sourced produce as well as dinner twice a week. They have a second site, Manorfon, with cabins, domes and nomads adjacent to Penbryn Beach. April-October from £335/week for two on a B&B basis.

< Home comforts on Yurt Farm.

< Yurt Farm.

Scotland

Russ Shea

< Huge skies and snowcapped peaks.

North of the border, the big country; a land where vistas are huge, snow-capped peaks bring awe and crystal pools that lure the swimmer never fail to draw a shocked intake of breath. Here seasons ring the changes, repainting canvasses thought familiar with fresh tones and adventure. Endless summer days on the north shore see a cursory half hour of dusk drift through before the sun reawakens, drawing the birds out of a confused slumber and once more into song. It may be a time of small swells for the surfer, but the bafflingly turquoise waters that lap against white sand fringes are a kayaker's paradise while high above, climbers scale sun-warmed faces, sheer walls shimmering under calloused fingers. Upland heath sees mountain bikes fast tracking along raised boardwalks, twisting through forest berms in an attempt to outpace winter's cold hand pulling up a white blanket to swathe the highlands and set fresh challenges. Waterfalls, once a source of fluid refreshment, now stand still under axe and crampon as the ice climber scales new heights. The high reaches of the Cairngorms offer the chance to bed in for the night under snow-packed canopies and star-filled skies; close by snowboarders and skiers play on the wide open slopes, leaning through arcing turns, launching off kickers. On the coast the short days are bathed in swell, beaches and reefs reawaken and the gathered surfers thank the god of new technology for the miracle of the modern wetsuit.

❯ There are fresh adventures and new challenges around every corner.

Environment

From the lowlands around Glasgow and Edinburgh it is a surprisingly short trek into the wild. The coastline is within easy access and the peaks of the highlands wait on the horizon. Ben Nevis in the Grampians stands as the UK's highest, at 4409 ft above sea level, while the huge granite peaks of the Cairngorms, the highest, coldest and snowiest plateaux, feature the remaining five of the highest six. While the snow may blanket a magnitude of sins, from toilet waste to rubbish, when it melts, the detritus remains so ensure you take *everything* back down the mountains with you.

Where winter sports once dominated, the summer seasons now see not only climbers and walkers, but a glut of mountain bikers heading for a profusion of quality trails and parks which have seen Scotland blossom as a player in the world MTB scene. Here again, the Foresty Commission has worked with riders on their successful 7Stanes project which has seen the development of a series of quality trails across Scotland's southern regions. The trails here and further afield have been mostly built and maintained to minimize their impact on the environment: from Fort William the boardwalks and trails of the Nevis range protect the upland heaths and boggy gullies from damaging erosion that could take decades to repair. Best to invest in a good map and stick to the designated trails; regrowth in these mountainous regions is a slow and fragile process.

On the north shore, Caithness is a wondrous playground of flat, sedimentary slabstone, perfect for reef formation. This section of coastline is ideal for experienced surfers, with the only environmental black-spot being the nuclear power station at Dounreay. Moving west into Sutherland the coastal landscape morphs into a series of dune-backed sandy bays, where sandbanks and rivermouths peel in isolation.

Thanks to the Land Reform Act and Scottish Outdoor Code, considerate and responsible wild camping is permitted across the majority of Scotland. Wild camping is governed by a set of rules and principles based on minimum impact to the environment and others as well as a bit of common sense. Key considerations include limiting your stay in any one spot to three nights to minimize damage to vegetation, clearing up after yourself and others less considerate, not lighting fires and being intelligent and informed when it comes to toilet hygiene. The excellent Mountaineering Council of Scotland website has a downloadable leaflet, 'Wild Camping, a Guide to Good Practice' with details on how to minimize your impact as well as setting out legal position. Check out mcofs.org.uk.

Climate

Although tempered by the UK's temperate maritime climate, the Scottish highlands can see some savage winter days. Venturing into the mountains in the depth of the cold season is best left to those who are well prepared and experienced. Temperatures can drop to below -10°C during the day and record night time readings have reached below -27°C. The weather changes quickly up here so be aware and be prepared. When winter winds come in from the north and east, snow often follows. For those lovers of wild swimming, be aware that spring meltwater can be very cold, and plunge pools may bring a bit of a shock to the system, while surfing at rivermouths may be appreciably colder than the nearby beach or reef. The warming vestiges of the North Atlantic drift passes the west and northern fringes of Scotland, bringing mild water temperatures in even the winter's full chill meaning line-ups will be less chilly than those found to the south in the North Sea. Expect a balmy 11 or 12°C in the summer, meaning a 4/3 mm is very comfortable but only 6 or 7°C in the winter means a 5/4 mm wetsuits, boots, gloves and hoods are pretty essential.

In summer sunscreen is essential and a high spf is recommended for climbing and walking. Ticks can be picked up while walking and cycling in heather and scrub, while midges can be a nuisance, especially when camping or on very still days. Check midgeforecast.co.uk.

Resources

7stanes.gov.uk Forestry Commission's excellent website detailing routes and resources available across their sites.

scottishmountainbike.com Trail maps and a forum.

mcofs.org.uk Mountaineering Council of Scotland provides invaluable advice for hill walkers, climbers, mountaineers, and ski tourers regarding access and conservation – check their site before heading off into the wild.

adventure.visitscotland.com The Scottish tourist board know what they're doing, the site offers a number of alternatives for those looking to explore the adventurous spirit of the country.

forestry.gov.uk Forestry Commission site with details on dedicated walks.

jmt.org Protecting Scotland's mountains, moorland, coast and woodland, John Muir Trust is a wild land conservation charity.

sais.gov.uk Avalanche information service.

treesforlife.org.uk Charity aiming to restore the Caledonian Forest.

cairngorms.co.uk Official website for the Cairngorms National Park.

news.bbc.co.uk/weather National and local weather forecasts.

mountainbothies.org.uk The invaluable Mountain Bothies Association.

Mountain biking Newcastleton

Provider	DIY
Skill level	Beginner-advanced
Time frame	From 2 hrs
Equipment	Mountain bike, helmet, appropriate clothing, tool kit and spares. Snacks and provisions – there are no café facilities on site
Exertion level	●●●●○

You're barely over the border before you're into the first of the Seven Stanes – a series of dedicated, quality mountain bike trail centres marked out across Scottish Forestry Commission land. Minding its own business in a quiet corner of Scotland's southern reaches, Newcastleton is probably the most over-looked and under-visited of the Stanes sites. But this is all part of the park's surprising charm, along with its two challenging trails, skills area and north shore bike park that is.

The extended and upgraded blue Caddrouns Trail is a great spot for those beginning to explore the pleasures of singletrack and without the pressure of numbers experienced at some other trails, you can take your time to enjoy it and really find your feet. Around half of the 3½ mile trail is singletrack and one of the most memorable sections is the 1¼ miles of Pouter Lampert. Snaking through the forest, the gradual climb brings on a sense of anticipation only matched by the exhilaration felt as the gradient reverses and you are sent back down through a blur of green and repetitious flashes of brown along the wide flowing singletrack, along boardwalks and, if you're ready to give it a go, the rock steps.

For more experienced riders, there is the 10-mile red trail which delivers fast, tight singletrack descents and short climbs as well as access to a challenging, technical north shore section for those who want to really push themselves. The trail links up with Caddrouns to share Pouter Lampert and guarantee a very satisfactory conclusion. For those in search of wider paths, the five miles Linns route sticks to forest roads but that doesn't mean it's all easy pedalling – the Linns Road descent is at a decent enough gradient to pick up a bit of pace and get the adrenaline pumping. Dropping down a gear or two – literally not metaphorically – it's on to the steep Linns Climb, shared with the red route. Nearing the top, a huge lump of granite is revealed, drawing the attention away from the oxygen deficit situation.

Each of the mountain bike centres feature their own 'stane', the Scots word for stone. Like a portal to Scotland, the stone sculpture that stands here, right on the border, has a hole through its centre allowing those with their feet firmly planted in England to peer through and see the Celtic countryside, with its promise of mountain biking possibilities, revealed.

Practicalities

Facilities at the trail head are limited. Aside from car parking and toilets/change facilities at Dykecroft visitor centre, there's nothing else here. Grab a map and hit the trails. In the borders, just 5 miles from England, the village of Newcastleton has broad Georgian streets and good amenities including a bank.

Transport 25 miles away, Carlisle is the handiest train station – from here ride the coast to coast Reivers Trail north, reivers-route.co.uk. Onward bus available Mon-Sat with telfordscoaches.com. No bikes.

Sleeping £££ Sorbietrees, TD9 0TL, T01387-375215, delivers comfortable farmhouse B&B with bike store and wash plus drying room a couple of miles from town. Set in 110 acres, **Rock UK**, Whithaugh Park, TD9 0TY, T01387-375394, offer group lodge-style accommodation – family lodges sleep 4-7. **Camping Lidalia**, TD9 0RU, T01387-375819, is a lovely little site on the edge of the village, open year round.

Eating & drinking The Olive Tree, Hermitage St, Newcastleton, is a family run café and bakery. The butcher sells local produce and meats.

Resources Bike hire is available nearby from **Rock UK**, Whithaugh Park, TD9 0TY, T01387-375394 – 1½ miles from trail head. See 7stanes.gov.uk for comprehensive details including trail maps for the 7 centres.

Also try On the other side of the border, head to Kielder Forest Park, home to the red-graded Lonesome Pine Trail.

∨ The 7stanes trails are well thought-out with clear markers to keep you on track.

> **Lowdown**

ⓘ Directory
Newcastleton, Dumfries & Galloway Dykecroft visitor centre, Dumfries & Galloway, TD9 0TD.

Ⓢ Prices
Free.

Ⓢ Season
Year round.

Ⓞ Don't miss
It's all about Pouter Lampert.

Ⓧ Avoid This is prime midge territory, cover up and ladle on the repellent to stop being eaten alive.

Surfing Pease Bay

Provider	DIY
Skill level	Beginner-advanced
Time frame	Sunrise to sunset
Equipment	Board, wetsuit (5 mm in winter plus boots, gloves and hood)
Exertion level	●●●○○

When a swirling low pressure system pin-wheels off the eastern seaboard of Canada and rolls past Iceland through the North Atlantic, the eyes of Scotland's many surfers are fixed on the weather map. As the depression sweeps through the northern reaches of the North Sea, so its spinning winds generate lines of swell that will come marching out of the Arctic, bearing down on the eastern coastline of the British mainland. Pease Bay, with its northeasterly aspect, lies straight in its path. With winds that blow in from the southwest, there's a chance that these waves will find an offshore breeze awaiting, a perfect formula for the many waveriders who gather on the sandy fringes to welcome the new day and the fresh swell.

Before Thurso was carried into the spotlight on the back of World Tour surf contests, Pease Bay was probably the most famous surfing beach in Scotland. It is the ancestral home of waveriding north of the border, a place where the earliest Scottish boardriders took to the sea and it is still at the very heart of an expanding scene almost 40 years later. This sandy bay is a big draw for those of all abilities and has been the site where many national titles have been decided. Looking down from the hills that watch over it, its allure is apparent. Peaks feather and break along its length while to the south a reefy point offers good righthanders on more challenging days in clean conditions. Surfers' cars and vans jostle for parking, whatever the tide, whatever the weather, for if wind and swell combine, no winter chill can keep the crew from these North Sea sand banks.

At low tide the reefs to the north and south of the bay become exposed, and beginners should stay near the sandy middle section.

Practicalities

Pease Bay rests between Eyemouth to the south and Dunbar to the north, both of which make good bases.

Transport Dunbar is the nearest railway station, 8½ miles to the north.

Sleeping £ The Anchorage B&B, Upper Houndlaw, Eyemouth, TD14 5BU, T01890-750307, eyemouthbb.co.uk. The stone Edwardian townhouse is a short walk from the harbour and town centre. Locally sourced breakfast with vegetarian option. £ Dive St Abbs, St Abbs, TD14 5PW, T01890-771945, offers simple but comfortable bunkhouse accommodation from £17.50/person. There is the great option of the **Press Mains Cottages** near Coldingham, TD14 5TS, T01890-771310, watchbadgers.co.uk. There are 4 cottages available to rent in a quiet, rural location.

Eating & drinking The Creel Restaurant, 25 Lamer St, The Old Harbour, Dunbar EH42 1HJ, T01368-863279, specializes in good quality locally sourced and organic produce.

Resources Puro Nectar Surf Shop, 104 High St, Dunbar, T01368-869810, is well stocked with a good range of equipment from boards, new and used, wetties, to clothes and accessories. Board hire is available as are surf lessons from £35/2 hrs with a BSA instructor, all equipment provided. South of Pease, **St Vedas Surf Shop**, Coldingham Bay, T01890-771679, is also well stocked and offers surf lessons from £35 as well as board and wetsuit hire for £9. See their site for tide information: stvedas.co.uk/tide_times.htm.

Also try Walk from Pease Bay to the unspoilt beauty of Cove Harbour, either at low tide along the shore or via the ¾ mile cliff-top path.

◄ Sam Christopherson – high lines on the East Coast

Surfing Belhaven

Provider	Coast to Coast Surf School
Skill level	Beginner-advanced
Time frame	2 hrs to full day
Equipment	Board, wetsuit and transport from Dunbar provided
Exertion level	●●●○○

Sitting in the clear blue line-up, golden sand shimmering in the summer sun, it's hard to believe that the bustling streets of Edinburgh are just a short hop away to the west. Bass Rock draws the eye, bobbing in the North Sea like a giant icing-topped cake. The shallows are filled with the frenetic energy of a surf lesson, yellow foamies speeding through the white water accompanied by whoops of excitement and smiles that stretch from ear to ear. Out

back a group of surfers exchange chit-chat, with one eye trained on the horizon, scanning for the next approaching set. But all goes quiet as the lines approach. Surfers paddle into position, manoeuvring on to the peak before an explosion of power sees the first accelerate on to the wave, elegantly popping to their feet as they begin to drop down the face, angling left into a graceful bottom turn which leads out on to the open face. The surfer trims and glides along the steep glassy wall, tracing a line along the groomed face, knees bending with the board rising and falling, momentum gained as the board accelerates onward. The thrill of the glide, open carving turns and the chase of the elusive barrel, this is what awaits those who graduate to the whitewater.

> Sam Christopherson Retro Glide.

∨ User-friendly Belhaven is a popular draw for the region.

c2csurfschool

Tony Marsh

Sam Christopherson has been running lessons at Belhaven since 2004, and his Coast to Coast Surf School has quickly become established as one of the best in Scotland. This beach was chosen due to the regular swells that arrive here from the passing low pressures, as well as the beginner friendly characteristics of the waves that break here. "The school was set up to provide high quality surf instruction," explains Sam, "introducing newcomers to ideal beginner beaches while emphasizing safety and wave etiquette." The main element in any beginners' environment is fun, but there is more to surfing than merely getting to your feet and riding to the beach – there is a beach culture and a set of rules that enhance safety and respect in the water. Wave priority, where to paddle out and the dangers of rip-currents are all part of a well-rounded learning experience. C2C is also conscious of the environment in which it operates, organizing beach clean-ups and campaigning on issues such as beach parking. "The Surf School has a new surf base next to Dunbar's train station and a surf café next door," says Sam. "We will be offering free surf lifts from the station to the beach for all our train customers." This means surfers from Edinburgh can hit the waves by rail, keeping their carbon footprint low by sharing a lift and the stoke out to Belhaven. "One of the good things about this region of the east coast is we have very long summer day light hours and consistent offshore wind, so we can make the most of any summer swells," explains Sam.

A forty-minute walk from the centre of Dunbar, Belhaven is a great spot for beginners although if you have never surfed before it is highly recommended you take lessons first. There are also peaks here to entertain more experienced purveyors of the glide.

Practicalities

The elegant seaside town of Dunbar has plenty of amenities as well as a growing surf community.

Transport On the East Coast main line, regular trains run to Dunbar from Edinburgh (27 mins) and Newcastle (60 mins) eastcoast.co.uk.

Sleeping On the cliffs, the family £££ **The Rocks**, Marine Rd, EH42 1AR, T01368-862287, experiencetherocks.co.uk, offers very comfortable rooms delivering views over the bay and Bass Rock. The bar has a good range of real ales while the restaurant focuses on local produce. In the beautiful **John Muir Country Park**, Belhaven Bay Caravan and Camping Park, EH42 1TS, T01368-865956, meadowhead.co.uk, is south of the beach. Open Mar-Oct with statics also available, it holds the David Bellamy gold award for conservation.

Eating & drinking The Creel Restaurant, 25 Lamer St, The Old Harbour, Dunbar EH42 1HJ, T01368-863279, specializes in good quality locally sourced and organic produce with a focus on seafood. **Coast Café**, Station Rd, is the C2C crew's café and is a great place to drop into for a warming bowl of soup or a sarnie. In the winter check for surf film nights, during the warmer months bands often pop in to play a set or two. For a cheap bite, Sam recommends the **Volunteer Arms**, Victoria St, named for the lifeboat crews.

Resources As well as a range of courses from basic lessons to sunset surfs and long weekends, C2C offers board and wetsuit hire from £20 for those who want to practise their newly acquired skills. **Puro Nectar Surf Shop**, 104 High St, Dunbar, T01368-869810, is well stocked with a good range of kit from boards, new and used, wetties, to clothes and accessories.

Also try For those who have progressed into the line-up, C2C offers a regular timetable of surf tours to some of Scotland's best waves, from long weekends in Thurso, to a week chasing down world-class breaks in the Hebrides during the Summer Solstice. Where better to hone those new-found skills, what better backdrop for the trim and glide than a golden Celtic evening on a North Shore beach.

> Lowdown

❶ Directory
Coast to Coast Surf School, Station Rd, Dunbar, EH42 1JX. T07971-990361, c2csurfschool.com.

❸ Prices
£35 for a 2-hr lesson, including transport from Dunbar and all equipment. A surf day is £60.

❸ Season
Mar-Nov.

❶ Don't miss
Named for the naturalist, conservationist and explorer, The John Muir Country Park covers a stunning stretch of East Lothian coastline and marshland between Dunbar Castle and Peffer Burn, a haven for wildlife and great for a stomp.

❽ Avoid The last weekend in Sep can be busy during the Dunbar Traditional Music Festival featuring traditional Scottish music to bluegrass and skiffle.

Mountain biking Glentress

Provider	DIY
Skill level	All
Time Frame	2 hrs +
Equipment	Mountain bike, helmet, map, provisions, appropriate gear and a repair kit/spare tube
Exertion level	●●●●○

Traditionally borders are a place of conflict. The arbitrary drawing of lines and divisions in a landscape fuelling jealous rivalries, bitter skirmishes, long fought battles and hard won feuds. The Scottish Borders territory, encompassing 1,800 sq miles of moorlands, uplands, wide plains and rocky coastline, is no exception. And while wars no longer rage here, deep in the heart of the Tweed Valley claret is spilled with a violent regularity by cross border raiders seeking to plunder the riches of the Glentress Forest. This is no battleground, rather a proving ground where skinned kneecaps and shins the colour of brooding skies are worn like badges of honour. This is a rolling landscape, cut by deep valleys and meandering burns, camouflaged beneath a blanket of towering Scots pines, shimmering

beech and dense ferns. This is Glentress, the feather in the cap of the 7Stanes and one of the best MTB venues the UK has to offer.

Those looking for the complete deal of challenging trails, epic rides and top notch facilities have arrived. Perennial award winner, the forest delivers four quality trails, a skills area as well as a freeride park, providing enough challenges and terrain to keep new off-road recruits, singletrack stalwarts and expert skill seekers happy. The all-weather trails here are well thought out, leaving from two main hubs – Buzzard's Nest and Osprey car park – which manages the ranks whose numbers swell in the summer months and pretty much any given weekend. Leaving from Osprey, the Glentress Red Route is the classic here for intermediate riders looking to push themselves. It delivers big on its promises of fast flowing descents like Spooky Wood, tough climbs throughout and obligatory challenges of rocks and rooty sections, with berms, jumps, log skinnies and northshore thrown in for good measure. The 11 miles trail is constantly evolving and currently stands at 65% singletrack cut with forest road. If you need to,

> ❯ Perennial award winner, Glentress delivers four quality trails, a skills area as well as a freeride park.

❮ The forest has more than 300,000 visitors a year, the majority of whom have a predilection for fat tyres and singletrack.

Wig Worland

photo: Wig Worland

sneak in a quick breather at the Pennels Vennel picnic benches – just whip out your camera and snap the views to justify your actions.

If you're new to singletrack or are looking to rekindle your love of mountain biking, the skills area is a must-go zone. The loop is short – just one mile – but packs in plenty of challenges to build confidence on unfamiliar terrain from short sections of raised timber trail to rock gardens. This is not just the domain of the novice, it's good for honing skills at any level. The 2½ miles Green Route that leaves from Buzzard's Nest is also ideal, combining a good mix of forest road, singletrack and epic views. The Blue Route takes it to the next level and after a forest road warm up from the trail head it's straight into singletrack, climbing alongside the majestic Douglas firs. The trail can be ridden as five miles or 10 miles taking in the upper loop (which can also be tackled alone from the Buzzard's Nest) and some sweeping descents. With technical sections this is not a soft option.

Experienced riders who revel in a challenge and want to stretch their legs can opt to tackle the Black Route which includes memorable sections like Britney Spears – a short sharp burst of descent which will leave you wanting to hit it one more time – do you see what they did there? The 18-mile trail is tough and technical, including a 427-ft ascent but the pay-offs are worth it. Take yourself off to the Hub Café and reward yourself with a slice of cake.

> **Lowdown**

ⓘ Directory
Glentress Forest, Peebles, EH45 8NB.

➎ Prices
Car parking from £3 to assist trail maintenance.

☉ Season
Year round.

ⓞ Don't miss
Coffee and cake at the Hub, brain child of former pro MTB champions Emma Guy and Tracy Brunger.

✖ Avoid
If you can, try to avoid weekends in the height of summer as this is the busiest time.

Practicalities

The Hub has everything you need from bike shop and café to changing facilities and showers. The towns of Peebles and Innerleithen are separated by about 5 miles and have a good split of accommodation and amenities between them – as well as about 50 miles of charted trails!

Transport Edinburgh Waverley train station, 25 miles to the north, has regular onward bus links to the forest with First, firstgroup.com – no bikes.

Sleeping ££ **Millbank B&B**, High St, Innerleithen, T01896-831399, is run by MTBers so has kit room, workshop and bike wash. **The Bike Lodge**, High St, Innerleithen, T01896-833836, thebikelodge.co.uk, is ideal for groups. Sleeping up to 6 people in 3 en suite rooms with living space and bike store. From £650/week. There are 2 okay campsites in Peebles close to the trails open Easter-Oct. **Crossburn Caravan Park**, EH45 8ED, T01721-720501, on the edge of town, and **Rosetta Holiday Park**, EH45 8PG, T01721-720770, basic facilities. There is 'posh' camping at **Glentress Forest Lodge**, Linnburn Farm, Peebles, EH45 8NA, T01721-721007. Comfortable 'wigwams' sleep up to 5. Bike storage. Open year round from £35/night for 2 people.

Eating & drinking Post ride, slump into **The Hub Café**, T01721-722104, at the main Osprey car park. Using fresh ingredients and local suppliers they serve up good honest grub. In nearby Peebles, **The Sunflower**, Bridgegate, T01721-722420, is run by mountain bikers, serving up home-baked goodies, as well as more substantial fare. Mon-Sat, 1000-1500 plus Thu-Sat 1800-2100.

Resources 7stanes.gov.uk is an excellent resource with detailed route info and mapping available to download. **The Hub Bike**, Osprey Car Park, Glentress Forest, T01721-721736, is well stocked with hardware, accessories and CyTech qualified mechanics who offer both services and repairs. Bike hire available (bring photo ID) – hardtail Konas from £22/day and demo fleet bikes from £40/day, helmets included. Booking advised. Skills courses available for all levels, including women-only tuition. Essentials full-day course from £99 includes lunch, afternoon tea and uplift to Buzzard's Nest car park. Covers all the key skills including control, braking, cornering and anticipating the trail.

Also try If you're looking for downhill, head to Innerleithen, a few miles southeast of Glentress. A staging post for the British Downhill Series, the trails here are graded extreme, so experienced riders only need apply. It is home to waymarked DH tracks and a red-graded XC trail. Uplift available with Uplift Scotland £32/day, booking essential, T07709-144299. 7stanes.gov.uk for maps and overviews.

Canyoning Falls of Bruar

Provider	Nae Limits
Skill level	All levels
Time frame	From a few hours to a full day
Equipment	All canyoning and safety equipment provided. Remember to bring a dry change of clothes
Exertion level	●●●●○

Water babbling over rock, tree-lined river banks where the moss grows thick, and the call of wild birds in the air; the waters that flow fast and clear through Perthshire have for centuries drawn visitors eager to experience its serenity, calm and natural beauty. But those in search of tranquillity are not alone. In the last 20 years the rivers have drawn a new sort of visitor, a visitor hungry for the throb of adrenaline in their veins, a visitor seeking the jaw-dropping force of nature as it surges across exposed granite and down plunging gorges, a visitor keen to try the sport that has taken Europe by storm: canyoning.

Eager to demonstrate that canyoning is very different from gorge walking, Nae Limits was set up in 2001, an adventure travel company that offers a range of canyoning experiences all of which guarantee to send pulses racing. "Canyoning is basically a vertical descent down the course of a mountainous river by any means possible," explains John Mason-Strang, who runs Nae Limits with his wife Kate, "that means sliding, jumping, abseiling, scrambling and whitewater swimming; it's fast paced and furious but also a great way to see the beautiful scenery that the river has to offer."

John, Kate and their team of instructors and guides run three different canyoning trips at a range of sites tailored to suit all ability – and energy – levels. Each trip starts with a full safety briefing, equipment fitting and introduction to canyoning to make sure everyone is informed, comfortable and safe throughout the course. Trying on wetsuits and buoyancy aids then testing out helmets and harnesses in the comfort of the adventure centre's warm, dry changing facilities, while essential, also

serves to get the heart beating faster with thoughts of the cold, wet and wild conditions to come.

From Pitlochry HQ, the guides lead the way, transporting the group to one of Nae Limits' exclusive canyoning sites where crowds and queueing just don't factor and the fun begins. From the rock sliding and small jumps of the Lower Bruar Canyon's 'Adrenaline Shot' to the big drop plunge pools, tricky traverses and massive rope lowers of the 'Bruar Extreme' there's something for everyone, although whatever level of trip you take, getting very wet is obligatory.

Walking down narrow muddy tracks between towering tree trunks, the sun dappling through the leaves, it's hard to believe what awaits you. However, before long you're stepping into a harness ready to abseil down a vertical rock face, sliding

◄ Abseiling down a vertical rock face into the heart of an 100 ft waterfall, all part of a day's work.

Nae Limits

Nae Limits

Practicalities

Less than half a mile away from Nae Limits' base in Ballinluig, Pitlochry is a picturesque town surrounded by woodland on the banks of the River Tummel and with the dramatic skyline of Ben Vrackie in the distance. Peppered with Victorian architecture, exciting independent shops, and a diverse range of restaurants and pubs, Pitlochry has more to offer than its neighbouring village so makes a better base if you are thinking of staying in the area. Accommodation is plentiful and ranges from self-catering cottages through to historic inns and high end hotels.

Transport   Pitlochry is served by a train station and coach service; citylink.com.

Sleeping   A 19th-century coaching house in the village itself, **££ The Ballinluig Inn**, PH9 0LG, T01796-482242, has 8 en suite bedrooms offering comfortable, simple accommodation, a roaring fire and a good choice of ales. For something special, try the **£££ East Haugh Country Hotel**, T01796-473121, easthaugh.co.uk – 4-star accommodation in a 350-year-old turreted stone house full of character. The bar and restaurant menus feature local produce only including ingredients from the vegetable garden, seafood from the Western Isles and, in season, local game shot by the chef. For a touch of the great outdoors, Nae Limits recommends **Faskally Campsite**, PH16 5LD, T01796-472007, faskally.com, on the outskirts of Pitlochry, a tranquil, pretty, relaxed site by the river, with space for tents and tourers as well as static caravans and holiday chalets.

Eating & drinking   The award-winning **Moulin Inn**, T01796-472196, complete with its own brewery, is a popular destination for good quality pub food and a great atmosphere, or try the **Port na Craig**, PH16 5ND, T01796-472777, a 17th-century inn and restaurant just a short riverside stroll away from the town centre, serving high end, locally sourced Scottish cuisine. John recommends **The Old Armoury**, T01796-474281, restaurant and tearooms using local, seasonal produce with a large garden, perfect for afternoon teas in the sunshine.

Resources   For information on what's around and about Pitlochry check out pitlochry.org.

Also try   If the Bruar Extreme canyoning experience isn't enough for you and you're after a double dose of adrenaline, Nae Limits also runs whitewater rafting excursions, where frantic paddling, screeching and flying high over river rapids as you catapult downstream are all the name of the game. Available year round on the River Tay and a wide range of other rivers when the time is right from £38.50/person.

down waterfalls, wading through rivers and slipping over wet granite to plunge deep into fresh, clear pools. Although high energy, there are pauses and slower sections on each excursion, giving you time to breathe before the next heart stopping leap or challenging climb.

Throughout every excursion one thing that remains consistent is the excitement, passion and infectious sense of adventure that Nae Limit's instructors exude, which is no coincidence. All of the company's staff are carefully selected for their positive attitude and love of the outdoors as well as their skills and experience. So it's no surprise to learn that the hard work they put in to making all their activities as enjoyable as possible has paid off, resulting in numerous awards for their adventure provision, including four-star accreditation from Visit Scotland. If you are looking for a more dynamic and exciting way to experience the beautiful Scottish countryside, canyoning with Nae Limits certainly fits the bill.

> **Lowdown**

❶ **Directory**
Nae Limits, Ballinluig nr Pitlochry, Perthshire, PH9 0LG, T08450-178177, naelimits.co.uk.

❸ **Prices**
From £45/person.

❂ **Season**
Apr-Oct.

❂ **Don't miss**
The 120-ft waterfall abseil on the full-day excursion; a must for adrenaline junkies.

❂ **Avoid**   Don't just turn up at the activity centre. Check your booking confirmation for the location you should be heading to.

Snowboarding Cairngorms

Provider	DIY
Skill level	Novice-experienced
Time Frame	1 day +
Equipment	Snowboard, boots, technical clothing, gloves, goggles, helmet. All can be hired
Exertion level	●●●●○

From here the couloir drops steeply away, channelling your field of vision down through the winding passage, the high white walls stark against the deep blue overhead. The light spindrift dances over the surface, giving the illusion of waves moving through the snowfield with the breeze. Thighs still burn from the hike, but the steady loping climb through the bleached landscape has been worth every step, for the view over the edge reveals a virgin run, unscarred by carving edge, unbroken by snaking lines. The joys of off piste hiking can bring the ultimate rewards and a little local knowledge goes a long way. A nod from your guide and the tension of goggles realigned, followed by the ritual of gloved fingers clapped together. Edging forward, the nose of the board breaks the surface as gravity begins its pull, that brief moment before acceleration and adrenaline kick in, weight skewed on back foot; floating, gliding, looking across the slope to nail that first arcing turn, that glistening rooster tail of crystals that splashes a spectrum across the building zephyr.

For those who think that bluebird days are a plane ride away, think again; the mountains of Scotland can provide classic riding. Whether you are a beginner on the nursery slopes, or a seasoned veteran of Alaskan heli-boarding, there's enough here to leave anyone with a broad grin and an aching body. As the UK's most successful snowboarder, Lesley McKenna knows a thing or two about the world's best boarding terrain, and for her the slopes around Cairngorm can be up there with the best. "My favourite run on Cairngorm is actually Aladdin's Couloir," says Lesley,

Russ Shea

◄ Classic bluebird days in the Cairngorms.

Practicalities

With a rich variety of terrains from heather moorlands and ancient pine forests to ice walls and a mountain range at its heart, the Cairngorms National Park was formed in 2003. With good amenities, Aviemore is a popular base.

Transport Aviemore train station is 8 miles from the mountain. Take the sleeper from London Euston and arrive at 0745 the next morning. Regular onward bus service: stagecoachbus.com.

Sleeping There are a number of hostels in the area. **£ The Lazy Duck Hostel**, Nethy Bridge, Invernesshire, PH25 3ED, T01479-821642, lazyduck.co.uk. One of the best hostels you could hope to find, open year round. Wood-clad bunkhouse with comfortable 'sleeping gallery' and wooden bunks, well-equipped kitchen, woodburner and Wi-Fi. The down side – it is small, sleeping 8, so gets full quickly. Apr-Oct. Low impact camping for 4 small tents also available, complete with hammock to chill out in. Twenty mins drive from Cairngorm, or just ski from the door. . .

Eating & drinking Grab a bite at the UK's highest restaurant, **Ptarmigan Restaurant**, T01479-861336, which converts local produce into warming soups and other hearty fare. 0900-1630 winter, 1000-1700 summer. **Mountain Café**, Grampian Rd, Aviemore utilizes some of the best local produce to create healthy, wholesome food. **The Ord Ban**, Rothiemurchus Centre, Inverdurie, PH22 1QH, T01479-810005, is all about seasonal cooking and local produce. **Woodshed Bar,** Coylumbridde Hotel, Aviemore, is the place to enjoy a bit of après-ski.

Resources The Snowboard School, Cairngorm, PH22 1RB, T08455-191191, thesnowboardschool.co.uk, offers lessons for all abilities. Based on level 3 of the Day Lodge, Cairngorm Mountain they are a not for profit organization working in partnership with Cairngorm Mountain Ltd. For backcountry guiding contact G2 Outdoor who also cover a few essential skills such as using transceivers and avalanche awareness.

Also try With a vast area of high plateau, steep sided glens and dramatic cliff lined corries, the Cairngorms with their sub-arctic eco-system, provide plenty of opportunity for high-level walking. Mountain Innovations offers a 2-day, 18-mile walk, incorporating 1500 ft of ascent though the spectacular mountain pass of Lairig Ghru. With the gold award for Green Tourism they have a 'leave nothing, take only photographs' policy and offer a £15 green travel discount for guests arriving by public transport. £295 Price inclusive of full board, transport to the mountains and transfers. **Mountain Innovations**, Boat of Garten, Invernesshire, PH24 3BN, T01479-831331, scotmountain.co.uk.

"a steep and narrow off-piste run to the west of the Head Wall. It is one of the best free-ride runs I have ever done if the snow is good." But she also advises anyone venturing off-piste to make sure they go with a good guide. They'll help you get away from the crowds, but also keep you safe in an environment where conditions can change amazingly quickly.

Cairngorm Mountain tops out at 3600 ft, and offers 18½ miles of pisted riding area with 11 lifts. The longest run is two miles but for those who prefer freestyling to freeriding, there is also the Vans Terrain Park located in the Ptarmigan Bowl near the top. With its mixture of kickers, rails and ramps, it offers a great variety of terrain. Cairngorm also benefits from a funicular railway that rises to a height of 3599 ft, giving access to the widespread runs, from the red and black runs down the West Wall across to the blue and green runs of the Coire Cas. While the snowfall in the Scottish resorts can sometimes be a little hit and miss in comparison with their continental cousins, with everything from fresh backcountry to miles of well-groomed piste, Cairngorm is proving an increasingly popular choice for those who want to minimize their carbon footprint but still leave footprints in the snow.

For those who are looking to find their feet on the large nursery slopes, The Snowboard School, part of Cairngorm Snowsports, is a not-for-profit organization with an excellent range of one-off lessons to full course packages available through the winter months to get you up and riding and away. If you have no idea and no gear, there is a great network of hire facilities where everything from goggles to boots, boards and jackets are available. Want to move on to the next level? Then there are lessons for all abilities whether you need to nail a simple Indy grab or master a McTwist. Day instruction and lift pass package from £63 for adults, or £79 inclusive of boots and board also.

< 18½ miles of pisted riding is on offer for those looking to minimize their carbon footprint but still leave footprints in the snow.

> **Lowdown**

❶ Directory
Cairngorm Mountain, Aviemore, Invernesshire, PH22 1RD, T01479-861261, cairngormmountain.co.uk.

❷ Prices
Adult lift pass from £20/half day, £96/4 day tickets, board and boot hire from £20.

❸ Season
Winter (check website for snowfall update).

❹ Don't miss
For the experienced, get off-piste with a good guide – it will open up a whole new Scottish boarding experience.

❺ Avoid
Never venture into the backcountry without a guide. There is an avalanche danger as well as the risk of entering dangerous terrain.

Winter climbing Cairngorms

Provider	Glenmore Lodge
Skill level	Intermediate-advanced
Time frame	2 days
Equipment	They can supply crampons, ice axe, helmet, plastic boots, climbing harness and all technical climbing equipment and hardware plus basic waterproofs. Ensure you have adequate warm clothing including thermals and insulating layers, decent waterproof jacket and over trousers, ski goggles, mittens and gloves, plus essentials including whistle, compass, map, head torch, survival bag
Exertion level	●●●●●

On the walk in to a climb it's easy for your mind to wander. Ambling under the summer sun, you look up the valley at the vertical walls rising ahead, and find yourself imagining what it must be like on the frigid, desiccated South Summit.

Striking out towards the Hillary Step, going for the wind-scoured summit of Everest, one foot trudging slowly in front of the other as you cross the roof of the world. Or to be faced with the Traverse of the Gods, clinging to the sheer, mighty, massive face of the Eiger, trying not to think of the Spider, the Exit Cracks, or dream of the Summit Icefield. What it must be like to hear the clatter and whizz of rocks skimming down the face, and to tuck in, hoping they're not heading your way. On this bright, balmy afternoon you try to imagine the technical ability required to stay alive, crampons scrabbling over rock and ice, spindrift blowing off the face, all the time focusing on making sure that every step is perfectly placed, every anchor is securely placed.

∨ Pausing for thought to drink in the vistas above Loch Morlich.

Glenmore Lodge

To be able to sample just what it might be like to push yourself out into the wild, to get a taster of what the high Alpine and Himalayan adventurers feel, that is what winter climbing in the Highlands of Scotland offers. If your mind is scrambling up vertical faces and taking on the technical challenges of climbing in the big white but your body is not yet equipped to follow, then Glenmore Lodge's Weekend Introduction to Winter Climbing is an ideal opportunity to cement a solid foundation and develop core winter climbing skills. Don't worry about being sent out to lead pitches on this weekend, it's about becoming a competent second and developing confidence in these challenging conditions. There is a two-person team with each instructor, meeting on the first morning to discuss experience levels and aims, enabling your instructor to plan the relevant programme. To get the most out of this course, you need to have experience of summer rock climbing, and a familiarity with winter hillwalking using crampons and ice axes is certainly an advantage, but if you're a little rusty there is a recap of core winter skills on the first morning. The specific aims of the two days include basic rope work, tying in to multiple point anchors and belaying. Climbing over a variety of mediums in crampons and with ice tools as well as climbing technique on ice and mixed ground is a core focus, as well as escaping from winter multi-pitch climbs.

Being on the hill in these extreme conditions presents specific challenges to the winter climber and there are inherent safety issues that are discussed. Avalanche awareness and the choice of safe route is a fascinating subject and is an ongoing topic out on the climb, as well during an evening talk. For those who have not yet committed to buying expensive equipment such as crampons and ice axes, Glenmore Lodge can supply equipment to try out, to help you make an informed purchase. The staff and other students are always a great source of advice on just what will fit your requirements. This is one of the great aspects of climbing courses, not only the essential skills gleaned from the tutors, but the social interaction with fellow students help make these weekends such great fun. There's even a pool and sauna at the Lodge, to help ease those aching muscles, or a climbing wall for those who just can't get enough.

> Getting to grips with ice-axe technique.

Glenmore Lodge

> Lowdown

❶ Directory
Glenmore Lodge, Aviemore, Inverness-shire, PH22 1QU, T01479-861256, glenmorelodge.org.uk.

❻ Prices
£320.

❽ Season
Winter.

❶ Don't miss
The 20 ft-high climbing wall back at the lodge, if your arms have anything left to give that is, or failing that the sauna.

❽ Avoid
Being cold on the mountains can be extremely serious, ensure you have adequate layers and warm clothing for the course.

Practicalities

Glenmore Lodge, Scotland's National Outdoor Training Centre, is based in the heart of the Cairngorms National Park, close to Glenmore Village, about 8 miles from Aviemore. They offer an all inclusive experience including equipment, accommodation and food and hold the gold award for Green Tourism, minimizing their impact and supporting a number of local and national environmental initiatives. The Glenmore Lodge Mountain Rescue Team works closely with and offers support to Cairngorm Mountain Rescue and RAF Search and Rescue.

Transport Trains run into Aviemore with direct services from London with GNER and a Scotrail sleeper service. There is also a service from Citylink, citylink.co.uk, and Megabus megabus.com, from Edinburgh and Glasgow. The number 34 bus leaves Aviemore from outside the railway station and police station at hourly intervals; travelinescotland.com. Transfers are available on arrival and departure days for those booked on courses, but need to be booked with the lodge in advance.

Sleeping All accommodation is provided at the Glenmore Lodge. Most rooms are twin and en suite and there is a kit drying room for wet gear. Extra nights can be booked at a cost of £25-31/person. In the grounds, self-catering chalets are also available sleeping 4 from £70 in bunks and twins.

Eating & drinking The Lochain Bar serves a wide variety of Scottish beers and whiskys, as well as meals prepared from locally sourced produce.

Also try Glenmore Lodge offers a full range of mountain sport and paddle courses for all levels. From Jan-Mar. For those with a good level of ski and hill fitness, they offer a 5-day introduction to ski mountaineering which covers skiing on and off piste, safely traversing mountainous terrain on skis plus navigation and route planning as well as technical sessions including avalanche awareness and belaying.

Snow Hole Expedition Cairngorms

Provider	Mountain Innovations
Skill level	Intermediate-experienced
Time frame	3 days
Equipment	Rucksack, good gloves and spares, technical jacket and trousers, goggles, sleeping bag and mat. Ice axe, crampons and other technical gear can be hired. Check website for full list
Exertion level	●●●●●

Paul Tomkins VS/Mountain Innovations

Patagonia, Winter 2009. The wind scours the surface of the mountain, a bleached white shroud descending with a tempest that burns exposed skin and tugs at flapping hoods. A howling wail fills the air, a resonance felt deep within chilled bones. "I knew that in these conditions, out here in Patagonia, survival was on a knife edge," says climber Alex Palmer. "A tent would not survive, it would be blow down and we would get hypothermia." Who knows how long the storm will last, how long the group will have to ride out the white-out. "It's a strange feeling knowing that if I wandered too far I could disappear and probably never find my way back. It's a sobering thought. Crawling back into the snow hole all was quiet and calm. It was like the violence raging outside didn't exist. It was our safe haven." Inside, the snow cave is an oasis. With the swirling night air at minus twenty on the mountain face, here, illuminated by candles, the ambient temperature sits just below freezing. Wrapped up in warm down, this cave carved into the mountains white crust is home. It is the difference between surviving and not.

Learning how to build a snow hole is not only an indispensable winter skill for the serious winter climber or walker, it is also a fun and rewarding challenge. Out on the Cairngorm/Ben Macdui plateau in somewhat Arctic conditions it is easy to imagine you are thousands of miles from civilisation as you trek onwards through the deep snow, wind biting at any exposed skin offered up. Snow holes here require snow of about 10 ft vertical depth, and there is some serious digging involved in sculpting out your cool retreat. The

snow holes built on this course are designed specifically for Scottish conditions, with a vaulted roof for good ventilation. Ambient temperatures on these mountains rarely drop below minus eight, so the design of the snow hole aids the venting of warm air to prevent the snow of the cave from reaching melting point, something you may not imagine is possible while you're working out in the chill constructing your communal mountainside accommodation. With body heat, cooking and lights it's amazing the warmth that can be generated but, as you learn, cooking and water melting creates carbon monoxide within the insulated cocoon so adequate ventilation needs to be maintained. It's all about location, location, location and up on this mountain, surveying is an essential skill – avalanche risk needs to be assessed and dangerous slopes avoided. Up here on the mountain, environmental issues are also addressed and the 'Pack it in and pack it out' principles are followed. With snow that

∧ Digging in for the night.

> Finessing the edges.

often lingers until September, and many sites lying close to water courses, issues like human waste are also addressed.

Overnighting in a snow hole is a uniquely rewarding experience. With the group tucked into the blue tinged candle-lit snow cave, only the stars of the Cairngorm skies linger outside in the night time cold to admire the fruits of their labours; the guide rustles up a cracking supper to enjoy in the cosy comfort of sleeping bags. Priceless.

Mountain Innovations run this excellent three-day and four-night course. Day one covers essential winter skills training, before embarking on a two day expedition where the fine art of designing and building your snow hole in a safe site is learnt. All relevant techniques and safety tips are passed on before everyone overnights in the communal snow hole. The days involve four to five hours of walking with a pack and there will be three hours of heavy digging so a good degree of fitness and stamina will be required. Those looking to embark on the adventure should have had some previous hill walking experience, preferably in winter though this isn't essential.

> Dinner in bed – just what you need after three hours of heavy digging.

Practicalities

Established in 1998 by Andrew and Rebecca, Mountain Innovations holds the Gold award for Green Tourism thanks to their 'leave nothing, take only photos' approach to the environment and offer a £15 green travel discount to those arriving by public transport. As a highly qualified mountaineer, Andy and his team offer a range of holidays through the year from mountain walking to navigation and winter skills. All courses are inclusive of full board and accommodation as well as transport to and from the hill and transport between Aviemore train station and the centre.

Transport Trains run into Aviemore with direct services from London with GNER and a Scotrail sleeper service. Mountain Innovations operate an onward transfer service.

Sleeping Aside from overnighting in the snow hole, all accommodation is provided at the Froach Lodge with 6 twin rooms, woodburner heated dining rooms and comfortable lounge with open fire. The lodge is low impact, radiators are fed from a biomass boiler fuelled by Scottish wood pellets and all biodegradable waste is composted, some of which is used to feed the veggie patch.

Eating & drinking On-site, tasty, wholesome 2-course evening meals are prepared making the most of home-grown organic ingredients while bread is baked daily. The fantastic home-made cakes that greet the returning party are devoured in minutes. For an evening night cap, relax in leather sofas by the open fire in the **Boat Hotel**'s bar with one of the local malts (boathotel.co.uk).

Also try Boat of Garten is also known as the Osprey Village, as it was here the birds reintroduced themselves in the fifties. They can be seen nesting at the RSPB Osprey Centre and hunting along the River Spey. Check out rspb.co.uk and search for Loch Garten where they have an osprey blog.

> **Lowdown**

ⓘ Directory
Mountain Innovations, Froach Lodge, Deshar Road, Boat of Garten, Invernesshire, PH24 3BN, T01479-831331, scotmountain.co.uk.

Θ Prices
£390.

⊙ Season
Jan-Mar.

⊙ Don't miss
The awesome views.

⊗ Avoid
Don't leave anything on the mountain – even an apple core.

Mountain biking Coast to Coast

Provider	Scottish Mountain Bike Guides
Skill level	Intermediate-advanced
Time frame	7 days
Equipment	Mountain bike, helmet, basic tools and spares, inner tubes, bike pump, multi tool, appropriate clothing
Exertion level	●●●●●

Turning your back on the natural pleasures afforded by Fort William may initially feel alien, after all, this is an area renowned for its mountain biking potential, championship quality terrain and charted downhill territory. But pushing off you feel legs, cramped too long under office desks, and deadlines begin to unfurl. Shoulders relax and feelings of uncertainty disappear as the Great Glen Cycle route leads you away from the thronging hum of adventurists and deep into forest, letting the calming waters wash over you as you skirt the great inland lakes, weaving your way to the head of Loch Ness. Day one, 31 miles down, another 162 miles to go. Legs warmed up and ready to ride.

The Coast to Coast is an epic week-long expedition bisecting Scotland west to east, taking in classic high mountain passes, miles of technical, heart thumping singletrack and silent wooded glens as you navigate the stunning green and purple mottled terrain on offer between Fort William and Montrose. "The Coast to Coast gives you a taste of everything that Scottish mountain biking has to offer," says an enthusiastic Phil McKane, experienced SMBLA trails leader and owner of Scottish Mountain Bike Guides who run the tour.

Gauging abilities, encouraging you on, day two sees you guided into the Corrieyarick Pass – a climb of some 2559 ft up an 18th-century military road leading out from Fort Augustus. But according to the usual rules of engagement, what goes up, must come down and the pass does so in grand style, delivering around 12 miles of descent with the odd hairpin bend thrown in for good measure. As well as bagging a Munro, taking in the royal pleasures of Balmoral and spending a day burning round the

Cairngorms, the seven day mission also manages to find time to spend a morning exploring the Lagan Wolftrax trail centre which delivers some of the most challenging routes in the country. With legs weary and souls recharged, the final day of the odyssey descends into Montrose. Having absent-mindedly brushed a hand over the waters of Loch Eil at the journey's start, dipping at least a toe in the frigid North Sea that washes the shores of the bay here seems like a fitting conclusion. Coast to Coast, done.

Practicalities

The tour is all inclusive from transfers to Glasgow at the start and end of the journey, quality bunkhouse accommodation, qualified guide with good local knowledge, luggage transfer – the support crew delivers baggage to each overnight stop. Overnight your bikes are prepped for the next day's journey by support elves and any problems fixed.

Transport Transfers are organized from Glasgow train stations – Queen St station if coming from the north or east, Central if coming from the south or west.

Sleeping Included for the duration, but at the end of the tour **£ Glasgow Hostel**, Park Terrace, T0141-3323004, is a handy pit stop with secure bike store, drying room, Wi-Fi access and the silver award for Green Tourism.

Eating & drinking Majority of meals for the duration of the trip are catered for and included but it is worth packing some high energy snacks if you need a quick refuel en route.

Also try For a wilderness MTB experience, try the 3-day self-sufficient expedition of Ben Nevis and the Mamore Mountains. The 47-mile tour explores testing terrain that lies in the shadows of Scotland's highest peak involving 4-6 hrs of challenging riding each day. The nights are spent camping wild, which means coming to terms with using a bike trailer is a real necessity. £145 for the 3-day trip includes guiding, transfers and the majority of meals, rope in 2 mates and get it booked.

⌄ This week-long expedition delivers a taste of everything that Scottish mountain biking has to offer mixed with a decent dose of escapism.

> Lowdown

❶ **Directory**
Scottish Mountain Bike Guides, Largs, Scotland, KA29 0WX, T01475-740414, scottishmountain bikeguides.com.

❷ **Prices**
£525.

❸ **Season**
Year round.

❹ **Don't miss**
The Laggan Wolftrax Trails Centre Centre midway though the journey – fast flowing, technical singletrack, boulder fields, slab features, the works.

❺ **Avoid**
If you want to steer clear of the bunkhouse experience, don't forget to upgrade to B&B digs for the duration – an extra £75.

Kite surfing Fraserburgh

Provider	Synergy
Skill level	All
Time frame	2-day entry level IKO course, 2-days on the level 3 IKO course
Equipment	All kite surfing and safety equipment provided. Remember to bring a warm dry change of clothes including a hat and gloves at any time of year
Exertion level	●●●●●

For many, a blustery autumn day in Aberdeenshire is a cue to batten down the hatches, but for the dedicated few it's a reason to pack the van and head to the coast, raring to harness the power of the wind and skim across the sea.

When the exposed sand dunes of Fraserburgh Bay meet with the full force of the North Sea's strength and combine with northerly winds the resulting conditions are kite surfing heaven. From huge jumps to high-powered racing, surfing the waves to freestyle competitions, a cluster of vans and a handful of onlookers can be found almost every day of the season looking on in awe as colourful canopies skilfully speed back and forth across the bay.

Although known as one of the best spots to kite surf in Scotland and popular with advanced practitioners, Fraserburgh Bay remains relatively uncrowded making it the perfect place to learn and progress on calmer days. Run by Mark Davies and Maggie Cleeve, Synergy caters for all ability levels whether you want to get the hang of the basics on one of their entry level courses or take your skills up a level, ride upwind or progress to jumping with an advanced level qualification. All the courses are International Kite Organization (IKO) accredited and Mark and Maggie are both fully qualified instructors with years of experience and bags of enthusiasm.

On top of that, their in-depth knowledge of the local landscape and thorough understanding of the winds mean that if it's not working in Fraserburgh, or even if it's working too well, they're ready to get everyone to the best spot for their needs, ensuring that students get the most out of their course, whatever the conditions.

< Catching a lift.
∨ East of Fraserburgh there are deserted spots to explore.

Practicalities

Known locally as 'The Broch', Fraserburgh is one of the country's major fishing ports, 40 miles north of Aberdeen. As a residential, working community the usual high street shops are to hand as well as a fair few pubs and bars to have a pint in. Not a glut of accommodation or restaurants to choose from, but if you are happy to travel there are a number of places nearby.

Transport The nearest train station to Fraserburgh is in Aberdeen, an hour's drive away. Stagecoach Bluebird run a regular service to the town — for more information on services and a timetable call T01346-517000.

Sleeping Recommended by Synergy, **££ the Tufted Duck**, T01346-582481, in the nearby fishing village of St Comb, has views over Fraserburgh Bay, comfortable rooms and restaurant serving fresh produce. Dedicated wet room also. Just outside Fraserburgh the **££ Lonmay Old Manse**, T01346-532227, offers 5-star Scottish tourist board rated accommodation set in the heart of the Aberdeenshire countryside. **Marric Cottage**, Fraserburgh, T01651-806015, is a small, 1-bedroom self-catering cottage.

Eating & drinking The restaurant at the **Tufted Duck**, T01346-582481, serves locally sourced Scottish cuisine.

Resources Synergy Kites, synergykites.com, sell new and ex demo/school equipment online. Their website is a great resource for kite surfers with an excellent spot guide.

Also try If you don't fancy getting wet, take to 3 wheels and give kite buggying a go. See synergykites.com.

> **Lowdown**

ⓘ Directory
Synergy, 1 Logie Lodge, Crimond, Fraserburgh, AB43 8SQ, T07981-793066, synergykitesports.com.

ⓢ Prices
From £130/person for the 6-hr IKO level 1 course.

ⓢ Season
Apr-Oct.

ⓞ Don't miss
The essential hot drink at the beach café to thaw yourself out.

ⓧ Avoid
The rip current in front of the main boardwalk from the car park. Walk towards the town a little way so you don't get sucked out.

Climbing The Highlands

Provider	Scotch on the Rocks Guiding
Skill level	Novice-experienced
Time frame	5 days

Equipment 1:50 000 OS map, compass (Silva – type 4 recommended), waterproof jacket, waterproof trousers, hat and gloves, boots and climbing shoes, climbing helmet, warm outdoor wear, day rucksack, rucksack liner (bin liner), small first aid kit/blister kit, water bottle or vacuum flask, head torch, gaiters, toiletries and sun cream, notebook and pens. Lunches can be provided. Technical climbing equipment provided

Exertion level ●●●●○

Wispy clouds race by overhead, torn ribbons of white against the huge blue expanse. The rough texture of the rock is warm to the touch in the afternoon sun, lichens dapple the vertical slabs while tussocks of grass stand proud in glorious isolation on windswept ledges or belligerently wedged into shaded cracks. Looking up the wide expanse of face at the tiny trace of rope stretching away into the ether, the Highlands of Scotland can feel as dominating and awe-inspiring as the Lhotse face on Everest, but in a way it is. Climbing is all about taking on personal challenges, pushing boundaries and progressing to the next level, and out here in the vast skyline of the rugged summits and jagged peaks, there are plenty of comfort zones to climb out of.

When learning to climb one enters an educational environment unlike any other, it is the world's biggest, and most vertical classroom. Every day is unique, every challenge differs from hour to hour, and the Highlands open vista makes for a glorious backdrop from which every person takes away something special. "Every course has a different highlight," explains Bill Strachan, the founder of Scotch on the Rocks. "Often people are completely amazed when they wake up in the morning with a view across the Cairngorm Plateau if we've been camping. More often than not it's the unexpected chance encounters that people feel are the highlights, looking down on whales when climbing on the sea cliffs of Skye, seeing a broken spectre

❮ On the brink.

Scotch on the Rocks

Scotch on the Rocks

◄ "Torridon has some of the oldest rocks in the world and makes for great climbing." Bill hard at work on sandstone crag Seana Mheallan making the Crack of Ages look easy.
∨ Abseiling off the Inaccessible Pinnacle on the Skye Ridge, "It's a good day out," says Bill. "Attainable by most folk as long as they have a head for heights!".

Scotch on the Rocks

Practicalities

The vibrant city of Inverness is the administrative hub of the Highlands so has excellent transport links and amenities.

Transport Inverness train station is a main Scottish hub and well served with onward connections and bus links. Scotch on the Rocks provides transport out to the hill/crag from your accommodation to minimize their carbon footprint.

Sleeping Just by the train station, the modern, and somewhat stark £ **Inverness Youth Hostel**, Victoria Drive, IV2 3QB, T01463-231771, syha.org.uk, is a handy pre-expedition overnight stop off with dorms and private rooms. **£££-££ Ness Bank B&B**, Ness Bank, IV2 4SF, T01463-232939, on the river's edge is 5 mins' walk from the centre with the silver award for Green Tourism. Camping 3 miles west of the city centre and on the edge of the Beauly Firth, the pretty and simple **Bunchrew Caravan Park**, IV3 8TD, T01463-237802, is open to tents and tourers Mar-Nov with statics also available.

Eating & drinking You can pre-book a packed lunch with Scotch on the Rocks or stop by **The Old Town Deli**, Church St, and stock up on local goodies from fresh baked breads to cheese and meats to make your own crag-side feast. **Contrast Brasserie**, Glenmoriston Hotel, Ness Bank, T01463-223777, uses quality local produce — venison, steak, salmon, haggis — to create a somewhat chic dining experience. Excellent Sunday roasts around £10. Lunch and 'pre theatre menu' is a real bargain, 2 courses at £7. Just south of Inverness, the **Oakwood Restaurant**, Dochgarroch, T01463-861481, is a quirky little spot that specializes in fusing local produce, simple cooking, good prices and bonkers decor.

Also try The nearby Moray Coastline is home to a veritable bounty of surf spots. Lossiemouth is home to a long, flat northeasterly facing beach with various shifting peaks as well as a bit of low tide river mouth break. Works best in big northeasterly swells and popular when on due to proximity of Inverness and Elgin. NB Watch for rips. In Elgin, **Soul Fibre** surf shop, Batchen St, T01343-569103, offers equipment hire and advice. Don't head out into the Moray Firth alone.

when the cloud rolls in, hearing the stags rut in the glens. Often for me the highlight of a trip can be the feeling of satisfaction in completing something with a client when they have been so sure it was impossible, the Old Man of Stoer springs to mind."

For those new to the rock face, whether making the progression from an indoor wall or the virtual novice, a five-day course is the perfect way to ease into the world of outdoor climbing. There are many rope techniques to learn, the art of placing anchors, moving on the rock, gear choice and retreating from the crag. "All courses are tailored to the goals of each client or group," says Bill. "For example some may come along to experience climbing, others may wish to learn the skills to climb themselves, some may prefer a mix of climbing/walking/scrambling/navigation. During the course each day builds on the previous one, allowing participants to progress at their own pace and experience different climbing areas. Even when the weather is less than ideal there are plenty of options for gaining skills." By the end of a 5-day climbing course one of the key aspects learnt is the ability to recognize whether something is safe or not, one should feel confident, with the skills and knowledge to progress further. Then an appreciation of the challenges offered by the Highlands will truly unfold, and a real desire to sample more of what this region has to offer will prove irresistible.

> Lowdown

ℹ Directory
Scotch on the Rocks Guiding, 1 Mitchell's Lane, Inverness IV2 3HQ, T0141-416 4066, scotchontherocks guiding.co.uk.

💲 Prices
£90/day groups (£160/day individual).

☀ Season
All year.

✪ Don't miss
This region offers an amazing assortment of experiences from walking, hiking, climbing and bouldering.

✖ Avoid
Boots are critical, never embark on a course in brand new footwear that hasn't been broken in.

Surfing Thurso

Provider DIY	
Skill level Intermediate-advanced	
Time frame Sunrise to sunset	
Equipment Board, wetsuit (5 mm in winter plus boots, gloves and hood)	
Exertion level ●●●●●	

The view from the sea wall encompasses a huge vista, enclosed by low curling headlands. The arc of the horizon collides with the vertical edge of the Orkney Isles, the Old Man of Hoy standing proud along the angular fringe. To the west, nestled in the corner, the harbour lies quiet, its white lighthouse sleeping in the autumn sun. To the east, the river mouth drains into the bay under the castle battlements, brown waters dancing as they jitter towards the waiting brine. But all these elements are lost amid the rolling thunder and the plume of white spray that rises into the air as another set of waves bears down on the edge of the huge slabstone reef that lies in front, centre stage, demanding attention. There is nothing in this picture postcard setting that can rival the waves of Thurso East when it comes to physical presence.

< The might of Thor's River.

Demi Taylor

> **Lowdown**

💲 **Prices**
Free.

🌡 **Season**
Year round.

⊕ **Don't miss**
Tempest Café is a great place to warm up after a surf.

✖ **Avoid**
Never get out of your depth when it comes to the conditions, the waves here are powerful.

Demi Taylor

> Dune-backed Dunnet Bay.

But it is only from the eastern side of the bay that the waves can be fully appreciated. The farmyard at Thurso East offers the perfect perspective to the wrapping right hand walls that spin in cylindrical perfection towards the river mouth, spilling whitewater rushing through the flat, kelpy shallows of dark Caithness rock. It is this smooth, angled substrate that creates the perfect foil for powerful North Atlantic swells, allowing the powerful lines to break and peel along the hard stone reef in an unending, hollow wall. Surfers speak of Thurso in hushed reverence. It is a wave that demands respect, a truly world-class challenge that breaks in one of Britain's most isolated points. Yet the rewards lure contenders from across the globe to charge winter swells with the hardy locals, trading waves in the line-up and stories in the pub after.

Thurso East breaks through the tides, but needs a wind from the southeast to produce offshore days. Swell direction dictates the complexities of wave characteristics on any given day, but anything from a straight westerly through to a northerly will wake the sleeping reef. The paddle out can be deceptively easy, a deep channel combines with the river's flow to carry the surfer out into the line-up, but the wave size can deceive and even small swells pack a powerful punch. On a big day the locals will be riding big boards, a signal that these barrels carry with them a Hawaiian property that demands respect. Virgin travellers would do well to sit and watch, gain some added knowledge before rushing in. Respect the locals and you'll find a friendly bunch, cross them and you'll find a chill reception waiting. The term 'world class' is much abused in surfing, 'Pipeline-like' has lost its true impact, but experience Thurso breaking on a ten-foot offshore day and you'll know that both terms sit comfortably in any descriptive sentence you could muster when recalling the scene to friends back home.

Practicalities

Thurso town has all the local amenities needed including banks, supermarket and petrol stations. The pubs are 'lively' on the weekend and there is always the (in)famous nightclub to sample. Ferries leave from Scrabster Harbour for the Orkneys, but there is also a rival service that operates from Gills Bay. If heading out west make sure you fill up first in town as there are no opportunities out of town.

Transport Thurso train station is in the town centre with decent links to the rest of Britain, usually via Inverness. Those travelling north from England usually hop aboard the sleeper train with scotrail.co.uk – Euston, London to Thurso takes around 17 hrs with one or two changes. Public transport along the north shore is not brilliant or a viable option on a surf trip. Try Dunnets, T01874-893101, for car hire from Thurso station.

Sleeping **££ Pentland Lodge House**, Granville St, Thurso, KW14 7JN, T01847-895103, pentlandlodgehouse. co.uk. Excellent B&B with great views over Thurso Bay to see whether Thurso East is breaking. Large rooms and locally sourced breakfasts. Centrally located with parking. **£ Sandra's Backpackers**, 24/26 Princes St, Thurso, T01847-894575, sandras-backpackers.co.uk. Centrally located hostel with bunks, a double/twin room and family rooms. Kitchen, limited Wi-Fi and no curfew. A traditional resting spot for surfers on a tight budget. While there are campsites in Thurso town (**Campbell Caravan Hire**, Main Rd, T01847-893524), the simple, wild **Dunnet Bay Caravan Club** site, KW14 8XD, T01847-821319, nestling behind the sand dunes to the east, is a bit special and feels like a real escape. Overlooking the beach and open Mar-Oct.

Eating & drinking **The Captain's Galley**, The Harbour, Scrabster, T01847-894999, captainsgalley.co.uk, serves amazing seafood, straight off the boats. Their policy is to serve the freshest possible locally sourced produce, all of which is non-pressure stock species and only when in season. Quality food in a restaurant run with a strong environmental and ethical agenda that you would expect from a Green Tourism gold standard bearer.

Resources Tempest Surf shop, The Harbour, Thurso, KW14 8DE, T01847-892500, stocks a decent range of surf hardware. No board hire available, you'll need to bring your own.

Also try If Thurso is an ambition still to be realized, there are many amazing beaches nearby. Dunnet Bay has miles of golden sand backed by huge grassy dunes. The waves here are much more beginner friendly, but never surf alone.

Surfing Melvich

Provider DIY	
Skill level Beginner-intermediate	
Time frame Sunrise to sunset	
Equipment Board, wetsuit (5 mm in winter plus boots, gloves and hood)	
Exertion level ●●●○○	

The towering dunes stand watch, marram grass wafting in a light breeze that whistles down the low valley, ruffling the peaty waters that wind their way into the ocean. The waves that peel along the river mouth at Melvich beach hold a magical, mesmeric quality. Unlike the metronomic barrels offered up by the hard cold reefs of Caithness, here in Sutherland the waves are formed on shifting, moving sandbars; natural sculptures groomed by tides and currents as they ebb and flow through the rhythmic cycles of days passing and seasons changing. A myriad of factors combine to dictate the waves peeling here on any given day, each wrapping wall ridden is unique, a fleeting moment in time and space that can never be recaptured but may live in the memory eternally.

The river's ceaseless momentum has worn a passage through the eastern edge of the bay while the western headland is dotted with cottages. On a westerly to northwesterly swell the lines find an easy destination in the sandy shallows here. Today the waves are head high and ruler topped, a mane of spray leaving a fine rainbow-tinged vapour trail as the right hand walls reel away from the river channel toward the beach. On a lucky day a visiting waverider may be greeted by an empty line-up, save for a lone seal bobbing by the channel, waiting for a passing salmon to ambush. This is a place to come and get away from the hustle and bustle of the world, to forget about the nine to five. Up here deadlines, budgets, reviews, exams, are all lost in a bigger picture; one where cetaceans may break the surface as they pass outback, where perfect walls reel past as you paddle back out in the channel. Whether summer or winter, low tide or high, sitting

on the peak as a seven-wave set approaches, Melvich offers another unique day in the shifting sands of time and tide.

Melvich breaks all through the tides, and is offshore in southerly winds. Beginners can get waves on the beach, the river mouth is more challenging especially in a bigger swell. Wave quality varies with the build up of sand over and between the bouldery triangle near the eastern end of the beach. Parking is available on the eastern side of the Halladale river behind the dunes near the Big House, and also on the western side above the dunes. The water quality here is generally excellent. Watch for rips, especially in bigger swells.

∧ Travelling west, the geography of Sutherland creates plenty of opportunities.

Practicalities

Crossing from Caithness to Sutherland along the A836, Melvich is an unassuming entrance.

Transport Forsinard, 20 mins south, and Thurso 18 miles east, are the nearest railway stations, with connections via Inverness and Dingwall.

Sleeping **££ The Melvich Hotel**, Melvich, Sutherland, KW14 7YJ, T01641-531206, melvichhotel.co.uk. Overlooking the bay, the new owners have an ongoing programme to bring this great building back to former glories. They champion locally sourced produce with a specials menu changing daily and featuring locally caught seafood and locally reared meats. Bar also. **£ Sharvedda B&B**, Strathy, KW14 7RY, T01641-541311, sharvedda.co.uk, on the road to Strathy Point. This comfortable, cosy B&B serves up locally sourced brekkies and has views over the countryside. Camping is available at the nearby **Craigdhu**

Campsite, Bettyhill, KW14 7SP, T1641-521273. Also check the **Halladale Inn**, T01641-531282, halladaleinn.co.uk, a short walk to Melvich with a chalet park and site for caravans and motorhomes.

Eating & drinking The **Farr Bay Inn**, by Betty Hill, KW14 7SZ, T01641-521230, is about creating good food using locally sourced produce at affordable prices. Bar food from £5.

Resources **Tempest Surf** shop, The Harbour, Thurso, KW14 8DE, T01847-892500, stocks the basics.

Also try Strathy is an excellent beachbreak and is one of the few places with shelter in a westerly wind, the huge headland here can make for surfable waves when other spots are blown out. Also if the swell is too big elsewhere, it may be more manageable here.

⌃ Melvich.

> **Lowdown**

 Prices
Free.

 Season
Year round.

 Don't miss
If the surf is flat, check out Smoo Cave in Durness.

 Avoid
Never surf alone up here, even if experienced.

Snowboarding Scotland: best of the rest

Provider	See details
Skill level	All
Time Frame	Dawn till dusk
Equipment	Snowboard, boots, technical clothing, gloves, goggles and helmet, all available for hire
Exertion level	●●●●○

Scotland is often bemoaned amongst the snowboarding community for its inconsistent snow but after a decent dump of fresh powder, it's easy to forget you are not in the Alps. Firing off a massive kicker in one of the great snow parks gives you just as big a buzz, while carving through the Back Corries at Nevis makes it hard to believe you are a couple of hours from Edinburgh or Glasgow. For beginners, it's an ideal destination for mastering the basics – all resorts are geared up to help you learn your toe from your heel edge, with fully accredited ski schools, board hire and patient instructors. Snowboarding in Scotland brings another dimension to our outdoor adventure playground. Just keep an eye on the weather charts and you can time your trip to hit those perfect days between January and April (ski-scotland.com).

White Corries, Meall a' Bhuiridh, Glencoe, Argyll
The area is based around a large basin with seven lifts and 19 runs. It is renowned as the best resort for freestyle snowboarders due to the excellent natural terrain here. Access from the bottom car park is by chairlift up to the Eagles Rest Café and from here up to the main area by the Plateau Poma. There is a good mix of runs with 12½ miles of piste, from a large nursery area through to a black run called Fly Paper, that they claim is the steepest and most challenging in Britain. A full day adult lift pass is £30. **Glencoe Mountain Resort**, Glencoe, Argyll, PH49 4HZ, T01855-851226, glencoemountain.co.uk. For lessons and hire check out Glencoe Mountain Snowsport School, T01855-851226, two-hour beginners' lesson from £25. **£ The Glencoe Independent Hostel**, Glencoe, near Ballachulish, Argyll, PH49 4HX, T01855-811906, offers hostel accommodation, an alpine bunkhouse, caravans and a log cabin.

Glenshee, Perthshire
Proud of its claim to be the largest resort in the UK, Glenshee boasts 21 lifts and 36 runs, spread over an area with 25 miles of piste. The resort spreads across three valleys with the longest single run being Glas Maol, at over 1¼ miles. While it doesn't have the reputation for the best freestyle terrain, there's room to get out and explore including the quarter pipe at Butcharts Coire and a couple of black runs. **Glenshee Ski Centre**, Cairnwell by Braemar, AB35 5XU, T01339-741320, ski-glenshee. co.uk. Full day adult lift pass is £25. Equipment hire from the centre £12/half day. Beginners' lessons with the SnowSports School from £18 for 1½ hours T01250-885255, cairnwellmountainsports.co.uk. **£ Gulabin Lodge**, Spittal of Glenshee, PH10 7QE, T01250-885255, gulabinlodge.co.uk, offer simple, comfortable bunkhouse accommodation at the foot of Ben Gulabin, around six miles south of the ski centre.

Nevis Range
Aonach Mor is Scotland's eighth highest mountain and boasts boarding up to 3900 ft and a season that may extend into April in certain years. It has 35 runs, the longest of which is 2½ miles of off-piste descent. The resort is fed by the gondola, which arrives at a large beginner-friendly area rich with green and blue runs. Take the lifts on up the mountain and access some rich riding terrain with plenty of red and black runs and a large

> Glenshee.
> Eyeing up the off-piste potential afforded by the Nevis range.

off-piste area known as the Back Corries. Always check with the ski-patrol before venturing into the backcountry, to get advice on avalanche risk and exit points. This is a great place to get a first taste of going off-piste with some good areas to explore. Freestylers can enjoy the Boardwise Park at the top. **Nevis Range Ski Centre**, Torlundy, Fort William, Invernesshire, PH33 6SQ, T01397-705825, snowsports.nevisrange.co.uk. A full zone day ski pass is £28 adult, or £18 for the beginners' area. A two-hour group lesson with the Snowsport School is £21 and a full day's hire of board and boots is £19. On the busiest days queues for hire can be long. **£ Snowgoose Mountain Centre**, Station Road, Corpach, Fort William, T01397-772467, highland-mountain-guides.co.uk, has self-catering apartments as well as a cracking alpine-style bunkhouse and hostel accommodation on offer although navigating the road around Loch Eli at the end of the day can be a bit of a faff.

The Lecht, Aberdeenshire

This small resort is ideal for beginners or those with families. It seems to have rebranded recently to 'Lecht 2090' as it is 2090 ft above sea level. Pretty consistent snow here, but there are also the six back up snow cannons should nature not feel like

playing. Located in the eastern Cairngorms, The Lecht rises up to 2700 ft, with 12 lifts and 18 pisted runs that extend for 12½ miles. The terrain here isn't exactly a freerider's paradise but The Falcon, Harrier, and Buzzard seem the most popular; for freestylers there is a halfpipe and funpark with kickers and rails built where conditions allow. Beginners have the benefit of a huge area fed by the Magic Carpet – a conveyer belt style lift. **Lecht 2090**, Corgarff, Strathdon, AB36 8YP, T01975-651440, lecht.co.uk. A day pass is £25 for an adult. For lessons and hire contact the centre: board and boot hire is £17, instruction £25 for a two-hour class. Clothing hire also available, on a first come first served basis – book in advance, T01975-651440 ext 7. Accommodation nearby is not an easy ask and your best bet is the small and oh, so perfectly formed **Lazy Duck Hostel**, PH25 3ED, T01479-821642, lazyduck.co.uk. 25 miles north of The Lecht on the A939, the wood-clad hostel sleeps eight. When the birds are laying there are free range eggs to enjoy and after a day in the mountains a sauna in which to warm away those aches and pains and admire your latest batch of war wounds or bruises of honour. Limited camping also available for the hardy or foolish…

∧ The Lecht.
∨ Powder.

∧ On edge above Fort William.
< Angus Leith, Glenshee.

Sea kayaking Summer Isles

Provider DIY

Skill level Intermediate-advanced

Time frame 6 days

Equipment All specialist sea kayaking equipment from kayaks to cagoules, tents, cooking and eating utensils are provided. Wetsuits are not provided or necessary, wear light weight, quick drying layers – not cotton and pack spares in case you do capsize! Sun block and insect repellent for midges

Exertion level ●●●●○

From Shetland and the Orkney Isles to the Outer and Inner Hebrides, the coastal waters of the Scottish Highlands are littered with archipelagos, skerries and outlying islands waiting to catch the adventurer's eye. A scattering of tiny island silhouettes lie almost forgotten close to the fringes of Coigach peninsula like a collection of delicious crumbs fallen into the sea as the nearby summits were pulled up to form the vast mountainous table top of Ben Mor Coigach. But their name alone, with all it promises is enough to inspire even the most tired office worker to pack their bags and head out on an expedition of new possibilities, or at the very least put in a holiday request form, pronto, for these are the Summer Isles.

Paddling through the channels and inlets around the outlying skerries of Eilean Flada Mor it is clear that these sandstone isles deliver every inch of the startlingly clear blue waters, white sand shores and peaceful, private paradise that their moniker suggests. Indeed only the main island Tanera Mor, lying a mile and a half off shore from Achiltibuie, is populated, just. Wilderness Scotland's expedition to the Summer Isles combines six days of sea kayak exploration with five nights of truly wild

> Exploring the sea caves of Tanera Beag.
> Pulling kayaks ashore on white sandy beaches.

< Navigating between the scatterings of land that make up the Summer Isles.

Tim Willis

Tim Willis

camping, under the stars and far from the madding crowds. Launching into the sheltered waters in the late afternoon, the first day's short paddle is just enough to reawaken dormant memories lying deep within muscles and sleeping joints. The first night's camp on the white sand shores reawakens the soul. Good job too because from here, the pace picks up with around 1½ miles of paddling a day, exploring coastlines, circumnavigating islands and their smaller siblings, passing resident seal colonies and sea cliffs scaled by itinerant colonies of climbers who lean precariously out into the breeze, impossibly attached by an invisible foot hold. Pulling kayaks ashore on uninhabited isles to push out on foot, you stretch out legs that have been holed up too long and get the occasional feeling you are being watched. Lying back post picnic to examine the clouds you may be lucky enough to catch a glimpse of this watchful presence, a sea eagle on the wing or a rare golden eagle riding the thermals.

The wild camping is an all-important element of the experience, giving you the freedom to explore places where those who are unable to give up their creature comforts fear to tread. It allows you to go off grid, to disconnect from the wider world and reconnect with yourself and your environment. You might find yourself picking mussels for a camp fire supper or perhaps combing the shoreline for kelp or seaweed delights. But what is certain is that you'll find yourself bedding down in some of the most spectacular of coastal locations. And if the weather doesn't hold, well you can always huddle together in the base camp tent around mugs of steaming coffee and other local potions to warm the soul.

> **Lowdown**

ℹ **Directory**
Wilderness Scotland, 3a St Vincent St, Edinburgh, EH3 6SW, T0131-625 6635, wilderness scotland.com.

$ **Prices**
From £575/person.

☀ **Season**
May-Sep.

○ **Don't miss**
Keep your eyes peeled, there is an abundance of marine life in these waters: seals, porpoises and dolphins.

✖ **Avoid** You need a minimum of 4 days paddling experience, preferably guided, for this expedition. Avoid booking a course you're not ready for – introductory courses in the lochs of the northwest Highlands are also available.

> Candy coloured kayaks, hulls wet from a morning's adventure glisten in the sun.

Practicalities

With the gold award for Green Tourism, Wilderness Scotland take their commitment to the environment and sustainable tourism seriously, contributing to a number of conservation organizations. The expedition cost includes transfers to and from Inverness, guiding, kayaking equipment and meals plus 5 nights camping including cooking equipment and 2-man tents but not sleeping bags and mats. Inverness has good transport links.

Transport Inverness is well served by its train station.

Sleeping Just by the train station, the modern, and somewhat stark **£ Inverness Youth Hostel**, Victoria Drive, IV2 3QB, T01463-231771, syha.org.uk, is a handy pre-expedition overnight stop off with dorms and private rooms. **£££-££ Ness Bank B&B**, Ness Bank, IV2 4SF, T01463-232939, on the river's edge is 5 mins walk from the centre with the silver award for Green Tourism.

Eating & drinking Contrast Brasserie, Glenmoriston Hotel, Ness Bank, T01463-223777, uses quality local produce – venison, steak, salmon, haggis – to create a somewhat chic dining experience. Excellent Sunday roasts around £10. Lunch and 'pre theatre menu' is a real bargain 2 courses at £7. Just south of Inverness, the **Oakwood Restaurant**, Dochgarroch, T01463-861481, is a quirky little spot that specializes in fusing local produce, simple cooking, good prices and bonkers decor.

Also try To the south, the white sand shores and daydream blue waters around the Isle of Barra create an arresting scene. Clearwater Paddling run their 'Wild Barra' trips where 3 nights of wild camping on the shores, under the stars and 3 nights in their lodge are combined with aquatic exploration of the island's lagoons, rocky coves, inlets and wildlife. May-Aug £585/person including lodge accommodation, kayak equipment and guiding. **Clearwater Paddling**, Barra, HS9 5XD, T01871-810443, clearwaterpaddling.com.

Walking Torridons

Provider	Hillways
Skill level	All levels
Time frame	6 days
Equipment	All canyoning and safety equipment provided. Remember to bring a warm dry change of clothes
Exertion level	●●●●○

In a nutshell, Munros are the loftiest of Scotland's peaks, mountains that reach and surpass the 3000 ft mark. There are currently 283 of them. There were until very recently 284, but one was demoted to the ranks of a mere Corbett (which rests in the 2500-2999 ft parameters). In 1889 The Scottish Mountaineering Club was formed by William Naismith – he of the Naismith's Rule fame, a formula devised to calculate the walking time of a route taking into account elevation and gain (the general rule of thumb being one hour to cover three miles plus 30 minutes for every 1000 ft of ascent). He was quickly joined by Sir Hugh Munro who tasked himself with the documentation of those mountains reaching over the magic 3000 ft marker. This he accomplished equipped with a crude altimeter, early mapping and a good deal of intuition. The definitive list of 'Munros' and their 'Corbett' cousins has been maintained and refined by a SMC private members club ever since, and while the status of mountains may rise and diminish with technology, the enthusiasm for bagging them certainly hasn't wavered, as documented by the list of 'Munro Compleatists' also watched over by the SMC.

With 35 years of walking, trekking and leading behind him, former Air Force navigator Keith Gault has a real passion for Munros – he has completed them, twice. So what better person to lead you on a six-day summer hill walking expedition of the north west Highlands. "The combination of sheer-sided individual mountains rising up from deep glens and the ever-present blue water of lochs combine to make Torridon a special destination." enthuses Keith.

< Beinn Allign in its winter jacket.

Keith Gault

Keith Gault

"The mountains just beg to be climbed!" Glacial erosion has helped to carve out the landscape; Torridon is all castellated ridges of sharply tiered sandstone, corries and glens whose appearance is softened by pockets of ancient Caledonian Pine. Between Kintail and Torridon lie some 50 Munros and 27 Corbetts. The six-day adventure will see you, weather permitting, summit the four highest peaks in the range, Beinn Allign, Ben Eighe, Siloh which stands separate above Loch Maree, as well as Keith's personal favourite Liathach. "This huge shapely bulk dominates the north side of Glen Torridon. The mountain is comprised largely of Torridonian sandstone that weathers into steep terraced cliffs that cascade down to the floor of the glen. High above Glen Torridon, a 4¼ mile roof-top ridge carries the walker along an amazing highway in the sky with expansive views in all directions. Westwards, the eye is drawn across Loch Torridon and out over the waters of the Minch towards the Outer Isles." Despite their steep sides and majestic architecture, the mountains are covered by an excellent network of good quality paths. "The greatest challenge is coping with the steep climbs and descents," says Keith reassuringly. And the tour is a holiday and a break as opposed to a boot camp, where taking in the natural environment is on an equal footing with climbing mountains. But if you do get to bag yourself a couple of Munros along the way, all the better!

∧ Slioch lies beyond the shores of Loch Maree.

> **Lowdown**

ⓘ **Directory**
Hillways, T07801-629350, hillways.co.uk.

ⓢ **Prices**
£450.

◉ **Season**
May (plus summer months as requested).

◉ **Don't miss**
The views from Beinn Allign – you can look across to the Isle of Skye or take in the fabulously wild Horns of Allign, ripe for some summer scrambling.

✖ **Avoid**
Don't get into trouble if spending a few days exploring the region alone. "Take heed of the weather forecast," says Keith, "and always be prepared to turn back if the going gets too tough or conditions deteriorate."

Practicalities

Torridon and the nearby village of Kinlochewe provide handy bases with accommodation from which to explore the area. There is no bank/cash machine in Torridon – Gairloch and Lochcarron have the nearest banks. The tour is inclusive of guiding, accommodation and food.

Transport Achnasheen is the nearest train station with bus links on to Torridon and Kinlochewe.

Sleeping Accommodation is included in the price of the tour but if you can't bear to leave this prime patch of wilderness and want to spend a few extra days exploring the region, there are a couple of good options. Backed by woodland the Green Tourism award holding **£££ The Torridon Hotel**, Achnasheen, Wester Ross, Scotland, IV22 2EY , T01445-791242, is on the southern edge of the loch and the budget blowing end of the scale. Their bolt-hole **Boat House** is modern with log burner in the lounge sleeping 6 from £825/week. At nearby Kinlochewe **£££-£ Kinlochewe Hotel**, IV22 2PA, T01445-760253, offers simple, comfortable B&B plus bunkhouse beds from £12.50/ night. At the base of Liathach, **£ Torridon Youth Hostel**, IV22 2EZ, T01445-791284, is in a cracking location Mar-Oct, also self-catering. **Torridon Campsite**, T01445-712345, on the edge of the village is basic, often boggy with a simple toilet /coin operated shower block, also open to the public. Year round. No charge, no booking. **Sands Caravan & Camping**, Gairloch, IV21 2DL, T01445-712152, is a lovely, informal, 55 acre site with pitches nestled in the dunes or providing views across the Minch, just pitch up at least 23 ft from your neighbours. Heated wooden wigwams also available for 'posh camping' option.

Eating & drinking The Torridon Inn, T01445-791242, prides itself on its local suppliers and creating home-made food from around £10. **Kinlochewe Hotel**, IV22 2PA, T01445-760253, serves up simple, tasty meals using local produce and suppliers.

Also try Northwest of Torridon, head out on a 'Shellfish Safari' with Ian McWhinney whose ancestors have been farming the land and fishing the waters of Gairloch since the 15th century. Trip from £17.50/person for 1¾ hrs. **Shellfish Safaris**, Dry Island Badachro, Gairloch, Rosshire, IV21 2AB. Stay at Dry Island, in their comfortable Creel Cabin. Nestled amongst the trees it also offers views across the loch from £200/week. They also offer B&B in **The Old Curing Station** from £40. Eat at **Badachro Inn**, on the shores of Gair loch, which makes the most of Ian's catch and has a good selection of real ales to wash it down with.

Swimming Fairy Pools, Skye

Provider	DIY
Skill level	Novice-advanced
Time frame	All day
Equipment	Towel, bathers (depending on season/hardiness wetsuit)
Exertion level	●●○○○

One of the largest of the Scottish Isles, the landscape of Skye is magical and nonsensical – a terrain dreamt up in a child's fevered imagination or created in a surrealist's mind. The Storr with their jagged Tolkien-esque spires, resemble those created by fingers patiently drip feeding wet sand into towers at the seashore. The green baize stretched tight along impossible contours is perforated by so many lochans and pools it appears the very fabric of the land may tear beneath too heavy a stride, a too carelessly placed walking boot. No uniform gold washing of coves and bays here, instead they are available in a pick

and mix range of shades to match moods from black to cream and even the duskiest of pinks. Then there are the waters that lap the shores here – even the conscience of a saint could not be clearer. And while the colour looks as though it has been shipped in specially from a fantasy Caribbean island, the lightning shivers that jolt through your body on entering assures you it has not. Nothing is ordinary here, nothing is dull.

The dark, bare summits of The Cuillin are used to taking centre stage, dominating the scene. With fire in their bellies, this snaking range of sharp, jagged toothed hills forced their way though the heart of Skye and upward for some 3248 ft to create the highest point on the island. The ridges are scarred by deep gullies and corries, the hills are riddled with burns and glens. Allt Coir a Mhadaidh rises in one such corrie or 'cauldron' high up in the hills. From here the burn weaves its magic across the

Andy Law

◀ Leaps of faith for the brave.

James Laver

James Laver

Andy Lew

◀ The deceiving colour of the waters casts a spell over would-be waterbabes, luring them in.

landscape, travelling west, drawing other sources to it, gathering momentum before turning its course south and feeding into Glen Brittle to continue its onward journey, joining the sea at Loch Brittle. And it is in this context that the Cuillin find themselves drifting into the background. Along the length of Allt Coir a Mhadaidh is a series of compelling cascades, smooth, sculpted pools and private pockets that will tempt even the most fervent of landlubbers to dip more than a toe in, such is the mesmerizing power of these fairy pools. As with the ocean that licks the island's shores, the fairytale aquamarine of these fresh water pools does enough to temporarily trick the senses into taking the plunge, making the true chill of the water difficult to fathom.

From the 'Fairy Pools' car park, the path leading up the valley and along the water's edge offers access to a series of sublime swimming holes which seem to signal their presence in coded flashes as clouds pass across the sun. Press on upstream to the enchanted twin pools, the higher of which is constantly washed, renewed and re-energized by a cascade, while the lower is a still oasis. Separating and joining the two is a submerged rock arch to swim beneath, eyes wide open, or leap from, eyes clamped shut. And when the swimming is over, you can pull yourself from the water's edge on to the rock ledges to absorb the sun's warmth and turn your eyes once again to the magnificent sight of the Cuillin towering behind.

On following the Allt Coir a Mhadaidh upstream, take the distinct left fork to explore some similarly sublime pools and impressive waterfalls of the neighbouring Allt Coir a Tairneilear.

> **Lowdown**

⊙ **Prices**
Free.

⊙ **Season**
Year round.

⊙ **Don't miss**
There are plenty of pools to enjoy here so push out to explore before selecting your perfect place for an energizing dip.

⊗ **Avoid**
The midges here are a hungry bunch during midge season, so don't loiter too long before taking the plunge.

Practicalities

The toll-free Skye Bridge connects the mind-blowing island with the mainland, spanning the Kyle of Lochalsh to Kyleakin. On the A87 which runs along the Isle's eastern flank, Portree is the island's capital. The Cuillins take centre stage on the island and although there is very little in the way of amenities around them, for the wild at heart there is more than enough.

Transport Apr-Oct capture the feeling of an island escape and make the crossing on the Glenelg-Kylerhea ferry, skyeferry.co.uk, £15 return for car and up to 4 passengers. On public transport it is a real mission: around 40 miles from Glenbrittle, the nearest train station is Kyle of Lochalsh on the mainland, connections from Inverness. Onward coach service to Sligachan Hotel with citylink. co.uk and bus to Carbost with stagecoachbus.com. From here it is another 7 miles hike or taxi ride.

Sleeping At the foot of the Cuillins and on the edge of Loch Brittle, **Glenbrittle Campsite**, Carbost, IV47 8TA, T01478-640404, dunvegancastle.com, is the showcase, an ideal spot from which to strike out and explore the swimming holes — just pack some decent hiking boots and follow Glen Brittle upstream. A perfectly simple site, the facilities are fairly basic but the showers are hot. The shop stocks a few basic provisions or you could always forage for your supper on the shoreline here. Hard stands and electric hook-up also, Apr-Sep. Inland from the campsite £ Glenbrittle SYHA, IV47 8TA, T01478-640278, has the silver award for Green Tourism. Open Apr-Sep. There is limited daytime access to the hostel if you're seeking shelter from the weather. **££ The Old Inn**, T01478-640205, offers simple, fairly basic B&B plus hostel accommodation. Its big selling point is that it has a decent enough bar with good atmosphere on site, the closest to the Fairy Pools.

Eating & drinking Just off the A863, the **Sligachan Hotel**, T01478-650204, is a bit of a trek. Formerly a place for 'gentlemen climbers' it is now home to a cracking little micro brewery where you can sup on an ale, a fine single malt or enjoy some top notch cooking. Camping and quality hotel accommodation also.

Resources skye.co.uk.

Also try As a member of Skye Mountain Rescue Team, Tony Hanly is pretty familiar with the terrain around here. What better person to lead you on a traverse of the Cuillin — the dark and challenging mountain range of bare, precipitous peaks and steep gullies. The 2-day course covers 11 Munros (mountains over 3000 ft in height) on the Black Cuillin with a possible overnight bivvy for that real wilderness feeling from £200.

Climbing Scotland: best of the rest

Provider	See info
Skill level	Various
Time frame	From 1 day
Equipment	Safety equipment provided, wear comfortable, appropriate clothing
Exertion level	●●●●●

Cast your eye over a relief map of Scotland and it appears as through the master draughtsman, caught in a moment of frustration, had scrunched the neat plans for the country into a ball and tossed them over his shoulder. Realizing his haste, he had carefully tried to unfold the drawing, ironing the crumpled sheet with his palms but the page remained creased. As daylight is cast over the surface, shade became great valleys and riverbeds, light converting to hills and towering mountaintops. Ideal terrain for climbers, a perfect adventure playground. It's little wonder then that Scotland's climbing heritage can be traced more than 300 years, in the 1600s Martin Martin documented a society built around climbing on the remote Hebridean isle of St Kilda. Climbing ability wasn't just about establishing a hierarchy and pecking order, it was about hunting and gathering, plucking sea birds from lofty cliff ledges to eat and trade.

The geography of the country means plenty of different rock types and challenges lending themselves to a wealth of styles. There is sports

> "D Gully Buttress" on the NE Face of Buachaille Etive Mor just above Hell's Wall which has uncharacteristically sloping holds. "Most of the rock is very positive with good edges and cracks for holds," explains Mike Pescod of Abacus Mountaineering. "The neighbouring Curved Ridge is climbed completely on spikes of rock that allow excellent hand holds for the entire climb."

climbing, bouldering, epic sea cliffs and wilderness ascents in remote settings and public climbs on road side crags, in fact there is something for just about every predilection and niche. And while climbing here may no longer be about filling your belly, it will certainly nourish the soul.

Am Buachaille Sea Stacks, Sutherland
Some 10 miles south of the fury of Cape Wrath lies Sandwood Bay. There is no access to the beach for vehicles, the only way in is by foot – from the car park at Blairemore it is a four-mile walk across exposed and often wet moorland but the rewards far outweigh the effort. Crossing the Sandwood crofting estate, managed by the John Muir Trust, and skirting the loch is in itself an epic experience of wilderness views while the beautiful beach is a remote expanse of dramatic dune-backed sand. On the western edge of the bay the sandstone sea stack Am Buachallie rises for some 213 ft and despite having trekked in to the bay and navigated the coastline, there is still one

< The magnificant Buachaille Etive Mor has been extruded from the surrounding landscape to dominate the head of Glen Coe valley.

more hurdle to overcome – a swim to the base of the stack through the frigid ocean channel. This is a total experience and is about more than just the climbing, it's about immersing yourself in your environment – literally. "This climb includes everything," says Paul Tattersall of Go Further Scotland. "A beautiful walk to a stunning and remote location; a walk around a rugged coast; a swim out to the stack; an exhilarating climb; a 164 ft abseil; and some breathtaking views." On the Stoer Peninsula, the 197 ft Torridonian sandstone Old Man of Stoer is another classic tidal sea stack with several quality multi-pitch climbs lying in wait. Tackle one of the serious multi-pitch routes with **Go Further Scotland**, T01445-771260, gofurtherscotland.co.uk, experienced climbers and guides from £220. Sheigra Rough Camping overlooks the beach. There are no facilities here, just a water pipe. Minimize your impact on this patch of paradise and enjoy.

Glen Coe, Highlands

Glaciation and millions of years of erosion have carved, finessed and moulded the volcanic and sedimentary strata of Glen Coe into an arresting mountainscape and, once the summer warmth has melted the snow and dried the hard faces, a proving ground for rock climbers. The entrance to Glen Coe is wild and spectacular. Having crossed Rannoch Moor, the A82 runs along the narrow valley floor squeezed between jagged peaks and the mountain ridge of Aonach Eagach that rises wavelike to create a solid impenetrable wall. For many, Buachaille Etive Mor, the aptly named Great Herdsman, ushers in the first tantalizing taste of what lies ahead – road-side crags, mountainous climbs and intense, vertical walls. Warmed by the early morning sun, Rannoch Wall with views across the moor is a good choice for mid-grade climbers seeking exposure. "Dominating the heads of Glen Coe and Glen Etive The Buachaille is home to a vast array of brilliant climbs at all grades," says IFMGA qualified Mike Pescod of Abacus Mountaineering who has spent the last 13 years climbing Scotland. "Some of the best climbing in Scotland is found here in a unique sense of space and grandeur. Deep chasms, sun-drenched slabs, intimidating walls and fine ridges are all found on the one hill." Abacus delivers 'designer' courses to suit the needs and wants of the individual from introductory sessions

to guided climbs in and around Glen Coe, and beyond. Prices for a day's climbing from £205/2 people includes instruction, guiding and technical equipment plus transport from Fort William. **Abacus Mountaineering**, Fort William, PH33 7LS, T01397-772466, abacusmountaineering.com. Stay in Fort William 16 miles north where there is a good selection of accommodation including the comfortable **Smiddy Bunkhouse**, Snowgoose Mountain Centre, Corpach, T01397-772467, with beds (including bedding) from £13/night. All that pine really makes you feel as if you're on some sort of Alpine expedition, living the dream.

Old Man of Hoy, Orkney

First ascended by Chris Bonington and co. in 1966 during a televized broadcast and first base jumped in 2008 by Tim Emmett, Gus Hutchinson Brown and Roger Holmes, this 449 ft red sandstone sea stack needs little introduction. An iconic landmark on the Thurso to Stromness ferry route, it is entirely surrounded at high tide by a sleepless sea that has slowly worn it away to create this isolated pinnacle and climbing gem. There are a number of routes to explore and for those already confidently seconding to a good standard, MIC climbing instructor Gary Smith of Get High offers an 'esoteric journey to climb the Old Man of Hoy, which ranks as one of the coolest climbing adventures in Britain.' T07921-312905, gethigh.co.uk, from £160/day. Ferry travel from Scrabster to Stromess with NorthLink Ferries, T0845-600 0449, northlinkferries.co.uk, and onward travel to Hoy, from the Norse for 'High island' with Orkney Ferries, T01856-872044, orkneyferries.co.uk. Hostel accommodation available at **Rackwick Youth Hostel**, KW16 3NJ, T01856-873535, April-September, from £10, camping also available on site.

▾ Paul descends the Old Man of Stoer.

▾ Old Man of Stoer.

▾ The weathered sandstone of Am Buachaille

◂ Sunset over Sandwood Bay, while the Herdsman watches on from a distance.

Canoeing Coast to Coast

Provider	Wilderness Scotland
Skill level	Intermediate
Time frame	4 days
Equipment	All canoeing and camping equipment provided. Remember to bring sleeping bags, mats, waterproof jacket and trousers, wellies and warm clothing
Exertion level	●●●●○

From the windswept, heather-coated foothills of Ben Nevis, to the deep blue waters of Loch Linhe, Fort William's granite fronted buildings and winding streets lined with pubs, restaurants and guest houses offer tourists a pleasant welcome. However, the town centre itself, set back from the loch's lapping shoreline by a busy dual carriageway, is not the primary draw of Fort William. Rather it is the settlement's convenient location that draws outdoors enthusiasts all year round, ready to hillwalk, climb and cycle their way through the Scottish Highlands. Marking the end of the West Highland Way, Scotland's oldest and most popular walk, Fort William is not just about land based activities, it is also the starting point for a classic coast to coast canoeing expedition.

Bisecting this Celtic land, Wilderness Scotland's Great Glen Adventure traverses the country's lochs and rivers from the sheltered waters of the Caledonian Canal in the west, to the River Ness, flowing out of Inverness and into the Beauly Firth in the east. The four-day open-top canoe excursion, led by experienced guides involves around seven hours of paddling a day so, while taking in the stunning scenery and unique perspective that paddling across Scotland provides, you can't help but develop your technique with laid back coaching building on your own skill set. While some of the paddling is straightforward, allowing you to breathe slow and take in the reflected landscape on the calm waters before your blade breaks the surface tension, some of the larger lochs can experience windy conditions and the

◄ Paddling Loch Ness.

exposed nature of the terrain means the route is necessarily flexible and adaptable. Then of course, there's the business of going through locks and while sometimes canoes can be towed, at other times you need to 'portage', or carry them. Day three usually involves the longest portage through six locks but your efforts are rewarded as you push out into the iconic waters of Loch Ness to hunt for fabled monsters lurking in the deep. "It's the whole experience that makes it special," explains Tim Willis, Wilderness Scotland's operations manager. "People who do the Great Glen Adventure take away a real sense of achievement, new skills and some incredible memories – staring up at Urquhart Castle as you paddle silently through the waters of Loch Ness is a magical feeling."

Wild camping each night is as much a part of the trip as the canoeing, with guides picking the best spots for a good night's rest after long days on the water. From the grassy shores of Loch Oich to the dense woodland below Invermoriston, each camping spot provides beautiful surroundings and a chance to really feel close to nature. And with all the exertion that paddling and pitching requires, food is an important part of the trip. Delicious meals are on the menu for breakfast, lunch and dinner, all designed to keep energy and morale levels high.

With all wild camping comes environmental responsibility, something the team at Wilderness Scotland takes very seriously. The company prides itself on its sustainable approach to adventure tourism, asking that group members share tents to minimize impact and ensuring that every campsite is left as it was found, with as little disruption as possible. This necessitates some mucking in, tidying up and clearing away, although the guides are generally happy to take on the lion's share.

On top of the en-route environmental awareness, Wilderness Scotland also does its bit to preserve the Highlands for future generations to enjoy. The company donates a percentage of its profits to three of Scotland's nature charities; The John Muir Trust, Trees for Life and the Scottish Wildlife Trust. As a result it is the only adventure travel company in Scotland to hold the Green Tourism Gold Award and has won many other awards in recognition of its commitment to sustainable tourism.

> **Lowdown**

ⓘ **Directory**
Wilderness Scotland, 3a St Vincent St, Edinburgh, EH3 6SW, T0131-625 6635, wildernessscotland.com.

⊙ **Prices**
£495/person.

☀ **Season**
May-Sep.

◎ **Don't miss**
The view of Urquhart Castle from Loch Ness is a spectacular sight and a real highlight.

⊗ **Avoid**
Littering, leaving gates open and generally disturbing the countryside when wild camping.

Practicalities

The largest town in the Scottish Highlands, Wilderness Scotland operates out of Fort William, also known as the Outdoor Capital of the UK. With its proximity to Ben Nevis, the Munros and the West Highland Way, Fort William is popular with all sorts of fresh air enthusiasts and, as a result, its specialist stores, activity providers and B&Bs aplenty mean it is the perfect base from which to explore the Highlands whether on foot, on wheels or on water.

Transport   Fort William is served by train, firstscotrail.com, and coach, citylink.com .

Sleeping   If you want a comfy bed before the expedition, there are plenty of places to chose from. £££ **Myrtle Guesthouse** is a characterful, elegant property with stunning views and spacious rooms, T01397-698042, £ **Glen Nevis SYHA**, PH33 6SY, T01397-702336, in the shadow of Ben Nevis should stir up your pre-trip excitement. With dorms and doubles available, it also has the silver award for Green Tourism.

Eating & drinking   The **Grog and Gruel**, recommended by the Wilderness Scotland crew is a popular, atmospheric pub in the heart of the town serving real ales and home cooked food. Alternatively, if you are looking for something special to reward all your efforts, Michelin starred chef Ross Sutherland cooks high end Scottish cuisine at the stylish and modern **Lime Tree**, T01397-701806. Be aware mains come in at around £20.

Resources   For information on what's around and about Fort William as well as advice on activities and providers check out vist-fortwilliam.co.uk.

Also try   From leisurely cycle ways and tree-lined trails to fast and rocky downhills, Fort William is the perfect place to give MTB a go. There are plenty of specialist stores, rentals, providers and expeditions on offer and information on the best trail to suit your ability level at ridefortwilliam.co.uk.

> Camping up lakeside.
⌄ Portage.

Mountain biking Fort William

Provider	DIY
Skill level	Intermediate-advanced
Time frame	All day
Equipment	Mountain bike, helmet, snacks, water, a map and a repair kit/spare tube
Exertion level	●●●○○

The timber boardwalk seems to draw you in, pull you forward as the mesmeric hum of wheels on slats resonates through the bike. The trail seems to hover above the ground, a narrow line traversing the scrub grass and heather, the blur of boulder, brooks and pools below. Banks that taunt you on faster, the weaving platform down the open side of the hill's expanse, ahead the dive into cover, snaking, dropping, gravel and jumps – out of the sun's glare into the wood's damp embrace. The challenge awaits, rock gardens with berms, steps, jumps and gaps. All before the safety of the car park and the chance to draw breath. And then the gondola again to the top, and a choice of which trail follow next, which gauntlet to take up.

The Nevis Range is a region steeped in outdoor tradition, from climbers to skiers to hikers to mountainbikers, the region is a canvas for all who seek adventure on high. The trails of this area are

> It's all about a sense of perspective.

⌄ The boardwalk cuts across the mountainside weaving a line of sheer enjoyment.

Andy McAndlish

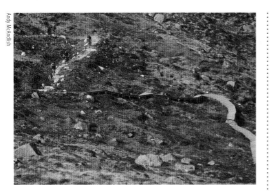

Andy McAndlish

world renowned, and range from fun cross-country to extreme grade downhill courses. Leanachan Forest is home to the Nevis Range Ski Centre, home of the Off Beat Course, the Nevis Red Trail and many more. The Off Beat Course is an orange extreme difficulty downhill, and has been a regular venue for World Cup events and World Championships. The trail is 1¾ miles long and will be a descent of four to five minutes for advanced riders, though a competent rider should be able to complete the course – just in their own time. The start of the course is fed by the gondola, before traversing the hill and dropping down into steeper sections that feature several smooth berms, rock gardens and rock slabs, into the trees over twisty natural terrain and a wall ride. The final stretch is the motorway with big step downs and gap jumps. Afterwards, if you've got anything left, why not try the Nevis Red Trail, a 3¼ mile trail that winds across Aonach Mor, it's a mixture of boardwalk, bedrock and gravel, with jumps, rock gardens with berms and gap jumps before finishing back in the car park in about 30 minutes.

The gondola uplift provides access to these, and other trails from 1015 until 1545 from mid-May to mid-September. These trails are pretty tough and it's recommended you use better quality off road mountain bikes for all but the gentle routes. Always wear your helmet, gloves and protective clothing, and make sure you check out all the trails on offer – they are improved every year with new sections opening up. Riders need to be 12 and above and everyone has to sign a Participation Statement and stick to a Code of Practice. The trails can be closed on certain days for track maintenance, bad weather or race days. Best check in advance. If the gondola is closed, there is still access to some of the lower trails.

Practicalities

As an outdoors hub, the area around Fort William thrives with amenities from hire centres and specialist shops to accommodation and decent spots to grab a bite and a glass of something reviving.

Transport Travelling through epic scenery, Fort William train station is well connected to Scotland's major cities.

Sleeping £ Snowgoose Mountain Centre, Station Rd, Corpach, Fort William T01397-772467, highland-mountain-guides.co.uk, has self-catering apartments as well as the cracking alpine style Smiddy Bunkhouse – all bedding included from £13/night. £ Glen Nevis SYHA, PH33 6SY, T01397-702336, in the shadow of Ben Nevis has dorms, doubles and the silver award for Green Tourism. Unsurprisingly, there are a number of campsites in the Fort William area but the handiest for the trails is Glen Nevis Camping and Caravan Park, PH33 6SX, T01397-702191, glen-nevis.co.uk, 4 miles from the Fort William centre. The site holds the gold David Bellamy Award for Conservation and is based at the foot of Ben Nevis. Open Mar-Oct, if you want to book there's a £10 additional fee (although more than 100 pitches are kept for roll ins). Also part of the Glen Nevis Estate, south of the campsite and on-site bar/café are the S/C Glen Nevis Holiday Lodges, Cottages and Caravans. Lodges are high end, sleeping up to 6 available Feb-Oct from £520/week while the cottages are cheaper.

Eating & drinking The Grog and Gruel, High St, Fort William is a decent, traditional CAMRA listed pub serving up quality home cooking and real ales to wash it down with. For a warm glow at altitude, the top station of Ben Nevis is home to the Snowgoose Restaurant and Bar with good fare created from local produce.

Resources Off Beat Bikes, High St, Fort William, T01397-704008, offbeatbikes.co.uk, offer bike hire directly at the trail head – XC from £12/half day, DH from £40/half day. Package with bike includes helmet, body armour and pads. Nevis Bike School, T01397-705825, offers guiding and coaching, whether you want improve your XC skills or May-Sep your DH skills from £30. For routes, information and mapping see: ridefortwilliam.co.uk and nevisrange.co.uk

Also try The Witches Trail includes sections from the World Cup Cross Country course. There are three marked trails to follow, the World Champs course is a red grade and is 5 miles, there's the 10 Under the Ben loop, another red grade than runs for 10 miles and the blue grade Broomstick Blue which is 3½ miles. Nevis Range has a map for sale that shows the routes or download from ridefortwilliam.co.uk.

> Lowdown

🌐 Prices
Gondola prices at nevisrange.co.uk.

☀ Season
Mid-May to mid-Sep.

✪ Don't miss
The four cross track.

✖ Avoid
Bring the right bike for the right course, the terrain is pretty serious so you'll be grateful for some decent suspension.

Surfing Tiree

Provider	Suds Surf School
Skill level	Beginner-advanced
Time frame	2 hrs to full day
Equipment	Board and wetsuit are provided
Exertion level	●●●○○

The dream is always a remote island, crystal blue waters lapping at white sand. Empty surf breaking under sun-bleached skies, while virgin beaches show no footprints but those you leave as you run to the water's edge, board under arm.

Islands have always occupied a special place in the surfing psyche. Perhaps this is because the wavering genome itself evolved on the archipelagoes across Polynesia, or because generations have been fed on decades of surf films that follow the adventures of island hopping ferals chasing the perfect ride off some mystical isle with names like Nias, Bali, Lombok, Reunion or Mauritius. However there are surfing destinations somewhat closer to home, just as dreamy and uncrowded as those found during the great explorations of the 1970s, just as promising and rewarding to those searching for a new surfing adventure away from the numbers. For those looking to broaden their surfing horizons, Tiree is the perfect destination.

The west coast of Scotland is a complex and convoluted coastline, with a myriad of islands and inlets buffering the mainland from the raw power of the North Atlantic's fury. Low-lying Tiree has long enjoyed a reputation as an excellent windsurf

◀ Living the dream on the Western Isles.

Howard Walker

Practicalities

Accommodation is more in demand and more expensive during the peak summer months, so if you'd like to come during this period book early. However the surf is best during spring and autumn, when the Atlantic delivers consistent swells in warm water. The main hub is Scaranish.

Transport Ferries operated by Caledonian MacBrayne run daily from the mainland during the summer and four times a week during the off season. The journey from Oban takes about four hours and goes via Coll. Costs per car approx £82 plus passengers. T0800-0665 000, calmac.co.uk.

Sleeping £ **Millhouse Hostel**, Cornaig, Tiree, T01879-220435. This is a newly converted barn with adjacent farmhouse near the old Tiree watermill. There are 2 large dorm rooms and 2 twin rooms, a wetsuit rack and kitchen area. Bike hire is also available. tireemillhouse.co.uk. £ **Cèabhar Guesthouse**, Sandaig, Tiree, PA77 6XQ, offers B&B with fresh local produce close to the beach at Sandaig. There are en suite singles and doubles, free Wi-Fi and mountain bikes to hire. ceabhar.com. **Balinoe Campsite**, Burnside Cottage, Cornaig, T01879-220399, info@wilddiamond.co.uk, lies in a sheltered spot on the southwest of the island. It can accommodate campervans, caravans and tents and has kitchen, shower and toilets. Considerate wild camping may be permitted but get permission from the nearest croft first.

Eating & drinking **Tiree Lodge Hotel**, T01879-220368, has great views over Gott Bay and offers lunches, evening meals, light snacks and refreshments. Also has one of the 2 public bars on the island. The Lodge offers a lively night out during the summer and weekends. Also at Gott Bay, the BYO **Elephant's End** menu features local produce. **The Farmhouse Café**, Balemartine, T01879-220107, is an informal spot and great place to grab a bowl of soup.

Resources Suds offers board and 5 mm winter wettie hire from £20/day, summer wetsuits and boards available to hire by the week also.

Also try If the waves are small, why not try stand up paddle surfing, or 'SUP'. Lessons are available from Suds who will provide all equipment needed. – 1½ hrs from £40. On calm days more experienced SUPers can book on to a 2-hr tour around the coast, getting you up close and personal with the marine life. If you've mastered the basics and want to practise your skills, hire a SUP from £20/day.

Pete Roberts

destination, but surfers too are being drawn there for the wide open beaches, clean glassy waves and empty breaks that await. Nestled on the southern fringes of the Inner Hebrides, bathed by the warm currents from the Gulf Stream, here lies a place where sunshine and swell co-exist.

The beaches along the north and west coast offer an open aspect to the swells generated in the North Atlantic by low pressures tracking across the open ocean. Breaks like Balevulin Bay, The Maze and The Green offer an enticement to get on the ferry and cross from the mainland. These breaks are pretty flexible, working on swells from the west and northwest or even big southwesterlies, and being an island, if there is swell running there will always be somewhere either offshore or sheltered. Suds, who operates his surf school here, has been enjoying the relaxed vibe on Tiree for years now. "The highlights of being a surfer here are surfing in quiet waves with just a few of your mates," he explains, "then heading in for a BBQ, fire and beers on the beach. The water quality and weather (it's sunny lots, honestly!) and not having to travel far between various facing beaches. We also enjoy consistent swell, even in summer."

With a population of only 400, this is a great place to escape the crowds, but it's certainly worth checking the weather charts and swell predictions before committing to the ferry ride. The island hasn't established a reputation as a classic windsurfing spot for nothing, and during the winter the winds can be too strong to surf.

∧ Empty peaks await Tiree wave hunters .

> **Lowdown**

ⓘ **Directory**
Suds Surf School,
Tiree, T07793-063849,
surfschool
scotland.co.uk.

Prices
One to one tuition is
£25/hr, courses are
£30/2½ hr session.

Season
Mar-Oct.

Don't miss
The prehistoric
Ringing Stone.

Avoid
If you like windsurfing
then the week of the
Tiree Wave Classic is
just for you – if not,
it'll be the one time
the island's beaches
get busy.

Surfing Scotland: best of the rest

Provider	DIY
Skill level	All breaks beginner-advanced
Time frame	Dawn till dusk
Equipment	Surfboard, wetsuit
Exertion level	●●●●●

Scotland, with its long summer days, consistent swell and classic autumn waves, is home to some of the best surf in the UK. Most beaches are not lifeguarded, so never surf alone and always keep an eye on conditions and rip currents.

∨ Quiet times and solo sessions.

Tim Nunn

Lewis, Hebrides

Some incredible waves can be found on the islands of Lewis and Harris. The beach at Europie, hemmed in by the Butt of Lewis to the north comes alive in all swells from northerly to westerly, and winds from the southeast are offshore. The sandbanks here produce hollow, powerful waves that work best from low to near high. At the southern end of the beach there is a sand-covered rocky bank that produces great waves at low tide. "Europie is a challenging, A-grade beach break," says Derek McCloud from Hebridean Surf Holidays. "It's very powerful, like big Hossegor." For more advanced surfers, the point breaks and reefs at Barvas and Bragar are a world-class challenge. Accommodation, hire and lessons are available through **Hebridean Surf Holidays**, 28 Francis Street, Stornoway, Lewis, HS1 2ND, T01851-840337. Caledonian Macbrayne runs a direct ferry from Ullapool to Stornaway, T0800-0665 000, calmac.co.uk.

Aberdeen

The three mile stretch of beach that runs to the north of the River Dee can seem like a pretty inhospitable place under the onslaught of winter winds and driving snow, but this beach at Aberdeen is the most likely spot where the first waves in Scotland were ridden. Certainly by 1966 there were wetsuitless surfers trading lefts and rights on their nine foot Mals, and the tradition has continued to this day, with Aberdeen being home to some of the country's hardiest surfers. There is a series of sand banks here that work through the tides, but the obvious high tide impediment is a series of controversial boulder groynes installed to prevent erosion. To the south of the river, Nigg Bay offers experienced surfers some excellent waves. Swells from the northeast, east or southeast will bring rideable fare with accompanying winds from the west being offshore. **Granite Reef**, 45 The Green, AB11 6NY, T01224-252752, granitereef.com, is the town's most established surf shop. They stock a good range of hardware, clothing and also run a surf school.

Greg Martin

Brims Ness, Caithness

Just west of Thurso, Brims is probably the most consistent wave in the whole of Scotland. It can be flat everywhere on the north shore, but still have a rideable wave here. It is home to three waves, The Bowl, The Cove and The Point. The Bowl is a shallow right that breaks over a flat slab reef, it's a fast and hollow wave really only suitable for experienced surfers. The crystal clear water makes it look like it's breaking in just inches of water, which isn't that far from the truth. The Cove is another right, slightly more forgiving, but still a challenge. Both will break in small westerly to northerly swells and are offshore in southerly winds, but if the swell kicks in they are transformed into serious grinding barrels. The Point is a left that breaks on the eastern fringe of this flat, slabstone headland. It needs a clean swell with a bit more power than the two rights, but the long hollow lefts can be classic on their day. This is a remote spot and best left to experienced surfers only. Turn right off the coast road between Thurso and Dounreay and follow the single track road towards the farm silos. Park respectfully in the farmyard.

The Broch, Fraserburgh

Fraserburgh is a no-nonsense working fishing port that has been home to waveriders since the 60s. This crescent-shaped sandy bay runs east from the town's harbour. Its north to northeasterly orientation means that it hoovers up any swell coming out of the Arctic, making it a very consistent spot, with plenty of room to spread out. The sandbanks provide some excellent peaks through the tides and southwesterly tradewinds are

◄ Valtos, Hebrides. Beware the rips and the isolation, this is Scottish wilderness surfing at its finest.

consistently offshore. The Broch is home to a vibrant surf scene with a committed and hardcore local crew, brochsurfclub.blogspot.com. **Point North East Surf Shop**, Cross St, T01346-517403, is run by long-time local charger Iain Masson and provides a full range of hardware and kit.

The Shit Pipe, Thurso

It's hard living in the shadow of a legend. Even though you may have virtues and qualities that would shine anywhere else, the limelight can so easily pass by. In Thurso Bay the world-class rights of Thurso East are a magnetic draw that bring surfers from across the globe to take on these reeling barrels, but across the channel, close by, sits another right hand reef known as the Shit Pipe. Legend has it the name derives from the colour of the water that leaches in from the river, but there is also a sewage outfall that occasionally discharges here. However, the wave itself has become the proving ground for local grommets, the place to earn their wings before they move on to the big beast. Shit Pipe needs a bigger swell to work, with a clean northwesterly bringing the reef to life. Long walling rights reel from the end of the reef out in front of the breakwater, all the way through to the beach. With an easy paddle back in the channel, this makes for an excellent session. In a classic swell, Shit Pipe may be all but empty as everyone heads for Thurso East, but if you feel you're not quite ready for the reef in front of the Castle, then the Shit Pipe may just be the best second best wave you've surfed in a long while.

▼ It's not-Shit Pipe, it's just overshadowed.

Greg Martin

Coasteering Oban

Provider	Hebridean Pursuits
Skill level	All levels
Time frame	3 hrs
Equipment	All coasteering equipment provided. Remember to bring a change of clothes
Exertion level	●●●○○

Two lone figures stand on a cliff edge. They breathe deeply, open-mouthed and smiling as they take in the scene around them. The late afternoon sunshine saturates the rock face and crisps the salt on their hands and faces. Below them cries of encouragement rise up from the water as the coloured helmets of the few gone before them bob in the current, hands gripping the gulley's edge and fresh water tickling their fingers. The figures take one last look at the beautiful Hebridean landscape, lit up, it seems, especially for them, before taking the plunge.

Coasteering may be growing in popularity in Scotland but it's still a fairly exclusive affair around Oban, where exploring the undeveloped tidal impact zone is reserved for those in the know. This makes it a different sort of coasteering to that which you might find elsewhere; one of blissful silences, empty landscapes and striking beauty, albeit with the same rush that comes from swimming, scrambling and plunging into the marine environment.

"We're lucky here in that we've got a whole adventure playground to ourselves; a vast and varied coastline which is hardly ever visited," explains Andy Spink, director of Hebridean Pursuits, an adventure company that offers coasteering trips among other activities.

Andy and his team of fully qualified instructors design each coasteering trip to suit the ability and desires of group they're taking out, focusing on beautiful beaches, challenging gullies or jaw-dropping jumps accordingly to make sure everyone comes away satisfied. "Coasteering is about pure enjoyment in an incredible natural environment," Andy concludes, "if we can give everyone that then we'll come away happy."

Practicalities

Sheltered from the Atlantic storms by the Inner Hebrides, Oban is a busy town and port, ferrying visitors back and forth to the islands. But it's more than just a stop off point. With its surprisingly mild climate, stunning views and culinary reputation as the seafood capital of Scotland, it's a draw for tourists in its own right and consequently there's plenty of accommodation, restaurants and facilities to make the most of. Hebridean Pursuits is based in the nearby village of Connel, just 10 mins away.

Transport Oban has a train station with 3 trains a day from Glasgow Queen St. Connel Station is on the same mainline connecting with Glasgow, firstscotrail.com. Once in Oban buses make it easy to get to Connel and other neighbouring villages. There are also regular ferry services to all of the Hebridean islands.

Sleeping ££ **The Oyster Inn**, T01631-710666, is a smart, clean and comfortable hotel in Hebridean Pursuits base village, serving locally sourced, traditional Scottish breakfasts. In nearby Oban, ££ **The Kimberley Villa**, T01631-571115, has great views, just minutes' walk from the town centre and harbour. The rooms are comfortable and a hearty Scottish breakfast is served every day. For self-catering, try ££ **Bracken Cottage**, T01631-770283, 3 miles outside of Oban. It's a small, warm and cosy cottage set in a pine forest. £££ **Barcaldine Castle**, T01631-720598, on the shores of Loch Creren, is a bona fide castle with views to Glen Coe.

Eating & drinking Famous for its seafood, the award-winning **Waterfront Restaurant**, T01631-563110, uses fish and seafood landed on the harbour front that very day. Another award-winner, **Ee-Usk**, T01631-565666, is perched on the water's edge with views over Oban Bay to Kerrera, Mull and the Morverns. A stylish restaurant serving local seafood and fish, it's popular with locals and visitors. Alternatively **The Barn**, T01631-571313, just outside Oban offers snacks and home-made meals.

Resources Andy Spink keeps a blog which shows off the region through his eyes; scotlandoutside.blogspot.com.

Also try Hebridean Pursuits has an outdoor pursuits house on Mull worth heading to if you fancy a real get-away. Self-catering accommodation in the wilderness with the option of trying your hand at kayaking, mountain biking, plunge pooling, gorge scrambling and wildlife spotting. hebrideanpursuits.com.

> Lowdown

❶ Directory
Hebridean Pursuits, Grosvenor Crescent, Connel, Oban, Argyll, PA37 1PQ, T01631-710317, hebrideanpursuits.com.

❷ Prices
From £40/person.

❸ Season
All year.

❹ Don't miss
The view of the Hebrides from McCaig's Folly, a spectacular coliseum-style structure that dominates the town.

❺ Avoid
Going alone. The tidal impact zone can be dangerous if you don't know what you're doing.

Swimming Inner Hebrides

Provider	SwimTrek
Skill level	All
Time frame	5 days
Equipment	Swimtrek provide hats and flippers (if required) as well as swim specific wetsuits on request. As well as appropriate outdoor clothing bring with you pre-tried goggles – one tinted, one clear lensed; swimmers; waterproof sunblock; dry bag; towels; walking boots, socks; midge net; sleeping bag; 20 litre day pack
Exertion level	●●●●○

The Gulf of Corryvreckan, the narrow strait that separates the Isles of Jura and Scarba by less than a mile is a complex stretch of huge tidal flows and racing currents. And if this weren't challenging enough, those currents conspire with the underwater topography of a towering pinnacle rising from the ocean floor to within a few yards of the surface and nearby terrifying abyss to transform these waters daily into a whirlpool. Excellent. And not just any old whirlpool, one that halted wild swimming stalwart, the late, great Roger Deakin on his odyssey of total immersion and nearly took the life of retreating writer George Orwell who was navigating this stretch in his boat. So yes, on reflection, perhaps this is not the most obvious choice of swimming destination. However during a few precious slack water moments, the threat lies dormant, allowing swimmers of a particular persuasion to prise willing bodies from the comfort of the accompanying escort boat and jump in. The promise of a turning tide helps to focus the attention on the job at hand and what follows next is a mad dash across the gulf. With adrenaline still pumping, the walk across uninhabited Scarba barely registers before the next challenge of the day unfolds.

SwimTrek's five-day tour of the Inner Hebrides isn't all knife-edge experiences. The expedition works up naturally to the biggest challenges, with a couple of mellow swims to help bodies and minds acclimatize. Aquatic adventures of the stroke and glide are equally matched by daily breathtaking hikes across the undulating terrain of the islands – the five-mile Evan's

∧ The waters of the Loch a' Bhaile-Mhargaid, Jura have gone towards the production of a fine single malt and a fine breed of swimmers.

∧ If you've conquered the Gulf of Corryvreckan, it definitely calls for a spot of celebration.

> **Lowdown**

❶ **Directory**
SwimTrek, Lansdowne Place, BN3 1FL, T01273-739713, swimtrek.com.

❸ **Prices**
£555.

❷ **Season**
Aug-Sep.

❶ **Don't miss**
Rising to a height of 2575 ft it is nigh on impossible to miss the stunning Paps of Jura.

❌ **Avoid**
The Gulf of Corryvreckan should only be attempted in quiet weather, at slack water, with local knowledge. This is not a challenge that should be undertaken lightly or solo.

Walk on the Wednesday takes you past the sleeping giants, the Paps of Jura before depositing you on the edge of Loch Tarbert, ready for a short refreshing swim. There is of course the option to 'pull a sickie' on most of the hikes and ride on the boat instead but you really do miss out on half the adventure.

The tour caters for a maximum of 11 people, accompanied by two guides and two boats. Daily hikes range between 1½-4½ miles with swims ranging between a manageable half mile to a more challenging mile and a half, but the boat is there if you want to take a break at any time.

Practicalities

The tour leaves from Craighouse on the Isle of Jura, finishing five days later back on the mainland at Craobh Haven, 20 miles south of Oban on the Craiginish peninsula. The trip includes all logistics, an escort boat, guides, the majority of food and all accommodation (camping). Bring your own sleeping bag.

Transport Getting there involves a number of connections but that adds to the 'expedition' feeling. From Glasgow, citylink.co.uk operates a bus service linking with the Kennacraig Ferry to Port Askaig, Islay, calmac.co.uk. A connecting ferry travel on to Feolin, Jura with an onward bus service to Craighouse. If you leave Glasgow at 0900, you should make Craighouse by 1700.

Sleeping With good onward transport links, overnight in Oban at £ Oban SYHA, Esplanade, PA34 5AF, T01631-562025, with views across the harbour, the bronze award for Green Tourism and reasonably priced full Scottish brekkies to boot.

Eating & drinking Meals are included for the most part except lunch and dinner on the first 2 days but seeing as you'll be camped up in the grounds of the Jura Hotel, Craighouse, it's churlish not to sample their cooking.

Also try Sign up for the annual Isle of Jura Fell Race which – taking in 16 miles, 7 mountains and 7500 ft of climbing – is one of the toughest tests in British fell running, jurafellrace. org.uk. Mere mortals can content themselves with walking to the summit of the Paps. Climb the highest, Beinn an Oir, the Mountain of Gold to be rewarded with views over Loch Tarbert to the north and Islay to the south.

Surfing Machrihanish

Provider	Clan Surf School
Skill level	Beginner-advanced
Time frame	Sunrise to sunset
Equipment	Board, wetsuit and transport from Glasgow provided
Exertion level	●●●○○

Mention this part of the Scottish coastline to most and someone is bound to pipe up about Macca, but mention the Kintyre Peninsula to a surfer and it'll muster an entirely different response. This 40-mile long finger of land is something of an anomaly, a waveriding dichotomy. Ask anyone and they'll tell you that there's no surf on mainland Scotland's west coast, after all Ireland blocks out swell from the west and the Hebrides hoover up waves from the north. There is however a small, distinct channel through which a solid northwesterly swell can thread to deliver surf to the beaches of Kintyre. With the myth well and truly busted, surfers from across Scotland have been heading for the western shores in increasing numbers.

Breaks on this western side are becoming something of a waveriding Mecca. From breaks like Caravans to Graveyards, through to the main beach at Machrihanish there are a variety of waves to be sampled and more local surfers arriving on the scene each year. For those not lucky enough to live on the doorstep of these spots, Clan in Glasgow runs day trips out to the beaches, providing tuition through their BSA qualified surf instructors. Swell direction is critical, and Clan is dialled into where there will be waves, when there will be beginner-friendly peelers and when there'll be pumping swell for the experienced waverider. The beach here is huge, a vast open sandy stretch to spread out along. The dune-backed bay provides plenty of peaks, with access from the northern Westport end, the middle via the airport terminal road, or the southern end at Machrihanish village.

> Surfing in the wild, wild west.

> Lowdown

ℹ Directory
Clan Surf, 45 Hyndland St, Glasgow, T0141-339 6523.

₴ Prices
£65 for a lesson, including transport from Glasgow and all equipment. £45 lesson and equipment only.

☀ Season
All year.

✪ Don't miss
Keep an eye out for the dolphins.

✗ Avoid
If you're going on a DIY mission, familiarize yourself with the lie of the land and make sure you are confident there will be waves waiting, it can be a long road home if not.

Practicalities

The peninsula clings on to the mainland by a thread, the A83 connecting the main towns of Tarbert and Campbeltown. Below lies the Mull, immortalized by Wings.

Transport Citylink operate a bus service from Glasgow to Campbeltown, around 5 miles east of the beach, taking just over 4 hrs. Clan do this trip in 2½ hrs.

Sleeping The showcase is the quiet, midge-free **Machrihanish Caravan and Camping Park**, PA28 6PT, T01586-810366. Less than a mile from the beach, the site is flat with well spaced pitches. Self-catering wooden wigwams sleeping up to 5 from £25/night for 2 – ideal if the westerlies kick in. Feb-Oct, Dec. Comfortable **Island View Cottage**, liveontheedge.co.uk, overlooks Westport Beach and sleeps 4 people, free Wi-Fi. From £310/week

Eating & drinking The Old Clubhouse, part of the new Dunes Golf Course, has a decent bar menu with a focus on Aberdeen Angus steak. Burgers from £7.50. Stock up on smoked, local fish for picnics at The Old Smoke House, The Roading, Campbelltown.

Resources Breaks Surf Shop, Longrow, Capmbeltown, PA28 6ER, T01586-550424, breakssurfshop.com, stocks all the essentials and offers equipment hire from £25/day. Surfcam: liveontheedge.co.uk/Surfcam.html.

Also try Just south of Campbeltown, explore Beinn Ghuilean on MTB via the Forestry Commission's 'Wee Toon Trail'. A 1½ mile beginner-friendly blue trail mixes easy climbs and descents, while the 1¼ mile red trail offers more challenges plus technical sections with berms, boardwalks and drop offs. Front suspension MTB hire with Breaks Surf Shop £15/day.

Paragliding Arran

Provider	Flying Fever
Skill level	All levels
Time frame	From a full day to a 5-day course
Equipment	All paragliding and safety equipment provided. Remember to bring a warm dry change of clothes
Exertion level	●●○○○

Standing on deck as the bow lunges through the metal grey sea, mountainous hunks of land rear into view on the horizon. The sun is starting to set behind the cloud bank throwing pink rays upwards and the first stars start to show, complemented by the lights of Brodick harbour. There's no doubt about it, Arran is a beautiful island from ground level, but its not a patch on the view from up high.

With a varied coastline, plenty of hills, rugged mountains and a windy climate, the Isle of Arran, in the Firth of Clyde, is a perfect place for paragliding, an experience which Flying Fever has been offering to visitors since 1993. Fully qualified instructor, tandem pilot and competitive paraglider Zabdi Keen started flying in 1989.

The process behind paragliding couldn't be simpler. You carry your paraglider in a rucksack up a hill, unroll the material and step forward into the wind. You feel a tug of air as it lifts the material off the ground to form a wing above your head and in a heartbeat your feet leave the earth. If after your first experience you want to take it further, a week-long course will show you the ropes so that you can learn how to do it on your own. Starting with ground handling, the course progresses through tandem flying, radio instruction and training techniques to gentle solo flights low down on the slopes, working up to take-off points higher up. Instructors also teach flying theory and airmanship. The course finishes with a final exam after which you get accreditation from the British Hanggliding and Paragliding Association.

From one-off tandem flights to fun days, elementary pilot courses to full season passes, Flying Fever has a range of options designed to get you up in the air as soon as possible. Based in Brodick, the company's team of instructors and tandem pilots take you through safety procedures and check equipment before gauging the wind conditions. Flying Fever's sites benefit from stunning views and because the island is only 19 miles long and 10 miles wide they are all within easy reach of base camp.

Practicalities

Brodick, where Flying Fever is based is one of the largest and busiest settlements on Arran, and is the main commercial centre and ferry port. With a wide range of tourist facilities and services available as well as plenty of restaurants, pubs and accommodation, it makes a handy base from which to explore and enjoy the island.

Transport Arran is served by ferry services from Ardrossan on the Scottish mainland, returns from £7.70 with calmac.co.uk. There is a train station at Ardrossan, firstscotrail.com, and can also be reached by coach from Glasgow.

Sleeping The Coastguard House, KA27 8SD, T07748-065623, sleeps 6 and has clifftop views and an open fire, from £375/week. **££ Alltan B&B** in Broderick, T01770-302937, offers modern, friendly accommodation with locally sourced breakfasts. **Seal Shore Camping**, T01770-820320, is a small, peaceful campsite with private beach 12 miles away from Brodick, with uninterrupted sea views out to Plaida island.

Eating & drinking Creelers, Home Farm, Brodick, KA27 8DD, T01770-302797, is well known on the island for its simple, delicious fare. For fine dining try **Eighteen69** in the Auchrannie Hotel, T01770 302234 – award winning contemporary Scottish cuisine.

Resources Flying Fever sells paragliding equipment and can source second hand kit if your purse strings won't stretch to buying brand new. flyingfever.net.

Also try Climbing Arran's tallest peak Goat Fell. It's a moderate climb that takes around 5 hrs but is well worth the hike; spectacular panoramic views await you at the summit, and on a clear day you could even see Ireland in the distance. It's a popular peak with a number of routes to climb. The easiest, main path sets out close to Brodick Castle in Cladach, leading through the forested grounds and contracting bare moorland before climbing the summit via the east ridge.

> **Lowdown**

ⓘ Directory
Flying Fever, Strathwhillan Farm, Strathwillan Rd, Brodick, Isle of Arran, KA27 8BQ, T01770-303899, flyingfever.net.

⊘ Prices
From £95/person.

⊘ Season
Mar-Oct.

❂ Don't miss
Sampling Arran's very own malt whisky at the Isle of Arran Distillery, arranwhisky.com.

⊗ Avoid
Just heading over for the day. Paragliding is weather dependent and the weather on Arran is unpredictable. Spend a few days on the island to make sure you get to take to the air.

Swimming Scotland: best of the rest

Provider	DIY
Skill level	All
Time frame	Dawn till dusk
Equipment	Bathers, towel, wetsuit depending on hardiness, a mug of something warm/warming and plenty of clothes to throw on post swim because it will undoubtedly be chilly
Exertion level	●●●○○

There are literally thousands of fresh water tarns and lochs across Scotland from petite and peaty lochans lying in wait on mountainsides to tempt the passing fell walker to the expansive bodies like Loch Lomond, which, covering an area of 44 sq miles is the country's largest. Then of course there are the rivers, salt water lochs and beaches cutting across the countryside and lining the coastline which add up to a whole lot of swimming potential. The Scottish Land Reform act also means that unlike in England and Wales you are free to access all inland waterways for passage but more importantly recreation, providing the Scottish Access Code is upheld – which basically means, reasonably, responsibly, respectfully and at your own risk. A pick of some of the best include:

Falloch Falls, Stirling

Follow the A82 north along the banks of Loch Lomond but don't let this vast expanse distract your eye too long as the real prize lies just up ahead. The Falloch river rises in the foot hills of Beinn a' Chroin before wending its way southwest and spilling into the head of Loch Lomond. On its course the spectacular Falls of Falloch plunge for some 33 ft and in their fury and relentless activity have carved a huge pool that just asks to be swum in. Locally known as Rob Roy's Bathtub, do not be fooled into thinking that the waters here are warm enough for a leisurely bathe, the temperature is always on the icy side. The falls are a popular picnic site, so this is no quiet escape but there is enough room for everyone to enjoy. The car park is signed from the road just north of Inverarnan and from here it is just a short 5 minutes walk. When in spate, seasoned kamikaze kayakers can occasionally be spotted making the

Mark Frogwell

∧ The Falls of Falloch.

drop, definitely something best left to experts. Stay at **Beinglas Farm Campsite**, Inverarnan, G83 7DX, T01301-704281, beinglascampsite.co.uk. The site is quiet – no noise after 2230 but if you've spent the day exploring the bens and lochs then that's ideal. In fact, the peak of Ben Glas provides a stunning backdrop to the site. Open year round with on-site bar and cosy wooden camping barns or 'wigwams' also available from £30/night for two – ideal if the weather looks set to turn.

Loch Ness, Highlands

Thanks to a certain monster said to be lurking within, this 23-mile-long stretch of inland water is possibly the most famous lake in the world. However, keen swimmer, don't let something like a potential bit of toe nibbling put you off! There are gently shelving access points to the dark depths of the loch right along the A82, and half way up Castle Urquhart with its car park makes a handy launch pad. On the eastern shore, the long single beach at Dores is another good spot to enjoy a dip. With a maximum depth of around 755 ft, this is not somewhere to stray out of your comfort zone or depth, besides, you never know who might be prowling in the dark waters below. **£££ Pottery House B&B**, Dores, IV2 6TR, T01463-751267, is a five-minute walk from the beach and edge of the loch and holds the gold award for Green Tourism.

Their hens provide the eggs for breakfast, the jams are home-made and rolls freshly baked. Grab a beer and a bite at the nearby Dores Inn.

Trinkie & North Baths, Wick

The sea pools dotted around the coastline of Britain are a testament to rewards reaped when man works with his environment. While some have been carved out by the hand of nature, most have been aided and abetted by those who enjoy them – sea wall construction to hold in the tide or an annual lick and polish. Wick on the wild north east coast is home to two such pools: North Baths lies just outside the harbour in Wick Bay while The Trinkie, from the Scottish word for trench was cut into the rocks on the exposed south east edge of the town some 70 years ago. Access via Wellington Avenue. The Friends of Trinkie and North have revived both of these pools, keeping the paint fresh, rebuilding walls and rekindling the town's love of a salt water dip. Overlooking the river, **Wick Caravan and Camping Site**, Riverside Drive, KW1 5SP, T01955-605420, is a 10-minute walk into town in a quiet secluded spot. April-October. Other decent tidal pools include: **Pittenweem**, **Fife** – west of the harbour the concrete tidal sea pool has been set into the vast rock reef that skirts the slim slice of golden sand here. Access via West Braes. **Portsoy**, **Moray Firth** – west of the harbour and easily accessed via Target Road, the salt water pool set into a large rock finger can be a decent spot for a splash – at high the sea floods right over the low concrete walls.

Gourock Outdoor Pool, Inverclyde

As you slip into this seawater pool looking across into the Argyll Hills, you notice that there is something different about it. Then you realize: that toe tingling chill that you expected to spread across your body in a northerly direction, numbing as it goes is indeed absent. While the River Clyde feeds the pool, its waters are tenderly filtered, cleaned and warmed to a somewhat nurturing 29°C. While this may seem like cheating to the hardy wild swimmer, it is also a somewhat welcome delight on a drizzly day when bruised clouds sweep the skyline. It is a proper community pool with diving boards, kids and pool parties. If you're after a quieter escape, then weekday mornings are best. From £3, The Pool, Albert Road, PA19 1PD, April-September.

Sheriffmuir Paradise Pool, Perthshire

East of Dunblane and Sheriffmuir, the walk through the fields leads to Wharry Burn. The plunge pool here, and the rock flume that feeds it have been gouged out and polished by the forces of time and motion. Eleven miles to the east, on the outskirts of Thornhill camp up at **Mains Farm Wigwams**, FK8 3QB, T01786-850753, mainsfarmwigwams.com, in wooden wigwams from £30/night. Tipi's also available from £50/night. Own bedding required. Pitches for tents and vans also available.

Coire Lagan, Isle of Skye

Starting out from the campsite above the beach on the shores of Loch Brittle the 5½ mile walk up to this corrie takes around three hours and ascends for nearly 1969 ft, the walking is not easy but the rewards are worth it. The clear pool dotted with aquatic flora has deep turquoise spots, like ink blots on a canvas, that draw the eye while its edges are cocooned by huge slabs, scree sloped, vertical peaks and jagged pinnacles often strewn with climbers in varying degrees of ascent. Reward your feet with a reviving paddle. Most of the path leading up is good although there are short scrambles to overcome. Return via the waterfall. Enjoy the simple delights of this wild western coast at **Glenbrittle Campsite**, Carbost, IV47 8TA, T01478-640404, dunvegancastle.com. The shop stocks a few basic provisions or you could always forage for your supper on the shoreline here. Hard stands and electric hook up also. April-September.

⌄ A spa pool experience of goggle-eyed delight is to be found beneath some of the less ferocious waterfalls.

Andy Law

Mountain biking Dalbeattie

Provider DIY	
Skill level All	
Time frame 2 hrs +	
Equipment Mountain bike, helmet, map, provisions, appropriate gear and a repair kit/spare tube	
Exertion level ●●●●○	

Dalbeattie has tried its hand at many things. Just back from the Solway Firth it has been a port and, drawing on the power of the free flowing River Urr, it thrived as a mill town. However it is granite that has defined it, shaped it and seen it thrive – the town wears it's grey coat with pride, glinting defiantly under a low autumn sun.

Like most of the 7Stanes, there are several levels of graded routes here, waymarked and charted through the working woodland owned and managed by the Foresty Commission. The skills

⌄ Phil Chapman pauses for though on the Hardrock trail.

section at the trail head has blue and red graded loops, with hints of black. A blast around should help you gauge your riding standard before committing to a route proper. With rock pavements, steps and slabs it is a good warm up to what lies ahead. And if this left you in any doubt, just to be clear, the riding, like the town is defined by granite.

The main event is the Hardrock Trail. Around two thirds of the 15½ mile red graded route is singletrack, of both the fast and flowing and the technical variety plus there are a number of seriously testing black rated features thrown in to make sure you're paying attention. The Slab is the biggie here – an intense nine mile section of angled granite that has been known to make grown men cry. Then there are the Terrible Twins, a dual slab section to overcome. It isn't as long as it's predecessor but it doesn't make it any less daunting. Fear not, you can bypass these features and swop them for some seriously fun singletrack instead.

If you're not quite ready for that, the 8½ mile Moyle Hill trail is a good alternative. After a few bone shaking traverses or two in the skills area, the raised timber trail crossing Richorn Plantation provides light relief. Steady climbs along the way are rewarded with views out over the Urr Valley. While much of the blue-graded route is forest road, it is interspersed with short stretches of singletrack, with the odd rooty section thrown in for good measure, great for gaining confidence and experience.

The green graded Ironhash Trail is a leisurely seven mile ride along wide forest roads, ideal for novices with barely a sniff of singletrack to navigate. As with all the routes here, it leaves from the trail head but gives more challenging features like Cloak Hill a wide berth. With some fun descents, this route should comfortably take no more than a couple of hours. It does however offer glimpses of The Slab and the wealth of challenges that are available when you're ready to progress.

Practicalities

In southwest Scotland, in the valley of the birch the town of Dalbeattie has been hewn from the granite landscape that surrounds it and saw it prosper. There is a good range of accommodation here and good facilities including some cracking smoke houses nearby if you have time to hunt them down. The River Urr flows past the western extremities of the town leading to the sea and Solway coastline

Transport Dumfries, 14 miles north east is the nearest station. Collection service £25 up to 6 people plus bikes for those staying at Gorsebank.

Sleeping Two miles north of Dalbeattie, **£ Urr Lodge**, Castle Douglas, DG7 3JZ, T01556-660490, provides comfortable, simple, affordable bunkhouse accommodation plus private rooms. On-site bike store and drying room plus free Wi-Fi access. A 5-mile ride from Dalbeattie, **££ Cowans Farm Guest House**, Kirkgunzeon, DG2 8JY, T01387-760284, delivers simple B&B accommodation in their modern barn conversion and have an on-site log cabin sleeping 3 that can be rented on a self-catering or B&B basis from £420/week. Drying room, bike store. There are a number of camp sites in the area. On the trails doorstep is **Gorsebank**, DG5 4QT, T01556-611634, set on the 80 acre equestrian farm. To keep the chill at bay they have heated wigwams sleeping 5 with raised sleeping benches, kitchen equipment plus timber tents – sleeping 3, from £20/night. On-site kitchen and dining room plus bike store and hire (see resources below). Open year round. **Kippford Holiday Park**, DG5 4LE2, T01556-620626, is close to the trail head and holds the David Bellamy Gold award for conservation. Camping plus statics and lodges available – from £17/pitch. On-site shop with fresh bread and local goodies. One mile from the 7Stanes trail, Islecroft, Mill St, DG5 4HE, T01556-612236, is a small site with bike lock up, just 5 mins from Dalbeattie town centre. Easter-Oct.

Eating & drinking The **Laurie Arms**, Haugh of Urr, T08721-077077, is worth sniffing out for its CAMRA listed selection of real ales and bar menu. A quick trip up the A711 towards Beeswing brings you to Loch Arthur Creamery and Farmshop.

Resources 7stanes.gov.uk is an excellent resource with detailed route info and mapping available to download. **Castle Douglas Cycle Hire**, Church St, Castle Douglas, T01556-504542, has a comprehensive range of hardware and accessories. Owned by a Cytech qualified mechanic you can be sure the quality is top notch – as are the servicing and repairs priced at £28/hr. Through **Gorsebank**, T01556-611634, ½ mile from the trail head, they also offer bike hire – hardtails, full suspension and even tandem bikes for lazy days – helmet and tool kit included from £12/4 hrs. Free parking, toilets and showers.

Also try This region of Dumfries and Galloway is rich in walking potential. The coast to coast Southern Upland Way spanning 212 miles and taking in some 80 summits is a commitment but in June, when the landscape is a wash of rich greens, is spectacular. southernuplandway.gov.uk for route planning. For a day's adventure, head out on the coastal path between Rockcliffe and Sandyhills. The 12 miles route is signposted from Rockcliffe village and delivers views out to the Isle of Man and across the Galloway coast.

> **Lowdown**

ⓘ **Directory**
The trail head is at Richorn, ½ mile south of Dalbeattie, DG5 4QU.

❸ **Prices**
Free/from £12/hr MTB hire.

❂ **Season**
Year round.

❂ **Don't miss**
A spot of star gazing in the nearby Galloway Forest. With minimal light pollution and 300 sq miles of forest to lose yourself in it is Britain's first Dark Sky Park.

❌ **Avoid**
You can easily bypass the black graded features on the Hardrock if you're not yet ready to tackle that amount of granite in one hit!

< For experts only: it might hurt when you fall on the Qualifier but not as much as your pride will if you don't give it a go.
∨ The alter ego of Dalbeattie – you don't have to get stuck between a rock and a hard place.

Best of the rest Scotland: activities

Mountain biking, Galloway Forest Park

The Galloway Forest Park spreads out over 300 sq miles and is a haven for wildlife from eagles soaring on high to deer and little-seen pine martens seeking shelter beneath great woodland canopies. Its edges corral the watery delights of burns, rivers, lochs, waterfalls and beaches, bunching the landscape into peaks, fells and hillocks – some blanketed in heather in an attempt to soften their rugged edges. With singletrack to explore and home to two of the 7Stanes, this woodland is also a haven for mountain bikers. Glen Trool delivers the 38 mile Big Country route, an enjoyable forest track and country road tour into the heart of the Galloway hills – there are climbs, but nothing too serious and the views over Loch Dee are certainly worth the effort. Also on offer here are two green routes – one long but mainly forest road, the other short but mainly singletrack – combined they shouldn't take more than three hours so you don't need to choose! Then there's the 5 mile blue graded trail, most of which is on clean, wide, purpose built singletrack with a long, swooping descent to finish on. For a change of scene and pace, Kirroughtree is all about testing, technical singletrack. There is a short, fun green route while Larg Hill is the next step in the grades; around half the trail is singletrack and can be ridden as either 6 mile or 8½ mile loop. The Twister takes it to another level with 10½ mile of technical, physical and mental challenges while Black Craigs is for experts only. Serious granite ridges and macking slabs combine with fast flowing singletrack. There is a skills area here by the trail head ideal for gaining confidence, working out problems and pushing yourself to the next level. Bike hire available at **The Break Pad**, Newton Stewart, DG8 7BE, T01671-401303, from £20/day.

Telemarking, Cairngorms

Curtseying your way down a mountain might seem like a strange concept and when you first start, it certainly isn't easy, but once you've executed the perfect telemark turn, it's like pure poetry. Free-hill skiing as it is otherwise known means just that, that your heels are not constricted by bindings and

> The Cairngorms are home to one of the most consistent snowfields in Scotland – ideal telemarking terrain.

only the front of your foot is locked on to your skis. Originally designed for getting around the snow-covered mountains and valleys of its fatherland Norway, telemarking is a great way to get out and explore the Cairngorms; those already versed in Alpine skiing should not find the transition too painful. The range provides the most consistent snow fields in Scotland and during particularly chilly years, the winter months which can stretch into April. Learn the art of telemarking with G2, g2outdoor.co.uk, £120 per two-hour session (based on two people plus £20 per additional person six max). If you've mastered the basics and want to push out on your own, **Aviemore Cross Country Ski Hire**, T01479-861253, in Glenmore forest rents equipment from less then £20/day.

Mountain biking, Mabie

Just south of Dumfries, Mabie is one of the full package 7Stanes combining quality riding for all levels with good on-site resources including on-site bike store and café. For those new to MTB, or just finding their singletrack feet, the green-graded five-mile Big Views and the longer more challenging blue graded Woodhead mix forest roads and sections of singletrack with a decent dose of cracking views. Or if you're looking for a route that really stretches your legs without having to test your technical abilities, Lochbank Loop serves up a 14-mile trail of quiet public and forest roads. For more experienced riders the Phoenix Trail is a classic that is all about the singletrack, combining technical climbs with sharp, rooty descents, flowing downills and tight berms. The Kona Dark Side bike park really is for experts only who want to test their skills on the insane elevated North Shore trail which in some places is less than the width of a helmet – which you'll definitely want to be wearing! **The Shed** at Mabie Forest, DG2 8HB, T01387-270275, is home to a quality MTB centre which has been at the heart of the scene here since the 80s. As well as on-site bike hire, they have an excellent café and bistro. Hardtails from £15/half day, full suspension from £20. Photo ID and deposit required.

Whitewater rafting, the River Tummel

When the dam releases, the full force of the River Tummel is a truly intense experience. Drifting somewhat serenely down stream at the start of your voyage you might find yourself glancing around, taking in the natural beauty of your surroundings. But don't get too comfortable, in the next breath the scene alters as the river picks up the pace and you buck your way through technical rapids. Waiting ahead is the Linn of Tummel, while it might be Gaelic for pool of tumbling stream, the reality is more like a two tier waterfall waiting to gobble you up. You may fall out, you will scream but the only way is down! The River Tummel is only raftable during the summer from June-September during scheduled dam releases. Rafting the Tay is available year round but is most fun when those melt waters kick in. **Nae Limits**, T08450-178177, run rafting trips on the Tummel from £50/person including transport to and from the site.

Walking Ben Nevis

No exploration of the Scottish landscape is really complete without a thorough examination of the mighty Ben Nevis. Rising from the shores of Loch Linnhe for 4410 ft it is not only Scotland's highest mountain but the highest point in Britain. The

Mountain Path that leads up from the Glen Nevis visitor centre is often rather sneerily referred to as the 'tourist trail' but this route, despite being walked by some 50,000 people a year is no mean feat, and the chance to tackle it is certainly not something to be sniffed at. To reach the summit, involves around 3-4 hours of fitness testing, if not technical, ascent along a broken, rock lined mountain track and a return journey to match. It is not a soft option. After sighting the true blue of Lochan Meall an t'Suidhe squeezed between the green of its sister summit and Cairn D'earg you're just under half way there; from here the path manages the gradient, zigzagging its way up the mountainside. The summit itself is no pinnacled point, rather a stretch of plateau which often lays on at least a dusting of snow to welcome the Munro-bagger. Treat the mountain with reverence, climb with due respect and you'll be rewarded with incredible vistas; lofty peaks, riven by deep valleys and lochs, a window to a world of possibilities.

Be aware that on reaching the summit, you will literally be standing on the roof of Britain and, having risen more than 4000 ft above sea level, the jackets off sunny day you experienced at the foot of the climb may in no way relate to what is actually happening on the summit, or even half way up for that matter. Every year people get caught out, underestimating the mountain factor. Winter conditions can occur between October-May (serious amounts of snow and ice where all but the properly equipped mountaineer could find themselves fighting for survival). Even in the warmer months, the weather can be alarming which is why it is advisable to only climb in fine stable weather unless properly equipped with appropriate cold weather clothing and the ability to navigate in extremely low visibility. See bennevisweather.co.uk before setting out.

∧ Screaming down the River Tummel.
∨ Julie Cartner, deep in the heart of Mabie Forest.

‹ Hanging on for grim death.

Best of the rest Scotland: sleeping & eating

Urban Angel, Edinburgh
Hanover St, E2 1DJ, and Forth St, EH1 2JS,
urban-angel.co.uk.

Urban Angel is a fresh, modern environment and having spread its wings with two locations, this lovely café-cum-deli is just that, serving up heavenly delights using the best seasonal, local, organic and fair trade goodies at good prices. The eggs Benedict brunch is a winner coming in just under £8, while lunch time fare ranges from sarnies and light salads to more substantial meals like the urban angel burger and fries £11. An ideal spot to find sanctuary in the city.

∧ Edinburgh's deli-cum café shaped city sanctuary.

Croft Organics, Skye
Skeabost Bridge, Portree, IV51 9PQ, T01470-532251,
croftorganicsofskye.co.uk.

Close to the shores of Loch Snizort Beag, with views out across green rolling countryside lies the welcoming organic croft. Camping in the field you are surrounded by meadow flowers and the beginnings of an orchard while butterflies flit and swallows dart overhead. They can even supply you with a tent if you turn up unprepared. If you'd rather something more substantial, they have a self-catering cottage to rent. John and Helen grow fresh organic produce on site and have free range eggs which they can supply you with and are part way through a conversion to receive full organic status from the Soil Association. But it doesn't stop

there, the green credentials of Croft Organics are impeccable. They have a wind turbine providing energy to their house and cottage, all detergents are eco-friendly, recycling and composting happen as a matter of course and, without seeming pious, they subtly ask guests to be conscious of water consumption. John is the knowledge, ask and he'll be able to recommend the best restaurants using the best local produce at any given time and usually knows a man who can source you fresh oysters and hand-dived scallops to cook up at home. If you want advice on inspiring island walks, as a former outdoors instructor, he's the man to point you in the right direction. Self-catering cottage sleeping 4 +1 with views over the croft from £275/week.

Kember and Jones, Glasgow
Byres Rd, G12 8TD, T0141-337 3851, kemberandjones.co.uk.

In the heart of Glasgow this is a cracking deli-cum café-cum fine food emporium. It makes a fine place for an early morning refuelling whether you're in need of a bowl of wholesome, home-made muesli topped with fresh berries and yoghurt or a stack of piggy pancakes topped with honeycomb. By lunchtime, their blackboard displays their daily seasonal specials from hearty soups to savoury tarts all made from the best ingredients.

Castle Creavie, Dumfries & Galloway
Kirkcudbright, DG6 4QE, T01557-500238,
castlecreavie.co.uk.

Set on a 300 acre working farm be under no illusion, this is no castle. Instead it is an idyllic spot where two well finished cottages wait for escapees. The Steading sleeps six from £320/week on a self-catering basis. The Cheese Loft sleeping two, is available for short breaks with B&B from £30/person or £25/person with breakfast goodies provided to cook at your leisure. Breakfast includes home baked bread as well as the farm's free range eggs and bacon – minimal food miles! Also on site, the Hayloft has been converted into a camping barn with pre-booked beds from

‹ Goodies laid out at Urban Angel.

£12/night. They encourage wildlife to flourish across their estate and create home-made goodies such as honey, jams and bread, They also have free range eggs available as well as home bred lamb, pork and bacon stored away in the freezer.

Applecross Campsite, Skye

Applecross, Strathcarron, IV54 8ND, T01529-744268, applecross.uk.com/campsite.

'With no mobile phone reception the emphasis here is on tranquility and relaxation!' There are some things you read in life that make your heart sing and that short statement on the Applecross website is one of those things. It's a statement of intent that sets the tone of the place – it says, we're cut off and proud and after all, that's its appeal. But it isn't just idle talk, the road in is an 'experience', even for the most adept of adrenaline seeking drivers. Or bike riders for that matter. An annual cycling event is held on this stretch which event organizers, Hands on Events refer to as, "The UK's biggest road climb at 2053 ft from sea level in just six miles". Which, yeah, I'm sure would be no big deal if the road was somewhat straight… But once you get there, the panic melts away. With views of the Inner Sound this sprawling six acres of open field camping limits itself to 60 tents or tourers meaning with 10 pitches per acre, there's plenty of room to spread out and ease jangled nerves. There are also wooden heated huts available for those who want to do posh camping. Open most of the year. To refuel, head to award winner, local produce champion and bar the **Applecross Inn**, T01520-744262 .

∨. Naughty never looked so good - Urban Angel's scrummy chocolate cake.

MacNeill/Urban Angel

Scarista House, Harris

Sgarasta Bheag, HS3 3HX, T01859-550238, scaristahouse.com.

On the south western reaches of this outer isle, overlooking a three mile stretch of beach, this Georgian manse feels as though it is lost in blissful isolation and time. The rooms are period and en suite while the library is home to a roaring fire and various resident creatures. Breakfasts are not ordinary either. The muesli and yoghurts are home-made, as are the jams and marmalade to spread thickly on home baked bread. Meanwhile the cooked breakfast ingredients – Inverawe kippers to Stornoway black pudding – reads like a who's who of local produce celebrities. B&B from £175. Three- and four-course dinners are also available from £39.50, which again serve up the best of what the local landscape can deliver be it local seafood, game, meat or some of their own home-grown organic veggies.

Wild Camping

The great outdoors.

Wild camping outside the parameters of a designated site, is one of life's real soul freeing experiences. And, thanks to the Land Reform Act and Scottish Outdoor Code, considerate and responsible wild camping is permitted across the majority of this Celtic landscape. Wild camping is governed by a set of rules and principles based on minimum impact to the environment and others as well as a bit of common sense. Some of the key points to remember when you've sought out your own piece of paradise are: stay no longer than three nights to limit damage to vegetation; clear up after yourself and others less considerate – remove all litter; fires pose a serious risk to the environment so don't spark up; toilet hygiene – if you've got to go, do so at least 30 yards from fresh or running water, burying your business properly where it will not damage the vegetation. A more complete overview on the wild campers' code can be found at the excellent Mountaineering Council of Scotland website: mountaineering-scotland.org.uk/leaflets/wildcamp. Find your perfect spot, pitch up and rest easy. In the morning steal silently away leaving no trace that you were ever there.

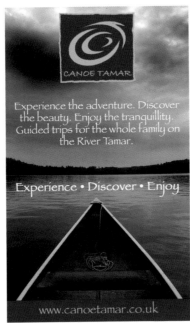

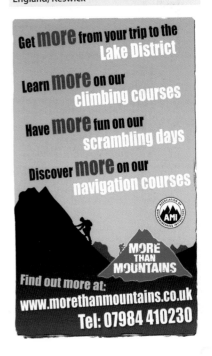

Directory

We're not afraid of advertising standards.

At Plas y Brenin we pride ourselves in the high standards we maintain. Across the board our entire staff work tirelessly to make sure every part of your course or holiday is absolutely first class.

Our highly qualified, vastly experienced and ever-enthusiastic coaches go out of their way to make sure you get the most from your visit, adopting a flexible, personalised approach to ensure you not only learn but you enjoy yourself too.

The huge fleet of boats and the equipment our stores provide modern and always well-maintained with all essential kit hire included in your course fee. Many courses even include dry-suit hire.

The on-site facilities are even more impressive. We are lucky enough to boast an indoor heated rolling pool, a suite of meeting rooms equipped with the latest AV equipment and our own private lake and rapids at the bottom of the garden. What's more, the views from the dining room and bar are simply breathtaking.

But our commitment to high standards doesn't stop there. Our catering and housekeeping staff are equally dedicated and enthusiastic too. As outdoor enthusiasts themselves they appreciate the important part a hot shower, a hearty meal and a comfy bed play in the overall experience, so they go out of their way to make sure you get just that. Every time.

We strongly believe this commitment to achieving and maintaining high standards sets us apart from other outdoor centres and we're not afraid to shout about it.

To experience our high standards for yourself simply telephone us on 01690 720214, e-mail us at brochure@pyb.co.uk or visit www.pyb.co.uk and we'll send you a free 72-page colour brochure.

PLAS Y BRENIN
Canolfan Fynydd Genedlaethol · The National Mountain Centre
www.pyb.co.uk

Plas y Brenin, Capel Curig Conwy LL24 OET Tel: 01690 720214 Fax: 01690 720394 www.pyb.co.uk Email: info@pyb.co.uk

Wales

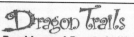

Dragon Trails

Rambles and Roasts in West Wales

Explore the spectacular scenery, history and wildlife of the Preseli hills and Pembrokeshire coast. Full board in Georgian country house. Delicious food and wine, log fires, daily guided walks. Weekly holidays April-June and Sept-Oct. Short breaks November-March.

For brochure ring Richard: 01600 750463 or visit www.dragontrails.com

Nationwide

Education/Courses

Equipment

Index

credits

Footprint credits

Project editor: Alan Murphy
Layout & production: Davina Rungasamy, Angus Dawson
Picture editor: Demi Taylor
Proofreader: Carol Maxwell
Series design: Mytton Williams

Managing Director: Andy Riddle
Commercial Director: Patrick Dawson
Publisher: Alan Murphy
Publishing managers: Felicity Laughton, Jo Williams
Digital Editor: Alice Jell
Design: Rob Lunn
Marketing: Liz Harper, Hannah Bonnell
Sales: Jeremy Parr
Advertising: Renu Sibal
Finance & administration: Elizabeth Taylor

Print

Manufactured in India by Nutech
Pulp from sustainable forests

Every effort has been made to ensure that the facts in this guidebook are accurate. However, travellers should still obtain advice from consulates, airlines etc about travel and visa requirements before travelling. The authors and publishers cannot accept responsibility for any loss, injury or inconvenience however caused.

Publishing information

Adventure Britain
1st edition
© Footprint Handbooks Ltd
May 2010

ISBN 978-1-906098-65-0
CIP DATA: A catalogue record for this book is available from the British Library

® Footprint Handbooks and the Footprint mark are a registered trademark of Footprint Handbooks Ltd

Published by Footprint
6 Riverside Court
Lower Bristol Road
Bath BA2 3DZ, UK
T +44 (0)1225 469141
F +44 (0)1225 469461
footprinttravelguides.com

Distributed in North America by
Globe Pequot Press